LATINOS AND THE LAW
CASES AND MATERIALS

By

Richard Delgado
University Distinguished Professor of Law & Derrick Bell Fellow
University of Pittsburgh School of Law

Juan F. Perea
Cone, Wagner, Nugent, Hazouri & Roth Professor of Law
University of Florida
Fredric G. Levin College of Law

Jean Stefancic
Research Professor of Law & Derrick Bell Scholar
University of Pittsburgh School of Law

AMERICAN CASEBOOK SERIES®

THOMSON
WEST

Mat #40368456

American Casebook Series and West Group are trademarks
registered in the U.S. Patent and Trademark Office.

© 2008 Thomson/West
    610 Opperman Drive
    St. Paul, MN 55123
    1–800–313–9378

Printed in the United States of America

ISBN: 978–0–314–16124–6

 *TEXT IS PRINTED ON 10% POST CONSUMER RECYCLED PAPER*

Acknowledgments

We thank Michael A. Olivas, Kevin R. Johnson, Rodolfo Acuña, and José Luis Morín for scholarly inspiration, and Steven W. Bender, Kevin R. Johnson, and Michael A. Olivas for a careful review of the contents. Ian F. Haney López offered many helpful suggestions, while librarians Michele Kristatis and Valerie Weis helped locate frustratingly obscure documents. We are grateful to our talented research assistants, Kara O'Bryon, William Godfrey, Tatyana Margolin, Marla del Vicente, and Chris Diamant for tireless performance and to faculty secretaries Jenna Cramer and Melissa Shimko for services too numerous to mention.

Centrum Institute for the Arts, in Port Townsend, Washington, provided a quiet, well-equipped setting for Stefancic and Delgado to work during a one-semester sabbatical. University of Pittsburgh law school deans Mary Crossley and David Herring, and University of Florida Levin College of Law dean Robert Jerry, encouraged and supported our work in unflagging fashion. The University of Pittsburgh law school's superb Document Technology Center prepared the manuscript with precision and dispatch.

We dedicate this book to Jean's father and grandparents and Richard's father, and Juan's mother and father, immigrants all.

*

Copyright Acknowledgments and
Reprint Permissions

Summary of Contents

PART SIX. CULTURAL STEREOTYPES AND HATE SPEECH

*

Table of Cases

The principal cases are in bold type. Cases cited or discussed in the text are roman type. References are to pages. Cases cited in principal cases and within other quoted materials are not included.

*

Table of Authorities

Page numbers of excerpted and quoted material are in bold type. Page numbers of cited material are in roman type. Works cited in cases are not included.

*

LATINOS AND THE LAW

CASES AND MATERIALS

*

The Black–White Binary Paradigm of Race:

Much current thought about race places two groups, blacks and whites, at the center and deems their relations constitutive of that concept. Other groups enter into the analysis only insofar as they succeed in analogizing their situation to that of one of the two main groups. Known as the black-white binary paradigm of race, this approach is fast losing favor. Most scholars today realize that Latinos are not just blacks with brown skins or white people with a good suntan. Understanding and dealing with their situation requires expanding one's approach beyond the one that earlier scholars used to understand black-white relations. It requires, for example, coming to terms with discrimination based on a foreign-sounding name, immigration status, accent, or inability to speak English, factors that rarely play a role in discrimination against blacks or Native Americans.

Critical Race Theory:

Another set of tools that we have found helpful are those of critical race theory, a legal movement that sprang up in the late 1970s when progressive lawyers realized that the heady gains of the sixties had stalled and were, in some cases, being rolled back. New approaches were needed to cope with the forms of colorblind, institutional, or unconscious racism that were developing and an American public that seemed increasingly uninterested in race. The body of critical race writing is large, but certain concepts are helpful in understanding Latino legal history. These include structural determinism (see the discussion of the black-white binary paradigm in Part Two), interest convergence (discussed in Part Two), resistance (in Parts Five and Nine), and the critique of colorblindness (in Part Four).

Postcolonial Theory:

While critical race theory has been developing in the United States, a second scholarly movement has been flowering on the other side of the world. Scholars in Asia and Africa, areas formerly under French, English, Portuguese, or Belgian control, as well as a few Latin American scholars, have been writing about a different form of subordination, namely colonialism and neocolonialism. These writers discuss issues such as the role of language, resistance, collaboration, and the struggle to maintain mental and psychic health in an occupied society.

Many themes from postcolonial literature find their way into this book. For example, Part Three discusses language issues and liberation. Part Seven builds on the writing of some of the postcolonials to analyze workplace issues and exploitation. And Part Six builds on postcolonial literature to understand media stereotypes of Latinos.

Internal Colony:

A related notion is that Latinos living in the United States are an internal colony. First introduced by Robert Blauner and Chicano scholar Rodolfo Acuña, the internal-colony model posits that the relation between white society and domestic Latinos resembles that of a colonial nation and its subjects. If one understands the dynamics of the settler-native relationship, one can discern many of the same dynamics in the situation of Latinos today. We shall make use of this theory at a number of points in this book.

As the reader will see, much seemingly unrelated law fits together when viewed from the perspective of one or more of these principles. For example, white self-interest, such as the needs of agribusiness, appears behind many of the shifts in this country's immigration laws and quotas. What might seem a relaxation of hard-line exclusion may, upon inspection, appear as a means to secure needed farm labor (interest convergence). Latino struggles to desegregate local schools and gain the right to a bilingual education resemble those of other colonized peoples to achieve self-sufficiency. Their efforts to combat harmful and degrading stereotypes in the media and at work reveal much about the role of speech and free expression in American law, which in turn illustrate much about how majoritarian law constructs citizenship and equal respect.

This book explores race and racism in a variety of settings: naturalization and citizenship; language rights; education; immigration; cultural stereotypes; and the workplace. It discusses rebellious lawyering, resistance, and the unique issues of Latinas. Its overarching goal is to enable the reader to make connections among race, history, legal doctrine, and social authority. The task is not easy, but we have attempted to provide the basic materials, notes, questions, and reading lists that will enable the reader to begin to understand a rich history and a complex and challenging present.

This casebook does not cover voting rights and criminal justice, which deserve separate books of their own.

A Note on Terminology:

Latinos are a diverse ("pan-ethnic") group, encompassing differing subgroups that vary by country of origin, date of arrival, degree of assimilation, English fluency, and much more.[1] Readers should keep this complexity in mind. Even when we make generalizations, such as "many Latinos/as regard Spanish as their mother tongue," you should remember that every such statement has many exceptions. For example, many speak an Indian language, such as Nahuatl, as their mother tongue; for Brazilians, it is Portuguese. Many second-generation Latinos have begun to lose their command of Spanish and speak English more proficiently. Others combine the two into "Spanglish," a discourse attractive to and adopted by some hip whites.

In referring to racial groups, we prefer "black" or "African American," "Latino" or "Latina," "Asian American," and "Indian" or "Native American." We do not use "Hispanic," since some readers do not

---

1. In a recent year, the makeup of the Latino group by place of origin was: Mexicans, 66.9%; Puerto Ricans 8.6%; Central or South Americans, 14.3%; Cubans, 3.7%; and other Hispanic, 6.5%.

like the way it emphasizes an association with the colonial nation, Spain, in derogation of the Indian forebears that most Latinos have. By the same token, we use "down" punctuation for the terms "whites," "blacks," and "critical race theory," since tradition does not compel capitalization and the trend among academic presses is to capitalize as little as possible. Where an author of one of the selections uses a different approach, we generally honor it, unless it introduces clear error (such as using the hyphenated form of "Mexican–American" or "Asian–American" to refer to individuals or groups). Finally, we generally use "Latino" as a noun referring to the group, and "Latino/a," as an adjective, for example in referring to the Latino/a religion.

*

Part One

LATINO HISTORIES

Chapter 1

MEXICAN AMERICANS

SECTION 1. THE UNITED STATES' CONQUEST OF MEXICO

In a peaceful revolution in 1821, Mexico achieved independence from Spain. Then, Mexico was approximately twice its current size, and included what is today Texas, California, Arizona, New Mexico, Nevada, and parts of Utah, Colorado, and Kansas. Soon afterward, American settlers began arriving in the Texas territories. During these early years, Mexicans were concerned about United States aggression, fears that were to prove entirely well founded.

By 1836, Anglo immigrants and "Tejanos"—former Mexicans living in Texas—had successfully fought for independence from Mexico. However, that country did not recognize Texas' claim to independence. In December 1845, Texas became a state under a joint resolution of Congress. For an account of the heavily United States-influenced move for Texan independence, see Rodolfo Acuña, *Occupied America: A History of Chicanos* 6–12 (3d ed. 1988).

THE WAR WITH MEXICO

President James K. Polk was a strong advocate for the annexation of Texas and, generally, for acquisition of Mexican territory. On the night Polk took office, he confessed his desire to acquire California, which was then part of Mexico. A short time later, he ordered General Zachary Taylor to march troops to the Rio Grande, which calculated to provoke Mexico. Although the boundary between the two countries was in dispute, it was understood to be at the Nueces River, 150 miles north of the Rio Grande. Polk had thus sent troops into an area understood, at least by Mexico, to be part of its territory. At least since Jefferson's presidency, the United States had coveted the Rio Grande and the valuable port city Matamoros, which provided access to the Gulf of Mexico. In 1846, Taylor's army advanced to the Rio Grande, very close to Mexican territory but still within the disputed zone between the two rivers.

"All that was needed," according to Howard Zinn, "was a military incident to begin the war that Polk wanted." As luck would have it, Polk received *two* such incidents: the murder of General Taylor's quartermaster as well as an attack by Mexicans upon one of Taylor's patrols that left sixteen Americans dead and the rest wounded and captured. Polk immediately sought war, declaring that "now, after reiterated menaces, Mexico has passed the boundary of the United States, has invaded our territory and shed American blood upon the American soil." See Howard Zinn, *A People's History of the United States* 147–51 (1995); Rodolfo Acuña, supra, 13. According to Zinn:

> The Mexicans had fired the first shot. But they had done what the American government wanted, according to Colonel Hitchcock [who served in Taylor's army], who wrote in his diary, even before those first incidents:

> I have said from the first that the United States are the aggressors. . . . We have not one particle of right to be here. . . . It looks as if the government sent a small force on purpose to bring on a war, so as to have a pretext for taking California and as much of this country as it chooses, for, whatever becomes of this army, there is no doubt of a war between the United States and Mexico. . . .

Zinn, supra, at 149.

Acuña summarizes the ensuing course of the war, which fully accomplished United States aims of expansion:

> The poorly equipped and poorly led Mexican army stood little chance against the expansion-minded Anglos. Even before the war Polk planned the campaign in stages: (1) Mexicans would be cleared out of Texas; (2) Anglos would occupy California and New Mexico; and (3) U.S. forces would march to Mexico City to force the beaten government to make peace on Polk's terms. And that was the way the campaign basically went. In the end, at a relatively small cost in men and money, the war netted the United States huge territorial gains. In all, the United States took over 1 million square miles from Mexico.

Acuña, supra, at 13.

Did white supremacy and racism toward the dark-skinned Mexicans play major roles in the run-up to the War with Mexico? Consider the following reading.

Reginald Horsman
Race and Manifest Destiny: The Origins of
American Racial Anglo–Saxonism
208–13 (1981)

The Anglo–Saxon blood could never be subdued by anything that claimed Mexican origin.

James Buchanan, February 14, 1845

The decisive years in the creation of a new Anglo–Saxon political ideology were from the mid–1830s to the mid 1840s. In these years American politicians and the American population were overwhelmed by a variety of influences, both practical and theoretical, which inspired a belief that the American Anglo–Saxons were destined to dominate or penetrate the American continents and large areas of the world. Americans had faith that they would increase in such numbers that they would personally shape the destiny of other areas.

The catalyst in the overt adoption of a racial Anglo–Saxonism was the meeting of Americans and Mexicans, in the Southwest, the Texas Revolution, and the war with Mexico. In confronting the Mexicans the Americans clearly formulated the idea of themselves as an Anglo–Saxon race. The use of *Anglo-Saxon* in a racial sense, somewhat rare in the political arguments of the early 1830s, increased rapidly later in the decade and became commonplace by the mid 1840s. The manner in which the Anglo–Saxon race was being isolated from other peoples was stated with clarity by Senator Benjamin Leigh of Virginia in January 1836 when opposing the abolitionist petitions. After pointing out that his fellow Congressmen had only to remember how the mobs of Cincinnati, Philadelphia, and New York had dealt with the few free Negroes in their midst to appreciate what would follow general emancipation, he candidly sketched the problem: "It is peculiar to the character of this Anglo–Saxon race of men to which we belong, that it has never been contented to live in the same country with any other distinct race, upon terms of equality; it has, invariably, when placed in that situation, proceeded to exterminate or enslave the other race in some form or other, or, failing in that, to abandon the country."

The idea of the Anglo–Saxon race as a distinct, all-encompassing force was expressed with increasing frequency in the late 1830s. In February 1837 William Gilpin wrote to his father from New Orleans that while the town was still Gallic in character the "Anglo–Saxon is pushing aside the Frenchman and eating him up. The big steamers ... are Anglo–Saxon, the huge stores and warehouses into which [goods] are piled have an Anglo–Saxon look and an Anglo–Saxon ship bears them hence. [Of] all the new part of the city, the only decent part is English." When Horace Bushnell, in August 1837, delivered an oration on the principles of national greatness, he used old and familiar arguments concerning America as a land saved for events of world significance; however, he used a new precision in writing of the origin of the people for whom the New World had been preserved. "Out of all the inhabitants of the world," he said, "... a select stock, the Saxon, and out of this the British family, the noblest of the stock, was chosen to people our country." In contrast, the Mexican state, he said, had started with fundamental disadvantages in the character of its immigrants. If the quality of the British people was changed into that of the Mexican, "five years would make their noble island a seat of poverty and desolation." For Bushnell, God had reserved America for a special people of Saxon blood.

By the 1830s the Americans were eagerly grasping at reasons for their own success and for the failure of others. Although the white Americans of Jacksonian America wanted personal success and wealth, they also wanted a clear conscience. If the United States was to remain in the minds of its people a nation divinely ordained for great deeds, then the fault for the suffering inflicted in the rise to power and prosperity had to lie elsewhere. White Americans could rest easier if the sufferings of other races could be blamed on racial weakness rather than on the whites' relentless search for wealth and power. In the 1830s and 1840s, when it became obvious that American and Mexican interests were incompatible and that the Mexicans would suffer, innate weakness was found in the Mexicans. Americans, it was argued, were not to be blamed for forcibly taking the northern provinces of Mexico, for Mexicans, like Indians, were unable to make proper use of the land. The Mexicans had failed because they were a mixed, inferior race with considerable Indian and some black blood. The world would benefit if a superior race shaped the future of the Southwest.

By the time of the Mexican War, America had placed the Mexicans firmly within the rapidly emerging hierarchy of superior and inferior races. While the Anglo–Saxons were depicted as the purest of the pure— the finest Caucasians—the Mexicans who stood in the way of southwestern expansion were depicted as a mongrel race, adulterated by extensive intermarriage with an inferior Indian race. Travelers delighted in depicting the Mexicans as an unimprovable breed and were particularly scathing about the inhabitants of Mexico's northern provinces. T. J. Farnham in 1840 wrote of the Californians as "an imbecile, pusillanimous, race of men, and unfit to control the destinies of that beautiful country." No one who knew "the indolent, mixed race of California," he argued, could believe they would long populate much less govern, the region. The mixed white and Indian races of California and Mexico "must fade away; while the mingling of different branches of the Caucasian family in the States" would produce a race which would expand to cover all the northern provinces of Mexico. "The old Saxon blood must stride the continent," wrote Farnham, "must command all its northern shores ... and ... erect the altar of civil and religious freedom on the plains of the Californias."

The Mexican Californians were constantly attacked as shiftless and ineffective. Richard Dana thought them "an idle, thriftless people" and asserted that nothing but the character of the population prevented Monterey from becoming a large town. "In the hands of an enterprising people," he said, "what a country this might be!" Lansford Hastings, in his famous emigrants' guide of 1845, characterized the Mexican inhabitants of California as "scarcely a visible grade, in the scale of intelligence, above the barbarous tribes by whom they are surrounded." This was not surprising, said Hastings. There had been extensive intermarriage and "as most of the lower order of Mexicans, are Indians in fact, whatever is said in reference to the one, will also be applicable to the other." Stereotypes that were to persist in American thinking long after the

1840s were firmly fixed in Hastings's work. A Mexican, he said, "always pursues that method of doing things, which requires the least physical or mental exorcise [sic], unless it involves some danger, in which case, he always adopts some other method." Writing of soldiers who were brought into California in 1842, he commented that they were "mere Indians," and that it was "with these wild, shirtless, earless and heart-less creatures, headed by a few timid, soulless, brainless officers, that these semi-barbarians, intend to hold this delightful region, as against the civilized world." The process of dehumanizing those who were to be misused or destroyed proceeded rapidly in the United States in the 1840s. To take lands from inferior barbarians was no crime; it was simply following God's injunctions to make the land fruitful.

In the Southwest there was even a tendency for American travelers to praise the Pueblo Indians in order further to debase the "mongrel" Mexicans. George Kendall, who was on the Texas–Santa Fe expedition, commented in his account of that sorry affair that "the *pueblos*, or town Indians of New Mexico, are by far the better part of the population." Most Mexicans, he said, were content if they could satisfy their animal wants, "and so they will continue to be until the race becomes extinct or amalgamated with Anglo–Saxon stock." Rufus Sage echoed Kendall: "There are no people on the continent of America, whether civilized or uncivilized, with one or two exceptions, more miserable in condition or despicable in morals than the mongrel race inhabiting New Mexico."

The scathing denunciations of the Mexican race encompassed the inhabitants of central Mexico as well as its outlying provinces, and these denunciations were not confined to writers from any one party or one region in the United States. Waddy Thompson of South Carolina, who went to Mexico in 1842 as minister for the Whig administration, advanced the familiar stereotype in his *Recollections*, which was published in 1847. While condemning aggressive expansionism and the rapacious spirit of acquisition which was developing in the United States, Thompson had no doubt at all of the ultimate result of the meeting of the Anglo–Saxon and the Mexican races. He objected to the means, not to the end. "That our language and laws are destined to pervade this continent," he wrote, "I regard as more certain than any other event which is in the future. Our race has never yet put its foot upon a soil which it has not only kept but has advanced. I mean not our English ancestors only, but that great Teuton race from which we have both descended."

To Thompson an essential element in Mexican weakness was the mixed population. Of seven million inhabitants, he wrote, only one million were white Europeans or their descendants. Of the others there were some four to four and one-half million pure-blooded Indians, and the rest of mixed blood. Thompson, like many others at this time, was easily able to envisage a mysterious disappearance of millions of people. "That the Indian race of Mexico must recede before us," he wrote, "is quite as certain as that that is the destiny of our own Indians." Negroes in Mexico Thompson characterized as "the same lazy, filthy, and vicious creatures that they inevitably become where they are not held in bondage." The general Mexican population Thompson characterized as "lazy, ignorant, and, of course, vicious and dishonest."

The American dismissal of the Mexicans as an inferior, largely-Indian race did not pass unnoticed in Mexico. Mexican ministers in the United States warned their government that the Americans considered the Mexicans an inferior people. The Mexicans realized both that their neighbors to the north were likely to invade their northern provinces, and that they would claim that this was justified because they could make better use of the lands. Mexicans who served as diplomatic representatives in the United States were shocked at the rabid anti-Mexican attitudes and at the manner in which Mexicans were lumped together with Indians and blacks as an inferior race.

The Texas Revolution was from its beginnings interpreted in the United States and among Americans in Texas as a racial clash, not simply a revolt against unjust government or tyranny. Thomas Hart Benton said that the Texas revolt "has illustrated the Anglo–Saxon character, and given it new titles to the respect and admiration of the world. It shows that liberty, justice, valour—moral, physical, and intellectual power—discriminate that race wherever it goes." Benton asked "old England" to rejoice that distant Texas streams had seen the exploits of "a people strung from their loins, and carrying their language, laws, and customs, their *magna carta* and all its glorious privileges, into new regions and far distant climes."

In his two terms as president of Texas, Sam Houston consistently thought of the struggle in his region as one between a glorious Anglo–Saxon race and an inferior Mexican rabble. Victory for the Texans and the Americans in the Southwest would mean that larger areas of the world were to be brought under the rule of a race that could make best use of them. Houston was less imbued with the harsh scientific racial theories that carried most Americans before them in the 1840s than with the romantic exaltation of the Saxons given by Sir Walter Scott and his followers.

———————

The racial character of the War with Mexico comes into even sharper relief when one considers the Americans' reluctance to fight England over the Oregon territory. While a war with Mexico would target a people presumed racially inferior, one with Britain would require Anglo–Saxons to fight fellow Anglo–Saxons. While the War with Mexico resulted in a conquest in which Americans could claim racial dominion, the latter confrontation resulted in an affirmation of shared Anglo–Saxon origins and a negotiated peace. Horsman, supra, at 220–21, 224–25.

SECTION 2. VIEWS OF AMERICAN POLITICIANS ON THE ANNEXATION OF MEXICO AND MEXICANS

Long before the war with Mexico, and even before that country gained its independence from Spain, American statesmen and commentators had expressed their longing for Mexican lands. Benjamin Franklin, for example, had identified Mexico and Cuba as targets for future American expansion; the Louisiana Purchase stimulated thoughts of further expansion. Earlier, President Jefferson had attempted to claim the Rio Grande as the southern boundary of Louisiana. For his part, President John Quincy Adams expressed his wish for one of the important Texas rivers, particularly the Rio Grande. In 1826, Mexico rejected his offer to buy Texas for $1 million, even though Anglo Americans had been rapidly settling in New Mexico and Texas. See Rodolfo Acuña, *Occupied America* 6–7 (1988); David J. Weber, *The Mexican Frontier 1821–1846: The American Southwest Under Mexico* 1–14 (1982).

Once the U.S. Army had crushed the Mexican forces, American leaders faced a serious quandry. Because of the reigning beliefs in white supremacy, the annexation of former Mexican lands, populated by dark-skinned Mexicans, posed a severe threat to the racial integrity of the United States. The prospect of incorporating undesirable, mixed-race Mexicans into the United States revolted many politicians.

Senator John C. Calhoun, for example, objected to the war and to the annexation of Mexican lands, because the United States would have to deal with "eight or nine millions of Mexicans, without a government, on [our] hands." *Cong. Globe*, 30th Cong., 1st Sess. 53 (1848). Calhoun may have coveted Mexican lands, but only if they contained few Mexicans: "[O]ur army has ever since held all that it is desirable to hold— that portion whose population is sparse, and on that account the more desirable to be held. For I hold it in reference to this war a fundamental principle, that when we receive territorial indemnity, it shall be unoccupied territory." *Cong. Globe*, 30th Cong., 1st Sess. 96 (Jan. 4, 1848).

During the same speech, on January 4, 1848, Calhoun feared that annexing Mexico would disrupt white racial purity and political control:

> The next reason which my resolutions [opposing the conquest of Mexico] assign, is, that it is without example or precedent, either to hold Mexico as a province, or to incorporate her into our Union. No example of such a line of policy can be found. We have conquered many of the neighboring tribes of Indians, but we never thought of holding them in subjection—never of incorporating them into our Union. They have either been left as an independent people amongst us, or been driven into the forests.

> I know further, sir, that we have never dreamt of incorporating into our Union any but the Caucasian race—the free white race. To incorporate Mexico, would be the very first instance of the kind of incorporating an Indian race; for more than half of the Mexicans are

Indians, and the other is composed chiefly of mixed tribes. I protest against such a union as that! Ours, sir, is the Government of a white race. The greatest misfortunes of Spanish America are to be traced to the fatal error of placing these colored races on an equality with the white race. That error destroyed the social arrangement which formed the basis of society. * * * And yet it is professed and talked about to erect these Mexicans into a Territorial Government and place them on an equality with the people of the United States. I protest utterly against such a project. * * *

Are we to associate with ourselves as equal, companions and fellow citizens, the Indians and mixed race of Mexico? Sir, I should consider such a thing as fatal to our institutions.

Cong. Globe, 30th Cong., 1st Sess. 96–98 (Jan. 4, 1848). Calhoun argued for calling a halt to the Mexican campaign and keeping only the sparsely populated lands in northern Mexico that the U.S. had already won.

Henry Clay too found the prospect of annexing Mexico appalling on racial grounds:

Does any considerable man believe it possible that two such immense countries, with territories of nearly equal extent, with populations so incongruous, so different in race, language, in religion and in laws, could be blended together in one harmonious mass, happily governed by one common authority?

Philip Anthony Hernández, *The Other North Americans: The American Image of Mexico and Mexicans, 1550–1850* at 246–47 (Ph.D. Diss. U. Cal. Berkeley 1974) (quoting speech of Henry Clay of Nov. 13, 1847 in Lexington, Kentucky).

Even ordinary Americans took this opportunity to express negative attitudes toward Mexicans. "Mexicans remained in the eyes of Americans what they were before the outbreak of hostilities—a distinctly inferior people whose racial characteristics offended the deeply held American assumptions on racial purity." Hernández, *supra*, at 203. Ultimately the annexation of only the northernmost, most sparsely populated parts of Mexico resolved these racial concerns.

SECTION 3.   THE TREATY OF GUADALUPE HIDALGO (1848)

The Treaty of Guadalupe Hidalgo of 1848 settled the war between the United States and Mexico, drawing the boundary line between the two countries at the Rio Grande and providing for the transfer of conquered territory from Mexico to the United States. Mexico ceded the long-coveted California, including the desirable port of San Diego, and a vast expanse that included present day Nevada, Arizona, New Mexico, and parts of Colorado and Utah. For this monumental acquisition, the United States paid the paltry sum of $15 million.

The government of Mexico, however, was concerned about the fate of Mexicans remaining in the conquered territories. It therefore bargained for protections for them and their property in what ultimately became Articles VIII and IX of the Treaty. See Richard Griswold del Castillo, *The Treaty of Guadalupe Hidalgo: A Legacy of Conflict* 38–42 (1990); Fernando Chacon Gomez, *The Intended and Actual Effect of Article VIII of the Treaty of Guadalupe Hidalgo: Mexican Treaty Rights Under International and Domestic Law* 22–38 (Ph.D. Diss. U. Mich. 1977).

Notwithstanding the document's importance in legal history, the Treaty of Guadalupe Hidalgo remains largely obscure and ignored. As historian David Weber puts it:

> The Treaty of Guadalupe Hidalgo is the key document of Mexican American history, for through it Mexicans living in the Southwest became Americans and were guaranteed "all the rights of citizens of the United States." Yet the treaty remains relatively unknown in the United States. In Mexico, on the other hand, since losers have a longer memory than victors, the treaty is still remembered with bitterness.

David J. Weber, *Foreigners in Their Native Land* 141 (1973).

The treaty's history is rife with indications of presidential and Senatorial unwillingness to deal with Mexicans on terms of equal citizenship, despite language in the treaty suggesting otherwise. It also betrays the United States' desire to facilitate the transfer of Mexican-owned lands to Anglo hands. In none of this were the parties in an equal bargaining position: The United States held a much stronger hand because of its successful military conquest; the Mexicans could bargain only to save face and for whatever concessions the United States was willing to recognize. See Weber, supra, at 141–42.

President Polk, when he first transmitted the draft treaty to the Senate, wrote that:

> To the tenth article of the treaty there are serious objections, and no instructions given to Mr. Trist contemplated or authorized its insertion. The public lands within the limits of Texas belong to that State, and this Government has no power to dispose of them or to change the conditions of grants already made. All valid titles to land within the other territories ceded to the United States will remain, unaffected by the change of sovereignty; and I therefore submit that this article should not be ratified as a part of the treaty.

V *Treaties and Other International Acts of the United States of America* 248 (Hunter Miller ed., 1937).

Article X, as drafted, provided that:

> All grants of land made by the Mexican government or by the competent authorities, in territories previously appertaining to Mexico, and remaining for the future within the limits of the United States, shall be respected as valid, to the same extent that the same grants would be valid, if the said territories had remained within the limits of Mexico.

Following Polk's recommendation, the Senate struck Article X from the Treaty. To quiet the protests of Mexicans, who feared that pre-existing land titles would not be honored in the absence of Article X, the United States issued a Statement of Protocol which provided the following:

> The American government by suppressing the Xth article of the Treaty of Guadalupe Hidalgo did not in any way intend to annul the grants of lands made by Mexico in the ceded territories. These grants ... preserve the legal value which they may possess, and the grantees may cause their legitimate (titles) to be acknowledged before the American tribunals.
>
> Conformable to the law of the United States, legitimate titles to every description of property, personal and real, existing in the ceded territories, are those which were legitimate titles under the Mexican law of California and New Mexico up to the 13th of May, 1846 and in Texas up to the 2nd of March, 1836.

Rodolfo Acuña, *Occupied America* 19–20 (3d ed. 1988) (quoting *Compilation of Treaties in Force* 402 (1899)).

Deleting Article X, however, would undermine the legitimacy of Mexican land grants by denying explicit recognition of ones made before the War and by declining to acknowledge the validity of Mexican practices and customs for designating land grants. Later, this was to prove quite important: During litigation over contested claims to land, the customs and practices of Mexican authorities were often held to be unenforceably vague under United States standards. Thus, by deleting Article X, Polk and the Senate made it much easier to take Mexican lands by making United States law and practice determinative and by dishonoring Mexican law and custom as the appropriate reference points for ascertaining the validity of land claims.

Articles VIII and IX contain important provisions regarding citizenship. Under Article VIII, Mexicans in the conquered territories enjoyed the right to remain in the United States and, either by election within one year or by continued residence within the United States, they "shall be considered to have elected to become citizens of the United States."

Revisions to Article IX of the draft treaty made plain the limited meaning of federal citizenship at the time and Congress's concerns about diminishing the racial purity of the United States. Under the original draft Article IX, those Mexicans who became United States citizens

> shall be incorporated into the Union of the United States, and admitted as soon as possible, according to the principles of the Federal Constitution, to the enjoyment of all the rights of citizens of the United States. In the meantime, they shall be maintained and protected in the enjoyment of their liberty, their property, and the civil rights now vested in them according to the Mexican laws.

The Senate amended the Treaty so that the final ratified version read:

The Mexicans * * * shall be incorporated into the Union of the United States and be admitted, *at the proper time (to be judged of by the Congress of the United States) to the enjoyment of all the rights of citizens of the United States according to the principles of the Constitution.*

See V *Treaties and Other International Acts of the United States of America* 219 (Hunter Miller ed., 1937) (emphasis added).

Rather than admit Mexicans into the Union "as soon as possible," the Senate made their admission discretionary, "at the proper time," in the judgment of Congress. The original language raised the frightening (to Anglos) prospect of Mexicans on an equal legal footing with whites. To avoid that prospect, the Senate gave Congress discretion to admit states containing Mexicans whenever Congress deemed it "proper."

A. ARTICLES VIII AND IX OF THE TREATY OF GUADALUPE HIDALGO (1848)

Article VIII:

Mexicans now established in territories previously belonging to Mexico, and which remain for the future within the limits of the United States, as defined by the present Treaty, shall be free to continue where they now reside, or to remove at any time to the Mexican Republic, retaining the property which they possess in the said territories, or disposing thereof and removing the proceeds wherever they please; without their being subjected, on this account, to any contribution, tax or charge whatever.

Those who shall prefer to remain in the said territories, may either retain the title and rights of Mexican citizens, or acquire those of citizens of the United States. But, they shall be under the obligation to make their election within one year from the date of the exchange of ratifications of this treaty: and those who shall remain in the said territories, after the expiration of that year, without having declared their intention to retain the character of Mexicans, shall be considered to have elected to become citizens of the United States.

In the said territories, property of every kind, now belonging to Mexicans not established there, shall be inviolably respected. The present owners, the heirs of these, and all Mexicans who may hereafter acquire said property by contract, shall enjoy with respect to it, guaranties equally ample as if the same belonged to citizens of the United States.

Article IX:

The Mexicans who, in the territories aforesaid, shall not preserve the character of citizens of the Mexican Republic, conformably with what is stipulated in the preceding article, shall be incorporated into the Union of the United States and be admitted, at the proper time (to be judged of by the Congress of the United States) to the enjoyment of all the rights of citizens of the United States according to the principles of

citizenship rights of white citizens or were to be treated as Indian inhabitants. Most government officials argued that Mexicans of predominantly Indian descent should be extended the same legal status as the detribalized American Indians. Mexicans, on the other hand, argued that under the Treaty of Guadalupe Hidalgo and international laws, the U.S. Government agreed to extend [to] all Mexican citizens—regardless of their race—the political rights enjoyed by white citizens. These rights were accorded to them on the basis of the international principle guaranteeing inhabitants of ceded territories the nationality of the successor state unless other provisions are made in the treaty of peace.

See Martha Menchaca, *Chicano Indianism: A Historical Account of Racial Repression in the United States*, 20 Am. Ethnologist 583, 584 (1993). Since 1812, when it became an independent nation, Mexico had granted full citizenship and political rights to Indians. Thus, at the time of U.S. conquest, Mexico maintained no formal racial restrictions on who could be a full citizen.

Once the United States annexed the northern half of Mexico, however, the meaning of the grant of citizenship in the Treaty to Mexicans was largely contingent on the Anglo–American perception of the race of particular Mexicans. Dark-skinned mestizos—the mixed-race Mexicans of Spanish and Indian ancestry so despised by white Anglos—were denied citizenship and meaningful political participation. The American treatment of Indians provided a paradigm for the treatment of visibly Indian Mexicans. Lighter-skinned Mexicans, by contrast, were treated as white and granted more political and citizenship rights. "Given the nature of the U.S. racial system and its laws, the conquered Mexican population learned that it was politically expedient to assert their Spanish ancestry; otherwise, they were susceptible to being treated as American Indians." See Menchaca, supra, at 587–89. Although the Treaty granted federal citizenship to all Mexicans who either elected it or who remained in the territories acquired by the United States, it was state citizenship that was significant for purposes of political participation, since the states defined qualifications for voting and access to education.

State and territorial legislatures discriminated against Mexicans who looked Indian and in favor of those who looked white. The California state constitution of 1849 granted the right to vote only to whites, consequently disenfranchising the vast majority of Mexicans, mestizos whose appearance revealed their Indian ancestry.

CALIFORNIA CONSTITUTION OF 1849 (ARTICLE II)

The debates of the Constitutional Convention made clear that "savage" Indians and blacks were not to receive the right to vote:

It was evident from the start of the convention that the Negro was not wanted in the new territory. At all events, it was agreed overwhelmingly that those Negroes already in the territory should not vote. The Indian was already in the state, but he should not be either a citizen or a voter. * * *

The delegates at Monterey in 1849 remained firm in their convictions that no persons other than whites should play any part in the governing of the state and proceeded to disenfranchise many of those individuals who had originally cast their ballots in the special election that put these very same delegates in their convention seats. Even an amendment that proposed to grant the right to vote to those Indians who had been citizens of Mexico and were taxed as owners of real estate, and expressly excepted all Negroes, was defeated by a vote of 22 to 21.

Robert F. Heizer & Alan F. Almquist, *The Other Californians* 96 (1971).

Which Californians would enjoy the privilege of voting was a major subject of debate at the convention. During this period, it was within the province of state power to determine voter qualifications. Accordingly, while the United States citizenship granted by the Treaty of Guadalupe Hidalgo might include federal citizenship for Mexicans of mixed Indian and Spanish ancestry, the Treaty's guarantee of federal citizenship offered no such guarantee of voting rights or political participation. The Treaty left these matters to the states. See Robert F. Heizer & Alan F. Almquist, *The Other Californians* 92–119 (1971). The convention ultimately agreed upon the following provision regarding suffrage:

> Section 1. Every white male citizen of the United States, *and every white male citizen of Mexico*, who shall have elected to become a citizen of the United States, under the treaty of [Guadalupe Hidalgo], * * * of the age of twenty-one years who shall have been a resident of the state six months next preceding the election * * * shall be entitled to vote at all elections which are now or hereafter may be authorized by law: *Provided*, That nothing herein contained, shall be construed to prevent the Legislature, by a two-thirds concurrent vote, from admitting to the right of suffrage, Indians or the descendants of Indians, in such special cases as such a proportion of the legislative body may deem just and proper.

Cal. Const. Art. II, § 1 (1849) (emphasis added).

Notes and Questions

1. Consider *People v. Hall*, 4 Cal. 399 (1854), in which the California Supreme Court ruled that the testimony of Chinese witnesses was not admissible against a white defendant. The same principles applied to Mexican–American mestizos.

In April, 1857, Manuel Domínguez, a mestizo, attempted to testify as a defense witness in a San Francisco courtroom. One of California's most distinguished citizens, Domínguez had served as a delegate to the Constitutional Convention and had signed the Constitution of 1849. By 1857, he was supervisor of Los Angeles County and a wealthy landowner. Notwithstanding his prominence, the judge dismissed him as a witness when the plaintiff's lawyer argued that Domínguez's Indian blood rendered his testimony inadmissible. See Heizer & Almquist, supra, at 131; Leonard Pitt, *The Decline of the Californios* 202 (1966).

2. Article II of the California Constitution raised intriguing questions about who would be considered a "white Mexican male" entitled to vote. In short, the state took the position that mestizos fell outside the polity. See Fernando Padilla, *Early Chicano Legal Recognition, 1846–1897*, 13 J. Popular Culture 564–74 (1979).

3. What are the implications of being a "white Mexican," under these early Anglo–American laws? What do you think the effect would be upon the unity of the Mexican community? Then? Now?

4. In *People v. De La Guerra*, 40 Cal. 311 (1870), the federal citizenship of a Mexican-origin California judge came into question. The court concluded that de la Guerra was entitled to U.S. citizenship under the Treaty of Guadalupe Hidalgo. It went on to affirm the state's power to define racial qualifications for voting under Article II. Accordingly, de la Guerra could be both a federal citizen and excluded from voting rights, if he was not deemed a "white male citizen of Mexico" under Article II. The court wrote that the "possession of all political rights is not essential to citizenship." Apparently, the state of California took it upon itself to make that determination.

5. Note that *De La Guerra* came down the same year, 1870, as the Fifteenth Amendment. That Amendment provides that the right of U.S. citizens "to vote shall not be denied or abridged by the United States or by any State on account of race, color, or previous condition of servitude." U.S. Const. Am. 15 (1870). What difference should the Fifteenth Amendment make in California's treatment of the suffrage of blacks, mestizos, and Indians?

6. In *In re Rodriguez*, 81 Fed. 337 (W.D. Tex. 1897), the court decided that a mestizo Mexican, who was neither a "free white person" nor a person of "African nativity" or "African descent" was nonetheless eligible for naturalization. For a detailed discussion of the racial requirements for naturalized citizenship, and Supreme Court decisions on the subject, see Ian F. Haney López, *White By Law: The Legal Construction of Race* (10th Anniv. ed. 2006) (discussing Supreme Court decisions on who was white and who was not).

C.   THE TREATY OF GUADALUPE HIDALGO AND LAND OWNERSHIP

Like the meaning of the federal citizenship promised in the Treaty of Guadalupe Hidalgo, another set of fundamental questions also arose. What would be the status of Mexican-owned real property after the transfer of sovereignty to the United States? How did approximately half of Mexico, owned by Mexicans through land grants made under Spanish and Mexican law, come to be owned by and integrated into the United States?

This massive transfer of land occurred in many ways. In Texas, many Mexicans were simply run off their lands by Anglos angered by their presence. The Treaty of Guadalupe Hidalgo did not apply to Texas, except to settle its southern boundary at the Rio Grande. See Article V, Treaty of Guadalupe Hidalgo, in V *Treaties and Other International Acts of the United States of America* 213, 315–16 (Hunter Miller ed., 1937). Texas had become a state in 1845, preceding the war and the Treaty. Describing the post-war situation in Texas, David Montejano writes:

> The American settlers, in speaking of Mexicans, constantly distinguished themselves as "white folks." Newcomers were sometimes surprised at the rights of Mexicans. Olmsted overheard one newcomer informing another American that he had seen a Mexican with a revolver and stating that they shouldn't be allowed to carry firearms. The other replied that it would be difficult to prevent it— "they think themselves just as good as white men." Around the Victoria area, Anglo–Americans had sharply distinct views of Germans and Mexicans: "They always employed German mechanics, and spoke well of them. Mexicans were regarded in a somewhat unchristian tone, not as heretics or heathen to be converted with flannel and tracts, but rather as vermin to be exterminated. The lady was particularly strong in her prejudices. White folks and Mexicans were never made to live together, anyhow, and the Mexicans had no business here. They were getting so impertinent, and were so well protected by the laws, that the Americans would just have to get together and drive them all out of the country."

David Montejano, *Anglos and Mexicans in the Making of Texas 1836–1986* at 29 (1987) (quoting Frederick Law Olmsted, *A Journey Through Texas; or, a Saddletrip on the Southwestern Frontier* 164, 245 (1860, reprinted 1969)).

Anglos acquired Mexican lands in other ways as well. White men would marry Mexican women from wealthy families and so become entitled to part of the Mexican family's land holdings. In addition, Mexican-owned lands were sold, usually at steep discounts, to cover taxes enacted by the new Anglo governors. See Montejano, supra, at 35, 37, 52; Arnoldo De León, *The Tejano Community* 1836–1900 at 14, 17 (1982).

United States policies also took their toll. Congress established tribunals that placed into question lands claimed under Mexican and Spanish grants preceding the war and the Treaty of Guadalupe Hidalgo. Congress established the California Land Claims Commission, a Surveyor General's office, and the Court of Private Land Claims to resolve previously undisputed land grants that were put into dispute by Congress after the war. The California Land Claim Act of 1851 established a commission, consisting of three appointed commissioners, whose purpose it was to ascertain the validity of private claims in California. 9 Stat. 631 (1851). Congress later established the office of Surveyor General of New Mexico, Kansas, and Nebraska. 10 Stat. 308 (1854). In 1891, Congress created the Court of Private Land Claims which eventually had jurisdiction to resolve land claims in the entire region. See 26 Stat. 854 (1891); 27 Stat. 470 (1893). The following excerpt describes these tribunals and their effect on the Mexicans living in the newly acquired territories.

Malcolm Ebright
Land Grants and Lawsuits in Northern New Mexico
34, 38–39, 45–50 (1994)

The only part of the [Treaty of Guadalupe Hidalgo] protecting land grant property rights after the Senate amendments was Article 8, which provided that "property of every kind now belonging to Mexicans ... shall be inviolably respected." Questions were left unanswered by Article 8 that had been resolved by Article 10, like the standard to be used in land grant adjudication * * *. The [law creating the California Land Claims Commission] placed the burden on the land grant owner to file a claim with the land board by 1853 or have his or her property declared public domain of the United States. This burden of initiating and proving a claim required the claimant to hire an attorney and to gather all the documents and testimony needed to support that claim. After the initial hearing, the land board's decision could be appealed to the federal district court where a new trial would take place. The district court's decision could also be appealed to the U.S. Supreme Court. If the claimant was finally successful there, they still had the burden of paying the cost of surveying their land and defending their survey before the Surveyor General's office.

This procedure transformed land grant owners into claimants who had to jump through numerous costly hoops before their property rights under the treaty were recognized. * * *

THE SURVEYOR GENERAL OF NEW MEXICO

The surveyor general's primary duty was to extend the federal public land survey system that provided for a checkerboard of townships, each containing thirty-six 640–acre sections. Once public land had been surveyed under this system, ownership could be obtained under the homestead and other laws that the surveyor general administered. The boundaries of land grants were not to be surveyed until after they were confirmed; even today large areas within land grants have not been surveyed. The American surveying system did not fit the arid Southwest, and Anglo property law was not understood by most Hispanos. Corruption of public officials and dishonesty of claimants under the United States land laws were additional factors preventing Hispanic land grant heirs from obtaining title to the land grants they occupied under the homestead and other similar laws. It was not unusual for enterprising Anglos to wrest from Hispanos their land grant property through fraud or manipulation of the land laws.

In addition to these problems, the scheme for adjudicating land grants under the surveyor general system was badly flawed. Hispanos did not understand or have any trust in the American system of land ownership. Although written evidence of title was not without importance under the Spanish and Mexican land systems, for Hispanos, possession was indeed nine-tenths of the law. Their use of the land was more important in establishing their ownership than were any documents. When called upon to bring their documents to Santa Fe and file claims with the surveyor general, most Hispanos demurred. Some feared that they would lose their documents if they turned them over to the surveyor general, while others felt they were adequately protected by the Treaty of Guadalupe Hidalgo and didn't need to file a claim. Most Hispanos never conceived of the possibility that the common lands of their community grants were in jeopardy because under their laws and customs, the common lands could never be sold. Since filing a claim entailed considerable expense, it was the questionable claim held by the speculator that was often filed first.

The surveyor general's responsibility concerning land grants was to report to Congress his recommendation as to whether claims should be confirmed or rejected by that body. * * *

THE COURT OF PRIVATE LAND CLAIMS

     * * *

The statute setting up the Court of Private Land Claims was not in itself a radical departure from the procedure followed in California to adjudicate land titles there, but differences in language between the two statutes were later used by the courts to justify a stricter, more technical approach under the 1891 Act. For example, the 1891 Act did not specifically mention custom as a factor to be considered by the court in making its decisions although custom would be implied under international law, a factor that was mentioned. Additionally the act required proof that every condition of a grant was performed within the time allowed and only a grant "lawfully and regularly derived from the Government of Spain or Mexico" was entitled to confirmation. * * *

The procedure in the Court of Private Land Claims heavily favored the government, resulting in numerous unjust decisions. As with the surveyor general system, the claimant before the land claims court had the burden of proving the existence of the grant and the performance of all its conditions. Previously, however, the claimant was aided by certain presumptions that eased the burden of proof, such as the presumption of the existence of a community grant from the existence of a settlement on the grant in 1846, the presumption of regularity of a grant, and the presumption of authority of a granting official. Under the Court of Private Land Claims, all three of these presumptions were eliminated. * * *

Although the adversarial climate favored the government in the Court of Private Land Claims, the decisions of the land claims court occasionally displayed a balanced approach that yielded a result favorable to the claimants. But in several instances, when the U.S. attorney appealed these decisions, the U.S. Supreme Court reversed, siding with the government and against the claimant. The most famous of these decisions concerned the ownership of the common lands of the San Miguel del Bado grant in San Miguel County. [Eds. The Supreme Court considered this grant in *United States v. Sandoval*, 167 U.S. 278 (1897). Contrary to Spanish and Mexican law, the Court decided that the common lands of a community grant were owned not by the community but by the Spanish or Mexican governments, such that title to such lands passed to the United States after 1848.] * * *

After the 1897 *Sandoval* decision, the land claims court rejected the common lands of every community grant that came up for adjudication. This vast acreage acquired by the United States now comprises most of the Carson and Santa Fe National Forests in northern New Mexico. But since the Court of Private Land Claims refused to apply the *Sandoval* decision retroactively, community grants confirmed before the *Sandoval* decision were able to retain their common lands.

Several other grounds were used by the Supreme Court and by the Court of Private Land Claims to reject perfectly valid grants. These included requirements that the grant be recorded in the Spanish or Mexican archives of New Mexico, that the grant be approved by the territorial deputation if made during the Mexican Period, and that there be strict compliance with each of the procedural steps of the grant: the petition, the grant, and the act of possession. But these technical reasons were seldom if ever the basis for a land grant rejection by Spain or Mexico. One situation in which Spanish or Mexican officials did reject a land grant due to a procedural defect was where notice to adjacent landowners, giving them the opportunity to object to the grant, had not been given. But United States courts rarely looked to see how the Spanish and Mexican governments had treated land grants in Hispanic New Mexico, despite the availability of numerous cases involving land grant disputes in the archives of New Mexico.

There were several grounds that did justify the rejection of land grants by Spanish and Mexican authorities. These included: (1) forgery of the documents, (2) insufficient proof that a grant had been made, (3) failure to notify owners of land adjoining the grant, (4) failure to meet a condition of the grant, (5) revocation of the grant by Spanish or Mexican officials, and (6) failure to settle the land four years after the grant was made, with continuous possession thereafter. These were grounds that would also justify United States courts in rejecting grants. For under international law, United States courts should have adjudicated land grants in the same manner as Spain and Mexico would have done. But instead, these courts often found it more expedient to rely on an obscure Spanish or Mexican law or commentary on Hispanic Law as the basis for a decision rather than seek the benefit of expert testimony on questions of Spanish and Mexican law.

* * *

Under the Mexican Colonization Law of 1824, individuals could receive grants of up to eleven leagues of land, about 48,000 acres. Many non-Mexican Americans found such large grants shocking. When Congressman William Carey Jones investigated the land situation in California in 1849, his report on the size of such grants astounded many of his readers:

> When the immigration [into California] began, the Americans, used to the freedom of the boundless west, looked with incredulous surprise at the great stretches of the best land in California owned by single individuals, grantees of the Mexican and Imperial Spanish Governments. The United States population had a poor opinion of the native Californians anyway and were not at all sure that the latter were anything but aliens with rights little better than the native Indians.

George Cosgrave, *Early California Justice* 25 (1948).

Sheer illegality played a role as well. Anglo–American squatters regularly staked out claims on Mexican-settled and owned land. Later, in litigations about the validity of Mexican land grants, the "avaricious squatters in their endless harassing of grant holders, had as their chief ally none other than the Government of the United States." Cosgrave, supra, at 27.

Land Grant Adjudications

As described above, Congress established three tribunals intended to adjudicate the validity of land ownership in the new territories conquered from Mexico. Many such adjudications wound up in the United States Supreme Court.

In *Fremont v. United States*, 58 U.S. (17 How.) 542 (1854), the Supreme Court upheld the validity of the title to land purchased by John Fremont, one of the Anglo military leaders who conquered California and later became a prominent national politician. Chief Justice Taney wrote that

> California was at that time in possession of the American forces, and held by the United States as a conquered country, subject to the authority of the American government. The Mexican municipal laws, which were then administered, were administered under the authority of the United States, and might be repealed or abrogated at their pleasure; and any Mexican law inconsistent with the rights of the United States, or its public policy, or with the rights of its citizens, were annulled by the conquest. Now, there is no principle of public law which prohibits a citizen of a conquering country from purchasing property, real or personal, in the territory thus acquired and held; nor is there any thing in the principles of our government, in its policy or its laws, which forbids it. The Mexican government, if it had regained the power, and it had been its policy to prevent the alienation of real estate, might have treated the sale by Alvarado [to

Fremont] as a violation of its laws; but it becomes a very different question when the American government is called on to execute the Mexican law. And it can hardly be maintained that an American citizen, who makes a contract or purchases property under such circumstances, can be punished in a court of the United States with the penalty of forfeiture, when there is no law of congress to inflict it. The purchase was perfectly consistent with the rights and duties of Colonel Fremont, as an American officer and an American citizen; and the country in which he made the purchase was, at the time, subject to the authority and dominion of the United States.

Botiller v. Domínguez
130 U.S. 238 (1889)

[Domínguez attempted to eject Botiller from the "Rancho Las Virgenes." The title of the plaintiff was a grant claimed to have been made by the government of Mexico to Domínguez, but no claim under this grant had ever been presented for confirmation to the board of land commissioners, appointed under the Act of Congress of March 3, 1851, (9 St. 631) "to ascertain and settle the private land claims in the state of California."

The California Supreme Court had decided that the federal statute creating the California Land Claims Commission was invalid.]

JUSTICE MILLER delivered the opinion of the court.

* * *

The question presented is an important one in reference to land titles in the state of California, and is entitled to our serious consideration. Although it has been generally supposed that nearly all the private claims to any of the lands acquired by the United States from Mexico, by the treaty of peace made at the close of the Mexican war, have been presented to and passed upon by the board of commissioners appointed for that purpose by the act of 1851, yet claims are now often brought forward which have not been so passed upon by that board, and were never presented to it for consideration. And if the proposition on which the Supreme Court of California decided this case is a sound one, namely, that the board constituted under that act had no jurisdiction of, and could not by their decree affect in any manner, a title which had been perfected under the laws of the Mexican government prior to the transfer of the country to the United States, it is impossible to tell to what extent such claims of perfected titles may be presented, even in cases where the property itself has by somebody else been brought before that board and passed upon. * * *

Two propositions under this statute are presented by counsel in support of the decision of the Supreme Court of California. The first of these is, that the statute itself is invalid, as being in conflict with the provisions of the [Treaty of Guadalupe Hidalgo], and violating the protection which was guaranteed by it to the property of Mexican citizens, owned by them at the date of the treaty; and also in conflict with the rights of property under the constitution and laws of the United States, so far as it may affect titles perfected under Mexico. The second proposition is, that the statute was not intended to apply to claims which were supported by a complete and perfect title from the Mexican government, but, on the contrary, only to such as were imperfect, inchoate, and equitable in their character, without being a strict legal title.

With regard to the first of these propositions it may be said, that so far as the act of Congress is in conflict with the treaty with Mexico, that is a matter in which the court is bound to follow the statutory enactments of its own government. If the treaty was violated by this general statute enacted for the purpose of ascertaining the validity of claims derived from the Mexican government, it was a matter of international concern, which the two states must determine by treaty, or by such other means as enables one State to enforce upon another the obligations of a treaty. This court, in a class of cases like the present, has no power to set itself up as the instrumentality for enforcing the provisions of a treaty with a foreign nation which the government of the United States, as a sovereign power, chooses to disregard. * * *

There is nothing in the language of the statute to imply any exclusion of [claims perfected under Mexican law] from the jurisdiction of the commission. * * *

Nor can it be said that there is anything unjust or oppressive in requiring the owner of a valid claim, in that vast wilderness of lands unclaimed and unjustly claimed, to present his demand to a tribunal possessing all the elements of judicial functions, with a guarantee of judicial proceedings, so that his title could be established if it was found to be valid, or rejected if it was invalid.

We are unable to see any injustice, any want of constitutional power, or any violation of the treaty, in the means by which the United States undertook to separate the lands in which it held the proprietary interest from those which belonged, either equitably or by a strict legal title, to private persons. Every person owning land or other property is at all times liable to be called into a court of justice to contest his title to it. This may be done by another individual, or by the government under which he lives. * * *

[T]here can be no doubt of the proposition, that no title to land in California, dependent upon Spanish or Mexican grants can be of any validity which has not been submitted to and confirmed by the board provided for that purpose in the act of 1851, or, if rejected by that board, confirmed by the District or Supreme Court of the United States.

Notes and Questions

1. The California commission, and later the Court of Public Land Claims, adopted procedures that often denied the validity of Mexican land

grants, either affirming the land titles of new Anglo–American owners of such lands or placing the land in trust for ultimate distribution or ownership by the United States government. For example, a judge might conclude that the Mexican authority granting a land claim lacked the power to do so, or might question the validity of Indian land claims under Mexican law (under Mexican law, Indians were citizens and entitled to land grants). American authorities required Mexican landowners to verify their ownership through detailed and extensive archival documents, often unavailable because of the destruction of crucial documents during the war by fires or governmental action. In addition, Mexican usage and custom were not respected, so that the descriptions of Mexican land grants were found to be "too vague" or "imprecise" when compared to Anglo–American land surveys. Finally, Mexicans who contested adverse rulings either initially or on appeal incurred heavy legal fees, which were regularly settled by giving their lawyer one-third to one-half of the original land grant. Through all of these means, Mexicans lost their lands, despite the promise in the Treaty of Guadalupe Hidalgo that the property of Mexicans remaining in the territories ceded to the United States would be "inviolably respected." See generally W. A. Keleher, *Law of the New Mexico Land Grant*, 4 N.M. Hist. Rev. 350–71 (1929); J. N.M. Bar Ass'n 5–26 (1904) (containing a brief history of the Court of Public Land Claims by the Hon. Wilbur F. Stone, Associate Justice of the Court of Public Land Claims); George Cosgrave, *Early California Justice* 25–32 (1948); Robert J. Rosenbaum, *Mexicano Resistance in the Southwest* 41 (1981).

In many ways, the results of the California commission and the Court of Private Land Claims speak for themselves. In California, of 848 land grant cases filed, 613 grants were upheld and 200 rejected, with the remainder disposed on other grounds. While not appearing devastating numerically, these outcomes do not reflect the enormous costs of securing them through litigation of multiple appeals. As one commentator put it "[t]he land grant procedure was a measure of oppression." Cosgrave, supra, at 32. As another commentator put it:

> Two effects of the California Land Claims Act had a catastrophic impact on the original California landholders. First, the imposition of the law called all land title in the state into question. During the years that it took to have claims considered and confirmed by the Land Claims Commission and the courts, landholders had no legal remedy against an army of "settlers" who staked claims on their rangeland. By the time some grantholders received patents to protect their lands, they had little left to protect. Second, the process of title confirmation under the California Land Claims Act placed an enormous financial burden on the claimants. Many lost their holdings as a result of the costs of litigation.

See Frederico M. Cheever, Comment, *A New Approach to Spanish and Mexican Land Grants and the Public Trust Doctrine: Defining the Property Interest Protected by the Treaty of Guadalupe Hidalgo*, 33 UCLA L. Rev. 1364, 1401–02 (1986). See also Ebright, supra, at 37.

In the Court of Private Land Claims, the results were equally devastating. According to Justice Stone, 301 land grant cases came before the court, contesting 36 million acres of land. Eighty-seven grants were confirmed, totalling about 3 million acres. Of 36 million acres claimed under original Mexican or Spanish grants, only 3 million acres, or one-twelfth of the total, remained under the control of Mexican grantees or their heirs. The remaining 33 million acres reverted to the public domain of the United States for disposal by the government. Commenting on the work of the court, Justice Stone wrote that "In addition to the benefits mentioned [greater stability in investment and finality of land titles], the reversion to the public domain of the general government of more than 30,000,000 acres of land comes like new cession of country to the United States—a region illimitable in the undeveloped wealth of its coal, metals, agriculture and health-giving climate." Stone, supra, at 26. It is little wonder, then, that "[t]he work of the land court, from its beginning until now, has received the highest commendation as well from the department of justice at Washington as from the Bar, the press and the people within its jurisdiction, whose interests are directly affected by its adjudications." Id.

2.   Consider whether the outcome would have been the same in the *Fremont* case if the ultimate owner of Alvarado's grant had been a Mexican, rather than Colonel Fremont. Alvarado, the Mexican from whom Fremont purchased the land, had failed to meet several requirements of Mexican law, including the failure to include a survey of the land grant. See, e.g., *United States v. Vallejo*, 63 U.S. (22 How.) 416 (1859) (Court reverses a grant of title where the grant is not found in original Mexican records); *United States v. Pico*, 27 Fed. Cas. 532 (1859) (claim of Mexican title rejected where unsupported by evidence from the Mexican archives). On the other hand, Mexican claimants won some of their cases. In *De Arguello v. United States*, 59 U.S. 539, 18 How. 539 (1855), the Court affirmed the grant to the Arguello family, but reduced its size. See also *United States v. Peralta*, 60 U.S. (19 How.) 343 (1856), affirming a land grant held by Mexicans.

3.   Why does the United States Attorney challenge these claims vigorously and often? What happens when he wins?

4.   Note the *Botiller* Court's holding that, even if the statute creating the California Land Claims Commission violated the Treaty of Guadalupe Hidalgo, the courts were bound to enforce it. What effect would you expect this to have with respect to subsequent acts of Congress dealing with the lands ceded under the Treaty of Guadalupe Hidalgo, such as the act creating the Court of Private Land Claims? What effect would you expect *Botiller* to have on enforcement of the Treaty's guarantees by Congress? By the courts?

5.   Consider the following assessment of the *Fremont* and *Botiller* cases:

   Moreover, the key example offered to support the notion that the judiciary "leaned so far in the direction of leniency" so as to demonstrate "the greatest readiness . . . to accept any substantial evidence" to confirm Mexican grants—the case of American pioneer and Bear Flag revolt leader John C. Fremont—supports rather than undermines the notion that Mexican grantees suffered discrimination in tribunals adjudicating Treaty rights. On the one hand were claimants like Fremont, an Anglo who possessed questionable papers documenting dubious title. Still the Supreme Court gave him the benefit of the doubt and confirmed his patent. On the other hand were claimants like Dominga Domínguez, a Mexican who possessed unquestionable papers documenting perfect title. Yet the Court brushed aside her claim because she had failed to make a timely application for a patent with the board of land commissioners, and refused to eject the French and Anglo squatters who had overrun her lands east of Mission San Gabriel, California.

In short, the indeterminate nature of the Treaty, and U.S. laws purporting to implement it, could be manipulated to promote the claims of grant holders when it suited the courts and to extinguish them when it did not.

Christopher David Ruiz Cameron, *One Hundred Fifty Years of Solitude: Reflections on the End of the History Academy's Dominance of Scholarship on the Treaty of Guadalupe Hidalgo*, 5 Sw. J.L. & Trade Am. 83, 97 (1998) (offering observations on historical interpretations of the Treaty and the need for new analysis by legal scholars).

6.   Judges often showed the influence of popular opinions of the times towards Mexicans and Indians. Supreme Court Justice Daniel, dissenting in *De Arguello*, described the character of Mexicans as "sunk in ignorance, and marked by the traits which tyranny and degradation, political and moral, naturally and usually engender." Consider the following comments from the Honorable Wilbur F. Stone, an Associate Justice of the Court of Private Land Claims:

Occasionally the court room at Santa Fe would be enlivened by a squad of Indians who had journeyed thither from their distant pueblos as witnesses for their grant. These delegations were usually headed by the governor of their tribe, who exhibited great pride in striding up to the witness stand and being sworn on the holy cross: wearing a badge on his breast, a broad red sash round his waist, and clad in a white shirt, the full tail of which hung about his Antarctic zone like the skirt of a ballet dancer and underneath which depended his baggy white muslin trousers, a la Chinese washee-washee.

The grave and imperturbable [sic] bow which the governor gave to the judges on the bench, in recognition of their equality with himself as official dignitaries, arrayed in that grotesque fashion, was enough to evoke a hilarious bray from a dead burro.

J.N.M. Bar Ass'n (1904), reprinting a brief history of the Public Claims Court by the Hon. Wilbur F. Stone. What were the chances that a judge expressing such attitudes would credit the testimony of American or Mexican Indian witnesses appearing before him?

7.   Given the ideology of Manifest Destiny, which sought Anglo–Saxon dominion over the desirable lands of Mexico and provided the rationale for the war against Mexico, are these outcomes of the work of the California commission and the Court of Private Land Claims surprising? Inevitable?

8.   Recall that the United States paid $15 million for the territories ceded in the Treaty of Guadalupe Hidalgo. "[T]he United States looked at the treaty as an enormous real estate deal; it expected to get clear title to most of the land it was paying for regardless of the property rights of Mexicans." Ebright, supra, at 30.

9. For a recent court decision remarkably different in its reasoning and conclusions, see *Lobato v. Taylor*, 71 P.3d 938 (2002) (Sup. Ct. of Co., en banc), cert denied, 540 U.S. 1073 (2003), enforcing easement rights dating back to the time of the United States conquest of Mexico. See *Lobato* in Part Nine infra.

10. The tradition of Mexican–American resistance to the conquest has continued well into the twentieth century. In *Rio Arriba Land & Cattle Co. v. United States*, 167 U.S. 298 (1897), the Supreme Court affirmed a decision by the Court of Private Land Claims holding that the common lands of the San Joaquin land grant belonged in the public domain of the United States and not to the community. This decision resulted in the loss of many thousands of acres to the Kit Carson and the Sangre de Cristo national forests. In the 1960s, Reies López Tijerina established himself as a Chicano activist and leader when he mounted a major protest against the United States' seizure of these lands. See Rodolfo Acuña, *Occupied America: A History of Chicanos* 340–41 (3d ed. 1988). For additional accounts of Tijerina's activism, see Richard Gardner, Grito! *Reies Tijerina and the New Mexico Land Grant War of 1967* (1970); Peter Nabakov, *Tijerina and the Courthouse Raid* (2d ed. 1970).

11. Some readers may consider these materials on land grants arcane and of minor significance. But these land grant adjudications constitute the "regularization" of the United States' conquest of Mexico. They are the means by which conquest was made to conform to, and appear normal under, United States law. The struggles of Mexican–American landowners and activists to preserve, or reclaim, ownership of their lands can be understood as civil rights struggles within the context produced by conquest.

SECTION 4. MEXICAN RESISTANCE TO CONQUEST IN THE SOUTHWEST

The struggles over the former land and people of Mexico did not proceed solely in the courts. Mexicans routed or displaced from their lands mounted armed, violent resistance. Much of this resistance can be understood as guerilla warfare against an oppressor. Much of it took place on the newly created border of the Rio Grande now dividing former Mexico in two. Consider the following excerpt.

Robert J. Rosenbaum
Mexicano Resistance in the Southwest
15–17 (1981)

Violent Resistance

When seen as a whole, the nineteenth century landscape of the Southwest appears dotted with brushfire conflicts between *mexicanos* and *americanos*. Some flared sharply and threatened to engulf whole towns and the surrounding countryside; isolated flashes of outrage, of just having had enough, left scorched spots like those along railroad tracks started by the hotboxes from passing trains. And in some places, violence smoldered constantly, leaving a perpetual atmospheric haze like the smog over Los Angeles.

Violence is not new to human societies; in fact, it seems to be a constant of the human condition. As political scientist Ted Robert Gurr observes, European states and empires through the past twenty-four centuries have averaged one year of violent disturbance in five, counting "important" disturbances only, and since 1945 violent attempts to overthrow governments have been more frequent than elections throughout the world.

The fact that mexicanos violently resisted Anglo American domination may come as a surprise. Resistance does not fit the myth of the speedy conquest; neither does it square with the stereotype of cowardly and inferior "meskins" nor the comforting belief in the benevolence and general attractiveness of the American way of life.

Equally important, however, in accounting for the omission of mexicano resistance from Anglo–American historic consciousness is the fact that uprisings never fundamentally threatened Anglo–American control; they never achieved a sufficient size or posed a severe enough threat to be recognized as revolutions.

Most of the literature about civil disorder and internal violence focuses on revolutions, the large-scale attempt to overthrow government, and either ignores urban riots and rural uprisings or dismisses them as insignificant expressions of frustration by the oppressed. Only recently have historians, anthropologists, and political scientists begun to examine these expressions of popular discontent as political activity—attempts by social groups to influence and determine matters that affect their common welfare.

During the course of the nineteenth century, mexicanos employed violence as one means for retaining some measure of self-determination in the face of an increasingly oppressive new regime. All incidents of political violence fall within the general category that Hobsbawm terms "peasant" or "primitive" rebellions, although several cases carried hints of other possibilities. The outbreaks divide into five types within Hobsbawm's "peasant" framework: Border Warfare, where the locale provided a unifying theme to all of the resistance even though each of the other types appeared; Social Banditry, the most basic and constant expression of hostility that was carried out by individuals who refused to submit and who enjoyed the support of their general communities; Community Upheavals, when tensions became sufficiently high and widespread to precipitate a "spontaneous" outbreak; Long–Term Skirmishing, where violent set-tos occurred at a low level of intensity but over a long period of time and Coordinated Rebellions.

LAW AND LAND

Friction between mexicano and americano involved race, language, religion, food, sex and almost every other conceivable cultural distinction. But the points where friction usually provoked violent resistance were law and land.

Anglo Americans brought their version of the English common law to the conquered territory. Mexicanos, particularly *los pobres*, accustomed to the more personalized and traditional procedures of the *alcaldes*, found Anglo law confusing. It was in English, in itself a problem, and the fact that Anglos blatantly manipulated legal codes and court procedures added to the mexicano's resentment. Law enforcement contributed a more pronounced level of anger. Mexicanos perceived their treatment by Anglo peace officers as capricious and unjust; the number of unpunished lynchings and killings of mexicanos by americanos gave stark evidence for the accuracy of this perception.

Land provided the other major stimulus for violence. Both Anglo and Hispanic competed for it. Fundamental differences in practices of land tenure and conceptions about proper land use, particularly the tensions inherent in the transformation of land into a saleable commodity, complicated the fundamental competition. And the terms of the Treaty of Guadalupe Hidalgo, guaranteeing property rights but not specifying how traditional Hispanic forms of land ownership were to be translated into modes compatible with American law, added to the confusion and increased distrust and hostility.

Thus, the confrontation between mexicano and americano is a history of conflict. The conflict was between cultures, and it occurred on two levels: Often conflict grew out of misunderstanding, as neither group understood the other's socially established structures of meaning; at least as often, however, conflict was between meanings—each understood the other well enough and that was precisely the problem. They didn't want the same things.

Western expansion and the frontier experience are often cited as the most distinctive feature about the United States and the source of the qualities that are identified as uniquely American. How accurate that interpretation is, is a matter of debate. But the history of the mexicano peoples in the Southwest leads to a somewhat different characterization. Because mexicanos followed an essentially peasant culture in their traditional homelands and were but recently severed from their mother country, the conflict between mexicano and americano emerges as the most European occurrence in the history of the trans-Mississippi West.

RESISTANCE: THE CORTINA WARS AND GREGORIO CORTEZ

While too many conflicts broke out to list here, at least a few deserve mention. The Cortina War, the saga of Gregorio Cortez, and Reies Tijerina and the New Mexico Land Grant War of 1967 are among the most significant acts of resistance following the United States War with Mexico. These and other conflicts grow directly out of the treatment of Mexicans at the hands of United States authorities and courts.

Robert J. Rosenbaum
Mexicano Resistance in the Southwest
42–49 (1981)

THE CORTINA WAR

Thirty-five years old in 1859, Juan Cortina was a man of mature vigorous years, from a prominent family, experienced in military affairs, and with a history of opposition to Anglo Americans. He was, in short, a natural leader of the society split by the new border. His family's property, the Espíritu Santo land grant, had been diminished by the Anglo courts. Cortina's pride rebelled against the gringo law officers whose arrogance rose as Anglo merchants and lawyers increased their inroads in the Valley. Twelve years under Anglo domination had built a volatile fund of anger and resentment in Cortina and his people that needed only a spark to ignite it into open war.

A law officer struck the spark. On July 13, 1859, in Brownsville, Cortina saw city marshal Bob Spears pistol-whipping a drunken vaquero who worked for Cortina's mother. He shot Spears and left town with the vaquero. Two months later, Cortina led an estimated sixty riders into Brownsville, where they released all of the mexicano prisoners in the jail, sacked the stores of particularly obnoxious merchants, and executed four Americans who had killed mexicanos and had gone unpunished.

Influential citizens, including the Mexican consul in Brownsville and Cortina's cousin, persuaded him to leave the city. Two days later, however, Cortina issued a proclamation that enumerated the grievances of his band and vowed that they would continue to fight for justice. Apparently, further pleas from mexicano residents of Brownsville convinced him to disband; in any event, Cortina did not strike again until Brownsville police captured one of his lieutenants, Tomás Cabrera. Regrouping, Cortina threatened to destroy the city if his man was not released. A joint force made up of Anglos and Mexican national guardsmen lent by the Liberal government, which did not want to disrupt U.S.-Mexican harmony, attacked Cortina on October 22. They suffered a resounding defeat. Cortina controlled the countryside and kept Brownsville under siege.

The arrival of the Texas Rangers inflamed the situation. In exasperation, the Rangers hanged Cabrera, despite earlier promises from Brownsville leaders that he would receive a fair trial. Cortina responded with a second proclamation and renewed his attacks. Mexicano riders swelled the size of his army. Noncombatants refused to help state officials and volunteered supplies to Cortina instead. Cortina's statements and actions won widespread approval from the people of the Border, and the combination of popular support and successful skirmishes kept Cortina master of the Rio Grande for the remainder of the year.

It took the U.S. Army to defeat the insurgents. Troops under Major S. P. Heintzelman accompanied by a force of Texas Rangers under

Colonel John S. Ford defeated the rebels at Rio Grande City on December 27, 1859. Sporadic fighting continued into the new year, but Cortina was now confined to sniping and harassing actions as he moved along both sides of the border pursued by American and Mexican troops. The aftermath of the rebellion saw Anglos, principally the Rangers, retaliate indiscriminately against all mexicanos in a fit of bloody terrorism.

Gringos called Cortina a bandit and attributed the uprising to the inherent characteristics of a vicious race who wanted plunder and the chance to "execute summary vengeance on all towards whom [they] had *private* grudges" (emphasis added). Americans on the Border were acutely conscious of being in the minority—numbering only three hundred against twelve thousand according to one contemporary estimate—and conscious of their disproportionate economic and political power. People occupying a privileged status often find it necessary to justify themselves in terms of the "natural" order of things and to attribute any signs of discontent to a biological or moral flaw of the complainers. But contemporary Anglo accounts of the uprising sometimes allowed traces of guilt or glimmerings of awareness of oppression to show through. Accounts of the Brownsville raid said that Cortina's raiders had shouted "Death to Americans; *viva la republica Mexicana*; and threatened to hold the Mexican flag on the staff of our deserted garrison," clearly attributing a political motive to the raiders. Another account explained the raid by saying: "under a polite exterior, the deepest, settled hatred exists in the Mexican mind towards us," an expression suggesting that there might be legitimate grievances against the newcomers.

Anglos made occasional lapses which hinted that Cortina and his followers were something other than bandits; Cortina asserted unequivocally that the movement aimed to bring justice to his people. The first proclamation, issued two days after the Brownsville raid, explained that in the name of "the sacred right of self-preservation" Cortina and his men were trying to "put an end to our misfortunes." Cortina laid the blame on a "secret conclave . . . [that] persecute[s] and rob[s] for no other crime than that of being of Mexican origin." Cortina described the Brownsville raiders as "clothed in the imposing aspect of our exasperation" and went on to warn that though they might have to lead a "wandering life . . . our personal enemies shall not possess our lands until they have fattened it with their own gore."

Cortina's two proclamations emphasize three major complaints: loss of land either through legal manipulation or through intimidation; the impunity with which Anglos killed Mexicans; and the arrogance of Anglo–American racism, "so ostentatious of its own qualities." While the grievances against the Anglos are expressed long and eloquently, the remedies are brief and vague. Beyond swearing to correct injustices and exterminate the "tyrants," the only specific proposal suggests that mexicanos "repose their lot under the good sentiments of the governor elect of the State, General Houston." A tragic aura, arising from phrases like "a wandering life" and "I am ready to offer myself as a sacrifice to your happiness," joins with the ill-defined proposals to give a hopeless quality to the undertaking. The grievances and the anger are real and powerful, but there is no corresponding conviction of hope for the future.

The Cortina War was planned and coordinated, widespread and momentarily effective: For three of the seven months that it lasted, Cortina controlled the Lower Rio Grande Border. It was a resistance movement that grew out of Border culture and was limited by Border culture as well. * * *

Many others also tried. Cortina was joined by other Border fighters who combined the dual roles of *enganchado* and *juarista* (a Benito Juárez supporter), and this double activity continued through the century, underscoring the regional sentiment in Border culture. But before there can be resistance movements, there must be people who are willing to resist. The essential materials for any form of resistance are individuals who refuse to submit, who will "break before they bend." The Border sheltered many proud people, and the most outstanding were remembered in ballads called *corridos*. The saga of Gregorio Cortez provides a good picture of the values and attributes that formed the basis for the resistance that came out of nineteenth-century Border culture.

THE SAGA OF GREGORIO CORTEZ

The story of Gregorio Cortez, who "defended his right with his pistol in his hand," captures much of the mexicanos' situation in Texas at the turn of the century. It began in 1901 with a brief flurry of gunfire and ended in 1913 after a legal fight waged by Hispanic Texans. The battle grew out of a confrontation between Anglo lawmen and a mexicano farmer. Set in a context of mutual mistrust and hostility, specific cultural problems—three errors in translation by a "bilingual" deputy named Boone Choate—touched off ten days of turmoil that reached epic proportions.

On June 12, 1901, Karnes County Sheriff W. T. (Brack) Morris, an experienced Texas peace officer, set out with two deputies in search of a "Mexican" horse thief. They were armed but unencumbered with a warrant. The lawmen learned that Gregorio Cortez, a rancher and farmer who had lived in the county for some eleven years, had recently traded a horse to a neighbor. Morris and his party went to question him, arriving as Cortez, his brother Romaldo, and their families were resting after the noon meal.

Whether Morris actually suspected Cortez or merely wanted information is not clear. Three mistakes by Choate, the translator, rendered the question academic.

The officers first spoke to Romaldo, asking if Gregorio was there. Romaldo turned, saying, *"Te quieren,"* literally, "You are wanted." In Spanish, this is a common way of saying "Somebody wants to talk to you." To a barely fluent Anglo deputy, it sounded very close to an admission of guilt.

Morris then asked, through Choate, if Cortez had traded a horse (*caballo*) to a man named Villarreal. Cortez said no, meaning that he had not traded a caballo but a mare, a *yegua*. Hearing the negative, Morris then told Choate to tell Cortez that he was going to arrest him and moved closer, drawing his gun. After Choate's translation, Cortez answered, "You can't arrest me for nothing," which Choate took to mean "No one can arrest me." Gunplay followed that left Morris dead on the spot and Romaldo fatally wounded.

Cortez became a hunted man. At first on foot, later mounted, he eluded posse after posse—some numbering over three hundred men—leading Texas authorities on a ten-day, five-hundred-mile chase toward Laredo—the border and safety. The lone Cortez almost made it; a vaquero betrayed him to the Texas Rangers as he rested, preparing to cross the Rio Grande at night.

A series of trials ensued that lasted almost four years. Cortez was charged with horse stealing and three counts of murder (Morris and two other lawmen). He was found not guilty by reason of self-defense for killing Morris, not guilty of horse theft, and not guilty of killing a posse member named Schnaebel. The Court of Criminal Appeals upheld his conviction for the murder of a man named Glover, however, and on January 2, 1905, Cortez entered Huntsville to serve a life sentence. Governor O. B. Colquitt pardoned him in 1913, and Cortez returned to the Border where he was born. He died in 1916, probably of natural causes, although both legend and family tradition maintained he was poisoned.

The saga of Gregorio Cortez is remarkable not only because it tells how one mexicano responded to a serious threat, but also because of the folklore that developed about him. * * *

Anglo Texans divided in their attitudes toward Cortez after his capture. Grudging admiration surfaced amidst the vituperative outpourings during the chase, and his conduct during the trial won many Anglos, including many of his pursuers, to his side. And Cortez was found not guilty of killing Morris, indicating that Anglos, too, thought that he had a right to defend himself.

On the other hand, many Anglos saw Cortez as a vicious specimen of a corrupt and inferior race. They called for his lynching, trumped up charges against him, abused and terrorized his family and other mexicanos. This sentiment remained alive throughout the era. One newspaper responded to the pardon with a vehement attack against the "chicken-hearted Governor" who had freed a "Mexican who took the lives of American citizens." * * *

Notes and Questions

1. See Américo Paredes's classic "*With His Pistol In His Hand*" (1958), for a definitive study of Gregorio Cortez and his role in Border folklore. Paredes writes, "[i]t was almost as if the Border people had

dreamed Gregorio Cortez before producing him, and had sung his life and his deeds before he was born." A Hollywood producer made Gregorio Cortez's story into a major motion picture entitled *The Ballad of Gregorio Cortez*. As one might expect, Juan Cortina also has a *corrido*, or ballad. See *Américo Paredes, Folklore and Culture on the Texas–Mexican Border* 27 (R. Bauman ed., 1993). See also Rodolfo Acuña, *Occupied America: A History of Chicanos* 43–47 (3d ed. 1988). For another account of the Cortina war, characterizing Cortina as a lawless bandit, see Walter Prescott Webb, *The Texas Rangers* 175–93 (1995 ed., © 1935).

SECTION 5.   MEXICAN AMERICANS' STRUGGLE AGAINST SEGREGATION

In addition to loss of lands, Mexican Americans and Puerto Ricans also faced racism and segregation in the areas where they lived. Jim Crow did not target only blacks; it also took aim at Latinos/as through segregated schools and other public facilities. Mexican Americans, particularly, used the courts to struggle against this widespread segregation. Many readers do not realize the extent to which Mexican Americans were subject to segregation and resisted that segregation in the courts. Consider the following excerpts.

Juan F. Perea
Buscando América: Why Integration and Equal Protection Fail to Protect Latinos
117 Harv. L. Rev. 1420, 1426, 1439–46 (2004)

SEGREGATION, EDUCATION, AND LATINOS

Spanish speakers, historically and in the present, have been treated as inferior and discriminated against by English-speaking America.* * *
* * *

Segregation was practiced throughout the Southwest to isolate Mexican–American children and to retard their educational progress. The purpose of the educational system was to reproduce the caste society of the Southwest, with Anglos at the top and Mexicans, Indians, and Blacks at the bottom. Equal education was inconsistent with the need for uneducated Mexican laborers. In the words of one Texas school superintendent: "Most of our Mexicans are of the lower class. They transplant onions, harvest them, etc. The less they know about everything else the better contented they are. . . . If a man has very much sense or education either, he is not going to stick to this kind of work." Anglo farmers, many of whom sat on school boards, used the schools to keep Mexicans uneducated, thereby guaranteeing a plentiful labor supply for their cotton fields.

Assimilation, conceived as one-way adaptation by persons of color to the norms of Whiteness and English monolingualism, was an important initial goal of American education for conquered peoples. Just as lessons supporting slavery and black inferiority were the most important lessons taught in schools to black children, lessons supporting conquest and subordination were the most important lessons taught in schools to Mexican children. Because Mexican culture and the Spanish language were perceived as major impediments to progress and learning, public schools made considerable efforts to exclude and eliminate the culture and language of Mexican students. According to Thomas Carter, "the full force of the educational system in the Southwest has been directed toward the eradication of both the Spanish language and the Spanish–American or Mexican–American cultures."

Wherever Mexicans lived in large numbers, segregation was the rule. Carey McWilliams described the segregated conditions in the California citrus belt:

> Throughout the citrus belt, the workers are Spanish-speaking, Catholic, and dark-skinned, the owners are white, Protestant, and English-speaking. The owners occupy the heights, the Mexicans the lowlands.... While the towns deny that they practice segregation, nevertheless, segregation is the rule. Since the Mexicans all live in jim-town, it has always been easy to effect residential segregation. The omnipresent Mexican school is, of course, an outgrowth of segregated residence. The swimming pools in the towns are usually reserved for "whites," with an insulting exception being noted in the designation of one day in the week as "Mexican Day".... Mexicans attend separate schools and churches, occupy the balcony seats in the motion-picture theaters, and frequent separate places of amusement.... The whole system of employment, in fact, is perfectly designed to insulate workers from employers in every walk of life, from the cradle to the grave, from the church to the saloon. [See Carey McWilliams, *Southern California Country: An Island on the Land* 219 (1946).]

Segregated schools for Mexican–American children were common in the Southwest. Often Mexican Americans and Blacks were grouped together, separate from Whites. Ironically, despite the fact that California's Education Code did not even mention them, Mexican–American children were the largest and most frequently segregated group in California's schools.

Juan F. Perea
The Black/White Binary Paradigm of Race:
The "Normal Science" of American Racial Thought
85 Cal. L. Rev. 1213, 1242–51 (1997); 10 La Raza L.J. 127 (1998)

Chicanos played an important role in fighting and ultimately overturning school segregation. In *Mendez v. Westminister School District of Orange County*, [64 F.Supp. 544 (S.D. Cal. 1946), *aff'd*, 161 F.2d 774 (9th Cir. 1947)] Gonzalo Mendez and several other Mexican–American parents challenged the long-standing and pervasive segregation of Mexican–

American children in Orange County. California's segregation statutes permitted school boards to establish separate schools for "Indian children ... and for children of Chinese, Japanese, or Mongolian parentage." Despite the absence of Mexican Americans from the statutory list, the parties "admitted that segregation *per se* is practiced in the above-mentioned school districts as the Spanish-speaking children enter school life and as they advance through the grades in the respective school districts." One commentator found it ironic that "the Code did not mention the group that was most commonly segregated by 1945: children of Mexican descent."

One of the State's arguments in *Mendez* was that the Supreme Court had authorized the segregation of the races under the "separate but equal" doctrine of *Plessy v. Ferguson*. District Judge McCormick found that the physical facilities, teachers and curricula of the segregated school for Mexican children were "identical and in some respects superior to those in the other schools." Accordingly, unlike many of the pre-*Brown* Black segregation cases, this case did not focus on the inequality of separate facilities, but rather on the inherent evil of state-sponsored segregation itself.

After concluding that segregation of Mexican–American children was inconsistent with California's Education Code, Judge McCormick considered the federal constitutional question. Relying on a prescient interpretation of equal protection and on the stigmatizing effects of segregation on children subject to it, he concluded that California's segregation of Mexican–American pupils violated the Equal Protection Clause. The judge wrote:

> "The equal protection of the laws" pertaining to the public school system in California is not provided by furnishing in separate schools the same technical facilities, text books and courses of instruction to children of Mexican ancestry that are available to the other public school children regardless of their ancestry. A paramount requisite in the American system of public education is social equality. It must be open to all children by unified school association regardless of lineage.

In this remarkable paragraph, the court rejects the entire underpinning of the Supreme Court's opinion in *Plessy v. Ferguson* and foreshadows the reasoning of the Court in *Brown v. Board of Education*. Where *Plessy* had reified segregation by disclaiming the Court's power to act to remedy social inequality, the *Mendez* opinion conveys a powerfully different understanding of equality that ultimately prevails in *Brown*.

The *Mendez* court also anticipated *Brown*, and rejected *Plessy*, in its understanding of the role of public education and the stigmatizing meaning and purpose of segregation:

> The evidence clearly shows that Spanish-speaking children are hindered impeded in learning English by lack of exposure to its use because of segregation, and that commingling of the entire student body instills and develops a common cultural attitude among the

school children which is imperative for the perpetuation of American institutions and ideals. It is also established by the record that the methods of segregation prevalent in the defendant school districts foster antagonisms in the children and suggest inferiority among them where none exists.

The United States Court of Appeals for the Ninth Circuit upheld Judge McCormick's decision on narrower statutory grounds.

Legal scholars and the general public recognized the importance of the *Mendez* decision. A Note on the *Mendez* case in the *Yale Law Journal* commented, regarding *Plessy*'s "separate but equal" doctrine, that

> a recent district Court decision [*Mendez*] . . . has questioned the basic assumption of the *Plessy* case and may portend a complete reversal of the doctrine. . . . Modern sociological and psychological studies lend much support to the District Court's views. A dual school system, even if "equal facilities" were ever in fact provided, does imply social inferiority.

Another Note on the *Mendez* case, in *Columbia Law Review*, commented on its significance:

> The segregation of races has not previously been considered a denial of equal protection so long as equal facilities were made available to the members of both groups. . . .
>
> Attacks on segregation based on the equal protection clause of the Fourteenth Amendment have been equally unsuccessful. If the physical facilities available to each group are substantially equal, the courts have followed the traditional view that the humiliation engendered by relegation to an inferior social status is not in itself indicative of discrimination. The court in the instant case breaks sharply with this approach and finds that the Fourteenth Amendment requires "social equality" rather than equal facilities.

Both of these notes, but particularly the former, recognize the importance of *Mendez* in furthering the cause of racial justice and desegregation for Blacks. On appeal, Thurgood Marshall, Robert L. Carter, and Loren Miller filed an *amicus* brief on behalf of the NAACP urging the desegregation of Orange County's schools. Robert L. Carter, Assistant Special Counsel of the NAACP, apparently used this brief as a dry run of the argument that segregation was unconstitutional *per se*. Carter noted that cases pending in Oklahoma, Texas, Louisiana and South Carolina involving segregated schools "may require a Supreme Court ruling in the near future on the constitutional issue of the *Mendez* case." The NAACP's efforts in support of the Mexican–American plaintiffs in these cases provide an example of early coalition between Blacks and Latinos/as to defeat white racism and Jim Crow as inflicted upon Latinos/as. Mexican–American plaintiffs also sued to desegregate the Texas schools in the *Delgado v. Bastrop* litigation, the first step leading to the defeat of school segregation in Texas.

Significantly, it was the *Mendez* decision that led to California's repeal of its school segregation statutes. Then Governor Earl Warren signed legislation repealing California's segregation statutes on June 14, 1947. This was, of course, the same Earl Warren who, as Chief Justice of the United States, would later pen the opinions in *Brown v. Board of Education* and *Hernandez v. Texas*. The sequence of events following *Mendez* might have provided a clue about what was to come when school segregation reached the Supreme Court.

Other segregation-era cases tell a powerful story of white racism against Mexican Americans and strong Mexican–American resistance in the courts. In *Lopez v. Seccombe*, [71 F.Supp. 769 (S.D. Cal. 1944)], for example, several leading Mexican–American and Puerto Rican citizens of San Bernardino, California, representing a class of 8,000 Mexican Americans, sued officials of San Bernardino to gain simple access to a public park. All persons of Mexican or Latin descent, including the plaintiffs, had "been excluded, barred and precluded" for several years from using a public park, playground, swimming pool, bathhouse and other facilities solely because of their Mexican and Puerto Rican ancestry. Apparently in response to contrary arguments by counsel for San Bernardino, the trial judge found it necessary to make a specific finding that the plaintiffs "are of clean and moral habits not suffering any disability, infectious disease, nor have they any physical or mental defect" that might justify the discrimination against them. The court concluded that segregation of San Bernardino's public park violated the Equal Protection Clause and issued a permanent injunction prohibiting the segregation of persons of Mexican and Latin ancestry.

———————

The Supreme Court finally considered discrimination against Mexican Americans in *Hernandez v. Texas*, decided two weeks before *Brown v. Board of Education*.

Hernandez v. Texas
347 U.S. 475 (1954)

CHIEF JUSTICE WARREN delivered the opinion of the Court.

The petitioner, Pete Hernández, was indicted for the murder of one Joe Espinosa by a grand jury in Jackson County, Texas. He was convicted and sentenced to life imprisonment. * * * [T]he petitioner, by his counsel, offered timely motions to quash the indictment and the jury panel. He alleged that persons of Mexican descent were systematically excluded from service as jury commissioners, grand jurors, and petit jurors, although there were such persons fully qualified to serve residing in Jackson County. The petitioner asserted that exclusion of this class deprived him, as a member of the class, of the equal protection of the laws guaranteed by the Fourteenth Amendment of the Constitution. * * *

In numerous decisions, this Court has held that it is a denial of the equal protection of the laws to try a defendant of a particular race or color under an indictment issued by a grand jury, or before a petit jury, from which all persons of his race or color have, solely because of that race or color, been excluded by the State, whether acting through its legislature, its courts, or its executive or administrative officers. * * * The State of Texas would have us hold that there are only two classes— white and Negro—within the contemplation of the Fourteenth Amendment. The decisions of this Court do not support that view. And, except where the question presented involves the exclusion of persons of Mexican descent from juries, Texas courts have taken a broader view of the scope of the Equal Protection Clause.

Throughout our history differences in race and color have defined easily identifiable groups which have at times required the aid of the courts in securing equal treatment under the laws. But community prejudices are not static, and from time to time other differences from the community norm may define other groups which need the same protection. Whether such a group exists within a community is a question of fact. When the existence of a distinct class is demonstrated, and it is further shown that the laws, as written or as applied, single out that class for different treatment not based on some reasonable classification, the guarantees of the Constitution have been violated. The Fourteenth Amendment is not directed solely against discrimination due to a "two-class theory"—that is, based upon differences between "white" and Negro.

As the petitioner acknowledges, the Texas system of selecting grand and petit jurors by the use of jury commissions is fair on its face and capable of being utilized without discrimination. But as this Court has held, the system is susceptible to abuse and can be employed in a discriminatory manner. The exclusion of otherwise eligible persons from jury service solely because of their ancestry or national origin is discrimination prohibited by the Fourteenth Amendment. The Texas statute makes no such discrimination, but the petitioner alleges that those administering the law do.

The petitioner's initial burden in substantiating his charge of group discrimination was to prove that persons of Mexican descent constitute a separate class in Jackson County, distinct from "whites." One method by which this may be demonstrated is by showing the attitude of the community. Here the testimony of responsible officials and citizens contained the admission that residents of the community distinguished between "white" and "Mexican." The participation of persons of Mexican descent in business and community groups was shown to be slight. Until very recent times, children of Mexican descent were required to attend a segregated school for the first four grades. At least one restaurant in town prominently displayed a sign announcing "No Mexicans Served." On the courthouse grounds at the time of the hearing, there were two men's toilets, one unmarked, and the other marked "Colored Men" and "Hombres Aqui" ("Men Here"). No substantial evidence was offered to rebut the logical inference to be drawn from these facts, and it must be concluded that petitioner succeeded in his proof.

Having established the existence of a class, petitioner was then charged with the burden of proving discrimination. To do so, he relied on the pattern of proof established by *Norris v. State of Alabama*, 294 U.S. 587. In that case, proof that Negroes constituted a substantial segment of the population of the jurisdiction, that some Negroes were qualified to serve as jurors, and that none had been called for jury service over an extended period of time, was held to constitute *prima facie* proof of the systematic exclusion of Negroes from jury service. This holding, sometimes called the "rule of exclusion," has been applied in other cases, and it is available in supplying proof of discrimination against any delineated class.

The petitioner established that 14% of the population of Jackson County were persons with Mexican or Latin American surnames, and that 11% of the males over 21 bore such names. The County Tax Assessor testified that 6 or 7% of the freeholders on the tax rolls of the County were persons of Mexican descent. The State of Texas stipulated that "for the last twenty-five years there is no record of any person with a Mexican or Latin American name having served on a jury commission, grand jury or petit jury in Jackson County." The parties also stipulated that "there are some male persons of Mexican or Latin American descent in Jackson County who, by virtue of being citizens, freeholders, and having all other legal prerequisites to jury service, are eligible to serve as members of a jury commission, grand jury and/or petit jury."

The petitioner met the burden of proof imposed in *Norris v. Alabama*, supra. To rebut the strong *prima facie* case of the denial of the equal protection of the laws guaranteed by the Constitution thus established, the State offered the testimony of five jury commissioners that they had not discriminated against persons of Mexican or Latin American descent in selecting jurors. They stated that their only objective had been to select those whom they thought were best qualified. This testimony is not enough to overcome the petitioner's case. * * *

Circumstances or chance may well dictate that no persons in a certain class will serve on a particular jury or during some particular period. But it taxes our credulity to say that mere chance resulted in their being no members of this class among the over six thousand jurors called in the past 25 years. The result bespeaks discrimination, whether or not it was a conscious decision on the part of any individual jury commissioner. The judgment of conviction must be reversed.

Notes and Questions

1. What view of the Equal Protection Clause does the U.S. Supreme Court embrace when it posits in *Hernandez* that "[t]hroughout our history differences in race and color have defined easily identifiable groups which have at times required the aid of the courts in securing equal treatment

under the laws. But community prejudices are not static, and from time to time other differences from the community norm may define other groups which need the same protection"? What role does the Court think race plays in defining Mexican Americans as a group? See Ian F. Haney López, *Race, Ethnicity, Erasure: The Salience of Race to LatCrit Theory*, 85 Cal. L. Rev. 1143 (1997) (arguing that a racial understanding of Latinos may be preferable and should at least be evaluated). See also Juan F. Perea, *The Black/White Binary Paradigm of Race: The "Normal Science" of American Racial Thought*, 85 Cal. L. Rev. 1213 (1997) (discussing prevalent binary conception of race as black or white).

2. Consider whether cases such as *Mendez* and *Hernandez* should appear in every book that discusses racism and segregation, especially constitutional law books. Could not the omission of cases in which Mexican Americans struggled against segregation lead many law students to conclude that the Mexican–American struggle against segregation has no place in our constitutional history? See *[Symposium]: Commemorating the 50th Anniversary of* Hernandez v. Texas, 25 Chicano–Latino L. Rev. 1 (2005); Richard Delgado, *Rodrigo's Roundelay:* Hernandez v. Texas *and the Interest Convergence Dilemma*, 41 Harv. C.R.-C.L. L. Rev. 23 (2006).

3. For a comprehensive study of *Hernández*, see *"Colored Men" and "Hombres Aquí":* Hernández v. Texas *and the Emergence of Mexican American Lawyering* (Michael A. Olivas ed., 2006).

4. For Robert Blauner:

Even informed Anglos [and blacks] know almost nothing about La Raza, its historical experience, its present situation, its collective moods. And the average citizen doesn't have the foggiest notion that Chicanos have been lynched in the Southwest and continue to be abused by the police, that an entire population has been exploited economically, dominated politically, and raped culturally. In spite of the racism that attempts to wipe out or, failing that, distort and trivialize the history and culture of the colonized, both expert and man in the street are far more aware of the past and present oppression suffered by blacks.

See Robert Blauner, *Racial Oppression in America* 166 (1972). Blauner refers to this continuing omission as "academic colonialism" by white scholars who persist in ignoring the history and problems encountered by Mexican Americans.

Chapter 2

PUERTO RICO AND PUERTO RICANS

At the end of the Spanish–American War of 1898, approximately one million Puerto Ricans came under the jurisdiction of the United States. Since then, the U.S. has maintained an ambiguous relationship with Puerto Rico, the United States's "oldest colony." See generally José Trías Monge, *Puerto Rico: The Trials of the Oldest Colony in the World* (1997).

Although the war began in Cuba, United States politicians did not want the war to end until they had expelled Spain from Puerto Rico and annexed the island. In May, 1898, before the invasion of Puerto Rico in July of that year, the following exchange took place:

> Assistant Secretary of the Navy Theodore Roosevelt, in a personal letter to Senator Henry Cabot Lodge, wrote: "give my best love to Nannie, and *do not make peace until we get Porto Rico*." Lodge replied: "Porto Rico is not forgotten and we mean to have it. Unless I am utterly ... mistaken, the administration is now fully committed to the large policy that we both desire."

Selections from the Correspondence of Theodore Roosevelt and H.C. Lodge, 1884–1918 (1925), quoted in *The Puerto Ricans: A Documentary History* 89 (Kal Wagenheim & Olga Jimenez de Wagenheim eds., 1994).

The United States coveted Puerto Rico for a number of reasons. The ideology of Manifest Destiny, which had played such an important role in the conquest of Mexico, continued to fuel United States expansion. Puerto Rico was seen as an important location for military reasons, as an important way to control the Gulf of Mexico and the canal connecting the Gulf to the Pacific. Important business reasons also underlay the conquest. The war occurred during a time of economic hardship, and the United States sought new markets for its increasing surpluses of goods. The hope of expanding markets was amply fulfilled, as today Puerto Rico is a major overseas trading partner of the United States. See Ediberto Roman, *Empire Forgotten: The United States's Colonization of Puerto Rico*, 42 Vill. L. Rev. 1119, 1149 (1997).

Prior to the invasion, Puerto Ricans recognized the threat posed by their "dangerous neighbor":

The American nation is a dangerous neighbor, especially for Cuba, the Dominican Republic, and Puerto Rico. We must trust very little in her statements. We must not fall asleep, and must keep watchful eyes on the Florida Channel. Anglo–American traditions are not the most reassuring.

There you have Mexico, invaded and dismembered, due to the greed of the Colossus. There you have Nicaragua, where they arrived one day, stirring troubles and difficulties. The North American Republic is too powerful to relax her pressure on the weak Latin American Republics.

On the alert, then ... the United States urgently needs to establish a position in the Antilles. In 1891, they talked and acted in this direction, without beating about the bush.

Translated from *La Democracia, 1894, No. 1030*, quoted in Wagenheim & Jimenez de Wagenheim, supra, at 85.

The Spanish–American War ended with the Treaty of Paris of 1898, which ceded Puerto Rico and the Philippines to the United States.

SECTION 1. THE TREATY OF PARIS (1898)

Article I:

Spain relinquishes all claim of sovereignty over and title to Cuba. * * *

Article II:

Spain cedes to the United States the island of Porto Rico and other islands now under Spanish sovereignty in the West Indies, and the island of Guam in the Marianas or Ladrones.

Article III:

Spain cedes to the United States the archipelago known as the Philippine Islands * * *.

The United States will pay to Spain the sum of twenty million dollars ($20,000,000) within three months after the exchange of the ratifications of the present treaty. * * *

Article IX:

Spanish subjects, natives of the Peninsula, residing in the territory over which Spain by the present treaty relinquishes or cedes her sovereignty, may remain in such territory or may remove therefrom, retaining in either event all their rights of property, including the right to sell or dispose of such property or of its proceeds; and they shall also have the right to carry on their industry, commerce and professions, being subject in respect thereof to such laws as are applicable to other foreigners. In case they remain in the territory they may preserve their allegiance to the Crown of Spain by making, before a court of record, within a year from the date of the exchange of ratifications of this treaty, a declaration of their decision to preserve such allegiance; in default of which declaration they shall be held to have renounced it and to have adopted the nationality of the territory in which they may reside.

The civil rights and political status of the native inhabitants of the territories hereby ceded to the United States shall be determined by the Congress.

* * *

Treaty of Paris, reprinted in 11 *Treaties and Other International Agreements of the United States of America 1776–1949*, at 615–19 (Charles I. Bevans ed., 1974).

Notes and Questions

1.   Notice the difference in language between Article IX of the Treaty of Guadalupe Hidalgo and Article IX of the Treaty of Paris. Consider Judge José Cabranes's suggestion that, "For the first time in American history, in a treaty acquiring territory for the United States, there was no promise of citizenship . . . [nor any] promise, actual or implied, of statehood. The United States thereby acquired not 'territories' but possessions or 'dependencies' and became, in that sense, an 'imperial' power." José A. Cabranes, *Citizenship and the American Empire* 20 (1979) (quoting J. Pratt, *America's Colonial Experiment* 68 (1950)). Do you agree with this comment?

2.   Note the distinction that Article IX makes between "Spanish subjects, natives of the [Iberian] Peninsula," and "native inhabitants of the territories." Only the Spanish could elect to retain their Spanish citizenship, not the predominantly *criollos* (creoles) who were citizens under the former Spanish rule. Thus the "native inhabitants" lost their Spanish citizenship and became subject to the will of Congress in defining their "civil rights and political status."

3.   According to Rubin Francis Weston:

Those who advocated overseas expansion faced this dilemma: What kind of relationship would the new peoples have to the body politic? Was it to be the relationship of the Reconstruction period, an attempt at political equality for dissimilar races, or was it to be the Southern "counterrevolutionary" point of view which denied the basic American constitutional rights to people of color? The actions of the federal government during the imperial period and the relegation of the Negro to a status of secondclass citizenship indicated that the Southern point of view would prevail. The racism which caused the relegation of the Negro to a status of inferiority was to be applied to the overseas possessions of the United States.

Rubin Francis Weston, *Racism in U.S. Imperialism* 15 (1972).

4.   For a recent treatment of the colonial status of Puerto Rico, see Pedro A. Malavet, *America's Colony: The Political and Cultural Conflict Between the United States and Puerto Rico* (2004).

SECTION 2.   CONSTRUCTING POLITICAL STATUS

THE FORAKER ACT OF 1900 AND THE *INSULAR CASES*

Treaties answer only the most basic questions of national sovereignty over disputed territory, leaving many questions unaddressed. In the case of Puerto Rico, the Treaty of Paris declared only that the civil and political rights of Puerto Ricans would be determined by Congress.

In 1900, Congress passed the Foraker Act, 31 Stat. 79 (1900), entitled "An Act Temporarily to provide revenues and a civil government for Porto Rico, and for other purposes." Arnold Leibowitz describes the Act as follows:

> President McKinley's Puerto Rican policy, which was incorporated in the Foraker Act of 1900, established a civil government in which the key roles would be given to Americans appointed by the President. There would be a Governor appointed by the President, an 11–man Executive Council (with a majority being Statesiders), 35 elected Puerto Ricans in the House of Delegates (whose laws were subject to Congressional veto), and an elected Resident Commissioner who spoke for Puerto Rico in the U.S. House of Representatives but who had no vote there.

Arnold H. Leibowitz, *Defining Status: A Comprehensive Analysis of United States Territorial Relations* 141–42 (1989).

In an important series of cases referred to as the *Insular Cases*,[1] the Supreme Court wrestled with the issue of the status of the Puerto Rico territory. *Downes v. Bidwell* concerned the constitutionality of the Foraker Act's tax provisions. The court's discussion of the status of Puerto Rico and its relationship to the United States had, and continues to have, enormous significance.

Downes v. Bidwell
182 U.S. 244 (1901)

[This was an action by Downes against the collector of the port of New York to recover taxes of $659.35 paid on oranges imported from Puerto Rico in November, 1900, after passage of the Foraker Act.]

JUSTICE BROWN announced the conclusion and judgment of the court:

This case involves the question whether merchandise brought into the port of New York from Porto Rico since the passage of the Foraker act is exempt from duty, notwithstanding the 3d section of that act which requires the payment of "15 per centum of the duties which are required to be levied, collected, and paid upon like articles of merchandise imported from foreign countries." * * *

In the case of *De Lima v. Bidwell* just decided, we held that, upon the ratification of the treaty of peace with Spain, Porto Rico ceased to be

---

1.   DeLima v. Bidwell, 182 U.S. 1 (1901); Downes v. Bidwell, 182 U.S. 244 (1901); Dooley v. United States, 182 U.S. 222   (1901); and Armstrong v. United States, 182 U.S. 243 (1901). See Leibowitz, supra, at 143 n.66.

a foreign country, and became a territory of the United States, and that duties were no longer collectible upon merchandise brought from that island. We are now asked to hold that it became a part of the United States within that provision of the Constitution which declares that "all duties, imposts, and excises shall be uniform throughout the United States." Art. 1, § 8. If Porto Rico be a part of the United States, the Foraker act imposing duties upon its products is unconstitutional, not only by reason of a violation of the uniformity clause, but because by § 9 "vessels bound to or from one state" cannot "be obliged to enter, clear, or pay duties in another."

The case also involves the broader question whether the revenue clauses of the Constitution extend of their own force to our newly acquired territories. The Constitution itself does not answer the question. * * *

[I]t can nowhere be inferred that the territories were considered a part of the United States. The Constitution was created by the people of the United States, as a union of states, to be governed solely by representatives of the states; and even the provision relied upon here, that all duties, imposts, and excises shall be uniform "throughout the United States," is explained by subsequent provisions of the Constitution, that "no tax or duty shall be laid on articles exported from any state," and "no preference shall be given by any regulation of commerce or revenue to the ports of one state over those of another; nor shall vessels bound to or from one state be obliged to enter, clear, or pay duties in another." In short, the Constitution deals with states, their people, and their representatives.

* * *

It is sufficient to say that * * * Congress has been consistent in recognizing the difference between the states and territories under the Constitution. * * *

Indeed, the practical interpretation put by Congress upon the Constitution has been long continued and uniform to the effect that the Constitution is applicable to territories acquired by purchase or conquest, only when and so far as Congress shall so direct. * * *

We are also of opinion that the power to acquire territory by treaty implies, not only the power to govern such territory, but to prescribe upon what terms the United States will receive its inhabitants, and what their status shall be in what Chief Justice Marshall termed the "American empire." There seems to be no middle ground between this position and the doctrine that if their inhabitants do not become, immediately upon annexation, citizens of the United States, their children thereafter born, whether savages or civilized, are such, and entitled to all the rights, privileges and immunities of citizens. If such be their status, the consequences will be extremely serious. Indeed, it is doubtful if Congress would ever assent to the annexation of territory upon the condition that its inhabitants, however foreign they may be to our habits, traditions,

and modes of life, shall become at once citizens of the United States.
* * *

[I]n Johnson v. McIntosh, 8 Wheat. 543, 583, it was said by [Chief Justice Marshall]:

"The title by conquest is acquired and maintained by force. The conqueror prescribes its limits. Humanity, however, acting on public opinion, has established, as a general rule, that the conquered shall not be wantonly oppressed, and that their condition shall remain as eligible as is compatible with the objects of the conquest. Most usually they are incorporated with the victorious nation and become subjects or citizens of the government with which they are connected. The new and old members of the society mingle with each other; the distinction between them is gradually lost, and they make one people. Where this incorporation is practicable humanity demands, and a wise policy requires, that the rights of the conquered to property should remain unimpaired; that the new subjects should be governed as equitably as the old; and that confidence in their security should gradually banish the painful sense of being separated from their ancient connections and united by force to strangers.

"When the conquest is complete, and the conquered inhabitants can be blended with the conquerors, or safely governed as a distinct people, public opinion, which not even the conqueror can disregard, imposes these restraints upon him; and he cannot neglect them without injury to his fame and hazard to his power." * * *

It is obvious that in the annexation of outlying and distant possessions grave questions will arise from differences of race, habits, laws, and customs of the people, and from differences of soil, climate, and production, which may require action on the part of Congress that would be quite unnecessary in the annexation of contiguous territory inhabited only by people of the same race, or by scattered bodies of native Indians.
* * *

Whatever may be finally decided by the American people as to the status of these islands and their inhabitants,—whether they shall be introduced into the sisterhood of states or be permitted to form independent governments,—it does not follow that in the meantime, awaiting that decision, the people [of Puerto Rico] are in the matter of personal rights unprotected by the provisions of our Constitution and subject to the merely arbitrary control of Congress. Even if regarded as aliens, they are entitled under the principles of the Constitution to be protected in life, liberty, and property. This has been frequently held by this court in respect to the Chinese, even when aliens, not possessed of the political rights of citizens of the United States. * * * We do not desire, however, to anticipate the difficulties which would naturally arise in this connection, but merely to disclaim any intention to hold that the inhabitants of these territories are subject to an unrestrained power on the part of Congress to deal with them upon the theory that they have no rights which it is bound to respect.

Large powers must necessarily be intrusted to Congress in dealing with these problems, and we are bound to assume that they will be judiciously exercised. That these powers may be abused is possible. But the same may be said of its powers under the Constitution as well as outside of it. Human wisdom has never devised a form of government so perfect that it may not be perverted to bad purposes. It is never conclusive to argue against the possession of certain powers from possible abuses of them. It is safe to say that if Congress should venture upon legislation manifestly dictated by selfish interests, it would receive quick rebuke at the hands of the people. * * *

Patriotic and intelligent men may differ widely as to the desireableness of this or that acquisition, but this is solely a political question. We can only consider this aspect of the case so far as to say that no construction of the Constitution should be adopted which would prevent Congress from considering each case upon its merits, unless the language of the instrument imperatively demand it. A false step at this time might be fatal to the development of what Chief Justice Marshall called the American empire. Choice in some cases, the natural gravitation of small bodies towards large ones in others, the result of a successful war in still others, may bring about conditions which would render the annexation of distant possessions desirable. If those possessions are inhabited by alien races, differing from us in religion, customs, laws, methods of taxation, and modes of thought, the administration of government and justice, according to Anglo–Saxon principles, may for a time be impossible; and the question at once arises whether large concessions ought not to be made for a time, that ultimately our own theories may be carried out, and the blessings of a free government under the Constitution extended to them. We decline to hold that there is anything in the Constitution to forbid such action.

We are therefore of opinion that the island of Porto Rico is a territory appurtenant and belonging to the United States, but not a part of the United States within the revenue clauses of the Constitution; that the Foraker act is constitutional, so far as it imposes duties upon imports from such island, and that the plaintiff cannot recover back the duties exacted in this case.

JUSTICE WHITE, with whom concurred JUSTICE SHIRAS and JUSTICE MCKENNA, uniting in the judgment of affirmance:

* * *

While * * * there is no express or implied limitation on Congress in exercising its power to create local governments for any and all of the territories, by which that body is restrained from the widest latitude of discretion, it does not follow that there may not be inherent, although unexpressed, principles which are the basis of all free government which cannot be with impunity transcended. But this does not suggest that every express limitation of the Constitution which is applicable has not force, but only signifies that even in cases where there is no direct command of the Constitution which applies, there may nevertheless be restrictions of so fundamental a nature that they cannot be transgressed, although not expressed in so many words in the Constitution. * * *

In the case of the territories, as in every other instance, when a provision of the Constitution is invoked, the question which arises is, not whether the Constitution is operative, for that is self-evident, but whether the provision relied on is applicable. * * *

From these conceded propositions it follows that Congress in legislating for Porto Rico was only empowered to act within the Constitution and subject to its applicable limitations, and that every provision of the Constitution which applied to a country situated as was that island was potential in Porto Rico.

* * *

There is in reason, then, no room in this case to contend that Congress can destroy the liberties of the people of Porto Rico by exercising in their regard powers against freedom and justice which the Constitution has absolutely denied. There can also be no controversy as to the right of Congress to locally govern the island of Porto Rico as its wisdom may decide, and in so doing to accord only such degree of representative government as may be determined on by that body. There can also be no contention as to the authority of Congress to levy such local taxes in Porto Rico as it may choose, even although the amount of the local burden so levied be manifold more onerous than is the duty with which this case is concerned. * * *

It may not be doubted that by the general principles of the law of nations every government which is sovereign within its sphere of action possesses as an inherent attribute the power to acquire territory by discovery, by agreement or treaty, and by conquest. It cannot also be gainsaid that, as a general rule, wherever a government acquires territory as a result of any of the modes above stated, the relation of the territory to the new government is to be determined by the acquiring power in the absence of stipulations upon the subject. * * *

The general principle of the law of nations, already stated, is that acquired territory, in the absence of agreement to the contrary, will bear such relation to the acquiring government as may be by it determined. To concede to the government of the United States the right to acquire, and to strip it of all power to protect the birthright of its own citizens and to provide for the well being of the acquired territory by such enactments as may in view of its condition be essential, is, in effect, to say that the United States is helpless in the family of nations, and does not possess that authority which has at all times been treated as an incident of the right to acquire. Let me illustrate the accuracy of this statement. Take a case of discovery. Citizens of the United States discover an unknown island, peopled with an uncivilized race, yet rich in soil, and valuable to the United States for commercial and strategic reasons. Clearly, by the law of nations, the right to ratify such acquisition and thus to acquire the territory would pertain to the government of the United States. Johnson v. McIntosh, 8 Wheat. 543, 595, * * *. Can it be denied that such right could not be practically exercised if the result would be to endow the inhabitants with citizenship of the United States and to subject them, not only to local, but also to an equal proportion of national, taxes, even although the consequence would be to entail ruin on the discovered territory, and to inflict grave detriment on the United States, to arise both from the dislocation of its fiscal system and the immediate bestowal of citizenship on those absolutely unfit to receive it? * * *

When the various treaties by which foreign territory has been acquired are considered in the light of the circumstances which surrounded them, it becomes to my mind clearly established that the treaty-making power was always deemed to be devoid of authority to incorporate territory into the United States without the assent, express or implied, of Congress, and that no question to the contrary has ever been even mooted. * * *

It is, then, as I think, indubitably settled by the principles of the law of nations, by the nature of the government created under the Constitution, by the express and implied powers conferred upon that government by the Constitution, by the mode in which those powers have been executed from the beginning, and by an unbroken line of decisions of this court, first announced by Marshall and followed and lucidly expounded by Taney, that the treaty-making power cannot incorporate territory into the United States without the express or implied assent of Congress, that it may insert in a treaty conditions against immediate incorporation, and that on the other hand, when it has expressed in the treaty the conditions favorable to incorporation they will, if the treaty be not repudiated by Congress, have the force of the law of the land, and therefore by the fulfillment of such conditions cause incorporation to result. It must follow, therefore, that where a treaty contains no conditions for incorporation, and, above all, where it not only has no such conditions, but expressly provides to the contrary, that incorporation does not arise until in the wisdom of Congress it is deemed that the acquired territory has reached that state where it is proper that it should enter into and form a part of the American family.

Does, then, the treaty [of Paris] contain a provision for incorporation, or does it, on the contrary, stipulate that incorporation shall not take place from the mere effect of the treaty and until Congress has so determined?—is then the only question remaining for consideration. * * *

It is to me obvious that [Articles II, IX, and X of the Treaty of Paris] do not stipulate for incorporation, but, on the contrary, expressly provide that the "civil rights and political status of the native inhabitants of the territories hereby ceded" shall be determined by Congress. * * *

The result of what has been said is that while in an international sense Porto Rico was not a foreign country, since it was subject to the sovereignty of and was owned by the United States, it was foreign to the United States in a domestic sense, because the island had not been incorporated into the United States, but was merely appurtenant thereto as a possession. * * *

Conceding, then, for the purpose of the argument, it to be true that it would be a violation of duty under the Constitution for the legislative department, in the exercise of its discretion, to accept a cession of and permanently hold territory which is not intended to be incorporated, the presumption necessarily must be that that department, which within its lawful sphere is but the expression of the political conscience of the people of the United States, will be faithful to its duty under the Constitution, and therefore, when the unfitness of particular territory for incorporation is demonstrated, the occupation will terminate. * * *

MR. JUSTICE HARLAN, dissenting:

* * *

The idea prevails with some—indeed, it found expression in arguments at the bar—that we have in this country substantially or practically two national governments; one to be maintained under the Constitution, with all its restrictions; the other to be maintained by Congress outside and independently of that instrument, by exercising such powers as other nations of the earth are accustomed to exercise. It is one thing to give such a latitudinarian construction to the Constitution as will bring the exercise of power by Congress, upon a particular occasion or upon a particular subject, within its provisions. It is quite a different thing to say that Congress may, if it so elects, proceed outside of the Constitution. The glory of our American system of government is that it was created by a written constitution which protects the people against the exercise of arbitrary, unlimited power, and the limits of which instrument may not be passed by the government it created, or by any branch of it, or even by the people who ordained it, except by amendment or change of its provisions. 'To what purpose,' Chief Justice Marshall said in Marbury v. Madison, 1 Cranch, 137, 176, 2 L. ed. 60, 73, 'are powers limited, and to what purpose is that limitation committed to writing, if these limits may, at any time, be passed by those intended to be restrained? The distinction between a government with limited and unlimited powers is abolished if those limits do not confine the persons on whom they are imposed, and if acts prohibited and acts allowed are of equal obligation.'

The wise men who framed the Constitution, and the patriotic people who adopted it, were unwilling to depend for their safety upon what, in the opinion referred to, is described as 'certain principles of natural justice inherent in Anglo–Saxon character, which need no expression in constitutions or statutes to give them effect or to secure dependencies against legislation manifestly hostile to their real interests.' They proceeded upon the theory—the wisdom of which experience has vindicated—that the only safe guaranty against governmental oppression was to withhold or restrict the power to oppress. They well remembered that Anglo–Saxons across the ocean had attempted, in defiance of law and justice, to trample upon the rights of Anglo–Saxons on this continent, and had sought, by military force, to establish a government that could at will destroy the privileges that inhere in liberty. They believed that the establishment here of a government that could administer public affairs according to its will, unrestrained by any fundamental law and without regard to the inherent rights of freemen, would be ruinous to the liberties of the people by exposing them to the oppressions of arbitrary power. Hence, the Constitution enumerates the powers which Congress and the other departments may exercise,—leaving unimpaired, to the states or the People, the powers not delegated to the national government nor prohibited to the states. That instrument so expressly declares in the 10th Article of Amendment. It will be an evil day for American liberty if the theory of a government outside of the supreme law of the land finds lodgment in our constitutional jurisprudence. No higher duty rests upon this court than to exert its full authority to prevent all violation of the principles of the Constitution.

Again, it is said that Congress has assumed, in its past history, that the Constitution goes into territories acquired by purchase or conquest only when and as it shall so direct, and we are informed of the liberality of Congress in legislating the Constitution into all our contiguous territories. This is a view of the Constitution that may well cause surprise, if not alarm. Congress, as I have observed, has no existence except by virtue of the Constitution. It is the creature of the Constitution. It has no powers which that instrument has not granted, expressly or by necessary implication. I confess that I cannot grasp the thought that Congress, which lives and moves and has its being in the Constitution, and is consequently the mere creature of that instrument, can, at its pleasure, legislate or exclude its creator from territories which were acquired only by authority of the Constitution.

* * *

[I]t is suggested that conditions may arise when the annexation of distant possessions may be desirable. 'If,' says that opinion, 'those possessions are inhabited by alien races, differing from us in religion, customs, laws, methods of taxation, and modes of thought, the administration of government and justice, according to Anglo–Saxon principles, may for a time be impossible; and the question at once arises whether large concessions ought not to be made for a time, that ultimately our own theories may be carried out, and the blessings of a free government under the Constitution extended to them. We decline to hold that there is anything in the Constitution to forbid such action.' In my judgment, the Constitution does not sustain any such theory of our governmental system. Whether a particular race will or will not assimilate with our people, and whether they can or cannot with safety to our institutions be brought within the operation of the Constitution, is a matter to be thought of when it is proposed to acquire their territory by treaty. A mistake in the acquisition of territory, although such acquisition seemed at the time to be necessary, cannot be made the ground for violating the Constitution or refusing to give full effect to its provisions. The Constitution is not to be obeyed or disobeyed as the circumstances of a particular crisis in our history may suggest the one or the other course to be pursued. The People have decreed that it shall be the supreme law of the land at all times. When the acquisition of territory becomes complete, by cession, the Constitution necessarily becomes the supreme law of such new territory, and no power exists in any department of the government to make 'concessions' that are inconsistent with its provisions. The authority to make such concessions implies the existence in Congress of power to declare that constitutional provisions may be ignored under special or embarrassing circumstances. No such dispensing power exists in any branch of our government. The Constitution is supreme over every foot of territory, wherever situated, under the jurisdiction of the United States, and its full operation cannot be stayed by any branch of the government in order to meet what some may suppose to be extraordinary emergencies. If the Constitution is in force in any territory, it is in force there for every purpose embraced by the objects for which the government was ordained.

* * *

In my opinion Porto Rico became, at least after the ratification of the treaty with Spain, a part of and subject to the jurisdiction of the United States in respect of all its territory and people, and that Congress could not thereafter impose any duty, impost, or excise with respect to that island and its inhabitants, which departed from the rule of uniformity established by the Constitution.

Notes and Questions

1. After *Downes v. Bidwell*, what exactly was the status of Puerto Ricans?

2. Is the Court correct that the general public would necessarily "rebuke" invasive federal legislation regarding the territory? What if the general public didn't care, especially after time passed? How much does the general public know about Puerto Rico and its continuing status? Consider these points when you read the more modern cases reproduced infra.

3. What exactly makes it valid for Congress to decide what parts of the Constitution apply to conquered territory? Doesn't the principle of enumerated powers make Congress subject to the Constitution always, and unable to make it discretionary? Reread Justice Harlan's dissent on these points.

4. "Former President Harrison pointed out that the perplexing question was related to the status of the new possessions 'and to the rights of their civilized inhabitants who have elected to renounce their allegiance to the Spanish Crown, and either by choice or operation of law have become American—somethings—what? Subject or citizen? There is no other status since they are not aliens any longer, unless a newspaper heading that recently attracted my attention offers another. It ran thus: 'Porto Ricans not citizens of the United States *proper*.' Are they citizens of the United States *improper*, or improper citizens of the United States?' " Weston, supra, at 190–91.

5. Efren Rivera Ramos described the United States's climate of opinion:

> The ideology of expansion at this stage was predicated on a certain vision of order, tied to the rationality of capital and the market and to the institutions of liberal government, a vision obsessed with stability as the cornerstone of progress, but stability conceived as the unquestioned acceptance of hierarchy and subordination under the normalizing control of the institutions of capital, patriarchy, racism, and elitist representative politics. This vision of order would be used repeatedly as a justification for outright intervention in the internal affairs of the Caribbean and Central America and even for the establishment of diverse forms of prolonged political and military control. * * * The discourse of the Insular Cases incorporated many of the notions that constituted what I have termed the "ideology of expansion".

See Efrén Rivera Ramos, *The Legal Construction of American Colonialism: The Insular Cases (1901–1922)*, 65 Revista Jurídica U.P.R. 225, 226–27, 284–89 (1996). Consider the opinions in *Downes* and the ways in which they reflect the "ideology of expansion." Recall, as well, the majority's reliance on the language of conquest from *Johnson v. McIntosh*.

6. For an argument that the *Insular Cases* create the possibility of territorial deannexation, in response to the Civil War crisis of secession, see Christina Duffy Burnett, *Untied States: American Expansion and Territorial Deannexation*, 72 U. Chi. L. Rev. 797 (2005).

Justice White's position, in his concurring opinion in *Downes v. Bidwell*, ultimately became the controlling view, as expressed in the following case.

Balzac v. People of Porto Rico
258 U.S. 298 (1922)

CHIEF JUSTICE TAFT delivered the opinion of the Court.

These are two prosecutions for criminal libel, brought against the same defendant, Jesus M. Balzac, on informations filed in the district court for Arecibo, Porto Rico, by the district attorney for that district. Balzac was the editor of a daily paper published in Arecibo, known as "El Baluarte," and the articles upon which the charges of libel were based were published on April 16 and April 13, 1918, respectively. In each case the defendant demanded a jury. The Code of Criminal Procedure of Porto Rico grants a jury trial in cases of felony, but not in misdemeanors. The defendant, nevertheless, contended that he was entitled to a jury in such a case, under the Sixth Amendment to the Constitution, and that the language of the alleged libels was only fair comment, and their publication was protected by the First Amendment. His contentions were overruled; he was tried by the court, and was convicted in both cases and sentenced to five months' imprisonment in the district jail in the first, and to four months in the second, and to the payment of the costs in each. The defendant appealed to the Supreme Court of Porto Rico. That court affirmed both judgments. * * *

[The Court decided that, based on federal statute, it had jurisdiction over appeals from the Supreme Court of Puerto Rico.]

We have now to inquire whether that part of the Sixth Amendment to the Constitution, which requires that in all criminal prosecutions, the accused shall enjoy the right to a speedy and public trial, by an impartial jury of the state and district wherein the crime shall have been committed, which district shall have been previously ascertained by law, applies to Porto Rico. Another provision on the subject is in Article 3 of the Constitution providing that the trial of all crimes, except in cases of impeachment, shall be by jury; and such trial shall be held in the state where the said crimes shall have been committed; but when not committed within any state, the trial shall be at such place or places as the Congress may by law have directed. The Seventh Amendment of the Constitution provides that in suits at common law, when the value in controversy shall exceed twenty dollars, the right of trial by jury shall be preserved. It is well settled that these provisions for jury trial in criminal and civil cases apply to the Territories of the United States. * * * But it is just as clearly settled that they do not apply to territory belonging to the United States which has not been incorporated into the Union. It was further settled in Downes v. Bidwell, 182 U.S. 244, and confirmed by Dorr v. United States, 195 U.S. 138, that neither the Philippines nor Porto Rico was territory which had been incorporated in the Union or become a part of the United States, as distinguished from merely belonging to it; and that the acts giving temporary governments to the Philippines and to Porto Rico had no such effect. The *Insular Cases* revealed much diversity of opinion in this Court as to the constitutional status of the territory acquired by the Treaty of Paris ending the Spanish War, but the *Dorr* case shows that the opinion of Mr. Justice White of the majority, in *Downes v. Bidwell*, has become the settled law of the court. The conclusion of this court in the *Dorr* case, 195 U.S. at 149, was as follows:

We conclude that the power to govern territory, implied in the right to acquire it, and given to Congress in the Constitution in Article 4, § 3, to whatever other limitations it may be subject, the extent of which must be decided as questions arise, does not require that body to enact for ceded territory, not made part of the United States by congressional action, a system of laws which shall include the right of trial by jury, and that the Constitution does not, without legislation and of its own force, carry such right to territory so situated.

The question before us, therefore, is: Has Congress, since the Foraker Act of April 12, 1900 (31 Stat. 77), enacted legislation incorporating Porto Rico into the Union? Counsel for the plaintiff in error give, in their brief, an extended list of acts, to which we shall refer later, which they urge as indicating a purpose to make the island a part of the United States, but they chiefly rely on the Organic Act of Porto Rico of March 2, 1917, known as the Jones Act.

* * *

The section of the Jones Act which counsel press on us is section 5. This in effect declares that all persons who under the Foraker Act were made citizens of Porto Rico and certain other residents shall become citizens of the United States. * * * Unaffected by the considerations already suggested, perhaps the declaration of section 5 would furnish ground for an inference such as counsel for plaintiff in error contend, but under the circumstances we find it entirely consistent with nonincorporation. When Porto Ricans passed from under the government of Spain, they lost the protection of that government as subjects of the king of Spain, a title by which they had been known for centuries. They had a right to expect, in passing under the dominion of the United States, a status entitling them to the protection of their new sovereign. In theory and in law, they had it as citizens of Porto Rico, but it was an anomalous status, or seemed to be so in view of the fact that those who owed and rendered allegiance to the other great world powers were given the same designation and status as those living in their respective home countries so far as protection against foreign injustice went. It became a yearning of the Porto Ricans to be American citizens, therefore, and this act gave them the boon. What additional rights did it give them? It enabled them to move into the continental United States and becoming residents of any State there to enjoy every right of any other citizen of the United States, civil, social and political. A citizen of the Philippines must be naturalized before he can settle and vote in this country. Not so the Porto Rican under the Organic Act of 1917.

In Porto Rico, however, the Porto Rican can not insist upon the right of trial by jury, except as his own representatives in his legislature shall confer it on him. The citizen of the United States living in Porto Rico cannot there enjoy a right of trial by jury under the federal Constitution, any more than the Porto Rican. It is locality that is determinative of the application of the Constitution, in such matters as judicial procedure, and not the status of the people who live in it. * * *

The jury system needs citizens trained to the exercise of the responsibilities of jurors. In common-law countries centuries of tradition have prepared a conception of the impartial attitude jurors must assume. The jury system postulates a conscious duty of participation in the machinery of justice which it is hard for people not brought up in fundamentally popular government at once to acquire. One of its greatest benefits is in the security it gives the people that they, as jurors, actual or possible, being part of the judicial system of the country, can prevent its arbitrary use or abuse. Congress has thought that a people like the Filipinos, or the Porto Ricans, trained to a complete judicial system which knows no juries, living in compact and ancient communities, with definitely formed customs and political conceptions, should be permitted themselves to determine how far they wish to adopt this institution of Anglo–Saxon origin, and when. Hence the care with which * * * the United States has been liberal in granting to the islands acquired by the Treaty of Paris most of the American constitutional guaranties, but has been sedulous to avoid forcing a jury system on a Spanish and civil law country until it desired it. We cannot find any intention to depart from this policy in making Porto Ricans American citizens, explained as this is by the desire to put them as individuals on an exact equality with citizens from the American homeland, to secure them more certain protection against the world, and to give them an opportunity, should they desire, to move into the United States proper, and there without naturalization to enjoy all political and other rights.

* * * The Constitution of the United States is in force in Porto Rico as it is wherever and whenever the sovereign power of that government is exerted. This has not only been admitted, but emphasized, by this court in all its authoritative expressions upon the issues arising in the *Insular Cases*, especially in the *Downes v. Bidwell* and the *Dorr* cases. The Constitution, however, contains grants of power, and limitations which in the nature of things are not always and everywhere applicable and the real issue in the *Insular Cases* was not whether the Constitution extended to the Philippines or Porto Rico when we went there, but which ones of its provisions were applicable by way of limitation upon the exercise of executive and legislative power in dealing with new conditions and requirements. * * *

On the whole, therefore, we find no features in the Organic Act of Porto Rico of 1917 from which we can infer the purpose of Congress to incorporate Porto Rico into the United States with the consequences which would follow. * * *

The judgments of the Supreme Court of Porto Rico are affirmed.

SECTION 3.   PUERTO RICAN CITIZENSHIP

In the 1917 Jones Act, Congress enacted a bill of rights for Puerto Rico granting United States citizenship to Puerto Ricans. In Section 5 of the Jones Act, "all citizens of Porto Rico, as defined by [the Foraker Act] ... are hereby declared, and shall be deemed and held to be, citizens of the United States." However, this grant of citizenship was far from full. According to Senator Foraker, the United States citizenship of Puerto Ricans did not intend to recognize any individual rights they might have, but rather to "recognize that Puerto Rico belongs to the United States of America." Foraker also commented:

> We considered very carefully what status in a political sense we would give to the people of [Puerto Rico], and we reported that provision not thoughtlessly.... We concluded ... that the inhabitants of that island must be either citizens or subjects or aliens. We did not want to treat our own as aliens, and we do not propose to have any subjects. Therefore, we adopted the term "citizens." *In adopting the term "citizens" we did not understand, however, that we were giving to those people any rights that the American people do not want them to have.* "Citizens" is a word that indicates, according to Story's work on the Constitution of the United States, allegiance on the one hand and protection on the other.

See Cabranes, supra, at 37 (quoting 33 *Cong. Rec.* 2473–74 (1900) (remarks of Sen. Foraker)).

Consider the role race and racism played in defining the meaning of United States citizenship for Puerto Ricans:

Rubin Francis Weston
Racism in U.S. Imperialism
194–201, 204 (1972)

DEMOCRATS AND PUERTO RICAN CITIZENSHIP

During fourteen years of Republican administration, American citizenship for the Puerto Ricans was denied. When the Democrats gained control of the House in 1912, they immediately started to act on various proposals to give American citizenship to the Puerto Ricans. A report on a bill to provide citizenship to the Puerto Ricans pointed out that under the Foraker Act of 1900 it was sometimes argued that Puerto Ricans were citizens of the United States. The basis of the argument was Section 1891 of the Revised Statutes which declares that "the Constitution and all laws of the United States which are not locally inapplicable shall have the same force and effect within all the organized territories and in every territory hereafter organized or elsewhere within the United States." Some Americans, however, contended that in the meaning of Section 1891 the Puerto Ricans were not citizens and "that the extension of the Constitution and laws over the island would not of itself have the effect of constituting the inhabitants thereof citizens of the United States." Many inhabitants of the states under the Constitution were not citizens, "as for instance Chinese, Indians, and others." Although the argument in favor of Puerto Rican citizenship had been presented, the Supreme Court had refused to "hold either that the Constitution of the United States extends over the island of Puerto Rico in all respects and for all purposes, or that the inhabitants thereof are citizens of the United States." It was the purpose of the proposed bill to confer American citizenship upon the Puerto Ricans collectively, "subject only to the condition that each take the oath of allegiance and receive a certificate." Those who did not wish American citizenship would not be forced to become citizens.

The debates in the House of Representatives on the question of American citizenship for the Puerto Ricans revolved around the racial questions. "Considering all the conditions with Haiti, Santo Domingo, Central America and elsewhere," Representative Joseph G. Cannon did not believe that Puerto Ricans were competent for self-government. The United States already had her hands full in taking care of all the aforementioned countries. The Illinois congressman felt that the Puerto Ricans did not "understand, as we understand it, government of the people, and by the people," because they had a different language. He contended that "75 or 80 per cent of those people are mixed blood in part and are not the equal to the full-blooded Spaniard and not equal, in my judgement, to the unmixed African, and yet they were to be made citizens of the United States."

Representative James L. Slayden of Texas opposed the bill on grounds similar to those expressed by Representative Cannon. He took exception to the view that the hybrid, a cross between the blacks and whites or between the brown and whites, was "less well fitted for self-government than the full-blooded African Negro." According to his observations, the Negro had not shown any moderate success in government "hybrid or thoroughbred." Haiti was used as an example of an almost completely black country not able to govern itself successfully. Cuba and the Dominican Republic were cited as countries of hybrids unable to sustain republican forms of government. Slayden believed that the problem was not in language but in color, and that Representative Cannon would certainly have been more accurate if he had said that "as a whole, they have a different color." That would better have explained what he conceived to be their incapacity, for "color in this matter is more important than language." The representative declared that the climate and geography of Puerto Rico were not conducive to Anglo–Saxon government because "the Tropics seem to heat the blood while enervating the people who inhabit them." According to Slayden, the United States was already in "an awkward situation with reference to . . . Porto Rico . . . and every member of the House" knew it. They were charging the United States "with inconsistency and worse . . . they prove it." He continued, "They know that we tax them without permitting representation in our Congress, something that was a crime when done by the British Parliament, but which does not appear so wicked when we play the role of King George and his Parliamentarians." Representative Slayden concluded by saying that "many people in this country who want to sever the tie that binds us to tropical and alien people take that position, because they see in it danger for us." They agreed that people inhabiting lands within 20 degrees of the equator could "neither comprehend nor support representative government constructed on the Anglo–Saxon plan."

Representative James Mann of Illinois observed that if the Puerto Ricans were made citizens, they could "demand admission into the Union with greater force and with better logic." To admit into the Union as a state with the "deciding power in the Senate if not in the House a people who were somewhat . . . strange" to the internal problems of the United States and its civilization was not to be desired.

Outside Congress influential persons expressed similar views to those expressed on the floor of the House. The former governor of Puerto Rico, R.H. Post, said, "The granting of citizenship to all of the inhabitants of Porto Rico, although but a step in the direction of complete assimilation, is still a step, and would tend to commit us to eventual statehood for Porto Rico, and might be construed as indicating that it was the policy of the United States that extraneous territory occupied by foreign races falling under the influence of the United States will eventually be admitted as sovereign States of the Union."

Outlook in its editorial policy agreed that the Puerto Ricans had legitimate grievances but asserted, "Statehood would not be of advantage to the United States and of doubtful advantage to Porto Rico." It was opposed to blanket naturalization because "it puts Porto Rico in the line to become first an organized territory and eventually a State in the Union, and raises hope of this ultimate statehood ... a consummation very undesirable both for them and for us...."

William Hayes Ward, editor of the *Independent*, wrote that he could not sympathize with a nation "which demands a special racial," intellectual, or educational "standard for citizenship or the ballot." The doctrine was aristocratic, and full democracy was "safer than aristocracy" since democracy always had the future. "Give the ballot to the ignorant and you will educate them, for you will have to. The ballot to the negro in the South gave the South the public school system, and so justified all the risk we took in the act." Ward supported unconditional statehood for Puerto Rico.

Supporters of the bill, such as Representative Henry A. Cooper of Wisconsin, believed that the people of Puerto Rico were civilized and entitled to citizenship in the United States. As evidence of their civilization, Cooper pointed to the fact that they voluntarily freed their slaves, taxing themselves $30,000,000 to compensate the owners. They were entitled to citizenship because under the Constitution the United States could not hold people in subjection to its laws for an indefinite period unless they were citizens. Since the United States was committed to hold Puerto Rico forever because of the Panama Canal, citizenship was the only logical status for the inhabitants of the island.

Representative Elmer A. Morse, also of Wisconsin, noted that the Negro population was not much larger, if any, "in Puerto Rico than in the great State of South Carolina." It was his belief that "while the quality of citizenship" was not as high as it should be, the people should be given the privilege of American citizenship.

The Senate failed to act on this bill in 1912. In 1913 Resident Commissioner Louis Muñoz Rivera observed, "My countrymen, having waited since 1898 for a measure of absolute and ample self-government, do expect today more than ever before that their hopes will soon be realized, Congress granting them American citizenship together with a law creating two elective houses, and investing them, through their representatives in both chambers, with power to make their laws and to regulate all their local matters."

It was with a degree of renewed hope that the Puerto Ricans welcomed the success of the Democrats at the polls in 1912. Democratic control of Congress and the Executive Department suggested that the concept of democratic expansion, long advocated by the party, would be applied to Puerto Rico.

President-elect Woodrow Wilson seemed to agree with the resident commissioner when he said, "No doubt we shall successfully enough bind Porto Rico ... to ourselves by ties of justice and interest and affection ... We can satisfy the obligation of generous justice toward the people of Porto Rico by giving them ample and familiar rights and privileges accorded our own citizens in our own territories...."

The Congress has never been noted for haste in its actions on civil and political rights, and Puerto Rican citizenship was no exception. When Congress took up the question of civil government for Puerto Rico, it was acting to replace a fourteen-year-old "Act Temporarily to Provide Revenue and Civil Government for Porto Rico and for Other Purposes." Serious debate on the bill, however, was not begun until 1916. Resident Commissioner Rivera, speaking in support of the citizenship bill before the House of Representatives, observed that the Republican party by decreeing independence for Cuba had gained glory for itself. The Democratic party was bound by the "principles written into its platforms and by recorded speeches of its leaders to decree liberty for Porto Rico." The bill under consideration could not "meet the earnest aspirations" of Puerto Ricans because it was "not a measure of self-government ample enough to solve definitely" the basic political problems or to match the national reputation of the United States—a reputation which had been established by "successful championship for liberty and justice throughout the world." From this viewpoint, the Puerto Ricans were willing to accept statehood as a step in the right direction and as "a reform paving the way for others more acceptable and satisfactory," which should come later provided the Puerto Ricans could demonstrate the capacity to govern themselves. To that capacity it was his "pleasant duty to assure Congress that the Porto Ricans" would "endeavor to prove their intelligence, their patriotism and their full preparation to enjoy and exercise a democratic regime."

The commissioner supported the measure only because he felt that it was the best that could be hoped for at that time. It was his opinion that Puerto Rico deserved better treatment. He pointed out that the behavior of the Puerto Ricans in the past was a testimony in favor of good behavior in the future. In spite of the Latin blood that predominated, there had never been a revolution or "an attack against the majesty of law." There was not sufficient reason to justify "American statesmen in denying self-government" to Puerto Rico and thereby compromise the basic American principle of popular sovereignty:

> ... My countrymen ... refuse to accept a citizenship of an inferior order, a citizenship of the second class, which does not permit them to dispose of their own resources nor to live their own lives nor to send to this Capital their proportional representation ... Give us statehood and your glorious citizenship will be welcome to us and to our children. If you deny us statehood, we decline your citizenship, frankly, proudly, as befits a people who can be deprived of their civil liberties, but who, although deprived of their civil liberties, will preserve their conception of honor....

Commissioner Rivera observed that the bill "authorized those who do not accept American citizenship to so declare before a court of justice, and thus retain Porto Rican citizenship." The bill further provided that "no person shall be allowed to register as a voter in Porto Rico who is not a citizen of the United States." Rivera objected to this provision:

> My compatriots are generously permitted to be citizens of the only country they possess, but they are eliminated from the body politic; the exercise of political rights is forbidden them; by a single stroke of the pen they are converted into pariahs and there is established in America on American soil, protected by the Monroe Doctrine, a division into castes like the Brahamans and Sudras of India. The Democratic platform of Kansas City declared 14 years ago, "A nation can not long endure half empire and half republic, and imperialism abroad will lead rapidly and irreparably to despotism at home." These are not Porto Rican phrases reflecting our Latin impressionability; they are American phrases, reflecting the Anglo–Saxon spirit, calm in its attitude and jealous—very jealous—of its privileges.

Inquiring into some of the probable reasons why Puerto Rico had not been given self-government, he found it could not be the fact that two races coexisted on the island of Puerto Rico because "in America more than ten states had a higher percentage of Negroes in their population than Porto Rico." It was not the lack of adequate numbers, for Puerto Rico was more populous than eighteen other states. After examining the probable reasons, he concluded that the reason behind the denial of self-government was based on the desire of office seekers "determined to report to their superiors that the Porto Ricans were unprepared for self-government."

The resident commissioner could not conceive of a people being denied the rights of self-government on purely racial grounds. His efforts to compare the racial situation in Puerto Rico with the situation in several of the Southern states was not a valid comparison. In Puerto Rico there had been considerable racial interbreeding while in the United States this practice was kept at a minimum, and in many areas by law. The incorporation of a large population of mixed races was potentially dangerous to existing racial patterns in the United States.

The importance of these racial implications was pointed up by Representative Joseph Cannon, who felt that

> when you talk about a people competent for self-government, certain things are to be taken into consideration. One is the racial question ... Porto Rico is populated by a mixed race. About 30 per cent pure African. I was informed by the army officers when I was down there that when the census was taken every man that was a pure African was listed and counted as such, but that there was 75 to 80 per cent of the population that was pure African or had an African strain in their blood ... Will anybody say that I am abusing the African. I am not any more than I am abusing the Filipino or the Moros; and I am certainly not abusing the African in the United States ... But the Commissioner from Porto Rico said that this bill is not as liberal as

he wanted it, and he hoped more and more would be given, and as I listened to his remarks I thought he was referring to Statehood. God forbid that in his time or my time, there should be statehood for Porto Rico as one of the United States.

Cannon hoped that Puerto Rico would not be admitted to statehood within the next three generations because the "people of Porto Rico did not have the slightest conception of self-government." He would vote against the pending bill because in the two hundred or three hundred years that the British had been in Jamaica, where there was also a large percentage of African blood, they had not been able to prepare the natives for self-government. In the United States the situation was reversed, for there were "10,000,000 people lately enslaved, who have made very great progress, but they were in contact with 90,000,000 of people who have proved their competency for self-government of the Caucasian race. . . ."

Commissioner Rivera replied that Puerto Rico

deprived of its national sovereignty depends upon the generosity and chivalry of the American lawmakers . . . It is very unfortunate that a Porto Rican is obliged to hear on this floor remarks offensive to the dignity of his native land. . . . It is not our fault that we are compelled to come here and ask for the enactment of legislation, of a constitution, which, should be our undeniable right to make, according to American principles ourselves. I must conclude, declaring emphatically that I am as proud to be Porto Rican as the gentlemen from Illinois is proud of being an Illinoisan, and as every gentleman on this floor is proud to be an American.

Representative Simeon D. Fess of Ohio saw in the Puerto Rican bill an attempt to do for Puerto Rico something that had not been done previously by Anglo–Saxons for non-Anglo–Saxons—giving them "the best form of local government" that the United States could outline for them and at the same time giving them United States citizenship. * * *

Americans in positions to influence or to establish policy were not very generous in giving to the Puerto Ricans rights usually given to Americans. For the first third of the twentieth century they rationalized the inconsistency of their treatment of the Puerto Ricans on the basis of cultural differences. In the final analysis, race emerged as the determining factor in establishing policy. That policy assumed that the Puerto Ricans were radically different from the Anglo–Saxons and were unassimilable into the American body politic. To the Puerto Ricans, the frustrations caused by this policy created a reciprocal dislike for Americans who gave out their culture and democracy in "a most patronizing manner." America's treatment of Puerto Rico was observed in Latin America and had some effect on attitudes toward the United States. According to one observer, the American treatment of Puerto Rico resulted from the concept of harmonious racial interbreeding brought by the Spanish to their American colonies, a concept completely alien to Anglo–Saxons. The term *Latin America* connoted cultural fraternity, and this did not serve to weaken the wall separating the United States from Latin America in general and Puerto Rico in particular. The difference in concepts added new buttresses to the wall in the form of factors unassimilable for the United States and recalcitrant to all absorption.

Notes and Questions

1. Notice that the United States citizenship of Puerto Ricans does not include the right to vote for President or Vice President because Puerto Rico is not a state. As stated in *Balzac*, however, Puerto Ricans have the right to move to a mainland state. Once they achieve residency there, they can exercise all the rights of any state citizen, including the right to vote.

In Sanchez v. United States, 376 F.Supp. 239 (D.P.R. 1974), Ada Flores Sanchez, a resident of Puerto Rico, attempted to challenge her ineligibility, despite her United States citizenship, to vote in elections for the President and Vice President of the United States. The judge held that:

> The constitutional challenge in this instance is plainly without merit. Although plaintiff is a U.S. citizen, under the Constitution of the United States the President is not chosen directly by the citizens, but by the electoral colleges in the States and the District of Columbia. * * *

> Today, electors are chosen by popular vote on State-wide tickets and State legislatures generally determine the qualifications for presidential electors. * * * [T]he Constitution does not, by its terms, grant citizens the right to vote, but leaves the matter entirely to the States.

> Although citizenship may be a prerequisite of voting, the right to vote is not an essential right of citizenship. * * *

> This Court * * * is of the opinion that it is inexcusable that there still exists a substantial number of U.S. citizens who cannot legally vote for the President and Vice President of the United States. However, until the Commonwealth votes for Statehood, or until a constitutional amendment is approved which extends the presidential and vice presidential vote to Puerto Rico, there is no substantial constitutional question raised by plaintiff. * * *

See also Leibowitz, *Defining Status*, at 149.

2. Puerto Ricans have continued to challenge their inability to vote for President and Vice President. Their results have been uniformly unsuccessful. In a recent decision, Igartúa-De La Rosa v. United States, 417 F.3d 145, 147–48 (1st Cir. 2005) (en banc), the court reasoned as follows:

> The constitutional claim is readily answered. Voting for President and Vice President of the United States is governed neither by rhetoric nor intuitive values but by a provision of the Constitution. This provision does not confer the franchise on "U.S. citizens" but on "Electors" who are to be "appoint[ed]" by each "State," in "such Manner" as the state legislature may direct, equal to the number of Senators and Representatives to whom the state is entitled. U.S. Const. art. II, § 1, cl. 2; see also id. amend. XII.

> * * *

Puerto Rico—like the District of Columbia, the Virgin Islands, and Guam—is not a "state" within the meaning of the Constitution. Puerto Rico was not one of the original 13 states who ratified the Constitution; nor has it been made a state, like the other 37 states added thereafter, pursuant to the process laid down in the Constitution. U.S. Const. art. IV, § 3, cl. 1. Nor has it been given electors of its own, as was the District of Columbia in the Twenty–Third Amendment.

* * *

As Puerto Rico has no electors, its citizens do not participate in the presidential voting, although they may do so if they take up residence in one of the 50 states and, of course, they elect the Governor of Puerto Rico, its legislature, and a non-voting delegate to Congress. Like each state's entitlement to two Senators regardless of population, the make-up of the electoral college is a direct consequence of how the framers of the Constitution chose to structure our government—a choice itself based on political compromise rather than conceptual perfection.

That the franchise for choosing electors is confined to "states" cannot be "unconstitutional" because it is what the Constitution itself provides. Hence it does no good to stress how important is the "right to vote" for President.

The court also rejected the argument that international treaties required the United States to grant Puerto Ricans the right to vote in federal elections.

3. Consider the future implications of such diluted citizenship for Puerto Ricans. How would you expect Congress to treat Puerto Rican island residents, who have no voting representation in Congress and no vote for the President?

SECTION 4. THE EVOLUTION OF COMMONWEALTH STATUS FOR PUERTO RICO

In 1950, Congress passed Public Law 600, which created a "compact" granting limited powers to Puerto Rico. Public Law 600, and its implementation, culminated in Puerto Rico's current status as a "Commonwealth." Consider the following excerpt.

Ediberto Roman
Empire Forgotten: The United States's Colonization of Puerto Rico
42 Vill. L. Rev. 1119, 1151–56 (1997)

THE CREATION OF THE COMMONWEALTH

In 1943, forty-five years after the initial occupation, the first major legal efforts were made to address the Puerto Rican people's lack of autonomy. Here again, the United States, uncomfortable with the role of colonizer, continued its denial and eventually developed a new euphemism for the term "colony": "commonwealth" status.

During the same period that the United States was endorsing self-determination principles in the Atlantic Charter, the Puerto Rican people cried out for an end to colonialism. After fifty years of U.S. control, the Puerto Rican legislature, relying upon the United States's declarations in the Atlantic Charter, demanded that Congress terminate "the colonial system of government ... totally and definitely." Shortly after that demand, President Roosevelt initiated the first of what was to become the trademark U.S. response to the Puerto Rican plea for autonomy—congressional or executive department hearings to review the status issue. President Roosevelt's committee proposed amendments to the Jones Act and forwarded a proposed bill to Senator Tydings for introduction before Congress. Tydings had sympathetically observed:

> [I]f you are willing to have help of a kind and have no real voice in the government of the nation to which you are appended, why, then, that is one thing.
>
> * * *
>
> If I were a Puerto Rican that would not satisfy me, just as it did not satisfy George Washington, Thomas Jefferson, and Simon Bolivar.

Roosevelt's initiative resulted in the enactment of laws that would produce the next changes in Puerto Rico's governmental structure, but which ultimately amounted to only a modicum of autonomy for the Puerto Rican people. In 1947, a year after the Philippines was given independence, Congress passed legislation that granted the Puerto Rican people the right to select a governor of their own choosing and empowered the governor to appoint executive officials.

In 1950, Congress enacted Public Law 600, which, in the form of a "compact" between the United States and Puerto Rico, granted the people of Puerto Rico further powers, including the right to organize a government and adopt a constitution. As will be addressed below, the use of the term "compact" assisted the United States in appeasing Puerto Rican and international calls to end the colonial status of Puerto Rico. Unfortunately, the use of "compact," and the representations by U.S. officials concerning the new status, left both the international community and the Puerto Rican political spectrum in a state of turmoil concerning the true status of the territory, an occurrence that has fostered the maintenance of the status quo.

Sections 1 and 2 of Public Law 600 provided that a referendum would be submitted to the Puerto Rican people to determine if they wished to organize their own government pursuant to a constitution of their own choosing. Although these provisions suggest that Puerto Rico was to be granted autonomy, the rest of the act made clear that Puerto Rico was not free from U.S. control. Specifically, Public Law 600 provided that if the Puerto Rican people adopted a constitution, the President would transmit it to Congress "if [the President found] that such constitution conform[ed] with the applicable provisions of this Act and of the Constitution of the United States." Further, House Report 2275 on Public Law 600 confirms Congress's intent to keep Puerto Rico a U.S. possession:

This bill does not commit the Congress, either expressly or by implication, to the enactment of statehood legislation for Puerto Rico in the future. Nor will it in any way preclude a future determination by the Congress of Puerto Rico's ultimate political status.

* * *

The United States has never made any promises to the people of Puerto Rico, or to Spain from whom Puerto Rico was acquired, that Puerto Rico would eventually be admitted into the Union.

Consistent with its intended imperialistic tenor, Public Law 600's proposed referendum failed to provide the Puerto Rican people with options other than colonial or commonwealth status, as the choice of "permanent" association with a "federal union" was posed in a yes-or-no referendum. The referendum was thus not a statement of the Puerto Rican peoples' freely expressed will. In any event, in 1951 a referendum was held in Puerto Rico to approve Public Law 600. A second referendum was held to approve the constitution. In March of 1952, by virtue of Public Law 447, Congress, after amending portions, approved the Puerto Rican Constitution and revoked inconsistent provisions of the Jones Act.

In the summer of 1952, the Puerto Rican Constitution and the Commonwealth of Puerto Rico were born. The first popularly elected Puerto Rican governor, Luis Muñoz Marin, attempted to give some real teeth to Puerto Rico's new status. Tracking the introductory remarks of the law, Muñoz Marin argued that Public Law 600 transformed the relationship between the Puerto Rican people and Congress to one which could not be altered without the consent of each of the contracting parties. By virtue of this so-called compact, the Puerto Rican people acquired a certain amount of local autonomy. The autonomy bestowed upon Puerto Rico by its parent state, however, was unquestionably limited and revocable, as is the case in a classic colonial relationship. In fact, all of the parties involved, including Muñoz Marin, accepted that the United States maintained complete control over Puerto Rico and could even revoke the Puerto Rican Constitution.

Public Law 600's use of the term "compact" also allowed the United States to address a potential international embarrassment that it might soon face concerning Puerto Rico. As a signatory to the U.N. Charter, which specifically endorsed self-determination, the United States faced the potential of increasing international scrutiny. Specifically, the United States faced the dilemma of being a member of an international organization that promoted self-determination and could therefore criticize the United States concerning Puerto Rico. The United States responded by ingeniously using the compact language of Public Law 600 and the territory's new status to avoid international condemnation. * * * Puerto Rico's political status remained unchanged as a result of the creation of the commonwealth status despite the United States's statements to the international community concerning Puerto Rico.

* * *

SECTION 5.   THE CURRENT STATUS
OF PUERTO RICANS

Bearing in mind the status of Puerto Rico as defined by the *Insular Cases*, *Balzac*, and subsequent developments, it should come as no surprise that recent U.S. Supreme Court rulings have left Puerto Ricans living on the island with second class citizenship.

Califano v. Torres
435 U.S. 1 (1978)

PER CURIAM.

Certain benefits under the Social Security Act, as amended in 1972, are payable only to residents of the United States, defined as the 50 States and the District of Columbia. The District Court for the District of Puerto Rico held in these cases that this geographic limitation is unconstitutional as applied to persons who upon moving to Puerto Rico lost the benefits to which they were entitled while residing in the United States. The Secretary of Health, Education, and Welfare, responsible for the administration of the Social Security Act, has appealed.

One of the 1972 amendments to the Social Security Act created a uniform program, known as the Supplemental Security Income (SSI) program, for aid to qualified aged, blind, and disabled persons. * * *

The exclusion of Puerto Rico in the amended program is apparent in the definitional section. Section 1611(f) of the Act * * * states that no individual is eligible for benefits during any month in which he or she is outside the United States. The Act defines "the United States" as "the 50 States and the District of Columbia." The repeal of the pre-existing programs did not apply to Puerto Rico. Thus persons in Puerto Rico are not eligible to receive SSI benefits, but are eligible to receive benefits under the pre-existing programs. [The SSI benefits are significantly larger.]

Appellee Torres received SSI benefits while residing in Connecticut; the benefits were discontinued when he moved to Puerto Rico. Similarly, appellees Colon and Vega received benefits as residents of Massachusetts and New Jersey, respectively, but lost them on moving to Puerto Rico.

Torres filed a complaint in the District Court of Puerto Rico claiming that the exclusion of Puerto Rico from the SSI program was unconstitutional, and a three-judge court was convened to adjudicate the suit. Viewing the geographic limitations in the law as an interference with the constitutional right of residents of the 50 States and the District of Columbia to travel, the court searched for a compelling governmental interest to justify such interference. Finding none, the court held [the statutes] unconstitutional as applied to Torres. Torres v.

Mathews, 426 F.Supp. 1106.[4] Soon after that decision, appellees Colon and Vega also sued in the Puerto Rico District Court. Relying on the *Torres* decision, a single judge enjoined the Social Security Administration from discontinuing their SSI benefits on the basis of their change of residency to Puerto Rico.

In Shapiro v. Thompson, 394 U.S. 618 (1969) and Memorial Hospital v. Maricopa County, 415 U.S. 250 (1974), this Court held that laws prohibiting newly arrived residents in a State or county from receiving the same vital benefits as other residents unconstitutionally burdened the right of interstate travel. As the Court said in *Memorial Hospital*, "the right of interstate travel must be seen as insuring new residents the same right to vital governmental benefits and privileges in the States to which they migrate as are enjoyed by other residents." Id. at 261.

In the present cases the District Court altogether transposed that proposition. It held that the Constitution requires that a person who travels to Puerto Rico must be given benefits superior to those enjoyed by other residents of Puerto Rico if the newcomer enjoyed those benefits in the State from which he came. This Court has never held that the constitutional right to travel embraces any such doctrine, and we decline to do so now. Such a doctrine would apply with equal force to any benefits a State might provide for its residents, and would require a State to continue to pay those benefits indefinitely to any persons who had once resided there. And the broader implications of such a doctrine in other areas of substantive law would bid fair to destroy the independent power of each State under our Constitution to enact laws uniformly applicable to all of its residents.

If there ever could be a case where a person who has moved from one State to another might be entitled to invoke the law of the State from which he came as a corollary of his constitutional right to travel, this is surely not it. For we deal here with a constitutional attack upon a law providing for governmental payments of monetary benefits. Such a statute "is entitled to a strong presumption of constitutionality." "So long as its judgments are rational, and not invidious, the legislature's efforts to tackle the problems of the poor and the needy are not subject to a constitutional straitjacket." Jefferson v. Hackney, 406 U.S. 535, 546 (1972).[7]

---

4. The complaint had also relied on the equal protection component of the Due Process Clause of the Fifth Amendment in attacking the exclusion of Puerto Rico from the SSI program. Acceptance of that claim would have meant that all otherwise qualified persons in Puerto Rico are entitled to SSI benefits, not just those who received such benefits before moving to Puerto Rico. But the District Court apparently acknowledged that Congress has the power to treat Puerto Rico differently, and that every federal program does not have to be extended to it. Puerto Rico has a relationship to the United States "that has no parallel in our history." Examining Board v. Flores de Otero, 426 U.S. 572, 596 (1976). Cf. Balzac v. Porto Rico, 258 U.S. 298 (1922); Dorr v. United States, 195 U.S. 138 (1904); Downes v. Bidwell, 182 U.S. 244 (1901). * * *

7. At least three reasons have been advanced to explain the exclusion of persons in Puerto Rico from the SSI program. First, because of the unique tax status of Puerto Rico, its residents do not contribute to the public treasury. Second, the cost of including Puerto Rico would be extremely great— an estimated $300 million per year. Third,

The judgments are reversed.

JUSTICE BRENNAN would affirm.

JUSTICE MARSHALL would note probable jurisdiction and set these cases for oral argument.

Harris v. Rosario
446 U.S. 651 (1980)

PER CURIAM.

The Aid to Families with Dependent Children program (AFDC) provides federal financial assistance to States and Territories to aid families with needy dependent children. Puerto Rico receives less assistance than do the States. Appellees, AFDC recipients residing in Puerto Rico, filed this class action against the Secretary of Health, Education, and Welfare (now the Secretary of Health and Human Services) in March 1977 in the United States District Court for the District of Puerto Rico; they challenged the constitutionality of 42 U.S.C.A. §§ 1308 and 1396d(b), claiming successfully that the lower level of AFDC reimbursement provided to Puerto Rico violates the Fifth Amendment's equal protection guarantee.

We disagree. Congress, which is empowered under the Territory Clause of the Constitution, U.S. Const., Art. IV, § 3, cl. 2, to "make all needful Rules and Regulations respecting the Territory ... belonging to the United States," may treat Puerto Rico differently from States so long as there is a rational basis for its actions. In Califano v. Torres, 435 U.S. 1 (1978) (*per curiam*), we concluded that a similar statutory classification was rationally grounded on three factors: Puerto Rican residents do not contribute to the federal treasury; the cost of treating Puerto Rico as a State under the statute would be high; and greater benefits could disrupt the Puerto Rican economy. These same considerations are forwarded here in support of §§ 1308 and 1396d(b)* and we see no reason to depart from our conclusion in *Torres* that they suffice to form a rational basis for the challenged statutory classification.

We reverse.

JUSTICE BRENNAN and JUSTICE BLACKMUN, not now being persuaded that the Court's summary disposition in Califano v. Torres, 435 U.S. 1 (1978), so clearly controls this case, would note probable jurisdiction and set the case for oral argument.

JUSTICE MARSHALL, dissenting.

inclusion in the SSI program might seriously disrupt the Puerto Rican economy. * * *

* For example, the Secretary estimates that the additional cost of treating Puerto Rico as a State for AFDC purposes alone would be approximately $30 million per year, and, if the decision below were to apply equally to various other reimbursement programs under the Social Security Act, the total annual cost could exceed $240 million.

The Court today rushes to resolve important legal issues without full briefing or oral argument. The sole authority cited for the majority's result is another summary decision by this Court. The need for such haste is unclear. The dangers of such decisionmaking are clear, however, as the Court's analysis is, in my view, ill-conceived in at least two respects.

The first question that merits plenary attention is whether Congress, acting pursuant to the Territory Clause of the Constitution, U.S. Const., Art. IV, § 3, cl. 2, "may treat Puerto Rico differently from States so long as there is a rational basis for its actions." No authority is cited for this proposition. Our prior decisions do not support such a broad statement.

It is important to remember at the outset that Puerto Ricans are United States citizens and that different treatment to Puerto Rico under AFDC may well affect the benefits paid to these citizens. While some early opinions of this Court suggested that various protections of the Constitution do not apply to Puerto Rico, see, *e.g.* Downes v. Bidwell, 182 U.S. 244 (1901); Balzac v. Porto Rico, 258 U.S. 298 (1922), the present validity of those decisions is questionable. We have already held that Puerto Rico is subject to the Due Process Clause of either the Fifth or Fourteenth Amendment and the equal protection guarantee of either the Fifth or the Fourteenth Amendment. The Fourth Amendment is also fully applicable to Puerto Rico, either directly or by operation of the Fourteenth Amendment. At least four Members of this Court are of the view that all provisions of the Bill of Rights apply to Puerto Rico.

Despite these precedents, the Court suggests today, without benefit of briefing or argument, that Congress needs only a rational basis to support less beneficial treatment for Puerto Rico, and the citizens residing there, than is provided to the States and citizens residing in the States. Heightened scrutiny under the equal protection component of the Fifth Amendment, the Court concludes, is simply unavailable to protect Puerto Rico or the citizens who reside there from discriminatory legislation, as long as Congress acts pursuant to the Territory Clause. Such a proposition surely warrants the full attention of this Court before it is made part of our constitutional jurisprudence.

Califano v. Torres, 435 U.S. 1 (1978) (*per curiam*), the only authority upon which the majority relies, does not stand for the proposition the Court espouses today. * * * While the plaintiffs in that case had also challenged the provision on equal protection grounds, the District Court relied entirely on the right to travel, and therefore no equal protection question was before this Court. The Court merely referred to the equal protection claim briefly in a footnote. * * * Observing that Puerto Rico's relationship with the United States was unique, the Court simply noted that the District Court had "apparently acknowledged that Congress has the power to treat Puerto Rico differently, and that every federal program does not have to be extended to it." That Puerto Rico has an unparalleled relationship with the United States does not lead ineluctably to the legal principle asserted here. At most, reading more into that single footnote of dictum than it deserves, *Califano v. Torres* may suggest that under the equal protection component of the Due Process Clause of the Fifth Amendment, Puerto Rico may be treated differently from the States if there is a rational basis for the discrimination when Congress enacts a law providing for governmental payments of monetary benefits. That is a more limited view than is asserted in this case, but even that position should be reached only after oral argument and full briefing.

I also object to the Court's reliance on the effect greater benefits could have on the Puerto Rican economy. This rationale has troubling overtones. It suggests that programs designed to help the poor should be less fully applied in those areas where the need may be the greatest, simply because otherwise the relative poverty of recipients compared to other persons in the same geographic area will somehow be upset. Similarly, reliance on the fear of disrupting the Puerto Rican economy implies that Congress intended to preserve or even strengthen the comparative economic position of the States vis-a-vis Puerto Rico. Under this theory, those geographic units of the country which have the strongest economies presumably would get the most financial aid from the Federal Government since those units would be the least likely to be "disrupted." Such an approach to a financial assistance program is not so clearly rational as the Court suggests, and there is no citation by the Court to any suggestion in the legislative history that Congress had these economic concerns in mind when it passed the portion of the AFDC program presently being challenged. Nor does appellant refer to any evidence in the record supporting the notion that such a speculative fear of economic disruption is warranted. In my view it is by no means clear that the discrimination at issue here could survive scrutiny under even a deferential equal protection standard.

Ultimately this case raises the serious issue of the relationship of Puerto Rico, and the United States citizens who reside there, to the Constitution. An issue of this magnitude deserves far more careful attention than it has received in *Califano v. Torres* and in the present case. I would note probable jurisdiction and set the case for oral argument. Accordingly, I dissent from the Court's summary disposition.

Notes and Questions

1. Consider the Court's disposition of these important issues in brief per curiam opinions. Do the courts and Congress treat the people of Puerto Rico fairly? Do the issues presented justify more thorough consideration, and possible reconsideration? Why has that not happened?

2. Does the Court's use of the permissive rational basis standard of review in reviewing the unequal treatment of Puerto Rican residents make sense? How can Congress treat an entire group of people defined by Puerto Rican ancestry less generously than and differently from other Americans?

In other settings, the Court has held that classifications based on national origin are subject to strict scrutiny. See Hernandez v. Texas, 347 U.S. 475 (1954); cf. Korematsu v. United States, 323 U.S. 214 (1944); Hernandez v. New York, 500 U.S. 352, 371 (1991).

3. If you were Puerto Rican, living on the island, what would you do? What are your choices in order to get representation?

4. Might you recall that the United States itself began as a colony of England and achieved independence only through armed struggle?

Chapter 3

CUBANS AND CUBAN AMERICANS

Between 1959 and 1990, nearly 700,000 Cubans emigrated to the United States in three waves. See Silvia Pedraza, *Cuba's Refugees: Manifold Migrations*, in *Origins and Destinies: Immigration, Race and Ethnicity in America* 267 (Silvia Pedraza & Rubén Rumbaut eds., 1996). The first wave began in 1959 when Fidel Castro's revolution triumphed over the regime of Fulgencio Batista and continued until 1962. During this period, approximately 248,000 Cubans migrated to the United States. The second wave began in 1965 and ended in 1973. Approximately 297,000 Cubans migrated during these years. The third wave migrated during 1980–81, the period of the Mariel boatlift. Nearly 125,000 Cubans migrated during this period. Maria Cristina Garcia, *Havana USA* 13, 43, 46 (1996).[1]

The group characteristics of each wave of Cuban exiles were significantly different from each other. According to Silvia Pedraza "the Cuban migration is characterized by an inverse relation between the date of departure and social class of the immigrants." Pedraza, supra, at 264. The first wave of immigrants consisted largely of the Cuban elite: educated, professional and upper-and middle-class Cubans. The refugees who arrived during the second wave tended to be working-class: small merchants, workers, and craftsmen. The third wave of Cuban refugees was younger, predominantly male, working class and included a higher proportion of Blacks than the prior waves. For detailed descriptions of the Cuban migrations, see Pedraza, supra, at 263–79; Garcia, supra, at 13–80.

In addition, the reception accorded the different waves of Cuban immigrants also differed. The social outcomes for each wave of immigrants were a function both of the characteristics of migrants themselves—their education and skills—and of the attitude of the country receiving them. The first wave of Cuban immigrants received, for the most part, a welcoming environment and significant federal and state assistance. Later waves of Cuban immigrants arrived in an environment

---

1. As of the 2000 Census, the total Cuban population of the United States was 1,241,685, 3.5 percent of the Latino/Hispanic population.

that welcomed and assisted them less, making their adjustment to the United States more difficult and less successful economically.

As mentioned, upper-class, elite Cubans were the first to leave during the first major wave of migration. These Cubans were well educated and represented disproportionately the professional, managerial, and middle classes. They included doctors, lawyers, engineers, educators, executives, business owners and other professionals. However, their exit from Cuba was not easy:

> By the end of 1961, the exit process had become a long and tedious affair. Potential emigres had to fill out numerous forms and submit to lengthy inquisitions. After 1960, airline tickets had to be purchased with U.S. currency; Cubans who did not have American dollars had to wait until friends or relatives in the U.S. sent them the proper currency by postal money order. Even after they received the money, there was a waiting list for seats on airlines. At the airport, members of the Cuban state police carefully inspected every piece of luggage and often subjected passengers to dehumanizing personal searches. Jewelry and other expensive goods had to be turned over to friends or relatives staying in Cuba or be confiscated by the police. The exit process, most emigres believed, was a form of psychological harassment, which continued even as they boarded their flights: it was not uncommon for people to be removed from planes awaiting takeoff and detained for further questioning. Travelers knew that until the plane crossed over into U.S. air space, they could be recalled.... Most exiles [] arrived at Miami International Airport penniless, with no idea as to where to take their families, much less where to find a job.

Maria Cristina Garcia, *Havana USA*, supra at 17–18.

Over time, the United States government responded to the plight of Cuban exiles. In 1960, President Eisenhower granted $1 million dollars to assist in resettlement efforts for Cuban refugees. Later, the Eisenhower administration created the Cuban Refugee Emergency Center (known as "Freedom Tower") in Miami to coordinate private and public relief efforts. In his statement accompanying a report on the Cuban Refugee Problem, Eisenhower declared:

> This latest exodus of persons fleeing from Communist oppression is the first time in many years in which our nation has become the country of first asylum for any such number of refugees. To grant such asylum is in accordance with the long standing traditions of the United States. Our people opened their homes and hearts to the Hungarian refugees four years ago. I am sure we will do no less for these distressed Cubans.

Statement by the President on Releasing a Report on Cuban Refugee Problems, Jan. 18, 1961, Doc. 431, Public Papers of the Presidents, Dwight D. Eisenhower, 1960–61.

SECTION 1. THE CHANGING RESPONSE TO CUBAN EXILES

EXCERPTS FROM 1961 SENATE HEARINGS

In 1961, the U.S. Senate held hearings on the problems associated with the sudden influx of Cuban refugees into the Miami, Florida area. The following excerpts from testimony given during these hearings illustrate the real complexity and hardship faced in Miami both by the newly arrived Cuban exiles and their American hosts. Most of the exiles arrived with no economic resources nor command of English, rendering many of their professional skills impracticable in their new setting. Many well-trained Cuban doctors and lawyers were among the refugees who fled to the United States. One aspect of the human tragedy of this exile was the dislocation of these Cuban professionals in the United States, where they were not able readily to resume practicing their professions because of differences in training and language. Both private and public efforts sought to alleviate their manifest hardship.

STATEMENT OF HON. ROBERT KING HIGH, MAYOR OF THE CITY OF MIAMI, FLORIDA

I should like to point out one of the ways in which Miami has met some of the problems brought about by the professional man and woman who came to this country to flee communistic tyranny.

In January of this year (1961) the faculty of the School of Medicine of the University of Miami, directed by Dr. Ralph Jones, chief of the department of internal medicine of the medical school, and the faculty in exile of the University of Havana initiated a continuing series of post graduate educational programs for exiled physicians from Cuba. The primary purpose of these programs of postgraduate education is to enable Cuban physicians who have been forced to flee their native land to utilize their professional knowledge and skill—

(1) To support themselves and their families during the time they must live in exile.

(2) To help this country meet its very considerable need for more physicians (particularly in federal, state, county, and municipal medical institutions).

(3) To contribute in every possible way to advancing the cause of democracy and freedom in this hemisphere.

Two intensive bilingual postgraduate medical educational programs, each 3 months in length, have been completed and more than 600 exiled physicians have participated in them. Seventy percent of the physicians who have participated in these programs have now passed the American medical qualifying examinations of the Educational Council for Foreign Medical Graduates, and have received certificates which make it possible for them to work as physicians in American hospitals.

More than 80 percent of the physicians who received a qualification certificate at the completion of the first course are now working as physicians in government hospitals, in state and city public health departments, on the faculty of medical schools, and so forth, in various parts of the country. These men are now supporting themselves and their families and making their contribution to the health and welfare of this society.

The results of the American medical qualifying examination which was given at the end of the second postgraduate course have become available in the past few days, and more than 100 physicians are now being placed in positions in various parts of the country which previously could not be filled with qualified physicians.

The need for these programs continues. A third course, in which 200 to 300 physicians will participate, will be initiated next week.

Following the example of the School of Medicine, similar programs have been initiated in the Schools of Law and Economics of the University of Miami, and one postgraduate program for exiled Cuban dentists has been completed despite the fact that the university has no dental school.

Again, Mr. Chairman, the suggested panel group would be asked to give special attention to the professional groups.

In essence, these bilingual postgraduate educational programs have demonstrated how an institution of higher learning can effectively preserve and utilize the great knowledge, special skills, and fine minds of members of the learned professions who are forced into exile by Communist tyranny. This had been done with appropriate dignity, tact, and courtesy. It has produced bonds of friendship between faculties and professional peoples of two cultures which will never be broken. It stands on the basis of solid accomplishment, as an example of how education can be put to work to reduce the tragedy of life in exile, and to advance the cause of democracy.

Statement of Hon. Robert King High, Mayor of the City of Miami, Florida, in *Hearings Before The Subcommittee to Investigate Problems Connected with Refugees and Escapees*, Judiciary Committee, U.S. Senate, 87th Cong. 1st Sess. 45–46 (1961), reprinted in *Cuban Refugee Programs* (Carlos E. Cortes ed., 1980).

The Retraining of Cuban Lawyers

Cuban lawyers, trained in the civil tradition derived from Spain, and speaking Spanish, could not adapt easily to the common-law tradition of legal practice in the United States and the fairly exclusive practice of law in English. The American Bar Association (ABA) and the University of Miami attempted to help former Cuban lawyers to engage in meaningful employment. The ABA appointed a special committee to deal with the refugee problem. The committee attempted to persuade law firms and private corporations of all kinds to hire Cuban lawyers as "law clerks, librarians, file clerks, messengers, or in some other capacity." The committee recognized "that it would be extremely difficult to find work of a legal nature for more than a limited number of the Cuban lawyers; not many U.S. law firms have a Latin–American practice and most corporations who have business in Latin America were already fully staffed from a legal standpoint."

See Statement of the Special Committee to Cooperate with Cuban Lawyers in Exile, American Bar Association, in Hearings Before The Subcommittee to Investigate Problems Connected with Refugees and Escapees, Judiciary Committee, U.S. Senate, 87th Cong. 1st Sess. 293, 294 (1961) (Appendix) reprinted in *Cuban Refugee Programs* (Carlos E. Cortes ed., 1980).

In February 1961, the University of Miami established a special training program for Cuban lawyers. Its objectives were as follows:

1.   To provide the Cuban lawyer with a basic knowledge of United States law and legal institutions to enable him to increase his opportunities of securing law-related employment in the United States with educational institutions, corporations, law firms, and government agencies; the objective is not to prepare him for the practice of law.

2.   To provide the Cuban lawyer with a basic knowledge of United States law which will enable him, upon his return to Cuba, to communicate more effectively with his United States counterpart in international legal practice.

3.   To provide the Cuban lawyer with a knowledge of United States legal institutions, a knowledge of the role of law in American life, thereby giving him insights into our basic democratic values, insights that can be transmuted to Cuba when democratic life is restored.

Early in the Program a number of Cuban lawyers labored with the thought that one of the Program's objectives was to prepare them for law practice. Every reasonable effort was made to negate this thought; it is believed that the message was effectively communicated that the licensing laws of all states require United States citizenship, and normally three years full-time legal training in an approved United States law school.

See John C. Chommie, *The University of Miami Program for Cuban Lawyers: A Report*, 5 Inter–Am. L. Rev. 177, 181 (1963).

Notes and Questions

1.   Note the apparent success of bilingual education for Cuban doctors. Why is bilingual education so controversial today?

2.   Do such programs constitute affirmative action? Why or why not?

3. Consider the hardship faced by Cuban lawyers. American-trained lawyers would face similar hardship if they faced sudden exile in a civil law jurisdiction that was not English-speaking.

Inevitably, however, within the Miami region, the presence of thousands of Cubans and the relief efforts, of which only they were the beneficiaries, generated tensions. Consider the following testimony during the Senate Hearings:

STATEMENT OF JUANITA GREENE, REPORTER, MIAMI HERALD

In Miami today there is resentment concerning the Cuban refugees, and it is growing. Much of it can be ignored, because it generates from "soreheads" who are generally resentful of everything. Some of it can be attributed to fear of strangers. Most of us in Miami now know the meaning of that Greek word, "xenophobia." As a newspaper reporter who has tried to be as objective as a human being who likes Cubans can be, I believe there are some legitimate causes for some of the resentment. I mention them not only because they appear legitimate, but because they seem possible of solution.

First of all, in Dade County, Cuban refugees are eligible for more relief than are our own-American needy. The maximum grant allowed a refugee family is $100. Certainly that is not too much, in my opinion. But the maximum allowed our own elderly is $66. Our dependent-children families get only $81 a month, regardless of the number of children. And our employable but unemployed workers who have exhausted their unemployment compensation or who were not entitled to it, get nothing.

Cuban relief goes to any Cuban refugee in need, and he does not have to wait weeks and months before receiving his first check, as our American needy must. Cuban refugees also were the first to get surplus food. And only because the Federal Government was giving it to the Cubans did our own local and State welfare agencies decide it could be of use to some of our American needy.

The second legitimate complaint, as I see it, is that Cuban refugees are taking away the jobs of some of our American workers. There are no statistics to prove or disprove this. But I know of many Cuban refugees who are working, many at lowly, ill-paid jobs. These were jobs formerly held by Americans. You will be hearing other witnesses with specific information on this question.

The third complaint involves our school systems. In many classrooms in public and parochial schools, the number of Spanish-speaking students—who speak no English—outnumbers the number of English-speaking students. Educators admit this holds the whole class back, especially because few of the teachers are bilingual. Otherwise tolerant parents call the Herald to complain that their children are being held back scholastically because of the flood of refugee children into the classrooms.

Resentment in Miami appears highest among our Negro population. Negroes in the South, like the refugees who fled Cuba, perhaps know more than the rest of us about fear and persecution. While they fight to achieve full freedom, they say they see strangers welcomed with open arms and given respect and assistance still denied the Negro. And all this is done in the name of freedom and democracy. Our Negro leaders point out that mulattoes and Negroes of Cuban origin attend white schools in Dade County. A Negro minister remarked recently that perhaps the American Negro could solve the school integration problem by teaching the children to speak only Spanish.

* * *

Another very touchy thing—we happen to be a southern city, with a large Negro population that has some very enlightened, well, what some people would call enlightened leaders, who are working for equal opportunity for the Negro in Miami. And some of them are a bit outspoken about the fact that here, in the name of freedom and democracy is a group of foreigners that is given not only more assistance but more dignity than their own American group.

Statement of Juanita Greene, Reporter, Miami Herald, in *Hearings Before The Subcommittee to Investigate Problems Connected with Refugees and Escapees*, Judiciary Committee, U.S. Senate, 87th Cong. 1st Sess. 73, 77 (1961) reprinted in *Cuban Refugee Programs* (Carlos E. Cortes ed., 1980).

Other witnesses also testified about hardship suffered by local residents, perhaps most acutely by the African–American community:

STATEMENT OF ARTHUR H. PATTEN, JR., MEMBER OF THE
COUNTY COMMISSION, DADE COUNTY, FLORIDA

[T]hose who are seeking employment (particularly in the colored areas of Dade County) cannot find it as a result of the fact that the jobs are simply not there, and many of those jobs, they are finding out now, are actually held by Cuban refugees. Many of these colored people have actually been relieved of their employment and have been replaced with cheaper Cuban help.

The tourist industry, the hotel workers, and so forth, do not come under the Federal minimum wage laws, and, consequently, those hotel entrepreneurs who can employ Cuban help at whatever salary they are willing to work for, and without any controls relative to a minimum wage, are doing so, and they are hiring those people at whatever subsistence those people are willing to take. Many of those hotels (I would say the vast majority of them) and many other businesses throughout this country have taken advantage of the fact that we have now in the locale a dependent group of people who will take jobs at almost any wage in order to provide for their needs. I think that this employment problem is one of the major factors prevalent here as a result of the Cuban influence.

Statement of Arthur H. Patten, Jr., Member of the County Commission, Dade County, Florida., in *Hearings Before The Subcommittee to Investigate Problems Connected with Refugees and Escapees*, Judiciary Committee, U.S. Senate, 87th Cong. 1st Sess. 49, 53 (1961) reprinted in *Cuban Refugee Programs* (Carlos E. Cortes ed., 1980).

STATEMENT OF H. DANIEL LANG, EXECUTIVE DIRECTOR,
GREATER MIAMI URBAN LEAGUE

A Negro minister and community leader appraised the situation as follows: "The Negro is on the lowest rung of the economic ladder and finds himself systematically being pushed out of a job to make room for Cubans, who themselves are trying to find freedom." He further stated that they, the Cuban refugees, see evidences in the undemocratic treatment of the Negro which buttresses the undemocratic situation from which they fled. He then remarked if the statement that the Negro lags culturally, and this is acting as a barrier to their being admitted to the school of their choice and on the other hand it is reported that there is a difference in the culture of the Cubans, plus the difference in language, and yet they are being admitted to the school of their choice in their neighborhood; this differential in treatment [then] becomes a source of frustration for the Negro. As a final comment, he stated the manner in which the Cubans are handled—and here he alluded to the fact that Negro leadership and institutions like the church have not been called on for assistance in the refugee problem—denies the Negro an opportunity to make a positive contribution to a cause that the Negro has great sympathy for. An educator—Negro—while expressing concern for the Cuban refugee in stating that training or retraining is necessary for their employment, there was some question as to the preferential treatment being given by the board of public instruction in providing training opportunities for the Cubans with no cost for materials and supplies, and the same opportunities were not being made available to Negroes.

As I have observed and talked with people and listened at group meetings and discussions, it is generally felt that the Cuban refugee and the treatment he is getting poses a threat to their economic security, and I add it is plain to see that frustrations and hostilities are present. Perhaps the only reason that there is not open conflict is the fact that the Cubans and Negroes live in different neighborhoods separated by a number of blocks and several main arteries of transportation. They resent the attention given to the problems of the Cubans, economic health and welfare (in Dade County, public assistance is not given on the basis of need, only through the categories or when there is a medical reason why the person can't work). The American worker without unemployment compensation has nowhere to turn. They question why they receive special treatment as a group when they plan only to remain until the situation in Cuba changes to their satisfaction.

Statement of H. Daniel Lang, Executive Director, Greater Miami Urban League, in *Hearings Before The Subcommittee to Investigate Problems Connected with Refugees and Escapees*, Judiciary Committee, U.S. Senate, 87th Cong. 1st Sess. 129, 131–32 (1961), reprinted in *Cuban Refugee Programs* (Carlos E. Cortes ed., 1980).

Notes and Questions

1. Does the situation described above help us understand present-day conflict between blacks and Latinos?

2. Is the resentment stemming from the presence of a large number of foreigners to some extent inevitable? In what ways is the resentment Cubans faced comparable to, or distinguishable from, that confronting undocumented Mexican immigrants today?

3. To what extent is the popular resentment a function of the relative privilege that Cuban exiles were perceived to enjoy?

THE CUBAN REFUGEE PROGRAM

The Cuban Refugee Program was a multifaceted program that provided financial, relocation, and educational assistance to Cuban refugees. Its purposes appear in the following Senate Report:

Senate Report No. 989, Sept. 12, 1961
U.S. Code Cong. & Admin. News 1791–93 (1961)

* * *

The proposed "Migration and Refugee Assistance Act of 1961" would:

* * *

2. Establish specific authority to assist Cuban refugees who have come to the United States. Heretofore this assistance has been carried out through contingency authority and funds under the foreign aid program.

3. Provide the President with authority to meet unexpected refugee, escapee, and migration problems by using not to exceed $10 million in any fiscal year out of his foreign aid contingency fund.

* * *

There follow brief descriptions of each of the programs authorized by the bill.

* * *

4. ***Assistance to Cuban refugees in the United States***—Aid to Cuban refugees has been made the responsibility of the Department of Health, Education, and Welfare. The program has been operated under Section 451(c) of the Mutual Security Act of 1954, as amended, and has been financed out of the President's contingency fund under that act.

Federal authorities have cooperated with the State of Florida, the city of Miami, and Dade County. Private voluntary agencies and institutions, together with private citizens, have played an important role. Of the 136,000 nonnaturalized Cubans in the United States, about 50,000 have registered as 'refugees' in Miami. The purpose of the Federal programs has been not only to aid individual refugees but to relieve the burden upon the communities in Florida where the refugees have been located. During the past 7 months about 26,000 persons have been helped with cash assistance in the amount of $3.2 million. Nearly 40,000 have been given medical attention. Surplus food has been made available to about 18,000 persons. Almost 8,000 persons have been resettled in virtually every State of the Union and Puerto Rico at a cost of about $800,000. Over 900 children unaccompanied by parents or other responsible persons have been cared for at a cost of about $700,000. Federal authorities have contributed almost $800,000 to Dade County's school budget, and loans in the amount of $175,000 have been made to nearly 400 Cuban students attending 51 colleges in 22 States. Assistance has been furnished in a variety of ways to help adult refugees find jobs and to train them to employ skills, which they already possess, in some useful way in the United States.

Refugees are continuing to find their way out of Cuba and programs of assistance to them must continue. It is expected that these programs will cost the Federal Government in the neighborhood of $25.8 million during the fiscal year 1962.

5. *Authorization for emergencies involving refugees, migrants, and escapees*—Section 2(c) of the bill would authorize the President to use not to exceed $10 million in any fiscal year in order to meet unexpected refugee and migration developments when the President determines such use to be important to the national interest. Experience since World War II teaches that international tensions and Communist efforts to increase such tensions will result in escapee and refugee problems. These situations may arise suddenly and it is impossible to predict where trouble may come. The bill recognizes the necessity of being prepared for such eventualities by the inclusion of the emergency provision just referred to.

* * *

As described in the preceding report, Congress passed the following legislation:

Migration and Refugee Assistance Act of 1962
P.L. 87–510; 76 Stat. 121 (June 28, 1962)

* * *

Sec. 2.

* * *

(b) There are hereby authorized to be appropriated such amounts as may be necessary from time to time—

* * *

(2) for assistance to or in behalf of refugees designated by the President (by class, group, or designation of their respective coun-

tries of origin or areas of residence) when the President determines that such assistance will contribute to the defense, or to the security, or to the foreign policy interests of the United States;

(3) for assistance to or in behalf of refugees in the United States whenever the President shall determine that such assistance would be in the interest of the United States: *Provided*, That the term "refugees" as herein used means aliens who (A) because of persecution or fear of persecution on account of race, religion, or political opinion, fled from a nation or area of the Western Hemisphere; (B) cannot return thereto because of fear of persecution on account of race, religion, or political opinion; and (C) are in urgent need of assistance for the essentials of life;

(4) for assistance to State or local public agencies providing services for substantial numbers of individuals who meet the requirements of subparagraph (3) (other than clause (C) thereof) for (A) health services and educational services to such individuals, and (B) special training for employment and services related thereto;

(5) for transportation to, and resettlement in, other areas of the United States of individuals who meet the requirements of subparagraph (3) (other than clause (C) thereof) and who, having regard for their income and other resources, need assistance in obtaining such services; and

(6) for establishment and maintenance of projects for employment or refresher professional training of individuals who meet the requirements of subparagraph (3) (other than clause (C) thereof) and, who, having regard for their income and resources, need such employment or need assistance in obtaining such retraining.

(c) Whenever the President determines it to be important to the national interest, not exceeding $10,000,000 in any fiscal year of the funds made available for this under the Foreign Assistance Act of 1961, as amended, may be transferred to, and consolidated with, funds made available for this Act in order to meet unexpected urgent refugee and migration needs.

* * *

Notes and Questions

1. Did the Migration and Refugee Assistance Act constitute affirmative action, as we understand it today?

2. Would it be constitutional today? If your response to this question is no, consider what changed in our constitutional law to yield that result.

Over time, the Cuban community has been remarkably successful in producing an economic enclave enjoying a high level of prosperity in Miami and in integrating itself into the economy of Florida. The economic success of the Cuban exiles can be understood as a result of two factors: the education and social capital many of the emigres brought with them, and the federal assistance they received, exemplified by the Cuban Refugee Program. See Maria Cristina Garcia, *Havana USA* 2 (1996).

In addition to the Cuban Refugee Program, the Cuban Adjustment Act of 1966, see infra, aimed to facilitate the acquisition by Cubans of legal permanent resident status, which, in turn, facilitated their acquisition of employment and eventual citizenship.

Lyndon B. Johnson
Remarks at the Signing of the Immigration Bill
Liberty Island, New York, Oct. 3, 1965

Asylum for Cuban Refugees

So it is in that spirit that I declare this afternoon to the people of Cuba that those who seek refuge here in America will find it. The dedication of America to our traditions as an asylum for the oppressed is going to be upheld.

I have directed the Departments of State and Justice and Health, Education, and Welfare to immediately make all the necessary arrangements to permit those in Cuba who seek freedom to make an orderly entry into the United States of America.

Our first concern will be with those Cubans who have been separated from their children and their parents and their husbands and their wives and that are now in this country. Our next concern is with those who are imprisoned for political reasons.

And I will send to the Congress tomorrow a request for supplementary funds of $12,600,000 to carry forth the commitment that I am making today.

* * *

I want all the people of this great land of ours to know of the really enormous contribution which the compassionate citizens of Florida have made to humanity and to decency. And all States in this Union can join with Florida now in extending the hand of helpfulness and humanity to our Cuban brothers.

The lesson of our times is sharp and clear in the movement of people from one land to another. Once again, it stamps the mark of failure on a regime when many of its citizens voluntarily choose to leave the land of their birth for a more hopeful home in America. The future holds little hope for any government where the present holds no hope for the people.

And so we Americans will welcome these Cuban people. For the tides of history run strong, and in another day they can return to their homelands to find it cleansed of terror and free from fear.

Over my shoulders here you can see Ellis Island, whose vacant corridors echo today the joyous sound of long ago voices.

And today we can all believe that the lamp of this grand old lady is brighter today—and the golden door that she guards gleams more brilliantly in the light of an increased liberty for the people from all the countries of the globe.

The following report describes the rationales for passage of the Cuban Adjustment Act, which made it easier for Cuban refugees to become permanent residents eligible for citizenship without having to leave the United States.

House Report No. 1978, Sept. 1, 1966
U.S. Code Cong. & Admin. News 3792 (1966)

* * *

The purpose of the bill, as amended, is to permit natives or citizens of Cuba who were inspected and admitted or paroled into the United States, subsequent to January 1, 1959, to apply for adjustment of status to permanent resident status and to have the status adjusted in the discretion of the Attorney General if they are otherwise eligible to receive an immigrant visa and be admissible into the United States. On approval of an application for adjustment, the Attorney General is authorized to create a record of the alien's admission for permanent residence as of the date of approval of the application.

GENERAL INFORMATION

Existing law, section 245(c) of the Immigration and Nationality Act, provides that natives of any country of the Western Hemisphere, or of any adjacent island named in section 101(b)(5) of the Immigration and Nationality Act, are precluded from applying for adjustment to permanent resident status while in the United States. This bill exempts only those refugees from Cuba, who are natives or citizens of Cuba, from the restriction against adjustment of status in the United States.

This legislation is permissive; thus, a refugee from Cuba may avail himself of this option if he desires to achieve permanent resident status, as the first step toward becoming an American citizen.

The Immigration and Naturalization Service reports that as of August 1, 1966, 165,000 refugees from Cuba are in the United States without permanent resident status. Approximately 81,000 are in a parolee status; approximately 47,000 admitted as nonimmigrants before the U.S. consuls withdrew from Cuba on January 3, 1961, are in an extended voluntary departure status; and 36,000 have arrived since resumption of the airlift on December 1, 1965.

* * *

The only recourse available to a refugee from Cuba under existing law in order to change to immigrant status is the awkward procedure of leaving the United States for an indefinite period of time in order to secure an immigrant visa at a U.S. consular office abroad and then reentering as a permanent resident. In addition to the great expense to the refugee, there is the burden placed upon U.S. consular offices in contiguous countries which do not have the staff to handle a large volume of immigrant visa applications from persons residing outside of their consular districts. Nevertheless, since January 1, 1959, approximately 75,000 Cubans have departed from this country in order to secure immigrant visas and reenter the United States as permanent residents.

Adjustment of status, through enactment of this legislation, would, the committee was informed, reduce the Government's expenditures in behalf of the Cuban refugees and will aid in their resettlement by enhancing their opportunity to qualify for employment in all areas of the Nation.

* * *

This legislation merely relieves the refugee of the burden of following a circuitous route to permanent resident status.

There are many precedents for this type of legislation. The Congress has been consistent in its willingness to approve legislation to aid persecuted peoples of the world. Most recently, the Congress has approved legislation in behalf of the Hungarian refugees (Public Law 85–559); admission of refugee-escapees who were within the mandate of the United Nations High Commissioner for Refugees (Public Law 86–648); and for refugees from communism from countries outside the Western Hemisphere (Public Law 89–236).

The Cuban Adjustment Act
P.L. 89–732; 80 Stat. 1161 (Nov. 2, 1966)

An Act to adjust the status of Cuban refugees to that of lawful permanent residents of the United States, and for other purposes.

* * *

Notwithstanding the provisions of section 245(c) of the Immigration and Nationality Act, the status of any alien who is a native or citizen of Cuba and who has been inspected and admitted or paroled into the United States subsequent to January 1, 1959 and has been physically present in the United States for at lest two years, may be adjusted by the Attorney General, in his discretion and under such regulations as he may prescribe, to that of an alien lawfully admitted for permanent residence if the alien makes an application for such adjustment, and the alien is eligible to receive an immigrant visa and is admissible to the United States for permanent residence. Upon approval of such an application for adjustment of status, the Attorney General shall create a record of the alien's admission for permanent residence as of a date thirty months prior to the filing of such an application or the date of his last arrival into the United States, whichever date is later. The provisions of this Act shall be applicable to the spouse and child of any alien described in this subsection, regardless of their citizenship and place of birth, who are residing with such alien in the United States.

* * *

Consider the following case, applying the Cuban Adjustment Act:

Matter of Masson
12 I. & N. Dec. 699 (BIA 1968)

Respondent, a native of Cuba, who in 1936 at age 7 was taken by his parents to Haiti, the country of his citizenship, where he lived until his admission into the United States as a visitor on July 5, 1964, is statutorily eligible for adjustment of status under the provisions of section 1 of the Act of November 2, 1966, notwithstanding he is not a refugee.

The proceedings have been certified to us by the special inquiry officer for review and final decision. Respondent has been under a final order of deportation since June 24, 1965. At a reopened hearing on March 14, 1967 respondent submitted an application on Service Form I–485A for adjustment of status to that of a permanent resident under the Act of November 2, 1966 [the Cuban Adjustment Act]. His application for permanent residence was approved by the special inquiry officer who thereafter certified the case to us.

Respondent is a 39–year-old married male alien, a native of Cuba and a citizen of Haiti. He was born in Cuba, but at the age of seven, in 1936, he was taken to Haiti by his parents, where he lived until entering the United States at San Juan, as a visitor on July 5, 1964. Deportability is conceded and thus is not in issue.

The sole question presented is whether respondent, who is a native of Cuba but who is not a refugee, is eligible to have his status adjusted under the Act of November 2, 1966. Respondent's "Application by Cuban Refugees for Permanent Residence" is filed under the provisions of Section 1 of the Act, which states as follows:

> Notwithstanding the provisions of section 245(c) of the Immigration and Nationality Act, the status of any alien who is a native or citizen of Cuba and who has been inspected and admitted or paroled into the United States subsequent to January 1, 1959, and has been physically present in the United States for at least two years, may be adjusted by the Attorney General, in his discretion and under such regulations as he may prescribe, to that of an alien lawfully admitted for permanent residence if the alien makes an application for such adjustment, and the alien is eligible to receive an immigrant visa and is admissible to the United States for permanent residence. * * *

It seems clear as pointed out by the special inquiry officer that the purpose of the Act of November 2, 1966 was to grant benefits to those Cubans who had fled as refugees from the Fidel Castro government of Cuba. Indeed, the bill enacted into law was headed "Cuban Refugees–Status." A careful review of the legislative history of the Act as contained in U.S. Code Congressional and Administrative News, 1966,

Volume three, starting at page 3792, refers constantly to granting relief to Cuban refugees.

However, the exact wording of the Act is specific, clear and unambiguous in stating that the status of any alien who is a native or citizen of Cuba and who has been inspected and admitted, etc., is entitled to the benefits of the Act. Nowhere in the Act itself is the word "refugee" used. Respondent is a native of Cuba; he was inspected and admitted to the United States subsequently to January 1, 1959, and has been physically present in the United States for at least two years, and meets the other requirements of section 1 of the Act of November 2, 1966 as set forth above. When the exact wording of the Act itself does not limit the benefits provided therein to refugees we do not believe it is possible for us to read such word into the Act simply by referring to the alleged purposes of the Act, and the legislative history thereof.

For these reasons we will affirm the order of the special inquiry officer granting respondent's application for adjustment of status to that of a permanent resident under the Act of November 2, 1966.

ORDER: It is directed that the order of the special inquiry officer of January 19, 1968 granting respondent permanent residence under the Act of November 2, 1966 (P.L. 89–732), be approved.

Notes and Questions

1. The Cuban Adjustment Act "was taken by generations of Cuban–Americans and many politicians to be an open-ended entitlement to [Legal Permanent Residence] status for virtually all Cubans who could make it to U.S. soil." D. Martin, A. Aleinikoff, H. Motomura & M. Fullerton, *Forced Migration Law and Policy* 737 (2007).

2. Would such legislation be constitutional today? Consider the arguments for and against constitutionality.

3. Consider the relevance of the Cold War in motivating these enactments benefitting Cuban exiles. To what extent do these federal enactments prove Professor Derrick Bell's theory of "interest convergence," which postulates that civil rights gains only occur when they are in the interest of the white majority? What majoritarian interests may this legislation have served? See Derrick Bell, Brown v. Board of Education *and the Interest Convergence Dilemma*, 93 Harv. L. Rev. 518 (1980).

The third major wave of Cuban immigrants occurred between April and October of 1980. Known as the Mariel boatlift, approximately 125,000 Cubans arrived in the United States during 1980–81. In April, 1980, the Cuban government announced that Cubans who wished to leave the island were free to emigrate from the Cuban port of Mariel. The announcement also urged departing Cubans to contact their relatives in the United States for transportation to the U.S. These announcements resulted in a huge flotilla of boats, numbering hundreds, traveling from the United States to Mariel to pick up friends and relatives who wanted to leave. In addition to family members, however, vessel owners were also forced to transport persons expelled from Cuba for various reasons, including those with physical or mental disabilities and approximately 26,000 with criminal records. Initially, diplomatic efforts aimed to curtail the flow of refugees, but these efforts proved largely unsuccessful. In the end, the U.S. Coast Guard interdicted vessels at sea and returned their occupants to Cuba. See Maria Cristina Garcia, *Havana USA*, supra at 60–79; Stephen H. Legomsky, *The USA and the Caribbean Interdiction Program*, 18 Int'l J. Refugee L. 677, 683–84 (2006) (on Cuban interdiction).

In contrast to the first two waves of Cuban refugees, these refugees tended to be working-class and dark-skinned. While the presence of Cubans with disabilities and criminal records came to dominate media accounts of the "marielitos," most of those with criminal records had been incarcerated for relatively minor offenses, such as extravagant behavior, gambling, or drug or alcohol addiction. Some had been convicted of offenses that would not be considered such at all in the United States—such as homosexuality.

Although initially this third wave of refugees was met with compassion and relief efforts, as soon as it became known that it contained convicts and disabled persons, public attitudes became decidedly negative. Press depictions of the "marielitos" emphasized the criminal element among them, even though this was a small percentage of the Cubans who arrived. About eighty percent of the Mariel refugees had no criminal history at all. Over time, many Marielitos were imprisoned in detention camps spread throughout the United States. Several riots over their indefinite and continuing detention led to negative media accounts. Even Cuban refugees of the prior generations, who initially had compassion for their plight, distanced themselves from these refugees.

Another significant exodus of Cubans by boat occurred in 1994. These were the "balseros." The Coast Guard was active in intercepting these vessels too, and interdicted over 37,000 Cubans. In a stunning departure from the policies underlying the Cuban Adjustment Act of 1966, the Clinton administration ordered that detained Cubans be held at the United States naval base in Guantanamo, Cuba or other safe havens:

> Today, I have ordered that illegal refugees from Cuba will not be allowed to enter the United States. Refugees rescued at sea will be taken to our naval base at Guantanamo, while we explore the possibility of other safe havens within the region. To enforce this policy, I have directed the Coast Guard to continue its expanded effort to stop any boat illegally attempting to bring Cubans to the United States. The United States will detain, investigate, and, if necessary, prosecute Americans who take to the sea to pick up Cubans. Vessels used in such activities will be seized.

The President's News Conference, Aug. 19, 1994, William J. Clinton, *Public Papers of the Presidents*, 1994, vol. II, p. 1477.

As a result of this policy change, 30,000 Cubans were detained at Guantanamo and another 8,000 in Panama. See Maryellen Fullerton, *Cuban Exceptionalism: Migration and Asylum in Spain and the United States*, 35 U. Miami Inter–Am. L. Rev. 527, 564 & n.250 (2004); Maria E. Sartori, *The Cuban Migration Dilemma: An Examination of the United States' Policy of*

Temporary Protection in Offshore Safe Havens, 15 Geo. Immigr. L.J. 319, 344 (2001).

In 1995, responding to the problem of 20,000 Cubans still detained at Guantanamo, the Clinton administration initiated another major shift in policy. Rather than receive safe haven, interdicted Cubans would be returned to Cuba:

> Still, that left tens of thousands of young men at Guantanamo who were becoming increasingly frustrated and desperate. Senior United States military officials warned me that unrest and violence this summer were likely, threatening both those in the camps and our own dedicated soldiers.

> But to admit those remaining in Guantanamo without doing something to deter new rafters risked unleashing a new massive exodus of Cubans, many of whom would perish seeking to reach the United States. To prevent that situation and to settle the migration issue, I took action. The Cuban rafters who were brought to Guantanamo last summer will be admitted to the United States * * *. Those Cubans rescued at sea while illegally trying to enter the United States will be taken back to Cuba. Under our generous program of legal immigration, 20,000 Cubans from Cuba will be allowed to enter and reside in the United States every year from now on. And we'll continue to provide assistance to Florida to help resettle those Cuban migrants.

Remarks to the Cuban–American Community, June 27, 1995, William J. Clinton, *Public Papers of the Presidents*, 1995, vol. I, p. 954. Consider the following case, dealing with the constitutional and statutory rights of Cubans placed in safe haven:

Cuban American Bar Ass'n, Inc. v. Christopher
43 F.3d 1412 (11th Cir. 1995)

Birch, Circuit Judge:

This case requires us to address the following issues: (1) whether Cuban and Haitian migrants temporarily provided safe haven at the United States naval base at Guantanamo Bay, Cuba, and at the United States military installations in Panama, may assert rights under the Immigration and Nationality Act, the 1951 United Nations Convention Relating to the Status of Refugees, the Cuban Adjustment Act, the Cuban Democracy Act and the Constitution of the United States. * * *

On August 8, 1994, Fidel Castro announced that the Cuban government would no longer forcibly prevent emigration from Cuba by boat. Castro's new policy encouraged thousands of Cubans to board makeshift rafts and boats to escape Cuba and head for the shores of the United States. While many were lost at sea, approximately 8000 Cubans arrived in the United States safely.

In an effort to quell this influx of migrants and to save the rafters' lives, on August 19, 1994, the President of the United States ordered the United States Coast Guard to intercept watercraft carrying persons fleeing from Cuba and bound for the United States' border and to transport these persons to the American naval base at Guantanamo Bay, Cuba. The United States leases its military base at Guantanamo Bay from sovereign Cuba under a lease agreement negotiated in 1903.

In August, 1994, the United States government began negotiating with the Cuban government to halt the flow of migrants to the United States. These diplomatic negotiations culminated on September 9, 1994, in an accord with the Cuban government. In this accord, the United States agreed it would allow Cuban migrants to enter the United States only by applying for immigrant visas or refugee admittance at the United States Interests Section in Havana, Cuba. A minimum of 20,000 persons are to be allowed to migrate legally to the United States each year, not including immediate relatives of United States citizens who are under no numerical restrictions. However, in conjunction with this international agreement, the Attorney General also ordered that no Cuban who had accepted safe haven in Guantanamo Bay or Panama would be allowed to apply for a visa or for asylum in the United States from safe haven.

Currently, Cuban migrants have three options with respect to their residence: (1) they may remain in safe haven; (2) they may repatriate to sovereign Cuba voluntarily; or (3) they may travel to a third country willing to accept them. While more than 1000 Cubans have requested voluntarily to be returned to Cuba, the Cuban government has restricted the return of Cuban nationals and has delayed the voluntary repatriation process. Persons who repatriate to Cuba voluntarily may then apply for asylum through the regular channels commencing at the United States Special Interests Section in Havana, Cuba.

The United States government's expressed desire is not to maintain these migrants for an indefinite period of time or against their will. The government's position is that it could return the migrants to Cuba legally without a migrant's request. However, the government has offered the Cuban migrants safe haven for as long as the migrants wished. All Cuban migrants volunteering to repatriate execute a form approved by the United Nations High Commissioner for Refugees ("UNHCR") and meet with a representative from UNHCR before returning.

* * *

In addition to UNHCR, humanitarian groups such as Amnesty International, Inc., the U.S. Committee for Refugees, and Church World Service (Immigration and Refugee Service) as well as legal organizations such as the Ad Hoc group of Cuban–American Attorneys, have been allowed to visit the migrants at the base. However, as the numbers of migrants and the length of the stay in safe haven have increased, problems have erupted. Many Cuban migrants have climbed over barbed wire and jumped from treacherous cliffs into the bay in attempts to swim the mile or so back to sovereign Cuba. Still others have scaled fences and braved a mine field in order to reach their homeland. During early December, 1994, many were injured during riots at the camps, particularly in Panama. The risk of violence and danger, both to the migrants and to the military personnel charged with their care, has grown. While the United States has begun negotiating with other countries to accept migrants from safe haven and has continued with the voluntary repatriation program, problems continue.

Since consummation of the accord, the Attorney General has exercised her discretion to parole into the United States Cuban migrants who have sponsors in the United States and are (1) over the age of 70; (2) who are ill; or (3) who are unaccompanied minors (under the age of 13). She has also begun to consider, on a case-by-case basis, the possible parole of other Cuban children at Guantanamo Bay who are accompanied, but who may suffer severe hardship if they remain in safe haven. Over 20,000 Cubans currently remain in safe haven at Guantanamo Bay and at military installations in Panama.

* * *

[The court described the history of and conditions of Haitian refugees also in safe haven at Guantanamo.]

* * *

We now consider the following issues on appeal:

1.   Whether the Cuban or Haitian migrants in safe haven outside the physical borders of the United States have any cognizable statutory or constitutional rights.

2.   Whether the Cuban Legal Organizations or HRC have a First Amendment right to associate with migrants held in safe haven outside the physical borders of the United States for the purposes of engaging in political speech, and if so, whether the government engages in impermissible viewpoint discrimination violative of any First Amendment rights of the individual migrants or the Cuban Legal Organizations or HRC by restricting the legal organizations' access to the migrants for the purposes of legal consultation.

* * *

STATUTORY AND CONSTITUTIONAL RIGHTS OF MIGRANTS IN SAFE HAVEN

The Cuban migrants and the Haitian migrants are asserting statutory rights under the Immigration and Nationality Act, ("INA") and the Refugee Convention. The individual Cuban plaintiffs in safe haven also assert rights under the Cuban Refugee Adjustment Act, 8 U.S.C. § 1255, and the Cuban Democracy Act, 22 U.S.C. §§ 6001–6010. The individual Haitian unaccompanied minor plaintiffs assert rights against discriminatory parole decisions under 8 U.S.C. § 1182. Additionally, the individual Cuban plaintiffs advance claims to Fifth Amendment rights of due process, and the individual Haitian migrants are asserting Fifth Amendment rights to due process and equal protection of the laws.

a.   *Status of Guantanamo Bay*

* * *

The district court here erred in concluding that Guantanamo Bay was a "United States territory." October 31 Order at 9. We disagree that "control and jurisdiction" is equivalent to sovereignty. See Agreement for the Lease to the United States of Lands in Cuba for Coaling and Naval Stations, Feb. 26, 1903, U.S.-Cuba, T.S. No. 418 (distinguishing between sovereignty of the Republic of Cuba over the leased land and the "control and jurisdiction" granted the United States). * * *

[W]e again reject the argument that our leased military bases abroad which continue under the sovereignty of foreign nations, hostile or friendly, are "functional[ly] equivalent" to being land borders or ports of entry of the United States or otherwise within the United States. Therefore, any statutory or constitutional claim made by the individual Cuban plaintiffs and the individual Haitian migrants must be based upon an extraterritorial application of that statute or constitutional provision.

b. *Extraterritorial Application of Legislation and the Constitution*

If the migrants have been provided rights by statute, we need not reach the constitutional questions urged upon us. However, because the Cuban Legal Organizations and HRC struggle to re-assert statutory claims foreclosed by *HRC II* and *Sale v. Haitian Ctrs. Council, Inc.*, 509 U.S. 155 (1993), and fail to assert new meritorious statutory claims, we reach the constitutional issues as well.

We decided in *HRC II*, 953 F.2d at 1510, * * * that the very same statutes and treaties regarding repatriation, Article 33 of the Refugee Convention, and the INA, specifically, 8 U.S.C. § 1253(h) and 8 U.S.C. § 1158(a) do not apply extraterritorially. In *HRC II*, we unequivocally held that the interdicted Haitians could not claim any rights under sections 1253(h) or 1158(a). We further concluded that

> the interdicted Haitians [on Coast Guard cutters and at Guantanamo Bay] have *none of the substantive rights*—under ... the 1967 United Nations Protocol Relating to the Status of Refugees, the Immigration and Naturalization Service Guidelines, the Refugee Act of 1980, the Immigration and Nationality Act, or international law— that they claim for themselves or that the HRC claims for them.

HRC II, 953 F.2d at 1513 n.8 (emphasis added). These laws, which govern repatriation of refugees, bind the government only when the refugees are at or within the borders of the United States. Therefore, the claims asserted by the migrants under the INA and under Article 33 continue to be untenable.

The individual Cuban plaintiffs attempt to utilize the Cuban Refugee Adjustment Act, 8 U.S.C. § 1255, and the Cuban Democracy Act, 22 U.S.C. §§ 6001–6010, to assert the right of the Cuban migrants to seek parole and asylum in the United States. While these acts acknowledge the political climate in Cuba, provide for economic sanctions for dealing with Cuba, and allow for certain rights for Cubans who reach the United States, they do not address the rights of Cuban migrants to enter or to seek entry to the United States initially, nor do they confer directly any rights upon the Cuban migrants outside the United States. Hence, neither of these acts can be relied upon by the individual Cuban plaintiffs to assert a right against repatriation or to seek parole or asylum in the United States from safe haven.

* * *

2. *First Amendment Rights of the Cuban Legal Organizations and HRC*

* * *

Neither the Cuban nor the Haitian migrants have any of the statutory or constitutional rights claimed here that might sustain the attorneys' claims to right of association, and "associational freedom in no way implies a right to compel the Government to provide access to those with whom one wishes to associate." Id. Hence, it would be not only improper, but also "nonsensical," for us to hold today that attorneys for either migrant group suddenly possess "a right of access to the interdicted [migrants] for the purpose of advising them of their legal rights." Id.

* * *

While we have determined that these migrants are without legal rights that are cognizable in the courts of the United States, we observe that they are nonetheless beneficiaries of the American tradition of humanitarian concern and conduct. In the context of the refugees' world of today (e.g., Bosnia and Rwanda) this is significant. While these migrants are faced with difficult conditions, the demonstrated concern of groups like the Cuban Legal Organizations and HRC and the goodwill of their military rescuers and caretakers will hopefully sustain and reassure them in their quest for a better life.

Nevertheless, we cannot contravene the law of this circuit and of the Supreme Court of the United States in order to frame a legal answer to what is traditionally and properly a problem to be addressed by the legislative and executive branches of our government. See *Perez-Perez*, 781 F.2d at 1479. "Although the human crisis is compelling, there is no solution to be found in a judicial remedy." *Sale*, 113 S. Ct. at 2567 (quoting Haitian Refugee Ctr. v. Gracey, 809 F.2d 794, 841 (D.C. Cir. 1987) (Edwards, J., concurring)).

Notes and Questions

1.　The U.S.'s interdiction policy continues at this writing. However, because the Cuban Adjustment Act continues in force, the combined policies have yielded an unusual result, known as "wet foot-dry foot:"

> Those [Cubans] who get far enough to set foot on dry land in the United States are usually allowed to remain and eventually obtain full residence status under the [Cuban Adjustment] Act. Those caught before landing, even close to shore in U.S. territorial waters, are sent back to Cuba,

after a special form of credible-fear screening. Today, Guantanamo is used to temporarily house those Cubans deemed ineligible to be returned to Cuba due to such a fear of persecution.

D. Martin, A. Aleinikoff, H. Motomura & M. Fullerton, *Forced Migration Law and Policy* 739 (2007). The following article provides an account of the wet foot dry foot policy:

Yves Colon
Touching Land Defines Who Stays, Goes
Miami Herald, June 30, 1999, at A15

Wet foot or dry foot.

That's the short version of United States policy when it comes to Cuban refugees. If they're caught in the water, they're sent back to Cuba. If they touch ground, they get to stay. "Everybody knows you have to make landfall," said Dan Geoghegan, assistant chief of Border Patrol in Miami.

That crucial difference must have been clear in the minds of the six men who jumped from their skiff into the ocean off Surfside Tuesday. Only two made it to shore. The others were taken to the cutter Farrallon just off shore where an INS asylum officer will conduct interviews that might dictate whether they're sent to Cuba or to the U.S. Naval Base at Guantanamo Bay, Cuba.

Simple policy

Most of the time, the policy is clear cut: Dry foot means they stay. Wet foot means they go back. But just five months ago, some Cubans muddied it a bit when they made it to a patch of partially submerged mangroves off Key Largo. Their 16–foot wooden boat had run aground in three feet of water. Two of them made it 100 yards from shore. Only one was able to walk out.

Although their feet were touching the same ground, the State Department and the INS decided that only the one who walked out of the water would be allowed to remain in the United States. "There are unique circumstances around every landing," Geoghegan said. "The strict interpretation of the wet-foot policy is that other alien was still in the water. The interpretation found that one had made landfall."

Allowing Cubans who make it to land to stay in the United States has been around for nearly 40 years, put into practice shortly after Fidel Castro took power. Five years ago, dehydrated and dazed rafters found after days at sea aboard makeshift vessels made of wood, barrels, tubes and even Styrofoam were a common sight in the Florida Straits. The number of rafters began dwindling after the United States changed its policy on Cuban migration in 1995 after 30,000 had made it to South Florida.

The change: Only those who made it to U.S. soil would be allowed to stay. Those caught at sea are interviewed, with many returned to Cuba.

The number of Cubans smuggled to this country is growing dramatically, the Border Patrol believes. During the current fiscal year, which has three months remaining, border patrol agents have caught 1,550 Cubans, compared to 615 during the last fiscal year.

Cuban exiles and others who watched the unfolding drama on television Tuesday afternoon quickly showed sympathy for the six men who tried to reach land. Protests broke out at several locations over the Coast Guard's tactics of keeping the men from shore.

Following rules

Coast Guard officials, however, said they acted properly according to their consistent policy.

"The Coast Guard has a policy of using the minimum amount of force necessary to enforce U.S. law and to keep our people safe. The Coast Guard is very concerned about the fate of people at sea, but we also have to enforce U.S. law. We'll do an investigation and we'll make the facts known as we come by them," said a statement issued by Coast Guard Lt. Ron LaBrec.

Notes and Questions

1. What might account for the radical shift in policy toward Cuban refugees from the 1960s to the present?

2. Consider the media characterization of Cuban Americans as a "model minority." Is this accurate? Is it only partially accurate? Does the label obscure the poverty and relatively harsh treatment accorded recent generations of Cuban immigrants?

3. Consider the disparate treatment received by undocumented Mexican and undocumented Cuban immigrants. If a Cuban immigrant makes it to land, he will receive preferential treatment under the Cuban Adjustment Act. Undocumented Mexicans who arrive in the United States, also on dry land, are subject to deportation, and recently have been the objects of public persecution and negative scrutiny by the media. Is this state of affairs constitutional? Consider the following case:

Romero v. United States Immigration and Naturalization Service
399 F.3d 109 (2d Cir. 2005)

JACOBS, CIRCUIT JUDGE.

Francisco Romero, a citizen of Mexico, petitions this Court to review a February 13, 2002 order of the Board of Immigration Appeals ("BIA"), denying his request for cancellation of removal under the Immigration and Nationality Act of 1952 ("INA") and ordering his voluntary departure from the United States. Romero argues: (i) that his right to equal protection is violated because the Nicaraguan Adjustment and Central American Relief Act ("NACARA"), Pub. L. No. 105–100, Title II, 111

Stat. 2160, 2193–201 (1997), permits cancellation of removal for similarly situated persons from a list of countries that does not include Mexico.

* * *

Romero entered the United States without inspection in or about February 1991, at or near San Ysidro, California. In 1995, Romero went through a marriage ceremony with Evelyn Ramos, a United States citizen. * * * The administrative file indicates that Romero's petition for adjustment of status was denied in March of 1998; that the basis of denial was the couple's failure to appear at a hearing regarding certain suspicious circumstances of the marriage; and that Romero received notice of that determination, but never appealed it.

In October 1999, the INS issued a Notice to Appear for removal proceedings, alleging that Romero was removable pursuant to INA Section 212(a)(6)(A)(i), as "an alien present in the United States who had not been admitted or paroled." Represented before the IJ by one Reverend Robert Vitaglione, Romero conceded removability, but requested cancellation under NACARA. Although Romero further conceded that he was not eligible for relief under NACARA, he argued that NACARA violates "the equal protection rights of all aliens." In December 2000, the IJ determined that Romero was ineligible for cancellation of removal, noted that it lacked jurisdiction to consider the constitutional challenge to NACARA, and granted Romero the right to depart voluntarily. The BIA affirmed the IJ's ruling.

NACARA directs (*inter alia*) that the Attorney General adjust the status—to that of lawful permanent resident—of any alien who: (i) is a national of Cuba or Nicaragua; (ii) has been continuously present in the United States since December 1, 1995; and (iii) filed for permanent resident status before April 1, 2000. NACARA § 202(a)-(b). The government concedes that under NACARA Romero would be entitled to adjustment of his immigration status to that of a lawful permanent resident if he were a national of Cuba or Nicaragua. Romero contends that his ineligibility for adjustment of status violates principles of equal protection, because NACARA affords relief for nationals of certain countries, of which Mexico is not one.

"[T]he power to expel or exclude aliens [i]s a fundamental sovereign attribute exercised by the [g]overnment's political departments largely immune from judicial control." Rojas–Reyes v. INS, 235 F.3d 115, 122 (2d Cir. 2000); see also Giusto v. INS, 9 F.3d 8, 9 (2d Cir. 1993) ("Congress has plenary authority to regulate matters of immigration and naturalization. . . ."). "[T]he most exacting level of scrutiny that we will impose on immigration legislation is rational basis review. Under this review, legislation will survive a constitutional challenge so long as there is a facially legitimate and bona fide reason for the law." *Rojas-Reyes*, 235 F.3d at 122.

We are not the first federal court of appeals to consider whether NACARA's preferential treatment of particular nationalities runs afoul of equal protection principles. Our sister courts that have considered this issue have repeatedly held that NACARA is supported by "facially legitimate and bona fide reason[s]." Id. See, e.g., Pinho v. INS, 249 F.3d 183, 190 (3d Cir. 2001) ("The special exemptions ... for members of these extremely identifiable groups bear[ ] at least a rational relationship to the legitimate government interests of foreign relations, national security policy, and compliance with on-going government programs."); Ram v. INS, 243 F.3d 510, 517 (9th Cir. 2001) (explaining that aliens from the NACARA countries took unusual risks in escaping oppressive regimes and war-torn countries, and holding that "this decision to favor aliens from specific war-torn countries must be upheld because it stems from a rational diplomatic decision to encourage such aliens to remain in the United States"); Appiah v. INS, 202 F.3d 704, 710 (4th Cir. 2000) (holding that "NACARA easily withstands constitutional challenge" and explaining that Congress intended to honor pre-existing understandings with certain groups of aliens). At least one court of appeals has considered—and rejected—the under-breadth argument that Romero makes in his petition to this Court. See Ashki v. INS, 233 F.3d 913, 920 (6th Cir. 2000) ("Although the NACARA exemptions clearly do not cover all aliens who will face hostile conditions in their homelands, this fact does not make these exemptions irrational.").

We agree with the reasoning of our sister courts, and we hold that NACARA's preferential treatment of Cubans and Nicaraguans over Mexicans meets the standards we apply to immigration decisions made by the political branches of government.

* * *

For the foregoing reasons, the ruling of the BIA is affirmed and Romero's petition is denied.

Notes and Questions

1. Note that the Court uses only rational basis review to test the constitutionality of the NACARA statute. Is that appropriate, considering the explicit national-origin distinctions the statute draws? What standard of review would you expect to apply to a national-origin classification? What would be the outcome if a stricter standard of review applied?

2. Congress asserts, and Courts accept, the "plenary power" of Congress over immigration matters as a sufficient reason for judgments of who gets preferential treatment. Why should Congress have such a power to treat differentially persons who want to be in the United States?

Part Two

LEGAL STATUS, NATURALIZATION, AND CITIZENSHIP

Are Latinos a race? An ethnic group? A series of national origin groups? All of these? The following chapters address a number of issues related to the group's legal and social status. They also consider how Latinos and Latinas figure into the American equation—that is, issues of citizenship and belonging. Chapter 4 takes up the group's status in the law; Chapter 5, their social recognition and treatment at the hands of others, especially the dominant group. Chapter 6 ponders questions of citizenship, naturalization, and relationships with other nonwhite minorities.

The reader interested in these matters should see also Part Five: Immigration, Six: Stereotypes, and Nine: Latina Feminism, parts of which deal with similar issues of identity.

The most casual study of the legal and social identities of Latinos reinforces the constructedness of race and ethnicity. Racial groups, such as African Americans, whites, Latinos, and Asians correspond to no objective, immutable category laid down by nature or God. Human beings share at least 99.9 percent of their genetic material. The relatively minor physical differences in skin color, hair texture, and eye shape that demarcate what we call races do not correspond to anything that one might reasonably consider important—not intelligence, personality, character, or moral virtue—or distinctively human.

Yet, societies and legal systems seize on relatively minor physical differences and imbue them with great significance. We call them into existence, in other words, by our decision to recognize and act upon them. Without our conscious acts of choice, "Latino," "African American," or "white," would not exist.

The reader should revisit the role of choice after reading the following materials.

Chapter 4

LEGAL STATUS OF LATINOS

SECTION 1. LATINOS AND THE U.S. CENSUS

Latinos are a diverse group. In fact, the category itself is somewhat artificial, in the sense that most Latinos and Latinas do not think of themselves as such until they move to this country. Before that, in their homelands, they were simply Mexicans, Guatemalans, or Venezuelans.

The 2000 Decennial Census (the most recent) counted 35.3 million Latinos (a number that has now grown to well over 40 million), excluding the 3.8 million Latinos in Puerto Rico. The largest group is of Mexican heritage (about 66 percent in 2002), followed by Puerto Ricans (8.6 percent), Central and South Americans (14.3 percent), and Cubans (3.7 percent). Most Latinos live in seven states—California, Texas, New York, Florida, Illinois, Arizona, and New Jersey in that order of numerosity. Latinos of Mexican descent tend to live in the West, most Puerto Ricans in the Northeast, and Cubans in Florida. East Los Angeles has the highest proportion of Latinos outside Puerto Rico—well over 90 percent. See Steven W. Bender, *Comprende?: Celebrating the Spanish All Americans Know* (forthcoming 2008).

In the 2000 Census, the Office of Management and Budget (OMB) renamed the former "Hispanic" category "Hispanic or Latino." Individuals who identified with this group then encountered a box where they could check Latino as their ethnicity. Then, further down, they had an opportunity to choose a race, such as White, Black, American Indian, Asian, or Other. A large number who checked the Latino box selected "Other" as their race. For an explanation of the OMB's reasoning in adopting this approach, see Office of Management and Budget, *Revisions to the Standards for the Classification of Federal Data on Race and Ethnicity*, Nov. 2, 2000, http:// www.census.gov/population/www/ socdemo/race/Ombdir15.html; see also Kenneth Prewitt, *Racial Classification in America: Where Do We Go from Here?*, 134 Daedalus 5 (Winter 2005); Clara E. Rodriguez, *Changing Race: Latinos, the Census, and the History of Ethnicity in the United States* (2000).

In previous versions of the Census, which is taken every 10 years, the government adopted a wide variety of approaches to counting Latinos, ranging from no category at all, to categorization as a race, to categorization as an ethnicity with the respondent selecting a race. See *OMB Revisions*, supra.

Prewitt, who served as director of the Census from 1998 to 2001 notes that "Across two centuries, particular categories have come and gone in response to an ever-shifting mix of political, scientific, and demographic considerations," and that in 1790 slaves were included in the count because the slaveholding states, via the "three-fifths" clause, had made their fractional representation a nonnegotiable demand at the Constitutional Convention. Prewitt notes that subsequent events, such as wars of conquest, including the War with Mexico, added new territories expanding who needed to be counted. Id.

The civil rights revolution of the 1960s prompted the Equal Employment Opportunity Commission (EEOC) in 1964 to identify four minority groups—Negroes, Spanish Americans, American Indians, and Asian Americans. The next 1970 census followed suit, but modified the EEOC classification by changing Spanish American/Hispanic to an ethnicity. OMB formalized this procedure in 1977 and went further by asking those who selected Hispanic as their ethnicity to identify with one of the primary racial groups, American Indian/Native Alaskan, Asian, African American, and white. The 1980 and 1990 census maintained this categorical structure intact.

In the years leading up to the 2000 Census, the multiracial movement campaigned for a "multiracial" category, while others urged a separate classification for persons of Middle Eastern origin. Still other advocates urged disaggregating the white group to provide special niches for Greek Americans and other ethnic whites. The Census Bureau's response was to add a "mark one or more" instruction, so that respondents could check membership in as many racial and ethnic categories as they saw fit, resulting in a grid of over one hundred potential categories.

How did Latinos respond when faced with this bewildering complexity? Recent data collected by the American Community Survey showed that:

58.5   percent of Latinos indicated that their race was white alone.
35.2   percent indicated that it was "some other race" alone.
 1.6   percent indicated black or African American alone.
 3.6   percent indicated they were of two or more races.
 1.2   percent indicated that they were either American Indian and Alaska Native alone, Asian alone, or Native Hawaiian and Other Pacific Islander alone.

U.S. Census Bureau. *The American Community—Hispanics: 2004* (American Community Survey Reports, February 2007). See Ian F. Haney López, *How the Census Counts Hispanics*, 134 Daedalus 42 (Winter 2005) (criticizing the Bureau's refusal to recognize that many Latinos consider themselves a race).

SECTION 2. ARE LATINOS A RACE?
AN ETHNICITY? A CULTURE?

The U.S. Census provides for Latino self-identification in both ethnic and racial terms. Yet it does not allow them to select "Latino" as a race, but only an ethnicity. Was this wise? Does it place Latinos at a disadvantage vis-à-vis other groups, such as African Americans or Asian Americans, in asking for social benefits? The following excerpt addresses this question.

Ángel R. Oquendo
Re-Imagining the Latino/a Race
12 Harv. BlackLetter J. 93, 93–98, 103–07, 109–10 (1995)

This excerpt condemns "racial" subcategories, such as "Black Hispanics" and "White Hispanics," which have been increasingly gaining currency, and ultimately suggests that such categories should be rejected. First, they project onto the Latino/a community a divisive racial dualism that, much as it may pervade U.S. society, is alien to that community. Second, they presuppose an independent objective concept of race capable of meaningfully classifying individuals as "Black" or "White."

Categorizing on the basis of physical features, of course, is an accepted practice in the United States. In fact, this society has primarily used physiognomy to create the "Hispanic" category. Yet what really unites Latino/as is their unique history of oppression. Unlike other immigrant groups, the largest Latino/a groups—Mexicans and Puerto Ricans—did not come into the United States via Ellis Island; they entered through the brutal process of U.S. imperial expansion. They were militarily attacked, invaded, colonized, and annexed. This common experience has caused them to form a unified community, which now includes other people of Latin American ancestry.

Another factor that bonds the Latino/a community is their common language. Not all Latino/as in the United States speak Spanish, but they all have some connection with it. If they do not speak Spanish themselves, then it is the language of their ancestors. Because they share a language, Latino/as constitute a race in the sense proposed by Spanish philosopher Miguel de Unamuno. In fact, in categorizing Latino/as, the "Anglo" majority has emphasized this common linguistic heritage more than physical appearance. For instance, the derogatory term that cuts across the different Latino/a groups is "spik"—which emphasizes how Latino/as "speak" rather than how they look. More significantly, the anti-Latino/a movement has coalesced politically in reaction to the "English only" movement, which attacks their linguistic identity.

A NEW CATEGORIZATION

Soy Mexicana
soy Mexican–American

soy American of Spanish Surname (A.S.S.)
soy Latina
soy Puerto Riquena
soy Cocoanut
soy Chicana

In 1978, during my last high school year in Puerto Rico, I took the SAT. Any test can be intimidating, but one that measures aptitude can make you feel insecure and challenged. These feelings were accentuated in my case because the exam was in English, and more important, was administered by an organization from the United States.

I was nervous, in part, because I was being tested by the people who kept us afloat with their massive economic support, who from afar made important decisions for us, and who generally were successful where we had failed. When they came to our land, they were well-off and they ran many of the large companies. In contrast, when we went to their land, we were poor, did the most menial jobs, and scored the lowest on intelligence tests. Therefore, the test had a greater meaning for me. It symbolized America's continuing dominion and control over Puerto Rico. I was determined to wage a battle that I could ultimately win.

* * *

Yet I was caught off guard even before the examination began. While I was filling out the personal information part, I was asked to identify myself racially. This struck me as odd for two reasons. I had never been asked such a question before, * * * and I had never thought of myself in terms of race, even though I was aware of the concept of racial differences. I knew about the history and reality of racism, yet I did not see myself as a member of a particular race.

Fortunately, the SAT authorities were wise or benevolent enough to include "Puerto Rican" among the multiple choices and thus spared me a potentially profound existential dilemma. I had no need to check the color of my skin, feel the texture of my hair, visualize my facial features, or call to mind the physiognomy of my family and relatives. With a sense of relief, I checked the box labeled "Puerto Rican" and moved on.

At the time, I was only a kid facing an unexpected situation. Today, having now lived in the United States for over fifteen years, I have come to regard this kind of questioning as normal. In fact, until recently, I considered myself beyond astonishment with respect to issues of racial categorization. I thought that I would always find a box simply labeled "Puerto Rican," "Hispanic," "Latino," "Spanish Surnamed," or even "Other" with which I could feel comfortable.

However, racial categories have changed in the last few years. I am referring to the relatively recent tendency to subcategorize the category for Hispanics. Ever more often, surveys add to that category the following clarification "(Black and White)"—sometimes "(regardless of race)"—and qualify the White as well as the Black category with the parenthetical "(non-Hispanic)." So the list usually reads as follows:

"White (non-Hispanic)," "Black (non-Hispanic)," "Hispanic (Including White and Black Hispanics)," "Asian–American," "American Indian," and "Other."

A true bureaucrat's paradise! Granted, the Hispanic category is still being made available to me. But it is more difficult for me to embrace that category with all the added attachments and qualifications. I wonder if I am being told that there is something problematic about my category? Is the message that it, unlike other categories, needs further explanation? Is it implied that after all I do belong objectively to a race but that I am being given a break as a Latino/a for some undisclosed reason? The next step will probably be to create separate classifications for Black Hispanics and White Hispanics and to force Latino/as to choose. The quandary that I narrowly escaped as a child will thus be returning with a vengeance.

The Term "Latino/a"

* * *

The term "Hispanic" has been rejected by some because of its association with Spanish colonial power. They prefer "Latino" because it lacks any such connotation and is more inclusive and descriptive. * * * "Latino" is short for "latinoamericano." Like its English counterpart, the term refers to the people who come from the territory in the Americas colonized by Latin nations, such as Portugal, Spain, and France, whose languages are derived from Latin. People from Brazil, Mexico, and even Haiti are thus all "latinoamericanos." Individuals who are decendants of the former British or Dutch colonies are excluded.

"Iberoamericanos," in contrast, are individuals who come from American lands once occupied by Portugal and Spain, the two countries on the Iberian peninsula. Brazilians and Mexicans are iberoamericanos, but not Haitians or any of the citizens of countries once claimed by France, Britain, or the Netherlands. Finally, "hispanoamericanos" are persons from the former colonies of Spain in the "New World." The expression "Hispanic" probably derives from "hispanoamericanos."

An informal interpretation of the term "Latino" would take it to be equivalent to "hispanoamericano" or "iberoamericano." In other words, it may be used in a narrower sense to denominate only those who come from the former colonies of Spain and Portugal. In the United States, it appears to be employed in the narrowest sense to identify the children of the former Spanish possessions in the Americas.

The strict interpretation of "Latino" is more inclusive than the term "Hispanic," encompassing as it does those people who are descended from the onetime possessions of not only Spain, but also Portugal and France. However, "Latino" enthusiasts would probably exclude these people from the category because they use it to cover only people from what was once the Spanish empire in America. Therefore, in practical application, the term "Latino" is no more inclusive and descriptive than "Hispanic."

That the term "Latino" should be favored over "Hispanic" because the latter is linked to the brutal Spanish colonization of America is puzzling. "Latino," in the informal sense, is just as bound up with the Spanish colonial enterprise. The formal interpretation of Latino is associated with the similarly objectionable Portuguese and French colonial projects, and both terms slight the rich African and Native American influence on the Latino/a community.

What I do find attractive about the expression "Latino" is, first, that it calls to mind the Latino/a struggle for empowerment in the United States. The leaders of this campaign support "Latino" because it came from the community. The Latino/a people are thus conceived of as not just acquiescing to their christening by the Anglo majority, but rather as giving themselves a name. The adoption of the term "Latino" could be regarded as part of a broader process of self-definition and self-assertion.

Second, "Latino" is a newer term that invites re-thinking and re-defining of what membership in this community is all about. This attitude of re-birth and of facing a new beginning is needed as the Latino/a community in the United States becomes larger and more diverse and strives to find itself. The third reason why "Latino" is a better term is because it is a Spanish word. It accentuates the bond between the Latino/a community and the Spanish language. Furthermore, in insisting upon being called by its Spanish name, the Latino/a community is demanding recognition and respect for its culture.

* * *

The Poverty of the Concept of Race

Now, what if the racial dualism bias of the subcategorization were remedied? In other words, what if the re-categorization included specifying that the category Hispanic includes all races and perhaps clarifying that the categories "White," "Black," "Asian American," "Native American," and "Other" do not include "Hispanics"? My bureaucrat could now say: "This is generally a racial classification. For policy reasons Hispanics must be treated separately, even though they do not constitute a distinct race. What we are doing is pulling Hispanics from their corresponding racial categories and artificially creating a separate category for them. The questionnaire simply reflects this reality."

The Office of Management and Budget, in its Statistical Directive 15—which regulates racial and ethnic categorization on federal forms and statistics—endorses this approach. Latino/as, like all other U.S. citizens, are taken to fall within one of the four racial groups: American Indian or Alaskan Native; Asian or Pacific Islander; Black; and White. As a separate matter, Directive 15 then divides ethnicity into "Hispanic Origin" and "Not of Hispanic Origin."

This whole approach is problematically premised on the existence of an independently meaningful concept of race that applies to all people, including Latino/as. The creation of a separate category for Latino/as is taken to be independent of their status as members of a particular race. They supposedly continue to be Black, White, or another color.

Yet, race is, at best, a highly vague category that generally classifies people in terms of the way they look. Spanish philosopher Miguel de Unamuno reports that the word "race," as used in almost every European language, comes from the Spanish or Castilean word *raza*, which means "ray" or "line." "In Castilla," Unamuno points out, "one speaks of a 'raza' of sun and each thread in a cloth is called a 'raza'." The modern term "race" apparently came to refer to a mark shared by people who are related by heritage. Not surprisingly, people with resembling physical traits, presumably due to a common genealogy, came to be seen as belonging to the same race.

* * *

To the extent that Latino/as physiognomically resemble each other and differ from other groups, they could be taken to constitute a "race." The physiognomic differences among Latino/as are probably not much greater than those among the members of other "racial" groups, such as "Whites" or "African Americans." In light of the inexorable vagueness of the concept of race, the idea of racial cohesion among Latino/as is just as plausible as the notion that Latino/as can be internally segregated by race. The concept of race is incapable of providing a meaningful basis for making significant distinctions between those who fall within and those who fall without a particular race. * * *

The Evils of the Concept of Race

Many have repudiated the concept of race not only because of its inaccuracy but also because of the sinister purposes it has served historically. Unamuno's rejection of "racial materialism" provides a case in point. Racial materialism focuses on material or physical characteristics in defining the concept of race. Unamuno denounces "the materialist cast that is usually given to the anthropological concept of race."

In a 1933 article (published on the Day of the Race, "El dia de la raza"—as Columbus Day is referred to in Spanish-speaking countries) Unamuno asserts that it is the racists who use this material concept of race and adds: "Today I feel an obligation to insist on this point, in light of the ... barbarity, actually savagery, attained by such racism, especially in Germany." He assails "the barbaric sense" given to the materialist concept of race by "the racists, those supposed Aryans of the gammadion and anti-Christian cross."

* * *

If racial categories, in addition to having no intelligible substance, serve mainly as an instrument of oppression, why not just eliminate them altogether? Why not go beyond deleting subcategories, such as "Black Hispanic" and "White Hispanic," etc.? I would argue that these general categories should not be simply quashed, but re-anchored on the cultural or spiritual life of peoples. By reconceptualizing themselves, excluded people will be better able to recapture their identities and to struggle for social justice. * * * Overt or crude racism, which is characterized by openly treating African Americans as inherently inferior, has been termed "old-fashioned" racism. The transition to the more subtle and covert forms of racism that prevail in modern society takes place as old-fashioned racism becomes less acceptable. The injury caused by racism cannot be segregated from the racial classification in place. In fact, racism is unjust because it only allows a person to be identified by empty racial categories. Hence racism not only deprives people of their income; it robs people of their soul.

In *Race, Ethnicity, Erasure: The Salience of Race to LatCrit Theory*, 85 Cal. L. Rev. 1143 (1997), Ian F. Haney López echoes Oquendo's call for Latinos to demand recognition as a race. Id. at 1146–47, noting that "we should ... use race as a lens ... through which to assess the Latino/a experience" and criticizing both the Census Bureau and the United States Supreme Court for failing to recognize Latinos as a separate race. See *Hernández v. Texas*, infra this chapter.

Professor Haney López takes issue with legal scholars who discuss Latinos in terms of ethnicity (a group of affinities and shared behaviors), not race. See, e.g., Paul Brest & Miranda Oshige, *Affirmative Action for Whom?*, 47 Stan. L. Rev. 855, 856, 883–90 (1995), pointing out that Latinos may be of any race—white, black, indigenous, or even Asian—and hence do not constitute a single race. See also Orlando Patterson, *The Race Trap*, N.Y. Times, July 11, 1997, at A27, urging that society stop using racial categories, whenever possible, and use ethnicity instead; Kwame Anthony Appiah, *In My Fathers House: Africa in the Philosophy of Culture* 45 (1992) (urging that we use "culture" instead). Since society racializes Latinos and often treats them in the unjust and disdainful way it treats groups, such as African Americans, for whom the term "race" clearly applies, avoiding the term for Latinos is an evasion. Haney López, *Race, Ethnicity*, supra, at 1153–54.

For more on Haney López's social constructionist views, see *White By Law: The Legal Construction of Race* (10th Anniv. ed. 2006), observing that society and the legal system construct races, including the white and the brown, through certain practices, including laws that recognize the right to marry, immigrate, and nationalize. On social construction generally, see Michael Omi & Howard Winant, *Racial Formation in the United States: From the 1960s to the 1990s* (2d ed. 1994). For the argument that Latinos may, at times, at least, benefit from identifying themselves as an ethnic or national-origin group, see Juan F. Perea, *Ethnicity and Prejudice: Reevaluating "National Origin" Discrimination Under Title VII*, 35 Wm. & Mary L. Rev. 805 (1994). See also Gloria Sandrino–Glasser, Los Confundidos: *De-Conflating Latinos/as' Race and Ethnicity*, 19 Chicano–Latino L. Rev. 69 (1998); Ian F. Haney López,

Protest, Repression, and Race: Legal Violence and the Chicano Movement, 150 U. Pa. L. Rev. 205 (2001).

SECTION 3. LATINOS AND THE JUDICIAL SYSTEM

In 1954, the Warren Court, under the leadership of former California governor Earl Warren, handed down one of the most significant legal decisions of the modern era, Brown v. Board of Education, 347 U.S. 483 (1954). One of a number of progressive Warren Court decisions, *Brown* held that separate but equal public schooling for black schoolchildren violated the Equal Protection Clause. A little-noticed decision, *Hernández v. Texas*, appears in U.S. Reports immediately before the better known *Brown*. Decided only two weeks before *Brown*, *Hernández* remains today one of a handful of U.S. Supreme Court decisions on Latinos' entitlement to sue for discriminatory treatment.

Hernández v. Texas
347 U.S. 475 (1954)

Reread the *Hernández* opinion in Part One, supra.

Notes and Questions

1. Are African Americans a race? Why or why not? Are Latinos a race? Why or why not? For the view that all races are social constructs, see Haney López, *White by Law*, supra.

2. In *Hernández*, the Supreme Court, without ruling on whether Latinos are a race, allows them to sue for discrimination in parts of the country where they can show local prejudice. The Court thus left open whether they can sue for violations of equal protection in parts of the country other than Jackson County, Texas, and, if so, whether they are entitled to sue as a class. The next excerpt addresses some of those questions for Mexican Americans.

3. For more discussion of *Hernández*, see *"Colored Men" and "Hombres Aquí:"* Hernández v. Texas *and the Emergence of Mexican American Lawyering* (Michael A. Olivas ed., 2006).

4. For discussion of a related incident, see Michael A. Olivas, *The "Trial of the Century" That Never Was: Staff Sgt. Macario Garcia, the Oasis Café, and WWII Veteranos*, in *WWII Latina/o Cultural Citizenship* (M. Rivas–Rodriguez ed., forthcoming 2008).

5. See Ian F. Haney López & Michael A. Olivas, *The Story of* Hernández v. Texas: *Jim Crow, Mexican Americans, and the Anti–Subordination Constitution*, in *Race and Law Stories* (R. Moran & D. Carbado eds., forthcoming 2008), arguing that the judiciary should interpret *Brown v. Board of Education* in light of the Supreme Court's emphasis in *Hernández* on group oppression, not racial classification.

Richard Delgado & Vicky Palacios
Mexican Americans as a Legally Cognizable Class under
Rule 23 and the Equal Protection Clause
50 Notre Dame Law. 393, 393–94, 405–15 (1975)

Long inured to their status as "the forgotten minority," few Chicanos find it surprising that, even after a decade of intensive civil rights activity on behalf of blacks, the status of Chicanos as a legally cognizable minority is still in doubt. Indeed, the law's failure strikes a familiar chord; almost every Chicano has experienced at some point in his life having the following reasoning applied against him: (1) Our firm (agency, school district) regards Chicanos as white; (2) we do not discriminate against whites; and (3) therefore, we do not discriminate against Chicanos. This argument rests, of course, on the premise that Chicanos are indistinguishable from members of the majority culture and race and are simply not a minority group for purpose of remedial action.

What is surprising is that in certain areas of civil rights litigation this same argument, albeit in a somewhat more sophisticated form, receives judicial approval. This chapter examines two of these areas: the status of Chicanos under equal protection doctrine and their status under Rule 23 governing class actions [as defined by the Federal Rules of Civil Procedure—*Eds.*].

Inability to avail themselves of "class" status severely limits Chicanos' ability to redress grievances through litigation. Class actions enable a single plaintiff or group of plaintiffs to sue on behalf of an entire class. This procedural device possesses the substantial advantages of economy and res judicata effect as well as considerable political and psychological impact. By the same token, access to equal protection coverage enables a plaintiff to give his complaint constitutional dimensions and thus, in certain circumstances, to secure a stricter standard of judicial review.

Are Chicanos a legally-definable class? Among the characteristics common to many Chicanos are: Spanish language as the mother tongue; Mexican ancestry; Spanish surname; a distinct culture and history; a genetic heritage that results in certain recurring physical traits; economic, educational, and political exclusion from the mainstream of American life; perception by Anglos, including many government agencies, as a minority; and perception by Chicanos themselves as a non-Anglo group.

The almost mystical significance given the Spanish language as the carrier of Chicano culture has drawn comment by a number of ethnologists and other social scientists. A Chicano university professor has written:

In the beginning was the Word, and the Word was made Flesh. It was so in the beginning, and it is so today. The language, the Word, carries within it the history, the culture, the traditions, the very life of [our] people.... We cannot even conceive of a people without a language, or a language without a people. The two are one and the same. To know one is to know the other.

The refusal of Mexican Americans to surrender their native tongue has at times meant the forfeiture of substantial benefits. In schools, for example, bilingualism has often been suppressed, and, if not suppressed, rarely recognized as an asset. Some states require the ability to speak English as a condition of voting or holding political office. Others require that court proceedings and legal notices be in English. Chicano persistence in retaining the use of Spanish in the face of such pressures testifies to the likelihood that Spanish usage is, and will continue to be, a partial—but highly reliable—index of membership in the Chicano class.

Another characteristic held in common by Chicanos is their ancestry. The precise characterization of this ancestry, however, has been the subject of controversy. In a study on Mexican–American education, the United States Commission on Civil Rights, which used the terms "Mexican American" and "Chicano" interchangeably, declared:

> [T]he term Mexican American refers to persons who were born in Mexico and now reside in the United States or whose parents or more remote ancestors immigrated to the United States from Mexico. It also refers to persons who trace their lineage to Hispanic or Indo–Hispanic forebears who resided within Spanish or Mexican territory that is now part of the Southwestern United States.

This definition suffers from overinclusiveness, since an individual of pure Scandinavian descent who was at one time a Mexican citizen but later immigrated to the United States would qualify as a Chicano. A more accurate definition of Chicanos in terms of ancestry would be "any individual residing in the United States who traces his lineage to Indo–Hispanic or Hispanic ancestors who are living or once lived in Mexico or the Southwestern United States." Such a definition excludes Mexican citizens still living in Mexico but includes those Mexican citizens who are registered aliens. The definition would also include descendants of the colonial Spaniards with little or no Indian blood who, like the Mexican alien, identify with the culture and social goals of the Mexican American. At the same time, the requirement that Hispanic forebears come from the Southwest excludes those of Spanish descent who settled on the East Coast of the United States, since they have generally been assimilated into the dominant society and rarely identify with the culture of the Mexican American.

An additional feature shared by many Chicanos is Spanish surname. The cultural fusion of the native Meso–Americans and the Spanish was such that at one time virtually all residents of the American Southwest carried Spanish surnames. But today not all Chicanos bear Spanish surnames, nor are all persons bearing Spanish surnames Chicano. Because of the practice of women taking the husband's surname, those Chicanas who have married Anglos no longer bear Spanish names. Similarly, the Spanish surname of a Chicano husband is carried by his Anglo wife, who may have little attachment to the Chicano culture. This blurring effect obviously increases as generations pass. It is nonetheless true that most Chicanos still bear Spanish surnames. This is due to the tendency of Chicanos, like most ethnic minorities, to limit social interaction to members of their own group. This ethnic closure results in a high incidence of ethnic intramarriage.

The most important of the ties which bind Chicanos is their culture. Culture has been termed the very essence of an individual's social identity. Marcos de Leon, a California educator, has characterized the function of the Chicano culture in the life of the individual member as "all encompassing." It comprises the group's ideas, habits, values, and institutions; it is the force that gives the group cohesion and direction. It supplies the system of beliefs that enables the group to establish social and political structures. Aesthetics also plays a part since culture includes the group's preferences with regard to the graphic and plastic arts, folklore, music, drama, and dance.

Culture, of course, manifests itself differently from community to community and even from individual to individual. Particularly in view of the geographic dispersion of Chicanos, it would be a mistake to assume that the existence of a common culture results in individuals who are carbon copies of each other. Nevertheless, the United States Commission on Civil Rights has found that "Mexican Americans share common traits, common values, and a common heritage which may be identified as components of a general Mexican American cultural pattern." This cultural pattern, the Commission concludes, "sets them apart as a distinct and recognizable group." * * * The unwillingness of the dominant society to recognize the rich culture of the Mexican American creates a tension in the lives of many Chicanos, who see themselves as forced to choose between retaining the traditions of their people and gaining the educational and economic benefits of participation in the dominant society. Most have chosen to keep their culture. However, they have had to do so at the price of being stereotyped as backward, inferior, or, at best, quaint.

* * *

An additional feature that binds Chicanos is their physical appearance. Anthropologists Benson E. Ginsberg and William S. Laughlin have written about ethnic populations and the effect of their isolation or mixture on their genetic pools. Regardless of what other implications may follow from the existence of a distinct gene pool, it is at least clear that many Chicanos share a phenotype of physical characteristics. This commonality in phenotype bolsters the identifiability of the Chicano class. In writing of the history of the Chicano in this country, one author tells of the halt brought to the migration of Mexican laborers into this country by Depression unemployment. To alleviate the pressures created by unemployment, the Government simply deported Mexican laborers by the carload. Their legal rights ignored, thousands fell victim to a dragnet established and enforced by federal, state, and local agencies. Even Chicanos who were United States citizens were summarily deported.

Merely looking "Mexican" sufficed. "Visual identification or stereotype" was the criterion generally employed.

For centuries, Anglos have associated a combination of brown skin and certain other physical traits with people of Mexican ancestry. *Recopilación de Leyes de los Reinos de las Indias*, a 1680 compilation of nearly 200 years of law dealing with the Indians of Meso–America, expressly recognized the existence of a new "race," the mestizo of the Americas. In more modern times, the United States Commission on Civil Rights has also noted the similarities in the appearance of Chicanos: "Many Mexican Americans exhibit physical characteristics of the indigenous Indian population that set them apart from typical Anglos. In fact, some Anglos have always regarded Mexican Americans as a separate racial group."

In the popular mind, Mexicans have long appeared "different" from whites. One study of community attitudes toward Chicanos in Chicago in the 1940s cites a number of examples illustrating these perceptions. One resident of an Italian neighborhood, for example, was quoted as saying, "I don't want my kids to associate with the Mexicans. God made people white and black, and he meant there to be a difference."

Though many of the references to the Chicano's brown color have in the past been negative, Chicanos have turned this derogatory reference into a source of pride and self-awareness, much the same way African Americans have done with the word "black." While this turnabout has done much to improve the Chicano's self-image and sensitize the Anglo to the feeling of pride Chicanos have about themselves, some still equate dark skin with inferiority. So long as this negative attitude persists, physical characteristics will continue to be another source of commonality among Chicano people.

Economic and political disenfranchisement is another aspect of life shared by Chicanos. Chicanos consistently suffer from underparticipation and over-participation in various social institutions. In public education, for example, Chicanos have one of the highest dropout rates of any ethnic group. Data compiled by the United States Commission on Civil Rights show that, if present trends continue, by the year 2000 only one-half of the Chicano school population will graduate from high school.

The reasons for this educational gap are not hard to find: poverty, language handicap, migrancy, and cultural insensitivity on the part of teachers and school administrators. Even when an individual Chicano manages to escape or surmount the effect of these factors and obtains a baccalaureate or graduate degree his efforts are typically not rewarded to the same extent as the Anglo's. Because of demands within his group as well as discriminatory attitudes in the larger society, success-oriented Chicanos have limited opportunities to take advantage of educational and occupational opportunities. Other studies show that minorities who attain a high level of education and enter the professions are likely to find their opinions not as highly valued by their colleagues as are opinions of members of the dominant culture.

Mexican Americans have also endured exclusion from the American mainstream in the employment area. In the Southwest, Chicanos have an overall unemployment rate about double that of whites. Chicanos are markedly underrepresented in the more prestigious and high-paying professions and in many of the trades. That unemployment in the Chicano sector is not merely a lingering residue of bygone discrimination is shown by the disproportionately high unemployment rate among Chicano teenagers.

Regional data indicate that the poverty many Chicanos suffer is severe enough to affect their health and longevity. One Chicano community reported an infant mortality rate five to six times the national rate for white infants. In many southwestern communities, Chicanos fall victim in disproportionate numbers to diseases associated with low socioeconomic conditions.

* * *

In certain areas, however, the Chicano can claim the dubious distinction of over-participation in American institutions. One such area is the courts and penal institutions; another, the military service. Reports of police brutality are much more frequent in barrio and ghetto neighborhoods. Chicano juveniles, like Chicano adults, fare poorly at the hands of the justice system. One New Mexico counselor testified before the Commission on Civil Rights that minor violations such as curfew offenses, stealing cantaloupes, and the like, were frequently overlooked in the case of Anglo children. When the violator was a Chicano youth, however, formal charges were frequently pressed and became part of the juvenile's official record.

Another area of Chicano overrepresentation is the military service. The Mexican–American male has been an active participant in the military; the casualty rate for Chicanos in the Vietnam war was over 50 percent higher than their proportion to the total population. This figure prompted Chicano observers to note that where government agencies have exercised diligence and sincerity in their search for minorities they have been met with success. Unlike jury commissioners and private employers, draft boards have had little difficulty finding "qualified" people. In Nueces County alone, over 75 percent of the men killed in Vietnam bore Mexican–American names.

In politics, despite a few isolated successes, the Chicano community as a whole remains largely voiceless. Most Mexican Americans are native born and they comprise the second largest minority in the nation. Yet political participation by Chicanos remains low and there are still relatively few elected officials from the Chicano sector. Among the reasons for this phenomenon are attempts by some to discourage Mexican–American voting. Chicanos in some areas have experienced such discouragement by means ranging from outright intimidation to laws which endeavor to make registration difficult.

* * *

A related indicator of class separateness is community attitudes that emphasize the ways in which a group's members are unlike members of the dominant society Chicanos, like other minority groups, can recount a wide variety of personal experiences in which they have been the targets of prejudice. A California school principal told the Civil Rights Commission that he always seated the Chicano students behind the Anglo students at graduation ceremonies because he felt it made for a "better looking stage." A California teacher explained that she asked an Anglo boy to lead a row of Chicano youngsters to an activity because his father was a rancher and the boy needed to get used to giving orders to Mexicans. Another educator reported that she calls on Anglo children to assist Chicano children who hesitate in recitation because the "American" pupil is more likely to give a correct response and because it is good educational practice to draw out "American" children and give them a feeling of importance by having them help the "Mexicans."

The mass media have also contributed to the formation of negative stereotypes of the Chicano people. Tomás Martinez has analyzed the way in which advertisers promote racism by portraying stereotypes such as the "Frito Bandito." Television and newspaper commercials presenting "typical Mexican villages" or Mexican outlaws reinforce the belief that Mexicans are lazy, unambitious persons in need of underarm deodorant. Such commercials, Martinez suggests, are not harmless jokes or portrayals of cartoon characters. They are caricatures, whose function is to reaffirm symbolically the inferior social status of Mexicans and Mexican Americans in the eyes of the American public. In so doing, the advertisements suggest to the audience that such comical, lazy, and unkempt people want what Anglos have by virtue of their superior culture. The advertisements encourage the viewer to purchase the product because it is the duty of a member of the superior culture.

* * *

The final index of the Chicano's separateness is the perception he has of himself and his people. Much of what the Chicano feels about himself can be learned from the terms he chooses to identify his cultural group. One such term which has come into use is *la Raza*. Although literally translated "the race," the phrase more properly connotes the cultural and historical ties which unite Spanish-speaking people. An early forerunner of this designation was "la Raza Cosmica," a phrase coined by the nineteenth-century philosopher Jose Vasconcelos, who believed that Mexicans would form the cosmic, ideal people because of their particular blood mixture. This theory is said to have been the Mexican response to Anglo–Nordic historians who considered the Mexicans inferior half-breeds. Matt S. Meier and Feliciano Rivera write of the term *la Raza* that it connotes "not racial but ethnic solidarity, and a sense of common destiny." Another commentator states: "La Raza has become more than a slogan: it has become a way of life for a people who seek to fully realize their personal and group identity; and obtain equality of rights and treatment as citizens of the United States." It is this sense of a common destiny which illustrates the feeling of community in the use of *la Raza*.

More and more Mexican Americans are choosing to refer to themselves as "Chicano." The word itself is said to be a shortened version of "Mexicano," pronounced perhaps at one time by the Mexican Indians as "Meh-chee-cano." This term has undergone a number of changes in meaning. Originally it was derogatory, and many older Mexican Americans still consider it pejorative and refuse to use it. Later it came into popular use among the more militant Chicanos, and to some it still connotes militancy. More recently, however, "Chicano" has been used by Mexican Americans as a symbol of awareness and pride in their ethnic identity. In *Chicano Manifesto* Armando Rendon writes:

> I am a Chicano. What that means to me may be entirely different from what meaning the word has for you. To be Chicano is to find out something about one's self which has lain dormant, subverted, and nearly destroyed.

Although Chicano problems are not new, Mexican–American self-awareness, so long unvoiced, is perhaps best expressed by activists in the Chicano movement. Rendon characterizes the revolt as "primarily an internal conversion," involving an expansion of the individual's personality, background, and future as the individual Chicano perceives that all Chicanos have traveled the same paths, suffered the same indignities, and undergone the same deprivation. He then realizes that while some may have adjusted and survived better than others by adopting the Anglo's ways, all are bound by "a common birthplace; a common history, learned from books or by word of mouth; and a common culture much deeper than the shallow Anglo reservoir." This growing realization increases the Chicano's sense of identity and unity with other Chicanos and strengthens his desire to work for the enhancement of equal opportunity for his people in every phase of American life.

Chicanos have a word to express the kinship they feel—*carnalismo*. The closest literal translation would be "brotherhood," but *carnalismo* expresses much more. Of *pachuco* origin, *carnalismo* carries with it the unique frame of reference the Chicano's history has given him.

Taken together, the class characteristics discussed thus far demonstrate that the Chicano falls outside the mainstream of American life for many purposes. He is not in any sense an "average" American. His heritage and ancestry, his present welfare and future goals are at variance with those of the dominant society. It is these variances that make the Chicano a separate and identifiable class.

Shortly after Delgado and Palacios wrote, the Supreme Court in Castaneda v. Partida, 430 U.S. 482 (1977) reaffirmed *Hernández* in a case arising from discrimination against Mexican Americans in Texas' grand jury selection process. Because a statistical pattern strongly suggested systematic exclusion and because "it is no longer open to dispute that Mexican Americans are a clearly identifiable class" (citing *Hernández*), the Latino plaintiff had made out a prima facie claim, even though his group was a "governing majority" in the area in question.

Notes and Questions

1. *The role of interest convergence.* Since American society had been discriminating against blacks and Latinos for centuries, why did the Supreme Court issue the two surprising rulings, *Brown* and *Hernández*, when it did? For leading African–American critical scholar Derrick Bell, the answer is clear, at least in regard to *Brown*. He points out that in 1954, the United States was in the early stages of a Cold War with the forces of worldwide communism. Competing for the loyalties of the uncommitted Third World, much of which was brown, black, or Asian, the U.S. could no longer tolerate a stream of adverse publicity when the world press splashed across its front pages stories of Southern incidents of brutality against black people peaceably going about their business.

According to Bell, American elites thus quietly arranged for a Supreme Court breakthrough to improve international appearances and win a public-relations victory. See Derrick Bell, Brown v. Board of Education *and the Interest Convergence Dilemma*, 93 Harv. L. Rev. 518 (1980). See also Mary Dudziak, *Cold War Civil Rights: Race and the Image of American Democracy* (2000).

2. What about the companion case, *Hernández v. Texas*? For the argument that *Hernández*, too, came about not out of a spasm of conscience or evolving Equal Protection thinking on the Supreme Court's part, see Richard Delgado, *Rodrigo's Roundelay:* Hernández v. Texas *and the Interest Convergence Dilemma*, 41 Harv. C.R.-C.L. L. Rev. 23 (2006). Delgado argues that fear of Latin American communism and people's movements, as well as concern over the domestic variety, fueled the decision in *Hernández*.

3. *The black-white binary paradigm of race.* Legal recognition of the rights and status of Latinos may have been slow in coming because the reigning black-white binary paradigm of race deems African Americans the prototypical civil rights plaintiffs, with other groups off at the margin somewhere. See Juan F. Perea, *The Black–White Binary Paradigm of Race: The "Normal Science" of American Racial Thought*, 85 Cal. L. Rev. 1213 (1997); Elizabeth Martinez, *Beyond Black/White: The Racisms of Our Time*, 20 Soc. Just. 22 (1993); Richard Delgado, *Rodrigo's Fifteenth Chronicle: Racial Mixture, Latino–Critical Scholarship, and the Black–White Binary*, 75 Tex. L. Rev. 1181 (1997); Deborah A. Ramirez, *Multicultural Empowerment: It's Not Just Black and White Any More*, 47 Stan. L. Rev. 957 (1995). This structural feature of civil rights discourse means that Latinos are far from the consciousness of most civil rights scholars and lawyers. It also impairs the ability to generalize from one group's experience to that of another. It can lead one to think that America made just one large historical mistake— slavery—when this casebook, for example, recounts many others. It can easily lead to what is called "exceptionalism," the belief that one group (generally blacks) has had experiences that render it unique, when in fact all

the groups are special. It can seduce the nonwhite group in the binary to overidentify with whites, overlooking possibly more fruitful coalitions with other groups of color. See Richard Delgado, *Derrick Bell's Toolkit: Fit to Dismantle That Famous House?*, 75 N.Y.U. L. Rev. 283 (2000). See also Manuel G. Gonzales, *Mexicanos: A History of Mexicans in the United States* (1999); Carlos Muñoz, *Youth, Identity, Power: The Chicano Movement* (rev. ed. 2007).

4. If courts recognize that a group, say Latinos, is entitled to sue for discrimination, does it immediately follow that it is thinking of the group as a race? See Athena Mutua, *Shifting Bottoms and Rotating Centers: Reflections on LatCrit III and the Black/White Paradigm*, 53 U. Miami L. Rev. 1177 (1999) (on black-white binary and its effect on legal actionability).

5. If courts permit a group to sue for *racial* discrimination, does it follow that they must permit it to sue as a class, assuming it satisfies the requirement of numerosity (over, say, 50 in number)?

Most authorities today hold that race is a social construct, rather than a biological fact or essence. In other words, society decides to seize on small physical differences in the way groups look in order to render them one-down, create a market of low-cost surplus labor, cut down the competition for jobs and slots in desirable schools, and so on.

Yet, the legal system has yet to pronounce Latinos, definitively, a race entitled to sue for discrimination as such (at least in the absence of proof of local discrimination, see *Hernández*, supra). Might it one day do so? Consider the following relatively recent Supreme Court opinion suggesting that it might, and that one's race is subject to constant contestation, evolution, and litigation.

Saint Francis College v. Al–Khazraji
481 U.S. 604 (1987)

JUSTICE WHITE delivered the opinion of the Court.

Respondent, a citizen of the United States born in Iraq, was an associate professor at St. Francis College, one of the petitioners here. In January 1978, he applied for tenure; the Board of Trustees denied his request on February 23, 1978. He accepted a 1–year, nonrenewable contract and sought administrative reconsideration of the tenure decision, which was denied on February 6, 1979. He worked his last day at the college on May 26, 1979. In June 1979, he filed complaints with the Pennsylvania Human Relations Commission and the Equal Employment Opportunities Commission. The state agency dismissed his claim and the EEOC issued a right-to-sue letter on August 6, 1980.

On October 30, 1980, respondent filed a *pro se* complaint in the District Court alleging a violation of Title VII of the Civil Rights Act of 1964 and claiming discrimination based on national origin, religion, and/or race. Amended complaints were filed, adding claims under 42 U.S.C. §§ 1981, 1983, 1985(3), 1986, and state law. * * *

    * * *

Section 1981 provides:

> All persons within the jurisdiction of the United States shall have the same right in every State and Territory to make and enforce contracts, to sue, be parties, give evidence, and to the full and equal benefit of all laws and proceedings for the security of persons and property as is enjoyed by white citizens, and shall be subject to like punishment, pains, penalties, taxes, licenses, and exactions of every kind, and to no other.

Although § 1981 does not itself use the word "race," the Court has construed the section to forbid all "racial" discrimination in the making of private as well as public contracts. Petitioner college, although a private institution, was therefore subject to this statutory command. * * * The issue is whether respondent has alleged *racial* discrimination within the meaning of § 1981.

Petitioners contend that respondent is a Caucasian and cannot allege the kind of discrimination § 1981 forbids. Concededly, McDonald v. Santa Fe Trail Transportation Co., 427 U.S. 273 (1976), held that white persons could maintain a § 1981 suit; but that suit involved alleged discrimination against a white person in favor of a black, and petitioner submits that the section does not encompass claims of discrimination by one Caucasian against another. * * *

Petitioner's submission rests on the assumption that all those who might be deemed Caucasians today were thought to be of the same race when § 1981 became law in the 19th century; and it may be that a variety of ethnic groups, including Arabs, are now considered to be within the Caucasian race.[1] The understanding of "race" in the 19th century, however, was different. Plainly, all those who might be deemed Caucasian today were not thought to be of the same race at the time § 1981 became law.

In the middle years of the 19th century, dictionaries commonly referred to race as a "continued series of descendants from a parent who is called the *stock*," N. Webster, An American Dictionary of the English Language 666 (New York 1830) (emphasis in original), "[t]he lineage of

---

1. There is a common popular understanding that there are three major human races—Caucasoid, Mongoloid, and Negroid. Many modern biologists and anthropologists, however, criticize racial classifications as arbitrary and of little use in understanding the variability of human beings. It is said that genetically homogeneous populations do not exist and traits are not discontinuous between populations; therefore, a population can only be described in terms of relative frequencies of various traits. Clear-cut categories do not exist. The particular traits which have generally been chosen to characterize races have been criticized as having little biological significance. It has been found that differences between individuals of the same race are often greater than the differences between the "average" individuals of different races. These observations and others have led some, but not all, scientists to conclude that racial classifications are for the most part sociopolitical, rather than biological, in nature.

a family," 2 N. Webster, A Dictionary of the English Language 411 (New Haven 1841), or "descendants of a common ancestor," J. Donald, Chambers' Etymological Dictionary of the English Language 415 (London 1871). The 1887 edition of Webster's expanded the definition somewhat: "The descendants of a common ancestor; a family, tribe, people or nation, believed or presumed to belong to the same stock." N. Webster, Dictionary of the English Language 589 (W. Wheeler ed. 1887). It was not until the 20th century that dictionaries began referring to the Caucasian, Mongolian, and Negro races, 8 The Century Dictionary and Cyclopedia 4926 (1911), or to race as involving divisions of mankind based upon different physical characteristics. Webster's Collegiate Dictionary 794 (3d ed. 1916). Even so, modern dictionaries still include among the definitions of race "a family, tribe, people, or nation belonging to the same stock." Webster's Third New International Dictionary 1870 (1971); Webster's Ninth New Collegiate Dictionary 969 (1986).

Encyclopedias of the 19th century also described race in terms of ethnic groups, which is a narrower concept of race than petitioners urge. Encyclopedia Americana in 1858, for example, referred to various races such as Finns, gypsies, Basques, and Hebrews. The 1863 version of the New American Cyclopaedia divided the Arabs into a number of subsidiary races; represented the Hebrews as of the Semitic race, and identified numerous other groups as constituting races, including Swedes, Norwegians, Germans, Greeks, Finns, Italians, Spanish, Mongolians, Russians, and the like. The Ninth edition of the Encyclopedia Britannica [1878–1881] also referred to Arabs, Jews, and other ethnic groups such as Germans, Hungarians, and Greeks as separate races.

These dictionary and encyclopedic sources are somewhat diverse, but it is clear that they do not support the claim that for the purposes of § 1981, Arabs, Englishmen, Germans, and certain other ethnic groups are to be considered a single race. We would expect the legislative history of § 1981, which the Court held in *Runyon v. McCrary* had its source in the Civil Rights Act of 1866, 14 Stat. 27, as well as the Voting Rights Act of 1870, 16 Stat. 140, 144, to reflect this common understanding, which it surely does. The debates are replete with references to the Scandinavian races, Cong. Globe, 39th Cong., 1st Sess., 499 (1866) (remarks of Sen. Cowan), as well as the Chinese, id. at 523 (remarks of Sen. Davis), Latin, id. at 238 (remarks of Rep. Kasson during debate of home rule for the District of Columbia), Spanish, id. at 251 (remarks of Sen. Davis during debate of District of Columbia suffrage), and Anglo–Saxon races, id. at 542 (remarks of Rep. Dawson). Jews, ibid., Mexicans, see ibid. (remarks of Rep. Dawson), blacks, *passim*, and Mongolians, id. at 498 (remarks of Sen. Cowan), were similarly categorized. Gypsies were referred to as a race. Ibid. (remarks of Sen. Cowan). Likewise, the Germans:

> Who will say that Ohio can pass a law enacting that no man of the German race ... shall ever own any property in Ohio, or shall ever make a contract in Ohio, or ever inherit property in Ohio, or ever come into Ohio to live, or even to work? If Ohio may pass such a law, and exclude a German citizen ... because he is of the German

nationality or race, then may every other State do so. Id. at 1294 (remarks of Sen. Shellabarger).

There was a reference to the Caucasian race, but it appears to have been referring to people of European ancestry. Id. at 523 (remarks of Sen. Davis).

The history of the 1870 Act reflects similar understanding of what groups Congress intended to protect from intentional discrimination. It is clear, for example, that the civil rights sections of the 1870 Act provided protection for immigrant groups such as the Chinese. * * *

Based on the history of § 1981, we have little trouble in concluding that Congress intended to protect from discrimination identifiable classes of persons who are subjected to intentional discrimination solely because of their ancestry or ethnic characteristics. Such discrimination is racial discrimination that Congress intended § 1981 to forbid, whether or not it would be classified as racial in terms of modern scientific theory. The Court of Appeals was thus quite right in holding that § 1981, "at a minimum," reaches discrimination against an individual "because he or she is genetically part of an ethnically and physiognomically distinctive sub-grouping of *homo sapiens*." It is clear from our holding, however, that a distinctive physiognomy is not essential to qualify for § 1981 protection. If respondent on remand can prove that he was subjected to intentional discrimination based on the fact that he was born an Arab, rather than solely on the place or nation of his origin, or his religion, he will have made out a case under § 1981.

SECTION 4.   COLONIAL STATUS, REAL AND METAPHORICAL: PUERTO RICANS AND OTHER DESCENDANTS OF U.S. CONQUEST

Reread Part One on the history of Puerto Rico.

Some authorities consider that all or most U.S. Latinos living in the mainland are, in effect, an internal colony. See, e.g., Richard Delgado, *Rodrigo's Corrido: Race, Postcolonial Theory, and U. S. Civil Rights*, 60 Vand. L. Rev. 1691 (2007); Rodolfo Acuña, *Occupied America: A History of Chicanos* vii-ix (2d ed. 1981). These writers highlight the similarities between the status and treatment of Chicanos in the Southwest or Puerto Ricans living in Northeast cities to that of colonized people under French or English rule in Africa or India. These similarities include intentional destruction of culture and language; deprivation of legal and political rights; and appropriation of labor, especially of the dangerous, low-paid variety. See generally Chantal Thomas, *Critical Race Theory and Postcolonial Development Theory: Observations on Methodology*, 45 Vill. L. Rev. 1195 (2000); Ramón Grosfoguel, *Colonial Subjects: Puerto Ricans in a Global Perspective* (2003).

Puerto Ricans living in Puerto Rico are not just metaphorically colonized. They are an actual colony, with many of the classic incidents of such—inability to vote for the president, vice president, or their own representative in Congress, inability to qualify for certain federal benefits, and extreme poverty, all tolerated by a government that prides itself on freedom and political equality for all. See Part One (Puerto Ricans), as well as the periodic reports of the U.N. Special Committee on the Situation with Respect to the Implementation of the Granting of Independence to Countries and Peoples (describing progress toward the decolonization of entities such as Guam, Puerto Rico, and the Virgin Islands). See also Balzac v. Porto Rico, 258 U.S. 298 (1922) (on the territory's colonial status); Pedro A. Malavet, *America's Colony: The Political and Cultural Conflict Between the United States and Puerto Rico* (2004).

José Luis Morín
*Latino/a Rights and Justice in the United
States: Perspectives and Approaches*
25–28 (2004)

Notwithstanding Justice John Marshall Harlan's dissent in *Downes*, which maintained that colonies and colonial subjects run contrary to the very spirit and letter of the U.S. Constitution (Downes v. Bidwell, 182 U.S. 244, 380 (1901)), the *Insular Cases*, and even the Supreme Court's decision in *Johnson v. McIntosh*, have never been overturned. They remain binding precedents in U.S. law, an affirmation of Puerto Rico's colonial status and a confirmation of second-class legal status for Puerto Ricans in contravention of the universal prohibition against colonialism established under international law. Moreover, U.S. Supreme Court decisions of more recent years reaffirm the denial of equal protection under the U.S. Constitution to Puerto Ricans in cases that cite the *Insular Cases* as the legal precedent (see, e.g., Califano v. Torres, 435 U.S. 1 (1978); Harris v. Rosario, 446 U.S. 651 (1980)).

Not surprisingly, all political parties in Puerto Rico presently denounce Puerto Rico's ongoing colonial situation. They have also made their dissatisfaction with the enduring U.S. colonial scheme known to the United Nations. As a result, since the 1970s, the United Nations committee responsible for the implementation of the decolonization process has recognized repeatedly the Puerto Rican peoples' right to the exercise of self-determination under U.N. standards for decolonization, standards that the United States has failed to meet. Indeed, it is abundantly clear from the Congressional Record that labeling Puerto Rico a "commonwealth" in the 1950s was never meant to change the political, economic, and social relationship between the United States and Puerto Rico.

Congress's authority over the island nation and its peoples remains absolute, and thus it maintains Puerto Rico as a U.S. colony. The United States retains complete power to unilaterally nullify all or parts of the Puerto Rican Constitution. In fact, the U.S. Congress actually eliminated Article 2, Section 20 on economic and social rights of the 1952 Commonwealth Constitution, overriding the work of the Puerto Rican Constitutional Convention. Puerto Ricans do not share equal rights with U.S. citizens in the United States: they serve and die in U.S. wars, but cannot vote for the President who can send them into battle; U.S. laws apply to Puerto Rico without the consent of Puerto Ricans; Puerto Ricans have no say in treaties and foreign affairs that affect them; Puerto Ricans have no voting representation in the U.S. Congress; trade, shipping, immigration, and monetary policies are all controlled by the United States; U.S. federal courts operate in English, rather than in the native language of Puerto Rico; and the "commonwealth" status continues out of compliance with United Nations decolonization requirements. This situation has led former Chief Justice of Puerto Rico José Trías Monge to conclude that "[t]here is no known noncolonial relationship in the present world where one people exercises such vast, almost unbounded power over the government of another."

Why the United States maintains colonies in the face of the worldwide repudiation of colonialism in the post-World War II era becomes apparent when one considers the enormous benefits that accrue to the U.S. government and U.S. corporate interests. Net profits from Puerto Rico to U.S. corporations surpass the profits of all other industrial countries, including the United Kingdom, Germany and Japan. Puerto Rico serves as a captive market for U.S. goods; its population is a source of low-wage labor; 14 percent of the land is used for U.S. military bases; and Puerto Ricans can be readily drafted or they volunteer to serve and fight in the U.S. military.

Contrary to popular beliefs, Puerto Rico is not an example of U.S. magnanimity or a model for Third World development. Puerto Rico is an impoverished nation with 60 percent of its people living below the poverty line. According to Trías Monge,

> Per capita income in Puerto Rico is still only about one-third of that of the United States and half of Mississippi. In the Caribbean, eleven other areas enjoy a higher per capita income: the Cayman Islands, Aruba, Montserrat, the Bahamas, Martinique, the American Virgin Islands, the British Virgin Islands, the Netherlands Antilles, Guadeloupe, French Guiana, and Barbados. The per capita income of the poorest of these areas is 20 percent higher than that of Puerto Rico.

Notes and Questions

1. Many Puerto Ricans are unhappy with their current second-class status and demanding change and an island-wide referendum to determine the island's future. See, e.g., Pedro Malavet, *America's Colony*, supra; José Trías Monge, *Puerto Rico: The Trials of the Oldest Colony in the World* (1997). See also Himilce Novas, *Everything You Need to Know About Latino History* (rev. ed. 2008). According to Malavet, the three options for Puerto Rico include statehood, independence, and commonwealth status. How likely is it that the United States would grant Puerto Rico statehood, if the inhabitants of that island requested it? Bear in mind that Congress delayed

New Mexico's recognition as a state until 1912 when English speakers became a majority; before that time it was a mere territory. All of the other territories the United States acquired as a result of the war with Mexico, including California and Arizona, had English-speaking majorities and gained statehood much earlier.

2.　If Puerto Rico achieved independence from the United States, what would it gain, and what would it lose? See generally Sanford Levinson, *Why the Canon Should be Expanded to Include the* Insular Cases *and the Saga of American Expansionism*, 17 Const. Comm. 241 (2000); Frances Olsen, *Civil Disobedience on Vieques: How Nonviolence Defeated the U.S. Military*, 16 Fla. J. Int'l L. 547 (2004).

3.　Puerto Rico's poverty and school dropout rates, etc., are alarmingly high. But certain minority populations of the continental United States, such as inner-city blacks or Latinos in the Texas border shanty-towns ("colonias") exhibit similar dismal statistics. Does this strengthen the argument, mentioned earlier, that they, too, are, in effect, internal colonies of the United States? See also Silvio Torres Saillant & Ramona Hernández, *The Dominican Americans* (1998); Felix M. Padilla, *Puerto Rican Chicago* (1987).

SECTION 5.　LATINOS AND WHITENESS: THE "OTHER WHITE" STRATEGY AND HYPOCRITICAL ASSIGNMENT TO THE WHITE GROUP

Before Latinos achieved even the patchwork of legal protection discussed above, many courts considered them white. As a result, during the first several decades of the twentieth century, they could not sue for racial discrimination under the then-rudimentary civil rights laws and the Equal Protection Clause of the Fourteenth Amendment. See Steven H. Wilson, *Brown over "Other White": Mexican Americans' Legal Arguments and Litigation Strategy in School Desegregation Lawsuits*, 21 L. & Hist. Rev. 145 (2003); Neil Foley, *Becoming Hispanic: Mexican Americans and the Faustian Pact with Whiteness*, in *Reflexiones 1997: New Directions in Mexican American Studies* 53 (1998).

Latino lawyers would often play into this pretense. See Wilson, supra; Foley, supra. See also Ian F. Haney López, *White Latinos*, 6 Harv. Latino L. Rev. 1 (2003) (deploring tendency of some members of the Latino community to cling to whiteness).

Faced with a desegregation decree from a local court, Anglo school boards in the Southwest would sometimes simply transfer Mexican–American schoolchildren to the black dominated school and declare the resulting mix "integrated"—fifty percent black, and fifty percent "white" (that is, Mexican American). Meanwhile, the remaining schools became even more Anglo-dominated than before. By the mid–1950s, Latino litigators were having second thoughts about this strategy, and the civil rights revolution of the 1960s would spell its end.

Anglo-dominated jury commissioners would often do the same. See Sanchez v. State, 156 Tex.Crim. 468, 243 S.W.2d 700, 701 (1951) ("Mexican people ... are not a separate race but are white people of

Spanish descent ...''). See *Hernández v. Texas*, discussed supra this chapter and in Part One, Chapter 1, § 5, in which a Texas county had been excluding Mexican Americans from jury service for many years. When a Mexican–American defendant challenged this exclusion, the state responded that it considered members of his group white and hence he had received a trial by a jury of his peers, i.e., white people. Although *Hernández* halted this practice, nominally at least, in the jury-trial arena, it continued in other areas, such as school assignment practices. Ariela J. Gross, *"The Caucasian Cloak": Mexican Americans and the Politics of Whiteness in the Twentieth–Century Southwest*, 95 Geo L.J. 337 (2007); Daniel A. Rochmes, *Blinded by the White: Latino School Desegregation and the Insidious Allure of Whiteness*, 13 Tex. Hisp. J.L. & Pol'y 7 (2007).

Citing evidence of separate bathrooms and other facilities in the Texas county in question, Professor Gross writes that "the breakthrough in *Hernández* was the court's acceptance of ... (the) argument that Mexicans were treated as nonwhite by Anglos despite the fact that they were actually white." For a somewhat sympathetic interpretation of the other-white strategy, see Thomas A. Guglielmo, *Fighting for Caucasian Rights: Mexicans, Mexican Americans, and the Transnational Struggle for Civil Rights in World War II Texas*, 92 J. Am. Hist. 1212 (Mar. 2006) (rejecting the charge that litigators who pursued this strategy were sellouts or white wannabes and noting that they abandoned the strategy as soon as was practicable).

The "Other White" strategy used to combat segregation. Still, Mexican–American litigators were hesitant to give up a litigation strategy that, on occasion, actually worked. In the "other white" strategy, Mexican–American lawyers would confront a local judge with statistical evidence of discrimination against their clients. They would then insist that that discrimination had no basis in state law. A state's education code, for example, might provide for separate schools for Indian or Asian schoolchildren. And under Plessy v. Ferguson, 163 U.S. 537 (1896), black children could be assigned to separate schools, so long as they were equal to the white ones. See Wilson, *Brown over "Other White,"* supra.

But if nothing in the code specifically allowed for segregating Mexican schoolchildren, Latino litigators would challenge the segregation as, in effect, against a white group—and hence not allowable under the state's statutory law. Discrimination against those other groups (blacks, Indians, etc.) might be permissible, this argument seemed to say, but not against us. Needless to say, this approach was not calculated to build strong bonds between Latinos and African Americans. See Benjamin Marquez, *The Politics of Race and Assimilation: The League of United Latin American Citizens 1929–40*, 42 W. Pol. Q. 355 (1989); George A. Martinez, *Latinos, Assimilation and the Law: A Philosophical Perspective*, 20 Chicano–Latino L. Rev. 1 (1999).

For the view that many Latinos saw themselves as "off-white," or both white and nonwhite, see Laura E. Gómez, *Manifest Destinies: The*

Making of the Mexican American Race 158–61 (2007). For Gómez, Latino self-identification is a function of collective struggle, class and income differences, and the extent of racism directed against them or their children.

SECTION 6. LATINOS AND LEGAL INDETERMINACY

A tenet of both critical legal studies and critical race theory is legal indeterminacy—the notion that a court, by invoking suitable precedent, can make a case come out practically any way it wants. The law is so open-ended, in other words, that social and political preferences can tilt a case any way the judge wishes.

The following selections by legal scholar George Martinez argue that the history of Latino (specifically Mexican–American) litigation supplies positive proof of this thesis:

George A. Martinez
*The Legal Construction of Race: Mexican
Americans and Whiteness*
2 Harv. Latino L. Rev. 321, 322–23,
326–28, 332–38, 342–44 (1997)

During slavery, the racial divide between black and white became a line of protection from the threat of commodification: whiteness protected one against being an object of property. Even after slavery ended, it continued to be a valuable asset, carrying with it a set of assumptions, privileges, and benefits. Given this, it is hardly surprising that minorities have often sought to "pass" as white—i.e., present themselves as white persons. They did so because they thought that becoming white insured greater economic, political, and social security. Becoming white, they thought, meant gaining access to a panoply of public and private privileges, while insuring that one would avoid being the object of others' domination.

In light of the privileged status of whiteness, it is instructive to examine how legal actors—courts and others—constructed the race of Mexican Americans. * * * In *Inland Steel Co. v. Barcelona*, an Indiana appellate court addressed the question of whether Mexicans were white. The court noted that the *Encyclopedia Britannica* stated that approximately one-fifth of the inhabitants of Mexico are whites, approximately two-fifths Indians and the balance made up of mixed bloods, blacks, Japanese, and Chinese. Given this, the court held that a "Mexican" should not necessarily be found to be a white person.

The Texas courts also considered the same question. In *In re Rodriguez*, a Texas federal court addressed whether Mexicans were white for purposes of immigration. At that time, the federal naturalization laws required that an alien be white in order to become a citizen of the United States. The court stated that Mexicans would probably be considered non-white from an anthropological perspective, but went on to note that the United States had entered into certain treaties with Mexico. Those treaties expressly allowed Mexicans to become citizens of the United States. Thus, the court held that Congress must have intended that Mexicans were white within the meaning of the naturalization laws. *In re Rodriguez* reveals how racial categories can be constructed through the political process. Through the give and take of treaty making, Mexicans became "white."

Other cases show how politics operated to turn persons of mixed blood into whites or the opposite. In immigration cases, mixed race applicants often failed to establish their whiteness. For example, in *In re Camille*, the court held that the son of a white Canadian father and an Indian mother was non-white, and therefore not eligible to naturalize. Similarly, in *In re Young*, the son of a German father and a Japanese mother was not a white person within the meaning of the immigration laws. If these cases stand for the proposition that mixed race persons were not white, Mexicans—a mixture of Spanish and Indian—should not have counted as white. The treaties nevertheless operated to turn them into whites.

The issue of the race of Mexican Americans also arose in connection with school segregation. In *Independent School District v. Salvatierra*, plaintiffs sought to enjoin segregation of Mexican Americans in the city of Del Rio, Texas. There, the court treated Mexican Americans as white, holding that Mexican Americans could not be segregated from children of "other white races, merely or solely because they are Mexicans." Significantly, the court did permit segregation of Mexican Americans on the basis of linguistic difficulties and migrant farming patterns.

Mexican–American jury participation and exclusion also show how the race of Mexican Americans is constructed. For example, in *Hernández v. State*, a Mexican American had been convicted of murder. He sought to reverse his conviction on the ground that Mexican Americans had been excluded from the grand jury and the petit jury, relying on cases holding that exclusion of blacks from jury service violated due process and equal protection. The court recognized only two classes as falling within the guarantee of the Fourteenth Amendment: the white race and the black race. It went on to hold that Mexican Americans are white for purposes of the Fourteenth Amendment. The court reasoned that to hold that the members of the various groups comprising the white race must be represented on grand and petit juries would destroy the jury system. Since the juries that indicted and convicted the defendant were composed of members of his race—white persons—he had not been denied the equal protection of the laws.

* * *

On review, the United States Supreme Court also imposed a group definition on Mexican Americans. The court held in *Hernández v. Texas* that "persons of Mexican descent" are a cognizable group for equal protection purposes in areas where they were subject to local discrimination—but not otherwise. Defining Mexican Americans in terms of the existence of local discrimination hinders Mexican Americans in asserting their rights because not every plaintiff can afford the expense of obtaining expert testimony to prove the local prejudice.

Similarly, in *Lopez Tijerina v. Henry*, the court refused to allow Mexican Americans to define themselves as a group. Plaintiffs sought to bring a class action on behalf of a class of "Mexican Americans" in order to secure equal educational opportunity unity in local schools. The court rejected the claim for class representation, holding that the term "Mexican American" was too vague and failed adequately to define a class within the meaning of Rule 23 of the Federal Rules of Civil Procedure, governing class actions. Since the class was not adequately defined, the court dismissed the class action complaint.

Class actions permit a lawsuit to be brought by large numbers of persons whose interests are sufficiently related so that it is more efficient to adjudicate their rights in a single action. As such, it may represent the only viable procedure for people with small claims to vindicate their rights. The *Lopez Tijerina* case, then, seems to be an example of a court refusing to allow Mexican Americans to define themselves so as to resist oppression.

Subsequently, other courts permitted Mexican Americans to sue as a class under Rule 23 by distinguishing *Tijerina* under the *Hernández* rationale that local prejudice rendered the class sufficiently identifiable. Thus, the courts defined Mexican Americans in terms of local prejudice, a definition which, for the reasons discussed above, operated to the disadvantage of Mexican Americans in their efforts to assert their rights under Rule 23.

* * *

Federal agencies also constructed the race of Mexican Americans. The federal government has long compiled census data on persons of Mexican descent. In 1930, the Census Bureau made the first effort to identify Mexican Americans. The Bureau used the term "Mexican" to classify Mexican Americans, placing it under the rubric of "other races," which also included Indians, Blacks, and Asians. According to this definition, Mexican Americans were not considered "whites." Interestingly, the Mexican government and the United States Department of State both objected to the 1930 census definition of Mexican. Thus, in the 1950 census Mexican Americans were classified as whites. The Census Bureau experience is significant in that it presents another example of how politics have influenced the construction of race. * * *

White identity traditionally has served as a source of privilege and protection. Since the law usually recognized Mexican Americans as white, one might have expected that social action would have reflected the Mexican American's privileged legal status as white. That, however, was not the case. Legal recognition of the Mexican American as white had only a slight impact on conduct. Far from having a privileged status, Mexican Americans faced discrimination very similar to that experienced by African Americans. Excluded from public facilities and neighborhoods and the targets of racial slurs, Mexican Americans typically lived in one section of town because they were not permitted to rent or own property anywhere except in the "Mexican Colony." Segregated in public schools, Mexican Americans also faced significant discrimination in employment. Mexican Americans were earmarked for exclusive employment in the lowest brackets of employment and paid less than Anglo Americans for the same jobs. Moreover, law enforcement officials have committed widespread discrimination against Mexican Americans, arresting them on pretexts and meting out harassment and penalties disproportionately severe compared to those imposed on Anglos for the same acts. In all these respects, actual social behavior failed to reflect the legal norms that defined Mexican Americans as white. Although white as a matter of law, that law failed to provide Mexican Americans with a privileged status.

At one point, discrimination against Mexican Americans in Texas became so flagrant that the Mexican Ministry of Labor declared that Mexican citizens would not be allowed to go there. * * * In response, the Texas legislature, on May 6, 1943, passed a resolution that established as a matter of Texas public policy that all Caucasians were entitled to equal accommodations. Subsequently, Mexican Americans attempted to rely on the resolution and sought to claim one of the traditional benefits of whiteness—freedom from exclusion from public places. In *Terrell Wells Swimming Pool v. Rodriguez,* Jacob Rodriguez sought an injunction requiring a swimming pool operator to offer equal accommodations to Mexican Americans. Plaintiff argued that he could not be excluded from the pool on the basis of his Mexican ancestry because that would violate the public policy expressed in the resolution condemning discriminatory practices against all persons of the white race. The court refused to enforce the public policy on the ground that the resolution did not have the effect of a statute. Thus, Mexican Americans could not claim one of the most significant benefits of whiteness—freedom from exclusion from public places.

* * *

The legal construction of Mexican Americans as white thus stands as an irony—thoroughly at odds with the colonial discourses that developed in the American Southwest. As happened in other regions of the world the colonizers engaged in epistemic violence—i.e., produced modes of knowing that enabled and rationalized colonial domination from the standpoint of the West.

In sharp contrast to their legal construction as white, writers and other Anglo opinion-makers plainly constructed Mexican Americans as irreducibly Other. The historian David Weber writes:

Anglo Americans found an additional element to despise in Mexicans: racial mixture. American visitors to the Mexican frontier were nearly unanimous in commenting on the dark skin of the Mexican mestizos, who, it was generally agreed, had inherited the worst qualities of Spaniards and Indians to produce a "race" still more despicable than that of either parent.

Similarly, another commentator described how Anglo Americans drew a racial distinction between themselves and Mexican Americans:

Racial myths about the Mexicans appeared as soon as Mexicans began to meet Anglo American settlers in the early nineteenth century. The differences in attitudes, temperament and behavior were supposed to be genetic. It is hard now to imagine the normal Mexican mixture of Spanish and Indian as constituting a distinct "race," but the Anglo Americans of the Southwest defined it as such.

Likewise, the dean of Texas historians, Walter Prescott Webb, wrote:

Without disparagement it may be said that there is a cruel streak in the Mexican nature, or so the history of Texas would lead one to believe. This cruelty may be a heritage from the Spanish of the Inquisition; it may and doubtless should be attributed partly to the Indian blood.

Through this discourse on the Mexican American, Anglo Americans also reformulated their white selves. Anglo judges, as we have seen, did the same, ruling that Mexicans were co-whites when this suited the dominant group—and non-white when necessary to protect Anglo privilege and supremacy.

George A. Martinez
Legal Indeterminacy, Judicial Discretion and the
Mexican–American Litigation Experience: 1930–1980
27 U.C. Davis L. Rev. 555, 555–59, 611–18 (1994)

* * *

Legal theorists have argued that judicial decisions are often not logically compelled but instead the result of conscious or unconscious policy choices. Accordingly, one of my goals is to demonstrate that courts' decisions either for or against Mexican Americans were often not inevitable or compelled. In so doing, policy choices of the courts are revealed and brought to the surface.

Exposing the exercise of judicial discretion and the lack of inevitability in civil rights cases is important for two reasons. At one level, it helps reveal the extent to which the courts have helped or failed to help establish the rights of Mexican Americans. At another, exposing false necessity in judicial decision-making by explaining how the decision might have gone another way—i.e., offering a counterstory—is important because it may help break down barriers to racial reform. Drawing on critical race theory, legal pragmatism, and the philosophy of science, I argue that providing judges with counterstories or alternative perspectives on civil rights issues is one way to help them overcome the "unthinking conviction that [their] way of seeing the world is the only one—that the way things are is inevitable, natural, just, and best." By acknowledging their limited perspective, judges can avoid serious moral error and promote justice in civil rights cases.

[The author comprehensively reviews dozens of cases dealing with public swimming pools, school desegregation, land grants, and bilingual education, concluding as follows—*Eds.*]

The cases indicate that a number of courts generally exercised their discretion by taking a position against Mexican Americans on key issues. For example, in the effort to desegregate public accommodations, the courts ruled against Mexican Americans where they might have done otherwise. Likewise, the judiciary chose to reject Mexican–American efforts to reclaim land. Similarly, with respect to the effort to desegregate the public schools, most courts exercised their discretion to permit the segregation of Mexican Americans for "benign" reasons—e.g., linguistic difficulties—or because the segregation was "merely" de facto. Finally, with respect to bilingual education, courts generally exercised discretion to limit access to bilingual and bicultural education.

Exposing the exercise of judicial discretion is vitally important because it helps reveal the extent to which the courts have helped, or failed to help, establish the rights of Mexican Americans. In this regard, the inescapable conclusion is that courts could have done significantly more to vindicate justice on behalf of this group.

Critical race scholars have argued that civil rights gains are cyclical and tend to be cut back. This chapter provides new support for that argument. The cases reveal that the rights of Mexican Americans were often cut back through the use of judicial discretion. For example, in the area of school desegregation, the early cases held that Mexican Americans could not be segregated solely on the basis of race. That right, however, was immediately limited because most courts allowed the segregation of Mexican Americans for "benign" reasons, and school boards often justified segregation on that basis. Similarly, after the Supreme Court decision in *Brown v. Board of Education*, most courts narrowly interpreted *Brown* to bar only de jure segregation. Thus, the Court's refusal to bar de facto segregation limited the rights of Mexican Americans. Finally, in the area of bilingual education, the courts construed earlier cases so as to limit the right to bilingual education.

Important as these conclusions are, they nevertheless hold out the hope of racial reform. Exposing the lack of inevitability in civil rights decision-making may help break down barriers to racial reform. Critical race scholars have argued that a significant barrier to racial reform is the majoritarian mindset. One has described this mind set as "the bundle of presuppositions, received wisdom, and shared understandings against a background of which legal [decision-making] takes place."

The view that judicial decision-making is highly influenced by the perspective and preconceptions of the judge, and that the perspective of the dominant group may present a barrier to racial reform, finds substantial support in the recent revival of pragmatism in legal philosophy. Pragmatists treat "thinking as contextual and situated." Thinking is "always embodied in practices—habits and patterns of perceiving and conceiving." Thus, pragmatists have recognized that one cannot view the world except through one's preconceptions. Applying this notion to legal decision-making, they have emphasized the importance of context and perspective to the act of judging. Significantly, pragmatists also have recognized that the dominant perspective can stand in the way of racial reform. Both critical race scholars and pragmatists offer a similar explanation for how this happens. The general idea is that the dominant perspective or mind set makes current social and legal arrangements seem fair and natural. Bringing this mind set to the bench, judges may commit moral error in civil rights cases because narrow habits of perceiving lead them to believe that the way things are is inevitable or just.

One way to help judges break down mind set, broaden their perspectives, and promote justice in civil rights cases, is to provide counterstories—i.e., explain how decisions were not inevitable. Through this process judges can "overcome ethnocentrism and the unthinking conviction that [their] way of seeing the world is the only one—that the way things are is inevitable, natural, just, and best" and thereby avoid moral error when deciding any civil rights case. Similarly, pragmatists have stressed that justice may be advanced only if judges try to grasp the world from perspectives that run counter to the dominant one. As Martha Minow has explained, the effort to take the perspective of another may help us see that our perspective is limited and that the status quo is not inevitable or fair. To break down narrow habits of perceiving that stand in the way of racial reform, lawyers and activists must stand ready to offer alternative perspectives or counterstories that explain how decisions were not inevitable.

Some commentators have questioned whether counterstories can transform the consciousness of the dominant group. Contrary to those commentators, however, the idea that generating alternative visions of reality can advance racial reform finds important support in the philosophy of science and contemporary philosophy of law. In this regard, it is helpful to consider Thomas Kuhn's classic account of scientific change. Kuhn argued that during periods of normal science, perception is dependent on conventional "paradigms." According to Kuhn, a scientific revolution occurs when there is a transition from one paradigm to another. Paradigm changes cause scientists to see the world differently. At times of scientific revolution, then, scientists experience shifts of perception—the scientists' perception of their environment must be reeducated. According to Kuhn, the transition between competing paradigms is a conversion experience that cannot be forced by logic.

Applying these notions to judicial decision-making, one leading pragmatist and philosopher of law, Judge Richard Posner, argues that major changes in law often result from a similar conversion process. Such conversion results from a perceptual shift where one comes to see the world differently. According to Judge Posner, this process explains the major shifts that have occurred in law, including the expansion and recognition of civil rights. Thus, the key turning points in American law simply reflect changing outlooks. Judges and lawyers began to look at legal doctrine in a new way. Providing judges with alternative perspectives or counterstories may help stimulate a paradigm shift in the area of race.

Beyond this, exposing the exercise of discretion through counterstories is one way to help insure that the Mexican–American experience is reflected in legal discourse. In this regard, feminists have argued that women's experience has not been recognized by the law. To solve the problem of women's exclusion from legal discourse, Robin West has suggested that women must flood the legal market with their own stories. In this way, legal discourse is forced to consider the perspective of women. For similar reasons, critical race scholars have emphasized the importance of telling the silenced stories and unrecorded perspectives of outsider groups. Thus, offering counterstories is one way to help insure that legal discourse takes accounts of the Mexican–American experience.

Finally, exposing the lack of inevitability in judicial decision-making may also promote a renewed sense of community. * * * As Richard Rorty has explained, when the contingent character of human projects is recognized, "[o]ur identification with our community—our society, our political tradition, our intellectual heritage—is heightened." This occurs "when we see this community as ours rather than nature's, shaped rather than found, one among many which men have made." Similarly, once the contingent character of judicial decision-making is fully recognized, it may generate a renewed sense of community—the community may be viewed as ours rather than nature's. With luck and effort, one day Mexicans and other outsiders will take their rightful place as full members of that community.

Notes and Questions

1. Is legal reasoning really indeterminate? Could a determined judge or a gifted defense lawyer make any case—even a simple speeding ticket—come out either way?

2. Martinez, in the two above selections, implies that the answer is yes, and that American courts ruled that Latinos were white when this was necessary to saddle them with some disadvantage. Conversely, they ruled that they were non-white when this was necessary for the very same purpose.

3. If this was once true, is it true today? See Soberal–Perez v. Heckler, 717 F.2d 36 (2d Cir. 1983), *cert. denied*, 466 U.S. 929 (1984) (holding that language discrimination taking the form of failure to provide Social Security information in Spanish does not constitute discrimination against an ethnic group—only a language group); Espinoza v. Farah Manuf. Co., Inc., 414 U.S. 86 (1973) (interpreting national origin discrimination narrowly under Section 1981).

Chapter 5

CULTURE AND IDENTITY

The legal system, of course, is not the only means by which Latino identity receives shape and content. Other forces are: choice; voluntary or coerced assimilation; racial mixture, intermarriage, and Indianism or mestizaje; and popular media and stereotypes (see Part Six: Cultural Stereotypes and Hate Speech). This chapter discusses some of these forces.

SECTION 1. CHOICE

Does one have a choice to be a Latino? Suppose one changes one's name and mode of dress, and refuses to speak Spanish. Is one then not a Latino? Or, suppose a white-looking person with a Latina mother one day decides to adopt a hyphenated last name, improve his or her Spanish, and identify with the group. Does that person become a Latino/a?

Ian F. Haney López
The Social Construction of Race:
Some Observations on Illusion, Fabrication, and Choice
29 Harv. C.R.-C.L. L. Rev. 1, 39–50 (1994)

THE MEAN STREETS OF SOCIAL RACE

The literature of minority writers provides some of the most telling insights into, and some of the most confused explorations of, race in the United States. Piri Thomas's quest for identity, recorded in *Down These Mean Streets*, fits squarely within this tradition of insight and confusion. Thomas describes his racial transformation, which is both willed and yet not willed, from a Puerto Rican into someone Black. Dissecting his harrowing experiences, piercing perceptions, and profound misapprehensions offers a way to disaggregate the daily technology of race. In the play of race, chance, context, and choice overlap and are inseverable. Nevertheless, I distinguish and explain these terms in order to explore the thesis that a race is best thought of as a group of people loosely bound together by historically contingent, socially significant elements of their morphology and/or ancestry.

CHANCE

The first terms of importance in the definition of race I advance are "morphology" and "ancestry." These fall within the province of chance, by which I mean coincidence, something not subject to human will or effort, insofar as we have no control over what we look like or to whom we are born. Chance, because of the importance of morphology and ancestry, may seem to occupy almost the entire geography of race. Certainly for those who subscribe to notions of biological race, chance seems to account for almost everything: one is born some race and not another, fated to a particular racial identity, with no human intervention possible. For those who believe in biological race, race is destiny. However, recognizing the social construction of race reduces the province of chance. The role of chance in determining racial identity is significantly smaller than one might initially expect.

The random accidents of morphology and ancestry set the scene for Piri Thomas's racial odyssey. Seeking better prospects during the depression, Thomas's parents moved from Puerto Rico to Spanish Harlem, where Piri and his three siblings were born. Once in the United States, however, the family faced the peculiar American necessity of defining itself as White or Black. To be White would afford security and a promising future; to be Black would portend exclusion and unemployment. The Thomas family—hailing from Puerto Rico of mixed Indian, African, and European antecedents—considered themselves White and pursued the American dream, eventually moving out to the suburbs in search of higher salaries and better schools for the children. Yet in their bid for Whiteness, the family gambled and lost, because even while the three other children and Piri's mother were fair, Piri and his father were dark skinned. Babylon, Long Island proved less forgiving of Piri's dark skin than Spanish Harlem did. In the new school, the pale children scoffed at Piri's claim to be Puerto Rican rather than Black, taunting Piri for "passing for Puerto Rican because he can't make it for white," and proclaiming, "[t]here's no difference . . . [h]e's still black." Piri's morphology shattered not only the family's White dream, but eventually the family itself.

While the family insisted on their own Whiteness as the crucial charm to a fulfilling life in the United States, Thomas, coming of age amid the racial struggles of the 1950s and himself the victim of White violence, fought the moral hypocrisy he saw in their claim to Whiteness. Piri unyieldingly attacked the family's delusion, for example challenging with bitterness and frustration the Whiteness of his younger brother José:

José's face got whiter and his voice angrier at my attempt to take away his white status. He screamed out strong: "I ain't no nigger!

You can be if you want to be.... But—I—am—white! And you can go to hell!''

But Piri persisted in attacking the family, one at a time:

"And James is blanco, too?" I asked quietly.

"You're damn right."

"And Poppa?"

... "Poppa's the same as you," he said, avoiding my eyes, "Indian."

"What kinda Indian," I said bitterly. "Caribe? Or maybe Borinquen? Say, José, didn't you know the Negro made the scene in Puerto Rico way back? And when the Spanish spics ran outta Indian coolies, they brought them big blacks from you know where. Poppa's got *moyeto* [Black] blood. I got it. Sis got it. James got it. And, mah deah brudder, you-all got it.... It's a played-out lie about me—us—being white."

The structure of this painful exchange casts a bright light on the power that morphology and ancestry wield in defining races. In the racially charged United States, skin color or parentage often makes one's publicly constructed race inescapable.

Piri's dark features and José's light looks are chance in the sense that neither Piri nor José could choose their faces, or indeed their ancestry. Still, what we look like is not entirely accident; to some extent looks can be altered in racially significant ways. In this respect, consider the unfortunate popularity of hair straightening, blue contact lenses, and skin lighteners. Most importantly, however, though morphology and ancestry remain largely matters of chance, those aspects of identity gain their importance on the social, not physical, plane. Consider, now, the operation of context.

CONTEXT

Given Piri's status as a Puerto Rican with ancestral ties to three continents, there is a certain absurdity to his insistence that he is Black. This absurdity highlights the importance of context to the creation of races. Context is the social setting in which races are recognized, constructed, and contested; it is the "circumstances directly encountered, given and transmitted from the past." At the meta level, context includes both ideological and material components, such as entrenched cultural and customary prejudices, and also maldistributed resources, marketplace inequalities, and skewed social services. These inherited structures are altered and altered again by everything from individual actors and community movements to broad-based changes in the economic, demographic, and political landscape. At the same time, context also refers to highly localized settings. The systems of meaning regarding morphology and ancestry are inconstant and unstable. These systems shift in time and space, and even across class and educational levels, in ways that give to any individual different racial identities depending upon her shifting location. I refer to context in order to explain the phrases "historically contingent" and "socially significant" in the definition of race proffered at the start.

Changes in racial identity produced by the shifting significance of morphology and ancestry are often profoundly disconcerting, as Piri Thomas discovered. In Puerto Rico, prevailing attitudes toward racial identity situated the Thomases, as a family not light enough to be Spanish but not so dark as to be black, comfortably in the mainstream of society. They encountered no social or economic disadvantages as a result of their skin color, and were not subjected to the prejudice that usually accompanies rigid racial constructs. However, the social ideology of race in the United States—more specifically, in New York in the late 1950s—was firmly rooted in the proposition that exactly two biological races existed. Such an ideology forced the Thomas family to define themselves as either White or Black. In the context confronting Piri, "[i]t would seem indeed that . . . white and black represent the two poles of a world, two poles in perpetual conflict: a genuinely Manichean concept of the world." Once in the United States, Thomas came to believe that he and his family were Black as a biological fact, irrespective of their own dreams, desires, or decisions. Yet, Thomas was not Black because of his face or parents, but because of the social systems of meaning surrounding these elements of his identity.

Consider how Thomas came to believe in his own Blackness. In a chapter entitled "How to be a Negro without Really Trying," Thomas recalls how he and his fair-skinned Puerto Rican friend Louie applied for a sales job. Though the company told Thomas they would call him back, they hired Louie to start Monday morning. Thomas's reflections bear repeating:

> I didn't feel so much angry as I did sick, like throwing-up sick. Later, when I told this story to my buddy, a colored cat, he said, "Hell, Piri . . . a Negro faces that all the time."
>
> "I know that," I said, "but I wasn't a Negro then. I was still only a Puerto Rican."

Episodes of discrimination drove Piri towards a confused belief that he was Black. Aching to end the confusion, Piri traveled to the South, where he hoped to find out for sure whether his hair, his skin, and his face somehow inextricably tied him, a Puerto Rican, to Black America. Working in the merchant marine between Mobile, New Orleans, and Galveston, Piri experienced firsthand the nether world of White supremacy, and the experience confirmed his race: Bullied by his White bosses, insulted by White strangers, confronted at every turn by a White racial etiquette of violence, Thomas accepted his own Blackness. "It was like Brew said," he reflected after his time in the South, "any language you talk, if you're black, you're black." Suffering under the lash of White racism, Thomas decided he was Black. Thomas's Blackness did not flow from his morphology but from traveling the mean streets of racial segregation. His dislocations suggest a spatial component to racial identities, an implication confirmed in Thomas's travel from Spanish Harlem, where he was Puerto Rican, to Long Island, where he was accused of trying to pass, to the South, where he was Black.

Piri and his family were far from the first to face the Manichean choice between White or Black. The Chinese, whose population in the United States rose fifteenfold to 105,465 in the twenty years after 1850, were also initially defined in those stark terms. Thus in Los Angeles circa 1860 the Chinese area downtown was called "Nigger Alley." During their first years in the United States, as Ronald Takaki observes, "[r]acial qualities that had been assigned to blacks became Chinese characteristics." Not only were the supposed degenerate moral traits of Blacks transferred wholesale to the Chinese, but in a fascinating display of racist imagination, Whites also saw a close link between Black and Chinese morphology. Takaki cites a commentator who argued that Chinese physiognomy indicated "but a sight removal from the African race," and he reprints a startling cartoon contrasting Anglo Uncle Sam with a Chinese vampire replete with slanted eyes, but also with very dark skin, woolly hair, a flat nose, and thick lips.

In California, where the racial imagination included Mexicans and Indians as well as Blacks, Chinese were considered not only in terms of Blackness but also in terms of every non-White race, every rejected and denigrated Other. This point furnishes yet more evidence for the theory that racial identity is defined by its social context. Consider the 1879 play *The Chinese Must Go* by Henry Grimm of San Francisco. Notice the language Grimm ascribes to the Chinese characters, discussing, predictably, their nefarious anti-American plot to destroy White labor through hard work:

> *Ah Choy:* By and by white man catchee no money; Chinaman catchee heap money; Chinaman workee cheap, plenty work; white man workee dear, no work—sabee?

> *Sam Gin:* Me heep sabee.

The Chinese in this Grimm play speak in the language that Whites associated with Indians and Mexicans, making Sam Gin sound remarkably like Tonto playing out the Lone Ranger's racial delusions. Thus, the Chinese were assigned not only their own peculiar stereotypes, like a fiendish desire to work for low wages, but also the degenerate characteristics of all the minorities loathed by Whites. Not coincidentally, three years after Grimm's play, the United States passed its first immigration law: The 1882 Chinese Exclusion Act. In a telling example of law reifying racist hysteria, and Supreme Court upheld the Chinese Exclusion Act in part by citing the threat posed by the Chinese to White labor. The first Chinese, like the Thomas family nearly a century later, entered a society fixated on the idea of race and intent on forcing new immigrants into procrustean racial hierarchies.

The racial fate of Piri and the Chinese turned to a large extent on the social setting into which they immigrated. That setting provides the social meanings attached to our faces and forebears, and for this reason I write that races are groups of people bound together by historically contingent, socially significant elements of their morphology and/or ancestry. A race is not created because people share just any characteristic, such as height or hand size, or just any ancestry, for example Yoruba or Yugoslav. Instead, it is the social significance attached to certain features, like our faces, and to certain forebears, like Africans, which defines races. Context superimposed on chance largely shapes races in the United States.

Choice in Context

Piri's belief that he is Black, and his brother José's belief in his own Whiteness, can in some sense be attributed to the chance of their respective morphology and the context of their upbringing. Yet, to attribute Thomas's racial identity only to chance and context grossly oversimplifies his Blackness. Thomas's father shared not only his social context, but his dark looks as well, making context and chance equal between them. Nevertheless, his father insisted on his Whiteness, and explained this decision to Piri as follows:

> I ain't got one colored friend ... at least one American Negro friend. Only dark ones I got are Puerto Ricans or Cubans. I'm not a stupid man. I saw the look of white people on me when I was a young man, when I walked into a place where a dark skin isn't supposed to be. I noticed how a cold rejection turned into an indifferent acceptance when they heard my exaggerated accent. I can remember the time when I made my accent heavier, to make me more of a Puerto Rican than the most Puerto Rican there ever was. I wanted a value on me, son.

Thomas's father consciously exaggerated his Puerto Rican accent to put distance between himself and Black Americans. Thomas himself also made conscious and purposeful decisions, choices that in the end made him Black. As Henry Louis Gates argues, "one must *learn* to be 'black' in this society, precisely because 'blackness' is a socially produced category."

Choice composes a crucial ingredient in the construction of racial identities and the fabrication of races. Racial choices occur on mundane and epic levels, for example in terms of what to wear or when to fight; they are made by individuals and groups, such as people deciding to pass or movements deciding to protest; and the effects are often minor though sometimes profound, for instance, slightly altering a person's affiliation or radically remaking a community's identity. Nevertheless, in every circumstance choices are exercised not by free agents or autonomous actors, but by people who are compromised and constrained by the social context. Choice, explains Angela Harris, is not uncoerced choice, "freely given, but a 'contradictory consciousness' mixing approbation and apathy, resistance and resignation." Nevertheless, in racial matters we constantly exercise choice, sometimes in full awareness of our compromised position, though most often not.

Perhaps the most graphic illustration of choice in the construction of racial identities comes in the context of passing. Passing—the ability of individuals to change race—powerfully indicates race's chosen nature. Not infrequently someone Black through the social construction of their ancestry is physically indistinguishable from someone White. Consider Richard Wright's description of his grandmother in *Black Boy*: "My grandmother was as nearly white as a Negro can get without being white, which means that she was white." Given the prevalent presumption of essential, easily recognized phenotypical differences, light-skinned Blacks exist at an ambiguous and often unacknowledged racial border between White and Black. Those in this liminal space often respond along a range from some few who cross the established color line by "passing" to those who identify strongly with their Black status.

For most people, the pervasive social systems of meaning that attach to morphology ensure that passing is not an option. Moreover, for those who do jump races, the psychological dislocations required—suspending some personal dreams, for example childbirth; renouncing most family ties, for instance foregoing weddings and funerals; and severing all relations with the community, for example, ending religious and civic affiliations—are brutal and severe. In addition, because of the depth of racial animosity in this society, passing may only succeed in distancing one from her community, not in gaining her full acceptance among Whites. In this sense, recall the words of Thomas's father: "I noticed how a cold rejection turned into an indifferent acceptance when they heard my exaggerated accent." Nevertheless, some people do choose to jump races, and their ability to do so dramatically demonstrates the element of choice in the micromechanics of race.

Passing demonstrates not only the power of racial choice, however, but the contingency of the choices people make, thereby reinforcing the point that choices are made in specific contexts. Choices about racial identity do not occur on neutral ground, but instead occur in the violently racist context of American society. Though the decision to pass may be made for many reasons, among these the power of prejudice and self-hate cannot be denied. Thomas's younger brother José reveals the racist hate within him in the same instant that he claims to be White. José shouts at Piri: "I ain't black, damn you! Look at my hair. It's almost blond. My eyes are blue, my nose is straight. My motherfuckin' lips are not like a baboon's ass. My skin is white. White, goddamit! White!"

José's comments are important, if painful to repeat, because they illustrate that a person's choice in the matter of race may be fatally poisoned by ambient racist antipathies. Nevertheless, notice that the context in which passing occurs constantly changes. For example, it may be that in the contemporary context passing as White increasingly does not in fact require that one look White. Recently, many Anglos, committed to the pseudo-integrationist idea that ignoring races equals racial enlightenment, have seemingly adopted the strategy of pretending that the minorities they are friendly with are White. Consider the words of a

White Detroit politician: "I seldom think of my girlfriend, Kathy, as black.... A lot of times I look at her and it's as if she is white; there's no real difference. But every now and then, it depends on what she is wearing and what we're doing, she looks very ethnic and very Black. It bothers me. I don't like it. I prefer it when she's a regular, normal, everyday kind of person." Even so, passing may be far less common today than it was a hundred years ago. One observer estimates that in the half-century after the Civil War, as many as 25,000 people a year passed out of the Black race. The context in which passing occurs constantly changes, altering in turn the range of decisions individuals face.

Despite the dramatic evidence of choice passing provides, by far the majority of racial decisions are of a decidedly less epic nature. Because race in our society infuses almost all aspects of life, many daily decisions take on racial meanings. For example, seemingly inconsequential acts like listening to rap and wearing hip hop fashion constitute a means of racial affiliation and identification. Many Whites have taken to listening to, and some to performing, rap and hip hop. Nevertheless, the music of the inner city remains Black music. Rapping, whether as an artist or audience member, is in some sense a racial act. So too are a myriad of other actions taken every day by every person, almost always without conscious regard for the racial significance of their choices. It is here, in deciding what to eat, how to dress, whom to befriend, and where to go, rather than in the dramatic decision to leap races, that most racial choices are rendered. I do not suggest that these common acts are racial choices because they are taken with a conscious awareness of their racial implications, or because they compel complete shifts in racial identity. Rather, these are racial choices in their overtones or subtext, because they resonate in the complex of meanings associated with race. Given the thorough suffusion of race throughout society, in the daily dance of life we cannot avoid making racially meaningful decisions.

[Eds. In other parts of his article, Professor Haney López applies his thesis directly to Latinos.]

Luis Ángel Toro
"A People Distinct from Others": Race and Identity in Federal Indian Law and the Hispanic Classification in OMB Directive No. 15
26 Tex. Tech. L. Rev. 1219, 1260–62, 1271–72 (1995)

Two Chicano Examples

A Mexican couple immigrates to the United States and has children. They receive a Census form in the mail and set about determining their own and their children's racial identity. Looking at the racial categories, the couple sees none that describe them. They do not view themselves as American Indians but as *mestizos*, persons of mixed European and indigenous heritage. They are not enrolled members of a recognized tribe, nor are they identified as Indians in the community in which they live. By the same token, neither are they identified as whites. In the "Hispanic origin" question, the couple sees "Mexican, Mexican American, or Chicano" specifically listed as a "Hispanic" group. They identify themselves as part of that group and as being of "Other" race on the race question.

This couple might identify their children in the same manner. Alternatively, they might believe that a "Mexican or Mexican American" is only someone who was born in Mexico. As immigrants, they may not be familiar with the term "Chicano." Since their children were born in the U.S., they answer the Hispanic origin question in the negative. Knowing that there are millions of people like their children in this country, and believing that there must be some place on the Census form for them, they think again about the race question. Obviously, their children are not white: Every day they face the avoidance behaviors and "microaggressions" exhibited by whites, designed to remind them that they are not part of that group. They do not believe that their children are part of the "Black" or "Asian/Pacific Islander" groups, so they think again about the American Indian category. Perhaps aware of the one drop rule that, at least culturally, defines as Black any person with any known African ancestor or trace of apparent African ancestry, they conclude that "community recognition" as Indian means being treated as nonwhite on the basis of apparent indigenous ancestry. Therefore, they mark their children as members of the "American Indian or Alaskan Native" race.

Now, suppose that a fourth generation Chicano is filling out a Census form. Spiritually uplifted by the cultural pride inherent in the concept of Aztlan [Eds. A mythical land from which all members of La Raza—the Mexican race—came], he identifies himself racially as " 'American Indian' " but answers "yes" to the Hispanic origin question, marking the "Mexican, Mexican American, or Chicano" box. To the respondent, this seems like a decent reflection of his *mestizo* identity. To the Census Bureau, it is a wrong answer.

Suppose now that this same fourth generation Chicano is responding to a question under the combined race/ethnic short format permitted under Office of Management and Budget (OMB) Directive No. 15. Choosing between the selections, "White, Hispanic" and "American Indian" is easy. The respondent selects "American Indian" as the response, because he has never been treated as a white person in his community, because "Hispanic" seems an inaccurate description of a Chicano culture that has a strong indigenous influence, and because in physical appearance, i.e., "racially," the respondent is far closer to being a Native American than a European.

       * * *

SOME GUIDELINES FOR REFORM

Federal Indian law, or more accurately, the indigenous traditions that the law has addressed, provides the solution to the dilemma the

OMB faces. By illustrating alternatives to bloodline as the touchstone of identity, and by recognizing "community identification," federal Indian law provides an alternate means of classifying cultural identity that does not depend on an inquiry into genealogy. The best solution to the dilemma revealed by the problems inherent in the "Hispanic" classification is for the government to *abandon the outdated racial ideology embodied in Directive No. 15 and replace it with questions designed to determine an individual's membership in a socially constructed, cultural subgroup*. These cultural subgroups, not defined by reference to a person's bloodline, would be familiar to most Americans: Chicanos or Mexican Americans, Blacks or African Americans, Korean Americans, and so on. Members of these groups recognize each other as sharing a common history and vocabulary of experience, even as they remain internally divided by class, gender, sexual orientation, and political belief—factors that Directive No. 15 does not attempt to measure.

Since the agency cannot grant formal, political recognition of the type that led the Supreme Court to permit the indigenous people such as the Shawnee to escape state taxation, the OMB would inquire into social interaction to determine whether the subgroup is generally recognized in society as a "people distinct from others." The agency would have to undertake a detailed survey of American culture to determine exactly how people identify themselves and how they are recognized in order to create a framework of socially recognized ethnic or cultural subgroups. The agency should give priority to group self-identification over outsider identification because outsiders may tend to lump together different groups based upon presumptions of shared characteristics of the groups. This tendency is illustrated by the way the Asian/Pacific Islander groups and the Hispanic groups are combined.

More would be gained than simply eradicating the classical scheme of racial hierarchy from U.S. law. When an individual's membership in a cultural subgroup is legally significant, the law should not be hindered by a classification scheme that misstates the person's cultural identity, nor should the collection of accurate statistics be hampered by a classification scheme that serves only to confuse and mislead those attempting to classify themselves on a government form.

Even in a regime that recognizes only the rights of individuals, minority groups need accurate definition. If the purpose of a given statute is to remedy past discrimination, the different histories of various groups might justifiably lead to different types of remedies. If the purpose of a statute is to assist a racially subordinated cultural community in building its own institutions, as with the Minority Business Enterprise (MBE) programs, such a goal is subverted when members of one group are permitted to masquerade as members of another and to hijack the meager resources allotted to these programs. If the purpose is simply to monitor the health of American society, it does not help to deny divisions in society that in fact exist.

Notes and Questions

1.   How does choice, by self or others, play a part in establishing one's racial identity? See, e.g., Kevin R. Johnson, *How Did You Get to be Mexican: A White/Brown Man's Search for Identity* (1999). Can society sometimes punish Latinos who choose to flaunt their Latinicity too openly? See People v. Zammora, 66 Cal.App.2d 166, 152 P.2d 180 (1944) ("Sleepy Lagoon" case which led, a short time later, to the Zoot Suit riots in which roving bands of servicemen and Anglo toughs beat East L.A. Latino youths wearing distinctive clothing).

2.   What role do Haney López and Toro allow for culture in determining racial identity? On the racialization of minority groups in California, see Tomás Almaguer, *Racial Fault Lines: The Historical Origins of White Supremacy in California* (1994).

3.   Related to choice is the role of struggle and resistance. Some scholars hold that the primary experience by which a group forges identity is struggle, particularly against oppression and racism. See, e.g., Ian F. Haney López, *Racism on Trial: The Chicano Fight for Justice* 250 (2003), writing that "injustice creates race" and that the Brown Power era of the 1960s gave rise to a new identity in many Latinos who became self-aware and politicized in response to police brutality and insensitivity on the part of school authorities. See also *Oscar "Zeta" Acosta, The Uncollected Works* (Ilan Stavans ed., 1996) (excerpted in Part Nine infra). Placing this key moment even earlier in time is Richard Delgado, *Rodrigo and Revisionism: Relearning the Lessons of History*, 99 Nw. U. L. Rev. 805 (2005).

4.   For examples of early Latino resistance, much antedating the sixties, see, e.g., Mary Romero, *El Paso Salt War: Mob Action or Political Struggle*, 16 Aztlan: Int'l. J. Chicano Stud. Res. 119 (1985); Rodolfo Acuña, *Occupied America: A History of Chicanos* 76, 96–97 (5th ed. 2004) (discussing Las Gorras Blanca, "the white caps'" role in reclaiming New Mexico land rights and protesting cultural co-optation in the nineteenth century). See also Part Nine: Rebellious Lawyering.

SECTION 2.   MULTIPLE IDENTITY

Can one be a Latino/a and something else? Are the major racial boxes, such as black, white, American Indian, and Asian, that society uses to categorize individuals and that individuals use to identify themselves, hermetically sealed? What about someone who is both Latino/a and female, or gay, or a single working mother? What is that person's identity? Is it single or multiple?

Leslie G. Espinoza
Multi-Identity: Community and Culture
2 Va. J. Soc. Pol'y & L. 23, 23–30, 32–34, 37–41 (1994)

American society forces individuals to label themselves by race and gender. Not surprisingly, race and gender are the categories that correlate to power. A person's race and gender correlate to the likelihood that one will have educational opportunity, be in a particular income class, be in prison, or be the victim of a violent crime. Race and gender identity are the ways in which we are taught to articulate ourselves.

Multi-identity is not an accepted concept in dominant discourse. That discourse is about being "for us or against us," a cowboy or an Indian, an American or an alien, a woman or one of the boys, black or white, Mexican or white, Asian or white, Other or white. The politics of dichotomous categorical identity require individuals to be placed into or to be forced to choose one particular defining identity. Once placed in that category, the individual is assumed to possess all the characteristics of that category, good and bad. Furthermore, that category is understood by its opposition to another category.

Understanding personal identity, however, often requires the expression of multiple and distinct defining categories and the recognition of a unifying concept—the individual person. Identity may thus seem a paradox. How can there be group identity where each individual is an amalgam of unique characteristics, where each community and culture is a mix? The tension between group and individual difference has caused trouble between those with the power to put others into categories such as race, gender, or sexual preference, and those individuals pushed into socially constructed group identities that are both overinclusive and underinclusive. The choice is to assimilate or to be pushed into some distinct category of "other," whether it fits or not. This neat, blanket packaging of people both reflects and perpetuates current power structures. Of course, in reality, most individual outsiders are comfortable with the messy ambiguity of identity—when we are not thinking about it. When we try to counter the socially imposed categories and the oppression they represent, we find that we lack a language to express that which we have learned through experience.

I am a Mexican, Irish, Jewish, Woman, Heterosexual, Aunt, Law Professor, Californian, Bostonian, Tucsonian, middle child, professional; multi-identity is something I have thought about at length. So much so that often when I try to talk about it, my thoughts seem to all come out in an analytical jumble—a potpourri of personal anecdotes and generalized theory. Yet in all my formulations of self, whether geographical, educational, professional, or familial, the major categories that override all else are race and gender. For me, race and ethnicity should be more complicated; but they are not. The politics of race in America define me as Mexican. It is the identity of social hierarchy. It is the politics of being pushed to the bottom. It is the erasure of the richness of my Mexican/Irish/Jewish mix, and a white-washing of the colorful complexity of meaning in each of my ethnic roots.

* * *

I am a teacher, as was my grandmother. Maria Espinoza Cisneros taught in the town of Pitiquito, Sonora, Mexico, at the turn of the century. The oldest of eight children, she fled the Mexican revolution in 1912, settling with her family in Chino, California. My grandmother was the matriarch of her extended family until she died in 1967. Her husband died when he was still young and my grandmother raised her five children through the Great Depression. I never heard my grandmother speak a word of English.

When we were small, she would sit us in her yard and tell us of the Mayan and Aztec kings. She would start sometime around 700 A.D. and recite their names and year of ascension. She would tell us of the Spanish conquest. She would proudly tell us that we were Mexican. The Mayan, Aztec, and Spanish, however, were only part of our heritage. Being Mexican meant to be mixed, to have Indian blood, to be Mestizo. Our Indian ancestors were from three tribes: the Pima, the peaceful poets of the desert; the Tarahumara, the mystics of Northern Mexico; and the Apaches, the warriors of the plains and mountains. Each separate identity combined to create a unique composite. We were a mosaic, each tile separately colored and textured, piecing together a whole identity.

I knew my grandmother, my Nana, in the last years of her life. She was a bent, tiny woman, with well over eighty years behind her. Her hair was like her ideas, always neatly folded in braids and carefully contained in what looked like a frail hairnet. The braids wove a pattern that gave every strand a sense of structure and a knowledge of place and belonging. The hairnet was invisible, and seen, all at the same time. When she was in the kitchen or crocheting in the living room, it was hard for me to imagine her a "schoolteacher." Yet, she easily assumed her teaching persona when it was time to instruct her grandchildren in their legacy. She had a confidence and assurance that, just as her braids and her ideas fit together with a puzzling strength, her own sense of self would not unravel.

My own hair is short, cropped, and a mess of curls. Like my ideas, it moves every which way. No pattern of braids folds neatly around my head; no organizing net holds everything in place. I find my role transitions equally disarrayed. I am the carefully assimilated, accentless law professor. I move in and out of my other identities, but not smoothly. Like my grandmother, I want to teach my students a legacy. I want to teach them how they can take the pieces of their past and meld them with their developing lawyer persona. This is difficult to do when the discourse of law requires a single hegemonic voice.

* * *

The problem, however, is that not all of us can learn new languages and keep our fluency in past languages. The story of social hierarchy has been one where the language of social power reinforces that power by muting other languages. Trying to hold on to disempowered identities causes dysfunctionality in the use of the newly learned language of power and assimilation. When race equality means color-blindness that bleaches the concept to mean "the same as white," or when gender equality means "same as men" resulting in language categories like "non-pregnant persons," then socially-imposed bias makes those of us with certain identities outsiders. Our consciousness, our way of knowing, through our overlapping identities, cannot coexist with the new language. Our earlier cultural voice is dominated and silenced.

Gender differences provide a concrete example of this type of domination. Women use a special socialized style of speech which Robin Lakoff calls "women's language." This language includes "hedges," "tag questions," and "qualifiers." For example, when asked, "What time is dinner?" women will tend to respond indirectly: "I think that it should be around seven" or "Perhaps seven would be a good time." Alternatively, women will look for affirmation, "Would seven be good?" or "Dinner is at seven, if that's OK?" or "Seven, isn't it?" They might even try to qualify their response: "Assuming you'll be home, seven." Women tend not to respond directly: "Dinner is at seven."

* * *

I am intrigued by my grandmother, the teacher. To be a great teacher, she must have had a love for learning. Yet she never learned, or rather admitted to learning, English. She embraced all the different and often warring cultures of her Mexican identity. To the day of her death, she called herself a Mexican—never an American. She seemed to understand the difference of multi-identity in a culture where acceptance means assimilation, and assimilation means the uni-identity, the uni-lingualism of the dominant culture.

Linguistic assimilation has served as a particularly effective instrument in cultural suppression and eventually obliteration. Language domination means that English must be learned in order to participate in the society. More important is the pressure to disuse, and even unlearn, other languages. In 1991, the United States Supreme Court in *Hernández v. New York* reinforced uni-lingual, cultural domination. The Court held that the prosecutor's use of peremptory challenges during jury selection to exclude all Spanish-speaking, Latino jurors was constitutional—even if the exclusions resulted in all potential Latino jurors being excluded. Of course, all the excluded jurors spoke English. Their infirmity was that they also spoke Spanish. They had taken the first step toward "American identity," but they were not yet trustworthy. The government argued that its challenge to Latino jurors was justified because one of the witnesses at the trial would be testifying in Spanish. The government did not believe that bilingual, Latino jurors would adhere to the official English interpretation.

In *Hernández*, the jurors were asked if they would abide by the official English translation. They answered that they would. The prosecutor argued, however, that the individual jurors questioned could not be believed. They hesitated and looked away when answering the question. The Supreme Court relied on this notion of individual exclusion to justify its decision. Bilingual Latinos could not be per se excluded. Indeed, bilingual, Latino jurors who promised to rely on the official translation could not be peremptorily challenged—unless they were not believed. As the prosecutor in *Hernández* testified:

I believe that in their heart they will try to follow [the official translation], but I felt there was a great deal of uncertainty as to whether they could accept the interpreter as the final arbiter of what was said by each of the witnesses.

In *Hernández*, the Court tears away the mask of inclusive justice. Ours is not an adjudicatory system where judgment includes the views of peers who speak the same language of multi-identity. Members of the Latino community must not only speak English to be jurors, they must cease to speak Spanish.

* * *

The lure to trade our identity for power is strong. We want to be jurors; we want to be lawyers; we want to be law professors. I have this dream. My grandmother and I are speaking Spanish. I wake up but cannot understand what we said. Over the years, I have lost my ability to speak Spanish.

It takes a lot of energy to hide our accents, our idioms, our language. We have to learn to shift between identities, without an overlap. And then comes a time when we feel secure enough in the mastery of the dominant language to experiment with transformative speech—to create a new combination of languages. But can we remember that original language of culture and community? Have we lost all authenticity? I think not. We can try to stay connected to each of our identities. If we become fragmented, if we lose memory, we can endeavor to recapture it. I now understand why my grandmother never spoke English. She wanted to make certain that if we lost our ability to speak in Spanish, we would not lose our ability to dream in Spanish.

Notes and Questions

1.   Can someone with multiple identity "fall between the cracks" of our system of antidiscrimination law? Imagine a Latina who works for a supervisor who dislikes Latinas. He gives them the worst work and never promotes them, because he thinks they are demanding, emotional, and undependable. He nevertheless treats white women favorably, since they remind him of his sisters and mother, and he finds their presence at work comfortable and satisfying. He also likes men of color, and enjoys taking to them about musical groups and sports on Monday.

One day a Latina, Maria, who has received bad work assignments and been passed over for promotion several times, files suit under federal antidiscrimination law. Might the company escape liability because the supervisor treats Latinos (that is, the men) and women (that is, those who are white) on average well, so that either form of suit—for racial or sex discrimination—would fail? See Richard Delgado, *Rodrigo's Sixth Chronicle: Intersections, Essences, and the Dilemma of Social Reform*, 68 N.Y.U. L. Rev. 693 (1993), discussing such "intersectional" cases. Unless the law progresses to the point where it recognizes complex, intersecting identities and discrimination based on them, many plaintiffs like Maria could easily go without relief.

2. Suppose a light-skinned person with an Anglo last name one day decides to highlight his Latino heritage. After changing his last name, way of dressing, and determining to speak Spanish with others as much as possible, he begins to experience discrimination. Could a defendant in such a case argue that the newly reborn Latino brought it on himself by taking on that identity when he had a choice not to?

3. Suppose that the same reborn Latino checks a box indicating minority identity in a college application. If the college learns how recent his conversion has been, may it disregard his minority identity and evaluate him as though he were white?

On the role of choice and multiple identity in legal determinations of minority status, see Suzanne Oboler, *Ethnic Labels, Latino Lives: Identity and the Politics of (Re)presentation in the United States* (1995); Ángel Oquendo, *Re-Imagining the Latino/a Race*, supra; Laura M. Padilla, *Intersectionality and Positionality: Situating Women of Color in the Affirmative Action Dialogue*, 66 Fordham L. Rev. 843 (1997). See generally Ilan Stavans, *The Hispanic Condition: Reflections on Culture and Identity in America* (1995).

See also Bennun v. Rutgers State University, 941 F.2d 154 (3d Cir. 1991) (a son of a Sephardic Jew and a Romanian mother could sue under Title VII because he was born in Argentina, lived a life immersed in Spanish and Latino ways, and considered himself Hispanic).

4. For additional discussion of *Hernández v. New York* (the Spanish-speaking juror case, see Part Three, Chapter 8, § 3B).

SECTION 3.   ASSIMILATION

Society pressures Latinos and Latinas to assimilate—to take on Anglo characteristics and behaviors and enact their Latino side as little as possible. Sometimes Latinos believe themselves bicultural—able to assume the traits and patterns of either culture, as the situation demands. A few Latinos support assimilation or think that it is not necessarily a bad thing. Consider the following excerpts:

Richard Rodriguez
Hunger of Memory: The Education of Richard Rodriguez
43–45 (1982)

I stand in the ghetto classroom—"the guest speaker"—attempting to lecture on the mystery of the sounds of our words to rows of diffident students. "Don't you hear it? Listen! The music of our words. '*Sumer is i-cumen in . . . .* ' And songs on the car radio. We need Aretha Franklin's voice to fill plain words with music—her life." In the face of their empty stares, I try to create an enthusiasm. But the girls in the back row turn to watch some boy passing outside. There are flutters of smiles, waves. And someone's mouth elongates heavy, silent words through the barrier of glass. Silent words—the lips straining to shape each voiceless syllable: *"Meet meee late errr."* By the door, the instructor smiles at me, apparently hoping that I will be able to spark some enthusiasm in the class. But only one student seems to be listening. A girl, maybe fourteen. In this gray room her eyes shine with ambition. She keeps nodding and nodding at all that I say; she even takes notes. And each time I ask a question, she jerks up and down in her desk like a marionette, while her hand waves over the bowed heads of her classmates. It is myself (as a boy) I see as she faces me now (a man in my thirties).

The boy who first entered a classroom barely able to speak English, twenty years later concluded his studies in the stately quiet of the reading room in the British Museum. Thus with one sentence I can summarize my academic career. It will be harder to summarize what sort of life connects the boy to the man.

With every award, each graduation from one level of education to the next, people I'd meet would congratulate me. Their refrain always the same: "Your parents must be very proud." Sometimes then they'd ask me how I managed it—my "success." (How?) After a while, I had several quick answers to give in reply. I'd admit, for one thing, that I went to an excellent grammar school. (My earliest teachers, the nuns, made my success their ambition.) And my brother and both my sisters were very good students. (They often brought home the shiny school trophies I came to want.) And my mother and father always encouraged me. (At every graduation they were behind the stunning flash of the camera when I turned to look at the crowd.)

As important as these factors were, however, they account inadequately for my academic advance. Nor do they suggest what an odd success I managed. For although I was a very good student, I was also a very bad student. I was a "scholarship boy," a certain kind of scholarship boy. Always successful, I was always unconfident. Exhilarated by my progress. Sad. I became the prized student—anxious and eager to learn. Too eager, too anxious—an imitative and unoriginal pupil. My brother and two sisters enjoyed the advantages I did, and they grew to be as successful as I, but none of them ever seemed so anxious about their schooling. A second-grade student, I was the one who came home and corrected the "simple" grammatical mistakes of our parents. ("Two negatives make a positive.") Proudly I announced—to my family's startled silence—that a teacher had said I was losing all trace of a Spanish accent. I was oddly annoyed when I was unable to get parental help with a homework assignment. The night my father tried to help me with an arithmetic exercise, he kept reading the instructions, each time more deliberately, until I pried the textbook out of his hands, saying, "I'll try to figure it out some more by myself."

When I reached the third grade, I outgrew such behavior. I became more tactful, careful to keep separate the two very different worlds of my day. But then, with ever-increasing intensity, I devoted myself to my studies. I became bookish, puzzling to all my family. Ambition set me apart. When my brother saw me struggling home with stacks of library books, he would laugh, shouting: "Hey, Four Eyes!" My father opened a closet one day and was startled to find me inside, reading a novel. My mother would find me reading when I was supposed to be asleep or helping around the house or playing outside. In a voice angry or worried or just curious, she'd ask: "What do you see in your books?" It became the family's joke. When I was called and wouldn't reply, someone would say I must be hiding under my bed with a book.

(How did I manage my success?)

What I am about to say to you has taken me more than twenty years to admit: *A primary reason for my success in the classroom was that I couldn't forget that schooling was changing me and separating me from the life I enjoyed before becoming a student.* That simple realization! For years I never spoke to anyone about it. Never mentioned a thing to my family or my teachers or classmates. From a very early age, I understood enough, just enough about my classroom experiences to keep what I knew repressed, hidden beneath layers of embarrassment. Not until my last months as a graduate student, nearly thirty years old, was it possible for me to think much about the reasons for my academic success. Only then. At the end of my schooling, I needed to determine how far I had moved from my past. The adult finally confronted, and now must publicly say, what the child shuddered from knowing and could never admit to himself or to those many faces that smiled at his every success. ("Your parents must be very proud. . . .")

David G. Gutiérrez
Walls and Mirrors:
Mexican Americans, Mexican Immigrants, and
the Politics of Ethnicity
73–78 (1995)

[Although]   few Mexicans were formally deported [during the Depression—*Eds.*], repatriation for most individuals and families was a traumatic, disorienting, and sorrowful course undertaken under extreme duress. Many of the repatriates believed that Mexicans had been unfairly blamed for events over which they had no control. Despised and vilified after spending ten, fifteen, or even twenty or more productive years as hard-working, though isolated, members of the American working class, Mexican immigrant workers seemed to bear the brunt of Americans' resentment about the economic catastrophe. A famous *corrido* of the period underscores the sense of injustice and ingratitude many Mexicans clearly felt. "Los Deportados" lamented,

Los güeros son muy malores	The Anglos are very bad fellows
se valen de la ocasión	They take advantage
Y a todos los mexicanos	And to all the Mexicans
nos tratan sin compasión	They treat us without pity
Hoy traen la gran polvareda	Today they bring great disturbance

y sin consideración	And without consideration
Mujeres, niños, y ancianos	Women, children, and old ones
nos llevan a la frontera,	They take us to the border,
nos echan de esta nación	They eject us from this country
Adiós paisanos queridos	Goodbye dear countrymen
Ya nos van a deportar	They are going to deport us
Pero no somos bandidos	But we are not bandits
Venimos a camellar.	We came to toil.

As "Los Deportados" expressed so poignantly, the political climate symbolized by the repatriation campaigns placed intense political and social pressures on the ethnic Mexican population of the United States, which continued even after hundreds of thousands of Mexican nationals and their children had returned to Mexico. The scapegoating that occurred at this time rekindled Americans' disdain for working-class Mexicans, and as always, their disdain was directed at Mexican Americans as well as the newer immigrants. For Americans of Mexican descent this situation was like the rubbing of salt in old wounds. Torn between their cultural ties, their nationality, and their awareness that American citizenship did not necessarily protect them from such excesses, Mexican Americans faced some tough decisions as to what their attitudes toward the repatriation campaigns ought to be. As in previous periods of increasing social stress, in the late 1920s and 1930s opinion among Mexican Americans (and the Mexican nationals who remained in the United States) on the complex issues intertwined with the repatriation crisis remained deeply ambivalent. Between the late 1920s and the mid–1930s, however, opinion and debate on these questions began to harden and polarize.

In the winter of 1921 an article by former Texas Congressman James L. Slayden appeared in an issue of the *Annals of the American Academy of Political and Social Science* that was devoted to Mexican immigration. A long-time observer of Mexican immigration trends in his state, Slayden proved to be one of the few Americans active in public life who was perceptive enough to recognize the deep impact mass Mexican immigration was having on the existing Mexican American population. From Slayden's point of view Mexican immigrants represented a threat to the existing Texas Mexican population not so much because immigrants competed with Mexican Americans for jobs and housing as because Anglo Texans generally refused to acknowledge any meaningful distinctions between Mexican Americans and Mexican immigrants. Whether one was a citizen of the United States made no difference: to white Texans a Mexican was a Mexican, and that was the end of it. As Slayden put it, "In Texas, the word 'Mexican' is used to indicate the race, not a citizen or subject of the country. There are probably 250,000 Mexicans in Texas who were born in the state but they are [defined as] 'Mexicans' just as all blacks are negroes though they may have five generations of American ancestors."

While Slayden was making his observations about the peculiarities of racial classification in Texas, some Mexican Americans in that state were themselves pondering the implications of their ambiguous status in American society. As migration from Mexico continued into the 1920s they began to chafe at the thought that Americans were equating them with immigrants who, in many cases, had just recently entered the United States from the interior of Mexico. Although most of these native-born Texas Mexicans harbored no ill will toward their immigrant neighbors, worsening economic conditions and the intensification of anti-Mexican sentiment among Anglo Americans caused many of them to wonder whether the new immigrants were undermining their already tenuous position in Texas society. Having lived in the United States their entire lives, and in many cases having served the United States as members of the armed forces in World War I, increasing numbers of Texas Mexicans began to take exception to Anglo Americans' nonchalant dismissal of them as mere Mexicans. They gradually concluded that the only way to stop this indiscriminate lumping of American citizens with newly arrived Mexican immigrants was to take a stand against continuing large-scale immigration from Mexico. This was a painful decision, but from their point of view prudence dictated that Americans of Mexican descent had to be concerned with the immediate well-being and future health of Mexicans already in the United States. Mexico would simply have to take care of its own.

Although similar sentiments had been heard in Mexican American communities since the 1850s, these attitudes took on new salience with the establishment of a different type of Mexican American organization in Texas in the years immediately after World War I. Having returned from service in the armed forces, many Mexican Americans were no longer content to accept treatment as second-class citizens. Consequently, in the early 1920s Mexican American community leaders in several Texas cities established a number of new civic organizations designed to protect and advance the interests of their people. The three largest of these new groups were El Orden Hijos de América (The Order of the Sons of America), El Orden Caballeros de América (The Order of the Knights of America), and the League of Latin American Citizens. Such groups were formed by lower-middle-class members of the Texas Mexican community, and their leaders were typically attorneys, restaurateurs, teachers, printers, and small entrepreneurs serving the Spanish-speaking community. By 1927 these groups had established an extensive network of chapters throughout the state of Texas. The Sons of America, for example, had councils in Somerset, San Antonio, Pearsall, and Corpus Christi. The Knights of America were active primarily in the San Antonio area, and the League of Latin American Citizens had established chapters in the south Texas towns of Harlingen, Brownsville, Laredo, Gulf, Penitas, McAllen, La Grulla, and Encino.

As their names indicated, these new organizations espoused a political perspective that departed significantly from the philosophies of older Mexican American voluntary associations, such as the *mutualistas* and honorific societies. Unlike earlier groups, which had based their organizations on the principle of mutual cooperation between Mexican immigrants and Americans of Mexican descent, from their inception the new organizations pointedly excluded non-American citizens from membership.

To these organizations, Mexican Americans were American citizens and thus should make every effort to assimilate into the American social and cultural mainstream. Although most were generally proud of their ethnic heritage, they believed that Mexican Americans had focused too much on maintaining their ethnicity and culture in the United States and, in the process, had hindered their progress as participating members of American society. Thus, while members of these new organizations continued to profess respect for Mexico and for their Mexican cultural heritage, they insisted that the best way to advance in American society was to convince other Americans that they too were loyal, upstanding American citizens. In keeping with these beliefs the new Mexican American organizations carefully cultivated what they considered to be an appropriate American public image by conducting their proceedings in English, by prominently displaying the American flag in their ceremonies, stationery, and official iconography, by singing such songs as "America" at their gatherings, and by opening their meetings with a recitation of the "George Washington Prayer."

The political agendas of the Sons of America, the Knights of America, and the League of Latin American Citizens all reflected these basic premises. For example, the by-laws of the Sons of America articulated the political assumptions and general plan of action by asserting, "As workers in support of the ideal that citizens of the United States of America of Mexican or Spanish extraction, whether native or naturalized, [we] have a broad field of opportunity to protect and promote their interests as such; [and are committed] to elevate their moral, social and intellectual conditions; [and] to educate them . . . in the proper extension of their political rights." Members hoped to implement these principles by organizing voter registration and poll-tax campaigns, by mounting battles against the segregation of Mexican Americans in public facilities, and by insisting on more adequate representation of Mexican Americans on Texas juries.

Such ideas quickly gained currency after some of the Texas-based groups were consolidated into a new, larger organization just before the Great Depression. After a preliminary series of meetings in 1927 and 1928 in which the terms of consolidation of the various organizations were negotiated, the League of United Latin American Citizens (LULAC) was officially founded at a meeting in Corpus Christi on February 17, 1929. The original delegates met again at Corpus Christi in May of that year to codify the objectives agreed to in principle at the founding convention. Drafting a constitution and a formal statement of principles they called "The LULAC Code," Texans Manuel C. Gonzales, Alonso S. Perales, Benjamin Garza, J. T. Canales, Luis Wilmot, and others agreed to a series of objectives that came to define the organization's basic philosophy and political program for the next sixty years. Foremost among these objectives was a pledge to promote and develop among LULAC members what they called the "best and purest" form of Americanism. They also resolved to teach their children English and to inculcate in them a sense of their rights and responsibilities as American citizens, and they promised to fight discrimination against Mexican Americans wherever they encountered it.

In many ways the new organization exemplified the integrationist strains of thought that had slowly evolved among some Mexican Americans over the previous years. LULAC's founders believed that Mexican Americans had for too long been denied the full enjoyment of their rights as American citizens and that it was now time to change the situation. Both LULAC's constitution and the LULAC Code emphasized that the best way to rectify the appalling conditions facing Mexican Americans was to organize as American citizens; thus LULAC's founders rejected outright the notion that they were merely Mexicans who happened to reside in the United States. Although LULAC members insisted that their organization did not represent a political club, most of the group's goals were clearly political in nature. Thus even though LULAC's by-laws specifically prohibited direct involvement in partisan elections, the group's leaders encouraged members to participate in politics and use their "vote and influence" to support "men who show by their deeds, respect and consideration for our people." They remained extremely sensitive to the anti-Mexican sentiment that was building up in Texas and other parts of the Southwest during the first years of the depression, however, and so from the outset were careful to disavow the use of political tactics that might be interpreted as radical. Despite such caution, they asserted their strong commitment to "destroy any attempt to create racial prejudices against [Mexican Americans], and any infamous stigma which may be cast upon them [by] demand[ing] for them the respect and prerogatives which the Constitution grants us all."

LULAC leaders consciously chose to emphasize the American side of their social identity as the primary basis for organization. Consequently, in pursuit of much-needed reforms they developed a political program designed to activate a sense of Americanism among their constituents. Considering themselves part of a progressive and enlightened leadership elite, LULAC's leaders set out to implement general goals and a political strategy that were similar in form and content to those advocated early in the century by W. E. B. Du Bois and the National Association for the Advancement of Colored People: for "an educated elite" "to provide the masses with appropriate goals and lift them to civilization." LULAC's political activities varied from chapter to chapter according to local political circumstances, but in general the organization adopted a three-pronged plan of attack in the 1930s and 1940s that strongly emphasized desegregated public education for Mexican American children; encouraged Mexican American citizens to register, pay their poll taxes, and vote; and supported aggressive local legal campaigns to combat discrimination against Mexican Americans in public facilities and on juries.

Although the depression constrained LULAC's organizing and prose-lytizing efforts, the organization proved remarkably successful in expanding its membership base after 1929. Utilizing "Flying Squadrons" of organizers who traveled to distant communities in cars or chartered buses, LULAC grew throughout the 1930s in Texas, and by the outbreak of World War II the organization had established viable chapters in New Mexico, Arizona, California, and Kansas. By the early 1940s LULAC claimed at least eighty dues-paying chapters nationwide, making it the largest and best-established Mexican American civil rights organization in the United States.

LULAC also proved remarkably successful in achieving many of its stated political goals. Indeed, despite the generally hostile political environment facing Mexican Americans during this era, LULAC scored a number of significant legal victories in Texas, and the organization assisted Mexican Americans in other states in mounting effective challenges against local discriminatory practices. From 1929 through World War II LULAC organized successful voter registration and poll-tax drives, actively supported political candidates sympathetic to Mexican Americans, and aggressively attacked discriminatory laws and practices in communities throughout Texas and the Southwest. More important over the long run, LULAC also achieved a number of notable legal victories in the area of public education. Following a strategy in which it focused its energies on legal challenges to discriminatory practices in one community at a time, LULAC began to chip away at the structure of the de jure segregation of Mexican American students. For example, in the organization's first legal challenge in 1930, LULAC lawyers brought suit against the Del Rio, Texas, School District for discriminating against Mexican American students. LULAC ultimately lost most of the major points contested in *Independent School District v. Salvatierra*, but the case was only the opening salvo in what proved to be a long legal struggle in which LULAC and other groups successfully argued that discrimination violated the equal-protection and due-process clauses of the Fourteenth Amendment to the U.S. Constitution. Similar LULAC efforts in the 1940s and 1950s built on this important precedent and helped Mexican Americans and other minority groups attack the separate-but-equal doctrine that was ultimately overturned in the famous *Brown v. Board of Education* case in 1954.

Ruben Navarrette, Jr.
A Darker Shade of Crimson: Odyssey of a Harvard Chicano
103–04 (1993)

It was in my sophomore year that I finally realized the development of a siege mentality among some minority students.

I witnessed, and to some degree facilitated, the subconscious dividing of the Harvard community in two camps. *Us* and *them*. We were advocates—progressive Chicano students who "knew who they were," embraced their culture, and were ready to uphold their sacred responsibility to *la comunidad* and sympathetic white liberal faculty who tried to ease our alienation. We were "down with brown." They were detractors—conservative politicians appealing for the votes of those who felt reversely discriminated against, professors frightened by classroom populations that were changing colors, newspaper columnists talking about merit who had forgotten that their first break in journalism had come from an influential uncle, and fellow Chicanos seeking acceptance by denouncing affirmative action benefits that they had already accepted. We considered Them to be all those who had never wanted Us to attend schools like Harvard in the first place and now wanted to limit our numbers or encumber our experience. We wanted to destroy a status quo that had systematically disenfranchised our parents and our parents' parents. They wanted to maintain that status quo and pined away for the good ol' days when one could go one's whole life and never encounter a Mexican as an equal. Mexican Americans at Harvard ... imagine!

If Us and Them were at war, then paranoia defined the battlefield. Those who were not friends were automatically enemies. Trust was a precious commodity, distributed sparingly. I was still convinced that there were inflexible standards for what constituted a Real Mexican. Instinctively, unscrupulously, I applied those standards to other Mexican Americans on campus, including those in RAZA, in a kind of ethnic litmus test to assess authenticity. I remember that, in my mind, authenticity implied loyalty. A foolish assumption of youth: Those *most* like you will not betray you.

What eventually ensued on our campus and, I would learn, on other college campuses around the country, was a messy game of ethnic "Truth or Consequences."

The exercise was conceived in difference. There were differences among the one hundred twenty-five Mexican–American undergraduates at Harvard just as there are differences among the twenty million Mexican Americans in the United States. Some students were from mixed marriages; some were not. Some were from upper middle-class families; some were not. Some had worked in the fields as children; some had not. Some spoke Spanish; some did not.

The exercise thrived in difference. The rules of the game were simple. The contestants might be two Harvard Chicanos, similar yet different. The difference is noted. It might be a difference in skin color, Spanish-speaking ability, religion, even political affiliation. At first glance, it appears unlikely that both people can be authentic. The difference dictates that one must be a real Mexican, the other a fraud. The objective of the game becomes for the contestants to each assert his or her own legitimacy by attacking the ethnic credibility of their opponent. *More ethnic than thou.* The weapons are whispers. A pointed finger. A giggle. A condescending remark from one to another.

"Oh, with your background, I don't think you'd understand my point...."

Owing to rigid, traditional—some might say stereotypical—conceptions of Mexican culture, *authentic* meant dark-skinned, Spanish-speaking, Catholic, lower-class, and loyal to family. So a young Mexican–American man with light skin and an Irish surname, or a young Chicana who votes Republican and whose mother is a college professor might both start off at a disadvantage. I remember a beautiful girl with a Mexican–American mother and a white father who, as a freshman, was told by a senior in RAZA that she might have difficulty being accepted, trusted by the group because of her mixed lineage. This, of course, after he slept with her. Sex, I learned early, is the oldest weapon of all.

Finally, the game ended in a cynical pool of hurt feelings and lost friendships. The winners, having savaged their opponent with slander, accusation, and innuendo, stood victorious; reward took the form of that elusive Harvard carrot, acceptance and respect. A reward, if not from the institution itself, at least from fellow Mexican Americans there.

The arguments against assimilation are straightforward: One loses touch with a rich ancestry. One loses the support of one's racial counterparts, and may even earn their contempt. See, e.g., Margaret E. Montoya, *Mascaras, Trenzas, y Greñas: Un/masking the Self While Un/braiding Latina Stories and Legal Discourse*, 17 Harv. Women's L.J. 185 (1994); Kevin R. Johnson, *"Melting Pot" or "Ring of Fire?": Assimilation and the Mexican–American Experience*, 85 Cal. L. Rev. 1259 (1997); Laura M. Padilla, *Social and Legal Repercussions of Latinos' Colonized Mentality*, 53 U. Miami L. Rev. 769 (1999). But see Linda Chavez, *Out of the Barrio: Toward a New Politics of Hispanic Assimilation* (1991).

SECTION 4. INDIANISM AND MESTIZAJE

A very high percentage of Latinos from Mexico and Guatemala have Indian blood. A much smaller percentage has black blood. Should they list their identity as Indian (or part-Indian) or black (or part-black)? If you look white but know your ancestry includes Indian or black blood, is it cowardly or dishonest to list oneself in any other way?

For example, one of the authors of this casebook (Delgado) is, as far as he knows, one-quarter Spanish, one-quarter Chichimec Indian, and one-half Slavic. Another of the authors (Perea) is Colombian, Costa Rican, and perhaps Nicaraguan Indian. The third author (Stefancic) is close to 100 percent Slavic and is married to a Latino male.

Perea grew up in the Washington, D.C. area. Stefancic grew up in an ethnic neighborhood in Cleveland, Ohio. Delgado grew up in the United States and Mexico.

Are all three Latinos? Is Stefancic white? White ethnic? Latina?

Many Latinos celebrate "mestizaje"—mixed blood. But not all do. See the following selections:

Siegfried Wiessner
¡Esa India! *LatCrit Theory and the Place of Indigenous Peoples*
Within Latina/o Communities
53 U. Miami L. Rev. 831, 837–39, 850–52 (1999)

If equal treatment, both in fact and in law, is our goal, it must be universal and it must be reciprocal and mutually granted. We must continue to be mindful of discrimination within our midst. If we do not respect the legitimate claims of others, we forfeit our own.

* * *

The indigenous peoples of the Western hemisphere are of flesh and blood. They have survived and continue to face an onslaught of massive attacks directed at the core of their existence. Their plight is not merely historical. It is a day-to-day occurrence of which we often are not aware, or wrongfully believe it exists only in foreign countries.

Conscious, and even more often, unconscious racism may infect the ranks of victim groups as well. I would like to share with you a personal example that highlighted the problem for me. A friend was driving a car in Miami, when a woman cut her off. Angry as hell and without even taking a close look at the inconsiderate "stupid" female driver, my friend blurted out "*¡Esa India!*" Now, my friend is from Chile, a country where very few Indians remain. My friend had never even met an *indio*, or, for that matter, an *india* in her country. She also now regrets the incident and has kindly agreed to have me share it with you. What it reflects, however, is an attitude of unreflected, yet pervasive scorn of native inhabitants of the hemisphere, which places indigenous peoples at the bottom of the social ladder, and which appears widespread among *criollas/os* not only in the Southern Cone, but throughout Latin America. Similar attitudes, I am told, are to be found in Mexico, Venezuela, and other parts of the Western hemisphere. They are a legacy of history—a history of suffering, physical and cultural genocide, conquest, penetration, and marginalization that has been endured by indigenous people in this hemisphere and beyond.

Still, indigenous peoples have not been stamped out. A majority of the population of Bolivia and Guatemala are *indios*. The indigenous people of Peru and Ecuador constitute more than forty percent of the population. In twelve countries, including Belize, Honduras, Mexico, and Chile, between five percent and twenty percent of the population are considered indigenous. Overall, approximately fifty million people maintain indigenous lifestyles. This population is growing in absolute and relative numbers, despite continuing attempts at physical extermination, the mass killings that never stopped, the disappearances, and the tortures. In civil wars, indigenous communities are often caught between the government and its armed forces on the one hand, and private armies or gangs on the other. Ethnocide was often committed through the theft of indigenous land, policies of assimilation and termination, public and private discrimination, and other severe deprivations of many kinds.

It bears repeating that the process of colonization has left indigenous peoples defeated and relegated to minor spaces and reservations, mere breadcrumbs of the land conceded by the dominant society. Indians were separated from the sacred land of their ancestors, with which they shared a deeply spiritual bond. Deprived of traditional environments, they were politically, economically, culturally, and religiously dispossessed. They became entrapped peoples, "nations within." The indigenous peoples aspire to leave this confinement, to extricate themselves from the trap, and to live lives of self-defined dignity and happiness. Indigenous peoples all over the world claim the right to live freely on their ancestral lands, to celebrate their culture and deeply-felt spirituality, and to move from cultural autonomy to economic autonomy, and to political self-government. At times they may even call for the ultimate option of secession.

* * *

Mexico is the battleground where it appears that indigenous peoples recently have taken up arms against the ruling elites. 85 percent of the Mexican population is *mestizo*, while ten million Mexicans are considered *indios*, primarily because of their language. These indigenous peoples, divided into fifty-three different *etnias*, have suffered degradation and severe deprivation of values. The Indian past is "in many ways glorified," but an enormous gap exists between the Mexican myth and its "operational code." The movement embodied by the *Ejército Zapatista de Liberación Nacional (EZLN)*, in the Mexican State of Chiapas, unites men and women from the Tojolobal, Tzeltal, Tzotzil, and Chol communities, all with Mayan roots, in the desire to confront the situation head-on. Since its inception, on January 1, 1994, the uprising has had military, political, and spiritual dimensions, and it has garnered considerable support, both inside and outside of Mexico. One year earlier thousands of *indios* had died needlessly in that very state, they had experienced "physical and spiritual hunger, lack of medical services, and a century and a half of discrimination." Their reasons for revolt and their demands were outlined in a document called the *Declaración de la Selva Lacandona*. The *indios* asked for autonomy, the democratization of the country's political life, the rule of law, and certain aspects of social justice. Negotiations, which began with much hope, have stalled, and the reaction to the uprising has become more violent. The "first post-modern revolution" faces a difficult road ahead.

* * *

Both on the regional and universal level, declarations on the rights and status of indigenous peoples are in the formative stage. Taken together with widespread state practice, pertinent customary law has emerged. Any international prescriptions regarding indigenous peoples should be structured in such a way as to maximize for the intended beneficiaries the access of shaping and sharing of all the values humans desire.

Martha Menchaca

Chicano Indianism: A Historical Account of
Racial Repression in the United States
20 Am. Ethnologist 583, 583–87, 599–600 (1993)

In this excerpt I describe forms of racial repression experienced by people of Mexican origin living under the legal system of the United States. I also document cases in which people of Mexican descent were compelled to argue that they should be treated as Caucasians in order to gain the legal rights of full citizens. Focusing on citizenship and racial legislation from 1848 to 1947, I argue that the U.S. legal system accorded privilege to whites and, conversely, legitimated the inferior treatment of racial minorities. Because Mexican-origin people were of mestizo descent (Spanish and Indian ancestry), they were placed in an ambiguous legal position. Their Indian ancestry linked them to people of color, subjecting them to heightened racial discrimination, while their Spanish ancestry linked them to whites, protecting them from the full impact of the racial laws of the period.

My fundamental aim is not to argue that Mexican-origin people are unaware of their indigenous past or that they have no indigenous historical consciousness. Rather, it is to show that they are among the dark-skinned people who historically have been discriminated against by this country's legal system. In embarking on this exploratory venture, I found it necessary to examine documents in which information about the racial repression of Mexican-origin people could be obtained. As primary sources, I consulted federal and state supreme court records and nineteenth-century citizenship legislation. These legal discourses illustrate more than a century of arguments used to justify racial discrimination in the United States.

U.S. VIOLATION OF THE TREATY OF GUADALUPE HIDALGO

Through annexation, conquest, and purchase, the United States acquired Mexico's northern frontier between 1845 and 1854. The four border states of California, Arizona, New Mexico, and Texas contained numerous small and large settlements of Mexican residents. Mexico also lost parts of its northern frontier that today include Nevada, Utah, parts of Colorado, and small sections of Oklahoma, Kansas, and Wyoming; these areas contained no Mexican settlements and remained under the control of indigenous peoples. At the termination of the Mexican–American War, the American states had the power to determine [state] citizenship eligibility requirements, a power given to them by the Constitution of the United States. As a consequence, the states were able to bar American Indians and all other racial minority groups from obtaining full citizenship privileges. The states proposed that only "free whites" (for example, whites who were not indentured servants or criminals) had all the desirable characteristics to receive such privileges. Because most political privileges could be acquired only by a citizen, individuals who did not qualify for citizenship received limited civil rights.

When the United States acquired Mexico's northern frontier, the mestizo ancestry of the conquered Mexicans placed them in an ambiguous social and legal position. In the U.S. government bureaucracy, it became unclear whether Mexicans were to receive the citizenship rights of white citizens or were to be treated as Indian inhabitants. Most government officials argued that Mexicans of predominantly Indian descent should be extended the same legal status as the detribalized American Indians. Mexicans, on the other hand, argued that under the Treaty of Guadalupe Hidalgo and international laws, the U.S. government agreed to extend all Mexican citizens—regardless of their race—the political rights enjoyed by white citizens. These rights were accorded to them on the basis of the international principle guaranteeing inhabitants of ceded territories the nationality of the successor state unless other provisions are made in the treaty of peace.

The Treaty of Guadalupe Hidalgo was exchanged and ratified in Queretaro, Mexico, on May 30, 1848, officially ending the Mexican–American War. It stipulated [many of] the rights of the inhabitants of the ceded territories (including the Indians), set the U.S.-Mexico border, and brought several binational agreements on economic relations to closure. However, Anglo–American legislators violated the treaty and refused to extend Mexicans full political rights. The legislators were able to disenfranchise many Mexicans by arguing that such people were of Indian descent and therefore could not claim the political privileges of white citizens.

Conflicting Racial Laws in the Conquered Territories

In 1848, with the end of the Mexican–American War, the United States politically disenfranchised all Indians of the Southwest by rescinding Mexico's racial laws in the newly conquered territories. Since 1812, Mexico had given Indians the right to claim citizenship and full political rights (*United States v. Lucero* 1869). Mexico also no longer practiced a legally based racial caste system. Thus, new racial restriction policies instituted in the conquered territories came to threaten the civil rights of the Mexicans because under U.S. laws, Indians and "half-breeds" were not considered citizens (Naturalization Act of 1790, ch. 3, sec. 1; see In re *Camille* 1880).

The eradication of Mexico's racial caste system had begun in the late 1700s when the Spanish crown resolved that generations of miscegenation had thoroughly blurred racial distinctions. In 1812, the legal basis of the racial ranking order was finally abolished. The racial caste system, which for two centuries had distinguished individuals on the basis of race, became nonfunctional for political and social purposes. Its gradual breakdown resulted from the growth of the mestizo population and the political power obtained by upper-class mestizos. By the turn of the nineteenth century, the mestizos had become the majority and were heavily represented in the upper classes.

Before the breakdown of the racial caste system, Mexico's population had been divided among Spaniards, *castas*, and Indians. Distinguishing the population on the basis of parental origin had been an adequate legal method of according economic privilege and social prestige to the Spaniards. The Spaniards included both *peninsulares*, individuals who had been born in Spain and were of full European descent, and *criollos*, who were also of full European descent but had been born in the New World. As miscegenation increased among the Spanish elite, the criollo category eventually came to be redefined. The castas were mestizos and other persons of mixed blood. The Indian category included only people of full indigenous descent.

Of the various racial groups, the Spaniards enjoyed the highest social prestige and were accorded the most extensive legal and economic privileges. The legal system did not make distinctions between peninsulares and criollos. Nevertheless, the Spanish crown instituted policies requiring that high-level positions in the government and the Catholic church be assigned to peninsulares, on the rationale that only peninsulares were fervently loyal to the Spanish crown. Exceptions were made when a new colony was established in the Americas and when a peninsular was unwilling to accept the appointment. It was required, however, that a criollo taking such an appointment be a son of peninsulares. Peninsulares were appointed to positions such as viceroy, governor, captain-general, archbishop, and bishop, whereas criollos were appointed to less prestigious positions, such as royal exchequer (treasurer, comptroller) and judge, and, after 1618, to mid-level administrative positions in the church (as priests or directors of schools).

The social and economic mobility of the rest of the population was seriously limited by the legal statuses ascribed to their ancestral groups. In theory, Indians were economically more privileged than mestizos because they held title to large parcels of communal land protected by the Spanish crown and the Catholic church. However, regardless of their landed property, the Indians were accorded little social prestige in Mexican society and were legally confined to subservient social and economic roles regulated by the Spanish elite. Most Indians were placed in *encomiendas* and *repartimientos* (Indian communities where land and labor were controlled by Spanish missionaries or government officials), Indian pueblos, or haciendas and were held in a perpetual state of tutelage. The mestizos enjoyed a higher social prestige than the Indians but were considered inferior to the Spaniards. They were also often ostracized by the Indians and the Spaniards, and they did not enjoy certain legal privileges accorded to those groups. For example, most mestizos were barred by royal decree from obtaining high-and mid-level positions in the royal and ecclesiastical governments. Moreover, the Spanish crown did not reserve land for the mestizos as it did for the Indians. For the most part, the only economic recourse most mestizos had was to enter the labor market or migrate toward Mexico's northern and southern frontiers. Each migrant who was the head of a household received 150 acres and exemption from taxation for a period of approximately ten years. After 1680, mestizos were occasionally allowed to become parish priests in Mexico's frontier settlements or in sparsely populated areas.

By the late 1700s, the rigid racial order had relaxed owing to changes in the interracial sexual and cohabitation practices of the Spanish elite. It had become common for upper-class Spanish males to take mestizo or Indian women as concubines and afterward legitimate their offspring. In such cases the racial status of the child became criollo and not mestizos. These criollos had the racial status of Spaniards but were not accorded the corresponding legal privileges. They were barred from positions reserved for the Spaniards of full European descent, and they suffered certain sanctions for marrying peninsular women. By the early 1800s, large numbers of criollos, mestizos, and Indians were becoming increasingly defiant of bounded social roles and were trespassing their borders with deliberate speed. Criollos attempted to pass for peninsulares in order to obtain more social privileges. Indians often passed for mestizos in order to obtain wage labor in the urban centers, mestizos passed for Indians as a means of acquiring the land titles of the Indians and mestizos who had amassed great fortunes tried to improve their social standing by passing for criollos. The blurring of the racial distinctions made it difficult for the Spanish crown to enforce the laws and the prescribed social norms, in particular because the majority of the population was indistinguishably mestizos.

The final blow to the racial order came about through the political defection of the masses. By the early 1800s, movements to liberate Mexico from Spanish colonial rule had erupted throughout the country, and as a consequence the Spanish crown attempted to avert revolutionary action by instituting the 1812 Spanish Constitution of Cadiz. The new constitution legally abolished the casta system and the racial laws. Theoretically, the constitution conferred on Spaniards, mestizos, and Indians the same political rights regardless of racial origin. The laws of Cadiz, however, were unable to avert the national independence movements. In 1821, the masses won the Mexican War for Independence and instituted a provisional constitution (the Plan de Iguala) reaffirming the racial philosophy of the Constitution of Cadiz. After the War of Independence, race could no longer be legally used to prevent Indians and mestizos from exercising citizenship rights. For example, it became common for mestizos and full-blooded Indians to be elected to the presidency. All subsequent Mexican constitutions ratified the spirit and language of the Constitution of Cadiz.

In northern Mexico, the frontier experienced the same legislative changes as the interior. Indians were considered Mexican citizens and were accorded full political rights. In New Mexico, southern Arizona, and California the acculturated Indians and the secularized mission Indians actively exercised those rights. In New Mexico numerous Pueblo Indians were elected to town and county political offices, and in California acculturated American Indians often held high-ranking posts in the military. Of course the new laws had limited effects on the majority of the American Indians, because Mexico held title to territories inhabited by unconquered indigenous populations. The majority of the Shoshone, Navajo, Apache, and Comanche Indians had not been conquered by the Mexican state. And the new legislation did not eradicate the Mexican elites' attitudes of racial and economic superiority toward the American Indians and mestizos.

When Mexico ceded its northern territory to the United States, then, it had already abolished all racial restrictions on citizenship. The Indians had theoretically been incorporated as Mexican citizens. In practice, of course, this legislation had not abolished racial prejudice and discrimination in Mexico, and the Indians continued to be stigmatized as uneducated people. However, the mestizo racial category had taken on a new social meaning. Because most of the population was mestizo, being mestizo had become a source of pride rather than a stigma. The European race continued to hold high social prestige in Mexico, but the masses no longer considered it the only prestigious racial group. In the legal domain, race could no longer be used as a civil rights barrier.

The racial policies of the United States, however, were less liberal than Mexico's. The United States at that time conferred full citizenship rights on "free whites" only. Thus, the states' constitutional right to deny Indians U.S. citizenship introduced the ideological and legal foundation for limiting the Mexican people's political rights. Moreover, government officials often used the Mexicans' indigenous heritage to undermine the civil rights language of the Treaty of Guadalupe Hidalgo. Article VIII of the treaty stated that the United States agreed to extend U.S. citizenship to all Mexican citizens, regardless of ancestry, who remained in the ceded territories. If individuals did not want U.S. citizenship, they had to so indicate within one year; otherwise they would become citizens automatically. Under Article IX the United States further agreed that Mexicans who chose to become U.S. citizens would have all the attendant rights. Article IX stipulated that "Mexicans who, in the territories aforesaid, shall not preserve the character of citizens of the Mexican Republic ... shall be incorporated into the Union of the United States, and be admitted at the proper time ... to the enjoyment of all the rights of citizens of the United States."

Regardless of the treaty, however, the U.S. government refused to ratify the racial equality laws of Mexico. When the annexed southwestern territories joined the Union, their state constitutions did not extend to American Indians the political rights guaranteed by the Treaty of Guadalupe Hidalgo and the Mexican constitution. And soon after the enactment of the treaty, controversy arose over the citizenship status of the Mexicans. The exclusionary Indian citizenship laws, endorsed by the southwestern legislators, became the legal basis for limiting the political rights of the Mexicans. [State] government representatives commonly argued that the language of the treaty and the U.S. Constitution was unclear as to whether Mexicans of Indian descent should be treated as American Indians or should be extended the privileges of whites.

Ironically, the political privileges that the Spanish and Mexican governments had previously given people in the Southwest were abolished by the U.S. racial laws. The Mexican mestizos and Indians entered a new racial caste-like order in which their civil rights were limited. Given the nature of the U.S. racial system and its laws, the conquered Mexican population learned that it was politically expedient to assert their Spanish ancestry; otherwise they were susceptible to being treated as American Indians. At the same time, as this historical blueprint suggests, it became politically expedient for American Indians to pass for Mexican mestizos if they wished to escape the full impact of the discriminatory Indian legislation.

The Denial of Citizenship for American and Mexican Indians

After ratification of the Treaty of Guadalupe Hidalgo, government representatives of the annexed region began to pass new racial-restriction citizenship laws. Most American Indians were prohibited from obtaining citizenship, and the anti-Indian legislation adversely affected the Mexicans of partial or full Indian descent. Unless a Mexican was predominantly white, he or she was subject to racial harassment. Those classified as Mexican Indians were not entitled to exercise full political rights or even basic civil rights: they were not allowed to vote, practice law, marry Anglo–American women, or run for political offices such as district judge. They were also subject to severe human rights infringements, such as being placed in debt peonage and being forced to live on reservations.

* * *

Court and legislative records from 1848 to 1947 reveal that the skin color of Mexican-origin people strongly influenced whether they were to be treated by the legal system as white or as non-white. During the nineteenth century, Mexican-origin individuals who were predominantly of Indian descent were subject to heightened racial discrimination. They were, for example, not allowed to become naturalized citizens if they were immigrants, to vote in the states of California and Arizona, to practice law in the state of Arizona, or to be exempted from segregationist legislation. The segregationist laws continued to affect darker-skinned Mexicans into the mid-twentieth century. * * * The legal records also indicate that *under the law* Mexican-origin people of predominantly Caucasian ancestry were ostensibly allowed to exercise the full political rights of citizens. * * * In the state of Texas, for example, local governments found alternative legal methods of discriminating against Mexicans who were identified as white. In the *Independent School District v. Salvatierra* court case, it was determined that "white Mexican students" could be legally segregated if they did not speak English.

* * *

In sum, the record reveals a history of racial repression and discrimination against members of the Mexican-origin community in the United States. Government officials used the people's indigenous ancestry to deny them equal citizenship rights and to keep them in a politically subordinate position. Indianism was used to construct an image of Mexican-origin people as inferior and therefore deserving of separate and unequal treatment. With respect to future scholarship on the racial history of the Chicano people, I trust that this exploration has demonstrated the value of using legislative and judicial records as evidence that this American minority group has experienced severe racial discrimination in the United States.

Notes and Questions

1. Might checking the Native American box on the Census questionnaire and similar forms be a plausible solution for Latinos puzzled by the array of racial categories, none of which seems to fit them? See Toro, supra.

2. Might U.S. Latinos/as with mixed blood make common cause with Native Americans on issues such as language and cultural rights, and the restoration of communal lands?

3. Many Latinos have black ancestors. See Taunya Lovell Banks, *Mestizaje and the Mexican Mestizo Self: No Hay Sangre Negra So There is No Blackness*, 15 S. Cal. Interdis. L.J. 199 (2006). Why does a culture that celebrates mestizaje and Indian blood not take pride in its black ancestry? See also Tanya Kateri Hernández, *Latino Inter–Ethnic Employment Discrimination and the "Diversity" Defense*, 42 Harv. C.R.-C.L. L. Rev. 259 (2007).

4. For a discussion of Spanish conquest, intermarriage, La Malinche, Aztec emperor Montezuma, and the future of Latino activism, see Gregory Rodriguez, *Mongrels, Bastards, Orphans, and Vagabonds: Mexican Immigration and the Future of Race in America* (2007).

Chapter 6

NATURALIZATION, CITIZENSHIP, AND RELATIONS WITH OTHER GROUPS

This chapter deals with a number of questions about belonging. Naturalization is the process by which an individual who is not a U.S. citizen becomes one.

Citizenship is the legal status most people associate with being "American" in the fullest sense—carrying the ability to vote, hold public office, own property, and obtain a U.S. passport.

A further question for a minority group, such as Latinos, is how it fits into the complex web of interactions that the various groups of color establish in relation to each other. For example, do Latinos and blacks have anything in common? Are they fighting for the same crumbs, and thus in opposition to each other? Are they members of the same society or brotherhood—the brotherhood of "people of color"?

Asian Americans, as well as Latinos, desire language rights, bilingual education, affirmative action, and more expansive immigration rules. Are they thus candidates for a fruitful coalition with Latinos?

As noted above, Latinos and Native Americans have many of the same objectives. What possibilities do you see for coalition with all these groups? With liberal whites? See the discussion of all these issues, infra.

SECTION 1. NATURALIZATION

The Treaty of Guadalupe Hidalgo, which ended the War with Mexico (see Part One, Chapter 1), provided that Mexicans living in the expansive new territory that now was part of the United States either return south of the redrawn border, many miles away, or remain where they lived. They had one year to make their decisions. See Richard Griswold del Castillo, *The Treaty of Guadalupe Hidalgo: A Legacy of Conflict* (1990); Christopher David Ruiz Cameron, *One Hundred Fifty Years of Solitude: Reflections on the End of the History Academy's Dominance of Scholarship on the Treaty of Guadalupe Hidalgo*, 5 Sw. J.L. & Trade

Am. 83 (1998); Guadalupe T. Luna, *On the Complexities of Race: The Treaty of Guadalupe Hidalgo and* Dred Scott v. Sandford, 53 U. Miami L. Rev. 691 (1999).

If they chose the latter (staying in what was now the United States), they would automatically become citizens of the United States, whether they liked it or not. This was the first, and crudest, form of "naturalization"—naturalization by treaty. Many Mexicans who had few ties to the United States and spoke little English became U.S. citizens this way.

The Treaty granted only one kind of citizenship, the federal kind. Mexicans remaining in California, Arizona, New Mexico, or Colorado, for example, did not automatically become citizens of those states. The states were free to devise their own rules for citizenship for such crucial matters as voting or holding public office. Since the federal government was relatively weak at the time, the grant of federal citizenship was less important than those of the states, so that the Treaty did relatively little to welcome former Mexicans into the American polity. The two types of citizenship created much confusion, both for the Mexicans and the native-born citizens of the states where they resided. See Menchaca, supra.

Revisit *In re Rodriguez*, supra Chapter 4, § 6, which considered the importance of skin color in judging a Mexican's qualification to become a citizen of the United States. Bear in mind that an early federal statute, enacted in 1790, limited naturalization to male persons of the white race. The statute, which remained on the books for nearly 150 years, was amended in 1870 to allow naturalization by "persons of African nativity . . . or descent." *In re Rodriguez*, somewhat anomalously, found the mestizo petitioner qualified for citizenship under the Treaty of Guadalupe Hidalgo.

Under the above-mentioned statute, federal courts in dozens of cases had to decide whether an Iranian, a Syrian, a person of mixed German and Japanese ancestry, a high-caste Hindu, or a light-skinned Japanese could become a citizen. See Ian F. Haney López, *White by Law: The Legal Construction of Race* (10th Anniv. ed. 2006).

What about Latinos? Most U.S. courts that considered the matter seem to have decided, sometimes reluctantly, that Mexican Americans, at least, were white. Why? Because the Treaty of Guadalupe Hidalgo granted them citizenship, and only whites could be citizens. Note the circularity of this reasoning.

Recall, as well, how the United States government quickly granted asylum to light-skinned Cubans fleeing the Fidel Castro takeover and later supplied them with financial aid and social services, with the result that the Cuban community in Miami today is relatively prosperous and middle class. Later arrivals were darker, poorer, had checkered criminal records, and were less anti-communistic. These newcomers received a much less favorable reception from the U.S. government, both before and after their arrival. See Part One (Cubans).

SECTION 2.   SOCIAL MEMBERSHIP

A.   THE EARLY YEARS

Even if early American courts somewhat grudgingly recognized Latinos' federal citizenship rights, society at large was not always so generous.

As war with the Mexicans loomed, the question arose how much of Mexico the United States should take. If it were to seize, for example, the northern two-thirds of that country, cities such as Monterrey, Guadalajara, and Mexico City would become part of the United States, much as Santa Fe and San Francisco actually did. The United States would gain many dark-skinned, Catholic, Spanish-speaking citizens.

Senator John C. Calhoun objected that this would change the country's racial composition for the worse and that our proper interest lay in the rich lands alone, not the Mexicans who lived on them. "Our army has ever since held all that it is desirable to hold," he wrote, namely "that portion whose population is sparse, and on that account the more desirable to be held. For I hold it in reference to this as a fundamental principle, that when we receive territorial indemnity, it shall be unoccupied territory." *Cong. Globe*, 30th Cong., 1st Sess. 96 (Jan. 4, 1848).

Calhoun went on to explain that the reason he wished to seize only the northern, thinly populated part of Mexico, was his fear that annexing more of that country would disrupt white supremacy in the United States. Id. at 96–98. See Part One, Chapter 1, for more such commentary.

The U.S. ended up seizing only the northernmost half of Mexico. Even so, the amount of land grabbed was vast, approaching in size the territory conquered by Alexander the Great.

Even before that, Anglos had begun streaming into the Southwest, where many of them encountered Mexicans for the first time. To their surprise, they found a Christian population, many of whom lived in orderly villages with irrigation, communal water rights, schools, churches, and government. Yet, they were sitting on some of the choicest real estate anywhere. They needed, of course, to be displaced. How to justify the incipient land grab? See Patricia N. Limerick, *The Legacy of Conquest: The Unbroken Past of the American West* (1987), and the following selection.

Reginald Horsman
Race and Manifest Destiny: The Origins of
American Racial Anglo–Saxonism
208–13 (1981)

Reread this excerpt in Part One supra.

The racial character of the War with Mexico becomes plainer when one considers the reluctance of the United States to fight England over the Oregon territory. A war with Mexico would be waged against a people thought racially inferior. But a war with Britain would require Anglo–Saxons to fight Anglo–Saxons. While the Mexican War resulted in a victory in which Americans could claim racial dominion, the latter confrontation resulted in an affirmation of Anglo–Saxon values and a negotiated settlement. Horsman, supra at 220–21, 224–25.

Notes and Questions

1.   Do all colonial societies paint the colonizers as intelligent, scientific, rational, and enlightened, and the natives as dark, superstitious, and child-like—in need of tutelage? Note how Rudyard Kipling's writings spoke about the "white man's burden," and how, in our time, even progressive movies such as "Mississippi Burning" feature a white hero who saves trembling, helpless blacks. See Richard Delgado, *Rodrigo's Corrido: Race, Postcolonial Theory, and U.S. Civil Rights*, 60 Vand. L. Rev. 1691 (2007).

For discussions of postcolonial theory, which contains this as a major theme, see, e.g., *The Post–Colonial Studies Reader* (Bill Ashcroft et al. eds, 2d ed. 2006). See Edward W. Said, *Orientalism* 1–6 (1978) (noting that after a time, all westerners writing on the Orient began to see that part of the world through the same lens—fetishistic, superstitious, cruel, and sensual).

2.   Do today's images of Latinos as lazy, musical, rhythmic, and romantic trace themselves to earlier ones you have read about? Do they perform the same legitimating function today? Specifically, do they reassure Anglos that Anglos deserve to be in charge, that Latinos are lazy and do not make good use of their opportunities? For the view that they do, and that these negative stereotypes serve important material interests, see Delgado, *Corrido*, supra, positing, in dialogue form, an explanation of how this works:

Richard Delgado
Rodrigo's Corrido: Race, Postcolonial Theory, and U.S. Civil Rights
60 Vand. L. Rev. 1691, 1722–25 (2007)

RAMON, SUSIE, AND A MOONLIT NIGHT

[Eds. The following is part of a conversation between "Rodrigo," a young firebrand, and "the professor," an older steadying hand.]

"Yes. And so imagine the scene. As in plantation society, you would have an Anglo family living in the big house. The Mexican crew would work in the fields and spend the nights in temporary shacks somewhere nearby. But these would be free people. Most of them would be male, many of them young. Some would be transient and would move with the crops. Others would settle down in semi-permanent quarters on the farm or a nearby town."

"I think I know what you are going to say. Society needed a taboo to keep everybody apart?"

"It did. Imagine that it's a moonlit night. Susie, the daughter of the farm family, is out for an after-dinner walk in the orchard. She comes across a 17–year-old field hand named Ramon. Bronzed from the sun and strong from outdoor work, Ramon is also a bright lad. Neither slave nor peon, merely exploited and underpaid, he has dreams and ambitions. He speaks English. He can sing and play the guitar. He knows how to fix things and make plants grow.''

"And so Susie and he strike up a friendship?''

"Yes. And that's what the mother and father most fear—Susie running away with a Mexican farmhand. They are both good looking and about the same age. They have a lot in common. Both are repressed. Susie hates the farm. Ramon hungers for something better. They form a bond.''

"And this is where the taboo comes in?''

"Yes. Multiply that situation by a thousand. You have early Anglos and their families working in close proximity to young, strapping Mexicans. This could easily lead to intimacy of two types: not only the romantic kind between the young daughters of the ruling family and the male farm workers, but also camaraderie between the Anglo supervisors and the Mexican farm hands. They are all about the same age. They have the same objectives—a healthy crop. They both understand and love nature and plants. Yet farm labor requires intense exploitation. Stoop labor. The short hoe. Broiling sun. Long hours. Low pay.''

"And so Anglo society coins a taboo,'' I said. "I can imagine what's in it. It would have to be pretty disparaging.''

"And it is. The taboo, as I mentioned, is triple. Its main components are three—dirt, sexuality, and jabber—attachment to a mysterious and unfathomable language. There are a few other components, but those are the main ones.''

"I'd like to hear about all three. I gather you think they work together?''

HOW THE TABOOS FUNCTION

"They do. Each of them—filth, hypersexuality, and jabber—separates dominant society from the Mexicans. And once in place, this separation would happen naturally. An Anglo wouldn't have to think about it every time.''

"I see what you mean,'' I said. "An overseer at a farm or ranch ordinarily might position himself about five or ten feet away from a worker. He's safe. Although the worker is potentially filthy, contagion and smell wouldn't travel that far. But he wouldn't get closer—close enough, for example, for the two to shake hands after completing a stage of the work.

"And little Susie, who knows in the back of her mind that Ramon is a potential sex maniac, might engage in repressed conversation with him on a moonlight night, but would make sure she has a ready escape route in case he gets too amorous. But what about jabber?''

"Jabber operates at a different level," Rodrigo replied. "Local authorities, including school boards, needed to do something with all those Mexican kids too young to work in the fields. The belief that they are a backward, superstitious people who will hang onto their culture and language justifies treating them that way in a host of settings. In school, for example, California authorities until fairly recently rationalized separate classrooms and schools for little Mexican kids on the ground that they needed special training because of their language deficiencies. And at worksites, it rationalized a kind of language-based hierarchy. Expert Latino fruit pickers, for example, could serve as low-level middlemen and foremen, but never crew chiefs. They could occupy minor supervisory roles because their knowledge of Spanish enabled them to give orders and discuss problems with the other workers. But their supposed inability to speak English—actually many spoke it quite well—excluded them from consideration as crew chiefs, because the chiefs needed, from time to time, to converse with the outside world and officials such as county agricultural agent or a clerk at a local fertilizer store."

"It seems to me that it also justifies suspicion," I added. "If a group is constantly jabbering away in a foreign language, it might easily be planning some form of resistance, maybe a strike for higher wages."

"Right," Rodrigo replied. "The planters were already uneasy about the exploitive conditions they imposed on their workers. Just as slaveowners in the South slept uneasily because they feared a slave rebellion, the Mexico farmhands might easily covet something better. Their speaking to each other in a foreign language fed this fear and justified harsh laws excluding farmworkers from unionization or coverage for workplace injuries."

José Luis Morín
*Latino/a Rights and Justice in the United
States: Perspectives and Approaches*
17–22 (2004)

THE ORIGINS OF LATINOS/AS IN THE UNITED STATES: AN ENCOUNTER WITH THE HISTORY OF U.S.-LATIN AMERICAN RELATIONS

Familiarity with the history of relations between the United States and Latin America is indispensable to unraveling the often forgotten events and circumstances that account for the Latino/a presence in the United States. In many instances, U.S. policies toward Latin America have been directly responsible for the influx of Latinos/as in the United States. But many today misconstrue that presence as one based solely on immigration when, in fact, Latinos/as inhabited what now comprises the Southwest and Western states of United States—approximately one-third of the continental United States—long before most other European settlement of North America.

Absent from the collective consciousness of most U.S. citizens are the wars of territorial conquests of the late 1800s. With the end of the

U.S.-Mexican War in 1848, Mexicans were subsumed along with the land that was previously sovereign Mexican territory into the United States. Following the United States' war with Spain in 1898, Puerto Ricans became subjects of the United States and their land a possession of the United States even though they had already achieved political autonomy from Spain in 1897. Thus, immigration alone does not account for the number of Latinos/as currently in the United States. In point of fact, recent census data reveals that three in five Latinos/as are U.S. born.

The conspicuous lack of awareness of this history provides fertile ground for the preservation of forms of prejudice and discrimination that inhibit the realization of full and equal rights and justice for Latinos/as.

IMPERIAL DESIGNS ON LATIN AMERICA

Before reviewing the early history of U.S. foreign policy toward Latin America, it is necessary to clarify that the United States, notwithstanding its anticolonial beginnings, occupies a place in history as one of the world's greatest empires and its ascent to this status was not accidental. By the end of the nineteenth century, the United States had successfully positioned itself as an imperial power with territorial possessions around the globe. It had also claimed a special dominant role over all of the Americas—a role that it maintains to the present. It is now well established that U.S. imperialism was not a passive endeavor, but a concerted effort to expand U.S. territorial reach for new markets and other economic, social, and political gains.

However much it has been couched in benevolent terms or justified in the name of spreading democracy, acquiring territories through wars of conquest places the United States squarely in the league of other imperial powers in world history that have engaged in the systematic violation of the right of self-determination of peoples. Indeed, as with all other imperial powers, the United States has used war and the threat of war as indispensable instruments to attain hegemony. Stated clearly, it is through conquest that the United States was able to wrest approximately half of the lands of Mexico and gain control over a series of island nations—including Puerto Rico, Cuba, the Philippines, Guam, and Hawaii—by the end of the 1800s.

The conquests of the 1800s were rooted in the longstanding and deeply held desires among many of the founders of the United States to construct an empire. As early as 1767, Benjamin Franklin articulated aspirations for the expansion of U.S. territory, including intentions to make Mexico and Cuba part of the United States. Thomas Jefferson contended that the United States "has a hemisphere to itself. It must have a separate system of interest which must not be subordinated to those of Europe." By the 1780s, Jefferson avowed that the Spanish empire should be taken over by the United States "peice by peice [*sic*]." These expansionist designs were not simply the whimsy of Franklin and Jefferson; they became an integral part of the ambitions of U.S. policymakers who followed. The goal of seizing other lands to advance U.S.

global economic and political interests could not be more plain than when in 1891 Secretary of State James Blaine in a letter to President Benjamin Harrison wrote, "I think there are only three places that are of value enough to be taken that are not continental.... One is Hawaii and the others are Cuba and Porto Rico [*sic*]."

THE RACIAL JUSTIFICATIONS FOR U.S. IMPERIALISM

U.S. domination over Latin American lands and peoples was made palatable and justifiable to the U.S. public in large measure through the perpetuation of racist ideologies. Manifest destiny, a dominant and influential belief system boldly advanced in the 1800s, touted the divine right of Anglo–Saxon U.S. citizens to territorial expansion based on purported racial and cultural superiority. The influence of the racist assumptions inherent in the notion of the "White man's burden" together with manifest destiny provided the requisite pretext for justifying Anglo–American dominance and territorial conquests.

Policymakers and the major news media coalesced around the idea that the United States was governed by persons of a superior race, religion, and culture distinguishable from all others, and, therefore, the United States was uniquely and rightfully entitled to claim dominance over other lands and other peoples. So deeply held were these beliefs that all non-Anglo Saxons, even those from Europe, were considered threats to the nation. By 1751, Benjamin Franklin voiced his beliefs about the racial and cultural threat that non-Anglo Americans posed, including German immigrants, who in his words "will shortly be so numerous as to Germanize us instead of our Anglifying them, and will never adopt our Language and Customs, any more than they can acquire our complexion."

In spite of the diversity of people and races in the United States in its early years—Native Americans, Europeans of different countries of origin, and Africans—prominent leaders and founders of the United States regarded the country as one only of and for Anglo Americans. John Jay in *The Federalist Papers* remarked that

> Providence has been pleased to give this one connected country to one united people—a people descended from the same ancestors, speaking the same language, professing the same religion, attached to the same principles of government, very similar in their manners and customs.

Very early in U.S. history, Latin Americans were singled out as racially inferior to Anglo–Saxon Americans. James Buchanan denounced "the imbecile and indolent Mexican race," and in the press, the *New York Evening Post* in the late 1840s categorized Mexicans as "*Indians—Aboriginal Indians.* Such Indians as Cortez conquered three thousand [*sic*] years ago, only rendered a little more mischievous by a bastard civilization.... They do not possess the elements of an *independent* national existence ... and they must share the destiny of their race."

As historian Howard Zinn documents, major U.S. newspapers and political leaders repeatedly championed the idea of Anglo superiority as justification for the conquests of Mexico. The *New York Herald* in 1847 stated unequivocally: "The universal Yankee nation can regenerate and disenthrall the people of Mexico in a few years; and we believe it is part of our destiny to civilize that beautiful country." Invoking God as further justification, Senator H. V. Johnson stated:

> I believe we should be recreant to our noble mission, if we refuse acquiescence in the high purposes of a wise Providence. War has its evils ... but however inscrutable to us, it has also made, by the Allwise Dispenser of events, the instrumentality of accomplishing the great end of human elevation and happiness.... It is in this view, that I subscribe to the doctrine of 'manifest destiny.'

Throughout the 1800s, words, cartoons, and photographs reinforced demeaning, negative stereotypes of the conquered peoples of Cuba, Puerto Rico as well as the Philippines and Hawaii. In an examination of the degrading representations of the peoples of these island nations in 1898, Frederic W. Gleach of Cornell University notes that "[r]acialization, infantilization, primitivization, and feminization were all used to construct our newly-interior Others as inferior to real Americans.... This was not a passing way of viewing them, but a persistent one—and a problematic one, even to the present."

The notion that Latin American peoples' own racial and cultural deficiencies rendered them unable to govern properly their own nations laid the foundation for a foreign policy grounded on achieving and maintaining U.S. hegemony over the Americas. The foreign policy initiative that enshrined U.S. hegemony is the Monroe Doctrine of 1823. It is a doctrine that many historians agree still remains influential in U.S.-Latin American relations. Racially negative characterizations of Latin Americans not only helped to rationalize the wars of conquest with Mexico and Spain in the 1800s, they were followed by U.S. government policies, practices, laws, and judicial decisions that relegated other Latin Americans subordinate to Anglo Americans.

U.S. acceptance of Latin Americans as representing a separate and inferior race rendered uncontroversial numerous military interventions throughout Latin America. In the case of Cuba, Orville H. Platt, author of the notorious Platt Amendment, vehemently opposed Cuba's incorporation into the United States because "The people of Cuba, by reason of their race and characteristic, cannot be easily assimilated by us.... Their presence in the American union, as a state, would be most disturbing." Since under U.S. policy Cubans were unworthy of incorporation into the union by virtue of their race, they could not be trusted with full political independence. As a result, the Platt Amendment of 1904 relegated Cuba to a neocolonial status and insured complete U.S. authority to intervene in Cuba's internal affairs, including control over Cuba's economy and politics. While the Platt Amendment was in effect

(1904–1932), the U.S. military forces invaded and/or occupied Cuba in 1906–1909, 1912, and 1917–1922.

Throughout the nineteenth century and into the twentieth century, Latin Americans were openly and continually depicted in Washington and throughout the United States as inferior and racialized "others," prone to uncivilized behavior, and undeserving of self-government. Simultaneously, the U.S. public was fed a steady diet of news stories and media portrayals that vividly reinforced in the hearts and minds of U.S. citizens that the U.S. government was acting benevolently and justifiably in pursuing its colonial agenda. Casting Latin Americans as racialized "others" helped to rationalize in the minds of the U.S. public their government's actions. It offered a vision of a government carrying out a benign mission among inherently inept peoples. Thus, U.S. policies were not to be interpreted as those of a colonial power acting in contravention of its own founding democratic principles, but in furtherance of those ideals. Professor Peter H. Smith explains that projecting the United States as a nation imbued with the higher goal of spreading democracy among these racially, culturally, and religiously backwards peoples was vital not only to justify and mobilize domestic support and resources for its imperial ventures, but to validate its actions to rival powers as well. In addition, he points out that the projection of lofty goals served to indoctrinate and thereby control the peoples of the subjugated societies themselves.

Racism and a racialized vision of the peoples of the developing world also proved useful in the establishment of a legal framework for the unequal application of the law toward Latinos/as in the United States. For example, in the case of Puerto Ricans, U.S. Supreme Court judgments governing the rights of Puerto Ricans have been compared to the condition of separate and unequal experienced by African Americans in the United States for more than half a century. Indeed, virtually the same group of Supreme Court justices responsible for *Plessy v. Ferguson*, 163 U.S. 537 (1896)—the case establishing the notorious legal doctrine of separate but equal—decided the *Insular Cases*, which continue to delimit the rights of Puerto Ricans. As with the *Plessy* case, the restrictions imposed on the rights of Puerto Ricans were grounded in the racist and racialized perceptions of Puerto Ricans and Latin Americans that prevailed throughout all branches of the U.S. government. Unlike *Plessy*, however, the *Insular Cases* have never been overturned, and as a result, significant restrictions on the most fundamental rights of the peoples of Puerto Rico are still applied.

During the Congressional debate about whether constitutional protections should be extended to Puerto Ricans in 1900, Puerto Ricans were characterized as follows:

> They are of the Latin race, and are of quick and excitable tempers, but they are at the same time patient, docile, frugal, and most of them industrious.

Given such characterizations, it is not surprising that Puerto Ricans were not accorded full constitutional rights, a condition that still exists today. As persons who collectively comprise a racially inferior group, the conclusion drawn was that Latin Americans present a danger to the dominant, White U.S. population and its institutions. As a consequence, it was imperative to restrict Latino/a rights through legislation and other legal obstacles to protect Anglo–American power and authority over the status and condition of Latinos/as in the United States.

B. THE WAR WITH SPAIN

A scant four decades after ending the War with Mexico, the United States acquired Puerto Rico and a few other possessions. Known as the "splendid little war," the Spanish American War saw the emergence of the United States as a full-blown, international imperialist power, and ushered in what historians call the American (viz, twentieth) century. See Sylvia R. Lazos Vargas, *History, Legal Scholarship, and LatCrit Theory: The Case of Racial Transformations Circa The Spanish American War, 1896–1900*, 78 Denv. U. L. Rev. 921, 923 (2001); see also Frank Burt Freidel, *The Splendid Little War* (1958); José A. Cabranes, *Citizenship and the American Empire: Notes on the Legislative History of the United States Citizenship of Puerto Ricans* (1979).

The war began in 1898 when Congress intervened in Cuba's second war of independence against Spain, which had broken out three years earlier. The American chapter of that war was brief and decisive. The Treaty of Paris, which marked its conclusion, ceded Puerto Rico, Guam, and the Philippines to the United States as "war indemnity"—i.e., booty. Cuba was not included, because the United States had earlier declared itself committed to Cuba's independence.

Discussions leading up to seizure made plain that Puerto Rico, once overrun, could not gain full admission to the United States because of its "racially and culturally foreign peoples," who would, at best, need a long period of tutelage before joining the Union. Lazos Vargas, supra at 929. The War also marked "the United States' first step to ... colonialism and empire." Id. at 929–30. In another round of conquest, the United States soon annexed the newly formed Republic of Hawaii, after white planters staged a coup against the Hawaiian King.

The resolution of the war plunged Puerto Rico into full-blown second-class citizenship, unable to vote in presidential elections, subject to the plenary power of Congress, exempt from the protections of the Uniformity Clause (which requires that all states be treated the same), and entitled only to those benefits that Congress deems adequate. These benefits may be less than those it makes available to citizens of other states, including reduced or nonexistent eligibility for food stamps, welfare, social security, and the minimum wage. See, e.g., Pedro Malavet, *America's Colony* (2004).

In addition, U.S. citizenship for those born in Puerto Rico and the other territories is less robust than that of those born in the mainland,

Hawaii, or Alaska, and is perhaps revocable at will. Lazos Vargas, supra at 936.

Statements by President William McKinley and Congress during and just before the Spanish–American War make plain that, like the earlier war with Mexico, it proceeded as part of a larger "civilizing mission." Lazos Vargas, supra, at 945. The same Anglocentric, Protestant framework that settlers and Congressional leaders espoused to justify taking over much of Mexico reappeared. Anglo society was efficient and modern; Catholic and Spanish society, repressed and backward.

The tropical people needed help. With the lead-in to the war, "came the awakening to the great fact that they had founded an empire" based on a superior self-identity. Henry Cabot Lodge, *The War With Spain* 234 (1970 c1899). That national identity and sense of higher purpose included a rhetoric, refined during the War, in which the United States would tame the tropical "barbarians," not for its own commercial benefit, but their own good. See Matthew Frye Jacobson, *Barbarian Virtues: The United States Encounters Foreign Peoples at Home and Abroad, 1876–1917* (2000). Did the war with "tropical people" have repercussions that endure today? See the following selection:

José Luis Morín
Latino/a Rights and Justice in the United States: Perspectives and Approaches
22–25 (2004)

U.S. CONQUESTS IN MEXICO AND PUERTO RICO

The two largest Latino/a populations in the United States today, Mexicans and Puerto Ricans, share a history linked inexorably to the U.S. imperial expansion of the 1800s. Familiarity with the historical experiences of these two groups is essential to understanding the treatment of Latin Americans who later came to the United States and the contemporary situation of Latinos/as.

Contrary to the depiction of Latinas and Latinos as primarily "illegal immigrants" to the United States, many Mexicans lived on the lands that presently comprise roughly one-third of the continental United States, including the present-day states of California, Texas, New Mexico, Arizona, Nevada, and parts of Colorado, Utah, and Kansas. At the end of the U.S.-Mexican War in 1848, approximately 75,000 Mexicans living on the lands acquired by the United States through the war were forced to decide whether to become U.S. citizens.

The conquest of these lands and the people who inhabited them was possible through the efforts of President James K. Polk. By stationing troops at the border with Mexico, Polk intentionally instigated hostilities with Mexico. In view of the vast territories and resources taken as part of the Treaty of Guadalupe Hidalgo that ended the U.S.-Mexican War, it was not unexpected that the purpose of a $15 million payment to Mexico at the conclusion of this war has been construed to have been nothing more than an attempt to legitimize a patent seizure of land in violation of the sovereignty of another nation. [Eds. See also Part One, Chapter 1, supra].

Drafted by a victorious U.S. government after Mexico's military defeat, the Treaty of Guadalupe Hidalgo of 1848 between the United States and Mexico failed to protect the rights of Mexicans who became U.S. citizens. Mexicans within the territories acquired by the United States were reduced to second-class citizenship, subjected to the loss of their lands in spite of preexisting land grants, and denied the right to vote and political representation.

Although the treaty in large measure did intend originally to extend full rights to Mexicans consistent with international law, in its final version the Treaty of Guadalupe Hidalgo was modified in significant ways to appease the concerns raised in Congress over the racial threat that Mexicans represented to Anglo–American rule. As a result, article IX of the treaty was amended to grant Congress the ultimate power to decide at what time Mexicans could be granted full rights as U.S. citizens. Article IX of the Treaty of Guadalupe Hidalgo (1848), thus, reads:

> The Mexicans who, in the territories aforesaid, shall not preserve the character of citizens of the Mexican Republic, conformably with what is stipulated in the preceding article, shall be incorporated into the Union of the United States and be admitted, *at the proper time (to be judged of by the Congress of the United States)* to the enjoyment of all the rights of citizens of the United States, according to the principles of the Constitution; and in the mean time, shall be maintained and protected in the free enjoyment of their liberty and property, and secured in the free exercise of their religion without restriction [emphasis added].

Any reference to protecting liberty and property in the treaty turned out to be disingenuous. Not only were full constitutional rights withheld in the amendment to article IX, article X of the Treaty of Guadalupe Hidalgo, anticipated to protect "[a]ll grants of land made by the Mexican government or by the competent authorities, in the territories previously appertaining to Mexico," was completely stricken from the final version of the treaty. This action insured that Mexicans with valid land grants would eventually lose lands to White settlers who systematically challenged and won title over those lands in court.

In 1898, the U.S. war with Spain—sold to the U.S. public by government officials and the news media as a crusade to end the brutality of Spanish colonial rule in Cuba—resulted in one colonial power replacing another. As with the Treaty of Guadalupe Hidalgo, the Treaty of Paris of 1898, which ended the war, fell short of granting equal rights to the peoples of the lands transferred to the United States as the spoils of war. Article IX of the treaty states that the U.S. Congress shall determine the "civil rights and political status of the native inhabitants of the territories ... ceded to the United States." The ceded territories included the Philippines, Guam, and other islands of the Pacific, as well as Puerto Rico. Fears about the "alien nations" that inhabited these territories and the possibility that they might contaminate U.S. society by incorporating these "mongrel" races into the United States ran rampant at the time. Hence, the U.S. government inserted language in the Treaty of Paris that insured that the inhabitants of these conquered lands could not exercise full citizenship and constitutional rights. [Eds. See also Part One, Chapter 2, supra].

In one of a series of cases known as the *Insular Cases*, the U.S. Supreme Court determined it impossible to confer full constitutional rights to Puerto Rico because its "alien races" are not ready for having "the blessings of a free government under the Constitution extended to them" (Downes v. Bidwell, 182 U.S. 244, 286 (1901)). The Court based its decision, *inter alia*, on the Doctrine of Conquest set forth in Johnson v. McIntosh, 21 U.S. 543, 590 (1823)—a racially-charged doctrine that justified the granting of title to land in North America to the far superior persons from the "civilized" nations of Europe over Native Americans, who were nothing more than "fierce savages." Creating a legal rationale for U.S. colonial expansion was of such importance that Justice Henry Billings Brown in the *Downes* case conceded that any other decision could "be fatal to the development of ... the American Empire" (Downes v. Bidwell, 182 U.S. 244, 286 (1901)).

As a result, the *Downes* case and subsequent U.S. Supreme Court cases have allowed the U.S. Congress to retain plenary (that is, absolute) power to determine the civil rights of Puerto Ricans and the political status of Puerto Rico. As an unincorporated territory—one of several territories that "belong to but are not a part of the United States" (Downes v. Bidwell, 182 U.S. 244, 287)—full and equal constitutional protections need not apply to Puerto Ricans.

In 1917, Puerto Ricans were made U.S. citizens with the passage of the Jones Act by the U.S. Congress. Yet U.S. citizenship—imposed without the consent of the Puerto Rican people and in disregard for the unanimous vote of the Puerto Rican legislature to preserve Puerto Rican citizenship—still did not guarantee full and equal protection under the U.S. constitution for persons residing in Puerto Rico. The U.S. Supreme Court in Balzac v. People of Porto Rico [*sic*], 258 U.S. 298 (1922), in fact, held that the right to a jury trial and other such rights under the U.S. Constitution are not applicable to the inhabitants of Puerto Rico unless granted by the U.S. Congress. The court's reasoning, which still stands today, is that Puerto Rico remains an unincorporated territory of the United States, even after the enactment of the Jones Act, and as such, the U.S. Congress retains plenary powers to determine the rights of Puerto Ricans under the Territorial Clause of the U.S. Constitution, article IV, section 3, paragraph 2.

For discussions of the role of contemporary images and stereotypes of Latinos in restricting Latinos' range of opportunities, see Part Six: Cultural Stereotypes and Hate Speech.

SECTION 3. INTERRACIAL TENSIONS AND RELATIONS

In most, if not all, colonial societies, the occupiers made use of native collaborators, often English- or French-speaking members of the educated class, to help them run the country. Often the colonials would give these "middlemen" civil service jobs in the colonial administration in return for their tacit agreement to help keep their countrymen in check and ward off any incipient rebellion.

In the American South, plantation owners would use light-skinned slaves as house servants, giving them light work in return for their agreement to help keep an eye on their darker-skinned counterparts in the fields and alert the master to any talk of escape or insurrection.

Has American society imposed any similar role on Latinos? Consider the following developments:

1.   The rise of the broker class. Rodolfo Acuña describes the rise of the "broker class" of upper-class, college educated Latinos who help U.S. corporations sell products, such as cigarettes, alcohol, or luxury items like cars, to their communities, or deliver votes to a political party. See Rodolfo Acuña, *Occupied America: A History of Chicanos* 357 (5th ed. 2004).

2.   The increase in tensions between blacks and Latinos. Noted by several commentators, e.g., Earl Ofari Hutchinson, *The Latino Challenge to Black America* (2007); Nicolas C. Vaca, *The Presumed Alliance: The Unspoken Conflict Between Latinos and Blacks and What It Means for America* (2004), might the new frictions between the two outgroups be a manifestation of the way majority society stirs up enmity between minority groups, so that they fight over patronage and small slights, neatly deflecting each other from a dominant society that oppresses them both?

See, e.g., Earl Ofari Hutchinson, *Black vs. Brown: The Blame Game*, L.A. Times, Nov. 25, 2007, at M1; Earl Shorris, *Our Next Race Question: The Uneasiness Between Blacks and Latinos (Colloquy)*, Harper's, Apr. 1996, at 55; Jack Miles, *Blacks vs. Browns: African Americans and Latinos*, The Atlantic, Oct. 1992, at 41; Richard Delgado, *Derrick Bell's Toolkit: Fit to Dismantle That Famous House?*, 75 N.Y.U. L. Rev. 283 (2000). See also Manning Marable, *Beyond Racial Identity Politics: Toward a Liberation Theory for Multicultural Democracy*, 35 Race & Class 120 (1993); Eric K. Yamamoto, *Rethinking Alliances: Agency, Responsibility, and Interracial Justice*, 3 UCLA Asian Pac. Am. L.J. 33 (1995).

On tensions among Latinos of different races, see Tanya Kateri Hernández, *Latino Inter–Ethnic Employment Discrimination and the "Diversity" Defense*, 42 Harv. C.R.-C.L. L. Rev. 259 (2007).

3. Consider also the way youth gangs senselessly feud with each other over honor and turf, e.g., Gregory Rodriguez, *Black vs. Brown: It's More about Class and Less about Color*, L.A. Times, Nov. 25, 2007, at M8; Megan Garvey, *L.A. County Targets Racial Gang War*, L.A. Times, Dec. 17, 2005, at B4; Aruna Lee, *Korean-Latino Relations Grow Icy*, New Amer. Media (News Analysis) (on-line, Mar. 12, 2007), excerpted infra.

When a member of one minority group discriminates against a member of another, can the victim sue for discrimination under state and federal laws? See Cardona v. American Exp. Travel Related Services, 720 F.Supp. 960 (S.D. Fla. 1989), in which a federal judge allowed a lawsuit brought by a Colombian worker charging that his employer favored Cubans. The case is excerpted in Part 7, infra.

Badillo v. Dallas County Community Action Comm., Inc.
394 F.Supp. 694 (N.D. Tex. 1975)

MEMORANDUM OPINION

WILLIAM M. TAYLOR, JR., CHIEF JUDGE.

The five individual plaintiffs in this case bring this suit under the Civil Rights Acts of 1866 and 1964, claiming that the defendant Dallas County Community Action Committee (hereinafter referred to as the "DAC") discriminated against them because of their Mexican–American national origin. In addition to seeking back pay, reinstatement, original job positions, and promotions allegedly improperly denied them, the plaintiffs also request preliminary and permanent injunctive relief designed to restrain the DAC from maintaining policies, practices or customs whose effect is to deny or deprive them of employment opportunities with the defendant on the basis of their national origin.

The individual plaintiffs also represent a class of people (divided into two sub-classes) which attempt to enjoin the defendant DAC from either intentionally or inadvertently discriminating against the plaintiffs on the basis of their national origin either with regard to employment opportunities, promotions, and terminations or with regard to the delivery and receipt of services offered to the Dallas Community by the defendant.

* * *

Although employment discrimination cases and other suits involving race and national origin discrimination never follow the usual and expected chain of events, the instant case has several peculiarities which distinguish it from even the normal Title VIII case. Typically, an employment discrimination suit pits an individual or group of unhired, or fired, or unpromoted minority plaintiffs against a white or Caucasian-controlled employer. However, in the instant case, a group of five individual Mexican–Americans sue in their own behalf and on behalf of other Mexican–Americans similarly situated with regard to the defendant DAC, alleging that the organization through Black officials sitting in middle or higher level management positions have either intentionally or inadvertently adhered to policies and employment decisions which effectively discriminated against the plaintiff Mexican–American DAC employees and job applicants on the basis of their national origin. Thus, the situation involves one minority group suing another minority for its discriminatory conduct.

* * *

* * * Badillo, the principal individual plaintiff, complained that his position as "job development specialist" with the Manpower program, was terminated only because of his keen interest in alleged discriminatory practices conducted by DAC officials against his fellow Mexican–Americans. In effect, he claimed that his termination resulted not from a failure to adequately perform his duties but in essence because Mrs. Morrison and other supervisory personnel within DAC discriminated against him on the basis of his national origin. The Manpower program involves the creation of employment centers and employment service units, for the purpose of providing disadvantaged enrollees in the program with education, vocational training, work experience, and job placement and counseling opportunities. Under 42 U.S.C. § 2737, community participation and cooperation is greatly stressed. In accordance with that philosophy, the plaintiff Badillo was hired to help create job opportunities, sponsored and administered as a comprehensive program by the DAC, for poverty level individuals in Dallas County.

The Director position of the DAC and other components, such as the Manpower program, held especial prominence in the eyes of DAC employees not only for its inherent political power, but in addition for the increased pay and job responsibilities connected with it. Mr. Medrano, another individual plaintiff, sought the Deputy Directorship of the DAC, after having been the director of a neighborhood service center and the Director of the Neighborhood Service System, the latter capacity of which he now maintains.

Closely associated with the Manpower comprehensive work and training program administered, coordinated, and evaluated overall by the DAC, are supportive and follow-up services necessary to assist disadvantaged individuals in achieving successful training, job experience and opportunities such as health services, day care for children, and transportation assistance. The outlying community houses with their staff of administrators, aides and other personnel are designed to effectuate those purposes in Dallas. Mrs. Cervantes, another plaintiff, served as a community house aid until May 19, 1972, when, as she claims, the DAC terminated her job position on account of her being a Mexican–American.

The other two individual plaintiffs had similar claims to the first three. Sepulvida claims that he was not promoted within the DAC organization because of his Mexican–American origin. In similar manner, Arredondo claims that his Mexican heritage illegally caused his not being hired at all by the DAC.

The goals and purposes Congress emphasized in the Economic Opportunity Act of 1964 when looked at in light of the claims made by the plaintiff herein introduce another paradoxical aspect to this lawsuit. From the statutory purpose provisions, it is clearly obvious that the DAC was created expressly to help or enhance the lives of Dallas' economically disadvantaged citizens, a target group which poignantly contains vast numbers representing minority cultures and races. Yet the lawsuit alleges that in spite of these laudatory purposes expressed in the statutes, the DAC nevertheless operates in such a way as to openly discriminate against the Dallas Mexican–Americans.

Because the DAC is an entity with only limited resources aimed at fighting social problems of almost unlimited dimensions, struggles among the various poverty groups—racial, ethnic, religious and political—which comprise the municipality's poor population exist. Naturally, the manner of distributing the scarce resources through programs administered by DAC officials is open to criticism. One apparent criticism has been the lack of exactness used by the DAC in its efforts of distribution. Minority groups' jealousies of their position relative to other minority recipients and their suspicions of the motivations of other needy groups give rise to much of the aforementioned criticism. In addition, those jealousies and suspicions cast political overtones to everything that DAC does. No doubt, many Mexican–Americans held these feelings toward Dallas' Black population since the Black population's larger absolute size and larger amount of impoverished members gave it an inherent claim to more services and jobs offered by the Economic Opportunity Act in general and DAC, in particular. The Court believes that the Mexican–American's concern over the amount of control the Dallas Black population had over DAC operations compounded the alleged legal reasons for this lawsuit.

Apparently, legitimate concern over their vested interests in the DAC poverty-oriented programs, as well as the political implications of such a suit, caused the individual plaintiffs to expand their own claims to include class-wide treatment of Mexican–Americans as a group. The appropriate definition of the class sought to be represented by the individual plaintiffs became subject of much debate during the early stages of the suit, especially as intervenors joined the plaintiff's list. The Court ruled under F.R. Civ. P. 23(b) that the complaint alleged in fact two subclasses: The first, designated as "class one" for purposes of this litigation, was defined to include:

> All past and present Mexican–American employees, agents, representatives of defendant including but not limited to all past and present Spanish surnamed employees, agents and representatives.

The second, designated as "class two," was aimed at the allegation that because of DAC's discriminatory conduct, poor Mexican–Americans in Dallas neither received nor had available to them the services, projects, and job opportunities offered city-wide to the rest of the disadvantaged. It included:

> All Mexican–American residents of the County of Dallas, Texas, including but not limited to all Spanish surnamed Americans residing in Dallas County, Texas, or who have resided in Dallas County, Texas, during any period from October, 1965, the date upon which defendant began its operations in Dallas County, Texas, until the present time.

After acknowledging the peculiarities of this case and realizing the importance its outcome has upon the usually forgotten, misplaced, and ill-treated of the City of Dallas, one nevertheless comes down to two crucial issues at hand. Insofar as the individual plaintiffs are concerned, did the DAC, its employees, and supervisory personnel discriminate against the plaintiffs by failing to hire them, promote them, or illegally fire them on the basis of their national origin? Insofar as the "class two" Mexican–American residents of Dallas County are concerned, did the DAC, its employees, and supervisory personnel discriminate against them by not making available on an equal basis its services and related programs? The facts introduced at trial provide a negative answer to the first question. As for the second, the answer is also no. The individual claims and the class claims will be treated in that order.

I.   Individuals

A.   Santos Badillo

Mr. Badillo applied for and was accepted by DAC for employment as a job development specialist in the Manpower segment of the defendant's operations. He started his $7,500 a year job on May 11, 1970, under the immediate supervision of Mrs. Edna Morrison, a Caucasian. Within a few weeks after his starting, Mrs. Morrison became aware of Mr. Badillo's spending work time in the office of the Field Director of Manpower Teams trying to find documents to substantiate his personal theory that Manpower and other DAC projects were discriminating against Mexican–Americans. Mrs. Morrison conferred with her superior and then issued a written reprimand to Mr. Badillo on June 11, 1970, advising, among other things, that he was not to proceed with his personal interests while on DAC time. The plaintiff remained undaunted and continued his investigatory work until Mrs. Morrison again found his work effort lacking. As a probationary employee—one who has three months within which to show his desire and ability for a given job with DAC—Badillo failed to meet the standard and was therefore fired on July 17, 1970.

Mrs. Morrison stated that the reason for his firing was "for cause" in that Mr. Badillo showed "poor judgment" in several instances, in that he disregarded his supervisors' directions, failed to follow normal procedures and instructions relating to the expected eight-hour work day, and lacked the correct attitude or loyalty toward the agency itself.

The reasons in support of Mrs. Morrison's firing Badillo were developed in numerous investigatory reports performed by the Office of

Economic Opportunity and the Equal Employment Opportunity Commission in response to the plaintiff's charge that the DAC discriminated against him.

Most of the factual details in this regard were developed by the O.E.O. reports, especially that of Mr. Alexander Porter which concluded in a letter to the plaintiff that "no discrimination could be shown in this instance and the DCCAC was justified in terminating your employment." The three subsequent reports, completed by Baglio, Kent and Martinez, all relied upon Porter's initial investigation to an important extent, but reached different results.

Although the Martinez report officially represented the O.E.O.'s final conclusions, it differed completely from the Porter and Kent versions and significantly from the Baglio report when it stated that the "facts warranted a finding of probable cause to credit his complaint of discrimination." The different conclusions reached by the four reports indicate two things to the court. First, that individuals can independently reach different conclusions about the same subject. And, that Mr. Badillo's constant and repetitious requests for reviews of unfavorable O.E.O. reports demonstrated his persistence in trying to obtain one final report adopting his version of the termination. That final report did appear, completed by Samuel Martinez, Director of Region VI of the O.E.O., a one-time defendant in this case until the court dismissed the claims against him under the doctrine of sovereign immunity. Martinez' posture in the case together with the thoroughness of the Porter report lead this court to put more emphasis and faith in the conclusions reached in the latter. The court makes the same conclusions with respect to the 1972 E.E.O.C. report made by Gene Renslow which supported Badillo's position.

Importantly Badillo's own testimony at trial supports these conclusions. Although being paid to perform an eight-hour day, Mr. Badillo testified that he only needed two hours to produce his quota of new job openings, and therefore only spent that much time on his job. The credibility of that statement was undermined when other evidence showed that the top "job development specialist" produced twice as many jobs as Badillo. Any bad faith on the DAC's part is also dispelled in the Court's mind when the record demonstrated that the DAC did not attempt to replace Mr. Badillo even though his position was not officially phased out.

As was most recently stated by the Fifth Circuit Court of Appeals sitting en banc, Congress, in adopting the Civil Rights Act of 1964, sought only to "give all persons equal access to the job market, not to limit an employer's right to exercise his informed judgment as to how best to run his shop." Willingham v. Macon Telegraph Company, 507 F.2d 1084 (5th Cir. 1975). In a very clear sense, the DAC had the right and perhaps even the obligation to terminate Mr. Badillo for his failure to devote his time and energy, at least to the extent of an eight-hour day, to performing his job with the correct attitude toward his superiors and

their rules without having the termination characterized as being preju-
dicially motivated. Mr. Badillo was adequately informed that his unauthorized studies performed during work time violated established DAC
procedure.

After continuing in his own way, contrary to his supervisors' directives, the decision to terminate him became necessary. It was justified
and was not discriminatory.

B.   Robert Medrano

Mr. Robert Medrano, the second individual to enter this lawsuit on
the plaintiffs' side, alleged that DAC's refusal in August, 1972, to
promote him from his position of Neighborhood Service System's Director to the job of Deputy Director of Field Services, the second highest
position in the DAC administration, was discriminatory on the basis of
national origin.

Medrano's work record with the DAC has been an exemplary one, so
much so that DAC still employs him in one of the most responsible
positions in its hierarchy. Since his initial job with the DAC, in the
Manpower component in 1968, Mr. Medrano had progressively occupied
more and more responsible job positions until the summer of 1972 when
he applied, along with approximately thirty other individuals, for the
Deputy Directorship. Indeed, because of his upward movement through
the DAC ranks from Manpower component employee, to Neighborhood
Service Center Director, to Administrative Assistant to the Executive
Director, had so closely paralleled that of Mr. Willis Johnson, a one-time
Director of DAC, Mr. Medrano felt discriminated against by not receiving
the promotion to Deputy Director.

When the Deputy Director position became vacant in 1972, Mr.
Willis Johnson took steps to fill it in a thorough, reasonable and non-
discriminatory manner. Initially, he named a screening committee on
May 11, 1972, for the purpose of reviewing applications from a wide and
varied number of places. Not only did it place advertisements for the
position in the *Dallas Morning News*, *Times Herald*, *In-Sepia News* and
El Sol de Texas (a Spanish-oriented newspaper) but, in addition, placed
notifications in all the DAC facilities in Dallas, notified other community
action agencies throughout the country and even contracted the Texas
Employment Commission.

The committee adopted the recommendation of an Assistant Director of the O.E.O. by choosing to follow "OEO Guidance 6901–1,
'Guide to Selecting the CAA Executive Director,'" for the selection
procedure to be used in filling the Deputy Director vacancy. Included in
those guidelines was an interviewing process. Of the thirty some applicants, only the ten finalists were selected for personal interviews by the
screening committee. Out of those finalists, four were of Mexican–
American origin.

The method by which the screening committee selected the ten
finalists began by dividing the applications into five random groups.

With the exception of the chairman, each committee member, separate from the other members, reviewed all groups of applications and selected what he or she considered were the two outstanding applicants in each group of five. Each committee member also rated the applications in order of preference. After tabulating the results of the ratings, the Chairman reviewed the resumes and then met with the committee to announce the finalist list and to discuss the desired objectives of the remaining selection steps.

Prior to the final interviews, the screening committee utilized OEO Guideline 6901–1 to formulate a standard set of questions in order to determine the qualifications of each remaining applicant with respect to the following criteria:

1. Goals, objectives, priorities

2. Program plans and budgets

3. Organization

4. Leadership ability and potential

5. Administrative capabilities, including depth and length of experience

6. Community support

7. Community change

8. Review and evaluation.

According to the suggested procedure contained in the OEO Guideline 6901–1, each member of the screening committee independently evaluated and awarded a numerical score with respect to the above selection criteria.

After totaling the scores of each applicant and arriving at the committee's preference list, the screening committee submitted it to Willis Johnson, Executive Director of DAC, who concurred with their conclusions that Lloyd Conley, the applicant from St. Louis, Missouri, was most qualified for the position. Of the top three finalists, Mr. Medrano finished third, with a score of 65.4. Mr. Conley scored a 77.6 and Mr. Henry Castillo, also of Mexican–American descent, finished second with a 69.4.

Mr. Medrano made many claims of fact that he hoped would support the conclusion that he was more qualified or equally as qualified as Mr. Conley. Although some of his stated facts bear relevance upon his seeking the Deputy Directorship, they by no means refute in this Court's mind the objective, reasonable conscientious job performed by the screening committee. It is true that Mr. Medrano had more work experience with the DAC, lived longer in Dallas, spoke two languages fluently, and had more contact with the Dallas poverty community. Nevertheless, Mr. Conley's appearance at trial assured the Court of his articulateness and leadership abilities. In view of Mr. Conley's impressive credentials, the Court finds the screening committee's decision to be well-founded.

In a hind-sight position as the present one, the Fifth Circuit in United States v. Jacksonville Terminal Company, 451 F.2d 418, 446 (1971), announced that in order for the Court to find that an individual was discriminated against that individual would necessarily have to present a prima facie case that the sought-after position was denied him, that it was available at the time of application, and that he was equally or more qualified than the ultimate recipient. Presented with that standard, the Court must conclude that Mr. Medrano's case is simply without merit.

C. Mrs. Andrea F. Cervantes

Mrs. Cervantes' claim arises out of her termination as a DAC Community House Aide on or about May 17, 1972, the subsequent explanations given for the occurrence, and the refusal of the DAC to hire her as an assistant director to a DAC summer program offered in 1972.

After hearing the evidence at trial, the Court concludes that Mrs. Cervantes lost her job due to the fact that a DAC budgeting move adopted in April, 1972, required the combination of the Community House component with the Neighborhood Services Program, thereby eliminating certain job categories, including those of Mrs. Cervantes and a Black peer of hers named Mrs. Butler. Placed in proper perspective, the real reason for Mrs. Cervantes' termination was not DAC discriminatory conduct but instead the simple misfortune of her having a job which ceased to exist. Although the immediate reason for her termination, as explained by her supervisor Mr. Medrano, was couched in terms of her lack of seniority, the real explanation, as pointed out above, was the natural consequence of an entity reorganizing itself. Any disparity in determining "seniority" between Mrs. Cervantes' case and other DAC employees at that time, is explained away as an inadvertent difference on the part of two different supervisors applying the same basic policy. This position is buttressed with evidence which showed that Allene Hardy, Willie Mae Butler, and Ruthie Ross—three Black Americans occupying positions with the Community House component—were also terminated within one month of Mrs. Cervantes. That fact coupled with the budgetary decision disproves any theory that Mrs. Cervantes' termination resulted from racial bias exhibited by her Black superiors toward herself and her fellow Mexican–Americans.

DAC's inadvertent or intentional bad faith with regard to Mrs. Cervantes is not involved here, as there was no evidence which showed that DAC retained "community house aide" positions after her dismissal and sought applications for the position. See McDonnell Douglas Corp. v. Green, 411 U.S. 792 (1973).

Mrs. Cervantes also contends that the DAC discriminated against her in the way it reviewed the circumstances surrounding her termination. According to the Personnel Policies and Procedures Manual effective in May 1972, and immediately thereafter until July 15, 1972, when they were amended, Mrs. Cervantes and any other aggrieved employee of DAC could request a review of their grievance. In Mrs. Cervantes' case, she requested and received an explanation from her supervisor, Mr. Medrano, for her termination. After having such a conference, an employee still dissatisfied with his or her situation was entitled to request a three-man grievance committee to review the matter within five days thereafter.

Not until December 8, 1972, some five months after her conference with Mr. Medrano, did Mrs. Cervantes contest or object in any way his explanation for her termination. At that time, she asked for further grievance proceedings. The Court finds that Mrs. Cervantes received all the necessary attention, explanation, and other procedures required of the DAC. Furthermore, no discrimination resulted against her in this regard.

Mrs. Cervantes' claims were compounded in and about the spring and summer of 1972 when the DAC allegedly discriminated against her by refusing to hire her as an assistant director for the 1972 Summer Program. Although Mrs. Cervantes did have some previous experience with a somewhat related summer program conducted by the Target Area Coordinating Council (TACC), this fact and the other evidence introduced at trial proved insufficient to establish that Mrs. Cervantes was equal to or superior to the men hired to head up the DAC 1972 Summer Program, as is required by the Jacksonville Paper standard. The evidence surrounding the ultimate selection of Mr. Victor Bonillo as the Assistant Director of defendant's 1972 Summer Program was incomplete and therefore proved inconsequential insofar as Cervantes' proposed theory attempted to tie his appointment with the discrimination against herself and other Mexican–Americans. Accordingly, the Court holds in favor of the defendant as to Mrs. Cervantes' claims.

* * *

II. Class aspects

Although the Court has found in favor of the defendant DAC as to the individual plaintiffs' claims, the class itself may still prevail on its own merits under the doctrine of Parham v. Southwestern Bell Telephone Co., 433 F.2d 421 (8th Cir. 1970). Primarily, the class contends that ever since the DAC's origin in 1965, its programs, facilities, and employment opportunities have not been advertised, or otherwise extended to the Mexican–American segment of Dallas' population. The class contends that this is an inequitable and discriminatory manipulation of the program. Implicit in that assertion is the parallel contention that part of the Dallas Black population, because of its large numbers and consequential occupation of influential positions within the DAC organization, has discriminated against the plaintiff class in the above-mentioned ways. Due to the importance the DAC holds in the lives of many of Dallas' impoverished citizens, this lawsuit naturally takes on political overtones which requires a close scrutiny and analysis of the evidence presented at trial. Much of the plaintiffs' case consists of their reliance upon DAC statistics.

In many employer discrimination cases, racial statistics are used as a basis for allocating the burden of proof. Typically, the theory advanced is that a total absence or very nominal number of Blacks in the work force or some departmental level thereof constitutes a permissible basis for a jury or judge to infer that the employer has discriminated. In some instances, that inference together with supporting facts and statistics will be strong enough to establish the plaintiff's prima facie case, thereby casting the burden upon the employer to disprove the inference with evidence either showing the lack of a discriminatory effort or showing a reasonable business necessity for such conduct. See Fiss, *A Theory of Fair Employment Laws*, 38 U. Chi. L. Rev. 235, 270 (1971).

The Fifth Circuit Court of Appeals has accepted the logic behind this standard, where a plaintiff initially demonstrates that a Caucasian-controlled employer has altogether failed to hire or promote Blacks or some other minority. The logical inference behind the legal shifting of the burden of proof also recognizes that an employer, for purposes of discrimination cases, intends the natural consequence of his acts. Thus, for example, if an employer, either intentionally or inadvertently, hires few or no minority members then the courts presume that he intends the natural consequence of his acts—i.e., employment discrimination.

From an examination of the Fifth Circuit opinions dealing with "discrimination statistics," one receives the impression that a plaintiff's ability to establish a prima facie case will usually depend upon other factors or evidence of an employer's discriminatory conduct in addition to statistical evidence. In most if not all cases where the burden of proof has shifted, "plus factors" of an employer's discriminatory policies—such as a biased seniority system or testing program—have been present.

In Johnson v. Goodyear Tire & Rubber Co., 491 F.2d 1364–73 (5th Cir. 1974), the plus factor evidence took the form of a program of "discriminatory testing," improper use of "high school diploma as a requirement for hiring," and a "discriminatory seniority system." In *Rowe*, supra, the plus factor drew upon the employer's history of having had a lay-off and rehiring policy based upon prior experience with the defendant, which naturally worked to the discriminatory disadvantage of Black employees who had no such experience. That pattern and practice had carried over into the then present employment decision making process in a subtle, yet discriminatory nature.

In the United States v. Hayes International Corp. case, 456 F.2d 112, 119 (5th Cir. 1972), the defendant's inconsistent use of a referral service for all new employees turned out to be the additional factor besides statistical proof. And recently, in Pettway v. American Cast Iron Pipe Co., 494 F.2d 211 (1974), the Fifth Circuit pointed out that the "statistical pattern" of racial stratification between and within the defendant's departments by the derogation of Black employees into lower-paying jobs "(should be) considered in light of the past intentional discrimination and the illegal testing requirement." Coupled together, the statistics and the plus factors presented a "prima facie case of present effect of past discrimination in the company's promotion and transfer process."

The sum total of these cases brings this Court to conclude that it is indeed the rare lawsuit where a plaintiff's proffer of statistical evidence lone is consequential enough to establish a prima facie case of discrimination and thereby cause the burden to shift to the defendant. * * *

A.   *Statistical Evidence*

The reasons for reviewing the effect statistical evidence has upon an employer's discrimination suit are several-fold. First, of all the evidence produced at trial by the plaintiff, the Court fails to see any "plus factors" of discriminatory conduct, policies, or procedures exhibited by DAC toward Dallas' Mexican–American population. Under a reading of the above cases holding in favor of the statistical evidence creating a prima facie case, that conclusion would require an unequivocal or "overpowering" showing of statistical proof of discrimination in order for this Court to find that the plaintiff class had carried its burden of making a prima facie case. Although an analysis of the statistical evidence presented in this case offers some sticky problems, the Court nevertheless concludes that the plaintiff class' statistics proved altogether insufficient to establish either a prima facie case or actual discrimination on the part of the DAC toward the Mexican–Americans.

* * *

In summary, the Court finds that the plaintiff has failed to establish a prima facie case of discrimination through a statistical evidence presentation. The burden of proof therefore did not shift to the defendant.

B.   *Other Evidence of Discrimination*

In addition to its discrimination claim based upon statistical evidence, the plaintiff class has also complained that the services provided by the DAC have been insufficiently advertised so as to attract and notify a proportionate number of Mexican–Americans. The Court also finds this claim to be without merit. The evidence points out that since 1970, three years before the filing of this lawsuit, the DAC printed one of its four employment promotional items in Spanish, announced job opportunities over several radio stations including KBUY, a Spanish speaking one, advertised opportunities in El Sol, a Spanish newspaper, as well as the two major Dallas daily newspapers. All these efforts show no discriminatory bias exhibited against the plaintiff class.

Part of the plaintiff's complaint in this subject area also claims that the location of all the DAC's twenty-two (22) Community Houses, with the exception of three in Spanish speaking areas, and the four (4) Community Centers are located in predominantly Black neighborhoods. Dallas County maps with color overlays depicting the density and location of Black and Mexican–American clusterings demonstrate no racial disparity on DAC's part. The Court finds that the location of the DAC facilities have been chosen for valid reasons.

The contention that an exorbitantly large number of DAC's inner city and outlying facilities are located in predominantly Black neighborhoods, although basically true on its face nevertheless fails to convey an accurate impression of the social make-up of the county. For one thing, several of the predominantly Black areas happen coincidentally to be the same location of higher density Mexican–American areas. Therefore, a service center, such as the one in West Dallas, may not only serve a predominant portion of Blacks, but in addition serve a similarly located, yet less dense neighborhood of Mexican–Americans. In light of the fact that Mexican–Americans constitute only 6.7% of Dallas' total population, the Court must also recognize that they are far more dispersed than the more numerous and more concentrated Black population. Instead of grouping together in one or two large areas, Mexican–Americans tend to form smaller neighborhood patterns often measured by several contiguous streets which are located within larger tracts having more concentrated mixtures of Blacks.

Once again the Court finds no discrimination or discriminatory effect practiced upon the poverty level Mexican–Americans by the DAC and its plan of offering O.E.A. structured programs to them. The pragmatics of operating such an organization reinforce this conclusion. Due to the constant change in personnel, uncertainty in long range financing, and burden in administering the individual programs, the Court realizes that the DAC would do little, if any, good if its primary worry concerned meeting specific ratio tests in every detail of its operation so as to preclude every possibility of its operations appearing to some minority recipients as discriminatory.

The attorneys for the defendant are directed to prepare and submit the appropriate form of judgment to the Court.

Aruna Lee
Korean-Latino Relations Grow Icy
New America Media, Mar. 12, 2007

Economic necessity is making Korean and Latino immigrants depend on one another. Yet, tensions, not warmer ties, seem to be growing. Aruna Lee is a writer for New America Media.

LOS ANGELES—Steve Cho, a Korean owner of a liquor store in the Pic–Union/Westlake neighborhood of Los Angeles and a member of the U.S. National Guard, likes to listen to Spanish music and is currently learning Spanish. He admits, however, that there is hardly any communication between Koreans and Latinos. Others say the separation runs even deeper.

In clubs, schools and the work place Koreans and Latinos are increasingly sharing the same spaces, and yet there is little interaction between them. One public high school teacher here noted that his

Korean and Latino students have "learned from their relatives to mutually ignore each other."

As the two communities continue to grow they are becoming more dependent economically on one another. In major cities across the U.S. it is now common to find Korean-owned establishments employing predominantly Latino workers. While this opens opportunities for cultural exchange it also often leads to serious, sometimes violent, misunderstandings.

"The building I live in is predominantly Korean," says Cho. In the next building nearly all of the residents are Latino. There are no links between residents of the two buildings, just the occasional glance and a resounding silence.

An article on Korean–Latino relations, in the Spanish-language daily, *La Opinion* listed some of the similarities between the two communities. Among them is the high population of foreign-born, Korean and Latino alike, many of whom struggle with English. This not only limits their ability to communicate with one another, but also to participate in the political process and integrate into mainstream society.

Alvaro Ramirez, who was born in Colombia and came to the US in 1996, told *La Opinion* he believes Koreans exploit the Latino community through the high prices of goods sold in local stores and the low wages paid to Latino employees.

According to Korean media in Los Angeles, which has one of the largest Korean and Latino populations in the country, nearly 60 percent of Koreatown's labor force is Latino.

Jae Hak Lee, a researcher at Koryo University in Seoul, Korea says his studies reveal that nearly 65 percent of Latino workers employed by Koreans say they have a negative view of their employers. Two out of three Latino employees say they would prefer to work for non-Koreans, who would have more respect for labor laws. In contrast, 74 percent of Korean business owners say they prefer to hire Latinos. Why the discrepancy? For some, the reason is cultural.

Many Korean immigrants tend to be entrepreneurs. They come from a society where a six-day work week is the norm; and because they often don't speak English they use their savings to open small businesses here. The size of the Latino labor force and a burgeoning Korean entrepreneurial sector make it a given that these two communities are going to rely on each other, particularly in cities like New York and Los Angeles.

Tensions between the two groups have been growing for several years. There has been a recent spike in court cases involving Korean business owners and their Latino employees. According to the New York-based National Mobilization Against Sweatshops, Latino immigrant workers filed a lawsuit against the Food Bazaar, a Korean supermarket chain for $1.5 million in unpaid wages.

Nine Latino workers claim they received no wages for the duration of their employment as grocery baggers. Forced to live off customer tips that amounted to $100–200 a week, they say they worked an average of 50 hours per week, and were fired without notice.

"Some Korean employers treat their Latino employees differently than Korean workers," says Danny Park at the Korean Immigrant Workers Alliance. "They've been known to fire workers without any notice."

One story that caught the attention of both communities was the killing of a Korean man in late January by his Latino employee after his boss apparently criticized him for not working hard enough.

The incident raised fears among Koreans, who are concerned over a repeat of the deadly Los Angeles riots of 1992, in which African Americans, angered by perceived racism from Korean storeowners, burned and looted Korean-owned establishments. This time, they say any riots that break out could be between Koreans and Latinos.

In 2002 a number of Latino employees were fired by their Korean employers after attempting to form a union. Last year many Latino workers expressed fear of losing their jobs after participating in mass rallies against planned immigration laws.

Growing tensions have spurred leaders in both communities to call for increased dialogue and promotion of cultural understanding. Charles Kim, executive director of the Korean American Coalition, says the Korean community needs to make more of an effort to understand the Latino community.

"Koreans need to change the way they see their Latino neighbors," says Kim.

Storeowner Steve Cho says that while community leaders and activists call for unity and understanding, the divide is clear and not going away in the neighborhoods.

"Ultimately," says Cho, "Latinos and Koreans have to get along. We have to learn to respect our mutual cultures and see each other as human beings."

Elena Shore of New America Media contributed to this article.

Notes and Questions

1.   For more discussion of workplace discrimination, see Part Seven: The Workplace.

2.   Are relations among outgroups as bad as they sound in *Badillo* and the Aruna Lee selection? If so, what is the solution?

3.   Can you name an issue on which all groups of color might join forces? If you answered, affirmative action, then affirmative action *for whom*? See the *Ho* case, discussed in Part Four, infra, that set Asians against blacks and Latinos over this very issue.

*

Part Three

LANGUAGE RIGHTS

In Parts Two and Nine, you read about some of the early forms of Latino/a resistance to Anglo domination, including indigenous revolts and land-grant conflicts in the Southwest. Another, quieter form of resistance takes a cultural turn and consists of maintaining a common language and culture in the face of homogenizing pressure.

This Part takes up two forms of such resistance, namely folk tales, corridos, and other narratives that tell of oppression and a people's never-ending struggle to be free of it. And a second manifestation consists of the determination to preserve the Spanish language at school, in the workplace, or when communicating with the government.

Chapter 7

LANGUAGE IN LATINO CULTURE

SECTION 1. LANGUAGE AS THE
EMBODIMENT OF CULTURE

Latinos are perhaps more attached to their language than is any other non-English-speaking immigrant or minority group. Compare *The Latino/a Condition* 557 (Richard Delgado & Jean Stefancic eds., 1998); Lupe S. Salinas, *Linguaphobia, Language Rights, and the Right of Privacy*, 3 Stan. J. C.R.-C.L. 53, 62 (2007), noting that this tenacity draws on a nearby border as well as concentrated settlements such as New York, San Antonio, and Dallas where Spanish is a lingua franca.

One reason for this deep attachment may be that language is the vehicle for transmission of culture. A host of tales, stories, songs, corridos (laments), actos, and street and improvisational theatre, much of it in Spanish, embodies the group's history and struggles against an Anglo society that seemed bent on destroying that culture at every turn. See also David G. Garcia, *Remembering Chavez Ravine: Culture Clash and Critical Race Theater*, 26 Chicano–Latino L. Rev. 111 (2006).

Many crucial events in Latino history—treatment at the hands of Texas Rangers, the struggles of undocumented immigrants, the exploits of guerrilla warriors and "social bandits," are recorded in Spanish only. The official histories are either devoid of them or contain sanitized accounts, from the victor's viewpoint, of what happened. Thus, a Latino/a child who grows up speaking only English, because school authorities and the surrounding culture discourage his learning and speaking Spanish, is cut off from events that may have shaped his own family and dictated its fortunes. The child is also cut off from a historical framework that can help the child understand the host of indignities, including playground chants and taunts, which come her way on account of her looks and last name. For a discussion of social banditry, see Eric J. Hobsbawm, *Primitive Rebels: Studies in Archaic Forms of Social Movement in the 19th and 20th Centuries* (1965).

What is lost when a group's history is recorded by another, more powerful, group speaking a different language? See the following excerpt by prominent historian Rodolfo Acuña giving one graphic example:

Rodolfo F. Acuña
Crocodile Tears: Lynching of Mexicans
HispanicVista.com, July 20, 2005

The U.S. Senate just the other day issued an apology for its history of inaction on lynchings. It acknowledged decades of obstruction. The Senate heard testimony from more than 150 descendants of lynching victims. More than 200 anti-lynching bills had been introduced, three passed the House and seven U.S. presidents lobbied for such laws. Tellingly, Congress has never apologized for slavery. It has been documented that a total of 4,742 Americans were lynched between 1882 and 1968. Of these 3,452 were African Americans.

Sen. Mary L. Landrieu (D–La.) sponsored the bill after she read James Allen's "Without Sanctuary: Lynching Photography in America." Beyond irony some right wing radio hosts have been hailing this action, comparing it to today's use of the filibuster by Democrats to prevent the life appointment of right wing judges.

Related to this action, I have received several interesting calls from reporters this week. A *Los Angeles Times* writer called me about information on *El Clamor Publico*, a Spanish-language newspaper published in Los Angeles from 1855–1859. It is the 150th anniversary of the paper and the *Times* wanted to acknowledge its existence.

On June 15, I received an Email from Armando Miguelez, one of the foremost experts on 19th Century Spanish language newspapers. Armando commented on an article published by the *Washington Post*, pointing to the irony of the Senate's actions. He observed that in a four-year period in the *El Clamor Publico* alone, he counted 80 linchamientos of Mexicans, Chileans, Peruvians, Indians and Blacks in California. It is doubtful whether the Allen book included this source and the figures do not include those of Spanish-language newspapers in Texas, New Mexico and Arizona. For example, the files at Tuskegee Institute, considered the most comprehensive count of lynching victims, lists the lynching of fifty Mexicans in the states of Arizona, California, New Mexico, and Texas.

William D. Carrigan and Clive Webb's "The Lynching of Persons of Mexican Origin or Descent in the United States, 1848 to 1928," has different figures. Between 1848 and 1928, according to Carrigan and Webb, mobs lynched at least 597 Mexicans. This does not include many incidents of other forms of mob violence. This is considerable, considering that the Mexican population was small in comparison to the Black population. Webb and Carrigan described how on November 16, 1928, four masked men broke into a hospital in Farmington, New Mexico. They seized Rafael Benavides who was dying of gunshot wounds and hanged him from a locust tree. Benavides was the last known lynching; not the last victim of mob violence.

As mentioned, many of the lynchings of Mexicans have been lost in the pages of Spanish-language newspapers such as *El Clamor Publico*.

Its publisher, Francisco Ramirez, espoused the return to Mexico movement. According to Ramirez, Mexicans could not find justice in the United States. On May 10, 1856, Ramirez wrote "California has fallen into the hands of the ambitious sons of North America who will not stop until they have satisfied their passions, by driving the first occupants of the land out of the country, vilifying their religion and disfiguring their customs." The *Clamor* described how Texans from El Monte threw hot tar on Diego Navarro's family home and broke into the house, dragged him out, and executed him, along with two other Mexicans whom they accused of being members of a rebel gang.

There was also the case of the Berreyesa family whose problems began with Bear Flaggers. They assassinated an elder Berreyesa and his two nephews in 1848. In July 1854 a band of Euroamericans dragged Encarnacion Berreyesa from his house while his wife and children looked on, and suspended him from a tree. When Berreyesa did not confess to the killings, vigilantes left him half dead and hanged Berreyesa's brother Nemesio.

The most flagrant act of vigilantism was at Downieville in 1851. A kangaroo court convicted a Mexican woman called Juanita who was pregnant and lynched her as 2000 miners looked on. She was the first woman hanged in California. Popular lore rationalized that Juanita was a prostitute (inferring that the lynching was lamentable but, after all, Juanita was antisocial). Years later her husband sued but was ignored by the courts.

Beyond the acknowledgment that these incidents happened, history has its lessons. For example, there is a difference between a senate filibuster to prevent the appointment of a racist judge and a filibuster to prevent the passage of a law to prosecute lynching.

There is also historical context. You would think that people would think about consequences such as unjust wars. Clark Clifford and Robert McNamara have admitted that the Vietnam War was wrong. Fifty years from now, will it make a difference if Congress admits that Americans were wrong for the U.S. imperial wars in the Middle East?

The lynchings were wrong then, and today the hatred and the terrorism of minutemen on the border draw from an American root: racism and violence at anytime or anywhere.

––––––––––

If Acuña is right, Mexicans and Mexican Americans were lynched at a frequency (given their then-small numbers) similar to that of blacks. But this fact was unknown to most mainstream historians, because the accounts appeared in community newspapers, which were in Spanish. See also William D. Carrigan & Clive Webb, *The Lynching of Persons of Mexican Origin or Descent in the United States, 1848 to 1928*, 37 J. Soc. Hist. 411 (2003); Walter Van Tillburgh Clark, *The Ox–Bow Incident* (1940).

Should Latino/a intellectuals and storytellers write in Spanish, for all or part of their work? Should they write for their people? Or should they aim for a crossover audience? Postcolonial scholars address a similar issue.

Richard Delgado
Rodrigo's Corrido: Race, Postcolonial
Theory, and U.S. Civil Rights
60 Vand. L. Rev. 1691, 1705–10 (2007)

"Writers like Ngugi wa Thiong'o, Chinua Achebe, Haunani–Kay Trask, Frantz Fanon, and Trinh Minh–Ha," Rodrigo began, "have been pointing out how the colonial subject forced to speak English or French loses touch with his own people. This happened, of course, with American Indian, Alaskan Native, and Australian aboriginal children sent to English-speaking boarding schools. But it can also happen to an adult writer such as Ngugi. If he writes in English or French, he ends up writing for an audience that consists of the occupying force and their relatives in the homeland. He chooses terms and issues that appeal to them and are understandable in light of their experience. He unconsciously softens his punches and tries to reach common ground with them."

"For the sake of argument," I said, "what's wrong with that? Isn't crossover what every writer wants?"

"It's of course important to appeal to European progressives, if only to speed the day when they leave. But, for Ngugi, it's a big mistake to write with them in mind. For the colonial language stealthily incorporates the worldview of the conquering nation. Terms like 'merit,' 'leader,' 'responsible government,' 'folk medicine,' and 'tribe' render the colonial subject one-down. It's very hard to make an argument for liberation using the language of the oppressor. All the terms carry meanings that other people have given them. You end up sounding irresponsible, quaint, or ridiculous."

"Derrick Bell once pointed out something similar, showing how litigation under American law leads public interest lawyers to sacrifice their clients' interests time after time."

"And that genius, Alan Freeman," Rodrigo added with alacrity, "showed how the very structure of antidiscrimination law rendered minorities worse off, even when they won. Girardeau Spann did, too."

"And I'm sure you have noticed how certain critical theorists use counterstories to displace master narratives such as without-intent-no-discrimination or the idea that colorblindness could ever be a coherent civil rights strategy. These narratives inform civil rights law so deeply that over time they come to seem commonplace and natural. But they are not—they shift burdens and presumptions in a way that keeps us always running uphill."

"Yes," Rodrigo said, scribbling something on a piece of paper and tucking it into his pocket. "Many race-crits, especially storytellers such as Derrick Bell and Patricia Williams are discontent with the dominant language of the law. Writing in a different key, or even a different language, might solve some of those problems."

"And for a broad theory of the role of language they can look to the work of Ngugi and other postcolonials who distrust the dominant language and dominant discourse."

"Exactly," Rodrigo said. "As Edward Said once said, the power to narrate is the power to destroy. Thus, resistance figures must tell and retell their stories. And many of those writers consciously ignore English or French, even though they know them well, and choose to write in a native language, even an oral one, with no written vocabulary or alphabet. Ngugi, for example, explains that when he criticized the racism of the colonial system, he won praises and prizes, and his novels were in all the syllabi. But when he started writing in a language understood by the peasants and questioning the very foundations of imperialism and foreign domination of the Kenyan economy and culture, he was sent to maximum security prison. For him, literature was a form of combat. Oh, and he wrote children's literature, too."

"Breathtaking," I said. "That would certainly give force. . . . "

"And a voice . . ." Rodrigo interjected.

"Right, to Latinos insisting on a legitimate role for Spanish. That language enables them to speak out against oppression and discrimination in a way that one can't—at least so readily—in English, the language of the very group that is oppressing them. A powerful insight, Rodrigo. Do other postcolonial writers say the same thing?"

"Many do. Braj B. Kachru writes 'The English language is a tool of power, domination and elitist identity, and of communication across continents.' I have the quote right here. This echoes the finding of contemporary Lat–Crit authors who write that Latinos are 'perhaps more attached to their language than any other non-English speaking immigrant or minority group.' "

"Hmm. Fascinating," I said. "I did not know that. Maybe that's because, as your friend Trinh Minh–Ha put it, 'Language is one of the most complex forms of subjugation, being at the same time the locus of power and unconscious servility.' I just brought that up on my laptop while you were speaking. And here's a cross-reference to Raja Rao. . . . "

"Another well known postcolonial author," Rodrigo interjected. "I've run across a lot of his writings."

"I'm not surprised. Rao says that the colonial subject who adopts the language of the conqueror 'has to convey in a language that is not one's own the spirit that is one's own. One has to convey the various shades and omissions of a certain thought-movement that looks maltreated in an alien language.' "

"In fact," Rodrigo replied, excitedly fishing a second piece of paper out of his pocket. "Simon During says much the same thing. I have it right here. 'For the post-colonial to speak or write in the imperial tongues is to call forth a problem of identity, to be thrown into mimicry and ambivalence.' "

"Trenchant," I exclaimed. "It reminds me of Frantz Fanon's words about psychiatric self-preservation. The native must take forceful action, or else he or she succumbs to despair and depression. Holding onto one's language could be a potent way of achieving mental health for the colonized subject such as the Latino."

"And with Latinos," Rodrigo exclaimed. "It may explain why the second generation, the children of the immigrants, do much worse than the first, with a high rate of drop out, drug-taking, arrest, and other forms of pathology. This could give ammunition to Latino and Asian bilingual activists seeking support for their programs. I have much more on this. Maybe when we talk about Latinos a little bit later, I'll bring it in."

"I hope you do," I said. "I don't know much about Latinos and the language controversy. I'm eager to learn. But I think you said you had a number of other themes."

SECTION 2. LANGUAGE AS A RECORD OF STRUGGLE

If history is always written by the victors, the counternarratives of a people who fought valiantly, but lost, can easily remain submerged, the story of their valiant struggles against overwhelming odds hidden from view. Worse yet, the victorious army's official historians may paint their resistance as futile, tricky, doomed, quixotic, or devious, when in fact it was heroic and an expression of a people's desire to be free.

Richard Delgado
*Rodrigo's Corrido: Race, Postcolonial
Theory, and U.S. Civil Rights*
60 Vand. L. Rev. 1691, 1738–41 (2007)

"Hundreds of *corridos, actos, cantares,* and laments—called *decimas,*" Rodrigo continued, "complain of swaggering, ruthless Anglo developers who cheated the Mexicans out of their ancestral lands, and white teachers and authority figures who insult them and treat them mean. *Corridos* tell of brutal Texas Rangers who shoot them for no good reason and white men who treat their women as sex objects and their men with disrespect. Américo Paredes, who taught at Texas, published several collections of this literature."

"Didn't a recent movie build on one of his themes?"

"Yes. *The Ballad of Gregorio Cortes.* It tells the story of a legendary Mexican–American outlaw who bravely defended his rights and challenged injustice at the hands of Texas authorities. Other tales and songs describe Mexican Americans' struggle to preserve their identity and affirm their rights as human beings. They tell of feisty heroes who refused 'to take it lying down,' but fought back against injustice and oppression. One group, known as the 'border corridos,' celebrates heroes who risk their lives '*defendiendo su derecho*'—defending their rights."

"These certainly sound like some of the postcolonial themes you mentioned earlier from the other side of the world."

"Yes. And the people sang these songs at events, such as weddings, and at work when no Anglo was listening. Oh, and before I forget. Some of the *corridos* describe *sin verguenza* (shameless) Anglo thieves and cattle rustlers."

"Exactly the opposite of the way Latinos were constructed in the Anglo imagination, as devious, thieving, shoot-you-in-the-back types."

"The literature does open one's eyes. One theme reappears frequently: It's how Anglo Americans claimed to be *cristianos* and approached you with an overwhelming sense of moral superiority. They established a system of law that was supposed to protect everyone's rights. Yet they ended up acting worse then the Comanches."

"Do any of the ballads mention lynching?" I asked. "You mentioned this earlier."

"Some of them do. They also describe many uprisings, such as the one resulting from El Plan de Diego and a resulting Anglo crackdown, another that occurred when Gregorio Cortes was finally arrested, and several that protested lynchings. One famous corrido, entitled *Los Sediciosos*, celebrates a 1915 uprising in which a large group of angry Mexicans battled a force of Anglos to avenge a host of indignities. Others celebrate Joaquin Murietta, a Robin–Hood type figure who stole from the rich and gave to the poor. Modern-day ballads celebrate braceros or fence-crossing, undocumented aliens who make it across the border, or even drug dealers who thumb their noses at Anglo authority figures."

"What about the themes you mentioned—filth, hypersexuality, and jabber?"

"They appear, too, sometimes accompanied by wonderment and a sense of irony. For example, one complains that Anglos consider Mexicans dirty, when it is they who desecrate the earth and pollute the streams. Later, community newspapers such as "El Clamor" presented an image of taste and refinement to counter the Yankee image of a group of stupid, coarse barbarians and 'greasers.' "

Juan F. Perea
Los Olvidados: *On the Making of Invisible People*
70 N.Y.U. L. Rev. 965, 965–71 (1995)

In his recent book, Latinos, Earl Shorris poignantly describes Bienvenida Petión, a Jewish Latina immigrant, who clings to her language and culture "as if they were life itself." When Bienvenida dies, it is "not of illness, but of English." Bienvenida dies of English when she is confined to a nursing home where no one speaks Spanish, an environment in which she cannot communicate and in which no one cares about her language and culture.

"Death by English" is a death of the spirit, the slow death that occurs when one's own identity is replaced, reconfigured, overwhelmed, or rejected by a more powerful, dominant identity not one's own. For Latinos, illness by English of varying degree, even death by English, is a common affliction, without known cure. It may be identified, however, by some of its symptoms.

The mere sound of Spanish offends and frightens many English-only speakers, who sense in the language a loss of control over what they regard as "their" country. Spanish also frightens many Latinos, for it proclaims their identity as Latinos, for all to hear. The Latino's fear is rational. Spanish may subject Latinos to the harsh price of difference in the United States: the loss of a job, instant scapegoating, and identification as an outsider. Giving in to this fear and denying one's own identity as a Latino is, perhaps, to begin to die of English.

Latino invisibility is, I believe, the principal cause of illness by English. When I write of Latino invisibility, I mean a relative lack of positive public identity and legitimacy. I believe invisibility in this sense is created in several ways. Sometimes we are rendered invisible through the absence of public recognition and portrayal. Sometimes we are silenced through prohibitions on the use of Spanish. Sometimes we are rendered politically invisible, or nearly invisible, through the attribution of foreignness, what I shall call "symbolic deportation." * * *

The media presentation of the Los Angeles riots in the spring of 1992 illustrates the creation of Latino invisibility by omission. * * *

SEARCHING FOR LATINOS IN THE BOOKSTORES

When I travel, I spend a lot of time in bookstores searching for books on Latino life and history. It is hard to find such books. Not that they do not exist, as I own many of them. Yet I have never found a bookstore with a section on Latinos. There must be at least one, somewhere, but I have not found it yet. Since bookstores never have a section of books on Latinos, I have to search through many corridors, many categories, to find what I want. * * * The absence of a Latino or Hispanic studies section in most bookstores demonstrates a point about racial and ethnic categories in popular and scholarly culture. The need to roam across various corridors and subjects to find books on Latinos is caused by the absence of recognition that Latinos constitute an important subject about which many books have been written. The absence of a section on Latino studies and the fairly random sprinkling of books on Latinos throughout sections of varying relevance to Latinos is a metaphor for our denied identity, our absence from the popular imagination. To place books on United States Latinos in the Latin American studies section [as many bookstores do] is to place us outside the borders of the

United States. It is symbolic deportation to the nations of Latin America together with symbolic exclusion from identity within the United States.

The difficulty of finding books on Latinos contrasts sharply with the relative ease of finding books on African Americans and their history. Most bookstores have an African–American or Black Studies section, the result of African–American demands for books on their history and literature. That African–American history and writing are so much easier to locate than Latino history demonstrates a much greater degree of public acknowledgement and legitimacy for black identity and the lack thereof with respect to Latino identity.

Latinos must voice similar demands for the books on our history and culture, so we are not such a well-kept secret. To be scattered widely among disparate disciplines is to dissipate Latino identity without category. It is a metaphor for the popular and scholarly denial of our identity. It is another form of Latino invisibility.

Notes and Questions

1.   How strongly do present-day Latinos feel about preserving the mother tongue? See Gregory Rodriguez, *The Overwhelming Allure of English*, N.Y. Times, April 7, 2002, at 3 (Wk. in Rev.), reporting that by the third generation, many Latinos are "English dominant" and struggle to understand or make themselves understood in Spanish. Despite the growth of Spanish-language radio and other media, "The big picture is that bilingualism is very difficult to maintain," especially in the third generation. Id. Rodriguez adds, however:

> At the same time, Spanish is certainly not going away in the regions of the country that serve as gateways to new immigrants. American-born Latinos can enjoy Latin–American soap operas or old-fashioned boleros on the radio. But like children of immigrants in the past, the descendants of today's newcomers will negotiate their work lives and create art and music in the language in which they are schooled. While bilingual education is often blamed for the persistence of Spanish in the United States, most such programs are designed to shift the child into English-speaking classes within three or four years.... Even in Miami, the nation's quintessential bilingual city, international corporations complain of a shortage of fully bilingual workers to conduct business with Latin Americans in professional Spanish.

2.   Perhaps because of the rapid growth of the Latino population, other writers are much more upbeat about the future of Spanish in the United States.

3.   On postcolonial theory, see Homi K. Bhabha, *Is Frantz Fanon Still Relevant?*, Chron. Higher Ed., Mar. 18, 2005; James T. Gathii, *Imperialism, Colonialism, and International Law*, 54 Buff. L. Rev. 1013 (2007); Latin American Subaltern Studies Group, *A Founding Statement*, 20 Boundary 2, Fall 1993, at 110.

Louis E.V. Nevaer
America the Bilingual
Pacific News Service, Oct. 12, 2004

When the Census Bureau announced in 2003 that Hispanics had surpassed African Americans as the nation's largest minority, it was more than a mere demographic fact: it was a formal declaration that the United States had become a bilingual nation.

For most of its history, America has had a no-nonsense social contract with the immigrant: you are welcome, provided you become "American." To enter the mainstream of American life, one had to speak English, lest he or she be marginalized in a "Little Italy," a "Chinatown" or any other working class ethnic ghetto. Throughout the 19th and 20th centuries, millions of immigrants signed on, some even changing their names upon arriving at Ellis Island to something that sounded more "American," and insisting that their American-born children speak only English.

By the second half of the 20th century, through sheer numbers, Hispanics had changed the terms of this contract, undermining the myth of the "melting pot." For the first time, there was a permanent resident population that, however proficient in English, refused to surrender its native language. In 1970, the Census Bureau created a new category to track this Spanish-speaking population: Hispanic.

Some critics decried "Hispanic" as an artificial construct. Others, most notably African Americans, saw something sinister: a deliberate attempt by white America to create divisions among blacks. There are today, after all, four major "black" Americans: African Americans, Hispanics of color (such as baseball great Sammy Sosa and the late diva Celia Cruz), West Indians (who reject an African–American label), and immigrants from Africa, who may call themselves by their country name (Nigerian American, for example) to avoid confusion with American-born African Americans. There are emerging identities: some dark-skinned Dominican and Puerto Rican youth in New York City have taken the term "Blatinos."

But forcing a political reading on Hispanic ascendancy ignores the role of the capitalist system in transforming the United States into a bilingual consumer market. Whereas in Canada, political legislation mandates that everything be in English and French, in the United States, it is American business that is largely responsible for the proliferation of Spanish.

For decades, American corporate executives have watched with awe the explosion in the Hispanic consumer market. Hispanics today control more than $600 billion in purchasing power; by 2010, this will reach $1 trillion. The rise in the economic power of Hispanics in the United States, and the way they identify themselves—by culture and language, not race—have created a consumer market that coexists alongside the larger "Anglophone" one.

These parallel economies have alarmed some English-speaking Americans. Joan Didion's description of the linguistic "problem" in her book "Miami" is familiar. "An entrepreneur who spoke no English could still, in Miami, buy, sell, negotiate, leverage assets, float bonds, and, if he were so inclined, attend galas twice a week, in black tie." Among Anglos, she writes, "there remained considerable uneasiness on the matter of language, perhaps because the inability or the disinclination to speak English tended to undermine their conviction that assimilation was an ideal universally shared by those who were to be assimilated."

Hispanics, without apology, refuse to "assimilate," if that means giving up their culture and language. When it comes to breakfast cereal, Hispanics collectively indicated their choice would be determined by which one advertises in Spanish: Post Raisin Bran or Kellogg's Corn Flakes. Corporate America listened.

Proof? Pick up the phone and call any customer service number and you are likely to hear, "Press one to continue in English," followed by "Oprima dos para español."

Welcome to the United States de América!

The lesson is obvious: the spread of Spanish throughout the United States, in fact, is consistent with Adam Smith's "invisible hand." Said Smith, "It is not from the benevolence of the butcher, the brewer, or the baker that we expect our dinner, but from their regard to their self-interest. We address ourselves, not to their humanity, but to their self-love, and never talk to them of our necessities, but of their advantages."

Corporate America cannot be faulted for attempting to secure a competitive edge by reaching out to customers in their language of choice. In a market economy, the seller speaks the language of the buyer, whether the buyer seeks a seat on an airplane for a cross-country flight, or life insurance.

We are, in fact, in the midst of a linguistic "crisis," as Spanish spreads and English remains in denial. (Consider this tantalizing fact: More New Yorkers get their news in Spanish from Jorge Ramos on "Noticiero Univision" than in English from Dan Rather on "The CBS Evening News.") From New York to Los Angeles, from Miami to Seattle, government is struggling to provide civil servants who speak Spanish—from police officers to social workers, from librarians to motor vehicle department clerks.

The last time language challenged America this way was in the 18th century. At that time, the Founding Fathers debated whether to make English or German the "official" language and, unable to decide, declined to make a choice, thus passing the buck onto us.

Yet, there comes a point when politics has to ratify economics. Until then, corporate America will continue to address, and seek to profit from, the greatest domestic reality of the 21st century: America the Bilingual.

Ilan Stavans
The Gravitas of Spanglish
Chron. Higher Educ., Oct. 13, 2000

slang, *n.* The grunt of the human hog (*Pignoramus Intolerabilis*) with an audible memory.—Ambrose Bierce

Once asked by a reporter for his opinion on *el espanglés*—one term used to refer to Spanglish south of the border—the Nobel Prize-winner Octavio Paz is said to have responded: "Ni es bueno ni es malo, sino abominable." Indeed, it is commonly assumed that Spanglish is a bastard jargon: part Spanish and part English, with neither *gravitas* nor a clear identity. It is spoken (or broken) by many of the approximately 35 million people of Hispanic descent in the United States, who, no longer fluent in the language of Cervantes, have not yet mastered that of Shakespeare.

The trouble with this view is that it is frighteningly nearsighted. Only dead languages are static, never changing. After the various forms of Chinese, English is the second most widely spoken language around the world today, with 350 million speakers; Spanish is the third, with 250 million. In the Americas, where English and Spanish cohabit promiscuously, Spanglish spreads effortlessly. "Tiempo is money," intones an advertisement running on a San Antonio radio station. Musicians and literati use Spanglish without apology in songs, novels, poems, and nonfiction—often merely sprinkling in a few words, but also using a full-blown dialect. Even on the campaign trail, George W. Bush's nephew, George P. Bush, can be heard at political rallies switching between Spanish, English, and, yes, Spanglish.

Not surprisingly, Spanglish has become a hot topic. For some time, I've been working on a lexicon of the language, and this semester I'm offering a course based on my research, "The Sounds of Spanglish." In historical and geographic scope, it is, I believe, the first of its kind and has drawn about 60 students (unusual for a small liberal-arts institution like Amherst College). The buzz the course and the dictionary have created on National Public Radio and in newspapers around the globe has brought home to me just how much interest the subject of Spanglish arouses these days. But it also generates anxiety—and even xenophobia. In the United States, it announces to some people an overall *hispanización* of society; abroad, it raises the specter of U.S. cultural imperialism and the creation of a "McLengua."

But a language cannot be legislated. It is the most democratic form of expression of the human spirit. Every attack serves as a stimulus, for nothing is more inviting than that which is forbidden. To seize upon the potential of Spanglish, it is crucial to understand the development of both Spanish and English.

Antonio de Nebrija, the first to compile a Spanish grammar, noted in the 15th century: "Siempre la lengua fue compañera del imperio." An imperial tool, indeed, with a clear-cut task: to spread the sphere of influence of the Catholic crown. But, as the ethnolinguist Angel Rosenblatt argued as far back as 1962, Spanish was never simply transplanted; instead, it adapted to the new reality. For more than 500 years, Spanish has twisted and turned in spontaneous fashion, from the Argentine Pampas to the rough roads of Tijuana. Today, it is as elastic and polyphonic as ever. A person in Madrid can communicate with someone in Caracas, but numerous nuances—from meaning to accent and emphasis—distinguish the two.

The verbal dimension of the Conquest is, I am convinced, a little-known aspect of the encounter between Europe and the pre-Columbian world that ought to be analyzed in detail. For the Conquest involved not only political, military, and social colonization; it was an act of linguistic subjugation, imposed on millions of Indian peoples who spoke such languages as Mayan, Huichol, and Tarascan in Mexico, and Arucanian, Guaraní, and Quechua in South America. The Spanish language spoken today on the continent that ranges from Ciudad Juárez to Tierra del Fuego is an acquired artifact. Of course, the fact that Sor Juana Inés de la Cruz and Jorge Luis Borges wrote their poems and stories in Cervantes's tongue doesn't mean that they wrote in translation. Their Spanish was as much theirs as it was the property of Benito Jerónimo Feijoo, Miguel de Unamuno, or Federico García Lorca. But their language, as such, arrived in the Americas in far different fashion than Spanish came to the Iberian Peninsula. It is no coincidence that 1492, the annus mirabilis in Iberian history, when Spanish began to be standardized and the Jews were expelled, was also the year that Columbus, and the language of Iberia, sailed the ocean blue.

It is in this period that Spanish became a language of power, a global language with an army, a language through which Catholic Spain concentrated its strength and announced itself as a well-delineated nation to other countries, spreading its world-view in northern Africa, Turkey, the Philippines, the Caribbean, and the Americas. But what was being imposed? The answer might surprise those critics of Spanglish who worry about linguistic impurity.

It was also in 1492 that Nebrija, a respected scholar at the University of Salamanca, published his *Gramática la lengua castellana*, the first grammar of the Spanish language, and his *Diccionario latino-español*. Shortly after, around 1495, he came out with the *Vocabulario español-latino*. The climate was ripe in Spain not only for the consolidation of Castile and Aragon into a single Catholic empire, but also for a unifying tongue that would help centralize political and social power. The so-called Reconquista of Muslim-held territory in Spain, which had started in the 11th century, was finally complete. But to become one, a nation needs a set of symbols, a shared history, a centralized power structure—and a single, commonly understood language. Castilian Spanish became that language.

By devoting himself to standardizing and cataloging the spelling, syntax, and grammar of Castilian Spanish, Nebrija legitimated a language whose speakers had only recently become self-conscious about its use. Over a period of several centuries, the vulgar Latin spoken in the peripheries of the Roman Empire, which was different from the classical Latin of authors like Ovid and Seneca, had evolved on the Iberian Peninsula into various dialects. Those, in turn, had been gradually absorbed by one, Castilian. The language of the New World was also penetrating Iberian Spanish. For example, the 1492 *Diccionario* contained the Latin term "barca" for a small rowboat; the 1495 *Vocabulario* listed the Indian term "canoa," from the Nahuatl, followed by the Latin definition.

* * *

Yet the soul-searching about the Spanish language has not extended to consideration of its role as an instrument of colonial control. That is because Spain is mired in a symbolic battle with the United States. Still smarting from the 1898 loss of Cuba, Puerto Rico, and the Philippines to U.S. influence, the Spanish take pride in the fact that their language is now the second-most-important tongue in the land of their former enemy. Noting Spain's importance in the American past, King Juan Carlos proudly announced during the Quincentennial of Christopher Columbus's "discovery" of the Americas that "España está al centro del pasado de los Estados Unidos." That same year, Puerto Rico, in a nationwide referendum, established Spanish as the island's official language—for which Spain awarded the Puerto Rican people the prestigious Príncipe de Asturias prize for extraordinary achievement. And only a few months ago, the prize went to branches of the academia in the Americas, in recognition of their efforts to preserve the language of Nebrija.

Small wonder that, in such an atmosphere, the melding of Spanish with English in Spanglish seems threatening.

Of course, English makes up the other part of Spanglish. The fact that Shakespeare's language has no official body like the Real Academia Española to protect it is reason to rejoice. Dictionaries have been produced by individuals unaffiliated with political causes, like Robert Cawdrey, Noah Webster, and, of course, Samuel Johnson—the insuperable Dr. Johnson—who remains a magisterial model.

In many ways, Johnson's *Dictionary of the English Language*, which first appeared in 1755, followed the same pattern as the Spanish dictionary, using quotations from canonical figures to put a word's usage in the proper context. In his introduction, Dr. Johnson noted that language was in constant mutation. Still, he said, his mission was to honor his country so "that we may no longer yield the palm of philology without a contest to the nations of the continent" and to give "longevity to that which its own nature forbids to be immortal."

But Johnson's task was not to promote the world-view of a state or empire. He was the quintessential individual. He argued against establishing an academy of the English language, lest "the spirit of English liberty" be hindered or destroyed. He believed the worst malady to afflict a language was spread by translators too prone to use foreign words, especially French, rather than colloquial alternatives. At the same time, he was open to foreign influences, tracing words to Greek, Roman, and other etymologies, and allowing for neologisms.

Even the creation of the *Oxford English Dictionary*, by far the most reputed lexicon in the English language, epitomizes individualism and openness. It was not an official group, but a university (and within it, Richard Chevenix Trench, then Dean of Westminster), that called in 1857 for a new dictionary to cure "the deficiencies of the language." Work by hundreds of people around the world began in 1878, and the actual publication of "125 constituent fascicules" took place from 1884 to 1928. While the endeavor was dedicated to Queen Victoria, and early copies were presented to King George V and to the president of the United States, it was, by all accounts, a nonofficial effort by Oxford University and the Clarendon Press. And it took as its objective categorizing words from English-language regions far and wide.

The birth of Spanglish per se is not too difficult to place in this history. From 1492 through the mid–19th century, the encounter of the Anglo–Saxon and Hispanic cultures produced a bare minimum of verbal miscegenation. The chronicles of conquest and conversion of Alvar Núñez Cabeza de Vaca, El Inca Garcilaso de la Vega, Gaspar Pérez de Villagrá, Fathers Eusebio Kino and Junípero Serra, and many others, for example, were primarily targeted at the Iberian Peninsula. They were composed in Castilian Spanish and colored by few regionalisms.

The linguistic picture changed dramatically in the 19th century in the region that is now the Southwestern United States. Between 1803, when Thomas Jefferson negotiated the Louisiana Purchase, and 1848, when the Treaty of Guadalupe Hidalgo signed over almost one-third of Mexico's land to the United States, Anglo arrivals created a dialogue between English and Spanish, beginning a tentative merging of the two tongues.

With the 1848 treaty, the Mexican people in the Southwest became, overnight, Americans. Curiously, however, no mention was made anywhere in the document of the inhabitants' *madre lengua*, although newspaper reports noted that Spanish was to be respected. Soon, however, English became the dominant tongue of business and diplomacy, although usage of Spanish in schools and homes did not altogether vanish. Then, with the Spanish–American War, and U.S. control over formerly Spanish colonies, the United States replaced the Spanish empire as a global power. The Spanish language was out, at least politically; English was in. Again, however, Spanish usage didn't altogether cease; it was kept alive in areas like Miami and New York, which were becoming magnets for immigrants.

Nevertheless, it was clear that the communication code was changing. From 1901 until the end of the millennium, dictionaries of Anglicisms were published with more and more frequency all across the

Hispanic world—a symptom of verbal cross-fertilization. Words like lasso, rodeo, amigo, mañana, and tortilla made it into English; mister and money into Spanish. Added to the mix, numerous Nahuatl words like *molcajete* (mortar), *aguacate* (avocado), and *huipil* (a traditional embroidered dress) are accepted by the Real Academia Española as "Americanismos."

Out of this potpourri comes Spanglish—a vital social code, whose sheer bravura is revolutionizing both Spanish and, to a lesser extent, English.

There isn't one Spanglish, but many. Issues of nationality, age, and class make a difference. The multiplicity is clear in the United States, where the lingo spoken by Cuban–Americans is different from so-called Dominicanish (Nuyorican) Spanglish. Localisms abound. There are not only geographical differences (Istlos, for instance, is Spanglish for East Los Angeles, Loisiada is New York's Lower East Side), but also ethnic ones (*chale* is a Chicano expression of disagreement, *chompa* is Nuyorican for jumper, Y.U.C.A. stands for Young Urban Cuban American in Florida).

"Ganga Spanglish," as I've heard the jargon spoken by urban youngsters, introduces other nuances, incorporating slang from other ethnic groups. Look at a sample of lyrics from the popular group Cypress Hill's album *Temple of Boom*. Ebonics, Chicano Spanglish, and L.A. Spanglish are intertwined:

> *Don't turn your back on a vato like me*
> *Cuz I'm one broke [expletive]*
> *In need*
> *Desperate! What's going on in the mente*
> *Taking from the rich not from my gente*
> *Look at that gabacho slipping*
> *Borracho from the cerveza*
> *He's sipping*
> *No me vale, madre*
> *Gabacho pray to your padre*
> *This is for the time you would*
> *Give me the jale.*

* * *

Here at Amherst, a few students and I did an experiment not long ago: We invited four Spanglish speakers of different backgrounds (Brownsville, Tex., Chicago, Los Angeles, and Miami) to meet for the first time; the only guideline was that they should not be formal, but communicate in a comfortable way. The result was astounding: As soon as the participants familiarized themselves with one another, the conversation flowed easily, although the speakers often felt compelled to define some terms; within 15 minutes, a sense of linguistic community was perfectly tangible.

Ebonics, or black English, provides an interesting comparative case study. Expressions like "I own know what dem white folk talkin bout" and "Hey, dog, whass hapnin?" are common among African–American youth, especially in ghettos across the country. This form of communication follows its own grammar and syntax. It is, for the most part, a spoken language nurtured by oral tradition, even though the poets and novelists of the Harlem Renaissance in the 1920's and their successors have transcribed it. And there is little doubt that Ebonics is an intraethnic slang used by members of a minority group to establish identity. It dates back to the age of slavery, and, embraced particularly by poor people in urban centers, is marked by class.

Spanglish, too, is often an intraethnic vehicle of communication, used in the United States by Hispanics to establish empathy among themselves. But the differences with Ebonics are sharp. For one thing, Ebonics is not a product of *mestizaje*, the cross-fertilization of two perfectly discernible codes; Spanglish is. Spanglish is also not defined by class, as people in all social strata, from migrant workers to politicians, academics, and TV anchors regularly use it, both in the United States and south of the Rio Grande.

Of course, the interchange between Ebonics and Spanglish has been strong, especially in rap music, where Latino pop stars often imitate their African–American counterparts. In literary works like Piri Thomas's 1967 memoir of a black Puerto Rican in Spanish Harlem, *Down These Mean Streets*, the hybrid street register also comes through.

* * *

It seems to me that, although Latino and Latin American intelligentsia look down on Spanglish, attitudes toward that language will change. The reason is simple: Spanglish won't go away. Instead, as time goes by, it will solidify its status. Indeed, it is already in the process of standardizing its syntax. The question is no longer, What is Spanglish? It is, Where is it going? Will it grow into a full-blown language? Is it likely to become a threat to Spanish, or even to replace it altogether? (English, our lingua franca, is obviously not at stake.) None of that is impossible, although the transformation is likely to take hundreds of years.

We are, clearly, at once witnesses and participants to radical change. Imagine if, by a miracle, Miguel de Cervantes was given a copy of Gabriel García Márquez's *One Hundred Years of Solitude*. How many Americanisms in it might be utterly impenetrable to him? Even if Spanglish never seizes its chances fully, the future of Spanish—and of English—will be affected by it.

The day may even come when a masterpiece of Hispanic identity, in order to be fully appreciated by millions of people, not only in the United States, but around the world, shall be composed in the vernacular: Spanglish. Then it will be translated into English for the uninitiated reader.

Notes and Questions

1.   If Spanish and English mutually enrich each other, with hundreds of words and phrases in common, could an Official English law ever be enforceable?

2.   For the view that languages, including English, are always evolving and constantly enriching and being enriched by other tongues, see Steven W. Bender, *Comprende?: Celebrating the Spanish All Americans Know* (forthcoming 2008).

3.   Latinos who are bilingual (speaking English and Spanish) earn much more than those who speak just one of these languages. See Salinas, *Linguaphobia*, supra, at 58.

SECTION 3.   LANGUAGE AND CULTURAL TRUST

Can language diversity be an essential precondition for cultural trust? See the following selection by scholar Margaret Montoya:

Margaret E. Montoya
Law and Language(s): Image, Integration and Innovation
7 La Raza L.J. 147, 148–53 (1994)

For many Chicanas and Chicanos, language introduced us to law, providing the earliest point of intersection with official rules, official regulations, and official prohibitions. The use of Spanish in the schools throughout the Southwest was widely prohibited and routinely punished. My father tells of being beaten in kindergarten for speaking Spanish. In *Culture and Truth*, Renato Rosaldo remembers his Tucson junior high school where students were made to grab their ankles while they were swatted for the crime of speaking Spanish. One of my University of New Mexico colleagues recalls that in a New Mexico town during the 1950s, if a student were overheard speaking Spanish, he/she would be forced to stand on tiptoes as the teacher drew a circle at the height of his/her nose. The student would be made to stand with his/her nose in the circle for the required length of time, enduring pain and humiliation for speaking Spanish.

Stories like these have normative consequences. As time passes, the necessity for cruel punishment attenuates. Our parents encourage us to speak English. Accomplished English speakers listen for and correct our accents. We hear and sometimes laugh at jokes about fractured English or comedy routines featuring Jose Jimenez, Speedy Gonzales, Paul Rodriguez, or Cheech Marin. We receive praise from teachers for speaking the over-corrected speech of the over-achiever. We learn to value the syntax, the cadence, and the accent of the monolingual English speaker. Over time these stories constrain our behavior, mold our values, and create our preferences. Over time Spanish, our mother tongue, becomes an "outlaw" language. * * * Being obliged to abandon your mother tongue, to surrender your primary language, to give up the language that you first learned as a baby, forces a rupture with your family, your community, and your history. * * *

Although bilingual when I arrived at law school, I had been well trained * * *. English was my public language. My memories from law school begin with one of the first cases I ever read. On page one of my criminal law casebook I met the only Chicana or Latina I would ever hear about during my law school education. The case dealing with infanticide was entitled *People of the State of California v. Josephine Chavez*. In addition to the appellate opinion, the casebook included copies of the actual Chavez Complaint, Warrant of Arrest, Jury Instructions, Verdict and Judgment, news reports of the Chavez arrest and trial from *The Fresno Bee*, the local newspaper, the relevant sections of the California Penal Code, and the author's commentary and analysis.

Josephine Chavez gave birth one night over the toilet in her mother's home without waking her year-and-a-half-old son, her brothers, sisters, or mother. She delivered, in the words of the opinion, with "the doors open and no lights ... turned on." The baby dropped into the toilet and Josephine cut the umbilical cord with a razor blade. She recovered the body of the baby, wrapped it in newspapers and hid it underneath the bathtub. She attended a carnival that evening and then ran away. Later she turned herself in to her probation officer.

The class wrestled with the legal issue: whether the baby had been born alive and was therefore subject to being killed by its mother. Finally, on the third day, I broke my silence and interjected what I thought were other equally relevant facts—her youth, her poverty, her fear of the pregnancy, her delivery in silence and in darkness.

My vivid recollection is that the classroom discussion about the Chavez case, like the appellate court opinion, was oblivious to the cultural, linguistic, or socio-economic context of the alleged crime. Perhaps this oblivion is not surprising for an opinion written in 1947, nor even perhaps for a law school discussion in the mid–1970s. However, I am sure that, even today, a classroom discussion of this case or others dealing with Outsider experiences would not emphasize the contextual information, especially if that contextualization required a language other than English.

So how are we today to make sense of this story? Can these tragic events be understood from the traditional perspective—a perspective that is monolingual and monocultural? How do we effectively explore Josephine Chavez's criminal intent, mens rea, diminished capacity, or examine the legal personhood of this dead baby unless we are prepared to draw on knowledge that is embedded in the life experiences of those who have been historically silenced? The linguistic and socio-cultural norms that control legal discussion, particularly within the classroom, impede the introduction of information about the experiences of subordinated groups. These norms impoverish the discussion within the classroom and stunt the creativity that can be brought to bear on the legal issues presented by the client's complex story. These constraints have legal and representational ramifications.

The effective representation of a bicultural client such as Josephine Chavez requires that we tell her story using language and knowledge that has been taboo in the traditional law school classroom. Our understanding of Josephine Chavez's motives and behavior is enhanced if we import words and concepts from Spanish into our analysis. Her story implicates information about *familia*, about *verguenza*, about *respeto*. The familial and cultural matrices that encode meaning are different in the two languages. The networks embedded in the words *familia* and family are defined differently and experienced differently. *Verguenza* may translate into shame but *verguenza* is experienced as more than shame. *Respeto* has different cultural parameters than the meaning we give to respect.

* * *

I have found that telling personal stories establishes a climate of trust with students. Reciprocity in self-disclosures creates an environment of safety for storytelling. So I work to incorporate narrative formats into my classroom and clinical teaching. I use narratives to teach students to listen to and interpret client stories, and, at times, tell their own stories. For example, I have taped a mock interview that * * * raises cultural and linguistic as well as ethical issues for discussion by law students in my clinical course. In the interview I play a Latina lawyer with limited facility in Spanish. The client Miguel "Caballo" Grado has suffered a back injury and is seeking assistance with an SSI claim. Soon after the interview begins, the client asks about my family background:

Client: Did you say it was Montoya?

Lawyer: ... my name is Margaret Montoya.

Client: *Donde* ... Where are you from?

Lawyer: Well, my dad's family, Los Montoya, is from the southern part of the state and my mother's family is from the northern part of the state.

Client: What's your dad's name?

Lawyer: Ricardo Montoya and, you know, they're from, he was from Santa Rita.

Client: Hmm, I knew a bunch of Montoyas who were all from Silver City, and I think the family was from Santa Rita.

Lawyer: Well, my grandfather's name was Felix Montoya ...

Client: No.

Lawyer: ... and my grandmother's name was Refugio Sierra.

Client: Hmm, that's interesting. Did ... You're telling me they're from Santa Rita, but did they live in Silver City too? Because I know *este* Modesto Montoya, Modesto Montoya there in Silver.

Lawyer: Oh, you know, Mr. Grado, I don't know a lot about, you know I know my dad's brothers and sisters, but ... I don't really know those one generation back, so I don't really know if there would have been....

As I proceed to share information about my family, the client attempts to locate me within his framework of names and geographic associations. In fact, the client and I spend over three minutes of the taped interview discussing my family connections. As the interview goes on, the client provides relevant information about his family's financial affairs. In a subsequent interview, after displaying some concern about providing this information, the client tells me that he has been treated by a *curandera*, a medicine woman who has given him massages and herbal tea medications.

Client: You know, I don't know how the Social Security is going to look at it, but I've been seeing a *curandera*.

Lawyer: Hmm.

Client: ... and uh, she's been doing wonderful stuff for my back—at least it lasts more than the pill does. Ah, she helps me with the massages and she does other things for me, gives me some potions if you will, and ah, they've been pretty effective so that I could get to bed at night.

Lawyer: I need to get more information ... the *curandera* is, hmm ... so she, does she do other things than give you a massage? You said that she gives you ...

Client: Well, she gives me some teas.

Lawyer: And what kind of teas does she ...

Client: Ah, various kinds of bark ... I know that I was having some problems with my bladder one time and she gave me some *popotillo* and then she gave me some *yerba buena*.

Lawyer: Yeah ... I don't know *popotillo*. *Yerba buena* is mint tea. Uh, I don't know *popotillo*.

Client: It's a ... It's a wild herb that grows out there and, ah, it's good for bladder infections and stuff like that and it really works great. It cleans your whole system out.

Lawyer: And you have told Dr. Fox [the treating physician] that in fact you're ...

Client: Umm, uh.

Lawyer: It's alright if you haven't. It's that I'm going to have to figure out how we use this information.

Client: Well, you know ... It's traditional to seek a *curandera*. There's nothing wrong with it. I really haven't mentioned it to him too much. Uh, I do not know how he would take it.

Lawyer: Sure.

Client: I don't know how up here, but down there, it's just, ah, you know anything that has to do with our culture and stuff is frowned upon . . .

The purpose of this simulated interview is to explore the following issues * * *: the impropriety of attorney disclosures when interacting with clients; client expectations about attorney behavior; techniques for gaining access to and interpreting legally relevant information that is culturally coded; and interviewing and counseling techniques for intra- and intercultural interactions. The deliberate and extended use of Spanish and English in the simulation and the interjection of details from the everyday lives of poor Latinos/as has yielded rich discussions about the representation and re-presentation of clients from subordinated populations.

* * *

* * * [It] is [also] an important form of resistance against cultural and linguistic domination. Reclaiming these "outlaw" languages, taboo knowledge, and devalued discourses is a stand against cultural hegemony. Telling stories through the language of the master and the language of the subversive subaltern allows us to examine how language can be regenerative of meaning.

The Josephine Chavez case has long had a grip on me because in the same way that I couldn't fully tell her story without resorting to Spanish, I couldn't then, and can't now, tell my story either. As a Latina, weaving meaning from both English and Spanish is a necessary process in the understanding of my subjectivities. To the extent that my identity is socially constructed, that identity is encoded through two linguistic codes. Reflecting on my subjectivities, de/constructing the forces that have acted to create my multiple identities, requires decoding through Spanish and English.

Gloria Anzaldúa has written about the psychological, sexual, and spiritual borderlands "physically present wherever two or more cultures edge each other, where people of different races occupy the same territory, where under, lower, middle, and upper classes touch, where the space between two individuals shrinks with intimacy." My contribution to academic discourse is my ability to extract meaning from the aesthetic, linguistic, and cultural borderlands of my existence and blend that meaning with traditional legal analysis. Indeed, this is the challenge for legal educators who identify with subordinated communities. It is time that we reclaim Spanish and other outlaw languages for use in the classroom and in legal scholarship and seize the opportunities these languages offer for pedagogical innovation.

Chapter 8

ENGLISH-ONLY AND BILINGUAL EDUCATION

Perhaps because of the close connection between language and culture/identity, the right to speak Spanish (and, sometimes, other non-English languages) is fiercely contested. Controversies rage in the following forums:

- In schools, where they take the form of struggles over bilingual education
- In dealings with the government
- In domestic law, such as child custody proceedings
- In workplaces, where employers sometime try to impose English-only rules for Spanish speaking workers

Workplace issues are covered in Part Seven, infra.

SECTION 1. BILINGUALISM AND OFFICIAL ENGLISH IN PUBLIC LIFE

Meyer v. Nebraska
262 U.S. 390 (1923)

While this court has not attempted to define with exactness the liberty thus guaranteed, the term has received much consideration and some of the included things have been definitely stated. Without doubt, it denotes not merely freedom from bodily restraint but also the right of the individual to contract, to engage in any of the common occupations of life, to acquire useful knowledge, to marry, establish a home and bring up children, to worship God according to the dictates of his own conscience, and generally to enjoy those privileges long recognized at common law as essential to the orderly pursuit of happiness by free men. The established doctrine is that this liberty may not be interfered with, under the guise of protecting the public interest, by legislative action which is arbitrary or without reasonable relation to some purpose within the competency of the state to effect. Determination by the Legislature of what constitutes proper exercise of police power is not final or conclusive but is subject to supervision by the courts.

The American people have always regarded education and acquisition of knowledge as matters of supreme importance which should be diligently promoted. The Ordinance of 1787 declares:

Religion, morality and knowledge being necessary to good government and the happiness of mankind, schools and the means of education shall forever be encouraged.

Corresponding to the right of control, it is the natural duty of the parent to give his children education suitable to their station in life; and nearly all the states, including Nebraska, enforce this obligation by compulsory laws.

Practically, education of the young is only possible in schools conducted by especially qualified persons who devote themselves thereto. The calling always has been regarded as useful and honorable, essential, indeed, to the public welfare. Mere knowledge of the German language cannot reasonably be regarded as harmful. Heretofore it has been commonly looked upon as helpful and desirable. Plaintiff in error taught this language in school as part of his occupation. His right thus to teach and the right of parents to engage him so to instruct their children, we think, are within the liberty of the amendment.

The challenged statute forbids the teaching in school of any subject except in English; also the teaching of any other language until the pupil has attained and successfully passed the eighth grade, which is not usually accomplished before the age of twelve. The Supreme Court of the state has held that "the so-called ancient or dead languages" are not "within the spirit or the purpose of the act." Latin, Greek, Hebrew are not proscribed; but German, French, Spanish, Italian, and every other alien speech are * * *.

It is said the purpose of the legislation was to promote civic development by inhibiting training and education of the immature in foreign tongues and ideals before they could learn English and acquire American ideals, and "that the English language should be and become the mother tongue of all children reared in this state." It is also affirmed that the foreign born population is very large, that certain communities commonly use foreign words, follow foreign leaders, move in a foreign atmosphere, and that the children are thereby hindered from becoming citizens of the most useful type and the public safety is imperiled.

That the state may do much, go very far, indeed, in order to improve the quality of its citizens, physically, mentally and morally, is clear; but the individual has certain fundamental rights which must be respected. The protection of the Constitution extends to all, to those who speak other languages as well as to those born with English on the tongue. Perhaps it would be highly advantageous if all had ready understanding of our ordinary speech, but this cannot be coerced by methods which conflict with the Constitution—a desirable end cannot be promoted by prohibited means.

* * *

As the statute undertakes to interfere only with teaching which involves a modern language, leaving complete freedom as to other matters, there seems no adequate foundation for the suggestion that the purpose was to protect the child's health by limiting his mental activities. It is well known that proficiency in a foreign language seldom comes to one not instructed at an early age, and experience shows that this is not injurious to the health, morals or understanding of the ordinary child.

* * *

Reversed.

English-only or official English laws are in effect in about half the states; these range from Arizona's heavy-handed law discussed later, to statutes little more intrusive than ones declaring the oriole the official bird. Whether draconian or mild, these laws give encouragement to racists and nativists ("Speak English, spic, it's the law"). Some federal and state laws mandate the provision of services or materials, such as ballot information, in languages other than English. These, too, inflame English language chauvinists. See the following materials.

S.I. Hayakawa
English is Key to Opportunities of American Life
Reading Eagle (Reading, Pa.), Mar. 20, 1990

Should English be designated the official language of the United States?

Are you surprised that I'm even asking that question?

Most people think that English already is our official language, but they're wrong. It isn't. Not yet anyway.

Let me tell you how I came to believe that English must be designated our official language.

I was born and brought up in Canada. Canada, as I am sure you know, has two official languages, English and French—a fact which most probably doubles the cost of government in time consumed and money spent.

My father, who studied English in a Japanese high school, settled in Canada after traveling and living for a period in the United States.

He was a serious student of Edgar Allan Poe. In our home, we had sets of books by Dickens, Thackeray, and O. Henry. So majoring in English seemed a natural thing for me to do for my bachelor's, master's and doctor degrees.

On my first visit to the United States in 1927, I was refused entry because of my Japanese ancestry. However, in 1929, I was awarded a graduate fellowship in English at the University of Wisconsin.

After I got my doctorate, the university hired me as a full-time professor of English. In 1954, I finally ceased to be the one foreigner in my family of an American wife and three children, when I was sworn in as an American citizen during naturalization ceremonies in Chicago.

As a professor of English, I continued to teach, write, and give lectures. Then suddenly, in the midst of wild student turmoil in the mid '60s, I found myself president of San Francisco State University. My handling of the crisis made me a hero—the tough guy who "faced down the radicals at State."

A few years after that, the good people of California elected me their U.S. senator. While many had been surprised that someone of Japanese ancestry had become a senator, I am the most surprised.

When I took office and began dealing with our national problems, one thing stood out above all ... And that is, that there are many barriers to effective communication which are entrenched in our society—prejudice, generation gaps, and social and economic inequality, to name a few.

I realized that the last thing we need to do in our country is to add a language barrier to all of these.

In fact, one effective way to help solve the problems we already have is to establish a common ground on which we can all come together. That common ground is our English language.

And so in 1981, I introduced a Constitutional Amendment in Congress to make English the official language of the U.S. government.

Thousands of citizens all across the country offered support. Since no organization existed at that time to represent the interests of these people and bind them together into a powerful force, great potential for citizen action was lost.

That's why, after I retired from the Senate in 1983, I founded U.S. English. * * *

U.S. English was founded on the principles that English must be made the official language of government and that the opportunity to learn English must be guaranteed to all the people of the United States.

U.S. English members understand the natural instincts and rights of people from all cultures to preserve their own customs and traditions.

However, we believe that this is the responsibility of families, churches, and private organizations, not the responsibility of government or public schools.

U.S. English has maintained from its inception that we must preserve our common bond through the enactment of a Federal English Language Amendment. And in order to mobilize our citizens in support of this drive, U.S. English has begun by pressing for State English Language Amendments.

In 1986, after being rebuffed by the California Legislature in our attempts to designate English the official state language, we went directly to the voters.

U.S. English members collected hundreds of thousands of signatures on petitions to put the official English issue on the ballot. It passed with 74 percent of the vote.

In 1988, we passed similar initiatives in Arizona, Colorado, and Florida—bringing the total number of states with laws protecting English to 17.

Unfortunately, certain groups who do not, or will not, understand U.S. English's motives for a common unifying language are challenging our victories with costly legal actions. So you see, even after we've won, we have to keep fighting to defend the role of English in our society.

Our long-range goal is to establish English as the official language of the United States.

However, U.S. English is not only concerned that we preserve and protect our common language, we are also committed to ensuring that all citizens have the opportunity to learn English.

To this end, we promote effective and cost-efficient methods of teaching English to limited English proficient students.

Our objective is to ensure that bilingual programs be designed to make teaching English the standard by which they are measured.

And what do all these people that enter into the American mainstream have in common? English—our shared common language!

English is the key to individual participation in the opportunities of American life.

It is the linchpin of a productive and efficient economy for us all. I hope you agree that we must preserve the precious bond that unites all Americans into one nation.

Juan F. Perea
Demography and Distrust:
An Essay in American Languages, Cultural Pluralism, and Official English
77 Minn. L. Rev. 269, 328–33, 335–38, 340–49 (1992)

American nativism and racism have targeted many groups throughout our history. Native Americans, African Americans, Mexican Americans, and Asian Americans, among other groups, have been subjected to unequal treatment and oppression because of their differences from the majority culture. * * *

America during 1910–1914 experienced growing nativism, as the nation groped for a sense of national unity. World War I focused this nativism: "The struggle with Germany ... called forth the most strenuous nationalism and the most pervasive nativism that the United States had ever known." Nativism takes aim at the ethnicity of "enemy people." Germans were deemed disloyal merely for being, acting, speaking, and reading like Germans. At the time, Germans were the largest national-origin group of immigrants in America, numbering more than 2.3 million persons. Germans had also been the largest non-English-speaking group of American colonists.

Loyalty was equated with conformity to the core English-speaking culture. Difference from that culture and difference of opinion were equated with foreign influence and subversion * * *. The wartime hysteria yielded unprecedented demands for conformity, embodied in the movement for "100 per cent Americanism." One hundred percent Americans, mostly members of the core culture, "felt sure that the nation would never be safe until every vestige of German culture had been stamped out." One writer on Americanization, echoing the words of John Jay in *The Federalist*, wrote that "[t]he war has taught us the need of a more united people, speaking one language, thinking one tradition, and holding allegiance to one patriotism—America." The wartime nativism led to the imprisonment, public flogging and lynching of Germans.

To Kill or Use Our German Press? asked the Literary Digest of May 11, 1918. Killing the German press would eliminate "enemy publications" assumed to be under German influence. Others argued that "[t]he best use to which German-language papers can be put in these days is communicating American sentiments to people who can not read English." Eliminating the German press went beyond rhetoric and into the law. A 1920 Oregon law prohibited publication of any foreign language newspaper unless it carried a full, conspicuous, and literal translation of all its contents. Such translation being prohibitively expensive, the law was intended to put the foreign-language press out of business. Advocates of such measures had forgotten "the service done by the foreign language press to the government during the war by aiding the loans and explaining the draft." They would silence not only the press, but also the German voice. The governor of Iowa banned the use of any language other than English "in all schools, church services, conversations in public places or over the telephone."

Killing the German culture in American society also meant killing it in the schools. * * * By 1919, fifteen states had banned the teaching of foreign languages, and required English to be the sole language of instruction in primary schools, both public and private. Illinois made English its exclusive language of instruction

> [b]ecause the English language is the common as well as official language of our country, and because it is essential to good citizenship that each citizen shall have or speedily acquire, as his natural tongue, the language in which the laws of the land, the decrees of the courts, and the announcements and pronouncements of its officials are made.

Although English was the dominant language of the country, apparently only Illinois, rather peremptorily, declared it the official language of the land.

A Nebraska statute prohibited teaching any language other than English to students who had not passed the eighth grade. In 1922 the Supreme Court of Nebraska affirmed the conviction of Robert Meyer, who had violated the statute by teaching biblical stories in German to a ten-year-old. * * * For the Nebraska court, as for many Americans past and present, a foreign mother tongue was "foreign to the best interests of this country." The pattern repeats itself often. The United States Supreme Court, more detached from the nativism of the time, reversed Meyer's conviction and found that the statute violated substantive due process rights under the Fourteenth Amendment. * * *

The war against Germany produced an unprecedented fear of German–American ethnicity, resulting in intensified demands for conformity with the core culture and the concomitant dismemberment of the German culture and language in America. A wartime crisis spawned intense social and legal suppression of ethnic traits associated with the enemy. America attempted to define her true identity as that of her core culture. The perception of foreignness * * * was once again equated with disloyalty and subversion. At roughly this same time, nativists sought to reinforce the core American culture through the immigration and naturalization laws.

OFFICIAL LANGUAGE POLICY ENACTED THROUGH THE IMMIGRATION AND NATURALIZATION LAWS

Despite the absence of federal laws declaring English to be the official language of our country, some federal laws do, in effect, produce this result. Our current federal immigration and naturalization laws require English literacy for naturalized citizenship, and literacy in any language for admission to the United States. In addition, the Immigration Reform and Control Act of 1986 required aliens newly legalized under its amnesty provision to demonstrate "minimal understanding of ordinary English" in order to become permanent resident aliens.

The English-literacy requirement for citizenship is of tremendous symbolic importance. It is an important expression of federal policy in favor of English. It is through our naturalization laws that, in clearest form, the nation spells out the criteria that must be met by those who would join the American nation.

English literacy has not, however, always been a requirement for citizenship. Nor has literacy of any kind always been a requirement for initial admission to the nation. The evolution of the English-language literacy requirement further demonstrates that nativism finds expression through language restrictions.

A strong popular movement favoring coerced assimilation occurred for the first time near the beginning of the twentieth century. Before this time, until around 1880, immigration to the United States had been open and unrestricted. Most assumed that American society would assimilate new immigrants. Indeed, because most of the immigrants until this time were from northwestern Europe, and especially from

Great Britain, Germany, and Scandinavia, traditional sources of the American population, their racial and cultural characteristics matched those of the existing population and they were able to assimilate with relatively little cultural friction.

By 1890, immigrants from these countries began to be outnumbered by immigrants from the countries of southern and eastern Europe: Italy, Poland, and the Austro–Hungarian empire. These new immigrants brought with them their distinctive cultural traits. In response to these new, culturally different immigrants, a strong popular movement, fueled by American nativism, developed in favor of restrictions on immigration to the United States.

The first goal of proponents of restricted immigration was a literacy test for immigrants that, in theory, would exclude a large proportion of those seeking admission * * * . The literacy test, "though ostensibly selective in history, would prove restrictive in operations." The purpose of the literacy test was clear: to exclude people whose ethnicity differed from that of the majority. Advocates of the test hoped that it would reduce immigration by twenty-five percent.

Opponents of the new European immigration tried three times, without success, to enact restrictive legislation that included a literacy requirement in some language for admission to the United States. Such legislation passed the Congress on three occasions. It was consistently vetoed by successive presidents because it was such a departure from prior, liberal immigration policy.

 * * *

Later, more effective restrictive legislation passed establishing numerical quotas for immigrants. The prevailing idea among advocates of quota restrictions was that national unity depended on racial "homogeneity," which appeared to mean preservation of the existing racial character of the country. Thus, one congressman argued that "[t]he trouble grows out of a country composed of intermingled and mongrelized people. The stability of a country depends upon the homogeneity of population." Another congressman coined the slogan, "one race, one country, one destiny." As the advocates of restriction saw it, the survival of constitutional democracy depended on the Nordic race: "If, therefore, the principle of individual liberty, guarded by a constitutional government created on this continent nearly a century and a half ago, is to endure, the basic strain of our population must be maintained."

These comments illustrate the theme, repeated throughout our history, that our national identity, unity, and loyalty to our government depend on uniformity—sometimes racial, sometimes linguistic. "Foreign influences," persons whose ethnicity differs from that of the majority, are perceived as a threat to the nation. America's supposedly uniform ethnicity had to be created and preserved through the law. In the case of the immigration laws, the idea was that national unity depended on racial purity and uniformity, with existing American races superior to any others seeking entry. An identical theme underlies the official

English movement's claim that national unity depends on linguistic uniformity or purity.

* * *

THE DEVELOPMENT OF LANGUAGE REQUIREMENTS FOR CITIZENSHIP

The first statutory requirement of English ability for naturalized citizenship appeared in 1906. The rationale was that a requirement of ability to speak English would improve the "quality" of naturalized citizens. The Commission on Naturalization of 1905 expressed the prevailing view: "[T]he proposition is incontrovertible that no man is a desirable citizen of the United States who does not know the English language." * * *

* * * The Nationality Act of 1940 also contained the requirement that an applicant for citizenship speak English. Section 304 of the Act stated: "No person . . . shall hereafter be naturalized as a citizen of the United States upon his own petition who cannot speak the English language."

In 1950, at the height of the national hysteria over the threat of communism, Congress stiffened the language requirements for naturalization. The Subversive Activities Control Act of 1950 amended section 304 to demand full literacy in English:

No person . . . shall hereafter be naturalized as a citizen of the United States upon his own petition who cannot demonstrate

(1) an understanding of the English language, including an ability to read, write and speak words in ordinary usage in the English language . . . , [and]

(2) a knowledge and understanding of the fundamentals of the history, and of the principles and form of government, of the United States.

These provisions of the naturalization statute remain essentially the same today.

The symbolic importance of an English literacy requirement for naturalization should not be underestimated. It is in the naturalization laws that the criteria for belonging to America, for participating in its government, are most clearly stated. As one leading commentator aptly stated it, "[a]n English literacy requirement . . . establishes that the United States is an English culture and that its citizens will have to learn English in order to participate fully in it. The very existence of a literacy test establishes the 'official' character of the language." To date, this represents the maximum degree to which English is officially and legally recognized as the language of the United States.

It is revealing that increased requirements for citizenship were enacted as part of the Subversive Activities Control legislation. Once again, "foreign" characteristics, this time lack of English literacy, were associated with disloyalty and "subversive activities." * * *

* * *

The legislation, just like the Alien and Sedition Acts, and with just as broad a legislative brush, aimed * * * to keep the "foreign influence" out of America. Supreme fear and distrust of "foreign" traits and the "foreign language" press led to legal restrictions designed to reinforce the identity of the core American culture. Nativism demands that only English-speaking Americans and the English-language press can be trusted. The English literacy requirement for citizenship remains the same today.

THE OFFICIAL ENGLISH MOVEMENT

From the panorama of the legal treatment of ethnicity and language several distinctive features of nativist movements stand out. Nativism tends to grow and flourish at times of national stress, often in response to unwelcome immigration or wartime. Nativism triggers restrictive laws aimed at persons whose ethnicity differs from that of the core culture, ostensibly to serve the goals of national unity or national security. Nativist movements seek to reinforce their narrow view of American cultural identity through the law by restricting cultural traits deemed "foreign." Another feature common to these movements is the desire to disenfranchise certain * * * aspiring Americans because of their difference from the core culture.

The official English movement of the 1980s is part of this tradition. Former Senator S.I. Hayakawa, acting through U.S. English, an organization he founded with Dr. John Tanton, sought an amendment to the Constitution making English the official language of the United States. Subcommittees of the Senate Judiciary Committee, in 1984, and the House Judiciary Committee, in 1988, conducted hearings on proposed official English amendments. Despite persistent efforts and publicity, proponents of official English have not yet succeeded in achieving a federal constitutional amendment.

* * *

The official English movement now appears to have a two-fold strategy: first, to obtain official English laws or constitutional amendments in the states, and, second, to enact a federal statute making English the official language of the federal government. Since the movement's ultimate goal is still a federal constitutional amendment, it appears that official English proponents will attempt to strengthen their position by arguing that the presence of many state laws and a possible federal statute increases or proves the necessity for a federal constitutional amendment.

The movement has been quite successful at the state level. [About one-half of the] states now have laws declaring English to be their official language. * * *

* * *

Through a federal constitutional amendment or statute, the movement seeks the elimination of bilingual ballots in state and federal elections. To accomplish this result, they must, in effect, persuade Congress to repeal certain provisions of the Voting Rights Act that require bilingual ballots under some circumstances. * * *

* * *

The official English movement belongs squarely within the matrix of modern American nativism. The cause of the official English movement is the immigration of people unpopular in the eyes of the majority. Its manifestations are those of earlier nativist movements: a desire, now abandoned, to restrict immigration; an appeal to national unity or, conversely, raising the familiar spectre of national disunity and the disintegration of American culture caused by new immigration; and, most important, the desire to disenfranchise certain Americans.

Many commentators agree that the cause of the official English movement is the large, and largely unwelcome, immigration of many Hispanics and Southeast Asians during recent decades. Since the repeal of national origin quotas in 1965, increasing numbers of immigrants have come from non-European countries, thus changing the racial and cultural balance carefully preserved by the prior quota system. In addition to legal immigration, a large influx of aliens took place from Latin America, many of whom subsequently were legalized during the amnesty offered in 1987 and 1988. * * *

Like all other immigrant groups, these immigrants have brought with them their native languages. The influx of Spanish-speaking Hispanic immigrants has antagonized many Americans. Immigrants from Southeast Asia have also encountered hostility, violence, and language restriction. The racial and cultural differences of recent immigrants from the core culture have not gone unnoticed.

Part of U.S. English's original program was to "control immigration so that it does not reinforce trends toward language segregation." The organization intended to lobby for legislation to restrict immigration that would reinforce the maintenance of certain languages, particularly Spanish, which, after English, is the second most-used language in this country. This means limiting the immigration of Hispanics, who are depicted as advocates of "language segregation." * * *

* * *

The official English movement renews the claim that national unity depends on ethnic purity—really conformity with the Anglo core culture—this time in the form of language. * * *

This perceived threat to the English language, however, is not supported by facts. English is ubiquitous. Between 94 and 96 percent of the American population is already English-speaking. Fully 85 percent of the population claims English as its mother tongue. Furthermore, English enjoys virtual hegemony as an international language of business, commerce, and interaction between nations. Given the national and international status of English, concerns about its deterioration (and ours), echoed throughout our history, are greatly overstated. Since fact does not support claims of deterioration of the English language, nor of national disunity, something else must be going on.

Since its inception, one of the official English movement's principal goals has been to eliminate bilingual, or more correctly, multilingual voting ballots. This can be accomplished only through the Congress's repeal, or refusal to extend, provisions in the 1975 amendments to the Voting Rights Act. * * *

Proponents argue that English-only ballots create incentives for citizens to learn English and to realize that they cannot enjoy full participation in American life without doing so. Furthermore, the argument runs, multilingual ballots impair the political process because they make some voters dependent on "interpreters or go-betweens," because they preserve "minority voting blocs," and because voters whose primary language is not English will not be "as fully informed as possible" when they go to the polls. Proponents of official English thus claim that multilingual ballots reduce political participation, a claim glaringly at odds with the obvious access to political participation that multilingual ballots provide to non-English speakers.

These arguments deserve brief response. First, English-only ballots create no meaningful incentive to learn English, particularly given the overwhelming existing social and economic incentives to do so. English-only ballots disenfranchise citizens who, for various reasons, have retained a language other than English. According to a 1982 study by the Mexican American Legal Defense and Educational Fund, seventy-two percent of monolingual Spanish-speaking citizens would be less likely to vote without the language assistance the Voting Rights Act requires. Similarly, monolingual citizens speaking other non-English languages also would be disenfranchised.

Second, voters who rely on American newspapers printed in languages other than English, such as the *Miami Herald*, which is published daily in both Spanish and English editions, can be fully informed about the issues in an election. The Supreme Court recognized as much when, in 1966, it upheld the Voting Rights Act in *Katzenbach v. Morgan*. The Court stated that ability to read or understand Spanish-language newspapers, radio, and television is as effective a means of obtaining political information as ability to read English.

The movement's concern about "minority voting blocs" defined by language both expresses fear of the political power of Hispanics and the offensive assumption that minority group members think alike and vote alike. If proponents of official English are truly concerned about ethnic voting blocs, they should also be equally concerned about English-speaking ethnic voting blocs. Their concern, however, is only about ethnicity, Hispanic or Asian, different from that of the core culture.

Furthermore, the movement vastly overstates the competence and political participation of members of the majority core culture. Only about half of all eligible voters usually vote. Are all voters "as fully informed as possible"? Why deny access to multilingual ballots to citizens who do care enough to vote? And why hold only minority voters to a standard of "being as fully informed as possible" for voting? The movement's arguments amount to saying that people who do not know English are too ignorant to make informed voting decisions, an offensive presumption common throughout our history.

As mentioned earlier, many states declare English their official language. Although some of these statutes are merely declaratory and have little more force than laws declaring the oriole the official bird or the columbine the state flower, some have real teeth. One of the more draconian of these state laws came before the Arizona Supreme Court:

Ruiz v. Hull
191 Ariz. 441, 957 P.2d 984 (1998)

OPINION

MOELLER, JUSTICE.

In October 1987, Arizonans for Official English (AOE) [succeeded in] a petition drive to amend Arizona's constitution to designate English as the state's official language and to require state and local governments in Arizona to conduct business only in English. * * * The Amendment, entitled "English as the Official Language," provides that "[t]he State and all political subdivisions of [the] State shall act in English and in no other language." The Amendment binds all government officials and employees in Arizona during the performance of all government business, and provides that any "person who resides in or does business in this State shall have standing to bring suit to enforce this article in a court of record of the State."

    * * *

In November 1992, the ten plaintiffs in this case brought an action in superior court [seeking] * * * a declaratory judgment that the Amendment violates the First, Ninth, and Fourteenth Amendments of the United States Constitution. The plaintiffs are four elected officials, five state employees, and one public school teacher. They are all bilingual and regularly communicate in both Spanish and English as private citizens and during the performance of government business. Plaintiffs allege that they speak Spanish during the performance of their government jobs and that they "fear communicating in Spanish 'during the performance of government business' in violation of Article XXVIII of the Arizona Constitution."

    * * *

DISCUSSION

Plaintiffs contend that the Amendment is a blanket prohibition against all publicly elected officials and government employees using any language other than English in the performance of any government business. Therefore, they reason that the Amendment is a content-based regulation of speech contrary to the First Amendment. Plaintiffs also argue that the Amendment constitutes discrimination against non-English-speaking minorities, thereby violating the Equal Protection Clause of the Fourteenth Amendment. AOE and the state defendants respond that the Amendment should be narrowly read and * * * construed as requiring the use of English only with regard to "official, binding government acts." They argue that this narrow construction renders the Amendment constitutional.

At the outset, we note that this case concerns the tension between the constitutional status of language rights and the state's power to restrict such rights. On the one hand, in our diverse society, the importance of establishing common bonds and a common language between citizens is clear. We recognize that the acquisition of English language skills is important in our society. * * *

     * * *

However, the American tradition of tolerance "recognizes a critical difference between encouraging the use of English and repressing the use of other languages." We agree that Arizona's rejection of that tradition by enacting the Amendment has severe consequences not only for Arizona's public officials and employees, but also for the many thousands of persons who would be precluded from receiving essential information from government employees and elected officials in Arizona's governments. If the wide-ranging language of the prohibitions contained in the Amendment were to be implemented as written, the First Amendment rights of all those persons would be violated, a fact now conceded by the proponents of the Amendment, who, instead, urge a restrictive interpretation in accordance with the Attorney General's narrow construction discussed below.

By this opinion, we do not imply that the intent of those urging passage of the Amendment or of those who voted for it stemmed from linguistic chauvinism or from any other repressive or discriminatory intent. Rather we assume, without deciding, that the drafters of the initiative urged passage of the Amendment to further social harmony in our state by having English as a common language among its citizens.

     * * *

PLAIN MEANING RULE

The Attorney General maintains that although the Amendment declares English to be Arizona's "official" language, its proscriptions against the use of non-English languages should be interpreted to apply only to "official acts of government." Ariz. Att'y Gen. Op. I89–009, at 5–

6. The Attorney General defines "official act" as "a decision or determination of a sovereign, a legislative council, or a court of justice." Id. at 7. Although he does not further explain what acts would be official, the Attorney General concludes that the Amendment should not be read to prohibit public employees from using non-English languages while performing their public functions that could not be characterized as official. The Attorney General opines that the provision "does not mean that languages other than English cannot be used when reasonable to facilitate the day-to-day operation of government." Id. at 10.

* * *

To arrive at his interpretation, the Attorney General takes the word "act" from § 3(1)(a) of the Amendment, which provides that, with limited exceptions, the "State and all political subdivisions of this State shall act in English and in no other language." The Attorney General proposes that the word "act" from § 3(1)(a) should be ascribed to the word "official," found in the Amendment's proclamation that English is the official language of Arizona. Therefore, the Attorney General interprets the Amendment to apply only to the official acts of the state and limits the definition of the noun "act" to a "decision or determination of a sovereign, a legislative council, or a court of justice." We agree with the Ninth Circuit that the former Attorney General's opinion ignores the fact that "act," when used as a verb as in the Amendment, does not include among its meanings the limited definition he proposed. Similarly, section 1(2) of the Amendment also describes English as the language of "all government functions and actions." The Amendment does not limit the terms "functions" and "actions" to official acts as urged by the Attorney General, and the ordinary meanings of those terms do not impose such a limitation. We agree with the district court that originally evaluated the challenges to the Amendment in *Yniguez*: "The Attorney General's restrictive interpretation of the Amendment is in effect a 'remarkable job of plastic surgery upon the face of the [Amendment].'"

We hold that by ignoring the express language of the Amendment, the Attorney General's proposed construction violates the plain meaning rule that requires the words of the Amendment to be given their natural, obvious, and ordinary meaning. By its express terms, the Amendment is not limited to official governmental acts or to the "formal, policy making, enacting and binding activities of government." Rather, it is plainly written in the broadest possible terms, declaring that the "English language is the language of ... all government functions and actions" and prohibiting all "government officials and employees" at every level of state and local government from using non-English languages "during the performance of government business." Amendment, §§ 1(2), 1(3)(a)(iv). * * *

LEGISLATIVE INTENT

We also believe the Attorney General's proposed construction is at odds with the intent of the drafters of the Amendment. The drafters perceived and obviously intended that the application of the Amendment would be widespread. They therefore inserted some limited exceptions to it. Those exceptions permit the use of non-English languages to protect the rights of criminal defendants and victims, to protect the public health and safety, to teach a foreign language, and to comply with federal laws. Amendment, § 3.2. Regardless of the precise limits of these general exceptions, their existence demonstrates that the drafters of the Amendment understood that it would apply to far more than just official acts.

For example, one exception allows public school teachers to instruct in a non-English language when teaching foreign languages or when teaching students with limited English proficiency. Such instruction by teachers is obviously not a "formal, policy making, enacting or binding activity by the government," the narrow construction urged by the Attorney General. The exceptions would have been largely, if not entirely, unnecessary under the Attorney General's proposed construction of the Amendment. When construing statutes, we must read the statute as a whole and give meaningful operation to each of its provisions.

In construing an initiative, we may consider ballot materials and publicity pamphlets circulated in support of the initiative. The ballot materials and publicity pamphlets pertaining to the Amendment do not support the Attorney General's limiting construction. In AOE's argument for the Amendment, Chairman Robert D. Park stated that the Amendment was intended to "require the government to function in English, except in certain circumstances," and then listed those exceptions set forth in section 4 of the Amendment. Chairman Park's argument then went on to state that "[o]fficially sanctioned multilingualism causes tension and division within a state. Proposition 106 [enacting the Amendment] will avoid that fate in Arizona." The Legislative Council's argument in support of the Amendment stated that the existence of a multilingual society would lead to "the fears and tensions of language rivalries and ethnic distrust." Arizona Publicity Pamphlet in Support of the Amendment, at 26. Therefore, the Amendment's legislative history supports a broad, comprehensive construction of the Amendment, not the narrow construction urged by the Attorney General.

AMBIGUITY

The Attorney General's interpretation would unnecessarily inject elements of vagueness into the Amendment. We feel confident that an average reader of the Amendment would never divine that he or she was free to use a language other than English unless one was performing an official act defined as "a decision or determination of a sovereign, a legislative council, or a court of justice."

Because we conclude that the narrow construction advocated by the Attorney General is untenable, we analyze the unconstitutionality of the Amendment based on the language of the Amendment itself.

English-Only Provisions in Other Jurisdictions

Although English-only provisions have recently become quite common, Arizona's is unique. Thus, we receive little guidance from other state courts. Twenty-one states and forty municipalities have official English statutes. However, most of those provisions are substantially less encompassing and certainly less proscriptive than the Amendment. The official English provisions in most states appear to be primarily symbolic. See, e.g., Puerto Rican Org. for Political Action v. Kusper, 490 F.2d 575, 577 (7th Cir. 1973) (noting that official English law appears with laws naming the state bird and state song, and does not restrict the use to non-English languages by state and city agencies). Indeed, the Amendment has been identified as "by far the most restrictively worded official-English law to date." M. Arrington, Note, *English Only Laws and Direct Legislation: The Battle in the States Over Language Minority Rights*, 7 L.J. & Pol. 325, 327 (1991). This observation is shared by other commentators—who note that the Amendment "is the most restrictive of the current wave of official-language laws," and "is so far the most restrictive Official English measure." See D. Baron, *The English–Only Question* 21 (1990), and J. Crawford, *Hold Your Tongue* 176 (1992).

* * *

Language is Speech Protected by the First Amendment

* * *

The First Amendment to the United States Constitution provides:

Congress shall make no law respecting an establishment of religion, or prohibiting the free exercise thereof; or abridging the freedom of speech, or of the press; or the right of the people peaceably to assemble, and to petition the government for a redress of grievances.

The First Amendment applies to the states as well as to the federal government. The expression of one's opinion is absolutely protected by the First and Fourteenth Amendments. [S]ee also Meyer v. Nebraska, 262 U.S. 390, 401 (1923) (stating that the United States Constitution protects speakers of all languages). The trial court held that the Amendment is content-neutral, and, therefore, does not violate the First Amendment. That ruling is flawed.

"Whatever differences may exist about interpretations of the First Amendment, there is practically universal agreement that a major purpose of that Amendment was to protect the free discussion of governmental affairs." Landmark Communications, Inc. v. Virginia, 435 U.S. 829, 838 (1978) (footnote omitted) (quoting Mills v. Alabama, 384 U.S. 214, 218 (1966)). * * *

Notwithstanding [some] limited exceptions, we find that the Amendment unconstitutionally inhibits "the free discussion of governmental affairs" in two ways. First, it deprives limited-and non-English-speaking persons of access to information about the government when multilingual access may be available and may be necessary to ensure fair and effective delivery of governmental services to non-English-speaking persons. It is not our prerogative to impinge upon the Legislature's ability to require, under appropriate circumstances, the provision of services in languages other than English. See, e.g., A.R.S. § 23–906(D) (providing that every employer engaged in occupations subject to Arizona's Workers' Compensation statutes shall post in a conspicuous place upon his premises, in English and Spanish, a notice informing employees that unless they specifically reject coverage under Arizona's compulsory compensation law, they are deemed to have accepted the provisions of that law). The United States Supreme Court has held that First Amendment protection is afforded to the communication, its source, and its recipient. Virginia State Board of Pharmacy v. Virginia Citizens Consumer Council, Inc., 425 U.S. 748, 756–57 (1976).

In his concurring opinion in *Barnes*, Justice Scalia stated, "[W]hen any law restricts speech, even for a purpose that has nothing to do with the suppression of communication . . . , we insist that it meet the high First–Amendment standard of justification." 501 U.S. at 576. The Amendment contravenes core principles and values undergirding the First Amendment—the right of the people to seek redress from their government—by directly banning pure speech on its face. By denying persons who are limited in English proficiency, or entirely lacking in it, the right to participate equally in the political process, the Amendment violates the constitutional right to participate in and have access to government, a right which is one of the "fundamental principle[s] of representative government in this country." See Reynolds v. Sims, 377 U.S. 533, 560 (1964). The First Amendment right to petition for redress of grievances lies at the core of America's democracy. McDonald v. Smith, 472 U.S. 479, 482–83, 485 (1985); United Mine Workers of America v. Illinois State Bar Assn., 389 U.S. 217, 222 (1967) (right to petition is "among the most precious liberties safeguarded by the Bill of Rights"). In Board of Education v. Pico, 457 U.S. 853, 867 (1982), the Court recognized that "the right to receive ideas is a necessary predicate to the recipient's meaningful exercise of his own rights of speech, press and political freedom."

The Amendment violates the First Amendment by depriving elected officials and public employees of the ability to communicate with their constituents and with the public. With only a few exceptions, the Amendment prohibits all public officials and employees in Arizona from acting in a language other than English while performing governmental functions and policies. We do not prohibit government offices from adopting language rules for appropriate reasons. We hold that the Amendment goes too far because it effectively cuts off governmental communication with thousands of limited-English-proficient and non-English-speaking persons in Arizona, even when the officials and employees have the ability and desire to communicate in a language understandable to them. Meaningful communication in those cases is barred. Under such circumstances, prohibiting an elected or appointed governmental official or an employee from communicating with the public violates the employee's and the official's rights. * * *

* * *

AOE argues that the "First Amendment addresses [the] content not [the] mode of communication." The trial court adopted this argument, concluding that the Amendment was a permissible content-neutral prohibition of speech. Essentially, *AOE* argues that strict scrutiny should be reduced in this case because the decision to speak a non-English language does not implicate pure speech rights, but rather only affects the "mode of communication." By requiring that government officials communicate only in a language which is incomprehensible to non-English speaking persons, the Amendment effectively bars communication itself. Therefore, its effect cannot be characterized as merely a time, place, or manner restriction because such restrictions, by definition, assume and require the availability of alternative means of communication.

* * *

EQUAL PROTECTION

Section One of the Fourteenth Amendment provides, in pertinent part, that "[n]o state shall ... deny to any person within its jurisdiction the equal protection of the laws." The right to petition for redress of grievances is one of the fundamental rights guaranteed by the First Amendment. A corollary to the right to petition for redress of grievances is the right to participate equally in the political process.

The Amendment is subject to strict scrutiny because it impinges upon the fundamental First Amendment right to petition the government for redress of grievances. The right to petition bars state action interfering with access to the legislature, the executive branch and its various agencies, and the judicial branch.

The trial court rejected plaintiffs' equal protection argument on the grounds that plaintiffs had not shown that the Amendment was driven by discriminatory intent. See Hunter v. Underwood, 471 U.S. 222, 229 (1985). Because the Amendment curtails First Amendment rights, however, it is presumed unconstitutional and must survive this court's strict scrutiny. *AOE* and the state defendants bear the burden of establishing the Amendment's constitutionality by demonstrating that it is drawn with narrow specificity to meet a compelling state interest.

* * *

As discussed previously, the compelling state interest test applies to the Amendment because it affects fundamental First Amendment rights. Even assuming *arguendo* that *AOE* and the state defendants could establish a compelling state interest for the Amendment (and they have not met that burden), they cannot satisfy the narrow specificity requirement. Under certain very restricted circumstances, states may regulate speech. However, the Amendment is not a "regulation." Rather, it is a general prohibition of the use of non-English languages by all state personnel during the performance of government business and by all persons seeking to interact with all levels of government in Arizona. The Amendment's goal to promote English as a common language does not require a general prohibition on non-English usage. English can be promoted without prohibiting the use of other languages by state and local governments. Therefore, the Amendment does not meet the compelling state interest test and thus does not survive First Amendment strict scrutiny analysis.

Finally, we note that any interference with First Amendment rights need not be an absolute bar to render it unconstitutional as violating equal protection; a substantial burden upon that right is sufficient to warrant constitutional protections. By permanently implementing a linguistic barrier between persons and the government they have a right to petition, the Amendment substantially burdens First Amendment rights. Therefore, the Amendment violates the Fourteenth Amendment's guarantees of equal protection because it impinges upon both the fundamental right to participate equally in the political process and the right to petition the government for redress.

Richard Rodriguez
Hunger of Memory: The Education of Richard Rodriguez
32–36 (1982)

This boy became a man. In private now, alone, I brood over language and intimacy—the great themes of my past. In public I expect most of the faces I meet to be the faces of strangers. (How do you do?) If meetings are quick and impersonal, they have been efficiently managed. I rush past the sounds of voices attending only to the words addressed to me. Voices seem planed to an even surface of sound, soundless. A business associate speaks in a deep baritone, but I pass through the timbre to attend to his words. The crazy man who sells me a newspaper every night mumbles something crazy, but I have time only to pretend that I have heard him say hello. Accented versions of English make little impression on me. In the rush-hour crowd a Japanese tourist asks me a question, and I inch past his accent to concentrate on what he is saying. The Eastern European immigrant in a neighborhood delicatessen speaks to me through a marinade of sounds, but I respond to his words. I note for only a second the Texas accent of the telephone operator or the Mississippi accent of the man who lives in the apartment below me.

My city seems silent until some ghetto black teenagers board the bus I am on. Because I do not take their presence for granted, I listen to the sounds of their voices. Of all the accented versions of English I hear in a day, I hear theirs most intently. They are *the* sounds of the outsider. They annoy me for being loud—so self-sufficient and unconcerned by my presence. Yet for the same reason they seem to me glamorous. (A romantic gesture against public acceptance.) Listening to their shouted laughter, I realize my own quiet. Their voices enclose my isolation. I feel envious, envious of their brazen intimacy.

I warn myself away from such envy, however. I remember the black political activists who have argued in favor of using black English in schools. (Their argument varies only slightly from that made by foreign-language bilingualists.) I have heard "radical" linguists make the point that black English is a complex and intricate version of English. And I do not doubt it. But neither do I think that black English should be a language of public instruction. What makes black English inappropriate in classrooms is not something in the language. It is rather what lower-class speakers make of it. Just as Spanish would have been a dangerous language for me to have used at the start of my education, so black English would be a dangerous language to use in the schooling of teenagers for whom it reenforces feelings of public separateness.

This seems to me an obvious point. But one that needs to be made. In recent years there have been attempts to make the language of the alien public language. "Bilingual education, two ways to understand . . .," television and radio commercials glibly announce. Proponents of bilingual education are careful to say that they want students to acquire good schooling. Their argument goes something like this: Children permitted to use their family language in school will not be so alienated and will be better able to match the progress of English-speaking children in the crucial first months of instruction. (Increasingly confident of their abilities, such children will be more inclined to apply themselves to their studies in the future.) But then the bilingualists claim another, very different goal. They say that children who use their family language in school will retain a sense of their individuality—their ethnic heritage and cultural ties. Supporters of bilingual education thus want it both ways. They propose bilingual schooling as a way of helping students acquire the skills of the classroom crucial for public success. But they likewise insist that bilingual instruction will give students a sense of their identity apart from the public.

Behind this screen there gleams an astonishing promise: One can become a public person while still remaining a private person. At the very same time one can be both! There need be no tension between the self in the crowd and the self apart from the crowd! Who would not want to believe such an idea? Who can be surprised that the scheme has won the support of many middle-class Americans? If the barrio or ghetto child can retain his separateness even while being publicly educated, then it is almost possible to believe that there is no private cost to be paid for public success. Such is the consolation offered by any of the current bilingual schemes. Consider, for example, the bilingual voters' ballot. In some American cities one can cast a ballot printed in several languages. Such a document implies that a person can exercise that most public of rights—the right to vote—while still keeping apart, unassimilated from public life.

It is not enough to say that these schemes are foolish and certainly doomed. Middle-class supporters of public bilingualism toy with the confusion of those Americans who cannot speak standard English as well as they can. Bilingual enthusiasts, moreover, sin against intimacy. An

Hispanic–American writer tells me, "I will never give up my family language; I would as soon give up my soul." Thus he holds to his chest a skein of words, as though it were the source of his family ties. He credits to language what he should credit to family members. A convenient mistake. For as long as he holds on to words, he can ignore how much else has changed in his life.

It has happened before. In earlier decades, persons newly successful and ambitious for social mobility similarly seized upon certain "family words." Working-class men attempting political power took to calling one another "brother." By so doing they escaped oppressive public isolation and were able to unite with many others like themselves. But they paid a price for this union. It was a public union they forged. The word they coined to address one another could never be the sound (brother) exchanged by two in intimate greeting. In the union hall the word "brother" became a vague metaphor; with repetition a weak echo of the intimate sound. Context forced the change. Context could not be overruled. Context will always guard the realm of the intimate from public misuse.

Today nonwhite Americans call "brother" to strangers. And white feminists refer to their mass union of "sisters." And white middle-class teenagers continue to prove the importance of context as they try to ignore it. They seize upon the idioms of the black ghetto. But their attempt to appropriate such expressions invariably changes the words. As it becomes a public expression, the ghetto idiom loses its sound—its message of public separateness and strident intimacy. It becomes with public repetition a series of words, increasingly lifeless.

Notes and Questions

1.   What degree of protection does speaking a foreign language receive in the U.S. Constitution? Is the First Amendment the most pertinent clause? See Antonio J. Califa, *Declaring English the Official Language: Prejudice Spoken Here*, 24 Harv. C.R.-C.L. L. Rev. 293 (1989).

2.   What are the strongest arguments for using English as the official language in public affairs and government? The strongest arguments against that policy? See William Bratton, *Law and Economics of English Only*, 53 U. Miami L. Rev. 973 (1999); Drucilla Cornell, *The Imaginary of English Only*, 53 U. Miami L. Rev. 977 (1999); James Crawford, *Hold Your Tongue: Bilingualism and the Politics of English Only* (1992).

3.   Is a single language essential to a nation's unity? Without one, will the country fly apart? Canada does experience tension over French language rights, but Switzerland, with three official languages, has been peaceful for several hundred years. See Samuel P. Huntington, *Who Are We?: The Challenges to America's Identity* 324 (2004); S.I. Hayakawa, *One Nation ... Indivisible?* (1985).

4.   English has long borrowed from other languages, including Spanish, French, Greek, German, and Latin. Is the pure English that the English-only

movement aspires to even a coherent goal? See Juan F. Perea, *Demography and Distrust: An Essay on American Languages, Cultural Pluralism, and Official English*, 77 Minn. L. Rev. 269 (1992).

5.   A few years after *Ruiz v. Hull* came down, Arizona voters tried again, voting for a somewhat less aggressive English-only law. See Brady McCombs, *Anti-illegal-immigration measures, official English pass with landslides*, Arizona Daily Star, Nov. 8, 2006.

SECTION 2.   BILINGUAL EDUCATION

Do schoolchildren and their parents have a right to public education in Spanish, for either all or part of the school day? Until about 1960, many public schools took a "sink or swim" position with Spanish-speaking students. They made plain to them that if they did not learn English quickly, they would fail. Many schools went even further, affirmatively discouraging the use of Spanish in schools, even on the playground. See, e.g., U.S. Commission on Civil Rights, *Mexican American Education Study, Report 3: The Excluded Student* (1972). In 1962 two researchers showed that bilingualism correlated with high intellectual performance, not the reverse, and with the advent of the civil rights movement and Brown Power, the focus shifted. E. Peal & W. Lambert, *The Relation of Bilingualism to Intelligence*, 76 Psychol. Monographs 1 (1962).

In 1968, the federal Bilingual Education Act, while not mandating bilingual education, provided federal funding for school districts that offered it. Relatively few did. Because the federal incentive induced few school districts to offer bilingual education voluntarily, much litigation, a sample of which appears below, followed.

Consider three situations:

A.   Latino and Anglo parents demand that their school district provide a bilingual-education option for their English-dominant children in which the students learn standard school subjects, such as history and mathematics, in both English and Spanish.

B.   Recent Latino/a immigrants demand that their school board provide education in Spanish to their children, who only speak that language, so that they do not fall behind in their academic subjects during the year or two it takes them to learn English. During this time, they also take intensive classes in the English language.

C.   Latino parents demand that their school board provide bilingual classes so that their children, who are bilingual, will retain that proficiency as they go through their entire school careers.

Which case would draw your interest as a constitutional lawyer? If you were an executive of a large American corporation? The following materials may help you make your decision:

Lau v. Nichols
414 U.S. 563 (1974)

Mr. Justice Douglas delivered the opinion of the Court.

The San Francisco, California, school system was integrated in 1971 as a result of a federal court decree. The District Court found that there are 2,856 students of Chinese ancestry in the school system who do not speak English. Of those who have that language deficiency, about 1,000 are given supplemental courses in the English language. About 1,800, however, do not receive that instruction.

This class suit brought by non-English-speaking Chinese students against officials responsible for the operation of the San Francisco Unified School District seeks relief against the unequal educational opportunities, which are alleged to violate, *inter alia*, the Fourteenth Amendment. No specific remedy is urged upon us. Teaching English to the students of Chinese ancestry who do not speak the language is one choice. Giving instructions to this group in Chinese is another. There may be others. Petitioners ask only that the Board of Education be directed to apply its expertise to the problem and rectify the situation.

The District Court denied relief. The Court of Appeals affirmed
* * *.

We granted the petition for certiorari because of the public importance of the question presented.

The Court of Appeals reasoned that "[e]very student brings to the starting line of his educational career different advantages and disadvantages caused in part by social, economic and cultural background, created and continued completely apart from any contribution by the school system." Yet in our view the case may not be so easily decided. This is a public school system of California and § 71 of the California Education Code states that "English shall be the basic language of instruction in all schools." That section permits a school district to determine "when and under what circumstances instruction may be given bilingually." That section also states as "the policy of the state" to insure "the mastery of English by all pupils in the schools." And bilingual instruction is authorized "to the extent that it does not interfere with the systematic, sequential, and regular instruction of all pupils in the English language."

Moreover, § 8573 of the Education Code provides that no pupil shall receive a diploma of graduation from grade 12 who has not met the standards of proficiency in "English," as well as other prescribed subjects. Moreover, by § 12101 of the Education Code (Supp. 1973) children between the ages of six and 16 years are (with exceptions not material here) "subject to compulsory full-time education."

Under these state-imposed standards there is no equality of treatment merely by providing students with the same facilities, textbooks, teachers, and curriculum; for students who do not understand English are effectively foreclosed from any meaningful education.

Basic English skills are at the very core of what these public schools teach. Imposition of a requirement that, before a child can effectively participate in the educational program, he must already have acquired those basic skills is to make a mockery of public education. We know that those who do not understand English are certain to find their classroom experiences wholly incomprehensible and in no way meaningful.

We do not reach the Equal Protection Clause argument which has been advanced but rely solely on § 601 of the Civil Rights Act of 1964, 42 U.S.C. § 2000d, to reverse the Court of Appeals.

That section bans discrimination based "on the ground of race, color, or national origin," in "any program or activity receiving Federal financial assistance." The school district receives large amounts of federal financial assistance. The Department of Health, Education, and Welfare (HEW), which has authority to promulgate regulations prohibiting discrimination in federally assisted school systems, 42 U.S.C. § 2000d–1, in 1968 issued one guideline that "[s]chool systems are responsible for assuring that students of a particular race, color, or national origin are not denied the opportunity to obtain the education generally obtained by other students in the system." 33 Fed. Reg. 4955. In 1970 HEW made the guidelines more specific, requiring school districts that were federally funded "to rectify the language deficiency in order to open" the instruction to students who had "linguistic deficiencies," 35 Fed. Reg. 11595.

By § 602 of the Act HEW is authorized to issue rules, regulations, and orders to make sure that recipients of federal aid under its jurisdiction conduct any federally financed projects consistently with § 601. HEW's regulations, 45 C.F.R. 80.3(b)(1), specify that the recipients may not

> (ii) Provide any service, financial aid, or other benefit to an individual which is different, or is provided in a different manner, from that provided to others under the program;

> * * *

> (iv) Restrict an individual in any way in the enjoyment of any advantage or privilege enjoyed by others receiving any service, financial aid, or other benefit under the program.

Discrimination among students on account of race or national origin that is prohibited includes "discrimination . . . in the availability or use of any academic . . . or other facilities of the grantee or other recipient." Id., § 80.5(b).

Discrimination is barred which has that *effect* even though no purposeful design is present: a recipient "may not . . . utilize criteria or methods of administration which have the effect of subjecting individuals to discrimination" or have "the effect of defeating or substantially impairing accomplishment of the objectives of the program as respect individuals of a particular race, color, or national origin." Id., § 80.3(b)(2).

It seems obvious that the Chinese-speaking minority receive fewer benefits than the English-speaking majority from respondents' school system which denies them a meaningful opportunity to participate in the educational program—all earmarks of the discrimination banned by the regulations. In 1970 HEW issued clarifying guidelines, 35 Fed. Reg. 11595, which include the following:

> Where inability to speak and understand the English language excludes national origin-minority group children from effective participation in the educational program offered by a school district, the district must take affirmative steps to rectify the language deficiency in order to open its instructional program to these students.

> Any ability grouping or tracking system employed by the school system to deal with the special language skill needs of national origin-minority group children must be designed to meet such language skill needs as soon as possible and must not operate as an educational deadend or permanent track.

Respondent school district contractually agreed to "comply with title VI of the Civil Rights Act of 1964 . . . and all requirements imposed by or pursuant to the Regulation" of HEW (45 C.F.R. pt. 80) which are "issued pursuant to that title . . ." and also immediately to "take any measures necessary to effectuate this agreement." The Federal Government has power to fix the terms on which its money allotments to the States shall be disbursed. Whatever may be the limits of that power, they have not been reached here. Senator Humphrey, during the floor debates on the Civil Rights Act of 1964, said: "Simple justice requires that public funds, to which all taxpayers of all races contribute, not be spent in any fashion which encourages, entrenches, subsidizes, or results in racial discrimination."

We accordingly reverse the judgment of the Court of Appeals and remand the case for the fashioning of appropriate relief.

After *Lau v. Nichols*, can a state decline to provide *any* bilingual education? Suppose it offers non-English speaking schoolchildren no classes at all in their home language, but does offer them intensive training in the English language. See the following excerpt on one state's effort to do more or less exactly that:

Kevin R. Johnson & George A. Martinez
Discrimination by Proxy:
The Case of Proposition 227 and the Ban on Bilingual Education
33 U.C. Davis L. Rev. 1227, 1227–29, 1231–32, 1235,
1237–38, 1244, 1246–58, 1261, 1263–64 (2000)

In 1998, the California voters, by a sixty-one to thirty-nine percent margin, passed Proposition 227, a ballot initiative innocuously known as "English for the Children." This measure in effect prohibits bilingual education programs for non-English speakers in the state's public school system. This pernicious initiative violates the Equal Protection Clause of the Fourteenth Amendment because, by employing language as a proxy for national origin, it discriminates against certain persons of Mexican and Latin American, as well as Asian, ancestry. By attacking non-English speakers, Proposition 227 discriminates on the basis of race by focusing on an element central to the identity of many Latinas/os.

In the face of constitutional and other challenges, the courts upheld the initiative but failed to sufficiently engage the core Equal Protection issue that the case raised. * * *

* * *

THE HISTORY OF DISCRIMINATION AGAINST PERSONS OF MEXICAN
ANCESTRY IN CALIFORNIA EDUCATION

A full understanding of Proposition 227 requires consideration of the long history of discrimination against persons of Mexican ancestry in California. Although most of the state was once part of Mexico, California has seen more than its share of racism directed at Mexican Americans and Mexican immigrants. Anti–Mexican sentiment also has pervaded other states in the Southwest, particularly Texas and Arizona. * * *

* * *

In addition to segregation in the public schools, Mexican Americans have also suffered from relatively low funding for schools in predominantly Mexican American neighborhoods. Failures in school desegregation litigation led the civil rights community to attack school financing schemes. Mexican Americans challenged school financing in two precedent-setting cases, *Serrano v. Priest*, and *San Antonio School District v. Rodriguez.*

* * *

However, in 1978, California voters approved Proposition 13, which drastically reduced property taxes in California by more than fifty percent. * * * By dramatically cutting local property taxes, the initiative instantly cut school budgets, with particularly onerous consequences for Latinas/os. * * * Ultimately, *Serrano* created a right without a remedy.

* * *

Bilingual Education

Limited English proficiency has proven to be an [additional] educational obstacle to many Mexican Americans and Mexican immigrants. * * * In response, Mexican Americans and other minorities have advocated that the public schools provide bilingual and bicultural education.

Over twenty-five years ago, the Supreme Court decided *Lau v. Nichols*. In *Lau*, Chinese students unable to speak English brought an action against the San Francisco School District, alleging that the lack of instruction in their native language violated Title VI of the 1964 Civil Rights Act. The Court held that the school district had violated the law prohibiting race discrimination by failing to provide an appropriate curriculum to resolve the English language difficulties.

Following *Lau*, in 1976, the California legislature enacted the Chacon–Moscone–Bilingual–Bicultural Education Act. This Act required that, among other things, California public schools must teach students in kindergarten through high school in a language they could understand. In 1987, however, Governor George Deukmejian ended mandatory bilingual education in California by vetoing a bill that would have continued the Chacon–Moscone Act. Although bilingual-bicultural education no longer is mandatory, districts could continue to receive funding for bilingual education if they provided instruction in accordance with the Chacon–Moscone Act.

* * *

Passed in 1994, Proposition 187 would have barred undocumented immigrant children from the public schools and excluded undocumented immigrants from a variety of public benefits, and would have disparately impacted the community of persons of Mexican ancestry in California. The initiative galvanized Latina/o voters in the state; they voted overwhelmingly against a law that Anglo voters decisively supported. Proposition 187 drew the attention of Congress, which in 1996, enacted welfare "reform" that eliminated eligibility of many legal, as well as undocumented, immigrants from various public benefits. Latina/o immigrants subsequently flocked to naturalize and become citizens in order to avoid the potential impacts of the new laws, as well as other onerous laws punishing noncitizens, and to participate in the political process to avoid such attacks in the future.

* * *

Moreover, the political retrenchment with respect to affirmative action directly challenged the status of racial minorities. Proposition 209, dubbed the "California Civil Rights Initiative," in fact dismantled affirmative action programs designed to remedy discrimination against the state's minority population and ensure diversity in employment and education. The electorate passed this law in the face of strong opposition from Latinas/os and African Americans. Coming on the heels of some high profile judicial decisions rolling back affirmative action, underrepresented minorities found it difficult to understand Proposition 209 as anything other than an attack directed at the them.

* * *

PROPOSITION 227: DISCRIMINATION BY PROXY

The Supreme Court has acknowledged that a court deciding whether an initiative violates the Equal Protection Clause may consider "the knowledge of the facts and circumstances concerning [its] passage and potential impact" and "the milieu in which that provision would operate."[106] It becomes clear after consideration of these factors that Proposition 227 at its core concerns issues of race and racial discrimination.

Language as an Anglo/Latina/o Racial Wedge Issue

The ability to speak Spanish has long been an issue in California. For much of the state's history, the public schools adhered to an English-only policy, with punishment meted out to children who braved speaking Spanish in the public schools. Sensibilities changed, however, and some school districts eventually began to offer bilingual education. Nonetheless, "[t]he debate over bilingual education has raged since the 1960s."

In *Lau v. Nichols*, the Supreme Court held that a school district violated provisions of the Civil Rights Act of 1964 that barred discrimination on the basis of race, color, or national origin. The school district violated this act because it failed to establish a program for non-English speaking students. Critical to our analysis, the Court treated non-English speaking ability as a substitute for race, color, or national origin. Other cases also have treated language as a proxy for race in certain circumstances. This reasoning makes perfect sense. Consider the impact that English-only rules have on Spanish, Chinese, and other non-English speakers. It is clear that such regulations will have racial impacts readily understood by proponents. "Given the huge numbers of immigrants who enter this country from Asian and Latin American countries whose citizens are not White and who in most cases do not speak English, criticism of the inability to speak English coincides neatly with race."[114]

* * *

With race at the core, the modern English-only and bilingual education controversies are closely related. Latinas/os resist the language onslaught as an attack on their identity. "[L]anguage minorities understand English-only initiatives as targeted at them.... Spanish ... is related [to] affective attitudes of self-identity and self-worth. Thus,

106. Reitman v. Mulkey, 387 U.S. 369, 378 (1967) (invalidating initiative that effectively offered state approval of private discrimination); see also Crawford v. Board of Educ., 458 U.S. 527, 543 (1982).

114. Bill Ong Hing, *Beyond the Rhetoric of Assimilation and Cultural Pluralism: Addressing the Tension of Separatism and Conflict in an Immigration–Driven Multira-cial Society*, 81 Cal. L. Rev. 863, 874 (1993). See also Christi Cunningham, *The "Racing" Cause of Action and the Identity Formerly Known as Race: The Road to Tamazunchale*, 30 Rutgers L.J. 707, 709–10 (1999) (discussing connection between culture and race).

language symbolizes deeply held feelings about identity and is deeply embedded in how individuals place themselves within society."[122]

The intensity of the language debate at times is difficult to comprehend unless one views the laws as symbolic attacks under color of law against minority groups. For example, California voters in 1986 passed an advisory initiative that had no legal impact but to declare English the official language of the state of California.[124]

* * *

[S]ymbolic action of this nature can have concrete long-term impacts. In 1990, Professor Julian Eule observed that recent efforts in Arizona, California, and Colorado declaring English the official language were largely "symbolic and offer little opportunity for courts to remedy the gratuitous insult" to non-English speakers. However, he predicted that such measures would be "invoked in efforts to terminate states' bilingual programs" and that "[a]ttempts to demonstrate that the initiatives are motivated by racial animus [as required by the Supreme Court's Equal Protection jurisprudence] will encounter . . . proof difficulties. . . ."

[T]his is precisely what has happened. State English-only laws were followed by English-only regulations in the workplace and, ultimately, attacks such as Proposition 227, on bilingual education. And, as we shall see, it proved difficult to establish that states enacted such laws with a discriminatory intent.

The Case of Proposition 227

Following closely upon "the gratuitous insult" to Latinas/os transmitted by voter approval of English-only measures in Arizona, California, and Colorado, proponents unveiled Proposition 227 in July 1997 * * *. Although not identifying Latinas/os by name, the measure's text and context leave little doubt that a motivating factor behind its passage was to attack educational opportunities for Spanish-speaking Latinas/os, especially Mexican immigrants.

The Language of the Initiative

The people targeted by Proposition 227 are identified in the official title of the measure. This title, English Language Education for Immigrant Children, was shortened by advocates during the campaign to English for the Children. In the "Findings and Declarations," Proposition 227 refers four times to immigrants or immigrant children. Mention is made of "*[i]mmigrant parents,*" who "are eager to have their children acquire a good knowledge of English"; the state's public school system, which has done "a poor job of educating *immigrant children*"; the "wast[e of] financial resources on costly experimental language programs whose failure . . . is demonstrated by the current high drop-out rates and

---

122. Sylvia R. Lazos Vargas, *Judicial Review of Initiatives and Referendums in Which Majorities Vote on Minorities' Demo-* *cratic Citizenship*, 60 Ohio St. L.J. 399, 445 (1999).

124. See Cal. Const. art. III, § 6.

low English literacy levels of many *immigrant children*"; and the resiliency of "[y]oung *immigrant children*," who "can easily acquire full fluency in a new language, such as English, if they are heavily exposed to that language."

* * *

In addition to the disparate impact on Latinas/os, the initiative places special burdens on them. First, Proposition 227 proclaims as public policy what every Latina/o immigrant in this country already knows: that English "is the national public language of the United States of America and the State of California . . . and is also the leading world language for science, technology, and international business, thereby being the language of economic opportunity." This statement is curious in light of the fact that Latina/o immigrants and citizens strive to—and in fact do—acquire English language skills.

Second, the heart of the measure, section 305, eliminates the right of Latina/o parents to choose how their children will acquire English language skills and imposes a one-size-fits-all approach:

> [A]ll children in California public schools shall be taught English by being taught in English. . . . [T]his shall require that all children be placed in English language classrooms. Children who are English learners shall be educated through sheltered English immersion during a temporary transition period not normally intended to exceed one year.

This flies in the face of this nation's firm tradition of protecting fundamental family decisions, such as the type of education the children should receive, from governmental interference.[147] Section 305 denies Latina/o parents the choice of having their children taught English through gradual exposure rather than through mandatory immersion. It also dismisses the views of bilingual education experts, many of whom believe that non-English-speaking children generally need years of study in a second language to become proficient enough to succeed in it academically.

Finally, section 310, which permits parents to petition for bilingual instruction, requires that the child's parent or guardian provide "written informed consent." Such consent, however, cannot be obtained in the time-tested manner, that is, by having the parent sign a consent form. Section 310 instead requires that a "parent or legal guardian *personally visit* the school to apply for the waiver." Imagine the reaction of Anglo parents if a provision of the California Education Code effectively required them, but not African American, Asian, or Latina/o parents, to personally visit a school before their children could opt out of mandatory education programs.

---

147. See, e.g., Pierce v. Society of Sisters, 268 U.S. 510 (1925) (invalidating state law requiring all children to attend public school).

Ballot Arguments

Like the language of the initiative, the Proposition 227 campaign often spoke softly and subtly about race. Most campaign materials did not squarely mention race. Opponents feared raising the claim of racial discrimination because of a possible backlash. The ballot arguments in the voters pamphlet, however, make clear that the initiative singles out Latinas/os. Despite paying homage to "the best of intentions" with which the architects of bilingual programs began their efforts, the proponents sharply criticize those programs and explicitly refer to persons of Latina/o (and no other) descent.

First, the Proposition 227 advocates proclaimed that "[f]or most of California's non-English speaking students, bilingual education actually means monolingual, SPANISH–ONLY education for the first 4 to 7 years of school." No mention is made of the type of education afforded any other group of students, whether African American, Asian, or white. Second, the argument identifies "Latino immigrant children" as "the principal victims of bilingual education," because they have the highest dropout rates and lowest test scores of any group.

Third, the proponents of the measure state that "[m]ost *Latino parents* [support the initiative], according to public polls. They know that *Spanish-only* bilingual education is preventing their children from learning English by segregating them into an educational dead-end." If Proposition 227 were truly race neutral, it would be unnecessary to invoke the alleged political opinions of Latina/o parents. Similarly, the rebuttal to the argument against Proposition 227 criticized the measure's opponents as the leaders of organizations whose members "receive HUNDREDS OF MILLIONS OF DOLLARS annually from our failed system of SPANISH–ONLY bilingual education."

Statements by Advocates

* * *

From the outset, the sponsors of Proposition 227 denied any racial animus. Ron Unz claimed to support Latina/o parents who kept their children out of bilingual classes and insisted that they learn English. To unveil Proposition 227, he went to Jean Parker Elementary School in San Francisco, where nearly a quarter-century earlier the family of Kinney Lau, an immigrant Chinese student, had successfully sued the city's school district to secure Lau's right to receive a bilingual public education. In media appearances, Unz asserted that Proposition 227 was neither anti-immigrant nor anti-Latina/o and proclaimed that any victory would be morally hollow without Latina/o support. All of which prompted some Latinas/os, such as California Assembly Speaker Antonio Villaraigosa, to regard Unz as "a decent guy, although we have different views of the world."

Three of the four principal spokespersons who joined Unz in sponsoring Proposition 227 were Latinas/os. Nevertheless, many statements made by supporters demonstrated an intent to single out Spanish-speaking Latinas/os in a way that would not be tolerated if aimed at Anglos. Unz, for example, unfavorably compared today's Latina/o immigrants to the European immigrants of the 1920s and 1930s. He acknowledged that the only group of children given large quantities of "so-called bilingual instruction are *Latino-Spanish speaking children*" and emphasized that Proposition 227 was "something that will benefit, most of all, *California's immigrant and Latino population.*" Responding to the argument that bilingual education helps immigrant pupils learn better by teaching them respect for their culture, he sharply responded that "[i]t isn't the duty of the public schools to help children maintain their native culture."

Emphasizing that she was a Latina supporter of Proposition 227, cosponsor Gloria Matta Tuchman played a similar role for Unz that Ward Connerly, an African American, did for Governor Wilson in the Proposition 209 campaign. She exuded the tough-love assimilationism of her father, who taught her that "Anglos did us a favor by making us learn English. That's why we are so successful." Although few would question the importance to immigrants of learning English, coerced assimilation, which too often calls upon immigrants to renounce their native language and other ties to their heritage, is another matter.

Ron Unz's comments demonstrate the pro-Proposition 227 campaign's efforts to attack Latinas/os by using Latina/o figureheads: "Gloria [Malta Tuchman] is the best possible spokesperson for something like this," Unz said. "Her ethnicity, her gender ... all those things play an important role." Unz called [Jaime] Escalante's support a 'tremendous boost' to his campaign.... Having the most prominent Latino educator serving as honorary chairman really just allows more of these Latino public figures to voice their true feelings on the issue, Unz said." "Unz says he hopes Escalante's support of the campaign will help shake loose support ... from California's GOP leaders...." Consequently, Latina/o supporters were used to serve anti-Latina/o ends.

* * *

The Results

At the June 1998 election, Anglos heavily supported Proposition 227 while Latinas/os strongly opposed it. Specifically, although the measure passed by a 61–39% margin, Latinas/os, according to exit polls, opposed the measure by a 63–37%, which was contrary to what the pre-election polls had predicted. The election results are generally consistent with survey results showing that over 80% of Latinas/os supported bilingual education.

* * *

The Discriminatory Intent Necessary for an Equal Protection Violation?

In *Valeria G. v. Wilson,* the district court rejected all challenges to Proposition 227. The court specifically held against the plaintiffs on an Equal Protection claim based on the argument that the initiative created a political barrier that disadvantaged racial minorities. In so doing, the court emphasized that, even if the measure had a disproportionate impact on a minority group, the plaintiffs failed to establish the necessary discriminatory intent for an Equal Protection challenge. According to the court, the plaintiffs did not attempt to satisfy this "burden [but claimed] that they [were] not arguing a 'conventional' equal protection claim."

An amicus curiae brief submitted in *Valeria G.* contended that Proposition 227 violated international law, including the Convention on the Elimination of All Forms of Racial Discrimination, thereby "impl[ying] that Proposition 227 was motivated by racial or national origin discrimination." Finding that the issue was not properly before it, the court simplistically asserted that a better education for limited English proficient children was the purpose behind the measure.

The district court's cursory analysis of whether the voters passed Proposition 227 with a discriminatory intent deserves careful scrutiny.

Does *Lau v. Nichols*, a case brought by Chinese speakers, apply when Spanish speakers bring a similar suit? Johnson and Martinez believe it should. See *Serna v. Portales*, below. See also the discussion of the No Child Left Behind Act, in Part Four, which may exert pressure (if only indirectly) on schools to mitigate or accommodate the language deficiencies of Latino students.

Serna v. Portales
499 F.2d 1147 (10th Cir. 1974)

HILL, CIRCUIT JUDGE.

Appellees in this class action are Spanish surnamed Americans seeking declaratory and injunctive relief against Portales Municipal School District for alleged constitutional and statutory violations committed under color of state law. In particular, appellees contend that appellant-school district has deprived them of their right to equal protection of the laws as guaranteed by the Fourteenth Amendment to the United States Constitution and of their statutory rights under Title VI of the 1964 Civil Rights Act, specifically § 601, 42 U.S.C. § 2000d. Jurisdiction is invoked under 28 U.S.C. § 1343.

Pertinent facts include the following. The City of Portales, New Mexico, has a substantial number of Spanish surnamed residents. Accordingly, a sizable minority of students attending the Portales schools are Spanish surnamed. Evidence indicates that many of these students know very little English when they enter the school system. They speak Spanish at home and grow up in a Spanish culture totally alien to the environment thrust upon them in the Portales school system. The result is a lower achievement level than their Anglo–American counterparts, and a higher percentage of school dropouts.

For the 1971–72 school year approximately 34 percent of the children attending Portales' four elementary schools, Lindsey, James, Steiner and Brown, were Spanish surnamed. The junior high school and senior high school enrollments of Spanish surnamed students were 29 percent and 17 percent, respectively. Unquestionably as Spanish surnamed children advanced to the higher grades a disproportionate number of them quit school.

Appellees in their complaint charge appellant with discriminating against Spanish surnamed students in ... failure to provide bilingual instruction which takes into account the special educational needs of the Mexican–American student; failure to hire any teachers of Mexican–American descent; failure to structure a curriculum that takes into account the particular education needs of Mexican–American children; failure to structure a curriculum that reflects the historical contributions of people of Mexican and Spanish descent to the State of New Mexico and the United States; and failure to hire and employ and administrators including superintendents, assistant superintendents, principals, vice-principals, and truant officers of Mexican–American descent. This failure to provide equal educational opportunities allegedly deprived appellees and all other similarly situated of their right to equal protection of the laws under the Fourteenth Amendment.

At trial appellees presented the following evidence to support their allegations. Until 1970 none of the teachers in the Portales schools was Spanish surnamed, including those teaching the Spanish language in junior and senior high school; there had never been a Spanish surnamed principal or vice-principal and there were no secretaries who spoke Spanish in the elementary grades.

Evidence was offered showing that in 1969 the report by Portales Municipal Schools to United States Commission on Civil Rights indicated that at Lindsey, the 86 percent Spanish surnamed school, only four students with Spanish surnames in the first grade spoke English as well as the average Anglo first grader. During an evaluation of the Portales Municipal Schools by the New Mexico Department of Education in 1969, the evaluation team concluded that the language arts program at Lindsey School "was below average and not meeting the needs of those children." Notwithstanding this knowledge of the plight of Spanish surnamed students in Portales, appellants neither applied for funds under the federal Bilingual Education Act, 20 U.S.C. § 880b, nor accepted funds for a similar purpose when they were offered by the State of New Mexico.

Undisputed evidence shows that Spanish surnamed students do not reach the achievement levels attained by their Anglo counterparts. For example, achievement tests, which are given totally in the English language, disclose that students at Lindsey are almost a full grade behind children attending other schools in reading, language mechanics and language expression. Intelligence quotient tests show that Lindsey students fall further behind as they move from the first to the fifth grade. As the disparity in achievement levels increases between Spanish surnamed and Anglo students, so does the disparity in attendance and school dropout rates.

Expert witnesses explained what effect the Portales school system had on Spanish surnamed students. Dr. Zintz testified that when Spanish surnamed children come to school and find that their language and culture are totally rejected and that only English is acceptable, feelings of inadequacy and lowered self esteem develop. Henry Pascual, Director of the Communicative Arts Division of the New Mexico Department of Education, stated that a child who goes to a school where he finds no evidence of his language and culture and ethnic group represented becomes withdrawn and nonparticipating. The child often lacks a positive mental attitude. Maria Gutierrez Spencer, a longtime teacher in New Mexico, testified that until a child developed a good self image not even teaching English as a second language would be successful. If a child can be made to feel worthwhile in school then he will learn even with a poor English program. Dr. Estevan Moreno, a psychologist, further elaborated on the psychological effects of thrusting Spanish surnamed students into an alien school environment. Dr. Moreno explained that children who are not achieving often demonstrate both academic and emotional disorders. They are frustrated and they express their frustration in lack of attendance, lack of school involvement and lack of community involvement. Their frustrations are reflected in hostile behavior, discipline problems and eventually dropping out of school.

Appellants' case centered around the testimony of L.C. Cozzens, Portales' superintendent of schools. Cozzens testified that for the 1971–72 school year out of approximately 80 applications for elementary school teaching positions only one application was from a Spanish surnamed person. Nevertheless, through aggressive recruiting Portales hired six Spanish surnamed teachers. At Lindsey a program was established to teach first graders English as a second language; and with the aid of federal funds a program was also established to serve the needs of pre-school Spanish surnamed children. At the high school level an ethnic studies program was initiated which would be directed primarily at the minority groups and their problems.

The faculty was encouraged *to* attend workshops on cultural awareness. Altogether over a third of the entire faculty attended one or more of these workshops.

After hearing all evidence, the trial court found that in the Portales schools Spanish surnamed children do not have equal educational opportunity and thus a violation of their constitutional right to equal protection exists. The Portales School District was ordered to:

> reassess and enlarge its program directed to the specialized needs of its Spanish surnamed students at Lindsey and also to establish and

operate in adequate manner programs at the other elementary schools where no bilingual-bicultural program now exists.

. . .

* * * investigate and utilize whenever possible the sources of available funds to provide equality of educational opportunity for its Spanish-surnamed students.

. . .

* * * increase its recruiting efforts and, if those recruiting efforts are unsuccessful, to obtain sufficient certification of Spanish-speaking teachers to allow them to teach in the district.

Appellants, in compliance with the court's order to submit a plan for remedial action within 90 days, thereafter filed a proposed plan. In essence the plan provided bilingual education for approximately 150 Lindsey students in grades one through four. Each group would be given instruction in Spanish for approximately 30 minutes daily. A Title VII bilingual program would be instituted for approximately 40 pre-school children. Practically all personnel employed for this program would be Spanish surnamed. At the junior high one Spanish surnamed teacher aide would be employed to help Spanish surnamed children experiencing difficulty in the language arts. At the high school a course in ethnic studies would be offered emphasizing minority cultures and their contribution to society. In connection with this program appellants applied to the State Department of Education for state bilingual funds. These funds would provide one bilingual-bicultural instructor for the school district's other three elementary schools, and one bilingual-bicultural teacher or teacher aide at the junior high school. Seeking other sources of funding was also promised as long as the control and supervision of the programs remained with the local board of education.

* * *

Appellees thereafter filed a Motion for Hearing to hear appellees' objections to appellants' program. The motion was granted and at the hearing, after stating their objections to appellants' proposed plan, appellees introduced their own proposed bilingual-bicultural program. After reviewing both parties' programs, the trial court entered final judgment, adopting and adding the following to its prior memorandum opinion:

I. Curriculum

A. Lindsey Elementary

All students in grades 1–3 shall receive 60 minutes per day bilingual instruction. All students in grades 4–6 shall receive 45 minutes per day bilingual instruction. These times are to be considered a minimum and should not be construed to limit additional bilingual training (i.e. the Title III self contained classroom for first graders with special English language problems).

A testing system shall be devised for determining the adequacy of the above established time periods with ensuing adjustments (either an increase or decrease in bilingual instruction) as needed.

B. James, Steiner and Brown Elementary

All Spanish-speaking students in grades 1–6 shall receive 30 minutes per day of bilingual instruction. This program should be made available to interested non-Spanish speaking students as funding and personnel become available to expand the bilingual instruction.

A bicultural outlook should be incorporated in as many subject areas as practicable.

Testing procedures shall be established to test the results of the bilingual instruction and adjustments made accordingly.

C. Junior High

Students should be tested for English language proficiency and, if necessary, further bilingual instruction should be available for those students who display a language barrier deficiency.

D. High School

An ethnic studies course will be offered in the 1973–74 school year as an elective. This course should be continued and others added in succeeding years.

The minimum curriculum schedule set forth in A through D above is not intended to limit other bilingual programs or course offerings currently available in the Portales school system or which will become available in the future.

II. Recruiting and Hiring.

A special effort should be made to fill vacancies with qualified bilingual teachers. Recruiting should be pursued to achieve this objective.

III. Funding

Defendants appear to have complied with the court's directive to investigate and utilize sources of available funding. Efforts should continue in seeking funding for present as well as future programs which will help achieve equality of educational opportunities for Spanish-surnamed students.

Appellants promptly appealed, positing two grounds for reversal. First, appellants suggest that appellees neither have standing nor are suitable parties under Rule 23 to maintain this suit as a class action; second, that failure to afford a program of bilingual instruction to meet appellees' needs does not deny them equal protection of the law when such needs are not the result of discriminatory actions.

Appellants' first argument is that appellees are not suitable parties under Rule 23 to maintain this suit as a class action. In particular, appellants argue that appellees have failed to show that there are questions of law or fact common to the alleged class and that the claims of the representative parties are typical of the claims or defenses of that class. We disagree. National origin discrimination in equal educational opportunities is the alleged basis for this lawsuit. As the complaint and supporting evidence point out, 26 percent of the Portales school population are Spanish surnamed. Nevertheless, prior to the lawsuit there were no Spanish surnamed board of education members, teachers, counselors, or administrators. Nor was any attempt made by Portales school personnel to provide for the educational needs of Spanish surnamed children. These allegations clearly raise questions common to the class which appellees represent and are typical of the claims of that class. We therefore are convinced that appellees fully meet the rigid requirements of Rule 23 and thus properly filed this suit as a class action.

* * *

Appellants next challenge the district court's holding that the Portales municipal schools denied appellees equal protection of the law by not offering a program of bilingual education which met their special educational needs. In light of the recent Supreme Court decision in Lau v. Nichols, 414 U.S. 563 (1974), however, we need not decide the equal protection issue. *Lau* is a case which appellants admit is almost identical to the present one. In *Lau* non-English speaking Chinese students filed a class suit against the San Francisco Unified School District. The facts showed that only about half of the 3,457 Chinese students needing special English instruction were receiving it. The Chinese students sought relief against these unequal educational opportunities which they alleged violated the Fourteenth Amendment. The district court denied relief, and the Court of Appeals affirmed, holding that there was no violation of the equal protection clause of the Fourteenth Amendment nor of § 601 of the Civil Rights Act of 1964. The Supreme Court, without reaching the equal protection clause argument but relying solely on § 601 of the Civil Rights Act of 1964, 42 U.S.C. § 2000d, reversed the Court of Appeals.

The Supreme Court notes that the State of California requires English to be the basic language of instruction in public schools. Before a pupil can receive a high school diploma of graduation he must meet the standards of proficiency in English. A student who does not understand the English language and is not provided with bilingual instruction is therefore effectively precluded from any meaningful education. The Court concludes that such a state imposed policy, which makes no allowance for the needs of Chinese-speaking students, is prohibited by § 601. The reason for this is that § 601 bans discrimination based "on the ground of race, color, or national origin" in "any program or activity receiving Federal financial assistance." In reaching its conclusion the Court relies heavily upon HEW regulations that require school systems to assure that students of a particular national origin are not denied the opportunity to obtain the education generally obtained by other students in the system. In particular the Court noted that HEW has ordered school systems to take remedial steps to rectify language deficiency problems.

> Where inability to speak and understand the English language excludes national origin-minority group children from effective participation in the educational program offered by a school district, the district must take affirmative steps to rectify the language deficiency in order to open its instructional program to these students. 35 Fed. Reg. 11595 (1970).

Finally, the Court reasons that because the San Francisco school district contractually agreed to comply with Title VI of the 1964 Civil Rights Act and all HEW regulations, the federal government can fix the terms on which its money allotments to that district will be disbursed. The case was accordingly remanded to the Court of Appeals for the fashioning of appropriate relief.

As noted above, the factual situation in the instant case is strikingly similar to that found in *Lau*. Appellees are Spanish surnamed students who prior to this lawsuit were placed in totally English speaking schools. There is substantial evidence that most of these Spanish surnamed students are deficient in the English language; nevertheless no affirmative steps were taken by the Portales school district to rectify these language deficiencies.

* * * While the trial court reached the correct result on equal protection grounds, we choose to follow the approach adopted by the Supreme Court in *Lau*; that is, appellees were deprived of their statutory rights under Title VI of the 1964 Civil Rights Act. As in *Lau*, all able children of school age are required to attend school. N.M. Const. Art. XII, § 5. All public schools must be conducted in English. N.M. Const. Art. XXI, § 4. While Spanish surnamed children are required to attend school, and if they attend public schools the courses must be taught in English, Portales school district has failed to institute a program which will rectify language deficiencies so that these children will receive a meaningful education. The Portales school curriculum, which has the effect of discrimination even though probably no purposeful design is present, therefore violates the requisites of Title VI and the requirement imposed by or pursuant to HEW regulations. *Lau*, supra.

Appellants argue that even if the school district were unintentionally discriminating against Spanish surnamed students prior to institution of this lawsuit, the program they presented to the trial court in compliance with the court's memorandum opinion sufficiently meets the needs of appellees. The New Mexico State Board of Education (SBE), in its Amicus Curiae brief, agrees with appellants' position and argues that the trial court's decision and the relief granted constitute unwarranted and improper judicial interference in the internal affairs of the Portales school district. After reviewing the entire record we are in agreement with the trial court's decision. The record reflects a long standing educational policy by the Portales schools that failed to take into consideration the specific needs of Spanish surnamed children. After appellants submitted a proposed bilingual-bicultural program to the trial court a hearing was held on the adequacies of this plan. At this hearing expert witnesses pointed out the fallacies of appellants' plan and in turn offered a more expansive bilingual-bicultural plan. The trial court thereafter fashioned a program which it felt would meet the needs of Spanish surnamed students in the Portales school system. We do not believe that under the unique circumstances of this case the trial court's plan is unwarranted. The evidence shows unequivocally that appellants had failed to provide appellees with a meaningful education. There was adequate evidence that appellants' proposed program was only a token plan that would not benefit appellees. Under these circumstances the trial court had a duty to fashion a program which would provide adequate relief for Spanish surnamed children. As the Court noted in Swann v. Charlotte–Mecklenburg Board of Education, 402 U.S. 1, 15 (1971), "once a right and a violation have been shown, the scope of a district court's equitable powers to remedy past wrongs is broad, for breadth and flexibility are inherent in equitable remedies." Under Title VI of the Civil Rights Act of 1964 appellees have a right to bilingual education. And in following the spirit of *Swann*, supra, we believe the trial court, under its inherent equitable power, can properly fashion a bilingual-bicultural program which will assure that Spanish surnamed children receive a meaningful education. See also Green v. School Bd., 391 U.S. 430 (1968); Brown v. Bd. of Education (II), 349 U.S. 294 (1955). We believe the trial court has formulated a just, equitable and feasible plan; accordingly we will not alter it on appeal.

The New Mexico State Board of Education stresses the effect the decision will have on the structure of public education in New Mexico. It is suggested that bilingual programs will now be necessitated throughout the state wherever a student is found who does not have adequate facility in the English language. We do not share SBE's fears. As Mr. Justice Blackmun pointed out in his concurring opinion in *Lau*, numbers are at the heart of this case and only when a substantial group is being deprived of a meaningful education will a Title VI violation exist.

See Morales v. Shannon, 366 F.Supp. 813 (W.D. Tex. 1973), *rev'd and rem'd*, 516 F.2d 411 (5th Cir. 1975), and the complex "Keyes litigation," e.g., Keyes v. School Dist. No. 1, 413 U.S. 189 (1973), generally upholding the right to foreign-language instruction, although on narrower grounds than that of *Lau v. Nichols* or *Serna v. Portales*. See Rachel Moran, *Bilingual Education as a Status Conflict*, 75 Cal. L. Rev. 321 (1987).

Later cases have found against Latino litigants, e.g., Otero v. Mesa County Valley School Dist., 408 F.Supp. 162 (D. Colo. 1975), *rev'd*, 568 F.2d 1312 (10th Cir. 1977) on various grounds. See also Valeria G. v.

Wilson, 12 F.Supp. 2d 1007 (N.D. Cal. 1998), *aff'd sub nom.* Valeria v. Davis, 307 F.3d 1036 (9th Cir. 2002), *pet. for reh'g en banc denied*, 320 F.3d 1014 (9th Cir. 2003), discussed in Johnson & Martinez, supra. Occasionally, Latino parents themselves oppose bilingual education. Are they misinformed?

See Ruben Navarrette, Jr., *A Bilingual–Education Initiative as a Prop. 187 in Disguise?*, L.A. Times, July 6, 1997, at M6. Columnist Navarrette writes that "bilingual education is back in the news" and that many Spanish-speaking parents oppose it and want their children's schools to replace it with English immersion classes. Fearing that their kids will "become mired in bilingual education," they applaud California's efforts to scale the program back via an English-only initiative entitled "English Language Education for Immigrant Children."

Navarrette writes that this attitude is common in "the MTV generation, at ease with English . . . no historical scars, no romantic connection to bilingual education as rectifier of linguistic wrongs, no hang-ups over 'the way it used to be,' [and] no hostility toward English."

Navarrette traces the "old refrain" to nostalgia for the Chicano Movement of the 1960s and the heady days of high school blow-outs.

Note

Navarrette holds that language is nothing special; Stavans, supra, that it is. Who is right?

SECTION 3.   LANGUAGE AND OFFICIAL COERCION

A.   DEFENDANTS WHO NEED LANGUAGE ASSISTANCE

When the state acts in a coercive capacity, such as when it summons someone before a court, must it provide an interpreter or other form of language assistance?

Negron v. New York
434 F.2d 386 (2d Cir. 1970)

IRVING R. KAUFMAN, CIRCUIT JUDGE:

We affirmed in open court the granting of Negron's petition for a writ of habeas corpus by Judge Bartels. Because the issue decided by us will have important precedential value, we now set forth the reasons for our holding that the lack of adequate translation for Negron of those portions of his 1967 Suffolk County murder trial which were conducted in English rendered the trial constitutionally infirm.

Negron, a native of Arecibo, Puerto Rico, first emigrated to this country sometime between 1963 and 1965, at which time he worked for several months as a potato packer, before returning to his homeland. In 1966 Negron returned here to the same employment, living on a small farm with three co-workers in Riverhead, New York. He had been in this country for the second time only a few months when on the afternoon of August 10, 1966, a verbal brawl between Negron and one of his house-mates, Juan DelValle, both of whom had consumed a substantial amount of alcohol, resulted in the fatal stabbing of DelValle.

Within an hour of DelValle's death Negron had been arrested and charged with murder. Subsequently Negron was convicted after a jury trial of murder in the second degree and sentenced on March 10, 1967, to from twenty years to life imprisonment. * * *

The government does not dispute that at the time of his trial, Negron, a 23–year-old indigent with a sixth-grade Puerto Rican education, neither spoke nor understood any English. His court-appointed lawyer, Lloyd H. Baker, spoke no Spanish. Counsel and client thus could not communicate without the aid of a translator. Nor was Negron able to participate in any manner in the conduct of his defense, except for the spotty instances when the proceedings were conducted in Spanish, or Negron's Spanish words were translated into English, or the English of his lawyer, the trial judge, and the witnesses against him were gratuitously translated for Negron into Spanish.

The times during pre-trial preparation and at trial when translation made communication possible between Negron and his accusers, the witnesses, and the officers of the court were spasmodic and irregular. Thus, with the aid of an interpreter, his, attorney conferred with Negron for some twenty minutes before trial at the Suffolk County jail. Negron's own testimony at trial, and that of two Spanish-speaking witnesses called by the state, was simultaneously translated into English for the benefit of the court, prosecution and jury by Mrs. Elizabeth Maggipinto, an interpreter employed in behalf of the prosecution. At the commencement of the trial, Mrs. Maggipinto translated for Negron the trial court's instructions with respect to Negron's right to make peremptory challenges to prospective jurors. And, during two brief recesses in the course of Negron's four-day trial, Mrs. Maggipinto met with Negron and Baker for some ten to twenty minutes and merely summarized the testimony of those witnesses who had already testified on denial and cross-examination in English. It also appears from the record that when Mrs. Maggipinto was not translating Spanish to English for the court, she would return to her home and remain there "on call." When she was present in the courtroom, she never translated English testimony for Negron while the trial was in progress.

To Negron, most of the trial must have been a babble of voices. Twelve of the state's fourteen witnesses testified against him in English. Apart from Mrs. Maggipinto's occasional *ex post facto* brief resumes—the detail and accuracy of which is not revealed in any record—none of this testimony was comprehensible to Negron. Particularly damaging to Negron's defense was the testimony of Joseph Gallardo, an investigator from the Suffolk County District Attorney's office. Gallardo testified both at the *Huntley* hearing and at trial—each time in English, although he also was able to speak Spanish—that on the morning after the death of DelValle, and after Gallardo had given him the *Miranda* warnings, Negron admitted that he "killed [DelValle] because he called me a cabron [cuckold]." Negron denied at the hearing and at trial that he had made any such statement. Negron's version of the killing was that DelValle had indeed insulted Negron—but DelValle, not Negron, then produced a kitchen knife. In an ensuing scuffle, DelValle was accidentally killed.

I.

We have recently had occasion to comment that there is surprisingly sparse discussion in the case law of the right to a translator or interpreter at criminal trials. We agree, however, with Judge Bartels that in the circumstances of this case "regardless of the probabilities of his guilt, Negron's trial lacked the basic and fundamental fairness required by the due process clause of the Fourteenth Amendment." Indeed, the government does not dispute the nearly self-evident proposition that an indigent defendant who could speak and understand no English would have a right to have his trial proceedings translated so as to permit him to participate effectively in his own defense, provided he made an appropriate request for this aid.

It is axiomatic that the Sixth Amendment's guarantee of a right to be confronted with adverse witnesses, now also applicable to the states through the Fourteenth Amendment, Pointer v. Texas, 380 U.S. 400 (1965), includes the right to cross-examine those witnesses as an "an essential and fundamental requirement for the kind of fair trial which is this country's constitutional goal." But the right that was denied Negron seems to us even more consequential than the right of confrontation. Considerations of fairness, the integrity of the fact-finding process, and the potency of our adversary system of justice forbid that the state should prosecute a defendant who is not present at his own trial. And it is equally imperative that every criminal defendant—if the right to be present is to have meaning—possess "sufficient present ability to consult with his lawyer with a reasonable degree of rational understanding." Otherwise, "[t]he adjudication loses its character as a reasoned interaction * * * and becomes an invective against an insensible object." Note, *Incompetency to Stand Trial*, 81 Harv. L. Rev. 454, 458 (1969).

However astute Mrs. Maggipinto's summaries may have been, they could not do service as a means by which Negron could understand the precise nature of the testimony against him during that period of the trial's progress when the state chose to bring it forth. Negron's incapacity to respond to specific testimony would inevitably hamper the capacity of his counsel to conduct effective cross-examination. Not only for the sake of effective cross-examination, however, but as a matter of simple humaneness, Negron deserved more than to sit in total incomprehension as the trial proceeded. Particularly inappropriate in this nation where many languages are spoken is a callousness to the crippling language handicap of a newcomer to its shores, whose life and freedom the state by its criminal processes chooses to put in jeopardy.

II.

Nor are we inclined to require that an indigent, poorly educated Puerto Rican thrown into a criminal trial as his initiation to our trial system, come to that trial with a comprehension that the nature of our adversarial processes is such that he is in peril of forfeiting even the rudiments of a fair proceeding unless he insists upon them. Simply to recall the classic definition of a waiver—"an intentional relinquishment or abandonment of a known right," Johnson v. Zerbst, 304 U.S. 458, 464 (1938)—is a sufficient answer to the government's suggestion that Negron waived any fundamental right by his passive acquiescence in the grinding of the judicial machinery and his failure to affirmatively assert the right. For all that appears, Negron, who was dearly unaccustomed to asserting "personal rights" against the authority of the judicial arm of the state, may well not have had the slightest notion that he had any "rights" or any "privilege" to assert them. At the hearing before Judge Bartels, Negron testified: "I knew that I would have liked to know what was happening but I did not know that they were supposed to tell me."

* * *

Moreover, Judge Bartels found it "obvious that the court and the District Attorney were fully aware of Negron's disabilities." The Supreme Court held in *Pate* that when it appears that a defendant *may* not be competent to participate intelligently in his own defense because of a possible mental disability, the trial court must conduct a hearing on the defendant's mental capacity. Negron's language disability was obvious, not just a possibility, and it was as debilitating to his ability to participate in the trial as a mental disease or defect. But it was more readily "curable" than any mental disorder. The least we can require is that a court, put on notice of a defendant's severe language difficulty, make unmistakably clear to him that he has a right to have a competent translator assist him, at state expense if need be, throughout his trial.

Bill Piatt
The Attorney as Interpreter: A Return to Babble
20 N.M. L. Rev. 1, 1–14 (1990)

Should an attorney serve as an interpreter for a non-English-speaking client in a criminal prosecution? Out of an apparent sense of duty to the court or client, some bilingual attorneys have been willing to assume that role. Moreover, trial courts which have imposed such an obligation upon counsel have generally been upheld on appeal. This excerpt examines the potential harm to the client, counsel, and the administration of justice when an attorney acts as an interpreter for a client in litigation.

As with other language rights issues, problems with interpreters develop because courts and counsel seem not to understand the significance of the interests at stake. The lack of a coherent recognition of language rights in this country and the absence of any United States Supreme Court decision defining the right to court interpreters add to the uncertainty. Yet, the use of interpreters is becoming increasingly important to the administration of justice. For example, in 1986, interpreted proceedings constituted 6 percent of all federal court hearings. Examining the issues that arise when an attorney is called upon to interpret for a client first requires some understanding of the nature of the right to an interpreter. An understanding of the extent to which an attorney-interpreter fulfills the obligation of zealous advocacy is also required.

Through the middle of the twentieth century, courts generally held that appointment of an interpreter in a criminal proceeding rested solely in the trial court's discretion. Even after a provision was enacted for the appointment of interpreters in criminal proceedings in the federal courts, such an appointment was still considered to be a matter of discretion. However, in 1970, the Second Circuit Court of Appeals in *United States ex rel. Negron v. New York*, determined that the sixth amendment's confrontation clause * * * requires that non-English-speaking defendants be informed of their right to simultaneous interpretation of proceedings at the government's expense. Otherwise, the trial would be a "babble of voices," the defendant would not understand the testimony against him, and counsel would be unable to cross-examine effectively.

The Court Interpreters Act of 1978 expanded the right to an interpreter in federal court. The Act requires judges to employ competent interpreters in criminal or civil actions initiated by the government in a United States district court. An interpreter must be appointed when a party or witness speaks only or primarily in a language other than English or suffers from a hearing impairment, so as to inhibit the person's comprehension of the proceedings. The Director of the Administrative Office of the United States Courts is required to prescribe, determine, and certify the qualifications of persons who may serve as interpreters. The Director maintains a list of interpreters and prescribes a fee schedule for their use.

Courts have repeatedly determined that no constitutional right guarantees an interpreter in civil or administrative proceedings. However, various state constitutional and legislative provisions do so, in most cases leaving the determination to the trial court's discretion. Under traditional views of zealous advocacy, counsel for a party with a language barrier should be ethically required to urge the Court to appoint an interpreter. Before turning to a discussion of counsel as interpreter, it is important to consider how counsel who is not also required to serve as an interpreter should ordinarily proceed regarding interpretation issues in litigation.

The first issue is whether a client is entitled to an interpreter. Courts will ordinarily not appoint one in the absence of a request to do so, but the failure of an attorney to request an interpreter for a qualifying client has been held to constitute ineffective assistance of counsel. A client need not be totally ignorant of the English language in order to be entitled to an interpreter. The federal test is basically whether the client speaks only or primarily a language other than English. Thus, even though a client may be able to function in English in a social conversation, he or she may still be entitled to an interpreter in litigation. Zealous advocacy would seem to require counsel to seek an interpreter when a language barrier may inhibit his or her client's comprehension of the proceedings or interfere with presentation of evidence on the client's behalf.

Counsel must also ensure that the interpreter is qualified. In the federal system, the Director of the Administrative Office of the United States Courts examines and maintains lists of certified interpreters; some states do as well. In the absence of such certification, an attorney should require the interpreter to demonstrate sufficient education, training, or experience to satisfy the trial judge that he or she can make a competent translation. Although interpreters with obvious conflicts of interest, such as a family relationship to a witness, may be allowed to serve, opposing counsel should identify such conflicts and object, in order to preserve a record for appeal.

Assuming the court appoints a competent, unbiased interpreter, counsel's work is still not done. Counsel should ordinarily insist on a simultaneous translation. Because the court reporter only transcribes the English dialogue, counsel should insist on a "first-person" translation to avoid a garbled record. Further, counsel should adamantly insist on having two interpreters in the courtroom. One would translate witness testimony and proceedings for the record. The other would facilitate communication between counsel and client, and advise counsel of any translation errors made by the first, or "court" interpreter. Finally, counsel should insist that interpreted testimony be tape-recorded for correcting errors at trial or for transmission with the record on appeal if necessary.

* * *

In some pre-*Negron* cases, courts encountered no difficulty in finding that the right to confront witnesses in a criminal proceeding was satisfied where defense counsel was bilingual, or understood the testimony even though the defendant did not. Thus, the presence of counsel who could communicate with clients in French, Italian, or Polish, as well as Spanish, was held to obviate the need for the appointment of an interpreter. The "bald assertion" that an attorney who was forced to act as the client's interpreter could not thereby function effectively as counsel was found to be without merit in a case with a Spanish-speaking defendant and bilingual counsel. By the same token, the presence of a bilingual judge was held to satisfy the constitutional right of a Spanish-speaking defendant to confront witnesses in a criminal proceeding.

* * *

The failure of courts to consider these issues can produce potentially severe consequences. Language minority clients may be convicted without the traditional safeguards afforded to English-speaking clients. Bilingual attorneys can be subjected to state-imposed sanctions for participation without objection in the process. Constitutional ramifications may come into play, as well. * * * Even though the Supreme Court has never recognized a constitutional right to an interpreter, and although lower courts have reached contradictory conclusions on the subject, the Supreme Court has found a due process right to state-furnished "basic tools," including psychiatric experts on behalf of indigents. Similarly, a showing of particularized need for an interpreter coupled with a showing as to why a bilingual attorney cannot fulfill the need should lead to a conclusion that the failure to appoint a separate interpreter violates due process. In addition, *Negron* teaches that confrontation clause and due process violations occur when a language minority client does not have an interpreter to confront adverse witnesses. *Negron* also refers to a standard of "simple humaneness." Counsel should invoke these concerns as well in resisting the dual appointment as attorney and interpreter.

Equal protection considerations also come to the fore. The only apparent reason why courts require counsel to also serve as interpreters is to save the money which would otherwise be paid by the court to independent interpreters. Assuming that such a scheme effectively deprives the client of either the attorney or the interpreter to which the client would otherwise be entitled, the situation appears analogous to equal protection problems identified by the Supreme Court where state court schemes denied indigent defendants appellate transcripts.

    * * *

Moreover, even though trial courts have received wide discretion to appoint as interpreters persons with obvious bias, inherent conflict issues stemming from the attorney-client relationship loom large. For example, the attorney who interprets for a client at trial may well end up testifying against the client on appeal if an issue as to the adequacy of the translation is raised. Even though the issue of effective assistance of trial counsel occasionally arises in criminal appeals, no good reason argues for counsel to agree to inject an additional potential area of conflict between themselves and clients.

These concerns are not limited to the attorney-client relationship at trial. For example, the entry of a guilty plea has traditionally been viewed as the waiver of constitutionally protected rights. These rights include the privilege against self-incrimination, the right to trial by jury, as well as the right to confront witnesses. Waiver of these rights cannot be presumed from a silent record. The waiver traditionally can only be made by the defendant personally and not by counsel. When a bilingual attorney agrees to interpret for his or her client at this stage of the proceedings, the attorney runs the risk of effectively testifying against his client if the issue on appeal is whether, because of the language barrier, the client made a knowing and intelligent waiver of the rights set forth above. In such an appeal, the client would be arguing no waiver could have occurred because the "interpreter," who had not been certified as such, did not effectively communicate to the defendant a sufficient understanding of the interests at stake to constitute a waiver. Upholding the plea in such a circumstance is tantamount to our courts, with the approval and participation of defense counsel, telling language minority defendants:

1. You have a right to confront your accusers;

2. That right is not lost if you can't understand your accusers;

3. That right is lost if you can't understand this inquiry as to whether you wish to waive the right to confront your accusers, because of interpretation errors by your own counsel.

* * *

Given the many serious problems that surface when counsel serve as interpreters for their own clients, one cannot help but wonder why the situation has continued. Monolingual judges may have been unaware of the inherent difficulties in the understanding of courtroom testimony and the presentation of an effective case in the presence of a language barrier. The lack of any United States Supreme Court decision defining the right to an interpreter undoubtedly adds to uncertainties. Viewing the situation somewhat less charitably, judges may have been aware of the difficulties, but chosen not to rectify them because of the same fear, apprehension, and hostility monolingual people exhibit toward a language and speakers they do not understand.

* * *

Whatever the motivations of court and counsel, it should now appear obvious that it is unfair to the client when his or her attorney must serve as interpreter in court. The client, obviously, cannot enter his or her own objection because of a lack of understanding of the language and the process. Thus it becomes incumbent upon counsel and the courts to protect the due process and confrontation rights of clients who are not fluent in English.

Gonzalez v. United States
33 F.3d 1047 (9th Cir. 1994)

DISCUSSION

Gonzalez claims that he was denied his right to a qualified court interpreter under the Court Interpreters Act, 28 U.S.C. § 1827 (1988), and that the lack of adequate interpretation more generally deprived him of certain Fifth and Sixth Amendment rights because he did not understand the nature and cause of the charges against him and the potential consequences of his guilty plea. He additionally argues that his attorney's failure to request a qualified interpreter to assist him in court proceedings, as well as his attorney's gross miscalculation of his likely sentence under the applicable United States Sentencing Guidelines, constituted ineffective assistance of counsel.

* * *

Lack of a Qualified Interpreter

Gonzalez traces his right to a qualified interpreter to the Court Interpreters Act, 28 U.S.C. § 1827 (1988), which states in relevant part:

> The presiding judicial officer ... shall utilize the services of the most available certified interpreter, or when no certified interpreter is reasonably available, as determined by the presiding judicial officer, the services of an otherwise qualified interpreter, ... if the presiding judicial officer determines on such officer's own motion nor on the motion of a party that such party (including the defendant in a criminal case) ...
>
> > (A) speaks only or primarily a language other than the English language ...
>
> *so as to inhibit* such party's comprehension of the proceedings or communication with counsel or the presiding judicial officer....

28 U.S.C. § 1827(d)(1) (emphasis added). Both the magistrate judge and the district court judge did quickly perceive that Gonzalez, whose primary language is Spanish, had some difficulties with English.

However, the statutory predicate for appointment of an interpreter is a finding by the presiding judicial officer, upon inquiry, that a non-primary English speaker's skills are so deficient as to "inhibit" comprehension of the proceedings. In accepting Gonzalez's guilty plea, the district court judge here specifically determined that Gonzalez's language difficulties did not constitute a "major" problem. This was a factual finding, and we review the cold record for clear error only.

While the subsequently-filed presentence report contained the information that Gonzalez was a naturalized U.S. citizen, had lived in the United States for twenty years, and had been a principal in and worked for a variety of businesses, at the time of its inquiry the district court certainly knew that Gonzalez had lived in Oregon for ten years, was buying his own home, and worked in the auto and truck sales business. At Gonzalez's arraignment, where the defendant was represented by appointed counsel Norman Linstedt, the magistrate judge had also conducted the following colloquy:

Court: Do you understand?

Gonzalez: Yeah, little bit.

Court: What is your problem, language problem?

Gonzalez: Well, no. I don't know how to read that much. I understand. I understand.

At Gonzalez's change of plea hearing, where Linstedt continued as his attorney, the district court judge examined Gonzalez with a string of questions about the rudiments of his offenses. For example:

Court: What did you do? Did you work with other people to buy drugs and sell them?

Gonzalez: I used the telephone.

Court: In addition to using the phone, what did you do?

Gonzalez: I worked with Forcelledo.

Court: Did you sell drugs to people?

Gonzalez: Yes.

Court: Did you deliver drugs to people?

Gonzalez: Yes.

Court: Was that drug cocaine?

Gonzalez: Yes.

. . .

Court: Where did you get the drugs you sold?

Linstedt: You worked for Forcelledo?

Gonzalez: Right.

Court: Did you ever sell cocaine to somebody?

Gonzalez: Yes.

Court: Where did you get that cocaine?

Gonzalez: Get it from Forcelledo.

The court continued briefly, then Linstedt interjected:

> I spent from about 7:00 o'clock this morning and any deficiency that he has in language, his wife is here and we fully discussed this and read all of these documents; and we have been doing the same thing for the last couple of months. As his lawyer, I am satisfied that his plea is an understanding plea and in his best interest if he did what he just told Your Honor he did.

The court concluded:

> [T]here is some language difficulty but not a major one. The record should reflect that he has been in court when other defendants have entered a plea of guilty and that he has been assisted by competent counsel who has fully advised him of his rights and that he has also been assisted also by his wife who is able to assist the attorney in explaining these matters to him.

Reviewing the record of the district court's *sua sponte* inquiry, we hold the district court did not clearly err in concluding that Gonzalez's comprehension was not sufficiently inhibited as to require an interpreter. The defendant's answers were consistently responsive, if brief and somewhat inarticulate, and he only occasionally consulted his attorney. In addition, although his lack of objection is not dispositive, Gonzalez never indicated to the court that he was experiencing major difficulty, despite the opportunities afforded him. We therefore conclude that

Gonzalez was not entitled to an interpreter under the provisions of the Court Interpreters Act. Cf. *Valladares*, 871 F.2d at 1566 ("To allow a defendant to remain silent throughout the trial and then . . . assert a claim of inadequate translation would be an open invitation to abuse.").

As a result, use of interpreters was a matter for the district court's discretion, see, e.g., *Mayans*, 17 F.3d at 1179, and especially in light of Gonzalez's failure to object we cannot say that the court abused its discretion here. See United States v. Yee Soon Shin, 953 F.2d 559, 561 (9th Cir. 1992); *Lim*, 794 F.2d at 471. Gonzalez's statutory and Fifth and Sixth Amendment claims based on lack of an interpreter fail as a result of these conclusions.

* * *

AFFIRMED.

REINHARDT, JUDGE, dissenting.

I dissent. Once again, "fairness and due process" take an unnecessary beating in the courts. How easy it would be to afford individuals the full rights Congress provided them. Instead, our careless and hasty treatment of criminal cases all too often makes it difficult for defendants to receive a fair trial.

Here, we narrowly, grudgingly, and erroneously apply the Court Interpreters Act, a statute designed to make certain that defendants understand what is happening to them during criminal proceedings. By reviewing the factual, but not the legal, basis for the district court's decision, the majority has created the misleading impression that the district court's casually, if not inadvertently, adopted approach to determining whether language difficulties inhibit a defendant's understanding constitutes an appropriate application of the Act.

Nothing in the legislative history or statutory language supports the narrow application of the Act by the district court. While the majority reaches the correct result with regard to the procedural default issue, I cannot endorse its failure to review *de novo* the district court's erroneous ruling. Although the majority's opinion limits itself to reviewing the district court's factual findings for clear error, my colleagues' haphazard treatment of Gonzalez's claim might lead another court to assume incorrectly that they have created a new legal standard for determining when an interpreter must be provided under the Act.

The language of the Act is reasonably clear. It provides:

The presiding judicial officer . . . shall utilize the services of the most available certified interpreter . . . if the presiding judicial official determines on such officer's own motion or on the motion of a party that such party . . .

(A) speaks only or primarily a language other than the English language . . . so as to inhibit such party's comprehension of the proceedings or communication with counsel or the presiding judicial officer.

28 U.S.C. § 1827(d)(1). It is quite evident what the Act requires in this case. As soon as the presiding judicial officer became aware that Gonzalez primarily spoke Spanish, he should have immediately conducted a full factual inquiry into whether language difficulties in any way inhibited the defendant's comprehension of the proceedings. As the Fifth Circuit noted in a case upon which the majority relies, "*any* indication to the presiding judicial officer that a criminal defendant speaks only or primarily a language other than the English language should trigger the application of Sections (d) and (f)(1) of the Court Interpreters Act." United States v. Tapia, 631 F.2d 1207, 1209 (5th Cir. 1980) (emphasis added).

In making its factual inquiry, the district court should have focused on a single question: did the fact that Gonzalez primarily spoke Spanish in any way "inhibit" his comprehension of the proceedings? That is what the plain language of the statute requires and, absent evidence to the contrary, a court must follow its common, everyday meaning. The common meaning of "inhibit" is "hinder." *Random House Dictionary of the English Language* 732 (1979). Thus, the statutory language could not be clearer: a judicial officer *must* appoint an interpreter whenever the party in question speaks only or primarily a language other than English, unless his comprehension of the proceedings is not hindered.

Although I believe that the majority was required to reverse under *any* standard, its error stems in large part from its unfortunate decision to review the district court's factual finding for clear error instead of reviewing its legal conclusions *de novo*. Had my colleagues properly reviewed the district court's legal conclusions under the appropriate standard, I believe they would not have voted to affirm the decision to deny Gonzalez the benefit of an interpreter. There is absolutely no indication in the statute or its legislative history that a defendant must have a "major" language problem to be granted an interpreter, and the district court erred in reading such an additional requirement into the Act. Congress mandated the appointment of interpreters *whenever* a "language-handicapped" defendant's comprehension of the proceedings is impaired because Congress concluded that the appointment of an interpreter represents "a fundamental premise of fairness and due process for all." H. Rep. No. 1687, 95th Cong. 2d Sess. 4 (1978), *reprinted in* 1978 U.S.C.C.A.N. 4652, 4654 (quoting Congressman Fred Richmond). Whether the defendant suffers from a major language problem is irrelevant under the statute. The only question, and the sole permissible inquiry, in the case of defendants like Gonzalez is whether the defendant's comprehension is impaired for purposes of the judicial proceeding. Any other inquiry is improper. * * *

The reason that Congress chose the standard outlined in the statute, and why the district court erred in applying a different one, is quite evident from what occurred below. Many people may be capable of speaking enough rudimentary English to function at a very basic level in this country but lack the ability to comprehend complex criminal proceedings. Others may speak English so fluently that, even though

English represents their second language, they can follow the most complicated of criminal proceedings. Congress presumably had the latter group in mind when it required that language difficulties "inhibit" the defendant's comprehension of the proceedings for an interpreter to be appointed. This provision is designed to prevent the appointment of an interpreter when one is wholly unnecessary rather than to subdivide those who cannot speak English fluently into groups with "major" or "minor" difficulties.

In this case, as the majority itself notes, the record indicates that both judges quickly perceived that Gonzalez did not speak English well, that the defendant's responses were "brief and somewhat inarticulate," and that he could not read English at all. Gonzalez's marked inability to respond to simple, direct questions provides a strong indication that language difficulties prevented him from fully comprehending the proceedings against him.

A defendant's full comprehension of criminal proceedings implicates cherished constitutional values. A failure to understand those proceedings leads to the most serious of consequences. Indeed, as in this case, a defendant's inability fully to comprehend the proceedings against him may determine their outcome.

Had the district court made the proper inquiry using the correct legal standard, we would have had a fully developed record to evaluate the defendant's claim. In this case, however, we do not. All we know is that the questioning was cursory and that the district judge found that the defendant did not have a "major" language problem. Because there is absolutely no basis for concluding that, under the proper statutory standard, this primarily Spanish-speaking defendant did not need an interpreter; we should reverse the district court's decision.

Notes and Questions

1. Most English Only advocates want to stop government from addressing its citizens in any language but English. But most such advocates are happy to have the state supply interpreters for criminal defendants who do not speak English. Why the inconsistency? See Susan Berk–Seligson, *The Bilingual Courtroom: Court Interpreters in the Judicial Process* (1990).

2. Suppose you did not speak Spanish, but wanted to pick it up speedily, say in three months, in order to work with an agency whose client base is largely Spanish speaking. Could you do so, and how?

3. If a judge or prosecutor thinks a criminal defendant speaks more English than he is letting on, how could he or she find out for sure?

4. In *Flores v. State*, 904 S.W.2d 129 (Tex. Crim. App. 1995), a Texas appeals court upheld the constitutionality of sentencing a Spanish-speaking defendant to jail rather than to a diversion-probation program that was conducted exclusively in English. Were the man's constitutional rights violated?

B. THE OPPOSITE CASE—JURORS WHO DO *NOT* NEED LAN-GUAGE ASSISTANCE

Suppose the opposite situation—a Spanish-speaking juror does not need to listen to the official translator because he or she is capable of understanding the testimony of a Spanish-speaking witness directly. May officials exclude him for that reason?

Hernandez v. New York
500 U.S. 352 (1991)

JUSTICE KENNEDY announced the judgment of the Court and delivered an opinion in which the CHIEF JUSTICE, JUSTICE WHITE and JUSTICE SOUTER join.

Petitioner Dionisio Hernandez asks us to review the New York state courts' rejection of his claim that the prosecutor in his criminal trial exercised peremptory challenges to exclude Latinos from the jury by reason of their ethnicity. If true, the prosecutor's discriminatory use of peremptory strikes would violate the Equal Protection Clause as interpreted by our decision in Batson v. Kentucky, 476 U.S. 79. We must determine whether the prosecutor offered a race-neutral basis for challenging Latino potential jurors and, if so, whether the state courts' decision to accept the prosecutor's explanation should be sustained.

* * *

I

The case comes to us on direct review of petitioner's convictions on two counts of attempted murder and two counts of criminal possession of a weapon. On a Brooklyn street, petitioner fired several shots at Charlene Calloway and her mother, Ada Saline. Calloway suffered three gunshot wounds. Petitioner missed Saline and instead hit two men in a nearby restaurant. The victims survived the incident.

The trial was held in the New York Supreme Court, Kings County. We concern ourselves here only with the jury selection process and the proper application of *Batson* * * *. After 63 potential jurors had been questioned and 9 had been empaneled, defense counsel objected that the prosecutor had used four peremptory challenges to exclude Latino potential jurors. Two of the Latino venirepersons challenged by the prosecutor had brothers who had been convicted of crimes, and the brother of one of those potential jurors was being prosecuted by the same District Attorney's office for a probation violation. Petitioner does not press his *Batson* claim with respect to those prospective jurors, and we concentrate on the other two excluded individuals.

After petitioner raised his *Batson* objection, the prosecutor did not wait for a ruling on whether petitioner had established a prima facie case of racial discrimination. Instead, the prosecutor volunteered his reasons for striking the jurors in question. He explained:

> Your honor, my reason for rejecting the—these two jurors—I'm not certain as to whether they're Hispanics. I didn't notice how many Hispanics had been called to the panel, but my reason for rejecting these two is I feel very uncertain that they would be able to listen and follow the interpreter. App. 3.

After an interruption by defense counsel, the prosecutor continued:

> We talked to them for a long time; the Court talked to them, I talked to them. I believe that in their heart they will try to follow it, but I felt there was a great deal of uncertainty as to whether they could accept the interpreter as the final arbiter of what was said by each of the witnesses, especially where there were going to be Spanish-speaking witnesses, and I didn't feel, when I asked them whether or not they could accept the interpreter's translation of it, I didn't feel that they could. They each looked away from me and said with some hesitancy that they would try, not that they could, but that they would try to follow the interpreter, and I feel that in a case where the interpreter will be for the main witnesses, they would have an undue impact upon the jury. Id. at 3–4.

Defense counsel moved for a mistrial "based on the conduct of the District Attorney," and the prosecutor requested a chance to call a supervisor to the courtroom before the judge's ruling.

Following a recess, defense counsel renewed his motion, which the trial court denied. Discussion of the objection continued, however, and the prosecutor explained that he would have no motive to exclude Latinos from the jury:

> [T]his case, involves four complainants. Each of the complainants is Hispanic. All my witnesses, that is, civilian witnesses, are going to be Hispanic. I have absolutely no reason—there's no reason for me to want to exclude Hispanics because all the parties involved are Hispanic, and I certainly would have no reason to do that. Id. at 5–6.

After further interchange among the judge and attorneys, the trial court again rejected petitioner's claim. Id. at 12.

On appeal, the New York Supreme Court, Appellate Division, noted that though the ethnicity of one challenged bilingual juror remained uncertain, the prosecutor had challenged the only three prospective jurors with definite Hispanic surnames. The court ruled that this made out a prima facie showing of discrimination. The court affirmed the trial court's rejection of petitioner's *Batson* claim, however, on the ground that the prosecutor had offered race-neutral explanations for the peremptory strikes sufficient to rebut petitioner's prima facie case.

The New York Court of Appeals also affirmed the judgment, holding that the prosecutor had offered a legitimate basis for challenging the individuals in question and deferring to the factual findings of the lower New York courts. * * * We granted certiorari, 498 U.S. 894 (1990), and now affirm.

II

In *Batson*, we outlined a three-step process for evaluating claims that a prosecutor has used peremptory challenges in a manner violating the Equal Protection Clause. 476 U.S. at 96–98. The analysis set forth in *Batson* permits prompt rulings on objections to peremptory challenges without substantial disruption of the jury selection process. First, the defendant must make a prima facie showing that the prosecutor has exercised peremptory challenges on the basis of race. Id. at 96–97. Second, if the requisite showing has been made, the burden shifts to the prosecutor to articulate a race-neutral explanation for striking the jurors in question. Id. at 97–98. Finally, the trial court must determine whether the defendant has carried his burden of proving purposeful discrimination. Id. at 98. * * *

A

The prosecutor defended his use of peremptory strikes without any prompting or inquiry from the trial court. As a result, the trial court had no occasion to rule that petitioner had or had not made a prima facie showing of intentional discrimination. This departure from the normal course of proceeding need not concern us. We explained in the context of employment discrimination litigation under Title VII of the Civil Rights Act of 1964 that "[w]here the defendant has done everything that would be required of him if the plaintiff had properly made out a prima facie case, whether the plaintiff really did so is no longer relevant." The same principle applies under *Batson*. Once a prosecutor has offered a race-neutral explanation for the peremptory challenges and the trial court has ruled on the ultimate question of intentional discrimination, the preliminary issue of whether the defendant had made a prima facie showing becomes moot.

B

Petitioner contends that the reasons given by the prosecutor for challenging the two bilingual jurors were not race neutral. In evaluating the race neutrality of an attorney's explanation, a court must determine whether, assuming the proffered reasons for the peremptory challenges are true, the challenges violate the Equal Protection Clause as a matter of law. A court addressing this issue must keep in mind the fundamental principle that "official action will not be held unconstitutional solely because it results in a racially disproportionate impact.... Proof of racially discriminatory intent or purpose is required to show a violation of the Equal Protection Clause." * * *

A neutral explanation means an explanation based on something other than the race of the juror. At this step of the inquiry, the issue is the facial validity of the prosecutor's explanation. Unless a discriminatory intent is inherent in the prosecutor's explanation, the reason offered will be deemed race neutral.

Petitioner argues that Spanish-language ability bears a close relation to ethnicity, and that, as a consequence, it violates the Equal Protection Clause to exercise a peremptory challenge on the ground that a Latino potential juror speaks Spanish. He points to the high correlation between Spanish-language ability and ethnicity in New York, where the case was tried. We need not address that argument here, for the prosecutor did not rely on language ability without more, but explained that the specific responses and the demeanor of the two individuals during *voir dire* caused him to doubt their ability to defer to the official translation of Spanish-language testimony.

The prosecutor here offered a race-neutral basis for these peremptory strikes. As explained by the prosecutor, the challenges rested neither on the intention to exclude Latino or bilingual jurors, nor on stereotypical assumptions about Latinos or bilinguals. The prosecutor's articulated basis for these challenges divided potential jurors into two classes: those whose conduct during *voir dire* would persuade him they might have difficulty in accepting the translator's rendition of Spanish-language testimony and those potential jurors who gave no such reason for doubt. Each category would include both Latinos and non-Latinos. While the prosecutor's criterion might well result in the disproportionate removal of prospective Latino jurors, that disproportionate impact does not turn the prosecutor's actions into a *per se* violation of the Equal Protection Clause.

* * *

* * * Unless the government actor adopted a criterion with the intent of causing the impact asserted, that impact itself does not violate the principle of race neutrality. Nothing in the prosecutor's explanation shows that he chose to exclude jurors who hesitated in answering questions about following the interpreter *because* he wanted to prevent bilingual Latinos from serving on the jury.

If we deemed the prosecutor's reason for striking these jurors a racial classification on its face, it would follow that a trial judge could not excuse for cause a juror whose hesitation convinced the judge of the juror's inability to accept the official translation of foreign-language testimony. If the explanation is not race neutral for the prosecutor, it is no more so for the trial judge. While the reason offered by the prosecutor for a peremptory strike need not rise to the level of a challenge for cause, *Batson*, 476 U.S. at 97, the fact that it corresponds to a valid for-cause challenge will demonstrate its race-neutral character.

C

Once the prosecutor offers a race-neutral basis for his exercise of peremptory challenges, "[t]he trial court then [has] the duty to determine if the defendant has established purposeful discrimination." Id. at 98. While the disproportionate impact on Latinos resulting from the prosecutor's criterion for excluding these jurors does not answer the race-neutrality inquiry, it does have relevance to the trial court's decision on this question. "[A]n invidious discriminatory purpose may often be inferred from the totality of the relevant facts, including the fact, if it is true, that the [classification] bears more heavily on one race than another." Washington v. Davis, 426 U.S. at 242. If a prosecutor articulates a basis for a peremptory challenge that results in the disproportionate exclusion of members of a certain race, the trial judge may consider that fact as evidence that the prosecutor's stated reason constitutes a pretext for racial discrimination.

In the context of this trial, the prosecutor's frank admission that his ground for excusing these jurors related to their ability to speak and understand Spanish raised a plausible, though not a necessary, inference that language might be a pretext for what in fact were race-based peremptory challenges. This was not a case where by some rare coincidence a juror happened to speak the same language as a key witness, in a community where few others spoke that tongue. If it were, the explanation that the juror could have undue influence on jury deliberations might be accepted without concern that a racial generalization had come into play. But this trial took place in a community with a substantial Latino population, and petitioner and other interested parties were members of that ethnic group. It would be common knowledge in the locality that a significant percentage of the Latino population speaks fluent Spanish, and that many consider it their preferred language, the one chosen for personal communication, the one selected for speaking with the most precision and power, the one used to define the self.

The trial judge can consider these and other factors when deciding whether a prosecutor intended to discriminate. For example, though petitioner did not suggest the alternative to the trial court here, Spanish-speaking jurors could be permitted to advise the judge in a discreet way of any concerns with the translation during the course of trial. A prosecutor's persistence in the desire to exclude Spanish-speaking jurors despite this measure could be taken into account in determining whether to accept a race-neutral explanation for the challenge.

The trial judge in this case chose to believe the prosecutor's race-neutral explanation for striking the two jurors in question, rejecting petitioner's assertion that the reasons were pretextual. In *Batson*, we explained that the trial court's decision on the ultimate question of discriminatory intent represents a finding of fact of the sort accorded great deference on appeal.

* * *

Deference to trial court findings on the issue of discriminatory intent makes particular sense in this context because, as we noted in *Batson*, the finding "largely will turn on evaluation of credibility." 476 U.S. at 98 n.21. In the typical peremptory challenge inquiry, the decisive question will be whether counsel's race-neutral explanation for a peremptory challenge should be believed. There will seldom be much evidence bearing on that issue, and the best evidence often will be the demeanor of the attorney who exercises the challenge. As with the state of mind of a juror, evaluation of the prosecutor's state of mind based on demeanor and credibility lies "peculiarly within a trial judge's province."

* * *

In the case before us, we decline to overturn the state trial court's finding on the issue of discriminatory intent unless convinced that its determination was clearly erroneous. It "would pervert the concept of federalism," *Bose Corp.*, supra, 466 U.S. at 499, to conduct a more searching review of findings made in state trial court than we conduct with respect to federal district court findings. As a general matter, we think the *Norris* line of cases reconcilable with this clear error standard of review. In those cases, the evidence was such that a "reviewing court on the entire evidence [would be] left with the definite and firm conviction that a mistake ha[d] been committed." United States v. United States Gypsum Co., 333 U.S. 364, 395 (1948). For instance, in *Norris* itself, uncontradicted testimony showed that "no negro had served on any grand or petit jury in [Jackson County, Alabama,] within the memory of witnesses who had lived there all their lives." 294 U.S. at 591 * * *.

We discern no clear error in the state trial court's determination that the prosecutor did not discriminate on the basis of the ethnicity of Latino jurors. We have said that "[w]here there are two permissible views of the evidence, the factfinder's choice between them cannot be clearly erroneous." The trial court took a permissible view of the evidence in crediting the prosecutor's explanation. Apart from the prosecutor's demeanor, which of course we have no opportunity to review, the court could have relied on the facts that the prosecutor defended his use of peremptory challenges without being asked to do so by the judge, that he did not know which jurors were Latinos, and that the ethnicity of the victims and prosecution witnesses tended to undercut any motive to exclude Latinos from the jury. Any of these factors could be taken as evidence of the prosecutor's sincerity. The trial court, moreover, could rely on the fact that only three challenged jurors can with confidence be identified as Latinos, and that the prosecutor had a verifiable and legitimate explanation for two of those challenges. Given these factors, that the prosecutor also excluded one or two Latino venirepersons on the basis of a subjective criterion having a disproportionate impact on Latinos does not leave us with a "definite and firm conviction that a mistake has been committed." United States v. United States Gypsum Co., supra, 333 U.S. at 395.

D

Language permits an individual to express both a personal identity and membership in a community, and those who share a common language may interact in ways more intimate than those without this bond. Bilinguals, in a sense, inhabit two communities, and serve to bring them closer. Indeed, some scholarly comment suggests that people proficient in two languages may not at times think in one language to the exclusion of the other. The analogy is that of a high-hurdler, who combines the ability to sprint and to jump to accomplish a third feat with characteristics of its own, rather than two separate functions. This is not to say that the cognitive processes and reactions of those who speak two languages are susceptible of easy generalization, for even the term "bilingual" does not describe a uniform category. It is a simple word for a more complex phenomenon with many distinct categories and subdivisions. Sánchez, Our Linguistic and Social Context, in Spanish in the United States 9, 12 (J. Amastae & L. Elías-Olivares eds. 1982); Dodson, Second Language Acquisition and Bilingual Development: A Theoretical Framework, 6 J. Multilingual & Multicultural Development 325, 326–327 (1985).

Our decision today does not imply that exclusion of bilinguals from jury service is wise, or even that it is constitutional in all cases. It is a harsh paradox that one may become proficient enough in English to participate in trial, see, e.g., 28 U.S.C. §§ 1865(b)(2), (3) (English-language ability required for federal jury service), only to encounter disqualification because he knows a second language as well. As the Court observed in a somewhat related context: "Mere knowledge of [a foreign] language cannot reasonably be regarded as harmful. Heretofore it has been commonly looked upon as helpful and desirable." Meyer v. Nebraska, 262 U.S. 390, 400 (1923).

Just as shared language can serve to foster community, language differences can be a source of division. Language elicits a response from others, ranging from admiration and respect, to distance and alienation, to ridicule and scorn. Reactions of the latter type all too often result from or initiate racial hostility. In holding that a race-neutral reason for a peremptory challenge means a reason other than race, we do not resolve the more difficult question of the breadth with which the concept of race should be defined for equal protection purposes. We would face a quite different case if the prosecutor had justified his peremptory challenges with the explanation that he did not want Spanish-speaking jurors. It may well be, for certain ethnic groups and in some communities, that proficiency in a particular language, like skin color, should be treated as a surrogate for race under an equal protection analysis. Cf. Yu Cong Eng v. Trinidad, 271 U.S. 500 (1926) (law prohibiting keeping business records in other than specified languages violated equal protection rights of Chinese businessmen); *Meyer v. Nebraska*, supra (striking down law prohibiting grade schools from teaching languages other than English). And, as we make clear, a policy of striking all who speak a given language, without regard to the particular circumstances of the trial or the individual responses of the jurors, may be found by the trial judge to be a pretext for racial discrimination. But that case is not before us.

III

We find no error in the application by the New York courts of the three-step *Batson* analysis. * * *

* * *

Affirmed.

Notes and Questions

1. Does the *Hernandez* opinion make sense? Did you read it with a growing sense of incredulity?

2. Juan Perea points out that the opinion betrays society's innate discomfort with speaking Spanish by making knowledge of the Spanish language a disqualifying trait for jurors in cases in which some of the testimony is expected to be in that language. He shows the incongruity of excusing jurors who can listen to the witnesses, thus gaining a first-hand acquaintance with the facts of the case, rather than to the official, stumbling translator. Juan F. Perea, Hernandez v. New York: *Courts, Prosecutors, and the Fear of Spanish*, 21 Hofstra L. Rev. 1 (1992).

3. Imagine a part of the country (say, Miami or San Antonio) where a majority of the residents are native Spanish speakers. Might jury commissioners dismiss native speakers of English from jury service on the ground that they might listen to the (rare) English speaking witness, rather than the translator?

4. Dismissal because of Spanish-speaking ability is not the only form of mistreatment Latino jurors receive. Sometimes prosecutors dismiss them because they believe them untrustworthy, stupid, or too easily swayed by the defense. See Roger Enriquez & John W. Clark, III, *The Social Psychology of Peremptory Challenges: An Examination of Latino Jurors*, 13 Tex. Hisp. J.L. & Pol'y 25 (2007); People v. Zammora, 66 Cal.App.2d 166, 152 P.2d 180 (1944).

C. DRIVING WHILE SPANISH-SPEAKING

Even more than the average citizen, many Latinos are dependant on automobiles to get to work. Hence, the ability to obtain a driver's license is a prime concern, particularly for recent immigrants. See, e.g., Kevin R. Johnson, *Driver's Licenses and Undocumented Immigrants: The Future of Civil Rights Law?*, 5 Nev. L.J. 213 (2004), discussing state rules that deny drivers' licenses to the undocumented.

But suppose that a state only administers its driver's license examination in English. Does doing so violate federal regulations forbidding funding recipients from discriminating against a protected group? In an Alabama case, a U.S. District Court enjoined the English-only drivers' license test, and the Eleventh Circuit affirmed. See Sandoval v. Hagan, 197 F.3d 484 (11th Cir. 1999).

In Alexander v. Sandoval, 532 U.S. 275 (2001), the Supreme Court reversed. Writing for the Court, Justice Scalia held that Title VI § 602 of the Civil Rights Act of 1964 creates no private right of action for disparate-impact regulations promulgated under it.

SECTION 4. LANGUAGE AND ECONOMIC COERCION

How far must manufacturers, marketers, and service providers go in providing foreign-language information and labeling? See Soberal–Perez v. Heckler, 717 F.2d 36 (2d Cir. 1983) (Social Security Administration had no duty to provide forms and services in Spanish; language by itself does not constitute a suspect class).

Ramirez v. Plough, Inc.
6 Cal.4th 539, 25 Cal.Rptr.2d 97, 863 P.2d 167 (1993)

KENNARD, JUSTICE.

We granted review in this case to determine whether a manufacturer of nonprescription drugs may incur tort liability for distributing its products with warnings in English only. Recognizing the importance of uniformity and predictability in this sensitive area of the law, we conclude that the rule for tort liability should conform to state and federal statutory and administrative law. Because both state and federal law now require warnings in English but not in any other language, we further conclude that a manufacturer may not be held liable in tort for failing to label a nonprescription drug with warnings in a language other than English.

I

Plaintiff Jorge Ramirez, a minor, sued defendant Plough, Inc., alleging that he contracted Reye's syndrome as a result of ingesting a nonprescription drug, St. Joseph Aspirin for Children (SJAC), that was manufactured and distributed by defendant. Plaintiff sought compensatory and punitive damages on theories of negligence, products liability, and fraud. The trial court granted summary judgment for defendant. On plaintiff's appeal, the Court of Appeal reversed.

Viewing the appellate record in light of the standard of review for summary judgments, we determine the relevant facts to be these:

In March 1986, when he was less than four months old, plaintiff exhibited symptoms of a cold or similar upper respiratory infection. To relieve these symptoms, plaintiff's mother gave him SJAC. Although the product label stated that the dosage for a child under two years old was "as directed by doctor," plaintiff's mother did not consult a doctor before using SJAC to treat plaintiff's condition. Over a two-day period, plaintiff's mother gave him three SJAC tablets. Then, on March 15, plaintiff's mother took him to a hospital. There, the doctor advised her to administer Dimetapp or Pedialyte (nonprescription medications that do not contain aspirin), but she disregarded the advice and continued to treat plaintiff with SJAC.

Plaintiff thereafter developed Reye's syndrome, resulting in severe neurological damage, including cortical blindness, spastic quadriplegia, and mental retardation.

First described by the Australian pathologist Douglas Reye in 1963, Reye's syndrome occurs in children and teenagers during or while recovering from a mild respiratory tract infection, flu, chicken pox, or other viral illness. The disease is characterized by severe vomiting and irritability or lethargy, which may progress to delirium and coma. * * * The disease is fatal in 20 to 30 percent of cases, with many of the survivors sustaining permanent brain damage. The cause of Reye's syndrome was unknown in 1986 (and apparently remains unknown), but by the early 1980's several studies had shown an association between ingestion of aspirin during a viral illness, such as chicken pox or influenza, and the subsequent development of Reye's syndrome. These studies prompted the United States Food and Drug Administration (FDA) to propose a labeling requirement for aspirin products warning of the dangers of Reye's syndrome. The FDA published a regulation to this effect on March 7, 1986. Unless extended, the regulation was to expire two years after its effective date. In 1988, the FDA revised the required warning to state explicitly that Reye's syndrome is reported to be associated with aspirin use, and it made the regulation permanent.

Even before the federal regulation became mandatory, packages of SJAC displayed this warning: "Warning: Reye Syndrome is a rare but serious disease which can follow flu or chicken pox in children and teenagers. While the cause of Reye Syndrome is unknown, some reports claim aspirin may increase the risk of developing this disease. Consult doctor before use in children or teenagers with flu or chicken pox." The package insert contained the same warning, together with this statement: "The symptoms of Reye syndrome can include persistent vomiting, sleepiness and lethargy, violent headaches, unusual behavior, including disorientation, combativeness, and delirium. If any of these symptoms occur, especially following chicken pox or flu, call your doctor immediately, even if your child has not taken any medication. REYE SYNDROME IS SERIOUS, SO EARLY DETECTION AND TREATMENT ARE VITAL."

These warnings were printed in English on the label of the SJAC that plaintiff's mother purchased in March 1986. At that time, plaintiff's mother, who was born in Mexico, was literate only in Spanish. Because she could not read English, she was unable to read the warnings on the SJAC label and package insert. Yet she did not ask anyone to translate the label or package insert into Spanish, even though other members of her household could have done so. Plaintiff's mother had never heard, seen, or relied upon any advertising for SJAC in either English or Spanish. In Mexico, she had taken aspirin for headaches, both as a child and as an adult, and a friend had recommended SJAC.

* * *

Defendant moved for summary judgment, submitting uncontradicted evidence of the facts as stated above. Defendant argued that it was under no duty to label SJAC with Spanish language warnings, that the English language label warnings were adequate, and that the adequacy of the English warnings was ultimately inconsequential in this case because plaintiff's mother did not read the warnings or have them translated for her. On the motion for summary judgment, the parties agreed that over 148 languages are spoken in the United States. Plaintiff adduced evidence that defendant realized that Hispanics, many of whom have not learned English, constituted an important segment of the market for SJAC, and that defendant had acted on this knowledge by using Spanish language advertisements for SJAC in Los Angeles and New York.

The court granted summary judgment. In its order granting the motion, the court stated that there was "no duty to warn in a foreign language" and no causal relationship between plaintiff's injury and defendant's activities. Plaintiff appealed from the judgment for defendant.

The [California] Court of Appeal reversed. It reasoned that although the question of duty is an issue for the court, the existence of a duty to warn here was undisputed, the actual dispute being as to the adequacy of the warning given. The court noted that the adequacy of a product warning is normally a question of fact, and that a defendant moving for summary judgment has the burden of proving an affirmative defense or the nonexistence of an element of the plaintiff's cause of action. Given the evidence of defendant's knowledge that SJAC was being used by non-English-literate Hispanics, and the lack of evidence as to the costs of Spanish language labeling, the reasonableness of defendant's conduct in not labeling SJAC with a Spanish language warning was, the court concluded, a triable issue of fact.

II

A

Defendant concedes, as it must, that a manufacturer of nonprescription drugs has a duty to warn purchasers about dangers in its products. For purposes of the summary judgment motion, it also concedes that it had a duty to warn purchasers of SJAC about the reported association between aspirin use and Reye's syndrome. The issue presented, then, is not the existence of a duty to warn as such, or the class of persons to whom the duty extends, but the nature and scope of the acknowledged duty. Specifically, the issue is whether defendant's duty to warn required it to provide label or package warnings in Spanish. * * *

* * *

Defining the circumstances under which warnings or other information should be provided in a language other than English is a task for which legislative and administrative bodies are particularly well suited. Indeed, the California Legislature has already performed this task in a variety of different contexts, enacting laws to ensure that California residents are not denied important services or exploited because they lack proficiency in English.

* * *

In defining the circumstances under which a foreign language must be used, the Legislature has drawn clear lines so that affected persons and entities, in both the private and public spheres, know exactly what is expected of them. In some instances, the Legislature has limited its mandate to the English and Spanish languages. * * * In other instances, the statute requires that a person who used a foreign language for an advertisement, sales presentation, contract negotiations, or similar purpose must continue to use that language in written agreements and disclosures. (E.g., Civ. Code, § 2945.3 [contract with mortgage foreclosure consultant to be "in the same language as principally used by the foreclosure consultant to describe his services or to negotiate the contract"]; id., § 1689.7 [home solicitation contracts to be in language "principally used in the oral sales presentation"]; Gov. Code, § 8219.5 [advertisement by notary public in language other than English shall include fee schedule and statement that notary is not an attorney and cannot give legal advice].)

These statutes demonstrate that the Legislature is able and willing to define the circumstances in which foreign-language communications should be mandated. Given the existence of a statute expressly requiring that package warnings on nonprescription drugs be in English, we think it reasonable to infer that the Legislature has deliberately chosen not to require that manufacturers also include warnings in foreign languages. The same inference is warranted on the federal level. The FDA's regulations abundantly demonstrate its sensitivity to the issue of foreign-language labeling, and yet the FDA regulations do not require it. Presumably, the FDA has concluded that despite the obvious advantages of multilingual package warnings, the associated problems and costs are such that at present warnings should be mandated only in English.

On this point, the FDA's experience with foreign-language patient package inserts for prescription drugs is instructive. Recognizing that "the United States is too heterogeneous to enable manufacturers, at reasonable cost and with reasonable simplicity, to determine exactly where to provide alternative language inserts," the FDA for a time required manufacturers, as an alternative to multilingual or bilingual inserts, to provide Spanish language transactions of their patient package inserts *on request* to doctors and pharmacists. (45 Fed. Reg. 60754, 60770 (Sept. 12, 1980)). But the FDA later noted that manufacturers were having difficulty obtaining accurate translations (46 Fed. Reg. 160, 163 (Jan. 2, 1981)), and eventually it abandoned altogether the patient package insert requirement for prescription drugs (47 Fed. Reg. 39147 (Sept. 7, 1982)).

Were we to reject the applicable statutes and regulations as the proper standard of care, there would be two courses of action open to us. The first would be to leave the issue for resolution on a case-by-case basis by different triers of fact under the usual "reasonable person" standard of care. This was the approach that the Court of Appeal adopted in this case. As a practical matter, such an open-ended rule would likely compel manufacturers to package all their nonprescription drugs with inserts containing warnings in multiple foreign languages because, simply as a matter of foreseeability, it is foreseeable that eventually each nonprescription drug will be purchased by a non-English-speaking resident or foreign tourist proficient only in one of these languages. The burden of including warnings in so many different languages would be onerous, would add to the costs and environmental burdens of the packaging, and at some point might prove ineffective or even counterproductive if the warning inserts became so large and cumbersome that a user could not easily find the warning in his or her own language.

The other alternative would be to use our seldom-exercised power to judicially declare a particularized standard of care, giving precise guidance on this issue. But this determination would involve matters that are peculiarly susceptible to legislative and administrative investigation and determination, based upon empirical data and consideration of the viewpoints of all interested parties. A legislative body considering the utility of foreign-language label warnings for nonprescription medications would no doubt gather pertinent data on a variety of subjects, including the space limitations on nonprescription drug labels and packages, the volume of information that must be conveyed, the relative risks posed by the misuse of particular medications, the cost to the manufacturer of translating and printing warnings in languages other than English, the cost to the consumer of multilingual package warnings in terms of higher prices for, or reduced availability of, products, the feasibility of targeted distribution of products with bilingual or multilingual lingual packaging, the number of persons likely to benefit from warnings in a particular language, and the extent to which nonprescription drug manufacturers as a group have used foreign-language advertisements to promote sales of their products. Legislation and regulations would no doubt reflect findings on these and other pertinent questions.

Lacking the procedure and the resources to conduct the relevant inquiries, we conclude that the prudent course is to adopt for tort purposes the existing legislative and administrative standard of care on this issue. * * *

        * * *

IV

We recognize that if a Spanish language warning had accompanied defendant's product, and if plaintiff's mother had read and heeded the warning, the tragic blighting of a young and innocent life that occurred in this case might not have occurred. Yet, as one court has aptly commented, "The extent to which special consideration should be given to persons who have difficulty with the English language is a matter of public policy for consideration by the appropriate legislative bodies and not by the Courts." (Carmona v. Sheffield (N.D. Cal. 1971) 325 F.Supp.

1341, 1342, *aff'd per curiam* (9th Cir. 1973) 475 F.2d 738.) We hold only that, given the inherent limitations of the judicial process, manufacturers of nonprescription drugs have no presently existing legal duty, within the tort law system, to include foreign-language warnings with their packaging materials.

The judgment of the Court of Appeal is reversed with directions to affirm the summary judgment for defendant.

Steven W. Bender
Consumer Protection for Latinos:
Overcoming Language Fraud and English–Only in the Marketplace
45 Am. U. L. Rev. 1027, 1029–36 (1996)

American law has little patience with immigrants who arrive unable to understand English. These immigrants face, at best, spotty accommodation of their language barrier: translation in the criminal courtroom, the voting booth, and the classrooms is usually assured, but availability elsewhere varies. As consumers, immigrants unable to understand English are left largely to the morals of the marketplace. Existing consumer protection regulation too often assumes that consumers are proficient in English or, if not, are accompanied in their transactions by an interpreter. Sadly, this gap in protection has made some Latinos/as and other language minorities the victims of choice for unscrupulous merchants who prey on their inability to understand the terms of the bargain.

Believing that non-English-speaking consumers deserve the same protection as other consumers, this selection advocates guarantees for their ability to strike informed bargains. * * * It proposes reforms to common law remedies and to statutory consumer protection to place more responsibility on businesses when they deal with language minority consumers. It also provides a model of self-regulation for merchants who desire to accommodate these consumers. Finally, it revisits President Kennedy's consumer "bill of rights" from the point of view of Latino/a consumers.

　　　* * *

Latino/a Demographics and Language Abilities

America's immigrant population constitutes the largest "of any society in world history." Immigrants from Mexico represent the largest single group, comprising over twenty-seven percent of all immigrants. Immigration from Mexico has itself been described as constituting "the greatest migration of people in the history of humanity." * * *

A substantial number of Latinos/as in America cannot speak English well or at all. Although Latinos/as learn English as fast as or faster than other past immigrant groups, the traditional pattern of English language acquisition extends to three generations: the first generation acquires some English ability but is mostly monolingual, the second generation is bilingual, and the third generation prefers English. One study determined that of those Latino/a immigrants born and raised in Mexico, eighty-four percent speak mostly Spanish in their American homes. Eighty-four percent of their grandchildren born in America, however, speak mostly English at home, while only four percent speak mostly Spanish.

Despite the normal English acquisition pattern, continued Latino/a immigration assures the presence in America's marketplace of millions of monolingual Spanish-speaking consumers (the Spanish–Only Consumer). As counted by the 1990 census, over seventeen million Americans speak Spanish at home. If these Spanish-speaking Americans were gathered in a single state, it would be the third most populous, after California and New York. Although slightly over half of these seventeen million Spanish-speakers reported that they can speak English very well, 1,460,145 reported that they were completely unable to speak English, and 3,040,828 reported that they do speak English, but "not well." These figures surely overstate the actual proficiency because those unable to speak English are often uncounted and those participating in the census are likely to exaggerate their language skills.

Although not measured by the census, the number of Latinos/as in America unable to read English probably exceeds that of Latinos/as unable to speak it. One estimate is that half of the Latino/a adults in America are functionally illiterate in English. Moreover, many monolingual Spanish-speaking Latinos/as in America cannot read Spanish. This circumstance is explained by illiteracy estimates in Mexico that range from seven to twelve to over twenty-five percent of the population. These illiteracy statistics in turn reflect studies that estimate the average number of years of formal education in Mexico as anywhere from four to less than seven.

Language Fraud and English–Only in the Marketplace

The Spanish-only consumer has become a victim of choice for unscrupulous merchants in America. Current frauds cover the full spectrum of the consumer marketplace: from telemarketing to home solicitation sales to the car lot. * * * In California, a satellite dish vendor marketing door-to-door was accused of targeting Spanish-speaking homeowners to take advantage of the language barrier. Other California operators targeted residents of East Los Angeles for home equity loan scams under which Latino/a homeowners unknowingly conveyed full title to their homes to the loan brokers. In 1993, an Oregon car dealer was accused of using Spanish-speaking employees to entice immigrant customers to sign contracts written in English that sold them unwanted extras such as extended warranties and credit insurance. Another Oregon car dealer misrepresented to a Spanish-speaking customer that an "as-is" warranty gave the customer a fifty-day period to rescind the purchase. Other reported market frauds include an Arizona scam directed at Latinos/as who did not understand the process of car insurance and registration, a New Jersey real estate scam that targeted recent immigrants with limited English skills, and exploitation by certain notary publics of Spanish speakers' belief that they are lawyers.

Besides exploiting the language barrier, unscrupulous merchants exploit Latino/a culture and the current anti-immigrant political climate. Take the example of a Mexican immigrant family targeted by a water purification company selling door-to-door. Preying on what one observer described as the Mexican people's "national, almost religious quest" for pure water, the company sold the family an overpriced, defective purification system for $5000. A mortgage secured the purchase price that accrues interest at thirty-six percent per annum. After paying $6000 of monthly installments toward the purchase price, the family discovered that they still had to pay several thousand dollars or face losing their home. When they complained to the seller that they were unaware of the mortgage and the high interest rate, the seller responded that if they complained to any government agency or appeared in court to contest a foreclosure their immigration status would be investigated. The climate created by California's Proposition 187 may cause any Latino/a, whether documented or not, to avoid dealing with the government for fear of harassment or abuse. Abusive market practices thrive in this anti-immigrant climate.

Bender goes on to discuss doctrines such as the duty to read, fraud in bargaining, unconscionable contracts, and cooling off periods. He notes how English-only laws although not squarely applicable to the consumer setting, nevertheless operate against the public interest and proposes legislation mandating effective disclosure. He also discusses the possible application of current civil rights laws to the consumer marketplace.

Notes and Questions

1. Which is more important to monolingual Spanish-speaking immigrants—the right to receive government services in translated form, or the right to receive product information in Spanish? In other words, is a bilingual marketplace or bilingual governmental services more essential, assuming it were possible to have just one?

2. In Hernandez v. Erlenbusch, 368 F.Supp. 752 (D. Ore. 1973) three Spanish-speaking patrons sued a tavern that forbade foreign languages from being spoken there. They also sued persons who assaulted them after leaving the tavern. The District Court held that the tavern's policy violated Spanish-speaking patrons' right to buy, drink, and enjoy what the tavern had to offer on an equal footing with English-speaking patrons. It also held that the discriminatory policy was not justified as a way of helping keep the peace in the bar, and awarded the plaintiffs a small judgment against the tavern owners and bartenders for humiliation and distress, and another against the defendants who assaulted them. See also Aviva L. Brandt, *Bar Sued on*

English–Only Rule, Seattle Times, Jan. 5, 1996, at B3 (discussing a Washington state bar that ejected Spanish speakers because Anglo patrons complained that they could be insulting them or making fun of their wives).

3. Why would the right to drink beer while conversing in Spanish receive legal protection and the right to buy aspirin for a sick child with warning labels in that language not? Is it because a pub, practically by definition, is a place of public accommodation? Because pharmaceutical companies have a strong lobby? Because beer-drinking is, for some, practically a civic rite that must be open to all on equal terms?

SECTION 5. LANGUAGE AND FAMILY LAW

Suppose a married couple, one of whom is Spanish-, the other English-speaking, break up. Should language abilities enter into the child-custody decision?

Southern Poverty Law Center
Immigrant Mother Gets Center's Legal Help
March 18, 2005

LEBANON, Tenn. March 18, 2005—Faced with losing custody of her child for not speaking English, an immigrant woman here is receiving legal assistance from the Southern Poverty Law Center.

In November, Wilson County Judge Barry Tatum ordered a single mother from Oaxaca, Mexico, to learn English or have her parental rights terminated.

The woman's 11–year-old daughter was placed with a foster family after allegations of neglect. The mother, who speaks Mixteco, a native dialect, but not Spanish, was given a Spanish translator for the proceedings. During the proceedings, she asked the judge for counseling. Instead, Tatum gave her a deadline of six months to learn English at a fourth-grade level.

The ruling caught the attention of the Center's legal department, which quickly decided to take on the case and all of the woman's legal costs.

"The judge's requirement that a mother learn a new language within a few months or risk permanent parental termination is a gross violation of the Tennessee and federal constitutions," said Center legal director Rhonda Brownstein.

Tennessee attorney Jerry Gonzalez, the mother's attorney here, said the Center's involvement provides a major boost to the case.

"She now has three attorneys representing her, plus the resources of a nationally recognized civil rights group," Gonzalez said. "The Center's attorneys are experts in this field. We will do everything humanly possible to protect her rights."

Gonzalez said the judge's decision to force the mother to learn English represents a larger cultural bias toward Hispanics and other immigrants in the court system.

"As a group, immigrants are certainly at a big disadvantage when it comes to court orders regarding custody than a person who has lived and worked in Lebanon, Tennessee, their whole life," he said.

Brownstein called the ruling a bigoted response to the immigrant community in Lebanon and the rest of the country.

"If the millions of immigrants who built this great nation over the generations had been required to learn English or lose their children," she said, "we'd have a country full of motherless children. It's nothing short of an outrage."

The new case reflects the Center's commitment to provide legal representation to society's most vulnerable members.

Dianne Jennings
Judge Orders Amarillo Mother to Speak English to Daughter:
Not Doing So Is "Abusing" Child, He Rules in Custody Case
Dallas Morning News, Aug. 29, 1995

A West Texas judge has created an uproar in Amarillo by ordering a bilingual mother to speak English to her child to better prepare her for school.

To do otherwise is "abusing that child" and "relegating her to the position of a housemaid," state District Judge Samuel C. Kiser told the naturalized U.S. citizen, according to the transcript of a child custody hearing this summer.

"When he was telling me I was raising a housemaid, I felt like I was out of Earth, like I was floating in space," the mother, Martha Laureano, said Monday afternoon.

Ms. Laureano, 29, was born in Mexico and moved to the United States at age 14.

The office clerk is fluent in Spanish and English. She wanted her five children to be bilingual, and when her 5–year-old daughter was younger, she and her then-husband, Timothy Garcia, agreed that he would speak English to her and she would speak Spanish, Ms. Laureano said.

The couple have divorced, and in a child custody hearing in which Mr. Garcia was seeking unsupervised visits with his daughter, he complained that the only English the child was learning was what he taught her.

Neither Mr. Garcia nor his attorney could be reached for comment Monday. Earlier, Mr. Garcia defended Judge Kiser.

"He was fair. He was fair to both of us," he said.

Judge Kiser also could not be reached for comment Monday.

At the hearing, Judge Kiser ordered unsupervised visits with the child and said, "The child will only hear English."

The judge's decision offended people throughout Amarillo, said Dr. Ramon Godoy, publisher of *El Mensajero*, a weekly Spanish-language newspaper. They are insulted by the reference to domestic workers, he said, and afraid that anyone who speaks another language is open to child abuse charges.

"What the judge is telling us is it's not all right to speak any language [other than English] at home," Dr. Godoy said.

Judge Kiser based his remarks on the need to prepare the child to compete in a primarily English-speaking educational system.

"If she starts first grade with the other children and cannot even speak the language that the teachers and the other children speak, and she's a full-blood American citizen, you're abusing that child," he said, according to the transcript.

"You start speaking English to that child because if she doesn't do good in school, then I can remove her because it's not in her best interest to be ignorant," he told Ms. Laureano.

In the transcript, the judge said the girl "is not bilingual. She only speaks Spanish...."

Ms. Laureano said the 5–year-old "is not completely bilingual, but I would say she understands most of the English." Her four school-age children do well in school, she said.

Mark Tabaoda, Ms. Laureano's new attorney, who said he speaks Spanish to his children, said he will ask for a new trial on the basis of "prejudice on the part of the judge" or appeal the decision.

In a written order, the judge "toned down," Mr. Tabaoda said, "saying that the mother will make every effort to make sure the child speaks the English language."

Judge Kiser studied in South America as a college student and has said he occasionally speaks Spanish to his children.

Although Mr. Tabaoda said he is afraid that his client may be held in contempt, Ms. Laureano said she is still speaking Spanish to her children.

"That's just natural," she said. "If I was to speak all English, I would be forcing myself."

Luis de la Garza, president of Grupo de Apoyo a Inmigrantes Latino Americano, a Dallas support organization for immigrants, said his group was contacted about the incident by Dr. Godoy and plans to send a delegation to Amarillo soon to demonstrate its support for Ms. Laureano and Amarillo's Hispanic residents.

"We're going to try to speak to the judge and see what's going on there," Mr. de la Garza said.

He said the judge's actions and comments are part of what he called a national anti-immigration sentiment that some say has been growing since the passage of Proposition 187 in California last year. The measure, which has yet to be implemented because of legal challenges, would restrict access to certain benefits by undocumented immigrants.

Mauro E. Mujica, chairman of the board of U.S. English, in Washington D.C., said, "While I certainly agree with the judge that it would be better for the child to learn English, we don't advocate becoming involved in personal matters."

"I think it would be the same case if they (the child's parents) had a problem with religion," Mr. Mujica said. "If, say, a mother wants to raise a child Jewish and a judge is telling the mother to also teach the kid the Catholic religion, I would have the same problem."

Mr. Mujica said his organization is interested in trying to get English adopted as the official language of government, but not in private matters.

Notes and Questions

1.   A judge could not order a married couple to speak English to each other if they preferred another language such as French or Spanish. So why could one think he or she could order a mother to speak English to a child? See Ellen Barry, *Learn English, Judge Tells Moms*, L.A. Times, Feb. 14, 2005, at A14.

2.   Suppose that a Latino male divorced an Anglo woman, in a state requiring proof of fault, for refusing to learn or speak Spanish. (Or the other way around). Would this be grounds for divorce?

3.   Is it "parental malpractice" if two Latino parents who are perfectly comfortable in Spanish refrain from speaking it at home because they want the children to grow up as "American" as possible, with the result that the children grow up monolingual English-speaking, have to work hard later to learn Spanish in school, and suffer ridicule and embarrassment because of their bad accent and stumbling grammar?

4.   On the rapid rate of English-language acquisition among Latino children, see Julia Preston, *Latino Immigrants' Children Found Grasping English*, N.Y. Times, Nov. 30, 2007, at A15.

SECTION 6.   LANGUAGE AND THE PERSONAL SPHERE

After California passed an Official English measure in 1986, various non-state agents took it upon themselves to enforce the law far beyond its intended scope. Workers in a host of sectors complained that their employers adopted English-only rules punishing them for speaking Spanish on the job, even during breaks. After Colorado passed such a measure in 1998, a school bus driver told a child that speaking Spanish on the bus was prohibited. Schoolchildren in that state told their Spanish-speaking classmates that they were now unconstitutional and had to leave the country. See Steven W. Bender, *Comprende?: Celebrating the Spanish All Americans Know* (forthcoming 2008). For a discussion of workplace English-only rules, see Part Seven, infra.

Part Four

EDUCATION

Prefatory Note on Resistance

Studies of oppressed or colonized people show that they everywhere resist their condition. In acts large and small, they show their dissatisfaction with colonial status and their desire to be free. Gandhi's program of nonviolent resistance liberated India from British rule in a scant quarter of a century. César Chávez borrowed some of his tactics in a successful national boycott and unionization drive on behalf of Filipino and Mexican farmworkers.

Postcolonial writers such as Albert Memmi, Edward Said, and Arundhati Roy write about how the colonial subject mounts resistance to the overlords by withdrawing support, working slowly, pretending not to understand, or by teaching his or her children about indigenous culture and knowledge instead of, or in addition to, the kind that the overlords force-feed them in the official school. Sometimes, resistance takes dramatic forms, such as sabotage, poisoning, arson, or armed rebellion. See, e.g., Herbert Aptheker, *American Negro Slave Revolts* (50th Anniv. ed., 1993); Jean–Paul Sartre, *Introduction* to Albert Memmi, *The Colonizer and the Colonized* (1991); Arundhati Roy, *War Talk* (2003); James C. Scott, *Weapons of the Weak: Everyday Forms of Peasant Resistance* (1985).

Latino Resistance to Miseducation

Latinos have mounted sharp and insistent resistance to their own subordination in every field covered in this book. The methods of resistance have included all those mentioned above, plus litigation. Nowhere is this more evident than in the field of education, where Latinos have staged school walkouts protesting culturally insensitive teachers and curricula. They have challenged segregated schools with petitions to school boards and in lawsuits. They have risen up against biased curricula, disrespect for their culture, and refusal to provide bilingual education. See Ian F. Haney López, *Racism on Trial: The Chicano Fight for Justice* (2003); Richard Valencia, *Chicano Students and the Courts* (forthcoming 2008) (describing litigation in all these

303

areas, plus school financing, special education, school closures, and high-stakes testing).

This Part covers a few topics in a long and rich history marked by resistance and cultural reaction. Schools are the means by which a society transmits culture. See Samuel Bowles & Herbert Gintis, *Schooling in Capitalist America: Educational Reform and the Contradictions of Economic Life* (1976); Paulo Freire, *Pedagogy of the Oppressed* (1970). So, a great deal is at stake, and change, when it comes, is apt to be slow and hard-won. On the ways in which mainstream culture constructs subalterns as weak—and makes sure they stay that way—see Edward W. Said, *Culture and Imperialism* (1993); Frantz Fanon, *Black Skin, White Masks* (1952); Rodolfo Acuña, *Occupied America: A History of Chicanos* (5th ed. 2004).

Juan F. Perea
*Buscando America: Why Integration and Equal
Protection Fail to Protect Latinos*
117 Harv. L. Rev. 1420, 1423–24, 1427–31 (2004)

Today, Latinos are more segregated by race, poverty, and language than any other ethnic group. Latinos, by far, have the highest high school dropout rates of any group. In 2000, the status dropout rate for Latino students was 27.8%, more than twice the rate for Blacks and four times the rate for Whites. Put another way, only 56% of Hispanics graduated from high school in 2000, while 88% of Whites earned high school diplomas. Latinos rank last among major U.S. racial groups in their average level of educational attainment. In 1997, Whites demonstrated by far the highest rate of college graduation (33%), followed by Blacks (14%), and then Latinos (11%). The college graduation rates of Blacks and Latinos fell even further behind those of Whites during the rest of the 1990s.

Many dismal statistics reflect the current effects of past and present discriminatory practices in Southwestern schools. For example, Latino students tend to be held back in school much more often than their peers, and are overrepresented in low-ability groups and classes. In 1986, Latino students were 13% more likely to be placed in classes for the educable mentally retarded than Whites.

The interesting questions are why integration has failed for Latino students, and why we as a society have chosen, and continue to choose, not to educate Latino students effectively * * *. One reason is that effective education demands recognition of and attention to the cultural particularity of Latinos. As one would guess intuitively, students learn best in the language they understand best, which for many but certainly not all Latino students is Spanish. Yet bilingual education in our schools—particularly the more effective type that seeks the maintenance of Spanish and the acquisition of English—runs directly counter to strong traditions of Anglocentric assimilation and homogenization, as well as majoritarian hostility toward Spanish speakers.

* * *

* * * Language is the carrier and vessel of culture, which in turn shapes language and perception. Language constitutes a primary symbol of cultural identification. For Mexican Americans and other Latinos, the Spanish language is a primary symbol of their culture. The same is true, of course, for English speakers. Otherwise, European Americans would not be so tied to English as the exclusive language of proper American identity.

Language use, dominance, and status must be recognized as dynamic sites of political struggle and subordination. Because of the United States's history of conquest and enslavement, the languages of the conquered and the enslaved—indigenous languages, African languages, Black English, and Spanish—carry the low status assigned to their historically subordinated speakers. As the language of the conquerors, English is obviously the dominant and most prestigious language in the United States. The relationship between the high status of English and the low status of Spanish illustrates the form of oppression Iris Marion Young labels "cultural imperialism: * * * the universalization of a dominant group's experience and culture, and its establishment as the norm.... The dominant group reinforces its position by bringing the other groups under the measure of its dominant norms."

Thus, it is the history of the relationships between peoples speaking different languages that enables us to understand more fully the status of a language and the layered meanings in language conflicts. The United States's aggressive war of conquest against Mexico from 1846 to 1848 and the ensuing colonization of formerly Mexican lands provide important context for understanding the current status of the Spanish language and the meaning of debates over its use in the United States. After the conquest, Mexican Americans struggled, and continue to struggle, with Anglos for the survival of their culture and language.

* * *

* * * New Mexico took sixty-two years to achieve statehood, longer than any other state in the Union. From approximately 1900 to 1912, the principal objections to New Mexico's statehood were the presence of Mexicans and the fact that most Mexicans spoke Spanish. Mexicans in the territory were deemed unfit for state citizenship and consequent participation in national politics. Senator Albert Beveridge, Chairman of the Senate Committee on Territories, strongly opposed New Mexico's admission for reasons of race and language. In the Senate report discussing statehood for the territory, Senator Beveridge wrote: "Since we are about to admit [New Mexico] as a state of the Union, the disposition of its citizens to retain their racial solidity, and in doing so to continue the teaching of their tongue, *must be broken up.*"

Puerto Rico came under the ambit of the United States through military occupation by U.S. forces during the Spanish–American War. Under the Treaty of Paris of 1898, Spain ceded control of the island to the United States. Like other colonial rulers, the United States was interested in educating the people of Puerto Rico primarily for the purpose of preparing them for the social and cultural transformation that would accompany colonial control. The goal of Americanization was "the substitution of one set of cultural traits for another."

The goal of the American administrators of Puerto Rico was to accomplish Americanization through the schools. Prior to U.S. intervention, Puerto Ricans were a Spanish-speaking people. In heavy-handed fashion, American authorities declared from 1900 to 1905 a strict English-only policy in schools that taught only Spanish-speaking students.
* * *

Although territorial expansion and colonialism seem to have receded as overt policy goals of the U.S. government, the legal, linguistic, and cultural ramifications of conquest, colonialism, and assimilationism continue. Cultural imperialism is evident in the continuing linguistic subordination of Spanish speakers in schools, workplaces, and the law. The persistence of linguistic subordination and the Supreme Court's inadequate recognition of language discrimination as race discrimination demands reconsideration of the Court's conceptual tools for understanding language difference and language discrimination.

Recently, the No Child Left Behind (NCLB) Act has provided for sanctions for low-performing schools. At the same time, it means that a student cannot count on earning a high-school diploma merely by passing all their classes for 12 years. Through periodic high-stakes testing, the law seeks to assume that all students gain core proficiencies. A few states provide testing material in foreign languages; most do not, citing the expense. See Reading School Dist. v. Department of Education, 855 A.2d 166 (Pa.Cmwlth. 2004) (NCLB does not mandate language accommodation).

The law requires states to track and assure the progress of minority groups and the disadvantaged, a requirement that might seem to demand that they shift funding patterns. Will this prompt reverse-discrimination lawsuits? Reconsider this question after you read the following materials on school funding. See Steven W. Bender et al., *Everyday Law for Latinos*, Chapter 3 (forthcoming 2008).

Chapter 9

SCHOOL FUNDING

Many school districts containing a high proportion of minority children are in low-income neighborhoods that generate low tax proceeds. As a result, the schools in these districts are often poorly funded with dilapidated buildings, little equipment, and the most inexperienced teachers. Latinos and other minorities have protested this unequal treatment, sometimes through litigation. Two large lawsuits with national implications challenged state schemes of school financing that relied largely on local proceeds, rather than statewide funding that might provide more nearly equal per-pupil spending.

San Antonio Independent School District v. Rodriguez
411 U.S. 1 (1973)

JUSTICE POWELL delivered the opinion of the Court.

This suit attacking the Texas system of financing public education was initiated by Mexican–American parents whose children attend the elementary and secondary schools in the Edgewood Independent School District, an urban school district in San Antonio, Texas. They brought a class action on behalf of schoolchildren throughout the State who are members of minority groups or who are poor and reside in school districts having a low property tax base. * * *

   * * *

The school district in which appellees reside, the Edgewood Independent School District, has been compared throughout this litigation with the Alamo Heights Independent School District. This comparison between the least and most affluent districts in the San Antonio area serves to illustrate the manner in which the dual system of finance operates and to indicate the extent to which substantial disparities exist despite the State's impressive progress in recent years. Edgewood is one of seven public school districts in the metropolitan area. Approximately 22,000 students are enrolled in its 25 elementary and secondary schools. The district is situated in the core-city sector of San Antonio in a residential neighborhood that has little commercial or industrial property. The residents are predominantly of Mexican–American descent: Approximately 90% of the student population is Mexican–American and over 6% is Negro. The average assessed property value per pupil is $5,960—the lowest in the metropolitan area—and the median family income ($4,686) is also the lowest. At an equalized tax rate of $1.05 per $100 of assessed property—the highest in the metropolitan area—the district contributed $26 to the education of each child for the 1967–1968 school year above its Local Fund Assignment for the Minimum Foundation Program. The Foundation Program contributed $222 per pupil for a state-local total of $248. Federal funds added another $108 for a total of $356 per pupil.

Alamo Heights is the most affluent school district in San Antonio. Its six schools, housing approximately 5,000 students, are situated in a residential community quite unlike the Edgewood District. The school population is predominantly "Anglo," having only 18% Mexican–Americans and less than 1% Negroes. The assessed property value per pupil exceeds $49,000, and the median family income is $8,001. In 1967–1968 the local tax rate of $.85 per $100 of valuation yielded $333 per pupil over and above its contribution to the Foundation Program. Coupled with the $225 provided from that Program, the district was able to supply $558 per student. Supplemented by a $36 per-pupil grant from federal sources, Alamo Heights spent $594 per pupil.

* * *

* * * [S]ubstantial interdistrict disparities in school expenditures found by the District Court to prevail in San Antonio and in varying degrees throughout the State still exist. And it was these disparities, largely attributable to differences in the amounts of money collected through local property taxation, that led the District Court to conclude that Texas' dual system of public school financing violated the Equal Protection Clause. The District Court held that the Texas system discriminates on the basis of wealth in the manner in which education is provided for its people. Finding that wealth is a "suspect" classification and that education is a "fundamental" interest, the District Court held that the Texas system could be sustained only if the State could show that it was premised upon some compelling state interest. On this issue the court concluded that "[n]ot only are defendants unable to demonstrate compelling state interests ... they fail even to establish a reasonable basis for these classifications."

* * *

The wealth discrimination discovered by the District Court in this case, and by several other courts that have recently struck down school-financing laws in other States, is quite unlike any of the forms of wealth discrimination heretofore reviewed by this Court. Rather than focusing on the unique features of the alleged discrimination, the courts in these cases have virtually assumed their findings of a suspect classification through a simplistic process of analysis: Since, under the traditional systems of financing public schools, some poorer people receive less expensive educations than other more affluent people, these systems discriminate on the basis of wealth. This approach largely ignores the hard threshold questions, including whether it makes a difference for purposes of consideration under the Constitution that the class of disadvantaged "poor" cannot be identified or defined in customary equal protection terms, and whether the relative—rather than absolute— nature of the asserted deprivation is of significant consequence. Before a State's laws and the justifications for the classifications they create are subjected to strict judicial scrutiny, we think these threshold considerations must be analyzed more closely than they were in the court below.

The case comes to us with no definitive description of the classifying facts or delineation of the disfavored class. Examination of the District Court's opinion and of appellees' complaint, briefs, and contentions at oral argument suggests, however, at least three ways in which the discrimination claimed here might be described. The Texas system of school financing might be regarded as discriminating (1) against "poor" persons whose incomes fall below some identifiable level of poverty or who might be characterized as functionally "indigent," or (2) against those who are relatively poorer than others, or (3) against all those who, irrespective of their personal incomes, happen to reside in relatively poorer school districts. Our task must be to ascertain whether, in fact, the Texas system has been shown to discriminate on any of these possible bases and, if so, whether the resulting classification may be regarded as suspect.

* * *

Only appellees' first possible basis for describing the class disadvantaged by the Texas school-financing system—discrimination against a class of definably "poor" persons—might arguably meet the criteria established in these prior cases. Even a cursory examination, however, demonstrates that neither of the two distinguishing characteristics of wealth classifications can be found here. First, in support of their charge that the system discriminates against the "poor," appellees have made no effort to demonstrate that it operates to the peculiar disadvantage of any class fairly definable as indigent, or as composed of persons whose incomes are beneath any designated poverty level. Indeed, there is reason to believe that the poorest families are not necessarily clustered in the poorest property districts. A recent and exhaustive study of school districts in Connecticut concluded that * * * the poor were clustered around commercial and industrial areas—those same areas that provide the most attractive sources of property tax income for school districts. Whether a similar pattern would be discovered in Texas is not known, but there is no basis on the record in this case for assuming that the poorest people—defined by reference to any level of absolute impecunity—are concentrated in the poorest districts.

Second, neither appellees nor the District Court addressed the fact that, unlike each of the foregoing cases, lack of personal resources has not occasioned an absolute deprivation of the desired benefit. The argument here is not that the children in districts having relatively low assessable property values are receiving no public education; rather, it is that they are receiving a poorer quality education than that available to children in districts having more assessable wealth. Apart from the unsettled and disputed question whether the quality of education may be determined by the amount of money expended for it, a sufficient answer to appellees' argument is that, at least where wealth is involved, the Equal Protection Clause does not require absolute equality or precisely equal advantages. Nor, indeed, in view of the infinite variables affecting the educational process, can any system assure equal quality of education except in the most relative sense. * * *

     * * *

However described, it is clear that appellees' suit asks this Court to extend its most exacting scrutiny to review a system that allegedly discriminates against a large, diverse, and amorphous class, unified only by the common factor of residence in districts that happen to have less taxable wealth than other districts. The system of alleged discrimination and the class it defines have none of the traditional indicia of suspectness: The class is not saddled with such disabilities, or subjected to such a history of purposeful unequal treatment, or relegated to such a position of political powerlessness as to command extraordinary protection from the majoritarian political process.

We thus conclude that the Texas system does not operate to the peculiar disadvantage of any suspect class. But in recognition of the fact that this Court has never heretofore held that wealth discrimination alone provides an adequate basis for invoking strict scrutiny, appellees have not relied solely on this contention. They also assert that the State's system impermissibly interferes with the exercise of a "fundamental" right and that accordingly the prior decisions of this Court require the application of the strict standard of judicial review. It is this question—whether education is a fundamental right, in the sense that it is among the rights and liberties protected by the Constitution—which has so consumed the attention of courts and commentators in recent years.

In Brown v. Board of Education, 347 U.S. 483 (1954), a unanimous Court recognized that "education is perhaps the most important function of state and local governments." What was said there in the context of racial discrimination has lost none of its vitality with the passage of time:

> Compulsory school attendance laws and the great expenditures for education both demonstrate our recognition of the importance of education to our democratic society. It is required in the performance of our most basic public responsibilities, even service in the armed forces. It is the very foundation of good citizenship. Today it is a principal instrument in awakening the child to cultural values, in preparing him for later professional training, and in helping him to adjust normally to his environment. In these days, it is doubtful that any child may reasonably be expected to succeed in life if he is

denied the opportunity of an education. Such an opportunity, where the state has undertaken to provide it, is a right which must be made available to all on equal terms.

This theme, expressing an abiding respect for the vital role of education in a free society, may be found in numerous opinions of Justices of this Court writing both before and after *Brown* was decided.

Nothing this Court holds today in any way detracts from our historic dedication to public education. We are in complete agreement with the conclusion of the three-judge panel below that "the grave significance of education both to the individual and to our society" cannot be doubted. But the importance of a service performed by the State does not determine whether it must be regarded as fundamental for purposes of examination under the Equal Protection Clause. * * *

Education, of course, is not among the rights afforded explicit protection under our Federal Constitution. Nor do we find any basis for saying it is implicitly so protected. As we have said, the undisputed importance of education will not alone cause this Court to depart from the usual standard for reviewing a State's social and economic legislation. It is appellees' contention, however, that education is distinguishable from other services and benefits provided by the State because it bears a peculiarly close relationship to other rights and liberties accorded protection under the Constitution. Specifically, they insist that education is itself a fundamental personal right because it is essential to the effective exercise of First Amendment freedoms and to intelligent utilization of the right to vote. In asserting a nexus between speech and education, appellees urge that the right to speak is meaningless unless the speaker is capable of articulating his thoughts intelligently and persuasively. The "marketplace of ideas" is an empty forum for those lacking basic communicative tools. Likewise, they argue that the corollary right to receive information becomes little more than a hollow privilege when the recipient has not been taught to read, assimilate, and utilize available knowledge.

A similar line of reasoning is pursued with respect to the right to vote. Exercise of the franchise, it is contended, cannot be divorced from the educational foundation of the voter. The electoral process, if reality is to conform to the democratic ideal, depends on an informed electorate: A voter cannot cast his ballot intelligently unless his reading skills and thought processes have been adequately developed.

We need not dispute any of these propositions. The Court has long afforded zealous protection against unjustifiable governmental interference with the individual's rights to speak and to vote. Yet we have never presumed to possess either the ability or the authority to guarantee to the citizenry the most *effective* speech or the most *informed* electoral choice. That these may be desirable goals of a system of freedom of expression and of a representative form of government is not to be doubted. These are indeed goals to be pursued by a people whose thoughts and beliefs are freed from governmental interference. But they are not values to be implemented by judicial intrusion into otherwise legitimate state activities.

* * *

Furthermore, the logical limitations on appellees' nexus theory are difficult to perceive. How, for instance, is education to be distinguished from the significant personal interests in the basics of decent food and shelter? Empirical examination might well buttress an assumption that the ill-fed, ill-clothed, and ill-housed are among the most ineffective participants in the political process, and that they derive the least enjoyment from the benefits of the First Amendment. * * *

* * * Every step leading to the establishment of the system Texas utilizes today—including the decisions permitting localities to tax and expend locally, and creating and continuously expanding state aid—was implemented in an effort to extend public education and to improve its quality. Of course, every reform that benefits some more than others may be criticized for what it fails to accomplish. But we think it plain that, in substance, the thrust of the Texas system is affirmative and reformatory and, therefore, should be scrutinized under judicial principles sensitive to the nature of the State's efforts and to the rights reserved to the States under the Constitution.

It should be clear, for the reasons stated above and in accord with the prior decisions of this Court, that this is not a case in which the challenged state action must be subjected to the searching judicial scrutiny reserved for laws that create suspect classifications or impinge upon constitutionally protected rights.

We need not rest our decision, however, solely on the inappropriateness of the strict-scrutiny test. A century of Supreme Court adjudication under the Equal Protection Clause affirmatively supports the application of the traditional standard of review, which requires only that the State's system be shown to bear some rational relationship to legitimate state purposes. * * *

Thus, we stand on familiar ground when we continue to acknowledge that the Justices of this Court lack both the expertise and the familiarity with local problems so necessary to the making of wise decisions with respect to the raising and disposition of public revenues. * * *

In addition to matters of fiscal policy, this case also involves the most persistent and difficult questions of educational policy, another area in which this Court's lack of specialized knowledge and experience counsels against premature interference with the informed judgments made at the state and local levels. Education, perhaps even more than welfare assistance, presents a myriad of "intractable economic, social, and even philosophical problems." The very complexity of the problems of financing and managing a statewide public school system suggests that "there will be more than one constitutionally permissible method of solving them," and that, within the limits of rationality, "the legislature's efforts to tackle the problems" should be entitled to respect. On even the most basic questions in this area the scholars and educational experts are divided. Indeed, one of the major sources of controversy concerns the extent to which there is a demonstrable correlation between educational expenditures and the quality of education—an assumed correlation underlying virtually every legal conclusion drawn by the District Court in this case. Related to the questioned relationship between cost and quality is the equally unsettled controversy as to the proper goals of a system of public education. And the question regarding the most effective relationship between state boards of education and local school boards, in terms of their respective responsibilities and degrees of control, is now undergoing searching re-examination. The ultimate wisdom as to these and related problems of education is not likely to be divined for all time even by the scholars who now so earnestly debate the issues. In such circumstances, the judiciary is well advised to refrain from imposing on the States inflexible constitutional restraints that could circumscribe or handicap the continued research and experimentation so vital to finding even partial solutions to educational problems and to keeping abreast of ever-changing conditions.

* * *

JUSTICE MARSHALL, with whom JUSTICE DOUGLAS concurs, dissenting.

* * *

In my judgment, the right of every American to an equal start in life, so far as the provision of a state service as important as education is concerned, is far too vital to permit state discrimination on grounds as tenuous as those presented by this record. Nor can I accept the notion that it is sufficient to remit these appellees to the vagaries of the political process which, contrary to the majority's suggestion, has proved singularly unsuited to the task of providing a remedy for this discrimination. I, for one, am unsatisfied with the hope of an ultimate "political" solution sometime in the indefinite future while, in the meantime, countless children unjustifiably receive inferior educations that "may affect their hearts and minds in a way unlikely ever to be undone." * * *

* * *

The appellants do not deny the disparities in educational funding caused by variations in taxable district property wealth. They do contend, however, that whatever the differences in per-pupil spending among Texas districts, there are no discriminatory consequences for the children of the disadvantaged districts. They recognize that what is at stake in this case is the quality of the public education provided Texas children in the districts in which they live. But appellants reject the suggestion that the quality of education in any particular district is determined by money—beyond some minimal level of funding which they believe to be assured every Texas district by the Minimum Foundation School Program. In their view, there is simply no denial of equal educational opportunity to any Texas schoolchildren as a result of the widely varying per-pupil spending power provided districts under the current financing scheme.

In my view, though, even an unadorned restatement of this contention is sufficient to reveal its absurdity. Authorities concerned with educational quality no doubt disagree as to the significance of variations in per-pupil spending. Indeed, conflicting expert testimony was presented to the District Court in this case concerning the effect of spending variations on educational achievement. We sit, however, not to resolve disputes over educational theory but to enforce our Constitution. It is an inescapable fact that if one district has more funds available per pupil than another district, the former will have greater choice in educational planning than will the latter. In this regard, I believe the question of discrimination in educational quality must be deemed to be an objective one that looks to what the State provides its children, not to what the children are able to do with what they receive. That a child forced to attend an underfunded school with poorer physical facilities, less experienced teachers, larger classes, and a narrower range of courses than a school with substantially more funds—and thus with greater choice in educational planning—may nevertheless excel is to the credit of the child, not the State. Indeed, who can ever measure for such a child the opportunities lost and the talents wasted for want of a broader, more enriched education? Discrimination in the opportunity to learn that is afforded a child must be our standard.

* * *

Despite the evident discriminatory effect of the Texas financing scheme, both the appellants and the majority raise substantial questions concerning the precise character of the disadvantaged class in this case.

* * *

I believe it is sufficient that the overarching form of discrimination in this case is between the schoolchildren of Texas on the basis of the taxable property wealth of the districts in which they happen to live. * * * [T]he children of a district are excessively advantaged if that district has more taxable property per pupil than the average amount of taxable property per pupil considering the State as a whole. By contrast, the children of a district are disadvantaged if that district has less taxable property per pupil than the state average. * * *

* * *

* * * I must once more voice my disagreement with the Court's rigidified approach to equal protection analysis. The Court apparently seeks to establish today that equal protection cases fall into one of two neat categories which dictate the appropriate standard of review—strict scrutiny or mere rationality. But this Court's decisions in the field of equal protection defy such easy categorization. A principled reading of what this Court has done reveals that it has applied a spectrum of standards in reviewing discrimination allegedly violative of the Equal Protection Clause. This spectrum clearly comprehends variations in the degree of care with which the Court will scrutinize particular classifications, depending, I believe, on the constitutional and societal importance of the interest adversely affected and the recognized invidiousness of the basis upon which the particular classification is drawn. * * *

Nevertheless, the majority today attempts to force this case into the same category for purposes of equal protection analysis as decisions involving discrimination affecting commercial interests. By so doing, the majority singles this case out for analytic treatment at odds with what seems to me to be the clear trend of recent decisions in this Court, and thereby ignores the constitutional importance of the interest at stake and the invidiousness of the particular classification, factors that call for far more than the lenient scrutiny of the Texas financing scheme which the majority pursues. Yet if the discrimination inherent in the Texas scheme is scrutinized with the care demanded by the interest and classification present in this case, the unconstitutionality of that scheme is unmistakable.

* * * [T]he fundamental importance of education is amply indicated by the prior decisions of this Court, by the unique status accorded public education by our society, and by the close relationship between education and some of our most basic constitutional values.

The special concern of this Court with the educational process of our country is a matter of common knowledge. Undoubtedly, this Court's most famous statement on the subject is that contained in *Brown v. Board of Education*:

> Today, education is perhaps the most important function of state and local governments. Compulsory school attendance laws and the great expenditures for education both demonstrate our recognition of the importance of education to our democratic society. It is required in the performance of our most basic public responsibilities, even service in the armed forces. It is the very foundation of good citizenship. Today it is a principal instrument in awakening the child to cultural values, in preparing him for later professional training, and in helping him to adjust normally to his environment....

* * *

Education directly affects the ability of a child to exercise his First Amendment rights, both as a source and as a receiver of information and ideas, whatever interests he may pursue in life. * * *

Of particular importance is the relationship between education and the political process. * * * Education serves the essential function of instilling in our young an understanding of and appreciation for the principles and operation of our governmental processes. Education may instill the interest and provide the tools necessary for political discourse and debate. Indeed, it has frequently been suggested that education is the dominant factor affecting political consciousness and participation. * * * But of most immediate and direct concern must be the demonstrated effect of education on the exercise of the franchise by the electorate. * * *

* * *

* * * Our prior cases have dealt essentially with discrimination on the basis of personal wealth. Here, by contrast, the children of the disadvantaged Texas school districts are being discriminated against not necessarily because of their personal wealth or the wealth of their families, but because of the taxable property wealth of the residents of the district in which they happen to live. The appropriate question, then, is whether the same degree of judicial solicitude and scrutiny that has previously been afforded wealth classifications is warranted here.

As the Court points out, no previous decision has deemed the presence of just a wealth classification to be sufficient basis to call forth rigorous judicial scrutiny of allegedly discriminatory state action. That wealth classifications alone have not necessarily been considered to bear the same high degree of suspectness as have classifications based on, for instance, race or alienage may be explainable on a number of grounds. The "poor" may not be seen as politically powerless as certain discrete and insular minority groups. Personal poverty may entail much the same social stigma as historically attached to certain racial or ethnic groups. But personal poverty is not a permanent disability; its shackles may be escaped. Perhaps most importantly, though, personal wealth may not necessarily share the general irrelevance as a basis for legislative action that race or nationality is recognized to have. While the "poor" have frequently been a legally disadvantaged group, it cannot be ignored that social legislation must frequently take cognizance of the economic status of our citizens. Thus, we have generally gauged the invidiousness of wealth classifications with an awareness of the importance of the interests being affected and the relevance of personal wealth to those interests.

When evaluated with these considerations in mind, it seems to me that discrimination on the basis of group wealth in this case likewise calls for careful judicial scrutiny. First, it must be recognized that while local district wealth may serve other interests, it bears no relationship whatsoever to the interest of Texas schoolchildren in the educational opportunity afforded them by the State of Texas. Given the importance of that interest, we must be particularly sensitive to the invidious characteristics of any form of discrimination that is not clearly intended to serve it, as opposed to some other distinct state interest. Discrimination on the basis of group wealth may not, to be sure, reflect the social stigma frequently attached to personal poverty. Nevertheless, insofar as group wealth discrimination involves wealth over which the disadvantaged individual has no significant control, it represents in fact a more serious basis of discrimination than does personal wealth. For such discrimination is no reflection of the individual's characteristics or his abilities. * * *

The disability of the disadvantaged class in this case extends as well into the political processes upon which we ordinarily rely as adequate for the protection and promotion of all interests. Here legislative reallocation of the State's property wealth must be sought in the face of inevitable opposition from significantly advantaged districts that have a strong vested interest in the preservation of the status quo * * *.

Nor can we ignore the extent to which, in contrast to our prior decisions, the State is responsible for the wealth discrimination in this instance. * * * [W]e have no such simple *de facto* wealth discrimination here. The means for financing public education in Texas are selected and specified by the State. It is the State that has created local school districts, and tied educational funding to the local property tax and thereby to local district wealth. * * *

In the final analysis, then, the invidious characteristics of the group wealth classification present in this case merely serve to emphasize the need for careful judicial scrutiny of the State's justifications for the resulting interdistrict discrimination in the educational opportunity afforded to the schoolchildren of Texas. * * *

Notes and Questions

1. *Brown v. Board of Education* held that providing public education is one of the most important functions of the modern state. Why, then, is not education a fundamental interest, so that the government must provide it on a roughly equal basis to all?

2. *Brown* also declared that without an adequate education, a child is unlikely to be able to exercise the full rights of a citizen, such as the right to an informed vote, the right to run for political office, and the right to a decent job. If education is not a constitutionally protected interest, does it not have a close "nexus" with other rights such as free speech that are constitutionally protected?

3. The poor are politically impotent and unrepresented. (When was the last time a poor person became president of the United States or even a member of the Senate?). Why, then, are they not a "suspect class" of insular minorities, so that legislation that compounds their isolation should receive strict judicial review comparable to that which the courts accord racial minorities? See United States v. Carolene Products Co., 304 U.S. 144, 153 n.4 (1938).

Formal education is very costly, with expenses totaling $472.3 billion in a recent year for public elementary and secondary schools alone. See Valencia, *Chicano Students and the Courts*, Chapter 3. It is also the single largest employer of people in the United States. Thus, the need to distribute the costs of education fairly is a major concern.

Latinos have a high dropout rate, higher than that of blacks, Asian Americans, Native Americans, or whites, perhaps, in part, because they have been short-changed in the funding of their schools. How much of that underfunding is due to school segregation? See infra, this chapter. And how much of that segregation is due to discrimination in the housing market? To discrimination in the job market? To racially selective immigration policies that for much of our history favored white Europeans? In bringing suits to equalize school funding, are Latino litigators trying to reverse the operation of broad social forces?

In Serrano v. Priest, 5 Cal.3d 584, 96 Cal.Rptr. 601, 487 P.2d 1241 (1971), the California Supreme Court reached a result contrary to that of the United States Supreme Court in *Rodriguez*.

The case arose when John Serrano, who grew up in a working class family, sent his son to first grade in Los Angeles, which was then a "property rich" district. Serrano was by then securely ensconced in the middle class, having earned a degree from California State University–Los Angeles and secured a job as director of social services at a county center for the handicapped. Concerned that his son would not receive a challenging education at his current school, Serrano moved his family to Whittier, and then Hacienda Heights, where his son attended an excellent school, even though the district was "property poor." A group of attorneys interested in challenging California's school finance scheme then recruited Serrano, whose personal stake was negligible in the ensuing litigation, even though he was ideologically committed to it. See Valencia, supra, Chapter 3.

Serrano v. Priest
5 Cal.3d 584, 96 Cal.Rptr. 601, 487 P.2d 1241 (1971)

SULLIVAN, JUSTICE.

We are called upon to determine whether the California public school financing system, with its substantial dependence on local property taxes and resultant wide disparities in school revenue, violates the equal protection clause of the Fourteenth Amendment. We have determined that this funding scheme invidiously discriminates against the poor because it makes the quality of a child's education a function of the wealth of his parents and neighbors. Recognizing as we must that the right to an education in our public schools is a fundamental interest which cannot be conditioned on wealth, we can discern no compelling state purpose necessitating the present method of financing. We have concluded, therefore, that such a system cannot withstand constitutional challenge and must fall before the equal protection clause.

Plaintiffs, who are Los Angeles County public school children and their parents, brought this class action for declaratory and injunctive relief against certain state and county officials charged with administering the financing of the California public school system. Plaintiff children claim to represent a class consisting of all public school pupils in California, "except children in that school district, the identity of which is presently unknown, which school district affords the greatest educational opportunity of all school districts within California." Plaintiff parents purport to represent a class of all parents who have children in the school system and who pay real property taxes in the county of their residence.

Defendants are the Treasurer, the Superintendent of Public Instruction, and the Controller of the State of California, as well as the Tax Collector and Treasurer, and the Superintendent of Schools of the County of Los Angeles. The county officials are sued both in their local capacities and as representatives of a class composed of the school superintendent, tax collector and treasurer of each of the other counties in the state.

The complaint sets forth three causes of action. The first cause alleges in substance as follows: Plaintiff children attend public elementary and secondary schools located in specified school districts in Los Angeles County. This public school system is maintained throughout California by a financing plan or scheme which relies heavily on local property taxes and causes substantial disparities among individual school districts in the amount of revenue available per pupil for the districts' educational programs. Consequently, districts with smaller tax bases are not able to spend as much money per child for education as districts with larger assessed valuations.

It is alleged that "As a direct result of the financing scheme ... substantial disparities in the quality and extent of availability of educational opportunities exist and are perpetuated among the several school districts of the State.... (Par.) The educational opportunities made available to children attending public schools in the Districts, including plaintiff children, are substantially inferior to the educational opportunities made available to children attending public schools in many other districts of the State...." The financing scheme thus fails to meet the requirements of the equal protection clause of the Fourteenth Amendment of the United States Constitution and the California Constitution in several specified respects.

In the second cause of action, plaintiff parents, after incorporating by reference all the allegations of the first cause, allege that as a direct result of the financing scheme they are required to pay a higher tax rate than taxpayers in many other school districts in order to obtain for their children the same or lesser educational opportunities afforded children in those other districts.

In the third cause of action, after incorporating by reference all the allegations of the first two causes, all plaintiffs allege that an actual controversy has arisen and now exists between the parties as to the validity and constitutionality of the financing scheme under the Fourteenth Amendment of the United States Constitution and under the California Constitution.

Plaintiffs pray for: (1) a declaration that the present financing system is unconstitutional; (2) an order directing defendants to reallocate school funds in order to remedy this invalidity; and (3) an adjudication that the trial court retain jurisdiction of the action so that it may restructure the system if defendants and the state Legislature fail to act within a reasonable time.

* * *

I

We begin our task by examining the California public school financing system which is the focal point of the complaint's allegations. At the threshold we find a fundamental statistic—over 90 percent of our public school funds derive from two basic sources: (a) local district taxes on real property and (b) aid from the State School Fund.

By far the major source of school revenue is the local real property tax. Pursuant to article IX, section 6 of the California Constitution, the Legislature has authorized the governing body of each county, and city and county, to levy taxes on the real property within a school district at a rate necessary to meet the district's annual education budget. The amount of revenue which a district can raise in this manner thus depends largely on its tax base—i.e., the assessed valuation of real property within its borders. Tax bases vary widely throughout the state; in 1969–1970, for example, the assessed valuation per unit of average daily attendance of elementary school children ranged from a low of $103 to a peak of $952,156—a ratio of nearly 1 to 10,000.

The other factor determining local school revenue is the rate of taxation within the district. Although the Legislature has placed ceilings on permissible district tax rates, these statutory maxima may be surpassed in a "tax override" election if a majority of the district's voters approve a higher rate. Nearly all districts have voted to override the statutory limits. Thus the locally raised funds which constitute the largest portion of school revenue are primarily a function of the value of the realty within a particular school district, coupled with the willingness of the district's residents to tax themselves for education.

Most of the remaining school revenue comes from the State School Fund pursuant to the "foundation program," through which the state undertakes to supplement local taxes in order to provide a "minimum amount of guaranteed support to all districts. . . ." With certain minor exceptions, the foundation program ensures that each school district will receive annually, from state or local funds, $355 for each elementary school pupil and $488 for each high school student.

Certain types of school districts are eligible for "bonus" foundation funds. Elementary districts receive an additional $30 for each student in grades 1 through 3; this sum is intended to reduce class size in those grades. Unified school districts get an extra $20 per child in foundation support.

* * *

Although equalization aid and supplemental aid temper the disparities which result from the vast variations in real property assessed valuation, wide differentials remain in the revenue available to individual districts and, consequently, in the level of educational expenditures. For example, in Los Angeles County, where plaintiff children attend school, the Baldwin Park Unified School District expended only $577.49 to educate each of its pupils in 1968–1969; during the same year the

Pasadena Unified School District spent $840.19 on every student; and the Beverly Hills Unified School District paid out $1,231.72 per child. The source of these disparities is unmistakable: in Baldwin Park the assessed valuation per child totaled only $3,706; in Pasadena, assessed valuation was $13,706; while in Beverly Hills, the corresponding figure was $50,885—a ratio of 1 to 4 to 13. Thus, the state grants are inadequate to offset the inequalities inherent in a financing system based on widely varying local tax bases.

* * *

III

Having disposed of these preliminary matters, we take up the chief contention underlying plaintiffs' complaint, namely that the California public school financing scheme violates the equal protection clause of the Fourteenth Amendment to the United States Constitution.

* * *

A

Wealth as a Suspect Classification

In recent years, the United States Supreme Court has demonstrated a marked antipathy toward legislative classifications which discriminate on the basis of certain "suspect" personal characteristics. One factor which has repeatedly come under the close scrutiny of the high court is wealth. "Lines drawn on the basis of wealth or property, like those of race (citation), are traditionally disfavored." (Harper v. Virginia State Bd. of Elections (1966) 383 U.S. 663, 668.) Invalidating the Virginia poll tax in *Harper*, the court stated: "To introduce wealth or payment of a fee as a measure of a voter's qualifications is to introduce a capricious or irrelevant factor." (Id.)

Plaintiffs contend that the school financing system classifies on the basis of wealth. We find this proposition irrefutable. As we have already discussed, over half of all educational revenue is raised locally by leaving taxes on real property in the individual school districts. Above the foundation program minimum ($355 per elementary student and $488 per high school student), the wealth of a school district, as measured by its assessed valuation, is the major determinant of educational expenditures. Although the amount of money raised locally is also a function of the rate at which the residents of a district are willing to tax themselves, as a practical matter districts with small tax bases simply cannot levy taxes at a rate sufficient to produce the revenue that more affluent districts reap with minimal tax efforts. For example, Baldwin Park citizens, who paid a school tax of $5.48 per $100 of assessed valuation in 1968–1969, were able to spend less than half as much on education as Beverly Hills residents, who were taxed only $2.38 per $100.

Defendants vigorously dispute the proposition that the financing scheme discriminates on the basis of wealth. Their first argument is essentially this: through Basic aid, the state distributes school funds equally to all pupils; through Equalization aid, it distributes funds in a manner beneficial to the poor districts. However, state funds constitute only one part of the entire school fiscal system. The foundation program partially alleviates the great disparities in local sources of revenue, but the system as a whole generates school revenue in proportion to the wealth of the individual district.

We do not find that decision relevant to the present action. Here, plaintiffs specifically allege that the allocation of school funds systematically provides greater educational opportunities to affluent children than are afforded to the poor. By contrast, in *Briggs* the court found no wealth-oriented discrimination: "There is no pattern such that schools with lunch programs predominate in areas of relative wealth and schools without the program in areas of economic deprivation." (Id. at 302.)

Furthermore, the nature of the right involved in the two cases is very different. The instant action concerns the right to an education, which we have determined to be fundamental. (See infra.) Availability of an inexpensive school lunch can hardly be considered of such constitutional significance.

Defendants also argue that neither assessed valuation per pupil nor expenditure per pupil is a reliable index of the wealth of a district or of its residents. The former figure is untrustworthy, they assert, because a district with a low total assessed valuation but a miniscule number of students will have a high per pupil tax base and thus appear "wealthy." Defendants imply that the proper index of a district's wealth is the total assessed valuation of its property. We think defendants' contention misses the point. The only meaningful measure of a district's wealth in the present context is not the absolute value of its property, but the ratio of its resources to pupils, because it is the latter figure which determines how much the district can devote to educating each of its students.

We realize, of course, that a portion of the high per-pupil expenditure in a district like Gorman may be attributable to certain costs, like a principal's salary, which do not vary with the size of the school. On such expenses, small schools cannot achieve the economies of scale available to a larger district. To this extent, the high per-pupil spending in a small district may be a paper statistic, which is unrepresentative of significant differences in educational opportunities. On the other hand, certain economic "inefficiencies," such as a low pupil-teacher ratio, may have a positive educational impact. The extent to which high spending in such districts represents actual educational advantages is, of course, a matter of proof.

But, say defendants, the expenditure per child does not accurately reflect a districts' wealth because that expenditure is partly determined by the district's tax rate. Thus, a district with a high total assessed valuation might levy a low school tax, and end up depending the same amount per pupil as a poorer district whose residents opt to pay higher taxes. This argument is also meritless. Obviously, the richer district is favored when it can provide the same educational quality for its children with less tax effort. Furthermore, as a statistical matter, the poorer districts are financially unable to raise their taxes high enough to match the educational offerings of wealthier districts. Thus, affluent districts can have their cake and eat it too: they can provide a high quality education for their children while paying lower taxes. Poor districts, by contrast, have no cake at all.

* * *

Finally, defendants suggest that the wealth of a school district does not necessarily reflect the wealth of the families who live there. The simple answer to this argument is that plaintiffs have alleged that there is a correlation between a district's per pupil assessed valuation and the wealth of its residents and we treat these material facts as admitted by the demurrers.

More basically, however, we reject defendants' underlying thesis that classification by wealth is constitutional so long as the wealth is that of the district, not the individual. We think that discrimination on the basis of district wealth is equally invalid. The commercial and industrial property which augments a district's tax base is distributed unevenly throughout the state. To allot more educational dollars to the children of one district than to those of another merely because of the fortuitous presence of such property is to make the quality of a child's education dependent upon the location of private commercial and industrial establishments. Surely, this is to rely on the most irrelevant of factors as the basis for educational financing.

* * *

Defendants, assuming for the sake of argument that the financing system does classify by wealth, nevertheless claim that no constitutional infirmity is involved because the complaint contains no allegation of purposeful or intentional discrimination. Thus, defendants contend, any unequal treatment is only de facto, not de jure. Since the United States Supreme Court has not held de facto school segregation on the basis of race to be unconstitutional, so the argument goes, de facto classifications on the basis of wealth are presumptively valid.

We think that the whole structure of this argument must fall for want of a solid foundation in law and logic. First, none of the wealth classifications previously invalidated by the United States Supreme Court or this court has been the product of purposeful discrimination. Instead, these prior decisions have involved "unintentional" classifications whose impact simply fell more heavily on the poor.

For example, several cases have held that where important rights are at stake, the state has an affirmative obligation to relieve an indigent of the burden of his own poverty by supplying without charge certain goods or services for which others must pay. In Griffin v. Illinois, supra, 351 U.S. 12, the high court ruled that Illinois was required to provide a poor defendant with a free transcript on appeal. Douglas v. California, supra, 372 U.S. 353, held that an indigent person has a right to court-appointed counsel on appeal.

* * *

B

Education as a Fundamental Interest

But plaintiffs' equal protection attack on the fiscal system has an additional dimension. They assert that the system not only draws lines on the basis of wealth but that it "touches upon," indeed has a direct and significant impact upon, a "fundamental interest," namely education. It is urged that these two grounds, particularly in combination, establish a demonstrable denial of equal protection of the laws. To this phase of the argument we now turn our attention.

* * *

The fundamental importance of education has been recognized in other contexts by the United States Supreme Court and by this court. These decisions—while not legally controlling on the exact issue before us—are persuasive in their accurate factual description of the significance of learning.

The classic expression of this position came in *Brown v. Board of Education*, which invalidated de jure segregation by race in public schools. The high court declared: "Today, education is perhaps the most important function of state and local governments. Compulsory school attendance laws and the great expenditures for education both demonstrate our recognition of the importance of education to our democratic society. It is required in the performance of our most basic public responsibilities, even service in the armed forces. It is the very foundation of good citizenship. Today it is a principal instrument in awakening the child to cultural values, in preparing him for later professional training, and in helping him to adjust normally to his environment. In these days, it is doubtful that any child may reasonably be expected to succeed in life if he is denied the opportunity of an education. Such an opportunity, where the state has undertaken to provide it, is a right which must be made available to all on equal terms."

The twin themes of the importance of education to the individual and to society have recurred in numerous decisions of this court. * * *

* * *

It is illuminating to compare in importance the right to an education with the rights of defendants in criminal cases and the right to vote—two "fundamental interests" which the Supreme Court has already protected against discrimination based on wealth. Although an individual's interest in his freedom is unique, we think that from a larger perspective, education may have far greater social significance than a free transcript or a court-appointed lawyer. "[E]ducation not only affects directly a vastly greater number of persons than the criminal law, but it affects them in ways which—to the state—have an enormous and much more varied significance. Aside from reducing the crime rate (the inverse relation is strong), education also supports each and every other value of a democratic society—participation, communication, and social mobility, to name but a few."

The analogy between education and voting is much more direct: both are crucial to participation in, and the functioning of, a democracy. Voting has been regarded as a fundamental right because it is "preservative of other basic civil and political rights...." (Reynolds v. Sims, supra, 377 U.S. 533, 562.) The drafters of the California Constitution used this same rationale—indeed, almost identical language—in expressing the importance of education. Article IX, section 1 provides: "A general diffusion of knowledge and intelligence being essential to the preservation of the rights and liberties of the people, the legislature shall encourage by all suitable means the promotion of intellectual, scientific, moral, and agricultural improvement." At a minimum, education makes more meaningful the casting of a ballot. More significantly, it is likely to provide the understanding of, and the interest in, public issues which are the spur to involvement in other civic and political activities.

The need for an educated populace assumes greater importance as the problems of our diverse society become increasingly complex. * * *

We are convinced that the distinctive and priceless function of education in our society warrants, indeed compels, our treating it as a "fundamental interest."

First, education is essential in maintaining what several commentators have termed "free enterprise democracy"—that is, preserving an individual's opportunity to compete successfully in the economic marketplace, despite a disadvantaged background. Accordingly, the public schools of this state are the bright hope for entry of the poor and oppressed into the mainstream of American society.

      * * *

Second, education is universally relevant. "Not every person finds it necessary to call upon the fire department or even the police in an entire lifetime. Relatively few are on welfare. Every person, however, benefits from education...."

Third, public education continues over a lengthy period of life— between 10 and 13 years. Few other government services have such sustained, intensive contact with the recipient.

Fourth, education is unmatched in the extent to which it molds the personality of the youth of society. While police and fire protection, garbage collection and street lights are essentially neutral in their effect on the individual psyche, public education actively attempts to shape a child's personal development in a manner chosen not by the child or his parents but by the state. "[T]he influence of the school is not confined to how well it can teach the disadvantaged child; it also has a significant role to play in shaping the student's emotional and psychological make-up."

Finally, education is so important that the state has made it compulsory—not only in the requirement of attendance but also by assignment to a particular district and school. Although a child of wealthy parents has the opportunity to attend a private school, this freedom is seldom available to the indigent. In this context, it has been suggested that "a child of the poor assigned willy-nilly to an inferior state school takes on the complexion of a prisoner, complete with a minimum sentence of 12 years."

* * *

We, therefore, arrive at these conclusions. The California public school financing system, as presented to us by plaintiffs' complaint supplemented by matters judicially noticed, since it deals intimately with education, obviously touches upon a fundamental interest. For the reasons we have explained in detail, this system conditions the full entitlement to such interest on wealth, classifies its recipients on the basis of their collective affluence and makes the quality of a child's education depend upon the resources of his school district and ultimately upon the pocketbook of his parents. We find that such financing system as presently constituted is not necessary to the attainment of any compelling state interest. Since it does not withstand the requisite "strict scrutiny," it denies to the plaintiffs and others similarly situated the equal protection of the laws. If the allegations of the complaint are sustained, the financial system must fall and the statutes comprising it must be found unconstitutional.

* * *

In sum, we find the allegations of plaintiffs' complaint legally sufficient and we return the cause to the trial court for further proceedings. We emphasize, that our decision is not a final judgment on the merits. We deem it appropriate to point out for the benefit of the trial court on remand that if, after further proceedings, that court should enter final judgment determining that the existing system of public school financing is unconstitutional and invalidating said system in whole or in part, it may properly provide for the enforcement of the judgment in such a way as to permit an orderly transition from an unconstitutional to a constitutional system of school financing. As in the cases of school desegregation and legislative reapportionment, a determination that an existing plan of governmental operation denies equal protection does not necessarily require invalidation of past acts undertaken pursuant to that plan or an immediate implementation of a constitutionally valid substitute. Obviously, any judgment invalidating the existing system of public school financing should make clear that the existing system is to remain operable until an appropriate new system, which is not violative of equal protection of the laws, can be put into effect.

By our holding today we further the cherished idea of American education that in a democratic society free public schools shall make available to all children equally the abundant gifts of learning. This was the credo of Horace Mann, which has been the heritage and the inspiration of this country. "I believe," he wrote, "in the existence of a great, immortal immutable principle of natural law, or natural ethics,—a principle antecedent to all human institutions, and incapable of being abrogated by any ordinance of man ... which proves the absolute right to an education of every human being that comes into the world, and which, of course, proves the correlative duty of every government to see that the means of that education are provided for all...." (Old South Leaflets V, No. 109 (1846) pp. 177–180 (Tenth Annual Report to Mass. State Bd. of Ed.), quoted in Readings in American Education (1963 Lucio ed.) p. 336.)

The judgment is reversed and the cause remanded to the trial court with directions to overrule the demurrers and to allow defendants a reasonable time within which to answer.

Notes and Questions

1. At the time *Serrano* came down in 1971, local property taxes supplied more than one-half the budget of California's school districts, with the balance coming from the state (about 35 percent) and the federal government (about 6 percent). Valencia, supra. In turn, the ability of a local school district to raise money depended on its tax base—the assessed valuation of real property inside its borders. This, of course, varied widely from district to district.

2. Were the attorneys in *Serrano* courting disaster when they approached him as their lead plaintiff? Note that he and his children were relatively well off, educationally. Would you have chosen a different class representative? Why or why not?

3. Why did the California Supreme Court respond sympathetically to arguments (education as a fundamental interest, poverty as a semi-suspect class) that the United States Supreme Court rejected only a short time later?

4. On remand, the plaintiffs won almost all the relief they requested. The California Supreme Court upheld the trial court's ruling in *Serrano II* a few years later, 18 Cal.3d 728, 135 Cal.Rptr. 345, 557 P.2d 929 (1976).

5. A short time later, the California legislature revised the state's school financing law in accord with *Serrano*. But two years later, the "taxpayer revolt" movement enacted Proposition 13 (1978), which radically limited the property tax rate throughout California, setting a uniform standard of one percent of market value. This measure devastated California's superstructure, including its schools.

6. Soon after the *Serrano* litigation came to an end, a wave of state litigation broke out across the country challenging both school funding and educational adequacy in various districts. This litigation achieved mixed results. See, e.g., Campaign for Fiscal Equity, Inc. v. New York, 100 N.Y.2d 893, 801 N.E.2d 326, 769 N.Y.S.2d 106 (2003).

7. Prior to the *Rodriguez* decision, Texas contained some of the deepest poverty, see, e.g., Jane E. Larson, *Free Markets Deep in the Heart of Texas*,

84 Geo L.J. 179 (1995), and some of the most poorly-funded schools in the country; Valencia, *Chicano Students and the Courts*, Chapter 3, and still does so today. What measures, other than those that failed to bring results in the *Rodriguez* litigation, would you advise to remedy the situation?

    8. For additional discussion of the connection between geographic politics, power, and school funding, see Michael A. Olivas, Brown *and the Desegregative Ideal: Location, Race, and College Attendance Policies*, 90 Cornell L. Rev. 391 (2005), pointing out how Latino litigators are using a "politics of place" to challenge unfair schooling options, rather than the route taken by *Brown*. Using disparate Texas funding in the border area (see note 7, above) and admissions points awarded for living in chosen California neighborhoods, Olivas shows how universities need to tailor their strategies to serve all disadvantaged students. On the background and story of *Rodriguez* and other cases, see Peter Irons, *The Courage of Their Convictions* (1988).

Chapter 10

UNDOCUMENTED SCHOOLCHILDREN

An even harsher situation than that of children in underfunded schools (see Chapter 1) faces undocumented schoolchildren in districts that exclude them from the public schools altogether or admit them only if they pay tuition.

Undocumented college students face a similar situation when public universities charge them out-of-state tuition even though they may have lived in the state most of their lives. At the time of writing, California allowed undocumented students to pay resident tuition if they qualified in other respects for the lower rate, for example by graduation from a California high school. See Sara Hebel, *Judge Upholds Immigrant–Tuition Law*, Chron. Higher Educ., Oct. 20, 2006. A federal statute enacted in 1996 provides that undocumented immigrants are not eligible, based on their residence in a state, for "any postsecondary benefit unless a citizen or national . . . is eligible for such a benefit." California took the position that its policy bases eligibility on high-school attendance and graduation, not residence in the state, and so does not violate the federal law.

Immigrants' rights have been on the country's front burner recently as they have not been in many years. On April 20, 2006, nearly two million protesters, most of them Latino, marched in dozens of cities to protest growing anti-immigrant sentiment and acts. The 1970s, during which some of the foundational cases deciding the fate of undocumented schoolchildren came down, were also a time of ferment, with economic uncertainty and severe inflation fueling much of it. Valencia, *Chicano Students and the Courts,*, Chapter 4. The following case stemmed from a 1975 Texas measure enacted during such a period. The measure prohibited the use of state funds to educate undocumented children.

Plyler v. Doe
457 U.S. 202 (1982)

JUSTICE BRENNAN delivered the opinion of the Court.

329

The question presented by these cases is whether, consistent with the Equal Protection Clause of the Fourteenth Amendment, Texas may deny to undocumented school-age children the free public education that it provides to children who are citizens of the United States or legally admitted aliens.

I

Since the late 19th century, the United States has restricted immigration into this country. Unsanctioned entry into the United States is a crime, and those who have entered unlawfully are subject to deportation. But despite the existence of these legal restrictions, a substantial number of persons have succeeded in unlawfully entering the United States, and now live within various States, including Texas.

In May 1975, the Texas Legislature revised its education laws to withhold from local school districts any state funds for the education of children who were not "legally admitted" into the United States. The 1975 revision also authorized local school districts to deny enrollment in their public schools to children not "legally admitted" to the country. These cases involve constitutional challenges to those provisions.

* * *

Our conclusion that the illegal aliens who are plaintiffs in these cases may claim the benefit of the Fourteenth Amendment's guarantee of equal protection only begins the inquiry. The more difficult question is whether the Equal Protection Clause has been violated by the refusal of the State of Texas to reimburse local school boards for the education of children who cannot demonstrate that their presence within the United States is lawful, or by the imposition by those school boards of the burden of tuition on those children. It is to this question that we now turn.

III

The Equal Protection Clause directs that "all persons similarly circumstanced shall be treated alike." But so too, "[t]he Constitution does not require things which are different in fact or opinion to be treated in law as though they were the same." The initial discretion to determine what is "different" and what is "the same" resides in the legislatures of the States. A legislature must have substantial latitude to establish classifications that roughly approximate the nature of the problem perceived, that accommodate competing concerns, and that account for limitations on the practical ability of the State to remedy every ill. * * * [W]e thus seek only the assurance that the classification at issue bears some fair relationship to a legitimate public purpose.

But we would not be faithful to our obligations under the Fourteenth Amendment if we applied so deferential a standard to every classification. The Equal Protection Clause was intended as a restriction on state legislative action inconsistent with elemental constitutional premises. Thus we have treated as presumptively invidious those classifications that disadvantage a "suspect class," or that impinge upon the exercise of a "fundamental right." With respect to such classifications, it is appropriate to enforce the mandate of equal protection by requiring the State to demonstrate that its classification has been precisely tailored to serve a compelling governmental interest. In addition, we have recognized that certain forms of legislative classification, while not facially invidious, nonetheless give rise to recurring constitutional difficulties; in these limited circumstances we have sought the assurance that the classification reflects a reasoned judgment consistent with the ideal of equal protection by inquiring whether it may fairly be viewed as furthering a substantial interest of the State. * * *

A

Sheer incapability or lax enforcement of the laws barring entry into this country, coupled with the failure to establish an effective bar to the employment of undocumented aliens, has resulted in the creation of a substantial "shadow population" of illegal migrants—numbering in the millions—within our borders. This situation raises the specter of a permanent caste of undocumented resident aliens, encouraged by some to remain here as a source of cheap labor, but nevertheless denied the benefits that our society makes available to citizens and lawful residents. The existence of such an underclass presents most difficult problems for a Nation that prides itself on adherence to principles of equality under law.

The children who are plaintiffs in these cases are special members of this underclass. Persuasive arguments support the view that a State may withhold its beneficence from those whose very presence within the United States is the product of their own unlawful conduct. These arguments do not apply with the same force to classifications imposing disabilities on the minor *children* of such illegal entrants. * * * Their "parents have the ability to conform their conduct to societal norms," and presumably the ability to remove themselves from the State's jurisdiction; but the children who are plaintiffs in these cases "can affect neither their parents' conduct nor their own status." Even if the State found it expedient to control the conduct of adults by acting against their children, legislation directing the onus of a parent's misconduct against his children does not comport with fundamental conceptions of justice.

* * *

Of course, undocumented status is not irrelevant to any proper legislative goal. Nor is undocumented status an absolutely immutable characteristic since it is the product of conscious, indeed unlawful, action. But § 21.031 is directed against children, and imposes its discriminatory burden on the basis of a legal characteristic over which children can have little control. It is thus difficult to conceive of a rational justification for penalizing these children for their presence within the United States. Yet that appears to be precisely the effect of § 21.031.

Public education is not a "right" granted to individuals by the Constitution. San Antonio Independent School Dist. v. Rodriguez, 411 U.S. 1, 35 (1973). But neither is it merely some governmental "benefit" indistinguishable from other forms of social welfare legislation. Both the importance of education in maintaining our basic institutions, and the lasting impact of its deprivation on the life of the child, mark the distinction. The "American people have always regarded education and [the] acquisition of knowledge as matters of supreme importance." We have recognized "the public schools as a most vital civic institution for the preservation of a democratic system of government," and as the primary vehicle for transmitting "the values on which our society rests." "[A]s . . . pointed out early in our history, . . . some degree of education is necessary to prepare citizens to participate effectively and intelligently in our open political system if we are to preserve freedom and independence." * * * In addition, education provides the basic tools by which individuals might lead economically productive lives to the benefit of us all. In sum, education has a fundamental role in maintaining the fabric of our society. We cannot ignore the significant social costs borne by our Nation when select groups are denied the means to absorb the values and skills upon which our social order rests.

In addition to the pivotal role of education in sustaining our political and cultural heritage, denial of education to some isolated group of children poses an affront to one of the goals of the Equal Protection Clause: the abolition of governmental barriers presenting unreasonable obstacles to advancement on the basis of individual merit. Paradoxically, by depriving the children of any disfavored group of an education, we foreclose the means by which that group might raise the level of esteem in which it is held by the majority. * * * The inability to read and write will handicap the individual deprived of a basic education each and every day of his life. The inestimable toll of that deprivation on the social economic, intellectual, and psychological well-being of the individual, and the obstacle it poses to individual achievement, make it most difficult to reconcile the cost or the principle of a status-based denial of basic education with the framework of equality embodied in the Equal Protection Clause. What we said 28 years ago in *Brown v. Board of Education*, still holds true:

> Today, education is perhaps the most important function of state and local governments. Compulsory school attendance laws and the great expenditures for education both demonstrate our recognition of the importance of education to our democratic society. It is required in the performance of our most basic public responsibilities, even service in the armed forces. It is the very foundation of good citizenship. Today it is a principal instrument in awakening the child to cultural values, in preparing him for later professional training, and in helping him to adjust normally to his environment. In these days, it is doubtful that any child may reasonably be expected to succeed in life if he is denied the opportunity of an education. Such an opportunity, where the state has undertaken to

provide it, is a right which must be made available to all on equal terms. Id. at 493.

B

These well-settled principles allow us to determine the proper level of deference to be afforded § 21.031. Undocumented aliens cannot be treated as a suspect class because their presence in this country in violation of federal law is not a "constitutional irrelevancy." Nor is education a fundamental right; a State need not justify by compelling necessity every variation in the manner in which education is provided to its population. But more is involved in these cases than the abstract question whether § 21.031 discriminates against a suspect class, or whether education is a fundamental right. Section 21.031 imposes a lifetime hardship on a discrete class of children not accountable for their disabling status. The stigma of illiteracy will mark them for the rest of their lives. By denying these children a basic education, we deny them the ability to live within the structure of our civic institutions, and foreclose any realistic possibility that they will contribute in even the smallest way to the progress of our Nation. * * *

IV

It is the State's principal argument, and apparently the view of the dissenting Justices, that the undocumented status of these children *vel non* establishes a sufficient rational basis for denying them benefits that a State might choose to afford other residents. The State notes that while other aliens are admitted "on an equality of legal privileges with all citizens under non-discriminatory laws," the asserted right of these children to an education can claim no implicit congressional imprimatur. Indeed, in the State's view, Congress' apparent disapproval of the presence of these children within the United States, and the evasion of the federal regulatory program that is the mark of undocumented status, provides authority for its decision to impose upon them special disabilities. Faced with an equal protection challenge respecting the treatment of aliens, we agree that the courts must be attentive to congressional policy; the exercise of congressional power might well affect the State's prerogatives to afford differential treatment to a particular class of aliens. But we are unable to find in the congressional immigration scheme any statement of policy that might weigh significantly in arriving at an equal protection balance concerning the State's authority to deprive these children of an education.

* * *

We are reluctant to impute to Congress the intention to withhold from these children, for so long as they are present in this country through no fault of their own, access to a basic education. In other contexts, undocumented status, coupled with some articulable federal policy, might enhance state authority with respect to the treatment of undocumented aliens. But in the area of special constitutional sensitivity presented by these cases, and in the absence of any contrary indication fairly discernible in the present legislative record, we perceive no national policy that supports the State in denying these children an elementary education. The State may borrow the federal classification. But to justify its use as a criterion for its own discriminatory policy, the State must demonstrate that the classification is reasonably adapted to *the purposes for which the state desires to use it.*" We therefore turn to the state objectives that are said to support § 21.031.

V

Appellants argue that the classification at issue furthers an interest in the "preservation of the state's limited resources for the education of its lawful residents." Of course, a concern for the preservation of resources standing alone can hardly justify the classification used in allocating those resources. The State must do more than justify its classification with a concise expression of an intention to discriminate. Apart from the asserted state prerogative to act against undocumented children solely on the basis of their undocumented status—an asserted prerogative that carries only minimal force in the circumstances of these cases—we discern three colorable state interests that might support § 21.031.

First, appellants appear to suggest that the State may seek to protect itself from an influx of illegal immigrants. While a State might have an interest in mitigating the potentially harsh economic effects of sudden shifts in population, § 21.031 hardly offers an effective method of dealing with an urgent demographic or economic problem. There is no evidence in the record suggesting that illegal entrants impose any significant burden on the State's economy. To the contrary, the available evidence suggests that illegal aliens underutilize public services, while contributing their labor to the local economy and tax money to the state fisc. The dominant incentive for illegal entry into the State of Texas is the availability of employment; few if any illegal immigrants come to this country, or presumably to the State of Texas, in order to avail themselves of a free education. Thus, even making the doubtful assumption that the net impact of illegal aliens on the economy of the State is negative, we think it clear that "[c]harging tuition to undocumented children constitutes a ludicrously ineffectual attempt to stem the tide of illegal immigration," at least when compared with the alternative of prohibiting the employment of illegal aliens.

Second, while it is apparent that a State may "not ... reduce expenditures for education by barring [some arbitrarily chosen class of] children from its schools," appellants suggest that undocumented children are appropriately singled out for exclusion because of the special burdens they impose on the State's ability to provide high-quality public education. But the record in no way supports the claim that exclusion of undocumented children is likely to improve the overall quality of education in the State.[25] As the District Court in No. 80–1934 noted, the

25. Nor does the record support the claim that the educational resources of the State are so direly limited that some form of "educational *triage*" might be deemed a

State failed to offer any "credible supporting evidence that a proportionately small diminution of the funds spent on each child [which might result from devoting some state funds to the education of the excluded group] will have a grave impact on the quality of education." * * *

Finally, appellants suggest that undocumented children are appropriately singled out because their unlawful presence within the United States renders them less likely than other children to remain within the boundaries of the State, and to put their education to productive social or political use within the State. Even assuming that such an interest is legitimate, it is an interest that is most difficult to quantify. The State has no assurance that any child, citizen or not, will employ the education provided by the State within the confines of the State's borders. In any event, the record is clear that many of the undocumented children disabled by this classification will remain in this country indefinitely, and that some will become lawful residents or citizens of the United States. It is difficult to understand precisely what the State hopes to achieve by promoting the creation and perpetuation of a subclass of illiterates within our boundaries, surely adding to the problems and costs of unemployment, welfare, and crime. * * *

VI

If the State is to deny a discrete group of innocent children the free public education that it offers to other children residing within its borders, that denial must be justified by a showing that it furthers some substantial state interest. No such showing was made here. Accordingly, the judgment of the Court of Appeals in each of these cases is

Affirmed.

Notes and Questions

1. Can you square *Plyler* with *San Antonio v. Rodriguez*, which held that education is not a fundamental interest? Note that both cases arose in Texas in a relatively short period.

2. What level of scrutiny did the Court, in fact, apply?

3. How did the Supreme Court handle the Texas "outlaw" theory that undocumented children are violators of federal immigration law?

4. How did the Court respond to the contention that Texas was just conserving limited funds?

———————

In contrast to school-finance litigation, which has produced mixed results, lawsuits challenging total exclusion of undocumented children

reasonable (assuming that it were a permissible) response to the State's problems. Id. at 579–581.

have generally succeeded. Why should partial exclusion—in the form of poorly funded, barely adequate education—be permissible, and total exclusion not?

For example, in 1994, the voters of California enacted Proposition 187, an anti-immigrant measure that would have made it illegal for undocumented persons to receive any public service, including nonemergency health care. It also would have excluded undocumented children from attending public schools. And it ordered state authorities, including teachers and health care workers, to report suspected undocumented children to federal immigration authorities. See, e.g., Linda S. Bosniak, *Opposing Prop. 187: Undocumented Immigrants and the National Imagination*, 28 Conn. L. Rev. 555 (1996).

A federal court struck down most of the measure in the *LULAC* opinion excerpted below. But the ideas behind the measure are not dead. Other states, and even towns, are taking advantage of the current fervor to propose Proposition 187 lookalikes. Other states are ignoring *Plyler* and denying enrollment to undocumented children. Colorado, for example, tried to pass a law that would have required schools to collect citizenship data on children. See Steven W. Bender et al., *Everyday Law for Latinos*, Chapter 6 (forthcoming 2008).

League of United Latin American Citizens [LULAC] v. Wilson
997 F.Supp. 1244 (C.D. Cal. 1997)

Pfaelzer, District Judge.

I.

Background

Proposition 187 is an initiative measure which was submitted to the voters of the State of California in the November 8, 1994 general election. The stated purpose of Proposition 187 is to "provide for cooperation between [the] agencies of state and local government with the federal government, and to establish a system of required notification by and between such agencies to prevent illegal aliens in the United States from receiving benefits or public services in the State of California." Prop. 187, § 1. The initiative's provisions require law enforcement, social services, health care and public education personnel to (i) verify the immigration status of persons with whom they come in contact; (ii) notify certain defined categories of persons of their immigration status; (iii) report those persons to state and federal officials; and (iv) deny those persons social services, health care and education.

A. *Procedural History Prior to the Enactment of the [Federal] Personal Responsibility and Work Opportunity Reconciliation Act of 1996 ("PRA")*

After Proposition 187 was passed, several actions challenging the constitutionality of the initiative were commenced in state and federal courts in California. Ultimately, five actions filed in the United States District Court were consolidated in this Court for purposes of pre-trial proceedings and trial (collectively, the "consolidated actions").

* * *

1.   The De Canas Tests

The question of whether the benefits denial provisions in sections 5, 6 and 8 are preempted by federal law is governed by the Supreme Court's decision in De Canas v. Bica, 424 U.S. 351 (1976) (holding that California statute prohibiting an employer from knowingly employing an alien who is not entitled to lawful residence in the United States was not preempted under federal law). In *De Canas*, the Supreme Court articulated three tests to be used in determining whether a state statute related to immigration is preempted. Pursuant to *De Canas*, if a statute fails any one of the three tests, it is preempted by federal law.

Under the first test, the Court must determine whether a state statute is a "regulation of immigration." Since the "[p]ower to regulate immigration is unquestionably exclusively a federal power," id. at 354, any state statute that regulates immigration is "constitutionally proscribed." Id. at 356.

Under the second test, even if the state statute is not an impermissible regulation of immigration, it may still be preempted if there is a showing that it was the "clear and manifest purpose of Congress" to effect a "complete ouster of state power—including state power to promulgate laws not in conflict with federal laws" with respect to the subject matter which the statute attempts to regulate. Id. at 357. An intent to preclude state action may be inferred "where the system of federal regulation is so pervasive that no opportunity for state activity remains." Under the second test, a statute is preempted where Congress intended to "occupy the field" that the statute attempts to regulate.

Under the third test, a state law is preempted if it "stands as an obstacle to the accomplishment and execution of the full purposes and objectives of Congress." *De Canas*, 424 U.S. at 363. Stated differently, a statute is preempted under the third test if it conflicts with federal law, making compliance with both state and federal law impossible.

2.   The Application of the Tests in Light of the PRA

* * *

b.   The benefits denial provisions are preempted because the PRA occupies the field.

The intention of Congress to occupy the field of regulation of government benefits to aliens is declared throughout Title IV of the PRA. Whatever the level of government extending the benefits and whatever the source of the funding for the benefits—federal, state or local—they are all included within the expansive reach of the PRA. The new law includes: statements of national policy regarding the denial of public benefits to illegal immigrants (8 U.S.C. § 1601); rules regarding immigrant eligibility for federal, state and local benefits, including definitions of the benefits covered (8 U.S.C. §§ 1611; 1621); a description of state legislative options in the area of immigrant eligibility for state or local benefits (8 U.S.C. § 1621(d)); and a system for verifying immigration status to determine eligibility for benefits and services (8 U.S.C. § 1642). Together, these provisions both demarcate a field of comprehensive federal regulation within which states may not legislate, and define federal objectives with which states may not interfere.

(1) The national immigration policy calls for the denial of public benefits to aliens.

* * * In a sweeping statement, Congress has announced that there is a "compelling government interest to remove the incentive for illegal immigration provided by the availability of public benefits." 8 U.S.C. § 1601. This policy statement concerning the relationship between welfare and immigration leaves no doubt that the federal government has taken full control of the field of regulation of public benefits to aliens.

(2) Specific provisions of the PRA demonstrate that Congress has occupied the field of regulation of benefits to aliens.

Congress has ousted state power in the field of regulation of public benefits to immigrants by enacting legislation that denies federal, state and local health, welfare and postsecondary education benefits to aliens who are not "qualified." 8 U.S.C. §§ 1611, 1621.

Any alien not a "qualified" alien is ineligible for any federal benefit. 8 U.S.C. § 1611(a). Federal benefits include "any ... welfare, health ... postsecondary education, food assistance ... or any other similar benefit...." 8 U.S.C. § 1611(c). Similarly, any alien not a "qualified" alien, a "nonimmigrant" under the INA, or an alien "paroled into the United States" under the INA is ineligible for any state or local benefit. 8 U.S.C. § 1621(a). The PRA defines "State or local benefit" in the same words used to define "Federal benefit." 8 U.S.C. § 1621(c).

(a) Sections 5 and 6 of Proposition 187 are preempted.

Federal, state or local public benefits, as defined in the PRA, include social services and health services, which are the same benefits covered by sections 5 and 6 of Proposition 187. See 8 U.S.C. § 1611(c)(1)(B). Because the PRA is a comprehensive regulatory scheme that restricts alien eligibility for all public benefits, however funded, the states have no power to legislate in this area. If the state cannot legislate to grant or deny public benefits, then certainly the state cannot promulgate regulations to effectuate that goal. The only regulations that California can promulgate now are regulations implementing the PRA. * * * Any further argument by the defendants that they can promulgate regulations to effectuate *Proposition 187* in accordance with federal law would be specious.

Congress has expressly exercised its authority to establish the procedure that must be followed in verifying immigrant eligibility for federal, state and local benefits. The states have no power to effectuate a scheme parallel to that specified in the PRA, even if the parallel scheme does not conflict with the PRA. The PRA explicitly directs the United States Attorney General to promulgate regulations setting forth the procedures by which a state or local government can verify whether an alien applying for a federal, state or local public benefit is a "qualified" alien for purposes of determining whether the alien is eligible for benefits under the PRA. 8 U.S.C. § 1642(a). California is bound to follow the verification procedures prescribed by the PRA.

Congress' intention to displace state power in the area of regulation of public benefits to immigrants is manifest in the careful designation of the limited instances in which states have the right to determine alien eligibility for state or local public benefits. * * *

(b) The PRA expressly defers to *Plyler v. Doe.*

Section 7 of Proposition 187 denies public elementary and secondary education to any child not "a citizen of the United States, an alien lawfully admitted as a permanent resident, or a person who is otherwise authorized under federal law to be present in the United States." § 7. The Court found section 7 invalid on the ground that in Plyler v. Doe, 457 U.S. 202 (1982), the Supreme Court held that a state cannot deny basic public education to children based on their immigration status. *LULAC*, 908 F.Supp. at 785.

The PRA provides strong support for this finding. As stated, the PRA is a comprehensive statutory scheme regulating alien eligibility for government benefits. It does not deny public elementary and secondary education to aliens, but it does specifically deal with the subject of basic public education. Section 1643 provides, "Nothing in this chapter may be construed as addressing alien eligibility for a basic public education as determined by the Supreme Court of the United States under Plyler v. Doe (457 U.S. 202 (1982))." 8 U.S.C. § 1643. Thus, although basic public education clearly must be classified as a government benefit, just as health care is, the PRA does not purport to deny it to non-qualified aliens. Proposition 187 cannot do that either under the present state of the law.

(c) Section 8 is preempted.

Section 8 of Proposition 187 denies public postsecondary education to anyone not a "citizen of the United States, an alien lawfully admitted as a permanent resident, in the United States, or a person who is otherwise authorized under federal law to be present in the United States." § 8. Section 1611 of the PRA denies federal postsecondary education benefits to any alien who is not a "qualified" alien. 8 U.S.C. § 1611. Section 1621 denies state and local postsecondary education benefits to any alien who is not a "qualified" alien, a nonimmigrant under the INA, or an alien paroled into the United States under section 212(d)(5) of the INA. 8 U.S.C. § 1621. For all practical purposes, the preemption analysis with respect to section 8 of Proposition 187 is the same as the analysis for sections 5 and 6. Congress has occupied the field of regulation of public postsecondary education benefits to aliens.

There is further evidence that Congress has occupied the field of regulation of public postsecondary education benefits to aliens. On September 30, 1996, Congress enacted the Illegal Immigration Reform and Immigrant Responsibility Act of 1996 ("IRA"). The IRA regulates alien eligibility for postsecondary education benefits on the basis of residence within a state. 8 U.S.C. § 1623(a). Because the IRA defines alien eligibility for postsecondary education, it also manifests Congress' intent to occupy this field.

3. The PRA preempts sections 5 and 6 because there is a conflict between these sections and the PRA.

Sections 5 and 6 of Proposition 187 deny public social services and health benefits to persons "in the United States in violation of federal law." §§ 5; 6. The PRA denies federal benefits to aliens who are not "qualified." 8 U.S.C. § 1611. The PRA denies state and local benefits to aliens who are not "qualified"; nonimmigrants under the INA; or aliens who are paroled into the United States under section 212(d)(5) of the INA for less than one year. 8 U.S.C. § 1621.

Without further definition, the term used in sections 5 and 6 of Proposition 187, "alien in the United States in violation of federal law," is vague. Before the Court's decision striking the classification scheme in subsection (b) of sections 5 and 6, the term "alien in the United States in violation of federal law" referred to the state classification scheme in subsection (b) for its definition. However, the Court struck subsection (b) because it was part of a state scheme to regulate immigration and was therefore preempted by federal law. Thus, the remaining term "alien in the United States in violation of federal law" now stands alone without a definition. It was argued that regulations conforming to federal law would supply this definition and thus validate the benefits denial provisions of sections 5 and 6. Without regulations, it is left to the Court to supply a definition.

The Court cannot interpret "alien in the United States in violation of federal law" in Proposition 187 as meaning a person who is not a "qualified" alien under the PRA. To do so would be contrary to the rules of statutory construction. Therefore, the term from sections 5 and 6, "alien in the United States in violation of federal law" conflicts with the classifications in the PRA, making compliance with both laws impossible. For this reason, sections 5 and 6 are preempted by the PRA pursuant to the third *De Canas* test.

A specific provision of the PRA clearly conflicts with Proposition 187. The PRA delineates which state or local public benefits are to be denied to aliens who are not "qualified." 8 U.S.C. § 1621(c). The Act provides several general exceptions that preserve immigrant eligibility for certain programs and services, creating plain conflicts with the broader prohibitions in Proposition 187. 8 U.S.C. § 1621(b). For example, this Court has concluded that "section 5 broadly denies any and all aid, services and programs administered or supervised by the state departments of social and health services." *LULAC*, 908 F.Supp. at 780. The Court also determined that section 6 of the initiative enacts a similarly broad proscription. See id. at 783. It is obvious that these provisions of Proposition 187 conflict with the more limited restrictions in the PRA.

* * *

III.

CONCLUSION

After the Court's November 20, 1995 Opinion, Congress enacted the PRA, a comprehensive statutory scheme regulating alien eligibility for public benefits. The PRA states that it is the immigration policy of the United States to restrict alien access to substantially all public benefits. Further, the PRA ousts state power to legislate in the area of public benefits for aliens. When President Clinton signed the PRA, he effectively ended any further debate about what the states could do in this field. As the Court pointed out in its prior Opinion, California is powerless to enact its own legislative scheme to regulate immigration. It is likewise powerless to enact its own legislative scheme to regulate alien access to public benefits. It can do what the PRA permits, and nothing more. Federal power in these areas was always exclusive and the PRA only serves to reinforce the Court's prior conclusion that substantially all of the provisions of Proposition 187 are preempted under *De Canas v. Bica*. Only sections 2, 3 and 10 are enforceable.

Notes and Questions

1. The federal district court in *LULAC II* (above) and a related case, *LULAC I* [LULAC v. Wilson, 908 F.Supp. 755 (C.D. Cal. 1995)], concluded that under *De Canas*, federal immigration law preempted Proposition 187's central provisions and, further, that these provisions flew in the face of *Plyler v. Doe* (the Texas school case, supra.)

2. Could you draft an anti-immigrant measure for a state or town that would stand up?

3. Would you want to?

4. See Joshua J. Herndon, *Broken Borders:* De Canas v. Bica *and the Standards that Govern the Validity of State Measures Designed to Deter Undocumented Immigration*, 12 Tex. Hisp. J.L. & Pol'y 31 (2006), arguing that Arizona's Proposition 200, a measure similar in aim to Proposition 187, but drafted to avoid some of its pitfalls, is constitutional.

Chapter 11

SCHOOL DESEGREGATION

Brown v. Board of Education
347 U.S. 483 (1954)

CHIEF JUSTICE WARREN delivered the opinion of the Court.

These cases come to us from the States of Kansas, South Carolina, Virginia, and Delaware. They are premised on different facts and different local conditions, but a common legal question justifies their consideration together in this consolidated opinion.

In each of the cases, minors of the Negro race, through their legal representatives, seek the aid of the courts in obtaining admission to the public schools of their community on a nonsegregated basis. In each instance, they have been denied admission to schools attended by white children under laws requiring or permitting segregation according to race. This segregation was alleged to deprive the plaintiffs of the equal protection of the laws under the Fourteenth Amendment. In each of the cases other than the Delaware case, a three-judge federal district court denied relief to the plaintiffs on the so-called "separate but equal" doctrine announced by this Court in Plessy v. Ferguson, 163 U.S. 537. Under that doctrine, equality of treatment is accorded when the races are provided substantially equal facilities, even though these facilities be separate. In the Delaware case, the Supreme Court of Delaware adhered to that doctrine, but ordered that the plaintiffs be admitted to the white schools because of their superiority to the Negro schools.

The plaintiffs contend that segregated public schools are not "equal" and cannot be made "equal," and that hence they are deprived of the equal protection of the laws. Because of the obvious importance of the question presented, the Court took jurisdiction. Argument was heard in the 1952 Term, and reargument was heard this Term on certain questions propounded by the Court.

Reargument was largely devoted to the circumstances surrounding the adoption of the Fourteenth Amendment in 1868. It covered exhaustively consideration of the Amendment in Congress, ratification by the states, then existing practices in racial segregation, and the views of proponents and opponents of the Amendment. This discussion and our own investigation convince us that, although these sources cast some light, it is not enough to resolve the problem with which we are faced. At best, they are inconclusive. The most avid proponents of the post-War Amendments undoubtedly intended them to remove all legal distinctions among "all persons born or naturalized in the United States." Their opponents, just as certainly, were antagonistic to both the letter and the spirit of the Amendments and wished them to have the most limited effect. What others in Congress and the state legislatures had in mind cannot be determined with any degree of certainty.

An additional reason for the inconclusive nature of the Amendment's history, with respect to segregated schools, is the status of public education at that time. In the South, the movement toward free common schools, supported by general taxation, had not yet taken hold. Education of white children was largely in the hands of private groups. Education of Negroes was almost nonexistent, and practically all of the race were illiterate. In fact, any education of Negroes was forbidden by law in some states. Today, in contrast, many Negroes have achieved outstanding success in the arts and sciences as well as in the business and professional world. It is true that public school education at the time of the Amendment had advanced further in the North, but the effect of the Amendment on Northern States was generally ignored in the congressional debates. Even in the North, the conditions of public education did not approximate those existing today. The curriculum was usually rudimentary; ungraded schools were common in rural areas; the school term was but three months a year in many states; and compulsory school attendance was virtually unknown. As a consequence, it is not surprising that there should be so little in the history of the Fourteenth Amendment relating to its intended effect on public education.

In the first cases in this Court construing the Fourteenth Amendment, decided shortly after its adoption, the Court interpreted it as proscribing all state-imposed discriminations against the Negro race. The doctrine of "separate but equal" did not make its appearance in this court until 1896 in the case of *Plessy v. Ferguson*, supra, involving not education but transportation. American courts have since labored with the doctrine for over half a century. In this Court, there have been six cases involving the "separate but equal" doctrine in the field of public education. In Cumming v. Board of Education of Richmond County, 175 U.S. 528, and Gong Lum v. Rice, 275 U.S. 78, the validity of the doctrine itself was not challenged. In more recent cases, all on the graduate school level, inequality was found in that specific benefits enjoyed by white students were denied to Negro students of the same educational qualifications. State of Missouri ex rel. Gaines v. Canada, 305 U.S. 337; Sipuel v. Board of Regents of University of Oklahoma, 332 U.S. 631; Sweatt v. Painter, 339 U.S. 629; McLaurin v. Oklahoma State Regents, 339 U.S. 637. In none of these cases was it necessary to re-examine the doctrine to grant relief to the Negro plaintiff. And in *Sweatt v. Painter*, supra, the Court expressly reserved decision on the question whether *Plessy v. Ferguson* should be held inapplicable to public education.

In the instant cases, that question is directly presented. Here, unlike *Sweatt v. Painter*, there are findings below that the Negro and white schools involved have been equalized, or are being equalized, with respect to buildings, curricula, qualifications and salaries of teachers, and other "tangible" factors. Our decision, therefore, cannot turn on merely a comparison of these tangible factors in the Negro and white schools involved in each of the cases. We must look instead to the effect of segregation itself on public education.

In approaching this problem, we cannot turn the clock back to 1868 when the Amendment was adopted, or even to 1896 when *Plessy v. Ferguson* was written. We must consider public education in the light of its full development and its present place in American life throughout the Nation. Only in this way can it be determined if segregation in public schools deprives these plaintiffs of the equal protection of the laws.

Today, education is perhaps the most important function of state and local governments. Compulsory school attendance laws and the great expenditures for education both demonstrate our recognition of the importance of education to our democratic society. It is required in the performance of our most basic public responsibilities, even service in the armed forces. It is the very foundation of good citizenship. Today it is a principal instrument in awakening the child to cultural values, in preparing him for later professional training, and in helping him to adjust normally to his environment. In these days, it is doubtful that any child may reasonably be expected to succeed in life if he is denied the opportunity of an education. Such an opportunity, where the state has undertaken to provide it, is a right which must be made available to all on equal terms.

We come then to the question presented: Does segregation of children in public schools solely on the basis of race, even though the physical facilities and other "tangible" factors may be equal, deprive the children of the minority group of equal educational opportunities? We believe that it does.

In *Sweatt v. Painter*, in finding that a segregated law school for Negroes could not provide them equal educational opportunities, this Court relied in large part on "those qualities which are incapable of objective measurement but which make for greatness in a law school." In *McLaurin v. Oklahoma State Regents*, the Court, in requiring that a Negro admitted to a white graduate school be treated like all other students, again resorted to intangible considerations: " . . . his ability to study, to engage in discussions and exchange views with other students, and, in general, to learn his profession." Such considerations apply with added force to children in grade and high schools. To separate them from others of similar age and qualifications solely because of their race generates a feeling of inferiority as to their status in the community that may affect their hearts and minds in a way unlikely ever to be undone. The effect of this separation on their educational opportunities was well stated by a finding in the Kansas case by a court which nevertheless felt compelled to rule against the Negro plaintiffs:

> Segregation of white and colored children in public schools has a detrimental effect upon the colored children. The impact is greater when it has the sanction of the law; for the policy of separating the races is usually interpreted as denoting the inferiority of the negro group. A sense of inferiority affects the motivation of a child to learn. Segregation with the sanction of law, therefore, has a tendency to (retard) the educational and mental development of Negro children and to deprive them of some of the benefits they would receive in a racial(ly) integrated school system.

Whatever may have been the extent of psychological knowledge at the time of *Plessy v. Ferguson*, this finding is amply supported by modern authority. Any language in *Plessy v. Ferguson* contrary to this finding is rejected.

We conclude that in the field of public education the doctrine of "separate but equal" has no place. Separate educational facilities are inherently unequal. Therefore, we hold that the plaintiffs and others similarly situated for whom the actions have been brought are, by reason of the segregation complained of, deprived of the equal protection of the laws guaranteed by the Fourteenth Amendment. This disposition makes unnecessary any discussion whether such segregation also violates the Due Process Clause of the Fourteenth Amendment.

Because these are class actions, because of the wide applicability of this decision, and because of the great variety of local conditions, the formulation of decrees in these cases presents problems of considerable complexity. On reargument, the consideration of appropriate relief was necessarily subordinated to the primary question—the constitutionality of segregation in public education. We have now announced that such segregation is a denial of the equal protection of the laws.

Notes and Questions

1. *Brown* affirmed the fundamental proposition that racial discrimination in public education violates the equal protection guarantee of the United States Constitution. In reversing *Plessy v. Ferguson* (the separate-but-equal decision), the Supreme Court emphasized the importance of a public education. But *Brown*'s reach extended beyond education. In the years after it came down, courts invalidated segregation in many other settings, ranging from city buses to golf courses, beaches, bathhouses, and swimming pools. For the view that *Brown* was really not so much about helping black schoolchildren as advancing America's Cold War interests, see Derrick Bell, Brown v. Board of Education *and the Interest–Convergence Dilemma*, 93 Harv. L. Rev. 518 (1980); Mary L. Dudziak, *Desegregation as a Cold War Imperative*, 41 Stan. L. Rev. 61 (1988).

2.   Was it a mistake for the Supreme Court to base part of its reasoning on social science evidence indicating that segregation scarred black schoolchildren, rather than a simple moral intuition?

3.   In his article cited above and in a succession of later pieces, Derrick Bell argues that the Supreme Court would have done better to reaffirm *Plessy v. Ferguson*, uphold segregated schools, but make school boards equalize school funding. Part of his argument is that the burden of desegregation fell on black schoolchildren bused long distances to unfriendly schools, and on the black community, which lost many teacher and school-administrator jobs when black schools closed in the wake of desegregation decrees. The community lost role models, community centers, and a source of solidarity, and their children ended up scattered and assigned to schools that did not understand them or teach their history or cultural contributions.

Is desegregation a similar disaster for Latinos?

SECTION 1.   LATINO SCHOOL DESEGREGATION ACTIVISM

Although Latinos have waged school desegregation struggles in practically every region, the longest and bitterest such efforts have taken place in the Southwest. Official segregation of Mexican American schoolchildren in inferior schools began shortly after the Treaty of Guadalupe Hidalgo ended the War with Mexico in 1848. Although no western or southwestern state seems to have enacted a statute mandating the separation of white and Mexican schoolchildren, as they did separating blacks, Indians, and sometimes Asian Americans, school authorities sent Mexican American children to separate schools out of custom and because Anglo parents did not want their own children attending school with them. According to Professor of Education Richard Valencia of University of Texas–Austin, Latinos brought 35 school desegregation cases in the state of Texas alone between the end of the War with Mexico and the modern era. Valencia, *Chicano Students and the Courts,* Ch. 2

With the increase in the Mexican-origin population nationwide, the segregation of Mexican schoolchildren became even more deeply entrenched between 1930 and 1971, when a U.S. Commission on Civil Rights report confirmed what everyone knew: Mexican schoolchildren attended schools with very few whites. *Mexican American Education Study, Report 1: Ethnic Isolation of Mexican Americans in the Public Schools of the Southwest* (1971). According to Harvard expert Gary Orfield, this separation has worsened in recent years, with the result that Latinos today are even more isolated in schools than African Americans. Gary Orfield, *Schools More Separate: Consequences of a Decade of Resegregation (The Civil Rights Project Report)* (2001).

Litigation, although plentiful, has not been the only strategy Latino parents and children have employed to secure the benefits of integrated schools. For example, in 1910, in San Angelo, Texas, Mexican Americans staged a school walkout to draw attention to deteriorated school facilities and inferior educational resources in the local schools for Mexicans. When the school board heard their complaints but refused to order integration, the parents boycotted their own school, to no avail. The civil rights decade of the sixties saw similar walkouts ("blowouts") in Los Angeles, Denver, and other cities with large Latino school populations.

SECTION 2.   LATINO SCHOOL DESEGREGATION LITIGATION

In a little-known story, Mexican American school desegregation efforts preceded *Brown v. Board of Education* by many years. One case in particular, Mendez v. Westminister, 64 F.Supp. 544 (S.D. Cal. 1946), *aff'd*, 161 F.2d 774 (9th Cir. 1947), paved the way for that better known decision by devising an early version of the very legal theory the black plaintiffs in *Brown* used to win relief.

The Latino struggle for desegregated schools began in 1925, when a Mexican American rancher living in Tempe, Arizona filed what appears to have been the first such lawsuit, *Romo v. Laird*, on behalf of his four children, aged seven to fifteen. By local custom, the Tempe Elementary School District required "Spanish–Mexican" children to attend the segregated Eighth Street School, which was staffed largely by student teachers from a local state teachers' college. The suit alleged that the teachers were "inferior in attainments, qualifications, and ability to teach as compared with the teachers ... in the other schools" attended by the white students. Romo sought permission to enroll his children in one of the white schools.

The authorities answered that they had been segregating the Mexican schoolchildren for pedagogical and linguistic reasons, which was permitted under state law. Segregation of black children because of their race was permitted, but that of Mexican children was not; thus the school district advanced these other nonracial reasons, Valencia, supra. The Superior Court judge agreed with Romo that his children were being taught by inferior teachers and ordered that the district permit them to enroll in a school that, in the words of an earlier case, is "as well equipped and furnished and presided over by as efficient corps of teachers as the schools provided for the children of other races." Dameron v. Bayless, 14 Ariz. 180, 182, 126 P. 273 (1912).

Although Romo is the first known Mexican American desegregation lawsuit, it exerted little impact, Valencia, supra. Because it was not a class action, only the Romo children benefited. The school board responded to the court order by hiring certified teachers to teach at the Eighth Street School, which remained segregated.

The best known early Latino desegregation lawsuit was *Independent School District v. Salvatierra*, which arose in Texas in 1930. *Salvatierra* began when a group of Mexican American parents challenged some proposed school construction that would have exacerbated school segregation in their district. As in *Romo*, the lawyer for the plaintiffs argued that Texas law permitted only segregation of black children. Mexican–American children were white, in their view, hence the district was violating state law by segregating them from the rest of the children. The trial judge agreed, and the district appealed. On appeal, the school district argued, in familiar fashion, that it was separating the Mexican–American children not for racial but for pedagogical reasons: About half of them joined their parents in picking cotton and working on ranches during part of the school year. When they returned to school, they were behind, thus efficient education required segregating them in a special school. They also had special "linguistic" needs requiring separation. The appellate court agreed with these reasons and reversed. LULAC attorneys appealed to the Supreme Court, which declined review.

Throughout the thirties and forties, Latino litigators challenged school segregation cases in a host of cases, including one in Lemon Grove, California. Most of these proceeded on the "other white" theory or, at any rate, on a theory other than racial discrimination. In 1945, all this began to change when Gonzalo and Felicitas Mendez, of Westminster, California, sent their children to enroll in the neighborhood school on the first day of the school year. The school, which with very few exceptions only admitted white children, denied them admission on the ground that they were deficient in English. In fact they spoke English perfectly well. The following case, which established for the first time that separate was not equal because segregation violated the Equal Protection Clause of the Fourteenth Amendment, was the result:

Mendez v. Westminister School District of Orange County*
64 F.Supp. 544 (S.D. Cal.1946), *aff'd*,
161 F.2d 774 (9th Cir. 1947)

[Gonzalo Mendez, William Guzman, Frank Palomino, Thomas Estrada and Lorenzo Ramirez filed suit against the Westminster, Garden Grove and El Modeno School Districts, and the Santa Ana City Schools, all located in Orange County, California. The plaintiffs claimed that segregation practiced by these schools against Mexican–American children was unconstitutional.]

McCormick, District Judge.

* * *

It is conceded by all parties that there is no question of race discrimination in this action. It is, however, admitted that segregation *per se* is practiced in the above-mentioned school districts as the Spanish-speaking children enter school life and as they advance through the grades in the respective school districts. It is also admitted by the defendants that the petitioning children are qualified to attend the public schools in the respective districts of their residences.

---

* Eds. For reasons unknown to us, the court opinions in this case consistently misspell the name of the town of Westminster. We have decided to use the correct spelling in this volume.

In the Westminster, Garden Grove and El Modeno school districts the respective boards of trustees had taken official action, declaring that there be no segregation of pupils on a racial basis but that non-English-speaking children (which group, excepting as to a small number of pupils, was made up entirely of children of Mexican ancestry or descent), be required to attend schools designated by the boards separate and apart from English-speaking pupils; that such group should attend such schools until they had acquired some proficiency in the English language.

The petitioners contend that such official action evinces a covert attempt by the school authorities in such school districts to produce an arbitrary discrimination against school children of Mexican extraction or descent and that such illegal result has been established in such school districts respectively. * * *

* * * The segregation exists in the elementary schools to and including the sixth grade in two of the defendant districts, and in the two other defendant districts through the eighth grade. The record before us shows without conflict that the technical facilities and physical conveniences offered in the schools housing entirely the segregated pupils, the efficiency of the teachers therein and the curricula are identical and in some respects superior to those in the other schools in the respective districts.

The ultimate question for decision may be thus stated: Does such official action of defendant district school agencies and the usages and practices pursued by the respective school authorities as shown by the evidence operate to deny or deprive the so-called non-English-speaking school children of Mexican ancestry or descent within such school districts of the equal protection of the laws?

* * *

* * * [A] violation by a State of a personal right or privilege protected by the Fourteenth Amendment in the exercise of the State's duty to provide for the education of its citizens and inhabitants would justify the Federal Court to intervene. State of Missouri ex rel. Gaines v. Canada, 305 U.S. 337. * * *

* * *

We therefore turn to consider whether under the record before us the school boards and administrative authorities in the respective defendant districts have by their segregation policies and practices transgressed applicable law and Constitutional safeguards and limitations and thus have invaded the personal right which every public school pupil has to the equal protection provision of the Fourteenth Amendment to obtain the means of education.

We think the pattern of public education promulgated in the Constitution of California and effectuated by provisions of the Education Code of the State prohibits segregation of the pupils of Mexican ancestry in the elementary schools from the rest of the school children.

Section 1 of Article IX of the Constitution of California directs the legislature to "encourage by all suitable means the promotion of intellectual, scientific, moral, and agricultural improvement" of the people. Pursuant to this basic directive by the people of the State many laws stem authorizing special instruction in the public schools for handicapped children. Such legislation, however, is general in its aspects. It includes all those who fall within the described classification requiring the special consideration provided by the statutes regardless of their ancestry or extraction. The common segregation attitudes and practices of the school authorities in the defendant school districts in Orange County pertain solely to children of Mexican ancestry and parentage. They are singled out as a class for segregation. Not only is such method of public school administration contrary to the general requirements of the school laws of the State, but we think it indicates an official school policy that is antagonistic in principle to §§ 16004 and 16005 of the Education Code of the State.

Obviously, the children referred to in these laws are those of Mexican ancestry. And it is noteworthy that the educational advantages of their commingling with other pupils is regarded as being so important to the school system of the State that it is provided for even regardless of the citizenship of the parents. We perceive in the laws relating to the public educational system in the State of California a clear purpose to avoid and forbid distinctions among pupils based upon race or ancestry except in specific situations[5] not pertinent to this action. Distinctions of that kind have recently been declared by the highest judicial authority of the United States "by their very nature odious to a free people whose institutions are founded upon the doctrine of equality." They are said to be "utterly inconsistent with American traditions and ideals." Hirabayashi v. United States, 320 U.S. 81.

Our conclusions in this action, however, do not rest solely upon what we conceive to be the utter irreconcilability of the segregation practices in the defendant school districts with the public educational system authorized and sanctioned by the laws of the State of California. We think such practices clearly and unmistakably disregard rights secured by the supreme law of the land.

"The equal protection of the laws" pertaining to the public school system in California is not provided by furnishing in separate schools the same technical facilities, text books and courses of instruction to children

5. [Eds. This footnote reproduces California's school segregation statutes.]

Sec. 8003. "Schools for Indian children, and children of Chinese, Japanese, or Mongolian parentage: Establishment. The governing board of any school district may establish separate schools for Indian children, excepting children of Indians who are wards of the United States Government and children of all other Indians who are descendants of the original American Indians of the United States, and for children of Chinese, Japanese, or Mongolian parentage."

Sec. 8004. "Same: Admission of children into other schools. When separate schools are established for Indian children or children of Chinese, Japanese, or Mongolian parentage, the Indian children or children of Chinese, Japanese, or Mongolian parentage shall not be admitted into any other school."

of Mexican ancestry that are available to the other public school children regardless of their ancestry. A paramount requisite in the American system of public education is social equality. It must be open to all children by unified school association regardless of lineage.

We think that under the record before us the only tenable ground upon which segregation practices in the defendant school districts can be defended lies in the English language deficiencies of some of the children of Mexican ancestry as they enter elementary public school life as beginners. But even such situations do not justify the general and continuous segregation in separate schools of the children of Mexican ancestry from the rest of the elementary school population as has been shown to be the practice in the defendant school districts—in all of them to the sixth grade, and in two of them through the eighth grade.

The evidence clearly shows that Spanish-speaking children are retarded in learning English by lack of exposure to its use because of segregation, and that commingling of the entire student body instills and develops a common cultural attitude among the school children which is imperative for the perpetuation of American institutions and ideals. It is also established by the record that the methods of segregation prevalent in the defendant school districts foster antagonisms in the children and suggest inferiority among them where none exists. One of the flagrant examples of the discriminatory results of segregation in two of the schools involved in this case is shown by the record. In the district under consideration there are two schools, the Lincoln and the Roosevelt, located approximately 120 yards apart on the same school grounds, hours of opening and closing, as well as recess periods, are not uniform. No credible language test is given to the children of Mexican ancestry upon entering the first grade in Lincoln School. This school has an enrollment of 249 so-called Spanish-speaking pupils, and no so-called English-speaking pupils; while the Roosevelt, (the other) school, has 83 so-called English-speaking pupils and 25 so-called Spanish-speaking pupils. Standardized tests as to mental ability are given to the respective classes in the two schools and the same curricula are pursued in both schools and, of course, in the English language as required by State law. In the last school year the students in the seventh grade of the Lincoln were superior scholarly to the same grade in the Roosevelt School and to any group in the seventh grade in either of the schools in the past. It further appears that not only did the class as a group have such mental superiority but that certain pupils in the group were also outstanding in the class itself. Notwithstanding this showing, the pupils of such excellence were kept in the Lincoln School. It is true that there is no evidence in the record before us that shows that any of the members of this exemplary class requested transfer to the other so-called intermingled school, but the record does show without contradiction that another class had protested against the segregation policies and practices in the schools of this El Modeno district without avail.

* * *

* * * [I]t should be noted that the omnibus segregation of children of Mexican ancestry from the rest of the student body in the elementary grades in the schools involved in this case because of language handicaps is not warranted by the record before us. The tests applied to the beginners are shown to have been generally hasty, superficial and not reliable. In some instances separate classification was determined largely by the Latinized or Mexican name of the child. Such methods of evaluating language knowledge are illusory and are not conducive to the inculcation and enjoyment of civil rights which are of primary importance in the public school system of education in the United States.

It has been held that public school authorities may differentiate in the exercise of their reasonable discretion as to the pedagogical methods of instruction to be pursued with different pupils.[7] And foreign language handicaps may be to such a degree in the pupils in elementary schools as to require special treatment in separate classrooms. Such separate allocations, however, can be lawfully made only after credible examination by the appropriate school authority of each child whose capacity to learn is under consideration and the determination of such segregation must be based wholly upon indiscriminate foreign language impediments in the individual child, regardless of his ethnic traits or ancestry

* * *

There are other discriminatory customs, shown by the evidence, existing in the defendant school districts as to pupils of Mexican descent and extraction, but we deem it unnecessary to discuss them in this memorandum.

We conclude by holding that the allegations of the complaint (petition) have been established sufficiently to justify injunctive relief against all defendants, restraining further discriminatory practices against the pupils of Mexican descent in the public schools of defendant school districts.

Notes and Questions

1. Note the remarkable parallel between the reasoning and language of *Mendez*, decided in 1947, and that of *Brown v. Board of Education*, which came down in 1954.

The court wrote:

Spanish-speaking children are retarded in learning English by lack of exposure to its use because of segregation, and that commingling of the entire student body instills and develops a common cultural attitude among the school children which is imperative for the perpetuation of American institutions and ideals.

It also wrote:

---

7. See *Plessy v. Ferguson*, 163 U.S. 537 (1896).

[T]he methods of segregation prevalent in the defendant school districts foster antagonisms in the children and suggest inferiority among them where none exists.

Mendez, supra at 14–15.

Do these words remind you of *Brown's* famous line, written nine years later?

To separate them [black schoolchildren] from others of similar age and qualifications solely because of their race generates a feeling of inferiority as to their status in the community that may affect their hearts and minds in a way unlikely ever to be undone.

Brown, supra at 494.

If so, the similarity may not be completely coincidental. The NAACP, which was then searching for legal theories to challenge segregation in Southern schools, sent a representative, Robert Carter, to observe the *Westminster* litigation. Impressed with the social science evidence the Mexican Americans used to establish the injury that segregated schooling inflicted on young minds, he urged his organization to investigate this promising avenue. See Juan F. Perea, *The Black/White Binary Paradigm of Race: The "Normal Science" of American Racial Thought*, 85 Cal. L. Rev. 1213 (1997); Charles Wollenberg, *All Deliberate Speed: Segregation and Exclusion in California Schools, 1855–1975* (1976); Charles Wollenberg, Mendez v. Westminster: *Race, Nationality and Segregation in California Schools*, 53 Cal. Hist. Q. 317 (1974).

Shortly after the Ninth Circuit affirmed the *Mendez* opinion, California Governor Earl Warren signed a bill outlawing all school segregation in that state. Warren went on to become Chief Justice of the United States Supreme Court, where he wrote the opinion in *Brown v. Board of Education*, including the ringing words you just read, a few years later.

The NAACP participated in the Ninth Circuit appeal with a brief that served as a "dry run" for Brown. See Perea, *Black/White*, supra at 1242–51.

2.   The attorney for the *Mendez* plaintiffs was David C. Marcus, a civil rights lawyer from Los Angeles. See Valencia, supra. Marcus had successfully litigated a successful swimming-pool case, Lopez v. Seccombe, 71 F.Supp. 769 (S.D. Cal. 1944), just a few years earlier. Why might the equal protection breakthrough occur first in a non-school setting, and in schools some time later? Is it because schools are transmitters of cultural knowledge and resistant to change, while swimming pools are not? See the discussion of postcolonial theory and resistance, earlier in this Part.

3.   The law reviews were quick to note the new decision and to speculate on its significance. Columbia Law Review, Harvard Law Review, Illinois Law Review, Minnesota Law Review, and Yale Law Journal discussed the case. In the words of one authority, "Mendez portended the legal and integrationist theories put forth by the lawyers in *Brown*." Valencia, supra.

4.   The *Mendez* opinion states that the district's schools were roughly equal in facilities and supplies. Studies conducted during this time show that they generally were not. See Valencia, supra, including photographs of "Mexican schools." The Mexican schools were inferior in teacher-pupil ratio, buildings, drinking fountains, classroom lighting, athletic facilities, band,

and many other respects. Id. Many lacked modern textbooks and had windows in need of repair.

After *Mendez,* the dam burst. Latino parents filed one successful school desegregation lawsuit after another, generally following the *Mendez* strategy and equal-protection theory, not the "other white" approach. E.g., Delgado v. Bastrop Independent School District, Civ. No. 388 (W.D. Tex. 1948); Cisneros v. Corpus Christi Independent School District, 324 F.Supp. 599 (S.D. Tex. 1970).

Unfortunately, little changed. In a story familiar from the black experience, white parents moved away ("white flight") to escape having their children attend school with Latinos. School boards engaged in obstruction, foot-dragging, and delay. Some even turned the Latinos' earlier "other white" strategy against them. Upon receiving an order by a federal or state judge to desegregate, they merely paired Mexican and black schoolchildren in one school and pronounced the resulting mix desegregated.

SECTION 3.   LATINO SCHOOL DESEGREGATION IN AN ERA OF MULTIRACIALISM

In many areas of the country, especially outside the Southwest, cities contain not just one large minority group—black or Latino, for example—but two or more. Imagine, for example, a large-city school district with 12 percent black schoolchildren, 30 percent Latinos, and 50 percent whites. How much racial separation is permissible in such a situation, and what would a remedy look like? And are Latinos a protected class under U.S. civil rights law?

Keyes v. School District No. One, 413 U.S. 189 (1973) answered some of these questions. Affirming the results of *Mendez v. Westminster* and *Hernandez v. Texas* (see supra), it held, unequivocally, for the first time, that Latinos were indeed a protected class under national civil rights law. It also provided guidelines for future courts considering the meaning of "segregated" in Northern or Western cities with large populations of both Latinos and blacks.

The long-running *Keyes* litigation began in 1969 when African–American plaintiffs attending Denver schools filed a complaint in the local Colorado federal district court. That court found that the district, which contained about 12 percent blacks, 16 percent Latinos, and 71 percent whites, "had engaged in an unconstitutional policy of deliberate racial segregation," 413 U.S. at 189. It also held that the two groups, blacks and Latinos, have wholly different origins from Anglos and different problems. The two minority groups do, however, share one historic feature: cultural and economic discrimination at the hands of whites, 313 F.Supp. at 69 (D. Colo. 1970).

The following Supreme Court decision affirmed most of the rulings below in an opinion that for the first time ruled on a desegregation case in the West or North. It also found intentional (de jure) segregation in the absence of a state statute, but based instead on pupil-assignment and school construction policies.

Keyes v. School District No. 1, Denver, Colorado
413 U.S. 189 (1973)

MR. JUSTICE BRENNAN delivered the opinion of the Court.

This school desegregation case concerns the Denver, Colorado, school system. That system has never been operated under a constitutional or statutory provision that mandated or permitted racial segregation in public education. Rather, the gravamen of this action, brought in June 1969 in the District Court for the District of Colorado by parents of Denver schoolchildren, is that respondent School Board alone, by use of various techniques such as the manipulation of student attendance zones, schoolsite selection and a neighborhood school policy, created or maintained racially or ethnically (or both racially and ethnically) segregated schools throughout the school district, entitling petitioners to a decree directing desegregation of the entire school district.

* * *

The District Court went on to hold that the proofs established that the segregated core city schools were educationally inferior to the predominantly "white" or "Anglo" schools in other parts of the district—that is, "separate facilities ... unequal in the quality of education provided." Thus, the court held that, under the doctrine of *Plessy v. Ferguson*, respondent School Board constitutionally "must at a minimum ... offer an equal educational opportunity," therefore, although all-out desegregation "could not be decreed, ... the only feasible and constitutionally acceptable program—the only program which furnishes anything approaching substantial equality—is a system of desegregation and integration which provides compensatory education in an integrated environment." The District Court then formulated a varied remedial plan to that end which was incorporated in the Final Decree.

* * *

We granted petitioners' petition for certiorari to review the Court of Appeals' judgment insofar as it reversed that part of the District Court's Final Decree as pertained to the core city schools. * * *

I

Before turning to the primary question we decide today, a word must be said about the District Court's method of defining a "segregated" school. Denver is a tri-ethnic, as distinguished from a bi-racial, community. The overall racial and ethnic composition of the Denver public schools is 66% Anglo, 14% Negro, and 20% Hispano. The District Court in assessing the question of *de jure* segregation in the core city schools, preliminarily resolved that Negroes and Hispanos should not be placed in the same category to establish the segregated character of a school. Later, in determining the schools that were likely to produce an inferior educational opportunity, the court concluded that a school would be considered inferior only if it had "a concentration of either Negro or

Hispano students in the general area of 70 to 75 percent." We intimate no opinion whether the District Court's 70%–to–75% requirement was correct. The District Court used those figures to signify educationally inferior schools, and there is no suggestion in the record that those same figures were or would be used to define a "segregated" school in the *de jure* context. What is or is not a segregated school will necessarily depend on the facts of each particular case. In addition to the racial and ethnic composition of a school's student body, other factors, such as the racial and ethnic composition of faculty and staff and the community and administration attitudes toward the school, must be taken into consideration. The District Court has recognized these specific factors as elements of the definition of a "segregated" school, and we may therefore infer that the court will consider them again on remand.

We conclude, however, that the District Court erred in separating Negroes and Hispanos for purposes of defining a "segregated" school. We have held that Hispanos constitute an identifiable class for purposes of the Fourteenth Amendment. Hernandez v. Texas, 347 U.S. 475 (1954). Indeed the District Court recognized this in classifying predominantly Hispano schools as "segregated" schools in their own right. But there is also much evidence that in the Southwest Hispanos and Negroes have a great many things in common. The United States Commission on Civil Rights has recently published two Reports on Hispano education in the Southwest. Focusing on students in the States of Arizona, California, Colorado, New Mexico, and Texas, the Commission concluded that Hispanos suffer from the same educational inequities as Negroes and American Indians. In fact, the District Court itself recognized that "[o]ne of the things which the Hispano has in common with the Negro is economic and cultural deprivation and discrimination." There is agreement that, though of different origins Negroes and Hispanos in Denver suffer identical discrimination in treatment when compared with the treatment afforded Anglo students. In that circumstance, we think petitioners are entitled to have schools with a combined predominance of Negroes and Hispanos included in the category of "segregated" schools.

* * *

Common sense dictates that racially inspired school board actions have an impact beyond the particular schools that are the subjects of those actions. This is not to say, of course, that there can never be a case in which the geographical structure of, or the natural boundaries within, a school district may have the effect of dividing the district into separate, identifiable and unrelated units. Such a determination is essentially a question of fact to be resolved by the trial court in the first instance, but such cases must be rare. In the absence of such a determination, proof of state-imposed segregation in a substantial portion of the district will suffice to support a finding by the trial court of the existence of a dual system. Of course, where that finding is made, as in cases involving statutory dual systems, the school authorities have an affirmative duty "to effectuate a transition to a racially nondiscriminatory school system." *Brown II*, supra, 394 U.S. at 301.

On remand, therefore, the District Court should decide in the first instance whether respondent School Board's deliberate racial segregation policy with respect to the Park Hill schools constitutes the entire Denver school system a dual school system. We observe that on the record now before us there is indication that Denver is not a school district which might be divided into separate, identifiable and unrelated units. The District Court stated, in its summary of findings as to the Park Hill schools, that there was "a high degree of interrelationship among these schools, so that any action by the Board affecting the racial composition of one would almost certainly have an effect on the others." And there was cogent evidence that the ultimate effect of the Board's actions in Park Hill was not limited to that area: the three 1969 resolutions designed to desegregate the Park Hill schools changed the attendance patterns of at least 29 schools attended by almost one-third of the pupils in the Denver school system. This suggests that the official segregation in Park Hill affected the racial composition of schools throughout the district.

* * *

III

The District Court proceeded on the premise that the finding as to the Park Hill schools was irrelevant to the consideration of the rest of the district, and began its examination of the core city schools by requiring that petitioners prove all of the essential elements of *de jure* segregation—that is, stated simply, a current condition of segregation resulting from intentional state action directed specifically to the core city schools. The segregated character of the core city schools could not be and is not denied. Petitioners' proof showed that at the time of trial 22 of the schools in the core city area were less than 30% in Anglo enrollment and 11 of the schools were less than 10% Anglo. Petitioners also introduced substantial evidence demonstrating the existence of a disproportionate racial and ethnic composition of faculty and staff at these schools.

On the question of segregative intent, petitioners presented evidence tending to show that the Board, through its actions over a period of years, intentionally created and maintained the segregated character of the core city schools. Respondents countered this evidence by arguing that the segregation in these schools is the result of a racially neutral "neighborhood school policy" and that the acts of which petitioners complain are explicable within the bounds of that policy. * * *

* * *

In the special context of school desegregation cases, we hold that a finding of intentionally segregative school board actions in a meaningful portion of a school system, as in this case, creates a presumption that other segregated schooling within the system is not adventitious. It establishes, in other words, a prima facie case of unlawful segregative design on the part of school authorities, and shifts to those authorities the burden of proving that other segregated schools within the system are not also the result of intentionally segregative actions. This is true even if it is determined that different areas of the school district should be viewed independently of each other because, even in that situation, there is high probability that where school authorities have effectuated an intentionally segregative policy in a meaningful portion of the school system, similar impermissible considerations have motivated their actions in other areas. We emphasize that the differentiating factor between *de jure* segregation and so-called *de facto* segregation to which we referred in *Swann* is *purpose* or *intent* to segregate. Where school authorities have been found to have practiced purposeful segregation in part of a school system, they may be expected to oppose system-wide desegregation, as did the respondents in this case, on the ground that their purposefully segregative actions were isolated and individual events, thus leaving plaintiffs with the burden of proving otherwise. But at that point where an intentionally segregative policy is practiced in a meaningful or significant segment of a school system, as in this case, the school authorities cannot be heard to argue that plaintiffs have proved only "isolated and individual" unlawfully segregative actions. In that circumstance, it is both fair and reasonable to require that the school authorities bear the burden of showing that their actions as to other segregated schools within the system were not also motivated by segregative intent.

This burden-shifting principle is not new or novel. * * *

* * *

Notes and Questions

1. Shortly after *Keyes*, Latino and black school desegregation came virtually to an end, the victim of conservative presidencies and Justice Departments, and courts willing to declare school districts desegregated if they had made good faith efforts to comply with desegregation decrees or if too few whites remained in the district to allow for meaningful desegregation, Valencia, supra. Today, a half century after *Brown* and *Mendez*, according to UCLA scholar Gary Orfield, the nation's schools are more segregated than ever, with Latinos the most segregated minority group. Segregation is apt to deepen even further with the Supreme Court ruling, in Parents Involved in Community Schools v. Seattle School Dist. No. 1, 127 S.Ct. 2738 (2007), that voluntary integration plans that take race into account are unconstitutional.

2. Not only have Latino schoolchildren suffered from underfinanced (see *Rodriguez*, supra) and racially segregated schools, they have seen disproportionate assignment to special education (mentally retarded) classes based on faulty diagnoses or inability to speak English. See Valencia, *Chicano Students and the Courts*, Chapter 4; Jorge C. Rangel & Carlos M. Alcala, *Project Report: De Jure Segregation of Chicanos in Texas Schools*, 7 Harv. C.R.-C.L. L. Rev. 307 (1972).

3. With a high dropout rate, the group sends fewer of its young to colleges or universities than any other group, including blacks. A high percentage of Latinos who do go on to college attend community or junior colleges offering only two-year Associate of Arts degrees. See Valencia, supra.

4. The new emphasis on high stakes testing and "accountability," stemming in part from the No Child Left Behind Act, has also exerted a harsh impact on Latino schoolchildren, some of whom are high-achieving scholars with high GPAs but nevertheless have trouble with the test. Id. at Chapter 9.

5. Despite the various hurdles mentioned above, a few Latino youth graduate from high school with good records and a desire to enroll in a four-year college. A later chapter discusses two aspects of their quest for a college degree—diversity and affirmative action in higher education.

Chapter 12

DISCRIMINATION IN PUBLIC SCHOOLS

Aside from barriers such as segregated schools, high-stakes testing, lack of bilingual programs, and consignment to EMR (educable mentally retarded) tracks, Latino schoolchildren have had to face outright, old-fashioned, in-your-face racism at the hands of school authorities.

Some of this racism manifested itself in punishing children who spoke Spanish, even on the playground. At other times, school authorities would treat Latino/a schoolchildren as though they were dirty or infested with lice or contagious diseases. And of course many treated them as slow learners, even when they were not, or were indeed gifted. See, e.g., Gilbert C. Gonzalez, *Chicano Education in the Era of Segregation* (1990); Charles Wollenberg, *All Deliberate Speed: Segregation and Exclusion in California Schools, 1855–1975* (1976); Thomas P. Carter, *Mexican Americans in School: A History of Educational Neglect* (1970).

The following selection summarizes some of these practices:

Juan F. Perea
*Buscando America: Why Integration and Equal
Protection Fail to Protect Latinos*
117 Harv. L. Rev. 1420, 1439, 1441–46 (2004)

Language-based subordination has particularly plagued Latinos in the educational system. In the realm of schooling, a variety of techniques have been and continue to be used to burden or exclude Spanish speakers. Some of these can be characterized as assimilative in nature—pressuring Spanish speakers to abandon their language and culture or to integrate into Anglo society as an underclass. Some of the techniques are not assimilative, but rather discriminatory—residential or educational segregation, or teacher prejudice against Spanish-speaking students. All of these techniques, intentionally or not, reflect and enforce a racist, subordinating attitude toward Latino students. * * *

* * *

* * * Mexican–American children were regularly retained in first grade for two or three years, which automatically placed them behind

360

their Anglo peers. While this retention policy was often justified for linguistic reasons, in many instances the linguistic competence of the children was tested in a hasty and inconclusive fashion, if at all. Today, Latinos continue to be held back in school much more often than their peers. Mexican–American students continue to be physically, culturally, and intellectually segregated even within supposedly integrated classrooms.

Teachers who intentionally or unintentionally accept and implement stereotypes of Mexican–American children perpetuate the subordination of Mexicans. The common assumptions that Chicano children are inherently culturally disadvantaged or that they come from a "simple folk culture" are racist judgments imposed on cultural differences. Another common stereotype is that Latino parents do not care about the education of their children.

Studies * * * demonstrate that Anglo teachers viewed their Mexican–American students as lazy and favored Anglo students in class participation and leadership roles. Such leadership opportunities, according to the teachers, were necessary to teach Anglos how to control and lead Mexicans. Many Anglo teachers and parents saw Mexican–American children as dirty and diseased. One teacher advocated mandatory baths for "dirty Mexican kids because it will teach them how nice it feels to be clean." Another teacher refused to let her Mexican–American students hug her without first inspecting their hair for lice. These obviously racist attitudes on the part of Anglo teachers only reinforced stereotypes of inferiority that subordinated Mexican–American children.

* * *

* * * One Texas school imposed an extensive disciplinary system for speaking Spanish. A student caught speaking Spanish was first detained for an hour or more. If the child spoke Spanish again, the principal spanked him. Repeat offenders who persisted in speaking Spanish might ultimately be suspended or expelled from school. Other punishments for speaking Spanish included physical abuse and public humiliation. These kinds of punishments were, and continue to be, meted out in schools with large Mexican–American populations. In jurisdictions that have repealed bilingual education by referendum, including Massachusetts, Arizona, and California, some educators are enforcing the new laws in the old ways by prohibiting the use of Spanish among students on school campuses.

Another facet of the educational campaign to extinguish native Spanish has been the persistent devaluation of bilingualism in general and of the native ability to speak Spanish in particular. Many teachers, perhaps most, see childhood bilingualism as a deficit and an impediment to learning. Many teachers also believe that Spanish-speaking or bilingual Mexican–American children speak no language at all. * * * These "no Spanish" rules and disparaging attitudes toward native Spanish speakers are part of a system of behavioral controls intended to banish manifestations of "Mexicanness" from the public schools.

Recent news reports about local legal disputes provide ample evidence of the continuing devaluation of bilingualism and Spanish-speaking ability in schools, workplaces, and courtrooms. For example, a Texas judge hearing a custody dispute threatened a Mexican–American mother with the loss of her daughter because she spoke Spanish at home:

> [Y]ou're abusing that child and you're relegating her to the position of a housemaid. Now get this straight. You start speaking English to this child because if she doesn't do good in school, then I can remove her because it's not in her best interest to be ignorant. The child will hear only English.

In this judge's eyes, a five-year-old Mexican–American girl who spoke Spanish was ignorant, incapable of good school performance, and destined to be a housemaid. His opinion states neatly the pervasive assumptions that knowledge of the Spanish language is no knowledge at all and that Mexicans are unintelligent and fit only for menial labor. More recently, a Nebraska judge warned that he would limit severely a Mexican–American father's rights to visit his daughter if he continued speaking to her in Spanish. The judge insisted that "[t]he principal form of communication ... is going to be English and not the Hispanic language."

In another recent case, a New York judge rejected a constitutional challenge to the poor quality of education provided to Latino youngsters who had dropped out of school by the eighth grade. The judge explained that completion of the eighth grade constituted a "sound basic education," because "[s]ociety needs workers in all levels of jobs, the majority of which may very well be low level." The judge's satisfaction with blatantly unequal education for Latino and Black students, and his blithe contentment with their futures in menial labor, echo the exploitative purposes for which Mexican–American education was originally designed.

The education of Mexican–American children in the Southwest provides a powerful illustration of Derrick Bell's interest-convergence hypothesis. For most of the twentieth century, Latinos and Blacks lacked quality education because their education was not in the interests of Whites, who needed them only as manual laborers. Whites were interested in educating Mexican Americans only for the purpose of teaching them to believe in their own inferiority and to be satisfied with roles as manual laborers; indeed, Anglos saw Latino education as a threat to their labor force and to their sense of White supremacy. The troubling question we must ask today is: to what extent has this basic dynamic changed? The maintenance of White privilege, and Brown and Black subordination, though no longer held as overt goals, are clearly observable in our unequal educational system and in our failure to enact meaningful reforms.

Notes and Questions

1.   Suppose that you and your elementary school class spent a month in a school in Mexico or Spain as part of an international exchange program. The first day there you learn that the school authorities are rabidly anti-English. Not only is it forbidden for the group to speak English anywhere on the school grounds, teachers enforce the rule by washing any member's mouth with soap caught speaking English, even in the lunchroom. How would you feel? Would you put up with it? Would you rebel? Call your parents to come and get you as soon as possible?

2.   Suppose that, in order to avail yourself of an important professional opportunity (and the promise of a big promotion), you need to learn a foreign language—say, Swahili or Arabic—in six months. In one program, you take concentrated classes in the language, but the rest of the day you are permitted to speak English, for example with your room-mate after going home in the evening. You can also watch your favorite news programs on TV and listen to your favorite songs in English. In the other program, you are forbidden from speaking, or listening to, English at all.

In which program do you think you would learn Arabic faster? In which one might you suffer a nervous breakdown?

3.   Suppose that the second program also required you to *think* in the foreign language—"It's sink or swim" the instructors say—and punished thinking in English by expelling anyone suspected of thinking in English after one warning. How do they know you are thinking in English? Never mind; they have their ways.

4.   Suppose that the foreign school allows a little English, but all the kids look down on the visitors from America. They make fun of them, make anti-American remarks, call them stupid "hicks," and draw unflattering cartoons of them made up to look like a cross-eyed Uncle Sam. They don't invite them to any of their parties or let them join in their study groups. They joke that the Americans are unclean and hold their noses when they pass them in the hallways. What kind of redress should they seek? Should they "laugh it off?" Suppose that the visit is not just for a month, but a year.

5.   On the racial impact of recent federal laws, especially No Child Left Behind, see Rachel F. Moran, *Sorting and Reforming: High–Stakes Testing in the Public Schools*, 34 Akron L. Rev. 107 (2000). Moran draws an analogy between the TV show, "Who Wants to be a Millionaire," where the multiple choice questions are geared toward white men, and America's recent obsession with high-stakes testing. She writes that the obsession is serving as an inexpensive way to "get tough on public schools," discusses a number of court challenges to high-school exit exams, and argues that the consequences of America's neglect of its children will not be light.

Chapter 13

HIGHER EDUCATION

If a Latino student successfully negotiates the various challenges discussed above (segregation, underfunded schools, a hostile curriculum, and so on) and graduates from high school, he or she may—sometimes in the face of a skeptical school counselor's advice—aspire to attend a four-year college or university. This chapter considers two higher education issues affecting Latino/a students—race-conscious admissions and the small number of Latino/a faculty. Issues not covered here include: the fate of ethnic studies departments; the attack on minority dorms, organizations, and theme houses; and hate speech on campus. The latter issue is covered in Part Six: Cultural Stereotypes and Hate Speech. Nor do we cover the "Dream Act," which in various incarnations aims to ease the status of long-term U.S. residents who entered the U.S. as children, including making them eligible for in-state college tuition.

SECTION 1. LATINO/A STUDENTS AND FACULTY

As one might imagine from the above readings, the number of Latinos/as who obtain Ph.D.s or J.D.s is very small. The number of professors of Latino descent is even smaller. In the legal professoriate, for example, as recently as 1976, the number of Latinos or Latinas teaching at the nation's law schools could fit around a medium-sized seminar room table. See Michael A. Olivas, *The Education of Latino/a Lawyers: An Essay on Crop Cultivation*, 14 Chicano–Latino L. Rev. 117 (1994). As we write, over 30 years later, Latinos make up about 3.7 percent of fulltime, tenure-track law professors—Mexican Americans, about one-fourth of that figure—at a time when the group constitutes over 14 percent of the United States population. The representation of Latinos and Latinas in other fields, with the exception of sociology, ethnic and Latino/a studies, and education, is equally small. Latinos make up about two percent of the nation's lawyers and judges.

In law, the growth, however slow and rocky, of the number of Latino/a lawyers has owed much to the efforts of Michael Olivas, of the University of Houston law school, who in the mid-nineties began a campaign to shame leading law schools into admitting more Latino students and hiring more Latino/a professors. Consider the following excerpt:

Michael A. Olivas
The Education of Latino/a Lawyers: An Essay on Crop Cultivation
14 Chicano–Latino L. Rev. 117 (1994)

I am regularly asked why Latinos do not fare better in school and society, usually by well-meaning colleagues who are genuinely troubled by the problem. Having spent eight years in the Catholic seminary studying for the priesthood, I tend to be an optimist and put the best gloss on any problem. So, for all the years I have been writing about the education of Latinos, I have always taken the high road; I have variously relied upon the reservoir of goodwill in the majority, counted upon colleagues to follow their own institutional self-interest in seeking and graduating Hispanic students, and encouraged need-based aid programs because in any such program, Latinos, who constitute one of the most impoverished communities, will more likely participate. I have delivered dozens of lectures, usually during Hispanic Awareness Weeks or Cinco de Mayo celebrations, exhorting my people to do well and encouraging institutional leaders to help my people.

But, like Reverend Leon Sullivan, who finally gave up on white South Africans, I have come to believe, reluctantly, that the majority of individuals in higher education and legal education do not think a problem exists, do not act as if a problem exists, or do not care about minority achievement. I say this knowing how sharply critical and pessimistic this will seem to many readers. However, I have come to believe that Anglo racism lies at the heart of the problem. Even the self-help I have urged and the patronage of a small number of majority colleagues cannot resolve the clear and long-standing legacy of historical racism toward Latino populations in the United States. For this proposition I could cite historical evidence, from the annexation of the southwestern United States, the colonization of Puerto Rico, the Bracero Program and "Operation Wetback" to the English-only movement and longstanding immigration practices. I could also cite more subtle practices, such as the heightened reliance on standardized testing and the indifference of elected officials to Hispanic communities. While the laundry list could continue, it advances no purpose. Instead, I choose one issue on which to focus my point: the need for more Latino lawyers and professors, especially law professors. I believe that this need for an increased Latino professoriate is the single most important key to any hope for increasing Latino educational access. * * * [T]hings have improved for Latinos, even to the point that a white backlash has began to surface. However, in several key respects, progress has stalled and educational data paint a starker portrait than would have been expected.

The Condition of Latino Education

At all levels, Latino students lag behind their Anglo and other minority peers. Hispanic students, including virtually every subgroup, do poorly in grade school, middle school, and high school, particularly in the transitions from one level to the other. Despite the increasing size of Hispanic populations, the key indicator of high school completion has worsened: high school graduation rates for Hispanics have dropped from 62.9% in 1985 to 54.5% in 1990. Comparable white rates were 83.6% in 1985 and 82.5% in 1990, and African–American rates were 75.6% and 77% in the same period. Even with large GED and adult basic education enrollments, Hispanic educational achievement data are discouraging. As Table 1 indicates, only 44% of Mexican Americans, 56% of Puerto Ricans, and 64% of Cubans had completed four years of high school. Figures for whites show 80% have completed at least four years of high school. The corollary data are even more striking: while virtually no adult Anglo (1.7%) has less than five years of schooling, 16% of adult Mexican Americans and 10% of adult Puerto Ricans do not even reach this minimal level.

These bleak data take their predictable toll on the Latino college-bound population. In 1990, 29.1% of Latino high school graduates went to college, an increase over the 1985 level of 26.1%. However, 39.4% of white graduates attended college, up from 34.4% in 1985. Also, Black graduate figures improved from 26.1% to 33% in the same time period. Naturally, these attendance figures depend on high school completion as a denominator, and thus the increased attendance rates show an improvement, but only for the shrinking percentage of high school graduates.

Although Latino college enrollments in the fifty states and Washington D.C. increased from 417,000 to 680,000 in the years between 1978–1988 and to 758,200 by 1990, their percentage of the total only increased from 3.7 to 5.2, and to 5.5 in 1990. Thus, the totals increased substantially, but as part of an ever-increasing number of students overall, totalling 13.7 million in 1990. In addition, Hispanics are disproportionately enrolled in two-year colleges, with 56% of all their enrollments in this sector compared with 38% for all students. These students are also extraordinarily concentrated in a small number of colleges.

TABLE 1. EDUCATIONAL ATTAINMENT BY HISPANIC GROUP
MEMBERSHIP OF PERSONS 25 YEARS AND OLDER,
1980–1990

	% Completed Less Than 5 Years of School			% Completed 4 Years or More of High School			% Completed 4 Years or More of College		
	1980	1985	1990	1980	1985	1990	1980	1985	1990
Hispanic Group									
Mex. American	20.1	17.1	15.5	38.1	41.9	44.1	4.9	5.5	5.4
Puerto Rican	14.1	12.8	9.7	45.9	46.3	55.5	5.6	7.0	9.7
Cuban	7.3	7.4	5.8	34.6	51.1	63.5	12.2	13.7	20.2
Whites	3.2	2.7	1.7	69.6	73.9	79.6	17.4	22.4	22.2

Hispanic Association of Colleges and Universities (HACU) data show that 115 of 3300 institutions in the U.S. enroll almost half the Hispanic students in the country. These 81 Hispanic-serving institutions, all of which have at least 25% Latino enrollments, include fifty two-year colleges and 31 four-year institutions.

In graduate education, Latinos experienced an actual numerical decline of 15.2% between 1986 and 1988, dropping from 46,000 graduate students to 39,000. No other group, Anglo or minority, experienced declining enrollments during this time. Lest observers think these students went on to professional schools, Hispanic professional school enrollments increased only from 2% in 1980 to 3.5% in 1988; in actual enrollments, the increase was from 5,000 to 9,000, with no increase from 1986 to 1988. Graduate Management Admissions Test (GMAT) data show that only 1.1% of all GMAT takers in 1988–89 were Chicano and only 0.7% were Puerto Rican.

Latinos certainly are not flocking to law school, the subject of inquiry here. Although 1990–91 data show a promising one-time leap for Mexican Americans and Puerto Ricans in the United States over the previous year, fewer Mexican Americans were enrolled in law school in 1989–90 than in 1981–82. Also, there was only a slight increase for Puerto Ricans; 450 law students enrolled in 1983–84 and increased to 483 in 1989–90. At present, 2582 Cubans and other Latinos are enrolled in law school, more than Mexican Americans and Puerto Ricans combined, even though the latter two groups comprise over 85% of the U.S. Latino population. As with their undergraduate counterparts, Latino law students are extraordinarily concentrated in a small number of institutions: Miami enrolls over 200 students, Texas enrolls over 170, and UCLA, Texas Southern, Houston, and Georgetown enroll over 100 each. The University of New Mexico, St. Mary's, St. Thomas and Texas Southern University have the greatest concentrations of Latino law students.

* * *

From Law School Admissions Test (LSAT) data, it is clear why Latino law school enrollments are flat or declining. In 1990, only 1.1% of all LSAT takers were Mexican American, 1.1% were Puerto Rican, and 2.5% were "other" Hispanics, predominantly Cubans. Only nine more Chicanos took the LSAT than did Puerto Ricans. For Chicanos, 71% of test takers applied to a law school; 41% were admitted and 88% of those admitted enrolled in 1991. Eighty-three percent of Puerto Ricans applied, 41% were admitted, and 58% enrolled. For "other" Hispanics, 74% applied, 55% were admitted, and 85% enrolled. For whites, who constituted 79% of the LSAT takers, 75% applied, 58% were admitted, and 81% enrolled. * * * These data should serve as an answer to affirmative action critics who suggest that minority students are given unwarranted breaks in the admissions process. White enrollments are at an all time high, and minority enrollments appear to have peaked.

In sum, from grade school to law school, Latinos lag in all academic achievement data. This is not due to immigration; social science research has carefully disaggregated data to reveal that even indigenous sub-groups do not fare well throughout the system. Clearly, much work remains to be done in this regard.

THE LATINO PROFESSORIATE

The extent of the problem is inadvertently revealed by Richard Chused's Society of American Law Teachers (SALT) survey, when he did not include Latino faculty due to the negligible number. When I began teaching law in 1982, there were twenty-two Latino law teachers in the fifty states and Washington D.C. in only a dozen different institutions. The first Mexican American law professor was Carlos Cadena, who taught at St. Mary's Law School from 1952 to 1954 and from 1961 to 1965. He was also co-counsel in *Hernandez v. Texas*, and is thought to be the first Chicano to have argued before the U.S. Supreme Court.

Similar inconsequential numbers exist in other fields of study, even fields where one would expect to find Latino scholars. According to the most recent figures from the Equal Employment Opportunity Commission (lamentably inadequate as they are), Hispanics constitute 1.5% of all faculty and just 1.1% of all tenured faculty. As paltry as these figures are, they mask an even more startling under-representation because these numbers include *all* fields of the professoriate and report all Latinos, even some who would be surprised to find themselves described on their colleges' books as minority faculty. I have found institutions that pad their figures shamelessly and that list retired, resigned, and temporary faculty as if they were active participants in institutional life. After teaching one special course as an adjunct on an extension campus for a university, I found myself listed seven years later in the institution's catalogue, and one law school lists an 80 year-old emeritus a decade later. Such examples are legion and overstate the true number of Latino faculty. Professors from Spain, Brazil, Portugal, and South America are routinely identified and misleadingly tallied as "minority" faculty. In several universities, Anglo women married to Latinos have also been counted. Association of American Law Schools (AALS) data do not disaggregate Puerto Rican law schools from totals, consequently misstating the number of Latino law faculty. While I do not intend to dissect racial enumeration practices, suffice it to say that institutions employ far too few Latino faculty, and employ far too many statistical tricks in their reporting, and both practices evidence bad faith.

Although Latinos in all fields are under-represented. I am going to use law faculty as an example, because I am most familiar with the practices in this area, and because law professors enjoy an influence in higher education beyond their small numbers. Moreover, the problems Latinos face in entering the teaching of law mirror those of minorities in the academy at large: exceedingly small numbers, arbitrarily employed hiring criteria, and sheer prejudice. With adjustments for different trade usages and academic customs, the case I now recite resembles that in most disciplines.

First, one starts with exceedingly small numbers: fewer than 100 of the over 5700 law teachers (less than 2%) in the approximately 175 accredited law schools in the fifty states and Washington D.C. are Latinos; of the 94, 51 are Mexican Americans, 17 are Puerto Ricans, 17 are Cuban, and the remainder are of "other" Latino origin.

Although law faculty positions are not as plentiful now as when law enrollments were soaring, a substantial number of vacancies are filled each year. In 1986–87, 570 law professors or 10% of the total law professoriate entered teaching. In the same year, only one new Latino entered law teaching, while one left for law practice and another was appointed to a state bench. Ground was lost. A recent study by the Society of Law Teachers (SALT) found that 34% of respondent law schools had no minority faculty, neither Latino nor black, while another 30% had only one. By the 1990s, things began to improve due to organized efforts of Latinos, and in 1991, a total of 22 new Latino law professors had been hired—equaling the total number of Latino law professors in 1981–82. However, even if one includes black and Puerto Rican law schools, only 7.5% of the law professoriate is minority.

These extraordinary data show the small extent to which minorities, especially Mexican Americans and Puerto Ricans, have entered the legal academy. Data gathered by the National Chicano Council on Higher Education (NCCHE) reveals that there are only six Chicano professors in higher education, seven physicists, twelve in chemistry, and proportionately greater numbers in sociology, psychology, Spanish, and bilingual education. By any measure, these numbers are appalling.

What about the supply side? In 1986–87, all minority law students constituted 10.6% of law enrollments; by 1992, the percentage had increased to 15%. Of these, 1512 or 1.3% were Chicanos, the same percentage of law enrollments as in 1975–76, when 1443 Mexican Americans were enrolled. To be sure, relatively few Latinos are in the law school "pipeline," but this can be misleading. First, the consumers (law schools) are also the producers; why is it that the schools do not see their responsibility to recruit and graduate more Latino lawyers? Second, even 1400 graduates a year produce a large pool of eligible Latinos over time that is certainly sufficient to produce more than the one Mexican-American lawyer hired to teach in 1986–87, or even the 22 hired in 1991, the high-water mark for Latino hiring.

Things have improved slightly, but not to the degree promised by the "Decade of the Hispanic." As previously noted, the numbers increased but only as a static, small percentage encased in an overall growth in law school enrollments. What went wrong? What can be done? Is law teaching the pantheon with law review membership and Supreme Court clerkships the essential requirements for entry, so that most Latinos are simply not qualified? Hardly. Considerable data have been gathered on new teachers, and their qualifications are indeed high. For example, of the 577 new law teachers hired in 1986–87, 38% had law review experience (compared with 48% of the total professoriate); 16% had been elected to Coif membership (the national honorary reserved for the top 10% of graduates); 10% held the L.L.M., an advanced graduate degree in law (compared with 23% of the total); and 14% had published a book. Interestingly, one-third had no legal experience before they entered teaching; 30% had not even passed a bar exam. It was not minority teachers who lowered the standards; the minorities hired statistically resemble their majority counterparts, and in the case of Latinos, outperform Anglo credentials.

By 1992 the credentials of Latino law professors exceeded those of all other faculty hired during the same period. Since 1986, with an average of over 300 new faculty hired each year, a consistent credential pattern has emerged: approximately 12% hold advanced degrees in law or other subjects, an average of one-third were on law review, over one-third reported no bar admission, approximately 90% had never published a book, and approximately one-third had no non-teaching law experience. However, Latinos in law teaching bested each of these "required credentials." Of the 94 Latinos in law teaching by 1992, 29% had advanced degrees, 47% were on law review, and 26% had clerked. The schools they attended included the most elite producer-schools, with Harvard, Berkeley, and Yale as the largest suppliers. In short, Latino faculty have exceeded the usual criteria for law teaching, constituting a statistical elite, and yet Latino faculty are employed at only 60 institutions of the 175 ABA/AALS law schools in the United States.

What is operating here? A powerful mythology permeates law hiring, as it does hiring in nearly all academic fields—that there are too few minority candidates for too few positions, and that they possess unexceptional credentials for the highly credentialed demand. I believe these data paint the opposite picture—that, for most schools, white candidates with good (but not sterling) credentials are routinely considered and hired, while the high-demand/low-supply mythology about minorities persists, in the face of a more-than-adequate supply.

Not only does this myth not square with available data, but the practices ignore the supply-side responsibility of law schools and the lack of marketplace alternatives for Latinos in other legal employment. After all, major firms and governments are no more accessible to Latinos than are law faculties. The explanation for the existence of these myths is available, however, it is an unpopular one because it entails racism, which permeates the academy as it does all of society.

That this is so should not surprise us, as higher education reflects our society, draws from it, and collaborates with it. After all, the legal road to *Brown v. Board of Education* was a series of higher education cases, suits in our lifetime that assaulted a segregated citadel. The poisonous residue of those practices remains. Many of today's senior faculty directly benefited from having it all to themselves, and by not having to compete—in school or the academic marketplace—with women or minorities. To a large extent, they still do not compete, particularly not with Latinos.

* * *

Michael Olivas devised a hard-hitting strategy aimed at exposing law schools that were delinquent in hiring Latino faculty. With the backing of the Hispanic National Bar Association, Olivas published an annual "dirty dozen" list of law schools that were either located in parts of the country with heavy Latino/a populations or that boasted of their status as "national" schools, yet whose faculties included no Latino or Latina. Many schools on his list hired Latino/a faculty within a few years, most of them insisting that his list had nothing to do with it. Olivas paid a price for his advocacy: A prominent scholar in two fields—higher education and immigration law—Olivas has never received an offer from a top school, even though many of his protégés and beneficiaries with less-stellar publishing records have moved right up the ladder.

Perhaps inspired by Olivas, a group of Latino/a faculty at the University of California–Berkeley (not the law school, but the university at large) published a "Latino Report Card" on their university's treatment of Latino/a faculty, grading them from A to F on various measures including hiring, mentoring, tenuring, and support of minority research. The university rated low grades on most of these measures. See Richard Delgado & Jean Stefancic, *California's Racial History and Constitutional Rationales for Race–Conscious Decision Making in Higher Education*, 47 UCLA L. Rev. 1521 (2000). See also Eugene E. Garcia & Julie Figueroa, *Access and Participation of Latinos in the University of California: A Current Macro and Micro Perspective*, 29 Soc. Justice 47 (2002).

As for Latino law students, in 2006–2007 the number of Mexican American J.D. students was 2,499; of Puerto Rican students 551; and "other Latinos" 5,514. The total J.D. enrollment for all students was 141,031. ABA Section on Legal Education. Legal Education Statistics, http://www.abanet.org/legaled/statistics/stats.html.

For further reflections from Olivas on the situation of minorities, especially Latinos, in higher education, see Michael A. Olivas, *Commentary: Reflections on Academic Merit Badges and Becoming an Eagle Scout*, 43 Hous. L. Rev. 81 (2006).

SECTION 2. LATINO/A STUDENTS AND RACE–CONSCIOUS ADMISSIONS: THE DEBATE OVER UNIVERSITY–LEVEL AFFIRMATIVE ACTION

If the road has been lonely for the Latino/a would-be academic, it has not been much easier for the 18–year old high school graduate seeking admission to a four-year school. Affirmative action, a program of race-conscious admissions that gives a boost based on one's ability, as a racial minority person, to contribute unique perspectives to the classroom, has been under constant fire since it arrived on the scene around 1970. Sometimes challenges emanate from conservative whites and their supporters, other times from another ethnic group concerned that gains for one group are coming at their expense. Sometimes they take the form of statewide initiatives banning the consideration of race. The following materials consider many of these issues.

RACE-CONSCIOUS ADMISSIONS

University-level affirmative action in admissions began in the late 1960s and early 1970s as liberal university administrators realized that the first wave of post-*Brown v. Board of Education* schoolchildren of color would soon be arriving at their institutions. Their student bodies were mostly white, and the new crop of Latino/a and black college applicants, although educated in integrated schools, in most cases lacked the standard criteria—high GPA and SAT scores—that university admissions officers looked for. Earlier, President Lyndon Baines Johnson had instituted affirmative action in federal hiring. Universities began applying some of the lessons learned in the job setting to their own admissions processes, relaxing their numerical requirements for minority candidates who demonstrated a strong intellect, an academic orientation, and community leadership.

These plans soon came under attack. In Regents of University of California v. Bakke, 438 U.S. 265 (1978), a white applicant to the University of California–Davis Medical School sued when the university rejected his application. Pointing out that his qualifications were higher than those of some of the black students who had won admission pursuant to a special admissions program that set aside a quota of seats for blacks (16 out of 100 in the entering class), he charged that his rejection violated constitutional norms.

Announcing the opinion of the Court, Justice Powell struck down the program on the ground that race operated as the determinative factor regarding the 16 set-aside seats, thus depriving whites of a chance to compete for each of the 100 openings in the first-year class. Powell nevertheless ruled that race could serve as a legitimate factor in university admissions so long as it was just one factor of many and the institution did not set aside slots exclusively for minorities.

Powell's ruling that racial diversity, properly used, could play a part in university admissions came increasingly into question as cases in other settings, such as Adarand Constructors v. Pena, 515 U.S. 200 (1995), City of Richmond v. J.A. Croson Co., 488 U.S. 469 (1989), and Podberesky v. Kirwan, 38 F.3d 147 (4th Cir. 1994), cast doubt on its vitality.

The following case is an early challenge to the Powell opinion and a possible harbinger of things to come:

Hopwood v. Texas
78 F.3d 932 (5th Cir. 1996),
cert. denied, 518 U.S. 1033 (1996)

JERRY E. SMITH, CIRCUIT JUDGE:

With the best of intentions, in order to increase the enrollment of certain favored classes of minority students, the University of Texas School of Law (the law school) discriminates in favor of those applicants by giving substantial racial preferences in its admissions program. The beneficiaries of this system are blacks and Mexican Americans, to the detriment of whites and non-preferred minorities. The question we decide today * * * is whether the Fourteenth Amendment permits the school to discriminate in this way.

We hold that it does not. The law school has presented no compelling justification, under the Fourteenth Amendment or Supreme Court precedent, that allows it to continue to elevate some races over others, even for the wholesome purpose of correcting perceived racial imbalance in the student body. "Racial preferences appear to 'even the score' . . . only if one embraces the proposition that our society is appropriately viewed as divided into races, making it right that an injustice rendered in the past to a black man should be compensated for by discriminating against a white." City of Richmond v. J.A. Croson Co., 488 U.S. 469, 528 (1989) (Scalia, J., concurring in the judgment).

* * * [W]e reverse and remand, concluding that the law school may not use race as a factor in law school admissions. * * *

I.

A.

The University of Texas School of Law is one of the nation's leading law schools, consistently ranking in the top twenty. Accordingly, admission to the law school is fiercely competitive, with over 4,000 applicants a year competing to be among the approximately 900 offered admission to achieve an entering class of about 500 students. Many of these applicants have some of the highest grades and test scores in the country.

Numbers are therefore paramount for admission. In the early 1990s, the law school largely based its initial admissions decisions upon an applicant's so-called Texas Index (TI) number, a composite of undergraduate grade point average (GPA) and Law School [Admissions] Test (LSAT) score. The law school used this number as a matter of administrative convenience in order to rank candidates and to predict, roughly, one's probability of success in law school. * * *

Of course, the law school did not rely upon numbers alone. The admissions office necessarily exercised judgment in interpreting the individual scores of applicants, taking into consideration factors such as the strength of a student's undergraduate education, the difficulty of his major, and significant trends in his own grades and the undergraduate grades at his respective college (such as grade inflation). Admissions personnel also considered what qualities each applicant might bring to his law school class. Thus, the law school could consider an applicant's background, life experiences, and outlook. Not surprisingly, these hard-to-quantify factors were especially significant for marginal candidates.

* * * For the class entering in 1992—the admissions group at issue in this case—the law school placed the typical applicant in one of three categories according to his TI scores: "presumptive admit," "presumptive deny," or a middle "discretionary zone." An applicant's TI category determined how extensive a review his application would receive. * * *

Applications in the middle range were subjected to the most extensive scrutiny. For all applicants other than blacks and Mexican Americans, the files were bundled into stacks of thirty, which were given to admissions subcommittees * * *. Each subcommittee member, in reviewing the thirty files, could cast a number of votes—typically from nine to eleven—among the thirty files. Subject to the chairman's veto, if a candidate received two or three votes, he received an offer; if he garnered one vote, he was put on the waiting list; those with no votes were denied admission.

Blacks and Mexican Americans were treated differently from other candidates, however. First, compared to whites and non-preferred minorities, the TI ranges that were used to place them into the three admissions categories were lowered to allow the law school to consider and admit more of them. In March 1992, for example, the presumptive TI admission score for resident whites and non-preferred minorities was 199. Mexican Americans and blacks needed a TI of only 189 to be presumptively admitted. The difference in the presumptive-deny ranges is even more striking. The presumptive denial score for "nonminorities" was 192; the same score for blacks and Mexican Americans was 179.

While these cold numbers may speak little to those unfamiliar with the pool of applicants, the results demonstrate that the difference in the two ranges was dramatic. According to the law school, 1992 resident white applicants had a mean GPA of 3.53 and an LSAT of 164. Mexican Americans scored 3.27 and 158; blacks scored 3.25 and 157. The category of "other minority" achieved a 3.56 and 160.

These disparate standards greatly affected a candidate's chance of admission. For example, by March 1992, because the presumptive denial score for whites was a TI of 192 or lower, and the presumptive admit TI for minorities was 189 or higher, a minority candidate with a TI of 189 or above almost certainly would be admitted, even though his score was considerably below the level at which a white candidate almost certainly would be rejected. Out of the pool of resident applicants who fell within this range (189–192 inclusive), 100% of blacks and 90% of Mexican Americans, but only 6% of whites, were offered admission.

The stated purpose of this lowering of standards was to meet an "aspiration" of admitting a class consisting of 10% Mexican Americans and 5% blacks, proportions roughly comparable to the percentages of those races graduating from Texas colleges. The law school found meeting these "goals" difficult, however, because of uncertain acceptance rates and the variable quality of the applicant pool. In 1992, for example, the entering class contained 41 blacks and 55 Mexican Americans, respectively 8% and 10.7% of the class.

In addition to maintaining separate presumptive TI levels for minorities and whites, the law school ran a segregated application evaluation process. Upon receiving an application form, the school color-coded it according to race. * * *

Finally, the law school maintained segregated waiting lists, dividing applicants by race and residence. Thus, even many of those minority applicants who were not admitted could be set aside in "minority-only" waiting lists. Such separate lists apparently helped the law school maintain a pool of potentially acceptable, but marginal, minority candidates.

B.

Cheryl Hopwood, Douglas Carvell, Kenneth Elliott, and David Rogers (the "plaintiffs") applied for admission to the 1992 entering law school class. All four were white residents of Texas and were rejected.

The plaintiffs were considered as discretionary zone candidates. Hopwood, with a GPA of 3.8 and an LSAT of 39 (equivalent to a three-digit LSAT of 160), had a TI of 199, a score barely within the presumptive-admit category for resident whites, which was 199 and up. She was dropped into the discretionary zone for resident whites (193 to 198), however, because Johanson [Professor Johanson, chair of the law school admissions committee] decided her educational background overstated the strength of her GPA. Carvell, Elliott, and Rogers had TI's of 197, at the top end of that discretionary zone. Their applications were reviewed by admissions subcommittees, and each received one or no vote.

    * * *

III.

The central purpose of the Equal Protection Clause "is to prevent the States from purposefully discriminating between individuals on the basis of race." It seeks ultimately to render the issue of race irrelevant in governmental decisionmaking.

Accordingly, discrimination based upon race is highly suspect. "Distinctions between citizens solely because of their ancestry are by their very nature odious to a free people whose institutions are founded upon the doctrine of equality," and "racial discriminations are in most circumstances irrelevant and therefore prohibited. . . . " Hirabayashi v. United States, 320 U.S. 81, 100 (1943). Hence, "[p]referring members of any one group for no reason other than race or ethnic origin is discrimination for its own sake. This the Constitution forbids." Regents of Univ. of Cal. v. Bakke, 438 U.S. 265, 307 (1978) (opinion of Powell, J.); see also Loving

v. Virginia, 388 U.S. 1, 11 (1967); Brown v. Board of Educ., 347 U.S. 483, 493–94 (1954). These equal protection maxims apply to all races. Adarand Constructors v. Pena, 515 U.S. 200 (1995).

In order to preserve these principles, the Supreme Court recently has required that any governmental action that expressly distinguishes between persons on the basis of race be held to the most exacting scrutiny. Furthermore, there is now absolutely no doubt that courts are to employ strict scrutiny when evaluating all racial classifications, including those characterized by their proponents as "benign" or "remedial."

Strict scrutiny is necessary because the mere labeling of a classification by the government as "benign" or "remedial" is meaningless....

Under the strict scrutiny analysis, we ask two questions: (1) Does the racial classification serve a compelling government interest, and (2) Is it narrowly tailored to the achievement of that goal? As the *Adarand* Court emphasized, strict scrutiny ensures that "courts will consistently give racial classifications . . . detailed examination both as to ends and as to means."

Finally, when evaluating the proffered governmental interest for the specific racial classification, to decide whether the program in question narrowly achieves that interest, we must recognize that "the rights created by . . . the Fourteenth Amendment are, by its terms, guaranteed to the individual. The rights established are personal rights." Shelley v. Kraemer, 334 U.S. 1, 22 (1948). Thus, the Court consistently has rejected arguments conferring benefits on a person based solely upon his membership in a specific class of persons.

With these general principles of equal protection in mind, we turn to the specific issue of whether the law school's consideration of race as a factor in admissions violates the Equal Protection Clause. The district court found both a compelling remedial and a non-remedial justification for the practice.

First, the court approved of the non-remedial goal of having a diverse student body, reasoning that "obtaining the educational benefits that flow from a racially and ethnically diverse student body remains a sufficiently compelling interest to support the use of racial classifications." Second, the court determined that the use of racial classifications could be justified as a remedy for the "present effects at the law school of past discrimination in both the University of Texas system and the Texas educational system as a whole."

A.

1.

Justice Powell's separate opinion in *Bakke* provided the original impetus for recognizing diversity as a compelling state interest in higher education. In that case, Allan Bakke, a white male, was denied admission to the Medical School of the University of California at Davis, a state-run institution. Claiming that the State had discriminated against him impermissibly because it operated two separate admissions programs for the medical school, he brought suit under the state constitution, Title VI, and the Equal Protection Clause.

Under the medical school's admissions system, the white applicants, who comprised the majority of the prospective students, applied through the general admissions program. A special admissions program was reserved for members of "minority groups" or groups designated as "economically and/or educationally disadvantaged." The university set aside sixteen of the one hundred positions in the entering class for candidates from the special program.

* * *

While Justice Powell found the program unconstitutional under the Equal Protection Clause and affirmed Bakke's admission, Justice Stevens declined to reach the constitutional issue and upheld Bakke's admission under Title VI. Justice Powell also concluded that the California Supreme Court's proscription of the consideration of race in admissions could not be sustained. This became the judgment of the Court, as the four-Justice opinion by Justice Brennan opined that racial classifications designed to serve remedial purposes should receive only intermediate scrutiny. These Justices would have upheld the admissions program under this intermediate scrutiny, as it served the substantial and benign purpose of remedying past societal discrimination.

Hence, Justice Powell's opinion has appeared to represent the "swing vote," and though, in significant part, it was joined by no other Justice, it has played a prominent role in subsequent debates concerning the impact of *Bakke*. * * *

* * *

We agree with the plaintiffs that any consideration of race or ethnicity by the law school for the purpose of achieving a diverse student body is not a compelling interest under the Fourteenth Amendment. Justice Powell's argument in *Bakke* garnered only his own vote and has never represented the view of a majority of the Court in *Bakke* or any other case. Moreover, subsequent Supreme Court decisions regarding education state that non-remedial state interests will never justify racial classifications. Finally, the classification of persons on the basis of race for the purpose of diversity frustrates, rather than facilitates, the goals of equal protection.

Justice Powell's view in *Bakke* is not binding precedent on this issue. While he announced the judgment, no other Justice joined in that part of the opinion discussing the diversity rationale. In *Bakke*, the word "diversity" is mentioned nowhere except in Justice Powell's single-Justice opinion. In fact, the four-Justice opinion, which would have upheld the special admissions program under intermediate scrutiny, implicitly rejected Justice Powell's position. * * *

Indeed, recent Supreme Court precedent shows that the diversity interest will not satisfy strict scrutiny. Foremost, the Court appears to have decided that there is essentially only one compelling state interest to justify racial classifications: remedying past wrongs. In *Croson*, 488 U.S. at 493 (plurality opinion), the Court flatly stated that "[u]nless [racial classifications] are strictly reserved for remedial settings, they may in fact promote notions of racial inferiority and lead to a politics of racial hostility."

* * *

Within the general principles of the Fourteenth Amendment, the use of race in admissions for diversity in higher education contradicts, rather than furthers, the aims of equal protection. Diversity fosters, rather than minimizes, the use of race. It treats minorities as a group, rather than as individuals. It may further remedial purposes but, just as likely, may promote improper racial stereotypes, thus fueling racial hostility.

The use of race, in and of itself, to choose students simply achieves a student body that looks different. Such a criterion is no more rational on its own terms than would be choices based upon the physical size or blood type of applicants. Thus, the Supreme Court has long held that governmental actors cannot justify their decisions solely because of race.

* * *

* * *

While the use of race *per se* is proscribed, state-supported schools may reasonably consider a host of factors—some of which may have some correlation with race—in making admissions decisions. The federal courts have no warrant to intrude on those executive and legislative judgments unless the distinctions intrude on specific provisions of federal law or the Constitution.

A university may properly favor one applicant over another because of his ability to play the cello, make a downfield tackle, or understand chaos theory. An admissions process may also consider an applicant's home state or relationship to school alumni. Law schools specifically may look at things such as unusual or substantial extracurricular activities in college, which may be atypical factors affecting undergraduate grades. Schools may even consider factors such as whether an applicant's parents attended college or the applicant's economic and social background.

For this reason, race often is said to be justified in the diversity context, not on its own terms, but as a proxy for other characteristics that institutions of higher education value but that do not raise similar constitutional concerns. Unfortunately, this approach simply replicates the very harm that the Fourteenth Amendment was designed to eliminate.

The assumption is that a certain individual possesses characteristics by virtue of being a member of a certain racial group. This assumption, however, does not withstand scrutiny. "[T]he use of a racial characteristic to establish a presumption that the individual also possesses other, and socially relevant, characteristics, exemplifies, encourages, and legitimizes the mode of thought and behavior that underlies most prejudice and bigotry in modern America." Richard A. Posner, *The* DeFunis *Case and the Constitutionality of Preferential Treatment of Racial Minorities*, 1974 Sup. Ct. Rev. 12 (1974).

To believe that a person's race controls his point of view is to stereotype him. The Supreme Court, however, "has remarked a number of times, in slightly different contexts, that it is incorrect and legally inappropriate to impute to women and minorities 'a different attitude about such issues as the federal budget, school prayer, voting, and foreign relations.' " Michael S. Paulsen, *Reverse Discrimination and Law School Faculty Hiring: The Undiscovered Opinion*, 71 Tex. L. Rev. 993, 1000 (1993) (quoting Roberts v. United States Jaycees, 468 U.S. 609, 627–28 (1984)).* "Social scientists may debate how peoples' thoughts and behavior reflect their background, but the Constitution provides that the government may not allocate benefits or burdens among individuals based on the assumption that race or ethnicity determines how they act or think." *Metro Broadcasting*, 497 U.S. at 602 (O'Connor, J., dissenting).

Instead, individuals, with their own conceptions of life, further diversity of viewpoint. Plaintiff Hopwood is a fair example of an applicant with a unique background. She is the now-thirty-two-year-old wife of a member of the Armed Forces stationed in San Antonio and, more significantly, is raising a severely handicapped child. Her circumstance would bring a different perspective to the law school. The school might consider this an advantage to her in the application process, or it could decide that her family situation would be too much of a burden on her academic performance.

We do not opine on which way the law school should weigh Hopwood's qualifications; we only observe that "diversity" can take many forms. To foster such diversity, state universities and law schools and other governmental entities must scrutinize applicants individually, rather than resorting to the dangerous proxy of race.

* * *

In sum, the use of race to achieve a diverse student body, whether as a proxy for permissible characteristics, simply cannot be a state interest compelling enough to meet the steep standard of strict scrutiny. These latter factors may, in fact, turn out to be substantially correlated with race, but the key is that race itself not be taken into account. Thus, that portion of the district court's opinion upholding the diversity rationale is reversibly flawed.

B.

We now turn to the district court's determination that "the remedial purpose of the law school's affirmative action program is a compelling

---

* [Eds. But see Richard Delgado, *Five Months Later (The Trial Court Opinion)*, 71 Tex. L. Rev. 1011 (1993) (replying to Paulsen).]

government objective." The plaintiffs argue that the court erred by finding that the law school could employ racial criteria to remedy the present effects of past discrimination in Texas's primary and secondary schools. The plaintiffs contend that the proper unit for analysis is the law school, and the state has shown no recognizable present effects of the law school's past discrimination. The law school, in response, notes Texas's well-documented history of discrimination in education and argues that its effects continue today at the law school, both in the level of educational attainment of the average minority applicant and in the school's reputation.

In contrast to its approach to the diversity rationale, a majority of the Supreme Court has held that a state actor may racially classify where it has a "strong basis in the evidence for its conclusion that remedial action was necessary." *Croson*, 488 U.S. at 500 (quoting *Wygant*, 476 U.S. at 277 (plurality opinion)). Generally, "[i]n order to justify an affirmative action program, the State must show there are 'present effects of past discrimination.'"

Because a state does not have a compelling state interest in remedying the present effects of past societal discrimination, however, we must examine the district court's legal determination that the relevant governmental entity is the system of education within the state as a whole. Moreover, we also must review the court's identification of what types of present effects of past discrimination, if proven, would be sufficient under strict scrutiny review.

1.

The Supreme Court has "insisted upon some showing of prior discrimination by the governmental unit involved before allowing limited use of racial classifications in order to remedy such discrimination." *Wygant*, 476 U.S. at 274 (plurality opinion of Powell, J.). In *Wygant*, the Court analyzed a collective bargaining agreement between a school board and a teacher's union that allowed the board to give minorities preferential treatment in the event of layoffs. A plurality rejected the theory that such a program was justified because it provided minority role models. Such a claim was based upon remedying "societal discrimination," a rationale the Court consistently has rejected as a basis for affirmative action. Accordingly, the state's use of remedial racial classifications is limited to the harm caused by a specific state actor.

The *Croson* Court further discussed how to identify the relevant past discriminator. Writing for the Court, Justice O'Connor struck down a minority business set-aside program implemented by the City of Richmond and justified on remedial grounds. While the district court opined that sufficient evidence had been found by the city to believe that such a program was necessary to remedy the present effects of past discrimination in the construction industry, the Court held:

> Like the "role model" theory employed in *Wygant*, a generalized assertion that there had been past discrimination in an entire

industry provides no guidance for a legislative body to determine the precise scope of the injury it seeks to remedy. It "has no logical stopping point." "Relief" for such an ill-defined wrong could extend until the percentage of public contracts awarded to [minority businesses] in Richmond mirrored the percentage of minorities in the population as a whole.

The Court refused to accept indicia of past discrimination in anything but "the Richmond construction industry."

In addition, in a passage of particular significance to the instant case, the Court analogized the employment contractor situation to that of higher education and noted that "[l]ike claims that discrimination in primary and secondary schooling justifies a rigid racial preference in medical school admissions, an amorphous claim that there has been past discrimination in a particular industry cannot justify the use of an unyielding racial quota." Such claims were based upon "sheer speculation" about how many minorities would be in the contracting business absent past discrimination.

Applying the teachings of *Croson* and *Wygant*, we conclude that the district court erred in expanding the remedial justification to reach all public education within the State of Texas. The Supreme Court repeatedly has warned that the use of racial remedies must be carefully limited, and a remedy reaching all education within a state addresses a putative injury that is vague and amorphous. It has "no logical stopping point."

The district court's holding employs no viable limiting principle. If a state can "remedy" the present effects of past discrimination in its primary and secondary schools, it also would be allowed to award broad-based preferences in hiring, government contracts, licensing, and any other state activity that in some way is affected by the educational attainment of the applicants. This very argument was made in *Croson* and rejected.

* * *

Strict scrutiny is meant to ensure that the purpose of a racial preference is remedial. Yet when one state actor begins to justify racial preferences based upon the actions of other state agencies, the remedial actor's competence to determine the existence and scope of the harm— and the appropriate reach of the remedy—is called into question. The school desegregation cases, for example, concentrate on school districts— singular government units—and the use of interdistrict remedies is strictly limited. See *Missouri v. Jenkins*; Milliken v. Bradley, 418 U.S. 717, 745 (1974) ("[W]ithout an interdistrict violation and interdistrict effect, there is no constitutional wrong calling for an interdistrict remedy."). Thus, one justification for limiting the remedial powers of a state actor is that the specific agency involved is best able to measure the harm of its past discrimination.

Here, however, the law school has no comparative advantage in measuring the present effects of discrimination in primary and secondary schools in Texas. Such a task becomes even more improbable where, as here, benefits are conferred on students who attended out-of-state or private schools for such education. Such boundless "remedies" raise a constitutional concern beyond mere competence. In this situation, an inference is raised that the program was the result of racial social engineering rather a desire to implement a remedy.

* * *

Even if, *arguendo*, the state is the proper government unit to scrutinize, the law school's admissions program would not withstand our review. For the admissions scheme to pass constitutional muster, the State of Texas, through its legislature, would have to find that past segregation has present effects; it would have to determine the magnitude of those present effects; and it would need to limit carefully the "plus" given to applicants to remedy that harm. A broad program that sweeps in all minorities with a remedy that is in no way related to past harms cannot survive constitutional scrutiny. Obviously, none of those predicates has been satisfied here.

* * *

In sum, for purposes of determining whether the law school's admissions system properly can act as a remedy for the present effects of past discrimination, we must identify the law school as the relevant alleged past discriminator. The fact that the law school ultimately may be subject to the directives of others, such as the board of regents, the university president, or the legislature, does not change the fact that the relevant putative discriminator in this case is still the law school. In order for any of these entities to direct a racial preference program at the law school, it must be because of past wrongs at that school.

2.

Next, the relevant governmental discriminator must prove that there are present effects of past discrimination of the type that justify the racial classifications at issue: * * *

* * *

* * * [K]nowledge of historical fact simply cannot justify current racial classifications. Even if, as the defendants argue, the law school may have a bad reputation in the minority community, "[t]he case against race-based preferences does not rest on the sterile assumption that American society is untouched or unaffected by the tragic oppression of its past." "Rather, it is the very enormity of that tragedy that lends resolve to the desire to never repeat it, and find a legal order in which distinctions based on race shall have no place." * * *

The *Podberesky* court rejected the hostile-environment claims by observing that the "effects"—that is, racial tensions—were the result of present societal discrimination. There was simply no showing of action by the university that contributed to any racial tension. Similarly, one cannot conclude that the law school's past discrimination has created any current hostile environment for minorities. While the school once did practice *de jure* discrimination in denying admission to blacks, the Court in *Sweatt v. Painter* struck down the law school's program. Any other discrimination by the law school ended in the 1960s.

By the late 1960s, the school had implemented its first program designed to recruit minorities, and it now engages in an extensive minority recruiting program that includes a significant amount of scholarship money. The vast majority of the faculty, staff, and students at the law school had absolutely nothing to do with any discrimination that the law school practiced in the past.

In such a case, one cannot conclude that a hostile environment is the present effect of past discrimination. Any racial tension at the law school is most certainly the result of present societal discrimination and, if anything, is contributed to, rather than alleviated by, the overt and prevalent consideration of race in admissions.

Even if the law school's alleged current lingering reputation in the minority community—and the perception that the school is a hostile environment for minorities—were considered to be the present effects of past discrimination, rather than the result of societal discrimination, they could not constitute compelling state interests justifying the use of racial classifications in admissions. A bad reputation within the minority community is alleviated not by the consideration of race in admissions, but by school action designed directly to enhance its reputation in that community.

Minority students who are aided by the law school's racial preferences have already made the decision to apply, despite the reputation. And, while prior knowledge that they will get a "plus" might make potential minorities more likely to apply, such an inducement does nothing, *per se*, to change any hostile environment. As we have noted, racial preferences, if anything, can compound the problem of a hostile environment.

The law school wisely concentrates only on the second effect the district court identified: underrepresentation of minorities because of past discrimination. The law school argues that we should consider the prior discrimination by the State of Texas and its educational system rather than of the law school. The school contends that this prior discrimination by the state had a direct effect on the educational attainment of the pool of minority applicants and that the discriminatory admissions program was implemented partially to discharge the school's duty of eliminating the vestiges of past segregation.

As we have noted, the district court accepted the law school's argument that past discrimination on the part of the Texas school system (including primary and secondary schools), reaching back perhaps as far as the education of the parents of today's students, justifies the current use of racial classifications. No one disputes that Texas has a history of racial discrimination in education. We have already discussed, however, that the *Croson* Court unequivocally restricted the proper scope of the remedial interest to the state actor that had previously discriminated. The district court squarely found that "[i]n recent history, there is no evidence of overt officially sanctioned discrimination at the University of Texas." As a result, past discrimination in education, other than at the law school, cannot justify the present consideration of race in law school admissions.

* * *

VI.

In summary, we hold that the University of Texas School of Law may not use race as a factor in deciding which applicants to admit in order to achieve a diverse student body, to combat the perceived effects of a hostile environment at the law school, to alleviate the law school's poor reputation in the minority community, or to eliminate any present effects of past discrimination by actors other than the law school. Because the law school has proffered these justifications for its use of race in admissions, the plaintiffs have satisfied their burden of showing that they were scrutinized under an unconstitutional admissions system. The plaintiffs are entitled to reapply under an admissions system that invokes none of these serious constitutional infirmities. We also direct the district court to reconsider the question of damages, and we conclude that the proposed intervenors properly were denied intervention.

Notes and Questions

1. What is the nature of a university's interest in diversity in *Bakke*? According to the *Hopwood* court why is diversity in a public law school not a compelling interest?

2. Why would universities value an educated minority elite? Postcolonial theory calls attention to the way in which colonial societies cultivated educated, English-speaking natives and gave them jobs in the civil service in return for their loyalty. Might white-dominated universities harbor similar ambitions, if only unconsciously? If so, affirmative action would advance white interests, not minority ones.

3. *Hopwood* epitomizes the thinking behind a ferocious conservative effort to overturn campus affirmative action waged by right-wing think tanks and litigation centers and still under way. Until the following case (*Grutter v. Bollinger*), conservative lawyers pretty much had their way, pursuing a carefully orchestrated campaign to reverse affirmative action very much reminiscent of the decades-long effort by the NAACP that led up to *Brown*, although, of course, in reverse. See, e.g., Jean Stefancic & Richard Delgado, *No Mercy: How Conservative Think Tanks and Foundations Changed America's Social Agenda* (1996).

4. In the wake of *Hopwood*, the Texas legislature, spurred by Latino legislators, instituted the "Ten Percent Plan" that aimed to counter the

harmful effects of that decision on diversity in the state's colleges and universities. The plan made every graduate of a public high school in Texas eligible to attend the University of Texas, regardless of his or her SAT score. See Marta Tienda & Sunny Niu, *Texas' 10–Percent Plan: The Truth Behind the Numbers*, Chron. Higher Ed., Jan. 23, 2004, at B10. The plan stemmed to some extent the drastic loss of minorities in Texas colleges and universities, although critics charged it was weakening the state's commitment to academic merit. California adopted its own four percent plan, with little better results.

Grutter v. Bollinger
539 U.S. 306 (2003)

[In the companion case of Gratz v. Bollinger, 539 U.S. 244 (2003), the Court struck down the University of Michigan's undergraduate admissions policy. The university's policy automatically attributed 20 points, one-fifth of the total points needed for admission, to "underrepresented minority" candidates. The Court held that this point attribution violated the equal protection clause and that this use of race by the university was "not narrowly tailored" to the goal of achieving educational diversity.]

JUSTICE O'CONNOR delivered the opinion of the Court.

This case requires us to decide whether the use of race as a factor in student admissions by the University of Michigan Law School (Law School) is unlawful.

The Law School ranks among the Nation's top law schools. It receives more than 3,500 applications each year for a class of around 350 students. Seeking to "admit a group of students who individually and collectively are among the most capable," the Law School looks for individuals with "substantial promise for success in law school" and "a strong likelihood of succeeding in the practice of law and contributing in diverse ways to the well-being of others." More broadly, the Law School seeks "a mix of students with varying backgrounds and experiences who will respect and learn from each other." In 1992, the dean of the Law School charged a faculty committee with crafting a written admissions policy to implement these goals. * * *

The hallmark of that policy is its focus on academic ability coupled with a flexible assessment of applicants' talents, experiences, and potential "to contribute to the learning of those around them." The policy requires admissions officials to evaluate each applicant based on all the information available in the file, including a personal statement, letters of recommendation, and an essay describing the ways in which the applicant will contribute to the life and diversity of the Law School. In reviewing an applicant's file, admissions officials must consider the applicant's undergraduate grade point average (GPA) and Law School Admissions Test (LSAT) score because they are important (if imperfect) predictors of academic success in law school. The policy stresses that "no applicant should be admitted unless we expect that applicant to do well enough to graduate with no serious academic problems."

The policy makes clear, however, that even the highest possible score does not guarantee admission to the Law School. Nor does a low score automatically disqualify an applicant. Rather, the policy requires admissions officials to look beyond grades and test scores to other criteria that are important to the Law School's educational objectives. So-called " 'soft' variables" such as "the enthusiasm of recommenders, the quality of the undergraduate institution, the quality of the applicant's essay, and the areas and difficulty of undergraduate course selection" are all brought to bear in assessing an "applicant's likely contributions to the intellectual and social life of the institution."

The policy aspires to "achieve that diversity which has the potential to enrich everyone's education and thus make a law school class stronger than the sum of its parts." The policy does not restrict the types of diversity contributions eligible for "substantial weight" in the admissions process, but instead recognizes "many possible bases for diversity admissions." The policy does, however, reaffirm the Law School's longstanding commitment to "one particular type of diversity," that is, "racial and ethnic diversity with special reference to the inclusion of students from groups which have been historically discriminated against, like African–Americans, Hispanics and Native Americans, who without this commitment might not be represented in our student body in meaningful numbers." By enrolling a " 'critical mass' of [underrepresented] minority students," the Law School seeks to "ensur[e] their ability to make unique contributions to the character of the Law School."

The policy does not define diversity "solely in terms of racial and ethnic status." Nor is the policy "insensitive to the competition among all students for admission to the [L]aw [S]chool." Rather, the policy seeks to guide admissions officers in "producing classes both diverse and academically outstanding, classes made up of students who promise to continue the tradition of outstanding contribution by Michigan Graduates to the legal profession."

Petitioner Barbara Grutter is a white Michigan resident who applied to the Law School in 1996 with a 3.8 grade point average and 161 LSAT score. The Law School initially placed petitioner on a waiting list, but subsequently rejected her application. In December 1997, petitioner filed suit * * * [alleging that the university] discriminated against her on the basis of race in violation of the Fourteenth Amendment; Title VI of the Civil Rights Act of 1964, 78 Stat. 252, 42 U.S.C. § 2000d; and Rev. Stat. § 1977, as amended, 42 U.S.C. § 1981.

Petitioner further alleged that her application was rejected because the Law School uses race as a "predominant" factor, giving applicants who belong to certain minority groups "a significantly greater chance of admission than students with similar credentials from disfavored racial groups." Petitioner also alleged that respondents "had no compelling interest to justify their use of race in the admissions process." * * *

   * * *

During the 15–day bench trial, the parties introduced extensive evidence concerning the Law School's use of race in the admissions process. Dennis Shields, Director of Admissions when petitioner applied to the Law School, testified that he did not direct his staff to admit a particular percentage or number of minority students, but rather to consider an applicant's race along with all other factors. Shields testified that at the height of the admissions season, he would frequently consult the so-called "daily reports" that kept track of the racial and ethnic composition of the class (along with other information such as residency status and gender). This was done, Shields testified, to ensure that a critical mass of underrepresented minority students would be reached so as to realize the educational benefits of a diverse student body. Shields stressed, however, that he did not seek to admit any particular number or percentage of underrepresented minority students.

Erica Munzel, who succeeded Shields as Director of Admissions, testified that " 'critical mass' " means " 'meaningful numbers' " or " 'meaningful representation,' " which she understood to mean a number that encourages underrepresented minority students to participate in the classroom and not feel isolated. * * * Munzel also asserted that she must consider the race of applicants because a critical mass of underrepresented minority students could not be enrolled if admissions decisions were based primarily on undergraduate GPAs and LSAT scores.

The current Dean of the Law School, Jeffrey Lehman * * * indicated that critical mass means numbers such that underrepresented minority students do not feel isolated or like spokespersons for their race. When asked about the extent to which race is considered in admissions, Lehman testified that it varies from one applicant to another. In some cases, according to Lehman's testimony, an applicant's race may play no role, while in others it may be a " 'determinative' " factor.

   * * *

Dr. Stephen Raudenbush, the Law School's expert, focused on the predicted effect of eliminating race as a factor in the Law School's admission process. In Dr. Raudenbush's view, a race-blind admissions system would have a " 'very dramatic,' " negative effect on underrepresented minority admissions. He testified that in 2000, 35 percent of underrepresented minority applicants were admitted. Dr. Raudenbush predicted that if race were not considered, only 10 percent of those applicants would have been admitted. Under this scenario, underrepresented minority students would have comprised 4 percent of the entering class in 2000 instead of the actual figure of 14.5 percent.

   * * *

We granted certiorari to resolve the disagreement among the Courts of Appeals on a question of national importance: Whether diversity is a compelling interest that can justify the narrowly tailored use of race in selecting applicants for admission to public universities. Compare Hopwood v. Texas, 78 F.3d 932 (CA5 1996) (Hopwood I) (holding that diversity is not a compelling state interest), with Smith v. University of Wash. Law School, 233 F.3d 1188 (CA9 2000) (holding that it is).

We last addressed the use of race in public higher education over 25 years ago. In the landmark *Bakke* case, we reviewed a racial set-aside program that reserved 16 out of 100 seats in a medical school class for members of certain minority groups. The decision produced six separate opinions, none of which commanded a majority of the Court. Four Justices would have upheld the program against all attack on the ground that the government can use race to "remedy disadvantages cast on minorities by past racial prejudice." (joint opinion of Brennan, White, Marshall, and Blackmun, JJ., concurring in judgment in part and dissenting in part). Four other Justices avoided the constitutional question altogether and struck down the program on statutory grounds. (opinion of Stevens, J., joined by Burger, C.J., and Stewart and Rehnquist, JJ., concurring in judgment in part and dissenting in part). Justice Powell provided a fifth vote not only for invalidating the set-aside program, but also for reversing the state court's injunction against any use of race whatsoever. The only holding for the Court in *Bakke* was that a "State has a substantial interest that legitimately may be served by a properly devised admissions program involving the competitive consideration of race and ethnic origin." * * *

Since this Court's splintered decision in *Bakke*, Justice Powell's opinion announcing the judgment of the Court has served as the touchstone for constitutional analysis of race-conscious admissions policies. Public and private universities across the Nation have modeled their own admissions programs on Justice Powell's views on permissible race-conscious policies. * * *

* * * [T]oday we endorse Justice Powell's view that student body diversity is a compelling state interest that can justify the use of race in university admissions.

The Equal Protection Clause provides that no State shall "deny to any person within its jurisdiction the equal protection of the laws." Because the Fourteenth Amendment "protect[s] *persons*, not *groups*," all "governmental action based on race—a *group* classification long recognized as in most circumstances irrelevant and therefore prohibited—should be subjected to detailed judicial inquiry to ensure that the *personal* right to equal protection of the laws has not been infringed." *Adarand Constructors, Inc. v. Peña* [supra]. * * *

We have held that all racial classifications imposed by government "must be analyzed by a reviewing court under strict scrutiny." This means that such classifications are constitutional only if they are narrowly tailored to further compelling governmental interests. * * *

* * * Although all governmental uses of race are subject to strict scrutiny, not all are invalidated by it. * * * When race-based action is necessary to further a compelling governmental interest, such action does not violate the constitutional guarantee of equal protection so long as the narrow-tailoring requirement is also satisfied. * * *

With these principles in mind, we turn to the question whether the Law School's use of race is justified by a compelling state interest. Before this Court, as they have throughout this litigation, respondents assert only one justification for their use of race in the admissions process: obtaining "the educational benefits that flow from a diverse student body." In other words, the Law School asks us to recognize, in the context of higher education, a compelling state interest in student body diversity.

The Law School's educational judgment that such diversity is essential to its educational mission is one to which we defer. The Law School's assessment that diversity will, in fact, yield educational benefits is substantiated by respondents and their *amici*. Our scrutiny of the interest asserted by the Law School is no less strict for taking into account complex educational judgments in an area that lies primarily within the expertise of the university. Our holding today is in keeping with our tradition of giving a degree of deference to a university's academic decisions, within constitutionally prescribed limits.

We have long recognized that, given the important purpose of public education and the expansive freedoms of speech and thought associated with the university environment, universities occupy a special niche in our constitutional tradition. In announcing the principle of student body diversity as a compelling state interest, Justice Powell invoked our cases recognizing a constitutional dimension, grounded in the First Amendment, of educational autonomy: "The freedom of a university to make its own judgments as to education includes the selection of its student body." From this premise, Justice Powell reasoned that by claiming "the right to select those students who will contribute the most to the 'robust exchange of ideas,'" a university "seek[s] to achieve a goal that is of paramount importance in the fulfillment of its mission." Our conclusion that the Law School has a compelling interest in a diverse student body is informed by our view that attaining a diverse student body is at the heart of the Law School's proper institutional mission, and that "good faith" on the part of a university is "presumed" absent "a showing to the contrary."

* * *

* * * As the District Court emphasized, the Law School's admissions policy promotes "cross-racial understanding," helps to break down racial stereotypes, and "enables [students] to better understand persons of different races." These benefits are "important and laudable," because "classroom discussion is livelier, more spirited, and simply more enlightening and interesting" when the students have "the greatest possible variety of backgrounds."

The Law School's claim of a compelling interest is further bolstered by its *amici*, who point to the educational benefits that flow from student body diversity. In addition to the expert studies and reports entered into evidence at trial, numerous studies show that student body diversity promotes learning outcomes, and "better prepares students for an increasingly diverse workforce and society, and better prepares them as professionals."

These benefits are not theoretical but real, as major American businesses have made clear that the skills needed in today's increasingly global marketplace can only be developed through exposure to widely diverse people, cultures, ideas, and viewpoints. What is more, high-ranking retired officers and civilian leaders of the United States military assert that, "[b]ased on [their] decades of experience," a "highly qualified, racially diverse officer corps . . . is essential to the military's ability to fulfill its principal mission to provide national security." * * *

* * *

Moreover, universities, and in particular, law schools, represent the training ground for a large number of our Nation's leaders. Sweatt v. Painter, 339 U.S. 629, 634 (1950). Individuals with law degrees occupy roughly half the state governorships, more than half the seats in the United States Senate, and more than a third of the seats in the United States House of Representatives. The pattern is even more striking when it comes to highly selective law schools. A handful of these schools accounts for 25 of the 100 United States Senators, 74 United States Courts of Appeals judges, and nearly 200 of the more than 600 United States District Court judges.

In order to cultivate a set of leaders with legitimacy in the eyes of the citizenry, it is necessary that the path to leadership be visibly open to talented and qualified individuals of every race and ethnicity. All members of our heterogeneous society must have confidence in the openness and integrity of the educational institutions that provide this training. As we have recognized, law schools "cannot be effective in isolation from the individuals and institutions with which the law interacts." Access to legal education (and thus the legal profession) must be inclusive of talented and qualified individuals of every race and ethnicity, so that all members of our heterogeneous society may participate in the educational institutions that provide the training and education necessary to succeed in America.

The Law School does not premise its need for critical mass on "any belief that minority students always (or even consistently) express some characteristic minority viewpoint on any issue." To the contrary, diminishing the force of such stereotypes is both a crucial part of the Law School's mission, and one that it cannot accomplish with only token numbers of minority students. Just as growing up in a particular region or having particular professional experiences is likely to affect an individual's views, so too is one's own, unique experience of being a racial minority in a society, like our own, in which race unfortunately still matters. The Law School has determined, based on its experience and expertise, that a "critical mass" of underrepresented minorities is necessary to further its compelling interest in securing the educational benefits of a diverse student body.

Even in the limited circumstance when drawing racial distinctions is permissible to further a compelling state interest, government is still "constrained in how it may pursue that end: [T]he means chosen to accomplish the [government's] asserted purpose must be specifically and narrowly framed to accomplish that purpose." * * *

     * * *

To be narrowly tailored, a race-conscious admissions program cannot use a quota system—it cannot "insulat[e] each category of applicants with certain desired qualifications from competition with all other applicants." Instead, a university may consider race or ethnicity only as a " 'plus' in a particular applicant's file," without "insulat[ing] the individual from comparison with all other candidates for the available seats." In other words, an admissions program must be "flexible enough to consider all pertinent elements of diversity in light of the particular qualifications of each applicant, and to place them on the same footing for consideration, although not necessarily according them the same weight."

We find that the Law School's admissions program bears the hallmarks of a narrowly tailored plan. As Justice Powell made clear in *Bakke*, truly individualized consideration demands that race be used in a flexible, nonmechanical way. It follows from this mandate that universities cannot establish quotas for members of certain racial groups or put members of those groups on separate admissions tracks. Nor can universities insulate applicants who belong to certain racial or ethnic groups from the competition for admission. Universities can, however, consider race or ethnicity more flexibly as a "plus" factor in the context of individualized consideration of each and every applicant.

We are satisfied that the Law School's admissions program, like the Harvard plan described by Justice Powell, does not operate as a quota. * * *

     * * *

That a race-conscious admissions program does not operate as a quota does not, by itself, satisfy the requirement of individualized consideration. When using race as a "plus" factor in university admissions, a university's admissions program must remain flexible enough to ensure that each applicant is evaluated as an individual and not in a way that makes an applicant's race or ethnicity the defining feature of his or her application. The importance of this individualized consideration in the context of a race-conscious admissions program is paramount.

Here, the Law School engages in a highly individualized, holistic review of each applicant's file, giving serious consideration to all the ways an applicant might contribute to a diverse educational environment. The Law School affords this individualized consideration to applicants of all races. There is no policy, either *de jure* or *de facto*, of automatic acceptance or rejection based on any single "soft" variable. Unlike the program at issue in *Gratz v. Bollinger*, the Law School awards no mechanical, predetermined diversity "bonuses" based on race or ethnicity. Like the Harvard plan, the Law School's admissions policy "is flexible enough to consider all pertinent elements of diversity in light of the particular qualifications of each applicant, and to place them on the same footing for consideration, although not necessarily according them the same weight."

* * *

What is more, the Law School actually gives substantial weight to diversity factors besides race. The Law School frequently accepts nonminority applicants with grades and test scores lower than underrepresented minority applicants (and other nonminority applicants) who are rejected. This shows that the Law School seriously weighs many other diversity factors besides race that can make a real and dispositive difference for nonminority applicants as well. By this flexible approach, the Law School sufficiently takes into account, in practice as well as in theory, a wide variety of characteristics besides race and ethnicity that contribute to a diverse student body. * * *

Petitioner and the United States argue that the Law School's plan is not narrowly tailored because race-neutral means exist to obtain the educational benefits of student body diversity that the Law School seeks. We disagree. Narrow tailoring does not require exhaustion of every conceivable race-neutral alternative. Nor does it require a university to choose between maintaining a reputation for excellence or fulfilling a commitment to provide educational opportunities to members of all racial groups. Narrow tailoring does, however, require serious, good faith consideration of workable race-neutral alternatives that will achieve the diversity the university seeks.

* * *

We acknowledge that "there are serious problems of justice connected with the idea of preference itself." Narrow tailoring, therefore, requires that a race-conscious admissions program not unduly harm members of any racial group. Even remedial race-based governmental action generally "remains subject to continuing oversight to assure that it will work the least harm possible to other innocent persons competing for the benefit." To be narrowly tailored, a race-conscious admissions program must not "unduly burden individuals who are not members of the favored racial and ethnic groups."

We are satisfied that the Law School's admissions program does not. Because the Law School considers "all pertinent elements of diversity," it can (and does) select nonminority applicants who have greater potential to enhance student body diversity over underrepresented minority applicants. * * *

We are mindful, however, that "[a] core purpose of the Fourteenth Amendment was to do away with all governmentally imposed discrimination based on race." Accordingly, race-conscious admissions policies must be limited in time. This requirement reflects that racial classifications, however compelling their goals, are potentially so dangerous that they may be employed no more broadly than the interest demands. Enshrining a permanent justification for racial preferences would offend this fundamental equal protection principle. We see no reason to exempt race-conscious admissions programs from the requirement that all governmental use of race must have a logical end point. The Law School, too, concedes that all "race-conscious programs must have reasonable durational limits."

* * *

We take the Law School at its word that it would "like nothing better than to find a race-neutral admissions formula" and will terminate its race-conscious admissions program as soon as practicable. It has been 25 years since Justice Powell first approved the use of race to further an interest in student body diversity in the context of public higher education. Since that time, the number of minority applicants with high grades and test scores has indeed increased. We expect that 25 years from now, the use of racial preferences will no longer be necessary to further the interest approved today.

In summary, the Equal Protection Clause does not prohibit the Law School's narrowly tailored use of race in admissions decisions to further a compelling interest in obtaining the educational benefits that flow from a diverse student body. Consequently, petitioner's statutory claims based on Title VI and 42 U.S.C. § 1981 also fail. The judgment of the Court of Appeals for the Sixth Circuit, accordingly, is affirmed.

* * *

Notes and Questions

1. Why, again, is academic diversity a compelling interest, according to *Grutter*?

2. For whose benefit are such programs, according to the Supreme Court?

3. How would Derrick Bell's interest-convergence approach explain *Grutter*?

4. How would postcolonial theory explain *Grutter*?

Shortly after *Grutter* came down, the attack on university-level affirmative action shifted to the state level, where many states followed the lead of California's right wing populist Ward Connerly in introducing voter initiatives declaring race-conscious decisionmaking illegal. In California in 1996, Connerly and his fellow activists had succeeded in passing Proposition 209, which banned the use of race in most governmental programs, including higher education. The proposition, which is still in effect at the time this book went to press, has greatly reduced the number of black and Latino undergraduate and professional school students throughout the state. The Ninth Circuit upheld the California version in Coalition for Economic Equity v. Wilson, 110 F.3d 1431 (9th Cir. 1997) as a race-neutral measure aimed at eliminating racial discrimination and favoritism. More such litigation seems likely.

For an incisive comment on the *Grutter* opinion, see Michael A. Olivas, *Law School Admissions After* Grutter: *Student Bodies, Pipeline Theory, and the River*, 55 J. Legal Ed. 16 (2005). Olivas criticizes several metaphors writers use to describe "the quest for minorities in college enrollments," including "the pool" and "the pipeline," both of which:

> are inapt, both because they misconstrue the nature of the problems . . . and because they misdirect attention. A pool is static, likely to turn brackish, and bounded. It requires restocking and resupply, and if it overflows . . . it is no longer a pool. Id. at 21.

Olivas also notes that the increasing number of applicants to law school will not translate into larger numbers of minorities, because of excessive relevance on the LSAT. He warns that *Grutter*'s 25–year prediction will not come to pass unless law schools ease their reliance on the test.

See also Rachel F. Moran, *Of Doubt and Diversity: The Future of Affirmative Action in Higher Education*, 67 Ohio St. L.J. 201 (2006), noting how the shared purpose of *Brown* is missing in recent Supreme Court jurisprudence, and the Justices are divided over whether diversity is a compelling interest. She nevertheless argues that *Grutter* moves beyond *Bakke* by linking racial diversity on campus with equality and community— i.e., with broad concerns about a healthy culture.

Girardeau A. Spann
Proposition 209
47 Duke L.J. 187, 188–92 (1997)

California's Proposition 209 is thrilling, seductive, and replete with naughty fascination. The recently adopted ballot initiative, which has amended the California Constitution to prohibit race-and gender-based affirmative action by agencies of the state, is thrilling in its defiance of current convention. Its populist rejection of the affirmative action concept is staggering in scope, and irreverent in demeanor. It seems to condemn all affirmative action programs—regardless of their remedial justification or prospective promise—in a brazen rebuke of the social policymakers who spent decades putting those programs in place. Moreover, Proposition 209 is seductive in its simplicity. It suggests that centuries of intractable race and gender injustice can be neutralized through the unadorned expedient of prospective neutrality. Although such a suggestion dismisses conventional wisdom on the complex nature of race and gender relations, Proposition 209 lays precocious claim to one of those liberated enlightenments that the uninitiated have yet to recognize as appropriate. Proposition 209 is also replete with the naughty fascination of forbidden temptation, because of the bewitching possibility that it might be merely a ruse. Formally denominated the "California Civil Rights Initiative," Proposition 209 pledges to advance the cause of race and gender equality. But like the separate-but-equal and gender protective regimes that preceded it, Proposition 209 may be just another discriminatory attempt to appropriate resources by those accustomed to having them, at the expense of those accustomed to having them taken away.

As a nation whose formulation of social policy is constitutionally constrained, we reflexively turn to the courts for constitutional resolution of our controversial social policy disputes. But it turns out that the Constitution has surprisingly little to say about the validity of Proposition 209. This fact is starkly demonstrated by the divergent judicial receptions that Proposition 209 has received to date. Shortly after the adoption of Proposition 209, a federal district court issued a temporary restraining order enjoining its implementation, finding a "strong probability" that Proposition 209 would ultimately be held to violate the Equal Protection Clause of the Constitution. A few months later a three-judge court of appeals panel reversed the district court, stating that "[a]s a matter of 'conventional' equal protection analysis, there is simply no doubt that Proposition 209 is constitutional." The discrepancy between these two adjudications is telling.

The divergent doctrinal arguments offered by the district court and the court of appeals seem plausible within the confines of the opinions that advance them, but like two ships passing in the night, neither opinion engages the arguments made by the other. The district court determined that Proposition 209 was likely to be unconstitutional because it treated race and gender preferences differently than it treated other preferences, such as preferences for veterans, athletes or alumni children. Accordingly, the district court held that Proposition 209 constituted a race and gender classification that was prohibited by the Equal Protection Clause of the Constitution. More specifically, the district court found that Proposition 209 restructured the political process in a way that made it more difficult for proponents of race and gender preferences to secure the preferences that they desired (they had to amend the state constitution) than it was for proponents of other types of preferences to secure the preferences that they desired (they needed only to secure the adoption of ordinary legislation or administrative regulations). The court of appeals, on the other hand, found that Proposition 209 could not violate the Constitution under "conventional" equal protection analysis because it required the same race and gender neutrality that the Equal Protection Clause itself required. Moreover, as a matter of "political structure" analysis, the court of appeals held that Proposition 209 did not impermissibly restructure the political process. The court found that any political burdens suffered by women and minorities ultimately resulted from the neutrality commands of the Equal Protection Clause, and not solely from the Proposition 209 prohibition on race and gender preferences.

Despite each opinion's facial plausibility, neither responds to the baseline assumptions [of] the other. The court of appeals opinion ignores that Proposition 209 applies meaningfully only to affirmative action that is *permitted* by the Constitution (unconstitutional affirmative action would be invalid even in the absence of Proposition 209). As a result, Proposition 209 is itself an impermissible race and gender classification. It is so because it treats race and gender preferences differently than it treats other preferences. And it is impermissible under the heightened scrutiny that is applied to race and gender classifications, because its justification for this differential treatment is to neutralize affirmative action preferences that are themselves constitutionally valid. These constitutionally valid affirmative action preferences are therefore doctrinally indistinguishable from other non-prohibited preferences, but Proposition 209 treats them in ways that are fatally different. Moreover, Proposition 209 treats race and gender preferences differently than other preferences precisely *because* they benefit race and gender minorities rather than groups like veterans, athletes or alumni children: this makes Proposition 209 discriminatory in the most traditional sense. The court of appeals response to the district court argument, therefore, is simply non-responsive.

But there is a similar problem with the district court argument. The district court asserts that Proposition 209 is itself a racial preference that restructures the political process in a discriminatory manner, but as the court of appeals points out, Proposition 209 treats all races and genders in precisely the same way. It is true that the *topics* addressed by Proposition 209 are constitutionally suspect race and gender groups, but Proposition 209 is utterly neutral in the way that it treats those constitutionally suspect groups: it bans all preferences regardless of whom they benefit or burden. As a result of this neutrality, Proposition 209 is not subject to heightened constitutional scrutiny, because it is not a race or gender classification at all and it cannot violate an Equal Protection Clause that does nothing more than demand equal treatment within race and gender groups. Although *Loving v. Virginia* arguably holds that a legislative classification can become a race or gender classification merely by using the topics of race or gender as the basis for classification, this aspect of *Loving* may simply be wrong. The district court response to the court of appeals argument, therefore, is simply non-responsive.

Each opinion views Proposition 209 from a different perspective, but neither perspective can realistically claim to be more constitutionally correct than the other. Each * * * merely reflects a different set of baseline assumptions and normative preferences concerning the desirability of affirmative action as a policy. The liberal black district court judge likes affirmative action as a means of combating the lingering effects of race and gender discrimination, but the conservative white court of appeals judges dislike affirmative action because it interferes with their desire for prospective race and gender neutrality. There is, however, nothing in the Constitution that is capable of resolving this social policy dispute without simply elevating one policy preference above the other for reasons of subjective normative appeal. The meaning of the Equal Protection Clause is simply indeterminate with respect to the constitutionality of Proposition 209.

This doctrinal indeterminacy is a signal that the judiciary does not have any productive role to play in the resolution of the current affirmative action debate. In a democracy, resolution of that debate is properly left to the politically accountable branches of government rather than to the politically unaccountable Supreme Court. * * *

───────────

One argument for affirmative action is that it is necessary to provide minority communities with role models. Is this a good argument for it? The following selection expresses doubts.

Richard Delgado
Affirmative Action as a Majoritarian Device:
Or, Do You Really Want to Be a Role Model?
89 Mich. L. Rev. 1222, 1223–26 (1991)

Have you ever noticed how affirmative action occupies a place in our system of law and politics far out of proportion to its effects in the real world? Liberals love talking about and sitting on committees that define, oversee, defend, and give shape to it. Conservatives are attached to the concept for different reasons: They can rail against it, declare it lacking in virtue and principle, and use it to rally the troops. Affirmative action is something they love to hate. The program also generates a great deal of paper, conversation, and jobs—probably more of the latter for persons of the majority persuasion than it has for its intended beneficiaries. Yet, despite its rather meager accomplishments and dubious lineage, a number of us have jumped on the bandwagon, maybe because it seemed one of the few that would let us on.

But should we? Lately, I have been having doubts, as have other writers of color. Scholars of color have grown increasingly skeptical about both the way in which affirmative action frames the issue of minority representation and the effects that it produces in the world. Affirmative action, I have noticed, generally frames the question of minority representation in an interesting way: Should we as a society admit, hire, appoint, or promote some designated number of people of color in order to promote certain policy goals, such as social stability, an expanded labor force, and an integrated society? These goals are always forward-looking; affirmative action is viewed as an instrumental device for moving society from state *A* to state *B*. The concept is neither backward-looking nor rooted in history; it is teleological rather than deontological. Minorities are hired or promoted not because we have been unfairly treated, denied jobs, deprived of our lands, or beaten and brought here in chains. Affirmative action neatly diverts our attention from all those disagreeable details and calls for a fresh start. Well, where are we now? So many Chicano bankers and chief executive officers, so many black lawyers, so many Native American engineers, and so many women physicians. What can we do to increase these numbers over the next ten or twenty years? The system thus bases inclusion of people of color on principles of social utility, not reparations or *rights*. When those in power decide the goal has been accomplished, or is incapable of being reached, what logically happens? Naturally, the program stops. At best, then, affirmative action serves as a homeostatic device, assuring that only a small number of women and people of color are hired or promoted. Not too many, for that would be terrifying, nor too few, for that would be destabilizing. Just the right small number, generally those of us who need it least, are moved ahead.

Affirmative action also neatly frames the issue so that even these small accomplishments seem troublesome, requiring great agonizing and gnashing of teeth. Liberals and moderates lie awake at night, asking how far they can take this affirmative action thing without sacrificing innocent white males. Have you ever wondered what that makes *us*—if not innocent, then ... ? Affirmative action enables members of the dominant group to ask, "Is it fair to hire a less-qualified Chicano or black over a more-qualified white?" This is a curious way of framing the question, as I will argue, in part because those who ask it are themselves the beneficiaries of history's largest affirmative action program. This fact is rarely noticed, however, while the question goes on causing the few of us who are magically raised by affirmative action's unseen hand to feel guilty, undeserving, and *stigmatized*.

Affirmative action, as currently understood and promoted, is also ahistorical. For more than 200 years, white males benefited from their own program of affirmative action, through unjustified preferences in jobs and education resulting from old-boy networks and official laws that lessened the competition. Today's affirmative action critics never characterize that scheme as affirmative action, which of course it was. By labeling problematic, troublesome, ethically agonizing a paltry system that helps a few of us get ahead, critics neatly take our eyes off the system of arrangements that brought and maintained them in power, and enabled them to develop the rules and standards of quality and merit that now exclude us, make us appear unworthy, dependent (naturally) on affirmative action.

Well, if you were a member of the majority group and invented something that cut down the competition, made you feel good and virtuous, made minorities grateful and humble, and framed the "minority problem" in this wondrous way, I think you would be pretty pleased with yourself. Moreover, if you placed the operation of this program in the hands of the very people who brought about the situation that made it necessary in the first place, society would probably reward you with prizes and honors.

Please do not mistake what I am saying. As marginalized people we should strive to increase our power, cohesiveness, and representation in all significant areas of society. We should do this, though, because we are entitled to these things and because fundamental fairness requires this reallocation of power. We should reformulate the issue. Our acquiescence in treating it as "a question of standards" is absurd and self-defeating when you consider that we took no part in creating those standards and their fairness is one of the very things we want to call into question.

Affirmative action, then, is something no self-respecting person of color ought to support. We could, of course, take our own program, with our own goals, our own theoretical grounding, and our own managers and call it "Affirmative Action." But we would, of course, be talking about something quite different. My first point, then, is that we should demystify, interrogate, and destabilize affirmative action. The program was designed by others to promote their purposes, not ours.

The Role Model Argument

Consider now an aspect of affirmative action mythology, the role model argument, that in my opinion has received less criticism than it deserves. This argument is a special favorite of moderate liberals, who regard it as virtually unassailable. Although the argument's inventor is unknown, its creator must have been a member of the majority group and must have received a prize almost as large as the one awarded the person who created affirmative action itself. Like the larger program of which it is a part, the role model argument is instrumental and forward-looking. It makes us a means to another's end. A white-dominated institution hires you not because you are entitled to or deserve the job. Nor is the institution seeking to set things straight because your ancestors and others of your heritage were systematically excluded from such jobs. Not at all. You're hired (if you speak politely, have a neat haircut, and, above all, can be trusted) not because of your accomplishments, but because of what others think you will do for them. If they hire you now and you are a good role model, things will be better in the next generation.

Suppose you saw a large sign saying, "ROLE MODEL WANTED. GOOD PAY. INQUIRE WITHIN." Would you apply? Let me give you five reasons why you should not.

REASON NUMBER ONE. Being a role model is a tough job, with long hours and much heavy lifting. You are expected to uplift your entire people. Talk about hard, sweaty work!

REASON NUMBER TWO. The job treats you as a means to an end. Even your own constituency may begin to see you this way. "Of course Tanya will agree to serve as our faculty advisor, give this speech, serve on that panel, or agree to do us X, Y, or Z favor, probably unpaid and on short notice. What is her purpose if not to serve us?"

REASON NUMBER THREE. The role model's job description is monumentally unclear. If highway workers or tax assessors had such unclear job descriptions, they would strike. If you are a role model, are you expected to do the same things your white counterpart does, in addition to counseling and helping out the community of color whenever something comes up? Just the latter? Half and half? Both? On your own time, or on company time? No supporter of the role model argument has ever offered satisfactory answers to these questions.

REASON NUMBER FOUR. To be a good role model, you must be an assimilationist, never a cultural or economic nationalist, separatist, radical reformer, or anything remotely resembling any of these. As with actual models (who walk down runways wearing the latest fashions), you are expected to conform to prevailing ideas of beauty, politeness, grooming, and above all responsibility. If you develop a quirk, wrinkle, aberration, or, heaven forbid, a vice, look out! I have heard more than once that a law school would not hire X for a teaching position because, although X might be a decent scholar and good classroom teacher, he was a little exuberant or rough around the edges and thus not good role model material. Not long ago, Margaret Court, the ex-tennis star and grand dame of English tennis officialdom, criticized Martina Navratilova as a poor role model for young tennis players. Martina failed Court's assessment not because she served poorly, wore a wrinkled tennis uniform, displayed bad sportsmanship, or argued with the referees. Rather, in Court's opinion, Martina was not "straight," not "feminine" enough, and so could not serve as a proper role model. Our white friends always want us to model behavior that will encourage our students and protégés to adopt majoritarian social mores; you never hear of them hiring one of their number because he or she is bilingual, wears dashikis, or is in other ways culturally distinctive.

REASON NUMBER FIVE (the most important one). The job of role model requires that you *lie*—that you tell not little, but big, whopping lies, and that is bad for your soul. Suppose I am sent to an inner city school to talk to the kids and serve as role model of the month. I am *expected* to tell the kids that if they study hard and stay out of trouble, they can become a law professor like me. That, however, is a very big lie: a whopper. When I started teaching law sixteen years ago, there were about thirty-five Hispanic law professors, approximately twenty-five of which were Chicano. Today, the numbers are only slightly improved. In the interim, however, a nearly complete turnover has occurred. The faces are new, but the numbers have remained the same from year to year. Gonzalez leaves teaching; Velasquez is hired somewhere else. Despite this, I am expected to tell forty kids in a crowded, inner city classroom that if they work hard, they can each be among the chosen twenty-five. Fortunately, most kids are smart enough to figure out that the system does not work this way. If I were honest, I would advise them to become major league baseball players, or to practice their hook shots. As Michael Olivas points out, the odds, pay, and working conditions are much better in these other lines of work.

Recently, the California Postsecondary Commission, concerned about the fate of minorities in the state's colleges and universities, had its statisticians compile a projection for all young blacks starting public school in California that year. That number was about 35,000. Of these, the statisticians estimated that about one half would graduate from high school, the rest having dropped out. Of those completing high school, approximately one out of nine would attend a four-year college. Of that number, about 300 would earn a bachelor's degree. You can form your own estimate of how many of this group, which began as 35,000, will continue on to earn a law degree. Thirty? Fifty? And of these, how many will become law professors? My guess is one, at most. But I may be an optimist.

Suppose I told the ghetto kids these things, that is, the truth. And, while I am at it, told them about diminishing federal and state scholarship funds that formerly enabled poor kids to go to college, about the special threat to assistance for minority college students, and about a climate of increasing hostility, slurs, and harassment on the nation's campuses. Suppose I told them, in short, what the system is really like, how the deck is stacked against them. What would happen? I would quickly be labeled a poor role model and someone else sent to give the inspiring speech next month.

WHY THINGS ARE THE WAY THEY ARE AND WHAT CAN BE DONE

The role model theory is a remarkable invention. It requires that some of us lie and that others of us be exploited and overworked. The theory is, however, highly functional for its inventors. It encourages us to cultivate nonthreatening behavior in our own people. In addition, it provides a handy justification for affirmative action, which, as I have pointed out, is at best a mixed blessing for communities of color.

As with any successful and popular program, I think we need only examine the functions served by the role model argument to see why our white friends so warmly embrace it. Demographers tell us that in about ten years, Caucasians will cease to be the largest segment of California's population. In approximately sixty years, around the year 2050, the same will happen nationally. While this radical demographic shift is occurring, the population also will be aging. The baby boomers, mostly white, will be retired and dependent on social security for support. These retirees will rely on the continuing labor of a progressively smaller pyramid of active workers, an increasing proportion of them of color. You see, then, why it is essential that we imbue our next generation of children with the requisite respect for hard work. They must be taught to ask few questions, pay their taxes, and accept social obligations, even if imposed by persons who look different from them and who committed documented injustices on their ancestors.

If you want the job of passing on *that* set of attitudes to young people of color, go ahead. You will be warmly received and amply rewarded. But you do not have to be a role model. You can do other more honorable, authentic things. You can be a mentor. You can be an "organic intellectual," offering analysis and action programs for our people. You can be a matriarch, a patriarch, a legend, or a provocateur. You can be a socially committed professional who marches to your own drummer. You can even be yourself. But to the ad, ROLE MODEL WANTED, the correct answer, in my view, is: NOT ME!

Notes and Questions

1. The proponents of Proposition 209 and its look-alikes in other states maintain that they are merely following in the footsteps of Martin Luther King, Jr. who urged that the content of a person's character, not his or her skin color, should determine the person's fate. Are they, in fact, his ideological descendants?

2. Is the role-model argument for university affirmative action faulty, as Professor Delgado maintains? What, if anything, differentiates the function of a model role and an organic intellectual?

3. Does a university education usually make a person more, or less, radical? More, or less, dedicated to advancing his or her community? More, or less, willing to take on the establishment?

4. On the way the early U.S. colonizers recruited a native Mexican elite to govern New Mexico and keep ordinary Mexicans and Indians in their racial place, see Laura E. Gómez, *Off-White in an Age of White Supremacy: Mexican Elites and the Rights of Indians and Blacks in Nineteenth Century New Mexico*, in *"Colored Men" and "Hombres Aquí"* (Michael A. Olivas ed., 2006).

5. For the argument that affirmative action at the law school level reduces the number of black lawyers, see Richard H. Sander, *A Systemic Analysis of Affirmative Action in American Law Schools*, 57 Stan. L. Rev. 367 (2004). See also Richard H. Sander, *The Racial Paradox of the Corporate Law Firm*, 84 N.C. L. Rev. 1755 (2006) (arguing that affirmative action in hiring at large corporate firms simply increases attrition later when black associates come up for consideration for partnerships). But see Ian Ayres & Richard Brooks, *Does Affirmative Action Reduce the Number of Black Lawyers?*, 57 Stan. L. Rev. 1807 (2005); Richard Delgado, *Rodrigo's Tenth Chronicle: Merit and Affirmative Action*, 83 Geo. L.J. 1711 (1995); id., *Rodrigo's Riposte: The Mismatch Theory of Law School Admissions*, 57 Syr. L. Rev. 637 (2007).

6. Some white liberal scholars, and a few blacks, argue that university affirmative action should be cut back to its core function, admitting blacks, and that Latinos and Asians should not receive consideration. See, e.g., Paul Brest & Miranda Oshige, *Affirmative Action for Whom?*, 47 Stan. L. Rev. 855 (1995); John D. Skrentny, *Inventing Race*, Pub. Interest, No. 146, Winter 2002, at 97; George A. Yancey, *Who is White?: Latinos, Asians, and the New Black/Nonblack Divide* (2003). But see Richard Delgado, *Locating Latinos in the Field of Civil Rights: Assessing the Neoliberal Case for Radical Exclusion*, 83 Tex. L. Rev. 489 (2004) (reviewing Yancey, supra).

Occasionally, an attack on one minority group's eligibility for affirmative action comes from a different minority group wishing to improve its own chances under the same program. In Ho v. San Francisco Unified School

District, 965 F.Supp. 1316 (N.D. Cal. 1997), Asian Americans successfully sued to block San Francisco from capping Asian–American enrollment at elite public programs such as Lowell High School. The court held that the school district's scheme constituted an impermissible racial classification, even though its purpose was to assure a rough proportionality among the races at the schools of a multiracial city.

*

Part Five

IMMIGRATION

Most readers know that the United States is a country of immigrants. Except for those of pure Native American ancestry—a very small number—most Americans trace their family's origins to somewhere else.

What, if anything, is different about the U.S. Latino population? The reader who has come this far will have more than an inkling of some of those differences. Cuban Americans arrived in three relatively recent waves of immigration aimed at putting some distance between themselves and their revolutionary homeland. Puerto Ricans became part of the U.S.—first as a colony, later a commonwealth—when this country ended its war with Spain. Many Mexican Americans trace their ancestry to an even earlier period—Conquest. See Part One supra.

And today we are in the midst of a massive wave of immigration, much of it undocumented, that has provoked sharp controversy and drawn into question the commitment of the United States to being a welcoming society for all—or virtually all—newcomers.

The following materials introduce you to some of these issues.

Chapter 14

IMMIGRATION IN LATINO AND ANGLO SOCIETY

This country's immigration laws have constituted, and continue to constitute, one of the most powerful forces shaping the Latino community. As mentioned earlier, a high proportion of Latinos owe their presence in the United States to immigration, either of themselves or their ancestors. With most of the rest, a kind of reverse-immigration explains their presence here: in the ironic words of an in-group slogan, the country "immigrated to us." That is, parts of the country that many Latinos live in, including most of the Southwest, were parts of Mexico or, in the case of Puerto Rico, Spain. They became U.S. territories, states, or colonies, through war and Conquest.

As the reader will see, official policy toward immigration, especially from Latin America, has varied greatly from one period to another. Some eras, such as the late 1800s and early 1900s, have been relatively welcoming toward immigrants of all sorts. Other times have seen outbreaks of "nativism" and even attacks by the Ku Klux Klan and similar white-supremacist organizations aimed at immigrants and immigration. During two periods, the United States launched broad-scale repatriation programs that sought to deport as many Latinos as possible, including longtime residents and even U.S. citizens. See, e.g., *Immigrants Out!: The New Nativism and the Anti–Immigrant Impulse in the United States* (Juan F. Perea ed., 1997).

Just as society at large is divided about Latino immigration, the Latino group is, as well, with long-term residents and citizens generally less favorably disposed to Latino immigration, particularly of the illegal variety, and more recently arrived Latinos favoring it.

Most Europeans, including the many millions who arrived through Ellis Island during the huge waves of immigration to the United States between 1890 and 1924, did relatively well. Aided by settlement house workers, family and friends who had arrived before them, as well as their own considerable talent and energy, they found housing, got jobs, and began learning English. Their children graduated from high school and attended community college or the City College of New York. Each generation was a little better off than the previous one, so that by the third or fourth generation, the descendants of those immigrants were practically indistinguishable from long-term residents whose predecessors had come over on the Mayflower. See Richard Alba & Victor Nee, *Remaking the American Mainstream: Assimilation and Contemporary Immigration* (2003).

SECTION 1. "AL NORTE"—WHY THEY COME, AND HOW

The wave of Latino immigrants washing over the United States during the last few decades, as many as 700,000 to one million each year and a total possibly exceeding twenty million, with one exception [first-wave Cubans fleeing Fidel Castro], has not followed this upward path. See Jeffrey S. Passel, *Size and Characteristics of the Unauthorized Migrant Population in the U.S.* (2006). As with earlier groups of immigrants, the first generation works hard, saves some money, and learns halting English. But their children are not doing well. Many of the sons and daughters of immigrants, particularly Mexicans, drop out of school at a high rate and suffer many types of psychological disorder, including depression, suicidal thoughts, and dependence on drugs. See, e.g., Alejandro Portes & Rubén G. Rumbaut, *Immigrant America: A Portrait* (3d ed. 2006); and *Legacies: The Story of the Immigrant Second Generation* 276–81 (2001).

The militarized border and recently enhanced security have only exacerbated their predicament. Because the newly reinforced border regime, with helicopters, pilotless drones, listening devices, ATVs, and police dogs, has greatly increased the risk of detection and deportation back to Mexico, "coyotes" (human smugglers) have upped their fees sharply. At the same time, enhanced security near San Diego and other large border cities makes crossing the border at those places difficult. Because the risk of detection is high, unauthorized entrants are forced into the less heavily fortified regions of Arizona, where desert heat and lack of water increase the risks of losing one's way, becoming dehydrated, and dying.

The new regime has changed the entrant's calculus in two ways, illustrating the Law of Unintended Consequences. First, it decreases the undocumented alien's opportunities to come and go. Previous generations of immigrants would get a job in the United States, save some money, and return to their home village in Mexico to spend some of it and get together with their friends and relatives, before returning to the U.S. for another cycle of work and saving.

With the increased risk of detection, less of this cycling is going on. Previously, an immigrant might get a job, for example, working in the fields of an agricultural state such as California or Washington. When the growing season ended, he or she would go back home for a few months, until the beginning of the new growing season, at which point he or she would cross the border again and search for a new job, sometimes with the very same planter.

Now, immigrants no longer return to Mexico during the off season. Fearful of being caught during a border passage, they remain in the U.S. the entire year. Seasonal agricultural labor no longer fills the bill; the undocumented worker now requires a year-round job because of the risks of border crossing. Hence, the expansion we have witnessed of undocumented Mexican and Central American laborers into sectors such as hotels, restaurants, construction, roofing, food processing, and gardening and landscaping. Also, the new crop of year-round workers is no longer limited to agricultural regions. Hence, the sudden increase in Latino population in parts of the country where few resided before, such as New England and the South.

A second major change has to do with the children of the immigrants. In former times, crossing the border was relatively safe, so that an adult couple would come across alone, leaving the children back home with relatives. They would plan to come for them later, after the couple had learned some English, moved into an apartment, secured jobs, made contact with friends in the U.S., and learned their way around. Then, they would send for the children.

Now, crossing the border is much more dangerous and costly than it was before, so that many adults are bringing their children with them the first time. This "premature assimilation" exposes the children to many risks. The parents, not knowing English and distrustful of local authorities, may be unaware that they could safely send their children to school or take them to a public health clinic if one of them develops a fever. They may begin relying on the children, who usually learn English more quickly than the adults, as translators, placing unnatural strains on the parent-children relationship. (The child wants to go outside and play soccer, the adult needs the child to be present during an employment interview or a session with the landlord to discuss a rotting staircase). See Alejandro Portes, *Address*, 11th Annual LatCrit Conference, Las Vegas, Nevada, October 6, 2006.

John Ross
Days of the Dead
CounterPunch, Nov. 1, 2005

It is the season of the Dead in Mexico. On the Dias de los Muertos (November 1–2), the people will remember their "difuntos" (dead) by building altars to honor their passing and travel out to the graveyards to clean up their tombs, bringing with them the cempaxeutl (marigold) flowers, a tub of turkey mole, the dead person's favorite booze and cigarettes and, of course, lively music so that the "calacas" (the skeletons or "calaveras") will rise up and dance.

This year, the party will be enlivened by 453 fresh "muertos" just arrived from the "Other Side" (the U.S.). 2005 has been an all-time record year for the number of reported Mexican and Central American migrant deaths along the 3000–kilometer border.

The tally of migrant deaths is coldly calculated to fit into each fiscal year—the figures are used to justify and project budget requests for what used to be called the U.S. Border Patrol and is now the ICE (Immigration and Customs Enforcement) division of the Department of Homeland Security. Regardless of the name changes, the agency will always be the "Migra" to millions of migrant workers.

From October 1st 2004 through September 30th 2005, 454 Mexican and Central American migrant workers died trying to get across the U.S. border, according to a just-released ICE count for the past fiscal year. How this figure is actually determined is a major mystery to Claudia Smith, director of the California Rural Legal Assistance advocacy program for migrant workers, who is convinced that many deaths simply escape the Migra's attention. The fiscal '04–'05 numbers are a significant increase over fiscal '03–'04 when 383 migrants perished. In both years, 60% of the death toll was taken in the merciless Arizona desert west of Yuma where hundreds fry each summer under the watchful eye of the ICE. 22 migrants died in the first three weeks of July alone.

Since 1995, when the Border Patrol enhanced operations in San Diego ("Operation Gatekeeper") and El Paso ("Operation Hold The Line"), the most popular crossings, it has been stated U.S. policy to up the risks of illegal immigration by driving the migrants to the most dangerous crossings along the border such as Arizona's notorious "corridor of death."

Many of this year's crop of the freshly-dead were guided to their demise by the economic and trade policies of both the Mexican and U.S. governments, particularly in the agricultural sector where the dumping of U.S. corn and other produce in Mexico under the provisions of the North American Free Trade Agreement (NAFTA) has forced upwards of 3,000,000 farm families off the land and into the migration stream, according to Agricultural Ministry stats. Since NAFTA was inked in 1992 (it kicked in 1994), nearly 5000 Mexican and Central American workers, many of them dislocated farmers, have lost their lives trying to get across this border to take a job no North American will work. On the bone parade, that's more than died on 9/11.

The Dead die in the surf trying to swim into San Diego. They drowned in the All–America Canal just outside of Mexicali and in the big muddy river that Mexico calls the Rio Bravo and the U.S. the Rio Grande. The Dead die bitten by rattlesnakes trying to get through south Texas and battered by fast-moving cars on busy border freeways. The Dead suffocate to death in locked truck trailers and boxcars stuck on sidings. The Dead die in smash-ups after high-speed chases with the Migra or else are shot down when they try to run. The Dead are gunned down by Arizona ranchers who advertise "human safaris." The Dead die beaten with baseball bats by border thieves or gangs of "polleros" (people smugglers) because they can't pay their fee.

They die frozen stiff as a log up in the Rumarosa Mountains buried under the snow. But most of all, the Dead die down there in the scorching desert below to which the Migra has herded them in order to up "the risks of illegal immigration." Sometimes all you find are bleached bones. Sometimes just torn clothes.

Many more of the migrants make it across the border than die in the passage and they spread out into every nook and cranny of the American Dream—7,000,000 undocumented workers at last count. But just like their comrades who ate it on the border, they die up there too. Some, like six family members from Zacatecas murdered in Georgia this October for the remittance money they were about to send home, are victims of American violence. Some just had bad luck like the two young Tzeltal boys from Ocosingo in the Zapatista zone who came home this month to Chiapas in cardboard caskets from New Orleans where Katrina cut them down.

Up there, the Dead die in industrial accidents, from sleeping out in the cold, from heart attacks or just a broken heart for the country they've been forced to leave behind. Mexico's 47 U.S. consulates processed 10,000 requests last fiscal year to send the Dead back home.

Getting the Dead home to Mexico is a tricky business. Away from the border, family and friends pay the cost of the coffin and the transport. On the border, because the Dead there are so often unaccompanied, the consulates will supply a coffin (often made of cardboard) and the airfreight—but because both come out of meager budgets, the bureaucrats shop for the best bargains. Aeromexico, the low bidder, is the designated carrier to get the Dead home.

The designation seems one of life's bitter ironies to Jorge Santibanez, director of the College of the Northern Border think tank in Tijuana. Aeromexico flies thousands of migrant workers into Hermosillo, Sonora each year, the jumping off point for the Arizona desert where so many of them will die.

Now Aeromexico has won a contract from Homeland Security to fly live indocumentados who have accepted voluntary departure free of charge from Tucson to Guadalajara and Mexico City. Santibanez's mordant if modest proposal made with a Day of the Deadish twist: since the undocumented never have a lot of suitcases, how about letting them bring the coffins of their dead brothers and sisters on board as part of their luggage?

But for 400 or so defunct indocumentados, there will be no free flight home to celebrate los Dias de los Muertos with their relatives and "cuates" (friends.) Laid out in a muddy potter's field behind the town cemetery in Holtville California, 120 miles east of San Diego and halfway to Yuma Arizona—the deadliest span along the dividing line—they comprise the largest congregation of unidentified dead on the border.

Buried beneath rough hewn markers and white wooden crosses donated by a local migrants coalition that read "No Olvidado" ("Not

Forgotten"), the graves of the children perhaps decorated with a decaying stuffed animal, the souls of these Juan and Juana Does are suspended in exile. They have, in a sense, at last become permanent residents.

About a third of the 3500 migrant workers who have died during 10 years of Operation Gatekeeper have never been identified, reports Claudia Smith—many may be Central Americans who tend to carry no identification because they have to transit Mexico and it is better to blend in there. Smith, who thinks the Migra is fudging the figures, has long advocated link-ups between the 24 county coroners whose jurisdictions extend from San Diego, California to Corpus Christi, Texas on the Gulf to more accurately identify those who die in the crossing.

Smith's persistence has paid off with the installation by Mexico's Foreign Ministry of a database that will allow the consulates to more accurately match up DNA samples from family members with those who are missing in action on the border.

This Day of the Dead, as has become the ritual, parishioners from St. Joseph's Catholic Church in Holtville and migrant advocates from San Diego will gather once again in the muddy bone yard where the unidentified migrants molder, with candles and food and song to remember the nameless and perhaps, despite the great distances between Holtville and home, as the party warms up, the calacas will get up and dance.

One more death on the border that may not get listed in the local obituaries this Day of the Dead: Immigration Reform, which died quietly this fall in Mexico City. Both Mexico City and Washington seem to have agreed there is little resonance on this issue in a U.S. Congress which is busily authorizing border walls and denying the undocumented a driver's license.

And there is even less down on a local level where the migrants are now denied hospital care in some states and barred from attending public universities and even being charged with trespassing just because they are in the U.S. Colorado Republican Tom Tancredo wants to shut down public libraries that have Spanish reading sections because the undocumented may be reading the books.

In such a malevolent atmosphere, immigration reform is not going to fly, admits Mexico's Foreign Minister Luis Ernesto Derbez, giving up a six year battle by the government of President Vicente Fox to reach an accord with Washington. "Immigration reform is dead," Derbez told reporters in the Mexican capitol last week, "at least until after 2008."

Alejandro Portes & Rubén G. Rumbaut
Legacies: The Story of the Immigrant Second Generation
276–80 (2001)

The first girl born in California in 2000 was born to Mexican parents. She was named Anayeli de Jesús. Her parents, Elena and Javier, came from Mexico in the 1990s looking for a better life and hope the same for their daughter: "To be a good student and to go to the university."—Kate Folmar and Scott Martelli, "The New Faces of Orange County's Future."

"If one takes out the Mexicans, there will be no evidence for segmented assimilation." This is a statement often heard among immigration specialists. It is buttressed by the size of the Mexican-origin population, by far the largest among contemporary immigrant groups, and by its low human capital. Some observers believe that signs of dissonant acculturation, low ambition, and the emergence of oppositional attitudes concentrate mainly among second-generation Mexicans. This is erroneous since other groups that have experienced negative modes of incorporation are also at risk. In different contexts, we have examined evidence to that effect among other sizable immigrant minorities, including Nicaraguans, Haitians, and post-Mariel Cubans.

Nevertheless, the Mexican immigrant population is defined by several attributes that make it unique and deserving of special attention. It is worth reviewing what these are and how they affect the second generation, particularly in the context of the ideological battles just discussed. In California, in particular, nativist and assimilationist policies have been directed primarily at Mexicans and their offspring with consequences that, as just seen, have been the opposite of those intended. The Mexican population of the United States is marked by three characteristics that make it unique:

It is the product of an uninterrupted flow lasting more than a century. Mexicans are the *only* foreign group that has been part of both the classic period of immigration at the beginning of the twentieth century and the present movement. Accordingly, Mexicans are also the only group among today's major immigrant nationalities to have spawned an earlier second and even third generation.

Mexicans come from the only less-developed country sharing a land border with the United States. This geographical contiguity has facilitated both labor recruitment and subsequent mass labor displacements, mediated by social networks. The facility of such movements across a land border accounts for the lower average human capital of Mexican immigrants relative to other groups, who come from even poorer but more distant countries.

Because of their numbers, poverty, and visibility, Mexican immigrants were targets of repeated waves of nativist hostility throughout the twentieth century. These attacks included organized government campaigns aimed at their repatriation or at forcefully preventing their settlement. Mexican immigrants have thus experienced a negative mode of incorporation not only at present but for over 100 years. Demand for Mexican migrant labor has been equally persistent, but the conditions under which it has been employed have been marked by the social inferiority and political vulnerability created by this negative context.

Results of our study offer abundant evidence of the consequences of these features. Mexican immigrants represent *the* textbook example of theoretically anticipated effects of low immigrant human capital combined with a negative context of reception. It is worth summarizing these results for what they tell us about the specific experiences of the group and, by extension, of those to be anticipated for other disadvantaged foreign minorities:

Adult Mexican immigrants not only receive low earnings, but their economic disadvantage also endures even after controlling for their human capital. Net of human capital factors, Mexican parents in our sample earn $1,910 less per year than other adult immigrants.

This economic disadvantage is compounded because whatever human capital Mexican immigrants possess has a lower return than that among more successful groups. Thus, years of U.S. residence do not increase incomes for Mexican parents in our sample, and knowledge of English yields a lower payoff than for immigrants from other countries.

Mexican parents are significantly more likely to report low bonds of solidarity and low levels of support from their co-ethnics, reflecting the weak communities that have emerged under their precarious conditions of arrival and settlement. Aspirations for their children are also significantly lower than for other groups.

Mexican–American children are the only Latin group in the sample to lack a positive nationality effect on fluent bilingualism, and they have the lowest average self-esteem. Controlling for other factors, Mexican origin makes no positive contribution to either adaptation outcome.

Mexican–American children are the most likely to have shifted self-identities away from any American label and toward an unhyphenated national (i.e., Mexican) identity. They are also the group most prone to racialize their national origin. Both trends reflect a strong process of reactive formation to perceived external hostility.

Reflecting their parents' low aspirations, Mexican–American children have significantly lower educational expectations than the CILS average and the lowest among Latin-origin groups. This disadvantage persists after controlling for other factors. Net of them, second-generation Mexican students are still 10 percent less likely to believe that an advanced college degree is within their reach than other students.

Corresponding to these low aspirations and cumulative disadvantages, Mexican-origin students are less likely to perform well in school. Their lower-than-average grades and test scores cannot be explained by individual, family, or school predictors. In junior high school, Mexican students fell behind a net 12 points in standardized math scores and 15 points in reading scores, after controlling for these predictors; they also had a significant net disadvantage in grades. This inferior performance continues in late high school, where Mexican–American students suffer a significant handicap after controlling for a wide array of individual and family factors.

These cumulative results clearly point to a difficult process of adaptation and to the likelihood of downward assimilation in many cases. The high optimism of parents and the superior school performance and lower dropout rates of second-generation Mexicans relative to their native-parentage peers only qualify this conclusion. This optimism and relatively better academic record reflect a residual immigrant drive that weakens with the passage of time under the continuous influence of an adverse social environment. It is worth emphasizing that the second-generation Mexican advantage is only observable in comparison with their native counterparts, that is, third-generation and higher Hispanics who perform even worse than the more recent arrivals. This comparison offers no grounds for expecting that academic performance will improve and dropout rates will decline over time.

* * *

The danger of downward assimilation for Mexican–American youths is only compounded by the policies that have captured the imagination of mainstream voters. For reasons already examined, nativism and forceful assimilationism yield programs that undermine successful adaptation by increasing dissonant acculturation or provoking an adversarial reaction. In light of the present evidence, there is no second-generation group for which selective acculturation is more necessary than for Mexican Americans. This would entail educational programs that combine learning of English and acculturation with preservation of Spanish and understanding and respect for the parents' culture. In particular, there should be ample external support for the immigrant family and for its incipient attempts at building strong community bonds. In many Mexican families, the *only* thing going for the children is the support and ambition of their parents. These aspirations should be strengthened rather than undermined.

From a long-term perspective, policies toward Mexican immigration advocated by the two mainstream ideologies discussed previously verge on the suicidal. Demand for Mexican migrant labor continues unabated, and its arrival is guaranteed by various legal loopholes and the strong social networks created over a century. Once here, however, migrant workers and their children are heavily discriminated against, blamed for their poverty, and subjected either to nativist ire or pressures toward immediate assimilation. The results are not hard to discern in the spectacle of the impoverished barrios of Los Angeles, San Diego, Houston, and other large southwestern cities and in consistent results from our study. * * *

José Luis Morín
*Latino/a Rights and Justice in the United
States: Perspectives and Approaches*
35–38 (2004)

Today, it is generally incontrovertible that the primary aim of U.S. policy toward Latin America historically was its maintenance of political and economic hegemony over the Americas. Tragically, this goal too often came at the expense of the human rights and dignity of peoples in Latin America. But it is also argued that the United States has not only reaped the benefits of its past domination over Latin America, but it also actively seeks to keep them in place through its present policies. After decades of consolidating its hegemony over the hemisphere, the United States in the post-Cold War era is able to deploy new justifications for the use of military force, and it utilizes global economic strategies to maintain its power over the region.

In its first military intervention in a Latin American country after the fall of the Soviet Union, the 1989 U.S. military invasion of Panama purported to fight the "war on drugs" by capturing the alleged drug-kingpin and head of state Manuel Antonio Noriega, a former C.I.A. operative who had been paid upwards of $200,000 annually from U.S. tax dollars. However, as an anti-drug initiative, this military invasion today is widely considered a failure. "Operation Just Cause had virtually no effect on drug trafficking," and in reality, Noriega turned out to be "a minor player in the narcotics business." Analysts have documented how the invasion had nothing to do with fighting a war against drugs and virtually everything to do with how Noriega became increasingly expendable to U.S. policy and interests by the late 1980s. In fact, Panama's new President, Guillermo Endara, had ties to the banks implicated in drug-money laundering. Further belying President George H.W. Bush's justifications of the "war on drugs" for the invasion, the U.S. government's General Accounting Office reported increases in drug activity in Panama two years after the invasion, noting that the country "continues to be a haven for money laundering."

The U.S. invasion of Panama endures today, along with past interventions, as another affront to human rights and international law. Critics charged that the U.S. military's use of excessive force caused the deaths of thousands of Panamanian civilians in violation of international law. Numerous human rights groups reported that disproportionate numbers of Panamanian civilians were killed as a result of the invasion, and at the United Nations, the U.N. General Assembly vehemently condemned the invasion as a "flagrant violation" of international law. In the post-Cold War era, the U.S. invasion of Panama became symbolic of U.S. intentions to consolidate its authority over the Americas. Past pretexts—such as spreading democracy or the fight against communism—have been replaced with new justifications for U.S. interventionism, such as the war on drugs.

But it is crucial to note that direct military intervention—however much an option for U.S. policymakers—is superfluous in view of the United States' current global economic supremacy. The North American Free Trade Agreement (NAFTA) and other U.S. efforts to promote the neo-liberal agenda of free trade, open markets, privatization, and economic global integration have provided an international framework that facilitates and continues the flow of economic benefits to the countries of the "North"—the United States, Western Europe, and Japan—often with diminishing returns and growing economic inequality for a vast number of developing nations of the "South"—Latin America, Africa, and Asia.

There is mounting evidence that the free trade policies promoted by the United States have actually led to uneven development, favoring developed countries to the detriment of developing nations. "The income gap between the fifth of the world's people living in the richest countries and the fifth in the poorest was 74–to–1 in 1997, up from 60–to–1 in 1990 and 30–to–1 in 1960. By 1997, the richest 20% captured 86% of world income, with the poorest 20% capturing a mere 1%." Throughout Latin America from the period of the 1980s to the 1990s, "the absolute number of people living under conditions of poverty swelled from 125 million to 186 million, an increase of 61 million, or nearly 50 percent."

With the expansion of U.S. corporate interests, the exploitation of human labor and resources in Latin America by U.S. multinational corporations at the expense of human rights, labor rights, and environmental rights of Latin Americans has become an increasing concern. Over the last decade, U.S. companies have been accused of engaging in illegal child labor and sweatshop practices and in creating gross environmental hazards in factories or *maquiladoras* that produce garments and other items for major U.S. corporations throughout Mexico, Central America, and the Caribbean. Free trade zones that offer tax breaks to global corporations in developing countries have frequently been cited for using repressive means "to keep free trade zones free of labor unions, as well as health and safety regulations." In El Salvador, U.S. clothing manufacturers have been able to pay as little as 33 cents an hour to factory workers.

As illustrated in a series of editorials in the *New York Times*, free trade, as it currently operates, provides an unfair advantage to U.S. business interests. Profits are harvested by developed countries on the backs of poverty-stricken nations. Huge sums in U.S. subsidies to the U.S. cotton and other industries virtually insure that developing nations will remain poor and unable to compete fairly with developed nations.

The model for development in Latin America touted by U.S. presidents has been NAFTA. Yet despite NAFTA's promise of economic development, poverty stands roughly the same in Mexico today—just over 50 percent—as it did in the early 1980s. But if one factors in population growth in Mexico, from 70 million to 100 million over the same period, Mexico can be considered worse off today with "19 million more Mexicans living in poverty than 20 years ago, according to Mexican government and international organizations.... What has become painfully clear in Mexico is that free trade—most famously NAFTA—has failed to lift the country out of poverty."

Indeed, nearly ten years after NAFTA began, a study sponsored by the Carnegie Endowment for International Peace concludes that "NAFTA has not helped the Mexican economy keep pace with the growing demand for jobs." The purported benefits of NAFTA for Mexico's poorest have not been realized. "Real wages for most Mexicans today are lower than they were when NAFTA took effect." Moreover, "NAFTA has not stemmed the flow of poor Mexicans into the United States in search of jobs; in fact there has been a dramatic rise in the number of migrants to the United States, despite an unprecedented increase in border control measures."

Nobel prize winner in economics Joseph E. Stiglitz has also voiced criticisms about the course that globalization has taken, noting that even in instances where growth has occurred in Mexico, "the benefits have accrued largely to the upper 30 percent, and have been even more concentrated in the top 10 percent. Those at the bottom have gained little; many are even worse off." Stiglitz attributes the present-day attitude of developed countries to the persistence of the colonial mentality that presumes they know what is best for developing nations, and that the United States is still affected by the historical legacy of "manifest destiny" and expansionism, and to an even greater extent, "by the cold war, in which principles of democracy were compromised or ignored, in the all encompassing struggle against communism."

Despite these criticisms, the United States is poised to begin another round of free trade initiatives throughout the Americas in the form of the Free Trade Area of the Americas and bilateral treaties with Central American countries. Considering the balance of power, it is questionable whether most Latin American countries truly have a choice in the matter.

Notes and Questions

1. Why would NAFTA, a free trade agreement, impoverish so many villagers and farmers?

2. On NAFTA as an immigration push factor, see *Free Trade, Migration, and Corn Crises*, Commerce/Economics News, Oct. 20, 2007.

3. On death at the border, see, e.g., Timothy Dunn, *The Militarization of the U.S.-Mexico Border, 1978–1992; Low–Intensity Conflict Doctrine Comes Home* (1996).

SECTION 2.   AN EXCEPTIONAL CASE: THE EARLY WAVE OF CUBAN IMMIGRANTS

An exception to the above story is the first wave of Cuban immigrants that arrived in Florida in the months following Fidel Castro's revolution in the 1960s and 1970s. In 1966 Congress passed the Cuban Adjustment Act giving Cuban refugees quick access to legal permanent residence, a status that would otherwise take years to achieve. Many of these early arrivals were wealthy, Caucasian-looking professionals, who feared that the new socialist regime would take away some of their assets and privileges. Pro-freemarket and opposed to communism, they soon became the darlings of the U.S. and Florida governments, which showered aid and social services on them, with the result that this group fairly quickly resumed the middle-and upper-middle class status they had enjoyed back home. Miami today owes much of its prosperity and cosmopolitan quality to these immigrants.

Subsequent waves of Cuban refugees, including a group known as the Marielitos who came to this country from the port of Mariel in 1980, arrived as part of a major exodus. Another took place in 1994 during the Rafter Refugee Crisis. The latter event caused President Clinton to order the return to the island all Cubans picked up and intercepted at sea. Some of the marielitos were mentally ill or had criminal records, hence were unwelcome in Castro's Cuba. Needless to say, their adjustment in the United States has been rockier than that of the first group.

See generally Part One, supra, for detailed discussion of the waves of Cuban migration and the Cuban Adjustment Act.

SECTION 3.   LATINO IMMIGRATION FROM THE PERSPECTIVE OF POSTCOLONIAL AND CRITICAL THEORY

What drives Latino immigration and popular resistance to it? As you go through these materials, ponder what they mean about social power and the Latino/a condition. Consider the following issues:

- *Shifts and changes.* The country's interest in Latino immigration shifts from one period to the next. What accounts for these changes? Derrick Bell posited that interest convergence accounted for *Brown v. Board of Education* and other black breakthroughs, and that to understand the twists and turns of black fortunes, one had to attend to what the self-interest of elite whites dictated at the time. In the same fashion, might the needs of agribusiness or of the manufacturing sector call the tune for Latino/a immigration?

- *"We're here because you're there."* Mexico, Guatemala, the Dominican Republic, Honduras, and El Salvador are some of the largest sending countries for Latino immigration, particularly of the working-class undocumented kind. Why is this so? These are also the Latin American countries where the United States has meddled most insistently, with coups, takeovers, and other, less overt grabs of a country's wealth and natural resources. Could the United States' former and present role as a colonialist power, paradoxically perhaps, explain the brutal poverty that afflicts much of Latin America and triggers the exodus of desperate villagers looking for work here in order to send part of their wages home?

- *The role of neocolonialism*: *Globalization and the "flat world."* Globalization has meant the diffusion of capital, raw materials, and finished products throughout the digitally-connected world, with Asian Indian entrepreneurs and billionaires establishing successful companies in Silicon Valley and American corporations setting up plants in Thailand and along the Mexican border called *maquiladores*. In fact, a prime tenet of the new global economy, embraced by U.S. liberals and freemarket conservatives alike, is that trade should be as unencumbered as possible by tariffs and other protective measures and restrictions.

What about the free movement of workers and bodies? The European Union has embraced open borders and free movement of workers seeking jobs in member countries. The United States has not, with the result that immigration is the one last holdout for U.S. globalization policy. Why has the United States not "gone the limit?"

- By the same token, consider the odd political alignment in the current debate about immigration policy. U.S. corporations, generally bastions of conservatism, favor relatively open immigration, while unions, liberals, and some paleoconservatives like Pat Buchanan oppose it. Why is that?

Patrisia Gonzales & Roberto Rodriguez
We Are All Zapatistas
Universal Press Syndicate, Jan. 2, 2004

The sacred fire shot high into the night sky in Temoaya, Mexico, at a gathering of indigenous peoples. It brought the eagle and the condor—native peoples from the north and south—to this ceremonial center of the Otomi nation in October 1993.

In front of the fire were the sacred Peace and Dignity staffs carried by runners via Alaska and Chile. Living in subservience was no longer an option. A large Chiapas delegation—symbolically representing the Quetzal of the Mayans—spoke with a sense of urgency. The fire roared even higher into the cold Otomi sky. It was a prelude to Jan. 1, 1994, the Zapatista insurrection, timed to coincide with the first day of implementation of the North American Free Trade Agreement (NAFTA). The Ejercito Zapatista de Liberacion (EZLN)—which had been building for a decade—chose that day to protest the brazen inhumanity and the unconstitutional nature of the agreement. The drive to implement it included the stripping of article 27 from the Mexican Constitution—which formerly protected the integrity of the nation's communal lands.

The year before, there had been a huge indigenous gathering at the sacred site of Teotihuacan, Mexico, on Oct. 11, 1992. Many had come to greet the runners carrying the sacred staffs and prayers from throughout the continent (Abya Yalla, Pacha Mama, Semanahuak, Turtle Island). Others were there to affirm their sovereignty in the face of 500 years of European occupation. Before that, there had also been a historic gathering of indigenous peoples in Quito, Ecuador.

Something was in the air. Rigoberta Menchu had been named the 1992 Nobel Peace Prize winner, and then came the United Nation's Decade of Indigenous Peoples. After the initial Zapatista insurrection shocked the world, support arrived from the four winds. "Todos somos Zapatistas"—"We are all Zapatistas"—became the mantra for its supporters worldwide, though everyone was sent home with the same message: Don't come here simply to help us. Fight for your own dignity. And thus everyone returned home, all with their own tasks.

For indigenous people worldwide, it was not about others, but about us. There had always been contact between indigenous peoples. But now, it was more sustained, affirming a historic acknowledgement that the continent is one. Whereas before, the enemies of indigenous peoples had been European colonizers and their descendants, the new enemy was U.S. multinational corporations, come to take the little communal and indigenous land, resources and sustenance that remained.

The Zapatista struggle was not just another political movement. It was the first struggle of the electronic age, and it was a new "flower war"—a poetic and humanistic war from deep within the Chiapas jungle, which the Zapatistas clearly won. Their "pasamontanas," their masks, gave indigenous people a face and a heart. A large part of that face was organizing and creating autonomous, self-governing municipalities or zones. While an indigenous rights law—guaranteeing land, cultural and language rights—remains elusive, the Zapatistas have changed the face of Mexico and the continent. They've also inspired the worldwide anti-globalization movement.

Since the initial uprising, the continent has seen other major indigenous uprisings from Bolivia to Peru to Ecuador and Guatemala. No one can predict whether the recently negotiated Central American Free Trade Agreement (between the United States, Nicaragua, Guatemala, El Salvador and Honduras) will trigger other indigenous (or even broader) uprisings, though what's certain is that the same NAFTA dynamic will be unleashed.

Close to 2 million campesinos have been displaced from their lands due to U.S.-subsidized agricultural imports (maize) flooding into Mexico. This has greatly accelerated a century-old uprooting and migration process to the cities and into the United States. NAFTA has also meant huge job losses in the U.S. manufacturing sector (estimated at 3 million).

At least a half-million have been certified by the U.S. government as NAFTA-related.

The recent turmoil and protests in Miami (against the Free Trade Area of the Americas) and in Cancun, Mexico, (against the World Trade Organization talks) indicate that forthcoming agreements are not a done deal. They call for handing the continent's and world's natural resources (including the DNA of all living things)—at the expense of environmental, wage, labor, safety and human rights laws—over to multinational corporations. If anything, these proposed agreements may be a prelude to a worldwide Zapatista insurrection based on respect for our sacred Mother Earth. That can't spell good news for the best-laid plans of the multinationals.

Tim Weiner
Mexico City Journal: Of Gringos and Old
Grudges: This Land Is Their Land
N.Y. Times, Foreign Section, Jan. 9, 2004, at A4

MEXICO CITY, Jan. 8—In the American South, William Faulkner once wrote, the past isn't dead. It isn't even past.

This may become truer the farther south one goes. In the United States, almost no one remembers the war that Americans fought against Mexico more than 150 years ago. In Mexico, almost no one has forgotten.

The war cut this country in two, and "the wound never really healed," said Miguel Soto, a Mexico City historian. It took less than two years, and ended with the gringos seizing half of Mexico, taking the land that became America's Wild West: California, Texas, New Mexico, Arizona, Nevada, Utah and beyond.

In Mexico, they call this "the Mutilation." That may help explain why relations between the nations are sometimes so tense. As President Bush prepares to fly down to Mexico from Texas, where the war began back in 1846, the debate here over how to relate to the United States is heating up once again.

The question of the day is the more than 20 million Mexicans who now live in the United States. But sensitivities about sovereignty surround every thorny issue involving Americans in Mexico. Can Americans buy land? Sometimes. Drill for oil? Never. Can American officers comb airports in Mexico? Yes. Carry guns as lawmen? No. Open and close the border at will? Well, they try.

To realize that the border was fixed by war and controlled by the victors is to understand why some Mexicans may not love the 21st-century American colossus. Yet they adore the old American ideals of freedom, equality and boundless opportunity, and they keep voting, by the millions, with their feet. In "a relationship of love and of hatred," as Mr. Soto says, bitter memories sometimes surface like old shrapnel under the skin.

Fragments of the old war stand in the slanting morning sunlight at an old convent here in Mexico City, a sanctuary seized by invading American troops in 1847, now the National Museum of Interventions, which chronicles the struggle. "The war between Mexico and the United States has a different meaning for Mexicans and Americans," said the museum's director, Alfredo Hernandez Murillo. "For Americans, it's one more step in the expansion that began when the United States was created. For Mexicans, the war meant we lost half the nation. It was very damaging, and not just because the land was lost.

"It's a symbol of Mexico's weakness throughout history in confronting the United States. For Mexicans, it's still a shock sometimes to cross the border and see the Spanish names of the places we lost." Those places have names like Los Angeles, San Francisco, San Diego, Santa Fe, El Paso, San Antonio; the list is long.

The war killed 13,780 Americans, and perhaps 50,000 or more Mexicans—no one knows the true number. It was the first American war led by commanders from West Point. These were men like Ulysses S. Grant and William Tecumseh Sherman, Robert E. Lee and Jefferson Davis. A little more than a decade later, Grant and Sherman battled Lee and Davis in the Civil War.

Historians are still fighting over how and why the battles of the Mexican War began. Some say it was Mexico's fault for trying to stop the secession of what was then (and to some, still is) the Republic of Texas. Some say it was an imperial land grab by the president of the United States. President James K. Polk did confide to his diary that the aim of the war was "to acquire for the United States—California, New Mexico and perhaps some other of the northern provinces of Mexico." When it was won, in February 1848, he wrote, "There will be added to the United States an immense empire, the value of which 20 years hence it would be difficult to calculate." Nine days later, prospectors struck gold in California.

Aftershocks still resonate from the Mexican War—or, as the Mexicans have it, "the American invasion." The students who walk through the National Museum of Interventions still gasp at a lithograph standing next to an American flag. It shows Gen. Winfield Scott riding into Mexico City's national square—"the halls of Montezuma," in the words of the Marine Corps Hymn—to seize power and raise the flag. He had followed the same invasion route as the 16th-century Spanish conquerors of Mexico. The American occupation lasted 11 months.

Many of the 75,000 Mexicans living in the newly conquered American West lost their rights to own land and live as they pleased. It was well into the 20th century before much of the land was settled and civilized. Now, that civilization is taking another turn. More than half of the 20 million Mexicans north of the border live on the land that once was theirs. Some 8.5 million live in California—a quarter of the population. Nearly half the people of New Mexico have roots in old Mexico. Mexico is, in a sense, slowly reoccupying its former property.

"History extracts its costs with the passage of time," said Jesus Velasco Marquez, a professor who has long studied the war. "We are the biggest minority in the United States, and particularly in the territory that once was ours."

José Luis Morín

Latino/a Rights and Justice in the United States: Perspectives and Approaches
28–35 (2004)

CONSOLIDATING HEMISPHERIC HEGEMONY

Beyond the assertions of U.S. power over Mexico and Puerto Rico, the history of U.S–Latin American relations abounds with examples of instances in which the U.S. government has sought to extend its political, economic and cultural domination. The forms of racism and paternalism evident in manifest destiny, the *Insular Cases*, and the other examples cited previously, have also been discernible in U.S. actions toward other Latin American countries. The seemingly countless number of U.S. interventions in Latin America's so-called "banana republics" reeks of condescension and paternalism.

The cornerstone of U.S. policy toward Latin America has been the Monroe Doctrine of 1823. As most of Latin America broke away from Spanish and Portuguese colonial rule by the 1820s, President James Monroe's administration moved quickly to stave off any additional interventions or colonization by other European powers, declaring such attempts "dangerous to our peace and safety." The Monroe Doctrine's silence on U.S. colonial aspirations opened the door for the rise of force against any alleged outside threat to U.S. interests in the hemisphere, and consequently, any obstacle in the way of achieving complete hegemony over the Americas.

To advance U.S. interests in the Americas, the 1904 Roosevelt Corollary to the Monroe Doctrine laid out the ground rules that justified U.S. military interventionism. In the words of Theodore Roosevelt:

> Chronic wrong-doing, or an impotence which results in a general loosening of the ties of civilized society, may in America, as elsewhere, ultimately require intervention by some civilized nation, and in the Western Hemisphere the adherence of the United States to the Monroe Doctrine may force the United States, however reluctantly, in flagrant cases of such wrongdoing or impotence, to the exercise of an international police power.

Of course, the "civilized nation" to oversee this extension of the Monroe Doctrine was the United States, and U.S. desires to intervene in Latin America were far from reluctant. Commonly referred to as the "Big Stick" doctrine, the Roosevelt Corollary to the Monroe Doctrine legitimized the use of U.S. armed force, but it did little to "civilize" or democratize the region. Between 1898 and 1934, the United States militarily invaded and/or occupied Latin American countries on more than thirty occasions and "despite high-minded rhetoric and ostensible nobility of purpose, not a single U.S. intervention led to installation of democracy."

In the Dominican Republic, U.S. military interventions begun under Theodore Roosevelt's administration spanned many decades and included the U.S. invasions and military occupations in 1903, 1904, 1914, 1916–1924, and 1965. These interventions provided direct control over the Dominican Republic's economy for the benefit of U.S. banking and commercial interests, most clearly evident in U.S. seizure of the customhouses. Instead of spreading democracy, U.S. policies supported brutal dictators, as in the Dominican Republic's Rafael Trujillo, who could safeguard U.S. business interests and profits. Into the later half of the twentieth century, the 1965 U.S. military occupation of the Dominican Republic guaranteed that the democratically elected government of Juan Bosch would never return, paving the way for Trujillo's right-hand man Joaquin Balaguer.

For the United States, adherence to the norms of international law was at best an afterthought. As U.S. power and control over the region grew, justifying violations of international law became increasingly insignificant to U.S. government leaders. In a moment of complete candor in reference to the intervention of Panama, Theodore Roosevelt offered no explanation other than "I took the Isthmus." From as early as the 1850s, the U.S. government preferred to recognize William Walker as the legitimate president of Nicaragua—a North American filibuster who orchestrated an illegal coup to install himself as president, declare English the official language, and legalize slavery—than to respect the rights of Nicaraguans to self-determination. Into the twentieth century, the United States abused its self-ordained "police power" to impose a brutally racist and autocratic U.S. military regime upon the people of Haiti during the U.S. occupation of Haiti from 1915–1934.

Having already significantly consolidated its hegemony by the 1930s, the United States moved toward a policy of acting as a "good neighbor," adopting a noninterventionist stance, in words if not deeds. This shift was based, in part, on the implementation of international agreements, most notably the Convention on the Rights and Duties of States adopted at Montevideo in 1933, that reinforced the concept of the equality of states and specifically declared in article 8 that "[n]o state has the right to intervene in the internal or external affairs of another." Although the "good neighbor" policy ostensibly sought to demonstrate U.S. intentions to act in accordance with international law in an effort to salvage its international reputation, the policy change was undercut, not by a return to overt military interventionism, but by U.S. resort to the installation of puppet governments and support for military dictatorships responsible for egregious human rights violations throughout Latin America.

In the name of fighting communism, U.S. policy took an especially brutal turn at the expense of human rights in Latin America. Similar to the neo-colonial relationship maintained with the Dominican Republic, the United States propped up and sustained ruthless dictators and oligarchs throughout Latin America. The Somoza family dynasty (1934–1979) in Nicaragua, a family "[t]hat seized most of the wealth, including a land area equal the size of Massachusetts" and the infamous "Fourteen Families" of El Salvador who still control almost 60 percent of the land were among the most notorious examples. In Cuba, the United States backed the government of Fulgencio Batista, a dictator who tolerated gross economic disparities, poverty, unemployment, illiteracy, and racial exclusion for the protection of U.S. business interests. In these and other instances throughout Latin America, repression became the means by which social unrest in the face of economic injustice was quelled. Latin American armies trained and financed by the United States became the surrogates for U.S. marines, who in earlier times were readily called upon to intervene.

BEHIND THE RHETORIC OF DEMOCRACY

It would appear inconceivable that the United States—a country founded in a war against colonialism—would seek to subjugate other peoples or undermine the very principles of democracy that it purports to spread. The contradiction between its stated principles and its hegemonic ambitions has been and continues to be a central theme in U.S. foreign policy. However, a now familiar pattern was established early on in Latin America: U.S. global economic interests usually supercede even its best intentions. A U.S. marine in the 1930s, Smedley Darlington Butler, memorialized his recollection of decades of U.S. interventionism as such:

> I spent thirty-three years, most of my time being a high class muscle man for big business, for Wall Street and the bankers. In short, I was a racketeer for capitalism.... I helped make Mexico, especially Tampico, safe for American oil interests in 1916. I helped make Haiti and Cuba a decent place for the National City Bank boys to collect revenue in. I helped in the raping of half a dozen Central American republics for the benefits of Wall Street. The record of racketeering is long. I helped purify Nicaragua for the international banking house of Brown Brothers in 1909–1912. I brought light to the Dominican Republic for American sugar interests in 1916.

But as Cornell University historian Walter LaFeber explains, U.S. business interests were not alone in this venture; the U.S government worked ceaselessly to support U.S.-based commercial enterprises. By establishing and maintaining a system grounded in the Monroe Doctrine, the U.S. government could always provide direct assistance—including the use of military force to protect U.S. corporate interests in the region.

Hegemony over the Western Hemisphere translated into securing a perpetual source of cheap and exploitable land, raw materials, human labor, and other resources. This held true as much for the Cold War era (1947–1989) as it did in earlier periods in U.S.-Latin American relations.

In 1950, George Kennan, the chief State Department official responsible for the Cold War containment policy, outlined the goals of U.S. policy toward Latin America during the Cold War in order of importance, as follows:

1.   The protection of our [*sic*] raw materials;

2.   The prevention of military exploitation of Latin America by the enemy; and

3.   The prevention of the psychological mobilization of Latin America against us.

To these ends, in 1954, the U.S. government through the C.I.A. and the United Fruit Company combined to topple the democratically-elected government of Jacobo Arbenz, who sought land reform for impoverished peasants in Guatemala. Although not a communist, the U.S. government considered Arbenz "soft" on communism, creating the necessary pretext for the coup. For decades, U.S.-backed, right-wing military juntas in Guatemala crushed the opposition and committed countless atrocities and killings among civilians, peasants, and indigenous peoples.

In El Salvador, the Salvadoran military engaged in bloody counterinsurgency operations backed by the U.S. government. Its mission to eliminate the opposition to the government resulted in innumerable deaths, including the assassinations of three U.S. nuns, a Catholic layperson, and Archbishop Oscar Romero in 1980; the massacre at El Mozote, where hundreds of men, women and children were slaughtered in 1981; and the murder of six Jesuit scholars, their housekeeper and her daughter in El Salvador in 1989. The U.S. government continued to provide military aid to the government of El Salvador even as the U.S.-trained Salvadoran soldiers, such as the Atlactl Battalion, were being implicated in these murders. In lieu of sending its own troops (that is, the use of the "Big Stick"), the U.S. government preferred a policy that allowed the local armed forces to assume the role of assassins, saboteurs, and terrorists to protect U.S. interests in the region.

The 1975 Select Committee to Study Governmental Operations with Respect to Intelligence Activities, known as the Church Committee report after Senator Frank Church, revealed the extent of U.S. covert operations in Cuba, Chile, the Dominican Republic, and the Congo, including plots to kill Fidel Castro and Patrice Lumumba. The Church hearings and other disclosures established that the C.I.A.'s *Freedom Fighting Manual* and the School of the Americas' *Study Manual* were published and distributed to Latin American military personnel for the precise purpose of training in sabotage and torture.

In yet another successful attempt at "regime change" in Latin America, the United States in 1973 helped depose the democratically-elected government of Salvador Allende in Chile. Recently declassified C.I.A. documents directly implicate President Nixon and then Secretary of State Henry Kissinger in the covert operations to destabilize the Allende government. In an exposé of Henry Kissinger's involvement in the events that took place in Chile, Christopher Hitchens observed that "the very name of Allende was anathema to the extreme Right in Chile, to certain powerful corporations (notably ITT, Pepsi Cola and the Chase Manhattan Bank) which did business in Chile and the United States, and to the CIA." General Augusto Pinochet—whose right-wing dictatorship unseated Allende's government and was recognized by the United States—has been accused of torture and other gross violations of human rights resulting in the deaths and disappearances of thousands of persons following the 1973 coup (see, e.g., *Regina v. Bartle*, House of Lords, 24 March 1999 [1999] 2 All ER 97, [1999] 2 WLR 827). U.S. support for authoritarian regimes in Argentina, Paraguay, and Brazil had similar aims: violence—including torture, "disappearances," "dirty wars," and other violations of the most basic human rights—was to be deployed against anyone who opposed the established order of repressive, rightwing regimes that protected U.S. interests in the hemisphere.

In the case of Nicaragua, U.S. disregard for the human rights of Latin Americans under international law could not be more glaring. In 1986, the International Court of Justice (ICJ or the World Court) voted overwhelmingly to condemn U.S. support of the "contra war" and the mining of the Nicaraguan harbor in Nicaragua as blatant violations of international law that, *inter alia*, endangered the lives and wellbeing of civilians and infringed upon Nicaragua's territorial sovereignty (Military and Paramilitary Activities (Nicaragua v. U.S.), 1986 I.C.J. 14 (June 27)). By any measure, such actions could be categorized as state-sponsored terrorism. The seriousness of U.S. violations against Nicaragua left the ICJ no option but to rule that the United States was obligated to make reparations to the Republic of Nicaragua for all the injuries caused to the country and its people, damage claims which had risen to $17 billion. In defiance of the World Court's decision, the U.S. government refused to recognize the court's jurisdiction, shunning all accountability under international law.

The resulting turmoil, death, and economic and social destruction left after decades of internal conflict in Central America cannot be underestimated:

> [T]he years from 1979–1991 turned out to be the bloodiest, most violent, and most destructive era in Central America's post–1820 history. The number of dead and "disappeared" varies according to different sources. The minimum number is 200,000 (40,000 in Nicaragua, 75,000 in El Salvador, 75,000 in Guatemala, 10,000 in Honduras and the frontier fighting in Costa Rica), but this is only an estimate. Millions have been displaced or made refugees. If a similar catastrophe struck the United States in proportion, 2½ million North Americans would die and 10 to 20 million would be driven from their homes.

Following this period of armed conflict in Central America, it was found that "[h]undreds of thousands of Central Americans (one out of four in the case of Salvadorans) have been uprooted by force, military pressure, or war destruction, becoming refugees either in their own countries or abroad." By the early 1990s, "more than a million Salvadorans and about 200,000 Guatemalan refugees resided in the United States alone . . . most of them children or young adults."

The connection between U.S. policy and many documented human right atrocities of that era has been well established by respected sources, including the international commission of inquiry established under the Accord of Oslo of 1994. The commission of inquiry, officially named the Commission for Historical Clarification, concluded:

> Whilst anti-communism, promoted by the United States within the framework of its foreign policy, received firm support from right-wing political parties and from various other powerful actors in Guatemala, the United States demonstrated that it was willing to provide support for strong military regimes in its strategic backyard.

Throughout the Cold War period, as Smith asserts, "[f]ear of the 'communist threat' may have been greatly exaggerated, as now appears in retrospect." In support for this assessment, the Commission for Historical Clarification found that

> at no time during the internal armed confrontation did the guerilla groups have the military potential necessary to pose an imminent threat to the State. The number of insurgent combatants was too small to be able to compete in the military arena with the Guatemalan Army, which had more troops and superior weaponry, as well as better training and co-ordination . . . the State deliberately magnified the military threat of the insurgency, a practise justified by the concept of the internal enemy. The inclusion of all opponents under one banner, democratic or otherwise, pacifist or guerrilla, legal or illegal, communist or noncommunist, served to justify numerous and serious crimes.

Thus, in hindsight it is plausible to conclude that U.S. policies in Latin America had less to do with fighting communism than with maintaining the old order in which U.S. economic interests could reign free to exploit Latin America's land, labor, and other resources. Certainly, U.S. support for brutal rightwing dictatorships belies any rhetoric about spreading freedom and democracy.

———————

In a little-known chapter of U.S. history, escaping slaves took the Underground Railroad south, not north, hoping to reach Mexico, which had repudiated slavery early in its history and was in the process of liberalizing its policy toward its indigenous population (again, long before the United States did). Mexico welcomed the former slaves, many of whom became permanent residents and Mexican citizens.

Debbie Johnson
Mexico's History of Standing Up Against Black Slavery
Voz de Aztlan News Service, Apr. 30, 2007

There is a long history of Mexicans welcoming and assisting Blacks fleeing American slavery. The fact of the matter is that when white "slave-hunting" militias would come into Mexico demanding that their "property"—the enslaved workers—be returned, many Mexicans rejected these pleas and were angered at the fact that these slave hunters would have the audacity to enter Mexico and attempt to impose their laws in a nation that had already banned slavery for moral and religious reasons.

As early as 1811, the Rev. Jose Morelos—a Mexican of African descent—led an all-Black army brigade to help fight for Mexican independence. In 1855 more than 4,000 runaway slaves were helped by Mexicans in Texas to escape and find freedom in Mexico. The Underground Railroad was not just into Canada. It went south as well.

Indeed, throughout three centuries, African slaves were joined by Mexicans in opposition to the exploitation of Africans by European immigrants—settlers—on the North American continent. Just a few examples of this long and rich history of solidarity are:

- In 1546, Mexico recorded the first conspiracy against slavery, which occurred in Mexico City among a coalition of enslaved Africans and indigenous insurgents.

- In 1609 in Vera Cruz, Mexico, Yanga established the first free pueblo of formerly enslaved Africans in the Western Hemisphere.

- In 1693 within the area of the "United States," which was in fact Mexican territory, an alliance between African runaways and rebellious indigenous tribes developed and resulted in considerable cooperation.

- In 1820, in Mexico, the pro-independence army commanded by Black Gen. Vicente Ramon Guerrero was joined and saved by the courageous Mexican indigenous leader Pedro Ascensio. This army won many battles in resisting French and American colonial wars of occupation.

- In 1836, during the battle of the Alamo, Mexican troops fought not only to keep the U.S. from annexing Texas, but also to abolish the dreaded practice of slavery carried out by pro-slavery white settlers. While the Mexican people did not have to join in this fight, they believed slavery was wrong, and they helped fight to stop it. Mexicans consistently took in and helped Black slaves who would run away from the U.S. Another "underground railroad"— this one south of the border—saved the lives and allowed the freedom of thousands of African people fleeing enslavement by European settlers.

- During the period before the Civil War, Mexican authorities refused to return enslaved runaways to the U.S. slaveholders. Aided by Mexicans in Texas, thousands of runaways escaped to freedom in Mexico. The U.S. government had to send 20 percent of its whole army to the Mexican border to try to stop this and intimidate the Mexican people, but the people continued to aid escaping slaves.

- In 1862, during the Civil War, at the same time French colonialists had invaded Mexico seeking to take over. However, at the battle of Puebla on May 5, the Mexican defenders, with the help of freed African slaves—this army was considered the complete underdog—defeated and turned back the French invasion. It was a great victory, now celebrated as Cinco de Mayo. This victory was also a blow to the slaveholders of the United States.

- One historical event, organized through the solidarity of Mexican, Blacks, indigenous and Asian people, was the "Plan de San Diego." This was intended as a general uprising by these peoples joined in the Southwest, initiated in an effort to regain the lands stolen in the U.S.'s aggression in the 1840s, which include California, Texas, New Mexico, Arizona and other states of what is now the U.S. Southwest. The plan actually addressed and recognized the contributions of Blacks, Asians and indigenous people by granting them freedom and autonomy. Although the plan was not successful, it revealed the long history of solidarity of peoples of color in struggle against those who would enslave them.

- In 1866, Mexican President Benito Juarez confirmed an 1851 land grant giving Black people in Mexico a sizeable place of refuge at Nascimiento.

In another chapter that is not as well known as it should be, the federal government instituted two large, formal guest-worker programs aimed at bringing to the United States large numbers of Mexican workers who were needed to harvest crops and work in war industries. Abuses were rife. During other periods, for example when the American economy was poor, the United States conducted large-scale roundups and expatriations of Mexican-looking people. See the following excerpt.

Gilbert Paul Carrasco
Latinos in the United States: Invitation and Exile,
in *Immigrants Out!*
The New Nativism and the Anti–Immigrant Impulse
in the United States
190–200 (Juan F. Perea ed., 1997)

Throughout the history of the United States, there have been periods of labor shortage and labor surplus. In times of labor shortage, the United States has enthusiastically welcomed immigrants to fill gaps in the labor pool. More often than not, however, available employment has been characterized by harsh working conditions, enormous amounts of physical labor, and minimal remuneration. In addition to abject working conditions, immigrants have also faced discrimination and resentment.

During periods of labor surplus or economic stress, immigrants in the United States have been subjected to particular cruelty. Americans, led by various nativist organizations and movements such as the Know–Nothing Party in the 1850s or, more recently, U.S. English or California's "Save Our State" campaign, have blamed immigrants for the country's economic woes. Such xenophobic bigotry has resulted in calls for anti-immigrant legislation (including restrictions on immigration for whichever immigrant group was targeted at the time), attempts to deny public services (including elimination of bilingual education for school-aged immigrants and the American citizen children of undocumented immigrants), and, ultimately, deportation.

Mexican immigrants have usually been the subject of these seesaw trends. One reason for this is that Mexico and the United States share a common border. The border between the two countries stretches for two thousand miles and is evidenced in some places by a fence, but at most points merely by an imaginary line in the sand or by the Rio Grande River. A border that has historically been easy to traverse, this proximity facilitates immigration, both legal and illegal, as well as expulsion.

Due to their great distance from the United States, Europeans historically could not make the journey to where their labor was needed (typically the southwestern United States) before the need was met. The only immigrants left within reach of the American Southwest were Mexicans and Asians. The Chinese and the Japanese have their own regrettable history of discrimination in the United States. The laws and policies that temporarily ended immigration from Japan and China left Mexico as the only source to fill the labor vacuum. Mexican laborers have since become the United States' disposable labor force, brought in when needed, only to fulfill their use and be unceremoniously discarded, a trend that has been recurring for over 150 years.

From the Gold Rush to World War I

Early migration into the United States was aided by negligible border restrictions and virtually no immigration laws. The first wave of Mexican laborers was drawn to California by the Gold Rush shortly after Mexico ceded California to the United States under the terms of the Treaty of Guadalupe Hidalgo in 1848. The Gold Rush drew people from all over the world, triggering rapid population growth. Because most people who flocked to California wanted to strike it rich in their own mines, unskilled manual labor was scarce and laborers were needed to work not only in Anglo-owned mines but also to construct the railroads and to farm in agricultural areas. The work was backbreaking, low-paying, and often dangerous, so it was difficult to find Anglos who would do it.

In addition to fulfilling labor demands Mexicans brought with them the knowledge of mining. Anglos came to California with dreams of striking it rich but had little practical experience or knowledge of how to do it. Anglos, however, soon acquired the knowledge, tools, and techniques of Latino miners.

Unfortunately for Latinos, a need for their labor and knowledge did not translate into good attitudes toward them. Popular accounts of Latinos during that period were influenced by manifest destiny, "scientific" theories of racial miscegenation, and the Mexican War. These accounts provided the Anglo miner with a negative stereotype of the Latino that led to discrimination and hostility. These hostilities took the form of threats, violence, and restrictive legislation directed against Mexicans and Mexican Americans. Examples of these hostilities include posters appearing in mining areas threatening violence to any "foreigners" who remained where "they had no right to be," vigilante groups expelling Latinos from mines claiming that mineral rights and wealth in America were reserved for "Americans," the imposition of a Foreign Miners' Tax Law, assaults and lynchings.

In addition to the negative stereotypes and misconceptions, anti-Latino attitudes were also fueled by greed for the much coveted gold. Latinos who labored in the fields, on the railroads, or in the mines of Anglos were not as persecuted and discriminated against as those who sought their own fortunes in the mines. Nevertheless, although nonminers were not as persecuted as miners, there are recorded incidents of whole towns being put to the torch, rioters shooting any Mexican in sight, random murders, and other vigilante actions throughout this period.

Even while Latinos were being persecuted, their labor was needed, especially in jobs that were low-paying and labor-intensive. Such jobs included ranching, agriculture (especially for crops such as cotton and sugar beets), laying the rails that traverse the Southwest (a task made harder because most of the terrain is desert, semidesert, and/or mountainous), and mining (where, although their knowledge of mining techniques proved invaluable, they received lower wages for the same work that their unskilled Anglo counterparts did).

There was such a demand for Mexican labor in some labor-intensive occupations that employers held Mexicans captive. One such industry was the Colorado sugar beet industry. Sugar beets require attention almost year-round and, therefore, need a semipermanent labor force. When farmers could not persuade Mexican laborers to stay year-round to perform the arduous labor, they resorted to coercion. Coercive tactics employed by farmers took different forms. One such tactic was to refuse to make final wage payments to their employees so that they were unable to leave; thus, they had to remain in the area until the following season to collect their pay. Essentially, farmers had a captive work force without rights of citizenship or the ability to leave.

World War I Through the Great Depression

Although there were periods of economic trouble in 1907 and 1921 when immigrants were blamed for many of the problems, Mexican immigrants were generally welcomed into the United States until the 1930s and the Great Depression. Prior to the Depression, U.S. immigration policies were aimed mainly at keeping out Asians and southern and eastern Europeans, while allowing Mexican laborers to immigrate. For example, within a year of the enactment of the most restrictive immigration legislation in U.S. history—the Immigration Act of 1917—the first foreign labor program was initiated.

In response to pressure from agricultural employers in the Southwest, Congress included provisions in the law that allowed entry into the United States of "temporary" workers who would otherwise be inadmissible under the Act. This temporary worker program, or the first *bracero* program as Kiser and Kiser called it, was enacted for the duration of World War I and was extended until 1922, four years after the war ended. Although this program did not include the Mexican government's proposals to guarantee the contracts of immigrant workers as did later bracero agreements, it was the blueprint upon which the later programs were based.

After the Depression began, Latinos found themselves unemployed and unwanted. Jobs that Latinos had been doing for years were no longer available, either because the jobs were no longer there or because they were being performed by Anglos who were forced to resort to that type of labor. Because Latinos were historically ill-paid, many had little or no financial reserves and had no choice but to go on welfare or other relief programs. Another result of the Depression was that Mexican workers and immigrants were no longer welcomed. In fact, they were so unpopular that many were driven from the country. For example, Latinos in Oklahoma were threatened with being burned out of their homes, in Indiana a mob forced railworkers to "give up their jobs," and in Texas signs were displayed warning Mexicans to get out of town.

As the Depression lingered and county, state, and federal budgets dwindled, governments sought ways to cut welfare costs. One method used was to deny welfare benefits to Mexican laborers. This action, labeled "fair and humane" by government agents, was a move to reduce the labor surplus and at the same time to reduce welfare rolls. No longer welcome in the United States, and with no way to sustain themselves, many Mexicans began a mass exodus to Mexico.

The Mexican migration was heralded by governments of various jurisdictions. They decided to expedite this process by sending lawful resident Mexican workers back to Mexico rather than carry them on the public welfare rolls; however, this decision was problematic for a variety of reasons. Legally, to expel Mexicans from the United States was as costly as keeping them afloat when their funds were depleted. Consequently, instead of using costly legal maneuvers such as public hearings and formal deportation proceedings, social workers resorted to betraying Mexicans by telling officials that they wanted to return to Mexico. This duplicitous tactic, of course, lowered the cost of expulsion considerably. It also, however, effectively deprived many of due process.

This treachery toward Latinos continued throughout the Depression. Tragically, some, if not most, of the repatriated Latinos were lawful permanent residents of the United States. They had lived in the United States for decades, establishing homes and roots. Another result of repatriation was that many families were separated. In some instances, either one or both parents was an "alien," but children, having been born and raised in the United States, were American citizens. In some cases, the children were allowed to stay in the United States while their parents were repatriated, but in many other cases such U.S. citizens were themselves "repatriated." By the end of the Depression, over 400,000 Latinos were "repatriated" to Mexico without any formal deportation proceedings, including thousands of American citizens.

These repatriation programs naturally sparked protest from the Mexican government. In response to the protests, the Los Angeles Chamber of Commerce issued a statement assuring Mexican authorities that the city was in no sense unfriendly to Mexican labor. The communique stated further that the repatriation policy was designed solely to help the destitute. This was supposedly the case when invalids were removed from County Hospital in Los Angeles and shipped across the border.

WORLD WAR II AND THE *BRACERO* PROGRAM

When the Great Depression ended at the onset of World War II, so did the labor surplus that the Depression had created. Agricultural growers in the Southwest, however, began as early as 1940 to petition agencies of the United States for permission to use foreign labor to fill labor shortages, a precedent established during World War I. Shortly after Mexico declared war on the Axis powers on June 1, 1942, the Department of State contacted it about the importation of labor. The Mexican government doubted that the labor shortage really existed and viewed the efforts of the State Department as a way of obtaining cheap labor.

Cognizant of the deportation and repatriation of Latinos during the Great Depression, the Mexican government, to protect its citizens from harsh treatment and discrimination, entered into a formal agreement with the United States. This protection was provided by a government-to-government accord signed on July 23, 1942. The Mexican Labor Program, or the Bracero Program as it is more commonly known, was first implemented on August 4, 1942 and was funded by the U.S. President's emergency fund. The Bracero Program was renewed on April 26, 1943.

Under the Bracero agreement, Mexico would permit its citizens to work in the United States for temporary, renewable periods under agreed-upon conditions. The conditions stipulated methods of recruitment, transportation, standards of health care, wages, housing, food, and the number of hours the braceros were allowed to work. There was even a stipulation that there should be no discrimination against braceros. A violation of these conditions was supposed to have resulted in the suspension of braceros' availability for the violating area. Unfortunately, the conditions were, for the most part, ignored by both the growers and the U.S. government; thus, migrant laborers were subjected to most oppressive working environments.

Braceros across the country were compelled to endure poor food, excessive charges for board, substandard housing, discrimination, physical mistreatment, inappropriate deductions from their wages, and exposure to pesticides and other dangerous chemicals. Although Texas was not the only state that violated the conditions of the agreement, discrimination toward braceros there was so bad that Texas lost its privilege to utilize bracero labor until after the war.

To illustrate how important bracero labor was, we need only look at the impact on Texas of losing braceros. To fill its labor needs, Texas was forced to recruit local Mexican Americans, college students, school children, and prisoners of war. As a result, the cotton wages in Texas rose 236 percent during the war years, contrasted with California, where cotton wages increased 136 percent.

The upshot of the Bracero Program was that the U.S. government provided growers with cheap labor. Agricultural growers preferred hiring braceros to American citizens for two reasons. First, growers were able to set the wages that would be paid braceros instead of basing their remuneration on the principle of supply and demand or on collective bargaining agreements. Second, braceros tended to be males who traveled alone, while Americans had their families with them, thus making it easier to provide transportation and housing for braceros.

A secondary effect of the Bracero Program was that it provided the United States with soldiers to fight the war. Although braceros were initially brought in to replace Japanese Americans who were sent to internment camps and Americans who went into the armed services or the defense industry, braceros additionally freed up many Mexican Americans for the armed services. Deferments were given to those who held defense industry jobs, few of whom were Mexican American, while workers in the agricultural industry, heavily staffed by Mexican Americans, were eligible for the draft. In short, Mexican Americans in the agricultural industry were sent off to the war while braceros were imported to replace them.

While in the armed forces, Latinos distinguished themselves as fierce and reliable soldiers. Throughout the course of World War II, no Latino soldier was ever charged with desertion, treason, or cowardice. The bravery of Latino troops was recognized in the many medals awarded to Mexican Americans, including the Congressional Medal of Honor (the United States' highest honor), the Silver Star, the Bronze Star, and the Distinguished Service Cross. Seventeen Mexican Americans received the Congressional Medal of Honor for action in World War II and Korea. These seventeen Latino soldiers represent the highest proportion of Medal of Honor winners of any identifiable ethnic group. Because Mexican Americans seem to have gravitated to the most dangerous sections of the armed forces, they were overrepresented on military casualty lists.

Ironically, when the Mexican soldiers returned home, they were treated no better than they had been before they left. In Texas, a funeral parlor in Three Rivers refused to bury Félix Longoria, an American soldier decorated for heroism, because he was of Mexican descent. This obviously racist action sparked a storm of controversy that ended with the intervention of then Texas Senator Lyndon B. Johnson, who secured burial for Longoria in Arlington National Cemetery. Sergeants José Mendoza López and Macario García, each awarded the Congressional Medal of Honor, were refused service in restaurants and diners because of their Mexican heritage.

Sergeant García, however, decided to challenge such discrimination against Latinos. García, after being told that he would not be served because he was a "Mexie," admonished the proprietor to serve him, declaring, "[if I am] good enough to fight your war for you, I'm good enough for you to serve a cup of coffee to." The merchant in charge of the diner refused to serve García and went so far as to attempt physically to remove García from the diner. García defended himself. The altercation ended with the arrival of the police. The police sent everyone home and ordered the diner closed for the night to end the incident. Later, after the incident was recounted over the national news, Sergeant García was arrested and charged with aggravated assault in an attempt by the city to save face.

After the war, American soldiers returned to work, ending the labor shortage. Growers in the agricultural industry were, nonetheless, reluctant to give up bracero labor. Under the influence of agribusiness, Congress kept the program alive. The pressure they brought to bear was not enough to keep the program going on indefinitely, however, and the Bracero Program came to an end in December of 1947. Nonetheless, despite the termination of the Bracero Program, the use of Mexican labor did not end.

For nine months after the end of the Bracero Program, while no agreement existed between the United States and Mexico, the number of undocumented workers in the United States increased dramatically. Both governments became concerned with the increase and pushed for renewed labor negotiations. These negotiations led to a new bracero agreement in August of 1949. In addition to providing labor to the

United States, the new bracero agreement stressed a reduction in the flow of undocumented workers from Mexico and the legalization of undocumented workers already in the United States. The program resulted in 238,439 undocumented workers being recruited into the work force between 1947 and 1951, when mass legalization ended. Mass legalization ended for two reasons. First, it was ineffective in stemming the tide of undocumented workers coming into the country. Most importantly, the enactment of Public Law 78 on July 12, 1951, in response to the outbreak of the Korean War, created a new bracero program.

Under the new program, the U.S. Department of Labor was given administrative control of migration and essentially became a labor contractor. Public Law 78 conferred on the Secretary of Labor the responsibility for the certification of the need for the braceros, for authorization of their recruitment in Mexico, for transportation of the braceros to the labor camps, for guaranteeing the terms of their labor contracts, and for setting the prevailing wage. The new bracero agreement also rectified some problems of the prior agreements. The braceros were to enter contracts for periods of time ranging from six weeks to six months instead of year-long contracts. The braceros were also guaranteed work for at least 75 percent of the time for which they had contracted, as well as being paid the wages set by the Secretary of Labor.

FROM THE KOREAN WAR TO "OPERATION WETBACK"

Public Law 78 did not stem the tide of undocumented workers. Further, immigration authorities started finding undocumented workers in industrial jobs, causing labor unions to proclaim undocumented traffic as destructive to their welfare. As a result of these complaints, on June 17, 1954, Herbert Brownell, Jr., the U.S. Attorney General, ordered a crackdown on illegal immigration and a massive deportation drive, "Operation Wetback."

This crackdown on illegal immigration and the ensuing process of deportation were left to the Commissioner of Immigration, Joseph P. Swing. Swing, a retired army general and reputed "professional, long-time Mexican hater," developed "Operation Wetback" along the lines of a military campaign. "Operation Wetback" was a two-fold plan that coordinated the border patrol to prevent undocumented aliens from getting into the United States while rounding up and deporting those who were already here.

"Operation Wetback" went beyond its scope, however, and Americans of Mexican descent were also deported, stirring up memories of the mass deportations of the 1930s. Many of those deported were denied the opportunity to present evidence that would have prevented their deportation. Between 1954 and 1959, "Operation Wetback" was responsible for over 3.7 million Latinos being deported. Of that number, an unknown amount were American citizens. In their haste to deport "illegals," only 63,500 persons were removed through formal deportation proceedings. The rest of the deportees left the United States "voluntarily."

In addition to violating the civil liberties of American citizens via questionable expulsions, "Operation Wetback" violated the human rights of the people being deported. Deportations were characterized by disrespect, rudeness, and intimidation. There were even reports of immigration officers "collecting fares" from persons being deported.

Ironically, the bracero program was in effect while "Operation Wetback" was being executed. Public Law 78 was extended until it finally was allowed to lapse in December of 1964. Although the bracero program was originally intended to be an emergency remedy for labor shortages during World War II, it survived the war by almost twenty years. Further, more braceros were hired in single years after the war than were hired during all of the years of the war combined.

MODERN LABOR PROGRAMS

Even after the bracero program ended, importation of Mexican labor continued under the McCarran–Walter Immigration Act of 1952. Under the Act, immigrants from Mexico were permanently admitted to the United States to ensure there would be enough laborers. To guarantee there would be a sufficient labor force available under the Act, the Department of Labor lowered the admission standards for Mexican workers just days before the expiration of Public Law 78 and the Bracero Program.

Although many Mexican citizens were issued visas, or "green cards," that would allow them to live and work in the United States, most preferred to reside in Mexico. These people, known as commuters because they traversed the border regularly to get to work, maintained the bracero lifestyle by working in the United States for days, weeks, or even months at a time, only to return to Mexico. As well as emulating bracero work patterns, these migrant workers performed similar jobs to the braceros' (i.e., low-skilled or service oriented). In 1977, there were approximately one million Mexican resident aliens in the United States, according to the Immigration and Naturalization Service. The actual number of commuters is unknown due to inaccurate records and varying numbers of commuters from day to day.

The McCarran–Walter Act also established a fallback Bracero Program. The "H–2 program" revived all the worst parts of the Bracero Program. Under the "H–2 program," the U.S. Department of Labor has power to admit foreign labor for temporary jobs if able, willing, and qualified domestic workers can not be found at the time and place where they are needed. Similar to the mistreatment suffered by workers in the Bracero Program, these migrants are totally dependent on the growers for employment. If the worker proves himself to be hard-working and faithful, he might be asked to return again the following year; if not, he can be deported without an appeal.

In 1986 the United States went through its most recent mass legalization program. The Immigration Reform and Control Act of 1986 (IRCA) gave legal status to undocumented persons who had been in the United States from January 1, 1982 to the time of application (between May 5, 1987 and May 4, 1988). Like the McCarran–Walter Act, the IRCA provided special status to migrant farmworkers. The IRCA offered legal status to special agricultural workers who could prove that they spent at least ninety "man-days" during a qualifying period doing agricultural work on specified crops. The end result of the IRCA was to legalize millions of undocumented workers and fill a labor shortage caused by the most recent immigrant expulsion, "Operation Jobs."

Another method of obtaining Mexican labor has been accomplished through the exportation of jobs. This phenomenon is euphemistically called the Border Industrialization Program or, as it is more familiarly known, the *Maquiladora* Program. The program is a system of concessions vis-à-vis Mexico that allows manufacturing and assembly plants or *maquilas* to be located in border towns in northern Mexico and exportation of their products directly to the United States. Other concessions granted by Mexico have included exemptions from labor and environmental regulations.

The exemptions granted by Mexico do more than help American companies enter Mexico; they help American companies exploit Mexican labor. The maquilas have proven to be a financial success, but only at the expense of Mexican laborers suffering under poor working conditions, inadequate wages, deteriorating environmental conditions, and the inability to take any legal actions against their employers.

History shows that whenever labor is needed, it is sought out in Mexico and discarded when the need is over, with little regard for Mexican Americans who are often ensnared in the same net. This was true with the U.S. repatriation programs during the Depression in the 1930s and "Operation Wetback" in the 1950s.

Due to intense exploitation suffered by migrant workers, their productive capacities are used up early in their lives and they have to be replaced by new waves of younger immigrants. For the United States, employment of migrant workers represents a significant savings in producing and reproducing "human capital" because they stay in the United States only temporarily. Even though the United States needs Mexican labor, migrant laborers arrive to face more than exploitation and brutal working conditions. They face racism, xenophobia, and discrimination. Although Latinos both within and outside the United States have come to recognize the American perspective that they are dispensable and disposable when the need for their labor diminishes, their struggle for human dignity continues, notwithstanding the seemingly inexorable cycle of invitation and exile.

Notes and Questions

1. If Carrasco's numbers are correct, the U.S. deported almost four million Mexicans in two xenophobic waves coinciding with hard times or anti-foreign fervor, all in a 20–year period. This total rivals in extent, if not in savagery, better known episodes of ethnic purging such as the Turkish war against the Armenians or the Serbian campaign against Bosnians in the recent war there. The United States has never admitted fault, even though many of those deported were United States citizens in good standing whose sole sin was looking Mexican. See Juan R. Garcia, *Operation Wetback: The Mass Deportation of Mexican Undocumented Workers in 1954* (1980).

2. What (if any) apology or reparation is due for these two broadscale deportation programs? See infra Section 5: Reparations and Apologies.

3. What does the cyclical use and exclusion of immigrants from Mexico and other Latin American countries say about the social construction of those groups? See Elvia R. Arriola, *International Human Rights, Popular Culture, and the Faces of Despair in INS Raids*, 28 Miami Inter–Am. L. Rev. 245 (1996).

4. On some of these issues, see Guadalupe T. Luna, *An Infinite Distance?: Agricultural Exceptionalism and Agricultural Labor*, 1 U. Pa. J. Lab. & Emp. L. 487 (1998). See also Julia Preston, *Short on Labor, Farmers in U.S. Shift to Mexico*, N.Y. Times, Sept. 5, 2007, at A1 (reporting that some U.S. farmers are opening farms in northern Mexico, where the supply of farm labor is more plentiful than it is in the U.S. because of recent immigration crackdowns).

5. For a glimpse of the life of an undocumented immigrant musician in San Francisco's Mission District, see the documentary film *Romantico* (2005).

SECTION 4.   DEBATES OVER IMMIGRATION

At the time we write, the conflict over Latino immigration is sharp, bitter, and shows no sign of reaching resolution any time soon. The controversy includes questions about the kind of society America wants to be, as well as factual disputes about, for example, whether immigrants hurt or help the U.S. economy or take jobs from blacks. It includes moral and historical issues, such as whether America owes reparations to Braceros (guestworkers) for unpaid wages, or to Mexican Americans unjustly deported during two waves of nativist hysteria. The following materials expose you to some of these questions.

A.   THE COSTS AND BENEFITS OF IMMIGRATION

Our current policy is to sharply curtail Latino immigration, particularly of the undocumented sort. What presuppositions underlie this policy? Do we believe that immigrants hurt the economy and drive up social welfare costs? Do we believe they are diluting the Anglo–Saxon heritage that made this country great? What are the costs and benefits of our current policy? The next selections address some of these questions.

Roger Lowenstein
The Immigration Equation
N.Y. Times Mag., July 9, 2006, at 36

The day I met George Borjas, cloistered in his office at the John F. Kennedy School of Government at Harvard while graduate students from Russia, India, China and maybe Mexico mingled in the school cafe, sipping coffee and chattering away in all their tongues, the United States Senate was hotly debating what to do about the country's immigration policy. Borjas professed to be unfazed by the goings-on in Washington. A soft-spoken man, he stressed repeatedly that his concern was not to make policy but to derive the truth. To Borjas, a Cuban immigrant and the pre-eminent scholar in his field, the truth is pretty obvious: immigrants hurt the economic prospects of the Americans they compete with. And now that the biggest contingent of immigrants are poorly educated Mexicans, they hurt poorer Americans, especially African Americans, the most.

Borjas has been making this case—which is based on the familiar concept of supply and demand—for more than a decade. But the more elegantly he has made it, it seems, the less his colleagues concur. "I think I have proved it," he eventually told me, admitting his frustration. "What I don't understand is why people don't agree with me."

It turns out that Borjas's seemingly self-evident premise—that more job seekers from abroad mean fewer opportunities, or lower wages, for native workers—is one of the most controversial ideas in labor economics. It lies at the heart of a national debate, which has been encapsulated (if not articulated) by two very different immigration bills: one, passed by the House of Representatives, which would toughen laws against undocumented workers and probably force many of them to leave the country; and one in the Senate, a measure that would let most of them stay.

You can find economists to substantiate the position of either chamber, but the consensus of most is that, on balance, immigration is good for the country. Immigrants provide scarce labor, which lowers prices in much the same way global trade does. And overall, the newcomers modestly raise Americans' per capita income. But the impact is unevenly distributed; people with means pay less for taxi rides and household help while the less-affluent command lower wages and probably pay more for rent.

The debate among economists is whether low-income workers are hurt a lot or just a little—and over what the answer implies for U.S. policy. If you believe Borjas, the answer is troubling. A policy designed with only Americans' economic well-being in mind would admit far fewer Mexicans, who now account for about 3 in 10 immigrants. Borjas, who emigrated from Cuba in 1962, when he was 12 (and not long after soldiers burst into his family's home and ordered them at gunpoint to stand against a wall), has asserted that the issue, indeed, is "Whom should the United States let in?"

Such a bald approach carries an overtone of the ethnic selectivity that was a staple of the immigration debates a century ago. It makes many of Borjas's colleagues uncomfortable, and it is one reason that the debate is so charged. Another reason is that many of the scholars who disagree with Borjas also hail from someplace else—like gardeners and seamstresses, a surprising number of Ph.D. economists in the U.S. are foreign-born.

Easily the most influential of Borjas's critics is David Card, a Canadian who teaches at Berkeley. He has said repeatedly that, from an economic standpoint, immigration is no big deal and that a lot of the opposition to it is most likely social or cultural. "If Mexicans were taller and whiter, it would probably be a lot easier to deal with," he says pointedly.

Economists in Card's camp tend to frame the issue as a puzzle—a great economic mystery because of its very success. The puzzle is this: how is the U.S. able to absorb its immigrants so easily?

After all, 21 million immigrants, about 15 percent of the labor force, hold jobs in the U.S., but the country has nothing close to that many unemployed. (The actual number is only seven million.) So the majority of immigrants can't literally have "taken" jobs; they must be doing jobs that wouldn't have existed had the immigrants not been here.

The economists who agree with Card also make an intuitive point, inevitably colored by their own experience. To the Israeli-born economist whose father lived through the Holocaust or the Italian who marvels at America's ability to integrate workers from around the world, America's diversity—its knack for synthesizing newly arrived parts into a more vibrant whole—is a secret of its strength. To which Borjas, who sees a different synthesis at work, replies that, unlike his colleagues, the people arriving from Oaxaca, Mexico, are unlikely to ascend to a university faculty. Most of them did not finish high school. "The trouble with the stories that American journalists write about immigration," he told me, "is they all start with a story about a poor mother whose son grows up to become...." and his voice trailed off as if to suggest that whatever the particular story—that of a C.E.O., a ballplayer or even a story like his own—it would not prove anything about immigration. What economists aim for is to get beneath the anecdotes. Is immigration still the engine of prosperity that the history textbooks describe? Or is it a boon to business that is destroying the livelihoods of the poorest workers—people already disadvantaged by such postmodern trends as globalization, the decline of unions and the computer?

THE LOPSIDED-SKILL-MIX PROBLEM

This spring, while militias on the prowl for illegal immigrants were converging on the Arizona border and, on the other side of the political fence, immigrant protesters were taking to the streets, I sampled the academic literature and spent some time with Borjas and Card and various of their colleagues. I did not expect concurrence, but I hoped to isolate what we know about the economic effects of immigration from what is mere conjecture. The first gleaning from the Ivory Tower came as a surprise. All things being equal, more foreigners and indeed more people of any stripe do not mean either lower wages or higher unemployment. If they did, every time a baby was born, every time a newly minted graduate entered the work force, it would be bad news for the labor market. But it isn't. Those babies eat baby food; those graduates drive automobiles.

As Card likes to say, "The demand curve also shifts out." It's jargon, but it's profound. New workers add to the supply of labor, but since they consume products and services, they add to the demand for it as well. "Just because Los Angeles is bigger than Bakersfield doesn't mean L.A. has more unemployed than Bakersfield," Card observes.

In theory, if you added 10 percent to the population—or even doubled it—nothing about the labor market would change. Of course, it would take a little while for the economy to adjust. People would have to invest money and start some new businesses to hire all those newcomers. The point is, they *would* do it. Somebody would realize that the immigrants needed to eat and would open a restaurant; someone else would think to build them housing. Pretty soon there would be new jobs available in kitchens and on construction sites. And that has been going on since the first boat docked at Ellis Island.

But there's a catch. Individual native workers are less likely to be affected if the immigrants resemble the society they are joining—not physically but in the same mix of skills and educational backgrounds. For instance, if every immigrant were a doctor, the theory is, it would be bad for doctors already here. Or as Borjas asked pointedly of me, what if the U.S. created a special visa just for magazine writers? All those foreign-born writers would eat more meals, sure, but (once they mastered English, anyway), they would be supplying only one type of service—my type. Bye-bye fancy assignments.

During the previous immigrant wave, roughly from 1880 to 1921 (it ended when the U.S. established restrictive quotas based on country of origin), the immigrants looked pretty much like the America into which they were assimilating. At the beginning of the 20th century, 9 of 10 American adults did not have high-school diplomas, nor did the vast majority of immigrants. Those Poles and Greeks and Italians made the country more populous, but they did not much change the makeup of the labor market.

This time it's different. The proportion of foreign-born, at 12 percent, remains below the peak of 15 percent recorded in 1890. But compared with the work force of today, however, the skill mix of immigrants is lopsided. About the same proportion have college degrees (though a higher proportion of immigrants are post-graduates). But many more—including most of the those who have furtively slipped across the Mexican border—don't have high-school diplomas.

The latest estimate is that the United States has 11.5 million undocumented foreigners, and it's those immigrants—the illegal ones— who have galvanized Congress. The sponsor of the House legislation, Representative James Sensenbrenner, a Republican from Wisconsin, says bluntly that illegals are bad for the U.S. economy. * * *

* * *

Another bill, the product of an alliance between John McCain and Edward Kennedy, [proceeds on the] premise is that if you legalize undocumented people and reinforce the borders, then whatever negative impact immigrants have on the labor market will go away. The theory is that newly minted green-card holders, no longer having deportation to fear, will stick up for their rights and for higher wages too. Interestingly, some big labor unions, like the Service Employees International Union, are supporters. But economists are skeptical. For one thing, after the U.S. gave amnesty to the nearly three million undocumented workers who were in the country in 1986, their wages didn't budge. Second, economists, as you might expect, say market forces like supply and demand, not legal status, are what determine wages.

* * *

If economists ran the country, they would certainly take in more immigrants who, like them, have advanced degrees. (The U.S., which is hugely dependent on foreigners to fill certain skilled occupations like scientific research and nursing, does admit a relative handful of immigrants each year on work visas.) Canada and Australia admit immigrants primarily on the basis of skills, and one thing the economists agree on is that high earners raise the national income by more than low earners. They are also less of a burden on the tax rolls.

With the exception of a few border states, however, the effect of immigration on public-sector budgets is small, and the notion that undocumented workers in particular abuse the system is a canard. Since many illegals pay into Social Security (using false ID numbers), they are actually subsidizing the U.S. Treasury. And fewer than 3 percent of immigrants of any stripe receive food stamps. Also, and contrary to popular wisdom, undocumented people *do* support local school districts, since, indirectly as renters or directly as homeowners, they pay property taxes. Since they tend to be poor, however, they contribute less than the average. One estimate is that immigrants raise state and local taxes for everyone else in the U.S. by a trivial amount in most states, but by as much as $1,100 per household per year in California. They are certainly a burden on hospitals and jails but, it should be noted, poor legal workers, including those who are native born, are also a burden on the health care system.

Parsing the Wage Gap

Economists focus on Mexicans not because many are undocumented but because, relative to the rest of the labor force, Mexicans have far fewer skills. And Mexicans and other Central Americans (who tend to have a similar economic background) are arriving and staying in this country at a rate of more than 500,000 a year. Their average incomes are vastly lower than those both of native-born men and of other immigrants.

Native-born workers: $45,400
All immigrants: $37,000
Mexican immigrants: $22,300

The reason Mexicans earn much less than most Americans is their daunting educational deficit. More than 60 percent of Mexican immigrants are dropouts; fewer than 10 percent of today's native workers are.

That stark contrast conveys, to economists, two important facts. One is that Mexicans are supplying a skill level that is much in demand. It doesn't just *seem* that Americans don't want to be hotel chambermaids, pick lettuce or repair roofs; it's true. Most gringos are too educated for that kind of work. The added diversity, the complementariness of skills, that Mexicans bring is good for the economy as a whole. They perform services that would otherwise be more expensive and in some cases simply unavailable.

The Americans who *are* unskilled, however, must compete with a disproportionate number of immigrants. One of every four high-school dropouts in the U.S. was born in Mexico, an astonishing ratio given that the proportion of Mexicans in the overall labor force is only 1 in 25. So it's not magazine writers who see their numbers expanding; it's Americans who are, or would be, working in construction, restaurants, household jobs, unskilled manufacturing and so forth.

That's the theory. But economists have had a hard time finding evidence of actual harm. For starters, they noticed that societies with lots of immigrants tend, if anything, to be more prosperous, not less. In the U.S., wages in cities where immigrants have clustered, like New York, have tended to be higher, not lower. Mississippi, on the other hand, which has the lowest per-capita income of any state, has had very few immigrants.

That doesn't necessarily mean that immigrants caused or even contributed to high wages; it could be they simply go where the demand is greatest—that their presence is an effect of high wages. As statisticians are wont to remind us, "Correlation does not imply causation." (The fact that hospitals are filled with sick people doesn't mean hospitals make you sick.) Maybe without immigrants, wages in New York would be even higher.

And certainly, wages of the unskilled have been a source of worry for years. From 1970 to 1995, wages for high-school dropouts, the group that has been the most affected by immigrants, plummeted by more than

30 percent, after adjusting for inflation. Look at the following averages (all for male workers):

> College graduates: $73,000
> People with some college: $41,000
> High-school grads: $32,000
> Dropouts: $24,800

These figures demonstrate a serious problem, at least if you care about wage inequality, and a quick glance at this list and the previous one shows that native-born dropouts are earning only a shade more than Mexicans working in this country. But that hardly proves that cheap Mexican labor is to blame. For one thing, economists believe that other factors, like the failure of Congress to raise the minimum wage, globalization (cheap Chinese labor, that is) and the decline of unions are equally or even more responsible. Another popular theory is that computer technology has made skilled labor more valuable and unskilled labor less so.

Also, when economists look closely at wage dispersion, the picture isn't wholly consistent with the immigrants-as-culprits thesis. Look again at the numbers: people at the top (college grads) make a lot more than average but from the middle on down incomes are pretty compressed. Since only dropouts are being crowded by illegal immigrants, you would expect them to be falling further behind every other group. But they aren't; since the mid–90's, dropouts have been keeping pace with the middle; it's the corporate executives and their ilk at the top who are pulling away from the pack, a story that would seem to have little to do with immigration.

This isn't conclusive either, Borjas notes. After all, maybe without immigrants, dropouts would have done much better than high-school grads. Economists look for the "counterfactual," or what would have happened had immigrants not come. It's difficult to tell, because in the real world, there is always a lot more going on—an oil shock, say, or a budget deficit—than the thing whose effect you are studying. To isolate the effect of immigrants alone would require a sort of lab experiment. The trouble with macroeconomics is you can't squeeze your subjects into a test tube.

MARIELITOS IN MIAMI, DOCTORS IN ISRAEL AND OTHER NATURAL EXPERIMENTS

The academic study of immigration's economic effects earned little attention before the subject started to get political traction in the 1980's. Then, in 1990, Borjas, who was on the faculty at the University of California at Santa Barbara, published a book, "Friends or Strangers," which was mildly critical of immigration's effects.

That same year, David Card realized that a test tube did exist. Card decided to study the 1980 Mariel boat lift, in which 125,000 Cubans were suddenly permitted to emigrate. They arrived in South Florida with virtually no advance notice, and approximately half remained in the

Miami area, joining an already-sizable Cuban community and swelling the city's labor force by 7 percent.

To Card, this produced a "natural experiment," one in which cause and effect were clearly delineated. Nothing about conditions in the Miami labor market had induced the Marielitos to emigrate; the Cubans simply left when they could and settled in the city that was closest and most familiar. So Card compared the aftershocks in Miami with the labor markets in four cities—Tampa, Atlanta, Houston and Los Angeles—that hadn't suddenly been injected with immigrants.

That the Marielitos, a small fraction of whom were career criminals, caused an upsurge in crime, as well as a more generalized anxiety among natives, is indisputable. It was also commonly assumed that the Marielitos were taking jobs from blacks.

But Card documented that blacks, and also other workers, in Miami actually did better than in the control cities. In 1981, the year after the boat lift, wages for Miami blacks were fractionally higher than in 1979; in the control cities, wages for blacks were down. The only negative was that unemployment rose among Cubans (a group that now included the Marielitos).

Unemployment in all of the cities rose the following year, as the country entered a recession. But by 1985, the last year of Card's study, black unemployment in Miami had retreated to below its level of 1979, while in the control cities it remained much higher. Even among Miami's Cubans, unemployment returned to pre-Mariel levels, confirming what seemed visible to the naked eye: the Marielitos were working. Card concluded, "The Mariel influx appears to have had virtually no effect on the wages or unemployment rates of less-skilled workers."

Although Card offered some hypotheses, he couldn't fully explain his results. The city's absorption of a 7 percent influx, he wrote, was "remarkably rapid" and—even if he did not quite say it—an utter surprise. Card's Mariel study hit the cloistered world of labor economists like a thunderbolt. All of 13 pages, it was an aesthetic as well as an academic masterpiece that prompted Card's peers to look for other "natural" immigration experiments. Soon after, Jennifer Hunt, an Australian-born Ph.D. candidate at Harvard, published a study on the effects of the return migration of ethnic French from Algeria to France in 1962, the year of Algerian independence. Similar in spirit though slightly more negative than the Mariel study, Hunt found that the French *retour* had a very mild upward effect on unemployment and no significant effect on wages.

Rachel Friedberg, an economist at Brown, added an interesting twist to the approach. Rather than compare the effect of immigration across cities, she compared it across various occupations. Friedberg's curiosity had been piqued in childhood; born in Israel, she moved to the U.S. as an infant and grew up amid refugee grandparents who were a constant reminder of the immigrant experience.

She focused on an another natural experiment—the exodus of 600,-000 Russian Jews to Israel, which increased the population by 14 percent in the early 1990's. She wanted to see if Israelis who worked in occupations in which the Russians were heavily represented had lost ground relative to other Israelis. And in fact, they had. But that didn't settle the issue. What if, Friedberg wondered, the Russians had entered less-attractive fields precisely because, as immigrants, they were at the bottom of the pecking order and hadn't been able to find better work? And in fact, she concluded that the Russians hadn't caused wage growth to slacken; they had merely gravitated to positions that were less attractive. Indeed, Friedberg's conclusion was counterintuitive: the Russians had, if anything, improved wages of native Israelis. She hypothesized that the immigrants competed more with one another than with natives. The Russians became garage mechanics; Israelis ran the garages.

MEASURING THE HIT TO WAGES

By the mid–90's, illegal immigration was heating up as an issue in the United States, prompting a reaction in California, where schools and other public services were beginning to feel a strain. But academics were coalescing around the view that immigration was essentially benign—that it depressed unskilled native wages by a little and raised the average native income by a little. In 1997, a panel of the National Academy of Sciences, which reviewed all of the literature, estimated that immigration during the previous decade had, at most, lowered unskilled-native wages by 1 percent to 2 percent.

Borjas didn't buy it. In 1999 he published a second, more strident book, "Heaven's Door." It espoused a "revisionist" view—that immigration caused real harm to lower-income Americans. Borjas argued that localized studies like Mariel were flawed, for the simple reason that labor markets in the U.S. are linked together. Therefore, the effects of immigration could not be gauged by comparing one city with another.

Borjas pointed out, as did others, that more native-born Americans started migrating out of California in the 1970's, just as Mexicans began arriving in big numbers. Previously California was a destination for Americans. Borjas reckoned that immigrants were pushing out native-born Americans, and that the effect of all the new foreigners was dispersed around the country.

The evidence of a labor surplus seemed everywhere. "If you wanted a maid," he recalled of California during the 90's, "all you had to do was tell your gardener, and you had one tomorrow." He felt certain that Mexicans were depressing unskilled wages but didn't know how to prove it.

After Borjas moved East, he had an inspiration. It was easy to show that high-school dropouts had experienced both lower wage growth and more competition from immigrants, but that didn't settle the point, because so many other factors could have explained why dropouts did poorly. The inspiration was that people compete not only against those with a like education, but also against workers of roughly the same experience. Someone looking for a first job at a McDonald's competes against other unskilled entry-level job seekers. A reporter with 15 years' experience who is vying for a promotion will compete against other veterans but not against candidates fresh out of journalism school.

This insight enabled Borjas to break down the Census data in a way that put his thesis to a more rigorous test. He could represent skill groups within each age as a point on a graph. There was one point for dropouts who were 10 years out of school, another for those who were 20 years and 30 years out. Each of these points was repeated for each decade from 1960 to 2000. And there was a similar set of points for high-school graduates, college graduates and so forth. The points were situated on the graph according to two variables: the horizontal axis measured the change in the share of immigrants within each "point," the vertical axis measured wage growth.

A result was a smattering of dots that on casual inspection might have resembled a work of abstract art. But looking closer, the dots had a direction: they pointed downward. Using a computer, Borjas measured the slope: it suggested that wages fell by 3 to 4 percent for each 10 percent increase in the share of immigrants.

With this graph, Borjas could calculate that, during the 80's and 90's, for instance, immigrants caused dropouts to suffer a 5 percent decline relative to college graduates. In a paper published in 2003, "The Labor Demand Curve *Is* Downward Sloping," Borjas termed the results "negative and significant."

But what about the absolute effect? Assuming businesses did not hire any of the new immigrants, Borjas's finding would translate to a hefty 9 percent wage loss for the unskilled over those two decades, and lesser declines for other groups (which also received some immigrants). As we know, however, as the population grows, demand rises and business *do* hire more workers. When Borjas adjusted for this hiring, high-school dropouts were still left with a wage loss of 5 percent over those two decades, some $1,200 a year. Other groups, however, showed a very slight gain. To many economists as well as lay folk, Borjas's findings confirmed what seemed intuitive all along: add to the supply of labor, and the price goes down.

To Card, however, what seems "intuitive" is often suspect. He became a labor economist because the field is full of anomalies. "The simple-minded theories that they teach you in economics don't work" for the labor market, he told me. In the 90's, Card won the prestigious Clark Medal for several studies, including Mariel and another showing that, contrary to theory, raising the minimum wage in New Jersey (another natural experiment) did not cause fast-food outlets to cut back on employment.

In a recent paper, "Is the New Immigration Really So Bad?" Card took indirect aim at Borjas and, once again, plumbed a labor-market surprise. Despite the recent onslaught of immigrants, he pointed out, U.S. cities still have fewer unskilled workers than they had in 1980. Immigrants may be depriving native dropouts of the scarcity value they might have enjoyed, but at least in a historical sense, unskilled labor is not in surplus. America has become so educated that immigrants merely mitigate some of the decline in the homegrown unskilled population. Thus, in 1980, 24 percent of the work force in metropolitan areas were dropouts; in 2000, only 18 percent were.

Card also observed that cities with more immigrants, like those in the Sun Belt close to the Mexican border, have a far higher proportion of dropouts. This has led to a weird unbalancing of local labor markets. For example, 10 percent of the work force in Pittsburgh and 15 percent in Cleveland are high-school dropouts; in Houston the figure is 25 percent, in Los Angeles, 30 percent. The immigrants aren't dispersing, or not very quickly.

So where do all the dropouts work? Los Angeles does have a lot of apparel manufacturers but not enough of such immigrant-intensive businesses to account for all of its unskilled workers. Studies also suggest that immigration is correlated with a slight increase in unemployment. But again, the effect is small. So the mystery is how cities absorb so many unskilled. Card's theory is that the same businesses operate differently when immigrants are present; they spend less on machines and more on labor. Still, he admitted, "We are left with the puzzle of explaining the remarkable flexibility of employment demand."

Card started thinking about this when he moved from Princeton in the mid–90's. He noticed that everyone in Berkeley seemed to have a gardener, "even though professors are not rich." In the U.S., which has more unskilled labor than Europe, more people employ housecleaners. The African–American women who held those jobs before the war, like the Salvadorans and Guatemalans of today, weren't taking jobs; they were creating them.

THE PERSONAL IS ECONOMIC

Though Card works on immigration only some of the time, he and Borjas clearly have become rivals. In a recent paper, Card made a point of referring to the "revisionist" view as "overly pessimistic." Borjas told Business Week that Card's ideas were "insane." ("Obviously I didn't mean he is insane; he is a very bright guy," Borjas clarified when we talked. "The idea that you can add 15 or 20 million people and not have any effect seems crazy.") Alan B. Krueger, an economist who is friendly with each, says, "I fear it might become acrimonious." Card told me twice that Borjas's calculations were "disingenuous." "Borjas has a strong view on this topic," Card said, "almost an emotional position."

Card is more comfortable with anecdote than many scholars, and he tells a story about his wife, who teaches English to Mexicans. In one class, she tapped on a wall, asking a student to identify it, and the guy said, "That's *drywall*." To Card, it signifies that construction is one of those fields that soak up a disproportionate number of Mexicans; it's a little piece of the puzzle. "Even when I was a kid in Ontario 45 years ago," he notes, "the tobacco pickers were Jamaicans. They were terrible jobs—backbreaking." Card is a political liberal with thinning auburn air and a controlled, smirky smile. His prejudices, if not his emotions, favor immigrants. Raised by dairy farmers in Guelph, Ontario, he remembers that Canadian cities were mostly boring while he was growing up. The ones that attracted immigrants, like Toronto and Vancouver, boomed and became more cosmopolitan.

"Everyone knows in trade there are winners and losers," Card says. "For some reason it doesn't stop people from advocating free trade." He could have said the same of Wal–Mart, which has put plenty of Mom-and-Pop retailers out of business. In fact, any time a firm offers better or more efficient service, somebody will suffer. But the economy grows as a result.

"I honestly think the economic arguments are second order," Card told me when we discussed immigration. "They are almost irrelevant."

Card's implication is that darker forces—ethnic prejudice, maybe, or fear of social disruption—is what's really motivating a lot of anti-immigrant sentiment. Borjas, a Hispanic who has written in blunt terms about the skill deficits of Mexicans, in particular arouses resentment. "Mexicans aren't as good as Cubans like him," Douglas S. Massey, a demographer at Princeton, said in a pointed swipe.

Borjas lives an assimilated life. He has a wife who speaks no Spanish, three kids, two of whom study his mother tongue as a foreign language, and a home in Lexington, a tiny Boston suburb. Yet his mind-set often struck me as that of an outsider—an immigrant, if you will, to his own profession.

When I asked the inevitable question—did his exile experience influence his choice of career?—he said, "Clearly it predisposed me." The seeds of the maverick scholar were planted the year before he left Cuba, a searing time when the revolution was swinging decisively toward Soviet-style communism. His family had owned a small factory that manufactured men's pants. The factory was shut down, and the family made ready to leave the island, but their departure was delayed by the death of Borjas's father. The son had to attend a revolutionary school, where the precepts of Marxism–Leninism were drilled into the future economist with notable lack of success. One day he marched in the band and drummed the "Internationale" in front of Fidel Castro and the visiting Yuri Gagarin, the Soviet cosmonaut. "Since that year I have been incredibly resistant to any kind of indoctrination," he told me—an attitude that surfaces in wry references to the liberal Harvard environs as the "People's Republic of Cambridge" and to American political correctness in general.

Borjas's family arrived with virtually no money; they got some clothing from Catholic Charities and a one-time stipend of, as he recollects, $100. His mother got a factory job in Miami, where they stayed several years. Then the family moved to New Jersey. He attended Saint Peter's College in Jersey City and got his Ph.D. at Columbia.

I asked him whether the fact that he was Cuban, the most successful Latin subgroup, had affected his views of other Hispanics. "Look, I've never been psychoanalyzed," he said with an air of resignation, as if he were accustomed to hearing such loaded questions. One thing Borjas shares with Card is a view that others treat immigration emotionally. But Borjas takes comfort not in anecdote but in empiricism. As he said to me often, "The data is the data."

IMMIGRANTS CAN BE COMPLEMENTARY

Economists on Card's side of the debate recognize that they at least have to deal with Borjas's data—to reconcile why the local studies and national studies produce different results. Card shrugs it off; even 5 percent for a dropout, he observes, is only 50 to 60 cents an hour. Giovanni Peri, an Italian working at the University of California, Davis, had a more intriguing response. Peri replicated Borjas's scatter diagram, and also his finding that unskilled natives suffer a loss relative to, say, graduates. He made different assumptions, however, about how businesses adjust to the influx of new workers, and as a result, he found that the absolute harm was less, or the gain was greater, for all native-born groups. By his reckoning, native dropouts lost only 1 percent of their income during the 1990's.

Peri's theory is that most of the wage losses are sustained by previous immigrants, because immigrants compete most directly with one another. It's a principle of economics that a surplus in one part of the production scheme raises the demand for every other one. For instance, if you have a big influx of chefs, you can use more waiters, pushing up their wages; if you have a lot of chefs and waiters, you need more Sub–Zeros, so investment will also rise. The only ones hurt, in this example, are the homegrown chefs—the people who are "like" the immigrants.

Indeed, workers who are unlike immigrants see a net gain; more foreign doctors increases the demand for native hospital administrators. Borjas assumes that a native dropout (or a native anything) is interchangeable with an immigrant of the same skill level. Peri doesn't. If enough Mexicans go into construction, some native workers may be hurt, but a few will get promotions, because with more crews working there will be a greater demand for foremen, who most likely will be natives.

Natives have a different mix of skills—English, for instance, or knowledge of the landscape. In economists' lingo, foreigners are not "perfect substitutes." (Friedberg also observed this in Israel.) In some cases, they will complement rather than compete with native workers. Vietnamese manicurists in California cater to a lower-price, less-exclusive market than native-run salons. The particular skills of an Italian designer—or even an economist—are distinct from an American's. "My work is autobiographical to a large extent," notes Peri, who got into the field when the Italian government commissioned him to study why Italy was losing so many professionals. The foreigners he sees in California are a boon to the U.S. It astonishes him how people like Sensenbrenner want to restrict immigration and apply the letter of the law against those working here.

This is a very romantic view. The issue is not so much Italian designers as Mexican dropouts. But many Mexicans work jobs that are unappealing to most Americans; in this sense, they are not exactly like natives of their skill level either. Mexicans have replenished some occupations that would have become underpopulated; for instance, 40,-000 people who became meat processors immigrated to the U.S. during the 1990's, shoring up the industry. Without them, some plants would have raised wages, but others would have closed or, indeed, relocated to Mexico.

ARE ALL DROPOUTS THE SAME?

I talked to half a dozen vintners and a like number of roofing-company owners, both fields that rely on Mexican labor, and frequently heard that Americans do not, in sufficient numbers, want the work. In the case of the vineyards, if Mexicans weren't available, some of the grapes would be harvested by machine. This is what economists mean by "capital adjusting." If the human skills are there, capital will find a way to employ them. Over the short term, people chase jobs, but over the long term jobs chase people. (That is why software firms locate in Silicon Valley.)

If you talk to enough employers, you start to gather that they prefer immigrant labor over unskilled Americans. The former have fewer problems with tardiness, a better work ethic. Some of this may be prejudice. But it's possible that Mexican dropouts may be better workers than our dropouts. In Mexico, not finishing high school is the norm; it's not associated with an unsuitability for work or even especially with failure. In the U.S., where the great majority do graduate, those who don't graduate have high rates of drug use and problems with the law.

The issue is charged because the group with by far the highest rate of incarceration is African–American dropouts. Approximately 20 percent of black males without high-school diplomas are in jail. Indeed, according to Steven Raphael, a colleague of Card's at Berkeley, the correlation between wages and immigration is a lot weaker if you control for the fact that so many black men are in prison. But should you control for it? Borjas says he thinks not. It's pretty well established that as the reward for legal work diminishes, some people turn to crime. This is why people sold crack; the payoff was tremendous. Borjas has developed one of his graphs to show that the presence of immigrants is correlated with doing time, especially among African Americans. Incarceration rates, he notes, rose sharply in the 70's, just as immigration did. He doesn't pretend that this is the whole explanation—only that there is a link. Card retorts: "The idea that the way to help the lot of African Americans is to restrict

Mexicans is ridiculous." Black leaders have themselves mostly switched sides. In the 20's, A. Philip Randolph, who led the Pullman Porters, spoke in favor of immigration quotas, but the civil rights establishment no longer treats immigration as a big issue; instead it tends to look at immigrants as potential constituents. (One person who takes issue with the prevailing view is Anthony W. Williams, an African–American pastor in Chicago who is running for Congress against Representative Jesse Jackson Jr. Black leaders have forsaken their mission, he told me. "Immigration will destroy the economic base of the African–American community.")

* * *

The economists do have political opinions, of course. Borjas leans to a system like Canada's, which would admit immigrants on the basis of skills. He also says that, to make sure the problem of illegals does not recur, the U.S. should secure its borders before it adjusts the status of its present illegals.

Advocates of a more open policy often cite the country's history. They argue that the racists of by-gone eras were not only discriminatory but also wrong. Card, for instance, mentioned an article penned by a future U.S. senator, Paul Douglas, titled "Is the New Immigration More Unskilled Than the Old?" It was written in 1919, when many people (though not Douglas) held that Jews, Slavs and Italians were incompatible with the country's Anglo and Teutonic stock. Nativism has always been part of the American scene, and it has tended to turn ugly in periods when the country was tired of or suspicious of foreigners. In 1952, quotas were maintained in a law sponsored by Senator Pat McCarran, a prominent McCarthyite. There remains today a palpable strain of xenophobia in the anti-immigrant movement. Dan Stein, president of the Federation for American Immigration Reform, remarked to me, rather meanly, "If someone comes here from China and they go swimming in a dangerous river, a sign in English is enough, but the Mexicans want it in Spanish." Ninety years ago, some signs were in German, as were 500 newspapers on American soil.

But U.S. history, as Borjas observes, can be read in two ways. For sure, earlier waves of immigrants assimilated, but America essentially closed the gate for 40 years. Antipathy toward Germans during World War I forced German Americans to hide all traces of their origins. The quotas of the 1920's were reinforced by the Depression and then by World War II. The country had time to let assimilation occur.

A reverse process seems to be occurring with Mexican Americans. Very few Mexicans came north in the decades after 1920, even though they were relatively free to do so. As recently as 1970, the U.S. had fewer than one million Mexicans, almost all of them in Texas and California. The U.S. did bring Mexican braceros to work on farms during the 1940's, 50's and 60's. The program was terminated in 1964, and immigration officials immediately noticed a sharp rise in illicit border crossings. The collapse of the Mexican economy in the 70's gave migrants a further push. Finally, Mexicans who obtained legal status were (thanks to the 1965 reform) able to bring in family members.

The important point is that, ultimately, there was a catalytic effect—so many Mexicans settled here that it became easier for more Mexicans to follow. One story has it that in a village in central Mexico people knew the price of mushrooms in Pennsylvania sooner than people in the next county over. Even if apocryphal, it illustrates what economists call a network effect: with 12 million people born in Mexico now dispersed around the U.S., information about job-market conditions filters back to Mexico with remarkable speed.

Now that the network is established, the exodus feels rather permanent; it is not a wave but a continuous flow. This has led to understandable anxiety, even among economists, about whether Mexicans will assimilate as rapidly as previous groups. Although second-generation Mexicans do (overwhelmingly) speak English, and also graduate from high school at far higher rates than their parents, Borjas has documented what he calls an ethnic "half-life" of immigrant groups: with each generation, members of the group retain half of the income and educational deficit (or advantage) of their parents. In other words, each group tends toward the mean, but the process is slow. Last year he wrote that Mexicans in America are burdened if not doomed by their "ethnic capital," and will be for several generations. In "Heaven's Door," Borjas even wrote forgivingly of the quota system enacted in the 20's, observing that it "was not born out of thin air; it was the political consensus . . . reached after 30 years of debate." These are distasteful words to many people. But Borjas does not advocate a return to quotas. His point is that Americans shouldn't kid themselves: "National origin and immigrant skills are so intimately related, any attempt to change one will inevitably change the other."

The Limits of Economics

Economists more in the mainstream generally agree that the U.S. should take in more skilled immigrants; it's the issue of the unskilled that is tricky. Many say that unskilled labor is needed and that the U.S. could better help its native unskilled by other means (like raising the minimum wage or expanding job training) than by building a wall. None believe, however, that the U.S. can get by with no limits. Richard B. Freeman of Harvard floated the idea that the U.S. simply sell visas at a reasonable price. The fee could be adjusted according to indicators like the unemployment rate. It is unlikely that Congress will go for anything so cute, and the economists' specific prescriptions may be beside the point. As they acknowledge, immigration policy responds to a host of factors—cultural, political and social as well as economic. Migrant workers, sometimes just by crowding an uncustomary allotment of people into a single dwelling, bring a bit of disorder to our civic life; such concerns, though beyond the economists' range, are properly part of the debate.

What the economists can do is frame a subset of the important issues. They remind us, first, that the legislated goal of U.S. policy is curiously disconnected from economics. Indeed, the flow of illegals is the market's signal that the current legal limits are too low. Immigrants do help the economy; they are fuel for growth cities like Las Vegas and a salve to older cities that have suffered native flight. Borjas's research strongly suggests that native unskilled workers pay a price: in wages, in their ability to find inviting areas to migrate to and perhaps in employment. But the price is probably a small one.

The disconnect between Borjas's results and Card's hints that an alchemy occurs when immigrants land ashore; the economy's potential for absorbing and also adapting is mysterious but powerful. Like any form of economic change, immigration causes distress and disruption to some. But America has always thrived on dynamic transformations that produce winners as well as losers. Such transformations stimulate growth. Other societies (like those in Europe) have opted for more controls, on immigration and on labor markets generally. They have more stability and more equality, but less growth and fewer jobs. Economists have highlighted these issues, but they cannot decide them. Their resolution depends on a question that Card posed but that the public has not yet come to terms with: "What is it that immigration policy is supposed to achieve?"

Tamar Jacoby echoes some of Lowenstein's findings:

The most important of those new realities [driving immigration] is the global integration of labor markets. Today's immigrant influx—second in volume only to the wave that arrived a hundred years ago—is not some kind of voluntary experiment that Washington could turn off at will, like a faucet. On the contrary, it is the product of changing U.S. demographics, global development, and the increasingly easy international communications that are shrinking the planet ... Between 2002 and 2012 ... the U.S. economy is expected to create some 56 million new jobs, half of which will require no more than a high school education. More than 75 million baby boomers will retire in that period. And declining native-born fertility rates will be approaching replacement level. Native-born workers, meanwhile, are becoming more educated with every decade. Arguably, the most important statistic for anyone seeking to understand the immigration issues is ... in 1960, half of all American men dropped out of high school to look for unskilled work, whereas less than ten percent do so now.

Tamar Jacoby, *Immigrant Nation*, 85 Foreign Affairs 50 (Nov./Dec. 2006).

Jacoby goes on to show that the shortfall of unskilled labor is showing up in sector after sector—construction, masonry, dry-wall installation, restaurant work—and is being filled by immigrant workers. Unless Americans change to accept lifetime jobs flipping hamburgers or bussing tables, the need for immigrant labor will only increase.

She also points out that the country's need for unskilled workers is increasing just as economic changes south of the border are "freeing up a supply of unskilled labor to meet these growing needs." Mexico is moving from subsistence agriculture to more advanced industries, yet it is not developing enough jobs to meet the demands of its fast-growing population. Id. And the market is efficient. Immigrants here communicate to compatriots back home that City A has jobs while the market in City B is flat. Id. The workers' calculus also encourages immigration: If one is going to be unemployed, it is better to be so in Mexico or Guatemala. Consequently, most immigrants to the United States are highly motivated to find work.

What of immigrants' net effect on the receiving country? Jacoby finds agreement "among economists that newcomers enlarge the economic pie." Foreign workers getting jobs in meatpacking plants or carpet factories use their wages to buy groceries and shoes for their children. On Saturday, they buy washing machines and then hire plumbers to install them in their apartments. The companies where they work are more likely to remain in the United States than move to a foreign country where labor is cheap. Over the last decade, immigrants filled more than half of all new jobs, and two-thirds in regions such as the Midwest and the South, making them responsible for much of the growth in those areas. In North Carolina, for example, immigrants filled one-third of new jobs in the past ten years and were responsible for 9.2 billion dollars in consumer spending.

Is all this good for the national economy? It is, Jacoby writes, when the immigrants represent "complementarity"—when they are as different as possible from the local workforce and offer a different set of skills (say, gardening) and interests (say, blue-collar jobs). When this is present, the newcomers not only do not depress wages, they generate jobs for current citizens as foremen, supervisors, and business managers. "More low-skilled construction workers mean more jobs and higher wages for plumbers, electricians, and architects. More service workers allow skilled Americans to spend more of their time doing more productive work: instead of staying home to cut the grass, the brain surgeon has time for more brain surgeries." Id.

Jacoby goes on to point out that complementarity also affects wage levels. Some opponents of immigration ask why employers do not recruit Americans by simply paying more. But a factory faced with higher wage costs may move overseas, making everyone in the region worse off. Moreover, "it hardly makes sense to lure an American to do a less productive job than he or she is capable of by paying more for less-skilled work." Finally, immigrants "often create jobs where none existed before." Id. Witness the growth of lawn-care businesses, manicure parlors staffed by Vietnamese women, or medium-priced restaurants selling excellent ethnic food.

The bottom line: Immigrants contribute about $700 billion, or 5.4 percent of GDP. Id.

See Daniel Altman, *Shattering Stereotypes About Immigrant Workers*, N.Y. Times, June 3, 2007, at 4 (Business), describing contribution of immigrants to various sectors of the U.S. economy and concluding that they are a net benefit and even increase the employment rate, because of "complementarity"—they offer a combination of skills and cost that other workers cannot match; see also René Galindo & Jami Vigil, *Are Anti–Immigrant Statements Racist or Nativist?*, 4 Latino Stud. 419 (2006).

Scholarly Debates and Issue-Framing

Recent scholarly books by academics and think-tank figures have vigorously debated the terms in which the nation should approach immigration. Huntington, supra, believes that the key problem with Latino immigration is the new arrivals' refusal to adopt America's core Anglo Saxon values. George Borjas echoes some of these concerns but adds an economic dimension: The new immigrants cost America more in social welfare costs than they contribute through their labor to our economy. George J. Borjas, *Heaven's Door: Immigration Policy and the American Economy* (1999) (Borjas is almost alone among economists in drawing this conclusion).

Others who take similar dim views of Latin American immigration include Victor Davis Hanson, *Mexifornia: A State of Becoming* (2003); Michelle Malkin, *Invasion: How America Still Welcomes Terrorists, Criminals, and Other Foreign Menaces to Our Shores* (2002); Michelle Malkin, *In Defense of Internment: The Case for Racial Profiling in World War II and the War on Terror* (2004); Patrick J. Buchanan, *The Death of the West: How Dying Populations and Immigrant Invasions Imperil Our Country and Civilization* (2002); Peter Brimelow, *Alien Nation: Common Sense About America's Immigration Disaster* (1995); and Arthur M. Schlesinger Jr., *The Disuniting of America: Reflections on a Multicultural Society* (rev. ed. 1998).

Hanson takes the position that Mexicans contribute little to California except for placing social and cultural demands on its infrastructure. Brimelow writes that heavy immigration is stressing our basic Anglo–European culture and traditions, while the immigrants' rapid birthrate is threatening to overwhelm its gene pool. Schlesinger doubts that multiculturalism and multiracialism, beyond a certain point, are good things. And Malkin, despite Latinos' low crime rate—see, e.g., Robert J. Sampson, *Open Doors Don't Invite Criminals*, N.Y. Times, Mar. 11, 2006, at A15; Kristin F. Butcher & Anne Morrison Piehl, *Why Are Immigrants'*

Incarceration Rates So Low? Evidence on Selective Immigration, Deterrence, and Deportation, National Bureau of Economic Research Working Paper 13229 (2007)—considers immigrants a threat to America's security.

Writings that defend immigration include the abovementioned works by Johnson and Hing; John Higham, *Strangers in the Land: Patterns of American Nativism, 1860–1925* (2002); Richard Alba & Victor Nee, *Remaking the American Mainstream: Assimilation and Contemporary Immigration* (2003); and Linda Chavez, *Out of the Barrio: Toward a New Politics of Hispanic Assimilation* (1991). These writers either paint multiracialism as a positive good (Johnson, Hing); argue that Latinos are assimilating rapidly and hence no threat to traditional American values (Johnson, Alba, Higham); or argue that Latino immigrants are likely to follow the traditional immigrant path of previous generations of European immigrants and thus likely to fit in, make contributions, and embrace Americanism and national values (all of the authors, to varying degrees). Kevin R. Johnson, in an article and forthcoming book, goes further than most by arguing for completely open borders. See *Open Borders?*, 51 UCLA L. Rev. 193 (2003); *Opening the Floodgates: Why America Needs to Rethink its Borders and Immigration Laws* (2007). By the same author: *Protecting National Security Through More Liberal Admission of Immigrants*, 2007 U. Chi. Legal F. 157.

Suggesting that critical race theory can help illuminate debates over immigration, see Stephen Shie–Wei Fan, *Immigration Law and the Promise of Critical Race Theory: Opening the Academy to the Voices of Aliens and Immigrants*, 97 Colum. L. Rev. 1202 (1997). Opposing the idea of a new bracero program, see Cristina M. Rodriguez, *Guest Workers and Integration: Toward a Theory of What Immigrants and Americans Owe One Another*, 2007 U. Chi Legal F. 219. See also Joseph H. Carens, *Aliens and Citizens: The Case for Open Borders*, 49 Rev. Pol. 251 (1987).

Bill Ong Hing
The Dark Side of Operation Gatekeeper
7 U.C. Davis J. Intern'l L. & Pol'y 121, 123–
24, 133–44, 146–47, 149, 150 (2001)

March 7, 2000. The bodies of the three men were pulled Monday from the snow-frosted mountains of the Cleveland National Forest, a busy corridor for illegal immigration from Mexico. Asked to identify one body, a young man in jeans and a cotton jacket was escorted from a Border Patrol truck and nodded "yes" to acknowledge that the victim had been part of his group of border-crossers.

Sick and cold illegal immigrants stumbled out of the Laguna Mountains all day Monday after a weekend storm dumped 6 to 8 inches of snow. Temperatures Sunday night plunged to lows of between 20 and 34 degrees.

Eight people who were rescued by fire workers near Mount Laguna on Monday could barely move, said assistant chief Dave

Strohte. They had been caught in the wet snow wearing only tennis shoes, cotton pants and light jackets, he said. "They were completely unprepared for this," Strohte said.

September 11, 1998. This weekend four migrants died in Imperial Valley. On Friday, the body of a man was found floating in the All–American Canal. On Saturday, a man died who had been in a coma since August, when he was found in the desert north of Calipatria. He was found with a core body temperature of 108 degrees. On Sunday, the Border Patrol came upon the body of woman near Ocotillo. Some of her group stayed with her body. Asuncion Hernandez Uriel died of heat stress. Also on Sunday, the decomposed body of Oscar Cardoso Varon was pulled out of the All–American Canal.

August 13, 1998. Seven partially-clad bodies were found by a ranch foreman about 40 miles north of the border, near the Salton Sea. The temperatures in the desert had been over 105 degrees, with a heat index of around 115 factoring in humidity. The group had been dead about five weeks and consisted of five men and two teenagers.

March 31, 1998. A winter storm at the end of March left four migrants dead: Serafin Andrade Regalado, 41; Remigio Salomon Barriento, 24; Jose Carmen Raya Hernandez, 24; and Bertha Carrillo Topete, 33. Up to a foot of snow had fallen and temperatures dropped to 22 degrees.

INTRODUCTION

Since the institution of the U.S. Border Patrol's Operation Gatekeeper along the Mexico–California border in 1994, [hundreds of] migrants have died crossing the San Diego County and Imperial County segments of the border, mostly from hypothermia, heat stroke, and drowning.* [An even larger number] have died attempting to cross the Arizona and Texas stretches of the border. These deaths are the direct result of the philosophy of "control through deterrence" embodied in Operation Gatekeeper. By closing off traditional corridors of entrance used by undocumented migrants, Operation Gatekeeper has pushed migrants into far more treacherous areas.

* * *

Smuggling

The "prevention through deterrence" strategy has bolstered the smuggling industry. As the INS stepped up operations, most migrants turned to smugglers. This helps explain why most migrants attempting unauthorized entry succeed despite significantly more agents and technology on the border. The [government] did not foresee the extent of this

---

* Eds. In 2003 the U.S. Border Patrol became part of the newly created agency called U.S. Customs and Border Protection. The Immigration and Naturalization Service (INS), along with the U.S. Customs Service, became Immigration and Customs Enforcement (ICE), the largest branch of the Dept. of Homeland Security.

effect. Former Commissioner Meissner said architects of a nationwide border crackdown expected that hostile terrain and deadly weather conditions in remote mountains and deserts along the 2,000 mile U.S.-Mexico frontier would act as a greater deterrent to illegal crossings than has been the case: "We knew there would be ... changes in smuggling patterns. But it has been surprising to *see* how quickly that's happened and in the numbers that it's happened." Yet, as early as 1995, the U.S. Commission on Immigration Reform noted that given the difficult terrain crossers faced after Gatekeeper, undocumented aliens "would need guides to cross such terrain, jacking up the cost of illegal entry." In fact, get tough campaigns like Operation Gatekeeper are creating new opportunities for sophisticated immigrant smuggling rings with ties to organized crime and drug traffickers. Tough policies benefit smugglers who have the transportation and communication capabilities to counter the most zealous efforts. Smugglers have increased their fees and have turned to more sophisticated smuggling tactics. For example, in the Tucson sector, the smuggling fees increased from $1,000 in 1996 to $1,350 in 1998. In the Douglas, Arizona area, in 1999 the typical charge to be smuggled through Douglas to Phoenix was $150; now the price range is $800 to $1,300. Similarly, in San Diego, smugglers charged about $300 prior to Gatekeeper for help in crossing and transportation to Los Angeles; now the charge is $800 to $1,200. In the view of one long-time observer:

> [T]he [smugglers] haven't priced themselves out of the market. Migrants desperate to get into the U.S. just take more time to save up what they need, or just borrow more money from relatives already based in the U.S. If they use a reasonably experienced [smuggler], most migrants can still get through on their first try. If they can't afford to use a [smuggler], many of the migrants must now try 3, 4, or 5 times.

Increased use of fraudulent visas to gain entry has also climbed. Since the institution of Gatekeeper, southwest border port of entry inspectors apprehended an increased number of persons attempting fraudulent entry. These fraudulent entry attempts at ports of entry include the increasing use of fraudulent entry documents and false claims to U.S. citizenship. The increase in attempts to enter with fraudulent documents, at a time when apprehension rates are up as well, further suggests that the impetus to cross is great.

Given increased apprehension rates, greater reliance on smugglers, and expanded use of fraudulent entry documents, one could hardly say that the [border authority] has done much to attain its primary goal of controlling the border through deterrence. * * * Unfortunately, these are not the only costs.

Human Costs

* * *

As Operation Gatekeeper closed the 14–mile Imperial Beach corridor, border-crossing traffic moved east. Frustrated crossers moved first to Brown Field and Chula Vista, and subsequently to the eastern sections of the San Diego sector. Brown Field and Chula Vista are communities within the San Diego sector. Brown Field is just east of the Imperial Beach area, near the Otay port-of-entry and next to an airfield called Brown Field. Before Gatekeeper began in 1994, crossers who had made a first attempt in the western-most sector were just as likely to make their second try in the same area; but that changed very quickly. By January 1995, only 14 percent made their second try near Imperial Beach. The illicit border traffic had moved "into unfamiliar and unattractive territory." * * *

The death statistics are revealing. In 1994, 23 migrants died along the California/Mexico border. Of the 23, two died of hypothermia or heat stroke and nine from drowning. By 1998, the annual total was 147 deaths—71 from hypothermia or heat stroke and 52 from drowning. Figures for 1999 followed this unfortunate trend, and in 2000, 84 were heat stroke or hypothermia casualties. The total death count along the entire border for the year 2000 was 499. Of those, 100 died crossing the desert along the Sonora–Arizona border.

Why the radical surge in deaths? The new routes are death traps. The correlation between increasing deaths and Gatekeeper's closure of the westernmost corridors is clear. The Border Patrol Chief has stressed that although the distances migrants must traverse in places like Texas are enormous, the eastern edge of the California–Mexico border contains the "more difficult terrain." In fact, the San Diego and El Centro sectors encompass three of the four places considered by the Border Patrol to be "the most hazardous areas:" East San Diego County, the Imperial Desert and the All–American Canal. The fourth is Kennedy County, Texas. The INS recognizes that the challenges of the new routes include rugged canyons and high desert, remote, desolate stretches, and risks of dehydration and exposure. Bersin noted:

> [Migrants] must now traverse extremely difficult terrain—deep canyons filled with rocky shrub, virtually no water and peaks that rise over 6,000 feet, or through deserts, picturesque but bleak and dangerous. Whereas they previously crossed in areas with almost immediate access to roads, it now is an arduous two to three day trek before they reach the roadways and freeways which give them expedited access to their final destination. Guides are therefore needed more than ever before....

Given the potential dangers of wildfires, falls, snakebites and animal attacks, one fire prevention chief cautioned that migrants would be "walking into areas where I won't send firefighters." And one assistant Border Patrol chief for the San Diego sector agrees: "Even if you take the weather out of it as a factor, the terrain is still rough—some of the roughest I've ever been in." In contrast, the 14 mile area from Imperial Beach to the base of the Otay Mountain, the less rigorous original route, was much easier. The eastern mountain route crossings can last anywhere from 12 hours to four days.

The topography and climate of the eastern terrain are daunting. The Otay Mountains are "extremely rugged, and include steep, often precipitous, canyon walls and hills reaching 4,000 feet." Extreme temperatures ranging from freezing cold in the winter to searing heat in the summer can kill the unprepared traveler. The Tecate Mountains are full of steep-walled canyons and rocky peaks that rise over 6,000 feet. Night-time temperatures can drop into the 20's and snow can fall to altitudes as low as 800 feet. From mid-October to mid-April, there is a greater than 50 percent probability of below-freezing temperatures. In January 1997, 16 migrants froze to death. The All–American Canal parallels the border for 44 of its 85 Imperial County miles. It is unfenced and unlighted, 21 feet deep and nearly as wide as a football field. It has strong currents and is one of the most polluted rivers in the United States.

Most of the deaths have occurred in California's Imperial Desert— one of the hottest spots in the world. Both the Imperial and Yuma deserts are part of the Sonora Desert, a 1,600 square mile area that straddles the border. The temperature on some August days in the Imperial Desert nears 130 degrees. From June through September the average high temperature in El Centro, about 50 miles west of the Arizona border and 10 miles north of the Mexican border, is over 100 degrees. Imperial County coroner investigator estimates the shortest route that migrants hike in the Imperial Valley is 10 miles. Of course, migrants going the desert route have already hiked through the Baja California side of the desert when they arrive at the border. The sand dune area in Imperial County, where many migrants are forced to cross, straddles the border and is 30 miles wide with dunes as high as 300 feet.

The Sonora Desert is the hottest of North America's five great deserts. The desert straddles the border (extending from northern Mexico to California and east through Arizona and New Mexico). It gets less than five inches of rainfall a year and is described by Edward Abbey, founder of Earth First, as encompassing "some of the hottest locations in the U.S.," where summertime daily high temperatures can average 107 degrees, and can climb as high as 125 degrees. The temperatures in the desert can fall below freezing in the winter. By contrast, in Chula Vista, directly south of the city of San Diego, the average maximum temperature in August in 74.8 degrees and the average minimum temperature in January is 44.5 degrees. Most experts agree that once temperatures start getting up around 115 to 120, people can die within a couple of hours without water.

* * *

* * * On June 18, a pregnant woman and five other migrants were reported missing in the desert by two companions, about 60 miles east of Tijuana. The survivors said that other members of the group had died in the heat, which had approached or exceeded 100 degrees. They had crossed about 40 miles west of El Centro. Articles of women's clothing, including shoes, were found in the search area, along with empty water bottles, but there was no sign of the missing migrants. On July 28 the body of a border crosser was found in a secluded Imperial Valley field. Next to him were two empty water bottles. He had been dead for a week; his age was estimated between 25 and 35. On August 24, Margarita Melchor Rangel, 27, died while trying to cross the desert near the Chocolate Mountain Navel Aerial Gunnery Range. When she became ill, several in her group lagged behind to stay with her, at times carrying her. Eventually she collapsed. On September 15, the decomposed body of 43–year-old Celia Flora Gonzalez Reyes, who had been missing in the desert for more than a week, was sighted by a Border Patrol pilot. Her partially clad body was found next to a bush. On the weekend of September 25, five bodies were found in the Imperial Valley—two decomposed in the All–American Canal and three in various stages of mummification in the desert near El Centro. The last reported death of 1998 was on December 29. The victim died of heat stress.

* * *

Ricky Macken, a coroner along the border who has examined such bodies, describes it this way:

> Two reasons [why people die in the desert. They] run out of water and [their] system shuts down because you have no fluids, or temperature becomes elevated to the point where it causes your organs to start failing. Whether it's heat stroke or dehydration, ultimately it has the same effect—organs start failing and then ultimately you die because your organs can't maintain the high temperature. Blood will thin out, and there may be blood pressure issues. Symptoms are light headedness, nausea, and people are sick to their stomachs and try to throw up but they can't, depending on whether they're suffering from dehydration or elevated temperature. Most people suffer from both because you just can't carry enough water. You can be consuming water constantly, and still your body will run low of fluids because it's so hot. Once the temperature rises to a certain level, the brain shuts down causing fainting. As this continues, if there's not medical intervention (forced fluids intravenously), through sweating you lose electrolytes that the body needs for organs to work properly, so you flush out necessary nutrients through sweat. This is what intravenous treatment cures. In some cases, it's at the point where you can't reverse the effects so they ultimately will die anyway. Some have been found alive, ambulances have been called, temperature was brought back down, but they still succumb because the organs have been damaged to the point where they cannot respond. By sun stroke, if they're caught soon enough before it becomes a critical medical situation, when they use intravenous treatment, the body responds rather rapidly. Usually it's a combination.

> As soon as they die, the body starts decomposing. Heat causes a more rapid breakdown of the tissues, so once life has stopped then the fluids start to settle and leak out of the organs. Bacteria within the body start doing their job. Stomach continues to do its job. You

have breakdown of tissues of muscles and stuff sped up by the temperature. Within a day or day and a half, people are already in moderate to advanced stages of decomposition. In normal 60–70 degrees temperature, someone can be left several days before it's noticeable. In 90 degrees, two days. In 100 degrees—decomposition starts within hours, noticeably within a day. In the 30 or 20 degrees, you may never notice decomposition, that's the purpose of refrigeration. In olden days, people used to bury people quickly because there was no refrigeration. Now if people die, they're refrigerated, so they'll last indefinitely. It doesn't replace embalming, because embalming preserves tissues. But if you just refrigerate and bury, then once they're put in the ground, decomposition process starts. After the people in the desert have been out for a week or so they will already appear mummified. When the body decomposes, it will bloat and then go back down once the gases generated by decomposing escape the body to a more natural appearance, and then it will quickly look mummified. All the fats in the body will purge out—most of the body is fat and water, so once breakdown takes place, people weigh about 50–60 pounds, even if they were 200 pounds before. That's how you can tell where the actual scene of death is, because fluids will permanently leave a mark. So even if the body has been moved, you can tell where they originally died.

Animals also eat the bodies. Any carnivorous animal in the wild like coyotes. Animals forage. Around there, its coyotes and vultures. Not every decedent has been eaten, but it's not unusual, especially not those who have appeared to be dead for several months. It's not advertised to the families, but yes, people are eaten.

Victims of hypothermia during the freezing months of winter, in the mountains or the desert, face a different set of symptoms. As their body temperature drops, symptoms get more severe:

98.6—95.0: Intense shivering, ability to perform complex tasks is impaired, fatigue, poor coordination, immobile and fumbling hands.

95.0—91.4: Violent shivering, difficult speaking, sluggish in thinking, amnesia starts to appear, starts to lose contact with environment, stumbling gait, feeling of deep cold and numbness.

91.4—87.8: Shivering decreases, in its place is muscle rigidity, erratic movement, thinking is not clear, [victim can't [. . .] stand] hallucinations, loses contact with the surroundings.

87.8—85.2: Rigid muscles, no shivering, very irrational, starts into a stupor, pulse and respiration slow, pupils start to dilate, skin is turning bluish, drowsiness.

85.2—78.8: Does not respond to words that are spoken, pulse is very erratic, reflexes do not function, victim will be only semiconscious, heart starts atrial fib[rilation] [rapid twitching of individual muscle fibers].

Below 78.8: Heart and respiratory failure, ventricular fib, probable brain and lung hemorrhage, apparent death.

Increasing environmental deaths are not limited to California. Up to this point, the use of extreme climate and topography to prevent illegal entries has been limited to California. The result is a much higher migrant death toll in California than in states like Texas, New Mexico and Arizona, which also share borders with Mexico. Increasingly, however, illicit border crossers from Baja California are being pushed into Arizona's Yuma desert, where they are also dying in unprecedented numbers. From the start, the goal was to push the undocumented foot traffic toward the terrain east of San Diego. By 1999, Gatekeeper expanded as far east as Yuma, Arizona, and border related deaths for Arizona soared from 18 in 1998 to 31 in 1999. More than 100 people died in the first ten months of 2000 crossing surreptitiously from Mexico to Arizona, already doubling the number who died in all of the previous year. Of the 106 deaths recorded in Arizona by October 2000, 65 were due to exposure to the heat, three from the cold and 38 to a variety of causes, including drownings. * * *

* * *

Border Patrol agents themselves acknowledge that the number of bodies recovered may indicate a much larger death toll. Many bodies simply have not been discovered in the rugged territory. As one Border Patrol official put it, "[w]e're often coming across skeletons and bodies that have been out there for who knows how long, so there are probably a lot more out there now." Moreover, the deaths reported by the Border Patrol do not include those who died on the Mexican side of the mountains or desert.

* * *

Causes of Continued Border Crossing

Given the harrowing conditions facing border crossers, one has to wonder why the migration pattern continued, and even increased, after the institution of Operation Gatekeeper. * * *

The Mexican Economy

The primary cause of the continued flow of undocumented migration from Mexico is economic. * * * On December 20, 1994, about two months after the institution of Gatekeeper, the Mexican peso was devalued, immediately plummeting 40 percent. The devaluation, which came on the heels of an ill-fated privatization of eighteen state-owned banks in 1992, threw Mexico into its worst economic crisis since the Great Depression. A million people lost their jobs and thousands of borrowers stopped paying their loans as annual interest rates neared 100 percent. Within six months, Mexico's annual inflation rate jumped to 90 percent, and 17 percent of the nation's 34 million workers could not find work for even 15 hours a week. Unemployment doubled and wages sank. Within a year, the peso had lost 50 percent of its value.

The attraction of the United States is obvious. The strong economy in the United States pays Mexican workers eight to nine times more than what can be earned in Mexico. As the Mexican Consul in Douglas, Arizona observes, "[t]hese are people trying to get a better job so they can provide for their families, so they can improve their lot." Specific aspects of the Mexican economy—lost value of the peso, cuts in federal spending, increased taxes, and slow job growth—have increased the pressure to migrate north. Extreme poverty has exacerbated the situation. In 1993, 31 percent of Mexicans were considered extremely poor; by 1996 the figure was 50 percent.

The situation calls into question the likely effectiveness of the installation of fences and rigorous terrain on migrant traffic. The reality is that people desperate for work go where they can find it. Even Border Patrol officials acknowledge that the "challenge" of border control in the Gatekeeper area of operation is the high motivation of most of the aliens crossing there, who "travel hundreds of miles over several days from interior sections of Mexico on their way to find jobs in cities throughout the U.S." The migrants and their smugglers have a higher motivation to enter than the Border Patrol has to close down the border. Human rights advocates who have interviewed the migrants sense a desperation to cross and warn, "if we mined the border, people would be blown to pieces trying to avoid the land mines as they continued to come." As one agricultural economist observes, "lots of folks still are successful at illegal entries. Most have invested enough to getting in that even three or four apprehensions does not discourage them." Given the current economic realities, even though the risks have increased, the potential gain from successfully crossing the border will always be greater than having nearly nothing back home. In a sense, the only choice for many crossers is to attempt the journey. * * *

* * *

The North American Free Trade Act (NAFTA) certainly has not been the short-term solution to the economic crisis in Mexico nor has it stemmed the flow of migrants north. In fact, NAFTA may have contributed to the flow by creating economic displacement in Mexico. * * * Apparently, jobs created in Mexico by NAFTA are not as numerous as the jobs eliminated thus far. * * * One agricultural economist observes that the process of integrating economies tends to stimulate migration in the short and medium term, generating a migration increase that lasts 5 to 15 years. * * *

* * *

Thus, the forces initiating and sustaining migration between Mexico and the United States are not necessarily those that most policymaker and citizens imagine. Undocumented migration is not simply driven by the lure of high wages nor by poverty and a lack of development in

Mexico. Migration may in fact be stimulated by economic growth and development that NAFTA was intended to encourage. The economic forces that cause legal and illegal migration are powerful. Without positive, long term changes in the root causes that prompt illegal migration such as improvements in the Mexican economy, or understanding the actual effects of trade accords, the "push" and "pull" factors will remain strong.

Notes and Questions

1.   If immigrants confer, as Lowenstein and Jacoby write, a small, but definite overall net benefit on the U.S. economy, is it fair to impose the horrific costs on them that Hing describes? Sensible? In our own self interest?

2.   Why would an undocumented immigrant be so highly motivated to come to the United States that he or she runs such a high risk of death or, at least, extreme discomfort, in order to immigrate here? See, e.g., Mario Villarreal & Daniel M. Rothschild, *The New Latin Quarter*, Wall St. J., Aug. 28, 2007, at A12; Alexander Cockburn, *Zyklon B on the U.S. Border*, The Nation, July 9, 2007, at 9 (on use of delousing agent).

3.   Latino immigrants are, by and large, a pious, law-abiding group. Nationally, Latinos make up about 15 percent of the jail population, roughly in accord with their share of the population and much lower than one might expect for such a young group (median age, 27.4, compared to the U.S. average of 36.6). They also pay Social Security and sales taxes in amounts that, according to economists, exceed the cost of the social services (schools, public hospitals, etc.) that they consume. These costs are low because Latinos are a relatively young, healthy group and fear that placing demands on or coming to the attention of the authorities will cause them to be deported. See Heidi Beirich, *Immigration: Getting the Facts Straight*, Intell. Rep., Summer 2007, at 37.

Why, then, do opponents of immigration complain that Latino immigrants are a scourge and a drain on society? See *Immigration Raid Leaves Sense of Dread in Hispanic Students*, N.Y. Times, May 23, 2007, at B7; *Immigrants Out! The New Nativism and the Anti–Immigrant Impulse in the United States* (Juan F. Perea ed., 1997).

B.   THE CONTEMPORARY DEBATE OVER IMMIGRATION POLICY

Among the writers who have weighed in on immigration, especially in recent years, are academics, on both sides of the equation, trying to reach a wide, crossover audience. The following selection describes some of the fault lines of the current debate.

Kevin R. Johnson
*An Essay on Immigration Politics, Popular Democracy,
and California's Proposition 187: The Political
Relevance and Legal Irrelevance of Race*
70 Wash. L. Rev. 629, 635–41 (1995)

Extremes mar the history of immigration law and policy in the United States. Nativist outcries target the leading immigrant group of the day, such as the Irish in the early and mid–1800s, the Chinese in the late 1800s, and Mexicans at various times in the twentieth century. One explanation for the fluctuations is the absence in immigration matters of the usual moderating influences on the political process. This results from the limited membership rights of immigrants in the community.

Immigrants, at least prior to naturalization, enjoy minimal input into the political process. Those lawfully in the country who have not become naturalized citizens, referred to in immigration jargon as lawful permanent residents, as well as undocumented immigrants, cannot vote. Although immigrant rights and some ethnic groups lobby aggressively for immigrants, their pull with politicians naturally is restricted by the electoral powerlessness of their constituency. * * *

Harsh immigration policies historically have been proposed by those searching for answers to the particular political, social, and economic woes of the day. In part because of the limited political power of the immigrant lobby, the proposals at various times—particularly times of crisis—have met only token resistance. This ready-made recipe for extremism may account for why immigration law and policy diverge so dramatically from other areas of public law.

Although the courts in other circumstances may serve as a moderating influence on political excesses that injure minorities, the judiciary not infrequently is deferential to the immigration decisions of the political branches of the federal government. The so-called plenary power doctrine, though it has suffered cracks in its armor in its 100–plus years of existence, still shields some rather extreme immigration judgments. While first employed to uphold laws passed by Congress generally excluding the immigration of Chinese, a version of the doctrine surfaced more recently in the Supreme Court's refusal to disturb the Executive Branch's decision to interdict and repatriate Haitians fleeing political violence. * * *

* * *

Political Correctness and Immigration

Because the political branches frequently have the final say on immigration law and policy, it is important to have a basic understanding of the position of various interest groups on immigration.

It is difficult to peg a so-called politically correct position for immigration or to pinpoint "liberal" and "conservative" positions on the issue. Some conservative elements of society have been extremely intolerant of immigrants at various times in U.S. history. Consistent with that tradition, Republican Patrick Buchanan, strenuously advocated an all-out effort to seal the U.S.-Mexico border * * *. In contrast, other conservative bastions with a more free-market orientation, including some business interests that desire a ready supply of low-wage labor, have called for fewer rather than more immigration restrictions.

* * *

Liberal ranks in the United States also historically have been divided on immigration. At various times in U.S. history, immigrants were readily integrated into urban Democratic political machines. Such integration occurred more easily when the immigrants could shed their "immigrantness" and become citizens with the right to vote. That, however, was something far easier accomplished by the predominantly European immigrants of past generations than for immigrants of color who have come in increasing numbers to the United States since 1965. With low naturalization rates for the largest group of immigrants—Mexican nationals—to the United States political, social, and economic assimilation has not been as smooth as it was for some previous immigrant generations. Still, the Democratic Party has voiced concern for immigrants' rights, often at the behest of certain ethnic activist groups.

At the same time, however, some traditional liberal interest groups historically have been deeply antagonistic toward immigrants and immigration. Organized labor, for example, was one of the strongest proponents of the racist Chinese exclusion laws of the late 1800s. Labor backed employer sanctions, bitterly opposed by immigrant rights and Latino activist groups, in the Immigration Reform and Control Act (1986). In recent years, some claiming sympathy with the interests of labor have advocated the need to limit immigration. A number of environmentalists have advocated immigration restrictions. Not surprisingly in light of the support of traditional liberal interest groups for immigration restrictions, many Democrats in recent years, including past President Clinton, advocated increased immigration enforcement measures.

Recently, the divide among liberals on the subject of immigration by some accounts has widened. Ethnic minority groups, historically in the Democratic fold, typify the dissension. On the one hand, Latino activist organizations generally have opposed restrictionist measures in no small part because the Latino community is composed of a sizable immigrant population, and the citizen component fears the adverse ripple effects of heightened immigration enforcement efforts. On the other hand, some African Americans have expressed reservations about the perceived negative impacts of immigration on their community. The much-publicized conflict in Los Angeles, California between the African–American and Korean immigrant communities is a tangible example of the concerns motivating African–American ambivalence toward immigration.

———

A number of books have urged cutbacks in Latino immigration or immigration in general, including Samuel P. Huntington, *Who Are We? The Challenges to America's Identity* (2004). The following passages describe the book and Professor Huntington's main thesis:

Kevin R. Johnson & Bill Ong Hing
National Identity in a Multicultural Nation:
The Challenge of Immigration Law and Immigrants
103 Mich. L. Rev. 1347, 1347–54 (2005)

The daunting question posed by the title of Samuel Huntington's *Who Are We?: The Challenges to America's Identity* is well worth asking. After commencing the new millennium with wars in Afghanistan and Iraq, U.S. military torture of Iraqi prisoners, indefinite detentions of U.S. citizens declared by the President to be "enemy combatants," and a massive domestic "war on terror" that has punished and frightened Arab, Muslim, and other immigrant communities, many Americans have asked themselves the very same question.

Professor Huntington's fear is that the increasingly multicultural United States could disintegrate into the type of ethnic strife that destroyed the former Yugoslavia during the 1990s, or, in less dramatic fashion, divided Quebec for much of the twentieth century. Forming a cohesive national identity with a heterogeneous population is a formidable task but, as Professor Huntington recognizes, critically important to the future of the United States.

* * *

In asking the nation to reconsider its immigration policies, Professor Huntington asks a question worth asking. Immigration frequently has provoked controversy in the United States and, even when not at the forefront, lurks ominously in the background of the discussion of many policy issues, from public benefits to affirmative action to driver's license eligibility for undocumented immigrants. * * * Although the nation often professes to be "a nation of immigrants" open to the "huddled masses," sporadic outbursts of anti-immigrant sentiment mar its history, dating as far back as the Alien and Sedition Acts of the 1790s.

Professor Huntington expresses fear about the impacts of immigrants—specifically Mexican immigrants—on the United States, its culture, and, most fundamentally, the "American" way of life. He sees immigration and immigrants as transforming a white-Anglo–Saxon cultural nation, * * * raising the specter of the fall of Rome. In expressing such fears, Professor Huntington ties immigration to critical aspects of national identity and sees the United States changing slowly but surely as new and different—culturally and otherwise—immigrants are coming in large numbers to the United States.

We agree with Professor Huntington that national identity is central to the discussion of immigration and immigrants. * * *

* * *

Immigration has contributed to the multicultural nature of the United States and transformed the nation and its civil rights agenda. The nation cannot ignore the impacts of immigration on national identity, race, and civil rights if it wants to avoid potential unrest from those opposing the transformations taking place—the vigilante groups in Arizona using violence to enforce the immigration laws, immediately come to mind—and immigrants who may resist efforts at forced assimilation, deportation, and other actions that adversely impact immigrant communities. To ignore the changes risks a domestic explosion like that which the nation has never seen.

* * * Law and policy should strive to foster integration of immigrants into U.S. society, for example, by seeking to eliminate the immigrant caste structure in the labor market. Unfortunately, law has often done the opposite, with distinctions between different groups of immigrants thwarting, if not facilitating, their assimilation into American social life.

* * * One glaring weakness of *Who Are We?* is that it fails to weigh the positive impacts of immigration and immigrants. Consequently, it resembles a cost-benefit analysis that focuses exclusively on costs.

* * *

Even though some observers have labeled Professor Huntington's arguments as racist, * * * Professor Huntington grounds his concerns with the changes caused by Mexican immigrants to the nation's culture, with a particular emphasis on language (Spanish rather than English) and religion (Catholic rather than Protestant). Although we fear and suspect that language, national origin, and religion in certain circumstances serve as convenient proxies for race, we take Professor Huntington at his word that race is not the core basis of his concern with Mexican immigrants. Unfortunately, the same cannot be said for all those who seek to reduce immigration from Mexico and some anti-immigrant activists who may invoke his arguments to attempt to justify restrictionist immigration laws and policies.

* * * [C]ontrary to the claim that a separatist Mexican nation is emerging in this country, *all* immigrants in fact do assimilate to a certain degree into U.S. social life. The available empirical evidence shows that, in the aggregate, immigrants from all nations, including Mexico, overwhelmingly participate in the labor market, learn English, exhibit high labor participation rates, are firmly committed to family, and participate in community life in ways comparable to other Americans. This is not surprising given that most immigrants come to the

United States because they embrace American political values and economic freedoms.

* * *

In certain respects, Professor Huntington suffers from a myopia, seeing only the aspects of history and the evidence that support his case. One aspect of U.S. history that he does not fully acknowledge is that assimilation of immigrants has persistently been viewed as a problem with the immigrants of any particular period. Early in this nation's history, for example, the claim was that German and Irish immigrants— later replaced by Chinese, Japanese, southern and eastern European, and later Mexican immigrants—were racially inferior and refused to assimilate into mainstream U.S. society. These claims were buttressed by the assertion that the current cohort of immigrants differed from the last group. Despite those claims, the assimilation process has in most respects been successful, and most observers see the past efforts to limit the immigration of "unassimilable" persons as unfortunate mistakes that mar, not elevate, the nation's proud history.

* * *

C. LOCAL ENFORCEMENT OF THE IMMIGRATION LAWS

Private groups and town councils sometimes have been unwilling to rely on federal authorities to enforce the immigration laws and have taken matters into their own hands. Vigilante groups with patriotic-sounding names like Minutemen patrol the border, corral Mexican-looking people whom they believe are guilty of trying to infiltrate the United States, and call in the authorities to make arrests. The Southern Poverty Law Center has been monitoring the situation for human-rights abuses and, in one case, successfully sued an Anglo rancher for harassing Latino immigrants who were passing through their region. See, e.g., Randal C. Archibold, *A Border Watcher Finds Himself under Scrutiny*, N.Y. Times, Nov. 24, 2006, at A1. The film *Walking the Line* (2005) offers a rich documentary of the lives of immigrants who cross the desert border illegally, as well as the U.S. citizen-vigilantes who track and pursue them and humanitarians who break the law by aiding the immigrants. See also Susy Buchanan, *Vigilante Justice*, Intell. Rep., Spr. 2007, at 40 describing the operations of border vigilantes and some of the groups and individuals who oppose them.

In other cases, towns and cities (sometimes in regions with very few Latino immigrants) have been enacting ordinances designed to discourage immigrants from settling there. Some of these new laws limit the number of unrelated people who can live in a rented apartment. Others forbid soliciting work on a street corner or outside a home improvement store. See, e.g., Alex Kotlowitz, *Our Town*, N.Y. Times Mag., Aug. 5, 2007, at 31, 33 (reporting that over 40 towns have enacted such laws); Thomas Beaumont et al., *Latinos Seek Security, Safety in Iowa*, Des Moines Register, Mar. 18, 2001, at A1. Still others attempt to make English the official language of the town or consider seceding from a town or region with too many immigrants. See Julia Preston, *Immigration is at Center of New Laws Around U.S.*, N.Y. Times, Aug. 6, at A12 (reporting state legislatures were considering 1,400 bills to control immigration). But see Ken Belson & Jill P. Capuzzo, *Towns Rethink Laws Against Immigrants*, N.Y. Times, Sept. 26, 2007, at A1 (towns reconsidering after their local economies suffered when Latinos moved out). See also the discussion, supra, of California's Proposition 187 and similar measures elsewhere that aim at discouraging Latino immigration by denying immigrants access to social services.

See http://www.minutemanproject.com, Jim Gilchrist's Minuteman Project, containing entries such as *No Way, No How But … Immigration Still Has "Momentum"* (July 30, 2007); *Turmoil in Tulsa: The Illegal Immigration Wreck* (July 12, 2007); *Hijacker Update* (July 2, 2007).

Paul Vitello
Rift Over Illegal Immigration Leads to Talk of Secession
N.Y. Times, Dec. 16, 2006, at B12

FARMINGVILLE, N.Y., Dec. 14—Assuming a new name has often been part of the immigration experience. Now this Long Island hamlet, bruised for a decade by its reputation as a place where illegal immigrant day laborers crowd into rooming houses, is considering a name change of its own.

Farmingville, or at least the more affluent half of it, where few if any of the new immigrants live, would have itself be known instead as the village of Oak Hills.

Some people here acknowledge this is a kind of white flight by incorporation—a maneuver pioneered 20 years ago when an enclave within the increasingly Hispanic community of Central Islip, in Suffolk County, broke off to become the village of Islandia.

But many of the homeowners here who have signed a secession petition in recent days say that they are not leaving Farmingville— Farmingville has left them.

Now known as an illegal immigrants' haven, the community has been the scene of frequent demonstrations by residents, and by groups that come periodically to taunt the day laborers. On CNN, Lou Dobbs marks Farmingville with pushpins regularly on the map of his continuing crusade against illegal immigration.

And then there is the movie. A documentary based on a 2000 attack in which two men beat two Mexican day laborers almost to death evinced a complex portrait of the community but left the overriding impression that Farmingville is a place without pity. The film, which won a Sundance Film Festival prize, is titled simply—and many here think unfairly—"Farmingville."

"It seems like every time something is said about Farmingville, it's a negative rather than a positive," said Del DeMarino, 63, a resident since 1972 who is the chief organizer of the Committee for an Incorporated Village. "It's just not possible to change that now."

Demographers say the majority of immigrants are now settling in suburbia, where frustration with perceived federal inaction against illegal newcomers has led to a variety of ad-hoc local initiatives. In Suffolk County, for example, there have been crackdowns on overcrowded rooming houses in Farmingville and other areas, and laws passed against employment of illegal immigrants, neither of which has had much effect.

Unable to build fences like the 700–mile one proposed for the Mexican border, a handful of unincorporated communities like Farmingville are seizing on self-rule as a tool of self-preservation—or, as some see it, self-segregation.

"We know what they're talking about when they say they want to separate from 'Farmingville'—they mean the Mexicans," said William White, a local resident who opposes the name change.

Mr. DeMarino, a salesman for a shipping company and active in local politics, said immigration was not his only motivation.

There are fingers of other ZIP codes and hamlets that lie across parts of Farmingville, and the new village would incorporate them, he said, "giving us one identity." There is also a state road improvement project about to begin, and an incorporated village may be able to wield more influence over it than an unincorporated area.

But as he steered his Jeep through streets of widely spaced homes, elaborately decorated for Christmas, on the wealthier side of Farmingville that would become Oak Hills, Mr. DeMarino acknowledged that it was mainly the "stigma thing."

"See that house?" he said, pointing to a two-story colonial-style home with a broad lawn. "That house has been on the market for eight months. He dropped the price three times. Nice house. But if you are trying to sell a house in Farmingville, you have a problem."

Asked if that might have more to do with the slowing real estate market, Mr. DeMarino said Farmingville's notoriety compounded the problem.

Hard by the Long Island Expressway, Farmingville is an unincorporated area in the Town of Brookhaven. According to the 2000 census, 8 percent of its 16,000 residents were Hispanic, up from 3 percent in 1990.

In what passes for downtown, a stretch of broad boulevard dividing the east and west sides of Farmingville, the storefronts feature an unusual number of Laundromats within a few short blocks (three), money-order vendors specializing in international transfers and inexpensive, footlocker-size luggage (two), and window advertisements in Spanish (innumerable).

Miriam Valenciano, who owns a small house behind the downtown district, was skeptical when told about the proposed name change. "You mean we'll have an upper-class Farmingville and a lower-class Farmingville," she said. "That's what it sounds like to me. I think it's a little derogatory."

Inside a variety store, a man who gave his name only as John bought large stacks of tickets from a New York State Lottery machine. "What about the taxes?" he said when asked about the Oak Hills proposal. "They start a new village, there's new taxes, right? I don't want nothing to do with it."

Advocates of the plan say residents of the new village would have to pay only a minimal amount in new taxes to cover clerical costs. Services like garbage collection, road maintenance and snow removal would probably be handled through a contract with the township, and are unlikely to significantly change most residents' tax bills.

Exact boundaries have not been determined, but the proposed village of Oak Hills—named for the oak trees that thrive in the sandy soil of this part of the island—would be a tract of land in the western half of Farmingville where homes sell for about $500,000 and up, according to local real estate agents. It would exclude houses in the eastern half that are generally valued about $100,000 less.

Many of those cheaper houses on the east side have been converted, often illegally, into makeshift apartments for the men who get picked up in trucks for construction and landscaping jobs each morning.

"I've got nothing against those people, they work hard, but I think we have a right to protect our property values," said Joseph Alfini, 53, a retired electrician who lives in the core of the proposed village. "The landlords who rent these rooms out, they cannot afford to buy houses over here. If we have our own building department, we can keep it that way."

The Rev. Alan Ramirez, a vigorous defender of the day laborers, said of the movement: "They don't need to change their name. What they need to change is their attitude of hostility toward their neighbors."

State law requires any new village to have a minimum of 500 inhabitants and a contiguous area of not more than five square miles; Oak Hills would probably have about 3,000 residents. Once petitions are signed by 20 percent of the registered voters within the proposed boundaries, a majority vote in an election referendum would establish the new village.

Farmingville's secessionists began collecting petitions last month and hope to hold an election early in the new year.

Mr. DeMarino, the leader of the campaign, was interviewed at his home the other day while a crew of three Spanish-speaking women cleaned his house. A member of [a local political] committee, he has run twice unsuccessfully for councilman in the Town of Brookhaven.

Asked whether he might like to be mayor of Oak Hills someday, Mr. DeMarino smiled and said, "I cannot entertain that notion at this time."

———————

See Jason Englund, *Small Town Defenders or Constitutional Foes: Does the Hazleton PA Anti-illegal-immigration Ordinance Encroach on Federal Power?*, 87 B.U. L. Rev. 883 (2007) (discussing over 60 local governments in 21 states that are pondering anti-immigrant measures).

Other communities are taking the opposite approach, designating themselves "sanctuary" cities or towns and requesting that the local police refuse to cooperate with immigration enforcement, considering it a primarily federal concern. See James Reel, *Sanctuary Leaders Renew Defense of Asylum Seekers*, Nat. Catholic Rep., April 5, 2002; Peggy O'Hare, *Sanctuary Policy Irks Some in HPD*, Houston Chron., May 8, 2003, at A31; Anthony Faiola, *Looking the Other Way on Immigrants: Some Cities Buck Federal Policies*, Wash. Post., April 10, 2007, at A1. See also Renny Golden & Michael McConnell, *Sanctuary: The New Underground Railroad* (1986).

A number of churches have done the same, while volunteer groups like the Border Angels, Samaritans, and Humane Borders leave water, food, and clothing in the desert for desperate immigrants trying to cross the trackless desert. See, e.g., http://www.borderangels.org/mission.html.

May local authorities enforce immigration laws by rounding up and arresting Latinos suspected of being undocumented aliens? Or does national legislation "pre-empt" local or state action in this area? See Part Four: Education; Joshua J. Herndon, *Broken Borders*: De Canas v. Bica *and the Standards that Govern the Validity of State Measures Designed to Deter Undocumented Immigration*, 12 Tex. Hisp. J. L. & Pol'y 31 (2006); De Canas v. Bica, 424 U.S. 351 (1976) (laying out a three-prong test to determine the constitutionality of state measures to control immigration). See also Michael A. Olivas, *Immigration-Related State and Local Ordinances: Preemption, Prejudice, and the Proper Role for Enforcement*, 2007 U. Chi. Legal F. 27.

Hazleton, PA, a "rust belt" town in northeast Pennsylvania with a depressed economy resulting from mine closures, experienced a wave of Latino immigration attracted by the low cost of housing and jobs in nearby farms and factories. When the schools bulged and the city struggled to keep up with the demand for services, the mayor pushed through an ordinance penalizing landlords that rented to undocumented immigrants and businesses that hired them. A lawsuit presenting the following issues was the result.

Mexican American Legal Defense and Education Fund
Memo-Letter to Hazleton, Pennsylvania City Government
July 12, 2006

Via First Class Mail & Electronic Mail

Hazleton City Council Members
1529 Terrace Blvd.
Hazleton, PA 18201

Re: *Illegal Immigration Relief Act Ordinance*

Dear Hazleton City Council Members:

On behalf of MALDEF, I urge you to vote against the Illegal Immigration Relief Act Ordinance (the "Ordinance"). MALDEF has grave concerns regarding the proposed city Ordinance that would revoke the business licenses of companies employing undocumented immigrants; impose $1,000 fines on landlords who rent to undocumented immigrants; and would make English the official language of the city. MALDEF believes that the Ordinance would not withstand a constitutional challenge for the reasons stated below.

Unless the city enforces the law solely against Latino immigrants, all residents including U.S. citizens will be required to "produce their papers" any time they "use ... property" in Hazleton or else the property owner may be liable for a fine of $1,000. The prohibition strikes at the core of essential values of privacy and decency and encourages discrimination and division. The ordinance could encompass use of churches, playgrounds, restaurants and other establishments.

States and local governments may not usurp the federal government's power to regulate immigration. State and local laws that attempt to regulate immigration, concurrently or in contravention with federal policy, have previously been struck down under the doctrine of preemption. *Hines v. Davidowitz*, 312 U.S. 52, 66–7 (1941).

Hines v. Davidowitz involved a Pennsylvania law that required aliens to register with the state, carry a state-issued registration card, and pay a small registration fee. The U.S. Supreme Court held that the law was preempted, stating that the regulation in question "is in a field which affects international relations, the one aspect of our government that from the first has been most generally conceded imperatively to demand broad national authority. Any concurrent state [and local] power that may exist is restricted to the narrowest of limits ..." Id. at 68. The power to regulate immigration is unquestionably a federal power because it is so "intimately blended and intertwined" with the government's international responsibilities. Id. at 66.

The Ordinance will require that all residents carry and produce their documentation at all times to avoid being denied services by landlords and businesses and assistance from local officials. The Ordinance will place burdens and obligations on perfectly law-abiding legal residents and will subject them to "indiscriminate and repeated interception and interrogation by public officials." Id. This Ordinance would interfere with the rights, liberties, and personal freedoms of Hazleton residents, including native-born United States citizens.

Another case addressing the issue is *League of United Latin American Citizens v. Wilson*, where a federal court in California held that federal law preempted Proposition 187's requirement that state agents discover, report and initiate the removal of non-citizens who were unlawfully present according to state created criteria. 908 F.Supp. 755 (C.D. Cal. 1995). Denying eligibility for benefits based on immigration status depends upon a verification process requiring untrained state agents to make independent determinations of immigration status to determine who qualifies for public services. The Court held that the power to determine immigration status is exclusively reserved to the Immigration and Naturalization Service and immigration judges pursuant to the Immigration and Nationality Act. See Id., 8 U.S.C. § 1252(b); 8 C.F.R. § 242.1(a).

Similarly, the proposed Ordinance amounts to a regulation of immigration because it requires businesses, landlords and government officials to determine an individual's immigration status before providing any kind of service. Businesses, landlords and local government officials lack the information and expertise to make independent determinations of an individual's immigration status. Permitting them to make these determinations incurs the risk that inconsistent and inaccurate judgments will be made by anyone who comes into contact with individuals they suspect are not legal immigrants.

English-Only Laws Have Been Found Unconstitutional

Courts have also struck down official English statutes similar to the one proposed in the Ordinance. The Supreme Court in *Meyer v. Nebraska*, 262 U.S. 390, 399 (1923) held that official English laws conflict with the United States Constitution. The Court struck down a Nebraska law that prohibited teaching school in any language other than English. In finding that the law violated the due process clause of the 14th Amendment, the Court concluded that the teacher's right to teach "and the right of parents to engage him so to instruct their children, we think, are within the liberty of the amendment." Id. at 400. The court stated that, "[t]he protection of the Constitution extends to all, to those who speak other languages as well as to those born with English on their tongue." Id. at 401. The Court recognized it would be highly advantageous to everyone.

Pennsylvania has a rich history of linguistic diversity. In *The American Bilingual Tradition* (1977), Heinz Kloss states that the presence of monolingual German speakers, for example, dates back to the American Revolutionary War. The use of languages other than English did not threaten unity then and does not in the present. None of the original thirteen colonies found it necessary to declare English as its official language. By and large, even though there have always been a variety individuals speaking languages other than English, no language has ever threatened the position of English. English is the common language of the United States and it is likely to stay that way.

The English–Only provision of the Ordinance will make it nearly impossible for legal residents with limited English proficiency to communicate with local government officials. The proposed English–Only provision offers no benefit to the city or any citizen or group of legal residents. Instead, the Ordinance may serve to reduce efficiency in the local government and create an environment that invites discrimination of non-English speaking residents whether legal or undocumented.

I do not believe that there is a sound basis in public policy for these measures. The ramifications of these policies go far beyond businesses and landlords who would be punished for "aiding and abetting" undocumented immigrants. The measure would create an atmosphere of fear and mistrust in the community, which ultimately puts everyone's safety at risk. The provision would also hinder the efforts of the local police to fight crime. For example, if an undocumented immigrant witnesses a crime but fears arrest or even the possibility of being reported to immigration officials, they may be less willing to assist police officers in reporting crimes, which would not only be detrimental to the victims of crime but to the public in general.

The stated purpose of the Illegal Immigration Relief Act Ordinance is to "deter and punish any illegal immigration in the City of Hazleton," but the reality is that local businesses and the community will be the ones punished by the Ordinance. The claim that, "Illegal Immigration is a drain on city resources. Every domestic incident, every traffic accident, every noise complaint, each time we send our police department, fire department or code enforcement officer to respond, it costs taxpayer dollars," is simply unfounded. There is no report that shows that undocumented immigrants are responsible for every "domestic incident," "every traffic accident" and "every noise complaint." Moreover, no credible evidence has been provided showing that illegal immigration leads to higher crime rates. Mere rumor, innuendo, and conjecture are no basis for sound public policy.

For these legal reasons and for the sake of community unity, I urge you to reject the proposed Ordinance.

Sincerely,

Ricardo Meza
Regional Counsel

See also *News Release: ACLU, MALDEF File Request for Temporary Restraining Order in Immigration Ordinance Challenge, Ordinance Will Go Into Effect May 22, 2007* (May 15, 2007) (noting that the two organizations will sue to stop an anti-immigrant law in Farmer's Branch, Texas similar to the one in Hazleton). Subsequently federal judge James M. Munley struck down the Hazleton ordinance as interfering with "a carefully drawn federal statutory scheme." Julia Preston, *Judge Voids Ordinances on Illegal Immigrants*, N.Y. Times, July 27, 2007, at A14; *Press Release: Federal Judge Strikes Down Hazleton's Anti–Immigration Ordinances as Unconstitutional*, PRLDEF (July 26, 2007). Hazleton vowed to appeal.

Not all border states or areas with heavy Latino immigration are declaring them unwelcome. See Lawrence Downes, *After an Anti–Immigrant Flare–Up, Texas Gets Back to Business*, N.Y. Times, April 2, 2007, at A22, noting that: "Everybody said that the nation's anti-immigrant fever was going to spread to Texas this year," but that it did not. State lawmakers proposed dozens of bills with an anti-immigrant slant, including one that would have taxed money transfers to Latin America and another that would have sued the federal government to recover monies spent on border enforcement. Another would have denied birthright citizenship to Texas-born children of undocumented immigrants.

"Their goal seemed to be to make immigrants' lives as miserable as possible, and to howl at Washington for not fixing the mess." Id. Downes goes on to note that "last week something strange . . . happened. The Legislature took a big step back from the immigration fights, as an unusual alliance rose up in support of humane, sensible reform." The alliance included pro-business Republicans, the ACLU, the National Council of La Raza, and the state attorney general who concluded that most of the bills "would not survive court scrutiny." It also included agricultural districts "with a lot to lose from attacks on immigrant labor" and representatives of the meatpacking industry. Id.

Notes and Questions

1. If, as most economists believe, immigration, even of the illegal kind, benefits the nation as a whole, see, e.g., Max Boot, *Immigration Exaggeration*, Pittsburgh Post–Gazette, Dec. 9, 2007, at G1, what if it ends up costing a particular state or region more than it can afford in the cost of social services? When California enacted the short lived Proposition 187, for example, the state was reeling from the effects of a recession, high unemployment, and the loss of revenues in the wake of Proposition 13, a tax-revolt measure. Despite the overtones of nativism and Mexican-hating in some of the Proposition's campaign literature, might not some California citizens who voted for it have had a valid point?

2. *Should* immigration policy and enforcement be an exclusively federal concern? If federal exclusivity is an aspect of national sovereignty, as the plenary power doctrine implies (see *Chae Chan Ping*, Part Five, Chapter 2, Section 1 infra), perhaps it is better that the nation speak as one voice, not many, on these matters. Do you agree?

3. During the first Bracero period in the 1940s, Texas treated the guest workers so poorly that Mexico demanded that the federal government exclude Texas from the national program. Might allowing small towns to

enact repressive anti-immigrant measures similarly endanger broad national interests?

4.   Are blue-collar immigrants an oppressed class, locked in a form of peonage? See Leticia M. Saucedo, *The Employer Preference for the Subservient Worker and the Making of the Brown Collar Workplace*, 67 Ohio St. L.J. 961 (2006). On the differing attitudes of old-time and newcomer Mexican Americans on immigration, see Juan Castillo, *Born Here, Born There*, Austin Amer.-Statesman, Nov. 11, 2007, at A1.

5.   On colleges and universities that deny educational benefits for undocumented immigrants, see Sara Hebel, *Arizona's Colleges are in the Crosshairs of Efforts to Curb Illegal Immigration*, Chron. Higher Ed., Nov. 2, 2007, at A15; Kris W. Kobach, *Immigration Nullification: In–State Tuition and Lawmakers Who Disregard the Law*, 10 N.Y.U. J. Legis. & Pub. Pol'y 473 (2007) (arguing that states should deny in-state, resident tuition to undocumented alien schoolchildren). See also *North Carolina's Community Colleges Told to Admit Illegal Immigrants*, Chron. Higher Ed., Nov. 27, 2007; *Debates Persist over Subsidies for Immigrant College Students*, N.Y. Times, Dec. 12, 2007, at A31.

D.   IS IMMIGRATION THE NEW FORM OF CIVIL RIGHTS?

Is immigration a civil rights issue? Is it the main civil rights issue of our time, beside which all other issues pale? Numerically, at least, the claim is plausible: Nearly one million undocumented aliens cross over to the U.S. every year, suffering untold hardship on the way and in the wake of their arrival. Or does civil right start only after they arrive here and suffer discrimination, for example in the labor market or at school? See Kevin R. Johnson, *The End of "Civil Rights" As We Know It?: Immigration and Civil Rights in the New Millennium*, 49 UCLA L. Rev. 1481 (2002):

> Emerging critical scholarship contributes to our understanding of the civil rights implications of immigration law and its enforcement. It analyzes how immigration generates, and will continue to generate, new civil rights controversies in the United States for the foreseeable future. The nation has only begun to appreciate how Mexican migration has impacted the entire nation, not just the southwestern portion of the country, and contributed to the creation of new civil rights controversies. For example, the ability to obtain a driver's license has civil rights implications for undocumented Mexican immigrants. Civil rights issues associated with border enforcement, language regulation, cultural difference, and notions of equal citizenship and full membership, in all likelihood will continue to arise. Importantly, the nexus between immigration and civil rights has tightened as the overlap between immigrant and minority status has grown after congressional repeal of the discriminatory national origins quota system in the federal immigration laws in 1965. Put differently, the great majority of today's immigrants are people of color. Civil rights remedies must adapt to ensure that discrimination on the basis of citizenship status does not effectively amount to

racial discrimination. To further complicate matters, increasing rates of interracial marriage, accompanied by growing numbers of mixed-race people, contributes to new and different civil rights concerns. Consequently, if truly committed to the antidiscrimination norm, civil rights law must change to address the nation's changing racial demographics. In short, the United States is bound to see the end of civil rights—and civil rights law—as we know it today.

See also George A. Martinez, *Immigration and the Meaning of United States Citizenship: Whitenesss and Assimilation*, 46 Washburn L.J. 335 (2007) (current debates over curbing immigration on the ground that Latinos do not assimilate are thinly veiled reassertions of a preference for whiteness and white norms); Julia Preston, *Lives are Growing Harder, Hispanics Say in Survey*, N.Y. Times, Dec. 14, 2007, at A29 (reporting Pew Hispanic Center study that showed many Latinos were concerned about the danger that they or a close friend or relative might be deported; nearly two-thirds said that the immigration debate has made life more difficult).

SECTION 5.   REPARATIONS AND APOLOGIES FOR PAST WRONGS

While the current debate proceeds, a similar set of issues is coming to the fore concerning reparations for past national actions that today, in retrospect, seem clearly wrong. These include the two massive repatriation efforts, including Operation Wetback, mentioned above, and the withholding of pay of workers under the second Bracero guest worker program. The United States has paid reparations to U.S. residents of Japanese descent interned in concentration camps during World War II and apologized to the Native Americans for some of the atrocities inflicted on them. See *When Sorry Isn't Enough: The Controversy over Apologies and Reparations for Human Injustice* (Roy L. Brooks ed., 1999). What about abusive treatment of Latinos?

Gregg Jones
Apology Sought for Latino "Repatriation" Drive in '30s
L.A. Times, July 15, 2003, Pt. 2, at 1

Emilia Castaneda remembers the first years of her life as being a typical Depression-era childhood—hard times leavened with simple joys in the East Los Angeles melting pot that was Boyle Heights.

Now 77, she still conjures up treasured snapshots in her mind's eye: the duplex on Folsom Street that her father bought with his earnings as a bricklayer; her Japanese American girlfriends; and the elementary school on Malabar Street where she recited the Pledge of Allegiance every morning.

For Castaneda, that world ended in nightmarish fashion one day in 1935. In a campaign carried out by Los Angeles County and city authorities, in cooperation with federal immigration officials, the Castanedas and hundreds of other families of Mexican descent were loaded aboard a train and moved to Mexico—part of a decade-long, nationwide effort to reduce unemployment and public welfare rolls by forcing more than 1 million Mexicans and Mexican Americans to leave the United States, scholars said.

State Sen. Joseph Dunn (D–Santa Ana) and a Los Angeles law firm are launching an effort this week to win reparations and an apology for victims of that largely forgotten campaign. Inspired by the Reagan administration's compensation of Japanese Americans who were interned during World War II—a program established under the threat of a class-action lawsuit—Dunn will preside over a Senate hearing today that will examine the 1930s removal of Mexicans and Mexican Americans.

Dunn is also preparing legislation that would extend the statute of limitations for victims who wish to file claims for damages, commission a state study and ask Congress to review the issue.

"It's important for us as a society to recognize the wrong that was committed," Dunn said. "The best approach would be for Congress to enact a reparations program similar to that which was done for victims of the Japanese American internment."

As part of the campaign, a class-action lawsuit is being prepared and could be filed as early as today in Los Angeles Superior Court, seeking unspecified damages from the city and county of Los Angeles, the state of California and possibly other defendants, said attorney Raymond P. Boucher, of the Los Angeles law firm of Kiesel, Boucher & Larson. The plaintiffs will allege that their constitutional rights were violated by the removal effort, Boucher said.

Scholars estimate that 60% of the people sent to Mexico in the 1930s "repatriation" campaign were U.S. citizens. One was Castaneda.

"Somebody could say, 'We were wrong for the injustices committed to you and apologize for what was done,'" said Castaneda, now a resident of Riverside. "Maybe other people who are still in Mexico would hear about this and would come back."

Civil rights advocates say the issue resonates far beyond the victims.

"We learn from lessons of the past," said Dale Shimasaki, former director of the Civil Liberties Public Education Fund, a program created by the Civil Liberties Act of 1988 to educate people about the Japanese American internment.

The foundation for Dunn's effort was laid by two Southern California scholars: Francisco Balderrama, a Cal State L.A. professor of Chicano studies and history, and Raymond Rodriguez, a retired history professor from Long Beach City College. They pooled their passion and years of research to write the 1995 book "Decade of Betrayal."

Many Mexican nationals who were forced to leave the United States in the 1930s had been encouraged to come here by industries in need of cheap, reliable labor.

By the eve of the Great Depression in the late 1920s, the subject of Mexican labor had become a point of regional political rivalry. Agricultural producers in the South had begun to advocate immigration quotas for Mexican nationals. But those same Mexican nationals had been an important source of labor in California's agricultural industry, which had emerged as competition for Southern agriculture.

The onset of the Depression, however, created far broader support for action against Mexican and Mexican American laborers. By 1930, worsening unemployment and growing demands for public aid brought a backlash.

In Washington, Republican President Herbert Hoover initiated a "repatriation" program in 1930. Federal support ended when Democrat Franklin D. Roosevelt took office in 1933, but state and local governments continued their efforts throughout the decade.

Across the country, Mexicans—or people suspected of being Mexican—were stopped on the streets and asked to show papers to prove their right to be in the United States. The campaign spread to pool halls, parks—such as Los Angeles' La Placita—and other gathering places.

Lengthy Documents

The organizers of the Los Angeles campaign—including county and city officials and business groups—generated hundreds of pages of documents in their effort, many of which were reviewed recently by The Times. By 1931, Los Angeles County officials estimated that 60,000 people were receiving public aid. More than 6,000 of them were listed as foreign nationals, most of them classified as "Mexicans," a term loosely used at the time to refer to Mexican nationals and Mexican Americans.

W.F. Watkins, a local supervisor for the federal Bureau of Immigration, described in a 1931 memorandum to superiors how the Welfare Office of the Los Angeles County Charities Department was attempting to cut its costs by arranging "the voluntary return to Mexico of indigent citizens of that country or those who are a burden upon the public here," with free transportation to the Mexican border. Railroads agreed to carry the deportees for half the usual fare, paid by California counties and cities.

With the first trains scheduled to leave in mid-February 1931, Watkins reported that "tentative plans contemplate the handling of additional trains each 10 days or two weeks following, depending upon conditions. Local officials hope to rid this locality of a great financial burden through the voluntary return of such aliens."

Documents suggest—and victims and scholars assert—that people were pressured and even threatened into joining the exodus. Organizers of the campaign planted stories in The Times and other publications that warned of a massive roundup by immigration authorities. In a June 17, 1931, memorandum to superiors in Washington, Walter E. Carr, the Los Angeles district director of immigration, blamed state and local authorities and groups such as the Los Angeles Chamber of Commerce for the stories.

Carr said "thousands upon thousands of Mexican aliens" had been "literally scared out of Southern California by the various propaganda and activities over which this service had no control."

In California and Michigan—where thousands of Mexicans and Mexican Americans worked in the fledgling automobile industry—there were proposals to summarily deport anyone who couldn't produce on demand evidence of legal entry into the United States.

To increase pressure on Mexicans and Mexican Americans to leave the United States, state, county and municipal governments denied employment on relief projects to out-of-work foreign nationals, and private businesses denied jobs to people "because they looked like aliens," Carr wrote.

"All of these matters were given wide publicity, not only in the public press, but through a whispering campaign which gathered strength as time went on until the Mexican population was led to believe, in many instances, that Mexicans were not wanted in California and that all would be deported whether they were legally here or not," Carr wrote.

Emilia Castaneda said she was too young to recall the early stages of the campaign. But she remembers well the hardships of the Depression and lining up to receive public aid, including a blue-checked dress that she called her Weber's dress because it reminded her of the wrapper on a loaf of Weber's bread.

The campaign against foreign labor put her father out of work. By the time her mother died of tuberculosis in May 1935, the family didn't have money to buy flowers for the grave.

Shortly afterward, her father informed Emilia and her older brother that "he had to return to Mexico," she said. "They were forcing us to return."

She remembers going in the darkness to the train station with a trunk packed with their belongings.

"We cried and cried," she said. "I had never been to Mexico. We were leaving everything behind."

They were packed onto a train that rumbled across the deserts of Arizona and New Mexico for what seemed to her like an eternity before arriving in El Paso and being ushered across the border into Mexico.

They returned to her father's home state of Durango. She was shocked by the poverty and primitive conditions as they moved from one relative to another, living in rooms with dirt floors, without plumbing or running water.

A New Life

Their relatives and classmates referred to them derisively as the *repatriadas*.

She had to drop out of school to help provide for the family—cooking and washing clothes for her father and brother and working as a domestic.

After mastering Spanish—a language she had been forbidden to speak back at her Malabar Street school—she began corresponding with her godmother in Los Angeles. Eventually, her godmother obtained a copy of Castaneda's birth certificate and sent it to her so she could show it to U.S. immigration officials when she tried to cross the border.

When the national economy needed workers during World War II, immigration attitudes changed and Castaneda returned in 1944 at age 17, catching a train from El Paso to Los Angeles. She found work at a candy factory and then a glass factory, and eventually married a co-worker in 1949.

Castaneda said she hopes that the campaign to publicize the issue will at least educate Americans about what happened to families like hers.

Dunn said the issue is still relevant because of the ongoing debate over immigration, especially during times of economic difficulty. "The deportation program of the 1930s is not a proud chapter in American history," Dunn said. "Hopefully, by acknowledging this, we can minimize the likelihood of unjustly treating future immigrants to this great nation."

Eric L. Ray
Mexican Repatriation and the Possibility for a Federal Cause of Action: A Comparative Analysis on Reparations
37 U. Miami Inter–Am. L. Rev. 171, 171–81, 195 (2005)

From 1929 to 1944, the United States government, with the cooperation of state and local governments, engaged in a program of mass deportations targeting Latino immigrants, primarily those of Mexican descent, known as the Mexican Repatriation.

Scholars have estimated that between 500,000 and 2 million Mexicans, mostly U.S. citizens or legal residents, were either forcefully deported or forcefully persuaded to leave the United States for Mexico. The policy, authorized by President Herbert Hoover, was instituted as a means to free up jobs for Americans suffering financially during the Great Depression. Hoover's policy of mass deportations was also fueled by a nationwide anti-immigrant hysteria.

Lacking concrete or convincing substance were the three facetious claims often used to justify or at least to rationalize banishing the Mexicans: Jobs would be created for "real Americans"; cutting the welfare rolls would save taxpayers money; and "those people" would be better off in Mexico with their "own kind."

On September 24, 2004, California Governor Arnold Schwarzenegger vetoed California Senate Bills (S.B.) 37 and 427, effectively ending any state cause of action for Mexican Americans seeking financial reparations from California for the injustices they sustained. * * *

Because the statute of limitations to file tort claims had closed, S.B. 37 would have opened a two-year window for victims to sue local California governments for damages, including loss of property, due to the illegal deportations. In his veto message to members of the California Legislature, Governor Schwarzenegger stated, "While I am very sympathetic towards victims who were involuntarily sent back to Mexico . . . , these individuals were able to pursue legal action within a fixed period of time."

S.B. 427 would have set up a privately funded, sixteen-member commission, to look into the role of local and state governments in deportation efforts such as immigration raids and coercive tactics. S.B. 427 would have required the commission to gather facts and conduct a study regarding the unconstitutional deportations of U.S. citizens, permanent residents or legal residents of Mexican descent.

In his veto message, Governor Schwarzenegger stated, "[t]he establishment of a new commission is not necessary. The Legislature and the Administration can create commissions to advise them without the need for legislation."

Governor Schwarzenegger's decision to veto both bills echoed a similar stance by former California Governor Gray Davis, who feared that an investigative commission and the prospect of financial awards would cost California millions of dollars in legal fees and reparation payments, which the state could not afford.

Prior to seeking legislative redress, victims of the California Mexican Repatriation efforts filed a class action lawsuit in Los Angeles Superior Court seeking damages from the State of California, Los Angeles City, County and the Chamber of Commerce for their roles in the unconstitutional program. However, the case was dismissed because the statute of limitations had passed.

Lawyers for those seeking reparations did not go after the federal government because the federal government, under President Franklin Delano Roosevelt, had stopped the federally-endorsed deportations in 1932. Though the federal government ended its public participation in the deportation program, local and state authorities continued the anti-Mexican deportation policies.

The question that warrants consideration is whether a cause of action lies against the federal government. At a minimum, the legal and legislative efforts in California may be used as a starting point for generating public support similar to that garnered for Japanese–Americans interned during World War II, which resulted in an official apology and reparations despite repeated rejections for a legal remedy.

* * *

THE VICTIMS OF MEXICAN REPATRIATION

In the 1910s and 1920s, "Mexicans were recruited to come as cheap labor for various industries. . . . " "Especially effective in attracting Mexican workers to the United States was the presence of American economic interests in Mexico." Mexican immigrants became invaluable participants in industries such as railroad construction, mining, steel, ranching and farming. The "key factor for American agriculturalists and industrialists was the Mexicans' willingness to work for low wages." Despite American interest in Mexican labor, and regardless of their reputation as "hardworking" and "law-abiding" people, they were always considered second class citizens. It was this sentiment that made Mexicans and their American-born children easy targets as scapegoats during the Great Depression.

Senator Dunn's research prior to introducing his bills to the California Legislature revealed that "[l]ocal, state and national officials were bombarded with demands 'to curtail the employment of Mexicans' and that they 'be removed from the relief rolls and shipped back to Mexico.' " The Great Depression sparked a nationwide anti-immigrant environment that the federal government could not ignore. In response, the federal government initiated the first raids in 1931, abducting persons of Mexican descent from public places without regard to citizenship or legal status. Soon after the federal government's role became public knowledge, local institutions, such as the Los Angeles County Board of Supervisors, followed suit, transporting tens of thousands of people of Mexican descent and their American-born children. States such as Michigan, Texas and Colorado eventually followed the California model. Although the deportations were technically considered voluntary, official local government reports found to the contrary.

Senator Dunn's research has uncovered that as many as 50,000 victims of Mexican Repatriation are still alive. The challenge of determining a more precise figure lies in that many of the deported never returned to the United States, and those who did are scattered throughout the country. Many stories survive, however: "[Ignacio] Pina was only six years old when U.S. immigration officers showed up at his Montana home, jailed his family for a week, then put them on a train to Mexico." "Latinos or those looking like Latinos were rounded up, put on flatbed trucks and driven to the border. Others were coerced into leaving on their own and lost their homes and property, government documents show."

The most common cause for deportation was being in the country illegally. However, as many as 60% of those deported were either legal residents or had been born in the United States, thus making them citizens. Once a person was rounded up, they had the option of seeking a deportation proceeding (which very few knew was an option), which were ridden with violations of basic human rights; or they could "voluntarily return to their own country."

THE UNITED STATES GOVERNMENT'S PARTICIPATION IN MEXICAN REPATRIATION

Deportation proceedings represented the United States government's most egregious participation in the Mexican Repatriation program. As the deportation system was structured during the early 1930s, immigration officers working for the Immigration and Naturalization Service (INS) exercised almost total control of the process, including the deportation proceedings. Raids and arrests proceeded without warrants and Latinos were not allowed to see anyone. "Without the opportunity to post bail, deportees languished in jail until the next deportation train was formed.... With the advent of the depression and abetted by the hue and cry to 'get rid of the Mexicans,' the situation grew worse as the Immigration Service swung into action."

In its 1932 report, the government's own Wickersham Commission stated, "the apprehension and examination of supposed aliens are often characterized by methods [which are] unconstitutional, tyrannic and oppressive."

INS specifically targeted Mexican barrios and colonias. "During the period from 1930 to 1939, Mexicans constituted 46.3 percent of all the people deported from the United States. Yet, Mexicans comprised less than 1 percent of the total U.S. population." "Since the Immigration Service was housed within the Department of Labor, it might be surmised that the Service had a vested interest in getting rid of as many Mexicans as possible." In a telegram to the U.S. Government Coordinator of Unemployment Relief, the spokesman for Los Angeles Citizens Committee for Coordination of Unemployment relief stated, "four hundred thousand deportable aliens U.S. Estimate 5 percent in this district [sic]. We can pick them all up through police and sheriff channels. Local U.S. Department of Immigration personnel not sufficient to handle [sic]. You advise please as to method of getting rid [sic]. We need their jobs for needy citizens."

The federal policy of freeing up jobs taken by Mexican workers was making its presence felt in local communities nationwide. The most celebrated raid initiated by the federal government, known as La Placita, set the tone of fear in Mexican communities throughout the country. On February 26, 1931, under the supervision of the director of the Immigration Service, Walter E. Carr, immigration agents from all over California gathered in Los Angeles to discuss a massive effort aimed at scaring immigrants into returning to Mexico. "The Placita site was chosen for its maximum psychological impact in the INS's war of nerves against the Mexican community." Uniformed agents swept through a crowded park on a sunny day and began lining Mexicans up. Those without proper documentation were detained.

* * *

Secretary of Labor William N. Doak and his agents were granted the authority to protect the country from illegal immigrants. Doak concluded that 400,000 illegal immigrants were eligible to be deported immediately—a staggering and unsupported number aimed at pleasing organized labor.... Although many of the immigrants may have been illegal, many of their offspring were born in the United States and were thus entitled to the full panoply of constitutional rights afforded to all American citizens. While these children were entitled to stay, the possibility of remaining in the United States as young children while their parents were deported to Mexico presented an unrealistic scenario. "Younger children who had no choice but to accompany their parents suffered wholesale violations of their citizenship rights. This accounts for the fact that approximately 60 percent of those summarily expelled were children who had been born in the United States and were legally American citizens."

Federal Cause of Action for Reparations: Defeating The Statute of Limitations

Individuals seeking reparations against the United States government face the hurdle of defeating the statute of limitations. There are, however, ways around this obstacle. To defeat the statute of limitations, plaintiffs seeking a cause of action against the federal government would need their time-barred claim equitably tolled, which would require proof that material, factual predicates to the plaintiff's cause of action against the defendant, the United States government, were inherently unknowable or concealed by the United States.

* * *

The plaintiffs in the Mexican Repatriation case will have to rely on the fact that they were not aware of the existence of liability. These plaintiffs could not have known of a deliberate plan by the United States government to rid the nation of Mexicans as part of a tactic aimed at satisfying the majority of Americans who looked to the federal government to address the Depression in some way. Further, "a plaintiff does not need to possess actual knowledge of all the relevant facts in order for the cause of action to accrue."

* * *

Equitable tolling in this case could be based on the fact that many of the victims of Mexican Repatriation were settled back in Mexico by the time the statute of limitations had expired. There would have been no way for them to file a claim against the United States. Further, communication during that period, particularly communication between repatriates and lawyers in the United States, would have been unfathomable. Many of those repatriates were forced to settle in rural areas where it would have been nearly impossible to make phone calls or send letters to lawyers in the United States. Also, at that time, it would have been economically impracticable for a repatriate to pursue litigation against state or federal authorities. The Great Depression placed a financial burden on Americans, and particularly burdened Mexican Americans, who were forced to leave the United States.

The victims of Mexican Repatriation with the best legal case—the children who were in fact American citizens—were too young at the time to pursue litigation, and their parents most likely lacked resources to act on their behalf.

For many victims of Mexican Repatriation, the concept of a legal battle against the federal and state governments was largely unknown until media attention over the last ten years brought the issue into the open. Similar public outcry and media attention led to the United States' efforts during the 1980s to apologize and make reparations to Japanese Americans who were forced to live in internment camps during World War II.

The plaintiffs in the instant case could also try to establish that the government was an active participant in the deportations and that they covered up their involvement. "The statute of limitations can be tolled where the government fraudulently or deliberately conceals material facts relevant to a plaintiff's claim so that the plaintiff was unaware of their existence and could not have discovered the basis of his claim." Ignorance of rights that should be known is not enough. Fraudulent concealment requires concrete evidence, such as documents that may have been destroyed, or knowledgeable witnesses who may be dead or unwilling to implicate themselves or the government in an embarrassing political scandal.

* * *

One of the great ironies of Mexican Repatriation was that many Mexicans were recruited to work in the United States when the industrial revolution hit full swing in the United States. When the Depression ravaged the United States, a Mexican workforce was no longer needed and those who originally sought their cheap labor abandoned them. Mexican labor became an integral part of the development of the United States as a financial power. They came to the United States to find a better life and to provide their children with a more promising future. Those American-born children who were denied their constitutional equal protection rights are still alive and deserve redress.

Ronald L. Mize, Jr.
Reparations for Mexican Braceros?
Lessons Learned from Japanese and African American Attempts at
Redress
52 Cleve. St. L. Rev. 273, 273–87, 291–94 (2005)

The U.S.-Mexico Bracero Program, 1942–1964, aimed originally to be a war-time labor relief measure that brought Mexican laborers to the United States to work in the agricultural and railroad industries. Over the past six years, I have conducted field research in Colorado and California with those who were most directly affected by the Bracero

Program—the Mexican workers. During the summer of 2002, my research formed the basis of expert testimony on behalf of Braceros in a class action lawsuit growing out of the Bracero savings program. The ten percent deducted from workers' paychecks is only the tip of the iceberg as it relates to how growers and the government systematically cheated Braceros out of wages and benefits. Illegal deductions for farm implements and supplies such as carrot ties, blankets, room, excessive board, and transportation charges were all commonly documented practices. My affidavit supported a claim of peonage/indentured servitude. The legal and other redress attempts on behalf of Braceros will be situated within the larger context of reparations (primarily Japanese internment reparations and African American attempts at redress for slavery) to compensate for past injustices.

REPARATION ATTEMPTS FOR JAPANESE–AMERICAN INTERNMENT AND AFRICAN–AMERICAN SLAVERY

Redress for past injustices has recently taken center stage. Reparations for Holocaust victims, Japanese internees, survivors and family descendants of the Tulsa race riots and Rosewood, Florida massacre, victims of apartheid in South Africa, Native American land usurpation and cultural genocide attempts, Korean "comfort women," and the descendants of U.S. chattel slavery are all current topics of public and legal discourse. * * * Reparations will never fully remedy past wrongs and the limited monetary settlements will never make up for the pain, suffering, humiliation, and outright physical and psychological torture embodied in these historical wrongs. But reparations claims should move forward. Requiring the collective conscience of a nation to come to grips with its sordid history and to allow those who were wronged to express publicly what they endured as the nation-state either looked away or more likely was complicit in promoting the wrongs, the public dialogue on reparations moves offending nations forward by forcing them to deal with a past they deem easy to forget. It also requires the nation to seriously examine the historical origins of contemporary racialized predicaments and lingering inequalities. From the successful reparations campaign for those who endured the Japanese internment camps, we can develop a proxy for other redress attempts to follow. From the repeatedly unsuccessful attempts at African–American reparations, we also can begin to recognize the long-standing roots of racial oppression and the interpersonal and institutionalized racisms that reparations claims are implicitly challenging.

Japanese Internment

During the Second World War, U.S. President Franklin Delano Roosevelt authorized Executive Order No. 9066 which allowed the Secretary of War to define military areas "from which any or all persons may be excluded, and with respect to which, the right of any person to enter, remain in, or leave shall be subject to whatever restrictions the Secretary of War or the appropriate Military Commander may impose in his

discretion." Though Executive Order No. 9066 never specifically identified people of Japanese descent as the target of exclusion, the order
quickly became solely applicable to the Japanese–American population
living on the West Coast. Restricted areas and enforced curfews led to
the eventual forced relocation and internment of approximately 120,000
innocent "prisoners of war" in ten "concentration camps" as FDR
referred to them. In the mid 1980s, *coram nobis* litigation reopened
earlier cases filed on behalf of Japanese internees who challenged the
curfew and detainment process. A class-action lawsuit, *Hohri et al. v.
U.S.*, intensive lobbying by the National Asian Pacific American Legal
Consortium (NAPALC) and the Japanese American Citizens League
(JACL), and a congressional commission eventually led to the passage of
H.R. 442. The Civil Liberties Act of 1988 provided for individual payments of $20,000 to each surviving internee and a $1.25 billion education
fund.

* * *

African-American Slavery

* * * The lessons to be learned from African–American slavery
redress attempts should not be confined to the most recent discourse on
reparations. The issue of reparations goes back to the Civil War era and
General William Tecumseh Sherman's now infamous promise to give
freed slaves in South Carolina and Georgia their "40 acres and a mule."
Reconstruction, particularly the development of the Freedmen's Bureau,
and its abandonment in what President Andrew Johnson referred to as
Restoration, points to the potentialities for full African–American inclusion in the racial realities of entrenched economic servitude as a way of
life in both the South and the North. The *Dred Scott* and *Plessy v.
Ferguson* decisions placed the legislative stamp of approval squarely on
the side of Black disenfranchisement, state sanctioned segregation and
an institution of racial supremacy doctrine. The civil rights revolution of
the 1960s sought to challenge the institutionalized racism, particularly
in the form of Jim Crow laws, by recognizing the historical origins of
racial inequalities and promoting social programs based on the ethos of
equal opportunity. History serves as the context for the contemporary
reparations debate. * * *

* * *

Though "Sherman's land" was eventually returned to its former
white landowners by President Andrew Johnson, other aspects of Reconstruction were moderately, yet temporarily, successful in ushering in
positive social change for freed women and men. The Freedmen's Bureau, established in March 1865 and continued for nearly five years
despite the vetoes of President Johnson, established schools for African–
American children, provided food, clothing, fuel, and medical care, and
oversaw the legal rights of the newly franchised. The Bureau also
oversaw "all the abandoned lands in the South and the control of all
subjects relating to refugees and freedmen." As W.E.B. Du Bois noted in

his essay on the Freedmen's Bureau, "Up to June, 1869, over half a million patients had been treated by Bureau physicians and surgeons, and sixty hospitals and asylums had been in operation. In fifty months of work 21,000,000 free rations were distributed at a cost of over $4,000,-000—beginning at the rate of 30,000 rations a day in 1865, and discontinuing in 1869."

* * *

Calls for redress were severely hampered by what I refer to as the lost 100 years of U.S. history where the rights of African Americans were systematically denied and the fruits of their labors duly deprived. The Jim Crow era saw a rise in the number of lynchings and incidents of racial violence, soaring rates of residential segregation throughout the nation, unequal and separate education systems, barriers to voting and attendant rights of full citizenship, and economic marginalization. From *Brown v. Board of Education* in 1954 to the Fair Housing Act of 1968, the Civil Rights era attempted to dismantle these Jim Crow institutions. The words of Lyndon Baines Johnson's June 1965 speech at Howard University, entitled "To Fulfill These Rights," embodies the liberal dilemma on the eradication of racism and partial acknowledgement and awareness of the legacy of slavery and the impact of the lost 100 years between the end of slavery and the civil rights revolution. LBJ stated: "You do not take a person who, for years, has been hobbled by chains and liberate him, bring him up to the starting line of a race and then say, "you are free to compete with all the others," and still justly believe that you have been completely fair. Thus it is not enough just to open the gates of opportunity. All our citizens must have the ability to walk through those gates." The dominant rhetoric of the time seemed to articulate closely with a call for reparations.

Yet, the Civil Rights Act of 1964 and the Equal Employment Opportunity provisions in the law never went so far as to guarantee a fair race or an equally accessible open door policy. Instead, it in theory barred individual acts of discrimination in hiring practices and required public and private institutions (though not all) to demonstrate efforts at building their own affirmative action program. * * *

Since 1989, Representative John Conyers (D–MI) has introduced H.R. 40, "The Reparations Study Bill," with the express intent of building upon "legal precedence [that] had long been established relative to the appropriateness of reparations by governmental entities in response to government-sanctioned human rights violations." It is important to note that in the 13 years that H.R. 40 has been introduced, it has never made it out of committee for a full House vote. * * *

A series of lawsuits against profiteers of slavery (led by initial class action lawsuit filed by Deadria Farmer–Paellmann on behalf of all descendents of slavery) represents the third component. The initial suit named three corporations, Aetna, CSX, and Fleet Boston for conspiracy, demand for an accounting, human rights violations, conversion, and unjust enrichment. * * *

Finally, the grassroots mobilization pressing for slavery reparations in cities such as Chicago, Milwaukee, Detroit, and Madison has put this issue in front of local communities and local governments have had to seriously grapple with past events they certainly would prefer to leave in the dustbin of American history. In Milwaukee, the city council voted in 2001 whether they would endorse a recommendation to the federal government to study the lingering effects of slavery. The vote eventually deadlocked but similar measures were introduced in Madison, Chicago, Cleveland, Dallas, Atlanta, and Detroit. In Chicago, Alderman Dorothy Tillman drafted a resolution that not only garnered the city council's support for H.R. 40, it also developed a reparations study commission at the local level. * * *

A major impediment limiting reparations for descendants of slavery is that the current claimants are not the direct victims, they are at least two generations removed from it. The Braceros' legal claims will certainly be seen in a different light due to the number of surviving victims. * * *

The U.S.-Mexico Bracero Program

From 1942 to 1964, the federal governments of the United States and Mexico arranged a set of accords that supplied U.S. agricultural growers, and for a brief time the railroad industry, with a steady stream of Mexican labor. Initially intended to serve as a war time relief measure, the temporary-worker arrangements continued until 1964. The vast majority of workers were sent to three states—California, Arizona, and Texas—but a total of thirty participated in the program.

The Bracero Program began on August 4, 1942, in Stockton, California, as a result of the U.S. government responding to requests by Southwestern agricultural growers for the recruitment of foreign labor. Though the specific link has not been directly demonstrated, it is certainly more than coincidence that only six months previously, thousands of Japanese farmers and farm laborers (mostly residing in California) were detained as suspected "dangerous enemy aliens" and eventually shipped off to one of ten internment camps. The agreement arranged between the federal governments of Mexico and the United States stated the following four terms that served as the general guidelines for its twenty-two-year existence:

1. Mexican contract workers would not engage in U.S. military service.

2. Mexicans entering the U.S. under provisions of the agreement would not be subjected to discriminatory acts.

3. Workers would be guaranteed transportation, living expenses, and repatriation along the lines established under Article 29 of Mexican labor laws.

4. Mexicans entering under the agreement would not be employed either to displace domestic workers or to reduce their wages.

* * *

From 1942–1947, no Braceros were sent to Texas because of the documented mistreatment of Mexican workers by Texan growers and other citizens. A series of assurances by the Texas state government were secured before growers were allowed to import labor from Mexico. The states of Colorado, Illinois, Indiana, Michigan, Montana, Minnesota, Wisconsin, and Wyoming were also blacklisted by the Mexican government, up until the 1950's, due to discriminatory practices documented in each of the states.

* * *

In regard to all four guidelines, the Bracero Program was lived out much differently by the workers than how the program was designed to work on paper.... The history of the Braceros documents how the safeguards "guaranteed" by the governments were rarely put into practice or poorly enforced. Workers were often powerless in their attempts to request those issues guaranteed to them in the standard labor contracts and the agreements made between both governments.

* * * Contrary to the established literature and U.S. government portrayals of the program, Galarza documented the lack of adequate housing, substandard wages, exorbitant prices for inedible food, illegal deductions for food, insurance, health care, inadequate transportation, and a lack of legal rights. Gamboa found in his study of Braceros working in the Pacific Northwest that "although the workers had contracts guaranteeing minimum job standards, their employers unilaterally established rock bottom and discriminatory wage rates. In doing so, growers reduced the workers to a state of peonage.... In addition, the farmers' reckless abandon of human considerations was shocking and led to numerous job-related accidents." * * *

* * *

REPARATIONS CAMPAIGNS AND ATTEMPTS AT BRACERO REDRESS

In the summer of 2002, I was contacted by legal counsel representing Braceros in a class action lawsuit. Most of the media coverage centered around the Bracero mandatory savings program. As the rule was explained in a 1946 Mexican government document: "In conforming with the established international rules and contracts, of the amount paid to the Mexican Braceros of their salary ten percent was deposited into a savings fund [in Mexican National Banks] for each worker." This money would not be returned to the Bracero until he fulfilled the conditions of his contract and had returned to Mexico. What many Braceros found upon returning was that their money was not available at *Banco Nacional de Credito Agricola, Banco de Mexico* (where the Braceros' funds were transferred from Wells Fargo Bank), or the other Mexican federal banks designated as holders of the Braceros' mandatory savings deductions.

To recoup losses suffered by Braceros during the Program, the struggle for redress is still in the beginning stages. In 2000, one bill was introduced into Congress by Rep. Luis Gutierrez (D–IL). Yet recognition of the bill, let alone broad based support, has been elusive up to this point. The lack of consistent lobbying efforts certainly makes the Braceros reparations case less tenable. Much of the work has been in the courts and that struggle still continues. Finally, the grassroots mobilization, particularly by former Braceros themselves, represents the most important impetus for igniting this issue into the public consciousness of not only the United States but also Mexico.

The Bracero Justice Act of 2002 (H.R. 4918), introduced by Rep. Luis Gutierrez (D–IL) is to date the only congressional acknowledgement of the role that the United States played in the savings program debacle. The bill, which will most likely wither in committee, sought to extend the statutes of limitations and waive U.S. sovereign immunity claims. If this action is going to be thrust onto the public stage, there is no question that it needs broader multiracial support and further reach in terms of not only the savings claim but also allowing for peonage and breach of contract suits. From my research, I contend that the ten percent savings program was just the tip of the iceberg in the ways that Braceros were consistently cheated out of wages and subject to illegal deductions. At this point the biggest barrier is silence. Placing the claims of former Braceros into public forums might break the silence both in the United States and Mexico.

The major Latino-serving organizations have been duly silent in their support for Bracero claims. The largest organization representing Latinos, the National Council of La Raza (NLCR), has offered letters in support of local Bracero justice campaigns but a full brief and a commitment to the issue is to date still lacking. Other organizations, such as the League of United Latin American Citizens (LULAC), can certainly do much more to rectify its historical neglect of Mexican immigration issues and improve its service and credibility to more than Hispanic middle and upper class by lobbying on behalf of Bracero claims. The Congressional Hispanic Caucus needs the support from Latino lobbying organizations as well as coalitional support from civil rights and immigrant rights organizations. This would help to focus the issue on larger human rights concerns.

But the majority of the movement on behalf of Braceros has been in the courts. The recent consolidation of cases and the ruling certainly bring us directly back to the reparations challenges to liberal law standards. The savings program suits warrant attention but a neglected set of allegations in *de la Torre v. U.S. et al.* relate to peonage and indentured servitude. My research documented that some Braceros were required to work beyond their contracted work period, workers were consistently subjected to physical and legal coercion as a precondition for work, the terms of the individual work contract were broken by almost every grower, enforcement of living and working conditions was nonexistent, the grievance procedure was cumbersome if not impossible, and work was marked by complete social isolation. A total of thirty-one counts were filed in the peonage suit, yet the district judge only discussed peonage in terms of those parties not accountable (in particular Wells Fargo Bank). On August 23, 2002 U.S. District Judge Charles Breyer ruled:

> The Court does not doubt that many braceros never received Savings Fund withholdings to which they were entitled. The Court is sympathetic to the Braceros' situation. However, just as a court's power to correct injustice is derived from the law, a court's power is circumscribed by the law as well. The plaintiffs are not entitled to any relief from the Mexican Defendants or Wells Fargo in a United States court of law. As currently pled, plaintiffs are not entitled to relief from the United States because their claims are time-barred.
> * * *
>
> * * *
>
> * * * The complaint alleges that plaintiffs did not know "the amount of money deducted from their wages." This language implies that plaintiffs did, in fact, know that some money was being deducted, just not how much. The other complaints also fail to allege that the braceros were ignorant of the fact that a portion of their wages was being withheld. In short, the complaints allege that the braceros knew that a portion of their wages was being withheld. Plaintiffs knew that money was withheld and that it was never refunded. That is, the braceros knew the facts underlying their injury and its cause. This knowledge is all that is required for the statue of limitations to begin to run. * * *

Simply stated, if the plaintiffs knew they were being cheated out of wages, then the statutes of limitations would bar the plaintiffs from seeking redress. Most of my research, not on the savings program, makes it quite clear that Braceros were unaware of what was being deducted from their paychecks (particularly when paystubs were in English and the Spanish speaking Bracero may not have even been able to read in their native language). No Bracero could recollect in any detail how much they were charged for mandatory deductions, nor could they specify what those deductions were. Breaches of contract were so numerous (from being required to stay beyond contracted period, underpaying workers, overcharging for items such as food and blankets, charging for non-chargeable items such as housing and transportation) there was no question that the peonage claim should have been duly considered above and beyond the savings deduction debacle. Judge Breyer felt the need to dismiss most claims of peonage against all parties but it is important to remember that no grower, association, or food processor was named in the list of defendants. * * *

Further pressure on behalf of Braceros comes directly from the former contract workers themselves. In the past two years, Braceros have been mobilizing in the Coachella Valley of California with the assistance of labor organizer Ventura Gutierrez. In Mexico, a march on capital of Mexico City first brought the savings program issue to the Mexican public (who are much more cognizant as a whole of the abuse that Braceros endured from 1942 to 1964). A more recent pilgrimage to the border, like the former march to the original soccer stadium where Braceros were processed during World War II, followed the earlier tracks north to the border recruitment centers. Though numbers of protesters are small, a critical mass is crucial to the success of social movements in not only organizing communities but also shedding a public eye by requiring increased media attention on this historical wrong. Hopefully this movement will move beyond just the savings program and shed light on all the ways in which the rights of Braceros were systematically denied.

Notes and Questions

1. Is the case for reparations to the unpaid Braceros stronger, or weaker, than the claim for black reparations arising from slavery? See Cruz v. United States, 219 F.Supp.2d 1027 (N.D. Cal. 2002), dismissing an action by World War II braceros for unpaid wages, on statute of limitation grounds.

2. What about reparations for Operation Wetback? See the selection by Gilbert Carrasco, supra.

3. What other plausible reparations claims on behalf of Latinos can you think of? On behalf of specific Latin–American countries? Colonies?

4. Would official apologies be almost as good as reparations and much more politically feasible?

5. Who would have standing to bring these claims? The aggrieved survivors? Their descendants? The attorney general of Mexico, say, or El Salvador?

Chapter 15

IMMIGRATION AND THE LAW

SECTION 1. THE BASIC STRUCTURE—PLENARY POWER AND THE ROLE OF CONGRESS

Plenary power means that U.S. courts have little role to play in determining who may immigrate to this country in the first place. But courts can have much to say about who gets to stay, on what terms, and with what due process rights when the authorities want to stop, arrest, detain, or deport them. This chapter outlines some of the issues in a large, complex body of law rife with contradictions, anomalies, and ironies.

Gonzales v. Reno
212 F.3d 1338 (11th Cir. 2000)

EDMONDSON, CIRCUIT JUDGE:

This case, at first sight, seems to be about little more than a child and his father. But, for this Court, the case is mainly about the separation of powers under our constitutional system of government: a statute enacted by Congress, the permissible scope of executive discretion under that statute, and the limits on judicial review of the exercise of that executive discretion.

Elian Gonzalez ("Plaintiff"), a six-year-old Cuban child, arrived in the United States alone. His father in Cuba demanded that Plaintiff be returned to Cuba. Plaintiff, however, asked to stay in the United States; and asylum applications were submitted on his behalf. The Immigration and Naturalization Service ("INS")—after, among other things, consulting with Plaintiff's father and considering Plaintiff's age—decided that Plaintiff's asylum applications were legally void and refused to consider their merit.

Plaintiff then filed this suit in federal district court, seeking on several grounds to compel the INS to consider and to determine the merit of his asylum applications. The district court dismissed Plaintiff's suit. [W]e affirm.

I.

In December 1993, Plaintiff was born in Cuba to Juan Miguel Gonzalez and Elizabeth Gonzalez. When Plaintiff was about three years old, Juan Miguel and Elizabeth separated. Elizabeth retained custody of Plaintiff after the separation. Juan Miguel, however, continued to have regular and significant contact with his son. Plaintiff, in fact, attended school in the district where his father lived and often stayed at Juan Miguel's home.

In November 1999, Elizabeth decided to leave Cuba and to take her son to the United States. In the pre-dawn hours of 22 November, Plaintiff and Elizabeth, along with twelve other Cuban nationals, left Cuba aboard a small boat. The next day, the boat capsized in strong winds and rough seas off the coast of Florida. Eleven of the passengers, including Elizabeth, died. Plaintiff, clinging to an inner tube, endured and survived.

Two days later, Plaintiff was rescued at sea by Florida fishermen and taken to a hospital in Miami for medical treatment. While Plaintiff was receiving medical treatment, the INS was contacted by Plaintiff's great-uncle: Miami resident Lazaro Gonzalez. INS officials decided, upon Plaintiff's release from the hospital, not to remove Plaintiff immediately to Cuba. Instead, the INS deferred Plaintiff's immigration inspection and paroled Plaintiff into Lazaro's custody and care.

Soon thereafter, Lazaro filed an application for asylum on Plaintiff's behalf with the INS. This application was followed shortly by a second application signed by Plaintiff himself. * * *

The applications were substantially identical. The applications stated that Plaintiff "is afraid to return to Cuba." The applications claimed that Plaintiff had a well-founded fear of persecution because many members of Plaintiff's family had been persecuted by the Castro government in Cuba. In particular, according to the applications, Plaintiff's stepfather had been imprisoned for several months because of opposition to the Cuban government. Two of Plaintiff's great-uncles also had been imprisoned for their political acts. Plaintiff's mother had also been harassed and intimidated by communist authorities in Cuba. The applications also alleged that, if Plaintiff were returned to Cuba, he would be used as a propaganda tool for the Castro government and would be subjected to involuntary indoctrination in the tenets of communism.

Plaintiff's father, however, apparently did not agree that Plaintiff should remain in the United States. Soon after Plaintiff was rescued at sea, Juan Miguel sent to Cuban officials a letter, asking for Plaintiff's return to Cuba. The Cuban government forwarded this letter to the INS.

Because of the conflicting requests about whether Plaintiff should remain in the United States, INS officials interviewed both Juan Miguel and Lazaro. An INS official, on 13 December, met with Juan Miguel at his home in Cuba. At that meeting, Juan Miguel made this comment:

[Plaintiff], at the age of six, cannot make a decision on his own. . . . I'm very grateful that he received immediate medical assistance, but he should be returned to me and my family. . . . As for him to get asylum, I am not allowing him to stay or claim any type of petition; he should be returned immediately to me.

Juan Miguel denied that Lazaro was authorized to seek asylum for Plaintiff; Juan Miguel also refused to consent to any lawyer representing Plaintiff. Juan Miguel assured the INS official that his desire for Plaintiff's return to Cuba was genuine and was not coerced by the Cuban government.

One week later, INS officials in Miami met with Lazaro, Marisleysis Gonzalez (Plaintiff's cousin), and several lawyers representing Plaintiff. At that meeting, the parties discussed Juan Miguel's request. Lazaro contended that Juan Miguel's request for Plaintiff's return to Cuba was coerced by the Cuban government. INS officials also inquired about the legal basis for Plaintiff's asylum applications; Lazaro replied this way: "During the time he's been here, everything he has, if he goes back, it's all changed. His activities here are different from those that he would have over there." * * *

On 31 December, an INS official again met with Juan Miguel in Cuba to investigate further Lazaro's claim that Juan Miguel's request had been coerced. At that meeting, Juan Miguel repeated that he desired Plaintiff's return to Cuba. Juan Miguel also reasserted that he was under no undue influence from any individual or government. The INS official—taking Juan Miguel's demeanor into account—determined that Juan Miguel, in fact, genuinely desired his son's return to Cuba.

The INS Commissioner, on 5 January 2000, rejected Plaintiff's asylum applications as legally void. The Commissioner—concluding that six-year-old children lack the capacity to file personally for asylum against the wishes of their parents—determined that Plaintiff could not file his own asylum applications. Instead, according to the Commissioner, Plaintiff needed an adult representative to file for asylum on his behalf. The Commissioner—citing the custom that parents generally speak for their children and finding that no circumstance in this case warranted a departure from that custom—concluded that the asylum applications submitted by Plaintiff and Lazaro were legally void and required no further consideration. Plaintiff asked the Attorney General to overrule the Commissioner's decision; the Attorney General declined to do so.

Plaintiff then, by and through Lazaro as his next friend, filed a complaint in federal district court seeking to compel the INS to consider the merits of his asylum applications. In his complaint, Plaintiff alleged, among other things, that the refusal to consider his applications violated 8 U.S.C. § 1158 and the Fifth Amendment Due Process Clause. The district court rejected both claims and dismissed Plaintiff's complaint. Plaintiff appeals.

II.

* * * We conclude that Plaintiff's due process claim lacks merit and does not warrant extended discussion. See Jean v. Nelson, 727 F.2d 957, 968 (11th Cir. 1984) (en banc) ("Aliens seeking admission to the United States . . . have no constitutional rights with regard to their applications. . . ."). Plaintiff's guardian ad litem claim, because Plaintiff was ably represented in district court by his next friend, also lacks merit and similarly does not warrant extended discussion. . . . We now turn, however, to a more difficult question: the district court's dismissal of Plaintiff's statutory claim.

III.

Plaintiff contends that the district court erred in rejecting his statutory claim based on 8 U.S.C. § 1158. Section 1158 provides that "[a]ny alien . . . may apply for asylum." * * *

The INS responds that section 1158 is silent about the validity of asylum applications filed on behalf of a six-year-old child, by the child himself and a non-parental relative, against the wishes of the child's parent. The INS argues that, because the statute does not spell out how a young child files for asylum, the INS was free to adopt a policy requiring, in these circumstances, that any asylum claim on Plaintiff's behalf be filed by Plaintiff's father. As such, the INS urges that the rejection of Plaintiff's purported asylum applications as legally void was lawful. According to the INS, because the applications had no legal effect, Plaintiff never applied at all within the meaning of the statute.

Guided by well-established principles of statutory construction, judicial restraint, and deference to executive agencies, we accept that the rejection by the INS of Plaintiff's applications as invalid did not violate section 1158.

A.

Our consideration of Plaintiff's statutory claim must begin with an examination of the scope of the statute itself. * * *

Section 1158 provides, in pertinent part:

Any alien who is physically present in the United States or who arrives in the United States (whether or not at a designated port of arrival and including an alien who is brought to the United States after having been interdicted in international or United States waters), irrespective of such alien's status, *may apply for asylum* in accordance with this section or, where applicable, section 1225(b) of this title.

* * *

* * * The important legal question in this case, therefore, is not whether Plaintiff *may* apply for asylum; that a six-year-old is eligible to apply for asylum is clear. The ultimate inquiry, instead, is whether a six-year-old child *has* applied for asylum within the meaning of the statute when he, or a non-parental relative on his behalf, signs and submits a purported application against the express wishes of the child's parent.

* * * [T]he statute does not identify the necessary contents of a valid asylum application. In short, although the statute requires the existence of some application procedure so that aliens may apply for asylum, section 1158 says nothing about the particulars of that procedure. See 8 U.S.C. § 1158.

B.

Because the statute is silent on the issue, Congress has left a gap in the statutory scheme. From that gap springs executive discretion. As a matter of law, it is not for the courts, but for the executive agency charged with enforcing the statute (here, the INS), to choose how to fill such gaps. See *Chevron*, 104 S. Ct. at 2793. Moreover, the authority of the executive branch to fill gaps is especially great in the context of immigration policy. See *Aguirre-Aguirre*, 119 S. Ct. at 1445. Our proper review of the exercise by the executive branch of its discretion to fill gaps, therefore, must be very limited. See Pauley v. BethEnergy Mines, Inc., 501 U.S. 680 (1991).

That the courts owe some deference to executive policy does not mean that the executive branch has unbridled discretion in creating and in implementing policy. Executive agencies must comply with the procedural requirements imposed by statute. See *Morton v. Ruiz*, 415 U.S. 199 (1974). Agencies must respect their own procedural rules and regulations. See id. at 1074; see also Hall v. Schweiker, 660 F.2d 116, 119 (5th Cir. 1981). And the policy selected by the agency must be a reasonable one in the light of the statutory scheme. *Chevron*, 104 S. Ct. at 2782. To this end, the courts retain the authority to check agency policymaking for procedural compliance and for arbitrariness. But the courts cannot properly reexamine the wisdom of an agency-promulgated policy. See SEC v. Chenery Corp., 332 U.S. 194 (1947) ("The wisdom of the principle adopted is none of our concern.").

In this case, because the law—particularly section 1158—is silent about the validity of Plaintiff's purported asylum applications, it fell to the INS to make a discretionary policy choice. The INS, exercising its gap-filling discretion, determined these things: (1) six-year-old children lack the capacity to sign and to submit personally an application for asylum; (2) instead, six-year-old children must be represented by an adult in immigration matters; (3) absent special circumstances, the only proper adult to represent a six-year-old child is the child's parent, even when the parent is not in this country; and, (4) that the parent lives in a communist-totalitarian state (such as Cuba), in and of itself, does not constitute a special circumstance requiring the selection of a non-parental representative. Our duty is to decide whether this policy might be a reasonable one in the light of the statutory scheme. See *Chevron*, 104 S. Ct. at 2782.

* * *

The INS determination that ordinarily a parent (even one outside of this country)—and, more important, *only* a parent—can act for his six-year-old child (who is in this country) in immigration matters comes within the range of reasonable choices. In making that determination, INS officials seem to have taken account of the relevant, competing policy interests: the interest of a child in asserting a non-frivolous asylum claim; the interest of a parent in raising his child as he sees fit; and the interest of the public in the prompt but fair disposition of asylum claims. The INS policy—by presuming that the parent is the sole, appropriate representative for a child—gives paramount consideration to the primary role of parents in the upbringing of their children. . . .

Critically important, the INS policy does not neglect completely the independent and separate interest that a child may have, apart from his parents, in applying for asylum. Instead, according to the INS policy, special circumstances may exist that render a parent an inappropriate representative for the child. Where such circumstances do exist, the INS policy appears to permit other persons, besides a parent, to speak for the child in immigration matters. So, to some extent, the policy does protect a child's own right to apply for asylum under section 1158 despite the contrary wishes of his parents.

    * * *

[One] final aspect of the INS policy also worries us some. According to the INS policy, that a parent lives in a communist-totalitarian state is no special circumstance, sufficient in and of itself, to justify the consideration of a six-year-old child's asylum claim (presented by a relative in this country) against the wishes of the non-resident parent. We acknowledge, as a widely-accepted truth, that Cuba does violate human rights and fundamental freedoms and does not guarantee the rule of law to people living in Cuba. Persons living in such a totalitarian state may be unable to assert freely their own legal rights, much less the legal rights of others. Moreover, some reasonable people might say that a child in the United States inherently has a substantial conflict of interest with a parent residing in a totalitarian state when that parent—even when he is not coerced—demands that the child leave this country to return to a country with little respect for human rights and basic freedoms.

Nonetheless, we cannot properly conclude that the INS policy is totally unreasonable in this respect. The INS policy does take some account of the possibility of government coercion: where special circumstances—such as definite coercion directed at an individual parent—exist, a non-parental representative may be necessary to speak for the child. In addition and more important, in no context is the executive branch entitled to more deference than in the context of foreign affairs. This aspect of the INS policy seems to implicate the conduct of foreign affairs more than any other. Something even close to a per se rule—that, for immigration purposes, no parent living in a totalitarian state has sufficient liberty to represent and to serve the true, best interests of his own child in the United States—likely would have significant consequences for the President's conduct of our Nation's international affairs: such a rule would focus not on the qualities of the particular parent, but on the qualities of the government of the parent's country. As we understand the legal precedents, they, in effect, direct that a court of law defer especially to this international-relations aspect of the INS policy.

* * *

CONCLUSION

As policymakers, it is the duty of the Congress and of the executive branch to exercise political will. Although courts should not be unquestioning, we should respect the other branches' policymaking powers. The judicial power is a limited power. It is the duty of the judicial branch not to exercise political will, but only to render judicial judgment under the law.

When the INS confronted Plaintiff's purported asylum applications, the immigration law of the United States provided the INS with no clear answer. The INS accordingly developed a policy to deal with the extraordinary circumstances of asylum applications filed on behalf of a six-year-old child, by the child himself and a non-parental relative, against the express wishes of the child's parents (or sole parent). The INS then applied this new policy to Plaintiff's purported asylum applications and rejected them as nullities.

Because the preexisting law compelled no particular policy, the INS was entitled to make a policy decision. The policy decision that the INS made was within the outside border of reasonable choices. And the INS did not abuse its discretion or act arbitrarily in applying the policy and rejecting Plaintiff's purported asylum applications. The Court neither approves nor disapproves the INS's decision to reject the asylum applications filed on Plaintiff's behalf, but the INS decision did not contradict 8 U.S.C. § 1158.

Chae Chan Ping v. United States
130 U.S. 581 (1889)

FIELD, J.

This case comes before us on appeal from an order of the circuit court of the United States for the Northern district of California, refusing to release the appellant, on a writ of *habeas corpus*, from his alleged unlawful detention by Capt. Walker, master of the steam-ship Belgic, lying within the harbor of San Francisco. The appellant is a subject of the emperor of China, and a laborer by occupation. He resided at San Francisco, Cal., following his occupation, from some time in 1875 until June 2, 1887, when he left for China on the steam-ship Gaelic, having in his possession a certificate in terms entitling him to return to the United States, bearing date on that day, duly issued to him by the collector of customs of the port of San Francisco, pursuant to [Section 4 of the Chinese Exclusion Act]. On the 7th of September, 1888, the appellant, on his return to California, sailed from Hong Kong in the steam-ship Belgic, which arrived within the port of San Francisco on the 8th of October following. On his arrival he presented to the proper custom-house officers his certificate, and demanded permission to land. The collector of the port refused the permit, solely on the ground that under the [Scott Act of 1888], the certificate had been annulled, and his right to land abrogated, and he had been thereby forbidden again to enter the United States. The captain of the steam-ship, therefore, detained the appellant on board the steamer. * * *

The appeal involves a consideration of the validity of the act of congress of October 1, 1888, prohibiting Chinese laborers from entering the United States who had departed before its passage, having a certificate issued under the act of 1882 as amended by the act of 1884, granting them permission to return. The validity of the act is assailed as being in effect an expulsion from the country of Chinese laborers, in violation of existing treaties between the United States and the government of China, and of rights vested in them under the laws of congress. * * *

But notwithstanding these strong expressions of friendship and good will [found in the treaties between the United States and China, including the Burlingame Treaty], and the desire they evince for free intercourse, events were transpiring on the Pacific coast which soon dissipated the anticipations indulged as to the benefits to follow the immigration of Chinese to this country. The previous treaties of 1844 and 1858 were confined principally to mutual declaration of peace and friendship, and to stipulations for commercial intercourse at certain ports in China, and for protection to our citizens while peaceably attending to their affairs. It was not until the additional articles of 1868 were adopted that any public declaration was made by the two nations that there were advantages in the free migration and emigration of their citizens and subjects, respectively, from one country to the other, and stipulations given that each should enjoy in the country of the other, with respect to travel or residence, the "privileges, immunities, and exemptions" enjoyed by citizens or subjects of the most favored nation. Whatever modifications have since been made to these general provisions have been caused by a well-founded apprehension—from the experience of years—that a limitation to the immigration of certain classes from China was essential to the peace of the community on the Pacific coast, and possibly to the preservation of our civilization there. A few words on this point may not be deemed inappropriate here, they being confined to matters of public notoriety, which have frequently been brought to the attention of congress.

The discovery of gold in California in 1848, as is well known, was followed by a large immigration thither from all parts of the world, attracted not only by the hope of gain from the mines, but from the great prices paid for all kinds of labor. The news of the discovery penetrated China, and laborers came from there in great numbers, a few with their own means, but by far the greater number under contract with employers, for whose benefit they worked. These laborers readily secured employment, and, as domestic servants, and in various kinds of outdoor work, proved to be exceedingly useful. For some years little opposition was made to them, except when they sought to work in the mines, but, as their numbers increased, they began to engage in various mechanical pursuits and trades, and thus came in competition with our artisans and mechanics, as well as our laborers in the field. The competition steadily increased as the laborers came in crowds on each steamer that arrived from China, or Hong Kong, an adjacent English port. They were generally industrious and frugal. Not being accompanied by families, except in rare instances, their expenses were small; and they were content with the simplest fare, such as would not suffice for our laborers and artisans. The competition between them and our people was for this reason altogether in their favor, and the consequent irritation, proportionately deep and bitter, was followed, in many cases, by open conflicts, to the great disturbance of the public peace. The differences of race added greatly to the difficulties of the situation. Notwithstanding the favorable provisions of the new articles of the treaty of 1868, by which all the privileges, immunities, and exemptions were extended to subjects of China in the United States which were accorded to citizens or subjects of the most favored nation, they remained strangers in the land residing apart by themselves, and adhering to the customs and usages of their own country. It seemed impossible for them to assimilate with our people, or to make any change in their habits or modes of living. As they grew in numbers each year the people of the coast saw, or believed they saw, in the facility of immigration, and in the crowded millions of China, where population presses upon the means of subsistence, great danger that at no distant day that portion of our country would be overrun by them, unless prompt action was taken to restrict their immigration. The people there accordingly petitioned earnestly for protective legislation.

In December, 1878, the convention which framed the present constitution of California, being in session, took this subject up, and memorialized congress upon it, setting forth, in substance, that the presence of Chinese laborers had a baneful effect upon the material interests of the state, and upon public morals; that their immigration was in numbers approaching the character of an Oriental invasion, and was a menace to our civilization; that the discontent from this cause was not confined to any political party, or to any class or nationality, but was well nigh universal; that they retained the habits and customs of their own country, and in fact constituted a Chinese settlement within the state, without any interest in our country or its institutions; and praying congress to take measures to prevent their further immigration. This memorial was presented to congress in February, 1879. So urgent and constant were the prayers for relief against existing anticipated evils, both from the public authorities of the Pacific coast and from private individuals, that congress was impelled to act on the subject....

The validity of [the Scott Act], as already mentioned, is assailed, as being in effect an expulsion from the country of Chinese laborers, in violation of existing treaties between the United States and the government of China, and of rights vested in them under the laws of congress. * * * Here the objection made is that the act of 1888 impairs a right vested under the treaty of 1880, as a law of the United States, and the statutes of 1882 and of 1884 passed in execution of it. It must be conceded that the act of 1888 is in contravention of express stipulations of the treaty of 1868, and of the supplemental treaty of 1880, but it is not on that account invalid, or to be restricted in its enforcement. The treaties were of no greater legal obligation than the act of congress. By the constitution, laws made in pursuance thereof, and treaties made under the authority of the United States, are both declared to be the supreme law of the land, and no paramount authority is given to one over the other. A treaty, it is true, is in its nature a contract between nations, and is often merely promissory in its character, requiring legislation to carry its stipulations into effect. Such legislation will be open to future repeal or amendment. If the treaty operates by its own force, and relates to a subject within the power of congress, it can be deemed in that particular only the equivalent of a legislative act, to be repealed or modified at the pleasure of congress. In either case the last expression of the sovereign will must control. * * *

[I]f congress has this power it is wholly immaterial to inquire whether it has, by the statute complained of, departed from the treaty or not; or, if it has, whether such departure was accidental or designed; and, if the latter, whether the reasons therefor were good or bad. * * * if the power mentioned is vested in congress, any reflection upon its motives, or the motives of any of its members in exercising it, would be entirely uncalled for. This court is not a censor of the morals of other departments of the government; it is not invested with any authority to pass judgment upon the motives of their conduct. When once it is established that congress possesses the power to pass an act, our province ends with its construction and its application to cases as they are presented for determination. * * *

There being nothing in the treaties between China and the United States to impair the validity of the act of congress of October 1, 1888, was it on any other ground beyond the competency of congress to pass it? If so, it must be because it was not within the power of congress to prohibit Chinese laborers who had at the time departed from the United States, or should subsequently depart, from returning to the United States. Those laborers are not citizens of the United States; they are aliens. That the government of the United States, through the action of the legislative department, can exclude aliens from its territory is a proposition which we do not think open to controversy. Jurisdiction over its own territory to that extent is an incident of every independent nation. It is a part of its independence. If it could not exclude aliens it would be to that extent subject to the control of another power. * * *

To preserve its independence, and give security against foreign aggression and encroachment, is the highest duty of every nation, and to attain these ends nearly all other considerations are to be subordinated.

It matters not in what form such aggression and encroachment come, whether from the foreign nation acting in its national character, or from vast hordes of its people crowding in upon us. * * * If, therefore, the government of the United States, through its legislative department, considers the presence of foreigners of a different race in this country, who will not assimilate with us, to be dangerous to its peace and security, their exclusion is not to be stayed because at the time there are no actual hostilities with the nation of which the foreigners are subjects. The existence of war would render the necessity of the proceeding only more obvious and pressing. The same necessity, in a less pressing degree, may arise when war does not exist, and the same authority which adjudges the necessity in one case must also determine it in the other. In both cases its determination is conclusive upon the judiciary. If the government of the country of which the foreigners excluded are subjects is dissatisfied with this action, it can make complaint to the executive head of our government, or resort to any other measure which, in its judgment, its interests or dignity may demand; and there lies its only remedy.

　　　* * *

The power of exclusion of foreigners being an incident of sovereignty belonging to the government of the United States as a part of those sovereign powers delegated by the constitution, the right to its exercise at any time when, in the judgment of the government, the interests of the country require it, cannot be granted away or restrained on behalf of any one.

Chae Chan Ping solidified the plenary power of Congress to regulate the status and conditions of Chinese laborers (and other aliens), regardless of treaty provisions. Congress, still gripped with the Sinophobia of the West Coast, went further in its legislative policing of the Chinese: The Geary Act represented the nadir in imposing humiliating conditions upon that unfortunate group.

An Act to Prohibit the Coming of Chinese Persons Into the United States

The Geary Act (1892)

Be it enacted by the senate and house of representatives of the United States of America in congress assembled, that all laws now in force prohibiting and regulating the coming into this country of Chinese persons and persons of Chinese descent are hereby continued in force for a period of ten years from the passage of this act.

Sec. 2. That any Chinese person or person of Chinese descent, when convicted and adjudged under any of said laws to be not lawfully entitled to be or remain in the United States, shall be removed from the United States to China, unless he or they shall make it appear to the justice, judge, or commissioner before whom he or they are tried that he or they are subjects or citizens of some other country, in which case he or they shall be removed from the United States to such country. * * *

Sec. 4. That any such Chinese person or person of Chinese descent convicted and adjudged to be now lawfully entitled to be or remain in the United States shall be imprisoned at hard labor for a period of not exceeding one year, and thereafter removed from the United States, as hereinbefore provided. * * *

Sec. 6. And it shall be the duty of all Chinese laborers within the limits of the United States * * * to apply to the collector of internal revenue of their respective districts * * * for a certificate of residence; and any Chinese laborer * * * who shall neglect, fail, or refuse to comply with the provisions of this act * * * shall be deemed and adjudged to be unlawfully within the United States, and may be arrested * * * and taken before a United States judge, whose duty it shall be to order that he be deported from the United States * * * unless he shall establish clearly * * * that by reason of accident, sickness, or other unavoidable cause he has been unable to procure his certificate, and to the satisfaction of the court, *and by at least one credible white witness*, that he was resident of the United States at the time of the passage of this act. * * *

Sec. 7. That immediately after the passage of this act the secretary of the treasury shall make such rules and regulations as may be necessary for the efficient execution of this act, and shall prescribe the necessary forms and furnish the necessary blanks to enable collectors of internal revenue to issue the certificates required hereby, and make such provisions that certificates may be procured in localities convenient to the applicants. Such certificates shall be issued without charge to the applicant, and shall contain the name, age, local residence, and occupation of the applicant, and such other description of the applicant as shall be prescribed by the secretary of the treasury. * * *

27 Stat. 25 (1892) (emphasis added).

––––––––––

The Geary Act established the first internal passport system based on race in American history. It also required testimony from a white witness for a Chinese laborer to establish residence. This imposed a nearly insuperable requirement for most Chinese to meet. A Chinese laborer, arrested because he lacked a certificate of residency, might well be deported unless he could produce a white witness to testify on his behalf.

The Chinese were quick to express their outrage. The Chinese minister in Washington expressed his revulsion, labeling the legislation as "a violation of every principle of justice, equity, reason and fair dealing between two friendly powers."

Immigration-control advocates today call for a national identity card. Would that be any different from the indignity inflicted on the Chinese?

Notes and Questions

1. With *Chae Chan Ping*, the United States Supreme Court determined that Congress has "plenary" (unreviewable) power to regulate the status of Chinese would-be laborers and, by implication, other aliens regardless of existing treaty obligations. Does this mean that Congress could, today, enact immigration rules for Mexicans that contravene the Treaty of Guadalupe Hidalgo? See the immediately following sections.

2. If "exclusion of foreigners [is] an incident of sovereignty belonging to the government of the United States" and "cannot be granted away or restrained on behalf of any one" (*Chae Chan Ping*, supra), how can cases like that of the Cuban boy, Elian Gonzales, even arise? Would not the last word be that of some sovereign official telling him or his parents that he may stay—or not?

3. For a recent rich, comprehensive work on plenary power doctrine and its many violations, see Natsu Taylor Saito, *From Chinese Exclusion to Guantanamo Bay: Plenary Power and the Prerogative State* (2007).

4. See Gregory Rodriguez, *Shades of Mexican*, L.A. Times, Sept. 3, 2007, at A21, noting that federal officials are investigating an Indian tribe charged with selling tribal memberships to illegal immigrants in search of U.S. citizenship. If a Mexican, Guatemalan, or Bolivian has Indian blood and is genetically related to members of an American tribe, is the membership-selling scheme a fraud?

Rights of Immigrants, Documented and Otherwise

A 1996 federal statute, The Personal Responsibility Act and Work Opportunity Reconciliation Act, restricted immigrants' eligibility for federal and state aid and welfare. Its explicit purpose was to promote self-sufficiency and discourage immigration. Even legal ("qualified") aliens were made ineligible for a host of benefits including food stamps and supplemental security income, Medicaid, and cash assistance for poor families with young children. See Steve Bender et al., *Everyday Law for Latinos*, Chapter 9 (forthcoming 2008).

The undocumented, of course, have the fewest rights of all. They may generally qualify for basic emergency medical aid, immunizations, school lunches, and other programs essential for public safety, such as fire fighting services and ambulance transportation in an emergency, but little else. For their rights to attend a U.S. college or university, see Part Four.

SECTION 2. "REVERSE IMMIGRATION" AND THE TREATY OF GUADALUPE HIDALGO

As mentioned in Part One, the Treaty of Guadalupe Hidalgo in 1848 ended the war between the United States and Mexico and redrew the boundary between the two countries at the Rio Grande River. The Treaty assured Mexicans who chose to remain in the United States that their property would receive protection and that they would enjoy the full rights of U.S. citizens. Yet, the mestizo ancestry of many Mexicans—now Americans—gave many state authorities pause. Mexicans enjoyed national (i.e., federal) citizenship, to be sure, but what of their right to vote in local elections, obtain state hunting and fishing licenses, and send their children to public schools? These incidents of state citizenship were slow in coming; some are still so today.

See Martha Menchaca, *Chicano Indianism: A Historical Account of Racial Repression in the United States*, 20 Am. Ethnologist 583, 584 (1993):

> When the United States acquired Mexico's northern frontier, the mestizo ancestry of the conquered Mexicans placed them in an ambiguous social and legal position. . . . [I]t became unclear whether Mexicans were to be accorded the citizenship rights of white citizens or (those of) Indian inhabitants. Most government officials argued that Mexicans of predominantly Indian descent should be extended the same legal status as the detribalized American Indians. Mexicans, on the other hand, argued that under the Treaty of Guadalupe Hidalgo . . . the U.S. Government agreed to extend [to] all Mexican citizens—regardless of their race—the political rights enjoyed by white citizens. These rights were accorded to them on the basis of the international principle guaranteeing inhabitants of ceded territories the nationality of the successor state unless other provisions are made in the treaty of peace.

Thus, dark-skinned mestizos so despised by American politicians and the general public alike received local treatment much like that of Indians. Lighter-skinned compatriots were treated as white. Menchaca, supra, at 587–89.

Western states were quick to formalize this dichotomy. California, for example, in its Constitution of 1849 (Article II) granted the right to vote only to whites, thereby disenfranchising not only African Americans and persons of Asian descent but the great majority of Mexicans of mestizo makeup. In People v. De La Guerra, 40 Cal. 311 (1870) the California Supreme Court, two decades after statehood and the Treaty of Guadalupe Hidalgo, struggled with the status of a Californian of a prominent family and Mexican descent. A former member of the Constitutional Convention that earlier framed the state's Constitution, de la Guerra had won election to a state judgeship.

The case arose when a fellow citizen (perhaps a disappointed judicial candidate) sought to disqualify de La Guerra from holding office on the ground that, as a former Mexican, he was not a U.S. citizen as his office required. The challenger also sought to disqualify him on the ground that the very state constitution he had helped draft denied state citizenship to nonwhites like him. To its credit, the California Supreme Court rejected the challenge and declared de la Guerra suitable to serve as judge. It did note, however, that "possession of all political rights is not essential to citizenship."

SECTION 3. IMMIGRATION CATEGORIES AND THEIR OPERATION

Robert S. Whitehill

Immigration: Let's Get the Basics Right First
Pittsburgh Post–Gazette, Oct. 31, 2006, at A10

As politicians seeking election debate the pros and cons of immigration reform and control, it might be helpful to understand the immigration landscape before we fence it in.

The most precious status that the United States can confer upon a person is citizenship. The road from entry to the United States as a nonimmigrant, through permanent residency, to naturalization, is long, arduous and complicated, yet many more people seek to become American citizens than are able.

Most of us acquire U.S. citizenship upon birth. Since the passage of the 14th Amendment immediately after the Civil War, all persons born in the United States automatically are citizens. In addition, and subject to complicated rules, children born outside of our borders to U.S. citizen parents also are citizens at birth.

As employers increasingly look to noncitizen talent to meet their human resources needs, a basic understanding of the immigration process—which legally transforms an individual worker from being an "alien" to being a "citizen"—is a virtual necessity. Under the U.S. immigration law, if one is a lawful alien, he or she is either an immigrant or nonimmigrant. The journey to citizenship for most aliens begins with a nonimmigrant status, and is not for the faint of heart. It requires patience, determination and often legal guidance.

Nonimmigrant status: An alien may lawfully enter the United States temporarily through a nonimmigrant visa. While there are dozens of nonimmigrant visa categories, one common characteristic is that each is limited in time and scope; none is permanent. Some allow employment, some do not. Some may be renewed for years, others may not be renewed at all. Some examples of nonimmigrant visas are visitor's visas, student visas, temporary worker visas, intracompany transferee visas, and exchange visitors visas. These visas are identified by letters and numbers from A to V, each one corresponding to a different definition under the Immigration and Nationality Act.

Immigrant status: A foreign citizen seeking permanent residence, and ultimately naturalization, must pursue an immigrant visa, of which there are four basic types: (1) employment-based, (2) family-based, (3) asylum-or refugee-based and (4) diversity lottery-based. Each of them may lead to permanent residency in the United States, colloquially known as having a "green card."

Permanent residency: Not all individuals holding approved immigrant visas will be eligible for the green card. Before individuals can become permanent residents, they must prove that they are "admissible," meaning that they are not subject to any disqualifying circumstances. There are numerous grounds of inadmissibility, including commission of crimes, engaging in terrorist activities, being subject to a foreign residence requirement and so on.

To give an example, Luís is a native and citizen of Guatemala. He is a researcher at a local institution and the fiancé of a U.S. citizen. Luís is in our country on a valid nonimmigrant visa that his employer has obtained for him. This nonimmigrant visa, a temporary worker visa (H–1B), allows Luís to work for the employer for a limited period of time (up to six years). Let's say that the employer petitions for an employment-based immigrant visa for Luís, and it is granted. If immigrant visas are available in his category and there are no grounds of inadmissibility, he can obtain a green card.

If Luís secures permanent residency (a green card), he has the right to live and work in the United States and to come and go across our borders pretty much as he pleases. Nonetheless, he remains an alien, not a citizen. Luís still would not be a citizen if he married his fiancée and acquired permanent residency here through her petition (a family-based petition). While permanent residency does give an alien substantial rights and freedoms, it is merely another step along the way to citizenship.

Naturalization: An alien who has been a permanent resident of the United States for a period of five years is eligible for naturalization. There are exceptions to this rule, the principal among them being that aliens who are married to American citizens and living in "marital union" with their citizen spouse are eligible to apply for naturalization after three years.

An alien who is eligible for naturalization is not obligated to seek U.S. citizenship and may remain a permanent resident of the United States indefinitely, unless he or she commits an offense that would cause his or her removal or inadmissibility—for example, a conviction of a serious offense, an aggravated felony, may very well subject one to removal.

The basic requirements for naturalization are:

- Permanent residency for five years (three if married to a U.S. citizen and living in marital union).

- Physical presence in the United States for one-half of the required period of time for naturalization (30 of the 60 months or 18 of the 36 months required for eligibility).

- Residence in the jurisdiction where naturalization is being filed for at least 90 days.

- The alien must be of "good moral character."

- Ability to read, write and speak simple English, and basic knowledge of U.S. history and government.

- Willingness and ability to take the U.S. Oath of Allegiance.

The intriguing irony is that while the process of naturalization is complex and difficult, new citizens generally have a much deeper appreciation of the value of citizenship than the

---

Who Can Be a U.S. Citizen?

Currently, anyone born in the United States is a U.S. citizen ("birthright citizenship") whether their parents are documented or not. Recently, however, right-wing groups have begun urging that this form of citizenship be restricted to those whose parents are U.S. citizens.

A person may also acquire citizenship through naturalization. One must make an application (lying is grounds for deportation) and undergo a background check to prove that one was lawfully admitted to the U.S., has no criminal record, and has satisfied the period-of-residency requirement (three or five years). One must also be of "good moral character," at least 18 years old, be able to speak basic English, and know basic civics information. Additional requirements apply to children of U.S. citizens born abroad. See Whitehill, supra.

Family Unification

A second policy of immigration law—family unification—has also come under attack recently. Conservatives argue that this just encourages birthright citizens to sponsor their parents, then their other relatives, and so on in an unending chain. See Whitehill, supra. Even when this method works, delays and backlogs can slow the process to a crawl. See Bender, supra. A "public charge" exclusion may be countered by an affidavit of support from the U.S. citizen who sponsors the immigrant. Id. Marriage-based petitions are subject to careful, intrusive questioning to guard against sham marriages. During the residency period, the would-be citizen is on trial, indeed; any departure from the straight and narrow can result in deportation. See id. (explaining "removal").

Kevin R. Johnson
*Race and the Immigration Laws: The Need for Critical
Inquiry* in *Crossroads,
Directions, and a New Critical Race Theory* 191–96
(F. Valdes, J.M. Culp & A. Harris eds., 2002)

RACIAL EXCLUSIONS IN THE IMMIGRATION LAWS REINFORCE
THE SUBORDINATION OF MINORITY CITIZEN

A peculiarity of U.S. immigration law sheds additional light on the
linkage between immigration law and the United States' domestic racial
sensibilities. Although the Equal Protection Clause generally requires
strict scrutiny of racial-and national-origin classifications, the Supreme
Court in 1889—in a decision followed to this day [Chae Chan Ping]—
upheld a federal law barring immigration to the United States by people
of Chinese ancestry and emphasized that Congress's *"determination is
conclusive upon the judiciary."* This pronouncement encapsulates what
became known as the "plenary power" doctrine; it puts near-complete
authority, or "plenary power," over immigration matters in the hands of
the political branches of government. Consequently, the majority may
use the political process to attack *non-citizens* in direct and express ways
that it cannot with respect to *citizens*. The differential legal protection of
citizens and non-citizens strongly suggests how society might treat
citizens who share the race of non-citizens if the existing legal safeguards were diluted or removed. This fear is real. As we have seen,
attacks on "aliens" often prove overly inclusive and result in attacks on
domestic minorities who are viewed as "foreign."

Racial exclusions in the immigration laws, which often are obscured
through a variety of means, tangibly injure U.S. citizens who share the
ancestry of the excluded groups. "When Congress declares that aliens of
Chinese or Irish or Polish origin are excludable on the grounds of
ancestry alone, it fixes a badge of opprobrium on citizens of the same
ancestry.... [Such exclusions have] *the effect of labeling some group of
citizens as inferior to others because of their race or national origin."*
President Harry Truman unsuccessfully vetoed the Immigration and
Nationality Act of 1952 for precisely this reason: The law carried forward
the national-origins-quota system favoring immigration from northern
Europe, which Truman found indefensible because of its premise that
"Americans with English or Irish names were better people and better
citizens than Americans with Italian or Greek or Polish names."

Recognizing such dangers, Mexican American activists consistently
have resisted the harsh attacks on immigration and immigrants that
adversely affect people of Mexican ancestry. Similarly, African American
leaders protested when the U.S. government callously denied entry to
black refugees facing death from the political and economic turmoil
gripping Haiti. Asian advocacy organizations likewise objected to restrictionist and welfare "reform" measures that adversely affected the Asian
immigrant community in the 1990s. These groups understand the link

between discrimination under the immigration laws and the respect (or lack thereof) of their domestic civil rights.

* * *

IMMIGRATION LAW 101: THE RACIAL IMPACT OF "NEUTRAL" LAWS

In passing the Immigration Act of 1965, Congress abolished the national-origins-quota system, a formulaic device created in 1924 to favor northern European immigration. The 1965 law, however, for the first time in U.S. history, imposed an annual limit (120,000 persons) on migration from nations in the Western Hemisphere. Supporters of this unprecedented limitation sought to put a lid on Latin American immigration. In the words of a blue-ribbon immigration commission: "In the years after World War II, as the proportion of Spanish-speaking residents increased, much of the lingering nativism in the United States was directed against those from Mexico and Central and South America.... Giving in to ... pressures as a price to be paid for abolishing the national origins system, Congress put into the 1965 amendments" the Western Hemisphere ceiling. Despite the anti-Latina/o plank, the 1965 Immigration Act often is trumpeted as a glowing civil-rights achievement.

After 1965, the racial demographics of the immigrant stream changed significantly. Due to a number of exceptions to the Western Hemisphere ceiling, the 1965 act failed significantly to curtail migration from Latin America. Increasing numbers of Latin Americans, as well as Asians, have immigrated to the United States since 1965. Their racial difference, combined with other social forces, contributed to the groundswell of restrictionist sentiment in the 1990s.

The Immigration Act of 1965 also imposed an annual numerical limit on immigrants from each nation. Today, this per-country quota of fewer than 26,000 creates lengthy lines for immigrants from developing nations, such as Mexico, the Philippines, and India, and relatively short, or no, lines for people from most other nations. In April 1999, for example, the U.S. government was granting fourth-preference immigrant visas (brothers and sisters of adult citizens) to citizens of the Philippines who had applied in November 1978, compared with June 1988 for all but a few nations. For third-preference immigrant visas (married sons and daughters of citizens), applications of Mexican citizens filed in September 1990 were being processed in March 1998, compared with July 1995 for applicants from most other nations. Thus, because of the per-country cap, similarly situated people may wait radically different amounts of time for admission simply because of their country of origin. Given the overlap between national origin and race, this system has racial effects.

Similarly, the immigration laws historically have allowed the exclusion of any non-citizen who is "likely at any time to become a public charge," an inadmissibility ground that Congress made more stringent in 1996. Under this provision, poor people can be denied entry into this country for no other reason than that they are poor. The law makes it more difficult for working-class and poor citizens and immigrants to bring family members to the United States and for low-income people to immigrate to this nation. This exclusion, which by far is the most frequently invoked substantive ground for denying a non-citizen entry into the United States, has a disproportionate effect on non-citizens of color from developing nations; it has long served as an important device in limiting immigration from Mexico.

In serving as a proxy for race, the public-charge-inadmissibility ground also shows the intersection of race and class in the immigration laws. Efforts are made to exclude poor Latin American migrants from joining the poor (in the aggregate) Latina/o community in this country. The poor from Asia are also denied entry. Although poor people from white nations are also excluded, the number affected is not nearly as great (because many white nations are economically developed and because people of color constitute a large majority of the world's population) as it is for potential immigrants of color. Class-based exclusions thus have racial effects.

Besides excluding racial and ethnic minorities through a number of devices, the immigration laws include a special built-in preference for white immigrants. In the Immigration Act of 1990, Congress responded to the shift in the racial demographics of immigration after 1965 by creating a "diversity" visa program that operates as an affirmative-action program for white immigrants. Although facially neutral, this complicated scheme in operation prefers immigrants from nations populated primarily by white people. It reserves visas for nationals from low-immigration countries, which includes most European nations, and denies visas to citizens of high-immigration nations such as Mexico, the Philippines, India, and China. Although it ostensibly seeks to promote "diversity" in the immigrant stream, the diversity-visa program is "an '*anti-diversity*' program; it causes the resulting population mix to be *less* [racially] diverse than it would otherwise be."

In sum, the modern immigration laws have adversely affected non-citizens of color. Although facially neutral, these laws limit the immigration of non-white people and detrimentally affect the ability of non-white U.S. citizens and immigrants to reunite families. They give positive preferences to prospective immigrants from "white" countries. None of the requirements, however, has been the subject of in-depth critical race analysis and commentary. Their discriminatory impact has been observed by immigration specialists, but without a thorough investigation of how they fit into the larger pattern of white privilege in the United States. These and many other features of the immigration laws deserve comprehensive critical inquiry.

RESPONSES TO MIGRATION FLOWS FROM DEVELOPING NATIONS:
TURNING OUR BACKS ON PEOPLE OF COLOR

Race is critically important to a full understanding of the United States' response to migrant flows from developing nations. Although many have lauded the Refugee Act of 1980 for creating an ideologically neutral right to apply for asylum, the law was motivated in part by the hope of limiting the number of Vietnamese refugees coming to the United States, whom the president had admitted liberally after the fall of Saigon in 1975. Consequently, the act included various provisions designed to prevent a repeat of a Vietnamese-style influx from other non-white countries or regions.

Since 1980, the U.S. government has gone to extraordinary lengths to halt other refugee flows. For example, fearing a mass-migration of poor Latino/as in the 1980s, the United States engaged in the practice of mass detention of Central American asylum-seekers, unlawfully encouraging them to forgo their legal right to apply for asylum. Many were detained in remote locations far from family, friends, and community and often unable to obtain legal counsel. Told by the Immigration and Naturalization Service that they could never obtain relief, hundreds of Central Americans waived the right to a hearing on their asylum claims and "voluntarily" returned to face possible political persecution in their native countries.

The United States' policy toward Haitian asylum-seekers achieved a new level of callousness. As the result of a military coup in September 1991, "hundreds of Haitians [were] killed, tortured, detained without a warrant, or subjected to violence and the destruction of their property because of their political beliefs. Thousands [were] forced into hiding." Fleeing the political violence, many Haitians began the desperate journey by boat to the United States. To halt the flow of refugees, President George Bush, in a policy later continued and aggressively defended by President Bill Clinton, began repatriating all Haitians in May 1992 without any attempt to determine (as required by international law) whether they might in fact be fleeing political persecution, which would make them eligible to remain in the United States. The Supreme Court upheld the executive branch's unprecedented Haitian-repatriation policy, without addressing the claim in the amici curiae brief submitted by the NAACP, TransAfrica, and the Congressional Black Caucus that the policy was racially discriminatory and that the Haitians were being subjected to "separate-and-unequal" treatment.

Evidence supported the claim of racial discrimination against the Haitians. People of color from Haiti apparently were the first refugees *ever* singled out for interdiction on the high seas by U.S. armed forces. (Later, after the much-publicized *Golden Venture* ran aground off the coast of New York in 1993, the United States extended interdiction to ships carrying Chinese migrants.) During roughly the same time, the United States continued to receive the relatively "whiter" Cubans, often embracing them with open arms as a way to condemn the government of Fidel Castro.

Similarly, the United States has steadfastly resisted migration flows from Mexico. Even though undocumented people come to the United States from all over the world, the near-exclusive focus of governmental and public attention has fallen on illegal immigration from Mexico. In the 1990s, well-publicized border-enforcement operations, little different from military sweeps, were aimed at sealing the U.S.-Mexican border and keeping undocumented Mexican citizens out of this country. The death toll of Mexican migrants has risen substantially. The efforts to exclude Mexican immigrants stigmatizes people of Mexican ancestry in the United States, who are in effect told that the nation has enough of "them."

The unprecedented militarization of the United States' southern border followed an anti-immigrant outburst in California, which (as with the Chinese exclusion laws a century before) became a leader in the anti-Mexican backlash. California voters in 1994 passed Proposition 187, an initiative designed, among other things, to kick undocumented children out of the public schools. This law "force[d] the immigration issue onto the national agenda in a way that had not occurred since the passage of the National Origins Quota Acts in 1924." The bitter initiative campaign revealed more generalized anti-Mexican American animus as well as anti-immigrant sentiment.

  * * *

CONCLUSION

The U.S. immigration laws reveal volumes about domestic racial subordination. Historically, those laws have been designed to keep out non-white "foreigners" who share or personify the ancestry of disfavored domestic minorities. Racial exclusion remains part and parcel of the immigration laws, although it generally operates more subtly than in the heyday of Chinese exclusion. To fully understand and dismantle white privilege one therefore must analyze carefully the relationship between the external and the internal exhibitions of racism, which requires a thorough analysis of how immigration law operates to exclude non-white racial minorities.

MODERN BRACEROS, GUEST WORKERS, AND THE ISSUE OF EXPLOITATION

As the reader will recall, during the First and Second World Wars, the U.S. enacted guestworker ("Bracero," from the word "brazos," meaning arms) programs to enable the country to fill jobs needed for the war effort. These temporary programs allowed employers to contract for large numbers of workers, subject to certain legal protections and procedures, some of them instituted at the insistence of the Mexican government and aimed at guaranteeing standards of health care, wages, housing, food, and number of hours of work. Discrimination and violation of contract terms were rife, however, and the jobs led nowhere. When their contracts ended or they were no longer needed, the braceros were obliged to return to Mexico. See Gilbert Paul Carrasco, *Latinos in the United States: Invitation and Exile*, in *Immigrants Out! The New Nativism and the Anti–Immigrant Impulse in the United States* 190–200 (Juan F. Perea ed., 1997).

Although the formal program came to an end in 1964, a current mechanism, called the H–2 visa program, allows U.S. employers to recruit workers in Mexico to fill jobs in sectors of the economy where sufficient American workers are unavailable. This program, too, has received heavy criticism. See the following Executive Summary of a recent report.

Southern Poverty Law Center
Close to Slavery: Guestworker Programs in the United States (Executive Summary)
1–2 (2007)

In his 2007 State of the Union Address, President Bush called for legislation creating a "legal and orderly path for foreign workers to enter our country to work on a temporary basis." Doing so, the president said, would mean "they won't have to try to sneak in." Such a program has been central to Bush's past immigration reform proposals. Similarly, recent congressional proposals have included provisions that would bring potentially millions of new "guest" workers to the United States.

What Bush did not say was that the United States already has a guestworker program for unskilled laborers—one that is largely hidden from view because the workers are typically socially and geographically isolated. Before we expand this system in the name of immigration reform, we should carefully examine how it operates.

Under the current system, called the H–2 program, employers brought about 121,000 guestworkers into the United States in 2005— approximately 32,000 for agricultural work and another 89,000 for jobs in forestry, seafood processing, landscaping, construction and other non-agricultural industries.

These workers, though, are not treated like "guests." Rather, they are systematically exploited and abused. Unlike U.S. citizens, guestworkers do not enjoy the most fundamental protection of a competitive labor market—the ability to change jobs if they are mistreated. Instead, they are bound to the employers who "import" them. If guestworkers complain about abuses, they face deportation, blacklisting or other retaliation.

Federal law and U.S. Department of Labor regulations provide some basic protections to H–2 guestworkers—but they exist mainly on paper. Government enforcement of their rights is almost non-existent. Private attorneys typically won't take up their cause.

Bound to a single employer and without access to legal resources, guestworkers are:

● routinely cheated out of wages;

- forced to mortgage their futures to obtain low-wage, temporary jobs;

- held virtually captive by employers or labor brokers who seize their documents;

- forced to live in squalid conditions; and,

- denied medical benefits for on-the-job injuries.

House Ways and Means Committee Chairman Charles Rangel recently put it this way: "This guestworker program's the closest thing I've ever seen to slavery."

Congressman Rangel's conclusion is not mere hyperbole—and not the first time such a comparison has been made. Former Department of Labor official Lee G. Williams described the old "bracero" program—the guestworker program that brought thousands of Mexican nationals to work in the United States during and after World War II—as a system of "legalized slavery." In practice, there is little difference between the bracero program and the current H–2 guestworker program.

The H–2 guestworker system also can be viewed as a modern-day system of indentured servitude. But unlike European indentured servants of old, today's guestworkers have no prospect of becoming U.S. citizens. When their work visas expire, they must leave the United States. They are, in effect, the disposable workers of the U.S. economy.

This report is based on interviews with thousands of guestworkers, a review of the research on guestworker programs, scores of legal cases and the experiences of legal experts from around the country. The abuses described here are too common to blame on a few "bad apple" employers. They are the foreseeable outcomes of a system that treats foreign workers as commodities to be imported as needed without affording them adequate legal safeguards or the protections of the free market.

The H–2 guestworker program is inherently abusive and should not be expanded in the name of immigration reform. If the current program is allowed to continue at all, it should be completely overhauled. Recommendations for doing so appear at the end of this report.

———————

The Report goes on to detail how the current program suffers many of the same problems that plagued the predecessor Bracero programs, including abusive and deceptive recruitment, extraction of high bribes in return for jobs, holding the "deportation card" over the heads of the workers so that they will not complain, wage and hour abuses, injuries without effective recourse, systematic discrimination, sexual harassment, substandard housing, and being locked up at night.

Notes and Questions

1. Is any formal guest work just a new type of slavery or peonage?

2. Suppose that the guest worker receives second-class wages and a low social status—but these are an improvement over conditions back home, in Oaxaca, say. Does this render them more acceptable?

3. If neo-colonial exploitation by the U.S. produced the poor conditions that guest workers are fleeing, is it reprehensible for this country to benefit from their cheap labor while they are here—or is it a tacit form of reparations and rough justice?

4. Some college students take jobs as nannies in England, or in the Peace Corps in Africa—all at low wages. Are they like braceros?

5. For further information on the bracero (guest worker) program, see Part Seven.

6. For the view that immigration advocacy is the new form of civil rights, see Kevin R. Johnson, *The End of "Civil Rights" As We Know It?: Immigration and Civil Rights in the New Millennium*, 49 UCLA L. Rev. 1481 (2002).

SECTION 4. RACIAL PROFILING

Racial profiling became a national issue in the late 1990s as civil liberties groups and criminologists called attention to the unusual number of nonwhite motorists stopped on the nation's highways. See David A. Harris, *Profiles in Injustice: Why Racial Profiling Cannot Work* (2002).

Yet, one form of racial profiling has been in practice long before this time. Border authorities receive judicial sanction for stopping vehicles suspected of transporting undocumented immigrants into the United States. Before that became common, two mass repatriation programs, the last officially entitled Operation Wetback in 1954 (the very year of *Brown v. Board of Education*), targeted Mexican-looking people for summary deportation. Being a United States citizen was no defense.

The Fourth Amendment, designed to restrain official searches and seizures and assure prior judicial oversight, requires probable cause and a good reason for the search and seizure or stop. The doctrine contains many exceptions: open fields, plain view, and hot pursuit to name a few. The following case considers two further exceptions—the "Terry stop" doctrine and an immigration exception:

United States v. Brignoni–Ponce
422 U.S. 873 (1975)

[The Border Patrol's traffic-inspecting operation in Southern California included a fixed checkpoint on a principal north-south highway near San Clement. During a bad-weather period, the checkpoint was closed, but two officers in a patrol car parked on the roadside not far away observed a passing car with three occupants who "appeared to be of Mexican descent." The officers stopped the car and questioned the occupants about their citizenship and, unsatisfied with their responses, arrested them and charged one, Mr. Brignoni–Ponce, with knowingly transporting illegal aliens. At the trial Brignoni–Ponce attempted to suppress the testimony of his fellow passengers as the fruit of an illegal, warrantless seizure. The trial court denied the motion, and Brignoni–Ponce was convicted. Justice Powell, writing for the Court, framed the issue as "whether a roving patrol may stop a vehicle in an area near the border and question its occupants when the only ground for suspicion is that the occupants appear to be of Mexican ancestry."]

II

The Government claims two sources of statutory authority for stopping cars without warrants in the border areas. Section 287(a)(1) of the Immigration and Nationality Act, 8 U.S.C. § 1357(a)(1), authorizes any officer or employee of the Immigration and Naturalization Service (INS) without a warrant, "to interrogate any alien or person believed to be an alien as to his right to be or to remain in the United States." There is no geographical limitation on this authority. The Government contends that, at least in the areas adjacent to the Mexican border, a person's apparent Mexican ancestry alone justifies belief that he or she is an alien and satisfies the requirement of this statute. Section 287(a)(3) of the Act, 8 U.S.C. § 1357(a)(3), authorizes agents, without a warrant,

> within a reasonable distance from any external boundary of the United States, to board and search for aliens any vessel within the territorial waters of the United States and any railway car, aircraft, conveyance, or vehicle. . . .

Under current regulations, this authority may be exercised anywhere within 100 miles of the border. 8 CFR § 287.1(a) (1975). The Border Patrol interprets the statute as granting authority to stop moving vehicles and question the occupants about their citizenship, even when its officers have no reason to believe that the occupants are aliens or that other aliens may be concealed in the vehicle. But "no Act of Congress can authorize a violation of the Constitution," *Almeida-Sanchez*, supra, 413 U.S. at 272, and we must decide whether the Fourth Amendment allows such random vehicle stops in the border areas.

III

The Fourth Amendment applies to all seizures of the person, including seizures that involve only a brief detention short of traditional arrest. As with other categories of police action subject to Fourth Amendment constraints, the reasonableness of such seizures depends on a balance between the public interest and the individual's right to personal security free from arbitrary interference by law officers.

The Government makes a convincing demonstration that the public interest demands effective measures to prevent the illegal entry of aliens at the Mexican border. Estimates of the number of illegal immigrants in the United States vary widely. A conservative estimate in 1972 produced a figure of about one million, but the INS now suggests there may be as many as 10 or 12 million aliens illegally in the country. Whatever the number, these aliens create significant economic and social problems, competing with citizens and legal resident aliens for jobs, and generating extra demand for social services. The aliens themselves are vulnerable to exploitation because they cannot complain of substandard working conditions without risking deportation.

The Government has estimated that 85% of the aliens illegally in the country are from Mexico. The Mexican border is almost 2,000 miles long, and even a vastly reinforced Border Patrol would find it impossible to prevent illegal border crossings. Many aliens cross the Mexican border on foot, miles away from patrolled areas, and then purchase transportation from the border area to inland cities, where they find jobs and elude the immigration authorities. Others gain entry on valid temporary border-crossing permits, but then violate the conditions of their entry. Most of these aliens leave the border area in private vehicles, often assisted by professional "alien smugglers." The Border Patrol's traffic-checking operations are designed to prevent this inland movement. * * *

Against this valid public interest we must weigh the interference with individual liberty that results when an officer stops an automobile and questions its occupants. The intrusion is modest. The Government tells us that a stop by a roving patrol "usually consumes no more than a minute." * * *

Because of the limited nature of the intrusion, stops of this sort may be justified on facts that do not amount to the probable cause required for an arrest. * * *

* * *

* * * [B]ecause of the importance of the governmental interest at stake, the minimal intrusion of a brief stop, and the absence of practical alternatives for policing the border, we hold that when an officer's observations lead him reasonably to suspect that a particular vehicle may contain aliens who are illegally in the country, he may stop the car briefly and investigate the circumstances that provoke suspicion. * * * The officer may question the driver and passengers about their citizenship and immigration status, and he may ask them to explain suspicious circumstances, but any further detention or search must be based on consent or probable cause.

* * *

The Government also contends that the public interest in enforcing conditions on legal alien entry justifies stopping persons who may be aliens for questioning about their citizenship and immigration status. Although we may assume for purposes of this case that the broad congressional power over immigration authorizes Congress to admit aliens on condition that they will submit to reasonable questioning about their right to be and remain in the country, this power cannot diminish the Fourth Amendment rights of citizens who may be mistaken for aliens. For the same reasons that the Fourth Amendment forbids stopping vehicles at random to inquire if they are carrying aliens who are illegally in the country, it also forbids stopping or detaining persons for questioning about their citizenship on less than a reasonable suspicion that they may be aliens.

IV

The effect of our decision is to limit exercise of the authority granted by both § 287(a)(1) and § 287(a)(3). Except at the border and its functional equivalents, officers on roving patrol may stop vehicles only if they are aware of specific articulable facts, together with rational inferences from those facts, that reasonably warrant suspicion that the vehicles contain aliens who may be illegally in the country.

Any number of factors may be taken into account in deciding whether there is reasonable suspicion to stop a car in the border area. Officers may consider the characteristics of the area in which they encounter a vehicle. Its proximity to the border, the usual patterns of traffic on the particular road, and previous experience with alien traffic are all relevant. They also may consider information about recent illegal border crossings in the area. The driver's behavior may be relevant, as erratic driving or obvious attempts to evade officers can support a reasonable suspicion. Aspects of the vehicle itself may justify suspicion. For instance, officers say that certain station wagons, with large compartments for fold-down seats or spare tires, are frequently used for transporting concealed aliens. The vehicle may appear to be heavily loaded, it may have an extraordinary number of passengers, or the officers may observe persons trying to hide. The Government also points out that trained officers can recognize the characteristic appearance of persons who live in Mexico, relying on such factors as the mode of dress and haircut. In all situations the officer is entitled to assess the facts in light of his experience in detecting illegal entry and smuggling.

In this case the officers relied on a single factor to justify stopping respondent's car: the apparent Mexican ancestry of the occupants. We cannot conclude that this furnished reasonable grounds to believe that the three occupants were aliens. At best the officers had only a fleeting glimpse of the persons in the moving car, illuminated by headlights. Even if they saw enough to think that the occupants were of Mexican descent, this factor alone would justify neither a reasonable belief that they were aliens, nor a reasonable belief that the car concealed other aliens who were illegally in the country. Large numbers of native-born and naturalized citizens have the physical characteristics identified with Mexican ancestry, and even in the border area a relatively small proportion of them are aliens. The likelihood that any given person of Mexican ancestry is an alien is high enough to make Mexican appearance a relevant factor, but standing alone it does not justify stopping all Mexican–Americans to ask if they are aliens.

The judgment of the Court of Appeals is affirmed.

Affirmed.

One year later, the Supreme Court in United States v. Martinez–Fuerte, 428 U.S. 543 (1976) held that the Border Patrol's practice of stopping vehicles briefly at fixed points near the border, where they would send some cars to a nearby area for additional inspection, was constitutional even though the basis of the suspicion was Mexican appearance.

Brignoni-Ponce, Martinez–Fuerte, and a number of subsequent lower court cases interpreting them in various settings inspired the Cheech Marin satirical movie "Born in East L.A" chronicling the misadventures of a true-blue American wrongfully deported to Mexico and his vain efforts to return to his home country.

It also inspired sociologist-lawyer Alfredo Mirande to ponder whether American law does not implicitly contain a "Mexican exception" to the Fourth Amendment.

Alfredo Mirandé
Is There a "Mexican Exception" to the Fourth Amendment?
55 Fla. L. Rev. 365, 367–76, 380–86, 388–89 (2003)

INTRODUCTION

The Fourth Amendment to the United States Constitution provides that,

> The right of the people to be secure in their persons, houses, papers, and effects, against unreasonable searches and seizures, shall not be violated, and no Warrants shall issue, but upon probable cause, supported by Oath or affirmation, and particularly describing the place to be searched, and the persons or things to be seized.

The Amendment is applicable to the states through the Fourteenth Amendment, and it governs conduct of federal and state governmental agents.

Though the Amendment does not categorically prohibit warrantless searches, it ostensibly protects the people from "unreasonable" searches and seizures. The Supreme Court has reaffirmed that warrantless searches are not only suspect but are presumed to be unreasonable. A "cardinal principle" of Fourth Amendment law is that "searches conducted outside the judicial process, without prior approval by judge or magistrate are per se unreasonable under the Fourth Amendment subject only to a few specifically established and well-delineated exceptions."

In reality, however, the per se rule has not been closely observed. Since *Terry v. Ohio*, the Court has carved out a number of exceptions, so that the exceptions may have swallowed up the rule. In a concurring opinion in *California v. Acevedo*, Justice Scalia commented that the * * * warrant requirement "had become so riddled with exceptions that it was basically unrecognizable." One commentator catalogued almost twenty exceptions, such as automobile, border, and exigent circumstance searches, as well as any searches incident to arrests.

In this Essay, I examine whether there is also a "Mexican exception" to the Fourth Amendment. While there is clearly a Border exception, warrantless searches and seizures of persons who are "Mexican looking" are commonplace and extend well beyond the Border.... A related question examined is whether non-resident aliens have sufficient connection to the United States to be considered one of "the people."

TENSION BETWEEN NATIONAL SOVEREIGNTY AND FOURTH
AMENDMENT PROTECTIONS

In 1990, the Supreme Court held that the Fourth Amendment does not apply to the search and seizure by United States agents of property owned by a nonresident alien and located in a foreign country. Respondent Rene Martin Verdugo–Urquidez, a citizen and resident of Mexico, was a suspected leader of a large and violent organization and a narcotics smuggler. Mexican officials, after consulting with U.S. marshals, apprehended Verdugo–Urquidez and took him to the Border Patrol station located in Calexico, California. United States marshals subsequently arrested Verdugo–Urquidez and transported him to a correctional center in San Diego for trial.

Following the arrest, DEA agents, working in cooperation with Mexican authorities, carried out a warrantless search of Verdugo–Urquidez's properties in Mexicali and San Felipe, Mexico, seizing documents believed to implicate him in drug trafficking, including a tally sheet which the government alleged reflected the quantities of marijuana smuggled into the United States.

The district court granted his motion to suppress the evidence, and * * * a divided panel of the court of appeals affirmed. * * *

The Supreme Court reversed. Writing for the majority, Chief Justice Rehnquist noted that the intent of the Fourth Amendment was to protect the public from arbitrary governmental action. "It was never suggested that the provision restrain the actions of the federal government against aliens outside of the United States territory." He added that there is no indication that the Framers intended to extend Fourth Amendment protections to activities of the United States aimed at aliens who were on foreign soil or in international waters.

The Chief Justice further maintained that "the people" was a "term of art" which "refers to a class of persons who are part of a national community or who have otherwise developed sufficient connection with this country to be considered part of that community." Verdugo–Urquidez * * * lacked sufficient connection with the United States to be considered one of "the people."

The Rehnquist majority added that there was no indication that the Framers intended the Fourth Amendment to serve as a restraint on actions by the Federal government against aliens outside the United States or in international waters. In fact, in 1798, just seven years after the amendment was ratified, Congress passed an act to "protect the Commerce of the United States," which authorized the President of the United States to "instruct the commanders of the public armed vessels which are, or which shall be employed in the service of the United States, to subdue, seize and take any armed French vessel, which shall be found within the jurisdictional limits of the United States, or elsewhere, on the high seas."

The Court also noted that the court of appeals' reasoning was contrary to the decision in the *Insular Cases*, which established that not every constitutional protection applies to governmental activity, even in areas where the United States has sovereign power. The Sixth Amendment right to jury trial, for example, was found to not be applicable in Puerto Rico, nor in the Philippines. In distinguishing *Verdugo-Urquidez* from *INS v. Lopez–Mendoza*, where a majority of the Justices assumed that the Fourth Amendment applied to illegal aliens in the United States, the Court noted that the question decided in *Lopez-Mendoza* was whether the exclusionary rule should be extended to civil deportation proceedings, not whether Fourth Amendment protections are extended to illegal aliens in this country. Even assuming that illegal aliens are entitled to Fourth Amendment protections, the Court felt the situation of illegals is different from that of Verdugo–Urquidez in that he had no "voluntary connection" with this country that would qualify him as one of the people.

In *Lopez-Mendoza*, INS agents arrested Adan Lopez–Mendoza, a citizen of Mexico, while he was working at a transmission repair shop in San Mateo, California. The proprietor of the shop refused to let agents interview his employees during work hours, but as one agent engaged the proprietor, another went to the back of the shop and started questioning Lopez–Mendoza, who provided his name, said he was from Mexico and had "no close family ties in the United States." The agent then placed him under arrest and took him to INS's offices. After additional questioning, Lopez–Mendoza admitted that he was a citizen of Mexico and had entered the United States without inspection. * * *

During a hearing before an Immigration Judge, Lopez–Mendoza moved to terminate the proceedings, arguing that he had been arrested illegally. The Judge held that the legality of the arrest was not relevant in a deportation proceeding. * * *

In a majority opinion authored by Justice O'Connor, the Court agreed, holding that credible evidence gathered in connection with peaceful arrests by INS officers does not have to be suppressed in an INS civil deportation hearing. Applying a balancing test, the Court concluded that the benefits of excluding reliable evidence from a deportation proceeding would not outweigh the social costs. * * *

* * *

Paraphrasing Justice Cardozo's famous quote, Justice O'Connor concluded that "[t]he constable's blunder may allow the criminal to go free ...., but he should not go free within our borders."

In *INS v. Delgado*, a case decided in the same term as *Lopez-Mendoza*, the Supreme Court held that "factory surveys" (raids) carried out by the INS were not seizures of the entire work force, and that questioning of individual workers did not constitute an impermissible detention or seizure. The decision rejected the Ninth Circuit Court of Appeals holding that "factory surveys" constituted "a seizure of the entire work force" and that the INS agents could not interrogate individuals absent reasonable suspicion that an employee was in the country illegally.

The agents had acted after obtaining two warrants after the INS showed probable cause that the Davis Pleating Plant in Southern California employed many illegal aliens, but neither search warrant contained the name of any illegal aliens. During the survey, armed INS agents were stationed near the building exits, as other agents moved throughout the factory and questioned workers at their work areas. The agents showed badges, had walkie-talkies, and carried arms, though they never drew their weapons.

Four employees * * * who were legal residents of the United States maintained that the factory raids "violated their Fourth Amendment right to be free from unreasonable searches [and] seizures and the equal protection component of the Due Process Clause of the Fifth Amendment."

In rejecting respondents' claims, the Court noted that the Fourth Amendment does not prohibit all contact between the police and citizens. * * * "Only when the officer, by means of physical force or show of authority, has restrained the liberty of a citizen may we conclude that a 'seizure' has occurred." * * *

The critical issue before the Court, therefore, was whether, under similar circumstances, a reasonable person would have believed that he was free to leave. In *Florida v. Royer*, Drug Enforcement Administration (DEA) agents approached the defendant at an airport and asked him for his airplane ticket and driver's license, which the agents then examined. In a plurality opinion, a majority of the Court agreed that the request and examination of the documents were "permissible in themselves." In *Brown v. Texas*, however, the Court held that physical detention without reasonable suspicion of misconduct violated his Fourth Amendment right to be free of unreasonable seizures.

The *Delgado* Court noted that the fact that most people will respond positively to such a request does not negate its consensual nature, "unless the circumstances of the encounter are so intimidating as to demonstrate that a reasonable person would have believed he was not free to leave if he had not responded...." Writing for the *Delgado* majority, Chief Justice Rehnquist noted that the way Respondents were questioned "could hardly result in a reasonable fear that [R]espondents were not free to continue working or to move about the factory." The Court, therefore, held that these were classic consensual stops that are not constitutionally prohibited.

In *United States v. Martinez–Fuerte*, the Supreme Court held that Border Patrol stops at permanent checkpoints operated away from the international border are constitutional. In rejecting Respondents' request to exclude evidence relating to the transportation of illegal aliens, the Court held that the operation of a fixed checkpoint need not be authorized in advance by a judicial warrant and that stops at "reasonably located checkpoints" may be made without any individualized suspicion that the particular vehicle contains illegal aliens.

While recognizing that checkpoint stops are in fact Fourth Amendment seizures in balancing the public interest in the practice of routine stops to control the flow of illegal aliens with the limited intrusion on Fourth Amendment rights, the Court concluded that the government interest was greater than the interests of individual citizens. * * * The stop may intrude on person's right to "free passage without interruption" to a certain extent, but it entails only a limited detention of travelers, and does not involve searching vehicles or its occupants.

* * *

ROVING PATROLS AND THE FOURTH AMENDMENT

The Border Patrol conducts three types of surveillance along inland roadways, all designed to detect the illegal importation of aliens. Permanent checkpoints, as in *Martinez-Fuerte*, are maintained at key intersections like the Temecula and San Clemente checkpoints in Southern California. Temporary checkpoints are also set from time to time at various locations. In addition, the Border Patrol operates roving patrols such as the one in *Almeida-Sanchez v. United States*.

In all three types of surveillance, automobiles are detained and searched without a warrant, without probable cause that the automobile contains aliens, and even without probable cause to suspect that the cars made a border crossing. The only justification for relaxing the constitutional protections afforded by the Fourth Amendment appears in section 287(a)(3) of the Immigration and Nationality Act, 66 Stat. 233, 8 U.S.C. § 1357(a)(3), which permits warrantless searches of vehicles "within a reasonable distance from any external boundary of the United States." The Attorney General's regulation, 8 CFR § 287.1, defines "reasonable distance" as being "within 100 air miles from any external boundary of the United States."

In *Almeida-Sanchez*, a Mexican citizen with a valid work permit was convicted because he knowingly received, concealed, and facilitated the transportation of a quantity of illegally imported marihuana. The only issue on appeal was whether the search of his automobile was unconstitutional.

Border Patrol agents stopped Almeida–Sanchez on California Highway 78, twenty-five miles north of the border. The highway runs East–West, north of Highway 80, and partly through an undeveloped area.

Although the Ninth Circuit acknowledged that the search of Almeida–Sanchez's vehicle was not a "border search," it upheld the search, based on section 287(a)(3) of the Immigration and Nationality Act. The Supreme Court held that the warrantless search of the Petitioner's automobile without probable cause or consent was a violation of the Fourth Amendment right to be free of "unreasonable searches and seizures." The search could not be justified on the basis of special rules applicable to automobile searches because there was no probable cause. Nor could the search be justified as an "administrative inspection," as the officers had no warrant or reason to think that Petitioner had crossed the border or committed an offense, and Petitioner did not consent to the search. In the majority opinion, Justice Stewart noted that "[i]t is undenied that the Border Patrol had no search warrant, and that there was no probable cause ... not even the 'reasonable suspicion' found sufficient for a street detention and weapons search in *Terry v. Ohio*, and *Adams v. Williams*."

* * *

In *United States v. Brignoni–Ponce*, two Border Patrol agents were working the San Clemente checkpoint on Interstate 5. As the checkpoint was closed because of inclement weather, the agents were checking northbound traffic from a parked patrol car. Because the road was dark, the officers used their headlights to illuminate the road.

The Court held that except at the border or its functional equivalents, officers on roving patrols or at fixed checkpoints may not stop vehicles, unless they are able to articulate specific facts, that along with rational inferences from such facts, create a reasonable suspicion that the persons who are in the vehicles are in United States illegally. Here the officers did not have reasonable suspicion, relying exclusively on the "Mexican ancestry of the occupants" of the vehicle.

RACIAL PROFILING

Although courts have consistently held that police stops based on race or national origin are impermissible, law enforcement continues to use race as a primary determinant in making automobile stops. In *United States v. Mallides*, defendant was convicted of aiding and abetting illegal entry of aliens. He appealed, arguing that the conviction resulted from evidence that was the product of an unlawful detention and thus should have been suppressed. The United States District Court for the Southern District of California affirmed the conviction. On appeal, the Ninth Circuit Court of Appeals reversed, holding that the fact that several "Mexican–American appearing" males were riding in a sedan at dusk, and "sitting erectly" would not justify stopping them on suspicion of being illegal aliens.

Police officers spotted defendant's older model Chrysler Imperial turning onto Airport Road in the city of Oceanside. Mallides' conduct was not suspicious or unusual. He did not drive erratically or behave in a suspicious manner. The facts upon which the officers based the stop was that "six Mexican–American appearing males were riding in a Chrysler Imperial at dusk, sitting erectly, and none turned to look at the passing patrol car."

* * *

The court held that because "[t]he stop and detention were illegal," the result of such illegal conduct is inadmissible. There is nothing inherently suspicious about six people together in a sedan, sitting erect, and "[t]he conduct does not become suspicious simply because the skins of the occupants are nonwhite or because they sit up straight or because they do not look at a passing police car."

Similarly, in *United States v. Sanchez–Vargas*, the defendant was convicted of bringing an alien into the United States illegally and for illegally transporting an alien within the United States. Border Patrol Agent Scott stopped Sanchez–Vargas while he was driving a light-colored vehicle in the vicinity of the Otay Mesa Port of Entry. Scott testified that minutes prior to the stop, he had received radio transmissions from two other agents. One agent had said he had seen three vehicles, a van, a pickup, and a light-colored car "driving through the international boundary fence west of the Otay Mesa Port of Entry." The second officer reported that he had observed the light-color auto, making two U-turns and that it was heading north. Agent Scott initiated a high-speed chase and subsequently apprehended Sanchez–Vargas.

The Court of Appeals held that Scott had justifiably "founded suspicion" to stop Sanchez–Vargas. All of the facts taken together, including the radio transmissions and his own personal observations gave Scott "specific and articulable facts sufficient to warrant an investigative stop of Sanchez–Vargas' vehicle."

* * *

Similarly in *Gonzalez-Rivera v. INS*, the Ninth Circuit Court of Appeals reversed the deportation order of Mario Gonzalez–Rivera, holding that Border Patrol Officers stopped the deportee solely on the basis of his Hispanic appearance and that the stop was an "egregious constitutional violation." Gonzalez–Rivera appealed to the Ninth Circuit after the Board of Immigration Appeals (BIA) reversed the Immigration Judge's (IJ) ruling that the Border Patrol agents stopped the deportee simply because of his "Hispanic appearance."

Gonzalez was riding in the car his father was driving. They were traveling north on Highway 805 near San Diego when two Border Patrol Agents stopped the car. The agents discovered that Gonzalez' father was in the United States legally, but Gonzalez could not produce documents showing he was so, as well. After arresting Gonzalez, the agents learned that he had entered the United States without inspection. * * *

At the deportation hearing, Gonzalez filed a written motion to suppress evidence, arguing that his detention, arrest, and interrogation, were "an egregious violation of his Fourth Amendment rights," because he was stopped simply based on his Hispanic appearance. At the hearing, * * * Officer Wilson testified that Highway 805 is a major corridor of alien smuggling, that almost everyone who travels the highway is of Hispanic origin, and that there was nothing wrong or suspicious about the vehicle or the way that Gonzalez was driving. On the stand, Wilson said he based the stop on the following factors:

> (1) Gonzalez and his father appeared to be Hispanic; (2) both of them sat-up straight, looked straight ahead and did not turn their heads to acknowledge the Border Patrol car; (3) Gonzalez' mouth appeared to be "dry"; (4) Gonzalez was blinking; and (5) both men appeared to be nervous.

However, * * * Wilson later changed his description and said "that when [Gonzalez and his father] saw us, they turned, they *turned and looked at us*, and right away turned their heads, and just sat straight." * * * The INS attorney stated that while "everybody who is wearing a cap is not an illegal alien, ... all [of] these facts put together, seem to indicate articulable facts, ... to make a reasonable stop."

The Ninth Circuit concluded that the officers stopped Gonzalez because of his Hispanic appearance and that all of the other alleged factors "for the stop were either fabricated or of such minimal probative value in determining whether Gonzalez and his father looked suspicious that no reasonable officer would have relied on them." The opinion noted that "[i]n *Brignoni-Ponce*, the Supreme Court held that 'Hispanic appearance alone is insufficient to justify a stop' " * * * and suppressed the evidence.

Rights, Membership, and Personhood

Whether there is a Mexican Exception to the Fourth Amendment is at once both complex and at the same time remarkably simple. While the federal courts have consistently held that in principle, Hispanic or Mexican appearance is not sufficient to justify a stop, they also have held that Hispanic appearance is one of several factors that may, in conjunction with other facts "taken together with rational inferences from those facts, reasonably warrant that intrusion."

The reality, of course, is that there is a Mexican Exception. Mexican appearing persons are routinely stopped with articulable facts that are consistent with law-abiding behavior such as driving on a highway within 100 air miles of the border, driving a late model sedan, wearing a cap, and driving a car that appears to be weighed down or has a number of passengers in it. Mexican-appearing persons are also placed in a catch–22 situation where either looking at the officers or not looking at the officers may be interpreted as suspicious conduct.

* * *

* * * Federal courts appear to be increasingly reluctant to extend basic due process and equal protection guarantees under the Constitution to all persons, including non-citizens. * * *

Since most undocumented persons are of Mexican origin, and since Mexican-appearing persons are often confused with Middle–Easterners, the increased security measures that have been implemented in the "Post–911 Era" have had an adverse impact on the Latino population in the United States. Mexican-looking persons thus face a double jeopardy in that their physical appearance makes them more vulnerable to being stopped both as suspected "illegal aliens" and as would-be terrorists.

* * *

The so-called Mexican Exception to the Fourth Amendment has vast implications for Latinos and all Mexican-appearing persons, regardless of place of birth, citizenship, or immigration status. As Justice Brennan noted in his eloquent dissenting opinion in *Martinez-Fuerte*,

> Every American citizen of Mexican ancestry and every Mexican alien lawfully in this country must know after today's decision that he travels the fixed checkpoint highways at the risk of being subjected not only to a stop, but also to detention and interrogation, both prolonged and to an extent far more than non-Mexican appearing motorists.

For a sampling of case law expanding law enforcement's search-and-seizure rights against Latinos, see, e.g., United States v. Verdugo–Urquidez, 494 U.S. 259 (1990) (holding that the Fourth Amendment does not apply when American authorities search the Mexican residence of a Mexican citizen who had no voluntary connection with the United States, find incriminating evidence, and then transport him involuntarily to the U.S. for trial on drug charges); INS v. Delgado, 466 U.S. 209 (1984) (upholding factory raid during which INS agents systematically went through ranks of workers inquiring as to their citizenship while other agents blocked each exit); United States v. Vallejo, 56 Fed. R. Evid. Serv. (Callaghan) 64 (9th Cir. 2001) (rejecting evidence of drug-courier profile supported only by a defendant's having no books or bookbags despite his claim of being on the way to school).

Notes and Questions

1. For an original poem capturing the country's multiracial quality and celebrating its Hispano heritage, see the following by Detroit-area professor-writer James Perkinson.

la raza

like the ojos de espiritu
of emanuel martinez

in resurrection of light
fireflies kiting across
cobalt canvas skies
like a penitente march
from santa cruz de la cañada
to the black señor of chimayó
chanting down drug flows in
the voice of black crows
and of old men in plastic-bag
raincoats
like mulatto ambrosio
groaning in knives and revenge
in catamarcan quarters after
an 1804 flogging for daring to read
like the guadalupe image on the
spear of hidalgo riddled with
bullets in atotonilco dust never
failing to rekindle the tonantzin
myth and a return of the color
brown from the grave
like a million feet on a thousand
streets stomping a quiet coming
against all the tancredo interdictions
otherwise
borders uncrossing barriers
in reverse of history
hands slapping flautas
pueblos remembering 1680
turquoise like an alchemic incarnation
of aztlan mountains and eyes
aflame with the pain of a
ken burns film and ironic
remember-the-alamo grins
richmond, new jersey taking
back its ban as the boards
go up and the town falls
in the fall air there is a
great golden grimace of maize
the smell of copal
the bells of lost battles
the death knells of white jealousies
and birth rates
a rising river of moreno silver
grape picker grins in rusty vans
pounding sonoran sands into
a new country
a pantry full of jalapeno reprisals
just waiting for anglo bellies
and hubris
and ranchero tunes
and looms full of navajo dreams

and yaqui visions
and zapatista confrontations
and chicano organizations
and the strong hands of a mestiza madre
stroking away the tears of a harsh century
the opening puertos of a new day
the stay of execution for a post-modern gaucho
living insurrection against the nafta night
bamba beats in the heat of concrete jungle streets
like a raza on its feet meeting its face
in the sun and maybe
just maybe
jesus was really an outlaw
coyote refusing every border
like a judge without
an empire to protect
like a rojo dawn
under an old sombrero

2. For a different poem celebrating Latino identity and cultural origins, see Rodolfo "Corky" Gonzales, *I Am Joaquin: An Epic Poem* (1967), in *Latino/a Thought: Culture, Politics, and Society* (Francisco H. Vázquez & Rodolfo D. Torres eds., 2003).

*

Part Six

CULTURAL STEREOTYPES AND HATE SPEECH

If, as noted earlier, race is a social construction, not a biological fact, media images and stereotypes are key means by which society decides the content of a category like "black" or "Latino." And if the social construction of a group is negative—say, stupid, immoral, lazy, and prone to criminal behavior—innocent members of the group are likely to be on the receiving end of a good deal of demeaning language, hate speech for short. The selections in this Part introduce you to these topics.

Chapter 16

CULTURAL STEREOTYPES
OF LATINOS

A stereotype is an image of a group, often demeaning, that occurs again and again in literature, song, and other cultural scripts. The line between a negative stereotype and hate speech is indistinct. Hate speech often invokes a stereotype, as when someone says, "You dirty Mexican. Get out of my sight." Writers often reserve the term "hate speech" for one-on-one vituperation, or sometimes a rain of negative remarks uttered within the hearing of someone who is unfree to leave, such as a child in the classroom or a worker in a workplace.

The dominant images (stereotypes) of a group may, of course, contain a grain of truth. The stereotype of the British royal family, for example, includes haughty behavior. And many of the group may, in fact, act that way on occasion, but perhaps not all. Is a stereotype any less damaging merely because it contains an element of truth? See generally Steven W. Bender, *Greasers and Gringos: Latinos, Law, and the American Imagination* (2003).

Richard Delgado & Jean Stefancic
Images of the Outsider in American Law and Culture:
Can Free Expression Remedy Systemic Social Ills?
77 Cornell L. Rev. 1258, 1258–60, 1273–81, 1288–91 (1992)

Outsider groups argue that free speech law inadequately protects them against certain types of harm. * * * We believe that conventional First Amendment doctrine is most helpful in connection with small, clearly bounded disputes. Free speech and debate can help resolve controversies over whether a school disciplinary or local zoning policy is adequate, over whether a new sales tax is likely to increase or decrease net revenues, whether one candidate for political office is a better choice than another. Speech is less able, however, to deal with systemic social ills, such as racism, that are widespread and deeply woven into the fabric of society. Free speech, in short, is least helpful where we need it most.

Consider racial depiction, for example. Several museums have featured displays of racial memorabilia from the past. One exhibit recently toured the United States. Filmmaker Marlon Riggs produced an award-winning one-hour documentary, *Ethnic Notions*, with a similar focus. Each of these collections depicts a shocking parade of Sambos, mammies, coons, uncles—bestial or happy-go-lucky, watermelon-eating—African Americans. They show advertising logos and household commodities in the shape of blacks with grotesquely exaggerated facial features. They include minstrel shows and film clips depicting blacks as so incompetent, shuffling, and dimwitted that it is hard to see how they survived to adulthood. Other images depict primitive, terrifying, larger-than-life black men in threatening garb and postures, often with apparent designs on white women.

Seeing these haunting images today, one is tempted to ask: "How could their authors—cartoonists, writers, film-makers, and graphic designers—individuals, certainly of higher than average education, create such appalling images? And why did no one protest?"

* * *

Mexican Americans

Images of Mexican Americans fall into three or four well-delineated stereotypes—the greaser; the conniving, treacherous bandido; the happy-go-lucky shiftless lover of song, food, and dance; and the tragic, silent, tall, dark, and handsome "Spanish" type of romantic fiction—which change according to society's needs. As with blacks, Asians, and Indians, most Americans have relatively few interpersonal contacts with Mexican Americans; therefore, these images become the individual's only reality. When such a person meets an actual Mexican American, he or she tends to place the other in one of the ready-made categories. Stereotyping thus denies members of both groups the opportunity to interact with each other on anything like a complex, nuanced human level.

During and just after the conquest, when the U.S. was seizing and then settling large tracts of Mexican territory in the Southwest, "Western" or "conquest" fiction depicted Anglos bravely displacing shifty, brutal, and treacherous Mexicans. After the war ended and control of the Southwest passed to American hands, a subtle shift occurred. Anglos living and settling in the new regions were portrayed as Protestant, independent, thrifty, industrious, mechanically resourceful, and interested in progress; Mexicans, as traditional, sedate, lacking in mechanical resourcefulness and ambition. Writers both on and off the scene created the same images of indolent, pious Mexicans—ignoring the two centuries of enterprising farmers and ranchers who withstood or negotiated with Apaches and Comanches and built a sturdy society with irrigation, land tenure, and mining codes.

In the late conquest period, depiction of this group bifurcated. Majority-race writers created two images of the Mexican: the "good" (loyal) Mexican peon or sidekick, and the "bad" fighter/greaser Mexican who did not know his place. The first was faithful and domestic; the second, treacherous and evil. As with other groups, the second ("bad") image had sexual overtones: the greaser coveted Anglo women and would seduce or rape them if given the opportunity. Children's books of this time, like the best-selling Buffalo Bill series, were full of Mexican stereotypes used to reinforce moral messages to the young: They are like this, we like that.

The first thirty years of this century saw heavy Mexican immigration of mainly poor workers. The first Bracero programs—official, temporary importation of field hands—appeared. With increasing numbers, white-only signs and segregated housing and schools appeared, aimed now at Mexicans in addition to blacks. With the increased risk of interaction and intermarriage, novels and newspaper writing reinforced the notion of these immigrants' baseness, simplicity, and inability to assimilate.

The movies of this period depicted Latins as buffoons, sluts, or connivers; even some of the titles were disparaging: for example, *The Greaser's Gauntlet*. Films featured brown-skinned desperadoes stealing horses or gold, lusting after pure Anglo women, shooting noble Saxon heroes in the back, or acting the part of hapless buffoons. Animated cartoons and short subjects, still shown on television, featured tequila-drinking Mexicans, bullfighters, Speedy Gonzalez and Slowpoke Rodriguez, and clowns—as well as Castilian caballeras, light-skinned, upper class, wearing elaborate dresses and carrying castanets.

World War II brought the need for factory and agricultural workers and a new flood of immigrants. Images softened to include "normal," or even noble, Mexicans, like the general of Marlon Brando's *Viva Zapata*. Perhaps realizing it had over-stepped, America diminished the virulence of its anti-Mexican imagery. Yet the Western genre, with Mexican villains and bandits, continues; and the immigrant speaking gibberish still makes an appearance. Even the most favorable novel and film of the post-war period, *The Milagro Beanfield War*, ends in stereotypes.

A few Anglo writers found their own culture alienating or sick and sought relief in a more serene Southwest culture. As with the Harlem Renaissance, these creative artists tended to be more generous to Mexicans, but nevertheless retained the Anglo hero as the central figure or Samaritan who uplifts the Mexican from his or her traditional ignorance.

How Could They? Lessons from the History of Racial Depiction

The depiction of ethnic groups of color is littered with negative images, although the content of those images changes over time. In some periods, society needed to suppress a group, as with blacks during Reconstruction. Society coined an image to suit that purpose—that of primitive, powerful, larger-than-life blacks, terrifying and barely under control. At other times, for example during slavery, society needed reassurance that blacks were docile, cheerful, and content with their lot. Images of sullen, rebellious blacks dissatisfied with their condition would have made white society uneasy. Accordingly, images of simple, happy blacks, content to do the master's work, were disseminated.

In every era, ethnic imagery comes bearing an enormous amount of social weight. Nevertheless, we sense that we are in control—that things need not be that way. We believe we can use speech, jiujitsu fashion, on behalf of oppressed peoples. We believe that speech can serve as a tool of destabilization. It is virtually a prime tenet of liberal jurisprudence that by talk, dialog, exhortation, and so on, we present each other with passionate, appealing messages that will counter the evil ones of racism and sexism, and thereby advance society to greater levels of fairness and humanity.

Consider, for example, the debate about campus speech codes. In response to a rising tide of racist incidents, many campuses have enacted, or are considering enacting, student conduct codes that forbid certain types of face-to-face insult. These codes invariably draw fire from free-speech absolutists and many campus administrators on the ground that they would interfere with free speech. Campuses, they argue, ought to be "bastions of free speech." Racism and prejudice are matters of "ignorance and fear," for which the appropriate remedy is more speech. Suppression merely drives racism underground, where it will fester and emerge in even more hateful forms. Speech is the best corrective for error; regulation risks the spectre of censorship and state control. Efforts to regulate pornography, Klan marches, and other types of race-baiting often meet similar responses.

But modernist and postmodern insights about language and the social construction of reality show that reliance on countervailing speech that will, in theory, wrestle with bad or vicious speech is often misplaced. This is so for two interrelated reasons: First, the account rests on simplistic and erroneous notions of narrativity and change, and second, on a misunderstanding of the relation between the subject, or self, and new narratives.

The First Reason—Time Warp: Why We (Can) Only Condemn the Old Narrative

The racism of other times and places does stand out, does strike us as glaringly and appallingly wrong. But this happens only decades or centuries later; we acquiesce in today's version with little realization that it is wrong, that a later generation will ask "How could they?" about us. We only condemn the racism of another place (South Africa) or time. But that of our own place and time strikes us, if at all, as unexceptional, trivial, or well within literary license. Every form of creative work (we tell ourselves) relies on stock characters. What's so wrong with a novel that employs a black who . . ., or a Mexican who . . .? Besides, the argument goes, those groups are disproportionately employed as domestics, are responsible for a high proportion of our crime, are they not? And some actually talk this way; why, just last week, I overheard . . .

This time-warp aspect of racism makes speech an ineffective tool to counter it. Racism is woven into the warp and woof of the way we see and organize the world—it is one of the many preconceptions we bring to experience and use to construct and make sense of our social world. Racism forms part of the dominant narrative, the group of received understandings and basic principles that form the baseline from which we reason. How could these be in question? Recent scholarship shows that the dominant narrative changes very slowly and resists alteration. We interpret new stories in light of the old. Ones that deviate too markedly from our pre-existing stock are dismissed as extreme, coercive, political, and wrong. The only stories about race we are prepared to condemn, then, are the old ones giving voice to the racism of an earlier age, ones that society has already begun to reject. We can condemn Justice Brown for writing as he did in *Plessy v. Ferguson*, but not university administrators who refuse remedies for campus racism, failing to notice the remarkable parallels between the two.

The Second Reason: Our Narratives, Our Selves

Racial change is slow, then, because the story of race is part of the dominant narrative we use to interpret experience. The narrative teaches that race matters, that people are different, with the differences lying always in a predictable direction. It holds that certain cultures, unfortunately, have less ambition than others, that the majority group is largely innocent of racial wrongdoing, that the current distribution of comfort and well-being is roughly what merit and fairness dictate. Within that general framework, only certain matters are open for discussion: How different? In what ways? With how many exceptions? And what measures are due to deal with this unfortunate situation and at what cost to whites? This is so because the narrative leaves only certain things intelligible; other arguments and texts would seem alien.

A second and related insight from modern scholarship focuses not on the role of narratives in confining change to manageable proportions, but on the relationship between our selves and those narratives. The reigning First Amendment metaphor—the marketplace of ideas—implies a separation between subjects who do the choosing and the ideas or messages that vie for their attention. Subjects are "in here," the messages "out there." The pre-existing subjects choose the idea that seems most valid and true—somewhat in the manner of a diner deciding what to eat at a buffet.

But scholars are beginning to realize that this mechanistic view of an autonomous subject choosing among separate, external ideas is simplistic. In an important sense, we are our current stock of narratives, and they us. We subscribe to a stock of explanatory scripts, plots, narratives, and understandings that enable us to make sense of—to construct—our social world. Because we live in that world, it begins to shape and determine us, who we are, what we see, how we select, reject, interpret, and order subsequent reality.

These observations imply that our ability to escape the confines of our own preconceptions is quite limited. The contrary belief—that through speech and remonstrance alone we can endlessly reform our-selves and each other—we call the *empathic fallacy*. It and its compan-ion, the pathetic fallacy, are both based on hubris, the belief that we can be more than we are. The empathic fallacy holds that through speech and remonstrance we can surmount our limitations of time, place, and culture, can transcend our own situatedness. But our examination of the cultural record, as well as postmodern understandings of language and personhood, both point to the same conclusion: The notion of ideas competing with each other, with truth and goodness emerging victorious from the competition, has proven seriously deficient when applied to evils, like racism, that are deeply inscribed in the culture. We have constructed the social world so that racism seems normal, part of the status quo, in need of little correction. It is not until much later that what we believed begins to seem incredibly, monstrously wrong. How could we have believed that?

* * *

Racism is not a mistake, not a matter of episodic, irrational behavior carried out by vicious-willed individuals, not a throwback to a long-gone era. It is ritual assertion of supremacy, like animals sneering and posturing to maintain their places in the hierarchy of the colony. It is performed largely unconsciously, just as the animals' behavior is. Racism seems right, customary, and inoffensive to those engaged in it, while also bringing them psychic and pecuniary advantages. * * *

What Then, Should Be Done? If Not Speech, What?

So, what can be done? One possibility we must take seriously is that nothing can be done—that race-based subjugation is so deeply embedded in our society, so useful for the powerful, that nothing can dislodge it. * * * However, we offer four suggestions for a program of racial reform. We do this while underscoring the limitations of our own prescriptions, including the near-impossibility of getting a society to take seriously something whose urgency it seems constitutionally unable to appreciate. First, society should act decisively in cases of racism that we do see, treating them as proxies for the ones we know remain unseen. Second, past mistreatment will generally prove a more reliable basis for remedial action (such as affirmative action or reparations) than future-or present-oriented considerations; the racism of the past is the only kind that we recognize and condemn. Third, whenever possible we should employ and empower minority speakers of color and expose ourselves to their mes-sages. Their reality, while not infallible and certainly not the only one, is the one we must heed if we wish to avoid history's judgment. It is likely to be the one society will adopt in thirty years.

Scholars should approach with skepticism the writings of those neoconservatives, including some of color, who make a practice of telling society that racism is ended. Finally, we should deepen suspicion of remedies for deep-seated social evils that rely on speech and exhortation. The First Amendment is an instrument of variable efficacy, more useful in some settings than others. Overextending it provokes the anger of oppressed groups and casts doubt on speech's value in settings where it is, in fact, useful. With deeply inscribed cultural practices that most can neither see as evil nor mobilize to reform, we should forthrightly institute changes in the structure of society that will enable persons of color—particularly the young—to avoid the worst assaults of racism. As with the controversy over campus racism, we should not let a spurious motto that speech be "everywhere free" stand in the way of outlawing speech that is demonstrably harmful, that is compounding the problem.

Because of the way the dominant narrative works, we should prepare for the near-certainty that these suggestions will be criticized as unprincipled, unfair to "innocent whites," wrong. Understanding how the dialectic works, and how the scripts and counterscripts work their dismal paralysis, may, perhaps, inspire us to continue even though the path is long and the night dark.

Reginald Horsman
Race and Manifest Destiny
208–13 (1981)

Reread Reginald Horsman, *Race and Manifest Destiny*, in Part One supra.

In *Greasers and Gringos* Professor Steven Bender examines some of the most common stereotypes of the Latino—the greaser, the lazy lover of siestas, the amorous Latin lover, the spitfire oversexed senorita, and the gangster. He also discusses the supposedly dirty Mexican and the dull, unintelligent Latino/a who is ill-equipped for any but the most menial work. Like Delgado & Stefancic, he shows how these stereotypes performed various functions for the majority group, including justifying discrimination, inferior schools, and denial of social services and opportunities for advancement. Steven W. Bender, *Greasers and Gringos*, supra.

Charles Ramírez Berg
*Bordertown: The Assimilation Narrative and the Chicano
Social Problem Film, in Latino Images in Film:
Stereotypes, Subversion, and Resistance*
(2002)

Not only is *Bordertown* an excellent illustration of the way the assimilation narrative overlaps with the Chicano social melodrama, it is also a paradigmatic example of the entire class of Chicano social problem films. Here, Robin Wood's delineation of the horror genre's normality-Monster conflict as symbolic of the tension between the Dominant and the Other will prove useful. Wood gives the formula for the basic horror film as "normality threatened by the Monster." Similarly, the basic formula for the minority social melodrama is the mainstream threatened by the margin. Indeed, the "problem" of the ethnic/racial problem films is the perceived threat the margin's very existence poses to the dominant. The dilemma ethnic/racial Others raise for the American mainstream is how to combine two essentially incompatible ideas: the dominant's desire to preserve and protect its identity as a superior, racially pure in-group by exclusionary practices, and the implementation of the democratic ideal that guarantees freedom, equality, and opportunity for all American citizens.

Bordertown follows the standard rags-to-riches-to-rags assimilation narrative. Johnny Ramírez, a tough kid from East Los Angeles, matures into a responsible adult and acquires ambition and dedication when, as the judge who delivers his law school's commencement address puts it, "he realized his opportunities and duties as an American citizen." Johnny dreams of being on the Supreme Court, but his first court appearance reveals him to be a miserable lawyer. He loses an easy case to rich socialite Dale Elwell (Margaret Lindsay), who is defended by an upper-crust lawyer friend. When he is called a "shyster" by the defense attorney, Johnny throws him to the ground, a violent outburst that has him disbarred.

Rejecting the entreaties of the parish padre to content himself with humble work in the Mexican Quarter, Johnny leaves Mamá and the barrio to obtain what he now understands to be the only things that matter in America: power and money. "A guy's entitled to anything he can grab," he tells his uncomprehending mother just before he goes, "I found that out. And I'm for grabbing from now on." Before long he is managing a casino for a bumbling but well-meaning Anglo proprietor, Charlie Roark (Eugene Pallette), in a Mexican bordertown. Though he rebuffs Charlie's wife's (Bette Davis) amorous advances, she falls so deeply in love with him that she secretly murders her husband to free herself for Johnny. When he still shows no interest in her, Marie frames him for Charlie's murder, jeopardizing his ongoing courtship of Dale. Marie's crack-up on the witness stand (in one of the most memorable scenes of Davis's career) frees Johnny to return to Dale. But alone on a deserted highway one night, she rejects his proposal. "Marriage isn't for us," she tells him. "You belong to a different tribe, Savage." Pulling free from his grasp, she accidentally runs into a passing car and is killed.

Johnny sells the casino, uses the money to endow a law school in the barrio and returns, in his words, "back where I belong ... with my own people."

[Consider] the narrative and ideological features of *Bordertown* that are common to the Chicano social problem films that followed.

Stereotypical Inversion. Hollywood films that try to boost ethnics often begin by denigrating Anglos (think, for example, what a band of oafish louts the Anglos in *Dances with Wolves* are). *Bordertown* is no exception, peopled as it is by frustrated, oversexed blondes (Marie); flighty, materialistic socialites (Dale and her "fast" crowd of idle rich thrill-seekers); harsh and inflexible authority figures who operate from a strict brown-and-white moral code that justifies their intolerance of others ("If you knew any law," the judge tells Johnny after his fight in the courtroom, "you'd still be mentally unfit to practice."); crude simpletons (like Johnny's boss, Charlie Roark); and gangsters (the group that eventually buys the casino from Johnny). Naturally the Chicano protagonist makes the sound ethical choice when he recoils from such a thoroughly venal Anglo universe and retires to the moral haven of the *barrio*.

This pattern is the basis for Anglo-centered social problem narratives—the stories about an Anglo protagonist fighting for social justice. In these films the white hero mediates between an oppressed Chicano and a monolithically hostile Anglo citizenry: Leslie Benedict (Elizabeth Taylor) versus the intolerant Texans in *Giant*; the idealistic law professor (Glenn Ford) pitted against a politically ambitious lawyer and an angry mob in *Trial*; and the cynical-but-courageous newspaper editor (Macdonald Carey) opposed to the racist townsfolk in *The Lawless*. And in a couple of Chicano-centered films (those with a Mexican–American protagonist) the stereotypical inversion is even more pointed. Except for a sympathetic sheriff, the Anglos in *My Man and I* are a band of chiselling low-lifes, and those in *A Medal for Benny* a community of hypocrites.

Stereotyping of Other Marginal Groups. In Hollywood films dealing with a particular ethnic or racial group, the three key elements are the Anglo mainstream, the minority group, and the relationship between them. Busily building that specific ethnic group up and knocking the Anglo down, these films generally partake in a strange kind of Other tunnelvision, losing sight in the process of their insensitive stereotyping of any but the focused-upon ethnic or racial group. (An extreme example is the positive portrayal of the Sioux in *Dances with Wolves* existing alongside the film's vicious, cardboard depiction of the Pawnees.) In *Bordertown*, though Marie's Chinese servant appears in only a handful of scenes, he is the stereotypical hopping, misarticulating (substituting *l*'s for *r*'s) Chinese presence. Marie herself is a variation on the stereotypical "easy" blond. Another example: Johnny may be a bad lawyer, but he is a lot better than his Mexican defense attorney. Johnny has to prompt him to move for a dismissal of charges after Marie's breakdown on the witness stand.

This practice in effect maps Others' relation to the mainstream. In *Bordertown*, for instance, Mexican Americans are marginal, Mexican nationals more so, and Chinese Americans even more so. Interestingly, both *Giant* and *My Man and I* place their poor white characters—Jett Rink (James Dean) in *Giant* and Mr. and Mrs. Ames (Wendell Corey and Claire Trevor) in *My Man and I*—further from the center than Mexican Americans.

The Male Chicano Protagonist. Hollywood follows the path of least resistance in constructing its heroes. In the rare instance of a film hero being an ethnic character, Hollywood is careful to make him as palatable to mainstream audiences as possible. This is done mainly in three ways: (1) by making the protagonist male, (2) by casting Anglos in ethnic and racial roles (Douglas Fairbanks in *The Mark of Zorro* [1920] and Tyrone Power in the 1940 remake), and (3) by giving the Other protagonist upper class status (Zorro is a member of the landed gentry; his rebellion is in essence the struggle of New World elites to wrest California from Spanish aristocrats). It should not be surprising, therefore, that only one of the protagonists of these social problem films (Esperanza in the progressive *Salt of the Earth*) is female. Since in Hollywood films an ethnic woman can only be an overprotective matriarch, the "other woman," or a harlot, this practice automatically relegates Chicanas to stereotypical roles.

The Overprotective Mamá. The naive, good-natured, long-suffering mother, like Johnny's, is the norm in these films, and the typical way ethnic mothers are portrayed in Hollywood movies in general. * * *

        * * *

The Absent Father. Anglo families are complete and ideal, ethnic families fragmented and dysfunctional. The father's absence, from *Bordertown* to *La Bamba*, is seldom explained. Once again, from the male-dominant point of view, the lack of an organizing paternal sensibility makes for an abnormal, structurally unstable family unit, subtly establishing the psycho-social reasons why ethnics are different from—and inferior to— the mainstream.

        * * *

        The Absent Chicana. Except for the protagonist's mother, Chicanas do not exist, and certainly not as someone our Chicano hero would be romantically interested in. The implied message: Chicanas are so inferior to Anglo women they may be omitted from consideration altogether. * * *

        Besides *Salt of the Earth*, only two films depict an all-Chicano romance. * * *

The Alluring but Flawed Gringa. In light of the above, the protagonist's only option for roman[ce] is with an Anglo woman. But given the pattern of stereotypical inversion and Hollywood's trepidation about portraying interracial love stories, she is bestowed with severe emotional and psychological problems (Dale Elwell is a materialistic snob and a bigot and Marie's sexual starvation drives her to lust and murder). As a result, the romance is sabotaged from the onset. Thus by the use of an insidiously contorted self-preserving logic, Anglo patriarchy maintains its genetic "purity" in part by negatively stereotyping Anglo women as childish miscreants. Thus Chuchu's fascination with the troubled Marie (Shelley Winters) in *My Man and I* is both inexplicable (what could she possibly have to offer him?) and ideologically nonthreatening (as a marginal bar fly, her mingling with and marrying a Mexican is of little consequence to the dominant).

        * * *

The Reductive Definition of Success. Even given that in the American system the range of opportunities available to its minority members has been severely restricted throughout history, the options presented to the Chicano protagonist—succeed and die (morally or actually) or fail and live (in squalor though in moral equanimity)—are simplified in the extreme. This sort of absolutism is standard given Hollywood's wish-fulfillment narratives that define success—the quest to become the boxing champ of the world, or a Supreme Court justice—as an all-or-nothing proposition. Posed in such totalizing terms, however, the number of "successes" the American system allows in the movies is minuscule (one per protagonist per film) and these films reveal that both in and out of the movies achieving success is all but impossible for most people.

Hollywood has been expounding, explaining and defending the exclusionistic logic of this fable for decades, selling audiences the illusion of success even as they swallow the bitter pill of (preferred, safe) failure. Nevertheless, Anglo audiences can at least obtain pleasure from their identification with the Anglo hero's success. Mexican–American audiences, on the other hand, must learn to identify with the Anglo hero in order to enjoy "the freedom of action and control over the diegetic world that identification with a [white] hero provides." To the extent that such marginal viewer identification works, it justifies, celebrates and naturalizes the WASP norm, and becomes a means of Other viewers approaching the mainstream and internalizing its values. * * *

And Hollywood's providing Mexican–American protagonists in the Chicano-centered social problem films (save for *Salt of the Earth*) does not really improve the situation. A principal reason is that the heroes in these movies do not enjoy the sort of unbridled success available to Anglo protagonists. They get a greatly scaled-down version of Anglo success or they get failure. Johnny Ramírez cashes in and returns to East L.A. ("To do what?" we may well wonder as the film ends.) In *Right Cross*, Johnny Monterez injures his right hand swinging at his Anglo "friend." This ends his fighting career, but domesticates him (somehow ridding him of his bad temper, his inferiority complex, and his "paranoia" about the WASP system). In the conclusion of *My Man and I*, Chuchu is freed from jail and wins the heart of his beloved: a troubled, alcoholic blond. Giving up his dream of boxing as a career, Tommy in *The Ring* burns his cape and gloves in an oil drum in his backyard. With Lucy's help, he learns to be satisfied with life in the *barrio*. In the Hollywood cinema, Anglo protagonists succeed by succeeding; in the Chicano social problem films, Mexican–American protagonists succeed by failing.

Finally, again except for *Salt of the Earth*, this either/or-ism denies Chicano characters the possibility of redefining success in less grandiose—and more personal and local—terms. Working in their neighborhoods or otherwise contributing to the incremental betterment of their people is seldom a "successful" option. * * *

When an Anglo hero, from Will Kane (Gary Cooper) in *High Noon* to Deckard (Harrison Ford) in *Blade Runner*, turns his back on the system and retreats from it, it signifies the ultimate heroism—the rugged individual rejecting a contemptible system. But when a Chicano makes the same rejection, he doesn't ride into the sunset with Grace Kelly or discover a new Eden with Sean Young, he returns to the *barrio*, often alone. The Chicano couldn't make it in the big time, not so much rejecting the system as rejected by it. Clearly, WASP heroes have what it takes to succeed and have the added luxury of electing to accept or deny the system that allowed them that success. Other heroes have only what it takes to fail.

* * *

To be sure, much more work remains to be done with these films. Individual close readings are needed to investigate more fully the Anglo-centered films (Good Samaritan narratives, more interested in their WASP heroes' redemption than in the fate of the Chicano characters) and the Chicano-centered ones (variations cut from the *Bordertown* template or about how Chicanos need to become "naturalized" to enter the mainstream).

And it's time for a full-blown appreciation of *Giant*, one of the most enlightened of all of Hollywood's wide-screen epics. Its female protagonist allows it to question some of the key principles of the dominant ideology: patriarchy, the imperialistic bent of America's westward expansion ("We really stole Texas, didn't we?" Leslie tells Bick [Rock Hudson] the day after she meets him. "I mean away from Mexico."), racism, the class system and the social construction of manhood. Most impressively, it argues that the betterment of *Tejanos* will come not by simply adjusting an existing system, but by intermarriage and the raising of Anglo consciousness. Dramatically, Leslie's aiding the impoverished Mexican–American ranch workers is important but ideologically it is secondary to the fact that Bick's son married Juanna, that Bick now has a *mestizo* grandson, and that (even if it's only at a familial level) Bick rejected racism. *Giant* is a fascinating anomaly—a long, sprawling, big-budget movie made in the regressive 1950s that follows through on its liberal program *and* was a critical and box office success.

Notes and Questions

1.   What is the functional theory of racial stereotypes?

2.   Why are the dominant stereotypes of Latinos, and of other minorities, for that matter, generally negative? Are the ones for Latinos worsening today, because of nativism and anti-immigrant sentiment? See Andres Oppenheimer, *Time to Hit Back Against Anti–Latino Bigotry*, Miami Herald, July 20, 2007.

3.   Can one write any text, such as a film, novel, or short story, without drawing on a stereotype, such as the flirtatious maid, the thuggish Italian gangster, or the father as wandering wallet-sap? Would one not have to start from scratch in creating a character and thus waste time and risk boring one's audience?

4. What is the solution to movies and novels that demean members of an ethnic group? Censorship? Voting "with one's feet" (i.e., not buying)? Boycotts and group pressure? In the last few years, a coalition of minority groups has been sporadically putting pressure on corporate television to reduce the amount of racial stereotyping in programming and to increase the number of actors of color. Is this a promising avenue?

5. Should writers and other creative artists be colorblind and treat characters of color like anyone else?

6. If a journalist or organization issues a "feel good" report or description of the Latino situation in the U.S. that stresses progress and a rosy future, is that harmful, too?

7. For discussion of the acclaimed movie "Lone Star," which treats immigration issues and Latino characters in an engrossing but dignified way, see Elvia R. Arriola, *LatCrit Theory, International Human Rights, Popular Culture, and the Faces of Despair in INS Raids*, 28 U. Miami Inter–Am. L. Rev. 245 (1997).

8. For more on Latino stereotypes, see Steven W. Bender, *Sight, Sound, and Stereotype: The War on Terrorism and its Consequences for Latinas/os*, 81 Or. L. Rev. 1153 (2002); David Langum, *Californios and the Image of Indolence*, 9 W. Hist. Q. 181 (Apr. 1978). See also Arnoldo De Leon, *They Called Them Greasers: Anglo Attitudes Toward Mexicans in Texas, 1821–1900* (1983); Richard Delgado & Jean Stefancic, *Understanding Words that Wound* (2004); *Latin Looks: Images of Latinas and Latinos in the U.S. Media* (Clara E. Rodriguez ed., 1997); *Chicanos and Film: Representation and Resistance* (Chon. Noriega ed., 1992).

SECTION 1. CULTURAL STEREOTYPING FROM A POSTCOLONIAL AND CRITICAL RACE THEORY PERSPECTIVE

Reread "Ramon, Susie, and a Moonlit Night," in Part Two, Chapter 6, supra, in which Rodrigo and his interlocutor-straight man "the Professor" discuss a theory of racial formation and stereotypes. Briefly, they decide that the dominant group uses a triple taboo to keep members of their group (such as young Anglo women) at a distance from Latinos in order to prevent interracial friendships from forming and interfering with profitable economic exploitation.

They then continue as follows:

Richard Delgado
Rodrigo's Corrido: Race, Postcolonial Theory, and U.S. Civil Rights
60 Vand. L. Rev. 1691, 1725–38 (2007)

RODRIGO'S EVIDENCE THAT THE TABOOS PERSIST AND ARE IN FULL FORCE TODAY

"That all has the ring of truth," I said. "Taboos like the ones you mentioned would enable Anglo overlords to assure that their supervisors, daughters, and friends kept their distance from the Mexicans. They would permit oppressive labor conditions to continue indefinitely. But what evidence do you have that these taboos remain in force today? I have never spent time in the fields and orchards of the Southwest, or any of the cities in the Midwest, Northeast, and South, for that matter, where large Latino immigrant populations have been forming. Do I need to accept your theory on faith?"

"Not at all," Rodrigo replied. "I've been gathering mountains of evidence. Do we have time?"

I looked at my watch, told Rodrigo we had over half an hour, and motioned to the waiter who quickly caught my eye.

"Would you gentlemen like some coffee or decaf?"

Rodrigo nodded vigorously and asked if they had cappuccino. The waiter said yes, of course, after which I asked if they could make it with decaffeinated beans. "No problem," he said, and departed. I noticed that he spoke with a slight Spanish accent and wondered if he might be an immigrant, documented or otherwise.

"Nice fellow," Rodrigo said. "Where were we?"

"You were going to outline your evidence for the three taboos. I assume you can't prove some sort of a founding meeting of chief taboo articulators?"

"Of course not," Rodrigo said, I thought a little sharply. "The elite leadership would not need to meet. The taboos would develop through an invisible, tacit process and a thousand conversations. A little like TV stereotypes, say, the Latina maid or black doorman. No group of Hollywood or broadcast executives sat down and said to each other, 'What kind of role would be good for Latinas to play? How about maids and domestic workers?' "

"So yours is not a conspiracy theory."

"Not at all. It's entirely descriptive. It shows how culture operates and how the ideas a society develops about Indians, blacks, and Latinos are not accidents but serve useful functions. With Latinos, they rationalize economic exploitation, mainly in the form of unfair labor practices. Today that means, among other things, keeping a large, floating population of Latino workers who are illegal and undocumented, just like colonial subjects, and a ready supply of cheap, easily exploited labor."

"That's more plausible," I said. "But what kinds of evidence do you have?"

"Several," Rodrigo replied. "I've dug up a lot from popular sources—stories, plays, movies, and other narratives circulating in the dominant society. But also from *corridos*, *actos*, skits, *cantares*, laments, and other tales of the Mexican people showing how they perceived that the Anglos thought of, and acted toward, them."

"A little bit like the slave narratives," I pointed out.

"Precisely," Rodrigo said. "Both bodies of literature, the slave narratives for blacks and the *corridos* for Latinos, performed much the same function. Each recorded what the subjugated people thought of their condition, of their work life, their hopes and dreams, and, especially, what they thought of their masters and they of them."

The waiter showed up, cups, saucers, and silver pots full of rich-smelling coffee in hand. "Enjoy," he said, "and let me know when you're ready for the check."

"We will," I said. Then, to Rodrigo: "Please go ahead. This is all very useful. I can use this if I teach that new class. It looks like a great way to organize the material."

"I can run through this fairly quickly," Rodrigo said. "As I mentioned, the Latino taboo consists of filth, hypersexuality, jabber, and a few others. Their purpose is to make sure that Anglos don't get too close. Close enough to supervise and give orders, but not enough to feel real kinship, real camaraderie, as might happen if Anglos and Mexicans worked closely side by side, at some hard job."

"Or in little Susie's case, close enough that she might feel sexual attraction toward 17–year old Ramon with his deep tan, strong body, and interesting dreams," I added.

"Exactly. And, in the case of jabber, the taboo justifies suspicion and close supervision."

"It occurs to me," I interjected, "that your taboo theory taps into a powerful social science insight that I teach every year, namely the social-contact hypothesis."

"I teach that, too."

"So we each know that many social scientists hold that the best way to counteract prejudice is to arrange that people of different types and skin colors work together in pursuit of common goals. Sports or the military are good examples. Or going to grade school with kids of other races."

"Right," I said. "The hypothesis, which formed the basis for institutional desegregation beginning in the sixties, holds that racism is a kind of mistake or cognitive error. The racist individual internalizes the notion that persons of a different race, say blacks, are unlike his group, say whites. They are untrustworthy, stupid, sexually lascivious, lazy, criminal, want to spend all day listening to loud music and hanging out with their friends on street corners, hassling white passersby, and so on."

"And so, by placing young people of different races together on a sports team or in a third-grade classroom, they learn that people of different ethnicities are much like them—some good, some bad. Some like loud music, others hate it."

"And that's how the taboo acquires its diabolical efficacy," I summarized. "Someone who fears a member of another race or thinks they will smell bad or want to have sex with you without your consent will not get close enough to have the easygoing conversations that the social-contact hypothesis requires. Relationships will remain formal and impersonal. They will enable the pre-existing hierarchy, white over brown, to remain intact forever, with little strain or pressure."

"And I have lots of data on the three components, if you are interested."

"I certainly am. Why don't you start?" I said.

Filth

"Have you heard the phrase, 'dirty Mexican'?" Rodrigo began.

I made a face. "Of course. Everyone has. It's the most common, and unfair, of the stereotypes. You hear it everywhere, almost as an epithet."

"It *is* unfair," Rodrigo said emphatically. "But a thousand plots, stories, and cultural references drive it home. It's also untrue. But you see it everywhere. Steven Bender's book says it—and its close relative, the 'greaser'—is one of the most common of the Latino stereotypes. Even relatively modern movies and stories reinforce it. Historians say they find it in practically every era. Mexicans particularly are invested with this awful image, which includes at least the following components: filthy, unclean, unshaven, never bathes, lacking in personal hygiene, and likely to give you a communicable disease. A number of legal opinions actually deemed Mexicans a nuisance. They proceeded under that theory, as though the very presence of a handful of brown-faced people was certain to bring noise, disorder and smells to a neighborhood."

"I read somewhere that early school authorities would separate Latino and Anglo children for this reason. In addition to rationalizing that separate education would benefit the Latino kids because of their linguistic difficulties, authorities would separate them in school because the Anglo parents would insist on it for hygienic reasons. They thought their kids would catch diseases or contract cooties or fleas."

"And of course the Mexican kids would, in fact, come to school in raggedy clothes, since a farmworker's wages would hardly allow the family to shop at Abercrombie and Fitch during a back-to-school sale." I recalled, idly, how the stylish Rodrigo ever since I had known him had dressed sharply. It must have galled him to think of generations of promising young Latino children growing up with a double handicap— unable to dress as sharply as their Anglo counterparts, and, as a result thought of as culturally or innately inferior, dirty, and prone to wallow in disease and filth.

"A handbook, entitled 'Your Maid from Mexico' provides guidance for wealthy Anglo families wishing to hire a Mexican maid. But it also provides rules for maids. Two-thirds of them have to do with being clean—using a toothbrush and deodorant, for example. And not touching the guests at a dinner party.

"And in today's anti-immigrant climate," Rodrigo continued, "you see evidence of the same thing. Immigration opponents cite, without any statistics whatsoever, the drain on emergency rooms, medical clinics, and other resources in regions with high rates of Latino undocumented immigration. This taps into the belief that Latinos are always getting sick and prone to suffer diseases and accidents and injuries. In fact, they are easily the country's youngest and healthiest racial group and visit doctors and emergency wards in lower proportions than anybody else. First we invest them with an unfair stigma, then we use it against them."

"A double bind," I commiserated. "And the heart-wrenching thing about it is that the stereotype comes about, in part, because of unfair and unsanitary living conditions that society imposes on the immigrants. If your migrant labor camp does not have running water or indoor toilets, as many do not, you will relieve yourself in the fields, behind a tree somewhere. If your camp lacks showers or hot water, you will not look, or maybe be, as clean as some Anglo family living in a suburban house with three bathrooms, each with a hot shower. If your mother has to wash your clothes in a river, they may not look as nice as the clothes of a schoolchild whose mother has a washer and dryer right in the kitchen."

"The taboo creates its own conditions of reinforcement, so that in time it comes to seem true, the way things are," Rodrigo concluded. "After a while, you see virtually every nativist writer—Buchanan, Skerry, Hanson, Brimelow, and Huntington—casually referring to the same things, as though they were well-known truths. The environmental justice movement points out that sewage treatment plants and toxic dump sites are disproportionately located in minority neighborhoods—which is true—and nobody bats an eye. Are we ready to move on to the next component?"

"I am," I said. "I gather that it's sexuality."

"It is," Rodrigo said. "It and filth work together. I'm sure, Professor, that you've known white people who are uncomfortable around blacks. They don't like to sit next to them on buses...."

"I see this all the time," I said. "You can get on a bus or train. The only vacant seat is next to a well dressed, middle-aged black commuter. There can even be a few people standing. None of them wants to take that seat."

"I've seen the same thing," Rodrigo seconded. "One time, I had just got back to the States after all those years in Italy. I was riding a bus around Manhattan and noticed an empty seat. When I pointed it out to an elderly rider, he shook his head and said he was getting off soon. The seat was next to a black executive, I gathered from his well tailored suit."

"And did the rider get off at the next stop?"

"No. I don't think he got off at all, and I rode the bus for several miles. I ended up taking the seat myself."

"And I'm sure you know a certain type of person, usually from the South, who won't shake the hand of a black person or will do so only reluctantly."

"I have a colleague like that," I said. "He'll take my hand for just a quick, perfunctory squeeze, then pull his own away like a scalded cat. I don't know whether he does this for everybody, or just me. I thought maybe he had a germ phobia."

"More likely, it's a man-of-color phobia," Rodrigo said, with a slight grimace. "Do you know about the writing of Joel Kovel?"

"I do. He's a famous contemporary social scientist who coined a psychodynamic theory of race. It's quite original and not at all flattering, especially to whites. He holds that many white people have embedded, deep in their psyches, devastating associations with blackness and black skins."

"Indeed. It's of course impossible to prove or disprove a psychoanalytically based theory, such as his or Freud's. But Kovel's theory does seem to work, at least on an explanatory level. He says some white folks equate black and brown skin with dirt and feces. They shy away from it, unconsciously, and are never comfortable with one of us. They can't see us as persons, just as symbols of something they have been taught since childhood not to play with. We're taboo. Don't go there."

"And you were saying that a similar dynamic operates in the case of Mexican sexuality?"

Hypersexuality

"Yes," Rodrigo replied. "Bender catalogs this stereotype as well. He finds several versions of it: the sex maniac Latino male lusting after white women, the ultimate prize; and the softer-edged soulful Latino lover, romantic and ready to break into song and serenade the Anglo princess on his guitar or take her dancing in the moonlight. For their part, Latina women are the lustful objects of Anglo men's desires."

"Neither type is one you would want to take seriously, or take on as a partner in business. You wouldn't want either romancing your daughter."

"And so, like the dirty stereotype, it operates to put a distance between Anglos and Mexicans, particularly Mexican men, such as the ones you would find around a migrant-labor camp or community."

"Or find in town on an errand. Or in grade school," I added. "I gather that's your point."

"It is. And a steady stream of movie plots, stories, TV comedies, and other tales build on the hypersexual Latino or Latina. They both prove the existence of the underlying taboo and reinforce it constantly, so that it doesn't weaken over time. And when Anglos have things well in hand, a second image, related to the first, takes its place."

"Which one is that?"

"Oh, it's the hapless, huddled figure who could not possibly be a sexual competitor. John–Michael Rivera writes that Anglos wanted Mexicans deferential, so they discouraged them from looking you in the eye. They taught them to walk in a shuffling gait and to wear loose clothes that allow no sharp definition of the body line. The sombrero, unlike the Texan ten-gallon hat, sat low on the head, limiting the user's horizon, particularly his view up."

"Telling," I said, shaking my head. "And these sexual taboos, do you see evidence of them operating today, as you did for the first component, filth?"

"Everywhere," Rodrigo replied. "Books by nativist writers such as Peter Brimelow, Pat Buchanan, Sam Huntington, Tom Tancredo, and Victor Davis Hanson all call attention to the fast breeding Latino immigrant. They warn of the swamping of superior Anglo genes by those of the swarthy Latinos and blacks."

"And in the current immigration debate," I seconded, "proponents of restrictive policies evoke the specter of a 'flood of immigrants' and our schools and institutions awash in all those new bodies. Some mean-spirited groups such as Federation for American Immigration Reform (FAIR) cite cases, which nobody else can prove or disprove, of immigrant Mexican women who sneak across the border while pregnant in order to give birth in a San Diego parking lot so that the baby will be an American citizen. Once one member of a family is a citizen, these nativists warn, the others will ride piggyback on Junior to gain the benefits of American citizenship themselves. You see this fear of Latino sexuality and reproduction everywhere."

We were both quiet for a moment, while the waiter came to ask if we would like refills of our coffee. We both nodded yes, and he disappeared.

"Are you ready for your third component? It had to do with language, did it not?" I asked.

Jabber

"Yes, it's jabber," Rodrigo replied. "This one holds that the Latinos operate in a different discourse world from ours. Their very language reinforces their exoticism. It sounds funny, with all those trills and rollings of the tongue. Good old-fashioned Americans cannot, of course, speak it, and it's unreasonable to suppose that we should learn it, as opposed to requiring the Mexicans to stop speaking it and use only English. But not only that, their weird language provides a cover for them to make jokes at our expense and leer at our women."

"Although Spanish is a world language with a literature that includes Cervantes, Lope de Vega, and other writers who rival Shakespeare and Byron, narratives and stereotypes put the Spanish speaker on the same plane as a group of uncivilized cannibals sitting around a boiling pot, discussing how to cook the well-meaning Western missionary. Not only that, they come so attached to their strange language that they are unwilling to learn English. They even expect us to provide ballots in Spanish so that they can vote in our elections without taking the trouble to learn our language and read campaign material written in it. Most unfair of them," I added ironically.

"It's not just an irony," Rodrigo added. "It takes on real historical force. For example, few civil rights scholars know that Latinos were lynched in the Southwest."

"They were?"

"Yes, in large numbers, and for many of the same reasons that blacks were—for acting uppity, for romancing Anglo women, and for harboring aspirations to get ahead."

"What do you mean by large numbers? I assume you mean more than one or two."

"Between four and five hundred. That's about one-tenth the number of blacks who were lynched, but the number of Latinos was much smaller, so the proportion is very similar."

"That's amazing," I said. "I had no idea."

"Nor do most people, and the reason is that the main accounts of these lynchings appeared in community newspapers, which were in Spanish. Until Rodolfo Acuña and other Spanish-speaking historians researched these accounts, hardly anyone knew how pervasive lynching of Mexican Americans in the Southwest was."

"And that may be one reason why Anglos, intentionally or not, suppress Spanish speaking among the Latino community and don't want the kids growing up speaking that language. It makes their own history too available to them and increases the chance that they might revolt against the established order. It makes sense," I added.

"Not just that," Rodrigo said. "Reducing the ability of the second generation of Latino immigrant kids to speak Spanish creates a divide between generations, in which the young cannot communicate with their elders. Many Latino histories, stories, legends, and tales...."

"Such as those in the *corridos* that you mentioned earlier," I interjected.

"Indeed. Those and others. Many of those tales are oral and have no written record. They are in danger of being lost if generations cannot communicate with each other. This may be one reason the second generation of Latino kids exhibits such a high dropout rate. They learn English, so that the majority culture is wide open to them, with its stereotypes, TV plots with Latino villains, and other depictions which teach self-hatred. A sensitive Latino child who does not speak Spanish has no defense against this vast cultural brainwash. Language represents continuity, struggle, and ultimately, self-preservation."

"I've read of contemporary attempts to interrupt a thread of Latino storytelling and cultural continuity," I said. "I bet you've seen these cases, too." (Rodrigo looked curious, so I went on). "In Lebanon, Tennessee, a small town whose Latino population had swelled recently, a judge in a custody hearing ordered a Latina mother, Felipa Berrera, to speak English to her 11–year-old daughter or run the risk of losing any connection—legally, morally, and physically—with her forever. Other cases treat mothers who teach their children Spanish as guilty of child abuse."

Rodrigo said, "I remember that case. The mother's native language is Mixtec, and she came from a poor area in central Mexico. Her predicament was more acute than might meet the eye. Once in the United States, Mixtecs rely heavily on their children, not just as babysitters but as interpreters. Taking away Bererra's child not merely traumatizes her as a mother, it also takes away her ability to communicate with the Anglo-speaking world."

"Just as Ngugi and some of the postcolonials you mentioned earlier write," I added. "It reminds me, too, of those record companies who discourage Latino recording artists from performing their music in Spanish. A *New York Times* article I was reading described one artist's capitulation to this regime as a case of 'having arrived.' The article would have done better to describe it as a case of linguistic colonialism, pure and simple."

"It would have," Rodrigo agreed. "But speaking of the postcolonials, do you remember how Rodolfo Acuña suffered criticism at the hands of fellow academics for framing the Latino condition that way?"

"You mean as an internal colony?"

"Right. It just occurred to me a large body of evidence weighs in his favor, namely that Latino people themselves see their situation that way. Not all, of course, but many do."

"You mean in literature, oral traditions, that sort of thing?" I asked.

"Exactly. On the other side of the world, postcolonial writers build on popular traditions. Writers here could do the same."

"Intriguing," I said. "A few black writers, such as Robert Allen, have adopted a postcolonial framework in writing about the black situation. Black Panthers, particularly Eldridge Cleaver, too. And Native American literature, both oral and written, addresses these ideas as well. But I'd love to hear about your Latinos."

A. CULTURE AND THE TREATMENT OF SUBALTERN PEO-PLE

Postcolonial writers in conquered nations describe how the colonial administrators invariably depict the natives as simple, ignorant, and happy with their subordinate condition. For example, Gayatri Spivak, Edward Said, and Reginald Horsman write about various aspects of how Western writers and journalists describe, and continue to describe, domestic minorities as ambitionless and in need of tutelage—or, in the case of Said, strange and exotic. Said points out that the power to narrate is the power to destroy. *Culture and Imperialism* xii (1993). Several writers comment on how the dominant group always paints the colonial power as intelligent, efficient, rational, and enlightened, and the natives as dark, superstitious, and childlike. E.g., John–Michael Rivera, *The Emergence of Mexican America: Recovering Stories of Mexican Peoplehood in U.S. Culture* (2006); Edward W. Said, *Orientalism* (1978); Bhikhu C. Parekh, *Colonialism, Tradition, and Reform: An Analysis of Gandhi's Political Discourse* 40–41 (1989). These stories ease the European's conscience, while communicating to the indigenous person that he is lucky to be governed by such enlightened overlords.

B. LANGUAGE, COLONIAL OR NATIVE

Minorities can be complicit in their own subjugation. In Africa and Hawaii, postcolonial writers such as Ngugi wa Thiong'o, Chinua Achebe, Haunani–Kay Trask, Frantz Fanon, and Trinh Minh-ha point out how the colonial subject forced to speak English or French loses touch with his own people. See *Corrido*, supra, and Part Three: Language Rights, supra.

This happened as well with American Indian, Alaskan Native, and Australian aboriginal children sent to official English-speaking boarding schools. But, these writers say, it can also happen to adults. If a writer such as Ngugi Thiong'o writes in the colonial language (usually French or English), he ends up writing, he says, for an audience that consists, primarily, of the occupying force and their compatriots back in the mother country. He chooses language and issues that resonate with them and their experience. He unconsciously disparages his own people and culture in an effort to reach common ground with his readers. Words like "merit," "responsible government," "progress," "folk medicine," and "tribe" render his own people one down and confirm his readers in their comfortable sense that the invasion did the natives, essentially, a favor.

For example, when Kenyan writer Ngugi criticized the racism of the colonial system, he won praises and prizes, and all his novels were in the school syllabi. But when he started writing in a language understood by the peasants and questioning the very foundations of the imperial system and foreign domination of the Kenyan economy and culture, he was sent to maximum security prison. *The World of Ngugi Wa Thiong'o* 23, 216 (Charles Cantalupo ed., 1993).

As another writer, Trinh T. Minh-ha, put it, "Language is one of the most complex forms of subjugation, being at the same time the locus of power and unconscious servility." See *Woman, Native, Other* 52 (1989). And Chinua Achebe, *Things Fall Apart* 14 (expanded ed. 1996) says that only the traditional tale or story can continue beyond the war and the warrior and "save our progeny from blundering like blind beggars into the spikes of the cactus fence." Id.

Richard Delgado & Jean Stefancic
Understanding Words that Wound
56–57, 63–66 (2004)

THE STRANGE CAREERS OF FOUR SPECIAL WORDS

Spic

As a derogatory word for Mexicans, Mexican Americans, and Puerto Ricans, *spic* is thought to have developed in the early 1900s. Since then, the term has expanded to encompass other Hispanic groups, including Central Americans, South Americans, and Caribbeans. At the end of the 1800s, *spic* was commonly used to describe Italians; perhaps the term grew out of the term spaghetti, a traditional Italian dish. Today, this use is no longer common, making its use for Latinos the dominant one. Another theory holds that *spic* derived from the phrase "No *spic* da Ingles," highlighting early Hispanics' heavy accents. Occasionally, *spic* has also meant the Spanish language. One book gave an example of a person who studies Spanish: "I've had two years of *spic*." Hemingway wrote, "I wish I could talk *spik*.... I don't get any fun out of asking that *spik* questions." No matter the origin, *spic*, like *greaser*, *wetback*, and *beaner*, currently is a highly offensive term for Latinos.

Spic probably came into its current use with the wave of Mexican immigrants entering the United States from the early to mid–1900s. Then, Mexicans were seen as a necessary evil, due to the need for docile servants and cheap labor. One U.S. border patrolman stated, "a lot of fellows got tied with a *spiggity* women.... I married a *spiggity* and I chose her above any dammed white woman. She'll do as she's told—never go out to a show unless I tell her to, and she'll be faithful, too." The border patrolman was not so fond of Mexican men, though. Those other *spics* were used to perform needed labor; they were a rough crowd.

While Latinos originally were welcomed as a source of cheap labor, the 1980s saw a change in American attitudes. White America began to fear that Latinos were taking jobs away from them, even though the jobs that a majority of the newcomers performed were ones that whites would consider below them. The anti-immigration movement gained strength. Racial literature opposing immigration trumpeted, "We need a real border.... We get the Spics.... Deportation—they're all going home." Neutral observers wrote that "[N]on-Hispanics in the United States fear that the country's rapidly growing Hispanic population will not adopt the language, customs, and viewpoint of the dominant, English-speaking culture. Some of these people fear that their way of life will be replaced by the 'foreign ways' of Hispanic Americans." During the redistribution of Philadelphia voting districts in the 1990s, one legislator worried that political power might fall into the hands of the Latino community:

"Look, I'm a white mother fucker from Philadelphia. And I don't want no more ... *Spics* in my district." In the movie *Saturday Night Fever*, the lead character, played by John Travolta, recognized that two Latino dancers should have won a dance contest over him and his partner; they were simply better dancers. Travolta's character commented, "The *spics* should of won."

The fear of Hispanic engulfment has spread to college campuses. At Boston College minority students received e-mails deploring "Monkeys and Apes" and informing them that "BC is for white men ... not *spicks*." Students at UC–Berkeley (Boalt Hall) Law School were called *spics*. Latin American students at Smith College were told that *spics* need to "quit complaining or get out." When Bernhard Goetz shot and killed a group of minority youths who approached him asking for money, his motivation was to "rid his neighborhood of spics...." A New Jersey man was charged with murder after killing a Latino boy as part of a game in which he got points for using his car to "pick off spics...." Before the Columbine High School killings, the infamous teen duo discussed their hatred of *spics* as reason for their actions.

Even Latinos of high status are not immune from name-calling. When television talk show host Geraldo Rivera went to Jonesville, Wisconsin, to tape a Ku Klux Klan rally, a Klansman called him a *spic*. A fight broke out, and both men were arrested.

* * *

RACIAL EPITHETS IN THE WORKPLACE

In the area of employment discrimination, Title VII is the leading federal statute. Title VII, and its state-law equivalents, prohibit discrimination on the basis of race or sex with respect to the "compensation, terms, conditions, or privileges of employment." Under them, employees can sue for discrimination, a hostile work environment, or disparate treatment.

A hostile work environment exists "[w]hen the workplace is permeated with discriminatory intimidation, ridicule, and insult that is sufficiently severe or pervasive to alter the conditions of the victim's employment." Conduct that is "merely offensive" and "not severe or pervasive enough to create an objectively hostile or abusive work environment—an environment that a reasonable person would find hostile or abusive—is beyond Title VII's purview." Title VII "comes into play before the harassing conduct leads to a nervous breakdown."[164] "Harassed employees do not have to be Jackie Robinson, nobly turning the other cheek and remaining unaffected in the face of constant degradation. They are held only to a standard of reasonableness."[165] The use of racial epithets must be so severe that it creates a pervasive environment; language that merely shows disrespect and prejudice is not enough.

164. Harris v. Forklift Sys., Inc., 510 U.S. 17, 21 (1993).

165. Torres v. Pisano, 116 F.3d 625, 631–32 (2d Cir. 1997).

To establish a pervasively hostile atmosphere, a victim must prove more than a few isolated incidents of racial animosity. It must appear either that a single incident was extraordinarily severe, or that a series of incidents was "sufficiently continuous and concerted" to have altered the conditions of her employment. Rarely is one racial epithet enough. In *Risinger v. Ohio Bureau of Workers' Compensation*,[170] the district court had found that being called *chink* on one occasion was not enough to find a hostile work environment. On review, the Sixth Circuit did not disagree, but found that the district made an improper factual finding. The victim had been called *chink* on more than one occasion so that a hostile workplace could be inferred. While no "magic number" of epithets must appear, the use of repeated racial epithets must be sufficiently pervasive to create an abusive milieu. For example, an employee who was referred to as *spic* several times by several employees established a "concerted pattern of harassment" in violation of Title VII.[173]

Where a racial epithet is hurled by a boss or supervisor, courts have been more willing to find a hostile work environment. "Perhaps no single act can more quickly alter the conditions of employment and create an abusive working environment than the use of an unambiguously racial epithet . . . by a supervisor in the presence of his subordinates."[174] A "reasonable Puerto Rican would find a workplace in which her boss repeatedly called her a 'dumb *spic*' and told her that she should stay home, go on welfare, and collect food stamps like the rest of the '*spics*' to be hostile."[175] And, in a major recent decision brought under a state statute similar to Title VII, the California Supreme Court affirmed a finding of discrimination in a case brought by seventeen Latino workers subjected to years of abuse and slurs at the hands of the Avis Corporation and three supervisors. The court also found that imposing liability for hate speech did not violate the First Amendment.[176]

When racial epithets are wielded by fellow employees, liability attaches to employers only if the victim can show that the employer knew or should have known about the harassment and failed to remedy the situation. When an employee complained of being called a *spic* by a fellow employee and the supervisor did nothing, a Title VII violation was found.[178] Of course, when an employee is called *spic* by both fellow employees and supervisors, employer liability is highly likely.[179]

When a racial epithet is not directly targeted at a particular employee, it can still satisfy the requirement of a hostile work environment. "[A] racial epithet need not be directed at a plaintiff in order to contribute to a hostile work environment."[180] Where the term *spic* was

170. 883 F.2d 475, 477 (6th Cir. 1989).

173. Snell v. Suffolk County, 782 F.2d 1094, 1103 (2d Cir. 1986).

174. Rodgers v. Western–Southern Life Ins. Co., 12 F.3d 668, 675 (7th Cir. 1993).

175. Tores, supra note 165, at 632–33.

176. Aguilar v. Avis Rent A Car System, Inc., 21 Cal. 4th 121, 980 P.2d 846, 87 Cal. Rptr. 2d 132 (1999).

178. Miller v. Kenworth of Dothan, 277 F.3d 1269, 1273 (11th Cir. 2002).

179. See Carrero v. New York City Housing Auth., 890 F.2d 569 (2d Cir. 1989).

180. Black v. Zaring Homes, Inc., 104 F.3d 822, 826 (6th Cir. 1997).

used in the presence of a Latina employee, this created a hostile work environment even though the epithet was not directed toward her.[181] Even when the term *chink* was used in front of a black employee, it contributed to a hostile work environment for that worker. But where a fellow employee used the term *kike*, not referring to the plaintiff nor in her presence, no hostile environment was found. "[I]t is a fact of life that social, ethnic, religious, and racial distinction are frequently drawn. The Archie Bunkers of this world, within limitations, still may assert their biased view. We have not yet reached the point where we have taken from individuals the right to be prejudiced, so long as such prejudice does not evidence itself in discrimination."[184] One court went even farther: "[Racial epithets] may provide ventilation for suppressed hostility and fear. Comradeship among soldiers and fellow workers is often based upon insults designed in part to disguise affection."[185]

To prove disparate *treatment* under Title VII, an employee must prove that he or she was subject to a materially adverse employment action (that is, firing, non-hiring, non-promotion) due to intentional discrimination. Intentional discrimination is proven if the employee can show that the action was taken because of the employee's race. Court cases have required more than just the use of racial epithets by a superior to show intent. A plaintiff must show that the discrimination "actually played a role in the employer's decisionmaking process and had a determinative influence on the outcome."[188] Intent was found in a case where an Asian professor was not promoted, and suffered other actions, after a supervisor had stated on a prior occasion, "two *Chinks*" in the pharmacology department are "more than enough." But intent was not found in another firing even though the employee had been called a *wop* by supervisors on numerous occasions. Use of *chink* to refer to an employee was merely a stray remark, "unconnected to the process by which the [plaintiff's] hours and job assignments were controlled."[191]

The courts, on the other hand, have had no problem when an employer punishes an employee for using a racial epithet. Whatever protection such speech has outside the workplace, it does not receive the same protection within it. Allowing otherwise would pose great difficulty for an employer attempting to maintain a non-hostile work environment. See also Part Seven, infra (on employment discrimination).

Notes and Questions

1. For further analysis of hate speech in the workplace, see Part Seven: The Workplace.

181. Collier v. RAM Partners, Inc., 159 F.Supp. 2d 889, 894–95 (D. Md. 2001).

184. Howard v. National Cash Register Co., 388 F.Supp. 603, 606 (S.D. Ohio 1975).

185. Snell v. Suffolk County, 611 F.Supp. 521, 528 (E.D.N.Y. 1985).

188. Reeves v. Sanderson Plumbing Prods., 120 S. Ct. 2097, 2105 (2000).

191. Nyugen v. Dobbs Int'l Services, Inc., 94 F.Supp. 2d 1043, 1049 (W.D. Mo. 2000).

SECTION 2.   MINORITY RESISTANCE (AND NONRESISTANCE) TO RACIAL STEREOTYPING

Tom Kuntz
Adios, Speedy: Not So Fast
N.Y. Times, Week in Review, Apr. 7, 2002, at 3

Ay caramba. The Cartoon Network just can't seem to stay out of the line of fire in the culture wars. Last year it angered Bugs Bunny purists by omitting racially insensitive cartoons from what would have been a complete marathon broadcast of the Wascally Wabbit's oeuvre.

Now it's Speedy Gonzales fans who are hot as jalapenos—over the plucky Mexican mouse's virtual absence from the cable network's broadcasts. In an interesting twist, Hispanics are among those leading the criticism. The Web site HispanicOnline.com, specializing in Latino news and entertainment, has posted articles taking the network to task for what many see as a cave-in to political correctness; the site also offers a link to a bring-back-the-mouse petition drive.

But the Cartoon Network says P.C. isn't the overarching reason the Looney Tunes star is scarce on the channel (not banned, it insists); rather, Speedy shorts don't make the rotation because they simply aren't a ratings winner among the channel's vast archive of more than 8,500 cartoons. Laurie Goldberg, a network spokeswoman, conceded, however, that part of the audience appeal problem is the toons' negative stereotypes—like Speedy's lazy cousin, Slowpoke Rodriguez—and their depictions of drinking and smoking, clear parent turnoffs.

Yet many Hispanics view Speedy as a positive ethnic reflection because he always outsmarts the "greengo" cat Sylvester, says Virginia Cueto, associate editor of the Florida-based HispanicOnline, who has been covering the issue for the English-language site. Noting that Cartoon Network International still shows Speedy regularly in Latin American nations, Ms. Cueto said the network's main concern in the United States "seems to be what non-Latinos would get from watching these cartoons," as if Hispanic preferences here don't matter.

And so people are peeved. Here are excerpts from the overwhelmingly pro-Speedy (and mostly anonymous) postings on HispanicOnline:

THIS is an Outrage!!! Viva la Mouse! Viva Speedy Gonzales!

Come on! What is America coming to? . . . I guess they'll censor "West Side Story" because they've offended us Puerto Ricans in Nueva York. Get a grip! . . . I say bring Speedy back and let those censored idiots eat frijoles!!

Demeaning? Pleeeease, we need to get over the stupid P.C. [expletive]. I am of Mexican parents and I have much better things to do than worry about Speedy G, unless of course he was in my house—then I would get Senor Sylvester to take care of him.

The problem I have with this is that they are basically saying they know better than Hispanics do and telling them they should be offended by Speedy when in fact most are not.

That little mouse is a hero.... How about banning Pepe LePew, for stinking and being French, or Boris and Natasha, for being Russian, or ... Rocky the Flying Squirrel for not being P.C. to squirrels.

What deee hell is all the rucus about. The leeettle mouse is one of the foniest mouses in all of Mejico. I have enjoyed the leeettle mouse and Slooowpoke for many yeeers. Now, weeee have Pokemon and his amigos. Weee need to bring back Speedy! ...

I am 30 years old and have found myself saying, "Arriba, Arriba, Ole, Ole" many times throughout my life. The little guy is in me. I have a small stuffed version of him in the back window of my car as I fly through the Houston highways! ...

I am shocked that this little guy is being questioned over all the other stuff on TV. Give him a break. He's a good, happy, zippy little guy that doesn't beat anyone up, and doesn't have to save the day. He just IS!

If you ask me, the cartoons depict "gringo" society (those crafty American cats ...) as a not-too-bright, conniving species that exploits anyone who happens to be handy. The Mexican mice are always content in their own pueblos, doing their own thing, and here come the gringos into Mexican turf, interfering and looking out for their own interests. And Speedy always wins! So who is being depicted negatively here?

Program note: The Cartoon Network says Speedy Gonzales can be seen on the channel in May, in "Daffy Duck's Fantasy Island." It says it is considering broadcasting Speedy cartoons late at night or on its sister Boomerang channel, which features classic cartoons.

Not all Latinos "laugh it off" when confronted with racial stereotypes and derogatory images. Some fight back. See David G. Garcia, *Remembering Chavez Ravine: Culture Clash and Critical Race Theater*, 26 Chicano–Latino L. Rev. 111 (2006).

Yolanda Broyles–Gonzáles
El Teatro Campesino: Theater in the Chicano Movement
xi, xii, 10, 19–20 (1994)

The numerous social and political struggles of the 1960s and the 1970s—such as the civil rights movement, the United Farm Workers movement, the antiwar movement, and the women's liberation movement—were intimately bound up with a multifaceted cultural renaissance. Perhaps the single most inspirational struggle for Chicanas/os was the David and Goliath standoff between the United Farm Workers Union and the agribusiness giants in California and other states. * * *

One manifestation of that spirit of activism was the Chicana/o theater movement, which spread across the Southwest, the Northwest, and the Midwest in the 1960s and the 1970s. In virtually all centers of Chicana/o population as well as on campuses everywhere, theater groups sprang up dedicated to portraying the life, heritage, and problems of Chicanas/os in this country.

Under the wing of the United Farm Workers Union based in Delano, California, El Teatro Campesino (The Farm Workers' Theater) emerged in 1965, conceived as a union tool for organizing, fund-raising, and politicizing. In its beginnings El Teatro Campesino performed numerous highly improvisational skits (called *actos*), which painted the exploitive living and working conditions of farmworkers in boldly satirical words and actions and underscored the need to unionize against the abuses of agribusiness. In addition to regular performances—often on the backs of flatbed trucks before farmworkers—the group also played college campuses and toured Europe repeatedly. A group viewed and appreciated by farmworkers simply as an effective organizational tool, became, curiously, idolized in intellectual circles and was converted into a Chicano icon for the academy. Today the name Teatro Campesino enjoys almost mythical status, even though the ensemble that established that reputation no longer exists. (El Teatro Campesino, Inc., exists only as a production company.) * * *

The *carpa* [Eds. tent show, often ribald, and forerunner of today's Teatro Campesino] played with full force into the 1950s and the early 1960s, a resilience probably attributable to its native and working-class roots, as well as its ability to speak to the daily reality of Mexican workers in an entertaining manner. This is the world of working-class performance inherited by El Teatro Campesino.

On numerous occasions Luis Valdez and other members of the Teatro Campesino ensemble have affirmed and reaffirmed their roots in the Rasquachi Aesthetic within the Teatro Campesino. ("Rasquachi" is rich in connotations and can be used to express affection or disaffection while referring to something earthy, unpretentious, gaudy, resourceful, etc.) Valdez indicates: "We evolved—in our own earthiness—characters that emerged from Cantinflas and the whole comic Mexican tradition of the carpa, the tent." The performing family of El Circo Escalante made a great impression on the young Valdez. The Escalantes were itinerant artists who at times lived from performance income and at other times from farm labor income. That was to become a model for the early Teatro Campesino.

* * *

Much of the transmission of the Mexican popular performance tradition happened not from the top down, as is often assumed by critics, but from the bottom up. This is evident not only in the collective work mode, which relied on the collective talents of a group, but also in the way farmworker audiences often gave the Teatro performance guidance or feedback. It was the farmworker audience, for example, that demanded of the Teatro Campesino a performance aesthetic foregrounding action. Valdez recalls how the Teatro grew in response to farmworker input: "When we started the Teatro, workers came up to us after performances and said, 'There's not enough action,' so we introduced more slapstick. We use even more slapstick when we perform for Mexican–American farmworkers than when we perform for a middle-class audience in New York." * * *

The human body, memory, and community are intertwined phenomena that came to bear on the carpa and Teatro Campesino oral culture of performance in yet other very significant ways. * * * Within an orally based culture, memory and the body are the sites of a community's self-knowledge. Memory in this context signifies a remembrance of lived experience within a community, usually one's directly lived experience combined with the greater communal historical experience transmitted to youth by elders in oral historical discourse. * * *

* * * Performers relied directly on the memory of the Mexican working-class community's experience within the dominant society. * * * A critical exploration of that social experience lay at the heart of all Teatro Campesino performance work. Teatro Campesino ensemble member Olivia Chumacero commented on the intimate and direct relationship of continuity between the individual's performance work and life experience: "You had to draw from yourself, from where you were coming from. Things came out from you, from what you thought, from where you were coming from, from what you had experienced in life. It was wonderful. It was not a mechanical learning of lines, word for word. Words that someone had put in your mouth. It was your life."

The creation of pieces within the Teatro was a collective process of discussion and improvisation, with the human memory as repository and foundation. The key within this collective process of creation is the body, or physical memory. Within the collective creation process creational faith is vested in the social wisdom of the body, a wisdom that emerges in the process of improvisation. Improvisation in the Mexican oral performance mode entails thinking something through with the body. * * *

* * *

Born of and for the working-class farmworker community, the Teatro Campesino's actos directly enacted the physical sociocultural memory of that community's experience. Memory indeed was the prime conduit for all performance work within El Teatro Campesino. And the power and instrumentality of memory, rooted in the community and in the body, made possible the immediacy, authenticity, and vitality characteristic of the ensemble's work.

Richard Delgado

Storytelling for Oppositionists and Others: A Plea for Narrative
87 Mich. L. Rev. 2411, 2411–22, 2429–40 (1989)

Everyone has been writing stories these days. And I don't just mean writing about stories or narrative theory, important as those are. I mean actual stories, as in "once-upon-a-time" type stories. Derrick Bell has been writing "Chronicles"; others have been writing dialogues, stories, and metastories. Many others have been daring to become more personal in their writing, to inject narrative, perspective, and feeling—how it was for me—into their otherwise scholarly, footnoted articles and, in the case of the truly brave, into their teaching.

Many, but by no means all, who have been telling legal stories are members of what could be loosely described as outgroups, groups whose marginality defines the boundaries of the mainstream, whose voice and perspective—whose consciousness—has been suppressed, devalued, and abnormalized. The attraction of stories for these groups should come as no surprise. For stories create their own bonds, represent cohesion, shared understandings, and meanings. The cohesiveness that stories bring is part of the strength of the outgroup. An outgroup creates its own stories, which circulate within the group as a kind of counter-reality.

The dominant group creates its own stories, as well. The stories or narratives told by the ingroup remind it of its identity in relation to outgroups, and provide it with a form of shared reality in which its own superior position is seen as natural.

The stories of outgroups aim to subvert that ingroup reality. In civil rights, for example, many in the majority hold that any inequality between whites and nonwhites is due either to cultural lag, or inadequate enforcement of currently existing beneficial laws—both of which are easily correctable. For many minority persons, the principal instrument of their subordination is neither of these. Rather, it is the prevailing mindset by means of which members of the dominant group justify the world as it is, that is, with whites on top and browns and blacks at the bottom.

Stories, parables, chronicles, and narratives are powerful means for destroying mindset—the bundle of presuppositions, received wisdoms, and shared understandings against a background of which legal and political discourse takes place. These matters are rarely focused on. They are like eyeglasses we have worn a long time. They are nearly invisible; we use them to scan and interpret the world and only rarely examine them for themselves. Ideology—the received wisdom—makes current social arrangements seem fair and natural. Those in power sleep well at night—their conduct does not seem to them like oppression.

The cure is storytelling (or as I shall sometimes call it, counterstorytelling). As Derrick Bell, Bruno Bettelheim, and others show, stories can shatter complacency and challenge the status quo. Stories told by underdogs are frequently ironic or satiric; a root word for "humor" is *humus*—bringing low, down to earth. Along with the tradition of storytelling in black culture, there exists the Spanish tradition of the picaresque novel or story, which tells of humble folk piquing the pompous or powerful and bringing them down to more human levels.

Most who write about storytelling focus on its community-building functions: stories build consensus, a common culture of shared understandings, and deeper, more vital ethics. Counterstories, which challenge the received wisdom, do that as well. They can open new windows into reality, showing us that there are possibilities for life other than the ones we live. They enrich imagination and teach that by combining elements from the story and current reality, we may construct a new world richer than either alone. Counterstories can quicken and engage conscience. Their graphic quality can stir imagination in ways in which more conventional discourse cannot.

But stories and counterstories can serve an equally important destructive function. They can show that what we believe is ridiculous, self-serving, or cruel. They can show us the way out of the trap of unjustified exclusion. They can help us understand when it is time to reallocate power. They are the other half—the destructive half—of the creative dialectic. Stories and counterstories, to be effective, must be or must appear to be noncoercive. They invite the reader to suspend judgment, listen for their point or message, and then decide what measure of truth they contain. They are insinuative, not frontal; they offer a respite from the linear, coercive discourse that characterizes much legal writing.

* * *

Storytelling and Counterstorytelling

The same object, as everyone knows, can be described in many ways. A rectangular red object on my living room floor may be a nuisance if I stub my toe on it in the dark, a doorstop if I use it for that purpose, further evidence of my lackadaisical housekeeping to my visiting mother, a toy to my young daughter, or simply a brick left over from my patio restoration project. No single true, or all-encompassing description exists. The same holds true of events, especially ones that are racially charged. Often, we will not be able to ascertain the single best description or interpretation of what we have seen. We participate in creating what we see in the very act of describing it.

* * *

How can there be such divergent stories? Why do they not combine? Is it simply that members of the dominant group see the same glass as half full, minorities as half empty? I believe more is at work; stories war with each other. They contend for, tug at, our minds. To see how the dialectic of competition and rejection works—to see the reality-creating potential of stories and the normative implications of adopting one story rather than another—consider the following series of accounts, each describing the same event.

A Standard Event and a Stock Story That Explains It

The following series of stories revolves around the same event: A black (or Latino, or Asian, or Indian) lawyer interviews for a teaching position at a major law school (school X), and is rejected. Any other race-tinged event could have served equally well for purposes of illustration. This particular event was chosen because it occurs on familiar ground—most readers of this chapter are past or present members of a university community who have heard about or participated in events like the one described.

The Stock Story

Setting: A professor and student are talking in the professor's office. Both are white. The professor, Blas Vernier, is tenured, in midcareer, and well regarded by his colleagues and students. The student, Judith Rogers, is a member of the student advisory appointments committee.

Rogers: Professor Vernier, what happened with the minority candidate, John Henry? I heard he was voted down at the faculty meeting yesterday. The students on my committee liked him a lot.

Vernier: It was a difficult decision, Judith. We discussed him for over two hours. I can't tell you the final vote, of course, but it wasn't particularly close. Even some of my colleagues who were initially for his appointment voted against him when the full record came out.

Rogers: But we have no minority professors at all, except for Professor Chen, who is untenured, and Professor Tompkins, who teaches Trial Practice on loan from the district attorney's office once a year.

Vernier: Don't forget Mary Foster, the Assistant Dean.

Rogers: But she doesn't teach, just handles admissions and the placement office.

Vernier: And does those things very well. But back to John Henry. I understand your disappointment. Henry was a strong candidate, one of the stronger blacks we've interviewed recently. But ultimately he didn't measure up. We didn't think he wanted to teach for the right reasons. He was vague and diffuse about his research interests. All he could say was that he wanted to write about equality and civil rights, but so far as we could tell, he had nothing new to say about those areas. What's more, we had some problems with his teaching interests. He wanted to teach peripheral courses, in areas where we already have enough people. And we had the sense that he wouldn't be really rigorous in those areas, either.

Rogers: But we need courses in employment discrimination and civil rights. And he's had a long career with the NAACP Legal Defense Fund and really seemed to know his stuff.

Vernier: It's true we could stand to add a course or two of that nature, although as you know our main needs are in Commercial Law and Corporations, and Henry doesn't teach either. But I think our need is not as acute as you say. Many of the topics you're interested in are covered in the second half of the Constitutional Law course taught by Professor White, who has a national reputation for his work in civil liberties and freedom of speech.

Rogers: But Henry could have taught those topics from a black perspective. And he would have been a wonderful role model for our minority students.

Vernier: Those things are true, and we gave them considerable weight. But when it came right down to it, we felt we couldn't take that great a risk. Henry wasn't on the law review at school, as you are, Judith, and has never written a line in a legal journal. Some of us doubted he ever would. And then, what would happen five years from now when he came up for tenure? It wouldn't be fair to place him in an environment like this. He'd just have to pick up his career and start over if he didn't produce.

Rogers: With all due respect, Professor, that's paternalistic. I think Henry should have been given the chance. He might have surprised us.

Vernier: So I thought, too, until I heard my colleagues' discussion, which I'm afraid, given the demands of confidentiality, I can't share with you. Just let me say that we examined his case long and hard and I am convinced, fairly. The decision, while painful, was correct.

Rogers: So another year is going to go by without a minority candidate or professor?

Vernier: These things take time. I was on the appointments committee last year, chaired it in fact. And I can tell you we would love nothing better than to find a qualified black. Every year, we call the Supreme Court to check on current clerks, telephone our colleagues at other leading law schools, and place ads in black newspapers and journals. But the pool is so small. And the few good ones have many opportunities. We can't pay nearly as much as private practice, you know. [Rogers, who would like to be a legal services attorney, but is attracted to the higher salaries of corporate practice, nods glumly.] It may be that we'll have to wait another few

> years, until the current crop of black and minority law students graduates and gets some experience. We have some excellent prospects, including some members of your very class. I'm sure you know Patricia Maldonado, who is an articles editor on your own journal.

Rogers: [Thinks: I've heard that one before, but says] Well, thanks, Professor. I know the students will be disappointed. But maybe when the committee considers visiting professors later in the season it will be able to find a professor of color who meets its standards and fits our needs.

Vernier: We'll try our best. Although you should know that some of us believe that merely shuffling the few minorities in teaching from one school to another does nothing to expand the pool. And once they get here, it's hard to say no if they express a desire to stay on.

Rogers: [Thinks: That's a lot like tenure. How ironic; there are certain of your colleagues we would love to get rid of, too. But says] Well, thanks, Professor. I've got to get to class. I still wish the vote had come out otherwise. Our student committee is preparing a list of minority candidates that we would like to see considered. Maybe you'll find one or more of them worthy of teaching here.

Vernier: Judith, believe me, there is nothing that would please me more.

In the above dialogue, Professor Vernier's account represents the stock story—the one the institution collectively forms and tells about itself. This story picks and chooses from among the available facts to present a picture of what happened: an account that justifies the world as it is. It emphasizes the school's benevolent motivation ("look how hard we're trying") and good faith. It stresses stability and the avoidance of risks. It measures the candidate of color through the prism of preexisting, well-agreed-upon criteria of conventional scholarship and teaching. Given those standards, it purports to be scrupulously meritocratic and fair; Henry would have been hired had he measured up. No one raises the possibility that the merit criteria employed in judging Henry are themselves debatable, chosen—not inevitable. No one, least of all Vernier, calls attention to the way in which merit functions to conceal the contingent connection between institutional power and the things rated.

The discussion gives little consideration of the possibility that Henry's presence on the faculty might have altered the institution's character, helped introduce a different prism and different criteria for selecting future candidates. The account is highly procedural—it emphasizes that Henry got a full, careful hearing—rather than substantive: a black was rejected. It emphasizes certain "facts" without examining their truth— namely, that the pool is very small, that good minority candidates have many choices, and that the appropriate view is the long view; haste makes waste.

The dominant fact about this first story, however, is its seeming neutrality. It scrupulously avoids issues of blame or responsibility. Race played no part in the candidate's rejection; indeed the school leaned over backwards to accommodate him. A white candidate with similar credentials would not have made it as far as Henry did. The story comforts and soothes. And Vernier's sincerity makes him an effective apologist for his system.

Vernier's story is also deeply coercive, although the coercion is disguised. Judith was aware of it but chose not to confront it directly; Vernier holds all the cards. He pressures her to go along with the institution's story by threatening her prospects at the same time that he flatters her achievements. A victim herself, she is invited to take on and share the consciousness of her oppressor. She does not accept Vernier's story, but he does slip a few doubts through cracks in her armor. The professor's story shows how forceful and repeated storytelling can perpetuate a particular view of reality. Naturally, the stock story is not the only one that can be told. By emphasizing other events and giving them slightly different interpretations, a quite different picture can be made to emerge.

[Following two other stories—the one told by the disappointed candidate himself, and the one told by the judge in his order dismissing John Henry's legal complaint—the discussion continues as follows— *Eds.*]

Al–Hammar X's Counter Story

None of the above stories attempts to unseat the prevailing institutional story. Henry's account comes closest; it highlights different facts and interprets those it does share with the standard account differently. His formal complaint also challenges the school's account, but it must fit itself under existing law, which it failed to do.

A few days after word of Henry's rejection reached the student body, Noel Al–Hammar X, leader of the radical Third World Coalition, delivered a speech at noon on the steps of the law school patio. The audience consisted of most of the black and brown students at the law school, several dozen white students, and a few faculty members. Chen was absent, having a class to prepare for. The Assistant Dean was present, uneasily taking mental notes in case the Dean asked her later on what she heard.

Al–Hammar's speech was scathing, denunciatory, and at times downright rude. He spoke several words that the campus newspaper reporter wondered if his paper would print. He impugned the good faith of the faculty, accused them of institutional if not garden-variety racism, and pointed out in great detail the long history of the faculty as an all-white club. He said that the law school was bent on hiring only white males, "ladies" only if they were well-behaved clones of white males, and would never hire a professor of color unless forced to do so by student pressure or the courts. He exhorted his fellow students not to rest until the law faculty took steps to address its own ethnocentricity and racism. He urged boycotting or disrupting classes, writing letters to the state legislature, withholding alumni contributions, setting up a "shadow" appointments committee, and several other measures that made the Assistant Dean wince.

Al–Hammar's talk received a great deal of attention, particularly from the faculty who were not there to hear it. Several versions of his story circulated among the faculty offices and corridors ("Did you hear what he said?"). Many of the stories-about-the-story were wildly exaggerated. Nevertheless, Al–Hammar's story is an authentic counterstory. It directly challenges—both in its words and tone—the corporate story the law school carefully worked out to explain Henry's non-appointment. It rejects many of the institution's premises, including we-try-so-hard, the-pool-is-so-small, and even mocks the school's meritocratic self-concept. "They say Henry is mediocre, has a pedestrian mind. Well, they ain't sat in none of my classes and listened to themselves. Mediocrity they got. They're experts on mediocrity." Al–Hammar denounced the faculty's excuse making, saying there were dozens of qualified black candidates, if not hundreds. "There isn't that big a pool of Chancellors, or quarterbacks," he said. "But when they need one, they find one, don't they?"

Al–Hammar also deviates stylistically, as a storyteller, from the others, including John Henry. He rebels against the "reasonable discourse" of law. He is angry, and anger is out of bounds in legal discourse, even as a response to discrimination. Judith and John Henry were unsuccessful in getting others to listen. So was Al–Hammar, but for a different reason. His counterstory overwhelmed the audience. More than just a narrative, it was a call to action, a call to join him in destroying the current story. But his audience was not ready to act. Too many of his listeners felt challenged or coerced; their defenses went up. The campus newspaper the next day published a garbled version, saying that he had urged the law faculty to relax its standards in order to provide minority students with role models. This prompted three letters to the editor asking how an unqualified black professor could be a good role model for anyone, black or white.

Moreover, the audience Al–Hammar intended to affect, namely the faculty, was even more unmoved by his counterstory. It attacked them too frontally. They were quick to dismiss him as an extremist, a demagogue, a hothead—someone to be taken seriously only for the damage he might do should he attract a body of followers. Consequently, for the next week the faculty spent much time in one-on-one conversations with "responsible" student leaders, including Judith Rogers.

By the end of the week, a consensus story had formed about Al–Hammar's story. That story-about-a-story held that Al–Hammar had gone too far, that there was more to the situation than Al–Hammar knew or was prepared to admit. Moreover, Al–Hammar was portrayed not as someone who had reached out, in pain, for sympathy and friendship. Rather, he was depicted as a "bad actor," someone with a "chip on his shoulder," someone no responsible member of the law school community should trade stories with. Nonetheless, a few progressive students and faculty members believed Al–Hammar had done the institution a favor by raising the issues and demanding that they be addressed. They were a distinct minority.

The Anonymous Leaflet Counter Story

About a month after Al–Hammar spoke, the law faculty formed a special committee for minority hiring. The committee contained practically every young liberal on the faculty, two of its three female professors, and the Assistant Dean. The Dean announced the committee's formation in a memorandum sent to the law school's ethnic student associations, the student government, and the alumni newsletter, which gave it front-page coverage. It was also posted on bulletin boards around the law school.

The memo spoke about the committee and its mission in serious, measured phrases—"social need," "national search," "renewed effort," "balancing the various considerations," "identifying members of a future pool from which we might draw." Shortly after the memo was distributed, an anonymous four-page leaflet appeared in the student lounge, on the same bulletin boards on which the Dean's memo had been posted, and in various mailboxes of faculty members and law school organizations. Its author, whether student or faculty member, was never identified.

The leaflet was entitled, "Another Committee, Aren't We Wonderful?" It began with a caricature of the Dean's memo, mocking its measured language and high-flown tone. Then, beginning in the middle of the page the memo told, in conversational terms, the following story:

> And so, friends and neighbors [the leaflet continued], how is it that the good law schools go about looking for new faculty members? Here is how it works. The appointments committee starts out the year with a model new faculty member in mind. This mythic creature went to a leading law school, graduated first or second in his or her class, clerked for the Supreme Court, and wrote the leading note in the law review on some topic dealing with the federal courts. This individual is brilliant, personable, humane, and has just the right amount of practice experience with the right firm.

> Schools begin with this paragon in mind and energetically beat the bushes, beginning in September, in search of him or her. At this stage, they believe themselves genuinely and sincerely colorblind. If they find such a mythic figure who is black or Hispanic or gay or lesbian, they will hire this person in a flash. They will of course do the same if the person is white.

By February, however, the school has not hired many mythic figures. Some that they interviewed turned them down. Now, it's late in the year and they have to get someone to teach Trusts and Estates. Although there are none left on their list who are Supreme Court clerks, etc., they can easily find several who are a notch or two below that—who went to good schools, but not Harvard, or who went to Harvard, yet were not first or second in their classes. Still, they know, with a degree verging on certainty, that this person is smart and can do the job. They know this from personal acquaintance with this individual, or they hear it from someone they know and trust. Joe says Bill is really smart, a good lawyer, and will be terrific in the classroom.

So they hire this person because, although he or she is not a mythic figure, functionally equivalent guarantees—namely first-or second-hand experience—assure them that this person will be a good teacher and scholar. And so it generally turns out—the new professor does just fine.

Persons hired in this fashion are almost always white, male, and straight. The reason: We rarely know blacks, Hispanics, women, and gays. Moreover, when we hire the white male, the known but less-than-mythic quantity, late in February, it does not seem to us like we are making an exception. Yet we are. We are employing a form of affirmative action—bending the stated rules so as to hire the person we want.

The upshot is that whites have two chances of being hired—by meeting the formal criteria we start out with in September—that is, by being mythic figures—and also by meeting the second, informal, modified criteria we apply later to friends and acquaintances when we are in a pinch. Minorities have just one chance of being hired—the first.

To be sure, once every decade or so a law school, imbued with crusading zeal, will bend the rules and hire a minority with credentials just short of Superman or Superwoman. And, when it does so, *it will feel like an exception*. The school will congratulate itself—it has lifted up one of the downtrodden. And, it will remind the new professor repeatedly how lucky he or she is to be here in this wonderful place. It will also make sure, through subtle or not-so-subtle means, that the students know so, too.

But (the leaflet continued), there is a coda.

If, later, the minority professor hired this way unexpectedly succeeds, this will produce consternation among his or her colleagues. For, things were not intended to go that way. When he or she came aboard, the minority professor lacked those standard indicia of merit—Supreme Court clerkship, high LSAT score, prep school background—that the majority-race professors had and believe essential to scholarly success.

Yet the minority professor is succeeding all the same—publishing in good law reviews, receiving invitations to serve on important commissions, winning popularity with students. This is infuriating. Many majority-race professors are persons of relatively slender achievements—you can look up their publishing record any time you have five minutes. Their principal achievements lie in the distant past, when aided by their parents' upper class background, they did well in high school and college, and got the requisite test scores on standardized tests which test exactly the accumulated cultural capital they acquired so easily and naturally at home. Shortly after that, their careers started to stagnate. They publish an article every five years or so, often in a minor law review, after gallingly having it turned down by the very review they served on as editor twenty years ago.

So, their claim to fame lies in their early exploits, the badges they acquired up to about the age of twenty-five, at which point the edge they acquired from Mummy and Daddy began to lose effect. Now, along comes the hungry minority professor, imbued with a fierce desire to get ahead, a good intellect, and a willingness to work 70 hours a week if necessary to make up for lost time. The minority person lacks the merit badges awarded early in life, the white professor's main source of security. So, the minority's colleagues don't like it and use perfectly predictable ways to transfer the costs of their discomfort to the misbehaving minority.

So that, my friends, is why minority professors

(i) have a hard time getting hired; and,

(ii) have a hard time if they are hired.

When you and I are running the world, we won't replicate this unfair system, will we? Of course not—unless, of course, it changes us in the process.

This second counterstory attacks the faculty less frontally in some respects—for example it does not focus on the fate of any particular minority candidate, such as Henry, but attacks a general mindset. It employs several devices, including narrative and careful observation—the latter to build credibility (the reader says, "That's right"), the former to beguile the reader and get him or her to suspend judgment (everyone loves a story). The last part of the story is painful; it strikes close to home. Yet the way for its acceptance has been paved by the earlier parts, which paint a plausible picture of events, so that the final part demands consideration. It generalizes and exaggerates—many majority-race professors are not persons of slender achievement. But such broad strokes are part of the narrator's art. The realistically drawn first part of the story, despite shading off into caricature at the end, forces readers to focus on the flaws in the good face the dean attempted to put on events. And, despite its somewhat accusatory thrust, the story, as was mentioned, debunks only a mindset, not a person. Unlike Al–Hammar X's story, it does not call the chair of the appointments committee, a much-loved senior professor, a racist. (But did Al–Hammar's story, confrontational as it was, pave the way for the generally positive reception accorded the anonymous account?)

The story invites the reader to alienate herself or himself from the events described, to enter into the mental set of the teller, whose view is different from the reader's own. The oppositional nature of the story, the manner in which it challenges and rebuffs the stock story, thus causes him or her to oscillate between poles. It is insinuative: At times, the reader is seduced by the story and its logical coherence—it is a plausible counter-view of what happened; it has a degree of explanatory power.

Yet the story places the majority-race reader on the defensive. He or she alternately leaves the storyteller's perspective to return to his or her own, saying, "That's outrageous, I'm being accused of...." The reader thus moves back and forth between two worlds, the storyteller's, which the reader occupies vicariously to the extent the story is well-told and rings true, and his or her own, which he or she returns to and reevaluates in light of the story's message. Can my world still stand? What parts of it remain valid? What parts of the story seem true? How can I reconcile the two worlds, and will the resulting world be a better one than the one with which I began?

Why Outgroups Should Tell Stories and Why Others Should Listen

Subordinated groups have always told stories. Black slaves told, in song, letters, and verse, about their own pain and oppression. They described the terrible wrongs they had experienced at the hands of whites, and mocked (behind whites' backs) the veneer of gentility whites purchased at the cost of the slaves' suffering. Mexican Americans in the Southwest composed *corridos* (ballads) and stories, passed on from generation to generation, of abuse at the hands of gringo justice, the Texas Rangers, and ruthless lawyers and developers who cheated them out of their lands. Native American literature, both oral and written, deals with all these themes as well. Feminist consciousness-raising consists, in part, of the sharing of stories, of tales from personal experience, on the basis of which the group constructs a shared reality about women's status vis-à-vis men.

This proliferation of counterstories is not an accident or coincidence. Oppressed groups have known instinctively that stories are an essential tool to their own survival and liberation. Members of outgroups can use stories in two basic ways: first, as means of psychic self-preservation; and, second, as means of lessening their own subordination. These two means correspond to the two perspectives from which a story can be viewed—that of the teller, and that of the listener. The storyteller gains psychically, the listener morally and epistemologically.

The member of an outgroup gains, first, psychic self-preservation. A principal cause of the demoralization of marginalized groups is self-condemnation. They internalize the images that society thrusts on them—they believe that their lowly position is their own fault. The therapy is to tell stories. By becoming acquainted with the facts of their own historic oppression—with the violence, murder, deceit, co-optation, and connivance that have caused their desperate estate—members of outgroups gain healing. The story need not lead to a violent act; Frantz Fanon was wrong in writing that it is only through exacting blood from the oppressor that colonized people gain liberation. Rather, the story need only lead to a realization of how one came to be oppressed and subjugated. Then, one can stop perpetrating (mental) violence on oneself.

So, stories—stories about oppression, about victimization, about one's own brutalization—far from deepening the despair of the oppressed, lead to healing, liberation, mental health. They also promote group solidarity. Storytelling emboldens the hearer, who may have had the same thoughts and experiences the storyteller describes, but hesitated to give them voice. Having heard another express them, he or she realizes, I am not alone.

Yet, stories help oppressed groups in a second way—through their effect on the oppressor. Most oppression, as was mentioned earlier, does not seem like oppression to those perpetrating it. It is rationalized, causing few pangs of conscience. The dominant group justifies its privileged position by means of stories, stock explanations that construct reality in ways favorable to it. The stories are drastically at odds with the way most people of color would describe their condition. Artfully designed parables, chronicles, allegories, and pungent tales can jar the comfortable dominant complacency that is the principal anchor dragging down any incentive for reform. They can destroy—but the destruction they produce must be voluntary, a type of willing death. Because this is a white-dominated society in which the majority race controls the reins of power, racial reform must include them. Their complacency—born of comforting stories—is a major stumbling block to racial progress. Counterstories can attack that complacency.

What is more, they can do so in ways that promise at least the possibility of success. Most civil rights strategies confront the obstacle of otherness. The dominant group, noticing that a particular effort is waged on behalf of blacks or Latinos, increases its resistance. Stories at times can overcome that otherness, hold that instinctive resistance in abeyance. Stories are the oldest, most primordial meeting ground in human experience. Their allure will often provide the most effective means of overcoming otherness, of forming a new collectivity based on the shared story.

Members of outgroups should tell stories. Why should members of ingroups listen to them? They should listen to stories, of all sorts, in order to enrich their own reality. Reality is not fixed, not a given. Rather, we construct it through conversations, through our lives together. Racial and class-based isolation prevents the hearing of diverse stories and counterstories. It diminishes the conversation through which we create reality, construct our communal lives. Deliberately exposing oneself to counterstories can avoid that impoverishment, heighten "suspicion," and can enable the listener and the teller to build a world richer than either could make alone. On another occasion, the listener will be the teller, sharing a secret, a piece of information, or an angle of vision that will enrich the former teller; and so on dialectically, in a rich tapestry of conversation, of stories. It is through this process that we can overcome enthnocentrism and the unthinking conviction that our way of seeing the world is the only one—that the way things are is inevitable, natural, just, and best—when it is, for some, full of pain, exclusion, and both petty and major tyranny.

Listening to stories makes the adjustment to further stories easier; one acquires the ability to see the world through others' eyes. It can lead the way to new environments. A willing listener is generally "welcomed with open arms." Listening to the stories of outgroups can avoid intellectual apartheid. Shared words can banish sameness, stiffness, and monochromaticity and reduce the felt terror of otherness when hearing new voices for the first time. If we would deepen and humanize ourselves, we must seek out storytellers different from ourselves and afford them the audience they deserve. The benefit will be reciprocal.

La Raza Law Students Association
Letter to Moot Court Honors Program
October 10, 2006

UCLA School of Law
405 Hilgard Avenue, Mailbox 7
Los Angeles, CA 90095

October 10, 2006

Dear Moot Court Honors Program Executive Board,

I write this letter of concern on behalf of the Raza community, as well as other students who have expressed strong concern, in response to the Fall 2006 Moot Court Honors Program Competition.

Moot Court is a unique and important opportunity for law students to obtain experience in appellate brief writing and oral argument. Understanding the influence that Moot Court has in the legal profession, students look forward to the Competition and dedicate themselves to doing well by taking the process very seriously. Unfortunately, this year's Competition incorporates language into a scenario that we find both offensive and as a degradation of the importance of the Moot Court experience.

The 2006–2007 Moot Court Executive Board developed a problem about a man named "El Guapo," a convicted child molester, which the "State of Patron" has filed an indictment against for continuous sexual abuse of a child. The problem includes "facts" such as that the "INS, in their infinite wisdom, chose to deport El Guapo, a convicted child molester, that same week on the condition that El Guapo's sentence for child molestation would be reinstated if El Guapo ever attempted to reenter the United States or was found with its borders" (p. 2). Further, the problem includes the words "Beefeater," to describe a hypothetical port of entry at the U.S./Mexico border, and "Agent Jack Daniels," the name of an INS agent who questions El Guapo.

Law school is a difficult and isolating experience for students in general. But it is even more isolating for students of color being that issues of race and ethnicity are not incorporated into the day-to-day curriculum, and are often times completely ignored. Thus, this fact coupled with the low numbers of students of color on campus, creates a hostile, exclusionary, educational environment. Hence, it is an even greater academic hindrance when such an environment is perpetuated by groups who use negative stereotypes about an ethnic community. Not only is the Mexican illegal immigrant in the Moot Court problem a convicted child molester, but every other fictional term created for this problem are names of well-known brands of liquor (Patron, Jack Daniels, Beefeater).

We believe that the "facts," as written, further criminalize and demonize Latina/o immigrants, and perpetuate the isolating and negatively charged environment in which students are attempting to academically survive within.

This is a blatantly racist and disrespectful display by the Moot Court Executive Board. It is insensitive that the Board would further the stereotype of Latinos (but especially of Mexicans) as lazy drunks who commit criminal acts, as implicated in this fact pattern. The reasonable inference would be that there is an association between Mexicans and drunks. Hence, utilizing such a racially charged fact pattern that perpetuates such negative stereotypes (a "Mexican" being a convicted child molester) adds nothing to this exercise and, in fact, only serves to hurt our communities of color as well as continue to feed racist notions to those who refuse to look past them.

We ask for the following, reasonable, remedies to a situation which truly is a disservice to the entire law school, participants and non-participants alike:

1. A re-written fact pattern removing ethnic identity of the parties involved in this problem

2. A public apology that addresses the use of such insensitive language in the problem

3. Develop a system of review in which the Program and their faculty advisor ensure that a situation, such as this, does not occur while still furthering the interests of the Competition

We look forward to your immediate response. If we do not hear from you by next Tuesday, October 17, 2006, we will take further measures. We thank you, in advance, for taking the time to address this issue.

Martha Casillas and five other officers, UCLA Law Student Associations of Color.

Ediberto Roman
Who Exactly is Living La Vida Loca?: *The Legal and Political
Consequences of Latino–Latina Ethnic and Racial
Stereotypes in Film and Other Media*
4 J. Gender, Race, & Justice 37, 37,
39–47, 49, 53–55, 63–65 (2000)

THE LATIN EXPLOSION

" 'It's big!' they scream. 'It's new!' they yelp. It's the 'Latin Explosion' and it's got everybody 'Livin' La Vida Loca!' " From the covers of national magazines such as *Newsweek, Time, People*, and *George* to *The Oprah Winfrey Show*, popular culture is gushing over the so-called "Latin boom." This boom purportedly signals a change for America.
* * *

* * *

EXPLOSION OR EXPLOITATION

As these headlines purport to depict, the national print media has decided that Latinas and Latinos have somehow arrived! [But have] the media has truly embraced Latinas and Latinos, or simply perpetuated the traditional stereotypes? While a cursory review of these stories and their titles would suggest a Latin renaissance of sorts, a closer examination will reveal otherwise. In fact, this so-called "Latin Boom" appears to be nothing more than a repackaged formula for classic stereotypes. The objectification and commodification of Latinas and Latinos in the Latin Boom continues to support the dominant culture's already skewed perception of this group—little has changed with these new, glitzy high-profile characterizations. Notwithstanding the widespread exposure, Latinas and Latinos are still largely portrayed as one of the following: (1) the hot-blooded sexy character—the macho man or sultry curvy vixen, (2) the gangster or gang-member, who is almost always a drug dealer, (3) the snazzy entertainer, or (4) the immigrant, often an illegal immigrant.

In an effort to recast society's perceptions, I go beyond what some have satirically termed the "Latin Exploitation" in the hopes of reclaiming Latina–Latino identity. I seek to confront the use of the dominant stereotypes in the media as they reinforce a biased and untrue perception of reality. In the same spirit of a number of works on other ethnic imagery, I seek to transform the perception of Latinas and Latinos away from the characteristic stereotypical portrayals.

This piece, however, will not simply expose the insidious stereotypes of Latinas and Latinos. It will undertake the more difficult task of drawing a nexus between the societal prejudice which leads to the stereotyping and the legal and political consequences that result from it. Specifically, I argue that these media images, myths, metaphors, and stereotypes play a critical role in establishing society's vision of Latinas and Latinos. In other words, these stereotypes serve to reinforce both the characterizations of Latinas and Latinos from the perspectives of both the dominant and the dominated. These stereotypes, in turn, foster and perpetuate two insidious and pernicious effects. First, these stereotypes have an external effect on non-members of the group, reinforcing society's perception or label of Latinas and Latinos as "outsider," "foreigner," or "other." This effect in turn fosters individual and institutionalized hatred and violence. A related external effect is that the stereotypes marginalize the group and silence discourse on issues of importance to the group. The second major insidious consequence of stereotyping is the internal effect on the stigmatized. This internal effect attributes a discrediting quality to the victim, which the victim struggles against but may eventually internalize as part of his or her self-image. Thus, the internal effect of stereotyping serves the hegemonic function of having the victim accept his or her negative attributes. The stereotype in essence forces the stigmatized group to reflect those qualities that are being stereotyped.

By examining the sociological, political and legal effects of stigma, I seek to demonstrate that while sticks and stones may break bones, words and labels *can and do* hurt in countless other and equally damaging psychological ways. I propose some solutions to the current portrayals of Latinas and Latinos—solutions, which I hope, will begin a dialogue concerning ways to address and rectify the wrongs of marginalizing and subordinating people of color through stereotyping.

THE PORTRAYAL OF LATINAS AND LATINOS IN FILM

* * *

Five films reveal how the film industry characterizes Latinas and Latinos in common stereotyped roles. The films are among the more popular films that purport to focus on Latinas and Latinos or issues of importance to the group. One of the following four categories is almost always emphasized: hot-blooded lover, gangster, entertainer or immigrant.

The first film examined is the film industry's, and arguably the dominant culture's, version of the Latin American dream. It is a tale of the attainment of great wealth despite a life begun in poverty, a classic "Rags to Riches" story—the film is *Scarface*. It is the story of a Cuban immigrant who flourishes in America, but ironically the title role is played by an Italian–American actor, Al Pacino. What is the key to this immigrant's success? He assassinates other Cubans and Colombians in order to move up the Latin corporate ladder of cocaine drug-dealing. He is the ambitious, hot-tempered, yet terribly romantic, family-oriented drug lord of Miami. He speaks with a Bronx-like accent, not a Spanish one. He kills, but is perplexed by the consequences he must face. Scarface struggles with his unfulfilled love for a blond white woman, who is the widow of his former Latino drug boss, whom Scarface killed. Scarface's right-hand man is the love-struck, hot-blooded, Cuban pretty boy, Manny Rivera, played by the only leading actor in the movie who is actually Cuban. Manny fails to protect Scarface in their first drug deal because he is busy talking to and touching a blond white woman in a bikini. Manny's fall occurs when he is smitten with Scarface's virginal sister Gina, who in the initial scene of the film is almost child-like, but who next appears in a nightclub having sex in the men's bathroom. Manny loves Gina; they get married. Scarface is jealous and kills Manny. Gina, in a fit of anger, attempts to seduce Scarface before she tries to shoot him. Unlike most classic American love stories, Scarface ends with blood, gore, cocaine, and murder.

The next film is a Latin film about redemption—a story of forgiveness and of change. *Carlito's Way*, set in the 1970's, is about a Puerto Rican who wants to own a car rental establishment, who is again played again by Al Pacino. The film is purportedly set in Spanish Harlem, on streets filled with stickball players and dancing fools. Carlos Brigand, a.k.a. Carlito, is an ex-con and former heroin dealer known as the "J.P. Morgan of Smack," but is somehow now impoverished. In one of the first scenes, Carlito meets the new kingpin, Rolando, who is, of course, a Latino. Carlito then has a reunion with his cousin, who is an ambitious drug dealer's assistant, "mule" or gofer. Carlito's naive cousin is killed by other Latinos in a drug deal. During that drug deal gone wrong, although initially unarmed, Carlito kills the four Latinos who killed his cousin. Carlito's right-hand man is Pachanga, an untrustworthy Latino criminal, who eventually betrays Carlito. There are other Latinos in the film, including Sasso, who is a club owner and compulsive gambler.

As with other Latinos in Hollywood, Carlito is also a romantic, who is in love with none other than a blond white woman. Carlito attempts to ride off into the sunset, but is killed by Benny Blanco, the new up-and-coming young drug dealer, who is, of course, Latino. Carlito's death is portrayed as inconsequential, because with the next hot-blooded Latino on the way, the stereotypical life of the Latino drug dealer continues.

Hollywood does not exclude Latinas. A popular film on Latina issues and Latina friendship is *Mi Vida Loca*. The title is not about Ricky Martin's song but a story of a group of Latinas' love and friendship. It is Hollywood's Latin version of *The Joy Luck Club*. Of course, however, the story revolves around Latina gang members. It is set in Echo Park, Los Angeles, California. While the story is truly about the Echo Park *Locas*, a Latina gang, the film claims that the most important character is *Suavecito*, a low-rider truck! In this tale, the lead is Sad Girl, a gang member, who fights another gang member and former best friend, Mousey, over the affection of Ernesto, otherwise known as Bullet, the father of both women's newborn babies. The women eventually bond because their love interest is killed in a drug deal. The women are later mentored by Giggles, who was the first "homegirl" to be incarcerated and who shocks the other homegirls by announcing that she's getting a job. This movie again confirms "mainstream" America's stereotypes about Latina and Latino urban gang life.

* * *

While some of these films have extremely powerful performances, films such as *American Me* nonetheless depict a series of stigmatizing portrayals. It is in light of these portrayals that a series of questions arise. Why are young Latinos virtually always depicted as gang members or drug dealers? Why do Latinos always fall in love with blond white women? Why are Latinas always so hot-blooded? Why are Latinos always love struck? These questions for the filmmakers could go on and on, but a couple of questions for the reader may be appropriate at this point: How many Latinas and Latinos have you met? How many were gang members, drug dealers, entertainers, or hot-blooded for that matter?

* * *

Stigma, Myths, and Stereotyping

In *Stigma,* sociologist Erving Goffman notes that "society establishes the means of categorizing persons and the complement of attributes felt to be ordinary and natural for members of each of these categories." He observes that the term "stigma" is an attribute of the stigmatized that is deeply discrediting. Labeling a person with a stigma signifies that that person "is not quite human." Through the assignment of stigma to certain groups, society exercises a variety of discriminatory practices, which effectively, and often subconsciously, reduce the life chances of the stigmatized persons. According to stigma theory, society constructs an ideology to explain the stigmatized group's inferiority and rationalize society's animosity towards it, animosity which is based on the differences highlighted by the stigma. The stigmatizing perspective subtly invites the viewer—society—to justify the stigmatizing viewpoint as "natural, universal, and beyond challenge"; it marginalizes other perspectives to bolster its own legitimacy in defining narratives and images. Likewise, to stereotype is to impose a trait or characterization that may be true of some members of a group upon all member of the group. Thus, both stigma and stereotype have the effect of promoting discrediting attributes as reality.

* * *

The Insidious and Pernicious Legal and Political Effects of Stereotyping

A.   The External Effects

Why should we be concerned with stereotypes? We need to be concerned about stereotypes because of their insidious and pernicious effects. These effects are both external, which affect societal perceptions, and internal, which affect the self-perception of those stigmatized. The first of the two primary concerns addressed here is that stereotypes directly effect society's perception of Latinas and Latinos. This is what I call the external effect. This outward effect of stereotyping perpetuates the presumption that Latinas and Latinos are outsiders, members of a community that is something other than American. As a result these outsiders are labeled as foreign and are to be treated differently than the rest of Americans. * * *

        * * *

This stereotyping of Puerto Ricans and Filipinos was not limited to Congressional debate. Scholars also contributed to the xenophobia. In a series of articles published in the *Harvard Law Review*, this fear of foreigners prevailed. One writer noted:

> Our Constitution was made by a civilized and educated people. It provides guaranties of personal security which seem ill adapted to the conditions of society that prevail in many parts of our new possessions. To give the half-civilized Moros of the Philippines, or the ignorant and lawless brigands that infest Puerto Rico, or even the ordinary Filipino of Manila, the benefit of such immunities ... would ... be a serious obstacle to the maintenance there of an efficient government.

Another writer argued that "[w]hat was appropriate in the case of some territories might not be in other cases. A cannibal island and the Northwest territory would require different treatment." Eventually these concerns and other more legitimate ones led Congress to decide to treat the two territories differently. The Jones Act of 1916 promised independence to the Philippines, and the Jones Act of 1917 granted a subordinated form of U.S. citizenship to the people of Puerto Rico.

Recent manifestations of the foreigner label is evidenced by the English-only movement. This movement is championed by an organization called U.S. English, whose goal is to establish English as this nation's official language. According to this group, the decline of English and the ascent of other languages results from a failure to assimilate. They believe that the ability to speak English is proof of one's loyalty to this country. As Professor Martinez has observed, if a person, including a Latina or Latino, fails to speak English that person has not assimilated and is therefore necessarily disloyal. Professor Perea similarly concluded that "official English is a movement fueled by prejudice and fear directed at Hispanics."

Other characterizations of the outsider or foreigner have also had the external effect of justifying individual and institutionalized violence. Two recent individualized race-based murders of Asian–Americans were justified by the murderers because the victims were "chinks," "Viet Cong," or "Vietnamese." * * *

        * * *

B.   *The Internal Effect*

The second major legal and political consequence of stereotyping is its effect on the stigmatized or stereotyped. This is what I describe as the internal effect. Here, stereotyping serves the hegemonic function of having the stigmatized accept the stigma. In his book on stigma, Erving Goffman observes that while the stigmatized individual tends to hold the same beliefs about identity that we do, "he may perceive, usually quite correctly, that whatever others profess, they do not really 'accept' him and are not ready to make contact with him on 'equal grounds.'" More importantly, Goffman notes that the stigmatized may even begin to accept the discrediting quality of the stigma. The stigmatized:

> has incorporated from the wider society [the standards that] equip him to be intimately [aware] of what others see as his failing, inevitably causing him, if only for moments, to agree that he does indeed fall short of what he really ought to be. Shame becomes a central possibility, arising from the individual's perception of one of his own attributes as being a defiling thing to possess, and one he can readily see himself as not possessing.

The role that stereotyping has on minorities' self-image is well documented. In 1967, President Lyndon B. Johnson appointed Illinois Governor Otto Kerner to head a Commission to investigate, among other things, the way in which the white media depicted minorities in its coverage of the civil disturbances during the 1960s. The Kerner Commission concluded that the media failed to depict the frustrations of minorities that engaged in the disturbances. In 1970, the United States Commission on Civil Rights concluded that racism resulted in the pervasive "perception of Whites as the only normal Americans." In 1977, the United States Civil Rights Commission recognized the role television played in forming such perceptions, and conducted a study of the portrayal of minorities on network television. The study concluded that when minorities were depicted on television they were usually shown in "token or stereotyped roles." Two years later, the Commission concluded in another study that racial stereotyping had in some instances "actually intensified." A 1993 study by an Advisory Committee to the U.S. Civil Rights Commission concluded that the unfair portrayal of minorities in electronic and print media has produced negative self-images for people of color. Recent articles have argued that stereotypical portrayals of minorities in the media serve to reinforce negative beliefs minorities hold about themselves. "The overwhelming research literature suggests that media distortions that negatively impact the self-esteem of African–American children may preclude them from achieving self-actualization or 'impede their ability to realize their personal and academic potential in American society.'"

The effect of stereotyping on the stigmatized can be aptly characterized as the success of white hegemony. Nineteenth century social and political theorist Antonio Gramsci defined hegemony as "the 'spontaneous' consent given by the great masses of the population to the general direction imposed on social life by the dominant fundamental group." "A dominant culture enjoys [the fruits of] hegemony when the dominant culture's point of view becomes 'common sense' to both the dominant and subordinated groups." Under hegemonic conditions, the subordinate groups 'wear their chains willingly.' Condemned to perceive reality through the conceptual spectacle of the ruling class, they are unable to recognize the nature and extent of their own servitude. Hegemony creates scenarios where opposition and difference are co-opted rather than silenced, and often modified and stripped of their critical content, thereby leaving the subordinate group in the same, if not worse, situation and continues the cycle of stigmatization.

Notes and Questions

1.   Can minorities effectively "talk back" to the system of media images that paint them in derogatory terms? How?

2.   Can minority celebrities like Spike Lee, Ricky Martin, and Cheech make a difference?

3.   What about sly, ironic theatre and stories that mock the prevailing majoritarian myths and images? Are they more effective than protest or efforts to pressure the media to change their tune?

4.   What about law school exams and Moot Court problems with stereotypical racial characters? Should law students (including whites) protest, as the UCLA students did? Or should they "laugh it off" rationalizing, perhaps, that they have more important things to do?

5.   Has the war on terror increased the virulence of ethnic stereotyping, even for non-Arabs and non-Muslims? See Steven W. Bender, *Sight, Sound, and Stereotype: The War on Terrorism and its Consequences for Latinas/os*, 81 Ore. L. Rev. 1153 (2002), noting that recently, nativists and some media representatives have begun to suggest that Latino immigrants may be a terrorist threat—even though only one Latino (Jose Padilla) has ever been charged with terrorism, Latin America has a very small Muslim population, and most terrorists to date have been well funded people who do not have to cross a burning desert to reach their target.

6.   For the view that the construction of Latino criminality, in the face of all the evidence that Latinos are a basically law-abiding group, amounts to state violence, see Mary Romero, *State Violence, and the Social and Legal Construction of Latino Criminality: From El Bandido to Gang Member*, 78 Denv. U. L. Rev. 1081 (2001).

7.   Delgado's *"Storytelling"* article contains a counterplay about the hiring of a black man. How would the account have gone if John Henry had been Juan Gonzales, a Latino candidate?

Chapter 17

HATE SPEECH AGAINST LATINOS/AS

SECTION 1. TYPES OF HATE SPEECH

Hate speech can be general—as in a racist tract or book, or a speech to a crowd—or targeted more narrowly to a single individual or small group. When the latter happens, does the legal system offer any redress?

Richard Delgado
Words That Wound: A Tort Action for Racial
Insults, Epithets, and Name–Calling
17 Harv. C.R.-C.L. L. Rev. 133, 133–40,
143–46, 148–49, 179–81 (1982)

In *Contreras v. Crown Zellerbach Corp.* the Washington Supreme Court held that a Mexican American's allegations that fellow employees had subjected him to a campaign of racial abuse stated a claim against his employer for the tort of outrage. The plaintiff alleged that he had suffered "humiliation and embarrassment by reason of racial jokes, slurs and comments" and that the defendant's agents and employees had wrongfully accused him of stealing the employer's property, thereby preventing him from gaining employment and holding him up to public ridicule. Focusing upon the alleged racial abuse, the court declared that "racial epithets which were once part of common usage may not now be looked upon as 'mere insulting language.' "

Eleven months later, the United States Court of Appeals for the Seventh Circuit in *Collin v. Smith* affirmed a federal district court's decision declaring unconstitutional certain ordinances of the Village of Skokie, Illinois, which had been drafted to block a demonstration by members of the National Socialist Party of America. The village argued that the demonstration, together with the intended display of Nazi uniforms and swastikas, would inflict psychological trauma on its many Jewish citizens, some of whom had lived through the Holocaust. The court of appeals acknowledged that "many people would find [the] demonstration extremely mentally and emotionally disturbing." Men-

593

tioning *Contreras*, the court also noted that Illinois recognizes the "new tort" of intentional infliction of severe emotional distress, which might well include the uttering of racial slurs. Nevertheless, the threat of criminal penalties imposed by the ordinance was held impermissibly to abridge the plaintiffs' First Amendment rights.

The concatenation of these two cases and the unsettled condition in which *Collin* leaves tort actions for racial speech suggest that reappraisal of these tort actions is in order. * * *

American society remains deeply afflicted by racism. Long before slavery became the mainstay of the plantation society of the antebellum South, Anglo–Saxon attitudes of racial superiority left their stamp on the developing culture of colonial America. Today, over a century after the abolition of slavery, many citizens suffer from discriminatory attitudes and practices, infecting our economic system, our cultural and political institutions, and the daily interactions of individuals. The idea that color is a badge of inferiority and a justification for the denial of opportunity and equal treatment is deeply ingrained.

The racial insult remains one of the most pervasive channels through which discriminatory attitudes are imparted. Such language injures the dignity and self-regard of the person to whom it is addressed, communicating the message that distinctions of race are distinctions of merit, dignity, status, and personhood. Not only does the listener learn and internalize the messages contained in racial insults, these messages color our society's institutions and are transmitted to succeeding generations.

The psychological harms caused by racial stigmatization are often much more severe than those created by other stereotyping actions. Unlike many characteristics upon which stigmatization may be based, membership in a racial minority can be considered neither self-induced, like alcoholism or prostitution, nor alterable. Race-based stigmatization is, therefore, "one of the most fruitful causes of human misery. Poverty can be eliminated—but skin color cannot." The plight of members of racial minorities may be compared with that of persons with physical disfigurements; the point has been made that

> [a] rebuff due to one's color puts [the victim] in very much the situation of the very ugly person or one suffering from a loathsome disease. The suffering . . . may be aggravated by a consciousness of incurability and even blameworthiness, a self-reproaching which tends to leave the individual still more aware of his loneliness and unwantedness.

The psychological impact of this type of verbal abuse has been described in various ways. Kenneth Clark has observed, "Human beings . . . whose daily experience tells them that almost nowhere in society are they respected and granted the ordinary dignity and courtesy accorded to others will, as a matter of course, begin to doubt their own worth." Minorities may come to believe the frequent accusations that they are lazy, ignorant, dirty, and superstitious. "The accumulation of negative images ... present[s] them with one massive and destructive choice: either to hate one's self, as culture so systematically demand[s], or to have no self at all, to be nothing.''

The psychological responses to such stigmatization consist of feelings of humiliation, isolation, and self-hatred. Consequently, it is neither unusual nor abnormal for stigmatized individuals to feel ambivalent about their self-worth and identity. This ambivalence arises from the stigmatized individual's awareness that others perceive him or her as falling short of societal standards, standards which the individual has adopted. Stigmatized individuals thus often are hypersensitive and anticipate pain at the prospect of contact with "normals." It is no surprise, then, that racial stigmatization injures its victims' relationships with others. Racial tags deny minority individuals the possibility of neutral behavior in cross-racial contacts, thereby impairing the victims' capacity to form close interracial relationships. Moreover, the psychological responses of self-hatred and self-doubt unquestionably affect even the victims' relationships with members of their own group.

The psychological effects of racism may also result in mental illness and psychosomatic disease. The affected person may react by seeking escape through alcohol, drugs, or other kinds of anti-social behavior. * * * The achievement of high socioeconomic status does not diminish the psychological harms caused by prejudice. The effort to achieve success in business and managerial careers exacts a psychological toll even among exceptionally ambitious and upwardly mobile members of minority groups. Furthermore, those who succeed "do not enjoy the full benefits of their professional status within their organizations, because of inconsistent treatment by others resulting in continual psychological stress, strain, and frustration." As a result, the incidence of severe psychological impairment caused by the environmental stress of prejudice and discrimination is not lower among minority group members of high socioeconomic status.

One of the most troubling effects of racial stigmatization is that it may affect parenting practices among minority group members, thereby perpetuating a tradition of failure. A recent study of minority mothers found that many denied the real significance of color in their lives, yet were morbidly sensitive to matters of race. Some, as a defense against aggression, identified excessively with whites, accepting whiteness as superior. Most had negative expectations concerning life's chances. Such self-conscious, hypersensitive parents, preoccupied with the ambiguity of their own social position, are unlikely to raise confident, achievement-oriented, and emotionally stable children.

In addition to these long-term psychological harms of racial labeling, the stresses of racial abuse may have physical consequences. Evidence suggests that high blood pressure is associated with inhibited, constrained, or restricted anger, and that insults produce elevation in blood pressure. American blacks have higher blood pressure levels and higher morbidity and mortality rates from hypertension, hypertensive disease, and stroke than do white counterparts. Further, there exists a strong correlation between degree of darkness of skin for blacks and level of stress felt, a correlation that may be caused by the greater discrimination experienced by dark-skinned blacks.

In addition to such emotional and physical consequences, racial stigmatization may damage a victim's pecuniary interests. The psychological injuries severely handicap the victim's pursuit of a career. The person who is timid, withdrawn, bitter, hypertense, or psychotic will almost certainly fare poorly in employment settings. An experiment in which blacks and whites of similar aptitudes and capacities were put into a competitive situation found that the blacks exhibited defeatism, half-hearted competitiveness, and "high expectancies of failure." For many minority group members, the equalization of such quantifiable variables as salary and entry level would be an insufficient antidote to defeatist attitudes because the psychological price of attempting to compete is unaffordable; they are "programmed for failure." Additionally, career options for the victims of racism are closed off by institutional racism— the subtle and unconscious racism in schools, hiring decisions, and the other practices which determine the distribution of social benefits and responsibilities.

Unlike most of the actions for which tort law provides redress to the victim, racial labeling and racial insults directly harm the perpetrator. Bigotry harms the individuals who harbor it by reinforcing rigid thinking, thereby dulling their moral and social senses and possibly leading to a "mildly ... paranoid" mentality. There is little evidence that racial slurs serve as a "safety valve" for anxiety which would otherwise be expressed in violence. * * *

    * * *

The Harms of Racial Insults

Immediate mental or emotional distress is the most obvious direct harm caused by a racial insult. Without question, mere words, whether racial or otherwise, can cause mental, emotional, or even physical harm to their target, especially if delivered in front of others or by a person in a position of authority. Racial insults, relying as they do on the unalterable fact of the victim's race and on the history of slavery and race discrimination in this country, have an even greater potential for harm than other insults.

Although the emotional damage caused is variable and depends on many factors, only one of which is its outrageousness, a racial insult is always a dignitary affront, a direct violation of the victim's right to be treated respectfully. Our moral and legal systems recognize the principle that individuals are entitled to treatment that does not denigrate their humanity through disrespect for their privacy or moral worth. This ideal occupies a high place in our traditions, finding expression in such principles as universal suffrage, the prohibition against cruel and unusual punishment, the protection of the Fourth Amendment against unreasonable searches, and the abolition of slavery. A racial insult is a serious transgression of this principle because it derogates by race, a characteristic central to one's self-image.

The wrong of this dignitary affront consists of the expression of a judgment that the victim of the racial slur is entitled to less than that to which all other citizens are entitled. Verbal tags provide a convenient means of categorization so that individuals may be treated as members of a class and assumed to share all the negative attitudes imputed to the class. They thus make it easier for their users to justify their own superior position with respect to others. Racial insults also serve to keep the victim compliant. Such dignitary affronts are certainly no less harmful than others recognized by the law. Clearly, a society whose public law recognizes harm in the stigma of separate but equal schooling and the potential offensiveness of the required display of a state motto on automobile license plates, and whose private law sees actionable conduct in an unwanted kiss or the forcible removal of a person's hat, should also recognize the dignitary harm inflicted by a racial insult.

The need for legal redress for victims also is underscored by the intentionality of racial insults. This intentionality is obvious: What other purpose could the insult serve? There can be little doubt that the dignitary affront of racial insults, except perhaps those that are overheard, is intentional and therefore most reprehensible. Most people today know that certain words are offensive and only calculated to wound. No other use remains for such words as "nigger," "wop," "spick," or "kike."

In addition to the harms of immediate emotional distress and infringement of dignity, racial insults inflict psychological harm upon the victim. Racial slurs may cause long-term emotional pain because they draw upon and intensify the effects of the stigmatization, labeling, and disrespectful treatment that the victim has previously undergone. Social scientists who have studied the effects of racism have found that speech that communicates low regard for an individual because of race "tends to create in the victim those very traits of 'inferiority' that it ascribes to him." Moreover, "even in the absence of more objective forms of discrimination—poor schools, menial jobs, and substandard housing—traditional stereotypes about the low ability and apathy of Negroes and other minorities can operate as 'self-fulfilling prophecies.' " These stereotypes, portraying members of a minority group as stupid, lazy, dirty, or untrustworthy, are often communicated either explicitly or implicitly through racial insults.

* * *

It is, of course, impossible to predict the degree of deterrence a cause of action in tort would create. But "for most people living in racist societies racial prejudice is merely a special kind of convenient rationalization for rewarding behavior." In other words, in racist societies "most members of the dominant group will exhibit both prejudice and discrimination," but only in conforming to social norms. Thus, "when social pressures and rewards for racism are absent, racial bigotry is more likely to be restricted to people for whom prejudice fulfills a psychological 'need.' In such a tolerant milieu prejudiced persons may even refrain from discriminating behavior to escape social disapproval." Increasing the cost of racial insults thus would certainly decrease their frequency. Laws will never prevent violations altogether, but they will deter "whoever is deterrable."

Because most citizens comply with legal rules, and this compliance in turn "reinforce[s] their own sentiments toward conformity," a tort action for racial insults would discourage such harmful activity through the teaching function of the law. The establishment of a legal norm "creates a public conscience and a standard for expected behavior that check overt signs of prejudice." Legislation aims first at controlling only the acts that express undesired attitudes. But "when expression changes, thoughts too in the long run are likely to fall into line." "Laws ... restrain the middle range of mortals who need them as a mentor in molding their habits." Thus, "If we create institutional arrangements in which exploitative behaviors are no longer reinforced, we will then succeed in changing attitudes [that underlie these behaviors]." Because racial attitudes of white Americans "typically follow rather than precede actual institutional [or legal] alteration," a tort for racial slurs is a promising vehicle for the eradication of racism.

     * * *

ELEMENTS OF THE CAUSE OF ACTION

In order to prevail in an action for a racial insult, the plaintiff should be required to prove that

> language was addressed to him or her by the defendant that was intended to demean through reference to race; that the plaintiff understood as intended to demean through reference to race; and that a reasonable person would recognize as a racial insult.

Thus, it would be expected that an epithet such as "You damn nigger" would almost always be found actionable, as it is highly insulting and highly racial. However, an insult such as "You incompetent fool," directed at a black person by a white, even in a context which made it highly insulting, would not be actionable because it lacks a racial component. "Boy," directed at a young black male, might be actionable, depending on the speaker's intent, the hearer's understanding, and whether a reasonable person would consider it a racial insult in the particular context. "Hey, nigger," spoken affectionately between black persons and used as a greeting, would not be actionable. An insult such as "You dumb honkey," directed at a white person, could be actionable under this formulation of the cause of action, but only in the unusual situations where the plaintiff would suffer harm from such an insult.

The plaintiff may be able to show aggravating circumstances, such as abuse of a position of power or authority or knowledge of the victim's susceptibility to racial insults, which may render punitive damages appropriate. The common law defenses of privilege and mistake may be applicable, and retraction of the insult may mitigate damages.

Virginia v. Black
538 U.S. 343 (2003)

In this case we consider whether the Commonwealth of Virginia's statute banning cross burning with "an intent to intimidate a person or group of persons" violates the First Amendment. We conclude that while a State, consistent with the First Amendment, may ban cross burning carried out with the intent to intimidate, the provision in the Virginia statute treating any cross burning as *prima facie* evidence of intent to intimidate renders the statute unconstitutional in its current form.

I

Respondents Barry Black, Richard Elliott, and Jonathan O'Mara were convicted separately of violating Virginia's cross-burning statute, § 18.2–423. That statute provides:

> It shall be unlawful for any person or persons, with the intent of intimidating any person or group of persons, to burn, or cause to be burned, a cross on the property of another, a highway or other public place. Any person who shall violate any provision of this section shall be guilty of a Class 6 felony.

> Any such burning of a cross shall be *prima facie* evidence of an intent to intimidate a person or group of persons.

On August 22, 1998, Barry Black led a Ku Klux Klan rally in Carroll County, Virginia. Twenty-five to thirty people attended this gathering, which occurred on private property with the permission of the owner, who was in attendance. The property was located on an open field just off Brushy Fork Road (State Highway 690) in Cana, Virginia.

When the sheriff of Carroll County learned that a Klan rally was occurring in his county, he went to observe it from the side of the road. During the approximately one hour that the sheriff was present, about 40 to 50 cars passed the site, a "few" of which stopped to ask the sheriff what was happening on the property. Eight to ten houses were located in the vicinity of the rally. Rebecca Sechrist, who was related to the owner of the property where the rally took place, "sat and watched to see what [was] going on" from the lawn of her in-laws' house. She looked on as the Klan prepared for the gathering and subsequently conducted the rally itself.

During the rally, Sechrist heard Klan members speak about "what they were" and "what they believed in." The speakers "talked real bad about the blacks and the Mexicans." One speaker told the assembled gathering that "he would love to take a .30/.30 and just randomly shoot the blacks." The speakers also talked about "President Clinton and Hillary Clinton," and about how their tax money "goes to ... the black people." Sechrist testified that this language made her "very . . . scared."

At the conclusion of the rally, the crowd circled around a 25–to 30– foot cross. The cross was between 300 and 350 yards away from the road. According to the sheriff, the cross "then all of a sudden . . . went up in a flame." As the cross burned, the Klan played *Amazing Grace* over the loudspeakers. Sechrist stated that the cross burning made her feel "awful" and "terrible."

When the sheriff observed the cross burning, he informed his deputy that they needed to "find out who's responsible and explain to them that they cannot do this in the State of Virginia." The sheriff then went down the driveway, entered the rally, and asked "who was responsible for burning the cross." Black responded, "I guess I am because I'm the head of the rally." The sheriff then told Black, "[T]here's a law in the State of Virginia that you cannot burn a cross and I'll have to place you under arrest for this."

Black was charged with burning a cross with the intent of intimidating a person or group of persons, in violation of § 18.2–423. At his trial, the jury was instructed that "intent to intimidate means the motivation to intentionally put a person or a group of persons in fear of bodily harm. Such fear must arise from the willful conduct of the accused rather than from some mere temperamental timidity of the victim." The trial court also instructed the jury that "the burning of a cross by itself is sufficient evidence from which you may infer the required intent." When Black objected to this last instruction on First Amendment grounds, the prosecutor responded that the instruction was "taken straight out of the [Virginia] Model Instructions." The jury found Black guilty, and fined him $2,500. The Court of Appeals of Virginia affirmed Black's conviction.

On May 2, 1998, respondents Richard Elliott and Jonathan O'Mara, as well as a third individual, attempted to burn a cross on the yard of James Jubilee. Jubilee, an African–American, was Elliott's next-door neighbor in Virginia Beach, Virginia. Four months prior to the incident, Jubilee and his family had moved from California to Virginia Beach. Before the cross burning, Jubilee spoke to Elliott's mother to inquire about shots being fired from behind the Elliott home. Elliott's mother explained to Jubilee that her son shot firearms as a hobby, and that he used the backyard as a firing range.

On the night of May 2, respondents drove a truck onto Jubilee's property, planted a cross, and set it on fire. Their apparent motive was to "get back" at Jubilee for complaining about the shooting in the backyard. Respondents were not affiliated with the Klan. The next morning, as Jubilee was pulling his car out of the driveway, he noticed the partially burned cross approximately 20 feet from his house. After seeing the cross, Jubilee was "very nervous" because he "didn't know what would be the next phase," and because "a cross burned in your yard . . . tells you that it's just the first round."

Elliott and O'Mara were charged with attempted cross burning and conspiracy to commit cross burning. O'Mara pleaded guilty to both counts, reserving the right to challenge the constitutionality of the cross-burning statute. The judge sentenced O'Mara to 90 days in jail and fined him $2,500. The judge also suspended 45 days of the sentence and $1,000 of the fine.

At Elliott's trial, the judge originally ruled that the jury would be instructed "that the burning of a cross by itself is sufficient evidence from which you may infer the required intent." At trial, however, the court instructed the jury that the Commonwealth must prove that "the defendant intended to commit cross burning," that "the defendant did a direct act toward the commission of the cross burning," and that "the defendant had the intent of intimidating any person or group of persons." The court did not instruct the jury on the meaning of the word "intimidate," nor on the *prima facie* evidence provision of § 18.2–423. The jury found Elliott guilty of attempted cross burning and acquitted him of conspiracy to commit cross burning. It sentenced Elliott to 90 days in jail and a $2,500 fine. The Court of Appeals of Virginia affirmed the convictions of both Elliott and O'Mara.

Each respondent appealed to the Supreme Court of Virginia, arguing that § 18.2–423 is facially unconstitutional. The Supreme Court of Virginia consolidated all three cases, and held that the statute is unconstitutional on its face. * * *

    * * *

II

Cross burning originated in the 14th century as a means for Scottish tribes to signal each other. See M. Newton & J. Newton, *The Ku Klux Klan: An Encyclopedia* 145 (1991). Sir Walter Scott used cross burnings for dramatic effect in *The Lady of the Lake*, where the burning cross signified both a summons and a call to arms. See W. Scott, *The Lady of The Lake*, canto third. Cross burning in this country, however, long ago became unmoored from its Scottish ancestry. Burning a cross in the United States is inextricably intertwined with the history of the Ku Klux Klan.

The first Ku Klux Klan began in Pulaski, Tennessee, in the spring of 1866. Although the Ku Klux Klan started as a social club, it soon changed into something far different. The Klan fought Reconstruction and the corresponding drive to allow freed blacks to participate in the political process. Soon the Klan imposed "a veritable reign of terror" throughout the South. S. Kennedy, *Southern Exposure* 31 (1991) (hereinafter Kennedy). The Klan employed tactics such as whipping, threatening to burn people at the stake, and murder. W. Wade, *The Fiery Cross: The Ku Klux Klan in America* 48–49 (1987) (hereinafter Wade). The Klan's victims included blacks, southern whites who disagreed with the Klan, and "carpetbagger" northern whites.

The activities of the Ku Klux Klan prompted legislative action at the national level. In 1871, "President Grant sent a message to Congress indicating that the Klan's reign of terror in the Southern States had rendered life and property insecure." In response, Congress passed what is now known as the Ku Klux Klan Act. President Grant used these new powers to suppress the Klan in South Carolina, the effect of which severely curtailed the Klan in other States as well. By the end of Reconstruction in 1877, the first Klan no longer existed.

The genesis of the second Klan began in 1905, with the publication of Thomas Dixon's *The Clansmen: An Historical Romance of the Ku Klux Klan*. Dixon's book was a sympathetic portrait of the first Klan, depicting the Klan as a group of heroes "saving" the South from blacks and the "horrors" of Reconstruction. Although the first Klan never actually practiced cross burning, Dixon's book depicted the Klan burning crosses to celebrate the execution of former slaves. Cross burning thereby became associated with the first Ku Klux Klan. When D.W. Griffith turned Dixon's book into the movie *The Birth of a Nation* in 1915, the association between cross burning and the Klan became indelible. * * *

From the inception of the second Klan, cross burnings have been used to communicate both threats of violence and messages of shared ideology. The first initiation ceremony occurred on Stone Mountain near Atlanta, Georgia. While a 40–foot cross burned on the mountain, the Klan members took their oaths of loyalty. This cross burning was the second recorded instance in the United States. The first known cross burning in the country had occurred a little over one month before the Klan initiation, when a Georgia mob celebrated the lynching of Leo Frank by burning a "gigantic cross" on Stone Mountain that was "visible throughout" Atlanta.

The new Klan's ideology did not differ much from that of the first Klan. As one Klan publication emphasized, "We avow the distinction between [the] races, ... and we shall ever be true to the faithful maintenance of White Supremacy and will strenuously oppose any compromise thereof in any and all things." * * * Violence was also an elemental part of this new Klan. By September 1921, the New York World newspaper documented 152 acts of Klan violence, including 4 murders, 41 floggings, and 27 tar-and-featherings. Wade 160.

Often, the Klan used cross burnings as a tool of intimidation and a threat of impending violence. For example, in 1939 and 1940, the Klan burned crosses in front of synagogues and churches. After one cross burning at a synagogue, a Klan member noted that if the cross burning did not "shut the Jews up, we'll cut a few throats and see what happens." * * *

The Klan continued to use cross burnings to intimidate after World War II. In one incident, an African–American "school teacher who recently moved his family into a block formerly occupied only by whites asked the protection of city police ... after the burning of a cross in his front yard." And after a cross burning in Suffolk, Virginia, during the late 1940's, the Virginia Governor stated that he would "not allow any of our people of any race to be subjected to terrorism or intimidation in any form by the Klan or any other organization." D. Chalmers, *Hooded Americanism: The History of the Ku Klux Klan* 333 (1980). These incidents of cross burning, among others, helped prompt Virginia to enact its first version of the cross-burning statute in 1950.

The decision of this Court in *Brown v. Board of Education*, along with the civil rights movement of the 1950's and 1960's, sparked another outbreak of Klan violence. These acts of violence included bombings, beatings, shootings, stabbings, and mutilations. Members of the Klan burned crosses on the lawns of those associated with the civil rights movement, assaulted the Freedom Riders, bombed churches, and murdered blacks as well as whites whom the Klan viewed as sympathetic toward the civil rights movement.

Throughout the history of the Klan, cross burnings have also remained potent symbols of shared group identity and ideology. The burning cross became a symbol of the Klan itself and a central feature of Klan gatherings. According to the Klan constitution (called the kloran), the "fiery cross" was the "emblem of that sincere, unselfish devotedness of all klansmen to the sacred purpose and principles we have espoused." And the Klan has often published its newsletters and magazines under the name *The Fiery Cross*.

At Klan gatherings across the country, cross burning became the climax of the rally or the initiation. Posters advertising an upcoming Klan rally often featured a Klan member holding a cross. Typically, a cross burning would start with a prayer by the "Klavern" minister, followed by the singing of Onward Christian Soldiers. The Klan would then light the cross on fire, as the members raised their left arm toward the burning cross and sang *The Old Rugged Cross*. Throughout the Klan's history, the Klan continued to use the burning cross in their ritual ceremonies.

For its own members, the cross was a sign of celebration and ceremony. During a joint Nazi–Klan rally in 1940, the proceeding concluded with the wedding of two Klan members who "were married in full Klan regalia beneath a blazing cross." In response to antimasking bills introduced in state legislatures after World War II, the Klan burned crosses in protest. See Chalmers 340. On March 26, 1960, the Klan engaged in rallies and cross burnings throughout the South in an attempt to recruit 10 million members. Later in 1960, the Klan became an issue in the third debate between Richard Nixon and John Kennedy, with both candidates renouncing the Klan. After this debate, the Klan reiterated its support for Nixon by burning crosses. * * * In short, a burning cross has remained a symbol of Klan ideology and of Klan unity.

To this day, regardless of whether the message is a political one or whether the message is also meant to intimidate, the burning of a cross is a "symbol of hate." And while cross burning sometimes carries no intimidating message, at other times the intimidating message is the *only* message conveyed. For example, when a cross burning is directed at a particular person not affiliated with the Klan, the burning cross often serves as a message of intimidation, designed to inspire in the victim a fear of bodily harm. Moreover, the history of violence associated with the Klan shows that the possibility of injury or death is not just hypothetical. The person who burns a cross directed at a particular person often is making a serious threat, meant to coerce the victim to comply with the Klan's wishes unless the victim is willing to risk the wrath of the Klan. Indeed, as the cases of respondents Elliott and O'Mara indicate, individuals without Klan affiliation who wish to threaten or menace another person sometimes use cross burning because of this association between a burning cross and violence.

In sum, while a burning cross does not inevitably convey a message of intimidation, often the cross burner intends that the recipients of the message fear for their lives. And when a cross burning is used to intimidate, few if any messages are more powerful.

III

A

* * * The hallmark of the protection of free speech is to allow "free trade in ideas"—even ideas that the overwhelming majority of people might find distasteful or discomforting. "[T]he government may not prohibit the expression of an idea simply because society finds the idea itself offensive or disagreeable * * * " The First Amendment affords protection to symbolic or expressive conduct as well as to actual speech.

The protections afforded by the First Amendment, however, are not absolute, and we have long recognized that the government may regulate certain categories of expression consistent with the Constitution. See, e.g., Chaplinsky v. New Hampshire, 315 U.S. 568 (1942) ("There are certain well-defined and narrowly limited classes of speech, the prevention and punishment of which has never been thought to raise any Constitutional problem"). The First Amendment permits "restrictions upon the content of speech in a few limited areas, which are 'of such slight social value as a step to truth that any benefit that may be derived from them is clearly outweighed by the social interest in order and morality.' " R.A.V. v. City of St. Paul, supra (quoting Chaplinsky v. New Hampshire, supra, at 572).

Thus, for example, a State may punish those words "which by their very utterance inflict injury or tend to incite an immediate breach of the peace." Chaplinsky v. New Hampshire, supra, at 572; see also R.A.V. v. City of St. Paul, supra, at 383 (listing limited areas where the First Amendment permits restrictions on the content of speech). We have consequently held that fighting words—"those personally abusive epithets which, when addressed to the ordinary citizen, are, as a matter of common knowledge, inherently likely to provoke violent reaction"—are generally proscribable under the First Amendment. Furthermore, "the constitutional guarantees of free speech and free press do not permit a

State to forbid or proscribe advocacy of the use of force or of law violation except where such advocacy is directed to inciting or producing imminent lawless action and is likely to incite or produce such action." Brandenburg v. Ohio, 395 U.S. 444, 447 (1969). And the First Amendment also permits a State to ban a "true threat" where the speaker means to communicate a serious expression of an intent to commit an act of unlawful violence to a particular individual or group of individuals. The speaker need not actually intend to carry out the threat. Rather, a prohibition on true threats "protect[s] individuals from the fear of violence" and "from the disruption that fear engenders," in addition to protecting people "from the possibility that the threatened violence will occur." Intimidation in the constitutionally proscribable sense of the word is a type of true threat, where a speaker directs a threat to a person or group of persons with the intent of placing the victim in fear of bodily harm or death. Respondents do not contest that some cross burnings fit within this meaning of intimidating speech, and rightly so. As noted in Part II, supra, the history of cross burning in this country shows that cross burning is often intimidating, intended to create a pervasive fear in victims that they are a target of violence.

B

The Supreme Court of Virginia ruled that in light of *R.A.V. v. City of St. Paul*, even if it is constitutional to ban cross burning in a content-neutral manner, the Virginia cross-burning statute is unconstitutional because it discriminates on the basis of content and viewpoint. It is true, as the Supreme Court of Virginia held, that the burning of a cross is symbolic expression. The reason why the Klan burns a cross at its rallies, or individuals place a burning cross on someone else's lawn, is that the burning cross represents the message that the speaker wishes to communicate. Individuals burn crosses as opposed to other means of communication because cross burning carries a message in an effective and dramatic manner.

The fact that cross burning is symbolic expression, however, does not resolve the constitutional question. The Supreme Court of Virginia relied upon *R.A.V. v. City of St. Paul*, to conclude that once a statute discriminates on the basis of this type of content, the law is unconstitutional. We disagree.

In *R.A.V.*, we held that a local ordinance that banned certain symbolic conduct, including cross burning, when done with the knowledge that such conduct would " 'arouse anger, alarm or resentment in others on the basis of race, color, creed, religion or gender' " was unconstitutional. * * * This content-based discrimination was unconstitutional because it allowed the city "to impose special prohibitions on those speakers who express views on disfavored subjects."

We did not hold in *R.A.V.* that the First Amendment prohibits *all* forms of content-based discrimination within a proscribable area of speech. Rather, we specifically stated that some types of content discrimination did not violate the First Amendment:

> When the basis for the content discrimination consists entirely of the very reason the entire class of speech at issue is proscribable, no significant danger of idea or viewpoint discrimination exists. Such a reason, having been adjudged neutral enough to support exclusion of the entire class of speech from First Amendment protection, is also neutral enough to form the basis of distinction within the class.

Indeed, we noted that it would be constitutional to ban only a particular type of threat: "[T]he Federal Government can criminalize only those threats of violence that are directed against the President . . . since the reasons why threats of violence are outside the First Amendment . . . have special force when applied to the person of the President." And a State may "choose to prohibit only that obscenity which is the most patently offensive *in its prurience—i.e.,* that which involves the most lascivious displays of sexual activity." Consequently, while the holding of *R.A.V.* does not permit a State to ban only obscenity based on "offensive *political* messages," or "only those threats against the President that mention his policy on aid to inner cities," the First Amendment permits content discrimination "based on the very reasons why the particular class of speech at issue . . . is proscribable."

Similarly, Virginia's statute does not run afoul of the First Amendment insofar as it bans cross burning with intent to intimidate. Unlike the statute at issue in *R.A.V.*, the Virginia statute does not single out for opprobrium only that speech directed toward "one of the specified disfavored topics." It does not matter whether an individual burns a cross with intent to intimidate because of the victim's race, gender, or religion, or because of the victim's "political affiliation, union membership, or homosexuality." Moreover, as a factual matter it is not true that cross burners direct their intimidating conduct solely to racial or religious minorities. * * * Indeed, in the case of Elliott and O'Mara, it is at least unclear whether the respondents burned a cross due to racial animus. * * *

The First Amendment permits Virginia to outlaw cross burnings done with the intent to intimidate because burning a cross is a particularly virulent form of intimidation. Instead of prohibiting all intimidating messages, Virginia may choose to regulate this subset of intimidating messages in light of cross burning's long and pernicious history as a signal of impending violence. Thus, just as a State may regulate only that obscenity which is the most obscene due to its prurient content, so too may a State choose to prohibit only those forms of intimidation that are most likely to inspire fear of bodily harm. A ban on cross burning carried out with the intent to intimidate is fully consistent with our holding in *R.A.V.* and is proscribable under the First Amendment.

IV

[In a brief Part IV, a different majority held that Virginia could not presume intent to intimidate from the mere burning of a cross. Instead, intent to intimidate would have to be shown in each case.]

Her Majesty the Queen v. James Keegstra
[1990] 3 S.C.R. 697

Present: DICKSON C.J. AND WILSON, LA FOREST, L'HEUREUX-DUBE, SOPINKA, GONTHIER AND McLACHLIN JJ.

ON APPEAL FROM THE COURT OF APPEAL FOR ALBERTA

The accused, an Alberta high school teacher, was charged under s. 319(2) of the Criminal Code with wilfully promoting hatred against an identifiable group by communicating anti-Semitic statements to his students. Prior to his trial, the accused applied to the Court of Queen's Bench for an order quashing the charge. The court dismissed the application on the ground that s. 319(2) of the Code did not violate freedom of expression as guaranteed by s. 2(b) of the Canadian Charter of Rights and Freedoms. The court, for want of proper notice to the Crown, did not entertain the accused's argument that s. 319(3)(a) of the Code violated the presumption of innocence protected by s. 11(d) of the Charter. Section 319(3)(a) affords a defence of "truth" to the wilful promotion of hatred but only where the accused proves the truth of the communicated statements on a balance of probabilities. The accused was thereafter tried and convicted. On appeal the accused's Charter arguments were accepted, the Court of Appeal holding that ss. 319(2) and 319(3)(a) infringed ss. 2(b) and 11(d) of the Charter respectively, and that the infringements were not justifiable under s. 1 of the Charter.

* * *

THE USE OF AMERICAN CONSTITUTIONAL JURISPRUDENCE

* * * I think it appropriate to address * * * the relationship between Canadian and American approaches to the constitutional protection of free expression, most notably in the realm of hate propaganda. Those who attack the constitutionality of s. 319(2) draw heavily on the tenor of First Amendment jurisprudence in weighing the competing freedoms and interests in this appeal, a reliance which is understandable given the prevalent opinion that the criminalization of hate propaganda violates the Bill of Rights (see, e.g., L.H. Tribe, *American Constitutional Law* (2d ed. 1988), at 861 n.2; K. Greenawalt, *Insults and Epithets: Are They Protected Speech?*, 42 Rutgers L. Rev. 287, at 304 (1990)). In response to the emphasis placed upon this jurisprudence, I find it helpful to summarize the American position and to determine the extent to which it should influence the s. 1 analysis in the circumstances of this appeal.

A myriad of sources—both judicial and academic—offer reviews of First Amendment jurisprudence as it pertains to hate propaganda. Central to most discussions is the 1952 case of Beauharnais v. Illinois, 343 U.S. 250, where the Supreme Court of the United States upheld as constitutional a criminal statute forbidding certain types of group defamation. Though never overruled, *Beauharnais* appears to have been weakened by later pronouncements of the Supreme Court (see, e.g., Garrison v. Louisiana, 379 U.S. 64 (1964); Ashton v. Kentucky, 384 U.S. 195 (1966); New York Times Co. v. Sullivan, 376 U.S. 254 (1964); Brandenburg v. Ohio, 395 U.S. 444 (1969); and Cohen v. California, 403 U.S. 15 (1971)). The trend reflected in many of these pronouncements is to protect offensive, public invective as long as the speaker has not knowingly lied and there exists no clear and present danger of violence or insurrection.

In the wake of subsequent developments in the Supreme Court, on several occasions *Beauharnais* has been distinguished and doubted by lower courts. Of the judgments expressing a shaken faith in *Beauharnais*, Collin v. Smith, 578 F.2d 1197 (7th Cir. 1978), *certiorari denied*, 439 U.S. 916 (1978), is of greatest relevance to this appeal. In *Collin*, the Court of Appeal for the Seventh Circuit invalidated a municipal ordinance prohibiting public demonstrations inciting "violence, hatred, abuse or hostility toward a person or group of persons by reason of reference to religious, racial, ethnic, national or regional affiliation" (p. 1199), and thereby allowed members of the American Nazi Party to march through Skokie, Illinois, home to a large number of Jewish Holocaust survivors.

The question that concerns us in this appeal is not, of course, what the law is or should be in the United States. But it is important to be explicit as to the reasons why or why not American experience may be useful in the s. 1 analysis of s. 319(2) of the Criminal Code. In the United States, a collection of fundamental rights has been constitutionally protected for over two hundred years. The resulting practical and theoretical experience is immense, and should not be overlooked by Canadian courts. On the other hand, we must examine American constitutional law with a critical eye, and in this respect La Forest J. has noted in R. v. Rahey, [1987] 1 S.C.R. 588, at 639:

> While it is natural and even desirable for Canadian courts to refer to American constitutional jurisprudence in seeking to elucidate the meaning of Charter guarantees that have counterparts in the United States Constitution, they should be wary of drawing too ready a parallel between constitutions born to different countries in different ages and in very different circumstances. . . .

Canada and the United States are not alike in every way, nor have the documents entrenching human rights in our two countries arisen in the same context. It is only common sense to recognize that, just as similarities will justify borrowing from the American experience, differences may require that Canada's constitutional vision depart from that endorsed in the United States.

Having examined the American cases relevant to First Amendment jurisprudence and legislation criminalizing hate propaganda, I would be adverse to following too closely the line of argument that would overrule *Beauharnais* on the ground that incursions placed upon free expression are only justified where there is a clear and present danger of imminent breach of peace. Equally, I am unwilling to embrace various categorizations and guiding rules generated by American law without careful consideration of their appropriateness to Canadian constitutional theory. Though I have found the American experience tremendously helpful in coming to my own conclusions regarding this appeal, and by no means reject the whole of the First Amendment doctrine, in a number of respects I am thus dubious as to the applicability of this doctrine in the context of a challenge to hate propaganda legislation.

First, it is not entirely clear that *Beauharnais* must conflict with existing First Amendment doctrine. Credible arguments have been made that later Supreme Court cases do not necessarily erode its legitimacy (see, e.g., K. Lasson, *Racial Defamation As Free Speech: Abusing the First Amendment*, 17 Colum. Hum. Rts. L. Rev. 11 (1985)). Indeed, a growing body of academic writing in the United States evinces a stronger focus upon the way in which hate propaganda can undermine the very values which free speech is said to protect. This body of writing is receptive to the idea that, were the issue addressed from this new perspective, First Amendment doctrine might be able to accommodate statutes prohibiting hate propaganda (see, e.g., R. Delgado, *Words That Wound: A Tort Action for Racial Insults, Epithets, and Name–Calling*, 17 Harv. C.R.-C.L. L. Rev. 133 (1982); I. Horowitz & V. Bramson, *Skokie, the ACLU and the Endurance of Democratic Theory*, 43 Law & Contemp. Probs. 328 (1979); Lasson, *op. cit.*, at 20–30; M. Matsuda, *Public Response to Racist Speech: Considering the Victim's Story*, 87 Mich. L. Rev. 2320, at 2348 (1989); Comment, Doe v. University of Michigan*: First Amendment—Racist and Sexist Expression on Campus—Court Strikes Down University Limits on Hate Speech*, 103 Harv. L. Rev. 1397 (1990)).

Second, the aspect of First Amendment doctrine most incompatible with s. 319(2), at least as that doctrine is described by those who would strike down the legislation, is its strong aversion to content-based regulation of expression. I am somewhat skeptical, however, as to whether this view of free speech in the United States is entirely accurate. Rather, in rejecting the extreme position that would provide an absolute guarantee of free speech in the Bill of Rights, the Supreme Court has developed a number of tests and theories by which protected speech can be identified and the legitimacy of government regulation assessed. Often required is a content-based categorization of the expression under examination. As an example, obscenity is not protected because of its content (see, e.g., Roth v. United States, 354 U.S. 476 (1957)) and laws proscribing child pornography have been scrutinized under a less than strict First Amendment standard even where they extend to expression beyond the realm of the obscene (see New York v. Ferber, 458 U.S. 747 (1982)). Similarly, the vigourous protection of free speech relaxes when commercial expression is scrutinized (see, e.g., Posadas de Puerto Rico Associates v. Tourism Co. of Puerto Rico, 478 U.S. 328 (1986)), and it is permissible to restrict government employees in their exercise of the right to engage in political activity (Cornelius v. NAACP Legal Defense and Educational Fund, Inc., 473 U.S. 788 (1985)).

In short, a decision to place expressive activity in a category which either merits reduced protection or falls entirely outside of the First Amendment's ambit at least impliedly involves assessing the content of the activity in light of free speech values. As Professor F. Schauer has said, it is always necessary to examine the First Amendment value of the expression limited by state regulation (*The Aim and the Target in Free Speech Methodology*, 83 Nw. U.L. Rev. 562, at 568 (1989)). To recognize that content is often examined under the First Amendment is not to deny that content neutrality plays a real and important role in the American jurisprudence. Nonetheless, that the proscription against looking at the content of expression is not absolute, and that balancing is occasionally employed in First Amendment cases (see Professor T. A. Aleinikoff, *Constitutional Law in the Age of Balancing*, 96 Yale L.J. 943, at 966–68 (1987)), reveals that even in the United States it is sometimes thought justifiable to restrict a particular message because of its meaning.

Third, applying the Charter to the legislation challenged in this appeal reveals important differences between Canadian and American constitutional perspectives. . . . Section I has no equivalent in the United States, a fact previously alluded to by this Court in selectively utilizing American constitutional jurisprudence. Of course, American experience should never be rejected simply because the Charter contains a balancing provision, for it is well known that American courts have fashioned compromises between conflicting interests despite what appears to be the absolute guarantee of constitutional rights. Where s. 1 operates to accentuate a uniquely Canadian vision of a free and democratic society, however, we must not hesitate to depart from the path taken in the United States. * * *

In sum, much is to be learned from First Amendment jurisprudence with regard to freedom of expression and hate propaganda. It would be rash, however, to see First Amendment doctrine as demanding the striking down of s. 319(2). Not only are the precedents somewhat mixed, but the relaxation of the prohibition against content-based regulation of expression in certain areas indicates that American courts are not loath to permit the suppression of ideas in some circumstances. Most importantly, the nature of the s. 1 test as applied in the context of a challenge to s. 319(2) may well demand a perspective particular to Canadian constitutional jurisprudence when weighing competing interests. If values fundamental to the Canadian conception of a free and democratic society suggest an approach that denies hate propaganda the highest degree of constitutional protection, it is this approach which must be employed.

* * *

FREEDOM OF EXPRESSION

* * *

Section 319(2) of the Code constitutes a reasonable limit upon freedom of expression. Parliament's objective of preventing the harm caused by hate propaganda is of sufficient importance to warrant over-riding a constitutional freedom. Parliament has recognized the substantial harm that can flow from hate propaganda and, in trying to prevent the pain suffered by target group members and to reduce racial, ethnic and religious tension and perhaps even violence in Canada, has decided to suppress the wilful promotion of hatred against identifiable groups. Parliament's objective is supported not only by the work of numerous study groups, but also by our collective historical knowledge of the potentially catastrophic effects of the promotion of hatred. Additionally, the international commitment to eradicate hate propaganda and Canada's commitment to the values of equality and multiculturalism in ss. 15 and 27 of the Charter strongly buttress the importance of this objective.

Section 319(2) of the Code is an acceptably proportional response to Parliament's valid objective. There is obviously a rational connection between the criminal prohibition of hate propaganda and the objective of protecting target group members and of fostering harmonious social relations in a community dedicated to equality and multiculturalism. Section 319(2) serves to illustrate to the public the severe reprobation with which society holds messages of hate directed towards racial and religious groups. It makes that kind of expression less attractive and hence decreases acceptance of its content. Section 319(2) is also a means by which the values beneficial to a free and democratic society in particular, the value of equality and the worth and dignity of each human person can be publicized.

Section 319(2) of the Code does not unduly impair freedom of expression. This section does not suffer from overbreadth or vagueness; rather, the terms of the offence indicate that s. 319(2) possesses definitional limits which act as safeguards to ensure that it will capture only expressive activity which is openly hostile to Parliament's objective, and will thus attack only the harm at which the prohibition is targeted. The word "wilfully" imports into the offence a stringent standard of *mens rea* which significantly restricts the reach of s. 319(2) by necessitating the proof of either an intent to promote hatred or knowledge of the substantial certainty of such a consequence. The word "hatred" further reduces the scope of the prohibition. This word, in the context of s. 319(2), must be construed as encompassing only the most severe and deeply felt form of opprobrium. Further, the exclusion of private communications from the scope of s. 319(2), the need for the promotion of hatred to focus upon an identifiable group and the presence of the s.

319(3) defences, which clarify the scope of s. 319(2), all support the view that the impugned section creates a narrowly confined offence. Section 319(2) is not an excessive impairment of freedom of expression merely because the defence of truth in s. 319(3)(a) does not cover negligent or innocent error as to the truthfulness of a statement. Whether or not a statement is susceptible to classification as true or false, such error should not excuse an accused who has wilfully used a statement in order to promote hatred against an identifiable group. Finally, while other noncriminal modes of combatting hate propaganda exist, it is eminently reasonable to utilize more than one type of legislative tool in working to prevent the spread of racist expression and its resultant harm. To send out a strong message of condemnation, both reinforcing the values underlying s. 319(2) and deterring the few individuals who would harm target group members and the larger community by communicating hate propaganda, will occasionally require use of the criminal law.

Notes and Questions

1. Is a tort action the best remedy for hate speech against a Latino/a or other minority group member, as Delgado suggests?

2. Tort actions operate after the fact—i.e., after the harm is done. A state or university may wish to take preventive action to deter this form of speech through statutes announcing that it is prohibited and punishable. What lessons do you draw from *Virginia v. Black* about the ability of states to prohibit pure speech not intermixed with action or threat?

3. Canada's Charter is patterned after the U.S. Constitution. Could U.S. courts uphold criminalization of hate speech, as Canada's highest court has done? Consider this question after reading the following case.

4. For hate speech at work, see Part Seven, Chapter 18A–B (discussing hostile-workplace remedies).

5. Hate speech at times may be redressable under laws pertaining to: threat, defamation, fighting words, capture audiences, and hate crimes. See Steven W. Bender et al., *Everyday Law for Latinos*, Chapter 5 (forthcoming 2008); Delgado & Stefancic, *Understanding Words That Wound*, supra.

SECTION 2. PUBLIC AND SEMI-PUBLIC REMEDIES FOR HATE SPEECH

New York Times v. Sullivan
376 U.S. 254 (1964)

JUSTICE BRENNAN delivered the opinion of the Court.

We are required in this case to determine for the first time the extent to which the constitutional protections for speech and press limit a State's power to award damages in a libel action brought by a public official against critics of his official conduct.

* * *

Respondent's complaint alleged that he had been libeled by statements in a full-page advertisement that was carried in the *New York Times* on March 29, 1960. * * *

* * *

Of the 10 paragraphs of text in the advertisement, the third and a portion of the sixth were the basis of respondent's claim of libel. They read as follows:

Third paragraph:

In Montgomery, Alabama, after students sang "My Country, 'Tis of Thee" on the State Capitol steps, their leaders were expelled from school, and truckloads of police armed with shotguns and tear-gas ringed the Alabama State College Campus. When the entire student body protested to state authorities by refusing to re-register, their dining hall was padlocked in an attempt to starve them into submission.

Sixth paragraph:

Again and again the Southern violators have answered Dr. King's peaceful protests with intimidation and violence. They have bombed his home almost killing his wife and child. They have assaulted his person. They have arrested him seven times—for "speeding," "loitering" and similar "offenses." And now they have charged him with "perjury"—a *felony* under which they could imprison him for *ten years . . . .*

Although neither of these statements mentions respondent by name, he contended that the word "police" in the third paragraph referred to him as the Montgomery Commissioner who supervised the Police Department, so that he was being accused of "ringing" the campus with police. He further claimed that the paragraph would be read as imputing to the police, and hence to him, the padlocking of the dining hall in order to starve the students into submission. As to the sixth paragraph, he contended that since arrests are ordinarily made by the police, the statement "They have arrested (Dr. King) seven times" would be read as referring to him; he further contended that the "They" who did the arresting would be equated with the "They" who committed the other described acts and with the "Southern violators." Thus, he argued, the paragraph would be read as accusing the Montgomery police, and hence him, of answering Dr. King's protests with "intimidation and violence," bombing his home, assaulting his person, and charging him with perjury. Respondent and six other Montgomery residents testified that they read some or all of the statements as referring to him in his capacity as Commissioner.

* * *

Because of the importance of the constitutional issues involved, we granted the separate petitions for certiorari of the individual petitioners and of the *Times.* 371 U.S. 946. We reverse the judgment. We hold that the rule of law applied by the Alabama courts is constitutionally deficient for failure to provide the safeguards for freedom of speech and of the press that are required by the First and Fourteenth Amendments in a libel action brought by a public official against critics of his official conduct. We further hold that under the proper safeguards the evidence presented in this case is constitutionally insufficient to support the judgment for respondent.

       * * *

* * * To avoid placing a handicap upon the freedoms of expression, we hold that if the allegedly libelous statements would otherwise be constitutionally protected from the present judgment, they do not forfeit that protection because they were published in the form of a paid advertisement.

II.

Under Alabama law, a publication is "libelous per se" if the words "tend to injure a person ... in his reputation" or to "bring (him) into public contempt"; the trial court stated that the standard was met if the words are such as to "injure him in his public office, or impute misconduct to him in his office, or want of official integrity, or want of fidelity to a public trust...." The jury must find that the words were published "of and concerning" the plaintiff, but where the plaintiff is a public official his place in the governmental hierarchy is sufficient evidence to support a finding that his reputation has been affected by statements that reflect upon the agency of which he is in charge. Once "libel per se" has been established, the defendant has no defense as to stated facts unless he can persuade the jury that they were true in all their particulars. Alabama Ride Co. v. Vance, 235 Ala. 263, 178 So. 438 (1938); Johnson Publishing Co. v. Davis, 271 Ala. 474, 494–495, 124 So. 2d 441, 457–458 (1960). His privilege of "fair comment" for expressions of opinion depends on the truth of the facts upon which the comment is based. Parsons v. Age–Herald Publishing Co., 181 Ala. 439, 450, 61 So. 345, 350 (1913). Unless he can discharge the burden of proving truth, general damages are presumed, and may be awarded without proof of pecuniary injury. A showing of actual malice is apparently a prerequisite to recovery of punitive damages, and the defendant may in any event forestall a punitive award by a retraction meeting the statutory requirements. Good motives and belief in truth do not negate an inference of malice, but are relevant only in mitigation of punitive damages if the jury chooses to accord them weight. *Johnson Publishing Co. v. Davis*, supra, 271 Ala. at 495, 124 So. 2d at 458.

The question before us is whether this rule of liability, as applied to an action brought by a public official against critics of his official conduct, abridges the freedom of speech and of the press that is guaranteed by the First and Fourteenth Amendments.

Respondent relies heavily, as did the Alabama courts, on statements of this Court to the effect that the Constitution does not protect libelous publications. Those statements do not foreclose our inquiry here. None of the cases sustained the use of libel laws to impose sanctions upon expression critical of the official conduct of public officials. * * * In deciding the question now, we are compelled by neither precedent nor policy to give any more weight to the epithet "libel" than we have to other "mere labels" of state law. N.A.A.C.P. v. Button, 371 U.S. 415, 429. * * * [L]ibel can claim no talismanic immunity from constitutional limitations. It must be measured by standards that satisfy the First Amendment.

The general proposition that freedom of expression upon public questions is secured by the First Amendment has long been settled by our decisions. The constitutional safeguard, we have said, "was fashioned to assure unfettered interchange of ideas for the bringing about of political and social changes desired by the people." Roth v. United States, 354 U.S. 476, 484. "The maintenance of the opportunity for free political discussion to the end that government may be responsive to the will of the people and that changes may be obtained by lawful means, an opportunity essential to the security of the Republic, is a fundamental principle of our constitutional system." Stromberg v. California, 283 U.S. 359. "[I]t is a prized American privilege to speak one's mind, although not always with perfect good taste, on all public institutions," Bridges v. California, 314 U.S. 252, 270, and this opportunity is to be afforded for "vigorous advocacy" no less than "abstract discussion." N.A.A.C.P. v. Button, 371 U.S. 415, 429. The First Amendment, said Judge Learned Hand, "presupposes that right conclusions are more likely to be gathered out of a multitude of tongues, than through any kind of authoritative selection. To many this is, and always will be, folly; but we have staked upon it our all." United States v. Associated Press, 52 F. Supp. 362, 372 (D.C. S.D.N.Y. 1943). * * *

* * *

Thus we consider this case against the background of a profound national commitment to the principle that debate on public issues should be uninhibited, robust, and wide-open, and that it may well include vehement, caustic, and sometimes unpleasantly sharp attacks on government and public officials. See Terminiello v. Chicago, 337 U.S. 1, 4; De Jonge v. Oregon, 299 U.S. 353, 365. The present advertisement, as an expression of grievance and protest on one of the major public issues of our time, would seem clearly to qualify for the constitutional protection. The question is whether it forfeits that protection by the falsity of some of its factual statements and by its alleged defamation of respondent.

Authoritative interpretations of the First Amendment guarantees have consistently refused to recognize an exception for any test of truth—whether administered by judges, juries, or administrative officials—and especially one that puts the burden of proving truth on the speaker. Cf. Speiser v. Randall, 357 U.S. 513, 525–526. The constitutional protection does not turn upon "the truth, popularity, or social utility of the ideas and beliefs which are offered." N.A.A.C.P. v. Button, 371 U.S. 415, 445. As Madison said, "Some degree of abuse is inseparable from the proper use of every thing; and in no instance is this more true than in that of the press." 4 *Elliot's Debates on the Federal Constitution* (1876), p. 571. * * *

    * * *

That erroneous statement is inevitable in free debate, and that it must be protected if the freedoms of expression are to have the "breathing space" that they "need ... to survive," N.A.A.C.P. v. Button, 371 U.S. 415, 433, was also recognized by the Court of Appeals for the District of Columbia Circuit in Sweeney v. Patterson, 76 U.S. App. D.C. 23, 24, 128 F.2d 457, 458 (1942), cert. denied, 317 U.S. 678. Judge Edgerton spoke for a unanimous court which affirmed the dismissal of a Congressman's libel suit based upon a newspaper article charging him with anti-Semitism in opposing a judicial appointment. He said:

> Cases which impose liability for erroneous reports of the political conduct of officials reflect the obsolete doctrine that the governed must not criticize their governors.... The interest of the public here outweighs the interest of appellant or any other individual. The protection of the public requires not merely discussion, but information. Political conduct and views which some respectable people approve, and others condemn, are constantly imputed to Congressmen. Errors of fact, particularly in regard to a man's mental states and processes, are inevitable.... Whatever is added to the field of libel is taken from the field of free debate.

Injury to official reputation affords no more warrant for repressing speech that would otherwise be free than does factual error. Where judicial officers are involved, this Court has held that concern for the dignity and reputation of the courts does not justify the punishment as criminal contempt of criticism of the judge or his decision. Bridges v. California, 314 U.S. 252. This is true even though the utterance contains "half-truths" and "misinformation." Pennekamp v. Florida, 328 U.S. 331, 342, 343, n.5, 345. Such repression can be justified, if at all, only by a clear and present danger of the obstruction of justice. If judges are to be treated as "men of fortitude, able to thrive in a hardy climate," Craig v. Harney, 331 U.S. 367 at 376, surely the same must be true of other government officials, such as elected city commissioners. Criticism of their official conduct does not lose its constitutional protection merely because it is effective criticism and hence diminishes their official reputations.

If neither factual error nor defamatory content suffices to remove the constitutional shield from criticism of official conduct, the combination of the two elements is no less inadequate. * * *

    * * *

There is no force in respondent's argument that the constitutional limitations ... apply only to Congress and not to the States. It is true that the First Amendment was originally addressed only to action by the Federal Government, and that Jefferson, for one, while denying the power of Congress "to controul the freedom of the press," recognized such a power in the States. See the 1804 *Letter to Abigail Adams* quoted in Dennis v. United States, 341 U.S. 494, 522, n.4 (concurring opinion). But this distinction was eliminated with the adoption of the Fourteenth Amendment and the application to the States of the First Amendment's restrictions. See, e.g., Gitlow v. New York, 268 U.S. 652, 666; Schneider v. State, 308 U.S. 147, 160; Bridges v. California, 314 U.S. 252; Edwards v. South Carolina, 372 U.S. 229, 235.

What a State may not constitutionally bring about by means of a criminal statute is likewise beyond the reach of its civil law of libel. The fear of damage awards under a rule such as that invoked by the Alabama courts here may be markedly more inhibiting than the fear of prosecution under a criminal statute. * * * And since there is no double-jeopardy limitation applicable to civil lawsuits, this is not the only judgment that may be awarded against petitioners for the same publication. Whether or not a newspaper can survive a succession of such judgments, the pall of fear and timidity imposed upon those who would give voice to public criticism is an atmosphere in which the First Amendment freedoms cannot survive. Plainly the Alabama law of civil libel is "a form of regulation that creates hazards to protected freedoms markedly greater than those that attend reliance upon the criminal law." Bantam Books, Inc. v. Sullivan, 372 U.S. 58, 70.

The state rule of law is not saved by its allowance of the defense of truth. * * *

A rule compelling the critic of official conduct to guarantee the truth of all his factual assertions—and to do so on pain of libel judgments virtually unlimited in amount—leads to a comparable "self-censorship." Allowance of the defense of truth, with the burden of proving it on the defendant, does not mean that only false speech will be deterred. Even courts accepting this defense as an adequate safeguard have recognized the difficulties of adducing legal proofs that the alleged libel was true in all its factual particulars. See, e.g., Post Publishing Co. v. Hallam, 59 F. 530, 540 (C.A. 6th Cir. 1893); see also Noel, *Defamation of Public Officers and Candidates*, 49 Col. L. Rev. 875, 892 (1949). Under such a rule, would-be critics of official conduct may be deterred from voicing their criticism, even though it is believed to be true and even though it is in fact true, because of doubt whether it can be proved in court or fear of the expense of having to do so. They tend to make only statements which "steer far wider of the unlawful zone." Speiser v. Randall, supra, 357 U.S. at 526. The rule thus dampens the vigor and limits the variety of public debate. It is inconsistent with the First and Fourteenth Amendments.

The constitutional guarantees require, we think, a federal rule that prohibits a public official from recovering damages for a defamatory falsehood relating to his official conduct unless he proves that the statement was made with "actual malice"—that is, with knowledge that it was false or with reckless disregard of whether it was false or not. * * *

* * *

Such a privilege for criticism of official conduct is appropriately analogous to the protection accorded a public official when he is sued for libel by a private citizen. In Barr v. Matteo, 360 U.S. 564, 575, this Court held the utterance of a federal official to be absolutely privileged if made "within the outer perimeter" of his duties. The States accord the same immunity to statements of their highest officers, although some differentiate their lesser officials and qualify the privilege they enjoy. But all hold that all officials are protected unless actual malice can be proved. The reason for the official privilege is said to be that the threat of damage suits would otherwise "inhibit the fearless, vigorous, and effective administration of policies of government" and "dampen the ardor of all but the most resolute, or the most irresponsible, in the unflinching discharge of their duties." Barr v. Matteo, supra, 360 U.S. at 571. Analogous considerations support the privilege for the citizen-critic of government. It is as much his duty to criticize as it is the official's duty to administer. See Whitney v. California, 274 U.S. 357, 375 (concurring opinion of Justice Brandeis). As Madison said, "the censorial power is in the people over the Government, and not in the Government over the people." It would give public servants an unjustified preference over the public they serve, if critics of official conduct did not have a fair equivalent of the immunity granted to the officials themselves.

We conclude that such a privilege is required by the First and Fourteenth Amendments.

III.

We hold today that the Constitution delimits a State's power to award damages for libel in actions brought by public officials against critics of their official conduct. Since this is such an action, the rule requiring proof of actual malice is applicable. While Alabama law apparently requires proof of actual malice for an award of punitive damages, where general damages are concerned malice is "presumed." Such a presumption is inconsistent with the federal rule. "The power to create presumptions is not a means of escape from constitutional restrictions," Bailey v. Alabama, 219 U.S. 219, 239; "[t]he showing of malice required for the forfeiture of the privilege is not presumed but is a matter for proof by the plaintiff. . . ." Lawrence v. Fox, 357 Mich. 134, 146, 97 N.W.2d 719, 725 (1959). Since the trial judge did not instruct the jury to differentiate between general and punitive damages, it may be that the verdict was wholly an award of one or the other. But it is impossible to know, in view of the general verdict returned. Because of this uncertainty, the judgment must be reversed and the case remanded.

* * *

As to the *Times*, we conclude that the facts do not support a finding of actual malice. The statement by the *Times*' Secretary that, apart from the padlocking allegation, he thought the advertisement was "substantially correct," affords no constitutional warrant for the Alabama Supreme Court's conclusion that it was a "cavalier ignoring of the falsity of the advertisement (from which), the jury could not have but been impressed with the bad faith of the *Times*, and its maliciousness inferable therefrom." The statement does not indicate malice at the time of the publication; even if the advertisement was not "substantially correct"—although respondent's own proofs tend to show that it was—that opinion was at least a reasonable one, and there was no evidence to impeach the witness' good faith in holding it. * * *

* * *

We also think the evidence was constitutionally defective in another respect: It was incapable of supporting the jury's finding that the allegedly libelous statements were made "of and concerning" respondent. Respondent relies on the words of the advertisement and the testimony of six witnesses to establish a connection between it and himself. Thus, in his brief to this Court, he states:

> The reference to respondent as police commissioner is clear from the ad. In addition, the jury heard the testimony of a newspaper editor … ; a real estate and insurance man … ; the sales manager of a men's clothing store … ; a food equipment man … ; a service station operator … ; and the operator of a truck line for whom respondent had formerly worked…. Each of these witnesses stated that he associated the statements with respondent…. (Citations to record omitted.)

There was no reference to respondent in the advertisement, either by name or official position. * * * Although the statements may be taken as referring to the police, they did not on their face make even an oblique reference to respondent as an individual. Support for the asserted reference must, therefore, be sought in the testimony of respondent's witnesses. But none of them suggested any basis for the belief that respondent himself was attacked in the advertisement beyond the bare fact that he was in overall charge of the Police Department and thus bore official responsibility for police conduct; to the extent that some of the witnesses thought respondent to have been charged with ordering or approving the conduct or otherwise being personally involved in it, they based this notion not on any statements in the advertisement, and not on any evidence that he had in fact been so involved, but solely on the unsupported assumption that, because of his official position, he must have been. * * *

* * *

* * * For good reason, "no court of last resort in this country has ever held, or even suggested, that prosecutions for libel on government have any place in the American system of jurisprudence." City of Chicago v. Tribune Co., 307 Ill. 595, 601, 139 N.E. 86, 88, 28 A.L.R. 1368 (1923). The present proposition would sidestep this obstacle by transmuting criticism of government, however impersonal it may seem on its

face, into personal criticism, and hence potential libel, of the officials of whom the government is composed. There is no legal alchemy by which a State may thus create the cause of action that would otherwise be denied for a publication which, as respondent himself said of the advertisement, "reflects not only on me but on the other Commissioners and the community." Raising as it does the possibility that a good-faith critic of government will be penalized for his criticism, the proposition relied on by the Alabama courts strikes at the very center of the constitutionally protected area of free expression. We hold that such a proposition may not constitutionally be utilized to establish that an otherwise impersonal attack on governmental operations was a libel of an official responsible for those operations. Since it was relied on exclusively here, and there was no other evidence to connect the statements with respondent, the evidence was constitutionally insufficient to support a finding that the statements referred to respondent.

The judgment of the Supreme Court of Alabama is reversed and the case is remanded to that court for further proceedings not inconsistent with this opinion.

Reversed and remanded.

Doe v. University of Michigan
721 F.Supp. 852 (E.D. Mich. 1989)

OPINION

COHN, DISTRICT JUDGE.

It is an unfortunate fact of our constitutional system that the ideals of freedom and equality are often in conflict. The difficult and sometimes painful task of our political and legal institutions is to mediate the appropriate balance between these two competing values. Recently, the University of Michigan at Ann Arbor (the University), a state-chartered university, see Mich. Const. Art. VIII, adopted a Policy on Discrimination and Discriminatory Harassment of Students in the University Environment (the Policy) in an attempt to curb what the University's governing Board of Regents (Regents) viewed as a rising tide of racial intolerance and harassment on campus. The Policy prohibited individuals, under the penalty of sanctions, from "stigmatizing or victimizing" individuals or groups on the basis of race, ethnicity, religion, sex, sexual orientation, creed, national origin, ancestry, age, marital status, handicap or Vietnam-era veteran status. However laudable or appropriate an effort this may have been, the Court found that the Policy swept within its scope a significant amount of "verbal conduct" or "verbal behavior" which is unquestionably protected speech under the First Amendment. Accordingly, the Court granted plaintiff John Doe's (Doe) prayer for a permanent injunction as to those parts of the Policy restricting speech activity, but denied the injunction as to the Policy's regulation of physical conduct. The reasons follow. * * *

* * *

The Policy established a three-tiered system whereby the degree of regulation was dependent on the location of the conduct at issue. The broadest range of speech and dialogue was "tolerated" in variously described public parts of the campus. Only an act of physical violence or destruction of property was considered sanctionable in these settings. Publications sponsored by the University such as the *Michigan Daily* and the *Michigan Review* were not subject to regulation. The conduct of students living in University housing is primarily governed by the standard provisions of individual leases, however the Policy appeared to apply in this setting as well. The Policy by its terms applied specifically to "[e]ducational and academic centers, such as classroom buildings, libraries, research laboratories, recreation and study centers[.]" In these areas, persons were subject to discipline for:

1. Any behavior, verbal or physical, that stigmatizes or victimizes an individual on the basis of race, ethnicity, religion, sex, sexual orientation, creed, national origin, ancestry, age, marital status, handicap or Vietnam-era veteran status, and that

    a. involves an express or implied threat to an individual's academic efforts, employment, participation in University sponsored extra-curricular activities or personal safety; or

    b. has the purpose or reasonably foreseeable effect of interfering with an individual's academic efforts, employment, participation in University sponsored extra-curricular activities or personal safety; or

    c. creates an intimidating, hostile, or demeaning environment for educational pursuits, employment or participation in University sponsored extra-curricular activities.

2. Sexual advances, requests for sexual favors, and verbal or physical conduct that stigmatizes or victimizes an individual on the basis of sex or sexual orientation where such behavior:

    a. involves an express or implied threat to an individual's academic efforts, employment, participation in University sponsored extra-curricular activities or personal safety; or

    b. has the purpose or reasonably foreseeable effect of interfering with an individual's academic efforts, employment, participation in University sponsored extra-curricular activities or personal safety; or

    c. creates an intimidating, hostile, or demeaning environment for educational pursuits, employment or participation in University sponsored extra-curricular activities.

* * *

The Policy by its terms recognizes that certain speech which might be considered in violation may not be sanctionable, stating: "The Office of the General Counsel will rule on any claim that conduct which is the subject of a formal hearing is constitutionally protected by the First Amendment.''

* * *

The Policy provided for progressive discipline based on the severity of the violation. It stated that the University encouraged hearing panels to impose sanctions that include an educational element in order to sensitize the perpetrator to the harmfulness of his or her conduct. The Policy provided, however, that compulsory class attendance should not be imposed "in an attempt to change deeply held religious or moral convictions." Depending on the intent of the accused student, the effect of the conduct, and whether the accused student is a repeat offender, one or more of the following sanctions may be imposed: (1) formal reprimand; (2) community service; (3) class attendance; (4) restitution; (5) removal from University housing; (6) suspension from specific courses and activities; (7) suspension; (8) expulsion. The sanctions of suspension and expulsion could only be imposed for violent or dangerous acts, repeated offenses, or a willful failure to comply with a lesser sanction. The University President could set aside or lessen any sanction.

* * *

Vagueness and Overbreadth

Doe initially moved for a preliminary injunction against the Policy on the grounds that it was unconstitutionally vague and overbroad and that it chilled speech and conduct protected by the First Amendment. The University in response said that the Policy has never been applied to reach protected speech and a preliminary injunction should therefore be denied. * * *

* * *

Doe claimed that the Policy was invalid because it was facially overbroad. It is fundamental that statutes regulating First Amendment activities must be narrowly drawn to address only the specific evil at hand. Broadrick v. Oklahoma, 413 U.S. 601, 611. "Because First Amendment freedoms need breathing space to survive, government may regulate in the area only with narrow specificity." NAACP v. Button, supra 371 U.S. at 433. A law regulating speech will be deemed overbroad if it sweeps within its ambit a substantial amount of protected speech along with that which it may legitimately regulate. Id. 413 U.S. at 612; Gooding v. Wilson, 405 U.S. 518, 521–22 (1972).

The Supreme Court has consistently held that statutes punishing speech or conduct solely on the grounds that they are unseemly or offensive are unconstitutionally overbroad. In *Houston v. Hill*, supra, the Supreme Court struck down a City of Houston ordinance which provided that "[i]t shall be unlawful for any person to assault or strike or in any manner oppose, molest, and abuse or interrupt any policeman in the execution of his duty." The Supreme Court also found that the ordinance was overbroad because it forbade citizens from criticizing and insulting police officers, although such conduct was constitutionally protected. Id. 482 U.S. at 460–65. The fact that the statute also had a legitimate scope of application in prohibiting conduct which was clearly unprotected by the First Amendment was not enough to save it. In *Gooding v. Wilson*, supra, the Supreme Court struck down a Georgia statute which made it a misdemeanor for "[a]ny person [to], without provocation, use to or of another, and in his presence … opprobrious words or abusive language, tending to cause a breach of the peace." The Supreme Court found that this statute was overbroad as well, because it punished speech which did not rise to the level of "fighting words," as defined in *Chaplinsky v. New Hampshire*, supra. * * * These cases stand generally for the proposition that the state may not prohibit broad classes of speech, some of which may indeed be legitimately regulable, if in so doing a substantial amount of constitutionally protected conduct is also prohibited. This was the fundamental infirmity of the Policy.

The University repeatedly argued that the Policy did not apply to speech that is protected by the First Amendment. It urged the Court to disregard the [accompanying] Guide as "inaccurate" and look instead to "the manner in which the Policy has been interpreted and applied by those charged with its enforcement." However, as applied by the University over the past year, the Policy was consistently applied to reach protected speech.

On December 7, 1988, a complaint was filed against a graduate student in the School of Social Work alleging that he harassed students based on sexual orientation and sex. The basis for the sexual orientation charge was apparently that in a research class, the student openly stated his belief that homosexuality was a disease and that he intended to develop a counseling plan for changing gay clients to straight. See Discipline File 88–12–21, described supra. He also related to other students that he had been counseling several of his gay patients accordingly. The student apparently had several heated discussions with his classmates over the validity and morality of his theory and program. On January 11, 1989, the Interim Policy Administrator wrote to the student informing him that following an investigation of the complaints, there was sufficient evidence to warrant a formal hearing on the charges of sex and sexual orientation harassment. A formal hearing on the charges was held on January 28, 1989. The hearing panel unanimously found that the student was guilty of sexual harassment but refused to convict him of harassment on the basis of sexual orientation. The panel stated:

> In a divided decision the hearing panel finds that the evidence available to the panel indicates that _____ did not harass students on the basis of sexual orientation under the strict definition of "The University of Michigan Policy on Discrimination and Discriminatory Harassment by Students in the University Environment." In accordance with First Amendment rights to free speech and the University's policy of academic freedom, _____ did not violate the policy by discussing either the origins or "curability" of homosexuality in the School of Social Work.

Although the student was not sanctioned over the allegations of sexual orientation harassment, the fact remains that the Policy Administrator—the authoritative voice of the University on these matters—saw no First Amendment problem in forcing the student to a hearing to answer for allegedly harassing statements made in the course of academic discussion and research. Moreover, there is no indication that had the hearing panel convicted rather than acquitted the student, the University would have interceded to protect the interests of academic freedom and freedom of speech.

* * *

The manner in which [this and other] complaints were handled demonstrated that the University considered serious comments made in the context of classroom discussion to be sanctionable under the Policy. The innocent intent of the speaker was apparently immaterial to whether a complaint would be pursued. Moreover, the Administrator generally failed to consider whether a comment was protected by the First Amendment before informing the accused student that a complaint had been filed. The Administrator instead attempted to persuade the accused student to accept "voluntary" sanctions. Behind this persuasion was, of course, the subtle threat that failure to accept such sanctions might result in a formal hearing. There is no evidence in the record that the Administrator ever declined to pursue a complaint through attempted mediation because the alleged harassing conduct was protected by the First Amendment. Nor is there evidence that the Administrator ever informed an accused harasser during mediation negotiations that the complained of conduct might be protected. The Administrator's manner of enforcing the Policy was constitutionally indistinguishable from a full blown prosecution. The University could not seriously argue that the policy was never interpreted to reach protected conduct. It is clear that the policy was overbroad both on its face and as applied.

Doe also urges that the policy be struck down on the grounds that it is impermissibly vague. A statute is unconstitutionally vague when "men of common intelligence must necessarily guess at its meaning." *Broadrick*, supra 413 U.S. at 607. A statute must give adequate warning of the conduct which is to be prohibited and must set out explicit standards for those who apply it. Id. "No one may be required at the peril of life, liberty or property to speculate as to the meaning of penal statutes. All are entitled to be informed as to what the State commands or forbids." Lanzetta v. New Jersey, 306 U.S. 451, 453 (1939). These considerations apply with particular force where the challenged statute acts to inhibit freedoms affirmatively protected by the constitution. Smith v. Goguen, 415 U.S. 566, 573 (1974). However, the chilling effect caused by an overly vague statute must be both real and substantial, Young v. American Mini Theatres, 427 U.S. 50 (1976), and a narrowing construction must be unavailable before a court will set it aside, Screws v. United States, 325 U.S. 91, 98 (1945).

Looking at the plain language of the Policy, it was simply impossible to discern any limitation on its scope or any conceptual distinction between protected and unprotected conduct. The structure of the Policy was in two parts; one relates to cause and the other to effect. Both cause and effect must be present to state a *prima facie* violation of the Policy. The operative words in the cause section required that language must "stigmatize" or "victimize" an individual. However, both of these terms are general and elude precise definition. Moreover, it is clear that the fact that a statement may victimize or stigmatize an individual does not, in and of itself, strip it of protection under the accepted First Amendment tests. * * *

* * *

During the oral argument, the Court asked the University's counsel how he would distinguish between speech which was merely offensive, which he conceded was protected, and speech which "stigmatizes or victimizes" on the basis of an invidious factor. Counsel replied "very carefully." The response, while refreshingly candid, illustrated the plain fact that the University never articulated any principled way to distinguish sanctionable from protected speech. Students of common understanding were necessarily forced to guess at whether a comment about a controversial issue would later be found to be sanctionable under the Policy. The terms of the Policy were so vague that its enforcement would violate the due process clause. See Cramp v. Board of Public Instruction, 368 U.S. 278, 285–88 (1961).

CONCLUSION

* * *

While the Court is sympathetic to the University's obligation to ensure equal educational opportunities for all of its students, such efforts must not be at the expense of free speech. Unfortunately, this was precisely what the University did. From the Acting President's December 14 memorandum forward to the adoption of the Policy and continuing through the August 25 hearing, there is no evidence in the record that any officials at the University ever seriously attempted to reconcile their efforts to combat discrimination with the requirements of the First Amendment. The apparent willingness to dilute the values of free speech is ironic in light of the University's previous statements of policy on this matter. In 1977, the Regents adopted the "Statement on Freedom of Speech and Artistic Expression: The Rights and Obligations of Speakers, Performers, Audience Members, and Protesters at the University of Michigan" (Statement) which "reaffirm[ed] formally [the University's] deep and lasting commitment to freedom of speech and artistic expression." The Statement provides in part that

> freedom of speech must not ordinarily be restricted, governed or curtailed in any way by content except where the law, as interpreted by the Supreme Court of Michigan or the Supreme Court of the United States, holds that such an expression does not fall within

constitutionally protected free speech. In all instances, the University authorities should act with maximum constraint, even in the face of obvious bad taste or provocation. The belief that some opinion is pernicious, false, or in any other way detestable cannot be grounds for its suppression.

Needless to say, the philosophy expressed in the Statement is diametrically opposed to that reflected in the Acting President's December 14 Memorandum. Apparently, no one involved in the drafting process noted the apparent inconsistency with the Regents' views as expressed in the Statement.

Throughout the case, the University's counsel strenuously urged that First Amendment concerns held a top priority in the development and administration of the Policy. Counsel repeatedly argued that the University interpreted the Policy to reach conduct such as racial slurs and epithets in the classroom directed at an individual victim. However, as the Court observed in its August 25, 1989 bench opinion,

> what we have heard here this morning ... from University counsel is a revisionist view of the Policy on Discrimination and Discriminatory Harassment by Students in the University Environment, and it is a view and interpretation of the Policy that was not in the minds of the legislators when it was adopted. And there is nothing in the record that has been presented to the Court which suggests that this was an appropriate interpretation of the policy.

Not only has the administrative enforcement of the Policy been wholly inconsistent with counsel's interpretation, but withdrawal of the Guide, see supra at 13, and the eleventh hour suspension of section 1(c), see supra at 8, suggests that the University had no idea what the limits of the Policy were and it was essentially making up the rules as it went along.

Richard Delgado
Campus Antiracism Rules: Constitutional Narratives in Collision
85 Nw. U. L. Rev. 343, 345–48, 383–86 (1991)

Persons tend to react to the problem of racial insults in one of two ways. On hearing that a university has enacted rules forbidding certain forms of speech, some will frame the issue as a First Amendment problem: The rules limit speech, something that the Constitution forbids without a very good reason. If one takes that starting point, several consequences follow. First, the burden shifts to the other side to show that the interest in protecting members of the campus community from insults and name-calling is compelling enough to overcome the presumption in favor of free speech. Further, there must be no less onerous way of accomplishing that objective. Other concerns rise to the fore: Will the enforcer of the regulation become a censor, imposing narrow-minded restraints on campus discussion? Finally, what about slippery slopes and line-drawing problems: If a campus restricts this type of expression, might the temptation arise to do the same with classroom speech or political satire in the campus newspaper?

Others, however, will frame the problem in radically different terms—as one of protection of equality. They will ask whether an educational institution does not have the power, to protect core values emanating from the Thirteenth and Fourteenth Amendments, to enact reasonable regulations aimed at assuring equal personhood on campus. If one characterizes the issue this way, other consequences follow. Now, the defenders of racially scathing speech are required to show that the interest in its protection is compelling enough to overcome the preference for equal personhood; and we will want to be sure that this interest is advanced in the way least damaging to equality. They, too, will raise concerns about the decisionmaker who will enforce the rules, but from the opposite standpoint: The enforcer of the regulation must be attuned to the nuances of insult and racial supremacy at issue, for example by incorporating multi-ethnic representation into the hearing process. Finally, a different set of slopes will look slippery. If we do not intervene to protect equality here, what will the next outrage be?

The legal analysis, therefore, leads to opposite conclusions depending on the starting point. But an even deeper indeterminacy looms: Both sides invoke different narratives to rally support. Protectors of the First Amendment see campus antiracism rules as parts of a much longer story: the centuries-old struggle of Western society to free itself from superstition and enforced ignorance. The tellers of this story invoke martyrs like Socrates, Galileo, and Peter Zenger, and heroes like Locke, Hobbes, Voltaire, and Hume who fought for the right of free expression. They conjure up struggles against official censorship, book burning, witch trials, and communist blacklists. Compared to that richly textured, deeply stirring account, the minority-protector's interest in freeing a few (supersensitive?) individuals from momentary discomfort looks thin. A textured, historical account is pitted against a particularized, slice-of-life, dignitary one.

Those on the minority-protection side invoke a different, and no less powerful, narrative. They see a nation's centuries-long struggle to free itself from racial and other forms of tyranny, including slavery, lynching, Jim Crow laws, and "separate-but-equal" schools. They conjure up different milestones—Lincoln's Emancipation Proclamation, *Brown v. Board of Education*; they look to different heroes—Martin Luther King, the early Abolitionists, Rosa Parks, and César Chávez, civil rights protesters who put their lives on the line for racial justice. Arrayed against that richly textured historical account, the racist's interest in insulting a person of color face-to-face looks thin.

One often hears that the problem of campus antiracism rules is that of balancing free speech and equality. But more is at stake than that. Each side wants not merely to have the balance struck in its favor; each wants to impose its own understanding of what is at stake. Minority protectors see the injury of one who has been subject to a racial assault as not a mere isolated event, but as part of an interrelated series of acts by which persons of color are subordinated, and which will follow the victim wherever she goes. First Amendment defenders see the wrong of silencing the racist as much more than a momentary inconvenience: Protection of his right to speak is part of the never-ending vigilance necessary to preserve freedom of expression in a society that is too prone to balance it away.

My view is that both stories are equally valid. Judges and university administrators have no easy, *a priori* way of choosing between them, of privileging one over the other. They could coin an exception to free speech, thus giving primacy to the equal protection values at stake. Or, they could carve an exception to equality, saying in effect that universities may protect minority populations except where this abridges speech. Nothing in constitutional or moral theory requires one answer rather than the other. Social science, case law, and the experience of other nations provide some illumination. But ultimately, judges and university administrators must *choose*. And in making this choice, we are in uncharted terrain: We lack a pole star. * * *

* * *

* * * Neither the constitutional narrative of the First, nor of the Thirteenth and Fourteenth, Amendments clearly prevails in connection with campus antiracism rules. Judges must choose. The dilemma is embedded in the nature of our system of law and politics: We want and fear both equality and liberty. * * *

Might a postmodern insight offer a possible solution to the problem of campus antiracism rules? Perhaps the speech by which society "constructs" a stigma picture of minorities may be regulated consistently with the First Amendment because it is different from most other forms of speech in function and effect. Indeed, regulation may prove necessary for full effectuation of the values of equal personhood we hold equally dear.

The first step is recognizing that racism is, in almost all its aspects, a class harm—the essence of which is subordination of one people by another. The mechanism of this subordination is a complex, interlocking series of acts, some physical, some symbolic. Although the physical acts (like lynchings and cross burnings) are often the most striking, the symbolic acts are the most insidious. By communicating and constructing a shared cultural image of the victim group as inferior, we enable ourselves to feel comfortable about the disparity in power and resources between ourselves and the stigmatized group. Even civil rights law contributes to this stigmatization: The group is so vulnerable that it requires social help. The shared picture also demobilizes the victims of discrimination, particularly the young. Indeed, social scientists have seen evidence of self-hatred and rejection of their own identity in children of color as early as age three.

The ubiquity and incessancy of harmful racial depiction are thus the source of its virulence. Like water dripping on sandstone, it is a pervasive harm which only the most hardy can resist. Yet the prevailing First Amendment paradigm predisposes us to treat racist speech as an individual harm, as though we only had to evaluate the effect of a single drop of water. This approach—corresponding to liberal, individualistic theories of self and society—systematically misperceives the experience of racism for both victim and perpetrator. This mistake is natural, and corresponds to one aspect of our natures—our individualistic selves. In this capacity, we want and need liberty. But we also exist in a social capacity; we need others to fulfill ourselves as beings. In this group aspect, we require inclusion, equality, and equal respect. Constitutional narratives of equal protection and prohibition of slavery—narratives that encourage us to form and embrace collectivity and equal citizenship for all—reflect this second aspect of our existence.

When the tacit consent of a group begins to coordinate the exercise of individual rights so as seriously to jeopardize participation by a smaller group, the "rights" nature of the first group's actions acquires a different character and dimension. The exercise of an individual right now poses a group harm and must be weighed against this qualitatively different type of threat. * * *

* * * Thus, a wealthy and well-regarded citizen who is victimized by a vicious defamation is able to recover in tort. His social "picture," in which he has a property interest, has been damaged, and will require laborious reconstruction. It would require only slight extension of this observation to provide protection from racial slurs and hate-speech. Indeed, the rich man has the dominant "story" on his side; repairing the defamation's damage will be relatively easy.

Racist speech, by contrast, is not so readily repaired—it separates the victim from the storytellers who alone have credibility. Not only does racist speech, by placing all the credibility with the dominant group, strengthen the dominant story, it also works to disempower minority groups by crippling the effectiveness of *their* speech in rebuttal. This situation makes free speech a powerful asset to the dominant group, but a much less helpful one to subordinate groups—a result at odds, certainly, with marketplace theories of the First Amendment. Unless society is able to deal with this incongruity, the Thirteenth and Fourteenth Amendments and our complex system of civil rights statutes will be of little avail. At best, they will be able to obtain redress for episodic, blatant acts of individual prejudice and bigotry. But they will do little to address the source of the problem: the speech that creates the stigma-picture that makes the acts hurtful in the first place, and that renders almost any other form of aid—social or legal—useless.

Could judges and legislators effectuate the suggestion that speech which constructs a stigma-picture of a subordinate group stands on a different footing from sporadic speech aimed at persons who are not disempowered? It might be argued that *all* speech constructs the world to some extent, and that every speech act could prove offensive to someone. Traditionalists find modern art troublesome, Republicans detest left-wing speech, and some men hate speech that constructs a sex-neutral world. Yet race—like gender and a few other characteristics—is different; our entire history and culture bespeak this difference. Thus, judges easily could differentiate speech which subordinates blacks or Latinos, for example, from that which disparages factory owners. Will they choose to do so? There is cause for doubt: Low-grade racism benefits the status quo. Moreover, our system's winners have a stake in liberal, marketplace interpretations of law and politics—the seeming neutrality and meritocratic nature of such interpretations reassure the decisionmakers that their social position is deserved.

Still, resurgent racism on our nation's campuses is rapidly becoming a national embarrassment. Almost daily, we are faced with headlines featuring some of the ugliest forms of ethnic conflict and the spectre of virtually all-white universities. The need to avoid these consequences may have the beneficial effect of causing courts to reflect on, and tailor, constitutional doctrine. As Harry Kalven pointed out twenty five years ago, it would not be the first time that insights born of the cauldron of racial justice yielded reforms that ultimately redounded to the benefit of all society.

Notes and Questions

1. If U.S. courts generally strike down speech codes while Canada's highest court has upheld them, might it be because U.S. courts invariably treat the issue as a First Amendment (i.e., free speech), rather than a Fourteenth Amendment (i.e., equality) problem?

2. *New York Times v. Sullivan* is perhaps the most famous declaration of the importance of protecting speech in order to promote democracy. Is hate speech at all like the type of speech the Supreme Court was concerned with in *New York Times v. Sullivan*—i.e., a kind of cultural criticism or dissent—or is it a different type of speech entirely?

3. Our system of free speech is subject to innumerable "exceptions" and special doctrines—libel, defamation, words of threat, copyright, plagiarism, disrespectful words uttered to a judge or other authority figure, military secrets, shouting fire in a crowded theater, etc. Why not an exception for hate speech that a group of toughs spew on a lone black undergraduate walking home late at night from the campus library?

4. Is face to face hate speech of the sort in question not speech at all, but more like a slap in the face?

5. With derogatory media stereotypes, the First Amendment probably stands as a barrier to legal action, for example to enjoin distribution of a virulently racist movie or record. What kinds of extralegal campaigns might prove effective? Consumer boycotts? Complaints to the F.C.C. or other licensing agency? Rallies and marches? See Bender, supra.

Part Seven

THE WORKPLACE (INCLUDING THE FIELDS)

Work can be satisfying and creative. It can also be dangerous, soul-killing drudgery. See, e.g., L.M. Sixel, *Hispanics Still Face More Deaths, Injuries on the Job*, Hous. Chron., Sept. 26, 2003. It can be autonomous, an expression of the self and personality, like representing a favorite client in a socially important case. It can be unfree and exploitive, done under compulsion, and the opposite of autonomous. Work makes use of people's very diverse talents—white collar, blue collar, artistic, musical, entrepreneurial, and professional. Many people work at different kinds of jobs during their lives. Consider, for example, a teenager who mows lawns for spending money as a high school student, works at a bookstore while in college, then after graduation attends business school and goes to work for a large corporation. Or, a Latino child may help his parents in the fields while young, attend many different high schools, and earn a scholarship to a state college. After graduating, the Latino ponders law school versus getting a job immediately to help his family.

In a capitalist system such as ours, workers typically do not take home the full value of what they produce. See Karl Marx, *Capital: A Critique of Political Economy* (1990 ed.), describing the surplus value theory of labor. Instead, the corporation or business owner, who has invested capital and undergone risk, takes a certain amount of it for profit. In some sectors of the economy, this skimming is more overt and the work conditions more exploitive than in others. For example, in the typical law firm, the work is hierarchical, but the manner by which those at the top of the hierarchy (the partners) exploit the talents of the underlings is veiled and socially accepted. But see *Law vs. Having a Life: Stanford Students Lead Lawyers in Requesting Reforms at Major Law Firms*, Journal Record (Oklahoma City), Apr. 12, 2007.

Latinos find employment in practically every sector of the economy, including the arts and the professions. But they concentrate most heavily in certain occupations such as farming and orchard work, gardening and landscaping, food processing, custodial work, house cleaning, construction, and the hospitality industry. (See Introduction to this volume for the percentages in various areas.) What accounts for this concentration in the blue-collar fields?

Along with African Americans, Latinos also make up a significant part of the U.S. military, perhaps because the formal rules and top-down structure reduce the amount of room for discrimination. See Charles Moskos, *How Do They Do It?: The Army's Integration Success Story*, New Republic, Aug. 5, 1991, at 16. On the way formal rules do, in fact, tend to discourage discrimination, see Richard Delgado, et al., *Fairness and Formality: Minimizing the Risk of Prejudice in Alternative Dispute Resolution*, 1985 Wis. L. Rev. 1359.

But the U.S. military is not always a racism-free haven. Consider the fate of 60 members of a New Mexico National Guard unit who, while serving at a base in Kuwait "were told to remove their shoes, socks and shirts so that military investigators could check them for gang tattoos." See *N.M. Guard Unit Alleges Racial Discrimination: Task force says Army searched soldiers for tattoos because they're Hispanic*, Assoc. Press, Apr. 23, 2007.

> Several members of the Rio Rancho-based Task Force Cobra alleged racial discrimination, saying the unit was targeted because of its large number of Hispanics. Army investigators, however, found that the tattoo search was lawful and not racially motivated, the Albuquerque Journal reported in a copyright story published Sunday. "I'm embarrassed to say that's how the Army is," said Adjutant Gen. Kenny Montoya, who commands the Army and Air National Guard in New Mexico. "They don't want to admit mistakes."

Subsequently, Montoya wrote to a senior officer requesting an apology to his unit. On receiving no answer, he wrote the following month to Gen. Peter Schoomaker, then-chief of staff of the Army. "Let me know how I can help our Army to end their discriminatory practices, both now and in the future," Montoya wrote. Again, he received no answer.

> The military forbids soldiers from membership in extremist gangs that advocate racial violence or hate crimes. Id. Later that month, an army investigator arrived at the Ali Al Salem base to conduct a "tattoo check," which included stripping down to their athletic shorts. When several refused, the agent threatened them with arrest. The Latino soldiers complained of its "Gestapo-like" check and said it made them feel un-American.

> As word of the search spread, a top Army lawyer expressed concern. "It is too easy for this to be viewed as a witch hunt, where all of the unit members are presumed guilty until proven innocent," Col. Ralph M.C. Sabatino, a judge advocate, wrote in an email a day after the search. "The fact that all of this is being done on the uncorroborated vague and nonspecific accusations of a soldier ... only exacerbates the problem." Id.

Notes and Questions

1.   If a high percentage of Latinos work at low-paid blue collar jobs such as meat packing, gardening, house cleaning, or crop picking, is that accidental or the result of a deliberate social policy? See Rebecca Smith & Catherine Ruckelshaus, *Solutions, Not Scapegoats: Abating Sweatshop Conditions for All Low-Wage Workers as a Centerpiece of Immigration Reform*, 10 N.Y.U. J. Legis. & Pub. Pol'y 555 (2007).

2.   If it is not accidental, what role does immigration policy play in it? See Part Five: Immigration; Ernesto Galarza, *Merchants of Labor: The Mexican Bracero Story* (1964); id., *Farmworkers and Agri-business in California 1947–1960* (1977), noting the role of immigration restrictions, beginning around 1965, combined with the ending of the Bracero program around that time, in creating a Latino undocumented "problem." Immigrant workers, like most farmworkers, receive little protection from U.S. law. See Steven W. Bender et al., *Everyday Law for Latinos* (forthcoming 2008).

3.   Educational authorities in previous years would blithely announce that Latino children only needed a few years of school because their role in life was to serve as domestics (in the case of the girls) and field hands (in the case of the boys), and that any more years of education would simply make them dissatisfied at those jobs. Today, no educational authority would admit to such thoughts. Still, Latinos today continue to receive inferior educations and to occupy the lowest types of job. Is that accidental? See Part Four: Education.

4.   Some Latinos/as strenuously insist that Latinos are not all alike and in particular that all are not blue-collar workers and gardeners, which is, of course, true. The ones who proclaim this most loudly are usually among the small percentage who are, in fact, white-collar office workers or middle-ranked professionals. Are "anti-essentialism," "intersectionality," and the insistence on a complex Latino group identity distancing moves by bourgeois Latinos ashamed of being identified in the public mind with janitorial work, crop-picking, backroom work at restaurants, and the like? On the rise of the suit-wearing, latte-sipping Latino broker class, see Rodolfo Acuña, *Occupied America: A History of Chicanos* 357 (5th ed., 2004). See also Part Two, Chapter 6, § 3: Interracial Tensions and Relations.

Chapter 18

EMPLOYMENT DISCRIMINATION

Review Part Five, Chapter 15 on the various immigration avenues available to Latinos hoping to find work in the United States.

SECTION 1. TYPES OF JOB DISCRIMINATION AND THEORIES OF RELIEF

Much of the case law of employment discrimination against Latinos takes place in connection with blue-collar work where the discrimination, unlike in higher-echelon jobs, is not at all subtle but glaring and overt. See, e.g., Carlos R. Soltero, *Latinos and American Law: Landmark Supreme Court Cases* 95 (2006) (commenting on the unusual number of cases that include evidence of supervisors referring to Latino workers as wetbacks, spics, taco ticos, or banditos). Still, the plaintiff does not always prevail. In the cases that follow, note the catalogue of reasons why: Because he or she is an undocumented alien; because the racism was not overt or concerted enough to qualify under hostile-workplace doctrine; because the discrimination was on the basis of language or noncitizenship, not race or national origin; because no federal statute covered the sort of work the employee (say a farmworker) performed, etc.

See, e.g., David L. Hudson, Jr., *Tales of Hoffman: A 2002 High Court Case Figures Prominently in Immigrant Rights Battle*, ABA J., Dec. 2006, at 12.

Hoffman Plastic Compounds, Inc. v. NLRB
535 U.S. 137 (2002)

CHIEF JUSTICE REHNQUIST delivered the opinion of the Court.

The National Labor Relations Board (Board) awarded backpay to an undocumented alien who has never been legally authorized to work in the United States. We hold that such relief is foreclosed by federal immigration policy, as expressed by Congress in the Immigration Reform and Control Act of 1986 (IRCA).

Petitioner Hoffman Plastic Compounds, Inc., custom-formulates chemical compounds for businesses that manufacture pharmaceutical, construction, and household products. In May 1988, petitioner hired Jose Castro to operate various blending machines that "mix and cook" the particular formulas per customer order. Before being hired for this position, Castro presented documents that appeared to verify his authorization to work in the United States. In December 1988, the United Rubber, Cork, Linoleum, and Plastic Workers of America, AFL–CIO, began a union-organizing campaign at petitioner's production plant. Castro and several other employees supported the organizing campaign and distributed authorization cards to co-workers. In January 1989, Hoffman laid off Castro and other employees engaged in these organizing activities.

Three years later, in January 1992, respondent Board found that Hoffman unlawfully selected four employees, including Castro, for layoff "in order to rid itself of known union supporters" in violation of § 8(a)(3) of the National Labor Relations Act. To remedy this violation, the Board ordered that Hoffman (1) cease and desist from further violations of the NLRA, (2) post a detailed notice to its employees regarding the remedial order, and (3) offer reinstatement and backpay to the four affected employees. Hoffman entered into a stipulation with the Board's General Counsel and agreed to abide by the Board's order.

In June 1993, the parties proceeded to a compliance hearing before an Administrative Law Judge (ALJ) to determine the amount of backpay owed to each discriminatee. On the final day of the hearing, Castro testified that he was born in Mexico and that he had never been legally admitted to, or authorized to work in, the United States. He admitted gaining employment with Hoffman only after tendering a birth certificate belonging to a friend who was born in Texas. He also admitted that he used this birth certificate to fraudulently obtain a California driver's license and a Social Security card, and to fraudulently obtain employment following his layoff by Hoffman. Neither Castro nor the Board's General Counsel offered any evidence that Castro had applied or intended to apply for legal authorization to work in the United States. Based on this testimony, the ALJ found the Board precluded from awarding Castro backpay or reinstatement as such relief would be contrary to Sure–Tan, Inc. v. NLRB, 467 U.S. 883 (1984), and in conflict with IRCA, which makes it unlawful for employers knowingly to hire undocumented workers or for employees to use fraudulent documents to establish employment eligibility.

In September 1998, four years after the ALJ's decision, and nine years after Castro was fired, the Board reversed with respect to backpay. Citing its earlier decision in *A.P.R.A. Fuel Oil Buyers Group, Inc.*, the Board determined that "the most effective way to accommodate and further the immigration policies embodied in [IRCA] is to provide the protections and remedies of the [NLRA] to undocumented workers in the same manner as to other employees." The Board thus found that Castro was entitled to $66,951 of backpay, plus interest. * * *

Hoffman filed a petition for review of the Board's order in the Court of Appeals. A panel of the Court of Appeals denied the petition for review. After rehearing the case en banc, the court again denied the petition for review and enforced the Board's order. We granted certiorari, 533 U.S. 976 (2001), and now reverse.

This case exemplifies the principle that the Board's discretion to select and fashion remedies for violations of the NLRA, though generally broad, is not unlimited. Since the Board's inception, we have consistently set aside awards of reinstatement or backpay to employees found guilty of serious illegal conduct in connection with their employment. In *Fansteel*, the Board awarded reinstatement with backpay to employees who engaged in a "sit down strike" that led to confrontation with local law enforcement officials. We set aside the award. * * *

Though we found that the employer had committed serious violations of the NLRA, the Board had no discretion to remedy those violations by awarding reinstatement with backpay to employees who themselves had committed serious criminal acts. * * *

     * * *

Our decision in *Sure-Tan* followed this line of cases and set aside an award closely analogous to the award challenged here. There we confronted for the first time a potential conflict between the NLRA and federal immigration policy, as then expressed in the Immigration and Nationality Act (INA). Two companies had unlawfully reported alien-employees to the Immigration and Naturalization Service (INS) in retaliation for union activity. Rather than face INS sanction, the employees voluntarily departed to Mexico. The Board investigated and found the companies acted in violation of the NLRA [and] directed the companies to reinstate the affected workers and pay them six months' backpay.

We affirmed the Board's determination that the NLRA applied to undocumented workers, reasoning that the immigration laws "as presently written" expressed only a " 'peripheral concern' " with the employment of illegal aliens. 467 U.S. at 892 (quoting De Canas v. Bica, 424 U.S. 351, 360 (1976)). "For whatever reason," Congress had not "made it a separate criminal offense" for employers to hire an illegal alien, or for an illegal alien "to accept employment after entering this country illegally." *Sure-Tan*, 467 U.S. at 892–893. Therefore, we found "no reason to conclude that application of the NLRA to employment practices affecting such aliens would necessarily conflict with the terms of the INA." Id. at 893.

With respect to the Board's selection of remedies, however, we found its authority limited by federal immigration policy. For example, the Board was prohibited from effectively rewarding a violation of the immigration laws by reinstating workers not authorized to reenter the United States. *Sure-Tan*, 467 U.S. at 903. Thus, to avoid "a potential conflict with the INA," the Board's reinstatement order had to be conditioned upon proof of "the employees' legal reentry." "Similarly," with respect to backpay, we stated: "[T]he employees must be deemed 'unavailable' for work (and the accrual of backpay therefore tolled) during any period when they were not lawfully entitled to be present and employed in the United States." "[I]n light of the practical workings of the immigration laws," such remedial limitations were appropriate even if they led to "[t]he probable unavailability of the [NLRA's] more effective remedies." Id. at 904.

* * *

It is against this decisional background that we turn to the question presented here. The parties and the lower courts focus much of their attention on *Sure-Tan*, particularly its express limitation of backpay to aliens "lawfully entitled to be present and employed in the United States." 467 U.S. at 903. All agree that as a matter of plain language, this limitation forecloses the award of backpay to Castro. Castro was never lawfully entitled to be present or employed in the United States, and thus, under the plain language of *Sure-Tan*, he has no right to claim backpay. The Board takes the view, however, that read in context, this limitation applies only to aliens who left the United States and thus cannot claim backpay without lawful reentry. The Court of Appeals agreed with this view. Another Court of Appeals, however, agrees with Hoffman, and concludes that *Sure-Tan* simply meant what it said, i.e., that any alien who is "not lawfully entitled to be present and employed in the United States" cannot claim backpay. We need not resolve this controversy. For whether isolated sentences from *Sure-Tan* definitively control, or count merely as persuasive dicta in support of petitioner, we think the question presented here better analyzed through a wider lens, focused as it must be on a legal landscape now significantly changed.

The *Southern S.S. Co.* line of cases established that where the Board's chosen remedy trenches upon a federal statute or policy outside the Board's competence to administer, the Board's remedy may be required to yield. Whether or not this was the situation at the time of *Sure-Tan*, it is precisely the situation today. In 1986, two years after *Sure-Tan*, Congress enacted IRCA, a comprehensive scheme prohibiting the employment of illegal aliens in the United States. As we have previously noted, IRCA "forcefully" made combating the employment of illegal aliens central to "[t]he policy of immigration law." It did so by establishing an extensive "employment verification system" designed to deny employment to aliens who (a) are not lawfully present in the United States, or (b) are not lawfully authorized to work in the United States. This verification system is critical to the IRCA regime. To enforce it, IRCA mandates that employers verify the identity and eligibility of all new hires by examining specified documents before they begin work. If an alien applicant is unable to present the required documentation, the unauthorized alien cannot be hired.

Similarly, if an employer unknowingly hires an unauthorized alien, or if the alien becomes unauthorized while employed, the employer is compelled to discharge the worker upon discovery of the worker's undocumented status. Employers who violate IRCA are punished by civil fines, and may be subject to criminal prosecution. IRCA also makes it a crime for an unauthorized alien to subvert the employer verification system by tendering fraudulent documents. * * *

Under the IRCA regime, it is impossible for an undocumented alien to obtain employment in the United States without some party directly contravening explicit congressional policies. Either the undocumented alien tenders fraudulent identification, which subverts the cornerstone of IRCA's enforcement mechanism, or the employer knowingly hires the undocumented alien in direct contradiction of its IRCA obligations. The Board asks that we overlook this fact and allow it to award backpay to an illegal alien for years of work not performed, for wages that could not lawfully have been earned, and for a job obtained in the first instance by a criminal fraud. We find, however, that awarding backpay to illegal aliens runs counter to policies underlying IRCA, policies the Board has no authority to enforce or administer. Therefore, as we have consistently held in like circumstances, the award lies beyond the bounds of the Board's remedial discretion.

* * *

Indeed, awarding backpay in a case like this not only trivializes the immigration laws, it also condones and encourages future violations. The Board admits that had the INS detained Castro, or had Castro obeyed the law and departed to Mexico, Castro would have lost his right to backpay. Castro thus qualifies for the Board's award only by remaining inside the United States illegally. * * *

We therefore conclude that allowing the Board to award backpay to illegal aliens would unduly trench upon explicit statutory prohibitions critical to federal immigration policy, as expressed in IRCA. It would encourage the successful evasion of apprehension by immigration authorities, condone prior violations of the immigration laws, and encourage future violations. However broad the Board's discretion to fashion remedies when dealing only with the NLRA, it is not so unbounded as to authorize this sort of an award.

Lack of authority to award backpay does not mean that the employer gets off scot-free. The Board here has already imposed other significant sanctions against Hoffman—sanctions Hoffman does not challenge. These include orders that Hoffman cease and desist its violations of the NLRA, and that it conspicuously post a notice to employees setting forth their rights under the NLRA and detailing its prior unfair practices. Hoffman will be subject to contempt proceedings should it fail to comply with these orders. * * *

The judgment of the Court of Appeals is reversed.

It is so ordered.

Espinoza v. Farah Mfg. Co.
414 U.S. 86 (1973)

MR. JUSTICE MARSHALL delivered the opinion of the Court.

This case involves interpretation of the phrase "national origin" in Tit. VII of the Civil Rights Act of 1964. [Eds. Title VII is the main federal statute forbidding workplace discrimination. See Bender, supra, at ch. 2. It makes it unlawful "to fail or refuse to hire or to discharge any individual ... with respect to his compensation, terms, conditions, or privileges of employment ... because of race, color, religion, or national origin." The law covers public employees, private employers with more than 15 employees, labor unions, and employment agencies. Id.] Petitioner Cecilia Espinoza is a lawfully admitted resident alien who was born in and remains a citizen of Mexico. She resides in San Antonio, Texas, with her husband, Rudolfo Espinoza, a United States citizen. In July 1969, Mrs. Espinoza sought employment as a seamstress at the San Antonio division of respondent Farah Manufacturing Co. Her employment application was rejected on the basis of a longstanding company policy against the employment of aliens. After exhausting their administrative remedies with the Equal Employment Opportunity Commission, petitioners commenced this suit in the District Court alleging that respondent had discriminated against Mrs. Espinoza because of her "national origin" in violation of § 703 of Tit. VII. The District Court granted petitioners' motion for summary judgment, holding that a refusal to hire because of lack of citizenship constitutes discrimination on the basis of "national origin." The Court of Appeals reversed. * * *

Section 703 makes it "an unlawful employment practice for an employer ... to fail or refuse to hire ... any individual ... because of such individual's race, color, religion, sex, or national origin." Certainly the plain language of the statute supports the result reached by the Court of Appeals. The term "national origin" on its face refers to the country where a person was born, or, more broadly, the country from which his or her ancestors came.

The statute's legislative history, though quite meager in this respect, fully supports this construction. The only direct definition given the phrase "national origin" is the following remark made on the floor of the House of Representatives by Congressman Roosevelt, Chairman of the House Subcommittee which reported the bill: "It means the country from which you or your forebears came.... You may come from Poland, Czechoslovakia, England, France, or any other country." We also note that an earlier version of § 703 had referred to discrimination because of "race, color, religion, national origin, or *ancestry*." The deletion of the word "ancestry" from the final version was not intended as a material change, suggesting that the terms "national origin" and "ancestry" were considered synonymous.

There are other compelling reasons to believe that Congress did not intend the term "national origin" to embrace citizenship requirements.

Since 1914, the Federal Government itself, through Civil Service Commission regulations, has engaged in what amounts to discrimination against aliens by denying them the right to enter competitive examination for federal employment. But it has never been suggested that the citizenship requirement for federal employment constitutes discrimination because of national origin, even though since 1943, various Executive Orders have expressly prohibited discrimination on the basis of national origin in Federal Government employment.

* * * Congress itself has on several occasions since 1964 enacted statutes barring aliens from federal employment. The Treasury, Postal Service, and General Government Appropriation Act, 1973, for example, provides that "no part of any appropriation contained in this or any other Act shall be used to pay the compensation of any officer or employee of the Government of the United States . . . unless such person (1) is a citizen of the United States."

To interpret the term "national origin" to embrace citizenship requirements would require us to conclude that Congress itself has repeatedly flouted its own declaration of policy. This Court cannot lightly find such a breach of faith. * * *

Petitioners have suggested that the statutes and regulations discriminating against noncitizens in federal employment are unconstitutional under the Due Process Clause of the Fifth Amendment. We need not address that question here, for the issue presented in this case is not whether Congress has the power to discriminate against aliens in federal employment, but, rather, whether Congress intended to prohibit such discrimination in private employment. Suffice it to say that we cannot conclude Congress would at once continue the practice of requiring citizenship as a condition of federal employment and, at the same time, prevent private employers from doing likewise. Interpreting § 703 as petitioners suggest would achieve the rather bizarre result of preventing Farah from insisting on United States citizenship as a condition of employment while the very agency charged with enforcement of Tit. VII would itself be required by Congress to place such a condition on its own personnel.

* * *

* * * There is no indication in the record that Farah's policy against employment of aliens had the purpose or effect of discriminating against persons of Mexican national origin. It is conceded that Farah accepts employees of Mexican origin, provided the individual concerned has become an American citizen. Indeed, the District Court found that persons of Mexican ancestry make up more than 96% of the employees at the company's San Antonio division, and 97% of those doing the work for which Mrs. Espinoza applied. * * *

* * *

Finally, petitioners seek to draw support from the fact that Tit. VII protects all individuals from unlawful discrimination, whether or not they are citizens of the United States. We agree that aliens are protected from discrimination under the Act. That result may be derived not only from the use of the term "any individual" in § 703, but also as a negative inference from the exemption in § 702, which provides that Tit. VII "shall not apply to an employer with respect to the employment of aliens outside any State...." 42 U.S.C. § 2000e–1. Title VII was clearly intended to apply with respect to the employment of aliens inside any State.

The question posed in the present case, however, is not whether aliens are protected from illegal discrimination under the Act, but what kinds of discrimination the Act makes illegal. Certainly it would be unlawful for an employer to discriminate against aliens because of race, color, religion, sex, or national origin—for example, by hiring aliens of Anglo–Saxon background but refusing to hire those of Mexican or Spanish ancestry. Aliens are protected from illegal discrimination under the Act, but nothing in the Act makes it illegal to discriminate on the basis of citizenship or alienage.

Affirmed.

MR. JUSTICE DOUGLAS, dissenting.

It is odd that the Court which holds that a State may not bar an alien from the practice of law or deny employment to aliens can read a federal statute that prohibits discrimination in employment on account of "national origin" so as to permit discrimination against aliens.

Alienage results from one condition only: being born outside the United States. Those born within the country are citizens from birth. It could not be more clear that Farah's policy of excluding aliens is *de facto* a policy of preferring those who were born in this country. Therefore the construction placed upon the "national origin" provision is inconsistent with the construction this Court has placed upon the same Act's protections for persons denied employment on account of race or sex.

In connection with racial discrimination we have said that the Act prohibits "practices, procedures, or tests neutral on their face, and even neutral in terms of intent," if they create "artificial, arbitrary, and unnecessary barriers to employment when the barriers operate invidiously to discriminate on the basis of racial *or other impermissible classification*." Griggs v. Duke Power Co., 401 U.S. 424, 430–431 (1971) (emphasis added). There we found that the employer could not use test or diploma requirements which on their face were racially neutral, when in fact those requirements had a *de facto* discriminatory result and the employer was unable to justify them as related to job performance. The tests involved in *Griggs* did not eliminate all blacks seeking employment, just as the citizenship requirement here does not eliminate all applicants of foreign origin. Respondent here explicitly conceded that the citizenship requirement is imposed without regard to the alien's qualifications for the job.

These petitioners against whom discrimination is charged are Chicanos. But whether brown, yellow, black, or white, the thrust of the Act is clear: alienage is no barrier to employment here. *Griggs*, as I understood it until today, extends its protective principles to all, not to blacks alone. Our cases on sex discrimination under the Act yield the same result as *Griggs*. See Phillips v. Martin Marietta Corp., 400 U.S. 542 (1971).

The construction placed upon the statute in the majority opinion is an extraordinary departure from prior cases, and it is opposed by the Equal Employment Opportunity Commission, the agency provided by law with the responsibility of enforcing the Act's protections. The Commission takes the only permissible position: that discrimination on the basis of alienage *always* has the effect of discrimination on the basis of national origin. Refusing to hire an individual because he is an alien "is discrimination based on birth outside the United States and is thus discrimination based on national origin in violation of Title VII." The Commission's interpretation of the statute is entitled to great weight.

* * *

Mrs. Espinoza is a permanent resident alien, married to an American citizen, and her children will be native-born American citizens. But that first generation has the greatest adjustments to make to their new country. Their unfamiliarity with America makes them the most vulnerable to exploitation and discriminatory treatment. They, of course, have the same obligation as American citizens to pay taxes, and they are subject to the draft on the same basis. But they have never received equal treatment in the job market. Writing of the immigrants of the late 1800's, Oscar Handlin has said:

> For want of alternative, the immigrants took the lowest places in the ranks of industry. They suffered in consequence from the poor pay and miserable working conditions characteristic of the sweat-shops and the homework in the garment trades and in cigar making. But they were undoubtedly better off than the Irish and Germans of the 1840's for whom there had been no place at all. *The Newcomers* 24 (1959).

The majority decides today that in passing sweeping legislation guaranteeing equal job opportunities, the Congress intended to help only the immigrant's children, excluding those "for whom there [is] no place at all." I cannot impute that niggardly an intent to Congress.

Manzanares v. Safeway Stores, Inc.
593 F.2d 968 (10th Cir. 1979)

SETH, CHIEF JUDGE.

The plaintiff brought this action for injunctive relief and damages under 42 U.S.C. § 1981 only. The plaintiff asserts that relief is sought " ... with respect to the unlawful employment practices of the defendant, Safeway Stores, Inc., ... and the unfair, discriminatory representation afforded to the plaintiff by defendant Teamsters Local...."

The plaintiff was discharged by Safeway, and charges of theft of Safeway property were brought against him. He was acquitted and Safeway rehired him but without the seniority he had before the incident, and without "back pay."

The plaintiff describes himself in the complaint as of "Mexican American descent," and alleges that " ... Anglo employees of the Company, who have admitted to thefts of Company property have been subjected to suspension rather than discharge ..."; also that the " ... defendant Union failed to represent the plaintiff as it represented its Anglo members in the past." This allegation apparently refers to grievance procedures sought to be instituted by plaintiff. Plaintiff alleged that the acts of both defendants " ... were perpetrated upon the plaintiff because of his race and/or national origin."

The defendants filed motions to dismiss for failure to state a claim. More particularly reference in the motions was made to the "national origin" allegations in the complaint and the assertions that the protection afforded by 42 U.S.C. § 1981 was applicable only to discrimination based on race, color, or alienage.

The trial court granted the motions to dismiss. The order states that it was concluded that national origin does not give "standing" for a section 1981 claim, " ... and upon the conclusion that relief under § 1981 is available only for discrimination only on the basis of race or color, ... "

Thus the sole issue on this appeal is whether the allegations in the complaint that plaintiff was discriminated against because he was of "Mexican American descent," and the employees who were alleged to have received different treatment were "Anglos," were sufficient to permit plaintiff to seek relief under 42 U.S.C. § 1981.

Of course, section 1981 makes no mention of race, national origin, or alienage. The only reference is that "all persons" shall have described rights and benefits of "white citizens." Thus the standard against whom the measure was to be made were the rights and benefits of white citizens. The measure is group to group, and plaintiff has alleged that the "group" to which he belongs—those he describes as of Mexican American descent—is to be measured against the Anglos as the standard. This is perfectly clear and well understood in the context, and in the geographical area concerned. The allegation is direct that discrimination was directed to members of his group, and to him individually because of his affiliation. We hold that this was sufficient to have withstood the motions to dismiss. In this holding we consider that Mexican American, Spanish American, Spanish-surname individuals, and Hispanos are equivalents, and it makes no difference whether these are terms of national origin, alienage, or whatever. It is apparent that a group so described is of such an identifiable nature that the treatment afforded its members may be measured against that afforded the Anglos.

Thus plaintiff has alleged that there has been or is discrimination against him by defendants by reason of the fact he is of Mexican

American origin, and this is a sufficient identification of a group within the protection of section 1981. The group to group comparison or contrast is made, and with the other allegations a cause of action is alleged. This is a failure of "any person" to have the rights of "white citizens."

* * *

In Valdez v. Van Landingham, No. 76–1373 (Tenth Circuit), we considered an allegation of discrimination arising from plaintiff's name. We stated in that opinion:

> ... The issue is whether a Spanish surname constitutes a "racial" class which is protected by section 1981. The term "race" in our language has evolved to encompass some non-racial but ethnic groups. This Circuit has recognized Spanish speaking or Spanish-surnamed Americans as a minority for purposes of sections 1981, 1983, and 1985(3).

The purpose of the Civil Rights Act of 1866 is apparent. See *The Civil Rights Cases*, 109 U.S. 3; Jones v. Alfred H. Mayer Co., 392 U.S. 409. The Supreme Court has made many references to "racial" discrimination in 1981 cases. We must read these cases that section 1981 is directed to racial discrimination primarily, but is not necessarily limited to the technical or restrictive meaning of "race." * * *

Section 1981 does not apply to sex or religious discrimination. A number of cases have held that "national origin" is not enough.

It is also clear from the cases that Title VII and section 1981 are not identical. The proof is different, at least as to discriminatory intent as to constitutional claims. The Court said: "We have never held that the constitutional standard for adjudicating claims of invidious racial discrimination is identical to the standards applicable under Title VII, and we decline to do so today." Thus there is a difference and in some instances the plaintiff has a choice between the two. That there is a difference, and that there may be a choice, does not in itself lead us to any particular conclusion in this case.

Again, there are no Title VII allegations in the case before us. Also the section 1983 and section 1985 cases are, of course, quite different by reason of the great difference in the wording of the sections, and the equal protection aspects thereof.

If "white citizens" means a race, which technically does not seem particularly clear, it would seem that a group which is discriminated against because they are somehow different as compared to "white citizens" is within the scope of section 1981. We cannot consider this as a "national origin" case and that alone. Prejudice is as irrational as is the selection of groups against whom it is directed. It is thus a matter of practice or attitude in the community, it is usage or image based on all the mistaken concepts of "race." Webster's Third New International Dictionary includes in a lengthy definition of race a class of individuals with common characteristics, appearance, or habits. Also, "In technical

discriminations, all more or less controversial and often lending themselves to great popular misunderstanding or misuse, RACE is anthropological ... implying a distinct physical type ...'' The allegations in this
case thus equate the prejudices to those based on race. The allegations
demonstrate that the defendants may be poor anthropologists, but the
prejudice is asserted to be directed against plaintiff in contrast to the
Anglos. This in our view is sufficient. * * *

* * *

We must hold that the trial court erred in granting the motion to
dismiss the complaint, and the case is reversed and remanded for further
proceedings.

Notes and Questions

1.   What attitude does the Supreme Court exhibit toward job-discrimi-
nation suits brought by noncitizens and illegal aliens?

2.   Note that under Title VII one can file a claim of discrimination in
one of two ways—by filing a charge with a local office of the E.E.O.C. within
180 days of the discriminatory incident, or with a local or state agency that
performs much the same function. One must prove either disparate treatment or disparate impact. See Bender, supra, at Chapter 2.

3.   With *Hoffman Plastics* compare EEOC v. Tortilleria "La Mejor,"
758 F.Supp. 585 (E.D. Cal. 1991), holding that an undocumented alien may
sue under Title VII and that federal immigration law (IRCA) does nothing to
alter that ruling.

4.   On the basis of the two Supreme Court cases, what trends would
you expect to find in lower-court opinions dealing with citizens of Latino
descent who suffer discrimination at work? Revisit this question after you
have read a sampling of these cases, immediately infra.

5.   Is the purpose of colonialism to extract profits; of immigration law,
to assure a steady supply of low-paid labor; and of employment discrimination law, to deny recovery except in the most egregious cases?

6.   After *Espinoza v. Farah* held that employers could discriminate on
the basis of noncitizenship (alienage), citizenship became a legitimate
BFOQ—a job requirement that would hold up and defeat a claim of discrimination. In other words noncitizenship, standing alone, would not serve as a
proxy or stand-in for race. The employer could refuse to hire or promote
noncitizens, who merely happened always to be Mexican or Dominican, and
get away with it. See Juan F. Perea, *Ethnicity and Prejudice: Reevaluating
"National Origin" Discrimination under Title VII*, 35 Wm. & Mary L. Rev.
805, 822 (1994). Congress partly reversed *Farah* when it enacted a new
immigration statute in 1986, prohibiting discrimination on the basis of
alienage but providing for criminal penalties for an employer who knowingly
hired an illegal alien.

7.   How can one square *Farah* with Yick Wo v. Hopkins, 118 U.S. 356
(1886) holding that the Equal Protection Clause forbade a San Francisco

ordinance that discriminated against Chinese-run laundries? Can Title VII allow what the Equal Protection Clause forbids?

8. And what about job discrimination on the basis of other proxies for race, such as language, accent, or a foreign-sounding name? The Supreme Court has yet to address these issues, see Perea, supra, while lower courts have treated them inconsistently:

A bilingual radio announcer who added occasional Spanish words to his English-language show was fired when a consultant determined that speaking Spanish hurt his station's ratings. The Ninth Circuit found for the station on the ground that English was a bona fide requirement in the broadcasting industry, Jurado v. Eleven–Fifty Corp., 813 F.2d 1406 (9th Cir. 1987). Height requirements that excluded most Latinos were found to satisfy the disparate-impact requirement, as well as was a pattern of excluding a majority of those with Spanish surnames. Bender, supra, at Chapter 2.

Discrimination on the basis of a foreign accent is generally legal. See infra (accent discrimination). See also Part Three (language discrimination).

A Puerto Rican statute barring noncitizens from obtaining engineering licenses was unconstitutional. See Examining Bd. of Engineers, Architects and Surveyors v. Flores de Otero, 426 U.S. 572 (1976).

Lopez v. Union Tank Car Co.
8 F. Supp. 2d 832 (N.D. Ind. 1998)

MOODY, DISTRICT JUDGE.

* * *

Plaintiff Robert Lopez was 46 years old at the time of his discharge on July 12, 1995. Lopez is of Hispanic descent, and suffers from polio and post-polio syndrome. At the time of his discharge Lopez was employed as a "layout draftsman/CAD operator" in Union's drafting department. Lopez had been employed by Union since October, 1977.

The person with overall supervisory responsibility for the drafting department is known as the Chief Draftsman. Beginning March 3, 1992, the Chief Draftsman was Dennis Chansler. According to Union, the Chief Draftsman is the "sole supervisor" in the drafting department and the only individual authorized to make hiring/firing decisions.

* * *

On [Lopez's employment] evaluation covering 1992, prepared by group leader Richard Benak, Lopez was rated 4.0 on a five-point scale. The form describes a 4.0 rating as "SUPERIOR (Far above expected performance.)" Prior to preparing that evaluation, Benak recommended to Chansler that Lopez be promoted to the designer position, but Chansler disagreed. On his evaluation covering 1993, also prepared by Benak, Lopez was rated 3.7. Benak had rated Lopez 3.96, but Chansler modified the rating. A 3.0 rating is "COMMENDABLE" (Achieves all key responsibilities.)

Lopez worked for Benak during the first six months of 1994, then for other group leaders. Chansler prepared Lopez's evaluation for 1994, and rated Lopez 2.82. A rating of 2.0 is "MARGINAL" (Performance acceptable but should improve).

In preparing the evaluation for 1994, Chansler deviated from his normal practice by not soliciting input from Benak. According to Chansler, he did not consult with Benak at least in part because Chansler believed that Benak had rated Lopez too highly in the past. The group leaders Chansler did consult with included Carl Carney, who regularly referred to Lopez as a "wetback" and who, in a June 1994 meeting including Chansler and other group leaders, announced "no spics allowed" when he entered the room and observed that Lopez was present.

On March 14, 1995, Lopez sent a memo to Philip Daum, Union's Chief Engineer, and Benjamin Damiani, Union's Vice President of Engineering, complaining that Chansler's evaluation was "not objective," "demeaning," and "meant to defame my ability as a layout draftsman." Daum and Lopez met and discussed the review on March 20, 1995. On March 21, 1995, a confidential memo written by Daum detailing "plans to achieve the Plant 1 staffing reduction goals" recommended reducing the drafting staff by two, including Lopez.

On April 8, 1995, Lopez filed a charge with the Equal Employment Opportunity Commission (EEOC) concerning Chansler's evaluation covering 1994. In or around May 1995, Chansler and Daum discussed reducing the size of the drafting department. Chansler decided to discharge four people, and identified eight candidates for discharge, one of whom was Lopez. Although Lopez initially was not one of the more likely candidates, by late May Chansler had decided to discharge Lopez. * * *

Lopez complained to Benak about harassing conduct directed at him by group leaders and other employees. Benak witnessed harassment of Lopez, including slurs such as "cockroach," "fucking Mexican" and "fucking spic." Benak observed numerous occasions when Lopez was criticized about his physical handicap, including comments about his arms. * * *

A plaintiff attempting to prove discrimination based upon a racially or ethnically hostile environment must establish not only the existence of harassment so severe and pervasive that it alters the terms and conditions of plaintiffs employment, from both a subjective and objective view, but also that plaintiffs employer acted negligently with respect to the harassment; that is, knew or should have known that it was taking place, and failed to take reasonable remedial action.

Union's motion for summary judgment is based on one ground: that because Lopez's supervisor, Dennis Chansler, denies any knowledge that "any employee made any comments regarding Plaintiffs age, disability and/or race/national origin," and Lopez admits that he never reported any derogatory comments to Chansler, Union had no knowledge of harassment and so cannot be found negligent in failing to act remedially.

* * *

Nevertheless, the court believes that Lopez has demonstrated that a question of fact exists whether Chansler had knowledge that Lopez's co-employees verbally abused Lopez. First, Lopez testified in his deposition that in 1987 or 1988 Chansler himself asked Lopez if he "was good at picking lettuce." Although this occurred before Chansler was promoted to the position where he had hiring/firing authority over Lopez, it occurred after Chansler became Lopez's group leader, a position where he had some authority to direct Lopez's work activities. This comment, in and of itself, is evidence of a hostile environment.

But more importantly, the "lettuce-picking" comment considered in conjunction with other evidence casts doubt on the credibility of Chansler's denial that he was not aware of any derogatory comments made by Lopez's co-employees. For example, Lopez also testified that at a meeting of group leaders called by Chansler after Chansler's promotion, a group leader named Carl Carney arrived late for the meeting and announced "no spics allowed." Lopez "waited for Mr. Chansler to say something. He did not say a word." In addition, before Chansler was promoted and obtained his own office, he worked "out in the open" with the others making it possible for him to hear any one of a number of racial slurs and other derogatory comments directed at Lopez.

Viewing the evidence in the light most favorable to Lopez, as the court must, there is a question of fact whether Chansler was aware of harassment directed at Lopez. As a result, Union is not entitled to summary judgment on this aspect of Lopez's suit.

Machado v. Goodman Manuf. Co.
10 F. Supp. 2d 709 (S.D. Tex. 1997)

ATLAS, DISTRICT JUDGE.

Plaintiff Eduardo Machado (Plaintiff) has brought this action against Defendants Goodman Manufacturing Company, L.P. and Goodman Holding Company, alleging that he was discriminated against on account of his national origin in violation of Title VII of the Civil Rights Act of 1964 * * *.

Eduardo Machado began working for Defendant Goodman Manufacturing Company, L.P., a manufacturer and distributor of air conditioning equipment, in January 1991 in the position of Regional Sales Manager for Mexico, Latin America, and the Caribbean. For four years, Plaintiff remained in this position, working out of his home in Miami, Florida.

During this period, while he was based in Miami, Plaintiff claims that he was never subject to discriminatory treatment in connection with his employment.

In March 1995, Plaintiff was promoted to the position of Vice President of International Sales, for which he was relocated to Houston,

Texas. After his relocation, Plaintiff claims that he began to suffer discrimination on the basis of his national origin, Cuban. In particular, Plaintiff asserts that he was subject to discriminatory remarks by another Goodman Vice President, Barry Watson, and that Watson's and other Goodman executives' discriminatory treatment of him created a hostile environment that was severe enough to compel Plaintiff ultimately to resign his position.

Plaintiff claims that his work environment became so hostile that, in June 1995, he sought and received permission from Thomas Burkett, Goodman's President and CEO, to return to Miami to perform his duties as Vice President from his home office. However, even after Plaintiff returned to Miami, he claims that Watson, who was apparently at that point made Plaintiff's supervisor, continued his discriminatory harassing behavior which interfered with Plaintiff's ability to perform his job. After complaining fruitlessly to Burkett of Watson's behavior, Plaintiff resigned in August 1995. Subsequently, Plaintiff brought this action alleging that he was subject to national origin discrimination that led to his constructive discharge.

* * *

First, Plaintiff complains about his treatment in connection with his promotion to Vice President of International Sales. For instance, he testifies that although he had been promised the position by the outgoing Vice President, [Burkett] was hesitant about placing Plaintiff in that position. Plaintiff submits evidence that Burkett advertised for the position in trade journals and made Plaintiff go through an interview in order to obtain the position. After attaining the position, Plaintiff states that he received less compensation than his predecessor, who was not Cuban, and was given a substandard office.

Plaintiff contends that after his move to Houston, he "was faced with fellow VPs who were disrespectful, undermined his authority, embarrassed him in front of clients, and made discriminatory comments regarding his national origin." For example, Plaintiff testifies that when he was preparing for a business trip to Asia to determine what new products the company should buy, another Vice–President, Peter Alexander, instructed him simply to "play dumb" and bring back brochures for the other managers to consider. In Thailand, one of the companies Plaintiff was scheduled to visit informed Plaintiff that, prior to his arrival, the company had received a phone call telling them that Plaintiff was not the decision maker for his company and that he was only there to look over equipment and pick up brochures.

Plaintiff submits evidence of several overtly discriminatory remarks made to him by Watson in front of other employees. On three separate occasions, Watson told Plaintiff that he did not want Cubans living in his neighborhood.[3]

---

3. Plaintiff testifies, "As I was looking for homes in the Houston area and getting information from my coworkers about different neighborhoods, [Watson] would jump

In May 1995, Plaintiff tendered a letter of resignation to Burkett, informing Burkett of the discriminatory treatment he believed he had experienced, including Watson's remarks about not wanting Cubans in his neighborhood.[4]

Burkett convinced Plaintiff not to resign and initiated an investigation into the alleged discriminatory comments by Watson. Defendants claim that Burkett took prompt remedial action, including threatening Watson with termination if his discriminatory conduct continued. * * *

After Watson was reprimanded, Plaintiff claims that Watson made another offensive remark referring to Plaintiff's national origin[5] and continued to harass him by interfering with his ability to perform his job and slighting him on various occasions in front of clients.[6]

Because he found his work environment so hostile, Plaintiff sought and received permission from Burkett in June 1995 to return to Miami to perform his duties as Vice President from his home office. Despite Plaintiff's problems with Watson, Burkett assigned Watson to supervise Plaintiff after his return to Miami. * * *

After his move back to Miami, Plaintiff testifies that Watson continued to humiliate him and interfere with Plaintiff's ability to perform his

into the conversation and say he did not want Cubans in his neighborhood." "He said, 'I don't want Cubans in my neighborhood, and I'm not going to tell you where I live.'" One of Machado's co-workers, James Plant, testifies that Watson told Machado that a subdivision they were discussing "didn't allow Cubans." Another co-worker wrote the following statement describing a similar incident:

> Ed Machado, Barry Watson and I were in my office discussing Ed's relocation to Houston. Ed inquired about the Woodlands and I provided some general information about housing, schools, etc. I told Ed that he should come out to the area and see what is available. I also told Ed that if he was considering a move to the north side of Houston there were other nice areas he should check such as Barry's subdivision. I asked Barry if he was aware of any houses for sale or lease in his neighborhood. Barry responded that he didn't want Cubans moving into the neighborhood. Barry then left my office. Ed shook his head and then left. Ed was very upset by Barry's remark, which I also perceived Barry's statement to be an ethnic slur.

4. In this letter, Plaintiff wrote the following:

> [I]t appears that the position [of Vice President] was in title only. In reality, not only have I not been allowed to make the decisions that the position calls for, I am no longer allowed the decision making authority of my previous position. To make matters worse, I have been looked down upon and treated with disrespect. I have had senior personnel make derogatory remarks such as "I don't want Cubans living in my neighborhood" and have been told to "shush" in the middle of an office meeting. Furthermore, prior to my departure to the Far East, I was told to "play dumb." During my visit in Thailand, I was told by the companies I visited that they were informed that I was not the decision maker and that I was only there to look over equipment and pick up brochures. As someone who has dedicated his whole life to this industry, this situation was not only very embarrassing, but extremely degrading.

5. Plaintiff testifies that at a dinner with clients at which Burkett was present, during a conversation about Cuban baseball, Watson remarked, "Don't talk about Cubans. Ed gets upset."

6. For example, Plaintiff testifies that Watson embarrassed him at a meeting with clients; Watson was sitting next to Plaintiff, but when photos of the client's product were being passed around the table, Watson reached around Plaintiff and passed the photos to the person sitting on the other side of Plaintiff. On another occasion, Watson agreed to attend a business lunch with Plaintiff and some clients, but Watson did not show up.

job. For example, Plaintiff testifies that Watson repeatedly intercepted faxes and international correspondence to and from Plaintiff and responded to letters addressed to Plaintiff. Plaintiff also presents evidence that Watson denied Plaintiff's expense report, in which Plaintiff sought reimbursement for expenses he incurred equipping his home office; Plaintiff claims that the company had reimbursed several non-Hispanic employees for such expenses. Watson also warned Plaintiff that his meal expenses for entertaining clients "far exceeded" the company limit; Plaintiff has submitted evidence that his expenses were no greater than those claimed by other employees, but that other employees did not receive the warning Watson gave Plaintiff.

Plaintiff complained repeatedly to Burkett about Watson's behavior, but Burkett dismissed his complaints as petty and denied that Watson's behavior continued to be discriminatory or prejudiced. Because he felt that, if he remained with the company, Watson would continue to subject him to a hostile work environment and Burkett would not take action to stop Watson's discriminatory behavior, in August 1995, Plaintiff resigned from the company. * * *

[The court denied the defendant's motion for summary judgment on the claim of harassment because of national origin, but granted it on the constructive discharge claim.]

Notes and Questions

1. Note that the plaintiff in *Machado,* a Cuban, experienced little racism in Miami, but things were quite different after he moved to Houston, even though he worked for the same company. What might have accounted for the change?

2. In *Lopez*, the plaintiff suffered a great deal of racial harassment, before finally going to the authorities, then suing. Was he negligent in not reporting the problem as soon as it arose?

3. Racial slurs and jokes, if pervasive, can establish a hostile work environment. See Torres v. Pisano, 116 F.3d 625 (2d Cir. 1997). But these must be severe and frequent. Bender, supra. Where co-workers are the source of the abuse, management is liable if it knew about it and refused to intervene. Id. Women may suffer workplace harassment that is both sexual and racial. See Part Eight.

4. Is "lettuce picking" referring to a Mexican office worker offensive? Why or why not? Do not Mexicans, in fact, pick much of the nation's lettuce?

5. For additional cases featuring hostile, insulting language at work, see Marroquin v. City of Pasadena, 524 F.Supp.2d 857 (S.D.Tex. 2007); Alvarado v. Shipley Donut Flour & Supply Co., Inc., 526 F.Supp.2d 746 (S.D.Tex. 2007) (including terms such as wetback, fucking Mexican, stupid, lazy, taco eater). See also Section B infra (Hostile Workplace Discrimination).

A. EMPLOYMENT DISCRIMINATION BASED ON ENGLISH–ONLY RULES AND SIMILAR REQUIREMENTS

Employment discrimination can also take the form of discrimination based on speaking Spanish, especially on a jobsite that has enacted an English-only rule. See Part Three, Chapter 8 (discussing English–Only rules in other settings, such as state government). The EEOC considers this a form of discrimination barred by Title VII. Many courts, however, take the opposite position.

García v. Spun Steak Company
998 F.2d 1480 (9th Cir. 1993)

O'Scannlain, Circuit Judge.

We are called upon to decide whether an employer violates Title VII of the Civil Rights Act of 1964 in requiring its bilingual workers to speak only English while working on the job.

Spun Steak Company ("Spun Steak") is a California corporation that produces poultry and meat products in South San Francisco for wholesale distribution. Spun Steak employs thirty-three workers, twenty-four of whom are Spanish-speaking. Virtually all of the Spanish-speaking employees are Hispanic. While two employees speak no English, the others have varying degrees of proficiency in English. Spun Steak has never required job applicants to speak or to understand English as a condition of employment.

* * * Appellees García and Buitrago are production line workers; they stand before a conveyor belt, remove poultry or other meat products from the belt and place the product into cases or trays for resale. Their work is done individually. Both García and Buitrago are fully bilingual, speaking both English and Spanish.

* * *

Prior to September 1990, these Spun Steak employees spoke Spanish freely to their co-workers during work hours. After receiving complaints that some workers were using their bilingual capabilities to harass and to insult other workers in a language they could not understand, Spun Steak began to investigate the possibility of requiring its employees to speak only English in the workplace. Specifically, Spun Steak received complaints that García and Buitrago made derogatory, racist comments in Spanish about two co-workers, one of whom is African American and the other Chinese American.

The company's president, Kenneth Bertelsen, concluded that an English-only rule would promote racial harmony in the workplace. In addition, he concluded that the English-only rule would enhance worker safety because some employees who did not understand Spanish claimed that the use of Spanish distracted them while they were operating machinery, and would enhance product quality because the U.S.D.A.

inspector in the plant spoke only English and thus could not understand if a product-related concern was raised in Spanish. * * *

In addition, Spun Steak adopted a rule forbidding offensive racial, sexual, or personal remarks of any kind.

It is unclear from the record whether Spun Steak strictly enforced the English-only rule. According to the plaintiffs-appellees, some workers continued to speak Spanish without incident. Spun Steak issued written exceptions to the policy allowing its clean-up crew to speak Spanish, allowing its foreman to speak Spanish, and authorizing certain workers to speak Spanish to the foreman at the foreman's discretion. * * *

In November 1990, García and Buitrago received warning letters for speaking Spanish during working hours. For approximately two months thereafter, they were not permitted to work next to each other. Local 115 protested the English-only policy and requested that it be rescinded but to no avail.

On May 6, 1991, García, Buitrago, and Local 115 filed charges of discrimination against Spun Steak with the U.S. Equal Employment Opportunity Commission ("EEOC"). The EEOC conducted an investigation and determined that "there is reasonable cause to believe [Spun Steak] violated Title VII of the Civil Rights Act of 1964, as amended, with respect to its adoption of an English-only rule and with respect to retaliation when [García, Buitrago, and Local 115] complained."

García, Buitrago, and Local 115, on behalf of all Spanish-speaking employees of Spun Steak, (collectively, "the Spanish-speaking employees") filed suit, alleging that the English-only policy violated Title VII. On September 6, 1991, the parties filed cross-motions for summary judgment. The district court denied Spun Steak's motion and granted the Spanish-speaking employees' motion for summary judgment, concluding that the English-only policy disparately impacted Hispanic workers without sufficient business justification, and thus violated Title VII.

[The court decided that Local 115 had standing to sue on behalf of the Spanish-speaking employees at Spun Steak.] * * * It is well-settled that Title VII is concerned not only with intentional discrimination, but also with employment practices and policies that lead to disparities in the treatment of classes of workers. See, e.g., Griggs v. Duke Power Co., 401 U.S. 424, 430–31 (1971). Thus, a plaintiff alleging discrimination under Title VII may proceed under two theories of liability: disparate treatment or disparate impact. While the disparate treatment theory requires proof of discriminatory intent, intent is irrelevant to a disparate impact theory. * * *

The Spanish-speaking employees do not contend that Spun Steak intentionally discriminated against them in enacting the English-only policy. Rather, they contend that the policy had a discriminatory impact on them because it imposes a burdensome term or condition of employment exclusively upon Hispanic workers and denies them a privilege of employment that non-Spanish-speaking workers enjoy. Because their claim focuses on disparities in the terms, conditions, and privileges of employment, and not on barriers to hiring or promotion, it is outside the mainstream of disparate impact cases decided thus far. * * *

[The Court concludes that "a disparate impact claim may be based upon a challenge to a practice or policy that has a significant adverse impact on the 'terms, conditions, or privileges' of the employment of a protected group under section 703(a)(1)."]

To make out a *prima facie* case of discriminatory impact, a plaintiff must identify a specific, seemingly neutral practice or policy that has a significantly adverse impact on persons of a protected class. The burden [then] shifts to the employer to "demonstrate that the challenged practice is job related for the position in question and consistent with business necessity." 42 U.S.C.A. § 2000e–2(k)(1)(A) (Supp. 1992). In this case, the district court granted summary judgment in favor of the Spanish-speaking employees, concluding that, as a matter of law, the employees had made out the *prima facie* case and the justifications offered by the employer were inadequate.

* * *

It is beyond dispute that, in this case, if the English-only policy causes any adverse effects, those effects will be suffered disproportionately by those of Hispanic origin. The vast majority of those workers at Spun Steak who speak a language other than English—and virtually all those employees for whom English is not a first language—are Hispanic. It is of no consequence that not all Hispanic employees of Spun Steak speak Spanish; nor is it relevant that some non-Hispanic workers may speak Spanish. If the adverse effects are proved, it is enough under Title VII that Hispanics are disproportionately [burdened].

The crux of the dispute between Spun Steak and the Spanish-speaking employees, however, is not over whether Hispanic workers will disproportionately bear any adverse effects of the policy; rather, the dispute centers on whether the policy causes any adverse effects at all, and if it does, whether the effects are significant. The Spanish-speaking employees argue that the policy adversely affects them in the following ways: (1) it denies them the ability to express their cultural heritage on the job; (2) it denies them a privilege of employment that is enjoyed by monolingual speakers of English; and (3) it creates an atmosphere of inferiority, isolation, and intimidation. We discuss each of these contentions in turn.

The employees argue that denying them the ability to speak Spanish on the job denies them the right to cultural expression. It cannot be gainsaid that an individual's primary language can be an important link to his ethnic culture and identity. Title VII, however, does not protect the ability of workers to express their cultural heritage at the workplace. Title VII is concerned only with disparities in the treatment of workers; it does not confer substantive privileges. See, e.g., García v. Gloor, 618 F.2d 264, 269 (5th Cir. 1980), *cert. denied*, 449 U.S. 1113 (1981). It is axiomatic that an employee must often sacrifice individual self-expression during working hours. Just as a private employer is not required to allow other types of self-expression, nothing in Title VII requires an employer to allow employees to express their cultural identity.

Next, the Spanish-speaking employees argue that the English-only policy has a disparate impact on them because it deprives them of a privilege given by the employer to native-English speakers: the ability to converse on the job in the language with which they feel most comfortable. It is undisputed that Spun Steak allows its employees to converse on the job. The ability to converse—especially to make small talk—is a privilege of employment, [especially] in an assembly-line job. It is inaccurate, however, to describe the privilege as broadly as the Spanish-speaking employees urge us to do.

The employees have attempted to define the privilege as the ability to speak in the language of their choice. A privilege, however, is by definition given at the employer's discretion; an employer has the right to define its contours. Thus, an employer may allow employees to converse on the job, but only during certain times of the day or during the performance of certain tasks. The employer may proscribe certain topics as inappropriate during working hours or may even forbid the use of certain words, such as profanity.

Here, as is its prerogative, the employer has defined the privilege narrowly. When the privilege is defined at its narrowest (as merely the ability to speak on the job), we cannot conclude that those employees fluent in both English and Spanish are adversely impacted by the policy. Because they are able to speak English, bilingual employees can engage in conversation on the job. It is axiomatic that "the language a person who is multi-lingual elects to speak at a particular time is ... a matter of choice." *García*, 618 F.2d at 270. The bilingual employee can readily comply with the English-only rule and still enjoy the privilege of speaking on the job. "There is no disparate impact" with respect to a privilege of employment "if the rule is one that the affected employee can readily observe and nonobservance is a matter of individual preference."

This analysis is consistent with our decision in Jurado v. Eleven–Fifty Corporation, 813 F.2d 1406, 1412 (9th Cir. 1987). In *Jurado*, a bilingual disc jockey was fired for disobeying a rule forbidding him from using an occasional Spanish word or phrase on the air. We concluded that Jurado's disparate impact claim failed "because Jurado was fluently bilingual and could easily comply with the order" and thus could not have been adversely affected.

The Spanish-speaking employees argue that fully bilingual employees are hampered in the enjoyment of the privilege because for them, switching from one language to another is not fully volitional. Whether a bilingual speaker can control which language is used in a given circumstance is a factual issue that cannot be resolved at the summary judgment stage. However, we fail to see the relevance of the assertion, even assuming that it can be proved. Title VII is not meant to protect against rules that merely inconvenience some employees, even if the inconvenience falls regularly on a protected class. Rather, Title VII protects against only those policies that have a significant impact. The fact that an employee may have to catch himself or herself from occasionally slipping into Spanish does not impose a burden significant enough to amount to the denial of equal opportunity. This is not a case in which the employees have alleged that the company is enforcing the policy in such a way as to impose penalties for minor slips of the tongue. The fact that a bilingual employee may, on occasion, unconsciously substitute a Spanish word in the place of an English one does not override our conclusion that the bilingual employee can easily comply with the rule. In short, we conclude that a bilingual employee is not denied a privilege of employment by the English-only policy.

* * *

Finally, the Spanish-speaking employees argue that the policy creates an atmosphere of inferiority, isolation, and intimidation. Under this theory, the employees do not assert that the policy directly affects a term, condition, or privilege of employment. Instead, the argument must be that the policy causes the work environment to become infused with ethnic tensions. The tense environment, the argument goes, itself amounts to a condition of employment.

The Supreme Court in Mentor Savings Bank v. Vinson, 477 U.S. at 66, held that an abusive work environment may, in some circumstances, amount to a condition of employment giving rise to a violation of Title VII. * * * Although *Vinson* is a sexual harassment case in which the individual incidents involved behavior that was arguably intentionally discriminatory, its rationale applies equally to cases in which seemingly neutral policies of a company infuse the atmosphere of the workplace with discrimination. The *Vinson* Court emphasized, however, that discriminatory practices must be pervasive before an employee has a Title VII claim under a hostile environment theory.

Here, the employees urge us to adopt a *per se* rule that English-only policies always infect the working environment to such a degree as to amount to a hostile or abusive work environment. This we cannot do. Whether a working environment is infused with discrimination is a factual question, one for which a *per se* rule is particularly inappropriate. The dynamics of an individual workplace are enormously complex; we cannot conclude, as a matter of law, that the introduction of an English-only policy, in every workplace, will always have the same effect.

The Spanish-speaking employees in this case have presented no evidence other than conclusory statements that the policy has contributed to an atmosphere of "isolation, inferiority or intimidation." The bilingual employees are able to comply with the rule, and there is no evidence to show that the atmosphere at Spun Steak in general is infused with hostility toward Hispanic workers. Indeed, there is substantial evidence in the record demonstrating that the policy was enacted to prevent the employees from intentionally using their fluency in Spanish to isolate and to intimidate members of other ethnic groups. In light of the specific factual context of this case, we conclude that the bilingual employees have not raised a genuine issue of material fact that the effect is so pronounced as to amount to a hostile environment.

We do not foreclose the prospect that in some circumstances English-only rules can exacerbate existing tensions, or, when combined with other discriminatory behavior, contribute to an overall environment of discrimination. Likewise, we can envision a case in which such rules are enforced in such a draconian manner that the enforcement itself amounts to harassment. In evaluating such a claim, however, a court must look to the totality of the circumstances in the particular factual context in which the claim arises.

* * *

We do not reject the [EEOC's] English-only rule Guideline lightly. We recognize that "as an administrative interpretation of the Act by the enforcing agency, these Guidelines . . . constitute a body of experience and informed judgment to which courts and litigants may properly resort for guidance." *Meritor*, 477 U.S. at 65. But we are not bound by the Guidelines. We will not defer to "an administrative construction of a statute where there are 'compelling indications that it is wrong.' "

We have been impressed by Judge Rubin's pre-Guidelines analysis for the Fifth Circuit in *Garcia*, which we follow today. Nothing in the plain language of section 703(a)(1) supports EEOC's English-only rule Guideline. . . . It is clear that Congress intended a balance to be struck in preventing discrimination and preserving the independence of the employer. In striking that balance, the Supreme Court has held that a plaintiff in a disparate impact case must prove the alleged discriminatory effect before the burden shifts to the employer. The EEOC Guideline at issue here contravenes that policy by presuming that an English-only policy has a disparate impact in the absence of proof. We are not aware of, nor has counsel shown us, anything in the legislative history to Title VII that indicates that English-only policies are to be presumed discriminatory. Indeed, nowhere in the legislative history is there a discussion of English-only policies at all.

* * *

In sum, we conclude that the bilingual employees have not made out a *prima facie* case and that Spun Steak has not violated Title VII in adopting an English-only rule as to them. Thus, we reverse the grant of summary judgment in favor of García, Buitrago, and Local 115 to the extent it represents the bilingual employees, and remand with instructions to grant summary judgment in favor of Spun Steak on their claims. * * *

Reversed and Remanded.

Note. A forceful dissent by Judge Stephen Reinhardt, arguing that "language is intimately tied to national origins" and that English-only rules symbolize rejection of an entire culture, is not included.

Notes and Questions

1. In Garcia v. Gloor, 618 F.2d 264 (5th Cir. 1980), a Texas lumber supply company discharged Hector García for violating the company's English-only rule. The Fifth Circuit affirmed the trial court's judgment that his discharge was not unlawful. García, who was bilingual, had no "privilege" to speak Spanish on the job if work rules provided otherwise. And since he could speak English if he chose, his use of Spanish was not an unalterable trait linked with his national origin.

2. The alleged justifications for English-only rules, while superficially plausible, do not withstand critical analysis. See, e.g., Maldonado v. City of Altus, 433 F.3d 1294 (10th Cir. 2006) (finding an English-only workplace requirement inadequately supported by a business necessity); Juan F. Perea, *English-Only Rules and the Right to Speak One's Primary Language in the Workplace*, 23 U. Mich. J.L. Reform 265 (1990).

Suppose an employer refuses to hire someone who speaks English perfectly well but has a strong foreign accent? Consider the following selection:

Beatrice Bich–Dao Nguyen
Accent Discrimination and the Test of Spoken English:
A Call for an Objective Assessment of the
Comprehensibility of Nonnative Speakers
81 Cal. L. Rev. 1325, 1325–42, 1345–48, 1352–53 (1993)

Immigrants from all parts of the world come to the United States in the hope of building a better life for themselves and their children. For them, America embodies a land of opportunity, extending to each and every immigrant the hope of attaining the American Dream. In return, these immigrants bring with them their cultures and languages, enriching this nation's diversity. As they settle into their new lives and learn the customs of their adopted country, these new Americans reveal their status as immigrants through their accents.

Every individual has an accent that "carries the story" of who she is and that may identify her race, national origin, profession, and socioeconomic status. Yet we generally refer to an accent to indicate a "difference from some unstated norm of nonaccent, as though only some foreign few have accents."[3] As immigrants move into the work force to pursue freedom, equality, and economic opportunity, they may encounter the barrier of accent discriminations—"a closed economic door based on national origin discrimination."[6]

3. Mari J. Matsuda, *Voices of America: Accent, Antidiscrimination Law, and a Jurisprudence for the Last Reconstruction*, 100 Yale L.J. 1329, 1330 (1991).

6. Fragante v. City of Honolulu, 888 F.2d 591, 596 (9th Cir. 1989), *cert. denied*, 494 U.S. 1081 (1990).

Fearing the stigma that accompanies a foreign accent, some immigrants have turned to speech tutors, private companies, and colleges to eliminate or reduce their accents, even when their accents do not impair comprehensibility. Immigrants' perceived need to eliminate all traces of their accents in order to obtain employment or advance their careers is unfortunate. * * * "To tell the minority group member that he must discard the characteristic manifestations of his national identity in order to have a truly equal and fair opportunity to compete for a job is to tell him that his identity has no place in American society."[10]

Courts recognize that discrimination against accent may function as the equivalent of discrimination against national origin, which is prohibited under title VII of the Civil Rights Act of 1964 ("title VII" or "the Act"). Specifically, the Ninth Circuit has stated:

> Accent and national origin are obviously inextricably intertwined in many cases. It would therefore be an easy refuge in this context for an employer unlawfully discriminating against someone based on national origin to state falsely that it was not the person's national origin that caused the employment or promotion problem, but the candidate's inability to measure up to the communications skills demanded by the job. We encourage a very searching look by the district courts at such a claim.[13]

In addition, the Equal Employment Opportunity Commission (EEOC) has declared that discrimination based on a person's manner of speech or accent may constitute national origin discrimination under title VII.

Employers have a countervailing right to require sufficient communication skills from employees.[15] Nevertheless, the consistency with which employers raise the "unintelligible English" defense in accent cases[18] and the readiness of courts to uphold it threaten to nullify title VII's protection against national origin discrimination by leaving the determination of intelligibility to the subjective assessment of employers and courts.

* * *

---

10. Stephen M. Cutler, Comment, *A Trait–Based Approach to National Origin Claims Under Title VII*, 94 Yale L.J. 1164, 1177–78 (1985).

13. Fragante, supra note 6, at 596.

15. Professor Matsuda defines the problem this way:

The puzzle in accent cases is that accent is often derivative of race and national origin. Only Filipino people speak with Filipino accents. Yet, within the range of employer prerogatives, it is reasonable to require communication skills of employ-

ees. The claim that accent impedes job ability is often made with both sincerity and economic rationality. How, then, should Title VII squeeze between the walls of accent as protected trait and speech as job requirement?

Matsuda, supra note 3, at 1348.

18. Employers raising this defense to explain adverse employment decisions argue, based on subjective assessments, that job applicants' accents would have impeded job performance because the applicants' spoken English is not sufficiently comprehensible.

TITLE VII AND ACCENT DISCRIMINATION

In passing title VII, Congress made the momentous pronouncement that sex, race, color, religion, and national origin are not relevant to the selection, evaluation, or compensation of employees. Except for religion, these categories share a single distinctive aspect: each is an immutable trait with which an individual is born and which is beyond her power to alter. Congress intended, therefore, to compel employers to focus on individual qualifications, rather than on group identification, in making employment decisions.

Accent as an Aspect of an Immutable Trait

None of the legislative debates or committee reports accompanying title VII discusses the issue of what constitutes discrimination on the basis of national origin. In an effort to fill this gap, the EEOC defines national origin discrimination as including the denial of equal employment opportunity to a person because of her actual or ancestral place of origin, or because she has the physical, cultural, or linguistic characteristics of a national origin group. This includes discrimination based on an accent associated with foreign birth. The EEOC has found, for example, that the use of "Fluency-in-English requirements, such as denying employment opportunities because of an individual's foreign accent, or inability to communicate well in English," may constitute national origin discrimination.

Evidence that adults generally retain their natural accents supports the EEOC's determination and furthers Congress' intent of prohibiting discrimination based on immutable traits. Research in language acquisition shows that most people retain their original accents when they acquire a second language after childhood. One study of 109 speakers found that an individual's age at the time of second language acquisition is critical to the retention of an accent: when a child acquires a new language before age seven, there is no accent transfer; from ages seven to nine, there is a strong likelihood of acquiring accent-free speech in the second language; from nine to eleven, chances drop to about 50%; and from adolescence onward, chances of accent-free second language acquisition are minimal. Consequently, when employers use accent as a hiring criterion, they are discriminating against a trait which may be beyond the individual's power to control and which is indicative of national origin, a classification protected under title VII.

The Structure of Title VII Litigation

A title VII plaintiff may prove discrimination under a "disparate treatment theory" or a "disparate impact theory." Although plaintiffs alleging accent discrimination can bring suit under either theory, cases arc typically brought and analyzed as disparate treatment claims.

* * *

* * * To establish a prima facie case of national origin discrimination, a plaintiff must prove (1) that she has an identifiable national origin, (2) that she applied and was qualified for the job for which the employer was seeking applicants, (3) that she was rejected despite her qualifications, and (4) that, after her rejection, the position remained open and the employer continued to seek applicants from persons of the plaintiff's qualifications. * * *

> * * *

The defendant, rather than rebutting the plaintiff's prima facie case, may justify explicit discrimination by invoking the bona fide occupational qualification (BFOQ) exception to disparate treatment. The courts have construed the BFOQ exception as an affirmative defense for which the employer bears the initial burden of production and the ultimate burden of persuasion. To qualify as a BFOQ, a discriminatory job qualification must "affect an employee's ability to do the job,"[42] and "must relate to the 'essence' or to the 'central mission of the employer's business.'"[43]

Disparate Impact Claims

Under a disparate impact theory, discrimination results when facially neutral employment policies and practices even-handedly applied to all employees and applicants have a disproportionate, negative effect on members of protected groups. Disparate impact doctrine thus focuses on policies or practices that constitute part of an employer's standard operating procedure, rather than on isolated or sporadic discriminatory actions. Consequently, claims under this theory must demonstrate that the employer's practices cause broader harm than the harm it caused to the plaintiff alone.

The plaintiff establishes a prima facie case by showing that the adverse effects of defendant's employment criteria fall in significant disproportion on the plaintiff's protected group. Once this disparate impact is established, the burden then shifts to the employer to show that it results from a "business necessity," that is, that the employer's challenged practice "bear[s] a demonstrable relationship to successful performance of the jobs for which it [is] used."[47] If the employer meets this burden, the plaintiff must show that "other ... selection devices, without a similarly undesirable ... effect, would also serve the employer's legitimate interest."[48]

The plaintiff need not prove discriminatory motive in making a disparate impact claim. The plaintiff thus bears a lighter burden of proof

---

42. UAW v. Johnson Controls, Inc., 111 S. Ct. 1196, 1205 (1991).

43. Id. (quoting *Dothard*, 433 U.S. at 333; Western Air Lines v Criswell, 472 U.S. 400, 413 (1985)).

47. Griggs v. Duke Power Co., 401 U.S. 424, 431 (1971); see also Albemarle Paper Co. v. Moody, 422 U.S. 405, 431 (1975) ("[D]iscriminatory tests are impermissible unless shown, by professionally acceptable methods, to be 'predictive of or significantly correlated with important elements of work behavior which comprise or are relevant to the job or jobs for which candidates are being evaluated.'") (quoting 29 C.F.R. § 1607.4(c)).

48. Albemarle Paper Co., 422 U.S. at 425 (discussing use of general ability tests in racial context).

than the plaintiff in a disparate treatment case, who must show discriminatory intent. * * *

The Puzzle of Accent Discrimination Cases in the Title VII Framework

Accent discrimination cases are distinct from race and gender discrimination cases, as well as from other national origin discrimination cases, because courts must expressly examine the trait in question and evaluate it in relation to a plaintiff's job qualifications. In contrast, the court in a race or gender discrimination case would consider the plaintiff's immutable trait only to determine if she were in a protected class and would never ask whether the plaintiff's race or gender made her competent for the job in question.

A major challenge in applying title VII to accent discrimination cases is the difficulty in determining which accents actually impede job performance and which "simply differ[ ] from some preferred norm imposed, whether consciously or subconsciously, by the employer."[52] Trial courts currently lack an objective method to accomplish this task. Instead, they rely heavily on the defendant employer's appraisal and on their own subjective assessment of the accent. [S]uch assessments are almost unavoidably tainted with the biases and prejudices that make accent discrimination an accepted phenomenon.

Speech and Cultural Stereotypes

Studies of speech evaluation show that we are particularly susceptible to cultural stereotypes. For example, linguists using "matched guise" tests have found that a listener attaches cultural meanings to an accent which derives from the stereotypes and prejudices that the listener holds towards the race or ethnic group associated with that accent. Although we may believe that certain accents are inherently more comprehensible or euphonious, our judgments stem from associations and cultural meanings imprinted on our unconscious minds. An accent that one culture denigrates as low-class, vulgar, or rough may be esteemed as interesting or pretty in another.

Such stereotyping also affects a listener's assessment of a speaker's intelligibility. Comprehension is as much a function of attitude as of variability. Research shows that language variability is inevitable and that moderate accent differences rarely impede communication when listeners are motivated and nonprejudiced. But when listeners succumb to bias, their ability to assess and comprehend speech diminishes. This affects employment decisions and reinforces the acceptance of accent discrimination.

Ready Acceptance of Accent Discrimination

While Americans generally disavow race or gender discrimination, many accept accent discrimination as reasonable. Criticism of individuals based on their accents is commonplace and elicits few protests. For

---

52. Matsuda, supra note 3, at 1352.

example, in 1988, the editors of the *San Jose Mercury News* recommended against voting for A.L. Hahn, a young Korean American who ran for city council in Santa Clara, California, despite their general agreement with Hahn on the issues. Among other reasons for withholding support, the editors stated that, although "[w]e like Hahn, ... we think his heavy accent ... would make it difficult for him to be an effective councilman."[62] One could hardly imagine a responsible newspaper making the same statement about an African American woman and declaring that her skin color or sex would impede her success as a council member. Yet, because Mr. Hahn's accent was at issue and not another immutable trait, the *San Jose Mercury News* appeared comfortable in making and publishing this discriminatory statement.

By accepting such seemingly neutral observations with regard to accent, one overlooks the damaging impact such discrimination has on accented individuals. Even though immigration continually changes the ethnic composition of the United States, accents are still an impediment, even a stigma, for those in schools, workplaces, and social settings. Because their English does not conform to the accepted norm, accented individuals are frequently subjected to off-color remarks, gibes, and ridicule, causing feelings of anger, insecurity, and shame. For example, Galo Conde, a New York City public school teacher who arrived in the United States from Colombia twenty years ago, says that others, including his students, have often snubbed him because of his accent. He says that "[s]ometimes native Americans act like they have never heard a person with an accent." Carmen Friedman, another Colombian immigrant, took classes to eliminate her accent after realizing it had not diminished during her five years in the United States. Although she could communicate effectively in English, she did not "want to feel uncomfortable every time [she] sa[id] something," or have her "accent hurt [her] self-esteem anymore."

Bias against accents also manifests itself in the employment context. * * * In one instance, a Dominican woman from Queens enrolled in accent-elimination classes after her managers complained, in otherwise positive job reviews, that they could not understand her because of her accent. The woman, a 48–year-old senior accountant, suspects that the criticism was a pretext to keep her from being promoted: she had received no such criticism previously in her twenty years with the employer, and a speech evaluation clinic found her speech easy to understand.

* * *

* * * Maria Delgado tells the same story, stating that "[i]f they don't happen to need a Hispanic or bilingual person, they don't hire me. They hire the American. Well, I'm American, too! I think it would help if my accent was not so obvious."[67]

---

62. *For Santa Clara Council*, San Jose Mercury News, Oct. 18, 1988, at 6B.

67. Peggy Landers, *Accent on Understanding*, Miami Herald, Mar. 6, 1986, at

* * *

Customer Preference

Bias against accented individuals and the ready acceptance of accent discrimination also led to wider judicial acceptance of the customer preference defense in accent discrimination cases. Courts in accent cases regularly approve customer preference defenses even though they have consistently rejected them in other types of title VII suits.

* * *

But when it comes to accent discrimination cases, the courts currently accept defenses with a disconcertingly familiar ring: "We have nothing against immigrants. We simply can't have someone with an accent doing this job. Our customers won't be able to understand her."[76]

In many jobs, of course, successful job performance will depend on the employee's ability to speak with a certain level of intelligibility. Nevertheless, employers often make such claims without any empirical foundation, incorrectly assuming the inability of customers to comprehend certain accents. Given the linguistic evidence that comprehension adjustments are relatively easy for motivated listeners, claims of customer preference should be supported at least by some evidence. The second problem is actual prejudice. An employer may associate an accent with negative traits, such as laziness or lack of intelligence, because the employer holds negative stereotypes and prejudices against a particular race or ethnic group. By accepting the customer preference defense without close scrutiny, the courts fail to determine whether customers actually have such preferences, and whether the defense is a pretext for prejudice against accented individuals.

Examples of Accent Discrimination

Fragante v. City & County of Honolulu

Manuel Fragante, then a sixty-year-old Filipino immigrant, applied for an entry-level Civil Service Clerk job at the City of Honolulu's Division of Motor Vehicles and Licensing (DMV). The position involved constant public contact, as well as clerical tasks. Mr. Fragante scored the highest of 721 test takers on the written Civil Service Examination, which tested word usage, grammar, and spelling. He was ranked first on a certified list of eligible candidates for two clerical positions.

1B.

76. Fragante v. City of Honolulu, 669 F. Supp. 1429, 1431–32 (D. Haw. 1987), *aff'd*, 888 F.2d 591 (9th Cir. 1989), *cert. denied*, 494 U.S. 1081 (1990), is one example:

The job [as a DMV clerk] is a difficult one because it involves dealing with a great number of disgruntled members of the public.... Fragante was bypassed because of his "accent."

... While Plaintiff has extensive verbal communication skill in English it is understandable why the interviewers might reach their conclusion. And while there is no necessary relationship between accent and verbal communication ... listeners stop listening to Filipino accents, resulting in a breakdown of communication.

Two DMV employees, the assistant licensing administrator and the division secretary, then interviewed Mr. Fragante. The interview consisted of a ten to fifteen minute conversation. The interviewers had no list of standard questions, but rather a "rating sheet" one of the interviewers had devised, which an expert in employment practices would later call the "worst" he had seen in his thirty-five years of experience in the field. Both interviewers reported difficulty in understanding Mr. Fragante because of his Filipino accent and determined that DMV patrons would have similar difficulty when speaking to Mr. Fragante over the telephone or at the information counter. Due to their judgment that Mr. Fragante's accent would interfere with his job performance, the interviewers gave him a negative recommendation. Mr. Fragante dropped from the top of the list of eligible candidates and was not offered the DMV job.

The district court upheld the employment decision, observing that:

> The job is a difficult one because it involves dealing with a great number of disgruntled members of the public. The clerk must deal with 200–500 people per day, many of whom are angry or complaining and who do not want to hear what the clerk may have to explain concerning their applications or in answer to their questions.[85]

The district court's remarks appear to condone the idea that anticipated customer preference may dictate whether an accented individual is hired. The court emphasized not whether Mr. Fragante was intelligible, but rather the intolerance of "disgruntled members of the public" and their unwillingness to deal with an accented individual. The Ninth Circuit accepted the district court's approach, noting the trial court's observation that "Fragante, in fact, has a difficult manner of pronunciation."[88] Relying on this statement, the Ninth Circuit affirmed the district court's decision on the ground that Mr. Fragante was passed over because of the "deleterious *effect* of his Filipino accent on his ability to communicate orally, not merely because he had such an accent."[89]

The problem in the opinions of the district court and the Ninth Circuit is that both courts deferred to the subjective assessments of the interviewers who spoke to Mr. Fragante. These interviewers had no formal training in interviewing, and they used rating sheets that were "vague," "inadequate," and "not clearly job related nor well defined."[90] The district court also relied on its own subjective assessment to determine, after listening to him in court, that Mr. Fragante "has a difficult manner of pronunciation."[91] The courts had no objective method of evaluating Mr. Fragante's accent or its impact on listeners. They found his accent deleterious to his ability to communicate without any empiri-

---

85. Fragante v. City of Honolulu, 699 F. Supp. 1429, 1431 (D. Haw. 1987), *aff'd*, 888 F.2d 591 (9th Cir. 1989), *cert. denied*, 494 U.S. 1081 (1990).

88. Fragante, 888 F.2d at 598.

89. Id. at 599.

90. Fragante, 699 F. Supp. at 1430. An industrial psychologist testified that the interview and the rating system were "entirely subjective and did not meet federal or any acceptable standards of collective decisionmaking." Id.

91. Id. at 1432.

cal evidence that customers would not understand him. Moreover, the courts' reliance on subjective assessments posed the real danger that prejudice, whether conscious or unconscious, may have entered into the evaluation of Mr. Fragante's accent.

* * *

ADDING AN OBJECTIVE ELEMENT TO ACCENT DISCRIMINATION CASES

In these and other race discrimination cases, courts have recognized the danger of prejudice that inheres when those with decision-making authority assess employees of another racial group in the absence of objective criteria. * * * Recall that in *Fragante* the district court acknowledged defects in the interviewing process but nevertheless sustained the interviewers' decision that Mr. Fragante's accent would impede his job performance, finding that the rating system was not discriminatory. The court, however, never questioned the subjectivity of the assessments. Moreover, both the district court and the Ninth Circuit ignored the very real possibility of speech and cultural stereotypes intruding into employment decisions in such situations.

This permissive approach to accent discrimination cases clashes with the close scrutiny courts give to subjective evaluations in the context of racial discrimination because of their inherent potential for prejudice. * * *

A Call for Objectivity and the Test of Spoken English

Cognizant of the dangers inherent in subjective evaluations of accent, this Comment argues that courts should shift to objective methods of evaluation. * * *

* * *

The Test of Spoken English

The Educational Testing Service (ETS) developed the Test of Spoken English (TSE) in order to provide a reliable measure of proficiency in spoken English, affording educational institutions, government agencies, and other organizations an objective means of assessing the linguistic ability of nonnative speakers of English. Academic institutions currently use TSE scores to evaluate the spoken English of applicants for teaching assistantships or other academic positions, while various professional licensing agencies use the scores for selection and certification purposes.

The TSE provides an objective evaluation of the spoken English of those who have learned English as a second language, regardless of their native language. Although the test is not targeted to any specialized language usage, its value as a predictor of language skills in the employment context has been proven in a variety of communication-intensive jobs.

* * *

The TSE is an effective tool that provides an objective method of evaluating an individual's accent. Such a testing method would address the subjectivity problem infecting the adjudication of current accent discrimination cases by eliminating the need to rely on the subjective assessments of employers and fact finders, thereby lessening the possibility of speech and cultural stereotypes affecting the outcome. Moreover, the TSE would aid courts in drawing a rational line between plaintiffs whose speech is insufficiently comprehensible for the performance of a particular job and those who merely possess accents different from the accepted norm.

Parties and courts in accent discrimination cases [should] use the TSE as an objective guide to determine whether a plaintiff's accent would impede her ability to perform a particular job. Introduction of the TSE would not fundamentally alter the structure of title VII litigation in accent discrimination cases; it would simply add an objective element to them. TSE scores that indicate sufficient language skills for a particular job should constitute evidence of discrimination, but not discrimination per se, while low scores could establish lack of discrimination or discriminatory intent.

Use of this objective test may have led to different results in the cases discussed above and would certainly influence the outcome of future cases. More important than the result in any particular case, however, would be the TSE's effect of moving courts away from reliance on subjective assessments of a plaintiff's accent and the associated danger of prejudice and negative stereotypes affecting the outcome of accent discrimination litigation.

Notes and Questions

1.   The English–Only workplace cases have drawn much commentary from legal academics. See, e.g., Cristina M. Rodriguez, *Language Diversity in the Workplace*, 100 Nw. U. L. Rev. 1689 (2006); Mark Colon, *Line Drawing, Code Switching, and Spanish as Second–Hand Smoke: English–Only Workplace Rules and Bilingual Employees*, 20 Yale L. & Pol'y Rev. 227 (2002); Juan F. Perea, *English-Only Rules and the Right to Speak One's Primary Language in the Workplace*, 23 U. Mich. J.L. Reform 265 (1990).

2.   Is the "free choice" argument that courts use to deny claims of bilingual employees (i.e., that being bilingual they could, if they chose, speak only English) fully convincing?

3.   Can a person who learns a foreign language as an adult ever lose his accent completely? Experience suggests that this is very difficult, if not impossible. Does the Fragante case impose an unreasonable requirement, then? The E.E.O.C. takes the position that an employer may not discriminate unless a worker's accent interferes materially with ability to perform the work.

4.   Is it true, as Nguyen writes, that we all speak with an accent, but that society deems some inferior and others superior?

5. Why should employers care what language Spanish (or French, for that matter) speakers use at work when communicating with each other, and not with the public?

6. May a city or state make U.S. citizenship a requirement for critical jobs such as peace officer? See Cabell v. Chávez-Salido, 454 U.S. 432 (1982), ruling that it may.

B. HOSTILE WORKPLACE DISCRIMINATION

Another type of discrimination, just now emerging in the case law, is "hostile workplace" lawsuits in which a worker alleges that an employer tolerated or created a racially oppressive environment for work. Needless to say, many courts have not welcomed such claims with open arms, especially when brought by Latino/as.

Reread *Lopez v. Union Tank Car* and *Machado v. Goodman Manuf. Co.*, in Section 1, supra.

Rivera v. College of DuPage
445 F. Supp. 2d 924 (N.D. Ill. 2006)

ELAINE E. BUCKLO, DISTRICT JUDGE.

Plaintiff, who is bilingual, has brought a two-count complaint against his employer alleging that his immediate supervisor instructed him on five occasions during a five-month period not to speak in Spanish to his fellow employees. After plaintiff complained to the College's human resources department, he alleges that his supervisor commented twice more about his Spanish-speaking, and that another supervisor also once instructed him not to speak Spanish. In addition, he alleges that he suffered "retaliatory reprisals" from his immediate supervisor, including that she (1) ridiculed the amount of food that he consumed (though this ridicule actually began over a year before his internal complaint); (2) once told him not to use a golf cart that was assigned to other workers; (3) once told him not to park his truck behind a particular building; (4) once told him not to allow a riding mower to continue running while not in use; (5) once told him not to clean a lawnmower in a particular location; (6) once told him not to read in a particular area during a break; (7) once told him not to listen to his personal stereo; (8) once told him not to use a workbench another employee had asked to have for himself; (9) gave him both verbal and written warnings about his display of a temper and his assistance to a student with car problems; and (10) flipped her middle finger at him on one occasion (though she had done this several times prior to his complaint), whispered to him that he was a "fucking asshole," and told him that he had an attitude problem.

Even taking the facts in the light most favorable to the plaintiff, and drawing all reasonable and justifiable inferences in his favor, as I am required, I must grant defendant's motion for summary judgment. Count I of plaintiff's complaint alleges he was discriminated against on the basis of his national origin because of the defendant's "English-only rule." However, the undisputed facts show that the eight times his supervisors instructed him to speak only in English did not constitute an "English-only rule." Neither plaintiff nor any other employee suffered any disciplinary write-up, loss of pay, suspension, or any other materially adverse employment action as a result of speaking Spanish.

Count II of plaintiff's complaint alleges that he was retaliated against after reporting to upper-level management that his immediate supervisor had instructed him not to speak Spanish. Rivera contends that he can use the direct method to show this retaliation because he can demonstrate that (1) he engaged in statutorily protected activity; (2) he suffered an action that would have been materially adverse to a reasonable employee; and (3) there is a causal connection between the two. While Rivera did engage in a statutorily protected activity by complaining to his supervisor, there is no evidence from which to infer a causal connection between his complaints and his supervisor's actions. Neither can Rivera proceed using the indirect method of proof. Rivera has presented no evidence of similarly-situated employees who did not complain about the purported "English-only" rule who were treated differently. Further, Rivera cannot show that he suffered a materially adverse action. To be materially adverse, an action must "have dissuaded a reasonable worker from making or supporting a charge of discrimination." Rivera was not terminated, suspended, demoted, docked any pay, or given undesirable work assignments after complaining about his supervisor's comments or filing an EEOC charge. Instead, his supervisor gave him comments and warnings about his job performance (which Rivera believes was an "unjustified higher level of scrutiny"), ridiculed the amount of food he ate, and on one occasion, made an obscene gesture at him and called him an obscene epithet. While these actions may have been stressful or hurtful to Rivera, they would not have dissuaded a reasonable employee from making a complaint.

In his response, plaintiff argues that his supervisor's policy prohibiting Spanish-speaking in the workplace created a hostile work environment for him. Setting aside the fact that neither his EEOC charge nor his complaint articulate this theory, the facts do not show that the supervisor's directions to speak English were so "severe or pervasive" as to constitute a hostile work environment. In considering whether conduct is severe or pervasive, I have considered "the totality of the circumstances, including the 'frequency of the discriminatory conduct; its severity; whether it is physically threatening or humiliating, or a mere offensive utterance; and whether it unreasonably interferes with an employee's work performance.' " While even eight comments over a few months' time may in some circumstances create such an environment, the conduct here was infrequent, it was not physically threatening, it did not amount to an "English-only policy," and it did not interfere with Rivera's work performance. It may have been inappropriate and subjectively offensive to Rivera (and may have had a greater impact on other employees who are not parties to this suit), but it did not rise to the level of a hostile work environment for him.

Notes and Questions

1. Note the considerable amount of harassment that the Latino plaintiff had to endure: His employer showed him the middle finger; whispered that he is a "fucking asshole"; ridiculed his eating habits (presumably, foreign food), and instructed him eight times not to speak Spanish. All this evidence did not rise to the level of "severe or pervasive" required under hostile-workplace law. For a more sympathetic view, see Machado v. Goodman Mfg. Co., 10 F. Supp. 2d 709 (S.D. Tex. 1997), reprinted supra, which was decided, in part, on hostile-workplace grounds. See also Valdez v. Big O Tires, Inc., 2006 WL 1794756 (D. Ariz.), making similar finding in case of worker repeatedly called "wetback," "sand nigger," and "stupid-ass beaner."

The law on immigration raids on factories and other workplaces is evolving. See Bender, supra, discussing Immigration and Nationalization Serv. v. Delgado, 466 U.S. 210 (1984) (workers under no duty to speak to agents or answer questions without a lawyer).

2. See also *Marroquin v. City of Pasadena* and *Alvarado v. Shipley Donuts*, cited in Section 1, supra, for examples of graphic, insulting language that courts found not to satisfy the requirements of a hostile-workplace suit.

C. WHEN ONE MINORITY GROUP DISCRIMINATES AGAINST ANOTHER

As with hostile-workplace law, which courts have been slow to recognize, at least in the case of Latinos, courts have been quick to discern discrimination between different groups of color. See Tanya Kateri Hernández, *Latino Inter–Ethnic Employment Discrimination and the "Diversity" Defense*, 42 Harv. C.R.-C.L. L. Rev. 259 (2007). Consider the following case of employment discrimination between Colombians and Cubans.

Cardona v. American Exp. Travel Related Services
720 F.Supp. 960 (S.D. Fla. 1989)

JAMES LAWRENCE KING, Chief Judge.

Before the court is the defendants' motion to dismiss the plaintiff's claim under 42 U.S.C. § 1981. Defendants move to dismiss for failure to state a claim upon which relief can be granted. After careful review of the defendants' motion, the plaintiff's response and the reply thereto, and the complaint, and being otherwise fully advised, the court denies the motion to dismiss.

In his complaint, the plaintiff alleges that he was discriminated against because of his race by the management employees of American

Express Travel Related Services Co., Inc. (American Express) during the course of his employment with American Express. The plaintiff, a Colombian by national origin, seeks declaratory and injunctive relief and damages, claiming that he was discriminated against in violation of Title VII of the Civil Rights Act of 1964 and 42 U.S.C. § 1981. The plaintiff alleges that management employees discriminated against him by passing him over for promotion in favor of less qualified employees of Cuban national origin, and subsequently fired him for voicing his opposition to this allegedly discriminatory policy. The plaintiff's claim stated in three counts: Count I seeks injunctive and declaratory relief and damages for discrimination under Title VII; Count II seeks injunctive and declaratory relief, including reinstatement to his former position, and damages under 42 U.S.C. § 1981; and Count III seeks actual and exemplary damages under § 1981.

The defendants, in their motion to dismiss, raise two issues, both pertaining to Counts II and III. First, the defendants claim that as a Colombian, the plaintiff is not a member of a protected race under § 1981, but rather is a member of the larger, protected group of Latins or Hispanics. Defendants argue that the plaintiff alleges that he was discriminated against in favor of other members of the same race, that is, Latins who happen to be of Cuban national origin rather than Colombian, and that therefore he has failed to state a claim under § 1981.

Second, the defendants assert that the plaintiff has failed to state a claim in light of Patterson v. McLean Credit Union, 491 U.S. 164 (1989). The substance of this ground for dismissal is that the plaintiff has not specifically alleged that he was denied any post-employment opportunity which would have changed the nature of his contractual relationship with American Express.

Race Discrimination Under § 1981

The plaintiff alleges in Counts II and III of his complaint that he was discriminated against because he is a Colombian by national origin and by ancestry and/or ethnic characteristics. The United States Supreme Court, in St. Francis College v. Al–Khazraji, 481 U.S. 604 (1987), held that while a claim of discrimination based solely on the place or nation of the claimant's origin is not sufficient to state a claim under § 1981, "Congress intended to protect from discrimination identifiable classes of persons who are subjected to intentional discrimination solely because of their ancestry or ethnic characteristics." Among the ethnic groups noted by the Court to be distinct races in its review of the legislative history of § 1981 are Latins, Mexicans, and Spanish. Also distinguished as separate races because of their ethnicity are Finns, Norwegians, and Swedes, who are traditionally considered to be members of the Scandinavian races. Other ethnic groups are given separate status under § 1981 merely because of their country of origin and the ethnicity associated with people from those countries.

The defendants claim that Colombians and Cubans are members of the Latin race, and that therefore § 1981 protections do not apply to discrimination between the two groups. The court is not persuaded by this argument, nor does it find that to be the Supreme Court's interpretation of the intent of § 1981.

The plaintiff claims that he was discriminated against because of his Colombian ancestry or ethnic background, as well as his national origin. Merely because he is a member of a larger group of Spanish speaking peoples that have come to be known as Latins does not remove from the plaintiff his ethnicity as a Colombian. Much as the Scandinavian peoples of Norway, Sweden and Finland retain their status as members of separate races because of their ethnicity, the people from the Spanish speaking countries of the Caribbean Basin, Central and South America all have unique ethnic characteristics that distinguish them from each other as separate races within the intent of § 1981. Just as Scandinavians from Finland may be discriminated against in favor of Scandinavians from Sweden, so too are Latins from one country, who have distinct ethnic and cultural characteristics, susceptible to being discriminated against in favor of Latins from another country. Language itself is not dispositive in defining ethnic groups: the Supreme Court distinguishes between Spanish speaking Mexicans, Spaniards and Latins; indeed, within the Spanish speaking Latin superset are Brazilians, who speak Portuguese. Accordingly, the court holds that a person of Colombian ancestry who claims that because of his ethnic background he was discriminated against in favor of employees of Cuban ancestry, who have little in common with Colombians other than the Spanish language as the tongue of their ancestral home, has stated a claim under § 1981.

Discrimination in Post Employment Promotions Under § 1981

Notwithstanding the plaintiff's status as a member of a recognized racial group entitled to protection under § 1981, the defendants move to dismiss his complaint on the grounds that § 1981 does not apply to post employment discriminatory conduct practiced by a private employer. The defendants rely on the Supreme Court's decision in Patterson v. McLean Credit Union, 491 U.S. 164 (1989), arguing that the plaintiff fails to state a claim because he does not specifically allege that the defendants denied him a promotion which would have resulted in a new contract between the plaintiff and the defendant.

The Court in *Patterson* took exception to the Court of Appeals' pronouncement that claims of racial discrimination in making promotions " 'fall easily within § 1981's protection.' " Id. Rather, the Court held a promotion discrimination claim to be actionable only where it stems from the denial of an opportunity for an employee to enter into a new contract with the employer. Whether a new contract opportunity exists depends on whether "the promotion rises to the level of an opportunity for a new and distinct relationship between the employee and the employer...."

The Court in *Patterson* did not hold that to state a claim under § 1981 a plaintiff must specifically plead that the discriminatory promotion practices of an employer denied the employee an opportunity to enter into a new contract with the employer. Rather, the Court held that it was error for the District Court to instruct the jury that the employee alleging discriminatory promotion practices need only show that she was better qualified than a white applicant who got the job, without requiring a showing of intentional discrimination. Id. The plaintiff Nelson Cardona has alleged that he was denied promotions through the intentional racial discrimination of the defendants. He has not stated the nature of those opportunities, but this court does not believe that Patterson requires him to so specifically plead. Nor does this court believe that it is required to dismiss the plaintiff's claim without giving him the opportunity to develop his claim and carry his burden of proving that he was discriminatorily denied new contract opportunities.

CONCLUSION

The plaintiff's claim can hardly be said to be frivolous as pleaded. On its face, the complaint alleges intentional racial discrimination by the defendant against the plaintiff, who is a member of an ethnic group distinct from those employees whom he claims received preferential treatment and promotions at his expense. It is readily conceivable that the plaintiff could develop and show facts which would prove that he was intentionally discriminated against because of his race, that as a result of this discrimination he was denied promotions, and that the opportunities he was denied would have resulted in new contracts with the defendant employer. Therefore, this court finds that the plaintiff has stated a claim for which relief may be granted under § 1981. Accordingly, it is

ORDERED and ADJUDGED that the defendants' motion to dismiss be, and the same is hereby DENIED.

DONE and ORDERED.

D. OTHER FORMS OF WORK-RELATED OR ECONOMIC DISCRIMINATION

Kevin R. Johnson
Driver's Licenses and Undocumented Immigrants:
The Future of Civil Rights Law?
5 Nev. L.J. 213, 213–20, 223–26, 231–32, 235–37, 239 (2004)

In the United States, efforts to end racial discrimination have generally proceeded under the banner of civil rights. * * *

As immigration has dramatically transformed the demographics of this nation, the United States today is seeing a new generation of civil rights grievances that will for the foreseeable future generate new civil rights controversies. The nation has only begun to appreciate how Mexican migration has changed the entire country, not just the region known as the Southwest. Issues associated with immigration and border enforcement, language regulation, cultural difference, and equal citizenship and full membership are arising with increasing frequency and will likely continue to do so.

The nexus between immigration and civil rights has tightened as the overlap between immigrant and minority status has grown. From the late 1800s through 1965, the U.S. immigration laws preferred immigrants from northern Europe. In 1965, Congress repealed the discriminatory national origins quota system, which greatly increased migration from the developing world.

The globalizing world economy has accelerated the demographic changes in the United States. It is much more likely today that labor travels across national borders than a century ago. Many people of color from developing nations migrate to the developed world for jobs. The international labor market has created workers with ties and allegiances to more than one nation. For example, associations of Mexican immigrants from the same town, but living in this country—known as hometown associations, have become politically active in both the United States and Mexico. Global citizens with transnational identities pose challenges to the nation-state as it previously existed.

Liberalization of the immigration laws, combined with globalization, has assured that the vast majority of immigrants to the United States since 1965 are people of color. Many major U.S. civil rights laws do not, however, address discrimination based on immigration status. Indeed, discrimination against immigrants often is legally acceptable. Although the law ordinarily tolerates discrimination against immigrants within limits, it generally condemns racial discrimination. For example, although the requirement that a police officer be a U.S. citizen has withstood legal scrutiny, a racial prerequisite would not. Conceptions of civil rights, as well as legal remedies, must adapt to ensure that discrimination on the basis of immigration status does not effectively amount to discrimination on account of race. In other words, the law must police governmental conduct based on immigration status to ensure that it does not serve as a proxy for race and allow for circumvention of the core ban on anti-discrimination.

* * *

[C]onsider a matter that appears routine to most U.S. citizens: the ability to obtain a driver's license. The denial of licenses to undocumented immigrants generally increases fears of arrest and deportation, limits access to jobs, and increases immigrant vulnerability to exploitation by unscrupulous employers. Without acknowledging the impacts of the state policy at stake, the United States Supreme Court in 2001 rejected a class action challenge brought by a lawful immigrant from Mexico who primarily speaks Spanish, to Alabama's new English language requirement for driver's license tests.[18]

18. See Alexander v. Sandoval, 532 U.S.
275 (2001).

The state laws governing immigrant eligibility for driver's licenses follow a fascinating trajectory. As anti-immigrant sentiment hit a fever pitch in the early 1990s, states began limiting undocumented immigrant eligibility for driver's licenses. Over the last decade, civil rights activists in many states have pressed for undocumented immigrant eligibility for driver's licenses. Opposition to the calls for restoration of driver's license eligibility intensified with the fears generated by the tragic loss of life on September 11, 2001, which was perpetrated by noncitizens, many of whom had state-issued driver's licenses.

* * *

DRIVER'S LICENSES AS A CIVIL RIGHTS ISSUE

In recent years, states across the nation, from Georgia to California and Idaho to Rhode Island, have experienced political controversy over whether undocumented immigrants should be able to obtain driver's licenses. In California, for example, Latina/o legislators pressed aggressively for several years for a law that would permit certain undocumented immigrants to be eligible for a license and, after the law was passed, political controversy continued. States with burgeoning Latina/o populations across the nation have seen similar controversies. About thirty states, including Arizona, Colorado, Florida, Georgia, and Virginia, currently limit driver's license eligibility to lawful immigrants.

* * *

National security concerns understandably took on new urgency in the wake of the horrible loss of life that occurred on September 11, 2001. * * * In response, many states tightened the rules for obtaining driver's licenses. Congress held hearings on the issue, ultimately introducing a bill that would have required states to issue high tech driver's licenses.

National identification cards previously had been rejected on civil liberties grounds, with the primary concern being that such identifications would give the government undue power to violate the privacy of individuals. In light of the public's apparent willingness to trade off civil liberties for heightened security, national identity card proposals enjoyed a revival after September 11. In a new world preoccupied with security, a national identity card once again surfaced as a serious policy option.

* * *

* * * Although no widespread problems of identity fraud had resulted from issuing licenses to undocumented immigrants, the California Legislature enacted a new law in 1993 making only citizens and lawful immigrants eligible for driver's licenses, thus denying them to undocumented immigrants. This law came shortly before voters overwhelmingly approved the anti-immigrant initiative known as Proposition 187, which was marred by a campaign with distinctly anti-Mexican overtones and came to be seen as the embodiment of the nativist outburst of the early 1990s. The driver's license bill was one of many hotly contested matters such as undocumented immigrant access to public benefits, public education, bilingual education, and language rights during a sustained period in which California's Latina/o community felt under attack.

* * *

Courts historically have been deferential to the federal government's decisions to discriminate against noncitizens. They also have given considerable latitude to the states in the treatment of immigrants so long as the treatment poses no direct conflict with federal policy and does not purport to regulate immigration. Although Supreme Court decisions suggest possible grounds for constitutional challenges to the laws barring undocumented immigrants from obtaining a driver's license, to this point no court has actually invalidated a law.[44]

* * *

* * * All states and all drivers presumably would rather have licensed, safety-tested, drivers on the road than unlicensed drivers. State and local governments, concerned with safety and costs of medical care and emergency services for accidents, generally would support expanding eligibility for driver's licenses for public safety reasons. For precisely these types of reasons, the City of San Jose opposed passage of the California law in 1993 that denied licenses to undocumented immigrants:

> We believe the safety of the public is not served by denying driver's licenses to an entire segment of the population. It is to California's advantage to ensure that drivers are licensed and have proven their skills and knowledge of the vehicle code. By prohibiting licensing, registration and insuring of some immigrants, the public will be exposed to greater numbers of unsafe drivers. Further, the bill will not result in a curtailment of illegal immigration into California. . . .

Liability insurance companies naturally would favor maximizing the number of holders of driver's licenses, which in turn would improve driver safety and increase the market for insurance.

* * *

Criminal Justice Implications

The lack of an identification deeply affects the nature of undocumented immigrants' interactions with law enforcement officers. Lacking a license, an undocumented immigrant may want to avoid any interaction with the police and worry about possible deportation from the country for something as minor as a burned out taillight. Fear of deportation runs especially deep in immigrants with roots in the United States, such as those with U.S. citizen children; if deported, they may face loss of family, friends, and a job.

---

44. See John Doe No. 1 v. Georgia Dep't of Public Safety, 147 F. Supp. 2d 1369, 1376 (N.D. Ga. 2001); see also Lauderbach v. Zolin, 41 Cal. Rptr. 434, 439 (Cal. Ct. App. 1995) (holding that state could deny driver's licenses to immigrants without Social Security numbers who were unlawfully in the country but not to immigrants without Social Security numbers who were lawfully in the country).

Driving without a license is a crime in many states and, under certain circumstances, can result in deportation of an immigrant under the immigration laws. The Supreme Court has held that a state law may constitutionally allow for the arrest of a person for a minor traffic violation. Resisting arrest and other crimes resulting in possible deportation are more likely to occur as well if an undocumented immigrant fears arrest and deportation.

In some states, driving without a license may also be grounds for impoundment of the motor vehicle. At the same time, driving is a necessity for many people, including undocumented immigrants, who live and work in the United States. Consequently, we should assume that some undocumented immigrants will drive with or without a driver's license. It has been estimated that hundreds of thousands of unlicensed (and thus uninsured) drivers regularly drive in the state of California.

* * *

Efforts in recent years to enforce driver's license laws have adversely affected undocumented Latina/o immigrant workers. For example, in a small Kentucky town that had seen a rapid growth in its Latina/o population, local police, in the name of public safety, set up roadblocks on the road to a poultry processing plant, which employed many undocumented Mexican immigrants, to verify driver's licenses and motor vehicle registrations; many arrests resulted and the Immigration and Naturalization Service instituted deportation proceedings against some immigrants.

Thus, police practices make driver's licenses all the more important for Latina/o immigrants. * * * To facilitate law enforcement, many state and local police departments have worked for years to gain the trust and respect of the undocumented immigrant community. Effective law enforcement requires a good relationship between police and the immigrant community. To help encourage immigrants to cooperate with police, many departments prohibit officers from inquiring into the immigration status of any person—victim, witness, or perpetrator—and have resisted any involvement in immigration enforcement. Indeed, after September 11, some local police departments refused to cooperate with the federal government in interviewing Arab and Muslim noncitizens because of local policies precluding the inquiry into the immigration status of any person. In a system in which undocumented immigrants are denied driver's licenses, arrests for lack of a license will appear to the immigrant community as if the police are enforcing the immigration laws; such perceptions will thwart law enforcement efforts to gain the trust and cooperation of that community.

* * *

Driver's Licenses in the Supreme Court: Alexander v. Sandoval (2001)

To this point, the courts, including the United States Supreme Court, have not been particularly sensitive to the importance of driver's licenses to the immigrant community. In 1990, Alabama passed a law making English the official state language, which prompted the state to stop driver's testing in languages other than English. Previously, Alabama had administered examinations in over a dozen languages for more than twenty years.

In *Alexander v. Sandoval*, the Supreme Court failed to consider the racial and national origin impacts of Alabama's new requirement that driver's license testing be in English. This is true despite the fact that the new policy's disproportionate impact on minority communities. The Court decided the class action brought by Martha Sandoval, a legal immigrant from Mexico, on procedural grounds—that an implied private right of action did not lie under Title VI of the Civil Rights Act of 1964—and emphasized that it did not decide "whether the courts below were correct to hold that the English-only policy had the effect of discriminating on the basis of national origin."

The Alabama testing requirement did not expressly target immigrants or Latina/os. However, one could certainly understand that Alabama's change in its driver's license law to bar testing in any language other than English would primarily affect foreigners, including Latina Spanish speakers such as Martha Sandoval. The communities that would be affected reasonably should have been known to the law's supporters given the close nexus between immigration status, national origin, and English language proficiency in modern U.S. society. Nor was it a coincidence that the law was enacted at a time of high Latina/o immigration to the United States when nativist sentiment ran high.

In *Sandoval*, the Supreme Court wrestled with whether private parties could sue to enforce the provisions of a major civil rights law. The serious civil rights issues at stake to Latina/o immigrants were lost in legalisms. It was left for another day to analyze the discriminatory impacts of driver's license eligibility requirements.

* * *

THE EXPANSION OF CIVIL RIGHTS: IMMIGRATION, ALIENAGE, AND RACE

Immigration has transformed the United States and likely will continue to do so for the foreseeable future. After the elimination of racially discriminatory immigration laws in 1965, the flow of immigrants to the United States has been dominated by people of color from the developing world. * * * These immigrants share some of the same civil rights concerns as citizens of color in the United States. As the driver's license controversy reveals, however, immigrants have their own specific civil rights concerns.

* * *

Debates on issues like driver's license eligibility are not simply differences of opinion on matters of neutral public policy. Rather, the issues amount to a fight for status mobility in the United States. Latina/os, through measures seeking to ensure access to identification documents and to public universities, hope for access to the full amenities of social and economic life in the United States. One can expect these issues to increase with regularity due to a growing Latina/o, and immigrant, population working and living in the United States and seeking full membership.

* * *

The driver's license issue touches something deep for undocumented immigrants who live and work in the United States and seek some recognition of their membership in the national community. The controversy exemplifies the marginalized status of undocumented immigrants. A new Jim Crow has emerged, with undocumented immigrants filling segregated jobs and living in segregated housing, with the denial of an identification facilitating segregation. Through a variety of legal mechanisms, undocumented immigrants, many of them people of color, lose full memberships in U.S. society. Ensuring it for all contributing members of the national community who live and work within its boundaries may well be the pressing social issue of the next millennium.

Christopher David Ruiz Cameron
The Rakes of Wrath: Urban Agricultural Workers
and the Struggle Against Los Angeles's Ban
on Gas–Powered Leaf Blowers
33 U.C. Davis L. Rev. 1087, 1089–99 (2000)

During a year and-a-half of contentious debate, Los Angeles adopted, then amended, an ordinance banning the use of any "gas powered blower" to remove grass and leaves from lawns and walkways. Each violation of the ordinance is punishable by a fine not to exceed $100—a sum that represents about ten percent of a gardener's average monthly income of $1000. Other California cities and towns joined Los Angeles by enacting their own laws banning leaf blowers.

I argue that the leaf blower ban is to urban agriculture what the dreaded short hoe was to farm agriculture—namely, a way to enforce Latina/o invisibility and to subvert attempts by Latinas/os to assimilate into Anglo society. A farm worker using a short hoe must bend over to work. Stooping not only wrenches the back, but also ensures that the laborer, usually a Mexican immigrant, works without having to be seen, or heard, in the case of the leaf blower ban. . . . Indeed, like the short hoe, the leaf blower ban was sold to the public not as a means of racial oppression, but rather as benign guidance. Prominent advocates of the ban argued that, by foregoing gas-powered blowers in favor of rakes or brooms to ply their trade, Latina/o gardeners would pollute the environment less and actually lead healthier, more spiritually fulfilling lives.
* * *

SUBORDINATION OF LATINA/O GARDENERS

Tending the front and back yards of the landed gentry of Los Angeles is the work of as many as 65,000 Latina/o immigrants, nearly all of them men. By any measure, their work does not pay well. The average gardening crew, consisting of two to three men, charges $15 to $25 per yard and works ten to twenty yards per day. At these rates, the average gardener earns $250 per week, $1000 per month, and $12,000 per year. He works eight to twelve hours a day, six days a week, without overtime, paid vacation, or health insurance. If he does not work, then he does not get paid.

* * *

An important tool of the gardener's trade is the gasoline-powered blower, used to remove grass and leaf trimmings from freshly mowed lawns, clipped hedges, and wind-blown walkways. A twelve-pound machine, the blower is strapped to the gardener's back. Working with a nozzle attached to a lead hose, the gardener blows the trimmings into piles that he can conveniently sweep up and dispose of before he loads his pickup truck and drives off to the next job.

Gardeners estimate that it takes two to three times longer to clean a yard using rakes and brooms than it does to use a single leaf blower. Hiring more men for the crew might accomplish the task in less time, but many experienced gardeners believe that even long-time clients would balk at paying more. One gardener estimated that having to give up the leaf blower would cost him out $250 per month, a sum equal to as much as one fourth of an average gardener's income.

During the 1980s and 1990s, the sights and sounds of backpack-carrying Latino men using gas-powered blowers became familiar to Californians living in cities and suburbs the length of the state. Indeed, the notion of hiring professional hands to do work that dad, brother, or the neighbor's kid used to perform for pocket change was something new. Once a luxury confined to the enclaves of the rich and famous, hiring gardeners soon spread even to the homes and apartments of the middle class. In metropolitan Los Angeles, the hired gardener became common not only in the affluent communities of Bel Air, Brentwood, and Pacific Palisades, but also in such working-class communities as Lakewood, a community developed during the 1950s to house aerospace and defense plant workers. When the hired gardener arrived, so did his leaf blower.

Not everyone welcomed this transformation. By 1996, more than forty California cities and towns had passed ordinances banning or restricting the use of leaf blowers. Many residents complained about the noise and dust created by power mowers, motorized weed-whackers, and gas-powered leaf blowers. In Los Angeles, they made a well-publicized attempt to do something about it.

* * *

* * * Only in Hollywood can a handful of celebrities garner attention for a cause that might otherwise be ignored by an indifferent municipal electorate. So the Association of Latin American Gardeners of Los Angeles had to prepare to respond to testimony from television stars who spoke not only in their roles as residents of Los Angeles's affluent Westside, but also in their capacity as "experts" on the deleterious effects of gas-powered leaf blowers.

With a flair all their own, the celebrities offered three arguments. First, they argued that the devices are bad for the environment. * * *

* * *

Second, the celebrities argued that gas-powered blowers are bad for the gardeners' physical health. Meredith Baxter ticked off statistics about the dangers of using the devices, which she claimed expose gardeners to fire, smoke, and noise hazards. * * *

Third, the celebrities argued that the machines are bad for the gardeners' *spiritual* health. Julie Newmar suggested not only that the gardeners were ignoring the threat to their own health, but also that manufacturers of blowers were exploiting gardeners' ignorance. She told one newspaper: "These men are shuffling to the tunes of their manipulator. Your souls are being bought. The corruption should be banned. This is destructive technology run amok. I can't work in my office at my job anymore. Millions of people work at home. Don't we count?"

* * *

Latino gardeners and their allies responded to each of these arguments. As to the argument that blowers are bad for the environment, Adrian Alvarez, president of the association, conceded the point. But Alvarez contended that an outright ban was a smokescreen for discrimination against the Latino men who do physically demanding work of gardening. He said it was not a solution "when you deprive people of a fundamental tool" in earning a living. Alvaro Huerta, general secretary of the association, added: "[The ban is part of a] series of attacks against the Latino immigrant. All they want to do is work, and [the City Council] is creating this hostility."

Taking sides with the gardeners, a number of elected officials were more to the point. State Senator Richard Polanco compared the government's regulation of pollution by gardeners to its regulation of pollution by automobile manufacturers and concluded that Latinas/os were being singled out for disparate treatment. "We have not banned cars when we wanted them to be quieter or cleaner.... We simply force manufacturers to make quieter, cleaner cars. But when it comes to the tools of poor, immigrant gardeners, they just ban their tools. That is fundamentally unfair and wrong."

* * *

As to the argument that the machines are bad for gardeners' health, Alvarez rejected the notion that city officials should substitute their judgment for that of the workers themselves. "We're tired of the classism, the paternalism, the implication and assumption that gardeners can't think on their own," he said.

Finally, as to the argument that gas-powered blowers are bad for gardeners' spiritual health, the gardeners responded with a public demonstration of their own high moral standards. Invoking the commitment to nonviolent civil disobedience of Cesar Chavez and the United Farm Workers, the association organized barefoot marches along downtown streets to City Hall to make the point that laws passed there had caused them suffering; they circled City Hall carrying brooms; they held a candlelight vigil for one of their own who died in an automobile accident while returning from a protest. A particularly sobering moment came when a group of gardeners vowed to fast until death on the grounds of City Hall unless the mayor and the Council took action to address their grievances. Disaster, not to mention a public relations nightmare, was averted when the association and city officials worked out a compromise under which the Council agreed to help the gardeners find replacement machines. * * *

* * *

Legal and Extralegal Action: Before the Courts and in the Streets

Latino gardeners did not limit their resistance to lobbying lawmakers. Adopting a creative mixture of traditional and nontraditional political, legal, and extralegal tactics, they also took their case before both the courts and the court of public opinion. [Their] nontraditional tactics—the barefoot march, the broom sweep, the candlelight vigil for a fallen comrade, the hunger strike—set a high moral tone and probably had at least three positive effects. First, they delayed for about a year and-a-half implementation of the City Council's initial adoption of a leaf blower ban, which may have persuaded officials to reduce violations of the new law from misdemeanor to infraction status. Second, these tactics won a modest pledge by the Council to help gardeners search for alternative tools, such as the electric blower. Third, and perhaps most important, they brought together dispersed Latina/o workers, who otherwise would suffer the indignities of their collective oppression without even knowing each other. To the extent the gardeners had any latent political power, they learned that they could only exercise it by working together.

The results of using traditional legal tactics were more mixed. On the one hand, a challenge that the leaf blower ordinance lacked a rational basis under equal protection principles was rejected. This was unfortunate, because the argument made eminent sense. Whereas in the past Los Angeles had merely limited the use of other noisy and smelly tools of the gardeners' trade, such as lawn mowers and weed whackers, to certain hours of the day, the city was now banning the use of gas-powered leaf blowers at all times within 500 feet of any residence. Rejecting Los Angeles's reasons for regulating the use of leaf blowers differently from other equipment, at least one other city considered choosing time-of-day rather distance limits.

On the other hand, a challenge that the ban on "gas-powered" leaf blowers did not affect equipment powered by *methanol*, a mixture of gasoline and alcohol, was sustained. As a result, the tickets of two gardeners who each had been fined $270 for using methanol-powered leaf blowers were dismissed. The judge found the law to be indeterminate, a factor that, in this instance anyway, worked in favor of Latino gardeners. Association general secretary Huerta hailed the ruling not only as a victory, but also as an opportunity for further resistance. "Finally, justice prevails. We feel this is going to be very problematic for the city because they don't know if we have one methanol leaf blower out there or 10,000."

By mixing nontraditional and traditional tactics, the gardeners were able to call attention to their cause. This, in turn, helped them persuade lawmakers to reduce the severity of the ban, and perhaps, helped persuade the courts to construe ambiguities in the ordinance in favor of the gardeners.

Notes and Questions

1. Can a neutral, across-the-board requirement, like a state rule requiring documented status for a driver's license, be discriminatory if it denies a group like Latinos something necessary for livelihood? If Latinos are the main, or only, group so disadvantaged? See Alexander v. Sandoval, 532 U.S. 275 (2001) (raising but not deciding this question).

2. Is a rule against leaf blowers discriminatory if the only, or main, group that uses them is Latinos? Is it a simple environmental rule that we should all applaud, keeping down the noise in otherwise peaceful neighborhoods like Beverly Hills?

3. Why can't the marketplace take care of the leaf-blower problem— home owners who don't mind loud leaf blowers could hire gardeners who use them, and ones who do mind, would not?

4. Why doesn't society enact rules against noisy UPS trucks that also double park; embassy workers who scoff at parking regulations; and church congregations that double park and block intersections on Sunday?

5. Latina workers suffer all the types of employment discrimination mentioned in this Part, and, in addition, sexual harassment. See Part Eight infra; *Sexually Harassed Florida Farmworkers Get Justice*, SPLC Rep., Spring 2007, at 8 (describing successful lawsuit Southern Poverty Law Center brought on behalf of Latina farmworkers).

Chapter 19

FARM LABOR

Understanding struggles on behalf of farmworkers requires keeping in mind immigration policy (see generally Part Five supra), the Bracero program (see Part Five, Chapter 14, § 3), and the role of colonialism in maintaining a system of class oppression. One should remember Latinos' close connection to lands, especially in the Southwest, that were once theirs and that passed to U.S. control after an imperialist war against the weak new nation of Mexico. See Parts One and Two, supra.

Farmworkers' rights are inextricably tied up with César Chávez and the United Farm Workers movement. Consider the following selection by Chicano historian Rodolfo Acuña:

Rodolfo Acuña
Occupied America: A History of Chicanos
324–27 (3d ed. 1988)

THE ROAD TO DELANO: CREATING A MOVEMENT

Many Chicanos have incorrectly labeled the second half of the 1960s as the birth of the Chicano movement. Mexicans in the United States have responded to injustice and oppression since the U.S. wars of aggression that took Texas and the Southwest from Mexico. Middle-class organizations generally spoke for the community, since its members had the education, money, and stability to maintain more or less permanent associations. Established Anglo power brokers also recognized these organizations.

By the mid–1960s, traditional groups such as LULAC [League of United Latin American Citizens] and the G.I. Forum, along with recently formed political groups such as MAPA [Mexican American Political Association] and PASSO [Political Association of Spanish–Speaking Organizations], were challenged. For better or worse, the established Mexican–American associations had served as agents of social control, setting the norm for conduct. The rise of cultural nationalism challenged the acceptance of assimilation as a goal. Sectors of youth, women, and more militant activists were skeptical of traditional methods of struggle and advocated direct action. They also questioned the legitimacy of established leaders.

For the most part, LULAC and Forum leaders at first rejected "street politics"—marches, walkouts, confrontations, civil disobedience, and so on. Over the years their ties with the system tightened. At the same time, the civil rights, antinuclear, and anti-Vietnam movements, along with community action programs, legitimated an ideology of confrontation, creating a new awareness among Chicanos that resulted in a demand for self-determination by *los de abajo* (the underdogs) and youth. Also important was that sectors of the North American left, as well as government agencies, no longer dealt with established groups exclusively but recognized more militant Chicano organizations. This, for a time, broke the monopoly of the Mexican American middle class. Moreover, rank and file members of LULAC and the Forum grew closer to the new Chicano agenda.

CÉSAR CHÁVEZ AND THE UNITED FARM WORKERS

César Chávez gave the Chicano movement a national leader. In all probability Chávez was the only Mexican American to be so recognized by the mainstream civil rights and antiwar movements. Chávez and farm workers were also supported by the center Mexican American organizations along with the left.

On September 8, 1965, the Filipinos in the Agricultural Workers Organizing Committee (AWOC) struck the grape growers of the Delano area in the San Joaquín Valley. Filipino workers had been encouraged by a victory in the spring of 1965 in the Coachella Valley, where the U.S. Labor Department announced the *braceros* would be paid $1.40 an hour. The domestic pickers received 20¢ to 30¢ an hour less. Joined by Mexicans, the Filipinos walked out, and ten days later they received a guarantee of equivalent pay with braceros. When the Filipinos requested the same guarantee in the San Joaquín Valley, growers refused, and led by Larry Itlong, they voted to strike. The strike demands were simple: $1.40 an hour or 25¢ a box. The Di Giorgio Corporation became the major target. The rank and file of the National Farm Workers Association (NFWA) voted on September 16 to join the Filipinos. The termination at the end of 1964 of Public Law 78 significantly strengthened the union's position.

Chávez emerged as the central figure in the strike. Born in Yuma, Arizona, in 1927, he spent his childhood as a migrant worker. His father had belonged to farm labor unions and Chávez himself had been a member of the National Farm Labor Union. In the 1940s he moved to San Jose, California, when he married Helen Fávila. In San Jose Chávez met Father Donald McDonnell, who tutored him in *Rerum Novarum*, Pope Leo XIII's encyclical which supported labor unions and social justice. Through Father McDonnell Chávez met Fred Ross of the Community Service Organization (CSO). He became an organizer for the CSO and learned grass-roots strategies. Chávez rose to the position of general director of the national CSO, but in 1962 he resigned, moving to Delano, where he began to organize his union. Chávez went door to door visiting farm workers. Delano was chosen because of its substantial all-year farm-worker population; in 1968, 32 percent of the 7,000 harvest workers lived and worked in the Delano area year round.

Chávez concentrated his efforts on the Mexican field hands, for he knew the importance of nationalism in solidifying an organization. He carefully selected a loyal cadre of proven organizers, such as Dolores Huerta and Gil Padilla, whom he had met in the CSO. By the middle of 1964 the NFWA was self-supporting.

A year later the NFWA had some 1,700 members. Volunteers, fresh from civil rights activities in the South, joined the NFWA at Delano. Protestant groups, inspired by the civil rights movement, championed the cause of the workers. A minority of Catholic priests, influenced by Vatican II, joined Chávez. Anglo–American labor belatedly jumped on the bandwagon. In Chávez's favor was the growing number of Chicano workers living in the United States. Over 80 percent lived in cities, and many belonged to unions. Many, in fact, belonged to big labor such as the United Auto Workers (UAW).

The times allowed Chávez to make his movement a crusade. The stabilization of a large part of the Mexican American workforce made the forging of an organization possible. And, finally, the end of the bracero program took a lethal weapon from the growers.

The most effective strategy was the boycott. Supporters were urged not to buy Schenley products or Di Giorgio grapes. The first break-through came when the Schenley Corporation signed a contract in 1966. The Teamsters unexpectedly refused to cross picket lines in San Francis-co. Rumors of a bartenders' boycott reached 75–year-old Lewis Solon Rosenstiel, Schenley's president, who decided that a settlement was advisable. Soon afterward Gallo, Christian Brothers, Paul Masson, Alma-den, Franzia Brothers, and Novitiate signed contracts.

The next opponent was the Di Giorgio Corporation, one of the largest grape growers in the central valley. In April 1966, Robert Di Giorgio unexpectedly announced he would allow his workers at Sierra Vista to vote on whether they wanted a union and who would represent them. Di Giorgio did not act in good faith and his agents set out to intimidate the workers.

With the support of Di Giorgio the Teamsters opposed the farm workers and bid to represent the workers. Di Giorgio, without consulting the NFWA, set the date for the election. The NFWA urged its followers not to vote, since it did not have time to campaign or to participate in establishing the ground rules. It needed enough time to return eligible voters to the Delano area. Out of 732 eligible voters only 385 voted; 281 voters specified that they wanted the Teamsters as their union agent. The NFWA immediately branded the election as fraudulent and pres-sured Governor Edmund G. Brown, Sr., a friend of Di Giorgio, to investigate the election. Brown needed the Chicano vote as well as that of the liberals who were committed to the farm workers. The governor's investigator recommended a new election, and the date was set for August 30, 1966.

That summer an intense campaign took place between the Teamsters and the NFWA. A state Senate committee investigated charges of communist infiltration of the NFWA; the committee found nothing to substantiate charges. As the election neared, Chávez became more somber. He had to keep the eligible voters in Delano, and he had the responsibility of feeding them and their families as well as the army of strikers and volunteers. The Di Giorgio campaign drained the union's financial resources. Some weeks before the strike vote, Chávez reluctantly merged the NFWA and AWOC into the United Farm Workers Organizing Committee (UFWOC).

Teamsters red-baited the UFWOC and circulated free copies of Gary Allen's John Birch Society pamphlet. The UFWOC passed out excerpts from *The Enemy Within*, in which Robert Kennedy indicted James Hoffa and the Teamsters in scathing terms; association with the Kennedy named helped. Finally the vote was taken. The UFWOC won the election, 573 votes to the Teamsters' 425. Field workers voted 530 to 331 in favor of the UFWOC. Soon afterward the Di Giorgio Corporation and the UFWOC signed a contract.

Other growers proved to be more difficult. In 1967 the Giumarra Vineyards Corporation, the largest producer of table grapes in the United States, was targeted. When Guimarra used other companies' labels to circumvent the boycott, in violation of the Food and Drug Administration rules, the union boycotted all California table grapes. Boycott activities spread into Canada and Europe. Grape sales decreased significantly. Some of the slack was taken up by the U.S. Defense Department. In 1966 U.S. troops in Vietnam were shipped 468,000 pounds of grapes; in 1967, 555,000 pounds; in 1968, 2 million pounds; and by 1969, more than 4 million pounds. Later the U.S. Defense Department spent taxpayers' money to buy large quantities of lettuce when the union boycotted this product. In the summer of 1970 the strike approached its fifth year. In June 1970 a group of Coachella Valley growers agreed to sign contracts, as did a majority of growers. Victories in the San Joaquín Valley followed.

After this victory the union turned to the lettuce fields of the Salinas Valley, where growers were among the most powerful in the state. During July 1970 the Growers–Shippers Association and 29 of the largest growers in the valley entered into negotiations with the Teamsters. Agreements signed with the truckers' union in Salinas were worse than sweetheart contracts: They provided no job security, no seniority rights, no hiring hall, and no protection against pesticides.

Many growers, like the Bud Antle Company (a partner of Dow Chemical), had dealt with the Teamsters since the 1950s. In 1961, in return for a $1 million loan, Antle signed a contract with the truckers. By August 1970 many workers refused to abide by the Teamster contracts and 5,000 walked off the lettuce fields. The growers launched a campaign of violence. Jerry Cohen, a farm-worker lawyer, was beaten unconscious. On December 4, 1970, Judge Gordon Campbell of Monterey County jailed Chávez for refusing to obey an injunction and held him without bail. This arbitrary action gave the boycott needed publicity. Dignitaries visited Chávez in jail; he was released on Christmas Eve.

By the spring of 1971 Chávez and the Teamsters signed an agreement that gave the UFWOC sole jurisdiction in the lettuce fields and that allowed George Meany, president of the AFL, and the Teamsters president, Frank Fitzsimmons to arbitrate the situation. Throughout the summer and into the fall, however, growers refused to disqualify Teamster contracts and gradually the situation became stalemated.

The fight with the Teamsters hurt the UFWOC since it turned its attention from servicing contracts. Chávez refused help from the AFL for professional administrators, believing that farm workers had to learn from their own mistakes. According to *Fresno Bee* reporter Ron Taylor, although Chávez was a patient teacher, he did not delegate authority and involved himself with too much detail. Farm workers had never had the opportunity to govern themselves and Chávez had to build "ranch committees" from the bottom up. This took time and the corporate ranchers who ran agribusiness had little tolerance for democracy.

———————

Reread Carrasco, *Latinos in the United States*, in Part Five: Immigration, supra. On the farmworker movement, see generally Steven W. Bender, *One Night in America: Robert Kennedy, César Chávez, and the Dream of Dignity* (2008); Richard Griswold del Castillo & Richard A. Garcia, *César Chávez: A Triumph of Spirit* (1995); Ernesto Galarza, *Merchants of Labor: The Mexican Bracero Story* (1964).

Notes and Questions

1. If you were (are?) a Mexican American, how would you feel about the lands that were formerly Mexico?

2. How would you feel about the farmworkers' fight for adequate wages, field sanitation, reasonable work hours, and protection from harmful pesticides and fertilizers?

3. Without a steady flow of undocumented workers, field produce would cost a great deal more, the cost of living would rise, and inflation might set in. Do you think that most Americans realize this?

4. Are low-wage agricultural workers subsidizing the American economy—or hurting it as some maintain?

5.　Most farm labor does not fall under federal labor or occupational health and safety law. See Miriam C. Wells & Don Villarejo, *State Structures and Social Movement Strategies: The Shaping of Farm Labor Protections in California*, 32 Pol. & Soc'y 291 (2004). Why not? See Bender, supra; Guadalupe T. Luna, *An Infinite Distance? Agricultural Exceptionalism and Agricultural Labor*, 1 U. Pa. J. Lab. & Emp. L. 487 (1998).

6.　Why was farm labor the last form of work to gain the benefits of unionization? Until the bracero program ended in 1964, growers could obtain any number of low-paid contract workers, whose terms and salaries were set in advance. Did easy access to bracero guestworkers discourage collective action and unionization among farmworkers? See Kitty Calavita, *Inside the State: The Bracero Program, Immigration, and the I.N.S.* (1992); María Herrera–Sobek, *The Bracero Experience: Elitelore versus Folklore* (1979).

7.　On sexual harassment of Latina farmworkers, see Rebecca Clarren, *The Green Motel*, 15 Ms., Summer 2005, at 40; *News Release: E.E.O.C., Jury Orders Harris Farms to Pay $994,000 in Sexual Harassment Suit by E.E.O.C.*, Jan. 21, 2005.

Why Is Mexico So Poor?

Relatively few workers leave rich, developed countries in search of a better life. But many leave poor Latin American countries in hopes of making a new start north of the border. Why are these sending countries so poor that every year hundreds of thousands of their citizens cross the border illegally, risking death in the desert in search of jobs in America's fields and cities?

See *"We're here because you were there"* in Part Five, Chapter 14, § 3, supra, raising this question. In the case of Mexico, part of the answer may be that a colonial war of aggression robbed that nation of the richest one-half of its territory, a land grab approaching in size the territory that came under the control of Alexander the Great.

For more than a century, U.S.-backed coups and other forms of meddling in Latin American governance and economy kept the region weak. See, e.g., José Luis Morín, *Latino/a Rights and Justice in the United States: Perspectives and Approaches* (2004), describing U.S. policy of keeping Latin America weak, keeping investors from European nations at bay, and conspiring with a wealthy, light-skinned elite class in those countries to manipulate economic relations to the advantage of American corporate interests and siphon off the area's raw materials and natural resources. The North American Free Trade Agreement [NAFTA], a 1992 economic pact between the U.S., Canada, and Mexico, has done little to ease Mexican's poverty and may have deepened it, especially in the small-farm sector. See Ralph R. Reiland, *NAFTA: Winners and Losers*, Pittsburgh Trib. Rev., Jan. 29, 2007. See the following selection for an analysis of why this may have happened.

Kevin R. Johnson
Free Trade and Closed Borders: NAFTA and Mexican
Immigration to the United States
27 U.C. Davis L. Rev. 937, 938–43, 964, 967–69, 976–78 (1994)

Immigration touches upon deeply controversial questions concerning race, class, ethnicity, culture, language, and national identity. As the context of the current public dialogue on the issue suggests, concern with immigration often has been roughly correlated with the nation's economic well-being. * * * In light of the many complex and controversial issues raised by immigration, as well as increased migration pressures resulting from the growing interdependence of the world economy, it is not surprising that one prominent immigration scholar has predicted that, "in the United States, immigration policy will become *the* civil rights issue of the 21st century."

The much-publicized North American Free Trade Agreement (NAFTA), a tripartite trade pact between the United States, Canada, and Mexico, also [has] stirred up a good deal of controversy. Arguments about NAFTA touched on unusually sensitive concerns—strikingly similar in tone to those raised by immigration—such as economics, race, and class. Free trade proponents immediately, seemingly reflexively, embraced the trade accord, while liberal interest groups almost universally condemned it. On one side, economists and business interests almost unanimously backed the accord as economically beneficial for all nations involved. On the other side, organized labor claimed that NAFTA would encourage employers to flee the United States to re-establish operations in Mexico, resulting in a loss of "American jobs." Some environmental groups, emphasizing Mexico's allegedly lax environmental standards, criticized the treaty's adverse impact on the environment.

Like immigration, international trade, especially so-called free trade, periodically has provoked controversy in the United States. NAFTA certainly was not the first time that free traders and protectionists locked horns. Nonetheless, the vehemence of the debate, to the surprise of many, for a time appeared to place the prospects of a fledgling Presidency in jeopardy.

At least initially, the heated political discourse about immigration and NAFTA was disconnected. Those debating the issues did not view the trade agreement and immigration as related. In part, this was a result of the fact that, in negotiating the trade agreement, the United States excluded the subject of labor migration from the bargaining table. Consequently, while NAFTA provides for a reduction of restraints on trade with the hopes of increasing commerce between the three nations, it for the most part does not deal with the flow of people between those same nations. In fact, NAFTA authorizes each member nation to restrict immigration from other member nations into its territory and to take whatever steps necessary to ensure border security. Until it came time for Congress to consider whether to ratify the trade agreement, the anomaly of NAFTA's endorsement of free trade and closed borders went largely undiscussed, if not unnoticed.

* * *

In my view, NAFTA opponents advocating the linkage of immigration and NAFTA correctly argued that the trade agreement implicated migration issues and might well affect future migration from Mexico to the United States. For many reasons, most notably history and geography, the trade/migration separation is a false dichotomy in the context of U.S.-Mexico relations. Such issues are deeply interwoven into the fabric of all relations between the two nations. Of course, the political feasibility of dealing with migration issues in NAFTA is an entirely different matter. In the United States at least, political necessities not infrequently prohibit sensible policies.

I part company with the restrictionists/protectionists in prescribing how labor migration should have been treated in NAFTA. Freer movement between member nations modelled on the European Union, formerly known as the European Community, might have proven more compatible with trade and other goals than allowing migration restrictions to remain. Despite the United States and Mexico's refusal to address the relationship between trade and migration issues, continuing tension between NAFTA's free trade goals and the United States restrictionist immigration policies eventually might result in the relaxation of restraints on migration from Mexico. * * *

* * *

III. The False Dichotomy: Separation of the Flow of Trade From the Flow of People in NAFTA

In the formulation of NAFTA, the flow of capital between the member nations was discussed in isolation of the flow of people between the member nations. It is not entirely clear why the separation is appropriate. True believers in the free market presumably would prefer the free flow of both labor and trade. Historically, however, protectionists have opposed the free flow of both for parochial economic reasons.

* * *

Economists, sociologists, anthropologists, political scientists, and the like would feast on any attempt to explain the willingness to allow free trade and the concomitant resistance to free immigration. It undoubtedly tells us something about ethnocentrism, racism, and classism in the United States. It further suggests that persons may fear difference and change brought by new and different people joining the community. It also suggests that factors other than grand economic theory influence political stands.

In concrete terms, why is it that in the United States "open trade" borders are more politically palatable than "open people" borders? Consider briefly a few possibilities. The migration of people into the United States may raise a number of different concerns than the flow of trade or alienable capital. First, the migration of people may be more permanent than the flow of trade. As the immigration enforcement problems suggest, immigrants, illegal or not, often remain in the United States indefinitely and have a lasting impact on the nation. While the flow of products and capital may be prominent, trade may raise less enduring concerns.

Second, and perhaps more important, foreign capital, though implicating issues of power and control, is less visible to the average citizen than the presence of different types of people. Many of the new immigrants to this nation, legal or not, are viewed—literally and figuratively—as different in terms of race, class, and ethnicity by the majority. Many are from different cultures and speak different languages. Citizens may feel uncomfortable with changes, even if only perceived ones, wrought by the new immigrants. Nation-states' aversion to labor migration may result from the fear that it will change the "national identity." Fear of change brought by different people may be more visible than that brought by the infusion of more fungible capital or products. Even the changes contemplated by NAFTA triggered popular concern in the United States. Still, trade does not raise issues of class, race, and ethnicity as directly and deeply as immigration.

* * *

Free market principles suggest that a restrictionist NAFTA allowing member states to make every effort to curtail illegal immigration into their respective territories may not represent sound economic policy. As the European Union recognized, free movement of persons, services, and capital as factors of production further economic aims. It surely is anomalous to avoid discussing labor migration in a trade agreement when pre-existing labor migration between the nations has been so substantial for so long a period of time, when the issue has been such a source of diplomatic tension among the nations, when the migration results from economic disparities between the nations, and when the migration has unquestionable economic consequences for both nations. Moreover, as the European Union example suggests, the treatment of labor migration issues in a trade agreement may simply be a concession to the inevitable relaxation of immigration barriers between member nations, *at least when the trade partners are contiguous nations*. At some point, freer immigration from Mexico to the United States may result from similar pressures. Freer trade, particularly in the short term, seems most likely to encourage migration as the market readjusts.

* * *

CONCLUSION

In recent years, the focal point of diplomatic tension between the United States and Mexico often has been illegal immigration from Mexico to the United States. However, NAFTA, the most significant agreement between the two nations in decades, studiously avoided this most difficult question. Political realities, domestic in nature, simply made it impossible to take advantage of the historic opportunity to address migration issues that had troubled the nations for much of the twentieth century. From the U.S. perspective, any agreement on the subject would have a restrictionist flavor necessary to placate domestic pressures. These concessions probably would have been unacceptable to Mexico in light of its countervailing domestic pressures.

One may only speculate about what the post-NAFTA future holds with respect to migration between the United States and Mexico. If the experience of the European Union provides any guidance, NAFTA may have the unintended effect of breaking down the barriers to migration between the nations without any mass migrations. This seems unlikely, however, unless there is significant economic growth in Mexico.

As President Clinton learned and history teaches, it may be difficult to convince a domestic audience that changes should be made for the long-run common good, even though some may suffer in the short term. This was a difficult task with respect to obtaining approval for a NAFTA dealing almost singularly with core trade issues. Deeply ingrained cultural and other values in the American populace made domestic acceptance of a freer flow of people from Mexico much more problematic.

In conclusion, the United States and Mexico missed an important window of opportunity to address an issue that has troubled relations between them for many years. Rather than deal directly with migration questions in hopes of making a coherent plan for the future, the nations buried their heads in the proverbial sand and hoped that matters will improve. Only time will tell whether this was the correct tack to take.

José Luis Morín
*Latino/a Rights and Justice in the United
States: Perspectives and Approaches*
38–41 (2004)

[T]he primary U.S. government objective in Latin America, past and present, has been to create and maintain a system that assures U.S. economic and political hegemony. The historical events outlined in this chapter have had a profound impact on Latinos and Latinas, including the following:

THE ESTABLISHMENT AND FORTIFICATION OF
A DOMINANT-SUBORDINATE PARADIGM

U.S. imperial conquests and interventionist policies have established a dominant-subordinate paradigm that persists to the present. The current global economic configuration maintains a system advantageous to U.S. government and corporate interests that had its origins in the hegemonic aspirations of the United States' earliest leaders. The consequences of U.S. hegemony over the Americas have been lasting and dramatic. Today, Latin American countries remain impoverished and, therefore, vulnerable to continued exploitation and subordination, nearly as easily as they were in the 1820s. The single-minded pursuit of U.S. foreign policy goals and economic interests has often blinded the U.S. government to the human suffering and the violations of sovereignty and other rights resulting from its own actions. The covert and overt use of force and direct and indirect forms of intervention throughout the region have become so regular as to have become normalized as a matter of U.S. policy.

From "manifest destiny" to "free trade," U.S. policies toward Latin Americans have been repeatedly couched in benign terms, but its under-currents of paternalism and its human, economic, social, and environmental costs to Latin America are undeniable. While Latin America's social and economic troubles are also attributable to widespread and unrelenting corruption in many Latin American countries, it is equally true that the United States has traditionally played a key role in undermining democracy in support of corrupt and brutal regimes that sustained inequalities and hardships in their respective countries.

For much of its 71–year rule, the Institutional Revolutionary Party (PRI) in Mexico, for instance, engaged in fraudulent elections and other kinds of illegal, corrupt, and undemocratic behavior. Yet the United States government readily lent support for many of Mexico's leaders, including former President Carlos Salinas de Gotari, whose brother was implicated in illegal drug trafficking and who himself has been under a cloud of suspicion of corruption since the end of his term in office in 1994.

Accountability also rests with the United States for the many ruthless Latin American dictators it has sponsored over the years, including Somoza in Nicaragua, Trujillo in the Dominican Republic, Strossener in Paraguay, the Duvaliers in Haiti, Pinochet in Chile, and military regimes in Argentina and Brazil. Given this record, it is no wonder that Latin America remains weak and impoverished.

The powerful forces of globalization, as they function presently, more often than not promote poverty and unfair treatment of Latin American workers, peasants, and indigenous peoples, placing ever-increasing pressure on the poor of Latin America to immigrate to the United States in hope of a better life. U.S. free trade policies actually appear to be worsening conditions in Latin America and are the cause of an increase of Latin American immigrants into the United States who are desperate for work.

Consistent with the theory of "push and pull" factors—"factors that cause a population to move out of an area (push) and into a new area (pull)"—dire economic conditions that exist in Latin America provide a potent "push" incentive for Latin Americans to leave for the United States, as the economically dominant and powerful country where jobs and opportunities are purportedly abundant. Latin Americans will continue to try to migrate to the United States, where in turn, they are also susceptible to exploitation as low-wage factory or agricultural workers. Studies of the apparel industry in the United States show that U.S.

companies continue to draw on or "pull" Latin American immigrants to the United States into industries where they serve as a source of cheap and exploitable labor.

The dominate-subordinate paradigm that characterizes U.S.-Latin American relations fulfills two major functions: (1) it keeps Latin America and its peoples poor and vulnerable to exploitation, and (2) it provides for a steady steam of immigrants from Latin America to meet the needs of U.S. businesses vying for cheap labor. The failure of U.S. policy to have a positive impact on economic development in Latin America will result invariably in increases in Latino/a immigration.

The Racialization of Latin Americans

In the pursuit of its foreign policy objectives, the United States has often been indifferent to the human rights and well-being of Latin Americans. The United States has not been immune to the hubris common to previous imperial powers that have believed that they knew what was best for the world. Powerful ideas about race, including the grand allure of manifest destiny, shaped not only U.S. foreign policy, but how the United States was to view Latin Americans. The absence of concern for the human rights of Latin Americans by the U.S. government, as much as it is rooted in its hegemonic ambitions, is also rooted in racist and racialized perceptions of Latin Americans. The racialization of Latin Americans as racially inferior not only served to justify U.S. conquests and policies, it helped rationalize the subsequent subordination of Mexicans and Puerto Ricans in the United States, establishing the pattern of treatment for Latinos/as who followed. [T]his racialized image of Latin Americans formed the basis for prejudice and discrimination for all other Latinas and Latinos.

U.S.-Latin American Linkages and Their Consequences

Globalization and migratory patterns are likely to continue to strengthen linkages between Latinos/as in the United States and their native homelands. This phenomenon will make Latinos/as an ever-growing part of the future of the United States, U.S.-Latin American relations, thus, become an essential part of understanding the Latino/a experience in the United States today.

Latin Americans have endured an arduous historical trajectory. Centuries of colonialism, plunder, and exploitation have left a legacy that is present today. Vast economic and social inequalities and injustices still mar the Latin American landscape, with the effect of globalized corporate power on Latin America being but one example of how foreign interests and profits supercede the needs and concerns of contemporary Latin Americans and U.S. Latinos/as.

In his classic work *Open Veins of Latin America*, Eduardo Galeano poignantly reminds us of the impact of U.S. colonialism and neocolonial policies over time:

Along the way we [Latin Americans] even lost the right to call ourselves Americans, although the Haitians and the Cubans appeared in history as new people a century before the *Mayflower* pilgrims settled on the Plymouth coast. For the world today, America is just the United States; the region we inhabit is a sub-America, a second-class America of nebulous identity. ([1973] 1997, 2)

Indeed, the possibility of Latin Americans achieving the full realization of the right to chart their own historical course, to determine their own social and cultural identity, and to control their own economic development appears as elusive as ever in contrast to the power of the North American behemoth. This reality presents equally difficult challenges for Latinos/as in the United States.

Notes and Questions

1. For more on NAFTA as a push factor sparking increased immigration from newly impoverished regions of Mexico, see Part Five, Chapter 14, § 1.

2. The newly emerging field of environmental racism also considers farmworker and rural-life issues. See, e.g., Roberto Lovato, *A New Latino Agenda for the 2008 Election*, The Nation, Oct. 29, 2007; Lisa N. Foderaro, *Report Finds Farmworkers Unaware of Many Job Protections*, N.Y. Times, Oct. 24, 2007, at A1. See also Luke W. Cole & Sheila R. Foster, *From the Ground Up: Environmental Racism and the Rise of the Environmental Justice Movement* (2001); Regina Austin & Michael Schill, *Black, Brown, Poor & Poisoned: Minority Grassroots Environmentalism and the Quest for Eco–Justice*, 1 Kan. J.L. & Pub. Pol'y 69 (1991).

Part Eight

LATINA FEMINISM

Before the mid-1990s, one rarely encountered the written term "Latino/a" or even "Latina." A few careful speakers would refer to the Latino group as including Latinos and Latinas, but more would refer to it collectively as "Latinos," realizing, perhaps, that in Spanish a group-term such as "Colombianos" or "Cubanos" is understood to refer to members of both sexes, that is, is gender-inclusive. Then, the publication of a major text, *The Latino/a Condition*, spurred the legal community, at least, to adopt the term, ending in "o/a" when using it as an adjective. Many, if not most, writers, however, today continue to use "Latino," ending in the masculine vowel "o" to indicate the large group, as, for example, in the expression "the Latino community." This casebook, in fact, employs this approach.

The lag that one sees in linguistic usage mirrors a parallel one in the world of law and social policy. Latinas have long advocated feminist positions, even if this entailed asserting themselves against men of their group. But their advocacy has only coalesced into a movement and come to public attention in recent years.

Small numbers may have contributed to Latinas' invisibility. The legendary "machismo" (exaggerated masculinity, accompanied by female subjugation) of some Latin men may have cost the group the benefits of emerging Latina talent and voices. And some Latinas' reticence about targeting their own men over issues such as domestic violence, sexism, and lack of support for such feminist issues as reproductive freedom, university education for Latina women, and fulltime careers may have muted some Latinas' voices and contributions.

Whatever the causes may have been, they have largely been overcome. Latina voices appear in the nation's newspapers and law reviews. Latinas litigate their rights in court and advocate for them before state legislatures across the land.

Latinas share an interest in all the concerns and issues that this casebook covers—education, immigration, the workplace, stereotypes, and language rights—and in these areas their interests generally align with those of Latino men.

But in some areas, Latinas have interests that diverge from those of men. This chapter treats some of them—hierarchy and heterosexism in Latino circles or in the community of color at large, essentialism and intersectionality, childbearing and family life, domestic abuse and violence, and caretaking and elder care. The area is in rapid transition; the contents of a casebook on Latinos and the law several years from now will probably look very different in this respect.

Notes and Questions

1. Are Latina issues different from those affecting Latinos? From those affecting women in general? Reconsider your answers after you read this chapter.

2. For general information on Latinas, see *Latinas in the United States: A Historical Encyclopedia* (Vicki L. Ruiz & Virginia Sánchez Korrol eds., 2006); *Latina Issues: Fragments of Historia(ella) (herstory)* (Antoinette Sedillo López ed., 1999); *Twice a Minority: Mexican American Women* (Margarita Melville ed., 1980); Celina Romany, *Ain't I a Feminist?*, 4 Yale J.L. & Feminism 23 (1991); *Beyond Stereotypes: The Critical Analysis of Chicana Literature* (María Herrera–Sobek ed., 1985).

SECTION 1. TWO PROBLEMS FOR LATINAS: PATRIARCHY IN THE LATINO COMMUNITY; INDIFFERENCE AND NEGLECT IN THE WOMEN'S MOVEMENT

Adelaida R. Del Castillo
Gender and Its Discontinuities in Male/Female Domestic Relations: Mexicans in Cross–Cultural Context, in *Chicanas/Chicanos at the Crossroads: Social, Economic and Political Change* 211–13 (David R. Maciel & Isidro D. Ortiz eds., 1996)

Traditionally, gender in culture has been assessed through a sex/gender dichotomy in which the former is a biological given and the latter a cultural construction. As such, gender in culture is expressed through individuals who are bearers of prescribed male/female social roles. In the past, gender roles have been identified, described, and explained by anthropologists through the observation of the patterned, recurrent, and typical, contributing to the reification of predictable and fixed gender roles. This approach offers a binary frame of reference, which posits the oppositional (he's strong, she's weak, etc.) as universal in male/female gender-based norms and relegates all other gendered possibilities to the realm of the exceptional, the unexplainable, or the deviant. For although tradition may express expected practices, beliefs, and cultural ideals, it cannot account for cultural flexibility, contradiction, and indeterminacy.

According to gender-based norms, the family in Mexico is hierarchical in structure, asymmetrical in social and gender relations, genealogical in patterns of residence, and loyal to the family in its moral economy.

According to the traditional ideal, men have authority over women, the husband has authority over his wife as does the brother over his sister; and while the older have authority over the younger, the father remains the ultimate authority over the household and family matters.

It is significant that Mexico's most distinguished authors and pundits (mostly males) have also had something to say about the character, status, and gender-based norms of the Mexican male and female, thus contributing to the social construction of sex/gender ideology in Mexican society. Their conceptualizations cannot go unnoticed because they are probably more widely read internationally than any other literature of social scientific significance. The most notable of these authors is Nobel Prize laureate Octavio Paz. Through the use of various forms of literary license, Paz offers insights into the character and motives of the *macho* by positing a dialectical relationship between men and women. "The ideal of manliness is never to 'crack,' never to back down. Those who 'open themselves up' are cowards.... Women are inferior beings because, in submitting, they open themselves up. This inferiority is constitutional and resides in their sex, their submissiveness, which is a wound that never heals." For Paz, the sexual encounter itself speaks to a sociomoral asymmetry between the sexes, reified in physiology: "The *macho*, the male ... rips open ... the female, who is pure passivity, defenseless against the exterior world." Thus, a woman who transcends passivity is a cultural anomaly representative of gender chaos. Here, also, Paz offers a portrayal of the bad woman, *la mala mujer*, which serves logocentric propositions of unchaste female behavior in a Mexican context. The *mala mujer*, he tells us, is a woman who does not conform to the traditional female ideal and assumes male attributes such as the independence of the macho. Mexican gender ideology, its observations and portrayals, expresses cultural ideals of gender-appropriate behavior which may or may not have correlations in actual behavior.

If female subordination is a serious problem in the Mexican family, what about in Latino/a families in the United States? See the following selection:

Beatriz M. Pesquera & Denise A. Segura
With Quill and Torch: A Chicana Perspective on the American Women's Movement and Feminist Theories, in *Chicanas/Chicanos at the Crossroads: Social, Economic and Political Change* 233–45 (David R. Maciel & Isidro D. Ortiz eds., 1996)

We asked Chicana informants to describe ways in which the American Women's Movement has addressed or not addressed Chicana concerns. Ninety-five women answered this question; six women did not reply. Over half of the informants indicate that Chicana concerns have been somewhat addressed (53.5 percent) by the American Women's

Movement, whereas 38.6 percent feel these needs have not been addressed. Only two women feel that the American Women's Movement has addressed Chicana concerns.

Eighty-two women provided in-depth, written responses in support of their answers. Their responses range from acknowledging the importance of the American Women's Movement to forceful critiques of race-class biases. The latter sentiment prevails both among women who feel that the American Women's Movement has somewhat addressed and those who feel that it has not addressed Chicana concerns. The major difference between these two groups of women is the tenor of the critique; that is, women who feel that the movement has not addressed Chicana concerns articulate more intense antagonism, harsher criticism, and less acknowledgment of benefits gained.

Chicanas tend to portray the American Women's Movement as articulating the issues of relatively privileged, well-educated, middle-and upper-class white women. Informants argue that the social origins of movement activists hindered the development of issues relevant to women outside a narrow social milieu. For example, one respondent noted that "by its very historical origins, the movement has emphasized middle-class to upper-class concerns" (Chicana faculty member, 34 years old). This informant's criticism of the lack of diversity within the movement echoes that of other women of color and many white feminist scholars.

Informants object to what they perceive as a marked tendency within the American Women's Movement to present itself in global terms (i.e., The Women's Movement). Chicanas in Mujeres Activas en Letras y Cambio Social (MALCS) feel that this attitude obscures important racial/ethnic and class differences among women: "The women's movement that stands out in my mind is the 'second wave,' which occurred during the 1960s. This movement was primarily a 'white, middle-class movement' that openly called for the liberation of women. Although the movement seemed to speak in universal liberation terms (for all women), it systematically excluded the concerns of non-white women, as it failed to consider issues of race, class, and cultural oppression" (Chicana faculty member, 40 years old).

Another informant stated that "the movement has failed to adequately address classism and racism and how it impacts on women as a class and in dealing with our areas of common concern [i.e., women and the family]. I think we have been used to present a collective voice on behalf of women but have not been extended the same degree of importance in areas that concern us differently, i.e., class and race issues. In other words, white women also have to overcome their own prejudices as they try to overcome prejudice altogether" (Chicana graduate student, 24 years old). Like other women who feel that the American Women's Movement has somewhat addressed Chicana concerns, this informant recognizes that the movement often articulates issues pertinent to many women (e.g., the family). What she and others object to is the movement's failure to "adequately address" how other forms of inequality, in particular, race/ethnicity and class, condition women's lives. She and the other informants take exception to the manner in which the Women's Movement postulates stances on behalf of all women without considering these differences. Ultimately, she challenges white women to confront their own race and class privileges side-by-side with the struggle to eradicate sexism.

In general, the women who feel that the Women's Movement has somewhat addressed and those who feel that it has not addressed Chicana concerns object to an analysis of oppression that grants primacy to gender. They argue that overreliance on a gender critique inhibits the development of a more inclusive perspective sensitive to the ways in which race/ethnicity and class, as well as gender, shape the Chicana experience. As another Chicana observed, "The Anglo–American women's movement addresses the dominant culture's sexist practices but many times failed to address the development of our present economic system and how that brought about the division of labor, the social class differences, and the racist institutions" (Chicana graduate student, 32 years old). This woman acknowledges the need to eradicate sexism, but argues for the incorporation in the discussion of class and race/ethnicity as well.

Many women also voice disapproval of the "liberal-reformist" tendencies they feel predominate within the movement. They argued that the American Women's Movement should be less dedicated to finding ways to integrate women into a male-dominated world and more devoted to developing strategies to end structures of inequality and exploitation produced by American capitalism. These perceptions are captured in the response of one Chicana: "The reluctance of the dominant NOW-type feminism in the United States to face up to the reality of racism and class-based problems facing Chicanas has been the main obstacle to feminist concerns for Chicana issues. At the root of this problem is the narrow definition of feminism that is based on sex differences and not a problem of domination" (Chicana graduate student, 29 years old). This woman, like many of the informants, did not distinguish between the various segments within the American Women's Movement. While this overgeneralization may have contributed to the harsh tone of the critique, it is important to note that women who made this distinction tended to voice similar criticisms; for example, "The Women's Movement addressed the specific concerns that affect us as a race and/or class only when we demanded it, but only temporarily. There were few changes in white middle-class women's ideology and practice among the women's rights groups and women liberationists" (Chicana graduate student, 30 years old). This woman, like other informants, combines the different branches of the American Women's Movement in her critique to emphasize how the omission of Chicana concerns cuts across political and ideological alignments of feminists within the American Women's Movement.

Despite their criticism of the American Women's Movement, nearly all the informants endorse the key maxim: eradicating female subordination is essential. Many women credit the movement's critique of patriarchy with influencing their own development as Chicana feminists. They acknowledge that Chicanas benefit from the struggle against patriarchy. Despite this view, a majority feel that the gains netted from this particular struggle are inadequate and largely incidental: "All women of all races are helped when a woman, or any group of women, defies stereotypes and promotes a progressive agenda or idea. But Chicana-specific concerns are not usually what 'the larger agenda' of the Women's Movement is about" (Chicana faculty member, 39 years old). In words reminiscent of Chicana feminists in the 1960s and 1970s this woman contends that the American Women's Movement has not placed a high priority on Chicana concerns. * * *

Not only is the previous informant critical of the direction taken by the Women's Movement, she also questions its effectiveness to advocate for women outside the social mainstream. She, like most of the women in this study, contends that social policies to redress gender inequality have not significantly improved the life chances of most Chicanas. In general, Chicanas are poorer, less educated, and employed in the lowest-paying jobs vis-à-vis white women, as well as men. Sex discrimination in training and job access is but one barrier Chicanas face. They also experience discrimination based on their race/ethnicity and culture.
  * * *

While many women indicate that the American Women's Movement had been moving toward a more inclusive agenda, others feel that Chicana feminist efforts have been almost completely ignored. Their view is typified by the sentiment expressed by one respondent, who wrote that "women of color, particularly Chicanas themselves, have struggled as a group since the late 1960s and early 1970s to raise their/our own issues as women from an oppressed nationality group in the United States. Our fight within the predominantly white, middle-class 'women's movement' has been to address the issues of class and race, as *inextricable* [respondent's emphasis] to our gender issues" (Chicana graduate student, 27 years old). This informant articulates the widespread feeling that white feminists need to acknowledge that Chicanas have been actively challenging patriarchy and racial/ethnic and class oppression. * * * The term "Chicana" embraces political activism, ethnicity, and gender; therefore, Chicanas do not order their oppression hierarchically. Hence, their articulation of a triple-oppression approach that considers race/ethnicity and class, as well as gender.
  * * *

Chicanas' critiques of the American Women's Movement led them to conclude that they should articulate their own issues: "We need to do this—as Chicanas. We can't expect the white women to understand us in a cultural sense—though they may be able to understand us sociologically in a larger sense" (Chicana faculty member, 43 years old). This woman voices a sentiment heard throughout this group—that neither white women nor Chicano men know how to liberate Chicanas. Moreover, there is no compelling reason for them to do so, inasmuch as they derive privileges from the continued subordination of Chicanas.

Feminist Theory and Chicana Concerns

In this study, many women feel that feminist theories are less relevant to Chicanas than to the American Women's Movement. Forty-eight women (47.5 percent) indicate that feminist theory/scholarship has not incorporated the particular circumstances of Chicanas, while forty-two women (41.6 percent) feel it has somewhat incorporated them. Only two women contend that feminist theory has incorporated the particular circumstances of Chicanas. Nine women did not provide information on this issue.

The women who assert that feminist theory has not incorporated and those who assert that it has somewhat incorporated the particular circumstances of Chicanas describe it as grounded in a narrow range of experiences without a global vision. Echoing the voices of early Chicana feminists, the informants also discuss a range of exclusionary practices within feminist scholarship that limits Chicana voices. While [one informant] acknowledges recent efforts to include women of color, she, like the majority of the informants, asserts that these discussions typically overlook Chicanas. One result of this omission is Chicanas' alienation from American feminism and antagonism toward "white" feminists, who often act as "gatekeepers," limiting access to research and publication outlets necessary to the development of Chicana feminist discourse.

Even more objectionable to Chicana feminists than their exclusion is their inclusion as an "externalized other," whose experiences are appended to theory rather than centered at its heart. As one informant states, "Feminist scholars (excluding Chicanas) rarely talk about Chicanas or care to do any research on us. When we are included in any feminist theory we are used to substantiate a theory on white women. Generally theories are designed to explain the power relations between white males and females and then the experiences of Chicanas are forced into these theoretical frameworks" (Chicana faculty member, 31 years old). As an afterthought [she conceded] many feminist seminars offer a single session which will touch on "women of color" in general. This respondent, like most of the other women surveyed, speaks from personal experiences with Women's Studies courses (e.g., as student, faculty or staff member). Her words display frustration with the misrepresentation of Chicanas and their token inclusion in feminist writings.

Other informants focused attention on recent attempts by women of color to bring the theoretical and political issues to the forefront. One, for example, declared that "unfortunately, it seems that true change in the intellectual debate as well as the political territory comes about only when spearheaded by Chicanas themselves. Chicanas and U.S. Third–World women (i.e., other 'minority' women) have shifted the debate and political agendas through political action, scholarship, cultural/artistic activity, and journalism. . . . There remains, of course, all the work to do which will end only when racism and sexism (and class oppression) are obsolete'' (Chicana graduate student, 27 years old). This informant emphasizes that, by and large, inclusion of women of color in feminist theory has been by women of color themselves. Their goal is a praxis addressing multidimensional forms of Chicana oppression.

Chicanas who discussed the incorporation of Chicana concerns into feminist theories voiced considerable cynicism regarding possible underlying motivations. Their view is captured in the response of one MALCS member, who observed, ''I predict that it will become more 'fashionable' to hype the 'Hispanic' presence in the United States and the white feminist academics will give lip service to Chicana issues. Their appropriation of our concerns, however, will only serve their interests and diffuse our own voices'' (Chicana graduate student, 36 years old). The respondent notes that research on Chicanas is becoming more popular. Yet, she and most of the informants harbor deep misgivings that research on Chicanas will be expropriated by white feminists and to a lesser extent by other non-Chicana scholars who are employed in significantly greater numbers in the academy than are Chicanas, as is noted by several scholars. Study informants fear that non-Chicana scholars will secure recognition more readily for Chicana studies research than the Chicanas who initiated this line of inquiry. This is a particularly sensitive issue for Chicanas who feel they have spent years developing research on their communities.

Consistent with this apprehension, Chicanas in this study and others report that their research is often treated with skepticism in academic departments and denied publication in established research outlets. * * *

Study informants' critiques of feminist theories reveal a myriad of ideological and political contradictions. Chicanas are caught in the contradiction of seeking a feminist praxis while experiencing alienation from feminists' theories and feminist theoreticians. They are torn between criticizing feminism's lack of theoretical synthesis while denying the ability of white feminists to capture the essence of Chicana subjectivity. Chicana feminism, then, is struggling to wrestle free of these contradictory locutions to create a discourse that speaks to their multifaceted reality.

Despite their apprehensions and criticisms, most Chicanas view feminist theories as useful building blocks to develop their scholarship. As two informants noted, ''I believe feminist theory addresses the circumstances of women in general and addresses some of the circumstances of Chicanas (e.g., scholarship that deals with sexism, patriarchy, male dominance and control over women, economic and legal oppression of women)'' (Chicana faculty member, 26 years old); and, ''It is true that a close reading of feminist theory gives us a base from which we can develop our own theories and scholarship reflecting the Chicana/Latina reality" (Chicana graduate student, no age given). Informants value approaches analyzing the social construction/reproduction of gender, but they tend to favor broader analytic frameworks grounded on women of color outside the U.S. context. * * *

* * *

Women's Studies, Women's Centers, and Chicana Needs

An important facet of American feminism is the institutionalization of Women's Studies programs and women's centers at colleges and universities. These programs typically aim to provide support for women, offer courses on women, and support research on women. The extent to which these programs and centers meet Chicana needs is largely unknown. This is important to examine, because it provides another indicator of American feminism's sensitivity to Chicanas.

We asked informants whether or not Women's Studies programs and women's centers existed on their campus and the extent to which they feel they meet the needs of Chicanas. Over three-fourths of the informants (76.2 percent) indicate that there is a Women's Studies program on the campus (10.9 percent of the informants indicated that their campus did not have a Women's Studies program; 12.9 did not reply). More than half of these women (56.4 percent) feel these programs do not meet Chicanas' needs. * * *

* * *

Conclusion

Women in this study overwhelmingly criticize American feminism for failing to incorporate their concerns adequately within feminist theories, political agendas, and institutionalized programs. They oppose American feminism's tendency to "universalize" the experience of white middle-class women and to either ignore or subsume racial/ethnic, culture, and class differences among women to a general theory of women's common oppression. Many of these women acknowledge the importance of the struggle against patriarchy, but feel this addresses only one dimension of Chicana oppression.

Chicanas contend that the class privilege and racial advantage shared by white middle-class feminists often blind them to Chicana concerns. They advocate "deconstructing" American feminism, to account for ways the tripartite axes of stratification shape women's experiences and demarcate relations of power and privilege in American society.

Chicanas interpret reality through a "triple-oppression lens" rooted in their experiences as Chicanas in the United States. By a triple-oppression lens, we mean that Chicanas simultaneously experience reality as members of a historically oppressed group, with a culture distinct from that of the dominant culture. Furthermore, their location in the class structure is mediated by their racial/ethnic status. The social construction of a Chicana perspective, or worldview, is filtered through their racial/ethnic/class status. As a result, Chicanas' interests as women are distinct from and at times contradictory to those articulated within American feminism.

Notes and Questions

1.   Patriarchy and female subordination operate in mainstream Anglo culture, as well. What is different about the version that haunts the Latino community? See Maureen Ebben & Norma Guerra Gaier, *Telling Stories, Telling Self: Using Narratives to Uncover Latinas' Voices and Agency in the Legal Profession*, 19 Chicano–Latino L. Rev. 243 (1998). See also Elizabeth M. Iglesias, *Rape, Race, and Representation: The Power of Discourse, Discourses of Power, and the Reconstruction of Heterosexuality*, 49 Vand. L. Rev. 869 (1996).

2.   Is female subordination an ideology, as Del Castillo suggests, or merely a convenient rationalization some men employ to keep their women servile and under control? See Peggy McIntosh, *White Privilege and Male Privilege: A Personal Account of Coming to See Correspondences Through Work in Women's Studies* (1988); *This Bridge Called My Back* (Cherríe L. Moraga & Gloria E. Anzaldua eds., expanded & rev. 3d ed. 2002).

3.   Is machismo necessarily to be deplored, or does it have a positive side? See Gabriel S. Estrada, *The Macho Body as Social Malinche*, in *Velvet Barrios: Popular Culture and Chicana/o Sexualities* 41 (Alicia Gaspar de Alba ed., 2003).

4.   In *The Mexican Corrido: A Feminist Analysis* (1990), María Herrera–Sobek demonstrates how Mexican–American folk tales relegate women to a small number of archetypal roles, such as good mother, brave soldier, virginal inspiration, and lover, all of which tap deep psychological and cultural needs—by men. Are corridos "machismo lite"?

SECTION 2.   HETEROSEXISM

A group that is intensely patriarchal and macho is likely to be heterosexist and intolerant of sexual minorities, as well. Of course, mainstream society is not perfect in this regard, either. But the kind of rejection and ridicule that some sectors of the Latino community visit on gays and lesbians of color often takes on an even harsher edge than that which finds a home in society at large. The following passages explore this dimension:

Elvia R. Arriola
Gendered Inequality: Lesbians, Gays, and Feminist Legal Theory
9 Berkeley Women's L.J. 103, 110–12, 140–43 (1994)

In the late nineteenth century, * * * a series of Supreme Court decisions reflected society's continued tolerance of racial classifications. This tolerance was epitomized by the view that a racial classification is constitutional as long as each class is treated "equally"—a view that persisted for over fifty years. The infamous *Plessy v. Ferguson* articulated this vision of group-based equality.

Another version of group-based equality emerged several decades later, in the now famous footnote four to *United States v. Carolene Products Co.* While the Court in *Carolene* upheld a "reasonable" piece of state legislation, it warned that courts might, on occasion, have to exercise an antimajoritarian check on legislative powers when a law discriminates against "discrete and insular minorities."

* * *

The rhetoric surrounding the group-based model often obscures the public policy that undergirds its close relative, the individual-regarding or "irrelevancy" model of equality. This model reminds individuals and governments that under the Constitution certain personal traits are not legitimate classifying criteria. To this end, the rhetoric of irrelevancy argues that equality means never considering one's race, sex, religion, or national origin for classification purposes. * * *

* * *

Suppose that an employer pays all women the same wage. However, he places white women in the front office jobs because the clientele is mostly white, and relegates blacks and hispanics to the back room. Meanwhile, he sexually harasses the white women. Would a black woman denied a front office job have any right to challenge the employer on the basis of racism, or sexism, or both? What about a white woman? Is one issue more important than the other?

In another hypothetical, an Asian employer prefers to hire hispanics and Asians over blacks or whites. How do we assess this kind of preferential treatment when our standard paradigms of analysis usually see whites as oppressors and all minorities as victims? Is this a case of the so-called problem of reverse discrimination? What about when an employer hires Mexican nationals over Mexican–Americans because the latter are more likely to question working conditions and wages?

Finally, suppose that a white male employer fires a black lesbian after she rebuffs his sexual advances. Is this discrimination on the basis of race, gender, or sexual identity, or some combination of the three? * * * Claims of discrimination brought by lesbians of color face two obstacles under current discrimination analysis. First, the categories of race and gender may be viewed as distinct and separate. Second, the category of sexual identity is not even recognized as a basis of legally remediable discrimination. Faced with a claim by a woman of color, a court could determine that although the categories of race and sex apply, these categories have not been shown to bear any clear relationship to each other. This type of determination was made in *Munford v. James T. Barnes, Inc.*, a case brought by a black woman whose white male supervisor demanded that she have sex with him. She repeatedly refused. The sexual harassment carried racial overtones. Limited by conventional legal reasoning, the court in *Munford* failed to see how racism and sexism intersected in this case. It held instead that the race discrimination claim was "far removed" from the sexual harassment claim.

For a lesbian of color, the same methodology that fails to recognize a claim of racialized sexual harassment, or gendered racial harassment, also denies her claims of homophobic sexism. The firing of a black lesbian, as illustrated in the hypothetical above, presents a complex picture of identity and discrimination. Yet, the source of the problem is not complex; it is simple, though subtle—she is being fired because she has defied white male supremacy, and is a victim of anti-lesbian sexism.

The holistic/irrelevancy model recognizes the role of unconscious attitudes and the ways that interrelated factors create unique, compounded patterns of discrimination and affect special social identities. In doing so, it rejects the idea of arbitrarily separating out categories to address discrimination in our society. Instead, this model understands discrimination as a problem that arises when multiple traits and the stereotypes constructed around them converge in a specific harmful act. Traditional categories then become points of departure for a deeper, more subtle analysis that explores the historical relationships between certain social groups, as well as an individual's experience within each of these groups.

This model is holistic because it looks to the whole harm, the total identity. It is an irrelevancy perspective because it assumes that one trait or several traits operating together create unfair and irrelevant bases of treatment. Thus, under a holistic/irrelevancy model, the theory and practice of non-discrimination law become tools for mediating social conflict by challenging the power of deeply ingrained cultural attitudes that perpetuate cycles of oppression for certain social groups.

* * *

We need new models that acknowledge the reality of identity and personhood, notwithstanding that an individual may not fit rigid, dichotomized categories such as "masculine" or "feminine." The governing paradigms encourage the courts to ignore social reality and to refuse to extend existing and relevant legal protections to lesbians and gays. Courts have refused to extend these protections to lesbian and gay litigants because anti-gay discrimination merges questions of conduct with identity. The courts' refusal reflects the legal culture's insistence that discrimination occurs within distinct and separate categories. This categorization denies the complexity of individual identity, thereby preventing society from embracing the richness of its cultural diversity.

Discrimination harms not only the individual but society as a whole. Equality theorists should recognize the public policy underlying existing paradigms: respect for one's total identity. This public policy demands respect for traits such as gender, sexuality, race, class, age, and ethnicity. Each trait is important to one's moral worth, yet none provides justification for the denial of equal rights under the law.

Francisco X. Valdes
Queers, Sissies, Dykes, and Tomboys: Deconstructing the
Conflation of "Sex," "Gender," and "Sexual Orien-
tation" in Euro–American Law and Society
83 Cal. L. Rev. 1, 12, 14–15, 102–10, 154,
159–61, 354–55, 358–60 (1995)

Because sex, gender, and sexual orientation are central concepts in our society's sex/gender system, their histories and meanings are significant and complex. However, the conflation of this trio, and its effects, have gone largely unnoticed both in law and society. The conflation comprises three constructs: sex, gender, and sexual orientation. The first leg of this triangle is the conflation of sex and gender; the second, that of gender and sexual orientation. The third is the conflation of sex and sexual orientation.

The first leg, conflating sex and gender, holds that every person's sex is also that person's gender. This leg, or its disruption, produces "sissies" and "tomboys." The second leg, conflating sex-derived gender and sexual orientation, is less familiar, at least initially. This leg is the generally recognizable linkage between "queers" and "sissies" on the one hand, and "dykes" and "tomboys" on the other, suggesting that some correlation between sex-determined gender and sexual orientation *is* at work.

The conflation's third leg may be the least familiar, but is discernible and demonstrable nonetheless. The conflation of sex and sexual orientation is shown by the way in which sexual orientation is directly surmised by the sameness or difference of sex[es] within a coupling: a sameness of sex within a coupling results directly in conclusions of homosexual orientation for each participant whereas a difference of sexes within a coupling produces conclusions of heterosexual orientation.

In this conflationary scheme, "sex" refers to external genitalia, usually as observed at birth, while "gender" signifies the composite of personal appearance and social behaviors, characteristics and roles imputed to all persons at birth on the basis of sex. These attributes are organized into an active/male and passive/female paradigm that extends both to social *and* sexual identities. In other words, the conflationary manifestation or performance of sex-determined gender, in the form of "active/male" or "passive/female" personality, is expected and demanded in both social ("public") settings as well as in sexual ("private") relations. In this scheme, "sexual orientation" effectively represents the sexual dimension or performance of gender: sexual orientation denotes the sense and enactment of erotic desire or personality, which is cast as either "active" or "passive" under the sexed and gendered dictates of the active/passive paradigm. Moreover, in the active/passive hierarchy of this scheme, masculinity structurally is valorized over femininity and cross-sex couplings structurally are valorized over same-sex couplings. The conflation's sex/gender ideology therefore is heteropatriarchy—the intertwining of androsexism and heterosexism to validate malecentric and heterocentric biases.

As these socio-legal definitions indicate, the conflation of the three constructs begins with and pivots on "sex," and on its assignment at birth. And because gender is deduced from and fixed by sex, this conflationary scheme constructs the social and sexual dimensions of "gender" as both deductive and intransitive. It bears emphasis that these basic definitions, and their anchoring to active/passive ideology, are entrenched in Euro–American history, and they continue to prevail in the United States as a matter of clinical practice, cultural custom and legal doctrine.

* * *

The conflation today remains as firmly entrenched in sexual minority communities as it is in mainstream American society and its legal culture. This entrenchment is exemplified by the continuing sway of identifications like "butch" or "femme" or "queen" that project various conflationary configurations of sex, gender, and sexual orientation. And, though the butch-femme debate is often most directly associated with lesbian identity, its sex/gender issues extend to gay male identity as well because both female and male same-sex couples necessarily confront male/husband and female/wife roles and issues defined by traditionalist active/passive standards.

For instance, both female and male same-sex couples frequently encounter queries from friends, relatives, or acquaintances in the sexual majority asking, "Who plays the 'wife's' role?" This query, in effect, seeks to determine who is the "butch" and who is the "femme"; in other words, who conforms and who does not—who is socially *and* sexually gender typical and who is socially *and* sexually gender atypical. Of course, this query effectively signals underlying confusion (or incredulity) over the possibility that sex-determined gender and sexual orientation are not necessarily correlated or conflated either socially/publicly or sexually/privately.

Perhaps the most familiar example of the butch-femme issue in specifically gay male subculture might be the still-ubiquitous "drag" shows that glorify cross-dressing and other social gender-bending affectations as a means of representing sexual orientation to the audience. Much as we saw in the 1982 film, *Victor, Victoria*, these shows feature lip-sync impersonations of hyper-glamorous female performers, replete with wigs, makeup, gowns, and gestures. Major cities often have at least one establishment specializing in the presentation of this type of activity, and many other bars or lounges across the country include such fare in their regular entertainment schedules. Literally and normatively, these shows place gender squarely at center stage in the cultural life of communities apparently defined by sexual orientation, and thereby project active/passive traditions represented and reproduced jointly by the first and second legs of the conflation.

The ongoing butch-femme debate in lesbian communities, which contests the pros and cons of acting out sex-based gender roles socially and/or sexually within an all-female coupling, likewise attests to the conflation's hardiness. For example, JoAnn Loulan's groundbreaking surveys of lesbians throughout the country illustrate the phenomenon well: her most recent data show 44 percent of the 589 lesbians interviewed electing to adopt a socially and/or sexually gendered role within the relationship, with 19 percent identifying themselves as butch (the male role) and 25 percent as femme (the female role). The conflation thus persists among sizable segments of lesbian communities, coexisting with the growing recognition that butch-femme categorizing often serves to perpetuate androsexist as well as heterosexist images. In short, under the first and second legs of the conflation, internalized active/passive traditions regarding sex and gender continue to drive, at least in part, the personal[ized] constructions of sexual orientation among many lesbians living today.

In both male and female same-sex settings, the butch/femme/queen discourse manifests an awareness of and an acquiescence to official active/passive sex/gender themes and traditions, even when "bending" them. Among both the men and the women, sex is viewed as gender's determinant. Among both sexes, gender is understood to comprise social/public and sexual/private personality. Among both gay men and lesbians, social gender atypicality is associated with sexual gender atypicality. Thus, Leg One and Leg Two of the conflation remain jointly in place among both male and female segments of sexual minority communities.

In like vein, sexual minorities of color continue to live the conflation in much the same way that Eric Garber depicted in his study of early-to-mid–1900s Harlem. Indeed, the costumed events that Garber described now have evolved into the highly stylized recent innovation known as "voguing." Popularized by Madonna's 1990 pop music hit single, *Vogue*, this activity involves "striking a pose" which, more often than not, amounts to glamorized and exaggerated social gender posturing; the voguing balls of today, as with their earlier equivalents, are characterized by flamboyant social gender regalia and props.

The popularity of voguing and balls among African–American and Latino sexual minorities in New York City was depicted in movingly graphic detail in the 1990 film *Paris Is Burning*. The film documents the "houses" that play central roles in the production of balls; each is headed by a "mother" who directs his/her house's participation in the events. Participants compete in categories such as "Butch Queen," "Pretty Girl," and "Miss Cheesecake." One set of categories, "Realness," focuses on the ability of the competitors to emulate the subjects of the category; for instance, "Looking Like a Girl Going to School" or "Executive Man." In an especially revealing comment on these categories of competition, one participant explains that the object of the latter category is to "look like a real man, a straight man." Indeed, under the conflation's configuration and depiction of active/passive human identities and personalities, "real" men (and women) are "straight" men (and women).

Not surprisingly, then, social/public gender affectations provide much of the film's thematic centerpiece, attesting to the continuing vitality of the conflation's first and second legs even among youngsters unequipped to [re]cognize them: throughout the film, we repeatedly encounter young males in interviews and escapades who self-identify as gay, and who uniformly conceive and articulate that sexual identity by adopting in both outlandish and discreet ways the social/public attributes associated with femininity. This film, in fact, portrays individuals for whom sex-determined gender and sexual orientation are indistinguishable, and who live their lives *today* on that basis; these are persons who today define themselves as sexually and therefore socially cross-gendered, or vice versa, and who thereby apply to their beings and lives the active/passive dictates corresponding both to the first and to the second leg of the conflation.

Finally, there is Jacob's story. As an African American growing up in the southeast just as the integration of public schools was getting underway, Jacob was a star student who excelled both in academics and in extracurricular activities. Fearful that his "effeminate mannerisms" (coupled with his apparent lack of interest in girls) and general timidity toward sports might label him as gay, Jacob used his studies and activities to insulate himself from suspicion: he deflected any questioning of his closeted [homo]sexuality by raising his "bookworm" persona as a shield. Additionally, he steered clear of any association with the "hardcore faggots" in his high school, characterizing the group as "very effeminate acting." As Jacob's story indicates, for him as well as for his peers among both the "faggots" and nonfaggots, social effeminacy (in the form of mannerisms, activities, or talents) stood for, and therefore was interpreted as, same-sex desire. Social effeminacy, in other words, signaled and was tantamount to sexual effeminacy, and vice versa.

To avoid identification with the latter attribute of his personality, Jacob strategically deployed and disguised the former attributes of his personality. In doing so, Jacob displayed an intuitive understanding of the way[s] in which active/passive sex/gender traditions under the conflation's first and second legs operate[d] in tandem to shape his peers' and his family's [mis]perceptions of him, both socially and sexually. He intuited that society officially and culturally regards gender as deductive and intransitive; in turn, Jacob understood that his personal survival and prosperity depended on deflecting suspicion over his sexual/private personality which, by his own account, he consciously set out to do by disguising his apparently atypical or cross-gendered social/public personality.

Confirming this intuition, Jacob's calculated disguises succeeded. Though he engaged in same-sex liaisons throughout his high school years, Jacob was able to "pass for straight" in the eyes of both friends and family. In this way, Jacob enabled himself to avoid (some of) the stigma and prejudice heaped on persons who somehow—socially, sexually, or both—are deemed cross-gendered; persons who are devalued or denigrated because they personify the violation or disruption of one or more of the conflation's legs.

Both voguing and Jacob display yet again the way[s] in which contemporary sexual minorities—including those living in communities of color—comply with traditionalist sex/gender conceptions, even as they bend or break official or cultural sex/gender rules accompanying those conceptions. In both instances, sex was understood to fix gender. In both instances, gender was understood to encompass both social/public and sexual/private components. In both instances, gender transitivity that was social was associated with the sexual version. And, in both instances, society's problematization of gender atypicality socially and/or sexually was intuitively, if not intellectually, understood. Thus, while indulging, both socially and sexually, in various forbidden cross-gender attributes or activities, the individuals in these instances clearly were aware of— and accepted and accommodated—the official premises and the cultural power of the first and second legs of the conflation.

Although the history of the conflation in modern Euro–American culture presented above is necessarily oversimplified, it points to the inescapable conclusion that the conflation of sex, gender, and sexual orientation envelops our intellectual and attitudinal environment and shapes our personal and collective sensibilities. The conflation's embodiment and enforcement of active/passive sex/gender themes and traditions are so pervasive, so ingrained, so institutionalized, so internalized, that even our children unknowingly collect epithets like "queer," "sissy," "dyke," and "tomboy" in single, automatic breaths. These epithets, in turn, display how heteropatriarchy is imprinted in the collective psyche of each generation.

In short, this nation's sex/gender system is designed, built, and maintained precisely along the conflation's traditionalist active/passive fault lines, both socially and sexually. These official and cultural fault lines do not operate randomly: in practice, they operate to secure the social/public and sexual/private intransitivity of deductive gender, and thereby to secure the hierarchical imperatives that underlie and drive the Euro–American sex/gender system and its heteropatriarchal ideology. Unthinking schoolyard comments only reflect and confirm the conflationary system's continuing grip on the nation's senses, while underscoring traditionalist fear and loathing of social or sexual challenges to conflationary arrangements that (might) disrupt the sex/gender status quo.

In Latina/o cultures or settings, both within and beyond the United States, this conflationary dynamic and its sex/gender ideology are also present, and perhaps even more virulently so due to the prevalence of a strong "machismo" norm. Terms like "marimacha" and "maricon"— meaning dyke and queer, respectively—reflect and reify the conflation's sway over Latina/o sex/gender norms and sexual orientation identities:

the former connotes a mannish female, the latter an effeminate man. Both are devalued because they enact nonconforming combinations of sex, gender, and sexuality. Thus, as in Euro–American contexts, all three legs of the conflation operate, and in combination construct social and sexual identifications: sex establishes gender expectations, and gender a/typically is construed and mis/treated as homo/heterosexual orientation. As in Euro–American culture, social or sexual disruption of any leg is censured. Moreover, as these terms imply, Latina/o sex/gender hierarchies are not only heterocentric, they also are androcentric. Thus, as in the Euro–American sex/gender system, Latina/o ideals and values instill and demand conformity to the conflation's active/passive heteropatriarchal bent.

Accordingly, resistance to this conflation and its ideology must be recognized as central to the anti-subordination strategy of Queer legal theory. But this strategy also must guard against our prior internalization of conflationary beliefs or associations. In particular, concerns over gay male androsexism, and the dangers that it poses for Queer theorizing, should serve constructively to heighten our individual and collective vigilance against the potential for a wholesale or creeping influence of androsexism within Queer critiques. Because it counters the tradition of male supremacy that has run through Western history, this heightened vigilance may not come easily, but it is also not impossible. Indeed, by definition, the term "Queer" reflects and invokes this type of heightened awareness for sex/gender egalitarianism and against sex/gender imperialism. The key, then, is to live up to the standards of the term, and the challenge is to join in the fulfillment of the ideals underlying this commitment.

However, to do so we also must take into account other issues raised by Queer legal theory. American culture employs "queer" to denigrate persons suspected of being gay, but in recent years "Queer," has come to signify principally a rebellious resistance to heterosexist customs and precepts. As a result, "Queer" like "queer," tends to indicate minority "sexual orientation." But it need (and should) not be so: "Queer" is a description of consciousness regarding sexuality and its relationship to one's self and to one's culture. Thus, even though most persons who self-identify as Queer today probably are gay, lesbian, bisexual, or trans/bi-gendered, one *can* be gay or lesbian or bisexual or trans/bi-gendered without being Queer; Queer consciousness is neither innate nor uniform among sexual minorities. Likewise, Queer subjectivity may be articulated from a sexual majority position.

Queer legal theory likewise must and can avoid the similar danger of carelessly (or intentionally) reiterating the racist biases that, like androsexism, pervade our social and legal environments. The vigilance of Queer legal theory against racism is again especially important due to our cultural backdrop: the larger Queer social movement already has experienced problems with racial [dis]harmony because it has not (fully) excised racist overtones and undertones from its ranks. This failure excludes people of color from Queer venues, replicating and compounding the race divisions of the sexual majority. This failure thus demonstrates how deeply we are mired in acculturation, and how crucial it is for Queer legal theory to intercede during these formative times on behalf of Queers of color. Queer as legal theory, using Queer cultural politics and studies as its point of departure, has the opportunity and obligation to discontinue, interrupt, and condemn the replication of racism both in sexual minority cultural venues and legal projects.

This opportunity is also an obligation because the exclusion or marginalization of people of color within Queer settings is antithetical to the inclusiveness and expansiveness that is definitive and constitutive of Queerness. As in the case of androsexism, Queer undertakings proactively must show and apply a heightened sensitivity to, and an uncompromising opposition against, the omission of race, ethnicity, and class from Queer critiques. Queer as legal theory cannot tolerate or ignore any show of wholesale or creeping racism, ethnocentrism, or classism. The inclusiveness and egalitarianism of Queerness demand that Queer legal theory not ignore the lives and presence of Queers of color, of varying ethnic backgrounds, or of [dis]advantaged economic backgrounds: to do so would be to lend support to the oppression that subordinates groups based on race, ethnicity, or class more generally. As legal theory, the Queer enterprise must take a proactive stance toward race, ethnicity, and class, toward their particularized intersections with [homo/bi]sexuality, and toward their broader intertwining with sex/gender issues.

At the threshold—where we stand today—this concern therefore necessitates nothing less than a sustained effort to make the historic and unfinished fight against racism, ethnocentrism, and classism integral to Queer critiques of the law. This effort in turn requires an affirmative interrogation of why and how Queerness plays differently in different racial, ethnic, or class contexts, as much as it requires an interrogation of where and when racism, ethnocentrism, and classism—perhaps even of the unconscious type—confine Queer theorizing in arbitrary or unproductive ways. From the outset, Queer legal critiques therefore must take the time and make the effort expressly to discuss and expose the role of race, ethnicity, and class in the [mis]fortunes visited by the law on Queer (and other) lives. In this way, "Queer" as legal theory can avoid importing the assumed and imposed whiteness of "queer" as cultural epithet and also align itself with the greater anti-subordination civil rights movement for equality in color and class relations.

Finally, these notes make plain that the conflation's androcentric and heterocentric prejudice is replicated and disseminated not only through Anglo, but also through Hispanic, norms. For Latinas/os in the United States, and especially for those who identify as lesbian, gay, bisexual or trans/bi-gendered, this social combination is a "double whammy." In other words, Latina/o members of sexual minorities in the United States are socially and legally marginalized through the conflationary precepts and practices of the two systems that constitute our beings and structure our environments.

These notes thus make plain that this conflation concerns more than Queer legal theory; the conflation's impact specifically on Latina/o sexual minority communities implicates LatCrit theory as well. The conflation's heteropatriarchal biases are directly relevant to the anti-subordination mission of LatCrit theory because the LatCrit enterprise is explicitly and self-consciously dedicated to the cause of social justice for *all* Latinas/os; LatCrit theory insistently embraces and celebrates the multiple diversities of "Latinas/os," rejecting both single-axis analyses that essentialize Latinas/os as well as internal and external ideologies of subordination. Because the conflation's promotion of androsexism and heterosexism subordinates many Latinas/os, these notes suggest that LatCrit theory and Queer legal theory share a common interest in the transformation of today's sex/gender system, a transformation that unites the QueerCrit and LatCrit goals of a just post-subordination society. These notes, in sum, invite LatCrit interrogation of this conflation, an interrogation that properly is deemed integral to the LatCrit anti-subordination agenda.

Notes and Questions

1. What is different, if anything, about Latino/a heterosexism?

2. Is a Latina lesbian or a Latino gay man doubly disadvantaged vis-à-vis a straight white counterpart?

3. Do Latino/a gays and lesbians have more in common with the gay rights movement or the movement for black and brown civil rights? See *Chicana Lesbians: The Girls Our Mothers Warned Us About* (Carla Trujillo ed., 1991); Francisco X. Valdes, *Sex and Race in Queer Legal Culture: Ruminations on Identities & Inter-Connectivities*, 5 S. Cal. Rev. L. & Women's Stud. 25 (1995).

4. What do Latino/a gays and lesbians fear most—violence and intolerance based on their Latino looks and traits, or their sexual orientation?

SECTION 3. INTERSECTIONALITY AND ESSENTIALISM

Latinas are by their very nature "intersectional." Their identity is complex—they are both racial and sexual minorities. They sit, in other words, at the intersection of two legal categories—race and sex. Their identities and the range of sociolegal problems they encounter as they go through life are not the same as those that women, in general, encounter, nor the same as those that people of color, in general, encounter.

Does this really matter, or is it only of theoretical interest? The next selections suggest that society must attend to the special concerns of intersectional people if it wishes to render compete justice, of either the racial or the sexual kind.

Richard Delgado
Rodrigo's Sixth Chronicle: Intersections, Essences,
and the Dilemma of Social Reform
68 N.Y.U. L. Rev. 639, 639–47, 665–71 (1993)

I was returning to my office from the faculty library one flight below, when I spied a familiar figure waiting outside my door.

"Rodrigo!" I said. "It's good to see you. Please come in."

I had not seen my young protégé in a while. A graduate of a fine law school in Italy, Rodrigo had returned to the United States recently to begin LL.M. studies at a well-known school across town in preparation for a career as a law professor. An African–American by birth and ancestry, the talented Rodrigo had sought me out over the course of a year to discuss critical race theory and many other ideas. For my part, I had gratefully used him as a foil and a sounding board for my own thoughts.

"Have a seat. You look a little agitated. Is everything OK?" Rodrigo had been pacing my office while I was putting my books down and activating my voice mail. I hoped it was intellectual excitement and his usual high-pitched energy that accounted for his restless demeanor.

"Professor, I'm afraid I'm in some trouble. Do you have a few minutes? There's something I need to talk over with someone older and wiser."

"I'm definitely older," I said. "The other part I'm not sure about. What's happening?"

"There's a big feud going on in the Law Women's Caucus at my school. The women of color and the white members are going at it hammer and tongs. And like a dummy, I got caught right in the middle."

"You? How?" I asked.

"I'm not a member. I don't think any man is. But Giannina is an honorary member, as I think I mentioned to you last time. The Caucus has tried to keep its struggle quiet, but I learned about it from Giannina. And I'm afraid I really—how do you put it?—put my foot in the mouth."

"In your mouth," I corrected. Although Rodrigo had been born in the States and spent his early childhood here, he occasionally failed to use an idiom correctly, a difficulty I had observed with other foreigners. "Tell me more," I continued. "How did it happen? Is it serious?"

"It's extremely serious," said Rodrigo, leaping to his feet and resuming his pacing. "They were having a meeting down in the basement, where I went after class to pick up Giannina. We were going to catch the subway home, and I thought her meeting would be over by then. I stood at the door a minute, when a woman I knew motioned me in. That was my mistake."

"Are the meetings closed to men?"

"I don't think so. But I was the only man there at the time. They were talking about essentialism—as I've learned to call it—and the organization's agenda. A woman of color was complaining that the group never paid enough attention to the concerns of women like her. Some of the white women were getting upset. I made the mistake of raising my hand."

"What did you say?"

"I only tried to help analyze some of the issues. I drew a couple of distinctions, or tried to anyway. Both sides got mad at me. One called me an imperial scholar, an interloper, a typical male, and a pest. I got out of there fast. And now, no one will talk to me. Even Giannina made me move out of the bedroom. I've been sleeping on the couch for the last three nights. I feel like a leper."

A quarrel between lovers! I had not had to deal with one of those since my sons were young. "I'm sure you and she will patch it up," I offered. "You'd better—the two of you owe me dinner, remember?"

Rodrigo was not cheered by my joke nor my effort to console him. "I may never have Giannina's companionship again," he said, looking down.

"These things generally get better with time," I said, making a mental note to address the point later. "It's part of life. But if talking about some of these issues would help, I'm game."

In Which Rodrigo and I Review the Essentialism Debate and Try to Understand What Happened at the Law Women's Caucus

"The debate about essentialism has both a political and a theoretical component," Rodrigo began. "That book (Rodrigo nodded in the direction of *Yearning: Race, Gender, and Cultural Politics*, by bell hooks, lying open on my desk) and those articles pay more attention to the political dimension. But there's also a linguistic-theory component."

"You mean the early philosophical discussion about whether words have essences?" I asked, pausing a moment to offer Rodrigo a cup of steaming espresso. I pointed out the tray of ingredients and said, "Help yourself if it needs more cream and sugar."

"Exactly," Rodrigo replied, slurping his coffee. "The early anti-essentialists attacked the belief that words have core, or central, meanings. If I'm not mistaken, Wittgenstein was the first in our time to point this out. In a way, it's a particularly powerful and persuasive version of the antinominalist argument."

As always, Rodrigo surprised me with his erudition. I wondered how an Italian-trained scholar, particularly one so young, had managed to learn about Wittgenstein, whose popularity I thought lay mainly in the English-speaking world. "How did you learn about Wittgenstein?" I asked.

"He's popular in Italy," Rodrigo explained. "I belonged to a study group that read him. The part of his teaching that laid the basis for anti-essentialism was his attack on the idea of core meanings. As you know, he wrote that the meaning of a term is its use."

"I haven't read him in a while," I added hastily. "But you mentioned that the controversy's political side seems to be moving into the fore right now, which seems true. And I gather it's this aspect of the essentialism debate that you wandered into at school."

"In its political guise," Rodrigo continued, "members of different outgroups argue about the appropriate unit of analysis—about whether the black community, for example, is one community or many, whether gays and lesbians have anything in common with straight activists, and so on. At the Law Women's Caucus, they were debating one aspect of this—namely, whether there is one essential sisterhood, as opposed to many. The women of color were arguing that to think of the women's movement as singular and unitary disempowers them. They said that this view disenfranchises anyone—say, lesbian mothers, disabled women, or working-class women—whose experience and status differ from what they term 'the norm.' "

"And the others, of course, were saying the opposite?"

"Not exactly," Rodrigo replied. "They were saying that vis-à-vis men, all women stood on a similar footing. All are oppressed by a common enemy, namely patriarchy, and ought to stand together to confront this evil."

"I've read something similar in the literature," I said.

"I'm not surprised. In a way, the debate the Caucus was having recapitulates an exchange between Angela Harris, a talented black writer, and Martha Fineman, a leading white feminist scholar."

"Those articles are on my list of things to read. In fact," I paused, ruffling through the papers on my littered desk, "they're right here. I skimmed this one and set this other one aside for more careful reading later. I have to annotate both for my editors."

"Then you have at least a general idea of how the political version goes," Rodrigo said. "It has to do with agendas and the sorts of compromises people have to make in any organization to keep the group working together. In the Caucus's version, the sisters were complaining that the organization did not pay enough attention to the needs of women of color. They were urging that the group write an amicus brief on behalf of Haitian women and take a stand for the mostly black custodial workers at the university. While not unsympathetic, the Caucus leadership thought these projects should not have the highest priority."

"I see what you mean by recapitulation of the academic debate. Fineman and Harris argue over some of the same things. Not the specific examples, of course, but the general issues. Harris writes about the troubled relationship between black women and other women in the broader feminist mainstream, although she notes that many of the issues this relationship raises reappear in exchanges between straight and gay women, working-and professional-class minorities, black women and black men, and so on. She and others write of the way in which these relationships often end up producing or increasing disempowerment for the less influential group. They point out that white feminist theorists, while powerful and brilliant in many ways, nevertheless base many of their insights on gender essentialism—the idea that women have a single, unitary nature. They point out that certain feminist scholars write as though women's experiences can be captured in general terms, without taking into account differences of race or class. This approach obscures the identities and submerges the perspectives of women who differ from the norm. Not only does legal theory built on essentialist foundations marginalize and render certain groups invisible, it falls prey to the trap of over-abstraction, something the same writers deplore in other settings. It also promotes hierarchy and silencing, evils that women should, and do, seek to subvert.''

"Much the same goes on within the black community," I pointed out. "This community is diverse, many communities in one. Black neoconservatives, for example, complain that folks like you and me leave little room for diversity by disparaging them as sellouts and belittling their views as unrepresentative. They accuse us of writing as though the community of color only has one voice—ours—and of arrogating to ourselves the power to make generalizations and declare ourselves the possessors of all socio-political truth."

"I know that critique," Rodrigo replied. "It seems to me that they might well have a point, although it does sound a little strange to hear the complaint of being overwhelmed, smothered, spoken for by others, coming from the mouth of someone at Yale or Harvard."

"Like you at the Law Caucus, I found myself on the end of some stinging criticism. The critics write powerfully, and of course many in the mainstream loved their message—so much so that they neglected to read any of the replies. But let's get back to the feminist version, and what happened to you at the Law Women's meeting."

"Oh, yes. The discussion in many ways mirrored the debate in the legal literature and in that book." Rodrigo again pointed in the direction of the bell hooks book. "As you probably know, Harris's principal opponent in the anti-essentialism debate has been Martha Fineman, who takes black feminists to task for what she considers their overpreoccupation with difference. Their focus on their own unique experience contributes to a 'disunity' within the broader feminist movement that she finds troubling. It's troubling, she says, because it weakens the group's voice, the sum total of power it wields. Emphasizing minor differences between young and old, gay and straight, and black and white women is divisive, verging on self-indulgence. It contributes to the false idea that the individual is the unit of social change, not the group. It results in tokenism and plays into the hands of male power."

"And the discussion in the room was proceeding along these lines?" I asked.

"Yes," Rodrigo replied. "Although I had the sense that things had been brewing for some time. As soon as some of the leaders expressed coolness toward the black women's proposal for a day-care center, the level of acrimony increased sharply. A number of women of color said, 'This is just like what you said last time.' Some of the white women accused them of narrow parochialism. And so it went."

* * *

"Rodrigo, you might not know this because you've been out of the country for—what?—the last ten years?" Rodrigo nodded yes. "These issues are really heated right now. And they're not confined to feminist organizations. Many of the same arguments are being waged within communities of color. Latinos and blacks are feuding. And, of course, everyone knows about Korean merchants and inner-city blacks. Black women are telling us men about our insufferable behavior. We're always finishing sentences for them, expecting them to make coffee at meetings. Some of them with long memories recall how we made them march in the second row during the civil rights movement. We make the same arguments right back at them: 'Don't criticize, you'll weaken the civil rights movement, the greater evil is racism, we need unity, there must be common cause,' and so on. They're starting to get tired of that form of essentializing, and to point out our own chauvinism, our own patriarchal mannerisms and faults."

"Those are some of the things I got called at the meeting. It looks like I have company."

"We all need to think these things through. You and I could talk about it some more, if you think it would help. Can I offer you another cup of coffee?"

* * *

IN WHICH RODRIGO POSITS A THEORY OF SOCIAL CHANGE AND EXPLAINS THE ROLE OF OPPOSITIONAL GROUPS IN BRINGING IT ABOUT

* * *

"I think that virtually all revolutionary ideas start with an outsider of some sort," Rodrigo began. "We mentioned the reasons before. Few who operate within the system see its defects. They speak, read, and hear within a discourse that is self-satisfying. The primary function of our system of free speech is to effect stasis, not change. New ideas are ridiculed as absurd and extreme, and discounted as political, at first. It's not until much later, when consciousness changes, that we look back and wonder why we resisted so strongly."

"Revolutionaries always lead rocky lives. You'll see that too, Rodrigo, although I don't know if you classify yourself as one or not. All the pressure is in the direction of conforming, of doing what others do, in teaching, in scholarship, in fact in all areas of life."

Rodrigo shrugged off my counsel. "So, new ideas and movements come along relatively rarely. And when they do, they are beleaguered. For a long time, they garner little support. Then, for some reason, they acquire something like a critical mass. Society begins to pay attention. Now, the situation is in flux. The group now needs all the allies they can muster. They begin to make inroads and need to make more. They see that they are beginning to approach the point where they might be able to change societal discourse in a direction they favor."

"Including the power to define who is 'divisive,' " I added.

"That, too—especially that," Rodrigo said animatedly, seeing how my observation fit into the theory he was developing. He looked up with gratitude, then continued:

"At this point, they need all the help they can get. If they are you, they need Gary Peller and Alan Freeman. If they are feminists, they need Cass Sunstein. Earlier, they needed the religious right in their campaign against pornography. And so on. With a little growth in numbers, they may perhaps reach the point at which power begins to translate into knowledge. And knowledge, of course, is the beginning of social reform. When everyone knows you are right, knows you have a point, you are well on your way to victory."

"And for this the group needs numbers."

"Right. With them, they can change the interpretive community. They can remake the model of the essential woman, say, along lines that are genuinely more humane."

In Which Rodrigo and I Discuss the Role of Reformers and Malcontent Groups

"So, Rodrigo," I continued, "you are saying that new knowledge of any important, radical sort begins with a small group. This group is dissatisfied, but believes it has a point. It agitates, acquires new members, begins to get society to take it seriously. And it's at this point that the essentialism/anti-essentialism debate usually sets in?"

"Before it wouldn't arise. And later, when the large group is nearing its goals, it doesn't need the disaffected faction. So it's right at this midpoint in a social revolution—for example, the feminist movement—that we have debates like the one I got caught in the middle of."

"But you were saying before that the disaffected cell ought to sit out the revolution, as it were, and not just for its own good but for that of the wider society as well?"

"It should. And often such groups do, consciously or unconsciously. I'm just saying that when they do, it's usually not a bad thing."

"And this is because of your theory of knowledge, I gather, in which canonical thinking always gets to a point where it no longer works and needs a fundamental challenge?"

"And this, in turn, can only come from a disaffected group. Every new idea, if it has merit, eventually turns into a canon. And every canonical idea at some point needs to be dislodged, challenged, and supplanted by a new one."

"So maverick, malcontent groups are the growing edge of social thought."

"Not every one. Some are regressive—want to roll back reform."

"I can think of several that fit that bill," I said shuddering. "But you said earlier that the outsider has a kind of binocular vision that enables him or her to see defects in the bubbles in which we all live—to see the curvature, the limitations, the downward drift that eventually spells trouble. But earlier you used another metaphor. What was it?"

Rodrigo thought for a moment. "Oh, I remember. It was the role of hunger."

"I'd love for you to explain."

"It's like this." Rodrigo pushed aside his plate. "Change comes from a small, dissatisfied group for whom canonical knowledge and the standard social arrangements don't work. Such a group needs allies. Thus, white women in the feminist movement reach out to women of color; black men in the civil rights movement try to include black women, and so on. Eventually, the larger group makes inroads, changes the paradigm, begins to be accepted, gets laws passed, and so on."

"Can I take that plate?" I asked. Rodrigo passed it over, and I put it in the nonrecyclable bin outside my office along with the other remnants of our snack. "This is what you argued before, so I assume you're getting to your theory about hunger."

"Correct. But you see, as soon as all this happens, the once-radical group begins to lose its edge. It enters a phase of consolidation, in which it is more concerned with defending and instituting reforms made possible by the new consensus, the new paradigm of Foucault's Knowledge/Power, than with pushing the envelope towards more radical change. The group is beginning to lose binocular vision, the special form of insight most outgroups have, about social inequities and imbalances."

"And so the reform movement founders?" I asked. "We've seen many examples of that. As you know, legal scholarship is now extremely interested in that question. Many in the left are trying to discover why all our best intentions fail, why the urge to transform society for the better always comes to naught."

"I'm not sure I'd say the movement founders," Rodrigo interjected. "Rather, it enters into a different phase. I don't want to be too critical."

"But at any rate, it peters out," I said. "It loses vigor."

"But then, eventually, another group rises up to take its place. Often this is a disaffected subset of the larger group, the one that won reforms, that got the Supreme Court or Congress to recognize the legitimacy of its claims. It turns out that the reforms did not do much for the subgroup. The revolution came and went, but things stayed pretty much the same for it. So, it renews its effort."

"And that's what you meant by hunger?"

"In a way. Those who are hungry are most desperate for change. Human intelligence and progress spring from adversity, from a sense that the world is not supplying what the organism needs and requires. A famous American philosopher developed a theory of education based on this idea."

"I assume you mean John Dewey?"

"Him and others. He was a sometime member of the school of American pragmatists. But his approach differed in significant respects from that of the other pragmatists like William James and Charles Peirce. One was this. And so I'm thinking we can borrow from his theory to explain the natural history of revolutionary movements, applying what he saw to be true for individuals to larger groups."

"Where you think it holds as well?" I asked. "It's always dangerous extrapolating from the individual to the group."

"I think the observation does hold for groups, as well," Rodrigo replied. "But I'd be glad to be corrected if you think I am wrong. The basic idea is that groups that are victors become complacent. They lose their critical edge, because there is no need to have it. The social structure now works for them. If by intelligence, one means critical intelligence, we become dumber all the time. It's a kind of reverse evolution. Eventually society gets out of kilter enough that a dissident group rises up, its critical skills honed, its perception equal to that of the slave. It challenges the master by condemning the status quo as unjust, just as Giannina challenged me. Sometimes the injustices it points to are ones that genuinely need mending, and not just for the discontented group. Rather, they signal a broader social need to reform things in ways that will benefit everybody."

I leaned forward; the full force of what Rodrigo was saying had hit me. "So, Rodrigo, you are saying that the history of revolution is, by its nature, iterative. The unit of social intelligence is small; reform and retrenchment come in waves. This fits in with what you were saying earlier about the decline of the West and the need for infusion of outsider thought. And, it dovetails with other currents under way in environmental thought, economic thought—and, as you mentioned, in American political philosophy." * * *

Angela P. Harris
Race and Essentialism in Feminist Legal Theory
42 Stan. L. Rev. 581, 581–84, 587–89, 598–601 (1990)

In *Funes the Memorious*, Borges tells of Ireneo Funes, who was a rather ordinary young man (notable only for his precise sense of time) until the age of nineteen, when he was thrown by a half-tamed horse and left paralyzed but possessed of perfect perception and a perfect memory.

After his transformation, Funes

knew by heart the forms of the southern clouds at dawn on the 30th of April, 1882, and could compare them in his memory with the mottled streaks on a book in Spanish binding he had only seen once and with the outlines of the foam raised by an oar in the Río Negro the night before the Quebracho uprising. These memories were not simple ones; each visual image was linked to muscular sensations, thermal sensations, etc. He could reconstruct all his dreams, all his half-dreams. Two or three times he had reconstructed a whole day; he never hesitated, but each reconstruction had required a whole day.

Funes tells the narrator that after his transformation he invented his own numbering system. "In place of seven thousand thirteen, he would say (for example) *Máximo Pérez*; in place of seven thousand fourteen, *The Railroad*; other numbers were Luis Melián Lafinur, Olimar, sulphur, the reins, the whale, the gas, the caldron, Napoleon, Agustín de Vedia." The narrator tries to explain to Funes "that this rhapsody of incoherent terms was precisely the opposite of a system of numbers. I told him that saying 365 meant saying three hundreds, six tens, five ones, an analysis which is not found in the 'numbers' *The Negro Timoteo* or *meat blanket*. Funes did not understand me or refused to understand me."

In his conversation with Funes, the narrator realizes that Funes' life of infinite unique experiences leaves Funes no ability to categorize: "With no effort, he had learned English, French, Portuguese and Latin. I suspect, however, that he was not very capable of thought. To think is to forget differences, generalize, make abstractions. In the teeming world of Funes, there were only details, almost immediate in their presence." For Funes, language is only a unique and private system of classification, elegant and solipsistic. The notion that language, made abstract, can serve to create and reinforce a community is incomprehensible to him.

"We the People"

Describing the voice that speaks the first sentence of the Declaration of Independence, James Boyd White remarks:

It is not a person's voice, not even that of a committee, but the "unanimous" voice of "thirteen united States" and of their "people." It addresses a universal audience—nothing less than "mankind" itself, located neither in space nor in time—and the voice is universal too, for it purports to know about the "Course of human events" (all human events?) and to be able to discern what "becomes necessary" as a result of changing circumstances.

The Preamble of the United States Constitution, White argues, can also be heard to speak in this unified and universal voice. This voice claims to speak for an entire and united nation and to do so directly and personally, not in the third person or by merely delegated authority.... The instrument thus appears to issue from a single imaginary author, consisting of all the people of the United States, including the reader, merged into a single identity in this act of self-constitution. "The People" are at once the author and the audience of this instrument.

Despite its claims, however, this voice does not speak for everyone, but for a political faction trying to constitute itself as a unit of many disparate voices; its power lasts only as long as the contradictory voices remain silenced.

In a sense, the "I" of Funes, who knows only particulars, and the "we" of "We the People," who know only generalities, are the same. Both voices are monologues; both depend on the silence of others. The difference is only that the first voice knows of no others, while the second has silenced them.

* * *

We are not born with a "self," but rather are composed of a welter of partial, sometimes contradictory, or even antithetical "selves." A unified identity, if such can ever exist, is a product of will, not a common destiny or natural birthright. * * *

* * *

Race and Essentialism in Feminist Legal Theory

In feminist legal theory, the move away from univocal toward multivocal theories of women's experience and feminism has been slower than in other areas. In feminist legal theory, the pull of the second voice, the voice of abstract categorization, is still powerfully strong: "We the People" seems in danger of being replaced by "We the Women." And in feminist legal theory, as in the dominant culture, it is mostly white, straight, and socioeconomically privileged people who claim to speak for all of us. Not surprisingly, the story they tell about "women," despite its claim to universality, seems to black women to be peculiar to women who are white, straight, and socioeconomically privileged—a phenomenon Adrienne Rich terms "white solipsism."

Elizabeth Spelman notes:

[T]he real problem has been how feminist theory has confused the condition of one group of women with the condition of all.

... A measure of the depth of white middle-class privilege is that the apparently straightforward and logical points and axioms at the heart of much of feminist theory guarantee the direction of its attention to the concerns of white middle-class women.

The notion of a monolithic "women's experience" that can be described independent of other facets of experience like race, class, and sexual orientation I refer to in this essay as "gender essentialism." A corollary to gender essentialism is "racial essentialism"—the belief that there is a monolithic "Black Experience," or "Chicano Experience." The source of gender and racial essentialism (and all other essentialisms, for the list of categories could be infinitely multiplied) is the second voice, the voice that claims to speak for all. The result of essentialism is to reduce the lives of people who experience multiple forms of oppression to addition problems: "racism + sexism = straight black women's experience," or "racism + sexism + homophobia = black lesbian experience." Thus, in an essentialist world, black women's experience will always be forcibly fragmented before being subjected to analysis, as those who are "only interested in race" and those who are "only interested in gender" take their separate slices of our lives.

Moreover, feminist essentialism paves the way for unconscious racism. Spelman puts it this way:

> [T]hose who produce the "story of woman" want to make sure they appear in it. The best way to ensure that is to be the storyteller and hence to be in a position to decide which of all the many facts about womens lives ought to go into the story, which ought to be left out. Essentialism works well in behalf of these aims, aims that subvert the very process by which women might come to see where and how they wish to make common cause. For essentialism invites me to take what I understand to be true of me "as a woman" for some golden nugget of womanness all women have as women; and it makes the participation of other women inessential to the production of the story. How lovely: the many turn out to be one, and the one that they are is me.

In a racist society like this one, the storytellers are usually white, and so "woman" turns out to be "white woman."

Why, in the face of challenges from "different" women and from feminist method itself, is feminist essentialism so persistent and pervasive? I think the reasons are several. Essentialism is intellectually convenient, and to a certain extent cognitively ingrained. Essentialism also carries with it important emotional and political payoffs. Finally, essentialism often appears (especially to white women) as the only alternative to chaos, mindless pluralism (the Furies trap), and the end of the feminist movement. In my view, however, as long as feminists, like theorists in the dominant culture, continue to search for gender and racial essences, black women will never be anything more than a crossroads between two kinds of domination, or at the bottom of a hierarchy of oppressions; we will always be required to choose pieces of ourselves to present as wholeness.

* * *

[T]he paradigm experience of rape for black women has historically involved the white employer in the kitchen or bedroom as much as the strange black man in the bushes. During slavery, the sexual abuse of black women by white men was commonplace. Even after emancipation, the majority of working black women were domestic servants for white families, a job which made them uniquely vulnerable to sexual harassment and rape.

Moreover, as a legal matter, the experience of rape did not even exist for black women. During slavery, the rape of a black woman by any man, white or black, was simply not a crime. Even after the Civil War, rape laws were seldom used to protect black women against either white or black men, since black women were considered promiscuous by nature. In contrast to the partial or at least formal protection white women had against sexual brutalization, black women frequently had no legal protection whatsoever. "Rape," in this sense, was something that only happened to white women; what happened to black women was simply life.

Finally, for black people, male and female, "rape" signified the terrorism of black men by white men, aided and abetted, passively (by silence) or actively (by "crying rape"), by white women. Black women have recognized this aspect of rape since the nineteenth century. For example, social activist Ida B. Wells analyzed rape as an example of the inseparability of race and gender oppression in *Southern Horrors: Lynch Law in All Its Phases*, published in 1892. Wells saw that both the law of rape and Southern miscegenation laws were part of a patriarchal system through which white men maintained their control over the bodies of all black people: "[W]hite men used their ownership of the body of the white female as a terrain on which to lynch the black male." Moreover, Wells argued, though many white women encouraged interracial sexual relationships, white women, protected by the patriarchal idealization of white womanhood, were able to remain silent, unhappily or not, as black men were murdered by mobs. Similarly, Anna Julia Cooper, another nineteenth-century theorist, "saw that the manipulative power of the South was embodied in the southern patriarch, but she describes its concern with 'blood,' inheritance, and heritage in entirely female terms and as a preoccupation that was transmitted from the South to the North and perpetuated by white women."

Nor has this aspect of rape become purely a historical curiosity. Susan Estrich reports that between 1930 and 1967, 89 percent of the men executed for rape in the United States were black. * * * The rift between white and black women over the issue of rape is highlighted by the contemporary feminist analyses of rape that have explicitly relied on racist ideology to minimize white women's complicity in racial terrorism.

Thus, the experience of rape for black women includes not only a vulnerability to rape and a lack of legal protection radically different from that experienced by white women, but also a unique ambivalence. Black women have simultaneously acknowledged their own victimization and the victimization of black men by a system that has consistently ignored violence against women while perpetrating it against men. The complexity and depth of this experience is not captured, or even acknowledged, by * * * [an] essentialist approach re-creates the paradigmatic woman in the image of the white woman, in the name of "unmodified feminism." As in the dominant discourse, black women are relegated to the margins, ignored or extolled as "just like us, only more so." But "Black women are not white women with color." Moreover, feminist essentialism represents not just an insult to black women, but a broken promise—the promise to listen to women's stories, the promise of feminist method.

Notes and Questions

1.   Is feminism by its nature a concern of white women?

2.   Could it be otherwise?

3.   Does black feminism disempower Latinas and vice versa?

4.   Will every group leave some members unsatisfied and discontent?

5.   Angela Hooton, *A Broader Vision of the Reproductive Rights Movement: Fusing Mainstream and Latina Feminism*, 13 Am. U. J. Gender, Soc. Pol'y & L. 59 (2005), explains in concrete detail how the white elite leadership of the feminist movement focuses on "choice," thereby leaving many Latina issues unaddressed: limited access to providers, lack of health insurance, unequal treatment by providers, language barriers, and lack of information in Spanish, to name a few. The movement has also been critical of advocating a right to prenatal care, for fear it could lead to establishment of fetal rights. Latina activists are reorganizing and reframing all these issues, but with little aid from white women.

Rogers v. American Airlines
527 F.Supp. 229 (S.D.N.Y. 1981)

Plaintiff is a black woman who seeks $10,000 damages, injunctive, and declaratory relief against enforcement of a grooming policy of the defendant American Airlines that prohibits employees in certain employment categories from wearing an all-braided hairstyle. Plaintiff has been an American Airlines employee for approximately eleven years, and has been an airport operations agent for over one year. Her duties involve extensive passenger contact, including greeting passengers, issuing boarding passes, and checking luggage. She alleges that the policy violates her rights under * * * Title VII of the Civil Rights Act and under 42 U.S.C.A. § 1981 (1976), in that it discriminates against her as a woman, and more specifically as a black woman. She claims that denial of the right to wear her hair in the "corn row" style intrudes upon her rights and discriminates against her. * * *

The motion [by defendant to dismiss is] meritorious with respect to the statutory claims insofar as they challenge the policy on its face. The statutory bases alleged, Title VII and section 1981, are indistinguishable in the circumstances of this case, and will be considered together. The policy is addressed to both men and women, black and white. Plaintiff's assertion that the policy has practical effect only with respect to women is not supported by any factual allegations. Many men have hair longer than many women. Some men have hair long enough to wear in braids if they choose to do so. Even if the grooming policy imposed different standards for men and women, however, it would not violate Title VII. It follows, therefore, that an even-handed policy that prohibits to both sexes a style more often adopted by members of one sex does not constitute prohibited sex discrimination. This is because this type of regulation has at most a negligible effect on employment opportunity. It does not regulate on the basis of any immutable characteristic of the employees involved. It concerns a matter of relatively low importance in terms of the constitutional interests protected by the Fourteenth Amendment and Title VII, rather than involving fundamental rights such as the right to have children or to marry. The complaint does not state a claim for sex discrimination.

The considerations with respect to plaintiffs race discrimination claim would clearly be the same, except for plaintiff's assertion that the "corn row" style has a special significance for black women. She contends that it "has been, historically, a fashion and style adopted by Black American women, reflective of cultural, historical essence of the Black women in American society." "The style was 'popularized' so to speak, within the larger society, when Cicely Tyson adopted the same for an appearance on a nationally viewed Academy Awards presentation several years ago.... It was and is analogous to the public statement by the late Malcolm X regarding the Afro hair style.... At the bottom line, the completely braided hair style, sometimes referred to as corn rows, has been and continues to be part of the cultural and historical essence of Black American women." "There can be little doubt that, if Americans adopted a policy which foreclosed Black women/all women from wearing hair styled as an 'Afro/bush,' that policy would have very pointedly racial dynamics and consequences reflecting a vestige of slavery unwilling to die (that is, a master mandate that one wear hair divorced from one's historical and cultural perspective and otherwise consistent with the 'white master' dominated society and preference thereof)."

Plaintiff is entitled to a presumption that her arguments, largely repeated in her affidavit, are true. But the grooming policy applies equally to members of all races, and plaintiff does not allege that an all-braided hair style is worn exclusively or even predominantly by black people. Moreover, it is proper to note that defendants have alleged without contravention that plaintiff first appeared at work in the all-braided hairstyle on or about September 25, 1980, soon after the style had been popularized by a white actress in the film "10." Plaintiff may be correct that an employer's policy prohibiting the "Afro/bush" style might offend Title VII and section 1981. But if so, this chiefly would be because banning a natural hairstyle would implicate the policies underlying the prohibition of discrimination on the basis of immutable characteristics. In any event, an all-braided hairstyle is a different matter. It is not the product of natural hair growth but of artifice. An all-braided hair style is an "easily changed characteristic," and, even if socioculturally associated with a particular race or nationality, is not an impermissible basis for distinctions in the application of employment practices by an employer. The Fifth Circuit recently upheld, without requiring any showing of business purpose, an employer's policy prohibiting the speaking of any language but English in the workplace, despite the importance of Spanish to the ethnic identity of Mexican Americans. Garcia v. Gloor, 618 F.2d 264, 267–69. The court stated that Title VII

> is directed only at specific impermissible bases of discrimination-race, color, religion, sex, or national origin. National origin must not be confused with ethnic or sociocultural traits.... Save for religion, the discriminations on which the Act focuses its laser of prohibition are those that are either beyond the victim's power to alter, or that impose a burden on an employee on one of the prohibited bases....
> "[A] hiring policy that distinguishes on some other ground, such as grooming codes or length of hair, is related more closely to the employer's choice of how to run his business than to equality of employment opportunity."

Id. at 269.

Although the Act may shield "employees' psychological as well as economic fringes" from employer abuse, plaintiff's allegations do not amount to charging American with "a practice of creating a working environment heavily charged with ethnic or racial discrimination," or one "so heavily polluted with discrimination as to destroy completely the emotional and psychological stability of minority group workers. * * * " Id. If an even-handed English-only policy that has the effect of prohibiting a Mexican American from speaking Spanish during working hours is valid without a showing of business purpose, the policy at issue here, even if ill-advised, does not offend the law.

Moreover, the airline did not require plaintiff to restyle her hair. It suggested that she could wear her hair as she liked while off duty, and permitted her to pull her hair into a bun and wrap a hairpiece around the bun during working hours. * * * Plaintiff has done this, but alleges that the hairpiece has caused her severe headaches. A larger hairpiece would seem in order. But even if any hairpiece would cause such discomfort, the policy does not offend a substantial interest.

　　　* * *

This action is dismissed, except for plaintiff's claim of discriminatory treatment in the application of the grooming policy. * * *

Notes and Questions

1. Unless Title VII and other antidiscrimination statutes expand to include "intersectional" discrimination, individuals like the plaintiff in *Rogers* could easily fall within the gaps of a statutory scheme. See Paulette Caldwell, *A Hair Piece: Perspectives on the Intersection of Race and Gender*, 1991 Duke L.J. 365, discussing *Rogers v. American Airlines*.

2. With *Rogers* in mind, consider the following case:

A black woman arrives at work one day to learn that her new supervisor dislikes black women: He thinks they are feisty, hard to control, and lazy, and finds an excuse, eventually, to get rid of every one. He does not dislike all blacks, however. In particular, he likes black males, finding them rhythmical, musical, and good to talk with about sports on Monday. Nor does he dislike women in general—just black women. He finds white women ornamental and comforting, like his mother, and likes having them around.

Eventually the black woman tires of her poor treatment, learns of the supervisor's pattern of mistreatment of workers like her (black and female) and resolves to sue. If she rests her case on antidiscrimination statutes and case law coined with blacks in mind, she could easily lose: The employer can point out, truthfully, that he does not dislike blacks in general, in fact promotes and hires black men fairly and justly. Suppose, then, that she sues under sexual discrimination law. Again, she confronts a similar hurdle: The employer does not discriminate against women and, indeed, can show that he treats many women (the white ones, that is) with scrupulous fairness.

As a result, the black woman, who ironically suffers a dual disadvantage, could easily lose her case. Whichever body of doctrine she marshals could end up failing to protect from her the kind of "intersectional" discrimination she faces at work. What could you, as her lawyer, do in this situation?

See Trina Grillo, *Anti-Essentialism and Intersectionality: Tools to Dismantle the Master's House*, 10 Berkeley Women's L.J. 16 (1995); Margaret E. Montoya, Mascaras, Trenzas, y Greñas: *Un/masking the Self While Un/braiding Latina Stories and Legal Discourse*, infra this chapter.

3. On workplace issues and sexual harassment on the job, see Part Seven; see also E.E.O.C. v. Hacienda Hotel, 881 F.2d 1504 (9th Cir. 1989).

SECTION 4. CRITICAL LATINA FEMINISM

An emerging Critical Latina Feminism takes up issues like those above, as well as workplace harassment of Latinas and finding a voice for Latinas in the world of law schools and legal scholarship. The following selections are samples of this growing literature.

Maria L. Ontiveros
Three Perspectives on Workplace Harassment of Women of Color
23 Golden Gate U. L. Rev. 817, 817–28 (1993)

For women of color, sexual harassment is rarely, if ever, about sex or sexism alone; it is also about race. For us, racial epithets are spoken in sexist terms, and sexual or sexist comments involve our race and or our culture.

* * *

THE HARASSER

Since workplace harassment is a power dynamic, women of color serve as likely targets because they are the least powerful participants in the workplace. Unlike white women, they are not privileged by their race. Unlike men of color, they are not privileged by their gender. Although a white man might harass any woman, a man of color is not likely to feel that he has the prerogative to harass a white woman. He may feel that he is not able to harass her because of his lack of racial status or because he knows he could be subject to a disproportionate reaction stemming from society's deep-seeded, historical fears of attacks on white women by non-white men. If the harasser is a man of color, then, the victim is likely to be a woman of color. Harassers may also prefer those women of color, such as Latinas and Asian American women, whom they view as more passive and less likely to complain.

Additionally, racism and sexism can blend together in the mind of the harasser * * *. The types of statements used and actions taken incorporate the unique characteristics of women of color, subjecting each race and ethnicity to its own cruel stereotype of sexuality. Harassment of African American women incorporates images of slavery, degradation, sexual availability and natural lasciviousness. In *Brooms v. Regal Tube Co.*, the defendant showed the victim racist pornography involving bestiality, gave her pornographic pictures depicting an interracial act of sodomy and told her that she was hired for the purposes indicated in the photograph because it showed the "talent" of a black woman. In *Continental Can Co. v. Minnesota*, the harasser told his African American victim that, "he wished slavery days would return so that he could sexually train her and she would be his bitch."

A parallel stereotype portrays Asian American women as exotic, submissive, and naturally erotic. This attitude most likely grows out of the 1870's racist portrayal of all Asian women as prostitutes, seeking to enter the United States to engage in "criminal and demoralizing purposes." Unfortunately, these stereotypes still exist and affect women today. Hearings on sexual harassment sponsored by the California Women's Caucus included the testimony of an "Asian construction worker whose co-workers shoved a hammer between her legs, who was taunted with racial slurs, who was repeatedly grabbed on her breasts while installing overhead fixtures, and who was asked whether it was true that Asian women's vaginas were sideways."

In another case, a young Japanese American receptionist's harasser told her he had a foot fetish, stroked and kissed her feet, and kissed the nape of her neck. He told her, "I thought Oriental women get aroused by kissing the back of the neck." Finally, a Taiwanese–American banking executive won a settlement from a Los Angeles bank because, among other things, a co-worker said that she was best suited to a job as a "high-class call girl" and the bank's president once introduced her as "vice president in the real estate and sex department."

Like African American women and Asian American women, society considers Latinas naturally sexual [and] "hot-blooded." In addition, Latinas are often perceived as readily available and accessible for sexual use, with few recriminations to be faced for abusing them. Sonoma County District Attorney Gene Tunney has seen this perception become reality. In commenting on one case which typifies this situation he stated "we've become aware of people who have imported Mexican women, usually from rural villages in the middle of nowhere, and brought them here for sexual reasons. My suspicion is there is a lot of it going on."

Thus, race plays a critical role in workplace harassment of women of color because of the perspective of the harasser. In addition, the perspectives of at least two other key players affect the outcome of a harassment episode.

Women of Color as Members of the Minority Community

The community in which a woman lives and the culture in which she was raised influences her reaction to workplace harassment. For example, some women of color have been raised to be passive, defer to men and not bring attention to themselves. This may be particularly true in the traditional Asian value system that includes obedience, familial interest, fatalism, and self-control, and which tends to foster submissiveness, passivity, pessimism, timidness, inhibition and adaptiveness. Similar barriers may face Latinas growing up in a "macho" culture. For these women to resist an act aggressively or to pursue a legal remedy, these cultural issues must first be confronted.

Additionally, many women wrestle with feelings that they will be blamed for the harassment. For Asian American women, philosophies like "Shikata ga nai" and "If something happens to you, it is your fault for putting yourself in that position" exacerbate the guilt and self-doubt felt by any victim of workplace harassment. One Mexican immigrant victim of harassment, when asked why she did not report the harassment earlier, told a rape counsellor that "a woman who is raped in Mexico is the one at fault, maybe because her parents didn't watch her." Upon learning of the harassment, her husband denounced her as a permanent shame to her family.

Immigrant or illegal status and a lack of understanding of their legal rights further handicap women of color. * * * Marie DeSantis, a community advocate for Sonoma County Women Against Rape, notes that immigrant women are often victims of what she terms "rape by duress." They do not report such crimes because they are too intimidated by their fear of deportation, ignorance of their legal rights and presumed power of their employers. In the situation of the Mexican housekeeper, she stated that because she was here illegally and was paid by her employer, she had no place else to go. She worried that "He could have cut me up in a million pieces, and no one would have known."

The inability to understand the situation is further compounded by the differing ideas of sexuality which permeate different cultures. Sex is discussed less frequently and openly by Asian American women; sexual harassment is therefore not something to be discussed either. In fact, no words for "sexual harassment" exist in Japanese, Mandarin or Cantonese. In cultures that do not even have words to encompass the concept of sexual harassment, it is predictable that many women in those cultures are less likely to recognize harassing behavior when it presents itself.

Finally, victims recognize that accusations of workplace harassment will negatively implicate their cultures and likely bring adverse community response. For example, one Latina community worker was urged by two female co-workers (who had also been harassed and remained silent) to not report an incident of harassment "for fear that exposing the perpetrators would undermine their movement and embarrass the Latino community." This adverse community response may be especially painful for women of color, to whom community is particularly important.

The Clarence Thomas–Anita Hill hearings provide another example of negative community response with which many are familiar. As one author explained:

> Hill was attacked not only by white right-wing misogynists, but by African Americans who felt that she had stepped out of line by accusing a black man chosen by white racists for high office. It was demoralizing to see how the confrontation reinforced the perception that any woman who raises the issue of sexual oppression in the black community is somehow a traitor to the race, which translates into being a traitor to black men. It is particularly disheartening knowing that probably a lot of black people took this stance despite believing Anita Hill. They who decided that standing behind a black man—even one with utter contempt for the struggles of African Americans—is more important that supporting a black woman's right not to be abused.

The Legal System

Once an incident of workplace harassment becomes a lawsuit, the legal system provides the final construct of the event. The legal system's perception of women of color affects cases of workplace harassment brought by these women in at least three ways: judges and juries tend to disbelieve what they say; the dominant culture's construct of their sexuality influences the cases' outcomes; and the entire justice system misperceives relationships between men and women of color, thereby excusing discriminatory acts by men of color.

The story of a Mexican immigrant woman evidences the credibility problem. She told the Sonoma District Attorney that she believed her employer was "a doctor ... and that is a title of some esteem and high position in Mexico.... If you're a peasant girl, and it's your word against his, you don't have a chance."

African American women also have a hard time convincing the legal system that they are telling the truth. Judges have been known to tell jurors to take a black woman's testimony "with a grain of salt." A recent study of jury members in rape trials indicated the lack of credibility given black women's testimony. One juror said of black rape victims, "you can't believe everything they say; they're known to exaggerate the truth."

Even when women of color are believed, the dominant culture's construct of their sexuality influences their hearings and their results. As Professor Charles Lawrence wrote of the Hill–Thomas hearings,

> When the man on the street says, "I don't believe Hill's story," it is in part because he believes the old, oft-told story of "unchaste" black women. When Senator Orrin Hatch charges that her experience is the fantasy of a spurned woman, he is evoking this myth. When he implies that she tried to seduce Thomas by inviting him into her apartment, and when he reads the most lurid language in her account over and over again, all the while protesting his disgust, he is conjuring up these same racist images of the wanton black woman.

Penalties are affected because women of color are believed to have been "asking for it," to not be greatly affected by the abuse, or simply to not be worthy of the same legal protection given to the rest of society. One study concluded that defendants who assault African American women are less likely to receive jail time than those who assault white women. Another study found that assailants of African American women receive an average sentence of two years, compared to an average sentence of ten years for defendants who assault white women. One juror, sitting in the case of a rape of a black pre-teen, stated "being from that neighborhood she probably wasn't a virgin anyway."

A final problem occurs when the legal system misinterprets relationships between men and women of color. The so-called "cultural defense" has been used by people of color to explain why their action is understandable and even excusable in their culture, even when it offends American values.

In *People v. Chen*, a Chinese man, after learning of his wife's adultery, killed his wife by hitting her on the head eight times with a hammer. The defense argued that, in traditional Chinese culture, a man is often driven to violence upon hearing of his wife's infidelity, but, unlike this defendant, is stopped by someone in the community before he can actually hurt her. The court took this defense into account and sentenced him to five years probation. In another case, two Korean youths were acquitted on the charge of rape after arguing that the victim, a Korean woman, tacitly consented to the rape because her visit to bars with the men would communicate consent in Korea. Although many protested that these rulings misinterpreted Chinese and Korean social norms and views of justice, the legal system accepted them, thereby devaluing women of color in the process.

* * *

Courts, in attempting to accommodate different cultures, seem to privilege the race of the defendant while simultaneously divesting the victim of her gender. This misunderstanding of the relationships between people of color serves to excuse actions taken against women of color. Thus, like the credibility problems and stereotypes of sexuality, it causes the legal system to discount workplace harassment of women of color.

* * *

We need to reconstruct our perception of "sexual harassment" to face the issue of workplace harassment of women of color. This transformation must take place because the elements of a sexual harassment case are different and more onerous than those in a racial harassment case. Treating these cases as "sexual harassment," then, not only misstates the dynamic but also further disadvantages these women. Such a solution could be reached either by modifying the rules governing "sexual harassment" or by creating a new cause of action prohibiting discrimination against women of color *as* women of color.

* * * Deeply held notions of race, gender, identity, sexuality and power must be examined and reevaluated. Furthermore, this discovery must take place both within and across cultural and class boundaries. * * *

On sexual harassment in the fields, see *Sexually Harassed Florida Farmworkers Get Justice*, SPLC Rep., Spring 2007, at 8 (describing large settlement in case brought by Southern Poverty Law Center). On a similar incident in California, see Rebecca Clarren, *The Green Motel*, 15 Ms. 40, Summer 2005; E.E.O.C., Jury Orders Harris Farms to Pay $994,000 in Sexual Harassment Suit by E.E.O.C., Jan. 21, 2005 (press release) (describing same incident in which a farm supervisor raped and brutalized a vulnerable woman farm worker whose boss refused to believe her and take action).

Margaret E. Montoya
Mascaras, Trenzas, y Greñas: *Un/masking the Self While Un/braiding Latina Stories and Legal Discourse*
17 Harv. Women's L.J. 185, 186–92, 197–98, 200–02, 204–09,
214–17 (1994); 15 Chicano-Latino L. Rev. 1 (1995)

One of the earliest memories from my school years is of my mother braiding my hair, making my *trenzas*. In 1955, I was seven years old. I was in second grade at the Immaculate Conception School in Las Vegas, New Mexico. Our family home with its outdoor toilet was on an unpaved street, one house from the railroad track. I remember falling asleep to the earthshaking rumble of the trains.

* * *

We dressed in front of the space heater in the bedroom we shared with my older brother. Catholic school girls wore uniforms. We wore blue jumpers and white blouses. I remember my mother braiding my hair and my sister's. I can still feel the part she would draw with the point of the comb. She would begin at the top of my head, pressing down as she drew the comb down to the nape of my neck. "Don't move," she'd say as she held the two hanks of hair, checking to make sure that the part was straight. Only then would she begin, braiding as tightly as our squirming would allow, so the braids could withstand our running, jumping, and hanging from the monkey bars at recess. "I don't want you to look *greñudas*," my mother would say. "I don't want you to look uncombed."

Hearing my mother use both English and Spanish gave emphasis to what she was saying. She used Spanish to talk about what was really important: her feelings, her doubts, her worries. She also talked to us in Spanish about gringos, Mexicanos, and the relations between them. Her stories were sometimes about being treated outrageously by gringos, her anger controlled and her bitterness implicit. She also told stories about Anglos she admired—those who were egalitarian, smart, well-spoken, and well-mannered.

Sometimes Spanish was spoken so as not to be understood by Them. Usually, though, Spanish and English were woven together. "*Greñuda*" was one of many words encoded with familial and cultural meaning. My mother used the word to admonish us, but she wasn't warning us about name-calling: "*Greñuda*" was not an epithet that our schoolmates were likely to use. Instead, I heard my mother saying something that went beyond well-groomed hair and being judged by our appearance—she could offer strategies for passing *that* scrutiny. She used the Spanish word, partly because there is no precise English equivalent, but also because she was interpreting the world for us.

The real message of "*greñudas*" was conveyed through the use of the Spanish word—it was unspoken and subtextual. She was teaching us that our world was divided, that They–Who–Don't-Speak–Spanish would see us as different, would judge us, would find us lacking. Her lessons about combing, washing, and doing homework frequently relayed a deeper message: Be prepared, because you will be judged by your skin color, your names, your accents. They will see you as ugly, lazy, dumb, and dirty.

As I put on my uniform and as my mother braided my hair, I changed; I became my public self. My *trenzas* announced that I was clean and well cared for at home. My *trenzas* and school uniform blurred the differences between my family's economic and cultural circumstances and those of the more economically comfortable Anglo students. I welcomed the braids and uniform as a disguise which concealed my minimal wardrobe and the relative poverty in which my family lived.

As we walked to school, away from home, away from the unpaved streets, away from the "Spanish" to the "Anglo" part of town, I felt both drawn to and repelled by my strange surroundings. I wondered what Anglos were like in their big houses. What did they eat? How did they furnish their homes? How did they pass the time? Did my English sound like theirs? Surely their closets were filled with dresses, sweaters and shoes, *apenas estrenados*. [*Eds.* Hardly worn.]

I remember being called on one afternoon in second grade to describe what we had eaten for lunch. Rather than admit to eating *caldito* (soup) *y tortillas*, partly because I had no English words for those foods, I regaled the class with a story about what I assumed an "American" family would eat at lunch: pork chops, mashed potatoes, green salad, sliced bread, and apple pie. The nun reported to my mother that I had lied. Afraid of being mocked, I unsuccessfully masked the truth, and consequently revealed more about myself than I concealed.

* * *

Our school was well integrated because it was located in a part of town with a predominantly Latino population. The culture of the school, however, was overwhelmingly Anglo and middle class. The use of Spanish was frowned upon and occasionally punished. Any trace of an accent when speaking English would be pointed out and sarcastically mocked. This mocking persisted even though, and maybe because, some of the nuns were also "Spanish."

* * *

By the age of seven, I was keenly aware that I lived in a society that had little room for those who were poor, brown, or female. I was all three. I moved between dualized worlds: private/public, Catholic/secular, poverty/privilege, Latina/Anglo. My *trenzas* and school uniform were a cultural disguise. They were also a precursor for the more elaborate mask I would later develop.

Presenting an acceptable face, speaking without a Spanish accent, hiding what we really felt—masking our inner selves—were defenses against racism passed on to us by our parents to help us get along in school and in society. We learned that it was safer to be inscrutable. We absorbed the necessity of constructing and maintaining a disguise for use in public. We struggled to be seen as Mexican but also wanted acceptance as Americans at a time when the mental image conjured up by that word included only Anglos.

* * *

My participation in the Chicano student movement in college fundamentally changed me. My adoption of the ethnic label as a primary identifier gave me an ideological mask that serves to this day. This transformation of my public persona was psychically liberating. This nascent liberation was, however, reactive and inchoate. Even as I struggled to redefine myself, I was locked in a reluctant embrace with those whose definitions of me I was trying to shrug off.

When I arrived as a student at Harvard Law School, I dressed so as to proclaim my politics. During my first day of orientation, I wore a Mexican peasant blouse and cutoff jeans on which I had embroidered the Chicano symbol of the *águila* (a stylized eagle) on one seat pocket and the woman symbol on the other. The *águila* reminded me of the red and black flags of the United Farm Worker rallies; it reminded me that I had links to a particular community. I was never to finish the fill-in stitches in the woman symbol. My symbols, like my struggles, were ambiguous.

The separation of the two symbols reminds me today that my participation in the Chicano movement had been limited by my gender, while in the women's movement it had been limited by my ethnicity. I drew power from both movements—I identified with both—but I knew that I was at the margin of each one.

As time went on, my clothes lost their political distinctiveness. My clothes signified my ambivalence: Perhaps if I dressed like a lawyer, eventually I would acquire more conventional ideas and ideals and fit in with my peers. Or perhaps if I dressed like a lawyer, I could harbor for some future use the disruptive and, at times, unwelcome thoughts that entered my head. My clothing would become protective coloration. Chameleon-like, I would dress to fade into the ideological, political, and cultural background rather than proclaim my differences.

Máscaras *and Latina Assimilation*

* * *

For stigmatized groups, such as persons of color, the poor, women, gays, and lesbians, assuming a mask is comparable to being "on stage." Being "on stage" is frequently experienced as being acutely aware of one's words, affect, tone of voice, movements, and gestures because they seem out of sync with what one is feeling and thinking. At unexpected moments, we fear that we will be discovered to be someone or something other than who or what we pretend to be. Lurking just behind our carefully constructed disguises and lodged within us is the child whom no one would have mistaken for anything other than what she was. Her masking was yet imperfect, still in rehearsal, and at times unnecessary.

For Outsiders, being masked in the legal profession has psychological as well as ideological consequences. Not only do we perceive ourselves as being "on stage," but the experience of class-jumping—being born poor but later living on the privileged side of the economic divide as an adult—can also induce schizoid feelings. As first-year law students don their three-piece suits, they make manifest the class ascendancy implicit in legal education. Most Latinas/os in the legal profession now occupy an economic niche considerably higher than that of our parents, our relatives, and frequently that of our students. Our speech, clothes, cars, homes, and lifestyle emphasize this difference.

The masks we choose can impede our legal representation and advocacy by driving a wedge between self, our *familias*, and our communities. As our economic security increases, we escape the choicelessness and lack of control over vital decisions that afflict communities of color. To remain connected to the community requires one to be Janus-faced, able to present one face to the larger society and another among ourselves—Janus-faced not in the conventional meaning of being deceitful, but in that of having two faces simultaneously. One face is the adult face that allows us to make our way through the labyrinth of the dominant culture. The other, the face of the child, is one of difference, free of artifice. This image with its dichotomized character fails to capture the multiplicity, fluidity, and interchangeability of faces, masks, and identities upon which we rely.

* * *

Masking Within the Legal Environment

The legal profession provides ample opportunity for role-playing, drama, storytelling, and posturing. Researchers have studied the use of masks and other theatrical devices among practicing lawyers and in the law school environment. Mask imagery has been used repeatedly to describe different aspects of legal education, lawyering, and law-making. One distinctive example is John T. Noonan, Jr.'s analysis exposing the purposeful ambiguity and the duplicity of legal discourse.

Some law students are undoubtedly attracted to the profession by the opportunity to disguise themselves and have no desire or need to look for their hidden selves. Some, however, may resent the role-playing they know to be necessary to succeed in their studies and in their relations with professors and peers. Understanding how and why we mask ourselves can help provide opportunities for students to explore their public and private personalities and to give expression to their feelings.

Un/Masking Silence

* * *

My memories from law school begin with the first case I ever read in Criminal Law. I was assigned to seat number one in a room that held 175 students.

The case was entitled *The People of the State of California v. Josefina Chavez*. It was the only case in which I remember encountering a Latina, and she was the defendant in a manslaughter prosecution. In *Chavez*, a young woman gave birth one night over the toilet in her mother's home without waking her child, brothers, sisters, or mother. The baby dropped into the toilet. Josefina cut the umbilical cord with a razor blade. She recovered the body of the baby, wrapped it in newspaper, and hid it under the bathtub. She ran away, but later turned herself in to her probation officer.

The legal issue was whether the baby had been born alive for purposes of the California manslaughter statute: whether the baby had been born alive and was therefore subject to being killed. The class wrestled with what it meant to be alive in legal terms. Had the lungs filled with air? Had the heart pumped blood?

For two days I sat mute, transfixed while the professor and the students debated the issue. Finally, on the third day, I timidly raised my hand. I heard myself blurt out: What about the other facts? What about her youth, her poverty, her fear over the pregnancy, her delivery in silence? I spoke for perhaps two minutes, and, when I finished, my voice was high-pitched and anxious.

An African American student in the back of the room punctuated my comments with "Hear! Hear!" Later other students thanked me for speaking up and in other ways showed their support.

I sat there after class had ended, in seat number one on day number three, wondering why it had been so hard to speak. Only later would I begin to wonder whether I would ever develop the mental acuity, the logical clarity to be able to sort out the legally relevant facts from what others deemed sociological factoids. Why *did* the facts relating to the girl-woman's reality go unvoiced? Why were her life, her anguish, her fears rendered irrelevant? Engaging in analyses about The Law, her behavior, and her guilt demanded that I disembody Josefina, that I silence her reality which screamed in my head.

* * *

A discussion raising questions about the gender-, class-, and ethnicity-based interpretations in the opinion, however, would have run counter to traditional legal discourse. Interjecting information about the material realities and cultural context of a poor Latina's life introduces taboo information into the classroom. Such information would transgress the prevalent ideological discourse. The puritanical and elitist protocol governing the classroom, especially during the 1970s, supported the notion that one's right to a seat in the law school classroom could be brought into question if one were to admit knowing about the details of pregnancies and self-abortions, or the hidden motivations of a *pachuca* (or a *chola*, a "homegirl" in today's Latino gang parlance). By overtly linking oneself to the life experiences of poor women, especially *pachucas*, one would emphasize one's differences from those who seemed to have been admitted to law school by right.

Information about the cultural context of Josefina Chavez's life would also transgress the linguistic discourse within the classroom. One would find it useful, and perhaps necessary, to use Spanish words and concepts to describe accurately and to contextualize Josefina Chavez's experience. In the 1970s, however, Spanish was still the language of Speedy Gonzales, José Jimenez, and other racist parodies.

To this day, I have dozens of questions about this episode in Josefina Chavez's life. I yearn to read an appellate opinion which reflects a sensitivity to her story, told in her own words. What did it take to conceal her pregnancy from her *familia*? With whom did she share her secret? How could she have given birth with "the doors open and no lights ... turned on"? How did she do so without waking the others who were asleep? How did she brace herself as she delivered the baby into the toilet? Did she shake as she cut the umbilical cord?

I long to hear Josefima Chavez's story told in what I will call Mothertalk and Latina–Daughtertalk. Mothertalk is about the blood and mess of menstruation, about the every month-ness of periods or about the fear in the pit of the stomach and the fear in the heart when there is no period. Mothertalk is about the blood and mess of pregnancy, about placentas, umbilical cords, and stitches. Mothertalk is about sex and its effects. Mothertalk helps make sense of our questions: How does one give birth in darkness and in silence? How does one clean oneself after giving birth? How does one heal oneself? Where does one hide from oneself after seeing one's dead baby in a toilet?

Latina–Daughtertalk is about feelings reflecting the deeply in-grained cultural values of Latino families: in this context, feelings of *vergüenza de sexualidad* ("sexual shame"). Sexual experience comes enshrouded in sexual shame; have sex and you risk being known as *sinvergüenza*, shameless. Another Latina–Daughtertalk value is *respeto a la mamá y respeto a la familia. Familias* are not nuclear or limited by blood ties; they are extended, often including foster siblings and *comadres y compadres, madrinas y padrinos* (godmothers, godfathers, and other religion-linked relatives).

Josefina Chavez's need to hide her pregnancy (with her head-to-toe mask) can be explained by a concern about the legal consequences as well as by the *vergüenza* within and of her *familia* that would accompany the discovery of the pregnancy, a pregnancy that was at once proof and reproof of her sexuality. Josephine's unwanted pregnancy would likely have been interpreted within her community and her *familia* and by her mother as a lack of *respeto*.

I sense that students still feel vulnerable when they reveal explicitly gendered or class-based knowledge, such as information about illicit sexuality and its effects, or personal knowledge about the lives of the poor and the subordinated. Even today there is little opportunity to use Spanish words or concepts within the legal academy. Students respond to their feelings of vulnerability by remaining silent about these taboo areas of knowledge.

The silence had profound consequences for me and presumably for others who identified with Josefina Chavez because she was Latina, or because she was female, or because she was poor. For me, the silence invalidated my experience. I reexperienced the longing I felt that day in Criminal Law many times. At the bottom of that longing was a desire to be recognized, a need to feel some reciprocity. As I engaged in His/Their reality, I needed to feel Him/Them engage in mine.

Embedded in Josefina Chavez's experience are various lessons about criminal law specifically and about the law and its effects more generally. The opinion's characteristic avoidance of context and obfuscation of important class-and gender-based assumptions is equally important to the ideological socialization and doctrinal development of law students. Maintaining a silence about Chavez's ethnic and socio-economic context lends credence to the prevailing perception that there is only one relevant reality.

* * *

Over time, I figured out that my interpretations of the facts in legal opinions were at odds with the prevailing discourse in the classroom, regardless of the subject matter. Much of the discussion assumed that we all shared common life experiences. I remember sitting in the last row and being called on in tax class, questioned about a case involving the liability of a father for a gift of detached and negotiable bond coupons to his son. It was clear that I was befuddled by the facts of the case. Looking at his notes on the table, the professor asked with annoyance whether I had ever seen a bond. My voice quivering, I answered that I had not. His head shot up in surprise. He focused on who I was; I waited, unmasked. He became visibly flustered as he carefully described the bond with its tear-off coupons to me. Finally, he tossed me an easy question, and I choked out the answer.

This was one instance of feeling publicly unmasked. In this case, it was class-based ignorance which caused my mask[s] to slip. Other students may also have lacked knowledge about bonds. Maybe other students, especially those from families with little money and certainly no trust funds, stocks, or bonds, also would have felt unmasked by the questioning. But I felt isolated and different because I could be exposed in so many ways: through class, ethnicity, race, gender, and the subtleties of language, dress, make-up, voice, and accent.

For multiple and overlapping reasons I felt excluded from the experiences of others, experiences that provided them with knowledge that better equipped them for the study of The Law, especially within the upper-class domain that is Harvard. Not knowing about bonds linked the complexities of class-jumping with the fearful certainty that, in the eyes of some, and most painfully in my own/my mother's eyes, I would be seen as *greñuda*: dirty, ugly, dumb, and uncombed.

It was not possible for me to guard against the unexpected visibility—or, paradoxically, the invisibility—caused by class, gender, or ethnic differences that lurked in the materials we studied. Such issues were, after all, pervasive, and I was very sensitive to them.

Sitting in the cavernous classrooms at Harvard under the stem gaze of patrician jurists was an emotionally wrenching experience. I remember the day one of the students was called on to explain *Erie v. Tompkins*. His identification of the salient facts, his articulation of the major and minor issues, and his synopsis of the Court's reasoning were so precise and concise that it left a hush in the room. He had already achieved and was able to model for the rest of us the objectivity, clarity, and mental acuity that we/I aspired to.

The respect shown for this type of analysis was qualitatively different from that shown for contextual or cultural analysis. Such occurrences in the classroom were memorable because they were defining: Rational objectivity trumped emotional subjectivity. What They had to say trumped what I wanted to say but rarely did.

I have no memory of ever speaking out again to explain facts from my perspective as I had done that one day in Criminal Law. There was to be only one Latina in any of my cases, only one Josefina. While I was at Harvard, my voice was not heard again in the classroom examining, exploring, or explaining the life situations of either defendants or victims. Silence accommodated the ideological uniformity, but also revealed the inauthenticity implicit in discursive assimilation.

As time went on, I felt diminished and irrelevant. It wasn't any one discussion, any one class, or any one professor. The pervasiveness of the ideology marginalized me, and others; its efficacy depended upon its subtextual nature, and this masked quality made it difficult to pinpoint.

I had arrived at Harvard feeling different. I understood difference to be ineluctably linked with, and limited to, race, class, and gender. The kernel of that feeling I first associated with Josefina Chavez, that scrim of silence, remains within me. It is still my experience that issues of race, ethnicity, gender, or class are invisible to most of my white and/or male colleagues. Issues of sexual orientation, able-bodiedness, and sometimes class privilege can be invisible to me. I still make conscious choices about when to connect such issues to the topic at hand and when to remain silent. I'm still unclear about strategies and tactics, about being frontal or oblique.

Issues of race or gender are never trivial or banal from my perspective. Knowing how or when to assert them effectively as others react with hostility, boredom, or weariness can be a "crazy-making" endeavor. Sometimes it seems that every interaction requires that I overlook the terms of the discourse or that I affirmatively redefine them. My truths require that I say unconventional things in unconventional ways.

Speaking out assumes prerogative. Speaking out is an exercise of privilege. Speaking out takes practice.

Silence ensures invisibility. Silence provides protection. Silence masks.

Trenzas: *Braiding Latina Narrative*

* * *

The law and its practice are grounded in the telling of stories. Pleadings and judicial orders can be characterized as stylized stories. Legal persuasion in the form of opening statements and closing arguments is routinely taught as an exercise in storytelling. Client interviews are storytelling and story-listening events. Traditionally, legal culture within law firms, law schools, and courthouses has been transmitted through the "war stories" told by seasoned attorneys. Narrative laces through all aspects of legal education, legal practice, and legal culture. In these various ways the use of narrative is not new to the legal academy.

Only recently, however, has storytelling begun to play a significant role in academic legal writing. In the hands of outsiders, storytelling seeks to subvert the dominant ideology. Stories told by those on the bottom, told from the "subversive-subaltern" perspective, challenge and expose the hierarchical and patriarchal order that exists within the legal academy and pervades the larger society. Narrative that focuses on the experiences of Outsiders thus empowers both the storyteller and the story-listener by virtue of its opposition to the traditional forms of discourse.

Understanding stories told from different cultural perspectives requires that we suspend our notions of temporal and spatial continuity, plot, climax, and the interplay of narrator and protagonists. The telling of and listening to stories in a multicultural environment requires a fundamental re-examination of the text, the subtext, and the context of stories. The emphasis of critical scholarship (critical race theory, feminist jurisprudence, critical legal studies) on narrative affirms those of us who are Outsiders working within the objectivist orientation of the legal academy and validates our experimentation with innovative formats and themes in our teaching and in our scholarship.

Greñas: *Un/braiding Latina Narrative*

* * *

The Euro–American conquest of the Southwest and Puerto Rico resulted in informal and formal prohibitions against the use of Spanish for public purposes. So by situating myself in legal scholarship as *mestiza*, I seek to occupy common ground with Latinas/os in this hemisphere and others, wherever located, who are challenging "Western bourgeois ideology and hegemonic racialism with the metaphor of transculturation."

As Latinas/os we, like many colonized peoples around the globe, are the biological descendants of both indigenous and European ancestors, as well as the intellectual progeny of Western and indigenous thinkers and writers. As evidenced by my names, I am the result of Mexican–Indian–Irish–French relations. I am also the product of English-speaking schools and a Spanish-speaking community. Making manifest our mixed intellectual and linguistic heritage can counteract the subordinating forces implicit in the monolinguality and homogeneity of the dominant culture. While I reject the idea that personal narratives can or should be generalized into grand or universalistic theories, our stories can help us search for unifying identifiers and mutual objectives. For example, the deracination of language purges words of their embedded racism, sexism, and other biases.

Using Spanish /or other outlaw languages, dialects, or (patois) in legal scholarship could be seen as an attempt to erect linguistic barriers or create exclusionary discursive spaces, even among Outsiders with whom Latinas share mutual ideological, political, and pedagogical objectives. Personal accounts of humiliation, bias, or deprivation told from within the academy may sound to some like whining or may be perceived as excessive involvement with the self rather than with the real needs of the Outsider communities. As I have argued, this view would be seriously wrong. Instead, linguistic diversity should be recognized as enhancing the dialogue within the academy by bringing in new voices and fresh perspectives. Incorporating Spanish words, sayings, literature, and wisdom can have positive ramifications for those in the academy and in the profession, and for those to whom we render legal services.

Notes and Questions

1.   Which one wears the mask—a Latina trying to blend in during a law school class and pretend she has the same access to cultural information, for example about bonds and commercial paper, as the other students—or a Latina who has a little of such information but insists on addressing every question "from a Latina perspective"?

2.   Is workplace harassment of women of color different from that which targets white women?

3.   If one is a feminist of color, will the white-dominated feminist movement represent one's interests perfectly, or imperfectly? If the latter, what is the solution?

4.   Do all women have a single "essential" core group of issues and concerns that they share in common, so that the special issues of women of color are side-issues and distractions that should be placed on hold until society reckons with the large issues—patriarchy, sexual choice, reproductive freedom, etc.—that all women confront as women?

5.   Elvia R. Arriola, *Staying Empowered by Recognizing our Common Grounds*, 71 UMKC L. Rev. 447 (2002) discusses a Texas case [Esperanza Peace and Justice Center v. City of San Antonio, 316 F.Supp.2d 433 (W.D. Tex. 2001)] in which a newly conservative city council had ended the funding of a gay-lesbian art center directed by Latina lesbians. "The [successful] story of the Esperanza Center ... provides a ... lesson about the importance of coalitional critical thinking and ... practices," id. at 453. It also shows how right-wing thinking can trample on the rights of minorities, and how gay men can at times join with the right in opposing lesbian issues, id. at 454–55.

SECTION 5.   MARRIAGE, CHILDBEARING, AND FAMILY LIFE

Women of color, including Latinas, confront many problems that majority-race women do not have to deal with, at least so often. Some of these have to do with reproduction and family life. See *Latina Issues: Fragments of Historia(ella) (herstory)* (Antoinette Sedillo López ed., 1999).

Madrigal v. Quilligan
No. CV75–2057, slip op. (C.D.Cal., June 30, 1978), *aff'd* 639 F.2d
789 (9th Cir. 1981), reprinted in Dorothy Brown, *Critical
Race Theory: Cases and Materials* 102–11 (2003).

The rather subtle but underlying thrust of plaintiffs' complaint appears to be that they were all victims of a concerted plan by hospital attendants and doctors to push them, as members of a low socioeconomic group who tend toward large families, to consent to sterilization in order to accomplish some sinister, invidious social purpose. A careful search of the record fails to produce any evidence whatever to support this contention. It did appear that the hospital had received funds for the establishment of a family planning program, and that discussion and encouragement of alternative methods of birth control, including sterilization, were carried on in the outpatient prenatal care clinic. In the obstetrics ward, however, whenever a sterilization procedure was suggested or advised, it was done on the initiative of the individual employee. There was no hospital rule or instruction relative to the encouragement of patients to be sterilized and there was no evidence of concerted or conspiratorial action.

Consequently, this case in its present posture consists of ten separate and distinct claims against the individual doctors who actually performed the sterilization, and the liability of each must be determined by his own conduct.

ACTIONABLE CONDUCT UNDER § 1983

* * *

* * * In [a former] case the court was presented with precisely the type of "informed consent" to sterilization problem with which we are faced in the instant case. The court ruled there that in order for the defendant physician to be liable the absence of free and informed consent must be intelligibly communicated to the doctor. If he

negligently interpreted plaintiffs communications to indicate she consented to the operation, he is not liable under the standards enunciated in *Wood*, even if plaintiff did not intend to consent.

Liability, in this context, is predicated upon some conduct which is either malicious or is in wanton disregard of constitutional rights. There would be liability

... if ... [the doctor] determined that sterilization of the plaintiff was for her own good or the good of society and as a consequence of that belief ignored indications from the plaintiff that she did not consent to the operation, or if ... he attempted to take advantage of her mental and communication limitations to unduly influence her decision.... (Citations omitted)

With these legal principles in mind we turn to a consideration of the facts.

COMMUNICATION BREAKDOWN

This case is essentially the result of a breakdown in communication between the patients and the doctors. All plaintiffs are Spanish-speaking women whose ability to understand and speak English is limited. This fact is generally understood by the staff and most members have acquired enough familiarity with the language to get by. There is also an interpreter available whose services are used when thought to be necessary. But even with these precautions misunderstandings are bound to occur.

Furthermore, the cultural background of these particular women has contributed to the problem in a subtle but very significant way. According to the plaintiffs' anthropological expert, they are members of a traditional Mexican rural subculture, a relatively narrow spectrum of Mexican people living in this country whose lifestyle and cultural background derives from the lifestyle and culture of small rural communities in Mexico. He further testified that a cultural trait which is very important with this group is an extreme dependence upon family. Most come from large families and wish to have large families for their own comfort and support. Furthermore, the status of a woman and her husband within that group depends largely upon the woman's ability to produce children. If for any reason she cannot, she is considered an incomplete woman and is apt to suffer a disruption of her relationship with her family and husband. When faced with a decision of whether or not to be sterilized, the decision process is a much more traumatic event than it would be with a typical patient and, consequently, she would require greater explanation, more patient advice, and greater care in interpreting her consent than persons not members of such a subculture would require.

But this need for such delicate treatment is not readily apparent. The anthropological expert testified that he would not have known that these women possessed these traits had he not conducted tests and a study which required some 450 hours of time. * * * It is not surprising therefore that the staff of a busy metropolitan hospital which has neither the time nor the staff to make such esoteric studies would be unaware of these atypical cultural traits.

* * *

DOCTOR'S CUSTOM AND PRACTICE

Since these operations occurred between 1971 and 1974 and were performed by the doctors operating in a busy obstetrics ward, it is not surprising that none of the doctors [has] any independent recollection of the events leading up to the operations. They all testified, however, that it was their custom and practice not to suggest a sterilization procedure unless a patient asked for it or medical complications [were present that] would require the doctor, in the exercise of prudent medical procedures, to make such suggestion. They further testified that it was their practice when a patient requested sterilization to explain its irreversible result and they stated that they would not perform the operation unless they were certain in their own mind that the patient understood the nature of the operation and was requesting the procedure. The weight to be given to such testimony and the inferences to be drawn therefrom will be determined in the light of all the testimony relating to each doctor's conduct.

* * *

DOLORES MADRIGAL

The plaintiff Madrigal was born in a small town in Mexico and attended school there through the sixth grade. She does not read or speak English fluently. She had two children and after the birth of her second child she underwent a tubal ligation performed by Dr. Rutland. The medical file contains an early note that Mrs. Madrigal wished a tubal ligation. If this were so, she apparently changed her mind as she refused the suggestion several times prior to the operation. Presumably such a procedure was suggested because Mrs. Madrigal had suffered from a placenta previa during heir first pregnancy and from toxemia during her second. During labor, and having indicated that she did not wish a tubal ligation, her husband was called to the hospital. She overheard an interpreter telling him that because of the complications she might die in the event of a future pregnancy. She was then told that her husband had agreed to the operation and she was again presented with a consent form which she signed, inserting in her own handwriting therein a statement that she understood she was not going to have any more children. She complains that some pressure was put upon her to sign the consent, although Nurse Lang, who witnessed the signature, testified that she would not have witnessed a consent for sterilization if the patient had not verified her understanding of the nature of the operation and its consequences. In any event, there is no evidence that Dr. Rutland, who performed the operation, had any part in any overzealous solicitation for the sterilization, even if it had occurred. Dr. Rutland, on the other hand, testified that he speaks some Spanish and in accordance with his custom and practice would have explained the nature of the procedure, its permanency and its risks through an interpreter. In any event, he had before him the medical file which indicated an earlier desire on the part of the plaintiff for a tubal ligation and her written consent with the insertion of her own handwriting that she understood that the operation would prevent her from having children ever again.

I find that under the circumstances Dr. Rutland performed the operation in the bona fide belief that Mrs. Madrigal had given her informed and voluntary consent, and that his belief was reasonable.

MARIA HURTADO

Mrs. Hurtado is a forty-two year old Mexican American born in Mexico and has a sixth grade education. She has five living children and gave birth to three more who were born dead. She has had three cesarean sections and was given a tubal ligation by Dr. Neuman after the birth of her last child. Mrs. Hurtado contends that she was never informed about the nature and effect of the tubal ligation and nothing was ever said about it until she was in labor. She further states that the consent forms were brought to her during labor and she was not aware that she was signing a consent for tubal ligation. Although Mrs. Hurtado denies it, the hospital records indicate that she had made a request to the intern in the clinic some time before that she desired a tubal ligation. A similar note appeared in the medical record made by another doctor during another one of Mrs. Hurtado's clinical visits. At the time of her admission, she was examined by still another doctor to whom she again indicated her desire to have no more children. Consequently, consent forms were prepared and were signed by her before she had had any medication and before she was in active labor. Dr. Neuman, who performed the operation, testified that it was his custom and practice to always ask a patient who had indicated that she wanted a tubal ligation to again express her consent. In the light of the contrary evidence, Mrs. Hurtado's statement that she did not remember signing the consent for tubal ligation and had not been informed of its nature and results is simply not credible.

I find therefore that the evidence is insufficient to rebut the inferences drawn from the record, and that in any event Dr. Neuman was acting in a bona fide belief that Mrs. Hurtado had consented to the operation and that such belief was reasonable.

JOVITA RIVERA

This plaintiff was born in Mexicali, Mexico, in 1946 and came to the United States to live in 1968. She neither speaks nor understands the English language well. There have been five children of the marriage, one of whom was born dead. Mrs. Rivera obtained prenatal care at the Medical Center. At the time of her admission to the hospital she told the admitting doctor that she wanted her tubes tied. She had previously agreed with her husband that she would have her tubes tied after the fourth child. She understood, however, from her sister-in-law that this operation was reversible and that, at a later date if she decided she wanted more children, she could have tubes untied. She did not tell anyone at the hospital of this belief. While in labor, an emergency situation arose in which it became apparent that Mrs. Rivera could not deliver normally and a cesarean section was necessary within the next ten minutes in order to save the baby's life. Because of the emergency, a resident physician was called in to perform the operation. He again asked the plaintiff if she intended to have her tubes tied and she answered in the affirmative. Because of the emergency nature of the matter, no written consent was obtained from the plaintiff, but as a part of the cesarean section a tubal ligation was performed.

The doctor testified that it was not his practice to ask a patient about a sterilization procedure unless it was suggested by the patient herself or unless some medical reason for doing so arose. After it was determined that a cesarean section would have to be performed on Mrs. Rivera, and seeing the note in the hospital record indicating that she had previously asked to have her tubes tied, he again mentioned it to her and got an affirmative answer. The doctor further testified that he would never have performed a tubal ligation had he not fully believed that the plaintiff specifically asked for it.

From these facts, I conclude that the doctor was acting in good faith believing that he had an unequivocal consent and that such belief was reasonable under the circumstances.

* * *

HELENA OROZCO

Helena Orozco was born in Forth Worth, Texas, and speaks both English and Spanish. She has had four children by a previous marriage and two by her present marriage. She has, in addition, one adopted daughter. She received her prenatal care at the Medical Center and was, on many occasions, advised by personnel that she should have her tubes tied so that she would not have any more children because she had already had "too many cesarean sections." Her condition was further complicated by a ruptured hernia which someone attending her indicated would be a serious problem in the event of another pregnancy. She at first indicated that she did not want a tubal ligation but did consent to the cesarean. At a later time, however, she did sign her written consent because, she says, of the insistence of some member of the staff. The defendant Robert Yee performed the cesarean section, bilateral tubal ligation, and umbilical hernia repair, in reliance upon the written consent found in the file. There is no evidence which indicates that Dr. Yee was present or participated in obtaining the written consent, nor that he was aware that the plaintiff was in any way unwilling to have the operation. In fact, he testified that he would not have performed the sterilization procedures if he had any reason whatever to doubt the validity of the written consent.

I conclude therefore as to this defendant, Dr. Yee, that he was acting in the bona fide belief that he had the plaintiff's consent and that this belief was reasonable.

* * *

CONSUELO HERMOSILLO

This plaintiff was born in 1949 in Vera Cruz, Mexico, where she was educated through the eighth grade. She had three children, all born by cesarean section. It was at the birth of her third child that a tubal ligation was performed. She had received prenatal care at a County clinic where she was informed that it was advisable, after her third cesarean, to have a sterilization operation because of the risk of serious complications in further pregnancies. She testified that she did not want to give up having more children and that because of this advice given her at the clinic often came home crying. She then discussed the matter with her sister-in-law who told her that she had had her tubes tied and that she thought she could later have them untied. Such a belief was never mentioned to anyone at the hospital. In the early states of labor it appeared that Mrs. Hermosillo might be able to deliver normally but as the delivery progressed it became apparent that a cesarean section would be necessary, at which time she apparently signed a consent form for tubal ligation. Neither she nor the doctors have any specific recollection of what occurred at the time the consent was actually signed. The form, however, did contain a statement in her own handwriting in Spanish to the effect that she understood the nature of the operation. Both Dr. Muth, who performed the tubal ligation, and the senior resident physician, Allen Luckman, M.D., who assisted in the surgery, both testified that they would not have performed the sterilization process had they not believed that Mrs. Hermosillo had given a free and voluntary consent as indicated by the written form in the hospital record. The evidence amply supports the inference that Mrs. Hermosillo was thoroughly acquainted with the nature of the operation, except possibly for the undisclosed belief that despite what doctors told her she could have her tubes untied.

I conclude therefore that Mrs. Hermosillo was fully aware of the nature and effect of the tubal ligation although she had hoped for a normal delivery in which event such an operation would not have been done. But when it became apparent that a cesarean section was necessary she changed her mind and voluntarily consented and, in doing so, signed a consent form upon which the surgeon relied. I find that Dr. Muth performed the tubal ligation in the bona fide belief that Mrs. Hermosillo had consented and that his belief was reasonable under the circumstances.

* * *

A WOMAN'S DECISION WHILE IN LABOR

The plaintiffs have placed great reliance upon a New York psychiatrist who stated unequivocally that it would be impossible for a woman in labor, after suffering her first pain, to give an intelligent and knowing consent to a sterilization operation. Such a statement completely defies common sense. I prefer as more credible the testimony of the other doctors to the effect that whether a consent represented an informed and voluntary decision depended upon many facts, that a judgment could best be made by someone present at the moment the decision is made. One doctor testified that the fact that a woman was in labor might or might not affect her decision, depending upon the circumstances. There was further evidence that the attending physician was probably in the best position to make a judgment since he would be acutely aware of the necessity of having the patient's consent.

CONCLUSION

This case has not been an easy one to try for it has involved social, emotional and cultural considerations of great complexity. There is no doubt but that these women have suffered severe emotional and physical stress because of these operations. One can sympathize with them for their inability to communicate clearly, but one can hardly blame the doctors for relying on these indicia of consent which appeared to be unequivocal on their face and which are in constant use in the Medical Center.

Let judgment be entered for the defendants.

Perez v. Lippold
32 Cal.2d 711, 198 P.2d 17 (1948)

TRAYNOR, JUSTICE.

In this proceeding in mandamus, petitioners seek to compel the county clerk of Los Angeles County to issue them a certificate of registry (Civ. Code, sec. 69a) and a license to marry. (Civ. Code, sec. 69.) In the application for a license, petitioner Andrea Perez states that she is a white person and petitioner Sylvester Davis that he is a Negro. Respondent refuses to issue the certificate and license, invoking Civil Code section 69, which provides: " . . . no license may be issued authorizing the marriage of a white person with a Negro, mulatto, Mongolian or member of the Malay race."

Civil Code section 69 implements Civil Code section 60, which provides: "All marriages of white persons with negroes, Mongolians, members of the Malay race, or mulattoes are illegal and void." * * *
    * * *

Since the right to marry is the right to join in marriage with the person of one's choice, a statute that prohibits an individual from marrying a member of a race other than his own restricts the scope of his choice and thereby restricts his right to marry. It must therefore be determined whether the state can restrict that right on the basis of race alone without violating the equal protection of the laws clause of the United States Constitution. "Distinctions between citizens solely because of their ancestry are by their very nature odious to a free people whose institutions are founded upon the doctrine of equality." For that reason, legislative classification or discrimination based on race alone has often been held to be a denial of equal protection. . . . [The court cites the Japanese internment cases for the proposition that state governments cannot make distinctions based on ancestry in the absence of an emergency.]

A state law prohibiting members of one race from marrying members of another race is not designed to meet a clear and present peril arising out of an emergency. In the absence of an emergency the state clearly cannot base a law impairing fundamental rights of individuals on general assumptions as to traits of racial groups. It has been said that a statute such as section 60 does not discriminate against any racial group, since it applies alike to all persons whether Caucasian, Negro, or members of any other race. The decisive question, however, is not whether different races, each considered as a group, are equally treated. The right to marry is the right of individuals, not of racial groups. * * *

    * * * Race restrictions must be viewed with great suspicion, for the Fourteenth Amendment "was adopted to prevent state legislation designed to perpetuate discrimination on the basis of race or color." Any state legislation discriminating against persons on the basis of race or

color has to overcome the strong presumption inherent in this constitutional policy. * * * We shall therefore examine the history of the legislation in question and the arguments in its support to determine whether there are any exceptional circumstances sufficient to justify it.

California's first miscegenation statute was enacted at the same time as two other statutes concerning race. It has been held that these three statutes were *in pari materia* and therefore to be read together. The two companion statutes provided: "No black or mulatto person, or Indian, shall be permitted to give evidence in favor of, or against any white person. Every person who shall have one-eighth part or more of Negro blood shall be deemed a mulatto, and every person who shall have one-half of Indian blood shall be deemed an Indian." "No black, or mulatto person, or Indian, shall be permitted to give evidence in any action to which a white person is a party, in any Court of this State. Every person who shall have one eighth part or more of negro blood, shall be deemed a mulatto; and every person who shall have one half Indian blood, shall be deemed an Indian."

In 1854 this court held that Chinese (and all others not white) were precluded from being witnesses against white persons on the basis of the statute quoted above. People v. Hall, 4 Cal. 399, 404. The considerations motivating the decision are candidly set forth. "The anomalous spectacle of a distinct people (Chinese), living in our community, recognizing no laws of this State except through necessity, bringing with them their prejudices and national feuds, in which they indulge in open violation of law; whose mendacity is proverbial; a race of people whom nature has marked as inferior, and who are incapable of progress or intellectual development beyond a certain point, as their history has shown; differing in language, opinions, color, and physical conformation; between whom and ourselves nature has placed an impassable difference, is now presented, and for them is claimed, not only the right to swear away the life of a citizen, but the further privilege of participating with us in administering the affairs of our Government." For these reasons, therefore, "all races other than Caucasian" were held to be included in a statute referring only to a "black or mulatto person, or Indian."

California courts are not alone in such utterances. Many courts in this country have assumed that human beings can be judged by race and that other races are inferior to the Caucasian. Respondent's position is based upon those premises. He justifies the prohibition of miscegenation on grounds similar to those set forth in the frequently cited case of Scott v. State, 1869, 39 Ga. 321, 324: "The amalgamation of the races is not only unnatural, but is always productive of deplorable results. Our daily observation shows us, that the offspring of these unnatural connections are generally sickly and effeminate, and that they are inferior in physical development and strength, to the full blood of either race." * * * "It is stated as a well authenticated fact that if the issue of a black man and a white woman, and a white man and a black woman intermarry, they cannot possibly have any progeny, and such a fact sufficiently justifies these laws which forbid the intermarriage of blacks and whites, laying out of view other sufficient grounds for such enactments." Modern experts are agreed that the progeny of marriages between persons of different races are not inferior to both parents. Nevertheless, even if we were to assume that interracial marriage results in inferior progeny, we are unable to find any clear policy in the statute against marriages on that ground.

Civil Code section 60, like most miscegenation statutes, prohibits marriages only between "white persons" and members of certain other so-called races. Although section 60 is more inclusive than most miscegenation statutes, it does not include "Indians" or "Hindus"; nor does it set up "Mexicans" as a separate category, although some authorities consider Mexico to be populated at least in part by persons who are a mixture of "white" and "Indian." Thus, "white persons" may marry persons who would be considered other than white by respondent's authorities, and all other "races" may intermarry freely.

The Legislature therefore permits the mixing of all races with the single exception that white persons may not marry Negroes, Mongolians, Mulattoes, or Malays. It might be concluded therefrom that section 60 is based upon the theory that the progeny of a white person and a Mongolian or Negro or Malay are inferior or undesirable, while the progeny of members of other different races are not. Nevertheless, the section does not prevent the mixing of "white" and "colored" blood. It permits marriages not only between Caucasians and others of darker pigmentation, such as Indians, Hindus, and Mexicans, but between persons of mixed ancestry including white. If a person of partly caucasian ancestry is yet classified as a Mongolian under section 60 because his ancestry is predominantly mongolian, a considerable mixture of Caucasian and Mongolian blood is permissible. A person having five-eighths Mongolian blood and three-eighths white blood could properly marry another person of preponderantly Mongolian blood. Similarly, a Mulatto can marry a Negro. Under the theory that a Mulatto is a person having one-eighth or more of Negro ancestry, a person having seven-eighths white ancestry could marry a Negro. In fact two mulattoes, each of four-eighths white and four-eighths Negro blood, could marry under section 60, and their progeny, like them, would belong as much to one race as to the other. In effect, therefore, section 60 permits a substantial amount of intermarriage between persons of some Caucasian ancestry and members of other races. Furthermore, there is no ban on illicit sexual relations between Caucasians and members of the proscribed races. Indeed, it is covertly encouraged by the race restrictions on marriage.

Nevertheless, respondent has sought to justify the statute by contending that the prohibition of intermarriage between Caucasians and members of the specified races prevents the Caucasian race from being contaminated by races whose members are by nature physically and mentally inferior to Caucasians.

Respondent submits statistics relating to the physical inferiority of certain races. Most, if not all, of the ailments to which he refers are attributable largely to environmental factors. Moreover, one must take note of the statistics showing that there is a higher percentage of certain diseases among Caucasians than among non-Caucasians. * * * The categorical statement that non-Caucasians are inherently physically inferior is without scientific proof. * * * In any event, generalizations based on race are untrustworthy in view of the great variations among members of the same race. The rationalization, therefore, that marriage between Caucasians and non-Caucasians is socially undesirable because of the physical disabilities of the latter, fails to take account of the physical disabilities of Caucasians and fails also to take account of variations among non-Caucasians. The Legislature is free to prohibit marriages that are socially dangerous because of the physical disabilities of the parties concerned. The miscegenation statute, however, condemns certain races as unfit to marry with Caucasians on the premise of a hypothetical racial disability, regardless of the physical qualifications of the individuals concerned. If this premise were carried to its logical conclusion, non-Caucasians who are now precluded from marrying Caucasians on physical grounds would also be precluded from marrying among themselves on the same grounds. The concern to prevent marriages in the first category and the indifference about marriages in the second reveal the spuriousness of the contention that intermarriage between Caucasians and non-Caucasians is socially dangerous on physical grounds.

* * *

Respondent also contends that Negroes, and impliedly the other races specified in section 60, are inferior mentally to Caucasians. It is true that, in the United States, catalogues of distinguished people list more Caucasians than members of other races. It cannot be disregarded, however, that Caucasians are in the great majority and have generally had a more advantageous environment, and that the capacity of the members of any race to contribute to a nation's culture depends in large measure on how freely they may participate in that culture. There is no scientific proof that one race is superior to another in native ability. * * * In any event the Legislature has not made an intelligence test a prerequisite to marriage. * * *

Respondent contends, however, that persons wishing to marry in contravention of race barriers come from the "dregs of society" and that their progeny will therefore be a burden on the community. There is no law forbidding marriage among the "dregs of society," assuming that this expression is capable of definition. If there were such a law, it could not be applied without a proper determination of the persons that fall within that category, a determination that could hardly be made on the basis of race alone.

Respondent contends that even if the races specified in the statute are not by nature inferior to the Caucasian race, the statute can be justified as a means of diminishing race tension and preventing the birth of children who might become social problems. * * *

The effect of race prejudice upon any community is unquestionably detrimental both to the minority that is singled out for discrimination and to the dominant group that would perpetuate the prejudice. It is no answer to say that race tension can be eradicated through the perpetuation by law of the prejudices that give rise to the tension. * * *

Respondent relies on Pace v. Alabama, 106 U.S. 583, in which the United States Supreme Court held constitutional an Alabama statute imposing more severe punishment for adultery or fornication between a white person and a Negro than for such acts between individuals belonging to the same race. The Alabama statute also referred to intermarriage but the court considered the case as one dealing solely with adultery and nonmarital intercourse. We are not required by the facts of this case to discuss the reasoning of Pace v. Alabama except to state that adultery and non-marital intercourse are not, like marriage, a basic right, but are offenses subject to various degrees of punishment. * * *

It is contended that interracial marriage has adverse effects not only upon the parties thereto but upon their progeny. Respondent relies on Buck v. Bell, 274 U.S. 200, 47 S. Ct. 584, 71 L. Ed. 1000, for the proposition that the state "may properly protect itself as well as the children by taking steps which will prevent the birth of offspring who will constitute a serious social problem, even though such legislation must necessarily interfere with a natural right." That case, however, involved a statute authorizing sterilization of imbeciles following scientific verification and the observance of procedural guarantees. * * *

Respondent maintains that Negroes are socially inferior and have so been judicially recognized, and that the progeny of a marriage between a Negro and a Caucasian suffer not only the stigma of such inferiority but the fear of rejection by members of both races. If they do, the fault lies not with their parents, but with the prejudices in the community and the laws that perpetuate those prejudices by giving legal force to the belief that certain races are inferior. * * *

There are now so many persons in the United States of mixed ancestry, that the tensions upon them are already diminishing and are bound to diminish even more in time. Already many of the progeny of mixed marriages have made important contributions to the community. In any event the contention that the miscegenation laws prohibit interracial marriage because of its adverse effects on the progeny is belied by the extreme racial intermixture that it tolerates.

* * *

Even if a state could restrict the right to marry upon the basis of race alone, sections 60 and 69 of the Civil Code are nevertheless invalid because they are too vague and uncertain to constitute a valid regulation. * * *

Section 60 of the Civil Code declares void all marriages of white persons with Negroes, Mongolians, members of the Malay race or Mulattoes. In this section, the Legislature has adopted one of the many systems classifying persons on the basis of race. Racial classifications that have been made in the past vary as to the number of divisions and the features regarded as distinguishing the members of each division. The number of races distinguished by systems of classification "varies from three or four to thirty four." The Legislature's classification in section 60 is based on the system suggested by Blumenbach early in the nineteenth century. Blumenbach classified man into five races: Caucasian (white), Mongolian (yellow), Ethiopian (black), American Indian (red), and Malayan (brown). Even if that hard and fast classification be applied to persons all of whose ancestors belonged to one of these racial divisions, the Legislature has made no provision for applying the statute to persons of mixed ancestry. * * *

The only reference made in the statute to persons of mixed ancestry is the prohibition of marriages between a "white person" and a "mulatto." Even the term "mulatto" is not defined. The lack of a definition of that term leads to a special problem of how the statute is to be applied to a person, some but not all of whose ancestors are Negroes. * * * Even more uncertainty surrounds the meaning of the terms "white persons," "Mongolians," and "members of the Malay race."

If the statute is to be applied generally to persons of mixed ancestry the question arises whether it is to be applied on the basis of the physical appearance of the individual or on the basis of a genealogical research as to his ancestry. If the physical appearance of the individual is to be the test, the statute would have to be applied on the basis of subjective impressions of various persons. Persons having the same parents and consequently the same hereditary background could be classified differently. On the other hand, if the application of the statute to persons of mixed ancestry is to be based on genealogical research, the question immediately arises what proportions of Caucasian, Mongolian, or Malayan ancestors govern the applicability of the statute. Is it any trace of Mongolian or Malayan ancestry, or is it some unspecified proportion of such ancestry that makes a person a Mongolian or Malayan within the meaning of section 60? * * *

Section 69 of the Civil Code and section 60 on which it is based are therefore too vague and uncertain to be upheld as a valid regulation of the right to marry. * * *

In summary, we hold that sections 60 and 69 are not only too vague and uncertain to be enforceable regulations of a fundamental right, but that they violate the equal protection of the laws clause of the United States Constitution by impairing the right of individuals to marry on the basis of race alone and by arbitrarily and unreasonably discriminating against certain racial groups.

Let the peremptory writ issue as prayed.

Yvonne M. Cherena Pacheco
*Latino Surnames: Formal and Informal Forces in
the United States Affecting the Retention and
Use of the Maternal Surname*
18 T. Marshall L. Rev. 1, 2–4, 9–12,
14–17, 24–28, 33, 35, 37 (1992)

"Where is our history?
What are the names washed down the sewer
In the septic flood?
I pray to the rain
Give me back my rituals
Give back truth
Return the remnants of my identity
Bathe me in self-discovered knowledge
Identify my ancestors who have existed suppressed
Invoke their spirits with power . . ."

—Sandra Maria Esteves

Consider names, the difficulties which historically have confronted and continue to confront millions of Latino citizens and residents of the United States in their attempts to gain recognition of their complete names, and the impact of the failure of those attempts upon Latinas. Human beings generally receive names within their first days of life. Traditions regarding naming vary considerably from one culture to another, reflecting ancestral, religious, or linguistic customs. In any given state, the traditional naming patterns of the dominant culture or cultures will be reflected in the laws and the official behavior of that state.

The names originally given to a child usually reflect her parentage or lineage, clan membership, place of origin, as well as individual identity. Whatever the tradition within which the child is named, her name serves as the cornerstone of her identity as she grows toward maturity. Naming issues arise when the desire of the individual to be known by a particular name comes into conflict with social practice. Naming issues have a long history in North America, dating to at least colonial times. Enslaved Africans routinely were renamed by those who bought them, while Native American names quickly came to be shortened, mispronounced or translated into English or French. With the dominance of Anglo–Saxon culture well established from the beginning of the republic, European immigrants from other traditions had similar experiences of renaming, particularly if they hailed from Southern or Eastern Europe. What all of the victims of these practices had in common was their relative powerlessness, and the desire of those representing the dominant culture to force them to conform.

Very little has changed over the years regarding the value that an individual places on his name. Poet Sandra Maria Esteves seeks the true names of her ancestors in order to be able to name herself as an individual. In recent decades, women inspired by the feminist movement have asserted their right to retain their birth names after marriage, or to resume their use upon divorce or widowhood. At the same time, many couples have opted to combine their surnames after marriage to form a new, hyphenated version which is then borne by their offspring.

In the case of Latinos, the principal naming conflict centers on the use or non-use of a two-part surname representing the lineages of both parents. More precisely, the question is whether, as a practical matter, an individual living in the United States who has been named in the traditional Latin American style can retain both parental surnames, or must submit to use of the father's surname only. This issue has a special poignance for the Latina, because the application of the Anglo-cultural tradition to a traditional Latin surname eradicates the maternal or female identity of the individual.

* * *

Latin American Naming Tradition: The Form and the Substance

The Latina's name is made up of one or more given names together with a two-part surname (consisting of a patronymic and a matronymic), which is more than the traditional Anglo–American first name, middle name, and single surname combination. For the Latina, both parts of the two-part surname are considered essential in making her entire family name. The involuntary dropping of either part constitutes an unwanted name change and gives rise to the Latina's name issue. Many American individuals of all traditions prefer to use their complete name—the one given at birth, or during christening or formal naming. Among these are perhaps millions of Latinas in the United States, including both those who came to the United States from Latin America (i.e., Mexico, Central America, South America, and the Caribbean) and those born on the mainland.

The Latina positions both the paternal name and maternal name, respectively, in the place generally reserved in the North American custom for the single last name. For example, if an individual's name is Maria Iris Rivera Sancho then the name is ordered as follows:

(1) Maria, the given name or *nombre*;

(2) Iris, the *segundo nombre* or "second given name," not considered a middle name;

(3) Rivera, her paternal surname, known as the *primer apellido*, which translates as the "first last name"; and

(4) Sancho, the maternal surname, known as the *segundo apellido*, the "second last name."

The positioning indicates that Maria Iris is the daughter of a father named Rivera and a mother named Sancho. Sometimes the letter "y" (as the word "and") separates the *primer apellido* and the *segundo apellido*, e.g. Maria Iris Rivera y Sancho. However, each surname is considered part of the family name; one is not subordinate to the other. The position of the *primer* or *segundo apellido* indicates the paternal and the maternal order respectively. The Latina's birth name is made up of two names; her complete surname is used as a unit. In fact, until about 150 years ago, Spanish women did not take their husband's name after marriage. Today some of them retain both the mother's and the father's *apellidos*. For example, Sra. Leticia Maria Riosvega de Borrero's name indicates: her *primer nombre* is Leticia, *segundo nombre* Maria; her father's surname is Rios; her mother's surname is Vega; and she is married to one named Borrero.

It is not a novelty for an individual to use both paternal and maternal surnames nor is it an attribute solely belonging to one class, ethnic or racial group. In fact, by far the dominant custom throughout all of Latin America and Spain is to use both paternal and maternal surnames. For the Latina it is important culturally that both surnames be used; they represent both families to which the individual belongs. As the family unit is central to the identity of the individual so, too, is the name that each family unit bears. By custom, the use of both surnames is essential to self-identification. * * * The two names appear in all official documents such as birth certificates, baptismal certificates, marriage licenses, drivers' licenses, death certificates, professional licenses, etc. * * * Not all Latinos may be interested in using both paternal and maternal surnames but my purpose is to give that choice to all Latinos. * * *

Involuntary Name Changes: How and Why They Occur

* * * The Latino who emigrates to the United States finds himself caught between these two naming traditions—desiring to keep his Latino tradition but facing the opposition of a different dominant practice.

Although tradition or custom is not necessarily law, the custom of using the first, middle, and surname in the United States inhibits other name usage practices or at best ignores them. The customary becomes the familiar, the expected, the appropriate, and the legitimate, even it if does not take on the full force of law. No law in the United States restricts the use of surnames or precludes the Latina's right to cling to her full, original surname. Likewise, no official policy or other formal directive consciously sheds the *segundo apellido* or requires a Latina to depart from full adherence to familial traditions. Thus, if it is customary in the United States to have one surname, then the practice is to look for one surname for identifying an individual. When a Latino chooses to use the family name, which in the United States would be considered two surnames, the situation becomes problematic.

This pattern of legislative "benign neglect" does not mean that the United States is at all hospitable to the Latino naming tradition. In fact, cultural supremacy, bureaucratic laziness, racism and simple ignorance combine to make it exceptionally difficult for the Latino, as a practical matter, to obtain recognition for both last names. The United States' tradition of one surname is so well-entrenched that any deviation from it is immediately deemed awkward and odd, and subtle—but pervasive and quite powerful—forces will operate to change it. Actions by governmental units, by large and small private business organizations, by individual people—and ultimately by the Latina herself—will tend to drop the matronymic half of the surname, squeezing the Latina into the Anglo–Saxon mold. * * *

How does American society accomplish this? A variety of mechanisms operate simultaneously; even though no one of them in isolation could enforce the transformation, together they become nearly inescapable. Federal and state governments prefer using a single surname, despite lack of any statutory proscription against more. Administrative personnel may view those with multi-part surnames as un-American. * * * Government forms may have insufficient space to register a complete Latino name, and the instructions and format of the form may suggest that only a single word should be entered into the place for "last name." * * * Teachers may regularly refer to students by only a single last name. Military officers may likewise assume that a single word can suffice for a Latino soldier or sailor, as for an Anglo–Saxon, and the second last name is omitted. On alphabetical lists, on court papers, on government notices, the Latino can regularly anticipate inclusion of only the first half of his surname. No official rules require the shortening, but every Latino person in the United States has experienced it, and many have now grudgingly accepted the official system.

Even more than governmental action, the practices of private business and individuals reinforce the social norm of using a single last name. Telephone companies, banks, and credit agencies all act as if they expect every customer to adhere to the Anglo–Saxon style. If anyone objects, he could probably succeed, but many will not "rock the boat" when confronting a large, powerful organization. In applying for a job or for an apartment, a special incentive presses to conform. * * * To the Latino, it may seem more prudent to go along with the popular culture, to acquiesce in the name change, even at the cost of cultural identity.

* * *

The Impact of Involuntary Name Changes

* * * Although they overlap, three distinct types of problems are associated with the unwanted deletion of the second last name. Sometimes, these phenomena can be comical. But more often than not, they are serious and traumatic with long-range effects in economic, cultural, and personal terms.

Costs of Being Different

Costs are associated with simply being different, being reminded— every time someone says or writes your name—that your heritage derives from a culture unlike that of the numerically and economically dominant groups in the country. Three separate sub-themes emerge for the Latina.

First is the economic, social, and political disadvantage in perpetuating an identity at odds with the North American norm. Because peoples of British background were the principal early colonizers of the United States, a prejudice developed in favoring Americans with English-rooted names. Job opportunities benefited those with names that could be identified as English, and early immigrants, such as the Irish, the Italians, and the Eastern Europeans, felt the effects of discrimination in the struggle for employment. Eventually this type of discrimination lessened within the second and third generations as they have grown more homogeneous, especially socioeconomically. Although many immigrants kept their family names, significant numbers succumbed to the pressures of a name change.

Second, costs are associated with going in the opposite direction: attempting to conform to an Anglo–American society, assimilate into its practices, and adopt its naming patterns. When an individual simplifies or streamlines the family name, she may do so after a thorough assessment of the effects it will have on the individual and her culture. This assessment may include focusing on the origins of the family name, how the individual may see herself connected to that name, what impact changing the name or not being able to continue to use the name may have on the individual, and how the individual sees herself and therefore how she chooses to name herself.

One observer commented that the

> use of one's own name—and the misuse, modification, or appropriation by others—speaks volumes about "control" and "empowerment" in other aspects of one's life. An individual needs to rely on his sense of self and have the privacy that brings self-control and self-empowerment. For the individual to decide for himself what he should be named is a matter of privacy. The right as an individual to one's privacy is addressed in the term "personhood." The principle behind the term personhood, which was used by Professor Paul Freund, employs a rationale used in Justice Brandeis's dissenting opinion in *Olmstead v. United States*. Brandeis points out that the makers of the Constitution were favorable to the notion of the "pursuit of happiness." They recognized the significance of man's spiritual nature, of his feelings and of his intellect. They knew that only a part of the pain, pleasure, and satisfaction of life are to be found in material things. They sought to protect Americans in their beliefs, their thoughts, their emotions, and their sensations. They conferred, as against the Government, the right to be let alone—the most comprehensive of rights and the right most valued by civilized men. To protect that right, every unjustifiable intrusion by the Government upon the privacy of the individual, whatever the means employed, must be deemed a violation of the Fourth Amendment.

Costs of Not Being Accepted

The Latino and the Latino naming tradition are not merely treated as being "different" by the dominant society; they are treated as "inferior," subject to capricious, unwanted alteration to fit the expectations of mainstream society. Both racism and sexism play a role in this operation. Most members of the dominant society may respond that they are not racists, because they have never intended to treat those from the non-white races discriminatorily. * * * However, Americans who share a common historical and cultural heritage harbor many ideas, attitudes, and beliefs that attach significance to an individual's race and induce negative feelings and opinions about non-whites. Any unconscious racism or negative feelings towards Latinos may affect how members of the dominant society view the Latino name and whether or not they may "unconsciously" modify the name. By the same token, a society that has valued the male name more than the female is asked to value the way in which both the Latino and Latina prefer to use their name. In addition to the Latina, the Latino becomes a victim of sexism, when he is denied the usage of his maternal surname.

* * *

Costs of Being Compelled to Conform—Invisibility

Unfortunately, not much has been written about the plight of the women and men who have not been able to completely use the names which identify them. They have been made invisible. In Ralph Ellison's *Invisible Man*, the protagonist reflects:

> It is sometimes advantageous to be unseen, although it is most often rather wearing on the nerves. Then too, you're constantly being bumped against by those of poor vision. Or again, you often doubt if you really exist. You wonder whether you aren't simply a phantom in other people's minds. . . . It's when you feel like this that, out of resentment, you begin to bump people back.

Not having her complete name recognized is part of a greater reality of not being seen, for the Latina struggles with a denial of her identity that goes far beyond the loss of a name. The Latina remains invisible each time her life experience and her input are considered inferior, when her diversity and culture are not welcomed, and when she is discriminated against because she does not belong and her opinion does not matter.

* * *

It is never easy to attempt to reform a social practice that is as widespread, as subtle, and as basic as the dominant United States practice of insisting upon single-word surnames. This form of anti-Latino repression is so elusive and insidious that few people are even aware of it. This story boasts no overt villain, no blatantly racist government actions, no xenophobic community leaders attempting to resist Latino surnames, not even very many scrupulous clerks and form-filers who object to anything out of the ordinary. Instead, the Latina naming issue presents an unusually subtle phenomenon, which will have to be dealt with through concerted action by three different sets of actions.

First, the government will have to play a role. No name-purist statutes remain on the books, but official actions are still too unfriendly to the Latino tradition. Perhaps a persuasive argument for freedom in naming is that the government has other means of identifying an individual—i.e., use of social security number and the date and place of birth, together with the use of the family name. Additionally, if the use of a complete family name causes fear of an administrative nightmare, then that argument can be countered with the upgrading of data through the use of computer rather than manual collection of journal entries in books.

* * *

Second, society as a whole will have to be more accommodating. An imperfect "melting pot," society can do more to accommodate this form of diversity. Telephone books could regularly carry two last names. Newspapers could alter their conventions, and start referring to Latinos by two last names. All of us can be more aware of the Latino's preference and more respectful of it. Finally, and most importantly, the Latina herself must take the lead in promoting use of both surnames. She must clearly indicate her name preference to the world at large, consistently adopting the full Latin tradition and requesting that others do so, too. This will require effort, patience, and persistence—and quite often she will have to educate others about the reasons for her choice. * * *

Notes and Questions

1. Name as many ways as you can in which Latinas may be disadvantaged to a greater degree than Anglo women in the marital relation. See *Telling to Live: Latina Feminist Testimonios* (Luz del Alba Acevedo et al. eds., 2001); Ramón A. Gutiérrez, *When Jesus Came, the Corn Mothers Went Away: Marriage, Sexuality, and Power in New Mexico, 1500–1846* (1991).

2. *Perez v. Lippold* led, a few years later, to the Supreme Court decision in Loving v. Virginia, 388 U.S. 1 (1967). Why might the California case have come first?

3. Native American women until recently suffered a high rate of involuntary sterilization in U.S. government hospitals, often when they went into labor and went to the hospital for assistance in giving birth. See Relf v. Weinberger, 372 F.Supp. 1196 (D.D.C. 1974). The United States has never had an overpopulation problem. So, why all the sterilizations of minority women?

4. On Latina domestic workers, see Mary Romero, *Immigration, the Servant Problem, and the Legacy of the Domestic Labor Debate: "Where Can You Find Good Help These Days?"*, 53 U. Miami L. Rev. 1045 (1999). See also the following materials on violence in the home.

5. On the role of language in marriage, childrearing, divorce, and custody decisions, see Part Three: Language Rights.

SECTION 6. DOMESTIC AND SEXUAL ABUSE

Jenny Rivera

Domestic Violence Against Latinas by Latino Males: An Analysis of Race, National Origin, and Gender Differentials
14 B.C. Third World L.J. 231, 231–35, 240–47, 249–55, 257 (1994)

After about two months he started . . . hitting me again. This time I was going to do something, so I told Yolanda, my best friend. She said, and I'll never forget it, "So what, you think my boyfriend doesn't hit me? That's how men are." It was like I was wrong or weak because I wanted to do something about it. Last time he got mad he threatened me with a knife. That really scared me.

* * *

Although the general issue of domestic violence has received tremendous attention, the specific issue of violence inflicted upon Latinas by their spouses and male partners has not received comprehensively examination within the mainstream battered women's movement or elsewhere. This specific issue deserves consideration because differences of gender, race, and national origin shape Latinas' experiences with this form of violence.

Latinas' Experiences and Expressions of Male Violence

Racial and cultural differences are critical in analyzing and responding to the crisis of domestic violence. These differences are not merely cosmetic or superficial, much less mere grounds to support demands for assistance. Differences based on race and culture are both internal and external, and represent primary factors affecting the experiences of violence by women of color. Latinas are best situated to describe the nature of the violence against them by their male partners. The following excerpt reflects some of these feelings of anger, fear, and isolation:

I have never called the police here because [he] told me that they will deport us if I do. I've thought about learning some English, but between work and the kids there is hardly any time. So I've never really asked anybody for help. Anyway sometimes he goes months without hurting me and I try to forget about it and just work.

Latinas are differently situated from white and black women. They experience vulnerability and helplessness because of a dearth of bilingual and bicultural services from social service providers and shelters. In addition, Latinas may experience cultural isolation. These differences have led one researcher to conclude that Latinas need support services—targeted to their specific needs—to a greater extent than other battered women. Understanding the dynamic interplay of race and ethnicity in Latinas' lives first requires an analysis that focuses on the intersection of Latina experiences and needs.

* * *

Stereotypes: "El Macho" and the Sexy Latina

Historically, Latinos have been stereotyped as violent and alien.
* * * Latino males are believed to be irrational, reactive, hot-blooded,
passionate, and prone to emotional outbursts. "Macho" is the accepted—
and expected—single-word description of Latino men and male culture.
* * * For their part, Latinas are presented as both innocent virgins and
sexy vixens. Accustomed to a male-centered community, the Latina is
constructed as docile and domestic. In order to satisfy her hot-blooded,
passionate partner, however, the Latina must also be sensual and
sexually responsive. One commentator succinctly summarized these caricatures as they developed through film: "[They] established and repeated other stereotypes, including the violent-tempered but ultimately
ineffective Puerto Rican man; the mental inferior; the innocent, but
sensual Puerto Rican beauty; and the 'loose,' 'hot-blooded mama.' "

* * *

Within the Latino community, Latinas' identities are defined by
their roles as mothers and wives. By encouraging definitions of Latinas
as interconnected with and dependent upon status within a family unit
structure, the Latino patriarchy denies Latinas individuality on the basis
of gender. For Latinas, cultural norms and myths of national origin
intersect with these patriarchal notions of a woman's role and identity.
* * * Those within the Latino community expect Latinas to be traditional, and to exist solely within the Latino family structure. A Latina must
serve as a daughter, a wife, and a parent, and must place the needs of
family members above her own. She is the foundation of the family unit,
treasured as a self-sacrificing woman who will always look to the needs
of others before her own. The influence of Catholicism throughout Latin
America solidifies this image within the community, where Latinas are
expected to follow dogma and to be religious, conservative, and traditional in their beliefs. The proliferation of stereotypes, which are integral to
institutionalized racism, obstructs the progress and mobility of Latinas.
Assumptions about Latinas' intellectual abilities and competence are
formed on the basis of stereotypes, and justified by pointing to poor
educational attainment statistics. Unless these myths and misconceptions are dispelled, the reality of Latinas as targets of Latino violence
will remain unexplored, and Latinas' critical problems will remain un-
solved.

Legal Strategies

* * * Many of the strategies and responses to domestic violence
evidence a lack of understanding of the needs of Latinas and other
women of color. When Latinas are treated differently by law enforcement officials, are denied access to domestic violence shelters because of
language and cultural differences, or do not even take the first step of
seeking assistance because there is no place to turn, the domestic
violence movement fails.

* * *

Legislation

* * * The effectiveness of state and local legislation that criminal-
izes spousal abuse and marital rape must be evaluated by considering
the numerous obstacles that Latinas must surmount in order to exercise
their rights to security and protection. First, state law enforcement
officers and judicial personnel continue to reflect the Anglo male society.
Latinos and bilingual personnel are rarely found within the legal system,
and women continue to represent only a small percentage of the police
force. Second, the nature of the protection or sanctions set forth in state
laws notwithstanding, domestic violence legislation remains susceptible
to poor enforcement by police and judicial personnel. * * *

Law Enforcement

Law enforcement officials' failure to respond appropriately to violence against women has received harsh criticism as it affects women
and efforts geared toward ending domestic violence. * * * Discussions of
appropriate techniques and mechanisms for ensuring women's protection have failed to address Latinas. Instead, the debate has focused on
women as a monolithic class with similar patterns of conduct and
common concerns. When women of color have been considered, they
have been treated without reference to race-specific differences and
experiences. The treatment of women of color has focused primarily on
their economic status, and has lacked a detailed analysis of the role of
race—including the entrenched racism of law enforcement institutions
nationally. As a result, the different experiences and realities of women
of color are not considered when designing effective guidelines on enforcement in domestic violence situations. This absence creates the risk
that strategies aimed at all women will fail to address adequately the
needs of Latinas.

* * *

Latinos in the United States have had a long, acrimonious history of
interaction with local police and federal law enforcement agencies. This
history is marked by abuse and violence suffered by the Latino community at the hands of officers and dims the prospects of success of any
domestic violence enforcement strategy. * * * For example, Latinas are
suspicious of police who have acted in a violent and repressive manner
toward the community at large. In addition, a Latina must decide
whether to invoke assistance from an outsider who may not look like
her, sound like her, speak her language, or share cultural values.

* * *

A second factor is the failure of activists to consider the role of race
in police response. Officers often fail to make an arrest, minimize the
seriousness of the situation, or treat the woman as if she were responsible for the violence. Battered women's activists have criticized male
police officers for their sympathetic attitudes toward batterers. But they

rarely consider the race of the batterer, which is a relevant factor in the police response to a domestic violence situation. The history of aggression toward Latino males by police officers cannot be ignored, nor can the police's belief that violent behavior is commonplace and acceptable within the Latino community. No definitive research examines the impact of these stereotypes on arrest patterns, yet they are important factors in patterns of arrest for domestic violence.

* * *

* * * [I]f a Latina decides to go beyond her community and seek assistance from persons already considered representatives of institutional oppression, the community may view her acts as a betrayal. A Latina, therefore, may tolerate abuse rather than call for outside help. This hesitance to seek assistance provides the community with an excuse for ignoring or denying violence against Latinas, as well as for trivializing and resisting Latina activists' efforts to create a community strategy to end the violence.

Second, law enforcement officials may not give adequate consideration to calls received from poor neighborhoods and neighborhoods with significant populations of people of color, believing such work either highly dangerous or unrewarding. Although a misperception, this attitude engenders a sense within the community that seeking police assistance is futile.

The Criminal Justice System

Local prosecutors and judges react differently to domestic violence cases than to other criminal cases. They often treat these cases as inconsequential or private matters, ill suited to state intervention. Gender bias in the courts therefore results in the disparate treatment of domestic violence crimes compared to other crimes of violence.

* * *

Numerous obstacles based on language and culture must be removed in order for a Latina to use the criminal justice system effectively and ensure a criminal prosecution against her batterer. First, the shortage of bilingual and bicultural personnel—prosecutors, judges, clerks, and psychologists, all of whom are crucial and can influence the ultimate outcome of a Latina's case—creates a system unprepared to address claims by Latinas. Second, Latinas have limited resources to fill the gaps in available support services to assist them. Third, Latinas face racial and ethnic barriers. Neither white women victims nor white male batterers receive discriminatory treatment on account of their race. Latinas do. Latinas are devalued and dehumanized in this process, having no connection to those who have been assigned to prosecute and adjudicate their complaints. Fourth, the "cultural defense" raised by men in response to prosecution for killing their wives represents another barrier to Latinas. The defendant's theory in each of these cases is that violence against women is normal and sanctioned by the culture.

* * *

Such an approach, by requiring legal institutions to consider all relevant factors and to judge the defendant from his or her actual perspective, may initially appear inherently more fair and just. With violence against women, however, a cultural defense serves only to promote violence within the community. Even if violent actions against women are common in a particular culture in certain situations, legitimizing them only reinforces patriarchy, and exposes women to more of the same. It also runs counter to a legal system allegedly founded on the equality of all individuals.

Social Services

Social services, including counseling, assistance in securing entitlements and health coverage, and temporary or permanent housing for women who leave their homes, are especially critical for Latinas, whose access to and utilization of judicial and law enforcement remedies are also limited. Because of linguistic, cultural, and institutional barriers, Latinas have limited access to such services.

A recent study found that Latina shelter residents were the least likely to contact a friend, minister, or social service provider for assistance prior to entering the shelter. * * * [W]hen Latinas try to enter shelters, many are turned away because they speak little or no English. Indeed, the lack of bilingual and bicultural personnel represents a major barrier to Latinas' access to programs and shelters. Shelters without such personnel insist that they would do a disservice to Latinas by accepting them, because the language barrier would prevent personnel from providing Latinas with adequate services. Latinas are therefore denied access to shelters on the basis of national origin. Unfortunately, the shelter is often the only resource available to Latinas, thus compounding the negative impact of this exclusionary practice.

* * *

When accepted into a shelter, Latinas find themselves in foreign and unfamiliar surroundings, because a shelter rarely reflects a Latina's culture and language. For purposes of safety, women are often placed in shelters outside their community, which contributes to Latinas' sense of loneliness and isolation. Without bilingual and bicultural personnel and a familiar community environment, these shelters can provide only the barest, most temporary, services. Insensitivity based on racism or on a lack of knowledge about or exposure to other cultures, by both shelter personnel and other residents, further isolates Latinas and escalates their sense of unwelcomeness.

Nor do shelters facilitate the Latina's return to her own community. Because most lack Spanish-speaking personnel, the Latina cannot develop the skills and strengths necessary to escape the violence permanently and establish a new, independent life. These shelters currently provide only temporary, short-term services. They can scarcely hope to ameliorate the dependency and disempowerment that brought about the Latina's predicament in the first place. * * * Women of color should be placed at the center of feminist reform movements. The current lack of services available to Latinas reflects the consequences of failing to do so. * * *

Responses

The Latino community has not yet begun to develop a comprehensive strategy to end violence within itself. This failure reflects more than mere oversight. Historically, activists and leaders within the community have confronted racism and national origin discrimination with clear, focused strategies. Moreover, Latinos have vehemently opposed the characterization of those in their community as violent and uneducated. This commitment to equality and civil rights stops short, however, of addressing issues such as "women's rights" that are of specific importance to Latinas. Struggles within the Latino community to recognize the pervasiveness of domestic violence and its impact upon the lives of women and their families must continue. Unfortunately, demands for a community response to the violence have been met with insistence that such issues are private matters that cause division within the community and impair the larger struggle for equality. This approach skirts the real issue: Latinas are physically, emotionally, and psychologically abused on a daily basis by the men who are closest to them. These are not private matters—just as the lack of adequate health care, education, and living wages are not.

* * *

The development of strategies to address domestic violence must be grounded in the reality and experiences of all women, recognizing that there may be tensions and conflicts associated with developing reforms. It must be accepted that Latinas face multiple barriers because of their race, national origin, and gender; that this multiple discrimination factors into how Latinas experience and respond to domestic violence; and that institutional racism and patriarchal structures are interrelated in the experience of Latinas. A reform movement that recognizes these realities and experiences will acknowledge the need to work in unison, but only from a strong base. Latino community-based organizations must be strengthened and provided with the financial and political flexibility to develop and establish domestic violence shelters and services. The Latino community must place a high priority on domestic violence initiatives. The lives of women and the well-being of an entire community depend on it.

Aguirre-Cervantes v. INS
242 F.3d 1169 (9th Cir. 2001)

David R. Thompson, Circuit Judge:

Rosalba Aguirre–Cervantes ("petitioner"), a 19–year-old native of Mexico, petitions for review of an order of the Board of Immigration

Appeals ("BIA"), which vacated a decision by the Immigration Judge granting her request for asylum. Over many years, the petitioner was subjected to extreme abuse by her father. She contends this abuse constituted persecution, and that it occurred on account of her membership in a particular social group consisting of her immediate family, all of whose members were abused by her father. At the hearing before the Immigration Judge ("IJ"), the petitioner presented evidence that the country of Mexico was unable or unwilling to do anything about this abuse, and that if she returned to Mexico the abuse would likely continue.

The IJ concluded that the petitioner had satisfied the statutory requirements for asylum, but denied her request for withholding of removal. The INS appealed to the BIA, which agreed that the petitioner had suffered persecution but concluded that she was not eligible for asylum on the ground of persecution on account of membership in a particular social group.

The primary issue is whether the petitioner's immediate family, all of whose members lived together and were subjected to abuse by the petitioner's father, constitutes a protected particular social group under the asylum statute, 8 U.S.C. § 1101(a)(42)(A) (Supp. V 1999). We conclude that it does. We also conclude that the petitioner was persecuted by her father on account of her membership in that social group, that she has a well-founded fear of future persecution, and that Mexico is unable or unwilling to interfere with that persecution.

We grant the petitioner's petition for review and hold that she is eligible for asylum. We further hold that she is entitled to withholding of removal because she has established a clear probability of persecution if she returns to Mexico.

I

The petitioner lived in Michoacan, Mexico, with her parents and six of her nine siblings. Two of her brothers now live in the United States, and another sister lives with her grandfather in Michoacan.

In January 1998, at the age of 16, the petitioner left Mexico because of severe, repeated physical abuse by her father. She testified that from the time she was about three years old, her father beat her frequently and severely, sometimes daily and sometimes weekly. In administering these beatings, he employed a horse whip, tree branches, a hose and his fists. The petitioner suffered a dislocated elbow and lost consciousness as a result of some of this abuse, and bears various scars on her forehead, hand, arm and leg. Her father refused to allow her to seek medical treatment for any of the injuries he inflicted. Furthermore, she testified that her mother did not allow her to go to the police, telling her that her father had the right to do with her what he wanted. Several times, the petitioner went to live with her grandfather to escape her father's beatings, but each time her father came after her and forced her to return with him.

The petitioner testified that she was not aware of any shelters, agencies or children's services in Mexico that would help her. In addition, she testified that she believed the police would not have helped her even if she had been able to contact them. She related a story about two sisters whom she knew who were being physically and sexually abused by their father. Although they contacted the police for help, the police did little if anything, the sisters' circumstances did not change, and the father continued to abuse them.

Petitioner's father, Mr. Aguirre, abused not only the petitioner, but all of her siblings and her mother as well. He abused petitioner's mother (his wife) especially frequently during her pregnancies. The petitioner testified that whenever she tried to protect her mother by intervening, she was also beaten. In the last incident before she left Mexico, she heard her parents arguing and realized that her father was going to beat her mother. Knowing that her mother was healing from a cesarean delivery of her last child, she tried to protect her. Her father beat the petitioner severely and threatened to kill both her and her mother.

The petitioner presented evidence that in Mexico domestic violence is pervasive, officially tolerated, and in some areas legally approved. See John Makeig, *Spousal Abuse in Mexico, U.S. Examined*, Houston Chronicle, Sept. 28, 1997, at A41 [hereafter Makeig]; Bureau of Democracy, Human Rights and Labor, U.S. Department of State, Mexico—Profile of Asylum Claims & Country Conditions 5 (July 1997) [hereafter Mexico—Profile]. The State Department concluded that women who suffer domestic violence "are reluctant to report abuse or file charges, and even when notified, police are reluctant to intervene in what society considers to be a domestic matter." Mexico—Profile, p. 5. Evidence in the record further establishes that in Mexico there are very few shelters or social services available to domestic violence victims, and that few women avail themselves of these services. In addition, many child victims of domestic violence end up homeless and are among the more than 13,000 children living on the streets of Mexico City. U.S. Department of State, Country Reports on Human Rights Practices for 1997 585 (1998) [hereafter Country Reports].

The IJ found that the petitioner's testimony was "credible and consistent and detailed." The IJ ruled that she was a member of a social group of "victims of domestic violence," or of "the family which is a victim of domestic violence."

The BIA agreed with the IJ that the petitioner's severe abuse by her father constituted persecution. The BIA also credited "the [petitioner's] testimony in general" and stated that "[t]he determinative issue . . . is whether the harm experienced by the [petitioner] was, or in the future may be inflicted 'on account of' a statutorily protected ground." The BIA characterized the relevant social group as "Mexican children who are victims of domestic violence," and determined that such a group had not adequately been shown to be a particular social group for asylum purposes. The BIA reversed the decision of the IJ, and this petition for review followed.

II

BIA legal interpretations are reviewed de novo but generally are entitled to deference under Chevron, U.S.A. v. NRDC, 467 U.S. 837 (1984). In interpreting the Immigration and Nationality Act, the BIA is bound by this circuit's earlier decisions in cases originating within this circuit.

The BIA's factual findings are reviewed under a "substantial evidence" standard; a denial of asylum will be upheld if it is supported by reasonable, substantial and probative evidence in the record.

In general, we do not remand a matter to the BIA if, on the record before us, it is clear that we would be "compelled to reverse [the BIA's] decision if it had decided the matter against the applicant." If the ultimate outcome on an issue is clear on the record, remand is inappropriate, even if the BIA reasonably chose not to reach that issue.

The petitioner argued before the BIA that her immediate family constituted a particular social group entitled to protection under the asylum statute, 8 U.S.C. § 1101(a)(42)(A). The BIA, however, defined the group for which the petitioner sought protection as "Mexican children who are victims of domestic violence." The BIA did not address the question whether a family can be a particular social group for asylum purposes; accordingly, deference is not relevant. Rather, we review de novo the legal question of whether the petitioner's immediate family is a particular social group entitled to protection under 8 U.S.C. § 1101(a)(42)(A).

III

A. *Exhaustion of Administrative Remedies*

The INS argues that the petitioner did not exhaust her claim that she was persecuted on account of her family membership because this claim was not properly raised before the BIA. "Failure to raise an issue below constitutes failure to exhaust administrative remedies and 'deprives this Court of jurisdiction to hear the matter.'"

* * *

We conclude the petitioner exhausted her administrative remedies as to her family group claim, and we have jurisdiction to adjudicate that claim.

B. *A Family as a Particular Social Group*

To be eligible for asylum, an applicant must establish that she is a refugee. A refugee is a person "who is unable or unwilling to return to, and is unable or unwilling to avail himself or herself of the protection of," his or her country of nationality "because of persecution or a well-founded fear of persecution on account of race, religion, nationality, membership in a particular social group, or political opinion." 8 U.S.C. § 1101(a)(42)(A).

We have defined a "particular social group" as

a collection of people closely affiliated with each other, who are actuated by some common impulse or interest. Of central concern is the existence of a voluntary associational relationship among the purported members, which imparts some common characteristic that is fundamental to their identity as a member of that discrete social group.

Perhaps a prototypical example of a "particular social group" would consist of the *immediate members of a certain family*, the family being a focus of fundamental affiliational concerns and common interests for most people.

While our statement that the family is a prototypical example of a particular social group was not essential to the holding, we have confirmed the formulation in subsequent cases. For example, in Hernandez–Montiel v. INS, 225 F.3d 1084, 1091 (9th Cir. 2000), in which the particular social group was "made up of gay men with female sexual identities," we held that a particular social group "is one united by a voluntary association, including a former association, or by an innate characteristic that is so fundamental to the identities or consciences of its members that members either cannot or should not be required to change it." Additionally, we held that indigenous people comprising a large percentage of the population of a disputed area do not constitute a particular social group, in contrast to the immediate members of a certain family. Similarly, "a pattern of persecution targeting a given family that plays a prominent role in a minority group that is the object of widespread hostile treatment supports a well-founded fear of persecution by its surviving members."

* * *

Consistent with decisions from our circuit, our sister circuits and the BIA, we hold that a family group may qualify as a particular social group within the meaning of 8 U.S.C. § 1101(a)(42)(A). This is not to say, however, that every family group will qualify. Qualification will depend upon the circumstances of each case. The factors which lead us to conclude that the petitioner's family group qualifies as a "particular social group" are that the petitioner's family members are part of an immediate, as opposed to an extended, family unit; they now live or have lived together and are otherwise readily identifiable as a discrete unit; and they share the common experience of all having suffered persecution at the hands of the petitioner's father.

* * *

We decline the INS's suggestion that we delay our decision pending development of the proposed Rule. Family membership is clearly an immutable characteristic, fundamental to one's identity. Moreover, as noted in the summary accompanying the proposed Rule, the Rule's first three factors for determining whether a particular social group exists are drawn from *Sanchez-Trujillo*. In applying *Sanchez-Trujillo* to the present case, we have necessarily taken those factors into account. We have also considered the fourth, fifth and sixth factors of the proposed Rule and conclude that the petitioner's family satisfies them as well. Mexican society recognizes the family as a discrete unit, and members of a family view themselves as such. In the domestic violence context, Mexican society also treats members of a family differently from nonmembers because it regards violence within a family as a "domestic matter," rather than a matter for government intervention. Country Reports, p. 583; Mexico—Profile, p. 5. In sum, we have considered the factors specified in the proposed Rule and those factors support our conclusion that the petitioner is entitled to asylum protection as a member of a particular social group.

C. Persecution "On Account of" Group Membership

The INS concedes that the petitioner was persecuted. It does not concede, however, that she was persecuted "on account of" her family membership. See 65 Fed. Reg. 76,121, 76,133 (Dec. 6, 2000) (to be codified at 8 C.F.R. § 208.13(b)(1)). Establishing persecution on account of family membership is a burden the petitioner bears. She must present evidence, either direct or circumstantial, from which it is reasonable to conclude that her persecutor harmed her at least in part because of her membership in what we have held to be a particular social group, her immediate family. See *Elias-Zacarias*, 502 U.S. at 483. We conclude the petitioner carried this burden.

The petitioner presented extensive documentary evidence that domestic violence is practiced to control and dominate members of the abuser's family:

> Domestic violence is purposeful and instrumental behavior. The pattern of abuse is directed at achieving compliance from or control over the abused party. It is directed at circumscribing the life of the abused person so that independent thought and action are eliminated and so the abused person will become exclusively devoted to fulfilling the needs and requirements of the batterer. The pattern is not impulsive or out of control behavior. Tactics that work to control the abused party are selectively chosen by the perpetrator.

Family Violence Prevention Fund, Domestic Violence in Civil Court Cases 23 (1992). The perpetrator may abuse his children in part to coercively control his partner, as well. Id. at 49.

The undisputed evidence demonstrates that Mr. Aguirre's goal was to dominate and persecute members of his immediate family. He abused his wife and all of his children to whom he had access. There is no evidence that he ever acted violently toward any non-family member. The petitioner was most severely attacked by her father when she tried to defend her mother against abuse, particularly when her mother was pregnant. The petitioner's uncle also testified that two of the petitioner's brothers, who now live in the United States, fled Mexico because of frequent abuse by their father. It was the immediate family that was the target of Mr. Aguirre's assaults. It was established by abundant evidence—and undisputed—that it was the petitioner's status as a member of that family that prompted her beatings. The conclusion is inescapable that she suffered those beatings on account of her family membership.

* * *

D.   The Mexican Government's Inability or Unwillingness to Control the Persecutor

We next consider whether the petitioner established that the Mexican government was unable or unwilling to control Mr. Aguirre's abusive behavior.

When persecution is inflicted by a non-governmental entity, an applicant must be able to show that the persecutor was someone the government was "unable or unwilling to control." Sangha v. INS, 103 F.3d 1482, 1487 (9th Cir. 1997) (citing McMullen v. INS, 658 F.2d 1312, 1315 (9th Cir. 1981)). "Government action is not necessarily required; instead, police inaction in the face of . . . persecution [by nongovernmental groups] can suffice to make out a claim." Navas, 217 F.3d at 656 n.10 (citations omitted).

The BIA did not make a clear finding that the Mexican government was unable or unwilling to control Mr. Aguirre. The IJ, however, found that fact to be established, and the same evidence on that issue was before both the IJ and the BIA. In commenting on the documentary evidence, the BIA stated that the evidence "appears to establish that [in Mexico] 'the most pervasive violations of women's rights involve domestic and sexual violence which is believed to be widespread and vastly under reported.'" The BIA further noted that the U.S. State Department's Mexico—Profile stated that more than 13,000 children live on the streets of Mexico City, many of whom are victims of family violence and subsequently become involved with alcohol, drugs, prostitution and petty thievery. The BIA also cited the portion of the Mexico—Profile that reported "women are reluctant to report abuse or file charges, and even when notified, police are reluctant to intervene in what society considers to be a domestic matter."

In addition to the sources cited by the BIA, there was additional documentary evidence that domestic violence is widely condoned in Mexico and that law enforcement authorities are unwilling to intervene in such matters. As of 1997, in all but a few of Mexico's thirty-two states, it was "legal for husbands to use 'correction' discipline to handle wives and children." Makeig. At that time, Mexico City, with a population of 23 million, had only one battered women's shelter, with only eight beds, and battered wives' shelters existed in only five Mexican states. Id. This evidence demonstrates the government's inability or unwillingness to control the abusive behavior of domestic violence perpetrators like Mr. Aguirre and, indeed, its tacit approval of a certain measure of abuse.

Mexico—Profile, p. 5 (stating that "[a]lthough the [Mexican] Constitution provides for equality between the sexes, neither the authorities nor society in general respect this practice" and that domestic abuse that does not involve "cruelty or unnecessary frequency" is not considered a crime).

We conclude that any reasonable factfinder considering the evidence in this case would conclude that the Mexican government is unable or unwilling to control Mr. Aguirre's abusive behavior directed toward his immediate family. * * *

E.   Well–Founded Fear of Persecution

To be eligible for asylum, except in rare cases, the petitioner must establish that she has a well-founded fear of future persecution. We conclude the petitioner made this showing. The INS concedes that the petitioner suffered past persecution. A finding of past persecution creates a rebuttable presumption that the petitioner has a well-founded fear of future persecution. The INS may rebut this presumption by showing by a preponderance of the evidence that there has been "a fundamental change in circumstances such that the applicant no longer has a well-founded fear of persecution" in her home country, or by showing that the applicant "could avoid future persecution by relocating to another part of the applicant's country of nationality . . . and under all circumstances, it would be reasonable to expect the applicant to do so."

The "fundamental change in circumstances" ground for rebuttal replaces the former ground of changed country conditions. Under the former regulation, we stated that on a remand to the BIA, it generally could not look beyond the existing record to determine whether changed country conditions rebutted the presumption of a well-founded fear of persecution. We stated:

> In recent cases, we have made clear that on remand the BIA may not look beyond the existing record to determine whether changed country conditions rebut the presumption of a well-founded fear of future persecution. In fact, we have refused to remand where the petitioner is entitled to a determination of eligibility on the existing record. The reason for this rule is that a petitioner who was eligible for asylum when the BIA considered his case does not lose that eligibility as a result of the agency's failure to recognize it. Where the petitioner properly established his eligibility on the record made before the BIA, that eligibility must be accorded its proper legal effect.

Gafoor v. INS, 231 F.3d 645, 656 n.6 (9th Cir. 2000). Having set out the general rule in *Gafoor*, we then carved out a narrow exception to fit the particular circumstances of that case. Id. at 656.

The present case does not fall within *Gafoor*'s narrow exception. In that case we remanded to the BIA to permit it to consider whether a recent political coup that occurred after the petitioner filed his asylum application undermined the BIA's finding that the petitioner's well-founded fear of persecution was rebutted by a change in country conditions. No such relevant subsequent events are present in this case. Accordingly, the general rule applies. Pursuant to that rule, if we were to remand this case to the BIA, it could not look beyond the existing record to determine whether the presumption of a well-founded fear of future persecution was rebutted.

Confining ourselves to the existing record, it is clear that the presumption has not been rebutted. First, there is no evidence of a fundamental change in circumstances. The INS argues that because the petitioner is now 19 years old and no longer a minor, her circumstances may have fundamentally changed. However, the record does not indicate that her likelihood of persecution has changed simply because she is a few years older. Any reasonable fact finder would conclude that Mr. Aguirre would abuse her regardless of her age. He abuses both his wife and children of all ages and has threatened to kill both the petitioner and his wife, so clearly a family member's age is irrelevant to the likelihood of abuse.

Second, under the reasoning of *Gafoor*, if the petitioner were eligible for asylum when the BIA considered her case at the time she was 16, she should not lose that eligibility now that she is 19 just because of an erroneous ruling.

Third, the record does not contain any evidence that the petitioner could reasonably relocate within Mexico. When she previously tried to live with her grandfather, her father came after her and forced her to return home. Moreover, Mr. Aguirre has personal information about the petitioner that would assist him in tracking her down if she were to return to Mexico. She is still quite young and most likely would have to turn to relatives or family friends for assistance. Finding her would not likely prove difficult.

Considering all of the relevant circumstances, we are convinced that any reasonable factfinder would conclude that the petitioner's relocation away from her former home in Mexico would not effectively negate the likelihood of her future persecution by her father.

* * *

For these reasons, we grant the petition for review and grant withholding of removal. We remand to the Attorney General to exercise his discretion and determine whether to grant asylum.

Notes and Questions

1. Machismo, to the extent it continues in Latino culture, would seem to include superficially honorable, respectful treatment of women. Why, then, is domestic abuse so common? See Jenny Rivera, *Domestic Violence Against Latinas*, supra this chapter.

2.   On sexual harassment of Latinas generally, see Maria L. Ontiveros, *Fictionalizing Harassment—Disclosing the Truth*, 93 Mich. L. Rev. 1373 (1995); Maria L. Ontiveros, *Three Perspectives*, supra this chapter.

SECTION 7.   FAMILY CARE, CHURCH, AND CULTURE

Crying Out Loud, Some Years Nearly One Out of Five Young
Latinas Tries to Kill Herself. We Need to Understand Why
Houston Chron., Sept. 15, 2006, at B85

In 1961, when researchers first reported a disturbing pattern among young Latinas, it was treated as an ethnic concern.

Forty years later, the fact that almost a quarter of Hispanic girls in this country have tried to kill themselves is everyone's crisis.

Researchers need to better understand why so many girls want to die, and schools and nonprofits have to better help them cope.

Social workers have known about Latinas' exceptionally high rate of attempted suicide for decades, said psychiatrist Luis Zayas, a professor at Washington University in St. Louis. But the pattern's breadth was confirmed in 1995, when the Centers for Disease Control and Prevention first documented it in a national study.

Their finding: One out of five Latina teens had attempted suicide. Last year, the rates dropped for all teenagers, yet 15 percent of Latinas still reported trying to kill themselves, in contrast to 7 percent of white girls and 7 percent of black girls.

There's almost no literature to explain why this is. Researchers have found plenty of anecdotal explanations, as well as demographic risk factors: Fewer Latino youngsters have health insurance, for example. Latinos are also less receptive to seeking mental health care.

At home, Hispanic girls often are family translators and caretakers, while at school they try to fit into the competitive, sexualized and rebellious U.S. youth culture. Paradoxically, the dueling impulses within these young women represent mainstream values Americans most praise.

"Our view," Zayas and fellow researchers wrote in 1995 of the Latina attempted suicide rate, "is that it represents a major developmental struggle between the adolescent's need for autonomy . . . and her deep regard for family unity."

Zayas is now one year into a four-year study funded by the National Institutes of Health. He is exploring which young Latinas respond to these conflicts by trying suicide, and which resist. That grant should lead to other intensive efforts to grasp—and end—this self-destructive pattern.

"If we had rates of TB at this level," Zayas told the Kansas City Star, "we would have a national czar for prevention."

It's a good analogy. Now that Latinos are America's fastest-growing ethnicity and 42 percent of Houston's population, the well-being of young Latinas is a matter of public health.

The Mental Health Association of Greater Houston has recognized this, hiring two Spanish-speaking outreach specialists and offering mental health services in partnership with medical clinics. But schools, communities and Latino families also need education about suicide, said Lina Lopez, a psychiatrist with the University of Texas. Even adolescents whose suicide attempts don't succeed, Lopez points out, might influence their peers.

In school, work and the lives of future children, young Latinas' untreated suffering has far-reaching effects. For the health of the whole community, that pain needs to be better understood and treated.

Laura M. Padilla
Latinas and Religion: Subordination or State of Grace?
33 U.C. Davis L. Rev. 973, 973, 975, 977–
85, 988–97, 999–1000 (2000)

[R]eligion is not any one stable force across the vagaries of time and place ... [R]eligion encapsulates both the oppression practiced by Roman Catholicism's authoritative apparatus, as well as the resistance against such oppression mounted by dissident forces within that Church.

To illustrate, Catholicism has oppressed many women through its conservative insistence on male domination, yet devout Catholics have challenged that domination through liberation theology, including the *mujerista* theology described by Ada Maria Isasi–Díaz.

* * *

A question underlying my exploration is whether religion can liberate Latinas without unduly oppressing them. Answering that question is complicated by Latinas' cultural tendency to accept their fate of suffering with dignity, whether that suffering be religiously or culturally based. My exploration commences with background information on Latinas, religion, and culture. That provides the basis for deconstructing Latinas' relationship with Catholicism, including a discussion of how religion has served as both a source of subordination and strength. * * *

* * *

Latinas' cultural background is characterized by its reverence for family. Although such reverence has been implicated as a source of oppression, not all Latinas accept this charge. "Maintaining our families is an intrinsic part of our struggle. Therefore, we are not willing to accept fully the Anglo feminist understanding of the family as the center of women's oppression." Rather than blindly accepting others' pronouncements about what family should mean for them and the appropriate relationship between family and religion, Latinas must decide for themselves the significance of family.

Latinas' view of family also affects their religiosity. As mothers, Latinas are primarily responsible for inculcating religious values into their children. "It has been characteristic of the role of women, whether as mother or catechist, to instruct children in the faith, to see to it that they receive the sacraments. And to instill in them the values and virtues consonant with a good Christian life." Regardless of family status, religion is a central part of many Latinas' lives. Researchers consistently find that Latinas/os consider themselves very religious, with Latinas even more likely than their male counterparts to consider religion very important. The centrality of religion for Catholic Latinas/os is manifested through both orthodox doctrine and popular religiosity. The former is illustrated, for example, by many Latinas/os' belief in heaven, hell, the virginal birth of Jesus, and Jesus's resurrection, as well as Latinas/os' participation rates in sacraments such as baptism and Church weddings. The latter is illustrated in many ways, including through devotion to the Virgin Mary, a strong belief in the intercession of saints, and the habit, particularly among women, of lighting candles or establishing home altars.

Regardless of the formality of their religious beliefs, "Latinas' relationship with the divine is a very intimate one. This intimate relationship is a matter not only of believing that God is with us in our daily struggle, but that we can and do relate to God the same way we related to all our loved ones." In other words, Latinas' God is a personal, living God with whom they converse daily—upon awakening, while driving to work, booting up a computer, reprimanding children, and wondering how they will possibly get through another day. They can harm this divine relationship through apathy and excessive autonomy, thus distancing themselves from a God who could provide meaning in their lives. These sins of indifference and selfishness cause individual and collective harm by preventing Latinas from both living up to their potential and co-creating healthier communities. To avoid these sins,

> Latinas need to actualize our sense of *camunidades de fe* [faith communities] by setting-up communities which are praxis-oriented, which bring together personal support and community action, and which have as a central organizing principle, our religious understandings and practices as well as our needs.

* * *

Latinas/os and Religion in the Americas

Early settlement of the Americas was characterized by colonization, including religious colonization. The missionaries had many goals, including conquering indigenous populations in the name of God. While the goal of conquest was sometimes well meaning, the colonizers always acted in a dominating and intolerant manner that assumed both superior knowledge of what was right for the indigenous, and a conviction that local practices and religious beliefs had no redeeming qualities. The priests, even those who were genuinely concerned about the welfare of the indigenous, systematically destroyed the natives' religious traditions, thus wounding them at the most sacred level. This distinctive behavior deprived the indigenous of meaning and significance in their lives, leaving them spiritually untethered. In the process of converting natives in the name of "the one true God," the natives':

> [G]ods, their religion, and the ways of their ancestors were ... discredited, insulted, maligned, and totally destroyed.... Like other conquerors, the Christians burned the conquered people's temples and imposed their gods. But they refused any sharing, demanded the annihilation of local cults, and kept for themselves an absolute monopoly of the priesthood and the sacred. This radical opposition to everything that had been sacred to Indian people was the deepest source of their collective trauma.

Religious colonization thus resulted in complete devastation of a way of life and a belief system. In the process of purging everything valuable to the natives, the missionaries attempted to assimilate them to European standards. In addition to assimilating through religion, assimilation was attempted through education, intermarriage, and interbreeding, though often with the understanding that "they" could not truly be assimilated, and that "their" worth would always be calculated by the amount of European blood they had—the larger the amount, the more valuable.

Although the class system imposed in the New World dictated some forms of oppression, others were gender-based. All women, regardless of class, shared many forms of oppression and subordination, and no woman could exercise leadership within the Church.

> [A] poor, rural *india* shared with the *española* of the upper classes the prevailing norm of exclusion from participation in the new system. The universal function of women during this period was to serve in the home as procreators, housekeepers, wives and mothers. Other common grounds of exclusion shared *by indias* and *españolas* were the universal denial of participation in religion, government, and education.

Accordingly, all women were considered inferior to men, and native women were at a more extreme disadvantage. Yet in spite of the disdain with which Europeans viewed the indigenous and mestizos, particularly women, efforts at assimilation, including religious assimilation, continued. Religion's development in the New World became increasingly complicated, partly because of an interesting event that occurred shortly after the Spanish invasion. This event has directly affected Latinas/os throughout the Americas, and continues to shape their religious beliefs.

In the predawn hours of an early December day, the Virgen de Guadalupe (Virgin of Guadalupe) revealed herself to Juan Diego, a poor, dark *campesino* (farmer or countryman). She asked him to convey to the bishop her presence and her request that the bishop build a hermitage at the site where she revealed herself to Juan Diego. After Juan Diego complied with her request and was rejected by the bishop, she twice more revealed herself to Juan Diego, he continued to make the same request of the bishop, and the bishop continued to resist until Juan Diego's third interview with him. At that interview, as a sign from the Virgen, Juan Diego presented to the bishop brilliant flowers from the desolate hilltop where she had revealed to herself to Juan Diego. And as Juan Diego unfolded his white mantle to present the flowers, "she painted herself: the precious image of the Ever–Virgin Holy Mary, Mother of the God Téotl...." The bishop then believed and, in short order, the hermitage was built. Hundreds of millions of pilgrims have already journeyed to this site, and thousands continue to make the journey.

It is important to briefly discuss the ramifications of the Virgen story's symbolism and potential to liberate. By choosing to reveal herself to Juan Diego, a poor and oppressed Nahuatl Indian, the Virgen illustrated the importance of reaching and serving the oppressed, the downtrodden—those at the bottom. Juan Diego represented the people that had been conquered and whose religion had been dismantled—when the Virgen chose him, she chose someone who

> stands for every person whose self-dignity has been crushed, whose credibility has been destroyed, whose sense of worth has been trampled. As he will tell us himself, he is nothing; he is a bunch of dry leaves. He has been made to think of himself as excrement.... He no longer knows himself as he truly is, seeing himself only through others' eyes as totally worthless and useless.

The Virgen story replicates biblical teachings in which God favors the poor and outsiders. In the Old Testament, the Lord declares that He "will assemble the lame, and gather the outcasts, even those whom I have afflicted. I will make the lame a remnant and the outcasts a strong nation."

The Virgen story contains parallels to Christ's life as well. Just as the Virgen selected Juan Diego, a poor and marginalized *indio*, Christ frequently singled out the poor and the oppressed—outsiders—as his chosen people. For example, Jesus chose Mary Magdalene, a known prostitute, to be among his select company. Likewise, the Virgen chose Juan Diego to be her messenger, while Jesus chose poor fishermen from Galilee, certainly deemed outsiders, to be his disciples and messengers.
* * *

　　　* * *

The Virgen story additionally illustrates the potential for synthesis as a mode of liberation for Latinas because it respects elements of indigenous religion and culture while teaching Christianity. The Virgen told Juan Diego "[k]now and be certain in your heart, my most abandoned son, that I am the Ever–Virgin Holy Mary, Mother of the God of Great Truth, Téotl, of the One through Whom We Live, the Creator of Persons, the Owner of What is Near and Together, of the Lord of

Heaven and Earth." By using the names of Nahuatl Gods, the very same Gods who Spanish missionaries first disrespected and then dismissed, the Virgen acknowledges those Gods and thus grants them the respect that had formerly been stripped away from them. In the process, she neither discredits the natives' Gods nor denies the Christian God. Thus, she moves out of the "either/or, us or them" paradigm into a paradigm of acceptance. This contrasted with early conquerors' and missionaries' zeal for destroying all vestiges of the old religion and marked a new tolerance for alternate ways of seeing and believing. * * *

      * * *

Although Latinas/os have remained at the margins of Catholic leadership, with Latinas nearly invisible, the Church has gradually turned its attention to Latinas/os specific needs. For example, the Church has been involved in social justice issues affecting Latinas/os.

> It has at times provided extensive welfare services for the Mexican–American community, has sponsored citizenship classes and youth organizations, ... and has recently seen some of its clerical representatives demonstrate in picket lines on behalf of striking Mexican–American farm workers, directing antipoverty programs, and testifying on minimum-wage legislation before Congressional committees.

Although the Church has not uniformly embraced these causes, significantly, a critical mass within the Church has embraced them and been willing to take a controversial stand. This is consistent with the "Latino Religious Resurgence" which followed the Second Vatican Council, and allowed Latinas/os to proclaim a new role for their religion. * * *

Liberation theology in Latin America preceded and coincided with the development of the Latino Religious Resurgence in the United States. No discussion of Catholicism in the Americas would be complete without a brief introduction to liberation theology. One legal academic laid out the fundamentals of liberation theology as follows:

1) People's response to God is impeded by oppressive economic and social conditions.

2) Where the institutions we have in place create such oppressive conditions, we have a duty as Christians to do what we can to reform them.

3) Inherent in oppressive institutions is a class struggle between the beneficiaries and the victims of those institutions. The institutions cast the beneficiaries, like it or not, in the role of oppressors of the victims.

4) Reform of the institutions in question liberates the beneficiaries from their role as oppressors just as it liberates the victims from their role as persons oppressed.

5) Efforts to bring about such liberation have eschatological (religious and eternal) value even if their historical fruition is problematic.

More succinctly, Professor Araujo stated that "[o]ne goal of liberation theology is to reconcile human beings so that injustice and oppression caused by people and institutions are replaced with a more just society in which the dignity and the right to a flourishing human existence for all are respected. For Latinas/os, liberation theology and movements, which are similarly based on a desire to liberate subordinated persons from oppression, provide an opportunity for religion to be used as part of an antisubordination crusade. Because of movements like that embodied by liberation theology, 'Latin–American Catholicism in the past two decades has become identified in the popular imagination with progress and defense of human rights.' "

* * *

Women/Latinas Within the Church

[M]any hold religion responsible for perpetrating and maintaining a sense of inferiority, docility, and servitude among women. Because in religion the power to govern the institution resides chiefly with men, religion is considered patriarchy pure and simple. Catholicism, which directly excludes women from ordination, is considered, at least by some, patriarchy par excellence.

* * *

Judeo–Christian religions generally, and Catholicism specifically, are traditional patriarchal institutions which have subordinated and oppressed women. This subordination is rooted in the bible, and has been extended through biblical interpretation and subsequently developed Church doctrine and policy. In response to Eve's transgression in the first book of the bible, the Lord God said to woman, "I will greatly multiply your pain in childbirth, in pain you shall bring forth children; yet your desire shall be for your husband, and *he shall rule over you.*" Thus appears the first directive from God that man shall rule over woman. It is not the only such directive. The book of Ephesians orders that:

> Wives, be subject to your own husbands, as to the Lord. For the husband is the head of the wife, as Christ also is the head of the Church, He Himself being the Savior of the body. But as the church is subject to Christ, so also the wives ought to be to their husbands in everything.

In the *Book of Timothy*, Paul exhorted women to maintain certain roles.

> [L]et a woman quietly receive instruction with entire submissiveness . . . do not allow a woman to teach or exercise authority over a man, but to remain quiet. For it was Adam who was first created, and then Eve. And it was not Adam who was deceived, but the woman being quite deceived, fell into transgression. But women shall be preserved through the bearing of children if they continue in faith and love and sanctity with self-restraint.

Women also experience oppression at the hands of the Church through limits it places on their leadership, such as prohibiting their ordination as priests. * * * Thus, at a fundamental legal level, doors within the Church are closed to women. This not only officially limits women's roles in the Church, it sends a message about women's position and their [in]abilities.

Women are subordinated not only through biblical text and limited leadership opportunities, but also through interpretation of doctrine and Church policies that affect or limit women's rights. For example, the Catholic Church prohibits birth control, and abortion. That leaves Latinas few procreative options if they want to comply with Church doctrine.

* * *

Considering biblical teaching about women, limited Church-defined roles for women, and women's relative lack of power in the Church, it would be easy to conclude that within the religious realm, women are destined to a life of subordination. However, it would be inaccurate to accept that pronouncement and simply dismiss any hope for women within religious structures. "Contrary to some current stereotypes, women have always had a religious role for autonomous decisionmaking, especially in clergy-controlled Catholicism. While Latinas are generally not recognized as Church leaders, their role remains significant." * * *

* * *

* * * Women frequently hold leadership positions in grass-roots movements. Thus, to view Latinas as powerless in the Church oversimplifies a more complex dynamic. As noted,

> [S]uch a view leaves little room for differentiating between the institutionalized form of religion, on the one hand, and popular religiosity with its roots in the beliefs and traditions of the people, on the other. Upon a closer examination of how power unfolds, it becomes clear that women exercise a productive function in religion; one that subverts and transforms social values.

Even prior to recent feminists' assertions that Latinas play a significant unofficial role in religious life, others had acknowledged the importance of Latinas in the Church.

> When through lack of interest or numbers, the priests, sisters and other religious personnel [v]anish from Latino communities, or fail to provide adequate ministry it is business as usual for the local *"espiritista"* [spiritual healer], *"curandera"* [healer] and *rezadora* [prayer leader], as they continue . . . to give counsel so much needed in times of crisis. . . . Despite the patriarchy of the clergy, particularly within Catholicism, women's input continues to shape the transmission of social values among Latinas today. As in the past, the sustaining sources of popular religiosity are not the priests, nor even lay male leaders, but women.

Latinas accordingly are central in the transfer of religious and moral values, even if they are not formally recognized as religious leaders. * * *

* * *

Religion as a Source of Strength

* * *

Thus, religion becomes crucial as a solace for this world, and a beacon of hope for the next. Latinas can turn to the Lord with their problems, and seek the inner peace that is otherwise so elusive. * * *

In addition to engaging in one-on-one relationships with the divine, Latinas can and do come together in Church communities to grapple with common struggles. "[R]eligious communities, especially for women, have been among the most responsive groups in the church to issues of adult education, ministry to the poor, violence, and human rights." While gathering in community is crucial, an antisubordination agenda requires more—we must define the parameters of these communities to ensure that they are inclusive and that they address our specific needs through nonhierarchical means. * * *

* * * Although Latinas may not be formally recognized as Church leaders, it is common knowledge that their organizational work is crucial and they are often responsible for the day-to-day details which keep the Church operational and lively. However, because of cultural and religious upbringing, they normally do not expect, or receive, recognition for their work. Herein lies a paradox that may be partly responsible for the continuing subordination of Latinas—many Latinas do not want to create divisiveness within the Church, and will gladly perform any tasks asked of them, without asking for anything in return. This, in turn, makes it difficult to mount challenges to the Church's existing hierarchy and patriarchy. Yet it is crucial to assert that challenge.

* * *

Berta Esperanza Hernández-Truyol
Sex, Culture, and Rights: A Re/Conceptualization
of Violence for the Twenty–First Century
60 Alb. L. Rev. 607, 626–28, 632–34 (1997)

Much of the economic violence that is perpetrated on, and experienced by, Latinas as a group is a result of, and is perpetuated by, gendered cultural norms. Latinas are acculturated to be secondary, subordinate beings. *Marianismo*—a construct in which the Virgin Mary is the aspirational model—demands that a Latina must be *la buena mujer* ("the good woman"), and requires of women self-sacrifice, self-effacement, and self-subordination. The notion of *familismo* (family comes first) also keeps Latinas, right here within our own *fronteras* (borders), hiding behind the proverbial privacy closet door of family.

Familismo results in the expectation of Latinas to take the blows from husbands and fathers alike, and never to complain. Of course, many who are undocumented immigrants will not report violence against them, because they fear deportation for themselves or their families. As a result, they learn to suffer indignities and tolerate physical, sexual, and economic violence at the hands of their husbands and underground employers. Latinas endure such violence in their own homes, as well as in the homes of those for whom they work as nannies, housekeepers, and maids, because they are afraid that if they complain about or reject the sexual harassment, the underpayments, the humiliation, the rapes, and the insults that they suffer, they will be deported.

Economics and culture often clash in the demands they make of Latinas. Consider the complex, paradoxical messages given daily to all women in poverty. Society expects women to stay home and care for children, family and spouses, but the very same society demonizes them for the very same conduct if they happen to be in poverty and accept financial assistance from the state. The same conduct of stay-at-home care-taker goes from glorified to condemned and demonized depending on who is signing the paycheck, all the time for doing their jobs as mothers. This, too, is everyday economic violence.

* * * The international community must revision "violence" so that it offers women greater protection in the twenty-first century. Recognizing the close nexus between economic dependence and marginalization to physical victimization, I propose that the conceptualization of violence be developed, expanded, and transformed to embrace the indivisibility and interdependence of human rights. Such a re/conceptualization must embrace all three "generations" of rights: (1) civil and political rights (first generation); (2) social, cultural, and economic rights (second generation); and (3) solidarity rights (third generation).

As a prologue to re/constituting and re/conceptualizing violence, one useful blueprint/model to make the transition from the "A hit B" or "A shot B" to the less physically forceful but equally damaging forms of violence is the evolution (revolution) that transmogrified domestic violence from a private to a public act. In the past (and in some cultures in the present), it was believed that what happens between or among family members is a "private" matter. If a spouse hit his or her spouse or child, it was not a crime, but rather, business as usual within the family structure. Not too long ago, it was acceptable for a husband to keep his wife in line by using force. Courts even permitted a husband to beat his wife with a stick so long as it was no bigger than his thumb, the so-called "rule of thumb." It was believed that wives, like children, needed to be disciplined, controlled, and supervised not only physically, but also economically. Women were not allowed to deal in their own property. Municipal systems of law would not get into the business of forbidding violence in the home so as not to intrude in this private sphere of life. As a result, it was considered to be well outside the realm of the international legal system to reach such private individual conduct. In fact, until recently, states alone were subjects of international law; individuals were simply objects, and not subjects of it.

* * *

Recently, however, the United Nations has recognized that women's unequal status transcends the social and family spheres. Women's global disadvantages and marginalization also result from lack of access to economic development opportunities (in both the private and public sectors), denial of educational opportunities, and restriction from social and political participation. Scrutiny of women's condition reveals that their less-than-full citizenship status can be traced to both physical and economic violence. Such violence is often widely accepted, and even embraced, under the pretext of cultural normativity. Consequently, before women can achieve social and economic equality and engage in full political participation, societies world-wide must re/conceptualize the notion of violence. This reconceptualization must include all forms of injustice for women, including injustice beyond the hitting-or-shooting paradigm. It must include economic marginalization and acts of violence justified on the grounds of culture or traditional practices. Indeed, such a framework will facilitate and permit the recognition and understanding of the many intersections of the physical abuse and economic deprivation components in the construction of violence.

Thus, here are my suggestions on how to reconceptualize violence. On any matter, always ask the woman question: can or does the policy/practice/standard affect, facilitate, promote, or ignore violent consequences to women? This inquiry must recognize that such violent consequences can be direct or indirect, and physical as well as economic, emotional, psychological, social, educational, or political. Such a model requires women's comprehensive participation in the consideration of the consequences of the specific rules and practices. Indeed, in order to ensure that this model is truly inclusive, women must participate in the drafting process. In addition, the drafter must ask women if the proposal has an impact on their real lives. Indeed, women must participate in the process as both inquirers and inquired. The only effective way to eradicate violence against women is to understand its overt and subtle forms by deconstructing its causes and manifestations so that violence can be detected at the outset.

In looking at violence, we must expand our view from guns and fists to jobs and dignity. We need to ask those at the bottom of the economic ladder, the educational ladder, the health ladder and at the margins of the cultural borders what their needs are and how such needs can best be met. We must ask those who are not represented what their needs are. We must give a voice and render visible those who are unseen and unheard. We need to give the vote to those who have been denied access to the ballot box, and we must give dignity to the second sex—women of all races, colors, religions, sexualities, languages, national origins, and classes. A re/constructed paradigm must ask the necessary questions to bring those at the margins to the center of human rights talk. All this can be achieved through a re/conceptualization of violence that truly recognizes the needs of women around the world.

Notes and Questions

1. In the words of the old refrain, a woman's work is never done. What is different about a Latina's work?

2. Does our society glorify stay-at-home caretaking for women, or professional on-the-job success? Both? How does this play out for many Latinas?

3. Is religion a liberating or subordinating force in many Latinas' lives?

4. Why would a Latina, troubled by role conflicts, consider suicide? Have you ever done so, and if so, why?

5. How should feminists in one culture view a practice—wearing veils, genital cutting, rejecting of all abortions—that women in another culture seem to willingly embrace? Is women's liberation a universal value, or is it meaningful only within a given culture? See Antoinette Sedillo Lopez, *A Comparative Analysis of Women's Issues: Toward a Contextualized Methodology*, 10 Hast. Women's L.J. 347 (1999) (leaning toward the latter view).

SECTION 8.   WEALTH AND EARNING A LIVING

Workplace struggles, covered elsewhere in this volume, take on an additional dimension when one adds gender to the mix. The same is true for issues of land tenure. The following two selections illustrate a sampling of some of these issues.

Guadalupe T. Luna
"This Land Belongs to Me:" Chicanas, Land Grant Adjudication, and the Treaty of Guadalupe Hidalgo
3 Harv. Latino L. Rev. 115, 116, 118–22, 127–40 (1999)

MEXICANA AND CHICANA LINKAGES

During the negotiation of the Treaty of Guadalupe Hidalgo, the Mexican negotiators expressed concerns regarding the rights of landholders in the annexed territories. However, American negotiators dismissed such concerns. * * * Despite this dismissal, the fears of the Mexican negotiators that the property rights of the annexed Mexican land grantees would be abused would soon be confirmed. In fact, the ramifications of such abuses have continued to the present.

* * *

Following the war between the United States and Mexico, women in the annexed territories confronted a new legal regime. * * * While ancient Spanish law and Mexican civil law recognized the legal right of women to own and control property independent of patriarchal relationships, American common law significantly limited the property rights of women. Under the Mexican legal system, women owned and operated rural enterprises of varying sizes. * * * After the conquest, the Treaty of Guadalupe Hidalgo obligated the United States to protect the property interests of landholders residing in the annexed territories. Yet under American rule, Chicanas faced a legal system that, in contrast to the Mexican system, altered their legal identity by treating them as the property of their fathers, husbands, or brothers, relegating them to domestic roles and disregarding their legal identity as women. From the very beginning, they confronted threats to their status as landholders. The United States required the women, along with all other Mexican grantees, to present their claims of land ownership and to defend their validity.

* * * Secretary of State James Buchanan informed the grantees, that the "blessings" of Anglo–American law and institutions would protect their property and liberty interests. * * * Yet, *Mexicana* landholders were dispossessed of their property interests within a few years. In essence, the loss of their property reverted these woman back into the position of foreigners, so that Chicanas of the time, though promised protection, were instead excluded from enjoying the basic legal norms and fundamental rights that Buchanan invoked.

* * * The legal and historical record shows Chicanas facing legal rulings that created a new legal culture and hindered their full assimilation as equal participants into the new American culture and legal system. The imposed transformation altered their cultural and legal identity with far reaching consequences, including practically wiping out rural land ownership for contemporary Chicanas.

* * *

Spanish and Mexican Land Acquisition Law

Studying the stories of women who defended their property interests after the U.S. war with Mexico as part of the nation's legal history permits an examination of the impact that American property and land use laws had on *Mexicanas* and continue to have on Chicanas today. Such an examination further illustrates the profound impact of the conquest on the legal, social, economic, and political identity of the *Mexicana*.

Spanish Law and Women

* * *

During the Spanish period, women settlers were critical to Spain's colonization efforts in several ways, including helping to "establish and propagate civilization." Accordingly, as early as 1775, twenty-nine wives were included among the soldiers and settlers on an expedition into California. Before distribution of mission lands to settlers in the 1830s following Mexico's independence from Spain, colonial women played a central role in the mission economy. Missions were highly successful economic enterprises that produced a wide range of products, and engaged in domestic and foreign trade. Women were essential to the growth and care of missions as seamstresses, key keepers, storehouse managers, and housekeepers. * * *

Women and Mexican Law

After Mexico gained its independence from Spain, in 1821, Mexican civil law also recognized the legal identity of women outside of patriarchal relationships. Accordingly, the Republic of Mexico recognized the right of women to petition for land grants in its northernmost public domain. Women also worked on homesteads, headed families, worked as artisans, and, as in the Spanish period, served as "civilizing agents." Historians report that women headed more than 13% of Los Angeles households in 1844. In California, moreover, over sixty-six women received land grants. Because of their relationship to the land, these women had "greater privileges, benefiting from the land politics that enabled a significant number of them ... to own land and preside over the family economy on the ranchos."

* * *

Colonization Procedures in the Northern Provinces

Mexican colonization laws invited settlement in the Republic's northern territories, granting land in consideration for a purchase price, the escorting of friars, or military service. * * * Through a written petition, proposed grantees identified the quantity and location of the land they requested and consulted the district prefect or other local office. * * * Upon receipt of the *expediente*, the governor then advised the departmental assembly whether or not to recognize the award. The departmental assembly subsequently forwarded the package to the interior of Mexico. Finally, the grantee took legal possession of the land. * * *

Women were among the many that petitioned the Republic of Mexico for property. In one petition, for example, Romona Sanchez "represented herself as a *'desamparada mujer,'* an unprotected woman, who asked for the land, as *'un sitio valdio aproposito pa contener en el su ganado y hacer algunos labores pa subvenir a la mantencion de su familia'*, 'a vacant place, adapted to keep my cattle and carry on some husbandry for the maintenance of my family.'"

While the size of estates varied, several women owned substantial holdings that permitted them "self-reliance and more independence." * * * The sizeable holdings that women obtained from the Mexican Republic more than hints at the significance of Mexican women in developing and maintaining rural enterprises during this time period.

Inheritances

Whether by parental bequests or through marriages, inheritances also resulted in women's acquisition of property. For example, Maria Francesca Miranda's marriage to Don Antonio Ortega permitted her to recognize her pre-existing right to own property under Spanish and

Mexican law. In New Mexico, Bartolome Baca's will demonstrated a woman's pre-existing right to property ownership by declaring his wife as his sole executrix. Under community property law, the estate guaranteed his wife, Dona Maria de la Luz Chaves, a house with seventeen rooms, a chapel, a store, and numerous tracts throughout the region encompassing houses and various rural enterprises. While perhaps less striking than direct land grants, these cases demonstrate that *Mexicanas* were, under the Mexican system, granted the right to own real property.

Marriage Alliances

By the law of 1824, "foreigners were not only permitted but invited to settle as colonists on the vacant lands of the Mexican Republic." As long as foreign nationals declared loyalty to Mexico and met other stipulations required under its colonization laws, Mexico recognized their ownership status. In numerous instances, foreign nationals accordingly settled throughout the provinces and married *Mexicanas*. * * *

From the beginning, marriages with *Mexicanas* permitted foreign nationals to leverage and accumulate massive wealth, as a result of their closely knit kinship groups. The *Mexicanas* who married Anglo–Americans brought their husbands the full range of social class and status group benefits. Furthermore, marriage permitted the men to acquire greater amounts of land than individuals under the Republic's land grant laws. * * *

Aside from the obvious benefits to men, marriage also involved various forms of discrimination. * * * "Whether the Anglo married for love or security, he only expeditiously accepted his wife's culture, religion, and relatives." Professor Antonia Castaneda, moreover, contends that stereotypes of *Mexicanas* expedited land losses through their marriages with foreign nationals. *Mexicanas*, she asserts, were "defined both as women of easy virtue and inferiority," with a contrasting stereotype casting them as pure and good.

In a few instances, intermarriage also benefited the Mexican wives, though these benefits should not be overstated considering the costs of such alliances. Despite negative ramifications, marriages with foreign nationals sometimes permitted the women to hold onto their property. As an illustration, *United States v. Cazares* reports that James Dawson received a grant he entitled La Punta del Estero del Americano, on December 27, 1837.[85] On his land, Dawson built a house and "planted a large vineyard and an orchard with more than two hundred fruit trees, and had placed upon it cattle, horses. . . ." In a later litigation dispute, the court recognized that Dawson's widow "sufficiently proved the right of her deceased husband to petition for the land which she then occupied" and confirmed the widow's claim to the property. In this instance, her status as the wife of a foreign national ultimately protected her interest, particularly since her opponent was a Mexican male.

---

85. 25 F. Cas. 352 (N.D. Cal. 1855) (No. 14, 761).

Terms and Conditions of Land Grant Awards

Whatever the method of grant awards, once grantees received their award, they could neither alienate nor transfer their property without the consent of the Mexican government. * * * The land grant process created a contractual relationship between the Mexican Republic and grantees in which the parties mutually agreed to act under Mexican law. As long as grantees followed the dictates of the Republic's colonization laws, they were guaranteed property within Mexico's public domain.

* * *

The Treaty of Guadalupe Hidalgo

The Treaty of Guadalupe Hidalgo contractually obligated the United States to protect the country's newly acquired citizens. The Treaty provides in relevant part:

> In the name of Almighty God ... The United States of America, and the United Mexican States, animated by a sincere desire to put an end to the calamities of the war which unhappily exists between the two Republics, and to establish upon a solid basis relations of peace and friendship, which shall confer reciprocal benefits upon the citizens of both, and assure the concord, harmony and mutual confidence, wherein the two peoples should live, as good neighbors....[94]

In its "sincere desire" to terminate the "calamities of war," the Treaty of Guadalupe Hidalgo sought peace between the two nations. It also preserved the property rights of those residing in the annexed territories as they existed before the conquest.

Effective on July 4, 1848, the Treaty extended citizenship status to those persons remaining in the annexed territories, thereby further obligating the United States to protect and respect the property interests of the Mexican grantees. Accordingly, constitutional principles protected the grantees as any other citizen in the American Republic. However, over Mexico's objections, the United States deleted Article X from the Treaty before its final ratification. This article would have protected grantees who had yet to finish performing all conditions attached to their awards. Rather than permit grantees time to fulfill their contractual agreements with Mexico, U.S. negotiators lobbied against the provision, and the proposed Article X ultimately yielded to its critics. To alleviate Mexico's fears as to the impact of its deletion on affected land grantees, Congress responded with a Statement of Protocol on May 26, 1848:

> The American government by suppressing the Xth article of the Treaty ... did not in any way intend to annul the grants of lands made by Mexico in the ceded territories. These grants ... preserve

94. Treaty of Peace, Friendship, Limits, and Settlement with the United States of America and the Republic of Mexico, Treaty of Guadalupe Hidalgo, Feb. 2, 1848, U.S.-Mex., 9 Stat. 922.

the legal value which they may possess and the grantees may cause their legitimate [titles] to be acknowledged before the American tribunals.

Notwithstanding American proclamations regarding the legal rights of grantees, Congress promulgated various land acts with immediate consequences for grantees. The most important of these shifted onto land grantees the burden of demonstrating the validity of their claims of ownership. If unable to demonstrate the validity of a claim, the land grantee would be forced to yield his or her property interests to the public domain.

Elvia R. Arriola

Voices From the Barbed Wires of Despair: Women in the Maquiladoras, Latina Critical Legal Theory, and Gender at the U.S.-Mexico Border
49 DePaul L. Rev. 729, 755, 761–62, 764–68,
770–79, 782–85, 788–90, 792–93 (2000)

The problems at the U.S.-Mexico border that have expanded under NAFTA can be understood by looking closely at the maquiladoras for their impact on women's lives. * * * Examining how women from the interior of Mexico are affected by their jobs in maquiladoras provides a lens from which to appreciate the human rights and/or environmental concerns that have been raised about the maquiladoras in recent years. The gendered lens is especially useful because the opportunity to work in a maquiladora serves as a main attraction for poor Mexicans to migrate to the border.

* * *

The Maquiladoras: Licensed to Exploit, Profit, and Oppress

It is not difficult to pick out the setting of a maquiladora in a Mexican border city. Their physical infrastructure broadcasts power: state-of-the-art manufacturing, assembly and packing plants, modern industrial parks, huge truck parking facilities, powerful electric lights, massive water tanks, and in some, beautifully landscaped exteriors. The maquiladora zone is served by large highways, railroad tracks, and trucking terminals. Small airports serve trafficking between sister cities' twin plants. Guards and officials, who watch day, night, and weekends, police warehouses and assembly buildings surrounded by tall chain link fences. The atmosphere communicates efficiency and the import and export movement runs as smoothly as possible. The loud sounds of machinery can be heard from a few buildings even late on a Saturday, giving the impression of a twenty-four hour operation. Across the street, in contrast, stand rows and rows of tiny shacks mixed in with the occasional string of company houses on unpaved streets. Some of the shacks in the colonias are made of tar paper, cast off pieces of industrial waste, cement blocks, and cardboard. The nicer company houses are brightly painted, but all are hovels in comparison to the wealth and power that emanates from the small industrial city of maquiladoras.

As of April 1999, 4,235 maquiladoras were operating in Mexico. These industries were initiated as part of the Border Industrialization Program, a bi-lateral predecessor to NAFTA negotiated between Mexico and the United States in 1965. Their name derives from maquila that once referred to the miller's practice of keeping a portion of the grain as a form of payment. Today, the term maquiladora refers to the factories on Mexican soil that assemble raw material components of foreign-owned enterprises. Generally, maquiladoras share the following characteristics:

(1) being American subsidiaries or contract affiliates under Mexican or foreign ownership;

(2) principally engaged in the assembly of components (e.g., radio cassettes, television, small appliances), the processing of primary materials or the production of intermediate or final products;

(3) that import most or all primary materials and components from American plants and re-export them to the United States; and that

(4) are labor intensive.

* * *

Business merchants of the new "transnational capitalist class" have only praise for this booming industry whose draw to foreign investors is primarily the lowered production costs, i.e., the ability to pay workers in a devalued Mexican currency. * * * Management firms tout the benefits as (1) saving money by performing labor intensive manufacturing and repair operations; (2) enjoying the benefits of NAFTA for exports back into the United States and Canada; and (3) offering an attractive environment for manufacturing and repair operations.

Maquiladoras * * * employ over 1,000,000 workers in the borderlands alone, a trend which is only moving towards greater and faster development. Critics of the increased expansion argue that the impact of the maquiladora system on the workers is a very high price for modernization in Mexico. Indeed, to other critics the term maquis is a nickname for sweatshop, the "graveyard of American union labor,"[158] or a labor policy that ties women to the "bonds of patriarchy and capitalist exploitation."[159]

158. See Luis Alberto Urrea, *By the Lake of Sleeping Children: The Secret Life of the Mexican Border* 25 (1996).

159. Michelle Haberland, Abstract, Heading South: A Gendered Vision of the U.S. Textile and Garment Industries' Move to Mexico (visited Feb. 16, 2000), http:// www.lanic.utexas.edu/ project/labor95/haberland.html (criticizing a myopic view of maquiladoras women by United States labor as being only victims rather than workers with organizing consciousness whose issues must be addressed through the lenses of patriarchy and capitalism).

OPPRESSION ON THE BASIS OF GENDER

* * *

The maquiladora industry may be the late twentieth century's hallmark of an exploitive transnational capitalist system of production, trade economics, and employment whose success depends on the use and abuse of a highly feminized workforce which, in contrast to the sophisticated business elite that invests in maquiladoras, is poor, young, and uneducated. A typical maquiladora's population of workers is unlikely to benefit in any long lasting way from the experience of working for one of the thousands of bi-national or multinational factories currently supported under NAFTA and prior trade agreements between the United States and Mexico or other Japanese and European corporations. Because of the fragmentation of the production process, the work can be done rapidly, efficiently, and by individuals who have no skills prior to employment. The result is a system that offers little transferability of on-the-job skills and the ability to recruit an abundant labor force that, until recent decades, was largely excluded from the Mexican labor economy and that has traditionally been cheaper to employ than men.
* * *

Wages

* * *

The literature to the potential maquiladora investor makes clear that "reduced labor cost has always been an incentive for foreign companies to establish maquiladora operations in Mexico ... [and] wages for maquiladora laborers are often less than $1 an hour,"[167] an amount drastically lower than the minimum wages such an employer would have to pay under the United States labor laws. * * * A labor report guiding the future corporate investor notes that while nominal wages in Mexico have risen in recent years, the gains have been fully absorbed by inflation, and that for the maquiladora investor any increases in wages are offset by the devaluation of the peso with respect to foreign currencies.

* * *

* * * It is clear that the roughly 56% employment rate of women in the Mexican maquila is significantly higher than their 37% representation in the labor force, and their average wage of four dollars per day are key to NAFTA's success in turning Mexico into a manufacturing "export platform" of export products. * * * The job category statistics are also gendered. Women make up a higher percentage of the clothing and electronics industry while men make up the typical worker in the auto parts industry. Throughout Mexico the wage differential on the basis of gender always benefits men, with certain job categories showing an overall wage as high as 20%, 33%, and even 48% higher than women's

167. Frequently Asked Questions (FAQs) and Answers About Maquiladoras (visited Sept. 15, 1999), http://www. latinobeat.net/MexicoFAQ/html/mexfaq maq.htm.

wages. * * * In 1981, a maquiladora manager in Ciudad Juarez said, "Women have natural qualities that make them ideal for these positions. Their delicate hands endow them with finesse and precision. Moreover, the female psyche more easily endures the repetitive work."[178]

* * * The more than 50% per hour wage difference between male and female workers is a reflection of the "cheaper" wage for women produced by their doing "what is natural" to their "delicate fingers."

* * *

Terms of Employment

* * *

* * * The low pay is accompanied by job rankings, production quotas, and the longer "average" working hours. A recent study of the maquiladoras in Ciudad Juarez discovered as many as sixteen performance level categories, each having another fifteen to eighteen internal grades that were imposed on the workers. The study noted that such a system kept the "workers ... so busy competing with each other that they do not have the opportunity to organize collectively against management." Of course, "promotion" is illusory since the hierarchy of categories is primarily designed to bureaucratize the production process and to give management a better means of controlling the workers. Every step of the process includes an evaluation of "how much" a worker is producing. The more and the faster, the better, although "better" never translates into more money.

Job Rankings and Surveillance

* * *

* * * One way of assuring high productivity is to put the workers in teams or groups where all individuals perform the same task. The idea, described by one manager, is to have the workers "motivate one another to keep pace and work harder." * * * Also tied to the performance grading is the expectation that a worker should strive for the highest level of attendance or risk the stiff penalties resulting from absences.

* * *

Another plant manager confirmed the rigidity of such shop rules when he stated that "failure to show up for work amounts to a forfeiture of their privilege to work for us." * * *

* * *

Quotas: Driving the Worker to Produce More, More, and Even Faster

Management in the maquiladoras is fully aware of the benefits gained from being able to press the workers into higher and higher production levels, or as one manager put it being able to "double

178. Norma Iglesias Prieto, *Beautiful Flowers of the Maquiladora: Life Histories* *of Women Workers in Tijuana* 29 (Michael Stone & Gabrielle Winkler trans., 1997).

production every six weeks." It has to do with the absence of unionism. As this same manager put it, "we have a virtual haven for productivity, free of [collective] bargaining fetters. This is so much easier than in the U.S."

The quota system of production is the essence of job security for the maquiladora worker. The worker who does not demonstrate a consistent pattern of improvement in output risks losing her job because she never advances on the multiple performance grades and she could never dream of rewards or promotions: "What is important to them is meeting the quota. Yesterday a number of muchachas had to work from four in the afternoon until two in the morning."

In some factories the "piece work" system assures high levels of productivity. "Alma," who worked in a Tijuana maquiladora, described the system's impact:

> I had been working for six years in a textile maquiladora, where I nearly destroyed my kidneys and my eyes. I never earned a fixed salary. They paid me by the job, on a piecework basis, as they also call it. . . . You get used to it all, or at least we pretend to. At times we let ourselves be carried away by the noise or the music of the radios we all carry. It helps us forget the fatigue and the back pain we all have from working in front of the sewing machine. The moment came when I just couldn't take it any more and I quit, . . . I knew we were in for some hard times, but I never knew just how much. [Because of the currency devaluations] everything is priced out of sight, and I have to hustle to find another job, because every day things just get worse.
>
> —Alma, a maquiladora worker.

    * * *

The production level in actual numbers is dizzying and attests to the dehumanizing function of the assembly line as it breaks down tasks into smaller and smaller components effectively designed to turn the worker into another cog in the wheel of production. * * * Fast work by some workers can generate internal group conflict over productivity and get all workers in trouble with management:

> But then there were workers who had a fast pace, finishing with one half hour to spare. They wanted to rest so I can't really blame them. But you have to do it more carefully. In this case, the supervisor saw that these girls could finish faster. So, she personally raised the standard! To 410! She said we all had to do 410 per hour, which is ridiculous. We agreed among ourselves not to meet the standard . . . The managers got very angry . . . and reassigned us, breaking up the group.
>
> —Veronica Rivera, a maquiladora worker.

Average Workdays, Excellence, and Patronizing Responses

The maquiladoras thrive on the structure of a work week designed to produce the highest levels of output. While in the United States the average work week is thirty-eight to forty hours, in the maquiladoras the average is five to ten hours longer. * * * While overtime in the United States usually means a higher rate of pay, the only purpose of working beyond the average nine-hour workday in a maquiladora is to catch up on unmet quota standards. * * *

* * *

Workers who invent new and better methods of increasing production maintain high levels of productivity. They are never rewarded in any significant way, such as a wage increase, to reflect their talents or contributions to the company. Instead, managers typically display sexism and/or racism in their attitudes towards the Mexican worker whose labor is either inventive, reliable, or trustworthy. * * * Some plant managers would probably deny that their ways of "appreciating" the hard labor and talents of a Mexican worker who overcomes mechanical difficulties to meet the company's production demands are profoundly racist:

> That's one thing I like about Mexicans, they have pride; they don't want to be considered second-rate or third-rate. They want to be first so they put out for us.... The wire-stripping machines have a lot of downtime. I have this one Mexican boy ... He works in another building by himself on this machine that in the U.S. is always breaking down, it always has quality-control problems. There he is with his stereo headphones on listening to I guess Mexican disco or whatever. He's so ignorant, he thinks he's supposed to run the machine all day long. You'd never find someone like that in the States.
>
> —Unnamed Ciudad Juarez plant manager.

* * * The abundance of needy people looking for work at the border makes it easy for companies to absorb any turnover from frustrated and exhausted workers quitting their job. * * * Thus industry-wide practices designed to manipulate the workers' fears of losing their jobs becomes another aspect of the systemic abuse designed to maximize production and profits. One example is the use of threatened or contrived layoffs, together with intentional exploitation of the same skills. "I don't want him to get civilized. You hit them with pride. Mexicans are very prideful people. You may drop a subtle hint. You may hint that they are doing an inferior job. They'll get mad as hell and do a better job."

* * *

Gender at Work

The maquiladora industry is profoundly sexist. * * *

* * *

They hire women because men created more problems for them. We women are more easily managed. The bosses just have to express their concerns about production and we women, fools that we are, work even harder to protect their profits while we ourselves are dying of hunger.... [A] male worker wouldn't stand for it—he's more aggressive. Men organize themselves, and if they don't get what they want, they walk off the job, ... That's why they pull in any young girl to work. They train them and pay them the minimum wage if they can. The owners well understand this; they don't hire men because the maquildoras would not be as productive.

—Angela, a maquiladora worker.

Mexican Patriarchy, American Racism and Labor Division in the Maquiladoras

* * *

Given their traditional values, Mexican women have had little access to the experience of earning wages. Of course, similar to the history of women's labor in this country, that statement mostly pertains to the experiences of middle-class women. Like the United States, Mexico has its own longer history of peasant women working alongside their husbands in the fields, or of working-class mestizas earning a pittance of wages in the industrializing textile and tobacco factories in the nineteenth century. * * *

* * *

Plant managers who truly believe they are doing "good for Mexico" would apparently deny the charge of female exploitation since the Mexicana worker has been socially constructed into someone who is ignorant, has no skills, and can barely take orders without complaining. The belief system produces further sexualized racist attitudes about her, a young Mexican woman who, if not "saved" by maquiladora work, would choose more debasing work:

I mean, these girls don't have a lot of other options: stay at home, sell trinkets or candies on the street, work at a sewing factory, or, worst of all, prostitution.... The way I figure, these plants are good for Mexico because they ... offer the young women a chance to be something better. At Electro–Fixtures we have a slogan: "Working hard for EF is working hard for self-improvement."

—Unnamed Ciudad Juarez plant manager.

Choices about whom to employ and how to treat them are infused with gendered attitudes in the maquiladoras. Gender ideology is premised upon the division between male and female bodies and a culture's perceived differences in women's and men's talents and abilities based on these physical aspects. Researchers of the industry who have interrogated the workers and their employers note how young women are preferred for tasks that are delicate and monotonous, work assignments that draw directly upon the blatant stereotypes of a woman's physical form and her natural talents or her perceived demeanor—as docile, submissive, patient, and reserved. An image of the ideal maquiladora worker is created by a confluence of the historical fact of her dependency, cultural gender roles, and the sexually racist beliefs that these women are best suited for repetitive, tedious, and mindless work, while men should do the work requiring action, reason, endurance, and leadership. Gender attitudes further influence the manager's view of whether or not women can be promoted into positions of authority:

> It's just too much trouble. I can move women up a notch or two—you know, from operator to group chief and maybe even quality-control inspection. But, if I was to promote women into higher supervisory levels, well, the men, the Mexican males, would be terribly upset. I'm not against the idea of women doing that type of work, but my first duty is to maintain order in the plant. The attitude of the men here, let me just say that it does not give me a lot of room to move in.
>
> —Unnamed Ciudad Juarez plant manager.

* * *

Female Sexuality and Women's Bodies in the Maquiladoras: Sexual Harassment and Pregnancy Testing as Forms of Social Control

> Every day the girls go to work more and more decked out, and no sooner do we complain about something we don't like than the bosses tell us, "Arguing is not ladylike; if you get angry it makes you unattractive, and then we won't be fond of you."
>
> —Marta, a maquiladora worker.

* * *

Sexual Harassment

* * *

> The manager had his pets. In the beginning there was just one, then there were more. We all knew it because we all saw it happening. His pet was an operator, then after a while she became a supervisor. This happens a lot in the factories, but it depends on the woman.
>
> —Marta, a maquiladora worker.

One woman eventually quit from the pressure she felt from being sexually harassed by a supervisor and then being ignored in her complaints about the conduct by the personnel manager:

> I told him that I already had a friend and that I wasn't interested in a relationship with him.... He kept insisting and he became much more aggressive about it.... He started fondling me, at first making it look like it was an accident, you know, brushing his hand across my breasts. Then he started grabbing me from behind ... one time I almost cut my fingers on the belt, he startled me so. Finally, one night as I was leaving the plant ... he grabbed me in the parking lot and kissed me. He said something like, "If you don't give it to me I'll make sure you never work in Juarez again."

—Chela Delgado, former group chief at an electronics assembly plant.

Pregnancy Discrimination

Maquiladora owners also repress female sexuality. Because maintaining production levels is a key feature of the industry, the pregnant worker is seen as a threat to the business. Thus pregnancy-based sex discrimination throughout the industry is a virtual norm. Being able to keep one's job while pregnant is wholly dependent on being seen as a "good worker." A former line supervisor for a maquiladora in Tijuana explained that

> women workers received pregnancy tests. An infirmary always gave pregnancy tests because they wanted to make sure workers would work for at least a year.... Workers who became pregnant would have their probationary contracts "cut" after the first one or two months. The company would use the pretext that the workers were "bad elements," or say they had bad work records. The truth is that companies discriminate against pregnant workers because of the potential or expected loss of production, not because of the cost of maternity leave, as some companies argue.

* * *

From a policy perspective it is amazing that American employers, once they don the identity of the "transnational corporate producer," can so easily and brazenly practice what in this country is prohibited by the Pregnancy Discrimination Act of 1978. But transnational corporate investors justify the various methods used to screen for pre-employment pregnancy by stating that to end it would mean "exposing itself to substantial financial liabilities in the social security system for maternity benefits."

* * *

THE WORKING ENVIRONMENT OF A MAQUILADORA: HEALTH AND
SAFETY RISKS AS A TERM OR CONDITION OF EMPLOYMENT

* * *

The Hazards for Employees

Researchers have discovered that chemical production engages the highest level of risk for industrial accidents as compared to furniture making, metal fabrication, or non-electrical assembly. The most common risk factors generally include contact with actual instruments of production, physical plant conditions, and psychosocial conditions. * * *

> That work with acids is very exacting and dangerous, because if you don't mix the chemicals properly they can explode. Despite the hazardous nature of the work, and the fact that you must be specially trained to do it, they pay the same as for any other job, and they fail to recognize its critical importance.... One time there was an explosion and two co-workers were burned. * * * One of the

safety measures that we did have was goggles, but we rarely used them because they made us so hot, as the room has no ventilation.

—Gabriela, a former maquiladora worker.

Another major complaint of workers is the lack of adequate warnings for workers who might be exposed to toxic chemicals and substances. Julia Gonzalez complained that the maquiladoras "never translate chemical warning labels into Spanish."

* * *

The Environmental Impact of Maquiladora Activity in the Border Region

* * *

The intensity of maquila work, its repetitiveness and speed, make it highly dangerous to workers' health. Stress may also add risk to a worker's basic health or alertness for avoiding accidents on the job. * * * Workers fear losing their jobs, know that sexual harassment and monitoring of their sexual lives is just a part of the job, and are constantly being pressured to meet arbitrary production quotas. Of course, it is very difficult to establish a direct causal link between what the maquilas do and workers' health. It is even more difficult to create a causal link between the entire industry and the patterns it displays of sexist racism to the broader claims of environmental degradation at the border.

* * * Several factors also support the charge that the industry's disregard for basic occupational health and safety standards in the workplace is just an indicator of the maquiladoras' further disregard for the environmental consequences of their transnational activities. Those factors include the massive maquila expansion in the eighties, the increased migration to a region that has a fragile ecology and was never prepared for the fast development of an urban infrastructure, the public controversies, like the outbreak of anencephaly among dozens of borderland children in the Matamoros–Brownsville area, and the allegation that certain maquiladoras' disposal waste practices were responsible. Collectively, and against the backdrop of worker treatment, such factors have put the Mexican government in the environmental spotlight in recent years for its neglect of the border region.

While better policies have been issued in recent years by the Mexican government, and environmental groups are a constant feature at the border, the reputation that environmentalism is not a high priority to the Mexican government remains firm. The officials' inconsistent behavior does not help get rid of the reputation. In 1995, three hundred more maquiladoras were licensed at the border. In that same year, the Mexican government eliminated the regulations that required detailed environmental impact statements. In a survey among United States maquiladora investors in Tijuana, Mexico, 10% stated that a key reason for leaving the United States were the environmental laws, while 17% considered it an important factor. * * *

Notes and Questions

1. According to Professor Luna, how did Mexican women lose their former lands in the period after the war with Mexico?

2. In the view of Professor Arriola, what is wrong with maquiladoras, if the women who work there choose to do so because "it is the best game in town"? On extreme poverty on the U.S. side of the border, see Jane E. Larson, *Free Markets Deep in the Heart of Texas*, 84 Geo. L.J. 179 (1995).

3. The common view of Latinas is that of the stay-at-home Mom. How true is that?

4. Is international law an effective remedy for women's oppression? See Celina Romany, *Women as Aliens: A Feminist Critique of the Public/Private Distinction in International Human Rights Law*, 6 Harv. Hum. Rts. J. 87 (1993).

*

Part Nine

REBELLIOUS LAWYERING

At times, Latina or Anglo attorneys have taken the lead in the struggle for justice. At other times, lay people or lay lawyers have taken up the cause, researching the law, publicizing abuses, and setting the stage for struggle or litigation. At still other times, the storytelling tradition takes a legal dispute or injustice as its subject, singing or telling about it so that its memory lives on. At still other times, ordinary citizens break the law "on principle," inviting, as Martin Luther King did in his campaign of civil disobedience, official retribution. All of these roles could be considered part of what one author calls "rebellious lawyering."

SECTION 1. CONCEPTS OF REBELLIOUS LAWYERING

Gerald P. López
The Idea of a Constitution in the Chicano Tradition
37 J. Legal Educ. 162, 162–66 (1987)

I have lived and worked in various cities and on both coasts. But in some ways (and perhaps even against my will) L.A. is still home—the place where I was born and raised, and the place where my mother, sister, brother, and most of my extended family still live. What I now think about the world around me, not surprisingly, first came to life in the Chicano part of this city, East L.A. In my early East L.A. days, religion meant Catholic, fantasy meant cruising in your own car, glamour meant an ethnicized variation in some Hollywood theme, and fish meant Friday. No less important for a sports-crazy boy, baseball meant Koufax, and basketball meant Baylor and West and, yes, wanting desperately to beat the Celtics for the world championship. * * *

Two memories frame what a constitution meant for me in the tradition of East L.A. life. In one, I am four years old and in a car with my father and mother, canvassing the streets of East L.A., posting flyers on telephone poles. The flyers, in Spanish and English, urge everyone to vote for our candidate in an upcoming election. Like most Chicanos then and now, my parents were Democrats; the candidate was a Republican, the only one I was ever to see my family support. Even at four having to tell the world that "our candidate is a Republican" felt oxymoronic. But with his extraordinary dircctness, my father explained this switch in allegiance: he told me simply that the candidate would fight—fight both for what Chicanos were and for what we wanted.

In the other memory, I am with my family and thousands of other Chicanos in a park in East L.A. Fireworks, music, speeches, *gritos*, costumes, food and drink abound. Somehow these rituals, in all their ornamental and hyperbolic detail, expressed for me even at nine the collective pride I had come to anticipate and to savor on these patriotic occasions. After all, we were celebrating Cinco de Mayo in the park that day, and in remembering Mexico's small military victory over the French at Puebla, we were observing a moment that had come to signify something spiritually constitutive in the history of our people. My mom and dad even took time off from work—the highest tribute.

These memories obliquely yet accurately portray the idea of a constitution, not only in my early East L.A. days but, I think, in the Chicano tradition of living in this country. My father's reason, his *constitutional* reason, for backing a Republican candidate echoed a more general understanding in our community. Constitutions result from fighting. They establish social arrangements that express both in their original detail and in their ongoing adjustments what fighting continues to be about—not just in elections but in day-to-day living.

If ever you doubt this fighting, take a look through my eyes at the wear and tear on people like my relatives and friends here in East L.A., the homely heroes we Chicanos celebrate in our stories, ballads, and murals. Some of these people have been here for generations, anchored in our habits and ideas, learning from and teaching their grandparents and parents, their children and grandchildren what it means to be self-reliant as a people. Others only recently have arrived, undocumented and "unwanted," except of course to bus our tables, stitch together our clothes, harvest our food, clean our bathrooms, and care for our children. Old-timers and newcomers alike survive only to the extent that they quickly learn to temper the daily fighting with considerable self-irony. Laughter helps counter the fury, desperation, and resignation induced by so many events and so many people. * * *

Yet as important as transforming these arrangements was and is in the Chicano tradition, the Constitution itself had no particularly privileged place in our life in East L.A. or, for that matter, in the Chicano tradition generally. We did celebrate the Fourth of July as well as Cinco de Mayo; the celebrations were not in any crude sense rival observances. But the Cinco somehow expressed who we were, whereas the Fourth and its symbolic siblings, the flag and the Constitution, somehow all heralded the tradition of those with whom we regularly fought. Indeed, the language of the Constitution, particularly then and even now, does not readily afford an explanation for what seem to be the daily realities in Chicano life. To that extent our experience and the Constitution daily marginalize one another, sometimes threaten entirely to abandon each other.

In order literally to survive (to live *in* our history and *through* our practices), we Chicanos in East L.A. and elsewhere nurtured a separate tradition, parallel to the "grand tradition" of constitutional life in this country. For years most of us lived this non-converging tradition, as did our ancestors, only vaguely aware of the resistance it offered to what others would have us become. Over the past three decades, however, living this tradition has itself become a deliberate strategy in our efforts to define, *constitutionally*, what one can most importantly do with one's life. We now acutely appreciate that our tradition, like every other, necessarily represents one argument in the national and historical debate about the meaning of "American destiny."

In Chicano tradition the idea of a constitution differs at its roots from what a constitution means to most people, particularly the fortunate. In the grand tradition most believe that through a constitution we can lift our public life above the fallen and compromised realm of factional politics. Like all faiths, this idea of a constitution embraces rival interpretive dogmas. Living within the grand tradition are strict textualists and loose supplementers, proponents and opponents of judicial activism, those who believe in the structural rebellion expressed through this nation's two reconstructions and those who are skeptical of it. But all engaged in this ideological debate remain within the grand tradition insofar as they share the belief that, at our best and as a people, we can, through a constitution, somehow transcend conflict and heal by rising above our nature.

For all that may be honorable in this grand idea of a constitution, it contradicts Chicano experience in this country. Constitutions have been prominent in our life not for their healing but primarily for the injuries they have permitted and inflicted—in the workplace, on the streets, in the home, and in the minds and hearts of many a struggling and bewildered Chicano. And, if anything, factional politics become more prominent when the stakes get higher, as they frequently do whenever a constitution enters any political conversation. In our experience, constitutional interpretations and constitutional decisions reflect the provisional containment of fighting, not its transcendence. As Chicanos see it, through a constitution we in this country publicly announce that "for the moment, there's no battle here," not always confident the words will create, much less reflect, the reality.

Whatever world Madison presupposed in condemning factions as corruptions of a unified, public-spirited citizenry, today's national community aspires to a simple unity by regularly requiring non-converging traditions like our own to betray themselves. Chicanos know well the not-so-subliminal refrain: Vacate your history, your culture, your relationship to work, love, and others, and join with us as one in America's constitutional tradition. We even hear again these days, not always indirectly, that to be fully public-spirited we would have to change the very way we talk. Most Chicanos, after all, express their experience of the constitution in terms other than doctrinal, and often even in terms other than popular newsspeak or civics-babble. In this sense, we participate in the traditional national faith only inarticulately, through accounts that many find uneducated and confused and treat as somehow not quite part of constitutional discourse. In the eyes of the grand tradition, Chicano accounts of constitutional experiences and ideas somehow lack the "larger-than-life" quality, the "more-all-embracing-than-factional" spirit that distinguishes constitutional talk worth having—in scholarly journals, in the Supreme Court, and in New England town meetings.

Yet that very same talk others find constitutionally inarticulate ironically confirms, if only partially, why living in their own non-converging tradition offers Chicanos more than just a comforting familiarity. For those of us in the Chicano tradition, reminding ourselves through our daily language that we are not somehow "larger than life" through a constitution can be emancipating. We fight about a life constitutionally worth leading, and we know it. We fight with you and among ourselves, in our kitchens and in the fields, and in the formal constitutional battles we are increasingly entering. Chicanos live a dramatic, and often heated, conversation about things that matter, mundane and monumental. Our tradition embodies the continuity of our conflicts, and draws on their wisdom even as we continue to move against things as they are. At our best, we express in our practices an idea of a constitution at once far more aggressively skeptical and far more romantic than the grand tradition accommodates: we refuse to accept that you need believe in transcendence or else give up entirely.

* * *

Returning to the streets of this city reminds me that, over the years, Chicanos have made alliances and even some occasional friendships, most notably with people living in other non-converging traditions—Asians, feminists, Blacks, Native Americans, other Latinos, and certain members of both the intellectual community and the white working class. Still other moments on these very same streets convince me that, in some ways, each of us continues to find the other's nostalgia faintly ridiculous. You think our spiritual attachment to Cinco de Mayo quaint and quixotic; we think your attachment to the idea of a constitution in the grand tradition self-deluding. The truces we live by, in this city and in this country, apparently can't always disguise or alter residual sentiment.

I do not pretend that the idea of a constitution in Chicano tradition is radically discontinuous with all elements of the grand tradition. Our tradition certainly shares with classical republican thought the somewhat blurry image of a self constituted through others and through its relation to work, and of people making a living while simultaneously battling in public life. But unlike the grand tradition, Chicano tradition fights hard not to accept as settled the present arrangement of institutions and ideas. To acquiesce in what people now live and think would be to abandon the very spirit in us that rebels against all that has degraded our ancestors and contemporaries, and all that works even now, in newly emerging forms, to subordinate our descendants.

We won't celebrate the constitution's bicentennial in the grand tradition, and we'll be better for it.

Michael A. Olivas
"Breaking the Law" on Principle:
An Essay on Lawyers' Dilemmas, Unpopular Causes,
and Legal Regimes
52 U. Pitt. L. Rev. 815, 815–18, 820–26, 832–34, 846–54 (1991)

Martha Minow * * * identifies three risks inherent in the lawyer-client relationship that occur when the client breaks the law to pursue social, political, or legal change: a risk of nonrepresentation, where no accomplished lawyer will take the case; a risk of terminated representation, when ethical requirements may jeopardize an unpopular client's defense; and a risk of truncated representation, where the lawyer's choice of tactics may undermine the very premise of the client's grievance.

Consider the first risk. When unpopular clients break the law, they may face a difficult time in securing representation. If the client is wealthy, however, he or she will be able to secure counsel, however reprehensible or unpopular the crime. Minow does not argue the ethical or constitutional reasons for representation of politically-motivated offenders; rather her concern is that for the system to work saboteurs [must be ready] to challenge legal complacency, which in turn necessitates lawyers willing to commit themselves. * * *

In the United States, this willingness to test the legal barriers is essential to change. * * * The classic example is that of Martin Luther King, Jr., held in jail in Birmingham, Alabama. * * * Reverend King's incarceration had great moral and symbolic significance for his political agenda of overturning racial apartheid, and played out on national television, demonstrating how unjust public laws were for blacks. This and similar incidents led to a series of changes in civil rights laws.

In the second scenario, principled would-be law-breakers divulge to their attorney that they intend to break a law. Do lawyers have a "Tarasoff" duty to warn (or withdraw)? Minow poses the question in an example she cites, where a client that would import and distribute RU–486, the "abortion pill" available in Europe, could well violate Food and Drug Administration (FDA) regulations and be held in criminal contempt. Her analysis concludes that the Model Code allows the company's attorneys the discretion to serve their client without disclosing the intended lawbreaking. * * * If consulted before the client violates the law, the lawyer may advise the client on the likely or probable consequences of their proposed actions. In so doing, however, Minow warns, legal representation itself risks furthering a fraudulent scheme or ongoing crime.

Minow's third risk is a variation of T. S. Eliot's *Murder in the Cathedral*, doing what may be the right thing for the wrong reasons. This is a paradox of compelling stature, where a client's principles may preclude a defense that could minimize the very real personal harm that the client's conviction would cause. * * * [For example, the] famous civil rights litigator, William Kunstler, filed a suit against prosecutors and public officials in North Carolina, alleging harassment of Native Americans during a criminal investigation. He and his co-counsel held a press conference to draw public attention to the alleged harassment. The prosecutors sought sanctions alleging that Kunstler had filed the suit "for publicity, to embarrass state and county officials, to use as leverage in criminal proceedings, to obtain discovery for use in criminal proceedings, and to intimidate those involved in the prosecution of [the Indian activists]." Kunstler vowed, "I'm not going to pay any fine. I'm going to rot in jail if that's what I have to do to dramatize this thing." The same court also upheld Rule 11 sanctions against Julius Chambers, Director of the NAACP Legal Defense Fund (LDF), for charges stemming from an employment discrimination case brought by the LDF against the U.S. Army. The court reduced the $85,000 fine but upheld the sanctions, holding that the attorneys had not met their "responsibility to explore the factual bases for the clients' suits ... instead charging forward with the litigation in disregard of its manifest lack of merit." * * *

[For Minow], these three types of dilemma pose "genuine dangers," particularly if our system is not supple enough to consider principled claims or to accommodate pluralistic approaches to the law. * * * She urges an expanded role for "legal process" courses so that students learn "the historic traditions of lawyers defending people who break the law for political reasons." * * * Consider three further examples:

Case 1: The Case of Unaccompanied Refugee Children: Legal Clinics and the Risk of Cooptation

* * *

Thousands of unaccompanied children who have felt the violence in their Central American countries are being detained in refugee camps in the United States, most in shameful conditions without access to basic necessities of education, health care, or legal services. Because immigration procedures, including deportation, are considered civil rather than criminal proceedings, little process is due these alien children under the Constitution. Immigration law requires extraordinary legal advice, yet the Immigration and Naturalization Service (INS) has actively discouraged its detained aliens from getting it. Children are particularly vulnerable in the asylum process; nonetheless, at present, no statutory or common law right guarantees appointed counsel or guardians for children trapped in the immigration labyrinth.

* * *

[T]o stem the tide of Central American refugees and asylum seekers, the INS decided to detain these aliens in border facilities and tent-shelters. Earlier, many asylum seekers had been processed quickly in mass adjudications, often conceding their deportability and being sent back to their home country. Under this policy, unaccompanied children awaiting a decision were released to family members, church groups, or other community assistance organizations. The children were unaccompanied either because they had fled their country without adults, they were sent ahead by family members who had hoped to shield them from harm, or they had become separated from adults during flight. * * * The INS policy of detaining children and adults has led to an expansion of detention facilities in rural areas. INS figures for 1990–1991 show over 3,600 aliens in Texas detention facilities, and 2,500 alien children in California. Predictably, the facilities are ramshackle: one site in Texas has been sardonically dubbed "El Corralon" (The Corral), while another is a former Department of Agriculture pesticide storage facility. A study of the children in these facilities revealed that virtually all suffered from advanced and untreated cases of post-traumatic shock syndrome. * * * These children have virtually no access to health care or personal counseling, even though many have been severely traumatized by the war in their country, by the arduous and dangerous trip North, and by their incarceration here. The children are provided no educational services, even though every child in Texas is required to enroll in school during the school year. The centers have no libraries, teacher aides, or organized instruction. Like the adults, the detained alien children have little access to attorneys, telephones, or other legal means to prepare their cases.

* * *

Because the INS couches its actions in national defense terms ("securing our borders" and "intercepting drug trafficking"), little community outrage has been heard over these actions. The Red Cross has been coopted into operating one of the facilities, garbing the center with legitimacy, while community newspapers have been lulled into believing that the policy is humanitarian. * * * Further, INS officials counted on the remoteness of the camps, the economic incentive to the poor communities, and the distance from legal services to keep their practices from undergoing public scrutiny.

The practice of detaining alien minors has advanced two ulterior motives. First, to discourage other refugees from migrating to the United States. Second, authorities hoped to "bait" undocumented families into revealing themselves to authorities. As a result of these practices, family members in the United States, even those with permission to be in the country, have found it intimidating or impossible to locate their children. In *Flores v. Meese* and *Perez-Funez v. INS*, many of these INS practices concerning children came to light. In these cases, the courts found that the INS had acted to deprive unaccompanied alien minors of their rights to full hearings and due process. * * * In another case, the judge found "a persistent pattern and practice of misconduct," use of "intimidation, threats, and misrepresentation," and evidence of "a widespread and pervasive practice akin to a policy" concerning pressure on Salvadorans to concede their rights. * * *

As a result of the remote locations of the facilities, INS policies on transfer, availability of legal resources, and poor response by organized bars, legal assistance to unaccompanied children is virtually non-existent. For example, even though Laredo, Texas, is hundreds of miles away from San Antonio (the tenth largest city in the United States), over 80 percent of the San Antonio region immigration caseload is in Laredo. To make matters worse, no immigration judge lives in or is appointed on a regular basis in Laredo. Therefore, all hearings are consolidated into alternating weeks when a judge does ride the circuit. This irregular schedule precludes attorneys (most of whom live in San Antonio) from arranging their schedules to synchronize with those of the judges. A visiting federal judge found that aliens were not even provided adequate lists of legal services. For example, the list (in English) included names and numbers of lawyers who did not handle immigration cases, and failed to include a free legal assistance program. He characterized this and other practices as "bad faith." An ABA inspection team issued a report noting that legal services to detained aliens were "grossly inadequate." Even when courts have been persuaded that detained aliens have been deprived of basic legal information on their rights, and have ordered changes designed to increase information and services, the INS has "not diligently respected [injunctions and temporary restraining orders], nor were agents disciplined for failing to adhere to terms."

Most troubling has been the INS practice of transferring aliens as a means of depriving them of counsel. Because the policy of establishing rural detention centers virtually assures that the refugees and asylum seekers will not have access to counsel, transfer to one of them is tantamount to a deprivation of counsel. In a troubling decision, a United States district court upheld the practice, noting INS's discretionary authority to make custodial decisions. In several instances, transfers have even been made after counsel was retained or as a blatant attempt to deny counsel. The policies and practices of INS have ensured that legal services for detainees have been minimal or nonexistent.

* * *

The United States has been extraordinarily generous in extending refugee assistance to victims fleeing communism, and to victims of wars raging in countries that have been United States allies. However, actions carried out by client states or by clandestine United States operations exhibit a different history. Central American children, trapped between wars in their home countries and an immigration system in the United States that accords them no reasonable treatment, deserve special attention and protection. To do less is to continue a shameless, selfish, shortsighted policy.

Under these circumstances, what role may law schools play in ameliorating such a devastating situation? In Minow's terms, "law schools should pay greater attention to the social and economic conditions that might inspire [such] clients." Once the aliens are detained on this side of the border, however, clients' coerced concessions of deportability do not always leave much play-in-the-joints for fancy lawyering or maneuvering within the system. This very lack of options has resulted in Minow's first dilemma, that of the children, many of whom have meritorious asylum claims, not being able to obtain counsel in time to render significant assistance. * * * This may be traced in part to [the dearth] of immigration law [courses] being taught by American law schools. The Association of American Law Schools' 2006 data show approximately 180 full-time law teachers who teach in this field. It is likely that not all of the courses in immigration law would include substantial material on refugees, refugee rights, or unaccompanied children. Further, only a handful of refugee legal activists teach law on a full-time basis, and even fewer write the articles so critical to consciousness-raising and legal reform. In addition, clinical legal education is only partially suited to remedy such a legal system breakdown as these children experience.

* * *

However, at my own law school, we pooled our resources and agreed to try to provide clinical legal assistance. We decided to offer a between-semester clinical credit refugee project, with concentrated instruction in Houston, and a supervised field experience. We arranged for seven students to spend sixty hours in a week on a pro bono bar project in the Valley. Another fourteen students worked in Houston, trying to secure bond redetermination hearings and doing country research necessary for ongoing asylum cases. We sponsored conferences and coordinated course coverage so that more students could train as immigration lawyers. * * * Were we successful? It is hard to say. Student enthusiasm ran high, yet at two o'clock in the morning I could not help but wonder if we are simply legitimizing INS in its pernicious practices, and I recall the faces of the children who fled war only to wind up at El Corralon.

* * *

Case 3: "Oscar Z. Acosta, Chicano Lawyer"

In the early 1970s, two novels appeared that were widely read and admired, *The Autobiography of a Brown Buffalo* and *The Revolt of the Cockroach People* by Oscar Zeta Acosta, a lawyer in real life. Acosta became a counter-cultural hero, whose character later figured prominently in Hunter S. Thompson's popular "Fear and Loathing" series, where he became the wild Samoan attorney, Dr. Gonzo. Acosta's two novels have been widely studied by literary scholars, particularly emphasizing his search for identity as a Mexican American, and the bawdy, picaresque depiction of his life in the late 1960s, when Chicano political consciousness was awakened on campuses. * * *

* * *

In *Brown Buffalo*, he flees from his Legal Aid position and drives across the country and Mexico to find himself and discover his role in life. After a harrowing series of drug-and alcohol-related incidents, he returns to California, determined to become "Zeta, the world-famous Chicano lawyer who helped to start the last revolution." In *Revolt*, Acosta blends historical and political events into his narrative, having decided to become someone of importance:

> I will change my name. I will learn Spanish. I will write the greatest books ever written. I will become the best criminal lawyer in the history of the world. I will save the world. I will show the world what is what and who the fuck is who. Me in particular.

He then sets out on a variety of escapades, deftly meeting and incorporating figures from the times. He runs for Los Angeles County Sheriff; he defends Chicanos charged with political crimes; he testifies before the Los Angeles school board after a student walkout; he sues to get at the truth of a murdered reporter. These events and people become transmogrified into Acosta's tales in prose reeking of anger and a sense of the absurd. Acosta takes on a pseudonym, Buffalo Z. Brown, for its Mexican cultural antecedents and for the wistful significance of the American buffalo, doomed to extinction. As one scholar put it:

> The masks and use of fictionalization in ethnic autobiography are important keys to understand the intent and purpose of the autobiographer, for they help him to evaluate not only himself but also his race. In this particular case, *Brown Buffalo* represents the Chicano's confusion at the start of the Chicano Movement, while *Cockroach People* tells us where he is heading as a result of this Movement. The reader travels with Acosta in his search for an identity because he can relate so strongly with the human emotions the narrator experiences, while at the same time he learns and arrives at an understanding of the history and ideology of the Chicano Movement.

Although ostensibly fiction, Acosta's work, in several instances, draws from the author's real-life experience as a lawyer, as in the poignant portrait of the demoralizing work of a poverty lawyer, and in his handling of political cases, woven into *The Revolt of the Cockroach People*. One of these, *Castro v. Superior Court of Los Angeles County*, actually broke new ground and fits Martha Minow's classification of cases that need to be undertaken for their monkey-wrenching value. In his fictional treatment of the case, all hell is breaking out in East Los Angeles, home to a half-million Mexican Americans. This parallels history. On March 3, 1968, many high school students began a series of walkouts, and by the time the strike was over, a week later, the "blowouts" had given many young Chicano students their first taste of politics:

> Overnight, student activism reached levels of intensity never before witnessed. A few Mexican American student activists had participated in civil rights marches, anti-Vietnam War protests, and had walked the picket lines for the farmworker movement. But the high

school strike of 1968 was the first time students of Mexican descent had marched en masse in their own demonstration against racism and for educational change. It was also the first time that they had played direct leadership roles in organizing a mass protest!

Several leaders of the strike and ten students were indicted by a grand jury in June 1968 and became known locally as the "LA Thirteen." This entire episode is recounted by Acosta in *Revolt.* * * * Acosta and his co-counsel, in real life, attacked the indictments of the "LA Thirteen" on first amendment grounds, charging that the indictments were politically motivated, that the state educational code provisions under which they had been indicted were overbroad, and that both felony and misdemeanor counts should be dropped. The court of appeals agreed on all points, save the last, and preserved the misdemeanor counts. These misdemeanor counts had already been dismissed during collateral charges brought in municipal court, and the appeals court remanded for fact-finding on whether the District Attorney could press for further prosecution on the misdemeanors. When the charges were not refiled, victory for the "LA Thirteen" was complete. * * *

In *Castro*, Acosta had also challenged the racial composition of the grand jury, but with the decision in the writ proceeding, this issue was set aside. In another, similar case, however, Acosta advanced the argument that because it was a politically-motivated prosecution, the appeals court should quash the grand jury indictments on the grounds that the juror selection process was racist in its virtual exclusion of Mexican Americans. Acosta's data, for example, showed that in 1968, when 12.4 percent of Los Angeles County was Hispanic, only 3 grand jurors out of 171 serving that year were Hispanic, or 1.8 percent. This ratio of 6.9 available jurors to 1 juror called exceeded southern black grand juror ratios found discriminatory by the United States Supreme Court in earlier cases.

Los Angeles presented an additional feature in seating its grand juries, as each superior court judge was allowed to nominate two jurors. In 1969, 7 Hispanics had been nominated by 5 judges to the 189 positions. From 1959 to 1969, 25 of 1690 (2.8 percent) grand jurors in Los Angeles county courts were Hispanic. Acosta decided to subpoena the judges to find out why they had nominated so few Hispanics to their grand juries.

The trial court ruled against Acosta, finding that ten "Spanish-surnamed" persons had been nominated, of which a majority were Mexican American. "Therefore, it cannot be said that Mexican–Americans or persons with Spanish surnames were excluded from the 1969 grand jury." Acosta, however, wanted to depose the superior court judges, including the then-presiding judge, about their nominations, which, he argued, were too few for the percentage of Latinos in the Los Angeles population at large. * * * Acosta argued that, "as applied to a county containing over one-half million Spanish-surnamed persons, the peoples' 'explanations' of chronic tokenism in grand jury representation are inadequate, if not racist."

* * *

The state had asserted that the low level of education explained why so few Latino jurors had been chosen. Acosta offered counter evidence, drawing from United States Census data and other cases that a sixth-grade education was the minimum education necessary to be called for grand jury duty. As the appeals court noted, Acosta

> intended to show that, with very few exceptions, the judges of the respondent court were by reason of birth, education, residence, wealth, social and professional associations, and similar factors not acquainted with the qualifications of eligible potential grand jurors of petitioners' class and that they did not make an adequate effort to overcome this alleged deficiency.

The appeals court, having found for Acosta on this point, granted the writ.

* * *

This was Acosta's last major case before he disappeared off the coast of Mexico in May 1974. In December 1986, he was declared legally dead. In 1989, his son arranged to have his two novels reissued, so that a new generation of readers could appreciate Acosta's lawyering skills. Acosta fit neatly within Minow's typology of lawyers who, through their representation of unpopular clients and causes, force the system to confront its political underpinnings. The Chicanos who became Acosta's clients felt that they had pursued peaceful solutions to improve community conditions. When they exercised their first amendment rights, the full force of the Los Angeles police power, including the political aspirant District Attorney, was directed at them. Acosta's defense tactics, challenging the racial composition of the grand jury process and the racial bona fides of the judges in the appointment process, led to acquittals of the defendants in both trials on all the major charges. His combination of acute political instincts and deft lawyering did not compromise his clients' interests, and largely vindicated them. * * *

Notes and Questions

1.   López and Olivas suggest that a subordinated people should not be too respectful of the law. Do you agree? See Gerald P. López, *Reconceiving Civil Rights Practice: Seven Weeks in the Life of a Rebellious Collaboration*, 77 Geo. L.J. 1603 (1989). For further information on the fortunes of Latino children held unaccompanied (because their parents have been deported) in U.S. immigration detention centers, see Michael A. Olivas, *Unaccompanied Refugee Children: Detention, Due Process, and Disgrace*, 2 Stan. L. & Pol'y Rev. 159 (1990).

2. African–American figures such as Frederick Douglass and Thurgood Marshall have called the Constitution, essentially, a document from hell. López shares some of their skepticism. Do you?

3. López says that the Constitution means little to the Chicano community and can only acquire meaning through struggle and fighting. Do you agree that it is just a piece of paper until people infuse it with meaning through their blood, sweat, and tears?

4. Might street activism for immigrants' rights be the next incarnation of the civil rights movement? See Kevin R. Johnson & Bill Ong Hing, *The Immigrant Rights Marches of 2006 and the Prospects for a New Civil Rights Movement*, 42 Harv. C.R.-C.L. L. Rev. 99 (2007).

Richard Delgado
Rodrigo's Ninth Chronicle: Race, Legal Instrumentalism, and the Rule of Law
143 U. Pa. L. Rev. 379 (1994)

The waitress took our orders, first patiently explaining to my ebullient young friend how a certain Korean dish differed from one he had learned to like in his favorite restaurant in Chinatown. After she had gone, Rodrigo continued:

"Nice woman. Where were we? Oh, yes—the optimism-pessimism gap. What I realized on the flight home is that it's not enough simply to explain *why* our folks are on the whole less upbeat than Whites. We need a theory of what folks like us should *do*. Should we sit around in despair? Try harder? The principal purveyor of what we called 'bleak chic,' namely Derrick Bell, says that the situation is grim, but one must struggle anyway. Even though one knows in advance that the gains will be very slight, the effort must nevertheless be made. Yet he doesn't explain why, exactly."

"It seems to be an article of faith, a kind of existential commitment, something which gives life meaning, enabling us to carry on in an otherwise bleak and desolate world," I suggested.

"That's the interpretation I drew too, but then I began thinking we can go even beyond that. The theory I propose is not so much a replacement as a modification of Bell's. Under it, subordinated people would acknowledge that in many eras and in many courts, legal success is really not possible. At these times, it is best to look elsewhere for relief."

"To what Gerry Spann calls 'pure politics,'" I ventured, "mass marches, picketing, lobbying, the legislative arena—forums other than courts?"

"Exactly. And when these avenues seem foreclosed, when society as a whole seems to close its face to us, we can turn to our own sources, our own communities."

"That's self-help, cultural nationalism, building our own communities, looking to black colleges," I said in excitement. I could see the outlines of the long-awaited theory of social change forming, something that had eluded some of our finest minds. I longed to hear more. "And so, Rodrigo, you think that what's needed is an overarching theory to tell us which approach to use at any given moment. The interest convergence theory tells us that courts at times will be hostile or indifferent, but if I understand you correctly, that need not be a source of despair. Rather, it simply means that we should then look to other means for progress and succor."

"Exactly," Rodrigo replied. "We should look upon law as we would any other social institution, a tool that is useful for certain purposes and at certain times, but less so for other purposes or at different times. We need not succumb to the totalizing despair of some of our most eminent theorists, one that actually can prove enervating, despite my rather flip answer to the group this morning. Nor need we embrace the saccharine optimism of conventional civil rights theories grounded in liberalism and faith in progress. That's dangerous too, because it leads to disillusionment and burnout. We need a more sustaining approach, which my more pragmatic view provides. What do you think, Professor?" Rodrigo looked up cheerfully.

"I'd love to hear more details. But my first impression is that the idea has much promise. It has ties with a new legal movement, pragmatism. And it offers an approach to our condition that promises to be liberating—to avoid the Scylla and Charybdis of over-optimism on the one hand, and despair on the other. Do you have a name for your brain child?"

Rodrigo looked up and smiled, whether because of my question or because of the arrival of the waitress with a trayful of steaming, savory-smelling bowls, I could not tell. "Legal instrumentalism," he said. * * *

RODRIGO EXPLAINS AND DEFENDS LEGAL INSTRUMENTALISM AS A CIVIL RIGHTS STRATEGY

* * *

We traded morsels, and Rodrigo commented, "Mmmmm. Your stir fry is really good. So you think my theory has promise?"

"Emphatically so. I like its synthetic, umbrella quality, the way it allows for differentiation of strategy depending on the times and circumstances. And I especially like the—well, how shall I call it?—the mental health overtones. It promises a much more liberating way of looking at our civil rights progress and circumstances, one that avoids both false optimism and undue despair. But I'd love to know two things. First, how you thought of it. And second, how you would defend it against the charge of cynicism. You've already explained how it would work—we'd choose whatever tool seemed most promising at a given period in history. And I'd also like to know how you would respond to the accusation, one you are certain to hear leveled against you, that it goes against the rather noble ideal of the rule of law. If not frankly 'antilegal,' your theory verges on a demystification of law and litigation, for it seems to say, follow the law when that will work for you, and avoid or break it when it won't. There are precursors of your theory, and they are not all in good favor today.''

Legal Instrumentalism

Rodrigo paused to spear a last noodle stuck in the bottom of his cup, then continued. ''I know about Thrasymachus and that other dialogue, as well as some of their latter-day versions including 'By any means necessary.' But Socrates was not vindicating a system of laws that systematically oppressed a minority of its citizens, and so the tribunal that sentenced him to death was much more legitimate than ours, at least vis-à-vis him. Our Constitution excluded blacks, women, and those without property from the very beginning. It provided for the institution of slavery in no fewer than ten passages. And even when we abolished that institution a hundred years later, a system of Jim Crow laws kept our people in circumstances little better than those they had just escaped. It was not until yet another hundred years passed that separate but equal—legal apartheid—began to be repealed.'' We were not the first nation to repeal slavery—not even among the first ten.

''But surely, Rodrigo,'' I interjected, ''things have changed. And even if our system of civil rights laws is not perfect, does it not provide at least a degree of protection? What do we have that is any better? Anarchy?''

''Good points,'' Rodrigo replied mildly. ''I don't want to exaggerate. Sometimes the courts are our staunchest allies. But sometimes they are not. During these times we should look to other avenues. Otherwise one is just beating one's head against a stone wall.''

''What you called perseveration before.''

''Actually, your two questions turn out to be related. Legal instrumentalism occurred to me in reflecting on the idea of legitimacy and the way in which recent revolutionary leaders have viewed law. Few of the great ones held to any sort of romantic ideal. Gandhi, of course, considered the British system of laws and civil service entirely illegitimate and had little hesitation about ordering strikes and boycotts, even though they were technically illegal. Martin Luther King believed one had no obligation to obey unjust laws.''

''Although King did believe that one should be prepared to suffer punishment as a consequence,'' I interjected.

''To be sure. And in more recent times, the Black Panthers took a position very much like the one I am suggesting. Their leaders understood that the forces of law would often be arrayed against them, but that sometimes one could employ litigation, injunctions, and other legal strategies to make very real progress for the black community. Cesar Chavez and the farmworkers seem to have had a similar attitude. There is a long history of outsider groups seeing law in pragmatic terms, as sometimes legitimate and helpful, and at other times not."

"In more recent times, critical race theorists have been calling attention to the way this happens, not just in enforcement, police abuses, and the like, but also overtly in legal doctrine. They have been pointing out that wherever legal principles and rules conflict with the interests of the mighty, the law simply coins an 'exception.' In time, the loophole comes to be regarded as ordinary and usual, not even looked upon as an exception at all. Look at all the exceptions and special doctrines the law has carved out in the free speech area. These days, minorities, gays, and women are calling for hate-speech rules that would punish vicious name-calling and slurs. But our friends over at the ACLU consider this heresy and sue every university that enacts such a code. They argue that the First Amendment should be a seamless web, ignoring that we have literally dozens of exceptions that come into play in the case of speech that threatens powerful groups."

* * *

"So, you are saying that the rule of law in all its majesty never holds for us, but always for our adversaries or for empowered groups?"

"In general, yes," Rodrigo said. "Business necessity is a valid excuse for discrimination. The police can search or arrest you without a warrant if they can show good faith, which sometimes takes the form of simply pointing out that you were a black man walking or standing in the wrong neighborhood. Discrimination is permissible if it cannot be proved intentional. And the tax code, as everyone knows, contains so many exceptions for the activities of the rich that many who earn over one million dollars a year are able to escape paying taxes altogether."

"Your point, then, is that people of color should straightforwardly recognize that the law will often not protect them because it is designed to promote the interests of others, and that they should make the best of the situation."

* * *

"Yes. Minorities should invoke and follow the law when it benefits them and break or ignore it otherwise—when it gets in the way, is unresponsive, or is adverse to their interests. We should treat it like any other social institution, the highway department, for example. No one hesitates to call the highway department to task, to criticize it if it is always fixing the potholes on the other side of town and ignoring the ones in their neighborhood. No one speaks of the majesty of the rule of highway procedure or the grandeur of pothole fixing. If the department is doing its job, we leave it alone or give it a pat on the back. If it's not, we call it to account, or else work out some other way of getting the potholes fixed."

"Rodrigo, you are saying that social reformers should subsume law under their agenda, which is to achieve progress for minorities. Law-types approach things in just the opposite way, insisting on subsuming racial reform under law. Law people place law at the center, and then ask where racial justice should fit in. Should Martin Luther King be allowed to march in the face of an injunction? Should civil disobedience be countenanced? Should a white charged with discrimination be able to escape by showing a business necessity, or a lack of intent or causation?"

"I agree. We should demand the opposite—that race reform be placed in the center, following which we should ask where law fits in. That's the model I'm proposing, and does it not make just as much sense as the other approach?"

"It seems to me," I said, "that it all depends on what is uppermost in your mind, on what your objective is. The law-lover will subscribe to mythic, heroic views about the rule of law and insist that everything else be addressed within that framework. We, by contrast, will take a more utilitarian view of law, as the Panthers did. We'll ask: 'What can law do for us at this time and place?' "

"And that's the view I suggest under the rubric of 'legal instrumentalism.' We should demystify law, see it as the social institution it is: good for some things, less so for others. As we observed before, theory-fitting is everything. It makes no sense to use Gramsci to help you prepare a budget, nor law and economics to try to make this a fairer world for excluded groups. We should avoid counsels of despair. But, by the same token, we should disavow failed liberal programs that achieve too little because they promise too much. Hence, legal instrumentalism: try everything until you find what works."

* * *

SECTION 2. EXAMPLES OF REBELLIOUS LAWYERING

Rodolfo Acuña

Occupied America: A History of Chicanos
253–59 (3d ed. 1988)

World War II and the Chicano

Raúl Morin, in *Among the Valiant*, has documented the Chicanos' contribution to the war effort. Morin expressed the sense of betrayal that many Chicano soldiers [in World War II] experienced because of the racism at home. Morin wrote that 25 percent of the U.S. military personnel on the infamous Bataan "Death March" were Mexican Americans and that, in World War II, Mexicans earned more medals of honor than any other ethnic or racial group.

When the war began, about 2.69 million Chicanos lived in the United States, approximately one-third of whom were of draft age. According to Dr. Robin R. Scott, between 375,000 and 500,000 Chicanos served in the armed forces. In Los Angeles Mexicans comprised one-tenth of the population and one-fifth of the casualties.

Throughout the war Mexicans were treated as second-class citizens. For example, Sergeant Macario Garcia, from Sugarland, Texas, a recipient of the Congressional Medal of Honor, could not buy a cup of coffee in a restaurant in Richmond, California. "An Anglo–American chased him out with a baseball bat." The Garcia incident was not isolated.

The "Sleepy Lagoon" case (1942) and the zoot-suit riots (1943) insulted Mexicans throughout the United States. The events in Los Angeles generated sympathy and solidarity from as far away as Chicago. Angelenos as well as other North Americans had been conditioned for these events by the mass deportations of the 1930s. The war-like propaganda conducted during the repatriation reinforced in the minds of many Anglos the stereotype that Mexican Americans were aliens. The events of 1942 proved the extent of Anglo racism. Euroamericans herded Japanese Americans into internment camps. When the Japanese left, Mexicans became the most natural scapegoats.

During the war, Los Angeles became a magnet for the rapid migration of all races to the area. The mass influx overtaxed the infrastructure's ability to serve the expanding population. The Mexican *barrios*, already overcrowded, were the most affected, as the city's economic growth drew many Mexicans from other regions. Whites took higher paying defense jobs, while Mexicans assumed their place in heavy industry.

Mexicans occupied the oldest housing stock; segregation was common; and many recreational facilities excluded Mexican Americans. For instance, they could not use swimming pools in East Los Angeles and in other Southland communities. Often Mexicans and Blacks could only swim on Wednesday—the day the county drained the water. In movie houses in places like San Fernando, Mexicans sat in the balcony.

In this environment, a minority of Chicano youth between the ages of thirteen and seventeen belonged to *barrio* clubs that carried the name of their neighborhoods—White Fence, Alpine Street, El Hoyo, Happy Valley. The fad among gang members, or *pachucos* as they were called, was to tattoo the left hand, between the thumb and index finger, with a small cross with three dots or dashes above it. Many *pachucos* when they dressed up, wore the so-called zoot suit, popular among low-income youths at that time. Pachucos spoke *Spanish*, but also used *Chuco* among their companions. Chuco was the *barrio* language, a mixture of Spanish, English, old Spanish, and words adapted by the border Mexicans. Many experts indicate that the language originated around El Paso among Chicanos, who brought it to Los Angeles in the 1930s.

Although similar gangs existed among Anglo youth, Angelenos with little sense of history called gangs a Mexican problem, forgetting that the Euroamerican urban experience caused the gang phenomenon. The *Los Angeles Times*, not known for its analytic content, reinforced this stereotype and influenced the public with stories about "Mexican" hoodlums.

The "Sleepy Lagoon" case was the most notorious example of racism toward Chicanos in this era. The name came from a popular melody played by band leader Harry James. Unable to go to the public pool, Chicanos romanticized a gravel pit they frequently used for recreational purposes. On the evening of August 1, 1942, members of the 38th Street Club were jumped by another gang. When they returned with their home boys, the rival gang was not there. Later they witnessed a party in progress at the Williams Ranch nearby. They crashed the party and a fight followed.

The next morning José Díaz, an invited guest at the party, was found dead on a dirt road near the house. Díaz had no wounds and could have been killed by a hit-and-run driver, but authorities suspected that some members of the 38th Street Club had beaten him, and the police immediately jailed the entire gang. Newspapers sensationalized the story. Police flagrantly violated the rights of the accused and authorities charged twenty-two of the 38th Street boys with criminal conspiracy. "According to the prosecution, every defendant, even if he had nothing whatsoever to do with the killing of Díaz, was chargeable with the death of Díaz, which according to the prosecution, occurred during the fight at the Williams Ranch."

The press portrayed the Sleepy Lagoon defendants as Mexican hoodlums. A special committee of the grand jury, shortly after the death of José Díaz, accepted a report by Lt. Ed Duran Ayres, head of the Foreign Relations Bureau of the Los Angeles Sheriff's Department, which justified the gross violation of human rights suffered by the defendants. Although the report admitted that discrimination against Chicanos in employment, education, schooling, recreation, and labor unions was common, it concluded that Chicanos were inherently criminal and violent. Ayres stated that Chicanos were Indians, that Indians were Orientals, and that Orientals had an utter disregard for life. Therefore, because Chicanos had this inborn characteristic, they too were violent. The report further alleged that Chicanos were cruel, for they descended from the Aztecs who supposedly sacrificed 30,000 victims a day! Ayres wrote that Indians considered leniency a sign of weakness, pointing to the Mexican government's treatment of the Indians, which he maintained was quick and severe. He urged that all gang members be imprisoned and that all Chicano youths over the age of eighteen be given the option of working or enlisting in the armed forces. Chicanos, according to Ayres, could not change their spots; they had an innate desire to use a knife and let blood, and this inborn cruelty was aggravated by liquor and jealousy. The Ayres report, which represented official law enforcement views, goes a long way in explaining the events around Sleepy Lagoon.

The Honorable Charles W. Fricke permitted numerous irregularities in the courtroom during the trial. The defendants were not allowed to cut their hair or change their clothes for the duration of the proceedings. The prosecution failed to prove that the 38th Street Club was a gang, that any criminal agreement or conspiracy existed, or that the accused had killed Díaz. In fact, witnesses testified that considerable drinking had occurred at the party before the 38th Street people arrived. If the theory of conspiracy to commit a crime had been strictly pressed, logically the defendants would have received equal verdicts. However, on January 12, 1943, the court passed sentences ranging from assault to first-degree murder.

The Sleepy Lagoon Defense Committee had been organized to protect the defendants' rights. It was chaired by Carey McWilliams, a noted journalist and lawyer. McWilliams and other members were harassed and red-baited by the press and by government agencies. The California Committee on Un–American Activities, headed by State Senator Jack Tenney, investigated the committee charging that it was a Communist-front organization and that Carey McWilliams had "Communist leanings" because he opposed segregation and favored miscegenation. Authorities, including the FBI, conducted surveillance of the committee and support groups such as El Congreso de los Pueblos de Habla Español (the Spanish–Speaking Congress). The FBI viewed it as a Communist front, stating that it "opposed all types of discrimination against Mexicans."

On October 4, 1944, the Second District Court of Appeals reversed the lower court in a unanimous decision stating that judge Fricke had conducted a biased trial, that he had violated the constitutional rights of the defendants, and that no evidence existed that linked the Chicanos with the death of José Díaz.

After the Sleepy Lagoon arrests Los Angeles police and the sheriff's departments set up roadblocks and indiscriminately arrested large numbers of Chicanos on countless charges, most popular being suspicion of burglary. These arrests naturally made headlines, inflaming the public to the point that the Office of War Information became concerned over the media's sensationalism as well as its racism.

The tension did not end there. Large numbers of servicemen on furlough or on short-duration passes visited Los Angeles. Numerous training centers were located in the vicinity, and the glitter of Hollywood and its famous canteen attracted hordes of GIs. Sailors on shore leave from ships docked in San Pedro and San Diego went to Los Angeles looking for a good time. Most were young and anxious to prove their manhood. A visible "foe" was the "alien" Chicano, dressed in the outlandish zoot suit that everyone ridiculed. The sailors also looked for Mexican girls to pick up, associating the Chicanas with the prostitutes in Tijuana. The sailors behaved boisterously and rudely to the women in the Mexican community.

In the spring of 1943 several small altercations erupted in Los Angeles. In April marines and sailors in Oakland invaded the Chicano *barrio* and Black ghetto, assaulted the people, and "depantsed" zoot-suiters. On May 8 a fight between sailors and Chicanos broke out at the Aragon Ballroom in Venice, California, when some high school students told the sailors that *pachucos* had stabbed a sailor. Joined by other servicemen, sailors indiscriminately attacked Mexican youths. The battle cry was; "Let's get 'em! Let's get the chili-eating bastards!" Twenty-five hundred spectators watched the assault on innocent Chicano youths; the police did virtually nothing to restrain the servicemen, arresting instead the victims, charging them with disturbing the peace. Although Judge Arthur Guerin dismissed the charges for want of sufficient evidence, he warned the youths "that their antics might get them into serious difficulties unless they changed their attitudes." The press continued to sensationalize the theme of "zoot-suit equals hoodlum."

The "sailors riots" began on June 3, 1943. Allegedly, a group of sailors had been attacked by Chicanos when they attempted to pick up some Chicanas. The details are vague; the police supposedly did not attempt to get the Chicano side of the story, but instead took the sailors' report at face value. Fourteen off-duty police officers, led by a detective lieutenant, went looking for the "criminals." They found nothing, but made certain that the press covered the story.

That same night, sailors went on a rampage; they broke into the Carmen Theater, tore zoot-suits off Chicanos, and beat the youths. Police again arrested the victims. Word spread that *pachucos* were fair game and that they could be attacked without fear of arrest.

Sailors returned the next evening with some two hundred allies. In twenty hired cabs they cruised Whittier Boulevard, in the heart of the East Los Angeles *barrio*, jumping out of the cars to gang up on neighborhood youths. Police and sheriffs maintained that they could not establish contact with the sailors. They finally did arrest nine sailors, but released them immediately without filing charges. The press portrayed the sailors as heroes. Articles and headlines were designed to inflame racial hatred.

Sailors, encouraged by the press and "responsible" elements of Los Angeles, gathered on the night of June 5 and marched four abreast down the streets, warning Chicanos to shed their zoot suits or they would take them off for them. On that night and the next, servicemen broke into bars and other establishments and beat up Chicanos. Police continued to abet the lawlessness, arriving only after damage had been done and the servicemen had left. Even though sailors destroyed private property, law enforcement officials still refused to do their duty. When the Chicano community attempted to defend itself, police arrested them.

Events climaxed on the evening of June 7, when thousands of soldiers, sailors, and civilians surged down Main Street and Broadway in search of *pachucos*. The mob crashed into bars and broke the legs off stools, using them as clubs. The press reported five hundred "zoot suiters" ready for battle. By this time Filipinos and Blacks also became targets. Chicanos had their clothes ripped off, and the youths were left bleeding in the streets. The mob surged into movie theaters, where they turned on the lights, marched down the aisles, and pulled zoot-suit-clad youngsters out of their seats. Seventeen-year-old Enrico Herrera, after he was beaten and arrested, spent three hours at a police station, where he was found by his mother, still naked and bleeding. A twelve-year-old boy's jaw was broken. Police arrested over six hundred Chicano youths without cause and labeled the arrests "preventive" action. Angelenos cheered on the servicemen and their civilian allies.

Panic gripped the Chicano community. At the height of the turmoil servicemen pulled a Black off a streetcar and gouged out his eye with a knife. Military authorities, realizing that the Los Angeles law enforcement agencies would not curtail the brutality, intervened and declared downtown Los Angeles off limits for military personnel. Classified naval documents prove that the navy believed it had a mutiny on its hands. Documents leave no doubt that military shore patrols quelled the riot, accomplishing what the Los Angeles police could or would not do.

For the next few days police ordered mass arrests, even raiding a Catholic welfare center to arrest some of its occupants. The press and city officials provoked the mob. An editorial by Manchester Boddy on June 9 in the *Los Angeles Daily News* (supposedly the city's liberal newspaper) stated:

> The time for temporizing is past. . . . The time has come to serve notice that the City of Los Angeles will no longer be terrorized by a relatively small handful of morons parading as zoot-suit hoodlums. To delay action now means to court disaster later on.

Boddy's statement taken alone would not mean much; it could be considered to be just one man's opinion. But consider that before the naval invasion of East Los Angeles, the following headlines had appeared in the *Times*:

November 2, 1942: "Ten Seized in Drive on Zoot–Suit Gangsters"

February 23, 1943: "One Slain and Another Knifed in 'Zoot' Fracas"

March 7, 1943: "Magistrate 'Unfrocks' Pair of Zoot–Suiters"

May 25, 1943: "Four Zoot–Suit Gangs Beat Up Their Victims"

June 1, 1943: "Attacks by Orange County Zoot–Suiters Injure Five"

During the assault servicemen were encouraged by headlines in the *Los Angeles Daily News*, such as "Zoot Suit Chiefs Girding for War on Navy," and in the *Los Angeles Times*, such as "Zoot Suiters Learn Lesson in Fight with Servicemen." Three other major newspapers ran similar headlines that generated an atmosphere of zoot-suit violence. The radio also contributed to the hysteria.

Rear Admiral D. W. Bagley, commanding officer of the naval district, took the public position that the sailors acted in "self-defense against the rowdy element." Privately Bagley directed his commanders to order their men to stop the raids and then conducted a low profile cover-up. Sailors were, however, not the only vandals. Army personnel often outnumbered sailors. According to Commander Fogg, on June 8, 1943, hundreds of servicemen were "prowling downtown Los Angeles mostly on foot—disorderly—apparently on the prowl for Mexicans." By June 11, 1943, in a restricted memo, the navy and army recognized that the rioting resulted from "mob action. It is obvious that many soldiers are not aware of the serious nature of riot charges, which could carry the death sentence or a long prison term."

On June 16 the *Los Angeles Times* ran a story from Mexico City, headlined "Mexican Government Expects Damages for Zoot Suit Riot Victims." The article stated that "the Mexican government took a mildly firm stand on the rights of its nationals, emphasizing its conviction that American justice would grant 'innocent victims' their proper retribution." Federal authorities expressed concern, and Mayor Fletcher Bowron assured Washington, D.C., that there was no racism involved. Soon afterward Bowron told the Los Angeles police to stop using "cream-puff techniques on the Mexican youths." At the same time he ordered the formation of a committee to "study the problem." City officials and the Los Angeles press became exceedingly touchy about charges of racism. When Eleanor Roosevelt commented in her column that the riots had been caused by "longstanding discrimination against the Mexicans in the Southwest," on June 18 the *Los Angeles Times* reacted with the headline "Mrs. Roosevelt Blindly Stirs Race Discord." The article denied that racial discrimination had been a factor in the riots and charged that Mrs. Roosevelt's statement resembled propaganda used by the communists, stating that servicemen had looked for "costumes and not races." The article said that Angelenos were proud of their missions and of Olvera Street, "a bit of old Mexico," and concluded "We like Mexicans and think they like us."

Governor Earl Warren formed a committee to investigate the riots. Participating on the committee were Attorney General Robert W. Kenny; Catholic bishop Joseph T. McGucken, who served as chair; Walter A. Gordon, Berkeley attorney; Leo Carrillo, screen actor; and Karl Holton, director of the California Youth Authority.

The committee's report recommended punishment of all persons responsible for the riots—military and civilian alike. It took a left-handed slap at the press, recommending that newspapers minimize the use of names and photos of juveniles. Moreover, it called for better-educated and trained police officers to work with Spanish-speaking youth.

Little was done to implement the recommendations of the report, and most of the same conditions exist today in Los Angeles city and county. "The kid gloves are off!" approach of Sheriff Eugene Biscailuz has, if anything, hardened since the 1940s.

During World War II, police authorities sought to strengthen social control of the *barrios* and spied extensively on the Mexican community. Most available data on this phenomenon can be obtained through the federal Freedom of Information Act. Little is known about domestic spying at the local or state levels, since these government units are not required to provide copies of their reports to individuals or organizations.

Dr. José Ángel Gutiérrez has done pioneer research in this area. Through the Freedom of Information Act, he received documents proving that the FBI spied even on patriotic groups such as LULAC (League of United Latin American Citizens) and later the G.I. Forum. In 1941, the FBI's Denver Office reported on the LULAC chapter of Antonio, Colorado. Its officers included a county judge and a town marshal. The FBI also investigated respected leaders such as George I. Sanchez and Alonso Perales, reporting that the Mexican community distrusted Sanchez because he had converted to reformed Methodism.

In May 1946, the FBI infiltrated a Los Angeles meeting of LULAC. An informant asserted that participants had a long history of communist activity but made no effort to document the statement. Early in the 1950s, the FBI again investigated LULAC because it demanded racial integration. In Pecos, Texas, the FBI spied on the local LULAC council because a member wanted to be on the Selective Service Board. * * *

* * *

The Road to Delano: Creating a Moment

By the mid–1960s, Chicano militancy concerned growers and other employers. The purpose of immigration policy was to control not only Mexicans but Chicanos. After 1965, this policy became more restrictive, designed to regulate both the flow of workers and the wages paid. Essential to this strategy was the criminalization of Mexican labor, which devalued and degraded the work performed by Mexicans and Chicanos. Criminalization intensified the division of labor and resulted in Chicanos, to avoid discrimination, pecking down on the undocumented worker; it also justified increased use of police power against all Mexicans, whether documented or undocumented.

The first step in the criminalization process was the passage of restrictive legislation that directly affected the documented immigration of Mexicans. Liberals such as Senator Edward Kennedy sponsored legislation in 1965 designed to correct the past injustice of excluding Asians from legal entry. Nativists took the opportunity to broaden the legislation and, for the first time, placed Latin America and Canada on a quota system. The law specified that 170,000 immigrants annually could enter from the Eastern Hemisphere and 120,000 from the Western. Up to this time Mexico had been the principal source of Latin American immigration; the new law put a cap of 40,000 from any one nation. Unfortunately, few Chicanos or progressive organizations protested the law. And it was not until the 1970s that its full impact was felt; at that time it became a popular cause for progressives.

[For Acuña's account of César Chávez's farmworkers movement, see Part Seven, Chapter 19.]

Oscar "Zeta" Acosta
Autobiographical Essay,
in *Oscar "Zeta" Acosta: The Uncollected Works*
7–15 (Ilan Stavans ed., 1996)

* * * That really affected my whole thing with the result that, when I got out of the service, I attempted suicide. Naturally, I chickened out

like everybody else, but I ended up in psychiatry. I started school at San Francisco State and I started writing. I was majoring in creative writing and mathematics and I dug both of them. I had one more semester to go to get my degree in math but, by that time, I was halfway through a novel, so I dropped out to finish that and then intended to go back. I never did because by that time it was 1960, the Kennedy campaign and I got involved in that. I hadn't had a political thought up until then. I decided I didn't want to be either a mathematician or a professional writer after that involvement, but I did finish the novel and submitted it to three publishers, all of whom almost accepted it. They all said that I was great, earthy, poetic, the most brilliant unpublished writer in the world, but I was writing about Chicanos at that time—it was a Romeo and Juliet story of Okies and Chicanos in the valley—and that subject wasn't acceptable. So I decided I would write because that is what I am, a writer, but that I didn't want to have to write or to be a professional writer.

Since I was interested in politics and Chicanos, I decided to go to law school then work with Chávez and the farmworkers and be a union organizer. So I did it and got involved in the black civil rights movement for the next four years in San Francisco, but it wasn't really me. I told people that it wasn't just black and white, that there were Chicanos, too, and they laughed at me so I told them to go fuck themselves and they split. I graduated from San Francisco Law School, a night law school, in 1965. I was working at the *San Francisco Examiner* all of this time through college and law school as a copy boy, along with all of the political activity. When I got out, I took the bar exam and flunked it. It was the first time I had flunked an exam in my life and it was the third major trauma, so I ended up back with the psychiatrist. I studied for the bar again and passed it a couple of months later.

I became a legal aid lawyer in Oakland in a half-black, half-Chicano section. I hated it with a passion. I'd wake up in the morning and throw up. All we'd do was sit and listen to complaints. There were so many problems and we didn't do anything. We didn't have a direction, skills or tools.

After a year, I became totally depressed. I couldn't do anything, so I said fuck it to everything and I told the psychiatrist to shove it and to stick the pills up his ass. I said I'd been with him on and off for ten years and that I was still as fucked up as when I began, just taking ten times as many pills. I took off and ended up in Aspen.

I met some people who were pretty nice to me, including Hunter S. Thompson, the writer, and I started dropping acid and staying stoned most of the time and doing all kinds of odd jobs—construction work and washing dishes—and, within about three months my head was clear. I felt like I knew who I was, what I was and what I was supposed to do. I stayed there for about six months and then I was on my way to Guatemala to smuggle guns to the revolutionaries down there and to write about them. I got stopped in Juárez and thrown in jail. When I got out I called my brother who suggested that I go to Los Angeles. Well, I hated it. Being from up north, I was subjected to this old prejudice between Northern and Southern California, which was ridiculous. I asked my brother why I should go there and about a newspaper called *La Raza*. That was in January 1968. I arrived here in LA in February, intending to stay for a few months, write an article about it and then get out.

Then the high school walkouts occurred and I agreed to take a few misdemeanor cases. Two months later, thirteen of the organizers of the walkouts were busted on sixteen counts of conspiracy which could have resulted in forty-five years in prison for each of them. I agreed to take the case. It was my first major case, my first criminal case and here I am three years later. I haven't been able to get away and I don't think I ever will leave. This is it for me because I've gone through intensive changes in myself and my consciousness has developed about Chicanismo, La Raza, revolution and what we're going to do, so it looks like I'm here to stay. It seems to me that at some point in your life you have to make a stand, and I've decided that I might as well be here as anywhere else. This, East Los Angeles, is the capital of Aztlán, because there are more of us here than anywhere else.

To understand where I am you have to understand how the Chicano Movement has developed. In 1967 and 1968 young Chicano students, both in high school and college, began to identify as Mexican Americans. The first issue was what to call themselves. They began to organize coffee-houses and clubs but were mainly interested in the educational system. So, in March 1968, they had massive high school walkouts from four of the Mexican–American high schools in East Los Angeles. The result was numerous busts and that is when I became involved. Those walkouts were the first major activity by Chicanos as Chicanos in the history of this country. There had been labor groups and political-type groups, but there had never been any group organized to organize and politicize the community as Chicanos on broad-based issues. There are two million Chicanos here in Southern California. I think we're the largest ethnic minority in the Southwest—certainly here in Los Angeles we are. Statistically, we're the lowest in education, with an eighth-grade education being the median, and we're the lowest in housing and jobs. We have the problems here in Los Angeles and the Southwest that the blacks have throughout the country.

But the history of the Southwest is totally different from the history of the rest of the country, which is something that most people don't understand, and they don't understand that this historical relationship is what causes the attitudes that exist here today. They tend to see us as immigrants, which is absolutely wrong. We were here before the white man got here. The American government took our country away from us in 1848, when the government of Mexico sold us out. They sold not only the land, but they basically sold us as slaves in the sense that our labor and our land was being expropriated. The governments never gave us a choice about whether or not to be American citizens. One night we were

Mexican and the next day we were American. This historical relationship is the most important part of the present day relationships, but it's totally ignored or unknown or rejected by the Anglo society.

In 1968, when we started making a movement toward attaining better education and schools, we wanted the literature to reflect our heritage and our culture. We started meeting with school boards and the city council and we began to know the enemy. At that point I think that most of us believed we could integrate into the society and get a piece of the action, since nobody denied that we had problems. But now, three years later, there have been few changes. Now there are two assemblymen in the California legislature, one Congressman, and one member of the school board who are Chicanos, and that is it for a class that constitutes 13 percent of the population.

In 1968, our first problem was that of identity. As time went on we no longer questioned that. We had chosen a name—Chicano—whether we had Spanish or Indian blood, and we knew that we existed alone. That is, we relate to Mexico, but in a nostalgic way. We know that when the going gets rough, the Mexican government ain't going to do shit for us. And we know that no other aspect of the broad movement is going to do shit for us. They'll pay lip service, they'll condescend to us, but basically they're just as paternalistic to us as the white racist pigs. For example, I've spoken at numerous rallies for the Panthers, for Angela Davis, and every time I get the same bullshit treatment. I'm the last on the program with five minutes to speak and we get no offers of any real unity or working together.

I think that the Black Movement has been co-opted. Three years ago I used to know a lot of heavy blacks. They're just not around anymore. I'm talking about the Black Panthers. They're just rhetoric; they're just sucking in that money. They talk heavy as hell, but when it comes down to what they're fighting for I don't think even they know what they're fighting for because they're integrating into the society that they despise as fast as that society allows them to. I made this decision during Corky's trial.

Corky González is head of the Crusade for justice, which is based in Denver. He is also a poet, a street-fighter, a theorist and an organizer, and he is recognized by a lot of Chicanos as the boss, the leader. Chávez is like a grandfather to the Movement. We respect him and love him and would help him anytime he asked, but we don't feel that his progress, his ideology, is Chicano enough. César used the white liberal population quite a bit and, more than anything, this offends the average Chicano. It is bad because they take jobs that Chicanos should be taking and using them is the easy way out. There were probably more competent white militants three years ago than there were available Chicanos, but we feel that he should have trained his own people more as we do now.

Corky was on trial on a weapons charge arising out of the August 29, 1970, police riot here, where three people, including Rubén Salazar, were killed by the police. Corky had been trying to get away from the violence with his two children when the police busted him for a traffic violation, suspicion of robbery, and a concealed weapons charge. He was on a truck with a lot of people and we never denied that somebody on it had a loaded pistol, but it wasn't Corky. He wouldn't dare carry a goddamn gun around with him. He's a leader. He doesn't have to carry a gun for the same goddamn reason that Nixon doesn't have to. But we didn't stress that point at the trial for fear of alarming the jury and perhaps inflaming the press and cops. Why should we give them an excuse to shoot at Corky like they did at Rubén when they thought that he was a leader?

What I did stress in picking the jury was whether they would be prejudiced if Huey Newton testified for Corky. See, Huey had called and said he wanted to talk to me. I asked him if he'd come down and be a character witness for Corky. I thought it would be a great show of unity. Everybody said he would. Then, after I'd announced it all over town and picked a jury by hammering at that question, he wouldn't come or talk to me on the phone, so I have nothing more to do with the Black Movement. I'm talking about the professional revolutionaries, not the people.

I think in the past year or so the Chicano movement has begun to solidify. After the August 29th thing, there was the National Chicano Moratorium "non-violent march for justice" on January 31, 1971. It was against police brutality and repression and was non-violent until the end when fighting broke out and the cops swarmed out of the police station with everything, including twelve-gauge shotguns firing buckshot balls straight into the crowd. After two hours, one person was dead, thirty seriously injured, and there was about a half-million dollars' worth of damage, including seventy-eight burned police cars.

Things have gotten heavier since then and Chicano consciousness is spreading. Everybody in "El Barrio" is a Brown Beret. It's a concept, an idea. M.E.CH.A (Movimiento Estudiantil Chicano de Aztlán): the Chicano-student movement is also growing. Aztlán is the land we're sitting on now. The land where my forefathers lived hundreds of years ago before they migrated to the valley of Mexico. The Aztecs referred to the entire Southwest as Aztlán. Now the Chicano movement has no need for anyone else's ideas but our own. We have a way of life that we've learned from childhood. The concept of *la familia*, the respect for elders is not Sunday-school bullshit with us. It's part of our culture. A Chicano can no more disrespect his mother than he can himself. Which means he can, but at great cost to himself. The concept of community—of La Raza—isn't a political term to us as I feel it is to black and white radicals. The term brother is a social term to us, one we learn before we learn about politics.

We don't kid ourselves anymore. We know we're headed for a head-on collision with the rest of society. We're absolutely convinced of it and we're not being paranoid or nothing. We know that the main thing we want now is not better education or better jobs or better housing, because we know that they are not possible to achieve. It is not possible as the result of the history of human nature and the animal instinct against the races integrating in the liberal sense of the word.

You can't be a class or a nation without land. Without it, it doesn't have any meaning. It's that simple. So we are beginning to see that what we're talking about is getting land and having our own government. Period. It is that clear-cut. As to what land, that is still in the future. We have to develop the consciousness of land as the principal issue, just as three years ago we had to develop the consciousness of identity as the principal issue.

The black man came here as a slave. He is not of this land. He is so removed from his ancestry that he has nothing but the white society to identify with. We have history. We have culture. We had a land. We do feel solidarity with the American Indians because we are Indians. We have a total unification in ideology but no unification organizationally. I look upon them as my blood brothers. It is the Indian aspect of our ancestry that gives meaning to the term "La Raza." We are La Raza. Of course there is Spanish and European blood in us, but we don't always talk about it because it is not something that we are proud of. For me, my native ancestry is crucial. This consciousness is beginning to develop now, symbolized in the word *tierra*. We want our land back and this is what we are going to be fighting for.

I don't think you're going to see too much more of demonstrations against education or things of that sort. I think that has petered itself out. A lot of kids have gotten into OEO projects and school projects as a result of the movement, so they've been in college for a few years now and they are as hip to what's being taught in the colleges as the white radicals have been for some years now. They think it is a waste of time, that it takes away what little you have of your identity.

A perfect example is the National La Raza Law Students Association, here in Los Angeles, which I am pretty much associated with. The very first day they started school here on some OEO project I went in and spoke and told them, "Half of you will never be lawyers. Those of you that do are going to become so only because of your race. You got into these programs because you're Chicano. So you owe something to your Raza. Yet, I predict that in three years I'm going to be fighting 50 percent of you guys. You're going to be my enemies." They laughed. But it is a fact. This past year I've been working on these major cases of importance to Chicanos not only organizationally but legally, and often I've been unable to get the assistance of the Chicano law students. My prophecy to them has come true, except I was wrong in one respect. It is not 50 percent I'm fighting. It is about 75 percent. This is why I'm no longer pushing for more school programs, more handouts, more welfare. I think that will destroy the movement. They are attempting with those to do the same things they did to blacks.

For example, with the law students when I was doing this judges' thing in 1971, they didn't want to be associated with it because they were afraid that it might affect their future, their careers. That judges' thing was my third challenge to the Grand Jury system here. I was defending the "Biltmore Six," six young Chicanos who were busted for allegedly trying to burn down the Biltmore Hotel one night in 1970, when Reagan was delivering a speech. They were indicted by a Grand Jury and I contended that all Grand Juries are racist since all grand jurors have to be recommended by Superior Court judges and that the whole thing reeks of "subconscious, institutional racism." I was trying to get the indictments squashed on that basis.

To prove my contention I subpoenaed all 109 Superior Court judges in Los Angeles and examined them all under oath about their racism. After almost a year of work on this, the judge on that case, Arthur Alarcón, who is Mexican American, rejected the motion. The way it looks now, I think we're just about finished with that whole legal game.

I'm the only Chicano lawyer here. By that I mean the only one that has taken a militant posture, to my knowledge, in the whole country. When I got here I decided that if I was going to become anything legal I couldn't use the profession as it was. Lawyers are basically peddlers of flesh. They live off of other people's misery. Well, I couldn't do that. I made a decision that I would never charge a client a penny. As a matter of fact, I end up supporting some of my clients. I get money by begging, borrowing, and stealing. Sometimes I get a grant from some foundation like Ford. For a while I was under a Reggie program, although all I was doing was political, criminal work and they knew it. I don't even have an office. I'm in court practically every day.

I relate to the court system first as a Chicano and only seldom as a lawyer in the traditional sense. I have no respect for the courts and I make it clear to them from the minute I walk in that I have no respect for the system. That I'm against it and would destroy it in one second if I had the physical power to do it. The one thing I've learned to do is use criminal defense work as an organizing tool. That is my specialty. I organize in the courtroom. I take no case unless it is or can become a Chicano Movement case. I turn it into a platform to espouse the Chicano point of view so that that affects the judge, the jury, the spectators. We organize each case, set up defense committees, student groups, and use the traditional methods of organizing.

I think one thing I haven't mentioned enough yet, which is a very pertinent thing, is what drugs have done for me personally. I think psychedelic drugs have been important to the development of my consciousness. I don't think I'd have gotten to where I am without the use of these drugs. They've put me into a level of awareness where I can see myself and see what I'm really doing. Most of the big ideas I've gotten for my lawyer work have usually come when I am stoned. Like the Grand Jury challenge was the result of an acid experience. A lot of the tactics I employ I get the ideas for when I am stoned, which is not to say that I wouldn't get them if I wasn't stoned. A lot of my creativity has sprung from my use of these psychedelic drugs. And this doesn't just apply to me. When I got here to LA three years ago, I only knew one other guy who was taking acid. Guys were shooting heroin and they'd say to me "You dope addict. Are you crazy?" Now, just about all of my friends have tried or are taking acid. I think the acid experience is part and parcel of the radical Chicano Movement.

I don't have much contact with many of the other radical lawyers here. I think a lot of them are still finding themselves. Consequently, they'll often chicken out of something at the last minute. I think it's chickenshit, reactionary, and that they're the enemies of the people. I like them; they're nice guys, but it's too late for these personal things. Too many of them aren't doing the work that has to be done.

Now some of the Chicano law students are thinking of organizing a collective, but I've disagreed because I think it is looking to the future as any other lawyer would do. They are thinking in terms of money to make, cases to take. They're thinking of business. For me, to think of the future is inconsistent with my thinking of the present. It is only the present that is important. I think you develop yourself much more if you don't think of those things, if you think only of the job: defending Chicanos and organizing around the case.

Notes and Questions

1. Should oppressed people adopt some version of what Delgado calls "legal instrumentalism"—endorsing law when it is a useful tool and ignoring or criticizing it when it is not?

2. Did Acosta adopt this strategy, or did he marshal law itself in the aid of his cause? Did he do both? Would you? See Oscar Zeta Acosta, *The Autobiography of a Brown Buffalo* (1972).

3. Can one always, or generally do that, or is the deck stacked against one so that strengthening the rule of law by kowtowing to it on occasion will simply backfire against you when you need to change or criticize it?

4. Had you heard about the Sleepy Lagoon case and Zoot Suit riots? They are legendary in the Latino, especially the Chicano, community and as famous, in their way, as the Boston Tea Party or Paul Revere's ride in Anglo tradition. See People v. Zammora, 66 Cal.App.2d 166, 152 P.2d 180 (1944) (affirming conviction of Chicano youths for their part in the events at Sleepy Lagoon). See also Robert J. Rosenbaum, *Mexicano Resistance in the Southwest: The Sacred Right of Self–Preservation* (1981); Julian Samora, *Gunpowder Justice: A Reassessment of the Texas Rangers* (1979).

5. Should people of color consistently confront and challenge injustice and racism every time they encounter them, or would this prove exhausting and unfair?

6. Oscar Acosta envisions a "head-on collision with the rest of society" for Latinos as a result of advancing community consciousness and Chicanos' growing sense of being wronged. Is he referring merely to a legal or constitutional uprising, or something more? Were Martin Luther King, Jr. and Mohandas Gandhi revolutionaries, even though they both espoused

nonviolence? What about Acosta? Has his "collision" already taken place? Is it coming soon?

7. On the role of sixties-era militancy in shaping Latino self-awareness see Ian F. Haney López, *Racism on Trial: The Chicano Fight for Justice* (2003). For analysis of the role of institutional racism in the exclusion of Mexican Americans from juries in California, especially in the trial for the "LA Thirteen," see Ian F. Haney López, *Institutional Racism: Judicial Conduct and a New Theory of Racial Discrimination*, 109 Yale L.J. 1717 (2000).

8. On legal scholars and the struggle for racial justice, see, e.g., Gerald P. López, *Rebellious Lawyering: One Chicano's Vision of Progressive Law Practice* (1992); Richard Delgado, *The Rodrigo Chronicles: Conversations about America and Race* (1995). See also John–Michael Rivera, *The Emergence of Mexican America: Recovering Stories of Mexican Peoplehood in U.S. Culture* (2006); Nicolás Kanellos, *Heréncia: The Anthology of Hispanic Literature of the United States* (2002).

9. On brown balladeers who wrote of Latino authors and resisters, see, e.g., Americo Parédes, *"With His Pistol in His Hand:" A Border Ballad and Its Hero* (1958). On white folks who seek to disrupt white privilege and supremacy from within, see *Race Traitor* (Noel Ignatiev & John Garvey eds., 1996).

Paul Butler
Racially Based Jury Nullification: Black Power
in the Criminal Justice System
105 Yale L.J. 677, 679, 680, 698, 714–15, 723 (1995)

What role should race play in black jurors' decisions to acquit defendants in criminal cases? Consider trials that include both African–American defendants and African–American jurors. I argue that the race of a black defendant is sometimes a legally and morally appropriate factor for jurors to consider in reaching a verdict of not guilty or for an individual juror to consider in refusing to vote for conviction.

My thesis is that, for pragmatic and political reasons, the black community is better off when some nonviolent lawbreakers remain in the community rather than go to prison. The decision as to what kind of conduct by African Americans ought to be punished is better made by African Americans themselves, based on the costs and benefits to their community, than by the traditional criminal justice process, which is controlled by white lawmakers and white law enforcers. Legally, the doctrine of jury nullification gives the power to make this decision to African–American jurors who sit in judgment of African–American defendants. Considering the costs of law enforcement to the black community and the failure of white lawmakers to devise significant nonincarcerative responses to black antisocial conduct, it is the moral responsibility of black jurors to emancipate some guilty black outlaws. * * *

My goal is the subversion of American criminal justice, at least as it now exists. Through jury nullification, I want to dismantle the master's house with the master's tools. My intent, however, is not purely destructive; [it] is also constructive, because I hope that the destruction of the status quo will not lead to anarchy, but rather to the implementation of certain noncriminal ways of addressing antisocial conduct. Criminal conduct among African Americans is often a predictable reaction to oppression. Sometimes black crime is a symptom of internalized white supremacy; other times it is a reasonable response to the racial and economic subordination every African American faces every day. Punishing black people for the fruits of racism is wrong if that punishment is premised on the idea that it is the black criminal's "just deserts." * * *

I agree that criminal law enforcement constitutes a public good for African Americans when * * * locking up black men means that "violent criminals ... who attack those most vulnerable" are off the streets. [T]hen most people—including most law enforcement critics—would endorse the incarceration. But what about when locking up a black man has no or little net effect on public safety, when, for example, the crime with which he was charged is victimless? Putting aside for a moment the legal implications, couldn't an analysis of the costs and benefits to the African–American community present an argument against incarceration? I argue "yes," in light of the substantial costs to the community of law enforcement. * * *

[Eds. Professor Butler reviews the statistics on African Americans and the criminal justice system, and argues that a plausible interpretation of them is that criminal law is an instrument of white supremacy. He then argues that jury nullification, for a juror who holds this view, is morally proper for two reasons: because the "rule of law" is simply a myth for African Americans, and because African Americans do not have a fair say in the laws that govern them, because of systematic anti-black bias in the American democratic system.]

* * * Let us assume a black defendant who, the evidence suggests, is guilty of the crime with which he has been charged, and a black juror who thinks that there are too many black men in prison. The black juror has two choices: She can vote for conviction, thus sending another black man to prison and implicitly allowing her presence to support public confidence in the system that puts him there, or she can vote "not guilty," thereby acquitting the defendant, or at least causing a mistrial. In choosing the latter, the juror makes a decision not to be a passive symbol of support for a system for which she has no respect. Rather than signaling her displeasure with the system by breaching "community peace," the black juror invokes the political nature of her role in the criminal justice system and votes "no." In a sense, the black juror engages in an act of civil disobedience, except that her choice is better than civil disobedience because it is lawful. Is the black juror's race-conscious act moral? Absolutely. It would be farcical for her to be the sole colorblind actor in the criminal process, especially when it is her blackness that advertises the system's fairness.

At this point, every African American should ask herself whether the operation of the criminal law in the United States advances the interests of black people. If it does not, the doctrine of jury nullification affords African–American jurors the opportunity to control the authority of the law over some African–American criminal defendants. In essence, black people can "opt out" of American criminal law. * * *

* * *

In cases involving violent *malum in se* crimes like murder, rape, and assault, jurors should consider the case strictly on the evidence presented, and, if they have no reasonable doubt that the defendant is guilty, they should convict. For nonviolent *malum in se* crimes such as theft or perjury, nullification is an option that the juror should consider, although there should be no presumption in favor of it. A juror might vote for acquittal, for example, when a poor woman steals from Tiffany's, but not when the same woman steals from her next-door neighbor. Finally, in cases involving nonviolent, *malum prohibitum* offenses, including "victimless" crimes like narcotics offenses, there should be a presumption in favor of nullification. * * *

Why would a juror who is willing to ignore a law created through the democratic process be inclined to follow my proposal? There is no guarantee that she would. But when we consider that black jurors are already nullifying on the basis of race because they do not want to send another black man to prison, we recognize that these jurors are willing to use their power in a politically conscious manner. Many black people have concerns about their participation in the criminal justice system as jurors and might be willing to engage in some organized political conduct, not unlike the civil disobedience that African Americans practiced in the South in the 1950s and 1960s. It appears that some black jurors now excuse some conduct—like murder—that they should not excuse. My proposal, however, provides a principled structure for the exercise of the black juror's vote. I am not encouraging anarchy. Instead, I am reminding black jurors of their privilege to serve a higher calling than law: justice. I am suggesting a framework for what justice means in the African–American community.

———

Could Latino/a jurors use jury nullification to acquit young Latino defendants charged with minor crimes?

Since Paul Butler wrote his famous article, two further developments have taken place that illustrate minority disenchantment with the police and criminal justice system.

Snitching

In certain sectors of the black community, a vigorous, home-grown anti-snitching campaign, complete with rap songs, T-shirts, and intense peer pressure has sprung up. See, e.g., Jeremy Kahn, *The Story of a*

Snitch, The Atlantic, April, 2007, at 79; Alexandra Natapoff, *Snitching: The Institutional and Communal Consequences*, 73 U. Cin. L. Rev. 645 (2004).

Sanctuary and Water Bottles in the Desert

In the Latino community, and in certain circles of Anglo sympathizers, sentiment against Operation Gatekeeper and military-type enforcement of the border has coalesced into a powerful movement to aid desperate undocumented aliens reach their destination. Some churches and towns declare themselves "sanctuaries," where tired, frightened immigrants may obtain food and shelter without fear of legal consequences. Other groups leave water, food, and medical supplies in the desert where undocumented aliens struggling to reach U.S. cities may find them. See David A. Scharf, *For Humane Borders: Two Decades of Death and Illegal Activity in the Sonoran Desert*, 38 Case W. Res. J. Int'l L. 141 (2006); *Border Angels*, http://www.borderangels.org/mission.html (last visited April 4, 2007).

Corridos are beginning to sing the praises of coyotes, human smugglers who outwit border authorities and deliver their human charges safely to their destinations. A few, termed "narcocorridos," celebrate the exploits of drug dealers who escape the cops or succeed in eliminating a rival gang. See Guillermo E. Hernández, *What Is a Corrido?: Thematic Representation and Narrative Discourse*, http://www.chicano.ucla.edu/center/ events/whatisacorrido.html; Elijah Wald, *Narcocorrido: A Journey into the Music of Drugs, Guns, and Guerillas* (2000).

Notes and Questions

1. Is the sanctuary movement the present-day incarnation of Martin Luther King, Jr.'s religion-based program of black civil disobedience? Or is it a pointless exercise in trying to frustrate legitimate authorities merely doing their job?

2. Oppressed people have always sung and told about their predicament in tales and songs about injustice. These included the aforementioned corridos and black slave narratives. Are the narcocorridos any different? They do celebrate violence and bloodshed. But they assert, implicitly, that our drug laws are wrong and misguided and that drug dealers are merely honest businessmen trying to make a living. Do you agree?

3. Acosta was a notorious and frequent drug-user who believed that narcotics enhanced his consciousness, enabled him to see the outlines of mass oppression of his people, and be a better lawyer. Does that espousal help or hurt the cause for justice?

4. Storytelling has also caught on in the law, where a host of writers employ narrative, fiction, and other imaginative mediums to advance legal ideas. See, e.g., Derrick Bell, *Faces at the Bottom of the Well: The Permanence of Racism* (1992); Richard Delgado, *The Rodrigo Chronicles: Conversations about America and Race* (1995); Thomas Ross, *The Richmond Narra-*

tives, 68 Tex. L. Rev. 381 (1989). On the use of storytelling to mock, challenge, and subvert comfortable majoritarian myths and legal tales, such as without-intent-no-discrimination, see Richard Delgado, *Storytelling for Oppositionists and Others: A Plea for Narrative*, 87 Mich. L. Rev. 2411 (1989). On the use of simple observation to accomplish the same task, see Richard Delgado, *The Imperial Scholar: Reflections on a Review of Civil Rights Literature*, 132 U. Pa. L. Rev. 561 (1984); *The Imperial Scholar Revisited: How to Marginalize Outsider Writing, Ten Years Later*, 140 U. Pa. L. Rev. 1349 (1992).

5. Is a subversive story a form of "rebellious lawyering?" For the argument that social change requires legal change, which, in turn, requires displacing legal doctrines and narratives through energetic and well-told "counterstories," see Delgado, *Oppositionists and Others*, supra.

6. In recent years, a "Lat/Crit" movement has sprung up that considers some of the issues covered in this book, along with much else. The movement features an annual conference and sponsors field trips to foreign countries. See http://www.latcrit.org.

Gerald P. López
The Work We Know So Little About
42 Stan. L. Rev. 1, 1–10, 12–13 (1989)

I met someone not long ago who too many of us regrettably have come to regard as unremarkable, someone who might well find herself, along any number of fronts, working with a lawyer in a fight for social change. I'll call her María Elena. She lives with her two children in San Francisco's Mission District where she works as a housekeeper. She works as a mother too. And as a tutor of sorts. And as a seamstress. And as a cook. And as a support for those other women—those other Irish–American women, African–American women, Chinese–American women, and most especially those other Latinas—with whom she finds herself in contact. She works in much the same way as many other low-income women of color I've known over the years—women who surrounded me while I was growing up in East L.A., women who helped out in certain fights I participated in while practicing in San Diego, women who largely sustain various formal and informal grassroots efforts that a number of our law students now work with in those communities of working poor that line the east side of Highway 101 on the peninsula, from San Francisco through San Jose.

How María Elena and her children make it from day to day tells us all a great deal about where we live, whom we live with, and even about how peoples' actual experiences measure up to the "American dream"— a contrast that nowadays tends to get obscured and even denied around an election year. Indeed, our own lives are tied inescapably to the María Elenas in our communities. These women are important parts of our economy, indispensable parts of certain of our worklives, and even intimate parts of some of our households. In a very palpable way, María Elena's struggles implicate us. More perhaps than we acknowledge and more perhaps than feels comfortable, she and we help construct one another's identities. We're entangled.

Historically, you'd think that how the María Elenas of our communities make it from day to day should have played an obvious and central role in training those whose vocation is to serve as lawyers in the fight for social change. After all, the lives in which these lawyers intervene often differ considerably from their own—in terms of class, gender, race, ethnicity, and sexual orientation. Without laboring to understand these lives and their own entanglements with them, how else can lawyers begin to appreciate how their professional knowledge and skills may be perceived and deployed by those with whom they strive to ally themselves? How else can they begin to speculate about how their intervention may affect their clients' everyday relationships with employers, landlords, spouses, and the state? And how else can they begin to study whether proposed strategies actually have a chance of penetrating the social and economic situations they'd like to help change?

But, as my niece might say, "Get a clue!" Whatever else law schools may be, they have not characteristically been where future lawyers go to learn about how the poor and working poor live. Or about how the elderly cope. Or about how the disabled struggle. Or about how gays and lesbians build their lives in worlds that deny them the basic integrity of identity. Or about how single women of color raise their children in the midst of underfinanced schools, inadequate social support, and limited job opportunities. Indeed, in many ways both current and past lawyers fighting for social change and all with whom they collaborate (both clients and other social activists) have had to face trying to learn how largely to overcome rather than to take advantage of law school experience. What's ultimately extraordinary, I think, is that these relationships work at all and that we can even sometimes fully realize an allied fight for social change.

If you think this overstates all that together confronts the María Elenas of our communities and those lawyers with whom they work, take a brief glimpse through my eyes at María Elena's life and what it seems to say about any future relationship she might have with even the best lawyers. Thirty-one years old, she first set foot in this country a little over eight years ago. She came from Mexico with her husband, their two-year-old son, their three-month-old daughter, and no immigration documents. Not unlike thousands upon thousands of others, the family worked its way from San Diego, through Los Angeles, to Gilroy— picking flowers, mowing lawns, and harvesting fruit—surviving on the many day laborers' jobs that pervade the secondary labor market in this state and living in situations the rest of us would recoil from. Nearly two years later, they finally landed in the Mission District, expecting to reunite with some cousins and gain some stability. Instead, they found only confusing tales from various sources about how their *primos* had been deported after an INS factory raid in the East Bay.

More by force of habit than anything else, María Elena found herself trying to make do—hustling a place to live and her first job as a housekeeper. But the frustrations and indignities of undocumented life already had begun to take their toll on her husband. He couldn't find stable work; he couldn't support his family; he couldn't adjust to the sort of shadowy existence they seemed compelled to endure. Somewhere along the line, María Elena can't quite remember when, he just sort of withdrew from it all. From her, from the children, from trying. He wasn't violent or drunken. He just shrank into himself and didn't do much at all for months. And then one day when María Elena and the kids returned from grocery shopping, he was gone.

That was some four years ago and (it doesn't take much talking to María Elena to realize) many lonely, confused, hurt, angry, scared, and even guilty tears ago. It was also some 1,300–plus housekeeping days ago. For María Elena has come to realize the hard way that housekeeping for her and for so many other women of color no longer serves as the first and worst of jobs in a work career in the United States—as, for example, it once did in the late nineteenth century and still to some degree does for women from Western Europe. It's not that María Elena hasn't tried to find a job that pays better, that offers benefits and job security. She'd be interested, for example, in pursuing a recently publicized opening for some low-level industrial job, except that other Latinas have told her about the employer's so-called fetal protection policy—one that either endangers the health of future children or forces women to get sterilized. And she episodically searches for openings as a custodian and as an electronics assembler—jobs which most of us think of as being on the bottom rung of the job ladder, but which in most regards would be a step up for her and other housekeepers. She's found these jobs very hard to come by, however, except for the occasional openings on night shifts which her obligations to her kids just won't permit her to take.

Though she may be stuck in her job as a housekeeper, there's something unresolved and edgy about María Elena's daily existence. Things are always moving for her and her kids. Getting off to school and work. Coordinating the kids' return with a neighbor's afternoon schedule. Timing her own return with enough space to care for their needs and anxieties, particularly about school. Dealing with their illnesses while still honoring her housekeeping obligations. Often she drags her kids places others would not, and sometimes she leaves them alone when those of us who can afford the luxury of help would never consider it. She never has enough money to buy everything they see around them, but she tries to make sure they get what they need. When times get bad, they cut back. All in all, she seems to be a master of planned improvisation—about food, shelter, and medical care. You can feel her will and drive, and you can easily imagine her children's best efforts to help out. You can also sense, however, the interconnectedness of a range of difficult conditions any one of which might drive most of us to feeling that things had gotten out of control.

As if life weren't eventful enough, last year proved particularly epochal for María Elena and the kids. She decided to try to legalize their status in the United States through the provisions of the Immigration Reform and Control Act—the so-called amnesty program. It wasn't so much that the decision demanded that she resolve complex feelings about national allegiance; instead, it seemed to require that she make their lives vulnerable to law, to lawyers, and to government bureaucracy. For diffuse reasons, María Elena has come to regard law and lawyers as more dangerous than helpful. And time and again she has experienced governmental bureaucracies as inscrutable, senseless, and unchangeable. Even many of the lawyers and social service providers who advertised their willingness to help with legalization seemed, so far as she could tell, gouging, disorganized or both.

So, in her effort to retain some control over the situation, María Elena cautiously took advantage of a self-help program designed and delivered by a service organization which a number of her neighbors and local church groups had recommended as trustworthy and able. She found the program direct, accessible, and patient. In her words, "They kinda knew what we had to hear—you know, what we were going through, what we needed to do. From step one on." In this sense, she was lucky. For while some 70 percent of applicants both in the Bay Area and nationally undertook to complete their legalization applications on their own, most did not have the advantage of any effective outreach efforts, much less programs that spoke directly to their needs.

Still, María Elena experienced the message she heard about the law's demands as profoundly threatening and disorienting. * * * Like virtually every other undocumented worker, she had become expert at not leaving a paper trail. And she had found many people willing to accommodate her efforts to achieve a certain invisibility. Every one of her previous employers, for example, paid her in cash for her work— though perhaps not so much to protect her and her children, as to protect themselves, since they rarely paid minimum wage and never paid into social security for her housekeeping. Now, through some perverse irony, she was being told that she'd better hope that she hadn't been too good at covering her tracks.

* * * One former employer (a family of married doctors whose house and children María Elena cared for over a fifteen-month period) mistakenly feared that documenting María Elena's employment would expose them to criminal liability both for having employed an undocumented worker and for having not paid minimum wage or into social security. While the couple somewhat grudgingly wrote a short note on their personal stationery to help María Elena meet the application deadline, they refused a subsequent INS request—a quite standard one—for a notarized statement. So María Elena found herself again trying to talk the couple into helping—doing her best to explain the law, to avoid inadvertently antagonizing them, and to help them work through the embarrassment they seemed to fear in making a notarized admission.

* * *

So, like so many other people in her position, María Elena does her best to sort her way through the confusion. She's tried to reconcile the cautious advice of certain church and service organizations with the glitzy radio ads promoting private programs that guarantee green cards—all the time remembering to keep her ear to the ground for the ever-evolving rumors that make their way around the Mission. She heard somewhere that certain courses at community colleges and high schools have been or will be certified by the INS as meeting the ESL/Civics requirements. But she's found a number of schools increasingly cautious about promising anything, others suspiciously willing to promise too much, and most courses with waiting lists backed up seemingly forever. Meanwhile, to bring matters full circle, she's begun to sense that the employers she now works for would very much like her to get all this taken care of—so that they can know whether they can depend on her or have to hire another housekeeper.

For all her problems, María Elena just can't see herself seeking a lawyer's help, even at places with so positive a reputation as, say, the Immigrant Legal Resource Center, the Employment Law Center, or California Rural Legal Assistance. "Being on the short end and being on the bottom is an everyday event in my life," she says, half-smiling. "What can a lawyer do about that?" That doesn't make it all right, she admits. But she says she's learned to live with it—to deal with it in her own ways. In any event, lawyers and law all seem to conjure up for her big, complicated fights—fights that, as she sees it, would pit her against a social superior, her word against that of a more respected someone else, her lack of written records against the seemingly infinite amount of paper employers seem able to come up with when they must. Because she retains her sense of order by focusing on keeping her family's head above water, lawyers and law most often seem irrelevant to and even inconsistent with her day-to-day struggles.

Were María Elena alone in these sentiments, lawyers might have little cause for concern. But you may be surprised to learn that María Elena is scarcely unique in her views about lawyers and law—though, to be sure, some of her problems may well be peculiarly the product of her immigration status. In fact, we are beginning to discover that many other low-income women of color—Asian–Americans, Native–Americans, Latinas, Blacks—apparently feel much the same way as María Elena, even if they were born here and even when their families have been in this country for generations. Much else may well divide these women—after all, political and social subordination is not a homogeneous or monolithic experience. Still, their actions seem to confirm María Elena's impulses and their words seem to echo María Elena's own.

The little thus far uncovered about whether and how people translate perceived injuries into legal claims seems to confirm what apparently the María Elenas in our communities have been trying to tell us for quite some time, each in her own way. *Low-income women of color seldom go to lawyers, and they institute lawsuits a good deal less frequently than anybody else.* More particularly, they convert their experiences of oppression into claims of discrimination far less often than they (and everybody else) press any other legal claim. Indeed, most learn never even to call oppressive treatment an injury; if they do, many simply "lump it" rather than personally pressing it against the other party, much less pressing a formal claim through a lawyer. For all the popular (and I might add exaggerated) descriptions bemoaning how litigious we've all become, nearly all careful observers concede that low-income women of color seek legal remedies far too infrequently, especially when discriminated against at work. Partly as a result, they still seem to endure regularly the injustice and the indignities that those in high office insist just don't exist much in this enlightened era—at least not in their circles, where everyone seems to be doing just fine.

Most of us presume that this state of affairs bespeaks the unfortunate failure of these women constructively to use lawyers and law—an inability to serve their own needs. You know the litany as well as I do—it almost rolls off the tongue. Lack of information and knowledge about their rights. Limited resources for using legal channels. Limited understanding of the legal culture. * * * The anticipation of rejections by unresponsive agencies, the cost and unavailability of lawyers, the technical obstacles to pursuing causes of action all serve in advance as background assumptions deterring low-income women of color from pressing formal claims. But if you listen carefully to people like María Elena, you begin to realize that they're saying something else is also going on—something that both they themselves and the lawyers with whom they work often find even more difficult to overcome.

Apparently, in order to use law (particularly antidiscrimination law) and lawyers, many low-income women of color must overcome fear, guilt, and a heightened sense of destruction. In their eyes, such a decision often amounts to nothing less intimidating than taking on conventional power with relatively little likelihood of meaningful success. It also means assuming an adversarial posture toward the very same people and institutions that, in some perverse ways, you've come to regard as connected to you, at least insofar as they employ you when others will not (put aside at what wage, under what conditions, and with what benefits). And it seems inevitably to entail making your life entirely vulnerable to the law—with its powers to unravel the little you've got going for yourself and your family. * * *

Instead of using law and lawyers, most low-income women of color often deal with oppressive circumstances through their own stock of informal strategies. Sometimes they tend to minimize or reinterpret obvious discrimination. María Elena, for example, tells me she often chalks up bad treatment to personal likes or dislikes or denies that it could really be about her. * * *

Yet for the most part, these low-income women of color have fewer illusions about these strategies than you might first presume. They know that you can't explain away all discriminatory treatment and that you can't alter every oppressive situation through informal devices. And they even seem to sense that while they may perceive their own less formal approach to their problems as self-sustaining, it often turns out to be self-defeating. After all, they know better than the rest of us that too many of them still get paid too little, for too many hours of work, in terrible conditions, with absolutely no health benefits or care for their children, and with little current hope of much job mobility over the course of their lifetimes.

* * *

Somehow in the midst of all this, the María Elenas of our communities and at least the very best lawyers with whom they work still manage more than occasionally to make contact, to get things done, and even to find credible self-affirmation in the collective effort. In some instances, no doubt, they join together out of desperation. If you need help badly enough and if you want to help badly enough, you can often figure out ways to hook up and make the relationship other than dysfunctional. That endeavor is nothing to scoff at. It may well suggest how most things get done in this world, and it certainly says something about the human spirit under pressure.

At its best, this joint effort at fighting political and social subordination can be a story of magnificent mutual adaptation. At those times, both the María Elenas of our communities and those lawyers with whom they work face the enigma of their relationship head on. * * * Both depend on the other to make some sense of how their overlapping knowledge and skills might inform a plausible plan of action. Both try to connect their particular struggle to other particular struggles and to particular visions of the state and the political economy. And both inevitably challenge the other as together they put a part of themselves on the line. In short, when things go well they seem capable of favorably redefining over time the very terms that otherwise circumscribe their capacity to take advantage of one another's will to fight.

* * *

* * * Still, you should realize that legal education's historical disregard of practice with the politically and socially subordinated survives in all of us, even as some of us continue to try to break with this past. All of us (practitioners, teachers, students, other lay and professional activists) have learned, to one degree or another, not even really to notice inspired and imaginative work in fights against subordination, much less to study how it happens, how it might be taught, and what it might mean for us all. It's not simply that I think we have screwed-up views about lawyering for social change. More critically, we don't even treat it, because we don't even see it, as remarkably complex and enigmatic work—with multiple and even elusive dimensions, presenting massive conceptual and empirical challenges, and cultural and interpersonal dynamics more daunting and even more self-defining than we are accustomed to handling. Just as we have come to regard María Elena as too unremarkable to pay much attention to, so too have we come to understand working with her as like anything else in law, except (to be truthful) a lot more lightweight, formulaic, and intellectually vapid.

* * *

At the heart of the matter, we simply must come to realize that we all make those communities we call our own. That the problems of the María Elenas of this world are our problems, the future of María Elena's children is our future, and that the failure to share what clout we do exercise is ultimately our own failure, and a tragic and even dangerous one at that. We have a rare chance over the next several years to bring to life the systematic study of the work we know so little about, work that in many ways tells us precisely what we need most to know about ourselves—those sorts of things we'd often rather not hear, much less change. If we're big enough as people and honest enough as an institution, then in the near future María Elena and those others with whom she lives and labors might even come to recognize themselves as mattering—as systematically mattering—to the training we provide and the practice of law we help inspire.

Notes and Questions

1.　Is López right (Acosta, too) that lawyers for minority communities should live in those communities and send their kids to school there? If you were a legal assistance lawyer, would you live in the community your office serves? What if a deeply committed Anglo lawyer, working in a legal aid office that serves the Latino community, prefers not to live in that community but in an exciting, "hot" part of town with his Anglo friends? Should he seek another line of work?

2.　Suppose you are counsel to a group of disgusted radicals insistent on working for racial justice but impatient with the slow pace of change. They have attempted peaceful, law-abiding tactics such as sit-ins, letters to the editor, pamphlets, and organizing voter registration drives and gotten nowhere. The group is now considering introducing a secret virus into every computer in the United States that will disable it for one month, beginning on the fifth of May (Cinco de Mayo). Although they intend the virus to be merely a nuisance that will not do permanent harm, their action would, in fact, violate federal law. As their counsel, what do you advise the group? Would you warn them of the consequences of their proposed course of conduct, and let it go at that? Turn them in to the police? Resign as their lawyer?

3.　Re-read Patrisia Gonzales and Roberto Rodriguez, *We Are All Zapatistas*, in Part Five, Chapter 14, § 3, supra. Are the Latin American Indians entitled to rebel against illegitimate authority—including the United States government and multinational corporations? Would you help them?

A colonized people will eventually rebel against its condition. See Part Four, Prefatory Note and Part Six, Chapter 16, § 1, supra on postcolonial writings, including Frantz Fanon. Recall, as well, the material on the Puerto Rican nationalist movement in Part One. The United States today is the site of a slow-growing movement to restore ancient land rights, particularly in the Southwest, and land, water, fishing, grazing, and hunting claims.

Muneer I. Ahmad
Interpreting Communities: Lawyering Across Language Difference
54 UCLA L. Rev. 999, 999–1004, 1085–86 (2007)

As the rapid growth of immigrant communities in recent years transforms the demography of the United States, language diversity is emerging as a critical feature of this transformation. Poor and low-wage workers and their families in the aggressively globalized U.S. economy increasingly are Limited English Proficient, renewing longstanding debates about language diversity. And yet, despite a growing awareness of the challenges posed by limited English proficiency to the social, economic, political, and cultural well-being of poor immigrants today, relatively little attention has been paid to the role of language difference in poverty lawyering. This Article confronts the complexities of lawyering across language difference. Starting with the principal model for poverty lawyering—client-centeredness—it suggests the inadequacy of the model for meeting the challenges of language difference, particularly when an interpreter is interposed in the paradigmatic lawyer-client dyad. The nature of interpretation argues in favor of a more collaborative relationship among lawyers, clients, and interpreters than is often seen in poverty law practice. Specifically, it suggests that the disruption effected by the introduction of an interpreter may be more productive than is typically realized, and invites a normative reconceptualiztion of the traditional lawyer-client relationship. [It also urges] an emerging set of practices known as community interpreting, and [an] increased attention to cultural context, third-party relationships, and community [engagement].

INTRODUCTION

In Merced, California, a twelve-year-old Laotian boy serves as an interpreter for his Hmong-speaking mother and her English-speaking doctor, and inadvertently mistranslates the doctor's instructions for her prescription medications; the mother overdoses. In a jail in Prince William County, Virginia, a monolingual Spanish-speaking man is imprisoned for three months after criminal charges against him are dismissed, because no one comes to release him and he is unable to communicate with anyone in the facility. And a family court in Long Beach, California refuses to hear a divorce case because the indigent client failed to provide her own interpreter. Cases like these, in the health care system, the criminal justice system, and the courts, have begun to draw public attention to the ways in which inadequate attention to the country's growing language diversity increasingly jeopardizes life and liberty interests, particularly of poor people. And yet, as growth in immigrant communities dramatically alters the challenges faced by poverty lawyers, one of the critical sites for the protection and advancement of the interests of poor people—the lawyer-client relationship—remains largely unexplored in the context of language difference. This

Article examines the phenomenon of lawyering across language difference, the radical disruption it effects on the traditional lawyer-client relationship, and the fundamental challenges it poses to the prevailing, client-centered model of representation for poverty lawyering. Troubling though they may be, I argue that these disruptions and challenges pose important opportunities for poverty lawyers to reimagine a more open, dynamic, and porous lawyer-client relationship than exists in traditional lawyering theory and practice.

* * *

The core challenge to client-centeredness arises from the integral role of interpreters in the process of lawyering across language difference. Except in those limited circumstances where poverty lawyers are bilingual, interpreters figure prominently in the representation of Limited English Proficient (LEP) clients. Their very presence disrupts the one-lawyer, one-client, dyadic norm on which the client-centered model (and traditional lawyering more generally) is premised, and their active engagement injects the subjectivity of a third person—her thoughts and feelings, attitudes and opinions, personality and perception—into what previously had been the exclusive province of the lawyer and client. The paradigmatic direct bond of communication between lawyer and client is now mediated, and therefore modified, by another individual. As a result of this perceived intrusion and real disruption, many lawyers view interpreters with suspicion, and may wish to confine the interpreter's role to that of a machine, not unlike a telephone, merely transmitting "exact" translations, free of subjectivity, from one side to the other. And yet, when properly understood, the linguistic complexity and cultural embeddedness of interpretation reveal the lie of verbatim translation and underscore the inescapable subjectivity of all interpretation.

Once we acknowledge the subjectivity that inheres in interpretation, we can move in one of two directions: either to squelch that subjectivity and attempt to force the interpreter back into the fictive box of technology; or to embrace the subjectivity, draw it out further, scrutinize it rigorously, and engage it dialogically. Most lawyers, and the legal system as a whole, attempt the former. I argue unambiguously for the latter. By accepting the interpreter as a partner rather than rejecting her as an interloper, by resolving the dynamic of dependence and distrust in favor of collaboration, lawyers can enhance LEP client voice and autonomy while increasing their engagement in the communities from which their clients hail.

Moreover, by opening ourselves up to the active engagement of interpreters in the lawyer-(interpreter-)client relationship, we also expand our understanding of the universe of actors, contexts, and discourses that any lawyer-client relationship involves. The interpreter visibly marks outside influences, considerations, and concerns that animate all lawyer-client relationships. She literally embodies the third person who, by virtue of her effect on both the lawyer and the client, shapes and alters the content and form of lawyer-client communication. But even when the lawyer and client speak the same language, even when there is no interpreter present, *there is always a third person in the room*. Absent an interpreter, both lawyers and clients still draw upon or are otherwise influenced by actors and forces that, while not physically manifested in the interview room, profoundly affect the lawyer-client relationship. A client's pastor, family considerations, involvement in a community group, or concern for her reputation in the community may inform her views. Similarly, the expectations of a lawyer's supervising attorney, her professional aspirations, or her political commitments may shape the lawyer's perspective. These third-party influences operate invisibly within the confines of the client interview room. An examination of lawyering across language difference, however, can render them visible and thereby generate a more nuanced understanding of the lawyer-client relationship, one that more fully accounts for the social contexts in which the lawyer and the client reside.

The challenges of lawyering across language difference, properly understood, can help us begin to reconceptualize the lawyer-client relationship not as a closed system, as it is traditionally understood, but as a more porous, though still privileged, relationship in which a range of mediating forces is recognized, negotiated, and embraced.

* * *

Like its goals and methodologies, the challenges of and objections to community lawyering have been explicated by others. Two limitations in particular recur—the impact of such strategies on client autonomy, and the challenges of engaging in community lawyering strategies within the bounds of the rules of professional conduct. To be sure, these constraints are real, but as the literature in this area demonstrates, they are challenges to be managed, rather than absolute barriers to community lawyering.

The example of lawyering across language difference does not resolve these challenges. Rather, it presents particular permutations of them, and suggests ways of negotiating them. While lawyering across language difference does not necessarily compel community lawyering, at the same time, effective lawyering across language difference demands an orientation to lawyering that draws upon and is consistent with community lawyering practices. The potential of robust collaboration between lawyer, client, and interpreter thus suggests a far grander vision of lawyer engagement not only in the cases of clients, but in the struggles of communities.

CONCLUSION

The lawyer's role frequently has been analogized to that of an interpreter: fluent in two vocabularies, cultures, and modalities of expression, and charged with translating client interests into language and form intelligible by the law while translating the cultural idiosyncrasy of law into language intelligible by clients. Lawyering across language difference breathes new life into this metaphor, but also complicates it significantly by deepening our understanding of the nature of interpretation, the centrality and the difficulty of cultural analysis, and the irreducibility of mediating forces in the lives of our clients. As Gerald López has observed, interpreting makes us communitarians. It thrusts us into the lives of our clients, their social and political contexts, and their webs of relationships. It forces us to reckon with the communities to which our clients claim belonging, or which claim belonging of them. The more open and fluid lawyer-client relationship that results is both necessary to protect the agency and voice of the client, and, at the same time, threatening to them. This is nothing more, and nothing less, than the challenge of community.

SECTION 3.   CONTINUING STRUGGLES OVER LAND

Lobato v. Taylor
71 P.3d 938 (Colo. 2002) (en banc),
cert. denied, 540 U.S. 1073 (2003)

CHIEF JUSTICE MULLARKEY delivered the Opinion of the Court.

The history of this property rights controversy began before Colorado's statehood, at a time when southern Colorado was part of Mexico; at a time when all of the parties' lands were part of the one million acre Sangre de Cristo grant, an 1844 Mexican land grant. Here, we determine access rights of the owners of farmlands in Costilla County to a mountainous parcel of land now known as the Taylor Ranch. As successors in title to the original settlers in the region, the landowners exercised rights to enter and use the Taylor Ranch property for over one hundred years until Jack Taylor fenced the land in 1960 and forcibly excluded them. These rights, they assert, derive from Mexican law, prescription, and an express or implied grant, and were impermissibly denied when the mountain land was fenced.

* * *

We find that evidence of traditional settlement practices, repeated references to settlement rights in documents associated with the Sangre de Cristo grant, the one hundred year history of the landowners' use of the Taylor Ranch, and other evidence of necessity, reliance, and intention support a finding of implied rights in this case. While we reject the landowners' claims for hunting, fishing, and recreation rights, we find that the landowners have rights of access for grazing, firewood, and timber through a prescriptive easement, an easement by estoppel, and an easement from prior use.

In 1844, the governor of New Mexico granted two Mexican nationals a one million-acre land grant, located mainly in present-day southern Colorado (Sangre de Cristo grant), for the purpose of settlement. The original grantees died during the war between the United States and Mexico. The land was not settled in earnest until after the cessation of the war, and Charles (Carlos) Beaubien then owned the grant.

In 1848, the United States and Mexico entered into the Treaty of Guadalupe Hidalgo, ending the war between the two countries. Pursuant to the treaty, Mexico ceded land to the United States, including all of California, Nevada, and Utah; most of New Mexico and Arizona; and a portion of Colorado. The United States agreed to honor the existing property rights in the ceded territory. Relevant to the Sangre de Cristo grant, Congress asked the Surveyor General of the Territory of New Mexico to determine what property rights existed at the time of the treaty. On the Surveyor General's recommendation, Congress confirmed Carlos Beaubien's claim to the Sangre de Cristo grant in the 1860 Act of Confirmation.

In the early 1850s, Beaubien successfully recruited farm families to settle the Colorado portion of the Sangre de Cristo grant. He leased a portion of his land to the United States government to be used to establish Fort Massachusetts and recruited farmers to settle other areas. The settlement system he employed was common to Spain and Mexico: strips of arable land called *vara* strips were allotted to families for farming, and areas not open for cultivation were available for common use. These common areas were used for grazing and recreation and as a source for timber, firewood, fish, and game.

In 1863, Beaubien gave established settlers deeds to their vara strips. That same year, Beaubien executed and recorded a Spanish language document that purports to grant rights of access to common lands to settlers on the Sangre de Cristo grant (Beaubien Document). In relevant part, this document guarantees that "all the inhabitants will have enjoyment of benefits of pastures, water, firewood and timber, always taking care that one does not injure another."

A year later, Beaubien died. Pursuant to a prior oral agreement, his heirs sold his interest in the Sangre de Cristo grant to William Gilpin, who was Colorado's first territorial governor. The sales agreement (Gilpin agreement) stated that Gilpin agreed to provide vara strip deeds to settlers who had not yet received them. The agreement further stated that Gilpin took the land on condition that certain "settlement rights before then conceded . . . to the residents of the settlements . . . shall be confirmed by said William Gilpin as made by him."

In 1960, Jack Taylor, a North Carolina lumberman, purchased roughly 77,000 acres of the Sangre de Cristo grant (mountain tract) from a successor in interest to William Gilpin. Taylor's deed indicated that he took the land subject to "claims of the local people by prescription or otherwise to right to pasture, wood, and lumber and so-called settlement rights in, to, and upon said land."

Despite the language in Taylor's deed, he denied the local landowners access to his land and began to fence the property. * * *

The landowners claim rights to graze livestock, gather firewood and timber, hunt, fish, and recreate. * * * We conclude that the rights the landowners are claiming are best characterized as easements appurtenant to the land. We reach this conclusion from the evidence that under

Mexican custom access to common land was given to surrounding landowners, the evidence that this access was used to benefit the use of the land, and the presumption in favor of appurtenant easements.

The landowners argue that their settlement rights stem from three sources: Mexican law, prescription, and an express or implied grant from Beaubien.

Regarding the Mexican law claim, the landowners claim that community rights to common lands not only are recognized by Mexican law, but also are integral to the settlement of an area. The landowners further point out that in the Treaty of Guadalupe Hidalgo, the United States government agreed that the land rights of the residents of the ceded territories would be "inviolably respected." Under the landowners' theory, the treaty dictates that the court apply Mexican law to the Taylor Ranch and accordingly recognize the settlement rights.

The landowners further argue that use rights can be found via prescription. For this claim, they point to their regular use of the Taylor Ranch land for over one hundred years until the area was fenced in 1960.

Lastly, the landowners assert that their use rights were obtained by either an express or implied grant from Carlos Beaubien. For this claim, the landowners rely primarily on the Beaubien Document.

* * *

We [decide] that the landowners cannot claim rights under Mexican law. Their predecessors in title did not settle on the Sangre de Cristo grant until after the land was ceded to the United States and thus their use rights developed under United States law. Mexican land use and property law are highly relevant in this case in ascertaining the intentions of the parties involved. However, because the settlement of the grant occurred after the land was ceded to the United States, we conclude that Mexican law cannot be a source of the landowners' claims.

* * *

THE BEAUBIEN DOCUMENT

As evidence of a grant of rights from Carlos Beaubien, the landowners rely primarily on the Beaubien Document. The document was written by Beaubien in 1863, one year before his death.

One English translation of the document reads, in part:

Plaza of San Luis de la Culebra, May 11, 1863.

It has been decided that the lands of the Rito Seco remain uncultivated for the benefit of the community members (gente) of the plazas of San Luis, San Pablo and Los Ballejos and for the other inhabitants of these plazas for pasturing cattle by the payment of a fee per head, etc. and that the water of the said Rito remains partitioned among the inhabitants of the same plaza of San Luis and those from the other side of the vega who hold lands almost adjacent to it as their own lands, that are not irrigated with the waters of the Rio Culebra. The vega, after the measurement of three acres from it in front of the chapel, to which they have been donated, will remain for the benefit of the inhabitants of this plaza and those of the Culebra as far as above the plaza of Los Ballejos.... Those below the road as far as the narrows will have the right to enjoy the same benefit.... *[No one may] place any obstacle or obstruction to anyone in the enjoyment of his legitimate rights....* Likewise, each one should take scrupulous care in the use of water without causing damage with it to his neighbors nor to anyone. According to the corresponding rule, *all the inhabitants will have enjoyment of benefits of pastures, water, firewood and timber, always taking care that one does not injure another.*

(Emphases added.)

* * *

We find that the Beaubien document, when taken together with the other unique facts of this case, establishes a prescriptive easement, an easement by estoppel, and an easement from prior use.

Extrinsic evidence is relevant in interpreting the Beaubien Document. * * * Extrinsic evidence may reveal ambiguities in modern documents; that principle can be only more true with respect to the Beaubien Document. We are attempting to construe a 150 year-old document written in Spanish by a French Canadian who obtained a conditional grant to an enormous land area under Mexican law and perfected it under American law. Beaubien wrote this document when he was near the end of his adventurous life in an apparent attempt to memorialize commitments he had made to induce families to move hundreds of miles to make homes in the wilderness. It would be the height of arrogance and nothing but a legal fiction for us to claim that we can interpret this document without putting it in its historical context.

For the most part, the document is reasonably specific in identifying places where rights are to be exercised. That is not true with respect to the rights asserted by the landowners. The key language reads: "According to the corresponding rule, all the inhabitants will have enjoyment of benefits of pastures, water, firewood and timber, always taking care that one does not injure another."

Thus, given the specificity of other parts of the document, the lack of specificity in this sentence creates an ambiguity. We cannot determine from the face of the document what lands were burdened by the rights Beaubien conveyed to the first settlers.

We look to the extrinsic evidence in this case. Amici assert that the contrast between the specificity of the majority of the Beaubien Document and the casual reference to the settlement rights at the end of the document can best be explained by the events surrounding the execution of the document. Beaubien penned the document at a time when settlement was moving to the northern area of the grant, which lies northwest of the Taylor Ranch area. At that time, he wrote the Beaubien Document to establish common rights to the area in and around San Luis and at the same time memorialize settlement rights that had already been in existence in the more southern areas of the grant, where Taylor Ranch is located.

We agree with the amici. From the trial court findings, expert testimony, the documents associated with the grant, and a review of the settlement system under which Beaubien and the settlers were operating, we draw two conclusions. First, we conclude that the location for the settlement rights referenced in the Beaubien Document is the mountainous area of the grant on which Taylor Ranch is located. Second, we conclude that Beaubien meant to grant permanent access rights that run with the land.

We first discuss the location for the rights. The evidence in this case establishes that the reference to pasture, water, firewood, and timber in the Beaubien Document refers to access on the mountain area of the grant of which Taylor Ranch is a part.

* * *

There is also ample evidence that the document was meant to create permanent rights that run with the land. * * * Access to common areas was an integral feature of the settlement system under which the settlers and Beaubien were operating. Under Spanish and Mexican law, the government awarded community and private grants for the purpose of settling the frontier.

* * * Under colonial and Mexican law, the difference between a community grant and a private grant was that the common lands of the community could not be sold; the grantee of a private grant could sell the lands.

Expert reports submitted in this case reveal that Beaubien and the original settlers operated under this traditional system. Common areas were not only a typical feature but a necessary incentive for settlement.

As discussed above, because the Sangre de Cristo grant was part of the United States at the time permanent settlement began, this Mexican settlement tradition is not the source of the landowners' rights. However, because the settlers and Beaubien were so familiar with the settlement system, it is highly relevant in ascertaining the parties' intentions and expectations.

* * *

Thus, we conclude both that rights were granted and exercised from the time of settlement and that the Beaubien Document memorialized them. Moreover, we conclude that the location for the rights is the mountain portion of the grant of which Taylor Ranch is a part, and that the benefit and burden of these rights were meant to run with the land. * * * The law of implied easements recognizes that rights may be implied even though they were not properly expressly conveyed. This well-established area of property law is concerned with honoring the intentions of the parties to land transactions and avoiding injustice.

* * *

[The court concluded that the landowners had established a prescriptive easement, an easement by estoppel, and an easement from prior use.]

Having found that the landowners have implied profits in the Taylor Ranch, we now must address the scope of those rights. * * * We hold that the landowners have implied rights in Taylor's land for the access detailed in the Beaubien Document—pasture, firewood, and timber. These easements should be limited to reasonable use—the grazing access is limited to a reasonable number of livestock given the size of the vara strips; the firewood limited to that needed for each residence; and the timber limited to that needed to construct and maintain residence and farm buildings located on the vara strips.... We reject the landowner's claims for hunting, fishing, and recreation.

JUSTICE MARTINEZ dissenting only as to part II.C.

As the opinion by the chief justice correctly notes, this case involves the settlement rights of people who have been largely dispossessed of their rights in land when Taylor fenced the property. There is little dispute that the settlers enjoyed extensive rights in the lands that comprise the Taylor Ranch for about one hundred years. Rather, the dispute concerns the extent of the rights, if any, that survive when we construe settlement rights conceived in a different era pursuant to contemporary standards. In short, the difficulty of this case is that we must address the grave injustices imposed upon the settlers' successors in interest by interpreting documents from a different era, intended to reflect Beaubien's intent, through the perspective of modern property law. Nonetheless, equitable principles in our modern jurisprudence, properly construed and applied, permit us to recognize the rights of the settlers and their successors in interest.

Because I concur with the chief justice's analysis and conclusion that the landowners have access rights through a prescriptive easement, an easement by estoppel, and an easement from prior use, I join to make it the majority opinion and refer to it as such herein. * * * I believe that [the Beaubien] document cannot be read to limit the landowners' access rights to grazing, firewood, and timber. In my view, the imperfect nature of the Beaubien document requires us to look beyond that document to determine the full scope of the landowners' access rights. As a result, I would not limit the landowners' access rights; instead, based on the evidence in the record demonstrating that "settlement rights" encompassed more than grazing, firewood, and timber, I would also include access rights for fishing, hunting, and recreation through a prescriptive easement, an easement by estoppel, and an easement from prior use.

* * *

JUSTICE KOURLIS dissenting.

Although I have great sympathy for the historic and present plight of the landowners in this action, I cannot support the majority opinion for two reasons. First, it is my view that in 1863 Charles Beaubien attempted to make a community grant for the benefit of the inhabitants of the plazas of San Luis, San Pablo, and Los Ballejos. The law in effect at the time did not recognize such a grant and instead required individual identification of grantees. Hence, the Beaubien Document had no legal effect.

Second, I find no ambiguity either in the legal description in the Document or in the absence of grantee specificity. The legal description referred to the lands of the Rito Seco. The trial court found that the lands of the Rito Seco do not overlap with the current Taylor Ranch. There is no ambiguity; rather, the Document simply does not apply to Taylor Ranch. Additionally, the omission of grantee names was not an ambiguity: it was a clear attempt to create a communal grant, which was not legally recognized.

Because the Document is not ambiguous in any pertinent part, it cannot support an implication of rights not expressly set forth. Prescriptive easements, easements by estoppel, and easements from prior use do not apply to these facts.

* * *

In 1863, the year Charles Beaubien executed the Beaubien Document, under Colorado Territorial law, a document conveying any interest in real estate had to meet several formal requirements, including the requirements that it incorporate an accurate description of the property and the names of the grantees:

> the christian and surnames of the ... grantees ... and ... an accurate description of the premises, or the interest in the premises intended to be conveyed, and shall be subscribed by the party or parties making the same, and be duly proved or acknowledged, before some officer authorized to take the proof or acknowledgment of deeds, or by his, her or their attorney in fact.

The requirement that the document identify grantees by name is indicative of the territorial legislature's overt decision not to honor community grants that failed to mention specific grantees.

The Beaubien Document flatly fails to meet that requirement. The Beaubien Document does not give the christian and surnames of the grantees, instead only referring generally to the "community members" and "inhabitants" of specified villages. That omission is a legal deficiency that makes the document invalid as a conveyance under the operative law.

Compliance with real property law is a matter of substantial importance. In the early years of our history, the questions of who owned what and who could sell what were legitimate and pervasive concerns. As a citizenry, we clearly believed in the sanctity of private property and the ownership rights associated with it. * * *

The Beaubien Document, like every other real property transfer, must be held to the standards of the law in effect at the time it was executed in order to protect the certainty and marketability of property interests. The Document does not comport with those laws, and it, therefore, has no validity as to the landowners here.

* * *

American legal tradition has chosen to honor private property rights, sometimes to the detriment of communal rights. I have found no court that would recognize the easements that the landowners here urge. Because real property rights depend upon predictability and clarity of law, by attempting to do justice here in contravention of our precedent, we risk injustice elsewhere.

* * *

I do not believe that the landowners here have established their right to use the Taylor Ranch lands as they claim. They cannot, in my view, rely upon the Beaubien Document because it did not comply with the laws in effect at the time of its execution by failing to identify specific grantees. The document was not ambiguous, and therefore cannot support rights by implication. Further, none of the theories for implication of an easement apply to these facts.

REIES TIJERINA AND THE NEW MEXICO LAND GRANT WARS

The tradition of Mexican–American resistance to the conquest has continued well into the twentieth century. An early decision, *Rio Arriba Land & Cattle Co. v. United States*, 167 U.S. 298 (1897), concluded that the common lands of the San Joaquin land grant belonged in the public domain of the United States and not to the community. This decision resulted in the loss of many thousands of acres which are now contained within the Kit Carson and the Sangre de Cristo national forests. In the 1960s, Reies Tijerina established himself as a Chicano activist and leader when he mounted a major protest against the United States' seizure of these lands.

Rodolfo Acuña
Occupied America: A History of Chicanos
340–41 (3d. ed. 1988)

Reies López Tijerina, or *El Tigre*, was the most charismatic of the Chicano leaders. Born in 1926, in farm fields close to Fall City, Texas, he lived a marginal existence. The young man soon learned to hate his oppressors, especially Texas Rangers.

Tijerina became a preacher. He wandered into northern New Mexico, witnessing the poverty of the people there. [Tijerina] became interested in the land-grant question. He studied the Treaty of Guadalupe Hidalgo and became convinced that the national forest in Tierra Amarilla belonged to the *Pueblo de San Joaquín de Chama*. This was *ejido* land (communal or village land) that, according to Hispano–Mexican law, could not be sold and was to be held in common by the people. Villagers had the right to graze their animals and cut and gather timber in these forest lands. According to Tijerina, the U.S. government participated in frauds that deprived the people of the ejido lands. He got involved with the *Albiquiu* Corporation, an organization committed to the return of land grants to the New Mexicans.

In 1963 he incorporated *La Alianza Federal de Mercedes* (The Federal Alliance of Land Grants). It appealed to poor New Mexicans and to their lost dreams. The *Alianza* led marches on the state capital. On October 15, 1966, Tijerina and 350 members occupied the national forest campgrounds known as the Echo Amphitheatre and asserted the revival of the ejido rights of the Pueblo de San Joaquin de Chama, whose 1,400 acres lay mainly within the confines of the Kit Carson National Forest. In less than a week state police, sheriffs deputies, and Rangers moved in. On October 22 Alianza members took two Rangers into custody and tried them for trespassing and being a public nuisance. The Alianza court fined them and sentenced them to 11 months and 22 days in jail, and then "mercifully" suspended the sentence.

On November 6, 1967, Tijerina stood trial for the Amphitheatre affair. Original charges included conspiracy, but the jury threw it out. It did convict him of two counts of assault and he was sentenced to two years in a state penitentiary, with five years' probation.

Meanwhile, as the sentence was being appealed, Tijerina's actions alienated the establishment under the leadership of U.S. Senator Joseph Montoya. His support dwindled in New Mexico. Many followers were frightened by his growing militancy. Tijerina now entered Tierra Amarilla with the intention of making a citizen's arrest of District Attorney Alfonso Sánchez. A running gun battle followed and Tijerina was arrested. While on bail, he appeared at numerous protest rallies. Tijerina's uncompromising tactics gained him the admiration of militants and activists throughout the United States. In May and June 1968, Tijerina participated in the Poor People's Campaign, threatening to pull the Chicano contingent out if Black organizers did not treat them as equals. In the fall he ran for governor of New Mexico on the People's Constitutional party ticket.

Tijerina stood trial in late 1968 for the Tierra Amarilla raid. A key witness for the prosecution had been murdered. Tijerina defended himself. Much of the trial centered on the right to make a citizen's arrest. Tijerina proved his points, and the jury entered a verdict of not guilty.

In mid-February 1969 the Court of Appeals for the Tenth Circuit upheld the Amphitheatre conviction; Tijerina's lawyer immediately appealed to the Supreme Court. On June 5, 1969, *El Tigre* again attempted to occupy Kit Carson National Forest at the Coyote Campsite. His wife, Patsy, and some of the participants burned a few signs. Two days later the Rangers and police arrested several of the liberators. Tijerina allegedly pointed a carbine at one of the Rangers, when deputies threatened his wife. Authorities charged him with aiding and abetting the destruction of U.S. Forest Service signs and assaulting and threatening a federal agent. The court sentenced him to three years in the federal penitentiary. On October 13, Chief Justice Warren Burger refused to hear his appeal on the Amphitheatre case, and Tijerina went to prison. For seven months prison authorities isolated him from the other prisoners. Tijerina became a symbol, convicted of political crimes, rather than of crimes against "society." Tijerina was released in the summer of 1971.

U.S. General Accounting Office
Report to Congressional Requestors, Treaty of Guadalupe Hidalgo: Findings and Possible Options Regarding Longstanding Community Land Grant Claims in New Mexico
161–70 (2004)

CHAPTER 5: CONCLUDING OBSERVATIONS AND POSSIBLE CONGRESSIONAL OPTIONS IN RESPONSE TO REMAINING COMMUNITY LAND GRANT CONCERNS

Overview

As detailed in this report, grantees and their heirs have expressed concern for more than a century—particularly since the end of the New Mexico land grant confirmation process in the early 1900s—that the United States did not address community land grant claims in a fair and equitable manner. As part of our report, we were asked to outline possible options that Congress may wish to consider in response to remaining concerns. The possible options we have identified are based, in part, on our conclusion that there does not appear to be a specific legal basis for relief, because the Treaty was implemented in compliance with all applicable U.S. legal requirements. Nonetheless, Congress may determine that there are compelling policy or other reasons for taking additional action. For example, Congress may disagree with the Supreme Court's *Sandoval* decision and determine that it should be "legislatively overruled," addressing grants adversely affected by that decision or taking other action. Congress, in its judgment, also may find that other aspects of the New Mexico confirmation process, such as the inefficiency and hardship it caused for many grantees, provide a sufficient basis to support further steps on behalf of claimants. Based on all of these factors, we have identified a range of five possible options that Congress may wish to consider, ranging from taking no additional action at this time, to making payment to claimants' heirs or other entities, or transferring federal land to communities. We do not express an opinion as to which, if any, of these options might be preferable, and Congress may wish to consider additional options beyond those offered here. The last four options are not necessarily mutually exclusive and could be used in some combination. The five possible options are:

Option 1: Consider taking no additional action at this time because the majority of community land grants were confirmed, the majority of acreage claimed was awarded, and the confirmation processes were conducted in accordance with U.S. law.

Option 2: Consider acknowledging that the land grant confirmation process could have been more efficient and less burdensome and imposed fewer hardships on claimants.

Option 3: Consider establishing a commission or other body to reexamine specific community land grant claims that were rejected or not confirmed for the full acreage claimed.

Option 4: Consider transferring federal land to communities that did not receive all of the acreage originally claimed for their community land grants.

Option 5: Consider making financial payments to claimants' heirs or other entities for the non-use of land originally claimed but not awarded.

As agreed, in the course of our discussions with land grant descendants in New Mexico, we solicited their views on how they would prefer to have their concerns addressed. Most indicated that they would prefer to have a combination of the final two options—transfer of land and financial payment.

Potential Considerations in Determining Whether Any Additional Action May Be Appropriate

This report has detailed the principal concerns and contentions that grantees and their heirs and advocates have expressed, particularly since completion of the New Mexico community land grant confirmation process in 1904, about whether the property protection provisions of the 1848 Treaty of Guadalupe Hidalgo were implemented in a legal and fair manner. We have assessed these concerns and contentions based on extensive factual investigation and legal research and provided what we believe is the most thorough analysis undertaken to date of many of the most contentious issues surrounding the Treaty. With respect to grants and acreage, our analysis shows that the majority of the community land grants in New Mexico—over 68 percent—were confirmed under the Surveyor General and Court of Private Land Claims procedures, and that the majority of the acreage claimed under these grants—over 63 percent—was awarded. Our analysis also shows that 55 percent of the acreage claimed under both community and individual land grants in New Mexico combined was awarded under these procedures, rather than the 24 percent that is commonly reported in the land grant literature.

With respect to compliance with legal requirements, our analysis shows that the property provisions were carried out in accordance with all applicable U.S. laws and requirements, including the U.S. Constitution. First, because of the non-self-executing nature of the Treaty, Congress was required to enact legislation to put the provisions into effect. It did so in the 1854 and 1891 Acts establishing the Surveyor General and the CPLC procedures, respectively, and under U.S. law, any conflict between these statutes and the Treaty provisions (which we do not suggest exists) must be resolved in favor of the statutes. Another legally related issue of great concern to heirs, in part because it affected the disposition of more than 1.1 million acres of land, is the U.S. Supreme Court's 1897 decision in *United States v. Sandoval*. As discussed in this report, many heirs believe the *Sandoval* case was wrongly decided because the Court purportedly misapplied Spanish and Mexican law in holding that the sovereign (Spain, México, and later the United States), rather than communities, owned the common lands in community land grants. As our analysis explains, however, the Court had no authority under the 1891 Act to confirm grants based on the type of equitable rights involved in the *Sandoval* land grant claim and related cases; it could confirm only those grants "lawfully and regularly derived" under Spanish or Mexican law. As a matter of statutory interpretation, the Court found that these grants consisted only of grants held under legal, not equitable, title. As the Court explained in *Sandoval*, the grantees' concern was essentially a concern with the Congress' policy judgments in the 1891 Act itself, rather than with the courts' application of the act, and this concern could be addressed only by "the political department" of the U.S. government—that is, the Congress. As discussed in chapter 3, the California Commissioners had come to a similar conclusion regarding the nature and limits of their land grant confirmation authority, acknowledging that they were essentially carrying out political, rather than judicial, responsibilities. Heirs and scholars also have asserted that the confirmation procedures violated the requirements of due process of law under the U.S. Constitution. Our analysis shows, however, that the procedures satisfied these requirements as the courts had defined them at that time and even under modern-day standards. Finally, with respect to heirs' contention that the United States had a fiduciary duty, after their grants had been confirmed, to ensure that ownership of the lands remained with the heirs and was not transferred voluntarily or involuntarily, our analysis shows that the Treaty did not create such a duty and thus the United States acted properly in this regard.

The fact that the United States implemented the Treaty's property provisions in accordance with U.S. law may suggest that a predicate for taking additional congressional action at this time may be lacking and that further action may not be necessary or appropriate. In the absence of any legal violation for which relief might be warranted, taking action could set a precedent for resolving other sensitive disputes, and at least in the context of the Guadalupe Hidalgo claims, could be costly to taxpayers, depending on what action is taken. On the other hand, Congress may find that there are compelling policy or other reasons for taking at least some additional action. For example, as a matter of policy (or even law), Congress may disagree with the Supreme Court's *Sandoval* decision and decide that it should be "legislatively overruled," by addressing the affected grants in some way or taking other action. Congress, in its judgment, also may find that other aspects of the confirmation process in New Mexico provide a sufficient basis to support further steps on behalf of claimants. For example, Congress may wish to respond to the fact that, as detailed in this report, pursuing a land grant claim in New Mexico was inefficient and burdensome for many claimants, particularly compared with the more streamlined Commission process that Congress had established for California under the 1851 Act. As the New Mexico Surveyors General themselves reported during the first 20 years of their claims reviews under the 1854 Act, they lacked the legal, language, and analytical skills, and financial resources to review grant claims in the most effective and efficient manner. Moreover, unfamiliarity with the English language and the American legal system made claimants reluctant to turn over land grant documents and often required them to hire English-speaking lawyers, sometimes necessitating sale of part of their claimed land—for many, their principal resource—to cover legal expenses. In addition, because of delays in Surveyor General reviews and subsequent congressional confirmations caused by the intervention of the Civil War, concerns about fraudulent claims, and other reasons, some claims had to be presented multiple times to different entities under different legal standards. Finally, the claims process could be burdensome even after a grant was confirmed, because of the imprecision and cost of having the lands surveyed, a cost that grantees had to bear for a number of years. For these or other reasons, Congress may decide that some additional action is warranted.

Possible Congressional Options for Response to Remaining Concerns

With respect to your request for possible options to address remaining concerns about community land grant claims in New Mexico, our analysis and findings suggest a variety of possible responses, ranging from taking no additional action at this time to taking one or more additional steps. We describe five of these possible options below. If Congress decides that some additional action is warranted, we note that resolving specific land grant claims dating back to the 18th and 19th centuries would be a challenging task: among other things, it could require identification of the specific persons who were adversely affected by the confirmation process, determination of where the descendants of those persons are today, and an assessment of the relationship between those descendants and persons currently living on the affected land. We do not express an opinion as to which, if any, of these options might be preferable, and Congress may wish to consider additional alternatives. The five possible options are:

Option 1: Consider Taking No Additional Action at This Time

A first option could be for Congress to take no further action at this time regarding community land grants in New Mexico. As noted above, the majority of the community land grants in New Mexico were confirmed and the majority of acreage claimed under these grants was awarded. In addition, the procedures that Congress developed for confirming community land grants complied with applicable U.S. laws, including constitutional due process requirements. Although the confirmation processes could have been more efficient and less burdensome on claimants, U.S. citizens sometimes are subjected to inefficient and burdensome government procedures and yet do not receive compensation or other formal relief. Particularly given the high rate of confirmation of New Mexico land grants and the substantial passage of time since the confirmation process was completed 100 years ago, Congress may decide that no further official action is appropriate at this time.

Option 2: Consider Acknowledging Difficulties in Evaluating the Original Claims

If Congress decides for policy or other reasons that some type of additional response is appropriate, one alternative could be to make an official acknowledgment that the U.S. government could have evaluated community land grant claims in New Mexico in a more efficient and less burdensome manner and one that created fewer hardships for grantees. Acknowledgement of these difficulties could take many forms, ranging from a declarative statement to an apology by the U.S. government.

Option 3: Consider Creating a Commission or Other Entity to Evaluate and Resolve Remaining Concerns About Individual Claims or Categories of Claims

Another possible option for taking action in response to remaining land grant concerns, if Congress determines this is appropriate, could be for Congress to establish a commission or other entity to evaluate and resolve concerns about specific claims or categories of claims regarding New Mexico community land grants. Twenty-two congressional bills and resolutions reflecting this concept were introduced between 1971 and 1980, triggered in part by a 1967 raid of a county courthouse in northern New Mexico by land grant heirs and their advocates. Since January 1997, at least eight additional bills have been introduced to address New Mexico community land grant claims, most recently in 2001, and most of these also have involved creation of some type of commission. One of the bills, H.R. 2538, passed the House of Representatives in September 1998.

The commissions proposed in these bills generally have fallen into five basic categories, with differences in the composition of the commission, its duration, and the legal effect of any decisions or recommendations that the commission might issue. H.R. 9422, for example, the first bill introduced in 1971, would have created a three-member commission to serve a 5–year term. The commission's decisions would have been final except if disapproved by Congress. The commission would have been authorized to direct U.S. seizure of any privately owned lands in dispute and transfer of these lands to the respective community land grant. The 1971 bill also would have authorized $2.5 million for the expenses of the commission, $5 million for legal and professional assistance for petitioners, and a substantial $5 billion for land acquisitions. More recently, H.R. 2538, passed by the House in 1998, would have created a five-member commission with no specific term limit. After investigating and ruling on all pending claims, the commission was to report its decisions and recommendations to the President and Congress; Congress then was to decide whether to accept, reject, or modify the commission's recommendations, similar to its role regarding the Surveyor General confirmation recommendations. The 1998 bill would have authorized an appropriation of $1 million per year for fiscal years 1999 through 2007 to fund the commission's operations and a land grant study center. Most recently, Representative Tom Udall and 20 co-sponsors introduced H.R. 1823, the Guadalupe–Hidalgo Treaty Land Claims Act of 2001. Among other things, H.R. 1823 would have created a commission authorized to receive petitions from community land grant heirs in New Mexico and elsewhere, seeking determination of the validity of their grants under the Treaty. When its work was completed, the commission was to report its decisions to Congress and make recommendations regarding whether Congress should "reconstitute" certain grants—that is, restore the grants to full status as a municipality with "rights properly belonging to a municipality under State law"—or provide other relief to grant heirs. The bill would have set a 5–year deadline for submission of petitions and authorized an appropriation of $1.9 million per year for fiscal years 2002 through 2008 to fund the commission's work and that of a land grant study center.

One notable aspect of all of these bills was that they did not specify what legal standard the commission was to apply in reviewing land grant claims. The bills did not, for example, specify that the commission was to confirm a grant based on Spanish or Mexican law, usages, and customs—as in the 1854 Act—or only if title to the grant had been lawfully and regularly derived under Spanish or Mexican law—as in the 1891 Act. To make any such commission as successful as possible, it would be important for any congressional legislation creating such a commission to specify what laws or other standards are to be applied in reviewing claims.

Option 4: Consider Transferring Federal Land to Communities

Another possible option for responding to remaining land grant concerns, if Congress determines this is appropriate for policy or other reasons, could be for Congress to transfer federal land to communities that made claims to the Surveyor General or the CPLC under a community land grant but did not receive all of the acreage they claimed. This option has been reflected in some of the legislative proposals over the last 30 years, whereby federal land located within the grants' originally claimed boundaries would have been transferred to claimants. As agreed, in the course of our discussions with land grant descendants in New Mexico, we solicited their views on how they would prefer to have their concerns addressed, and this approach, which would address land grant heirs' claims of "lost" acreage most directly, was one of the two options preferred by grant heirs with whom we spoke. If Congress decided to adopt this option and there were no federal lands located within the originally claimed grant boundaries, alternate federal lands in New Mexico might be transferred or financial payment made in lieu of transfer.

Although the amount of federal acreage that might be affected under this option would depend on the specific grants at issue, preliminary surveys indicate that it could be substantial if all of the acreage originally claimed were now awarded. For example, according to Bureau of Land Management estimates, over half of the almost 1 million acres of land "lost" by three grants—the Cañón de Chama grant, the San Miguel del Vado grant, and the Petaca grant—is now owned by the federal government (the U.S. Forest Service), and thus potentially could be transferred to these grants. Appendix XII to this report shows the original claimed boundaries of these three grants and the present-day land ownership within those boundaries that could be at issue (see figures 9–11). Appendix XII also contains maps of five additional land grant claims for which we were able to locate preliminary surveys and which, if Congress adopted this option, it might decide to increase in size (see figures 12–14).

One other potential hurdle in implementing this option might be that any overlaps between claimed community land grant boundaries and the boundaries of existing Indian lands or additional aboriginal Indian lands would have to be resolved. For example, the Town of Cieneguilla land grant claim partially overlaps with the Pueblo of Picurís land grant, and the Don Fernando de Taos land grant claim conflicts with the Pueblo of Taos. Similarly, conflicts between the boundaries of claimed community land grants and confirmed land grants would have to be resolved. The original claimed boundaries of the San Miguel del Vado land grant, for example, overlap with the confirmed and patented boundaries of the Town of Las Vegas and Town of Tecolote land grants.

Option 5: Consider Making Financial Payments to Claimants' Heirs or Other Entities

A final possible option if Congress determines that additional action should be taken—and the other option favored by the land grant heirs with whom we spoke—could be for Congress to make payments to claimants for the "lost" use of land that was claimed but not awarded. If land were not being transferred to a community under Option 4, payment could be made for both past and future non-use; if it were being transferred, there could be payment only for past non-use. Congress might assign the task of determining payment amounts to the type of commission discussed under Option 3, again presumably based on a specified legal standard. Congress created a similar entity in 1946 in the Indian Claims Commission, which was authorized to address claims by making financial payments. Similarly, Congress created the Pueblo Lands Board to resolve Indian land claims in the 1920s and 1930s, through a combination land transfer/financial payment mechanism.

There likely would be a number of practical issues to be resolved in implementing this option, the first of which would be determining the criteria for payment. The amount might be determined on the basis of acreage alone, for example, or might also account for the value of the specific parcels at issue. A prime piece of agricultural property in a river valley, for instance, might be worth more than rocky hillside property. Likewise, the non-use of heavily wooded property with an abundance of wildlife might have a greater value than the non-use of property without those resources. A second practical issue to be resolved would be determining who should receive compensation. The individuals affected by adverse land grant decisions 100 years ago would have to be identified, as would the individuals who are their present-day descendants.

Finally, decisions would need to be made regarding possible restrictions on the permissible uses of any payments made. For example, funds might be directly distributed as cash payments to individual heirs, with no restrictions on how the funds could be used. Alternatively, payments might be made into some type of development trust fund, with money earmarked for specific activities. Over the past 10 years, Congress has established these types of trust funds for Indian tribes that lost land when dams were built on the Missouri River. A development trust fund could create the flexibility to provide assistance for a wide variety of activities, such as economic development, land acquisition, or educational programs. Trust fund monies also might be used to pay property taxes owing on community land grant common lands, thus providing an immediate benefit to grants that continue to be at risk of tax foreclosure. As discussed in chapter 4, the federal government had no legal obligation under the Treaty of Guadalupe Hidalgo to ensure continued ownership of community land grants once they were confirmed, including by payment of a land grant's property taxes to avoid forfeiture, but Congress may nevertheless decide that there are compelling policy or other reasons to provide financial assistance to these communities.

Summary

In summary, we have identified, as requested, a range of five possible options that Congress may wish to consider in response to remaining concerns regarding New Mexico community land grants. These options reflect our conclusion that there does not appear to be a specific legal basis for relief but that Congress may nonetheless determine that there are compelling policy or other reasons for taking additional action.

Notes and Questions

1.   Why did it fall to a non-lawyer, Lopez Reies Tijerina, to file the first modern land-grant claim?

2.   Why did not a radical Anglo lawyer or law student, inspired, perhaps, by Oscar Acosta's writings, file these claims?

3.   By the time Tijerina took action, American law schools were beginning to graduate numbers of Latino lawyers. Why did not one of them file the claim? Is it possible that their three years of law study "deschooled" them? See Peter Nabokov, *Tijerina and the Courthouse Raid* (2d ed. 1970); Malcolm Ebright, *Land Grants and Lawsuits in Northern New Mexico* (1994).

4.   Is the GAO correct that the U.S. wrongfully stole Mexican lands in the Southwest, but that nothing can be done?

5.   Is Ahmad right that a poverty lawyer, respectful of the community he or she represents, must engage that entire community as translator-interpreter in order to do justice to its goals and avoid doing it violence?

*

Index

References are to Pages

A

B

C

D

E

F

J

K

L

M

N

O

S

T

Texas: and applicability of the Treaty of Guadalupe Hidalgo, 19, 24; school financing system, 307–17; ten percent plan, 384–85

Tijerina, Lopez Reies, and New Mexico land grant war, 862–64. See also *Lopez Tijerina v. Henry*

Title VII: and accent discrimination, 658–67; and English-only rules, 652–58; and hair styles, 729–31; and national origin discrimination, 639–51; and racial epithets, 565–67

Trask, Haunani–Kay, and power of language, 209

Treaty of Guadalupe Hidalgo (1848), 15–34, 172–73, 175, 187; Article VIII, 17, 18; Article IX, 17–19; Article X, 16–17; and citizenship of Mexicans, 514–15; and federal citizenship, 17–18, 176; U.S. and land ownership, 23–34, 769–97, 864–71; violation of, 168–69

Treaty of Paris (1898), 50–51, 185, 187–88

Trinh, Minh–Ha, and power of language, 209, 210

U

U.S. Border Patrol. *See* Border Patrol

U.S. English, 231–32

U.S.-Mexico Bracero Program (1942–1964), 492, 496–97

UFWOC. *See* United Farm Workers Organizing Committee

unaccompanied refugee children, 814–17

Unamuno, Miguel, 110, 114

undocumented college students, 329

undocumented immigrants. *See* immigrants, undocumented

undocumented schoolchildren, 329–41; and free public education, 329–35

United Farm Workers Organizing Committee, 687–88

United Fruit Company, 426

United States: and anti-communism policy in Latin America, 424–25, 428; business interests in Latin America, 425–26, 428; and disregard of international law, 424–28; free trade policies of, 416–17; "good neighbor" policy of, 424; and human rights abuses of, 428; imperialism of, 8–9, 49–50, 61, 181–82, 186; interventions in Latin America, 693–96; labor market, shortages and surpluses of, 430–39; and Latin American relations, 423–28; nineteenth century racial policies of, 172–74; participation in Mexican repatriation, 490–91; policies toward Latin America, 180–85; support of dictators in Latin America, 694; war with Mexico (1846–1848), 8–13, 177–78, 421–23; war with Spain (1898–1900), 49–50, 185–89

United States v. Brignoni–Ponce, 525–29, 534

United States v. Lucero, 169

United States v. Mallides, 534–35

United States v. Martinez–Fuerte, 529, 533, 537

United States v. Sanchez–Vargas, 535

United States v. Sandoval, 27

United States v. Vallejo, 537

United States v. Verdugo–Urquidez, 531–32, 537

W

wealth discrimination, 308–17; as a suspect classification in school financing, 308–10, 321–24

wet foot dry foot policy. *See* Cuban migrants

white man's burden, 182

women of color, and workplace harassment, 732–37

women's movement, and Latinas, 699–706